"I have bought this book at least 20 times - it is by far my favorite baby present, grandparent present, parent of kids present, etc. How great to get something that does not add clutter but rather fun to a kids life. The indexes are EXCELLENT as are the directions and website references. Susan Peterson is very funny in person - she spoke to our MOPS group and was just excellent."

Louise Valente
Speech Pathologist
Co-owner of Pacific Coast Speech Services

"This is a wonderful resource that has all sorts of gems and suggestions. The book is well organized by county/region/type of place and the index gives you the option to search by price, area or specific place. Each entry has a detailed description of the place and gives suggestions about what to do, what is at the site, and even sometimes suggests what to do to prepare before you go (like books to buy about art so that the kids enjoy it more). Each entry also has a recommended age level which I think is really realistic. This woman really knows kids and obviously has gone to most of these sites (pretty amazing actually because there are so many!). I have a 4 year old and a 2 year old and have been using this book for the past year. It made my summer with the kids so much fun and I pull it out whenever we want to find some interesting place to go as a family . . . I HIGHLY recommend this book for families with children living or visiting soCal. It's been amazing for me since I didn't grow up in SoCal and all the usual travel guides like LonelyPlanet and RoughGuides don't have most of these places listed and aren't written for families . . . I'm in awe at the amount of work put into this book. Thank you Susan Peterson."

Tiffany F. Jones, PhD.
Associate Professor, History Department
California State University, San Bernardino

"It's 10:30 and I've already had five telephone calls from leaders thanking me for inviting you to the meeting last night, praising your fun-filled presentation, pleasant personality, great ideas, . . . Believe me, Susan, I have never looked so good. It's just not that easy to impress *or* entertain the "been there, done that" woman in Irvine. . . You may be sure that you have substantially improved the quality of Girl Scout field trips in Irvine so I feel confident that I can offer you the appreciation of the 1600 girls affected."

Mary Pearlman
Membership Development Director for Girl Scouts, Orange County

"Over 20 copies of *Fun and Educational Places to go With Kids* are continually checked out in the Orange County Public Library System; we can't keep them on the shelves! Children's librarians feel confident referring parents to this title. It's perfect for planning local inexpensive family outings."

Elke Faraci
Senior Administrative Librarian
Orange County Public Library System

"As a travel industry professional, I find Susan Peterson's book to be my #1 reference when designing group tours & outings for families in Southern California. Her easy-to-use guide, with its complete listing of activities by location, cost and age range, allows me to tailor every outing to meet each client's particular needs. Because she's an experienced mother of three I know I can trust her judgment, and that's why Pack the Kids will always pack her guide!"

Daniel McCollum
Director of Operations Pack the Kids Family Tour Adventures

AND EDUCATIONAL

TO GO WITH KIDS
AND ADULTS
IN SOUTHERN CALIFORNIA
SUSAN PETERSON

A comprehensive guide to Los Angeles, Orange,
Riverside, San Bernardino, San Diego,
Santa Barbara, and Ventura counties

Fun Places Publishing, California
www.funplaces.com

Toni-
Have fun!
Sus

Published by Fun Places Publishing
6124 Capetown Street
Lakewood, California 90713
(562) 867-5223
susan@funplaces.com
www.funplaces.com

ISBN 978-0-9833832-1-5

Printed in the United States of America

Tenth edition - April, 2014
Ninth edition - April, 2011
Eighth edition - April, 2009
Seventh edition - April, 2006
Sixth edition - June, 2003
Fifth edition - March, 2001
Fourth edition - October, 1998
Third edition - May, 1997
Second edition - May, 1996
First edition - May, 1995

ACKNOWLEDGMENTS

A 10th edition is reason for celebration, so - thank you! Thank you to you who are reading this guidebook for the first time; my hope is that it will give you a wealth of ideas of where to go with your kids and that you spend precious family time together (because kids actually *do* grow up fast). Thank you to you who have been faithful readers. I've had the pleasure of meeting and talking with many of you. May this edition continue to bless you in creating memories together and - there are GREAT new places to explore!

A special thanks is needed for the following people:

Lance - 30 years of being married to my best friend, best confidant, best supporter, best encourager, best partner - you are the best! Truly, thank you. Your faithfulness, steadfastness and thoughtfulness are such a testimony as to how well you love. And I appreciate your witty sense of humor, especially after long hours while working together. I'm the one that gets to do the fun stuff - go on the adventures to check out places for the book and speak to groups all over, and you get the pleasure of doing the computer work. Hmmm. Without you, there would be no book. I appreciate your computer expertise and sacrificial willingness to pull it all together. Thank you.

My three boys, whom I had the privilege (plus tears, trials and triumphs) to homeschool - Kellan, Bryce, and T.J. They have literally come along for the rides (mostly willingly). We all have been, and continue to be, richly blessed by purposing to spend time with each other.

Kellan, my oldest son, who is married to one of my favorite daughter-in-laws: I'm excited for you as you are graduated from seminary - you are going to be an awesome and really cool youth pastor! You are a gifted writer and speaker as you do both with conviction, passion, depth, humor and an extensive vocabulary. I so enjoy our talks, and the depth of them. I love seeing your life and faith unfold and grow deep roots as you intentionally choose God on a daily basis. You are my favorite.

Bryce, my middle son and married to my other favorite daughter-in-law: I'm proud that you are getting your doctorate in Criminal Justice, and prouder and more thankful of the man you've become. You are smart, a man of integrity, personable, and genuinely care for people and it shows. I'm so glad faith, family and keeping connected are important to you - all that says a lot about your character. And dad and I are thankful for skype! You are my favorite.

T.J., my youngest, who works as a karate instructor, goes on mission's trip to the jungles of Ecuador, and is finishing up college: Selfishly, I'm so pleased that you are still at home because I know that time is very short and dad and I want to continue to make the most of it. Communications is the perfect major for you as communicating and relationships have always been the most important things in your life. Your devotion and love for God shines as you seek hard after Him and seek to love your friends effectively. How wonderful to have a ring-side seat and even walk with you a bit on your journey. You are my favorite.

Thank you to those who worked with me in making phone calls and checking websites to verify every detail of information in these pages - I know it's not the fun part of the job, but I appreciate your help in making this edition so accurate. All the inaccuracies are mine. (Sorry for them!) Thank you to **Diana Clay** (you were my absolute rock in this - thank you!!!), Jewelene Pate, Heidi Grijalva, Jody Rouse, Kasey McKay, Krista Loon, Nancy Marentis, Tobi Ellis, Lis Golden-Morris, Janis Lacomb, Carrie Oswald, Kellan Peterson, Allura Cordova, and Liza Marentis. Thank you all *so* very much!! Many hugs!

Thank you to all of the people associated with places mentioned in this book that were so willing to talk with me, send me information, and enable my family to come and visit - thank you, THANK YOU, **THANK YOU!!**.

ABOUT THE AUTHOR:

I love my family, traveling (almost anywhere and everywhere), reading, walking, talking with friends, working out, speaking to groups, and just living life. I've been honored to be able go to Ecuador, into the jungle, the last 8 years on mission's trips, to continue relationships there with incredible people, to support our indigenous missionaries, and to serve and love by faith and action. I also get to "work" (i.e. spend time) with the young adults group at our church. I really like to explore new things, yet I have the same thing for lunch every day - go figure.

I would appreciate your ideas about and for this book. Do you have a wonderful place to go with kids that wasn't included in this edition? Please let me know and I'll share it in the next one. You can contact me at:

FUN PLACES TO GO WITH KIDS
email: susan@funplaces.com
www.funplaces.com

Share your experience with others by commenting on my Facebook page - photos, things you liked (or didn't like) about the attraction. My goal is for readers and adventurers to be prepared, experience new things, grow, enjoy family time and maybe even discover some new interests for your kids (and yourself).

www.facebook.com/funplacestogo

TABLE OF CONTENTS

INTRODUCTION and LEGEND EXPLANATION

In this world there are specifically fun places to go with kids, and there are places we go and bring our kids, anyhow. I think going shopping is great, but when my boys were younger, while I was looking at clothes, they thought it was fun to climb in the clothing racks and maybe even pull off a ticket or two to bring home as "prizes." That did not make for a fun family outing. I've tried to do the weeding for you so that anywhere you choose to go in this guidebook, whether it's an all-day outing or just for an hour, would be an enjoyable time for you and your child. Some places are obvious choices; some are places you might have simply forgotten about; some are hidden treasures; and some are new attractions.

The book is set up by county. Under each county, categories are listed alphabetically; and under each category, attractions are listed alphabetically. Note: The names of places in all capital letters used in a description (e.g., DISNEYLAND) are attractions listed separately elsewhere in the book and usually referenced by a page number. An explanation of what each category means is on the following pages simply titled, "What Do the Categories Mean?" If you still have a hard time figuring out in which category I have placed an attraction (and that is a strong possibility), look up the place in one of the four indexes in the back of the book: Name, City, Price, or Theme.

Next to most of the places described are symbols, meant to be at-a-glance guidelines. The **sun** indicates the average amount of time needed to see this attraction. You might decide you need more or less time - this is just a guideline. The **dollar signs and exclamation mark** are price guidelines. They incorporate *the entrance cost for one adult, a 10-year-old child, and the parking fee* (if there is one). If you have more than one child, or one who gets in for free, your cost will vary. **Ages** stands for recommended ages. It is meant to be an aid to help you decide if an attraction is appropriate and/or meaningful for your child. Some of the age restrictions, however, are designated by the place you visit. The **birthday cake** symbol represents an attraction that is a good place to 1) have a birthday party (the place may or may not have a separate party room), or 2) incorporate with a birthday party.

☀	=	15 minutes to 1 hour	!	=	FREE!
☀	=	1½ hours to half a day	!/$	=	FREE, but bring spending money.
☀	=	all day	$	=	1¢ - $5
			$$	=	$5.01 - $10
🎂	=	good for birthday parties	$$$	=	$10.01 - $20
			$$$$	=	$20.01 - $40
			$$$$$	=	over $40

GO Los Angeles Card and **GO San Diego Card** provide great deals in these and surrounding counties. See www.smartdestinatons.com for more info.

Discounts: Always check the attraction's website for online discounts. If you belong to AAA (i.e., Auto Club), ask if there is a discount for members.

Check www.CITYPASS.com for another way to save at some major attractions.

WHAT DO THE CATEGORIES MEAN?
(and other helpful information)
Each attraction in every county is listed under one, or more, of the following categories.

AMUSEMENT PARKS
Webster's definition of amusement is: "To cause to laugh or smile; entertainment; a pleasant diversion." So, from roller coasters to water slides - have fun!

ARTS AND CRAFTS
Children have creative urges and need a place to express themselves. Since art classes are offered in a dizzying array and with fluctuating times and prices, many of the places listed in these sections are paint-it-yourself ceramic studios to assist your young artists in developing their talents - move over Monet! There are other unique places listed, too, that aid in artistic endeavors. Note: Museums are also great resources for arts and crafts workshops.

BEACHES
Beaches are a *shore* bet for a day of fun in the sun. Along with sand and water play, some beaches have playgrounds, picnic tables, and waveless waters that make them particularly younger-kid friendly. Some also have paved pathways for biking, strolling, or rollerblading. These sections includes *just a few* suggestions of where to go beaching. Check the following website for more beaches and more beach information: www.beachcalifornia.com.

On a sad note, some beaches' waters get polluted, either temporarily or longer term. Before your visit, please contact Heal the Bay at (800) HEAL BAY (432-5229) / www.healthebay.org and see the rating/report card for that particular beach.

EDIBLE ADVENTURES
I am not a food critic. The places I mention have an "eatertainment" atmosphere and serve at least decent, if not delicious, food. From themed restaurants to high tea, from farmer's markets to a fun place to get an ice cream cone, the Edible Adventures sections cover some of the best. For a fairly comprehensive listing of tea rooms and customer reviews for Southern California (and beyond), look up www.teamap.com.

FAMILY PAY AND PLAY
The family that plays together, stays together. Indoor play areas, miniature golf courses, rock climbing centers, laser tag arenas, paint ball fields, indoor skateparks, and more, are great places to go to spend some special bonding time.

GREAT OUTDOORS
Contrary to popular belief, Southern California consists not only of concrete buildings, but also of the great outdoors. Explore the region's natural beauty by visiting open-space preserves, botanic gardens, nature centers, and a plethora of designed parks. Go take a hike - with your kids! For a complete listing of state-run parks, contact (916) 653-6995 / parks.ca.gov. Hiking is a favorite way to really see the fantastic outdoors of Southern California. Of the several websites to check for hiking trails one of my favorites is www.socalhiker.net.

Parks in Orange County have a fantastic resource with Michele Whiteaker's Nature Play Trips. Check out her website at www.funorangecountyparks.com. She describes each park in detail and has great photographs.

Enjoy almost 300 gardens nationwide for one membership price with a reciprocal membership program offered by American Horticultural Society. The program includes fifteen gardens just in Southern California! Members also receive the magazine, *The American Gardener*, discounted or free admission to flower and garden shows, the annual Seed Exchange, and special discounts on gardening products. See ahs.org for more info.

Also listed under the Great Outdoors sections are outdoor skateparks. Check www.socalskateparks.com or call your city hall to keep up on newly-opened skateboard parks.

MALLS
These sections are not necessarily to tell you where to go shopping, but rather to inform you of free kids' clubs, programs, and "shoppertainment" features that your local mall has to offer. We included just a few of our favorite unique malls, also. Be entertained, enjoy, and create - and maybe get in a little shopping, too!

MUSEUMS

There is a whole world of learning in the huge variety of museums in Southern California. Captivate kids' imaginations, heart even their hands by treating them to a visit. Here are a few tips about museums:

*Exhibits rotate, so be flexible in your expectations.

*If you really like the museum, become a member. Besides supporting the foundation, you'll reap benefits such as visiting the year round at no additional fee, being invited to members-only events, receiving newsletters, getting discounts on store mercha and lots more.

*The California Science Center in Los Angeles, Children's Museum at La Habra, Columbia Memorial Space Center, Discovery Science Center in Santa Ana, Kidspace Children's Museum, Natural History Museum of Los Angeles, Reuben H. Fleet Science C of San Diego, San Diego Natural History Museum, and Santa Barbara Museum of Natural History have reciprocal memberships exclude museums within 90 miles of the museum where membership was purchased. These memberships are also reciprocal - for the permanent exhibits only - with more than 300 other museums nation and worldwide. Check www.astc.org for more information.

*If you're a Bank of America cardholder know that you can get into 150 museums nationwide for free the first full weekend of month. The twelve great museums in Southern California are: Autry National Center, Birch Aquarium, Discovery Science Cente (Sundays only), Laguna Art Museum, The Living Desert, Los Angeles County Museum of Art, Museum of Latin American Ar Museum of Photographic Arts, Skirball Cultural Center, Palm Springs Art Museum, Riverside Art Museum, and San Diego M of Art. Check museums.bankofamerica.com for more details.

*If you're looking for a special present, most museum gift shops carry unique merchandise that is geared toward their specialty.

*Museums offer a fantastic array of special calendar events. Check their websites or get on a mailing list.

*Contact www.museumsusa.org for a wealth of info.

*Take a guided tour! You and your kids will learn a lot about the exhibits this way.

*Call first and ask if they are hosting a school field trip and if so, what time. Don't visit the museum then. Go whenever field t aren't as it will be less crowded then.

PIERS AND SEAPORTS

It ap*piers* that walking around seaport villages, looking at boats, fishing off piers, and taking a cruise are delightful ways to spe hours with your child.

POTPOURRI

The dictionary defines potpourri as: "A miscellaneous mixture; a confused collection." This accurately describes these sections Unique stores, cemeteries, libraries, Catalina Island, Tijuana, and more fill these pages. Whatever you do, there are a potpourri of to explore.

SHOWS AND THEATERS

How about a day (or evening) at the theater? The listings here include theaters that have performances specifically for children, planetarium shows, dinner and show productions, and musical extravaganzas.

TOURS

These groupings are all about insight into ordinary and unique places. Many tours are also offered under the museums sections few other sections. Note: See the Ideas and Resources section toward the back of the book for general tour ideas regarding a par profession or topic.

Tip: Many restaurants, especially chain restaurants, offer tours of their facility. I've listed some restaurants in the main sections book. The tours usually require a minimum number of participants (usually school-aged children), and could include a tour of kitchen, and a partial or full meal. Tours are usually free. I suggest that if you see a place you're interested in taking a tour of, call place and ask. They might not be set up to do it for the general public, but they might be willing to take your group around.

TRANSPORTATION

For a truly "moving" experience, take a journey with your child by bike, plane, train, automobile, ship, carriage, or another mod transportation. Note: There are numerous boating companies up and down the coastline. I've mentioned only a few, giving ju pertinent facts. Anchors away! Many beaches and parks have bike paths, so look under the Beaches sections and Great Outdoor sections for additional suggestions.

ZOOS AND ANIMALS

Kids and animals seem to go hand-in-hoof - both are adorable and neither is easy. Zoos, aquariums, farms, animal rescue fac and more are listed here. Animal lovers - these sections are for you!

MISCELLANEOUS TIDBITS

CAPTURE YOUR MEMORIES:
1. Camera / Smart phone - Capture these precious moments in a snap.
2. Video camera - Make movies involving the whole family. This is also a great way to document trips (remember to state the date and location) and interview kids, as well as get genuine reactions and impromptu stories, songs, and arguments.

SAFETY PRECAUTIONS (just a few to get you started):
1. Dress your kids in the same shirt (no, I don't mean one big shirt), or at least shirts of the same color (orange, yellow, and red are bright choices) when you go on an outing. I thought this would look silly, but while we did get stares and comments, I could find my kids at just a glance. If kids balk at wearing the same-colored shirt, invest in solid colored baseball caps. Not only can you spot your children quickly, but hats help shade their faces from the sun.
2. Dress kids in brightly colored or easily identifiable shoes. If someone should try to snatch your child, shoes are the hardest thing for a kidnapper to change.
3. Have a current picture of your child on your cell phone. In fact, take one on the day of your outing, in their outfits, for easy identification purposes.
4. Instruct your child where to meet and who to talk to (and not to talk to) in case you get separated from each other.

EXPECTATIONS:
1. Be Aware - Simply because you have a fun outing planned, whether it's going to the "happiest place on earth" or just an hour of play, please don't expect your child to necessarily enjoy every moment of it. Know and expect that your child will probably fuss about something, or seemingly nothing. Beware of the fun-stealers - tiredness and hunger. With younger children, visit places before or after nap time, and always bring food, even if you just ate.
2. Be Prepared - Call ahead and make sure the place you want to visit is open, especially if there is something that you particularly want to see. Also, check off your list of essentials from the next page; set realistic expectations for all participants; be flexible; and go for it!
3. Family Mottos - We didn't promise our kids that we'd take them on an outing. A promise, as any parent knows, cannot be broken; it is an absolute. A plan, however, can be altered depending on weather, circumstance, finances, and/or attitude! One of our family mottos is, "It's a plan, not a promise." Another one is, "Oh well." Feel free to use either or both as the situation warrants.

NEVER LEAVE HOME WITHOUT THESE ESSENTIALS

1) **SNACKS**: Always carry snacks and a water bottle with you and/or in the car. Listening to a child whine because he is hungry or thirsty can drive any sane parent over the edge. (And kids will not stop this endearing behavior until they actually get their food or drink!)

2) **MAP**: I would be lost without it! I have a GPS, but I also always carry a map because I like a bigger visual and the GPS isn't always accurate.

3) **TISSUES AND/OR WIPES**: For obvious reasons.

4) **QUARTERS**: A few quarters tucked away in a container in the car can come in handy for metered parking, arcade games, or purchasing those snacks I told you to pack but you forgot.

5) **TOYS/BOOKS/GAMES**: Keeping little fingers busy helps keep little hands out of trouble. (Check out the Educational Toys entry under the IDEAS and RESOURCES section on page 776.)

6) **iPods, iPads or a listening device**: They carry tunes that get kids singing instead of fussing. (And if kids cry really loud, just turn up the volume even louder!) We've found good storytelling CDs, in particular, to be a wonderful way to learn listening skills, use imaginations, and become educated. (See the IDEAS and RESOURCES section, on page 773, for some CD suggestions and resources.)

7) **FIRST AID KIT**: Fill it with the essentials, including band aids, ointment, adhesive tape, scissors, an ice pack, Benedryl, disposable gloves, a sewing kit, and Tylenol (both children's and adults').

8) **ROADSIDE EMERGENCY KIT**: This kit should contain jumper cables (know how to use them!), flares, a flashlight, batteries, extra drinking water, tools, matches, screwdrivers, wrenches, etc.

9) **JACKET**: Pack a light jacket or sweater for an unexpected change in weather or change of plans. Throw in a change of clothes, too, for little ones who spit up, for youngsters who don't always make it to the bathroom in time, and for those who have the gift of finding water wherever you go or for getting really dirty. (This tip could save your outing from being cut short.)

10) **BLANKET**: We use ours mainly for picnics, but it doubles as an "I'm cold" helper, and is handy for other emergencies.

11) **BACK PACK**: Even if your kids are still in the diaper/stroller stage, a back pack is great for storing snacks and water bottles, and keeping your hands free to either help your children or grab them before they dart away. Get the kids their own backpack, too, so they can carry their own snacks and souvenirs.

12) **SUNSCREEN**: With our weather, we almost always need it.

13) **CAMERA / CELL PHONE**: A picture is still worth a thousand words and brings to mind just as many memories.

14) **PORTABLE POTTY:** Caught somewhere without a potty around? Been there; done that; really not that fun. Adults might be able to hold it, but not so for little kids. My Carry Potty is just one brand available. (I will say from experience that boys just sometimes need a funnel and a bottle.)

15) **GROCERY BAG**: It holds trash, excuse me, I mean treasures, that kids collect such as rocks, sticks, and creepy crawly things. The bag helps keep your car clean and makes it easier to throw things away once you get home!

16) **CONTAINER**: A good thing to have if your kids are prone to motion sickness.

17) **A SENSE OF HUMOR!**: Some things (not everything!) will be funny later on. They will - I promise.

SOME IDEAS TO EXTEND THE MEMORIES OF YOUR OUTING

1. **PHOTO SHARING** - You, or your kids, can post photos on a favorite social network, write a caption, tag friends, and/or write a blog or a note so family and friends can share the experiences. When you travel to a new place, update your status, or tweet, to let others know where you are, what you're doing, and if you like it.

2. **JOURNALING** - Have your child write about the fun you have together. See my website, www.funplaces.com, for information on ordering the *Fun Places to go Journal*. Keep ticket stubs and brochures to attach them to journal pages. Use stickers for decorations.

3. **COLLECTIONS** - Collect key chains, refrigerator magnets, mugs, pencils, decks of cards, smashed pennies, or something else inexpensive from each place you go. Display them.
   A. Patches - I have collected patches and sewn them on a quilt; each of my boys has his own quilt or "travel blankets".
   B. Postcards - Ask your younger children, "What's the most fun thing you remember about this place?" and jot down the answers on the back of this inexpensive memory-keeper. Make older kids write out the answers themselves. Be sure you date the postcard. Keep all the postcards in a small, three-ring binder. Another option: If you're going away on a trip, bring stamps and mail the postcards home. Kids love to receive mail.

4. **EDUCATION** - Spend some time doing a little (or a lot of) research about a particular place, person, or time period before your visit. It will make your outing more meaningful and make a lasting impression upon your child. Think of your field trip as curriculum supplement! Call the attraction to get a brochure on it and/or do some online research. Other educational activities to enhance your outing include:
   A. Read stories - If you're going apple picking, for instance, read stories, or read about characters, that have something to do with apples, such as Johnny Appleseed, William Tell, Snow White, Adam and Eve, Sir Isaac Newton, and specifically, *The Giving Tree* by Shel Silverstein or *Ten Apples on Top* by Theo LeSieg.
   B. Theme books - There are thematic study books for almost every subject written. Teacher Created Materials, Inc. at (888) 434-4335 / www.teachercreated.com has over fifty, thematic unit study books available. Each book includes lessons and projects that incorporate math, arts and crafts, history, science, language arts, and cooking, into a study about one particular subject (i.e., weather, birds, the human body, holidays, and more).
   C. Spelling words - Give your child a spelling list pertaining to the attraction you're visiting.
   D. Maps - Have older children use a map to track your way to and from your outing - this is an invaluable skill, especially if they learn to do it correctly!
   E. Flash cards - Take photographs of the places you go. Put the photos on a piece of cardstock paper and write the facts about the attraction on the back. "Laminate" it with contact paper or clear packing tape. Use the cards as flash cards. Tip: If you're not a picture-taker, buy postcards instead.
   F. Use my *Fun Places to go Journal*. (See the back of the book for ordering information.)

These are just a few ideas - I'm sure you have many of your own!

5. **YOUR IDEAS -**

ROAD GAMES

"Are we almost there yet?" and "I'm bored!" (along with "I have to go to the bathroom!") are common cries from children (and adults) who are traveling. CDs, books, toys, electronic entertainment, and snacks all help to keep kids amused, as do car games. Here are just a few of our favorite games with brief explanations on how to play:

FOR THE YOUNGER SET:

MISSING LETTER ABC SONG - Sing the ABC song, leaving out a letter. See if your child can figure out what letter is missing. Now let your child sing (or say) the alphabet, leaving out a letter. Suggest correct (and incorrect) letters and see if your child agrees with you on what letter is missing. (Tip: Know your alphabet!)

MISSING NUMBER GAME - Count up to a certain number and stop. See if your child can figure out what number comes next. Now let your child do the counting. See if he/she agrees with what you say the next number should be.

COLOR CAR GAME - Look out the window for just red cars (or just blue or just green, etc). Each time your child sees a red car, he/she can shout "red!" (or "blue!" or "green!", etc.) Count together the number of cars of a particular color you see on your trip. Your child can eagerly share at night, "Daddy, we had a fifteen-red-car day!" A variation of this game is to count a particular type of car; VW Bugs is the popular choice for our family.

ABC WORD GAME - A is for apple; B is for bear; etc. Encourage your child to figure out words that start with each letter of the alphabet.

FOR OLDER CHILDREN:

ALPHABET SIGN GAME - Each person, or team, looks for a word outside the car (i.e., on billboards, freeway signs, bumper stickers, etc.) that begins with each letter of the alphabet. When the words are found, the person, or team, shouts it out. The words must be found in alphabetical order, starting with the letter A. Since words beginning with a Q, X, or Z are hard to find (unless you're near a Quality Inn, X-Ray machine, or a Zoo), players may find these particular letters used <u>in</u> any word. A word on a sign, billboard, etc, can only be used once, by one player or team member. Other players must find their word in another sign, billboard, etc. The first one to get through the alphabet wins! Warning #1: Try to verify that the word has been seen by more than just the player who shouted it out, or learn to trust each other. Warning #2: From personal experience: If the driver is competitive and wants to play, make sure he/she keeps his/her eyes on the road!

ALPHABET WORD GAME - This is a variation on the above game. Instead of finding words that begin with each letter of the alphabet, each player must look outside the car and describe his surroundings using letters of the alphabet, in sequential order. This game can be played fast and gets creative, depending on the quick-thinking skills of the people playing. Example: Someone who is on the letter "D" might look at the land and see dirt; a person looking for an "S" might say soil; someone else who is on the letter "G" might say ground. All are correct. Players may use the same point of reference as long as the exact same word is not used. Whoever gets through the alphabet first wins.

GHOST - (Or whatever title you choose.) The object of this game is to add one letter per turn and be in the process of spelling a word, without actually spelling out a word. Players take turns adding letters until someone either spells a word, or can't think of another letter to add without spelling a word. A player may try to bluff and add a letter that doesn't seem like it spells a word. If he gets challenged by someone asking what he is spelling, he must come up with a legitimate word. If he doesn't, he loses the round. (If he does have a word, however, than the challenger loses that round.) Whoever spells a word or can't think of a letter to add, gets a G. The second time he loses a round, he gets an H, etc. Whoever earns G-H-O-S-T (i.e., loses 5 rounds) is eliminated from the game. Example: Player 1 says the letter "B." Player 2 adds the letter "E." (Words must be at least 3 letters long to count as a word.) Player 3 says "T." Player 3 gets a G, or whatever letter-round he is on. He loses the round even if his intent was to spell the word "better" because "bet" is a word.

WORD SCRAMBLE - Make sure players have a piece of paper and a writing implement. Using a word on a sign or billboard, or using the name of the place you are visiting, see how many other words players can make out of it. To spice up the game, and add stress, set a time limit. Whoever has the most words wins. A variation is that letters are worth points: 2 letter words are worth 2 points, 3 letter words are worth 5 points, etc. The player with the most points wins. (Although a player may have fewer words, he/she could win the game by being long-worded.) Note: This game can be played for only a brief period of time by players who are prone to motion sickness.

FOR ALL AGES:

BINGO - This is the only game that you have to prepare for ahead of time. Make up bingo-type cards for each child. Cards for younger children can have pictures of things kids would typically see on their drive (although this depends on where you are traveling, of course): a blue car, McDonalds, a cow, a pine tree, etc. Cards for older children can have pictures, signs, license plates, and/or words that they would typically see on their drive: exit, stop, a traffic light, curvy road ahead, etc. Use magazines, newspapers, etc., and glue the pictures and words onto posterboard, one card per child. Tip: Have your kids help you prepare the cards as it's a fun project. Use raisins or M&M's as markers and when your child has bingo (or has seen a certain number of objects on his card), he can eat his reward. For those parents who intend to use the bingo boards more than once, "laminate" them with contact paper or clear packing tape. Put small pieces of velcro on a part of each picture or sign on the card and make (non-edible) markers that have the other part of velcro on them. (This will keep markers from sliding off the cards during sudden turns!) Keep the cards and markers together in a plastic baggy in the car.

20 QUESTIONS - This time-honored game has many variations. (Our version is usually called 40 Questions.) The basic rules are for one player to think of a well-known person, or at least someone well-known to your children, and for other players to ask questions about the person to try to find out his/her identity. Only yes or no answers can be given. Whoever figures out the mystery person, in 20 questions or less, wins. Tip: Encourage players to ask general questions first to narrow down the field. (Inevitably, my youngest one's first question was, "Is it George Washington?") Teach them to ask, for instance: "Is it a man?"; "Is he alive?"; "Is he real?"; "Is he a cartoon?"; "Is he on T.V.?"; "Is he an historical figure?"; "Is it someone I know personally?" You get the picture. For a variation of the game, think of an object instead of a person. (Tip: Tell the others players first, though, about the switch in subject matter.)

3 THINGS IN COMMON - This is a great thinking game that is easily adaptable for kids of all ages. One person names 3 words (or things) that have something in common. Everyone else takes turns guessing what that something is. Examples for younger children: #1) sky, ocean, grandpa's eyes (or whomever). Answer: Things that are blue. #2) stop sign, fire truck, Santa's suit. Answer: Things that are red. Examples for older kids and adults: #1) house, butter, horse. Answer: Things that have the word fly at the end of them. #2) chain, missing, sausage. Answer: Things that can end with the word "link." #3) tiger, nurse, sand. Answer: Kinds of sharks.

I'M GOING ON A PICNIC . . . - This game tests a player's abilities to remember things and remember them in order. Player 1 starts with the words, "I'm going on a picnic" and then adds a one-word item that he will bring. The next player starts with the same phrase, repeats player 1's item, and then adds another item, and so on. Play continues until one of the players can't remember the list of things, in order, to bring on a picnic. Example: Player 1 says, "I'm going on a picnic and I am going to bring a ball." Player 2 says, "I'm going on a picnic and I'm going to bring a ball and a kite." Variations of the game include adding items in alphabetical order or adding items beginning with the same letter.

THE PERSON NEXT TO US - Driving on the road, you glance at someone in the car next to you. Who is he? What kind of job does she have? Is he married? What are her hobbies? Where is he going, and why? Kids (and adults) can give a made-up answer to these, and an almost endless array of other questions. Include reasons in your response, such as "That man is a golfer because he has a good tan." I like playing this game at airports, too, albeit more quietly, while watching people disembark, especially those who are greeted by someone.

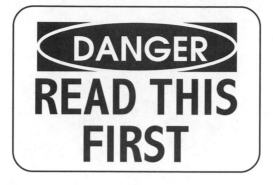

PLEASE be aware that although the facts recorded in this book are accurate and current as of April, 2014:

• HOURS CHANGE!
• EXHIBITS ROTATE!
• ADMISSION COSTS ARE RAISED WITHOUT FANFARE!
• PLACES CLOSE, EITHER TEMPORARILY OR PERMANENTLY!

To avoid any unexpected (and unpleasant) surprises:

Always, ALWAYS, *ALWAYS*
CALL BEFORE YOU VISIT AN ATTRACTION!!!

LOS ANGELES COUNTY

Ciudad de Los Angeles; City of Los Angeles; "City of Angels": This international city of Mexican heritage is one of extremes with its concrete jungles, acres of parkland, pockets of poverty, and renown cultural meccas. Almost 10 million people live in this county, which is a sprawling metropolis that encompasses the glitz of Hollywood, the incredible wealth of Beverly Hills, the quirkiness of Venice, the beach-city attitudes of Manhattan Beach and Malibu, the charm of Pasadena, the deserts of Lancaster, and the daily living of families in every community.

Brave the freeways to reach mainstream attractions such as Universal Studios Hollywood, California Science Center, Aquarium of the Pacific, Huntington Library, Magic Mountain, and the Music Center, as well as the numerous "smaller" jewels that make L.A. a gem of a place to visit.

—AMUSEMENT PARKS—

BUCCANEER BAY - SPLASH! LA MIRADA AQUATICS CENTER

(562) 902-3191 / www.splashlamirada.com
13806 La Mirada Boulevard, La Mirada

Arrgh - calling all scallywags (and non-scallywags) to come play and get wet at the family-friendly Buccaneer Bay. Piratey-themed, this clean and lovely small water park has three body slides (no raft slides) which riders must be 48". One is enclosed, short, straight, and very fast; another is longer and mostly enclosed; and the third is open, twisty, and meanders downward at a slower speed. Catch the gentle current at the circular river and grab an inner tube to float in it if you want. This river also has fountains on the side to get you extra wet and buckets overhead that fill up and pour over on floaters at random times.

A good-sized and colorful kiddie water playground makes up a third of the water park. Here, in zero depth waters, young ones (47" and under) can zip down several short slides, climb on the cargo nets, and squirt and play on the play equipment. And watch out below - the huge pirate's head on top of the play structure fills up with water and tips over, gushing down tons of water. Free life vests are available. An adjacent sprayground has water shooting up from the ground and raining down from above, as well as large tubs of water on short stands for kids to play with toy boats.

Splash! has two adjacent, swimming pools which are part of the La Mirada Aquatics Center. Open year round, one pool is for team competitions (swimming and water polo) and the other is for recreational swim (and lap swim, at times), so it is open to Buccaneer Bay attendees to also splash around and even shoot some hoops at the water basketball net.

Attractively landscaped, the water park is surrounded by rolling grassy hills and lawn dotted with palm trees. Ahoy mateys! Kids definitely enjoy playing in and on the landlocked, cutaway, large, wooden pirate ship and on the boulders that are designed to look like a skull. The skull has caves carved inside it, which are actually the eyeballs of the skull. Adults are invited to unwind in the fenced in hot tub.

No outside food/drinks (except bottled water) are allowed in, but the on-site snack bar offers an array of tasty food such as a cheeseburger ($4.95), grilled chicken sandwich ($6.95), and personal cheese pizza ($5.95), plus funnel cake and shaved ice. There are plenty of tables and chairs, lounge chairs, umbrellas, and nice, private cabanas for pool side relaxing. Music plays in the background. There is a small store here if you forget a bathing suit, sunscreen, or other sundries.

Note that nearby amenities include a park (see LA MIRADA REGIONAL PARK, pg. 69), a gymnasium, and a library.

Hours: Buccaneer Bay is open the end of May through mid-June and the month of September, Sat. - Sun., 10:30am - 5:30pm. Open daily, mid-June through Labor Day, 10:30am - 5:30pm. Recreational swim is open most of the year, Sat. - Sun. from noon - 5pm. It's open mid-June through Labor Day, Mon. - Fri., 1pm - 4pm; Sat. - Sun., noon - 4pm.

Price: Buccaneer Bay is $18.95 for adults; $13.95 for seniors and kids 47" and under; children 2 and under are free. After 3pm, tickets are $13.95 for everyone. Splash! recreational swimming is $3 for adults; $2 for ages 3 - 12. Annual passes are available for both places. Parking is free.

Ages: 2 years and up.

DRY TOWN WATER PARK AND MINING CO. - PALMDALE OASIS PARK AND RECREATION CENTER

(661) 267-6161 - water park; (661) 267-5100 - parks and rec / www.cityofpalmdale.org
3850-B East Avenue S, Palmdale

Is that a mirage? No, it really is a water park out here in the desert, surrounded by mountains! Mosey on beyond the weathered buildings grouped together to look like an Old West town (but with prettier landscaping) into the mid-sized water park. Note that a real, modern-day sheriff is always on duty here. Grab a tube and go down the three tube slides that jut out of a thirty-five-foot-high slide tower. Spin around (and around) on one of them, a vortex-like slide called the Devil's Punch Bowl, until you drop into the splash pool. Shoot down Dusty's Mineshaft Racer, a four-lane slide with mats. Take a ride in the circular, lazy river. Little Miners Camp is a children's water playground, ideal for youngsters to splash and play on the slides and colorful apparatus. Umbrella sprays, cargo nets, water hoses, and large water rings that shoot out water to walk through, plus a huge bucket that fills up with water and then tips over drenching those below, await here, too. Life jackets and tubes are available free of charge. Drier choices include a few arcade games, lounging areas, or indulging in a food break utilizing the concession stands. Locker rentals are $5. As always at water parks, wear water shoes of some kind as the pavement can get really hot.

The adjacent Oasis Park has a regulation competition swimming pool that is open year round. It also has a grassy area to let kids run (relatively) wild and a basin that is ideal for soccer and football. The recreation center has a gym with open play and a youth room with a large screen TV, foosball, ping pong, air hockey, basketball court, and other games.

Hours: The water park is open Memorial weekend through the end of August daily, 11am - 6pm. It is open the end of August through mid-September, weekends only, 11am - 6pm. It is open certain Fri. nights, 6:30pm - 9:30pm, too. Oasis Park is open daily. Call for pool hours.

Price: The water park, for Palmdale residents, is $16 for 48" and taller; $12 for seniors and kids 47" and under; children 2 and under are free. Admission for nonresidents is $21 for 48" and taller; $15 for seniors and kids. Discounts are offered for active military. Ask about twilight rates ($3 - $5 cheaper) offered during the week from 3:30pm - 6pm. Parking is free. The Oasis Park is free. The swimming pool at Oasis cost is about $2 per person.

Ages: 18 months and up.

PACIFIC PARK

(310) 260-8744 / www.pacpark.com - amusement park; www.smgov.net - parking
380 Santa Monica Pier, Santa Monica

The major kid-attraction on the Santa Monica pier is Pacific Park with its twelve family-oriented amusement rides, including six kiddie rides, that are all clustered tightly together. The rides include a huge Ferris wheel (130 feet high!), which gives a great view at the top for miles around; an historic carousel (with horses, camels, and lions); a roller coaster; spinning bumper cars; a pirate ship and a sea dragon that both swing back and forth like giant pendulums; Pacific Plunge, which launches riders forty-five-feet into the air over the ocean (at least a portion of it) before it drops; a scrambler; little sea planes; and a submarine ride for young sailors. A rock climbing wall, a mini bungee ride, and Gyro Loops (a 360-degree rotating ride/attraction) are also available. Lots of carnival-style and midway games are here, as are plenty of arcade games.

If your belly starts rumbling, grab a bite at oceanfront restaurants, snack bars, or ice cream shops. See SANTA MONICA PIER (pg. 160) for details about the pier and its other attractions.

Hours: All rides and games are up and running the end of May through Labor Day, Sun. - Thurs., 11am - 11pm (usually); Fri. - Sat., 11am - 12:20am. The rest of the year the hours fluctuate. Usually, a few rides, plus the Ferris wheel and some games, are operational during the week, noon - 7pm. Everything is open Fri., 6pm - midnight; Sat., 11am - midnight; Sun., 11am - 9pm. Call or check the website first!

Price: Individual rides cost $3 for the kiddie rides; $5 for the bigger kids' rides, each. An all-day rides wristband is $22.95 for 8 years and up; $15.95 for 7 years and under. Check online for discounts. AAA members and active military personnel receive discounts. Parking on or right next to the pier is $8 during the week; $15 on weekends. There is very limited metered street parking nearby.

Ages: 2 years and up.

RAGING WATERS

(909) 802-2200 / www.ragingwaters.com
111 Raging Waters Drive, San Dimas

What a cool place to be on a hot day! Raging Waters is out*rage*ous with its fifty acres of chutes, quarter-mile-long white-water rapids, slides, drops, enclosed tubes (which make these slides dark and scary), a wave pool, lagoons, and sandy beaches. The rides run the gamut from a peaceful, quarter-mile river raft ride in only three feet of water to the ultimate for daredevils, such as descending into Dr. Von Dark's Tunnel of Terror with its forty-foot drop, vertical banks, and 360° spins, all in total darkness. Or, plunge headfirst on High Extreme, a 600-foot ride off a 100-foot tower. Free fall off the Wedge where a feeling of near-zero gravity is terrifyingly fun. (I guess.) Jump in your tube and drop down Dragon's Den, a ten-story-high, twisting, enclosed flume that spins you around a gigantic bowl. Race against seven others in the huge slide (with bumps) of Raging Racer. Ride high and try your boogie boarding best at the waves from the Flow Rider wave machine and at the Wave Cove, where water surges and swells into waves every ten minutes, or so. There is even a small beach here.

The younger set reigns at the huge Kids Kingdom as they splash around in this water area designed just for them.

It has a big water play structure to climb on that shoots out water, plus tyke-size water slides, a maze of tubes and tunnels, showers under waterfalls, and a tire swing. The Little Dipper lagoon is also for youngsters, 48" and under, with its wading pools, shooting fountains, and waterfalls. Elementary-school-aged kids have their own, separate, fantastic, activity pool with slides, a ropes course, and Splash Island Adventure. The tropical-themed Island is a five-story treehouse with slides, water cannons, cargo nets, swinging bridges, and a huge bucket on top that spills over gallons of water. Holy smoke! The Volcano Fantasea is a smoking volcano with several enclosed slides oozing down its sides into hip-deep water and more water activities. For a challenge, use an overhead rope for balance while trying to cross a pool length on foam pads.

Life vests are available at no extra charge. Locker rentals are available, too. A picnic area is available just outside the main entrance gate. Outside food is not allowed inside, but there are several food outlets throughout the park. Hot tip: Wear water shoes, or sandals, because the walkways get very hot.

Hours: Open mid-May to mid-June and the first few weeks in September on weekends and holiday Mondays, 10am - 5pm or 6pm. Open mid-June through Labor Day, Mon. - Fri., 10am - 6pm or 7pm; Sat. - Sun., 10am - 7:30pm. Call first as hours fluctuate.

Price: $38.99 for 48" and taller; $28.99 for seniors and 47" and under; children 2 and under are free. Purchase season passes by May and save $'s, or purchase tickets online. Parking is $15.

Ages: 1½ years and up.

SIX FLAGS HURRICANE HARBOR

(661) 255-4111 or (818) 367-5965 / www.sixflags.com
26101 Magic Mountain Parkway, Valencia

This twenty-five-acre and twenty-three-slide water park is awash with amphibious fun set in a jungle and lagoons of a forgotten world. Older kids enjoy the thrill of the vertical drops, speed slides, body slides, open tube rides, and two of the tallest enclosed speed slides this side of the Mississippi. Stand in one of six upright launching tubes in Bonzai. Then, as the bottoms drop out, you'll experience a fifty-foot free fall in clear tubing, and then an additional 200 feet (!) in enclosed tubes (i.e. darkness), including twists and turns and a 360 loop. Taboo Tower, with its multiple slides, is sixty-five-feet high!! Reptile Ridge is another tower complex with five scary slides slithering from it. Tornado might just feel like the real deal with a seventy-five-foot drop through a huge opening of a 132-foot tunnel/funnel. Bamboo Racer pits six contestants against each other as they race down the slides into the water. The wave pool, with two-foot waves, is a hit for those practicing surfing techniques. A five-person raft ride is fun without being too scary, and the lazy, looping river ride in only three feet of water is great for everyone in the family. If you want to avoid some waiting in line, purchase a Flash Pass which saves your place, virtually, in line so you can play elsewhere and be line when the pass indicates its your time.

Relax in lounge chairs while your younger children play in Castaway Cove, a shallow pool with mini-slides, cement aquatic creatures, and a wonderful, fortress-like water play structure with waterfalls, swings, water-spurting gadgets, and more. Kids not only get a cove to call their own, but they get their own island at Splash Island. With rain curtains, slides, squirting fountains and water play platforms, they can happily play here all day. An activity pool, Lizard Lagoon, is great for swimming, plus it has a net for water volleyball and, of course, it also has several slides. Forgotten Sea Wave Pool has gentle waves to ride or just bob along. Check out the dive-in movies, too.

Food is available to purchase inside the Harbor as outside food is not allowed in. Hot tip: Wear water shoes, or sandals, as the walkways get very hot. Note: The Harbor shares the same parking lot as Magic Mountain.

Hours: Open Memorial Day to mid-June and in September on weekends only, 10:30am - 6pm. Open mid-June through Labor Day daily, 10am - 6pm or 7pm. Open weekends in July until 8pm. Hours vary a lot so check the calendar website or call first.

Price: $39.99 for 48" and taller; $31.99 for kids 47" and under; children 2 and under are free. Online tickets are discounted and season passes are a great deal. The Flash Pass is an additional $15. Parking is $20. Combo tickets for Hurricane Harbor and Magic Mountain are available.

Ages: 1½ years and up.

SIX FLAGS MAGIC MOUNTAIN

(661) 255-4111 or (818) 367-5965 / www.sixflags.com
26101 Magic Mountain Parkway, Valencia

Thrill seekers and/or roller-coaster aficionados consider action-packed Magic Mountain the most daring place to go with its more than forty-five rides and attractions geared mostly for kids 8 years and older. Nineteen roller coasters here range from the classic, wooden Colossus, to some of the world's tallest and fastest rides including Goliath, which is a 255-foot drop and Superman, which zips you 100 mph in seven seconds and then reverses the direction so mere humans zoom backwards! I was yelling for Superman at this point - the hero, not the ride. Lex Luthor: Drop of Doom is currently the world's tallest vertical drop with a 400-foot tower. Full Throttle is the world's tallest and fastest looping coaster. Scream is a floorless coaster that has a 150-foot initial drop, seven loops, and a top speed of 65 mph where riders, yes - scream. Ride the ultimate - Tatsu, with four inversions, zero gravity rolls, sharp dives, and more - all in one ride. This extreme theme park also boasts Deja Vu, a suspended coaster ride that plummets riders down a hill and, with a boomerang-style turn, back up. Riders are going forward and backward, so they don't know if they are coming or going! X2, yet another ripping coaster ride, spins its vehicles (360 degrees forward, backwards, and head-over-heels) independently of one another with sound and fire effects while going along the tracks. Green Lantern is the first vertical spinning coaster (with three 360-degree turns) in the U.S. And then there is Batman, one of the most popular rides as it combines more thrills and turns and loops than any Gotham City citizen can withstand. My stomach and I prefer to just watch some of these rides and not actually participate. If you don't want to wait in line, purchase a Flash Pass, which allows you to come back and board rides at a prescheduled time.

Other highlights here include the Log Ride, Jet Stream, and Tidal Wave (all very wet rides); bumper cars; Buccaneer, a swinging (like a pendulum) pirate ship for mateys to ride; Cyclone 500 for drivers to race around on a track; a raft ride (you will get wet); and scrambler. The Sky Tower is a "must-do" for all ages because it affords a 360-degree view of the park and the surrounding area.

A visit to Bugs Bunny World is ideal for the younger crowd, ages 2 to 8 years. Looney Tunes and Justice League characters are often here for hugs and pictures. The rides include a pint-size free fall, train ride, truck ride, balloon ride, pirate ship, Merrie Melodies carousel, four roller coasters (of course), and Tweety's Escape, which is a ride in an oversized bird cage. Another high-ranking attraction in this section is the Looney Tunes Lodge, a two-story funhouse. Visitors in here use cannons and other creative gadgets to shoot, drop, or hurl hundreds of foam balls through the air at one another. To complete this world is a fountain area where Looney Tunes statues spew out water.

Cyclone Bay is toward the back of the park, where specialty shops are the specialty. Cartoon Candy Company is an especially sweet stop as kids can watch fudge, caramel apples, and all sorts of mouth-watering delights being made before their very eyes. If it's real food that you're hankering for, try Mooseburger Lodge. In a forest-like setting, waiters and waitresses sometimes sing, a moose talks, and the dessert - chocolate "moose" - is served in an edible chocolate shell.

Although there are lots of grassy, shady areas to rest, Magic Mountain is spacious and hilly, so wear walking shoes. Believe it or not, educational field trips are offered here, such as Math & Science Day that focuses quite a bit on physics. Tip: Visit this Mountain on a Monday or Tuesday, if possible, as it is normally less crowded then. Note: If you want wet, summertime fun, check out SIX FLAGS HURRICANE HARBOR (pg. 4), which is right next door to Magic Mountain.

Hours: Open April through October daily, 10:30am - 6pm. Call for extended summer hours, usually 10:30am - 10pm, or later. Open the rest of the year weekends and holidays only, 10:30am - 8pm or 10pm. Definitely check the website calendar as hours fluctuate a lot.

Price: $67.99 for 48" and taller; $42.99 for kids 47" and under; children 2 and under are free. Discounts available through AAA and online. A Flash Pass, which allows priority boarding opportunities, costs $40 - $95, depending on the day and level of your pass, plus the price of an admission ticket. Parking is $20. Combo tickets for Magic Mountain and Hurricane Harbor are available.

Ages: 1½ years and up.

UNIVERSAL STUDIOS HOLLYWOOD

(800) UNIVERSAL (864-8377) or (818) 622-3750 / www.universalstudioshollywood.com

$$$$$

100 Universal City Plaza, Universal City

This huge, unique, Hollywood-themed amusement park is really one of the world's biggest and busiest motion picture and television studios. My personal advice is to go on the 50-minute, guided studio tram tour first, as lines get long later on. Each tram on the tour is outfitted with monitors that show numerous film clips, as well as how various sets and sound stages have been used in productions over the years. You'll go behind the scenes and through several of Hollywood's original and most famous backlots including Courthouse Square, Western facades, little Europe, and the set for *Desperate Housewives*. You'll also learn about the shows currently being filmed at Universal and see sound stages and lots of props, including parts of the town from *The Grinch* and the real (completely wrecked) airplane and detailed scene of devastation caused by the plane crash in *War of the Worlds*. Some of the elaborate special effects that you'll encounter along the way are furious dinosaurs attacking King Kong in enormous 3-D; the shark from *Jaws*; an earthquake in a subway station, where buildings collapse and a run-away big-rig crashes within inches of you, followed by fire and a flood coming toward you; an encounter with the undead from scenes of *The Mummy;* and a flash flood. Some of it can get a bit overwhelming for younger kids.

On an eight-passenger *Simpsons* ride the characters join you (kind of, as they are on screen) to experience an almost out-of-control roller-coasterish ride through Krustyland and, just like the TV show (characters voices and all), encounter wacky happenings, plus 4-D effects and the sensation of being immersed in the surroundings. Enjoy the building facades of the neighborhood of *Despicable Me* and then - put your goggles on and go on the 3-D motion simulator ride *Despicable Me: Minion Mayhem*, complete with super-villain, Gru, and his girls. Riders, or minions as they are now known, cruise and swerve through Gru's laboratory and then go through a minion training mission. Afterward (or before), play at the adjacent Super Silly Fun Land, a water play area with squirting fountains, splash pools, and huge buckets of water that overturn on unsuspecting guests. You will get wet. Tip: Bring a change of clothing. There is also a dry play area here where youngsters can climb on cargo nets, slide, and jump around, plus a themed ride with vehicles that spin and transport riders in the sky for a bird's eye view of Fun Land.

You can (or not) walk through the House of Horrors castle, a dimly lit labyrinth featuring original props with moving scarabs, a "waterfall" of scorpions, carnival-type mirrors, and real people in costume - Frankenstein, Wolf Man, and Chucky - that jump out to scare you. This attraction is not for the faint-hearted.

The Wizarding World of Harry Potter, featuring a replica of the Hogwarts Castle and the Forbidden Journey ride, is coming 2016(ish). The preshow queue, which will be an important component of the ride, will meander through the dungeon and the greenhouse, past the gallery of portraits (which will be entertaining), to a hologram of Dumbledore and then an audience-engaging conversation with Harry, Ron, and Hermoine. Then, onto the 3-D ride on which you'll move with the characters, becoming part of the action of soaring over the castle, playing a Quidditch match, evading an attack of a dragon, and sparring with the Dementors. A Central Park, on a much smaller scale than New York's, is also on the way that will be a landscaped resting area and a play area for kids.

Take the Starway (i.e., a really long escalator) to the lower lot where, if you are at least 46" tall, you can enter through the gates of Jurassic Park to river raft through the primordial forest. It starts off as a peaceful ride, but it ends up as a very wet, terrifying, face-to-face encounter with bellowing dinosaurs! You will get drenched. Ponchos are available for purchase at a nearby vending machine. Note that this ride has a single rider line which is usually faster than the regular line. The very short *Revenge of the Mummy* ride hurtles thrill-seeking passengers through dark (and cold!) Egyptian chambers and passageways as a ceiling of flame, skeleton warriors, and other ghoulish robotic figures, a few pyrotechnics, and laser images seek to terrify. The roller coaster ride also goes backwards for a brief duration. Be on the lookout for the Egyptian-dressed guys and females on stilts that walk around this ride area and scare unsuspecting people - fun to watch. Fight alongside Optimus on the 3-D *Transformers* ride, based on the movies. Your car jerks forward and back and up and down, as the mega sensory and special effects battle with gigantic animatronic robots that fight loudly play out all around you: It could be a transforming experience. Note: A parent who waits with a younger child while the other adult goes on the ride can then go to the front of the line instead of waiting in the line again. The nearby NBC Universal Experience room holds rotating exhibits of authentic props and wardrobe from past and present movies, including the DeLorean used in *Back to the Future*.

As the name Universal Studios is synonymous with quality productions, the live shows here are entertaining and highlighted with special effects. Animal Actors employ a lot of laugh-out-loud humor with a variety of well-trained animals including dogs, birds, cats, guinea pigs, ducks, and more. *Waterworld*, the "coolest" production here, and truly a favorite, has explosive stunts and special effects that blow you out of the water. The Special Effects Stage show reveals how sleight-of-sight effects were created and used in various Universal movies. See behind-the-camera work here with computer graphics and green screen technology, as well as the art of sound effects, and be a part of the half-hour show through audience participation. In a castle-like building, *Shrek* 4-D plays; a fifteen-minute animated show with the cast of *Shrek* that incorporates quite a few special effects to keep participants really feeling a part of the production, right down to the shaking and rocking theater seats. (Some stationary seats are available.)

Get an early start for your adventure at Universal Studios, and don't forget to bring your camera for some wonderful photo opportunities, especially with the many costumed characters around the park. If time is of the essence, or you don't like waiting, purchase a Front of the Line passe that allows guests to go to the front of line one time for each ride/attraction, plus priority and reserved seating at the shows. Lines that can take an hour, or more on busy days, can take only five minutes with this pass. Another speciality is the VIP Experience, which includes breakfast and lunch; exclusive back lot access, such as actually walking around sound stages and sets closed to the public; unlimited front of the line access to all rides and attractions; a personal tour guide; and more. Check out the adjacent

UNIVERSAL CITYWALK (pg. 175) for unusual shopping and dining experiences.

Hours: Open every day of the year. Open the majority of the year daily, 10am - 6pm. Summer and some holiday hours are usually Mon. - Fri., 9am - 9pm; Sat. - Sun., 9am - 10pm. Call for the day of your visit as hours fluctuate a lot. Tours are available at times in Spanish and Mandarin.

Price: $84 for 48" and taller; $76 for 47" and under; children 2 and under are free. Certain discounts available through AAA. Always check online, too, as many specials are offered. Front of the Line passes are $149 - $169, depending on the season. The VIP Experience is $349 per person. Annual passes are a really good deal here and sometimes Universal offers buy-a-day, get-a-year-free deal. Parking is $16; $10 after 3pm. Or, park near the Universal Station (www.metro.net) at 3913 Lankershim Blvd. (note that there are 773 free parking spaces there), cross the street, then take a free shuttle up to Universal Studios, saving driving time and a parking fee.

Ages: 3 years and up.

—ARTS AND CRAFTS—

AUNTIES CERAMICS

(626) 339-8916

116 E. Badillo Street, suite B, Covina

Create a unique gift at this ceramic art painting studio that stocks frames, holiday decorations, sports items, figurines, plates, refrigerator magnets, and more. Paints, brushes, stencils, and even design guidance, are included in the cost of your bisque piece. Aunties also offers classes on cleaning and painting greenware, and on painting porcelain dolls.

Hours: Open Mon. - Thurs., 10am - 5pm; Sat., 10am - 2pm. Closed Sun. and Fri.

Price: $5 per person to paint, plus the price of your piece and a firing fee.

Ages: 4 years and up.

COLOR ME MINE (Los Angeles County)

Beverly Hills - (310) 247-1226; Calabasas - (818) 222-4922; Encino - (818) 784-0400; Long Beach - (562) 433-4177; Los Angeles - (310) 410-9700; Montrose - (818) 542-6644; Pasadena - (626) 298-6765; Porter Ranch - (818) 363-8855; Redondo Beach - (310) 406-3068; Santa Monica - (310) 393-0069; Studio City - (818) 762-4434; Torrance - (310) 325-9968; Valencia - (661) 799-9266; Whittier - (562) 789-5600 / www.colormemine.com

Beverly Hills - 233 South Beverly Dr.; Calabasas - 23641 Calabasas Rd. at Courtyard Calabasas shopping center; Encino - 16350 Ventura Blvd., #B; Long Beach - 5269 East 2nd Str.; Los Angeles - 6081 Center Dr., #219 in the Howard Hughes Promenade; Montrose - 2280 Honolulu Ave.; Pasadena - 81 S. Fair Oaks Ave.; Porter Ranch - 19839 Rinaldi St.; Redondo Beach - 1509 Hawthorne Blvd. #105, in the South Bay Market Place; Santa Monica - 1335 4th St.; Studio City - 12080 Ventura Pl.; Torrance - 2627 Pacific Coast Hwy. in the Rolling Hills Plaza; Valencia - 24305 Town Center Dr., suite 190 at Westfield Town Center Mall; Whittier - 6711 A Greenleaf Ave.

Do your kids have an artistic flair? Or think they do? Color Me Mine is a delightful, cozy, paint-your-own ceramic store. Kids can express themselves by first choosing their own ceramic piece and then their own palette. White dinosaurs, dolphins, mugs, plates, and much more will be transformed into vibrant works of art that will be treasured forever, or at least a while. My boys were so intent on their artistry that the hours just flew by. Warning: This recreational activity can become quite addicting! Pieces are glazed and fired, then ready to be picked up in a few days. Each store has a computer that has 25,000 drawings that can be printed out and traced. Photos and logos can be added to your items, too.

If you won't come to the party, the party will come to you. Some stores offer Party in a Box or To Go Party packages that include a ceramic or bisque item per person and paints, plus brushes and palettes on loan. Glazed pieces can be picked up at the studio about a week after the party.

Note: The Encino and San Diego stores offer glass works and mosaics. Ask about other Color Me Mine's specialty classes. Some stores offer preschool classes, plus opportunities for boy and girl scouts to earn badges. See www.colormemine.com for a listing of all locations.

Hours: Most stores are open Sun. - Thurs., 11am - 9pm; Fri. - Sat., 11am - 10pm. Call your store first as hours vary.

Price: Studio painting rates fluctuate depending on the store; most charge $10 for the day for adults and $7 for ages 10 and under. Prices for mugs and vases start at $10.
Ages: 4 years and up.

THE LONG BEACH DEPOT FOR CREATIVE REUSE

(562) 437-9999 / www.thelongbeachdepot.org
320 Elm Avenue, Long Beach

This store has bins and jars and shelves filled with corks, baby food jars, egg cartons, buttons, bottlecaps, yarn, paper, cardboard, milk jugs, string, fabric, and more to create works of art, or at least to do art projects. Educators - take note! There is also an exchange area where you can take items if you leave some in return.

Get crafty, for free, every Saturday morning from 11am to 2pm. Bring whatever art projects you want to work on, gather round the tables together and meet other creative people. Purchase whatever supplies you need, or use the free ones on the tables. Sometimes a sewing machine is available, too. Come and enjoy making new friends while making eco-friendly gifts.

Hours: The store is open Mon. - Sat., 11am - 6pm. Close Sun. and holidays.
Price: Free for the Sat. morning "class"; bring $ for the shop.
Ages: 7 years and up.

PAINT A DREAM (Los Angeles County)

Palmdale - (661) 224-2000; Valencia - (661) 255-1177 / www.paintadream.com
Palmdale - 1233 Rancho Vista Blvd., in the Antelope Valley Mall; Valencia - 24201 Valencia Blvd., in the Westfield Valencia Town Center.

Pick it, plan it, paint it - perfect! Choose from an array of ceramics such as mugs, bowls, figurines, holiday items, sports items, plates, picture frames, Disney items, and much more. Create a design or just randomly paint your keepsake. Kids love participating in making something they will keep and maybe even use, or give away as a special gift. Paints, supplies, and firing are all included in the studio fee. Your masterpiece will be ready for pick up in about five days. Paint A Dream is a ideal location for field trips, scout groups, parties or celebrations of any kind. Check the website for special classes and events, such as Kid's Night, Family Night, and Ladies' Night. Tip: As both of these studios are in malls, see the mall's websites for other things to do at them.

Hours: Palmdale - Open Mon. - Fri., 10am - 9pm; Sat., 10am - 8pm, Sun., 11am - 6pm. Valencia - Open Mon. - Sat., 10m - 9pm; Sun., 11am - 6pm.
Price: $6 studio fee, plus the cost of your item.
Ages: 4 years and up.

PAINT 'N GLAZE

(562) 421-8000 / www.paintnglaze.com
3690 Studebaker Road, Long Beach

Do your kids have that glazed look in their eye? Then bring them to Paint 'N Glaze. This paint-it-yourself ceramic store is well supplied with an array of pieces to paint, so let your creative juices flow! Choose from mugs, vases, bowls, figurines, and more. My kids sometimes choose very interesting color combinations, but that is part of what makes their pieces so special. Designing your keepsake can take time, so be prepared to spend a few hours here. The studio price includes all of your paints, brushes, and stencils. Ask about summer classes and Parent's Night Out where kids can come and eat, paint a piece, and watch a movie while you and your beloved enjoy a night out.

Hours: Open Tues. - Thurs., 11am - 8pm; Fri. - Sat., 10am - 10pm; Sun., noon - 6pm. Closed Mon. and holidays.
Price: $8 per person studio fee, plus the cost of your product.
Ages: 4 years and up.

PAINT 'N' PLAY ART STUDIO

(626) 256-4848 / www.paintnplay2.com
418 S. Myrtle Avenue, Monrovia

This funky, contemporary art studio offers something for every artistic bent. It is also very kid-friendly. Shelves of boring, white ceramics are waiting to become vibrant, colorful masterpieces at the touch of a paintbrush (and some paint). The room goes back surprisingly far with tables that are set with paint-splattered cloths. A separate party area is toward the back. Choose from a large variety of pieces such as mugs, plates, vases, statues, coin banks, cookie jars, and novelty items. Paint, smocks, and help from the friendly staff are included in your price. Stencils, rubber stamps, and a design center are available to assist the artistically challenged.

Paint 'N' Play also offers classes for learning oil painting, working a potter's wheel, and sculpting with clay. Inquire about Mommy and Me workshops, school field trips, Girl Scout badge-earning programs, and other specialty events. The studio also offers To-Go kits and/or will come to your venue with all the supplies needed for a painting party. Note that the studio is located in Old Towne, so there are numerous fun shops to investigate. The Krikorian Theater is just four doors down, as well.

Hours: Open Tues. - Thurs., noon - 7pm; Fri., noon - 9pm; Sat. - Sun., noon - 7:30pm. Closed Mon. and holidays.

Price: There isn't a studio fee. The cost is the price of the piece, which start at about $16, plus about $6 for glaze. Acrylic-painted items may be taken home that day.

Ages: 4 years and up.

REDISCOVER

(310) 393-3636 / www.rediscovercenter.org
12958 W. Washington Boulevard, Los Angeles

Part warehouse, part studio, part lab - ReDiscover supplies the raw materials and kids supply the creativity. Bins and bins and shelves and shelves and walls are filled with recycled and reusable goods - cardboard, rubber bands, tubes, ribbon, pipe cleaners, tile pieces, beads, spools, tote bags, electronic components, jars, fabric, cork stoppers, buttons, doohickeys, thingamajigs and so much more! Beyond a place to do a craft project, although there is that element, ReDiscover the materials and support staff to make some pretty cool projects like making rope sandals, kites, ball runs, puzzles, games and contraptions of all sorts. Kids can also construct wood-making projects with usage of hammers, drills, nails and tools to make them, such as picture frames and go karts.

Youths - 2 to 18 - are invited to participate in school programs, field trips, drop-in workshops, free community events, and day camps. The Tinkering School camp is where big projects are put together - it's like having all the equipment in a well-stocked carpenter's garage at your fingertips. Educational programs can be adapted to any curriculum. Samples topics include Simple Machines, Life Cycles, Home and Habitat, and Music. Adults can get in on the action, too, with educators' workshops and Open Studio time. Open Studio is the time to come, design, explore and implement.

Hours: The warehouse is open for shopping and for Open Studio every Sat., 11am - 5pm.

Price: About $5 per person, per project. Field trips are about $175 per class of 25 students.

Ages: 4 years and up.

TRASH FOR TEACHING

(310) 527-7080 / www.trashforteaching.org
12815 S. Western Avenue, Gardena

This big, green (of course) building is where the saying, "One man's trash is another man's treasure" comes into play. The "trash" in this warehouse is huge bins and bins and more bins filled with all sorts of recyclable items and manufactured overruns or defects from over 200 companies that you get to recreate into art, or a project of some kind. Check out what their walls and partitions are made of - they practice what they preach. I love their mottos: "minimizing waster; maximizing education" and "filling minds instead of landfills". Not only does the company work with schools, but they offer any group or individual help in learning technology, physics, and to have fun by repurposing. They also host field trips, teacher training courses, corporate events and birthday parties. Every Sunday, 1:30am to 4:30pm, is a Spontaneous Creations Family Workshop with large scale and smaller scale projects to be undertaken and worked at on site. Essentially, it's a free-for-all creating time.

Hours: The warehouse is open Wed., 9am - 4pm; Sat., 9am - noon; Sun., 1:30pm - 4:30pm, or by appointment.

Price: The price of your materials - $2 a pound. Sunday family workshops are suggested donations of $5 per creator or $10 per family, which includes materials.

Ages: 3 years and up.

—BEACHES—

BELMONT SHORE BEACH or LONG BEACH CITY BEACH / BAYSHORE PLAYGROUND

(562) 570-3100 or (562) 570-3170 - beach; (562) 570-1715 - Bayshore Playground / www.longbeach.gov; www.beachcalifornia.com

15 39ᵗʰ Place, along Ocean Boulevard (off Livingston Dr.), Long Beach

This very long and fairly wide expanse of beach hugs the shoreline of the Pacific Ocean, with plenty of places to play, swim, and ride bikes along the paved pathway. (See pg. 209 for info on the bike trail). Along with the sand, there are lots of volleyball nets, a few palm trees, a specific dog zone (watch where you step), and Belmont Veterans Memorial Pier, featuring a place for fishing (no license required), a bait and tackle shop, a snack shop and an Aqua-link stop. (For just a few dollars, take the aqua-link, a.k.a. water taxi, around the waters, up to the Queen Mary and Shoreline Village.) Parking at the pier is $1 an hour; $10 max. Adjacent to the pier is an indoor, Olympic-size pool with stadium seating. There is also an outdoor pool at Belmont Plaza, a few beach-side restaurants next door, and tons of places to shop and eat just up the street.

South of the pier, starting around Bay Shore Avenue, is Bayshore Playground, Alamitos Bay Beach, and Peninsula Beach, which all interconnect. The small and popular Alamitos Bay Beach strip hugs the harbor near the yacht club and it has waveless waters, but check out the water quality. A small, enclosed playground at 14 54th Place has a few swings, slides, and talking tubes, plus an adjacent basketball court, roller hockey rink, racquetball court, and cement picnic tables under shade trees. Note: This is where Gondola Getaway (see pg. 210) is located.

> **Hours:** Open daily, 5am - 10pm.
> **Price:** Free
> **Ages:** All

CABRILLO BEACH

(310) 548-2645 or (310) 548-7554 / www.sanpedro.com

3720 Stephen M White Drive, San Pedro

This sometimes windy beach has a gated entrance, wonderfully wide sandy expanses, picnic tables, grass areas, barbecue pits, volleyball nets, and fire rings. It has a playground, too, with slides, climbing apparatus, swings, and a rock-like climbing structure. Beyond the breakwater is ocean surf; inside the breakwater is a gentle harbor. Check the water quality first at (800) 432-5229 or www.healthebay.org, as this beach has had a history of problems.

A paved, wheelchair-accessible trail runs from the parking lot across the beach to the water's edge at the tidepools. On wheels or by feet, take the sidewalk along the water to go out onto the rather long cement fishing pier. (Bring your own pole.) Although daring visitors walk the almost two miles on the rock jetty to the little lighthouse at the end, this is not advised. On the west beach, which is like a private little beach, you may hike the Cabrillo Coastal Park Trail that hugs the coastline. The trail, which is paved for a bit and then turns into a dirt pathway, dead ends at a gate barring entrance into Point Fermin Park.

See CABRILLO MARINE AQUARIUM (pg. 218), as this great, mid-size aquarium is adjacent to the beach (and it's inexpensive!). Ask about the seasonal grunion runs.

> **Hours:** Open daily, 5am - 10pm.
> **Price:** Parking is $1 an hour; $9 max, cash only. If you get here early enough, you can park for free on the street.
> **Ages:** All

COLORADO LAGOON

(562) 570-3215 / www.longbeach.gov

5119 E. Colorado Street & E. Appian Way, Long Beach

This half-mile stretch of lagoon water is fed through a large pipe from the ocean. The water quality is tested daily and usually deemed good, except after rain. Kids can swim the length of the lagoon, or a much shorter distance across it, from shore to shore. They can also jump off a wooden dock that spans across the water. Just beyond the sandy beach area is a grassy area. A playground, featuring a large plastic boat with slides and climbing apparatus, is shaded by a canopy. A few scattered picnic tables, shade trees, and barbecue pits make this an ideal location for a picnic.

Although the lagoon has residential quarters with a fairly busy street on one side of it, and a golf course on the other, we found it to be a relatively quiet place to spend the day. Lifeguards are on duty daily, mid-June through mid-September. See the Calendar entry (pg. 10) for information on the Colorado Lagoon Model Boat Shop for a first-rate, boat-building opportunity that's available only in the summer.

Hours: Open daily, 8am - dusk.
Price: Free
Ages: All

LEO CARRILLO STATE PARK AND STATE BEACH

(805) 488-1827 or (818) 880-0363 - beach; (800) 444-7275 - camping reservations / www.parks.ca.gov
35000 Pacific Coast Highway, Malibu

$$$$$

Leo Carrillo combines the best of everything that's enjoyable about the beach - a beautiful, sandy beach; good swimming and surfing; a few sea caves to carefully explore; lots of rocky points and rocks littering the beach; rich and fairly large tidepools; and lifeguards, seasonally. Camping near the beach (campsites are a five-minute walk from the beach, under the freeway) makes this one of our favorite campgrounds. Each campsite has a fire pit and picnic table, and usually an oak tree and some bushes at the perimeter. Some sites are creek side. Pack a sweater, even in the summer!

Hours: Open daily, 7am - 10pm.
Price: $12 per vehicle for day use. Camping is $45 a night, plus an $8 camping reservation fee. There are no hook-ups.
Ages: All

MANHATTAN BEACH

(310) 802-5000 / www.ci.manhattan-beach.ca.us
Manhattan Beach Boulevard, at the end of Manhattan Beach Pier, Manhattan Beach

!/$

This is definitely an iconic Southern California beach - great sand and wide stretches of it; waves for surfing; tons of volleyball courts for amateurs to play and where professional tournaments are held, including the Manhattan Beach Open; palm trees saluting the shore; a bike trail (see BIKE TRAIL: SOUTH BAY pg. 210); and a pier for fishing. See ROUNDHOUSE AQUARIUM (pg. 223) for information about the small aquarium at the end of the pier. There are numerous shops and restaurants within walking distance.

Hours: Open daily, sunrise - sunset.
Price: Free. Metered parking is $1.25 an hour.
Ages: All

MARINA BEACH or MOTHER'S BEACH

(310) 305-9545 or (310) 305-9503 / beaches.lacounty.gov; www.visitmarinadelrey.com
4101 Admiralty Way, Marina Del Rey

$$

This tiny patch of waveless water lagoon, where younger children can swim, is adjacent to a large marina. A half circle of sand has play equipment, such as a big pirate play boat, several swings, a tire swing, and slides. Lifeguards are on duty here in the summer. There are numerous picnic tables set up under a covered area right on the beach, near volleyball nets. It's pleasant scenery. Tip: A visit to the adjoining Cheesecake Factory makes it an extra fun (and tasty) excursion as does visiting the Farmer's Market that's here every Thursday morning. See MARINA DEL REY WATERBUS (pg. 213) for an inexpensive and fun water excursion, KIDS CLUB at Waterside Marina Del Rey (pg. 91) for free entertainment on Tuesday mornings, and FISHERMAN'S VILLAGE (pg. 159) for other activities in the immediate area.

Hours: Open daily, sunrise - 10pm.
Price: Free. Parking is usually 25¢ every 15 min. in the lots. Beach lots - Memorial Day - Labor Day, Mon. - Fri. is $8; Sat. - Sun., $10. Parking the rest of the year, Mon. - Fri. is $6; Sat. - Sun., $8.
Ages: Toddler to 8 years old.

MARINE PARK or MOTHER'S BEACH

(562) 570-3100 / www.longbeach.gov/park
5839 Appian Way, Long Beach

!/$

This beach is aptly nicknamed because it is a mother/child hang out. There are waveless waters in this lagoon-type setting, plus lifeguards, barbecues, a volleyball court and a good playground surrounded by a small, grassy park.

Hours: Open daily, sunrise - 10:30pm.
Price: Bring either lots of quarters for parking, or get here early to park on the street for free.
Ages: All

ROYAL PALMS STATE BEACH

(310) 305-9503 / beaches.lacounty.gov; www.sanpedro.com
1799 Paseo Del Mar, San Pedro

Park on the top of the bluff or drive down to the "beach." I put this word in quotes because there is precious little sand here, as the shoreline is composed of tons of rocks. Numerous tidepools are just beyond the parking lot, so you'll have a great day of exploring and searching for small marine organisms. My boys, of course, also loved climbing out on the rocks and the jetty. Note: A lifeguard is on duty here, too, in season. Tip: Come during low tide. We've also come during high tide, though, and watched the waves slam into the rocks and shoot high into the sky. Bring your camera!

One side of the beach has a cement patio with picnic tables (and restrooms) under the palm trees (hence the name of the park) that are snug up against the cliffs - very picturesque. A small playground is here, too.

Hours: Open daily, 6am - sunset.
Price: Free, although a toll booth is located here, too.
Ages: 4 years and up.

SANTA MONICA BEACH

Look up SANTA MONICA PIER / SANTA MONICA BEACH (pg. 160) for details.
Hours: Open daily, sunrise - sunset.
Ages: All

SEASIDE LAGOON

(310) 318-0681 / www.redondo.org/seasidelagoon
200 Portofino Way, Redondo Beach

Have a swimmingly good time at the gated Seaside Lagoon. This large saltwater lagoon, next to an ocean inlet and rock jetties, is heated by a nearby steam generating plant, so the average water temperature is seventy-five degrees. Warm, waveless waters, plus a lifeguard, make it an ideal swimming spot for little ones. A large water fountain sprays out water in the shallow end of the lagoon and there are a few slides in the deeper end. There is also a sandy beach area that semi-surrounds the swim area; grass areas that ring the sand; playgrounds with a big, plastic pirate ship and swings; barbecues; picnic tables; and a volleyball court. (Bring your own ball.) Tips: Bring your own beach chair and pack a picnic lunch. An easily-accessible snack bar is sponsored by RUBY'S (see pg. 25). Several other restaurants are in the immediate vicinity.

Hours: Open Memorial Day through Labor Day daily, 10am - 5:45pm.
Price: $6 for adults; $5 for ages 2 - 17; children under 2 are free. Season passes are available. Parking is $4.50 with validation.
Ages: All

VENICE BEACH

(310) 822-5425 / www.laparks.org; www.venicechamber.net
1800 Ocean Front Walk, between Washington Boulevard and Rose Avenue, Venice

I think Southern California's reputation of being offbeat, quirky, funky, etc., comes directly from Venice Beach. This area actually has a three-mile stretch of beach, but visitors also come to gawk at, and mingle with, the eclectic Venice population of street performers. These include jugglers (one juggler specializes in chain saws), musicians, artists, magicians, mimes, and fortune tellers, as well as people sporting unusual and colorful haircuts, and numerous tattoos, plus bikini-clad women (and men), skaters, and more. Self expression reigns. A hot spot here is Muscle Beach, where weight lifters of all levels pump iron. Venice Beach also has a bike path, playground, basketball courts, pagodas, volleyball courts, handball courts, shuffleboard, souvenir shops, a boardwalk, and restaurants. A cement skate park is here, too, complete with bowl, ramps, rails, and other street elements. A helmet and pads are required in the skate park.

Hours: Open daily, sunrise - sunset.
Price: Free, although parking may cost.
Ages: All

WILL ROGERS STATE BEACH
☼

$$$

(310) 457-9701 / www.beaches.lacounty.gov

17000 E Pacific Coast Hwy, Pacific Palisades

At almost two miles long, this lovely, clean stretch of beach offers wide sandy expanses, as well as lots and lots of volleyball courts, a playground, some fitness equipment, showers, a snack bar, and a bike trail/walkway that cuts through it. Note that the shoreline can sometimes be rocky. This beach is usually much quieter than its neighbor, Santa Monica Beach.

Hours: Open daily, sunrise - sunset.
Price: Parking is $6 - $12 during the summer (peak season); $4 - $9 during the winter.
Ages: All

ZUMA BEACH
☼

$$

(310) 457-2009 - beach; (818) 597-7361 - beach bus / beaches.lacounty.gov; www.ci.agoura-hills.ca.us - beach bus

30000 Pacific Coast Highway, Malibu

This is one of the biggest, busiest, and cleanest beaches in Southern California. Besides the miles of sand, good swimming, body surfing, lifeguard stations, volleyball courts, a swing set, snack bar, and ample parking, these ocean waters are often home to schools of dolphins that ride the waves. *This* is what Southern California beaches are all about! Tip: Catch the Beach Bus mid- June through mid-August, weekdays starting at 9:15am to Zuma Beach, #6. Pick up and drop off points are Lindero Canyon Middle School, Agoura High School and corner of Liberty Canyon and Agoura Rd. $2 each way - for all ages.

Hours: Open daily, sunrise - sunset.
Price: Parking in the lots is $3 - $10 a day in the summer; $3 - $8 in the winter. There is some free parking on PCH
Ages: All

—EDIBLE ADVENTURES—

94th AERO SQUADRON (Los Angeles County)
☀

$$$$

(818) 994 - 7437 / www.94thvannuys.com

16320 Raymer Street, Van Nuys

See 94th AERO SQUADRON (San Diego) on page 472 for details about this aviation-themed restaurant. At this location, the restaurant overlooks the Van Nuys airport.

Hours: Open Mon. - Thurs., 11am - 9pm; Fri. - Sat., 11am - 10pm; Sun., 9am - 3pm - brunch; 4pm - 9pm - dinner.
Ages: 4 years and up.

AMERICAN GIRL PLACE
☀

$$$$$

189 The Grove Drive at The Grove, Los Angeles

See AMERICAN GIRL PLACE (pg. 161) for details about this outing.

BELLADONNA GIFTS AND TEA ROOM
☀

$$$$

(661) 942-0106 / www.teamap.com

44054 10th Street West, Lancaster

Step in the door at Belladonna's (which translates as "beautiful lady") and relax - you are now on a mini-vacation. A small, renovated, purple, Victorian-style home has seven rectangular tables with a mixture of high-back chairs that seat a maximum of twenty-two total; walls that are decorated with hats (you may choose one to wear, if you wish); an eclectic arrangement of pictures; and whimsical decor. Enjoy the friendly service and settle down for a good cup of tea (choose from eighty-five flavors of loose leaf), freshly-made scones, and time to chat with your tea companion(s). This is how a tea experience should be!

Menu selections include (bottomless) tea and scone, $11.95; tea, sandwich, and scone, $16.50; and a full lunch, $23.95. The latter is served with tea; soup or a petite salad; tea sandwiches, such as turkey curry and black olives, chicken with walnut and cranberries, and cucumber with garden cream cheese; and a few desserts. The Princess Tea, for children, comes with a teacup full of fruit, peanut butter and jam tea sandwiches in heart shapes (it is the details that count!), sweetened tea (or another beverage), chocolate mousse, and another petite dessert, plus a tea keepsake all for $16.95. Scones are freshly made and the variety can include cranberry, apricot, and butterscotch with coconut.

The gift boutique is packed with tea sets, jewelry, decorative hand towels, gloves, tea accessories, and several other gift items.

Hours: Open Tues. - Fri., 10am - 5pm; Sat., 10am - 4pm, with the last seating at 2pm. Note that only full lunch is served on Sat. and the seatings are at 11am and 2pm. Closed Sun. and Mon. Reservations are highly suggested.

Price: Menu prices are listed above.

Ages: 5 years and up.

BENIHANA OF TOKYO (Los Angeles County)

Beverly Hills - (323) 655-7311; City of Industry - (626) 912-8784; Encino - (818) 788-7121; Santa Monica - (310) 260-1423; Torrance - (310) 316-7777 / www.benihana.com

Beverly Hills - 38 N. La Cienega Blvd.; City of Industry - 17877 Gale Ave.; Encino - 16226 Ventura Blvd.; Santa Monica - 1447 Fourth St.; Torrance - 21327 Hawthorne Blvd.

$$$$

Enjoy the "show" and the food at Benihana. With their choreographed cooking, the chefs prepare the food on a sizzling grill right in front of you, hibachi-style. Knives flash as the food is chopped up seemingly in midair, as well as on the frying table, with lightning speed - this is the show part. (Don't try this at home.) Although my kids are not normally prone to trying new foods, they readily taste new entrees here because the food is fixed in such an intriguing way. The onion ring volcano is especially cool!

Just some of the food choices include chicken - picante or hibachi with lemon; seafood - scallops, lobster tail, and tuna steak; steak - filet mignon or teriyaki steak; and fresh vegetables. Sushi is also available, but there's not much of a show with that entree. The communal tables seat up to ten people. Adult lunch prices range from $9 to $18; dinners, from $19 to $45. Kids' meals range from $10 to $13.25 for a choice of chicken, hibachi steak, or shrimp. Their meals also come with salad, shrimp appetizer, rice, and ice cream. Several Benihana locations have a koi pond and a traditional Japanese arched bridge as part of their outside decor.

Hours: Most locations are open daily for lunch, 11:30am - 3pm; for dinner, 5:30pm - 10pm. Call first as hours vary.

Price: Menu prices are listed above.

Ages: 5 years and up.

BUCA DI BEPPO (Los Angeles County)

(866) EAT BUCA (328-2822) for all locations; Claremont - (909) 399-3287; Encino - (818) 995-3288; Pasadena - (626) 792-7272; Redondo Beach - (310) 540-3246; Santa Clarita - (661) 253-1900; Santa Monica - (310) 587-2782; Universal City - (818) 509-9463 / www.bucadibeppo.com

Claremont - 505 West Foothill Blvd.; Encino - 17500 Ventura Blvd.; Pasadena - 80 West Green St.; Redondo Beach - 1670 South Pacific Coast Highway; Santa Clarita - 26940 Theater Dr.; Santa Monica - 1442 2nd St.; Universal City - 1000 Universal Studios Blvd., G101 (on Universal CityWalk)

$$$$

O Solo Mio! Eating at Buca Di Beppo (the name translated means, "Joe's Basement") is the epitome of Italian-style, family dining - good food, comfortable atmosphere for sitting and talking (boisterously so at times), and meals meant to be shared. In fact, many meals here come in two portion sizes - small, which feeds two or more, and large, which feeds four or more. (Single portions are also available.) The restaurant has other outstanding features that pay homage to Italian heritage. The walls are crammed with photographs and pictures of Italian people - actors and actresses, and a lot of just ordinary folk. (The Santa Monica location has 1,500 pictures!) Some pictures are like family portraits and other pictures feature people of all ages who don't have many clothes on. Paintings, art, statuary (some of it PG-13) also fill up the alcove walls, semiprivate room, and large rooms. Every spare inch is taken up with something that is purposefully kitschy and over-the-top, in a fun and colorful way. Italian music plays in the background.

The circular Pope's Room seats up to twenty people. The ceiling is painted, a la Sistine Chapel, and all of the pictures, art objects, and memorabilia are papal-oriented, including a bust of the present Pontiff. A favorite room, and you'll need to make a reservation, is the kitchen. Yes, the kitchen. Up to six people can eat at the one table in the kitchen while watching food being prepared and servers scurry back and forth. Note that some of the locations offer outside dining as well.

Menu prices can change according to location. Most menu choices, of the large size, include a pepperoni pizza ($24.99); spaghetti with meatballs ($29.99); stuffed shells with sausage, spinach, and ricotta cheese and Parmesan

($28.99); chicken parmigiana ($30.45), oven-baked salmon ($34.99); and much more. Single, lunch options can include cheese manicotti ($9.99); soup and salad ($6.99); baked ravioli ($9.99); and chicken limone ($12.99). Children's meals are $5.99 for a choice of mac and cheese, pizza, fettuccine Alfredo, or spaghetti.

Hours: Most locations are generally open Mon. - Thurs., 11am - 10pm; Fri. - Sat., 11am - 11pm; Sun., 11am - 9pm. Redondo Beach and Encino location aren't open for lunch. Call the specific restaurant for its hours.

Price: Menu prices listed above.

Ages: 4 years and up.

CAFE 50's

(310) 479-1955 - Santa Monica Blvd.; (323) 906-1955 - Vermont Ave. / www.cafe50s.com
11623 Santa Monica Blvd., Los Angeles; 850 N. Vermont Ave., Los Angeles

$$$

Well, shake it up, baby! This small hamburger joint is jumping with 50's memorabilia and atmosphere. The front room consists primarily of a soda counter (thirty-two types of shakes are offered) and a wall taken over by signed pictures of celebrities. Each red or green vinyl booth has a personal jukebox. For 25¢ you get two songs from the good old days. The walls and ceilings are crammed with nostalgic movie star posters, magazine covers, license plates, old-fashioned advertisement tin signs, serving trays, and pictures. Playing cards are another ceiling decoration. The rooms also boast bubble-gum machines, a case of signed sports paraphernalia, and glass displays of old TV collectibles such as Mickey Mouse ears, lunch boxes, box cartons, and more. On top of the lockers in the back room are board games that you can play - just ask. Besides the eye-catching decor, other entertaining features of this cafe include table top magic shows (usually on Sunday afternoons), and the "Food For Thought" newsletter packed with trivia, stories, jokes, and such.

Breakfast specialities include blueberry pancakes ($7.49), cheese blintzes with blueberry sauce and sour cream ($8.95), breakfast burritos ($9.79), and a variety of omelettes ($8.95 average). Lunch and dinner selections include appetizers of sweet potato fries ($6.95) and chili cheese fries ($5.95); salads such as Cobb ($11.95) and grilled chicken ($11.95); cheeseburgers ($7.29); hot dogs ($4.25); meatloaf ($9.95); and sandwiches such as a Monte Cristo ($9.95), BLT ($7.95), and patty melt ($8.50). Desserts, besides the shakes, include lemon-lime pie ($5.95), hot fudge chocolate cake ($5.95) and bread pudding ($4.79). Shake flavors include rocky road, orange dreamside freeze, apple pie, Butterfinger, and strawberry cheesecake for $4.79 each. Join the free Frequent Dining Club for great, free rewards. The Big Bopper never had it so good!

Hours: Both locations are open Sun. - Thurs., 7am - midnight; Fri. - Sat., 7am - 1am.

Price: See menu prices above.

Ages: All

CANDLELIGHT PAVILION DINNER THEATER

455 W. Foothill Boulevard, Claremont

$$$$$

See the entry for CANDLELIGHT PAVILION DINNER THEATER on page 179 for details.

THE CANDY FACTORY

(818) 766-8220 / www.thecandyfactoryla.com
12508 Magnolia Boulevard, N. Hollywood

$$$$

How sweet it is! The Candy Factory is one of the largest and oldest candy-making suppliers on the West Coast. The store does not actually have a lot of the finished product to purchase, but it has an abundance of the supplies needed, such as a wide variety of molds, flavorings, chocolates in every color (to melt), and lollipop sticks. Birthday parties are offered for ages 7 years and up for groups of fifteen to twenty-five. The $22.50 per person fee includes ninety minutes of making candy (and eating it) - swirling and pouring three chocolates and four molds (guitars, race cars, stars, and other fun shapes) and, while they're freezing, eating cake and drinking punch. Participants get deliciously messy and leave on a sugar high and with at least a pound of chocolate. My children offered (begged) to live at the Factory for a while - imagine that!

Hours: The store is open Tues. - Fri., 10am - 5pm; Sat., 10am - 4pm. Birthday parties are usually offered at 1:30pm or 2pm on the weekends. Open Sun. for private parties only. Closed Mon. and major holidays.

Price: Some prices are listed above.

Ages: 6 years and up.

CARNEY'S

Studio City - (818) 761-8300; West Hollywood - (323) 654-8300 / www.carneytrain.com
Studio City - 12601 Ventura Blvd.; West Hollywood - 8351 Sunset Blvd

Railroad the kids and take them to Carney's for a bite to eat on board passenger train cars. The West Hollywood location has a 1920's Union Pacific dining car. The Studio City location has two 1940's train cars and a caboose. Grab a burger - no chili ($3.55), hot dog with chili ($3.80), spicy Polish dog ($4.40), small chili fries ($2.95), chicken breast filet sandwich ($5.50), beef or chicken soft tacos ($3.25 each), Thai chicken wrap ($6.75), tuna salad ($7.25), or tuna melt ($5.50).

Hours: Studio City - Open Mon. - Thurs., 11am - 10pm; Fri. - Sun., 11am - midnight. West Hollywood - Open Sun. - Thurs., 11am - midnight; Fri. - Sat., 11am - 3am.

Price: Menu prices listed above.

Ages: All

CHARLIE BROWN FARMS

(661) 944-2606 / www.charliebrownfarms.com
8317 Pearblossom Highway, Littlerock

This innocuous-looking store appears to be a kind of old-fashioned general store. Walk through its doors, however, and you will be utterly amazed at the massive size of the store and the astonishing variety of goods offered here.

The immediate section has an impressive selection of more than 1,000 food items including nuts; dried fruits; pretzels and chips; locally-grown fruits and vegetables; a plethora of honey, molasses, and jams and jellies; sixty kinds of jerky; homemade cookies; ostrich eggs; soda flavors and brands that are no longer readily available; and so much more. The candy selection includes over 1,000 kinds - a multitude (over fifty) of flavors of saltwater taffy, plus brittle, horehound candies, chocolate, and hard-to-find speciality and novelty candies. Walk through room after room filled with vast assortments of everything under one major roof. One room is devoted to collectible, porcelain, and vinyl dolls - more than 1,000 of them. Another room is packed with games and toys, including reproductions of classics, collectibles, and newer ones, and too many choices of marbles. Another is devoted to hundreds of teapots, plus dishes, cookie jars, collectibles, and home products. Christmas ornaments and holiday decorations are available year round in a room toward the back. Another room features larger-than-life-size statues of pirates, penguin butlers, Betty Boop, cavemen, an old English phone booth, and more. Dinosaurs from miniature to life-size are ensconced in another room. There are also rooms filled with all things military; one for just gnomes; another for gift items; and much more! To sum up Charlie Brown Farms in a word - kitschy.

Outside there are large statues of knights, lions, dinosaurs, elephants, etc. Order your food at the counter and then sit indoors, with its Western ambiance, or outside, where you are surrounded by more large statues and creations. The decor is both odd and fun. The food is delicious with a choice of Texas barbecue tri-tip (this was my favorite), barbecued chicken, pulled pork, or baby back ribs, plus a choice of two sides for about $9.95. Or, order burgers of venison, ostrich, buffalo, or ground steak for an average of $7.95 per. Frog legs, alligator, wild boar, kangaroo, and rattlesnake meats are available at times, too. And that's just the beginning! There are also breakfast and sandwich wraps (average $7.95), bread bowls (about $6.95), a slew of salads to choose from (average $6.95), deli sandwiches (about $6.75), side orders (sweet potato fries, cowboy beans, garlic cheese fries, pepper bellies), plus the good stuff like shakes (choose from the fifty kinds offered), frozen custard, kettle korn, pie shakes (cherry pie shake, banana cream pie shake, etc.), deep-fried Oreos, Hawaiian shaved ice, funnel cakes and lots more. The coffee menu is also fairly extensive, of course.

Note that peach and other U-pic fruit orchards are just down the road.

Hours: Open daily, 8am - 8pm.

Price: Technically free, but bring money!!

Ages: 1½ years and up

CHUCK E. CHEESE'S (Los Angeles County)

www.chuckecheese.com

These popular indoor eateries and play lands for young kids offer token-taking kiddie rides and video and arcade games, as well as the all-important prize redemption centers. Many facilities also have play areas with tubes, slides, and ball pits. Chuck E. Cheese's, the costumed rat mascot, is usually walking around giving hugs and high fives.

An electronic version of Chuck E. performs several stage shows throughout the day.

Every child's favorite food is served here - pizza! A large cheese pizza is $15.99 and all-you-can-eat salad bar is $6.99. Other menu choices are buffalo wings, hot dogs, and sandwiches, plus dessert options of cinnamon sticks and apple dessert pizza. All purchases come with a few tokens, but kids always want more. Bring in their report cards (especially if they have good grades!) to redeem for extra tokens. Check out the website for online coupons, too. Note: This place is often noisy at peak lunch and dinner times, especially on weekends when crowds descend.

Hours: Most locations are open Sun. - Thurs., 9am - 10pm; Fri. - Sat., 9am - 11pm. Call for a particular location's hours.
Price: Free admission, but count on spending money on pizza and tokens.
Ages: 2 - 11 years.

DALE'S DINER

(562) 425-7285 / www.dalesdiner.com
4339 E. Carson Street, Long Beach

Hey Daddy-O! This small 50's diner is a really happenin' place. It's decorated with black and white checkered tile floor, turquoise vinyl seats, and a few special booths that look like they were made from the back section of cars from this era. Each table has its own small jukebox. At 25¢ for two songs, your kids can now be introduced to such classics as *Chantilly Lace* and *Purple People Eater*.

For breakfast, tasty morning choices include omelettes, with side dishes, ($8.95); a waffle, two eggs, bacon or sausage patty ($8.15); or blueberry flapjacks ($5.80). Kids' meals, for ages 9 and younger, include two oreo pancakes (about $5), or one egg and one pancake and a piece of bacon (about $4). The lunch and dinner menu offers a Cobb salad ($9.25), pork chops ($10.95), sirloin tip steak kabob ($12.25), deli sandwiches (average $8.45), hamburgers (average $7.65), and more. Top off your meal with a chocolate, vanilla, or cherry soda. Kids can choose a burger and fries, grilled cheese with fries, chili, or a pepperoni pizza for about $4.50. Beverages are extra. Come in sometime just for dessert and try a slice of freshly baked pie ($3.65); a malt, sundae, or float (average $4.85); or a scrumptious Brownie Saturday, which is alternating layers of brownies with vanilla ice cream, topped with hot fudge and whipped cream ($5.75).

Hours: Open Sun. - Thurs., 6am - 9pm; Fri. - Sat., 6am - 10pm. Closed Christmas.
Price: Menu prices are listed above.
Ages: All

ELISE'S TEA ROOM

(562) 424-2134 / www.elisestearoom.com
3924 Atlantic Avenue, Long Beach

This refined, yet welcoming and feminine tea room, off a main street in Long Beach, offers a pleasant respite and time to relax while enjoying a cup of tea. The decor is artfully arranged pictures on the walls and hutches filled with dolls and china plates and tea cups, plus lovely murals on the wall and ceiling. Tables are set with white linen tablecloths accompanied by matching padded chairs. A small shop selling tea paraphernalia and collectibles is located toward the back.

There are several types of "teas" to choose from - I've only listed a few of them. A scone with jam and a pot of tea is $7.25. Child's Tea with a heart-shaped (and kids notice these things!) peanut butter and jelly sandwich, a cookie, and tea or lemonade is $10.50. Full Tea consists of two scones with jam, six tea sandwiches, one petite dessert, and a pot of tea for $22.25. High Tea is the Full Tea, plus quiche and a house salad for $32.75. A sampling of the a la carte items include one scone ($2), one tea sandwich ($1.75), a small pot of tea ($3.25), and a bagel with red salmon pate and cream cheese ($9.95). Chicken salad is available for $11.95, and soup and salad for $9.50. There seems to be something at Elise's to fit everyone's budget and palate.

Hours: Open Tues. - Fri., 11am - 5pm; Sat., 10am - 5pm; Sun., noon - 4pm. Open the first Fri. until 9pm with some entertainment in conjunction with First Fridays Art Walk in Long Beach. Closed Mon., except for private parties. Reservations are suggested at all times and necessary on the weekends.
Price: Menu prices are listed above.
Ages: 5 years and up.

FAIR OAKS PHARMACY AND SODA FOUNTAIN

(626) 799-1414 / www.fairoakspharmacy.net

1526 Mission Street, South Pasadena

Fair Oaks is a small "store" with a quaint ambiance, located a few miles from Old Town Pasadena, which has lots of shops and restaurants. It is part pharmacy, that also sells retro collectibles, jewelry, and home accents; and part 1900's restaurant and soda fountain, complete with a marble counter top and antique fixtures. Both sides of the store are decorated with memorabilia, unique toys, and fun stuff to look at.

Lunch items include a grilled chicken sandwich ($10.95), roast beef sandwich ($8.95), chili cheese dog ($6.95), burger ($8.95), and chicken Caesar salad or Cobb salad ($10.95). The kid's menu includes grilled cheese sandwich ($5.50), hot dog ($4.50), hamburger ($6.50), and chicken fingers ($5.95) - add fries and a soda for an additional $3. Now for the good stuff - dessert. Ask the soda jerk (who is actually quite nice) to fix you an old-fashioned phosphate ($3.95); a chocolate, pineapple, or raspberry ice cream soda ($6.95); a hot fudge brownie topped with ice cream and whipped cream ($7.95); or a specialty drink. There is a small eating area inside, as well as a few tables and chairs outside.

Hours: The soda fountain counter, for desserts and beverages, is open Mon. - Sat., 9am - 9pm; Sun., 10am - 7pm. The kitchen, for meals, is open daily, 11am - 6pm. Closed Easter, Thanksgiving, and Christmas.
Price: Menu prices are mentioned above.
Ages: All

FARMERS MARKET

(323) 933-9211 / www.farmersmarketla.com   !/$$
6333 W. 3rd Street, Los Angeles

This unique outdoor market, originally founded in 1934 and almost unchanging in its "small-town" ambiance, is an eclectic mixture of more than sixty fresh food and produce vendors, and over twenty kitchens that make and sell all sorts of homemade domestic and international favorites. The market can be crowded, but it is a fun place to shop or enjoy lunch. Patrons can order their favorite ethnic food and eat at an outdoor table. Kids love stopping by Littlejohn's English Toffee House stall to watch (and sample) mouth-watering candy being made. At Magee's House of Nuts, they can see peanuts steadily pouring into a large machine behind glass, being churned around to make very fresh-tasting peanut butter. Across the way from the main marketplace, more than sixty-five retail stores offer unique clothing items and specialty gifts. Check the website for special events and celebrations at the market. See the entry for THE GROVE (pg. 94), for details about the uptown mall just across the road, the LOS ANGELES MUSEUM OF THE HOLOCAUST (pg. 131) and PAN PACIFIC PARK (pg. 77) which are just around the corner, too.

Hours: Open Mon. - Fri., 9am - 9pm; Sat., 9am - 8pm; Sun., 10am - 7pm. Closed major holidays.
Price: Free, but bring spending money. Parking is free for the first two hours with validation. It's $4 for the third hour and $1 for each additional 15 minutes. Parking is $2 for each 15 minutes without validation.
Ages: 2½ years and up.

FARMER'S MARKETS (Los Angeles County)

www.cafarmersmarkets.com; www.farmernet.com

Many cities host a weekly farmer's market. These markets usually consist of open-air (outside) booths set up for customers to purchase fresh produce, bakery goods, meats, and more - taste the difference! Freshly cut flowers are often available, too, as is entertainment of some sort. Indulge yourself and let your kids pick out "new" foods to try. The food and ambiance of a market is much more enticing than a grocery store. Call your local city hall or chamber of commerce, or check the above websites to see if there is a farmer's market near you. Here are just a few of the cities that I know of that host a market: Bellflower, Beverly Hills, Burbank, Calabasas, Cerritos, Coronado, Costa Mesa, Culver City, Encino, Gardena, Long Beach, Los Angeles, Malibu, Mission Valley, Monrovia, Montrose, Northridge, Ocean Beach, Oceanside (with llama rides!), Ojai, Oxnard, Pacific Beach, Pasadena, Pomona, Redondo Beach, Riverside, Santa Barbara, Santa Maria, Santa Monica, Studio City, Temecula, Torrance, Tustin, Ventura, Vista, and Westwood.

Price: Free
Ages: 5 years and up.

FARRELL'S ICE CREAM PARLOUR RESTAURANTS (Los Angeles County)

(661) 253-4FUN (4386) / www.mountasiafuncenter.com; www.farrellsusa.com $$$

21516 Golden Triangle Road inside the Mountasia Fun Center, Santa Clarita

This terrific family restaurant, with specialty desserts and celebratory ambiance, is located inside the MOUNTASIA FUN CENTER. See page 36 for all the fun this center has to offer. This location is smaller than other Farrells, but still packed with excitement and lots of candy and menu options. See page 247 for more details about the atmosphere, menu and prices.

Hours: Open Mon. - Thurs., noon - 9pm (open at 11am in the summer and on school breaks); Fri., noon - 11pm; Sat., 11am - 11pm; Sun., 11am - 9pm. Closed Thanksgiving and Christmas.
Price: Prices are listed above.
Ages: All

FOUR SEASONS TEA ROOM

(626) 355-0045 / www.4seasonstearoom.com

$$$$

75 North Baldwin Avenue, Sierra Madre

You are invited to take tea in one of two very sweetly decorated tea rooms, or on the outside patio. The rooms have just the right touch with a few old-fashioned pictures, and some greenery and lace outlining the windows. Antique furniture, beautiful china settings, soft music, and friendly service bespeak of a more genteel time. The covered outdoor patio has a trellis with vines and a gently bubbling fountain.

Afternoon Teas, $22, consist of scones that come fresh from the oven, accompanied by cream and raspberry jam; five finger sandwiches, such as egg salad, cucumber with dill butter, and chicken salad with cranberries; tea breads; a selection of dessert bites; and tea. Add a good-sized salad (now it's a Royal Tea) to the previous for a total of $28. Sandwich Tea, $17.50, includes five sandwiches and tea. Salad Tea, $17.50, come with a house salad and tea. Cream Tea, $17.50, is served with a scone and cream and jam, and a selection of petite desserts. The menu items change seasonally. (Hence the name of the tea room.) Note that Four Seasons offers only a few types of tea. Although the presentation is grown-up, children will rise to the occasion and enjoy it as well. Check the website for seasonal enter*tea*ment like Faerie Tale Teas, Murder Mysteries, and more.

Hours: Open Tues. - Fri., 11am - 4pm; Sat. the seatings are at 11am and 2:30pm. Reservations are recommended, especially for Fri. and Sat. Closed Sun., Mon., and holidays.
Price: Menu prices are listed above. There is usually a $7.50 minimum, per person.
Ages: 6 years and up.

FRESH BROTHERS

Beverly Hills - (310) 860-9400; Brentwood - (310) 826-0777; Calabasas - (818) 225-7555; Hollywood - (323) 962-6262; Manhattan Beach - (310) 546-4444; Marina del Rey - (310) 823-3800; Redondo Beach - (310) 374-5678; Santa Monica - (310) 656-6888; West Hollywood - (310) 652-5252; Westlake Village - (805) 777-8448. / www.freshbrothers.com

$$$

Beverly Hills - 250 S. Beverly Dr.; Brentwood - 11740 San Vicente Blvd.; Calabasas - 4751 Commons Way at The Commons; Hollywood - 1923 N. Bronson Ave.; Manhattan Beach - 2008 N Sepulveda Blvd.; Marina Del Rey - 4722 Admiralty Way; Redondo Beach - 407 N. Pacific Coast Hwy.; Santa Monica - 1447 Lincoln Blvd.; West Hollywood - 8613 Santa Monica Blvd.; Westlake Village - 180 Promenade Way.

Ciao means "hello" or "goodbye" in Italian. It's pronounced chow, which means "food". So, ciao - say hello to some good, Italian food at Fresh Brothers. This pizza place offers a variety of pizzas with various toppings and crusts, including skinny (half everything and on thin crust), deep dish and gluten free, as well as meatball sliders, buffalo wings, and create-your-own salad.

The reason I'm including this entry in the book, really, is because they offer kid's parties where kids can make their own pizzas. First, the kids get a personal pizza box that they decorate with stickers and markers. Then, they get to play with dough and make their own 7" pizza - with whatever toppings they want. The pizzas get baked, presented to each child in their box, and eaten! Drinks are included in the party and so is a Fresh Brothers t-shirt for each participant. Now, that's amore!

Hours: Call to schedule a party.
Price: The basic party package for twelve kids is $250. There are several add-ons available.
Ages: 4 years and up.

FRISCO'S CARHOP DINER

(626) 913-FOOD (3663) / www.friscos.com

$$$

8065 Gale Avenue, City of Industry

Pop quiz: What are skatetresses? Answer: Waitresses on skates! Frisco's has them, and lots more throwbacks to the 50's. The restaurant's prominent colors are hot pink and cool turquoise, along with white-and-black-checkered flooring. The walls and ceilings are painted blue with clouds that feature artists from the 50's (e.g., Jimmy Dean, Elvis, Marilyn Monroe, and others) with wings, as in heavenly angels. There are also some neon thunderbolts and a few 3-D images popping out. Other decor includes parking meters, traffic signals, dice, drive-in movie speakers, a juke box, and an old gas pump. Many of the booths have the front or back end of a car incorporated in them. The restaurants offer cruise nights, special events, and even live entertainment.

The food is a combination of American and Greek, served in a fifties-themed restaurant - and somehow it works! Breakfast selections include three eggs, plus home fries or hash browns or fresh fruit, for about $4.95; ribeye steak and eggs, $15.50; breakfast burrito, $6.95; and Belgian waffles, $6.95. Kids 12 years and under can choose from two pancakes or French toast, eggs, and bacon or sausage, plus a small drink for $5.95. Lunch options include a variety of burgers starting at $8; Greek salad, $8.50; lots of sandwich choices, such as turkey avocado melt on sourdough, $9.95; chicken souvlaki, $7.95; beef fajita pita, $9.69; gyro, $8.95; Baja chicken tacos, $8.95; and more. Kid's meals are $5.95 for a choice of burger, hot dog or corn dog, chicken strips, pizza, or grilled cheese, plus fries and a soft drink. Adult dinner choices, which are usually served with salad, baked potato, rice, french fries, or vegetable, and either garlic bread or pita bread, include BBQ full rack of ribs, $16.95; lemon garlic chicken, $13.95; and pizzas for an average of $10. Desserts include hot fudge or shakes, $4.95; and chocolate brownie a la mode, $3.95. Keep on cruisin'!

Hours: Open daily, 10am - 10pm.
Price: Menu prices are mentioned above.
Ages: All

GRAND CENTRAL MARKET

(213) 624-2378 / www.grandcentralmarket.com $$$
317 S. Broadway Street, Los Angeles

This is a fun, aromatic, cultural experience for kids who are used to shopping at a regular grocery store. There are more than forty stalls inside this covered structure that spans a city block. Everything from exotic fruits and vegetables to octopus, chicken feet, honeycomb tripe, chiles, fresh tortillas (made on-site), birch bark, shrimp powder, and lambs' heads are sold here. There are also meat stalls, restaurants, and bakeries. Stop here to shop and/or eat on your way to visit other fun and educational places listed in this book! See DOWNTOWN LOS ANGELES / GRAND PARK (pg. 167) for information on Grand Park and all the other places to go within this fairly immediate area.

Hours: Open daily, 9am - 6pm.
Price: Parking is free for one hour with validation, $2 for every fifteen minutes after that, $10 flat rate.
          Closed New Year's Day, Thanksgiving, and Christmas.
Ages: 3 years and up.

GYU-KAKU (Los Angeles County)

Beverly Hills - (310) 659-5760; Canoga Park - (818) 888-4030; Cerritos - coming soon; Los Angeles - (310) $$$$
234-8641; Pasadena - (626) 405-4842; Sherman Oaks - (818) 501-5400; Torrance - (310) 325-1437; Valencia -
(661) 254-2355 / www.gyu-kaku.com
Beverly Hills - 163 N. La Cienega Blvd.; Canoga Park - 6600 Topanga Canyon Blvd., suite 1010B in the Westfield Topanga
Center; Cerritos - coming soon; Los Angeles - 10925 W. Pico Blvd.; Pasadena - 70 W. Green St.; Sherman Oaks - 14457
Ventura Blvd.; Torrance - 24631 Crenshaw Blvd.; Valencia - 27025 McBean Parkway

Be your own chef at this restaurant that integrates Korean barbeque and Japanese-style grilling. Each table has its own grill in the center that uses hot coals which are replaced for you when necessary during your dinner. Place portions of specially marinated beef, chicken, pork, and seafood items to barbecue them just the way you like 'em. If cooking isn't one of your gifts, or you're not sure of how to do the pieces you selected, ask your server for tips and instructions. Food is part of the pleasure of being here and the other part is truly sharing a meal together in this intimate way.

Menu choices (from the Beverly Hills menu) include Kobe rib-eye steak, $23.95; short ribs, $7.95; filet mignon, $7.95; spicy pork, $4.95; chicken tenders, $3.95; lamb, $10.95; four pieces of butterfly shrimp with garlic, $5.95; salmon, $5.95; fried calamari, $5.95, and fried gyoza dumplings, $4.95. The wide selection of vegetables to grill directly or in tin foil include a mushroom medly, $4.95; Japanese sweet potato, $3.95; and broccoli with baked tofu, $3.95. Rice (and bibimbap), noodles (fried or ramen), soups and salads are also available. The food is tasty, especially with marinades and dipping sauces, and there is a communal feel to sharing a meal like this, kind of like sitting around a campfire. Kids meals are $9.50 for a sweet potato, sausage, corn, harami miso, rice, and small shaved ice with vanilla ice cream. Try big kid desserts such as grilled, cheese cake crepe, $5.95; s'mores, $2.95; black sesame or green tea ice cream, $1.95; or Lychee sorbet, $1.95. Note that menu choices do vary from location to location.

Hours: Most of the restaurants are open Mon. - Thurs., 3pm - 10:30pm; Fri. - Sat., 3pm - 11:30pm; Sun., 3pm - 9:30pm. The Beverly Hills, Canoga Park, Los Angeles, Pasadena, and Torrance restaurants are also open daily for lunch at 11:30 or noon. Call or check online first for hours for each restaurant.

Price: Menu prices are listed above.

Ages: 5 years and up.

HARD ROCK CAFE (Los Angeles County)

Hollywood - (323) 464-7625; Universal City - (818) 622-7625 / www.hardrock.com $$$$

Hollywood - 6801 Hollywood Blvd. at Hollywood & Highland Center; Universal City - 1000 Universal Center Dr. at Universal CityWalk

This has become the "in" place to eat and hang out if you are a rock 'n roll fan, or even if you're not. Each Cafe has its own unique music-related memorabilia displayed in the open and in glass cases covering the walls, but the essence of all the cafes is the same - to pay tribute to music industry legends and the hot artists of today, and to promote the environmental motto, "Save the Planet." Hard Rock Cafe is part restaurant and part museum, so before or after your meal take a walk around to see your favorite musician's guitar, record album, or stage costume on exhibit. And, oh yes, rock music is played constantly. Souvenir t-shirts and glasses bearing the Cafe's logo and location (as there are restaurants throughout the world) have become collectible items among Hard Rock Cafe enthusiasts.

The Cafe at UNIVERSAL CITYWALK (pg. 175), for instance, features a gigantic (seventy-eight foot) electric guitar out front. Inside are numerous guitars (one is covered with snake skin), a few saxophones (including a chandelier made of thirty-two of them), a cool-looking '57 Cadillac convertible spinning on a pedestal, a gleaming Harley Davidson motorcyde, gold records, autographed items, and an outfit worn by Elton John. This location also has outside, patio seating.

Menu items include Chinese chicken salad (about $11), burgers (average $11), barbeque ribs (about $22), fajitas (about $16), New York strip steaks (about $26), and sandwiches (average $11). Personal dessert favorites include chocolate chip cookie pie (about $5) and Heath Bar rainforest nut crunch sundae (about $6). Kids' meals are $8.95 each for a burger, hotdog, pasta, chicken tenders (shaped like guitars), or chicken salad. Most of their meals also come with fries and a beverage in a souvenir cup.

Hours: Open Sun. - Thurs., 11am - 10:30pm; Fri. - Sat., 11am - midnight.

Price: Menu prices are listed above. Certain discounts are available through AAA.

Ages: 5 years and up.

HOUSE OF BLUES GOSPEL BRUNCH (Los Angeles County)

(323) 848-5100 / www.houseofblues.com $$$$$

8430 Sunset Boulevard, Hollywood

Got the blues? Gospel Brunch at the renowned House of Blues is the cure. With its corrugated tin roof and weathered walls this unique building looks (deceptively) like an old shack, found in the poorer parts of the deep South. The three-story house's eclectic decor consists of bottlecaps imbedded in the walls, folk art done in various mediums, African designs on the wood beams, 3-D reliefs on the ceiling depicting Blues' artists (e.g., Aretha Franklin, Billie Holiday, and others), earth-tone colors mixed with splashes of bright colors, broken-in wooden tables and chairs, and lots more ambiance. The bars also have African masks and other cultural renderings.

The two-hour gospel brunch is a feast for the body, mind, and spirit. Indulge in eating some of the finest Mississippi Delta cuisine this side of, well, the Mississippi. Some of the southern-style, all-you-can-eat buffet items includes croissants; banana bread; corn muffins; omelets fixed any way you like 'em; bacon; sausage; shrimp; Greek salad; seasonal fresh fruit; breakfast potatoes; waffles with berries and whipped cream (and with or without fried chicken); fried chicken salad; Caesar salad; biscuits and gravy; grits; carved meats; maple glazed ham; brisket; smoke bbq chicken; Creole Chicken Jambalaya; and desserts, such as sticky buns, fresh cookies, or white chocolate banana bread pudding. Menu items are subject to change, but it's all finger-licking good!

The food is a precursor to the uplifting, high-energy, praise-the-Lord, hour-long concert that follows. The stage is on the first floor with a curtain that resembles a patchwork quilt. Above it are symbols of world religions. The upstairs section actually separates (think parting of the Red Sea) so visitors can look down onto the stage. If you are seated on the second floor towards the buffet area, you can either view the concert on the monitors, or get up and move toward the center railing that oversees the stage. Most people do not remain seated throughout the concert, anyway. They are standing up, dancing around, clapping their hands, singing along, and at times, even joining the musicians on stage.

Every week features different artists or groups from traditional ensembles and choirs to contemporary gospel that include nationally known singers to locally famous ones. It's a delicious and upbeat way for a family to spend a Sunday afternoon.

Dinner is served in this unique atmosphere nightly, starting at 5pm. There is a kid's menu available, too.

The House of Blues is home to numerous headliner concerts during the week. Check out the BLUES SCHOOLHOUSE (Los Angeles County) on page 162 for information on a school program.

Hours: The Gospel Brunch is served every other Sun. (usually the first and third Sun.) at noon. Get here earlier. Ask about holiday Sun., such as Easter and Mother's Day. Reservations are highly recommended.

Price: $42.50 for ages 13 and up; $34.50 for seniors; $21 for ages 5 - 12; children 4 and under are free. Parking is $10.

Ages: 5 years and up.

JOE'S CRAB SHACK (Los Angeles County)

City of Industry - (626) 839-4116; Long Beach - (562) 594-6551; Redondo Beach - (310) 406-1999 / www.joescrabshack.com

City of Industry - 1420 Azusa; Long Beach - 6550 Marina Drive; Redondo Beach - 230 Portofino Way

$$$$

If you're in a *crab*by mood, this is the restaurant for you! Most of the shacks really do resemble tacky-looking shacks - it's part of the charm. The servers must have fun because they sometimes dance on the tables and break out into song.

Outside the Newport Beach restaurant, for instance, is a collage of large, marine-related items such as a life-size carved wooden captain, a whale's tail, a surfboard, fishing nets, and a wooden alligator. Inside, a lot of stuff fills the walls and ceiling. From the corrugated tin roof hangs plastic seagulls, netting, crab and lobster decorations, animals made out of shells, surfer clothing, and small boats - you get the picture. The wall is completely covered with photographs of everyday people, some holding fish, some not. At almost any of the wooden tables, the waterfront view of the harbor is terrific.

Most of the meals are large enough to be shared; even the kid's meals are more than adequate. Crab is the featured specialty, but other foods are available. My oldest son fell in love with the crab cake sandwiches ($11.69). Other entrees include top sirloin and Malibu shrimp ($15.79); hamburger ($10.29); crab nachos - my favorite ($10.79); coconut shrimp ($14.69); Dungeness crab ($27.49); stuffed snapper ($18.29); steak ($14.99); chicken or shrimp Cobb salad ($11.59); and an appetizer of fried calamari with marinara ($7.89). One of the lunch specials is fish and chips, or bottomless soup and salad for $8.59. Kids' meals come with fries and are $4.99 for a choice of chicken fingers, corn dog, mini burgers, popcorn shrimp, pizza, or mac and cheese. They can even get snow crab for $9.99. Drinks are extra.

Hours: Open daily, 11am - midnight.

Price: Menu prices are listed above.

Ages: All

JOHNNY REBS' SOUTHERN ROADHOUSE (Los Angeles County)

Bellflower - (562) 866-6455; Long Beach - (562) 423-7327 / www.johnnyrebs.com

Bellflower - 16639 Bellflower Blvd.; Long Beach - 4663 Long Beach Blvd.

$$$$

This roadhouse restaurant serves up southern hospitality, as well as good ol' southern cookin'. Walk past the bales of hay and cow bells into the main room with its wood-beam ceilings, wooden tables and benches, and rustic ambiance. Large U.S. (and a few other) flags hang from the ceiling. The walls and counter tops are decorated with straw hats, old wash basins, musical instruments, license plates, old-fashioned kitchen gadgets and tools, and pictures of farms framed by shutters. Bluegrass music plays in the background.

The immediate attraction for kids (and adults) is the bowl of peanuts on each table because the peanut shells are to be thrown on the floor! (My floor looks like this too, sometimes. The only difference is that kids are allowed to do it here.) I have to mention that even the bathrooms fit into the Ma and Pa Kettle theme because they look like (nice) outhouses, and barnyard noises are piped in.

Our waiter, who wore a "long johns" shirt, served our beverages in canning jars. An extensive breakfast menu include grits ($2.60 a cup), omelettes (average $10), flapjacks ($6.75), catfish and eggs ($13), country ham and eggs ($12), BBQ beef or pork ($10), and a side order of biscuits and gravy ($4.75) and sausage ($3). Meals come with all the fixin's. The children's menu offers egg and toast, French toast, pancakes, or bacon and egg biscuit, for $2.99 to $5 each. The lunch menu is the same as the following dinner menu, only the portions are smaller, so prices are lower. Going along with the southern attitude toward food - anything tastes better when fried - choices include fried green tomatoes, okra, pickles, sweet potatoes, hushpuppies (i.e., fried cornbread), catfish, and chicken fried steak. Also, y'all may select ribs, hamburger, smoked tri-tip, pulled pork, blackened T-bone steak, stuffed Cajun sausage sandwich, chicken salad, and more. Dinner prices range from $13 to $27. The homemade desserts are delicious, especially the peach cobbler, key lime pie, and fried apple pie. Personal advice - don't even think about dieting, at least for the meal you eat here. Beverages include peach or cherry lemonade, mint julep, buttermilk, sodas, etc. The kids' menu, serving generous portions, offers chicken, grilled cheese sandwich, hamburger, mac and cheese, salmon, or beef ribs from about $4 to $9. Beverages are extra. "Put some south in your mouth" and grab some grub at Johnny Rebs'!

Hours: Open Sun. - Thurs., 7am - 9pm; Fri. - Sat., 7am - 10pm.
Price: Menu prices are listed above.
Ages: 2 years and up.

JOHN'S INCREDIBLE PIZZA CO. (Los Angeles County)

(909) 447-7777 / www.johnspizza.com
5280 Arrow Highway, Montclair
See JOHN'S INCREDIBLE PIZZA CO. (Orange County) (pg. 248) for details.
Hours: Open Mon. -Thurs.,11am - 10pm; Fri., 11am - 11pm; Sat., 10am - 11pm; Sun., 10am - 10pm.

KDB (Kitchen, Den, Bar)

10 Aquarium Way, Long Beach
See the entry for KDB on page 33 for information on this video-rich place to play and dine.

THE OLD SPAGHETTI FACTORY (Los Angeles County)

(626) 358-2115 / www.osf.com
1431 Buena Vista, Duarte

These elegant "factories" have posh, velvet seats in a variety of colors. The overhead fabric lamps are from a more genteel era. The old world antiques and the dark, rich furniture exudes a quiet, classy atmosphere. Yet, the restaurants are also very kid friendly. Old Spaghetti factories usually have a train or trolley car to eat in - this is a highlight. The franchised restaurants differ only in regional decor. For instance, the one in Riverside, being in a citrus city, has orange crate labels on the walls.

The food selection is focused on spaghetti (what a surprise!), with a large selection of sauces to choose from. Lasagna, tortellini, and ravioli are served here, as well. Dinner prices range from $10.75 (for "basic" spaghetti) to $13.50 (for jumbo crab ravioli). Kids' meals are $5.69 for a choice of mac and cheese, grilled cheese sandwich, and six 'sghetti meals with different sauces. Their meal comes with a salad, beverage, and dessert.

Hours: Most locations are open Mon. - Fri., 11:30am - 2pm and 5pm - 10pm (Fri. 'til 10:30pm or 11pm); Sat., noon - 11pm; Sun., 11:30am - 10pm. Hours may vary according to location - call first.
Price: Menu prices are listed above.
Ages: 4 years and up.

OLIVIA'S DOLL HOUSE TEA ROOM (Los Angeles County)

(310) 257-1199 - Lomita; (661) 252-1404 - general number / www.olivias4tea.com; www.oliviasdollhousetearoom.com
Lomita - 2051 Palos Verdes Dr. North; Los Angeles - 1450 S. Robertson Blvd.; Newhall - 22700 Lyons Ave.

Walk through the door into princess fantasyland. Each room in these small houses are tastefully decorated with classy flowery carpets, feminine wallpaper, lacy curtains, elegant furniture, frills, animated stuffed animals and dolls, and shelves and curios filled with collectable dolls and tea paraphernalia. Not a kitschy, cheap, glittery facade, Olivia's is the real deal - a little girl's (and big girl's!) dream come true for a private, dress-up tea party or any kind of celebration. (The website offers great visuals.)

The first part of the two-hour party is dress up, where young ladies get gussied up in gowns - and there are hundreds to choose from - and accessorize with feather boas, hats, gloves, parasols, and all kinds of jewelry, plus "diamond" tiaras. Each guest gets her hair in a up-do, befitting her new princess look, plus her make-up and nails done at the salon room with a long mirror and comfy stools. (Forget about little girls - this sounds like a mom's dream come true!) Each partygoer participates in a fashion show and gets her picture taken. Lemonade is served along with hors d'oeuvres (bite-size pizza, quiches, and cocktail weanies); finger sandwiches (turkey, tuna, egg salad, and peanut butter and jelly); and dessert (candy assortments, brownies, and a cookie). Party favors are doled out, too. The birthday girl gets very special treatment - a princess made to feel like a queen. Note that this is a great place for bridal and baby showers, too.

      Hours: Open only for private parties and by reservation.
      Price: Parties range between $335 - $375, depending on location, for 7 guests; additional guests are $25 each.
      Ages: 4 years and up.

POWELL'S SWEET SHOPPE (Long Beach)

(562) 434-6105 / www.powellssweetshoppe.com
5282 East 2nd Street, Long Beach

    See POWELL'S SWEET SHOPPE (Laguna Niguel) (page 250) for details. This location doesn't have a party room, but they still do parties!

      Hours: Open daily, 10am - 9pm.
      Price: Technically, free (but not a chance!)
      Ages: 2 years and up.

PROUD BIRD RESTAURANT

(310) 670-3093 / www.theproudbird.com
11022 Aviation Boulevard, Los Angeles

    Several airplanes have landed (as decor) outside this restaurant, which is fittingly located just a stone's throw from the Los Angeles International Airport. The planes include a P-38 Lightning, P-51 Mustang, and Bell X-I. Inside this elegant restaurant are hallways lined with aviation pictures and flight artifacts. The rectangular-shaped, main dining room has windows to see the field of planes in the "backyard," as well as planes actually landing and taking off from the airport. Tip: Choose a table near a window for the view.

    Adult entree lunches include grilled salmon with garlic mashed potatoes ($17), chicken Caesar salad ($15), Angus cheeseburger ($15), chicken scallopine ($15), and club sandwich ($14). Dinner choices include vegetarian pasta primavera ($23), beer battered fish and chips ($19), filet mignon ($35), prime rib ($27), shrimp scamp ($25), and lobster tail. Appetizers include spinach & artichoke dip and pita bread ($11) or calamari ($12 each). The kids' menu has grilled cheese sandwiches, hamburgers, fried shrimp, or chicken strips for about $8 each. Sunday brunches include everything from omelets and waffles to crab legs, and everything in between. Adults are $38; ages 4 to 12 are $17.50; ages 3 and under are free.

      Hours: Open Mon. - Sat., 11am - 3pm for lunch; Thurs. - Sat., 4pm - 8pm for dinner; Sun., 9am - 3pm for brunch, and 5pm - 8pm for dinner.
      Price: Menu prices are listed above.
      Ages: 5 years and up.

QUEEN MARY

1126 Queens Highway, Pier J, Long Beach

    See the entry for QUEEN MARY on page 146 for details.

ROCKET FIZZ SODA POPS AND CANDY SHOP (Los Angeles County)

Burbank - (818) 846-SODA (7632); Glendale - (818) 730-0233; Los Angeles (Westwood Village) - (310) 208-4509; Pasadena - (626) 449-SODA (7632); Sherman Oaks - (818) 981-9009; Valencia - (661) 253-FIZZ (3499) / www.rocketfizz.com
Burbank - 3524 Magnolia Blvd.; Glendale - 138 North Brand Blvd. Suite B; Los Angeles (Westwood Village)- 1067 Broxton Ave.; Pasadena - 111 West Green St.; Sherman Oaks - 14613 Ventura Blvd.; Valencia - 24300 Town Center Drive, Suite 103

    Looking for a uniquely flavored soda to perk up your taste buds? How about S'Mores, Cotton Candy, Mud Pie, Green Apple Jalapeno, Shirley Temple, Peanut Butter, Sweet Corn, Ranch Dressing, or Australian Style Hot Ginger Ale? There are literally hundreds more funky flavors well as a slew of traditional sodas to choose from. But that's not the only thing that brings customers in; it's also the huge array of nostalgic (and more current) candies, the unusual combos of flavors, and the novelty-type candies. Try salt water taffies, Gold Nugget gum, Toblerone, black licorice buttons, Charleston Chew, Necco wafers, bacon-flavored suckers, candy cigarettes, band aid bubble gum, and so many more. The shelves are also filled with collectible gifts, gag gifts, retro toys, and tin signs and colorful posters from yesteryear. The walk down Memory Lane isn't very far, after all.

Hours: Hours vary by store but all are open daily, usually around 10am until 9pm - 11pm, depending on the night and location of the store.
Price: Technically, free
Ages: 3 years and up.

RUBY'S (Los Angeles County)

(800) HEY RUBY (439-7829) - for all locations. Note that most of the phone numbers end in RUBY (7829): City of Commerce - (323) 382-RUBY; Long Beach - (562) 596-1914; Redondo Beach - (310) 376-RUBY; Rolling Hills Estates - (310) 544-RUBY; Whittier - (562) 947-RUBY; Woodland Hills - (818) 340-RUBY / www.rubys.com

City of Commerce - 100 Citadel Dr.; Long Beach - 6405 East Pacific Coast Highway in the Marketplace; Redondo Beach - 245 N. Harbor Dr. - (sit at the outdoor patio for an ocean view); Rolling Hills Estates - 550 Deep Valley Dr.; Whittier - 10109 Whittwood Lane; Woodland Hills - 6100 Topanga Canyon Blvd. at the Promenade Mall.

See the entry for RUBY'S (Orange County) on page 252 for details.

$$$$

SHOGUN (Los Angeles County)

La Verne - (909) 596-9393; Pasadena - (626) 351-8945 / www.restaurantshogun.com
La Verne - 2123 Foothill Blvd.; Pasadena - 470 N. Halstead St.

This Japanese-style restaurant has built-in tabletop grills where chefs prepare the food with rapid slicing and dicing movements (and cool tricks) in front of your eyes. (See BENIHANA on page 14, as it is a similar type of restaurant.) The "entertainment" is great and the food is delicious. Kids get a real kick out of the presentation, and are more likely to try "new" foods now that they've seen the unique way it has been prepared. Chicken, seafood, and steak are some of the menu selections. Lunch ranges from $9 to $21; dinners from $12 to $45. Kids' meals usually run from $7.95 to $9.95. (Kids are served the same meals as adults, just smaller portions.)

Hours: Open Mon. - Thurs., 11:30am - 10pm; Fri., 11:30am - 10:30pm; Sat., noon - 10:30pm; Sun., noon - 9:30pm.
Price: Menu prices listed above.
Ages: 4 years and up.

$$$$

SPEEDZONE

17871 Castleton Street, City of Industry
See the entry for SPEEDZONE on page 41 for details.

$$$

TYPHOON

(310) 390-6565 / www.typhoon.biz
3221 Donald Douglas Loop S, Santa Monica

This smallish restaurant is located on the second level of the Santa Monica airport, right off the runway, so the view of private planes landing and taking off through the huge glass windows is wonderful, and very pretty at nighttime. So, you can come here for the view.

And/or, you can come here for the bugs. This Asian fusion restaurant serves up unique dishes for adventurous eaters such as stir fry crickets with garlic - $11; Silk Worm Pupae, with 9 dipping sauces - $10; Manchurian Chambai ants on top of shoestring potatoes - $12; small, and Singapore-style scorpions (that have a crunchy taste) on shrimp toast - $12. Luckily (or not), the dishes are prepared in such a way that the bug taste is mostly covered up with spices and their food counterparts (toast, noodles, etc.), and the critters are fairly small. This, however, doesn't take away from bragging (or gagging) rights!

Other menu options include coconut curry chicken - $13; Chinese crispy duck - $18; moo shu pork - $13; Mongolian lamb - $20;. deep-fried, Thai-style frog legs - $11; soft shelled crab - $13; salmon filet - $24; and Vietnamese-style sandwiches - $11. Note that Typhoon is right down the street from the MUSEUM OF FLYING (pg. 137) and the Airplane Park.

$$$$

Hours: Open Mon. - Thurs., noon - 9:30pm; Fri., noon - 10pm; Sat., 5:30pm - 10pm; Sun., 11:30am - 9pm.
Price: Prices are listed above.
Ages: 5 years and up.

VINTAGE TEA LEAF

(562) 435-5589 / www.vintagetealeaf.com
969 E. Broadway, Long Beach

Classical music, bone china, lacy tablecloths, and a sophisticated, but homey, atmosphere in a Victorian-era tearoom make afternoon tea at Vintage Tea Leaf a real treat. You are first invited to go pick out your tea cup and saucer from a huge selection, guaren*tea*ing you'll find one to fit your personality, or mood. The Leaf features almost 100 kinds of tea to drink, each brewed just right. Feeling underdressed? Select a fancy hat and feather boa from the collection, then have a seat and settle in.

This tea house has a nice menu for its various tea "meals." For instance, the Vintage Tea of Decadence, $29, offers scones with lemon curd and Devon cream (and these are some of the best scones I've ever tasted - so moist!); soup or salad; four tea sandwiches (and there is a large selection to choose from); desserts; and a pot of tea. Only at tea places do you find such sandwich combinations as salmon, cream cheese, and lemon capers; mayonnaise and mixed berry jam on cranberry bread; etc. I need to be more adventurous while making sandwiches at home! Earl of Sandwich Tea, $22, is served with four tea sandwiches, scones and "toppings," and tea. Little Prince or Princess Tea, $16, comes with four peanut butter and jelly sandwiches; fruit cup; cupcake; and beverage. Soup, and scones with lemon curd and cream is $18. A pair of scones with Devon cream and lemon curd is $5. There is a minimum of $18 per person from 11:30am to 3pm.

The Vintage Tea Leaf also has a lovely gift shop with tea-related items.

Hours: Open Thurs. - Sun., 11:30am - 5pm. Closed Mon. - Wed. for private parties; closed New Year's Day, the week of the Long Beach Grand Prix, Thanksgiving, and Christmas.
Price: Some menu prices are listed above.
Ages: 3 years and up.

—FAMILY PAY AND PLAY—

ADVENTURE PLAYHOUSE

(818) 361-8741 / www.adventureplayhouse.com
1116 San Fernando Road, San Fernando

This big and long indoor play space has a few stand out offerings. A long, cylindrical, mega bounce has all sorts of obstacles to go up, over and through, plus a rock climbing wall; the tall slide is great; and the extra long elephant/lion/giraffe jumper is fun to walk and bounce through, plus it has inflatable obstacles inside. A smaller bounce for younger kids is a nice addition. A few toys for toddlers in the toddler section include the mini cars coasters, Little Tyke cars, soft foam blocks, and a mini ball pit. A teeter totter; a short, geometric climbing dome; kid-size tables and chairs; foosball tables; air hockey tables; space to shoot some basketball; and some run-around room make it a well-rounded place for slighter older kids, too. Socks are required for all participants. The inflatables and toys are all on carpet, while on a cement floor along one whole wall are benches and a few picnic tables.

Hours: Open Mon. - Thurs., 11am - 7pm; Fri., 11am - 8pm. Call for weekend hours as sometimes there are private parties and sometime there is open play time.
Price: $8 for ages 3 - 17 years; $5 for crawlers - 2 years old; adults are free.
Ages: 1½ - 9 years

ADVENTURE PLEX

(310) 546-7708 / www.adventureplex.org
1701 Marine Avenue, Manhattan Beach

Let's get physical! This adventure complex offers numerous classes for kids of all ages, including fitness programs, sports psychology, rock climbing, karate, pop star dance, coaching skills for teens, arts and crafts, homework tutoring, Mad Science programs, and more. Drop-ins are also welcome. For instance, come with your child to the Sports Court so he or she can pick up a game of basketball or volleyball. An indoor fitness center offers cardio equipment and free weights. Virtual fitness, with WII fitness, is also available to "play". Two, twenty-eight-foot-tall rock walls, located outside, are other appealing options. Kids, who must be at least 5 years old, learn skills, confidence, and even strategy planning by literally climbing the walls. A staff belayer is provided and so is safety equipment. Reservations are required. An adjacent ropes course is equally fun and challenging for kids at least 8 years old. A group of four or more is required in order to have the rock wall or ropes course available outside of open play hours.

The large, four-story indoor play structure, known as the Adventure Room, is a big draw and just plain fun for you and your child; mainly your child. Crawl through tunnels, go down slides, climb up ladders, play in the ball pit, bounce on the air bounces, bop through the soft foam obstacle course, and just get good and tired. There is a section for ages 3 years and under only, too. Socks are mandatory. An arts and crafts room, a classroom with internet access, a reading room (no library card needed) with books, an outdoor gardening area, and a cafe with indoor/outdoor seating complete this complex. The cafe offers a good array of turkey, tuna, chicken, or veggie sandwiches or wraps, and salads (average $9); and pizza (average $6.80 for a small). Kids' meals are also available for $5.85 for a choice of grilled cheese, quesadilla, chicken nugget or turkey hot dog. Note that MARINE AVENUE PARK (pg. 73) is located just across the way.

Hours: Drop-in sessions for the Sports Center (indoor sports games), general facility and Adventure Room are for two-hours, Sun. - Thurs., 10am - 6pm; Fri. - Sat., 10am - 7pm. Rock climbing is available daily, 9am - dusk. The ropes course is open Sat. - Sun., 11am - 4pm (depending on weather). Call first.

Price: Admission to the Adventure Room and Sports Courts is $10 for ages 3 and up and for one parent for two hours; $5 for ages 2 and under. Add another $8 to go onto the rock climbing wall, or pay $10 just for the rock wall. The ropes course is $15. The latter two activities are for two-hour increments. A day pass to the fitness center is $10. WII fitness is $5 for a half hour per individual; $10 for up to 4 people. Note that one hour before closing all admission is half off. Call for a class price list. Ask about membership prices.

Ages: 2 years and up, depending on the class or activity.

AGOURA HILLS / CALABASAS COMMUNITY CENTER ROCKWALL

(818) 880-2993 / www.ahcc.org
27040 Malibu Hills Road, Calabasas

$$$

Thirty-five-feet off the ground is pretty high up, and that's the top height of this rock climbing wall which has other different heights and slants. Just keep putting one hand and foot a little higher than the last placement, gripping the simulated rock outcroppings to reach your goal. If your child, or you, has never rock climbed before, take a class together to learn how to wear a harness, tie in, and belay. Come for a thirty-minute Try-A-Climb (with a belayer supplied), an after school program, and/or for a birthday party. Waivers are required for all climbers. Have a galactically good time here at a Cosmic Climb party where the rocks, the holds, and even the ropes glow neon colors under black lighting. Note that this is not a rock gym, but a few walls, in a separate area than the rest of the facility, with a very small amount of floor space. I like the price, though.

Hours: The Try-A-Climb is offered Tues., 5:30pm - 7:30pm; Wed., 4:30pm - 6:30pm; Sat. and Sun., 11am - 1pm. Open climbing is Mon., 6am - 10pm; Tues., 6am - 4:30pm and 5:30 - 10pm; Wed. - Fri., 6am - 10pm; Sat., 7am - 7pm; Sun., 7am - 6pm.

Price: Try-A-Climb is $7 for a half-hour. Open climbing daily rate (for 15 year olds and up tested climbers, or younger kids accompanied by a tested adult) is $7 per person; $10 for one parent and child 11 years and under. Class fees vary. Rental equipment is $4 for everything - harness and belay device, shoes and chalk bag.

Ages: 50 pounds and up.

AMY'S PLAYGROUND

(626) 799-0304 / www.amysindoorplayground.com
1115 Mission Street, Pasadena

$$

With its brick walls and with white fluffy clouds painted on the sky-blue ceiling, the atmosphere in this mid-sized, clean room is inviting. Amy's is a young child's haven that has four main play components - a structure with an enclosed, maze-like (think Habitrail) tube system that is great to climb up, crawl through (parents can, too, if you can), and slide back down; a large bounce house with a giant bounce slide; a playhouse with a kitchen; and a toddler section with foam shapes and blocks. There are a few other toys to play with and ride, too.

Bring your own food or purchase fruit cups, chips, or other snacks and a beverage at the register to enjoy at the indoor picnic tables. Remember to wear socks, or you can purchase them here for $1. A gift shop is also on the

premises.
  Hours: Open Mon. - Thurs., 10am - 6pm; Fri., 10am - 5pm. Open on weekends for private parties.
  Price: $9 for ages 2 and older; $7 for siblings and children under 2; adults are free.
  Ages: 1 - 8 years

THE ARC - ARCADIA ROCK CLIMBING GYM

(626) 294-9111 / www.arcadiarockclimbing.com

$$$$

305 N. Santa Anita Avenue, Arcadia

Like a good cliff hanger? Come climb the walls at this 6,000 square foot indoor rock climbing gym that is almost 80% bouldering. The walls are about thirty feet at the tallest and climbers need ropes and harness and a belayer, unless you (or an adult you bring) is certified to belay. You can also take a lesson to become a belayer. The bouldering is really cool with all the angles and cave-like exploration - kids and adults love this AND it's great exercise., and you don't need a belayer The Arc also offers a separate room for birthday parties, or meetings, and sleep-overs called Rock Inn with staffing, equipment and full gym access. Waivers must be signed for all climbers. Note that no children under 10 years old are allowed in gym after 6pm Monday through Friday.
  Hours: Open Mon. - Thurs., 10am - 10pm; Fri., 10am - 8pm; Sat. - Sun., 10am - 7pm. Closed New Year's Day, Thanksgiving, Christmas, and some other holidays.
  Price: A day pass is $15 for adults; $10 for ages 17 and under. Using a staff belayer, the cost is $25 an hour for the first person; $15 for each additional person - by appointment only. Shoes and harness rentals are $5.
  Ages: 5 years and up.

ARROYO MINIATURE GOLF

(323) 255-1506

$$

1055 Lohman Lane, South Pasadena

This older-style, nine-hole miniature golf course, adjacent to a real golf course, is a "hole" lot of fun. It has classic buildings such as a (small) castle, red barn, windmill, church and more, and just the right amount of difficulty. It's a good little course for practicing your short stroke game, so for the inexpensive price, practice, and fun of it, why not bring the kids and come play a couple of rounds?! There is a cafe on site, too, with burgers, etc.
  Hours: Open daily, 7am - 10pm.
  Price: $4 per person.
  Ages: 4 years and up.

AUTO CLUB RACEWAY AT POMONA

(800) 884-NHRA (6472) or (909) 593-7010 / www.nhra.com

$$$$

2780 Fairplex Drive at the Pomona Fairgrounds, Pomona

Start your engines! Host to several National Hot Rod Associations, with events beginning in February and ending in November, the quick track offers exciting races and 40,000 grandstand seats to accommodate fans. Pit passes are included with the purchase price of tickets, depending on the race.
  Hours: Call or check the website for a schedule.
  Price: Tickets range from $15 and up for adults for general seating, depending on the day, the event, and whether you want general or reserved seating. General seating can be as low as $10 for ages 6 - 12, and free for ages children 5 and under, depending on all the above factors.
  Ages: 5 years and up.

CALIFORNIA PAINTBALL PARK

(877) GIANT97 (442-6897) / www.thecaliforniapaintballpark.com

$$$$$

31050 Charley Canyon Road, Castaic

Line up your sights to play paintball at one of these ten playing fields sprawled over thirty-seven acres. Choose urban warfare, trenches, bunkers, or speedball fields, with theme-appropriate obstacles used to take cover at Tire Town, Spool Hill, Battle Castle, and others. Playing fields accommodate both beginner and advanced paintballers. Full face shields and ear protection are required. Old jeans and a long sleeve shirt, or camouflage clothing are suggested. Airsoft is available here as well. A parental waiver, available online, for youths 17 and under must be signed. There is also a shaded picnic area here.

Hours:	Open Sat. - Sun., 9am - 4pm.
Price:	$20 for airsoft or paintball walk ons with their own equipment; $50 for entry, plus airsoft gun and mask rental; $39 for entry, plus paintball gun, mask, chest protector, air and 400 rounds.
Ages:	Must be 10 years and up.

CHUCK E. CHEESE'S (Los Angeles County)

See the entry for CHUCK E. CHEESE'S (Los Angeles County) on page 16 for details.

DAVE & BUSTER'S (Los Angeles County)

Arcadia - (626) 802-6115; Los Angeles - (310) 846-9950 / www.daveandbusters.com

Arcadia - 400 S. Baldwin Ave. at Westfield Santa Anita Mall; Los Angeles - 6081 Center Dr. at the Promenade at Howard Hughes Center

See DAVE & BUSTER'S (Orange County) (pg. 258) for details. See the malls that they are located in for other attractions.

Hours:	Open Sun. - Wed., 11am - midnight; Thurs. - Sat., 11am - 1am.
Ages:	7 years and up.

FIELD OF FIRE

(661) 297-7948 / www.fieldoffire.com

23925 The Old Road, Newhall

Utilizing about eight acres, Field of Fire hits the mark with its four paintball fields studded with obstacles. Tanks, eighty foxholes, bushes, shacks, sand bags, and bunkers litter the field, while a 1,000-foot tunnel system goes under the field - how cool is that! A snack bar that serves burritos, chips, and beverages is also on the premises. Wear long sleeve shirts and jeans or camouflage clothing. A parental waiver, available online, must be signed for ages 17 and under.

Hours:	Open Sat. - Sun., 9am - 4:30pm.
Price:	$22 for walk on with own equipment for half a day; $28 for a full day. $30 for half a day of play with full equipment rental, including paintballs; $45 for a full day.
Ages:	Must be 10 years and up.

GIGGLES N' HUGS

Canoga Park - (818) 610 - HUGS (4847); Century City - (310) 553 - HUGS (4847); Glendale - (818) 956 - HUGS (4847) / www.gigglesnhugs.com

Canoga Park - 6600 Topanga Canyon Blvd., #2008 in the Westfield Topanga Plaza; Century City - 10250 Santa Monica Blvd., #155 in the Westfield Century City mall; Glendale - 3222 Glendale Galleria Way in the Glendale Galleria

You can play. You can eat. Or, you can play and eat (though not play with your food) all at the same place at Giggles N' Hugs. The play half of the really spacious room has several, good-sized, castle-like turrets to climb up into. The turrets are all connected to each other by crawl bridges, enclosed with cargo nets, on the second "story" of the castle. There is also a long, high-off-the-ground crawl bridge that connects to the Pirate boat. Play in the boat's large ball pit (parents, too!), and go down some short slides. The few other free-standing structures are also fun - one is platform that is lollipop themed and another has a longer, twisty slide. A small, enclosed toddler area has a tunnel and some soft blocks. There are also Little Tyke cars, big balls to play with, and other toys. Socks are required at all times. Music is playing in the background. Kids are loud and loving it all.

At Century City: This location's castle has a table and chairs inside, play space, and a slide. There are also sea dragons to play on; dragon murals; and a small room with a variety of toys to play on including a geodesic dome, mini merry-go-round, and see-saw. There is a fun playground just outside, too, at the mall.

A stand-out feature are the activities that all Giggles N' Hugs encourages by having various princesses and other characters and staff lead the children in singing, crafts, dancing, storytelling, magic shows, concerts, puppet shows, face painting, parachute games, or something else that kids like to join in on. This happens periodically on the stage or simply throughout the restaurant.

The restaurant half, divided by a dear, short fence, is truly a restaurant with tables and chairs along wonderful, fairytalish murals, and a few TV's. Menu choices include mostly high-end, organic foods, like breakfast panini ($9.95); blueberry pancakes, nutellacakes, or strawberry/banana waffles ($8.95); create your own omelette ($9.95); freshly made BBQ chicken pizza ($10.95); pesto penne ($11.95); New York steak sandwich ($13.95); Chinese chicken salad ($10.95); veggie wrap ($8.95); cheeseburger with fries ($10.95); wild Alaskan salmon ($15.95); cup of soup ($3.95); and sweet potato fries ($3.95). Kid's menu selections include New York steak bite ($7.50); chicken littles ($6.50); almond butter and nutella on whole wheat ($6.50); fruit plate ($5.95); build-your-own pizza ($7.50); and much more. Smoothies, ice blended drinks and espresso drinks are also available. This is not just a kid-friendly restaurant; this is a restaurant for kids and adults to <u>really</u> enjoy together.

At the Topanga Plaza location, just below Giggles N' Hugs, is a two-story(!) carousel and a play place for kids. Look up all the associated malls for what else they have to offer.

Hours: Open Mon. - Sat., 10am - 9pm; Sun., 10am - 7pm. Century City hours: Mon. - Thurs., 10:30am - 8pm, Fri., 10:30am - 10pm; Sat., 10am - 9pm; Sun., 10am - 7pm. Call first on weekends at all locations as they shut down for private parties.

Price: Entrance to Giggles N' Hugs is $10 ($9 at Century City) for kids who are walking; $5 for crawlers; babies and adults are free. Restaurant prices are listed above. Parking at Century City is $1 an hour for the first 3 hours.

Ages: 9 months - 8 years

GO KART WORLD AND SLICK CART RACING

(310) 834-3700 or (310) 834-3800 / www.gokartworld.com
21830 Recreation Road, Carson

Go full speed ahead on the six race tracks here. The Kiddie Track has electric-operated cars that go about three mph on an L-shaped track. This ride is for children over 3 years old and under 75 pounds. Mini Indie is for drivers at least 45" tall and goes about nine mph on a B-shaped track. A double-seater car can hold a driver who is at least 16 years old with a passenger who is at least 32" tall. The Bumper Car track is for drivers at least 43" tall. These cars can be individually manipulated to go forwards, backwards, and even spin all the way around. For a slick ride, drivers at least 56" tall can race on the Slick Track. We vote the Turbo Track the most-like-a-real-race-track ride. Race over and under passes and around banked, hairpin turns. Drivers must be at least 58" tall. The one-third-mile Super Trak is really super. It is two stories tall, strobe lit, and twenty-five feet wide with track space for up to twenty riders, with bank turns. All rides last four minutes. An electronic scoreboard keeps track of your time. If you have a group of ten or more, you may rent the track for a private party. A large (3,000 square feet) video and arcade game area, with redemption-playing games, is inside. Racers (and observers) can refuel at the Pit Stop Cafe, which offers pizza, chips, sodas, and more.

Hours: Open Sun. - Thurs., 10am - 10pm; Fri. - Sat., 10am - midnight.

Price: Each of the rides listed cost $6 per ride, or purchase 5 rides for $25. You may also purchase a wristband for $30 which allows sixty minutes of unlimited rides, with a minimum of 8 rides.

Ages: 3 years and up.

GOLF N' STUFF (Los Angeles County)

(562) 863-8338 / www.golfnstuff.com
10555 E. Firestone Boulevard, Norwalk

What course of action will you take? This big family fun center offers several different ways to have fun with four themed **miniature golf** courses designed with whimsical buildings like castles, Big Ben, a lighthouse, a tree house, a haunted mansion, a Western scene, and more, plus challenging obstacles- $8.50 for adults; one free child 3 years and under with each paying adult. Other attractions include **kiddie train -** $2.50 per rider; **Disc'O Thrill** (a huge flying disc ride that goes forward and back up a short roller coaster ramp while spinning around) - $6.25 a ride; **go-karts -** $6.25 for drivers, $3 for passengers; **bumper boats -** $6.25 for drivers, $3 for passengers; and **bumper cars -** $6.25 for drivers, $3 for passengers. Height restrictions apply for drivers and passengers. Look in the website for discount coupons and wristband specials, like two hours of unlimited attractions (not the arcade games) for $25.

Yes, there are also lots of arcade games to be played here along with a prize redemption area. I actually enjoy some of the interactive virtual reality games. This can keep you and the kids busy for hours - just bring quarters! A snack bar is on the premises, too, offering nachos, pizza, and hot dogs.

Hours: The golf course and arcades are open when school is in session, Mon - Thurs., 10am - 10pm (rides open 4pm - 9:30pm); Fri., 10am - midnight (rides open 4pm - 11:30pm); Sat., 10am - midnight (everything is open); Sun., 10am - 10pm (everything). Golf and arcade are open in the summer and school holidays Mon. - Thurs., 10am - 11pm (rides open noon - 10:30pm); Fri., 10am - midnight (rides open noon - 11:30pm); Sat., 10am - midnight (everything); Sun., 10am - 10pm (everything). Golf and rides begin to shut down about an hour before closing time.

Price: Attractions are individually priced above. Parking is $5 on Fri and Sat. after 6pm, but you then get $5 worth of tokens to use for games.

Ages: 4 years and up.

GUMMY THE BEAR

$$

(818) 363-9049 / www.gummythebear.com

17048 Devonshire Street, Northridge

It is lovely to have this much open play and run around space! The one huge room has two play houses (play rooms, actually - a kitchen and a bedroom); three big slides; and an enclosed, foam obstacle course on one side. A small bounce and Berenstain bear mural are along the back wall. There are small cars and trikes to ride around. There are also games on the circular benches around the poles that are painted to look like trees.

The other side of the room has a low wall with some comfy chairs and wooden picnic tables behind it. Immediately behind that is a long room/computer center with plenty of windows and raised desks and chairs. It holds computer monitors with internet access, so parents can combine work and play. Refreshments are available for purchase. Socks are required in the play area.

Hours: Open Tues. - Thurs., 10am - 7pm; Fri., 10am - 7:30pm. Open Sat. and Sun. for private parties. Closed Mon.

Price: $7.50 for 9 months - 12 years; adults are free.

Ages: 1 ½ - 7 years.

HANGAR 18 (Los Angeles County)

$$$$

Hawthorne - (310) 973-3388; Long Beach - (562) 981-3200 / www.climbhanger18.com

Hawthorne - 4926 W. Rosecrans Ave.; Long Beach - 2599 E. Willow St., Signal Hill

See HANGAR 18 (San Bernardino County) on page 407 for details about these 12,000 square foot indoor rock climbing gyms.

Hours: Both are open Mon. - Fri., 10am - 10pm; Sat. - Sun., 10am - 8pm.

Ages: 5 years and up.

HOLLYWOOD SPORTS COMPLEX

$$$$

(562) 867-9600 or (877) GIANT97 (442-6897); (562) 716-0487 - BMX / www.hollywoodsports.com; www.bellflowerbmx.com

9030 Somerset Boulevard, Bellflower

The huge, twenty-three acre paintball area has different fields sporting a variety of scenarios from movie sets with stone walls, buses, beat up automobiles, cargo nets, buildings, piles of tires, and so much more. One looks like something out of a *Terminator* movie (without even entering the fields!) with its futuristic/techno look. One paintball area features inflatable obstacles. Warriors, I mean players, run, hide, and generally try to ambush and shoot the enemy with paintballs while rock music plays in the background. (Getting hit can hurt.) There is also a speedball stadium, an airsoft field, and a separate area for beginners and kid's paintball games. Spectators can watch some of the action from a second-story observation deck. A target range for practice is here as well and the fields have lighting for nighttime play. A pro shop is on the premises for purchasing supplies. Note that paintballs for play here can only be purchased here. Wear old pants, a long sleeve sweatshirt, high-top boots or old tennis shoes, and protective clothing and mask.

Airsoft is a tactical game played with plastic bb's being shot from realistic-looking guns. A little softer, perhaps, than paintball and not as messy, players usually wear much the same gear as paintballers, and the military.

Hollywood Sports offers several packages just for groups such as Paintball Soft, where participants use a .50 caliber so the impact isn't as painful, it costs less, and is friendly to newcomers and younger players; Splatmaster, a jr. edition of paintball for players as young as 7 years old; and Lazer Splat, an outdoor laser tag game. (All of the adrenaline fun and none of the physical ouches from being hit!) Call or check the website for details and to make reservations. Groups can also use the three futsal courts, beach volleyball, the arcade, the banquet room, and the forty-foot rock climbing wall, which looks more like a mountain. It features several routes, ranging from easy (kind of) to difficult, including various angles of the rock face to climb.

The BMX track is well kept up and ready for action with all of its curves and hills. Riders must be active ABA members to race.

Hours: Open most of the year, Mon., Thurs. - Fri., 4:30pm - 9:30pm; Sat., 9am - 10pm; Sun., 9am - 8pm. Closed Tues. and Wed. Open extended hours in summer and on holidays. Call for BMX hours.

Price: Paintball field admission changes depending on the day: If you bring your own equipment, the price Mon. and Thurs. is $15 plus $11 for air; Fri., $18; Sat. - Sun., $38. If you need to rent, add on $14 for a gun and $6 for a mask to the previous prices and days. Note that full face protection is required for paintball. Walk-on airsoft prices are the same as paintball. Airsoft rentals are $30 for a gun and $6 for a mask. BMX is usually $12 to race; call for clinic prices.

Ages: Must be at least 10 years old to play paintball or airsoft.

IRWINDALE EVENTS CENTER ☼

(626) 358-1100 / www.irwindalespeedway.com $$$$

500 Speedway Drive, Irwindale

If your family likes fast cars, speed on over to a NASCAR, Speed Truck, Winston West, or USAC Midget and Sprint Cars event held at the speedway. This banked, one-half-mile super speedway track packs in thrills-a-minute for the racing enthusiast.

Hours: The season runs April through November. Races are held on Saturdays.

Price: Admission fees for regular events are usually $15 for adults; $5 for ages 6 - 12; children 5 and under free. Special event nights are $20 - $35 for adults; $10 for ages 6 - 12; children 5 and under are free.

Ages: 5 years and up.

JOHN'S INCREDIBLE PIZZA CO. (Los Angeles County) ☼

(909) 447-7777 / www.johnspizza.com $$$$

5280 Arrow Highway, Montclair

See JOHN'S INCREDIBLE PIZZA CO. (Orange County) (pg. 248) for details.

Hours: Open Mon. -Thurs.,11am - 10pm; Fri., 11am - 11pm; Sat., 10am - 11pm; Sun., 10am - 10pm.

JUMP 5150 ☼

(661) 295-5997 / www.jump5150.com $$$

28381 Constellation Road, Valencia

A pogo stick, a kangaroo, certain kinds of beans, and kids on a trampoline - all these are things that jump! Jump 5150 is an indoor trampoline place (so it pertains only to the last thing on the list) with a large, main room sporting wall-to-wall-to-floor-to-floor trampolines. It also features a trampoline dodgeball area, a foam pit, a party area, and a snack bar. Check out the website for information on dodgeball tournaments, fitness classes, Family Nights, and Little Jumpers, the latter of which is a time for just a parent and children 6 years and younger to jump. A waiver must be signed by a parent or legal guardian for all jumpers 17 years and under.

Hours: Open Tues. - Thurs., 3pm - 9pm; Fri., 10am - 11pm; Sat., 11am - 11pm; Sun., 11am - 9pm. Close Mon. and some holidays. Open longer during the summer and on some holidays.

Price: $9 an hour Tues. - Thurs. all day, and Fri. until 6pm (the second hour is free Tues. - Thurs.!); $11 an hour Fri. starting at 6pm through Sun.

Ages: 4 years and up.

THE JUMP AROUND ☼

(818) 993-JUMP (5867) / www.thejumparound.com $$

21515 Parthenia Street, Canoga Park

This place is made for kids (and adults) who love to jump around, which is every child I've ever met! Good, healthy physical activity is a great alternative to video games, and the weather isn't ever a factor. There are several, colorful, giant inflatables in this indoor playground that have slides, jumps, obstacle courses, a wall-climbing bounce, and a boxing ring where contenders wear oversized, blown-up gloves. Free foosball, air hockey, dual basketball, computer usage, satellite TV, and coffee (for adults) offer something fun for everyone. A toddler room has a little playhouse and toys geared for youngsters. All the action takes place in one big room. Socks must be worn at all times. There is a separate room for parties. Note that this facility allows "big" kids to have a party here, too - yea!

Hours: Open Mon. - Fri., 10am - 6pm, but call first to make sure a private party is not going on. Weekends are usually reserved for private parties.

Price: $7 for ages 2 - 15 for a two-hour session; $5 for walking toddlers - 2 years; infants and adults are free.

Ages: 3 years and up.

JUMPING GENIUS

(818) 347-KIDS (5437) / www.jumpinggenius.com
18327 Sherman Way, Reseda

   This spacious, indoor play area is bright and airy with charming murals. A child-sized spaceship, bus, train, and different shapes are some of the fun objects that kids can climb aboard or crawl through. The facility also has mini (really mini) coasters for young ones to roll down, a bounce house, giant bounce with slides, mini carousel, toys to ride on, a play house, infant area, tiny zip line, soft foam blocks, and a dress-up area with several costumes. Games include air hockey and ping pong. Most of all, Jumping Genius provides the room to let imaginations go wild. Note: Socks are required for kids and adults.

   Hours: Open Mon. - Thurs., 10am - 6pm; Fri., 9am - 8pm. Sometimes open play is offered on weekends, too, so call.
   Price: $9 for ages 6 months to 14 years for up to 3 hours of play; siblings are $7; adults are free. Last hour admission is $6 per child.
   Ages: 1 - 8 years.

JUMPING JACKS (Los Angeles County)

(909) 599-4199 / www.jumpingjacksparty.com
186 Village Court, San Dimas

   See JUMPING JACKS (Riverside County) on page 408 for details. This facility is 7,000 square feet larger (more jumping fun!) and it offers a glow-in-the-dark room with planet murals, plus a basketball court.

   Hours: Open play, family fun times are Tues., 10:30am - 1pm; Wed., 2pm - 5pm; Wed. - Thurs., 6pm - 9pm.
   Price: $8 per child for ages 2 and up; children under 2 with a paid sibling, and adults, are free.

JUMP 'N JAMMIN (Los Angeles County)

(626) 821-9120 / www.jumpnjammin.com
400 South Baldwin Avenue in the Westfield Santa Anita Mall, Arcadia

   See JUMP 'N JAMMIN (Orange County) (pg. 260) for details about this big and fun indoor play place.

   Hours: Open Mon. - Thurs., 10am - 6pm; Fri. - Sat., 10am - 8pm; Sun., 11am - 7pm. Closed Easter, Thanksgiving, and Christmas.
   Price: $12.95 for ages 2 and up; $5.49 for children 23 months or younger, or free with a full-price paid sibling; one adult is free with each paid child admission, additional adults are $3.
   Ages: 2- 12 years

K1 SPEED TORRANCE (Los Angeles County)

(310) 532-2478 / www.k1speed.com
19038 S. Vermont Avenue, Gardena

   See K1 SPEED (San Diego County) on page 486 for details. This location has an etched concrete racing surface, which is different from the asphalt on the other locations.

KDB (Kitchen, Den, Bar)

(562) 308-7529 / www.kdblongbeach.com
10 Aquarium Way, Long Beach

   KDB is a high-tech entertainment venue dedicated to over 130 latest (and greatest) interactive virtual reality, arcade games (like skee ball), and video games, many of them sports-oriented, plus motion simulator rides. A game prize redemption center is here, too. A real, ten-lane bowling alley; billiards tables; two bars with large screen TVs showing mostly sports; live entertainment for the older crowd; and the full-service, indoor-outdoor restaurant are also part of the scene.

   Food choices include appetizers of mac and cheese bites ($7) and shrimp ($9), and "real" food such as margherita pizza ($9), French dip ($10), turkey club sandwich ($9), hamburgers ($8), chopped Cobb salad ($10), beef short ribs ($15), Philly chicken wrap ($9), blackened shrimp and chicken fettuccine ($13), and more, including build your own pizza and your own burger, plus gluten-free items. Check the website for specials like Power Lunch during the week, 11am to 3pm - when you purchase a lunch entree you get either a $10 game card or one game of bowling and shoes for only $3 more. See THE PIKE AT RAINBOW HARBOR (pg. 175) and SHORELINE VILLAGE (pg. 161) for details about the other attractions in this immediate vicinity.

Hours: Open Sun. - Thurs., 11am - midnight; Fri. - Sat., 11am - 1am. Guests must be 21 years or older after 10pm.

Price: Menu prices are listed above. Bowling starts at $4 per person (depending on day and time); shoe rentals are $3.

Ages: 7 years and up.

KID CONCEPTS U.S.A.

(310) 465-0075 / www.kidconceptsusa.com
22844 Hawthorne Boulevard, Torrance

What a concept! The main feature within this 9,000 square-foot room is a good-sized, terrific, multi-level play structure. It has several tubes (large enough for adults to crawl through), slides, ball pits, a bounce room, obstacle courses, and lots of nooks and crannies to discover. Note: The black slide is really fast. Kids can also sit in a child-sized rocket ship or helicopter and "fly" away to parts unknown. (Doesn't that sound appealing sometimes?!) Although this area is well-ventilated, my kids got sweaty having such a good time. Wearing socks is a must!

A separate, upstairs section has interactive dance videos to get the kids moving, imitating the steps along with the beat. Below is a small costume section for dress up. Be an engineer using the train table. Play air hockey at .75¢ a game. Another small, separate area has a good array of soft foam blocks for building. The arts and crafts room is for your creative genius to create.

A room just for toddlers, painted in primary colors, has mats, little slides, tunnels and age-appropriate toys to play with and on. The party rooms are cutely-decorated. The toy store has a great selection of educational and fun toys. Check out the numerous classes and special events hosted here.

There is a sitting area, with tables and chairs, that you can just enjoy or use to eat at when ordering food from the cafe. It serves up delicious selections including regular pizzas ($5.99 for an individual pan cheese); specialty pizzas, such as barbecue chicken ($15.99 for a twelve-inch); chicken veggie pasta ($9.49); cream of broccoli soup ($3.99); a variety of salads ($8.99); hamburgers or turkey burgers with fries (about $7); angel hair pasta (about $9); fruit bowl ($5.99); zucchini sticks ($4.99); and brownies (about $1.99). Kid's meals are about $5 for a choice of pizza, chicken strips, a burger, grilled cheese, or a hot dog, plus fries and a drink.

Hours: Open Mon. - Thurs., 10am - 8pm; Fri. - Sat., 10am - 9pm; Sun., 10am - 6pm. Closed New Year's Day, Easter, Mother's Day, 4th of July, Thanksgiving, and Christmas.

Price: Two-hour sessions are $10 for ages 3 and up, with one free adult per child (additional adults are $4); $7 for ages 1 - 2; children under 1 are free with a paid child. Admission Mon. - Thurs., after 5pm is $7. Ask about prices for gym classes.

Ages: 9 months - 10 years.

KIDS AHOY

(818) 999-1533 / www.kidsahoyplayground.com
20929 Ventura Blvd. #28, Woodland Hills

Ahoy is a term used to call a ship or to attract attention. So, ahoy - ship out to this great, indoor, nautically-themed, play place. The large, carpeted room has so many fun elements your little mates won't know where to go first. The good-sized wooden ship in the center of the room is a good place to start with its boarding ladder and rope railings. It has an upper deck and a place to play below.

Alongside one wall is a play room with cargo netting, an obstacle course, slides, and steps for little people to climb up and then crawl through a tube that connects to an adjacent, duplicate, play room. Another one of these fun play rooms is on the opposite side wall, too. There is also a bounce house; lots of Little Tyke and other cars; a train table; two tire swings; an air hockey table; a short chalk board wall; free-standing, short slides; a playhouse; mini roller coasters; lots of books, plus kid-size table and chairs; and a small gated-off section for infants and toddlers with more toys just for them. Socks are required in all play areas.

The Galley is an open, adjacent space that's cutely decorated with painted fish, seahorses and paddles. It has a few Adirondack chairs and wooden picnic tables and benches. You are welcome to bring your own food. Note that there are a few picnic tables outside, as well.

Hours: Open Mon. - Thurs., 10am - 7pm; Fri., 10am - 6pm. Weekends are reserved for birthday parties.

Price: $8 for ages 9 months and up for kids who are playing; adults are free.

Ages: 9 months - 9 years.

KIDS CASTLE
(818) 565-5552 / www.kidscastleusa.com
2814 Empire Avenue, Burbank

    Outside, a dragon lounges on the top of the castle. Inside this amusement game castle, vivid and colorful cartoon-like images of a friendly dragon, plus all of his dragon friends, knights, and royal family completely cover all the walls and columns. Banners hang from the ceiling. The dimly-lit interior is packed with all kinds of family-friendly arcade and video games (many non-violent), a prize redemption area, a photo booth, a tilt-a-whirl type of ride, and a 1,600 square feet, multi-level, soft play area for younger kids that is also castle-themed. It features slides, tubes, obstacle courses, cargo climbing areas, and more.

    A good portion of the castle is given over to food, with plenty of seating (and several private party rooms). Menu choices include hot wings ($9.95); Greek salad ($7.50); grilled chicken sandwich or hamburger ($8.50); pizza ($13.95); fettuccine chicken alfredo ($13.50); and tilapia served with pasta ($15.95). The kid's menu offers chicken nuggets ($4.99), grilled cheese ($4.99), or individual pizza ($6.50). Have a fire-breathing good time!

    Hours: Open Mon. - Thurs., noon - 9pm; Fri. - Sun., 11am - 10pm.
    Price: Free general admission and free for the soft play area. Food prices are listed above. Games start at 2 credits each: $5 for 30 credits, $10 for 60 credits, etc. $1 for each new game card.
    Ages: 4 years and up.

KIDZONE WEST HILLS
(818) 704-1557 / www.kidzonewesthills.com
6729 Fallbrook Avenue, West Hills

    A gym just for kids! Kidzone is a large room offering lots of equipment and safety pads for kids to get physical and play creatively. A small, enclosed trampoline; mini exercise work-out machines; swings and ropes hanging from the ceiling; and climbing structures and toys - it's all about getting kids active while having fun doing it. See the website calendar for a schedule of classes.

    Hours: Open Mon. - Thurs., 10am - 6pm; Fri. - Sun., 10am - 7pm.
    Price: $12 for three hours; $10 for the first sibling. Ages 10 months and under are $8. Adults are free.
    Ages: 1 - 10 years.

LA BOULDERS
(323) 406-9119 / www.touchstoneclimbing.com/la-boulders
1375 E. 6th Street, #8, Los Angeles

    Bouldering is a form of indoor rock climbing without ropes or harnesses or such tall walls. Moving sideways, upside down, onto overhangs and archways, in a cave, and just up - bouldering is definitely a physically and mentally challenging sport as climbers solve "problems", which is what the routes are called. Come to learn the ropes of bouldering (so to speak), or advance your skills by signing up for a class on technique at this nicely-laid out bouldering gym with contemporary-looking walls. The staff is helpful and wants to see people succeed in their climbing endeavors. See DOWNTOWN LOS ANGELES / GRAND PARK (pg. 167) for information on Grand Park and all the other places to go within this fairly immediate area.

    Hours: Open Mon. - Thurs., 11am - 11pm; Fri., 11am - 10pm; Sat - Sun., 10am - 6pm.
    Price: A day pass is $20 per person; $15 on weekdays before 3pm. Shoes rentals are $4.
    Ages: 5 years and up.

LASER STORM (Los Angeles)
(310) 373-8470 or (310) 378-2265 / www.gablehousebowl.com
22501 Hawthorne Boulevard, Torrance

    Laser tag is taking kids (and adults) by storm! Power up your laser gun as two teams of up to thirty people compete against each other and "shoot" it out in a darkened room. Take cover behind neon-colored partitions, decorated with gak splats, as an opponent aims at you. Or, use the partitions as cover to stealthily sneak up on someone. The fifteen-minute games are action-packed, and all the running around can literally take your breath away! Note that there are two arenas here and that they are located right next to Gable House Bowl, which offers Rock and Glow bowling in addition to regular bowling. A full-service snack bar and arcade games are here, too.

Hours: Open during the school year, Mon., 3pm - 9pm; Thurs., 3pm - 10pm; Fri. - 3pm - 11pm; Sat., 10am - 11pm; Sun., 10am - 8pm. Closed Tues. and Wed. Open in the summer longer hours.

Price: Prices change depending on the day and time so check the website or call. Games Mon. - Fri. are generally $5 per person; Sat. - Sun., $6.

Ages: 6 years and up.

LEGO - MINI MODEL BUILD (Los Angeles County)

Canoga Park - (818) 884-8597; Glendale - (818) 549-0733 / shop.lego.com/en-US/MiniBuilds;

Canoga Park - 6600 Topanga Canyon Blvd. at Westfield Topanga mall; Glendale - 2148 Galleria Way at Glendale Galleria

See LEGO - MINI MODEL BUILD (San Diego County) on page 488 for info on this great, free LEGO mini model build. Timed tickets for entry into the store are available at each location. At the Glendale location, tickets are given out starting around 3pm; at Canoga Park, at 3:45pm. This leaves plenty of time for dinner and/or shopping.

Hours: The first Tues. of each month, 5pm - 7pm.
Price: Free
Ages: 6 - 14 years old, only.

LOLLIPOP DREAM

(818) 981-7446 / www.lollipop-dream.com

4006 Riverside Drive, suite 122 in Westfield Fashion Square, Sherman Oaks

Calling all princesses or girls who just like to dress up - Lollipop Dream is the place for you. The small retail store in the front has costumes, books, jewelry, and other fun items. The large backroom with lots of mirrors and fantasy wall murals, has a table with kid-size chairs in the center, plus vanity sets for make-up or face painting. The long wall closet holds over 200 costumes to play dress-up, along with tiaras, shoes, fairy wings, and other accessories. Lollipop Dream offers weekly walk-in events and monthly family special happenings, such as afternoon tea, story time, and happy hour (the fairytale kind), as well as being a great place for parties and even play dates. The staff dresses up, too, and helps direct the fun.

Hours: The store is open Mon. - Fri., 10am - 7pm; Sat., 10am -8pm; Sun., 11am - 6pm. Call or check the website for a schedule of events.
Price: Prices vary. An hour-long playdate during the week, for instance, is $15 per child for 2 - 9 children, which includes dressing up, face painting, a craft, and games.
Ages: 3 years and up.

MB2 RACEWAY (Los Angeles County)

(866) 986-RACE (7223) / www.mb2raceway.com

13943 Balboa Boulevard, Sylmar

Go cart yourself to this indoor go kart facility where the quarter-mile long racetrack has eleven turns. Keep control of the car and zoom around the turns, trying to beat other drivers' times. Kids must be at least 48" to drive.

Hours: Open Mon. - Thurs., noon - 10pm; Fri. - Sat., 11am - midnight; Sun., 11am - 8pm.
Price: Licensed drivers are $23 for a fourteen-lap race; juniors are $20 for a nine-lap race.
Ages: At least 48" tall.

MOUNTASIA FUN CENTER

(661) 253-4FUN (4386) / www.mountasiafuncenter.com

21516 Golden Triangle Road, Santa Clarita

Mountasia offers a mountain of fun for your family! Play either one of two **miniature golf** courses that feature a cascading waterfall. Note that the zebra course has a hole that goes under the waterfall and inside a cave, and that the elephant course has nine wheelchair friendly holes. Prices are $7.50 for ages 4 and up; $6.50 for seniors; children 3 years and under are free. Zip around the race track in **go karts** - $7.50 for a single or double car. Drivers must be at least 58" tall and passengers must be 42". Try to avoid getting wet (or go for it) in the **bumper boats** - $7.50 a ride; a passenger can ride for free. Height and age restrictions apply. Kids at least 48" tall and 6 years old can improve their batting average at the **batting cages**.

Inside Mountasia are family-oriented video and arcade games and a redemption center; a **rock climbing wall** ($7.50 for two climbs); and a spacious, future-city themed **lazer tag arena** where players put on vests and use their laser guns to "tag" opponents and score points ($7.50 per game). For fun eating, try **FARRELL'S ICE CREAM**

PARLOUR RESTAURANTS (with a huge ice cream and candy selection). See page 18 and 247 for details on this great, family-welcoming restaurant.

Hours: Open most of the year, Mon. - Thurs., noon - 9pm for Farrell's, arcade, and mini golf; and 2pm - 9pm for everything else; open the same on Fri. except until 11pm; Sat., 10am - 11pm (Farrell's opens at 11am); Sun., 11am - 9pm. All attractions are open in the summer and school breaks, Mon. - Thurs., 10am - 9pm; Fri. - Sat., 10am - 11pm; Sun., 11am - 9pm (Farrell's opens at 11am daily).

Price: Attractions are individually priced. Ask about unlimited play and Family Fun specials.

Ages: 4 years and up.

MULLIGAN FAMILY FUN CENTER - Torrance

(310) 325-3950 / www.mulligantorrance.com
1351 W. Sepulveda Boulevard, Torrance

    Fore a fun time of golfing come play at the two wonderful **miniature golf** courses that feature great add-ons such as a mining cave to go through, a haunted mansion obstacle, huge boulders to go under, a castle, an old West "town", a train and a fire house - $7.99 for adults, $5.50 for seniors and kids 10 and under. This center features also has **batting cages** - $1 for twelve pitches; **go-kart slic track** racing - $7 for drivers for a five-minute ride (drivers must be 56" and passengers 40") and $2.75 for passengers; **rookie go-karts** for ages 5 minimum, $5.50; **paddle boats** for ages 3 to 80lbs. - $3.50; glacier-looking **rock climbing** wall - $5.50 for two attempts; a small **kids play area** for young kids of a maximum 54" tall to climb (think gerbil habitat on steroids for the enclosed tubes), slide, jump, and play; **laser tag** - a hi-tech battle game in a 2,200-square-foot arena - $6; and the ever-present arcade games. A driving range is also here, as is a full-service snack bar serving nachos, pizza, hot dogs, and more.

Hours: Open Mon. - Thurs., noon - 8pm; Fri., noon - 10pm; Sat., 10am - 10pm; Sun., 10am - 9pm. The center is sometimes open longer during the summer and school breaks.

Price: Attractions are individually priced above. Ask about special package pricing or all-day passes.

Ages: 2 years through 54" tall for the play area; 4 years and up for miniature golf.

MULLIGAN FAMILY FUN CENTER - Palmdale

(661) 273-1407 / www.mulliganpalmdale.com
525 West Avenue P-4, Palmdale

    Do you have a Tiger in your house? A Tiger Woods, I mean. Practice a modified golf swing at the three themed, nine-hole **miniature golf** courses here - $6.49 for adults for all twenty-seven holes; $5.99 for seniors and children 10 years and under. A five-minute ride on a two-seater **go-kart** is $6.49 for drivers, who must be at least 56" tall, and $2.99 for passengers, who must be at least 40" tall. **Rookie go-kart**, where the driver must be a minimum 40" is $5. Get wet on **Blaster boats** (i.e., bumper cars in the water that are open seasonally) at $6.49 for drivers, who must be at least 44" tall, and $2.99 for passengers, who must be at least 44" tall. I always enjoy a round of **lazer tag** and this arena seems futuristic with neon colors and lights. The cost is $6.49. The **rock climbing wall** is $6.49 for three attempts. Instead of hanging on by a thread, try a rope, or at least the **Ropes Course**. This multi-level attraction looks like a play structure, but you are harnessed in while walking a ropes bridge, over a tightrope, and on an adventure trail - (i.e. more challenges). It costs $8.49 for one time use, but can be added to an unlimited all-day pass for an additional $5. Other attractions here include batting cages, a large game arcade area, and a snack bar.

Hours: Open most of the year, Mon. - Thurs., 2pm - 8pm; Fri., 2pm - 10pm; Sat., 11am - 10pm; Sun., 11am - 8pm. Open in the summer and on holidays longer hours, so call first.

Price: Individual attractions are listed above. Ask about special package pricing or park passes.

Ages: 4 years and up.

PAINTBALL U.S.A. CLOSE ENCOUNTERS

(800) 919-9237 / www.paintballusa.org
15112 Sierra Highway, Santa Clarita

    Play this version of Capture the Flag while armed with markers (i.e., guns) filled with paint. This makes the game a bit more colorful! You'll be placed on one of two teams. The object of the game is to get the flag from your opponent's base, while dodging paintballs by hiding behind objects such as bunkers and trees. There are fourteen fields here that incorporate bales of hay; huge wooden wheels; trenches; dunes; a maze; two that resemble real battlefields in the middle-East; ones with natural obstacles, such as trees and ravine; and man-made ones with buildings and inflatables. A referee is on the playing field to insure fair play and to help out. Each game lasts about twenty minutes.

After you're rested, go for another round. Tip: Wear pants and other clothing you don't care about, and shoes with good traction. Getting hit stings, so wear a padded shirt or multiply layers to help absorb the hits. Players 17 and under must have a waiver, which is available online, signed by a parent or guardian.

Participants can also play airsoft and infrared games (similar to laser tag, but played outside) here. In between games, enjoy shaded picnic facilities with BBQs - just bring your own food, or order pizza from the onsite cashier, as it can be delivered.

Hours: Open to the public, Sat. - Sun. and holiday Mon., 9am - 4pm. Groups of 25 or more can reserve play time during the week.

Price: If you have your own equipment, admission is $30 which includes all-day air. For rentals, prices are $40 for ages 10 - 17, which includes 200 paintballs; $45 for ages 18 and older.

Ages: 10 years and up, only.

PEEKABOO PLAYLAND

(323) 255-1400 / www.peekabooplayland.com
2030 Colorado Boulevard, Eagle Rock

This two-story, high-ceiling, airy home with lots of natural light has been converted to a sweet and casually elegant kid's play place. Stairs, with fencing all around, lead up to a big white bird to climb into, an entrance to a slide, and a large upper play area with a puppet theater, book nook, and plenty of toys and puzzles. Downstairs is a small ball pit, raised train tables, mini bounce, Little Tykes cars, mini slides, and a little kitchen room with a play oven, sink, and table. Kids can do Peekasso art projects once a week, here, too. There are couches for parents to relax and watch. All adults must wear socks, too.

Hours: Open Mon. - Thurs., 10am - 6pm; Fri., 10am - 5pm; open Sat. - Sun. for private parties only. Closed Thanksgiving and Christmas.

Price: $9 per child; $7 for siblings and children 1 and under; adults are free.

Ages: 1 - 8 years

PINT SIZE KIDS

(310) 339-7452 / www.pintsizekids.com
13323 Ventura Boulevard, Sherman Oaks

The mid-sized room with cement flooring is painted to look like a streets; a few Little Tyke cars and street signs add to the setting. Along the perimeter of the wide road are a few different little rooms, such as a workshop with Duplos and other toys; a medical center with doctor's coats, stethoscopes, an examining table, and toy body parts; a little kitchen with a play stove and frig, plus a table and chairs and painted fireplace; and a grocery store with a cash register, shelves with fake food, and bins of plastic fruits and veggies. A gated infant/toddler area has stuffed animals and toys for tots. A carpeted book nook in the front has plenty of books to peruse, a train table, and large stuffed animals to use as pillows.

This facility also offers a myriad of art, music, dance, sport and other classes geared for your pint-sized darlings. Wear socks as they are required.

Hours: Open Mon. - Fri., 9am - 6pm; Sat., 9am - noon.

Price: $12 for the first child, ages 9 months and up; $10 for siblings; parents are free.

Ages: 1 - 7

PLAY SOURCE

(818) 888-0899 / www.playsourceinfo.com
21921 Ventura Boulevard, Woodland Hills

This clean, spacious room, with various nature-oriented murals on each wall, has several large pieces of play equipment for younger kids, such as a bounce with a slide; an outer-space-themed structure with a few enclosed tunnels to crawl through (think large gerbil runs) and curvy slides; a short rock climbing wall with pads on the floor; and a playhouse with pretend kitchen implements. There are also Little Tyke cars; a short basketball net; balls; a little treehouse; an enclosed padded spot for littlest ones; tabletop toys and train sets; and lots of other building and educational toys. A few picnic tables (bring your own treats!) are located near the retail shop in the front of the play center. Please wear socks.

Hours: Open Mon. - Tues., 9am - 7pm; Wed. - Thurs., 9am - 8pm; Fri., 9am - 5pm. Open Sat. - Sun. for private parties only.

Price: $9 for the first child (9 months - 11 years); $7 for the first sibling; $5 for additional siblings; adults are free.

Ages: 6 months - 8 years

PUMP IT UP (Los Angeles County)

Torrance - (310) 533-9377; Van Nuys - (818) 994-1100 / www.pumpitupparty.com

Torrance - 1780 Oak Street; Van Nuys - 6862 Hayvenhurst Avenue, Unit B

See PUMP IT UP (San Diego County) on page 491 for details.

Hours: Torrance - Pre-K Open Jump is Mon. - Thurs., 10am - noon. All Ages Open Jump is Mon. - Thurs., noon - 2pm. Van Nuys - Open Jump is Tues. - Thurs., 3pm - 5pm.

Price: Both locations are $10 per child; adults are free.

ROCKREATION (Los Angeles County)

(310) 207-7199 / www.rockreation.com

11866 La Grange Avenue, Los Angeles

See the entry for ROCKREATION (Orange County) on page 264 for details. This location is a little smaller at 9,000 square feet.

Hours: The gym is open Mon. and Wed., noon - 11pm; Tues. and Thurs., 6am - 11pm; Fri., noon - 10pm; Sat. - Sun., 10am - 6pm. Closed major holidays. Climb Time is offered Sat. - Sun., 1pm - 3pm. Kids' Climb, for ages 6 - 12, is offered Mon., 4pm - 6pm; Sat. and Sun., 3pm - 5pm.

Price: $17 for adults for a day pass; $12 for ages 11 and under, but they must have a belayer. Rental equipment - shoes and harness - is an additional $7. Climb Time is $15 per hour. Kids Climb is $30 for the two-hour session - both include the necessary equipment. Reservations are needed.

Ages: 5 years and up.

ROLLING ROBOTS

Glendale - (818) 241-2308; Rolling Hills Estates - (424) 206-9466 / www.rollingrobots.com

Glendale - 1800 S. Brand Boulevard, #101; Rolling Hills Estates - 700 Silver Spur Drive

Does it get any cooler than building your own customized robot and then competing with it?? I think not! Rolling Robots is a store where you can purchase your own remote-controlled robot, (or car) including accessories and extras, then put it together at the store (or at home). Compete with other robots in the store's battle arena by maneuvering and crossing target spots on the arena floor so the robot's scanners light up and your bot score points. Of course, other robots try to block you from those spots. Games are about five minutes long. You can also just rent a robot to battle at the store for $3 a game. Weapons, a shield, and remote - you're ready to roll.

School or scout field trips, birthday parties, and summer camps (any group, really, with a minimum of ten people) can come for a few hours (or even weekly programs) and really learn robotics. The adjacent Robotics Lab room is the place to learn assembly and technology, and then actually build your robot. Birthday party kits include a battery-operated robot to assemble with a cardboard body, wheels, and movable arms.

Hours: Glendale - Open daily, 10am - 6pm. Rolling Hills - Open daily, noon - 6pm - usually by appointment.

Price: Robots start at $16.99 for a basic model with a cardboard body. Robot rentals are $3 a game.

Ages: 4 years and up.

ROUND1 BOWLING AND AMUSEMENT (Los Angeles County)

City of Industry - (626) 964-5356; Lakewood - (562) 408-2937 / www.round1usa.com; www.shoplakewoodcenter.com

City of Industry - 1600 S. Azusa Ave. Suite 285, in the Puente Hills Mall; Lakewood - 401 Lakewood Center Mall in Lakewood Center Mall

Lights! Action! Noise! And lots of it all! Talk about a place where kids (and adults) can be entertained for hours. On one side of the escalators (in the Lakewood Mall) are the twenty, trendy bowling lanes, each with their own screen to watch sporting events or music videos, while bowling. Distracting to me, but others love it. Bumper lanes are available for kids. Come at nighttime to play cosmic bowling, where the lanes are lit by neon lights. Five billiard tables are next to the alleys, as are two private rooms for karaoke (with songs available in English, Spanish, Chinese, Japanese and Korean); two ping pong tables (with netting over the doorway to help catch stray balls); dartboards; and a bar and cafe. The cafe serves 8" pizzas ($6.99), hamburgers ($4.49), nachos ($4.99), sweet potato fries ($3.49), buffalo chicken wings ($7.99), raviolis ($2.50) and more.

The other side of the escalator is taken over by over 200 of the newest and most popular arcade and video games in a rather large space. Redeem your tickets for some good prizes. Along with the games there is an entire section(!) of photo booths here in which to take pictures and then add cool extras to them. There are also a plethora of crane games with some big ticket items to win.

Elsewhere in Lakewood Center Mall (and immediately adjacent to it) are numerous eating options from sit-down restaurants to fast food and snack items. See LAKEWOOD CENTER KIDS CLUB (pg. 91) for other kid offerings in the mall.

Hours: Round1 is open daily, 10am - 2am; ages 18 and over only after 10pm.
Price: Bowling starts at $5 for one game during the day, during the week. Shoe rentals are $3.50. Karaoke starts at $15 an hour for up to six people, during the day, during the week, plus one order from the food menu. Billiards, darts, and ping pong start at $8 an hour.
Ages: 5 years and up.

SCOOTER'S JUNGLE (Los Angeles County)

El Segundo - (888) 516-1983; Valencia - (661) 877-4400 / www.scootersjungle.com
El Segundo - 606 Hawaii Street; Valencia - 28230 Constellation

See SCOOTER'S JUNGLE (Orange County) on page 265 for details. The Valencia location has three arenas, each geared for a different age group.

Hours: Most locations have such varied calendars, so check the websites. A few have regular times: El Segundo - Toddler Times are usually Tues. - Thurs., 10:30am - noon. Family Fun and All Ages are usually every other Wed. from 5:30pm - 8:30pm. Valencia - Toddler Times are usually Wed. - Thurs., 10:30am - noon.
Price: Family Fun Events at the El Segundo location is $9 per child; $4 for adults.
Ages: 2 years and up.

SHERMAN OAKS CASTLE PARK

(818) 756-9459 / www.laparks.org/shermanoaks_castlepk
4989 Sepulveda Blvd., Sherman Oaks

This Castle Park offers royal fun for the whole family. Adjacent to the parking lot is a small, outdoor eating area with picnic tables. Go through the castle onto grounds that are beautifully landscaped (palm and pine trees and plants) so puttin' around on the three majestic **miniature golf** courses is a real pleasure. All the fun elements are here - obstacles, hairpin turns, miniature buildings, themed holes, bridges, waterways, a gingerbread house, a lighthouse, and more. There are also nine **batting cages** (kids must be 8 years old, or at least 54" tall), over 100 arcade games surrounded by wall murals of a king and his subjects, a redemption center, and a full-service snack bar.

Hours: Open Mon. - Thurs., 10am - 11pm; Fri., 10am - midnight; Sat., 9am - midnight; Sun., 9am - 11pm. Open during the summer and school breaks, Mon. - Fri., 10am - midnight; Sat. - Sun., 9am - midnight.
Price: Miniature golf is $6.50 for the first round for adults; $5.50 for seniors and for children 5 - 12; ages 4 and under are free with a paying adult; $3 for replays for all ages. Pay only $3 a round for early bird specials on Sat. and Sun. morning, 9am - 10:30am.
Ages: 4 years and up.

SKY HIGH SPORTS (Los Angeles County)

Valencia - (661) 775-6300; Woodland Hills - (818) 346-6300 / Valencia - val.jumpskyhigh.com; Woodland Hills - woh.jumpskyhigh.com
Valencia - 28656 The Old Road; Woodland Hills - 6033 De Soto Avenue

See SKY HIGH SPORTS (pg. 266) for details about this fantastic, indoor trampoline place.

Hours: Open Sun. - Mon., 11am - 9pm; Tues. - Wed., 2pm - 9pm; Thurs., 2pm - 10pm; Fri. - Sat., 11am - midnight. The Woodland Hills location is open until 10pm (not 9pm). Both locations are open extended hours for holidays and open in the summer daily at 11am.
Price: $12 per person for the first hour; $6 an hour after that only Mon. - Thurs. (excluding holidays). Always check the website for specials.

Ages: 4 years and up.

SKY ZONE (Los Angeles County)

Covina - (626) 331-3208; Gardena (Torrance) - (310) 323-4500; Glendale - coming!; San Fernando Valley - coming!; Van Nuys - (818) 994-7777 or (800) 933-1247 / www.skyzone.com
Covina - 1314 North Azusa Ave.; Gardena - 1625 West 190ᵗʰ St.; Glendale - coming!; San Fernando Valley - coming!; Van Nuys - 7741 Hayvenhurst Ave.

How high can you jump? How long can you jump? (I can only last ten minutes.) Wall-to-wall trampolines, Sky Zone can test your limits, and take you beyond. The main room has over forty individual trampoline rectangles that form one big patchwork grid. And that doesn't include the angled trampolines on the walls which then have you literally bouncing off the walls. Toddlers have their own room to bounce in so they can join in on the fun.

The Foam Zone is an area to practice flips and tricks at your own risk, or just to jump into the soft foam block pit for the fun of it. Play dodgeball like never before - on a trampoline! There are several courts just for this game. Other sports offered here while trampolining include volleyball, and basketball on the few free-throw courts. For even more of a work-out join a Skyrobics or Skyburn class! You can also rest and watch others be active at tables and chairs both downstairs and up. A few arcade games are available to play, too.

You can't bring in outside food, but there are some snacks (and lots of candy) available for purchase. Sky Socks (with tread) are mandatory and available to purchase for $2. (Some locations include this sock fee in their admission price; some don't.) Waivers must be signed by a parent or legal guardian before jumping can commence. Always check the website for specials, deals, and classes including Toddler Time, Jumpapalooza, College Night, Hoppy Hour, SkyJam, Family Fitness, and more.

Hours: Open Tues. - Thurs., 3pm - 9pm; Fri., 3pm - 11pm; Sat., 10am - midnight; Sun., 10am - 9pm. Hours fluctuate by location. (Gardena location closes at 8pm, Sun. - Thurs.)
Price: Covina and Van Nuys: $9 for 30 min. for 40" and taller; $14 for 60 min., $19 for 90 min. $5 for 30 min. for 39" and below; $9 for 60 min. Gardena: $12 for 30 min.; $16 for 60 min.; $21 for 90 min. Prices fluctuate by location.
Ages: 3 years and up.

SPEEDZONE

(626) 913-9663 / www.speedzone.com
17871 Castleton Street, City of Industry

Ahhhh, the smell of gasoline and the sound of engines being revved! Although SpeedZone is advertised as a racing park for adults, kids can go full throttle here, too. The huge mural of formula race cars on the outside of the massive black-and-white-checkered building reinforce the park's intentions of being dedicated to speed, racing, and competition. The four tracks, along with their minimum height requirements are: Top Eliminator Dragsters, with 300-horsepower cars (4'8"); Grand Prix, with custom-scale-designed Formula One Racers (5' and have a driver's license); Turbo Track, a two-seater sidewinder racer which allows wheel-to-wheel racing with up to nineteen other drivers (5'); and Slick Trax, for a spin around the concrete track (5'). SpeedZone is the closest thing to professional racing available to the public. Kids between 42" and 54" are not left out - they have their own track called Lil' Thunder.

Two, eighteen-hole miniature golf courses are done in the racing theme motif and include paraphernalia such as gas pumps, tires, and guard rails, plus waterways and bridges. Inside, SpeedZone decor consists of racing flags, murals, photos, a few cars (on the floor and suspended from the ceiling), and signed memorabilia such as helmets and jumpsuits.

Enjoy American classic food in the Johnny Rockets restaurant. Meal choices include hamburgers ($7.99), grilled chicken breast sandwich ($8.99), chicken salad ($9.99), Philly cheesesteak ($9.99), chili cheese dog ($7.99), and a full selection of shakes and floats ($5.49). Kid's meals are $5.99 to $6.99 for a choice of two mini burgers, chicken tenders, or grilled cheese sandwich.

Keep the adrenaline pumping with more than 100 video, virtual reality, and arcade games in the Electric Alley, plus a prize redemption area. Play basketball or skee ball, or try virtual jetskiing, motocross, or downhill skiing. Mini-bowling (no shoe rentals needed!) is $3 per 5 frames. At the Daytona simulators, up to eight drivers can race against each other on the same track. A day at SpeedZone is not just another day at the races!

Hours: Open Mon. - Thurs., 11am - 10pm, racing opens at noon, Grand Prix at 6pm; Fri., 11am - midnight, racing opens at noon, Grand Prix at 6pm; Sat., 11am - midnight, racing opens at 11am; Sun., 11am - 10pm, racing opens at 11am. Open one hour earlier in the summer. All visitors at SpeedZone after 10pm must have a valid California driver's license.

Price: Free entrance. Top Eliminator - $16 for 3 races; Grand Prix - $7 for 3 laps; Turbo Track and Slick Trax are $7 each for 5 minutes. Lil' Thunder is $5 per race. Speedway miniature golf is $6 for adults; $5 for seniors; ages 5 and under are free with a paying adult.

Ages: 4 years and up for the restaurant and miniature golf; see above restrictions for driving cars.

TAC CITY AIRSOFT (Los Angeles County)

(626) 387-7717 / www.taccityairsoft.com
2208 Edwards Avenue, El Monte
$$$$

See TAC CITY AIRSOFT(Orange County) on page 267 for all details, including hours and pricing.

Ages: Minimum 10 years old.

TEMPEST FREERUNNING ACADEMY - Hawthorne

(310) 644-7686 / www.tempestacademy.com
3337 Jack Northrop Avenue, Hawthorne
$$$

See the Tempest Freerunning entry below for a full explanation about the academy. With all of the same ideas and physical challenges as the Northridge location, but almost twice the size, this facility is set up with different scenarios. A few colorful and crazy sections look like mazes - one is called Minecraft. The Antfarm space is unique in that one must crawl in and through some spots. One section looks like a cement, cubed building; another like a castle with stone-like walls and partitions with a fire escape; and another is all poles attached to each other for swinging on and around. These sections look so different under colored lights! A Santorini space has a beautiful mural of this city on a hill, which becomes 3-D with stairs jutting out of it, plus a balcony and poles. A trampoline area with a foam pit is here, as is a central, gymnastics spring floor. Read the below entry regarding classes and open gym.

Hours: Call or check online for a schedule of classes. Open gym time for adults is Mon. - Thurs., 8pm - 11pm; Sat., 3pm - 5pm. Open gym time for kids is Fri., 6pm - 9pm; Sat., 1pm - 3pm. The academy is generally open Mon. - Thurs., 4pm - 11pm; Fri., 4pm - 9pm; Sat., 9am - 5pm. It's closed Sun. and certain holidays.

Price: Open gym is $15 for adults per two or three-hour session; $20 for kids. Classes start at $100 a month for a, one-hour class once a week; $30 to drop in a class (must call in advance).

Ages: 6 years and up.

TEMPEST FREERUNNING ACADEMY - Northridge

(818) 717-0525 / www.tempestacademy.com
19821 Nordhoff Place, #115, Northridge
$$$

"Developed by the founders of Team Tempest and X-Games course designer Nate Wessel, our facility offers a real-world environment where you can learn everything from the basics of parkour to the advanced maneuvers and tricks of freerunning." (Quoted from the company's website.) Even if you don't know what the terms "freerunning" or "parkour" mean, if you have kids who enjoy X-treme sports (and/or you just want to physically wear your kids out), this innovative training facility is the place to take them. Both practices involved running; running up or scaling walls; wall spins; flips; vaulting over street elements; and other acrobatics and street stunts. Parkour is more regimented and direct than freerunning, which is a more free form and aesthetically-pleasing way of moving your body in motion.

Northridge location: Take all of the above and this is what you get with Tempest - a huge indoor warehouse-like facility (7,000 square feet) with different sections created to look and feel very unique. With columns, ledges, ramps, steps, benches, doorways, poles, and more, to run and jump on and over, one area has a fourteen-foot, warped wall (like a half pipe) designed and built for these sports; another is like a wildly colorful urban street scene; another has a blackboard along a long wall; yet another looks like a brick house. With a trampoline at one end and an eight-foot edge at the other, the huge foam pit (30 ft. long by 10 ft. wide by 6 ft. deep) is ideal for practicing flips. Another trampoline helps practitioners gauge just the right amount of bounce needed for certain tricks. A gymnastics spring floor is integrated into the center of the hardcore Parkour Park, giving some cushion to landings.

Is it safe? The sports lend themselves to physical extremes, but the qualified staff and coaches here do parkour and freerunning professionally (in competitions and for movies), so they train on the how tos and don't allow participants to go beyond what they've proven they can handle. At least seven classes are offered for different age brackets and abilities, from beginners to the advanced athlete. There is even a Tadpole class offered, for ages 6 to 8 years old. Tempest also offers open gym hours for participants to just run, practice, and experience parkour. The open gym times are separated by sessions for adults, 17 years and over, who have access to the entire gym; and sessions for kids, 16 years and under, which is a staff-monitored time where participants are allowed in certain areas of the gym and must be accompanied by a parent or legal guardian. Waivers must be signed. Come dressed in clothes that are comfortable to move in (not too tight and not really baggy), and wear gym shoes.

Hours: Call or check online for a schedule of classes. Open gym time for adults is Mon. - Thurs., 8pm - 11pm; Sat., 3pm - 5pm. Open gym time for kids is Fri., 6pm - 9pm; Sat., 1pm - 3pm. The academy is generally open Mon., 4pm - 11pm; Tues., 2pm - 11pm; Wed. - Thurs., noon - 11pm; Fri., 4pm - 9pm; Sat., 9am - 5pm. It's closed Sun. and certain holidays.

Price: Open gym is $10 for adults per two or three-hour session; $15 for kids. Classes start at $80 a month for a one-hour class, once a week; $25 to drop in a class (must call in advance).

Ages: 6 years and up.

THE PLAYROOM

(818) 784-PLAY (7529) / www.theplayroomvalley.com
14392 Ventura Boulevard, on the second floor of Oakridge Plaza, Sherman Oaks

This mid-size, clean, open, airy indoor play area and enrichment center, geared for younger children, has lots of colorful toys and equipment for kids. It has a small bouncer; short rock climbing wall; little ball pit; playhouse; little play gym; plenty of sturdy plastic cars to ride on; rockers; stand-alone slides; a wall of chalkboard; air hockey; small desks with puzzles and manipulatives; and a few mini roller coasters to roll down a little track. A nook with table and chairs offers a place for hungry visitors to chow down on food they bring in. Remember to wear socks!

Hours: Open Mon. - Fri., 10am - 6pm. Sat. - Sun. are usually reserved for private parties.
Price: $9 per child; adults are free.
Ages: 10 months - 5 years.

TOP OUT CLIMBING

(661) 288-1813 / www.topoutclimbing.com
26332 Ferry Court, Santa Clarita

Help your kids reach new heights in this beautiful, state-of-the-art indoor rock climbing gym. Topping at almost 12,000 square feet, Top Out offers two types of climbing - auto belay, which is an automated braking system so you can scale the walls without a partner, and bouldering. The bouldering area is the main emphasis of the gym, featuring a 100-foot long steep wall that wraps around, a twenty-foot high top out wall, and a fifteen-foot high freestanding boulder. Climb away! I'm a fan of this sport for all that does for participants, both in building up physical strength and agility, and in building up mental acuity - so good for kids and adults! A signed waiver must be filled out.

In the center of the gym is a lounge area with couches, benches, a pool table and free WiFi. This is the area for parties, too. A viewing deck with seating overlooks one of the bouldering areas. Yoga classes are offered on the second floor. Ask about rock climbing classes, recreational and competitive youth climbing teams, and special events.

Hours: Open Mon. - Fri., 11am - 11pm; Sat. - Sun., 10am - 7pm.
Price: A day pass is $16 for adults; $14 for military and students; $10 for ages 5 - 10 and under; children 4 and under climb for free with an adult. Rentals are $4 for shoes, $3 for a harness, or $6 for the full package.
Ages: 5 years and up.

ULTRAZONE (Los Angeles County)

Alhambra - (626) 282-6178; Sherman Oaks - (818) 789-6620 / www.lalasertag.com - Alhambra; www.zonehead.com - Sherman Oaks
Alhambras - 231 E. Main St.; Sherman Oaks - 14622 Ventura Blvd., suite 208

It's almost pitch black. You're going through mazes and tunnels trying to find your way to the enemy's base before your enemy finds you. Suddenly, ZAP - you get hit! You realize you've lost your power and now you have to recharge. Where *is* the recharging site? After getting lost several times you find it, and now your infrared sighting helps spy one of "them"! You fire, hit, and score one for your team!

Ultrazone, with over 5,000 square feet of high tech excitement, is the ultimate in laser tag. You carry your own equipment - a vest and laser gun - and play with up to forty-five people, or three teams. After a five-minute briefing, you'll play for twenty intense minutes in this futuristic-looking arena. The first game will wear you out, but it's just practice. Now that you've got a handle on how the game is played, go for a second round. Laser tag - there is fun to be had with a game this rad!

Notes: The Alhambra facility is a two-story arena. Both facilities have separate party rooms and a few arcade games in the lobby plus a snack bar.

Hours: Alhambra - Open most of the year, Wed. - Thurs., 3pm - 8pm; Fri., 3pm - midnight; Sat., 11am - 1am; Sun., 11am - 8pm. Closed Mon., Tues., and most major holidays. Sherman Oaks - Open Tues. - Thurs., 3pm - 10pm; Fri., 3pm - midnight; Sat., 10am - midnight; Sun., 10am - 10pm. Closed Mon. and certain holidays. Both are open extended hours during summer and on school breaks.

Price: Alhambra - $9 a game. Sherman Oaks - $9.50 a game. Ask about specials.

Ages: 6 years and up, or not afraid of the dark.

UNDER THE SEA

Burbank - (818) 567-9945; Culver City - (310) 915-1133 / www.undertheseaindoorplayground.com
Burbank - 2424 W. Victory Blvd.; Culver City - 3871 Grand View Blvd.

Murals of mermaids, octopuses, and even pirates submerge your children in a world of play at Under the Sea. This aquatically-themed indoor play area has bounce houses; multi-level structures with tubes and tunnels to crawl through; slides; a ball pit; soft play mats; Little Tykes™ cars; playhouses; free standing slides and soft play shapes; huge balls; air hockey; and a Baby Corner with a toddler swing, slide, and carousel. Socks are required in the play area. Ask about classes, including modern dance and Mommy & Me. You are welcome to bring your own food in and enjoy a meal at the picnic tables toward the entrance.

Hours: Open Mon. - Fri., 10am - 6pm. The Culver City location is open Tues. until 8pm. Both are open Sat. and Sun. for private parties only.

Price: Burbank - $9 for ages 9 months - 14 years; Culver City - $11. Adults are free at both locations.

Ages: 9 months to 8 years.

VALENCIA LASER BLAST

(661) 255-1600 / www.valencialaserblast.com
23460 Cinema Dr, Valencia

For some out-of-this-world fun, play laser tag in this 5,000 square foot, multi-level arena with spacey decor and shapes painted on the walls and on the maze-like partitions. There are also mirrors (to add confusion and fun), two platforms, three bases and a few mines to activate during this adrenaline-pumping game of tag.

The lobby has some arcade and video games, plus air hockey, basketball, skee ball, and more, with tickets and a prize redemption area. The snack bar serves good-tasting pizza ($11.95 for medium with pepperoni), Greek salads and yummy cupcakes. There are separate party rooms available.

Hours: Open most of the year, Tues. - Thurs., 3pm - 9pm; Fri., 3pm - 11pm; Sat., 10am - 11pm; Sun., 11am - 10pm. Open in the summer and holiday hours, Tues. - Thurs., noon - 10pm; Fri., noon - 11pm; Sat., 10am - 11pm; Sun., 11am - 10pm. Close Mon.

Price: $8.50 per game

Ages: 6 years and up.

VAN NUYS ICELAND

(818) 785-2171 / www.valleyskating.com
14318 Calvert Street, Van Nuys

Ice skating is fun. Bumper cars are fun. Bumper cars on ice are **really** fun! Several, electrically-powered cars are yours to glide and bump around on weekend afternoons. Of course you can always come and skate here, too. The rink offers pick-up hockey games, broomball (absolutely one of my favorite games!), walkers (for beginning skaters), classes, and Light Night sessions on Friday (8pm to 10pm) and Saturday nights (8:45pm to 11pm). These night sessions are skating to music and flashing lights (think disco) and/or watching a movie on their big screen. $10 includes everything, even skate rentals. It also has arcade games, a heated observation room, a pro shop, and two party rooms.

Hours: Open for bumper cars, Sat. - Sun., noon - 2pm. Call for skating sessions.

Price: Bumper cars are $5 per person for a five-minute ride. Skate sessions are $8 for ages 12 and up; $7 for kids; $3 for skate rentals.

Ages: 4 years and up. (Under 4 must be accompanied by a parent.)

WARPED PAINTBALL PARK / WARPED OPS AIRSOFT FIELD

(661) 450-9400 or (661) 450-9401 / www.warpedpaintballpark.com

34481 Ridge Route Road, Castaic

See AMBUSH PAINTBALL & AIRSOFT PARK (pg. 663) for information on this park as they are owned and operated by the same company. Spread over forty acres, Warped has six scenario fields and two tournament grade fields that include the Spool field, Graveyard field, Castle, the Jungle field, and the town of Baghdad, plus lots of natural obstacles such as hills and trees, as well as man-made ones such as a life-size tank and buildings.

Hours: Open Sat. - Sun., 9am - 4pm.

Price: $20 for full day of paintball or airsoft with your own equipment; $40 for all day admission plus rental equipment for both games.

Ages: 8 - 11 years for Splatmaster; 10 years and up for airsoft and paintball.

WE ROCK THE SPECTRUM KIDS GYM

Agoura Hills - (818) 991-KIDS (5437); Glendale - (818) 945-5444; Northridge - (818) 341-3818; Pasadena - (626) 304-2746; Santa Clarita - (661) 259-7949; Santa Monica - (310) 586-2629; Studio City - (818) 980-KIDS (5437); Tarzana - (818) 708-0860 / www.werockthespectrumkidsgym.com

Agoura Hills - 30315 Canwood St.; Glendale - 413 S. Central Ave., Unit E; Northridge - 19520 Nordhoff St., #18/19; Pasadena - 2381 E. Colorado Blvd.; Santa Clarita - 26063 Bouquet Canyon Rd; Santa Monica - 1909 Santa Monica Blvd.; Studio City - 4397 Tujunga Ave.; Tarzana - 5520 Crebs Ave.

This place does rock! More than "just" an indoor play place in that this colorful gym for kids encourages lots of movement with equipment to help facilitate just that. There is a rope ladder for climbing; wooden monkey bars; trampolines (with safety nets); mini exercise equipment; hula hoops; big balls; little slides; play tunnels; mini zip line; balance beam; and fun swings for all sizes, including a tire swing, sack swing, and plastic vehicle swings, hanging from the ceiling. All of this is on a padded floor. In this large room are also a small puppet theater, a train table, toys, dress up clothes, arts and crafts area, and puzzles at tables. There are adult-size tables, too. Some facilities also have a chalkboard, soft foam blocks, and more. Ask about classes, including those offered for kids with special needs. And give yourself a break by taking advantage of the Break Time program where you can leave your kids in care of the staff and go run errands, or just go.

Hours: Open daily - hours vary by location, but most are open at 9am and close between 6pm - 8pm. Sometimes private parties are held on weekends, so call first (of course!).

Price: $10 per child; siblings receive at 20% discount. An all-day pass is $15, which allows you in and out privileges of the facility. Adults are free. The Break Time program is $10 an hour with 1 hour minimum, 3 hours max for ages 2 and up, as well as those in special ed.

Ages: 6 months - 10 years. Different locations are geared for various ages - call first.

—GREAT OUTDOORS—

ABALONE COVE SHORELINE PARK

(310) 377-1222 - park; (310) 544-5260 or (310) 544-5264 - guided hikes / www.palosverdes.com/rpv/recreationparks

5970 Palos Verdes Drive South, Rancho Palos Verdes

This beautiful, cliff-side park on the Palos Verdes Peninsula has a grassy park area at the top and plenty of picnic tables. The ocean view (and sighting of Catalina on a clear day) is spectacular. This park is the only way down to Abalone Cove and the great tidepools at Portuguese Point, which you are welcome to explore on your own. (Ask for a tidepool map at the entrance.) A paved pathway follows along the street for a short while before veering downward. The quarter-mile dirt path is a bit more direct, as well as a bit steeper. Be prepared to carry your gear (chairs, towels, food, etc.). Lifeguards are on duty at the cove during the summer months. Fishing is allowed. Note: The WAYFARERS CHAPEL (on pg. 177) is directly across the street.

A variety of outdoor, educational, guided tours and hikes are offered, including a two-hour tidepool tour to discover small creatures native to California waters. Wear shoes with good tread as you must first hike down the trail, then cross a cobblestone beach to get to the rocky tidepool. And remember - wet rocks are slippery rocks! Your guide will explain all about the animals you see and ones that you may gently touch. Look for sea stars, sea slugs, sea urchins, crabs, octopuses, and mussels, and scan the ocean for seals and sea lions. Tours are given on days when low tides are one foot above sea level, or lower. Tips: Wear sunscreen and bring a water bottle.

Hours: Gates are open most of the year, Mon. - Fri., noon - 4pm; Sat., Sun., and holidays, 9am - 4pm. Gates are open Memorial Day through Labor Day daily, 9am - 4pm. Tours are given by reservation only and require a three-week advance notice. Closed New Year's Day, Thanksgiving, Christmas Eve, and Christmas Day.

Price: Parking is $5 per car; $15 per bus. No charge for seniors Labor Day - Memorial Day. Tours are $2 for adults; $1 for children 13 and under.

Ages: 4 years and up.

AIDAN'S PLACE - WESTWOOD PARK

(310) 473-3610 / www.laparks.org/dos/playground/accessibleplay.htm
1350 S. Sepulveda Boulevard, Los Angeles

Designed specifically for children of all abilities to play alongside each other, this large playground has several separate groupings of apparatus all on soft foam "flooring." The largest one, resembling colorful city buildings, has a conglomeration of platforms with lots of slides, ramps, twisted metal shapes, swings, and a short "rock climbing" wall. Another one has ramps, talking tubes, steering wheels, and some games attached to it. The fully-accessible cockpit is fun for all pilots and copilots.

The construction zone has three structures that look like trucks. The attached misters come on with the touch of a button. A covered sand pit has three diggers and an elevated sand area that is wheelchair accessible. There are lots of "extras" around the playground, too - a teeter-totter, a square springboard, and short, tube tunnels.

Aidan's Place is part of Westwood Park, which has a large grassy area, a basketball court, traditional playgrounds, picnic tables, wonderful shade trees, an indoor pool, huge sculptures toward the "back" of the park, and eight lighted tennis courts. Call (310) 477-5550 for information on playing at the Westwood Tennis Center - courts are usually $8 an hour. The pool is open year round (closed Mondays) for lap and recreation swim on weekends from 1pm to 5pm for $2.50 for adults; seniors and ages 17 and under are free. Call (310) 478-7019 for weekday times and more info.

Hours: Open Mon. - Fri., 8:30am - 10pm; Sat., 9am - 6pm; Sun., 10am - 5pm.
Price: Free
Ages: All

ANNENBERG COMMUNITY BEACH HOUSE and BACK ON THE BEACH CAFE

(310) 458-4904 - beach house; (310) 393-8282 - Back on the Beach Cafe / beachhouse.smgov.net; www.backonthebeachcafe.com
415 Pacific Coast Highway, Santa Monica

Though it has a private, somewhat exclusive feel, this beach and grounds are open to the public. A boardwalk-style walkway on the beach separates the beach from the pool and buildings. The wide and very clean beach sports fine sand; a lifeguard stand (and a lifeguard in the summer); six beach volleyball or beach tennis (a combo of volleyball, tennis and badminton) courts that are free to use or can be reserved for $10 an hour; part of the twenty-six mile bike path that runs from just north of here to all the way south to Torrance; and two beach soccer fields. There is also paddleboard rentals available and a small playground with some odd shapes to play on/with, a half sphere "rock" climbing wall, and swings.

On the other side of the walkway is a lovely, heated pool with plenty of lounge chairs under umbrellas and even some couches under the contiguous Pool House building awning. The Pool House has lockers, changing rooms, and a Rec Room that is open daily, mid-June through Labor Day (11am to 5pm) for playing a board game or ping pong, or relaxing with an ocean view. Next to the pool, one level up and separated by a fence, is a splash pad as well as a deck area with round tables and chairs under umbrellas and palm trees - a place to relax, read and watch the sand, surf and people.

A half-hour tour through the adjacent Marion Davies Guest House, originally built in the 1920's, is great for older kids and adults who are interested in the unique architecture and the stories of movie stars and other celebrities from that era.

The on-site, casual and beach-classy Back on the Beach Cafe has some indoor and lots of outdoor seating, and is right on the beach. A walkway allows easier access for strollers and wheelchairs. Menu options include: Breakfast - vegan scramble ($11.50); blueberry pancakes ($10.50); bananutella french toast - Nutella, bananas, crushed almonds, whipped cream ($12.75); granola sundae ($8.75); and a variety of omelettes with grilled potatoes and a mini scone ($12.75). Lunch - Greek salad ($11.75); chicken, apple, goat cheese salad ($13.25); Angus cheeseburger ($10.75); turkey burger ($11.75); steak sandwich ($14.25); California Reuben melt ($12.75); and fish tacos entree ($14.95). Starters - fried calamari ($13); seafood bisque ($8.75); and sweet potato fries ($4.75). Dinner - short ribs ($12); salmon mousse ($9); crab raviolis ($9); eggplant ($9); and skirt steak ($19). Desserts - cinnamon roll bread pudding; smore preserve with house-made graham cracker, dark chocolate fudge, and marshmallow brulee; and summer berry cobbler with vanilla ice cream for $8 each. Kid's menu - pasta ($7); blueberry pancake ($4); kosher hot dog with fries ($6.75); hamburger ($7.75); and chicken fingers ($8.75).

In the summer, reservations are available for the pool, parking, beach volleyball and "tennis" courts, beach soccer fields, and canopies.

Hours: The parking lot is open daily, 7am - 7pm (or 9pm, depending on the season). The beach and playground are open 24/7. The Beach House grounds - the courtyard, splash pad, and view deck - are open daily, 8:30am - about 8pm - depending on the season. The pool is open Memorial Day weekend, 10am - 6pm (pool passes go on sale starting at 9:30am); open the first few weekends in June and weekends in September, 11am - 5pm. It's open mid-June - Labor Day, Sat. - Mon., 10am - 8pm; Tues. - Fri., 10am - 6pm. The pool is also open Tues., 6:30pm - 9:30pm for 17 years and older. The Cafe is open daily, April - September, 8am - 8pm. It's open the rest of the year, Mon. - Fri., 8am - 3pm; Sat. - Sun., 8am - 4pm. Hours do fluctuate, so call first. Marion Davies Guest House tours are offered mid- June - Labor Day on the hour, Mon., Wed., Fri., Sat. - Sun., 11am - 2pm. It's open the rest of the year, usually, Fri. - Mon. at 11am, noon, and 1pm.

Price: Parking: April - October, $3 an hour, $12 a day; November - March, $3 an hour, $8 a day. The pool is $10 for adults; $5 for seniors; $4 for ages 1 - 17. Dollar Splash Day Mondays are only $1. The Beach House grounds - the beach areas, playground, courtyard, splash pad, view deck, and Marion Davies House - are free. Paddleboard rentals are $25 an hour.

Ages: All

ANTHONY C. BEILENSON PARK / LAKE BALBOA / PEDLOW FIELD SKATE ☀ PARK / SEPULVEDA DAM RECREATION AREA

(818) 756-8060 - park; (818) 756-9743 - Lake Balboa; (818) 756-9642 - sports center; (818) 654-5296 - skate park; (818) 756-9710 - Sepulveda Basin Wildlife Reserve; (818) 212- 4263 - Wheel Fun bike rentals / www.laparks.org; www.laparks.org/dos/horticulture/sepulvedabasin.htm; www.wheelfunrentals.com
6300 Balboa Boulevard, Encino

Is there anything you can't do at the massive Sepulveda Dam area? It is very spread out: On the east side of the street are three golf courses; on the west side is an enormous field with sixteen soccer fields, four lighted baseball diamonds, sixteen lighted tennis courts (and a backboard), lighted basketball courts, and lots of open space and gently sloping hills. The Encino Velodrome is also in this vicinity. A paved, relatively easy, ten-mile round-trip bike trail goes through and encompasses the east and west side of the park.

The favorite place to play is a little further north, just south of Victory Boulevard, near Lake Balboa at Anthony C. Beilsenson Park. This massive, shaded, boundless nautical-themed playground with rubberized and sand flooring is fantastic for all abilities! Wide ramps for wheelchairs have interactive play stations along the way with Braille boards, tic-tac-toe, sensory panels, talking tubes, and places to create music (or make noise) by playing bells and piano keys. The sprawling playground features boats, a lighthouse-shaped play structure, a tactile sea wall with fish and mosaics imbedded, slides of all heights - both open and enclosed, swings, raised sand play areas, sand diggers, and rocks to climb on, and metal shapes to spin and twirl on.

The adjacent twenty-seven-acre, man-made Lake Balboa, is made from reclaimed water and patrolled by lifeguards. Bring some old bread for the always-hungry ducks swimming around here. Numerous walkers take advantage of the 1.3-mile cement pathway that loops around the scenic lake - no bikes, blades, or skateboards are allowed. Bikes are allowed at the several other bike paths that wind throughout the park. Contact Wheel Fun Rentals if you'd like to rent a surrey, chopper, or another bike. Fishing is allowed at the lake. A license is required for those 16 years and older. Also, enjoy watching or racing electric, remote-controlled boats through the boating cove.

At Pedlow Field Skate Park, at 17334 Victory Boulevard, an enclosed, supervised, huge, cement skate park is a highlight. It includes handrails, steps, a funbox, plenty of ramps, a pyramid, and a waterfall (which is just the name of a ramp - there is no actual water). Safety gear - a helmet and knee and elbow pads - are required; citations are issued. Skaters 17 years and under must have a waiver signed by a parent or guardian.

Drive east through the park, past a golf course, and you'll reach the adjacent Woodley Park. One of its outstanding features is a model aircraft flying at the Apollo Field. Members of the San Fernando Valley Flyers club are often seen here, using (and fixing) their remote-controlled aircraft on a scale runway, and then flying them. See if you can tell the difference in the air between the models and the real planes coming to and from the nearby Van Nuys airport. Other park features include an archery range (short and long range), four cricket fields (come watch a game on the weekends, April through October), and 225-acres of a seemingly hidden Sepulveda Basin Wildlife Reserve, a refuge where an abundance of trees and other plants and animals (more than 200 species of birds!) dwell in a place so removed from yet smack in the middle of city life. At the reserve, located at 6350 Woodley Avenue, stroll the nature trails, walk to the eleven-acre lake created from reclaimed water, cross over bridges, try to shut out the noise of the streets that filter in, and enjoy. Call to join in on the monthly bird walks. Look up the JAPANESE GARDEN (pg. 66) as it is located in this area as well.

> **Hours:** The park and wildlife reserve are open daily, sunrise - sunset. The skate park is open Mon. - Fri., noon - dark; Sat., 10am - dark. The sports center is open Mon. - Fri., 9am - 10pm; Sat. - Sun., 9am - 5pm. Wheel Fun Rentals is open daily, 10am - sunset.
> **Price:** Free to the park, lake, skatepark, and reserve.
> **Ages:** All

APOLLO COMMUNITY REGIONAL PARK

(661) 940-7701 / parks.lacounty.gov
4555 W. Ave. G, Lancaster

This *space*ious park has three man-made lakes that are named after the astronauts from Apollo XI: Lake Aldrin, Lake Armstrong, and Lake Collins. The lakes are stocked seasonally with trout (November through April) and catfish (the rest of the year), and while there is not a fee for fishing, a California state fishing license is needed for those over 16 years of age. There is a floating dock, here, too. Popular spring and fall fishing derbies are held for both adults and children. Tip: Bring bread to feed the relentlessly friendly ducks and geese. This ritual alone took us over half an hour!

The park, though surrounded by the desert, is picturesque with its shade trees, bridges over portions of water, walking path, and plenty of run-around room. There is also a great abstract playground here, the kind that looks like abstract art, where creative play on the poles, colorful knobs, ropes, and more ensues. My kids were also intrigued by the glass-enclosed, well-built mock-up of a command module. The placard describes the dedication of the park to the Apollo program. (Don't you love sneaking in a history lesson?)

> **Hours:** Open daily, dawn - dusk.
> **Price:** Free
> **Ages:** All

ARATANI JAPANESE GARDEN

(909) 869-7659 / www.csupomona.edu
3801 W. Temple Avenue, on the campus of California State Polytechnic University, Pomona

Japanese gardens are steeped in tradition and symbolism. This 1.3-acre garden features plants of East Asia; a reflection pond with koi; a short waterfall; a little, bubbling stream; bridges; a sculptured rock garden; a small amphitheater; a patch of lawn with trees; and a paved pathway that winds throughout it all. Meant to be enjoyed and imbue visitors with a sense of peace, the garden succeeds in being a mini-retreat. Check out the Index by City in the back of this book to see what other attractions Cal Poly holds.

> **Hours:** Open daily, sunrise - sunset - campus days.
> **Price:** Free. Parking on campus can cost $5 for visitor's parking, or a few quarters for metered parking.
> **Ages:** All

AVERILL PARK

(310) 832-7328 / www.laparks.org; www.sanpedro.com
1300 South Dodson Avenue, San Pedro

This verdant, tranquil park has a series of linear, rock-lined streams and ponds that gently cascade into each other. A stone bridge and botanic-like garden add beauty to this area. The paved pathways on both sides of the stream have chain-link safety "ropes" and numerous trees - palm, bamboo, oak, banyan, and other shade trees. Picnic tables, small barbeques, and benches are tucked into nooks along the waterway. While ducks and turtles inhabit the waters, squirrels have free reign of the trees that cover one side of the hill. Grass covers the other side and the top. A picnic lunch here as a way of refreshing the soul.

Hours: Open daily, sunrise - sunset.
Price: Free
Ages: All

BALDWIN HILLS SCENIC OVERLOOK

(310) 558-5547 - visitor center; (310) 558-1444 - park / www.parks.ca.gov
6300 Hetzler Road, Culver City

Seemingly unending stone stairs that go straight up the hill - that's the tough part. Reaching the overlook and looking out over Los Angeles and, on a clear day, to the mountains beyond - that's the beauty of this park. Not for the faint of heart, but heart smart, the almost 300 steps up the 511-foot peak are not evenly or easily spaced as some are wider apart and some are taller to step up onto. Go up a little farther (you've already come this far) to the attractive visitor's center (which has a bathroom - bonus!). If don't want to go back down the same way, there is a one-mile trail at the east end of the center that winds back down via switchbacks that are still steep, but not as directly steep as the staircase. There is parking lot at the top, near the visitors center. Note that CULVER CITY PARK (pg. 53) is nearby.

Hours: Open daily, 8am - sunset. The visitor center is open Fri. - Mon., 9am - 4pm.
Price: Free. Parking is $6 in the lot, or try to find free street parking down below.
Ages: 8 years and up.

BELLFLOWER SKATE PARK and CARUTHERS PARK

(562) 866-5684 or (562) 804-1424 / www.bellflower.org
10500 Flora Vista Street at Caruthers Park, Bellflower

This 8,000 square-foot, supervision-free park features benches, ramps, rails, a curb, pyramid, snake run, hips, and bowls. A helmet and pads are encouraged. The adjacent, frequently-used Caruthers Park offers access to the bike path that runs along the riverbed (see BIKE TRAIL: LOS ANGELES RIVER TRAIL on page 209); large grassy areas; picnic tables; barbecue pits; swing sets and other playground equipment; an exercise/fitness course; and a wading pool for kiddies that's open the summer.

Hours: Open daily, sunrise - sunset.
Price: Free
Ages: All

BRAND PARK

(818) 548-2184 / www.lamountains.com
1601 W. Mountain Street, Glendale

The front part of this thirty-acre park is composed of green lawns, playgrounds, a few basketball courts, volleyball courts, and picnic tables. The back part, behind the museum and library, is a huge hilly area with miles of dirt and asphalt hiking trails (and for mountain bikers who like a real workout) that lead through a chaparral into the Verdugo Mountains and around a reservoir. An almost three-mile fire road "trail" starts on the asphalt road up the hill and to the left of the fire road fork. There is a great view from the top.

The park sees a lot of action on the weekends. Look up THE DOCTORS' HOUSE MUSEUM (on pg. 105), as it, and the beautiful adjacent Glendale Library, are located in the park.

Hours: The park is open daily, sunrise - sunset.
Price: Free
Ages: All

BROOKSIDE PARK - REESE'S RETREAT

(626) 744-4321 / www.ci.pasadena.ca.us
360 N. Arroyo Boulevard, Pasadena

This large - 62-acre - park is located in the middle of the Arroyo Seco, an eight-mile natural area with a river, wildlife, woods, meadows, trails, and much, much more. It is also just south of KIDSPACE MUSEUM (pg. 125). Its amenities include a fitness trail, five tennis courts, three baseball fields with stadium seating and lights, basketball court, soccer and football fields, and a wonderful, piratey playground.

Although there are two other playgrounds, the universally accessible, pirate-themed playground called Reese's Retreat, is kind of hidden, making it a more special find: It is near the Rose Bowl Aquatics Center. It features a large pirate boat that is anchored in blue padding with sea creatures emblazoned on them, including sharks at the end of the low planks. Play in, on, and under the boat with its periscopes, cannons, ropes and chains to climb, ramps, slides, swings, pirate maps, and sea creatures to ride. Just off this main area is a stack of cannon balls, a ride that sways back and forth, one that spins, and a shipwrecked water play area with a treasure chest that shoots water into an adjacent large sandbox. Bring buckets and shovels and expect the kids to get wet because of the little shallow pool area and small fountains.

Enjoy the trees, walking/running and bike trails, lots of grassy areas, picnic tables, and bbq areas and mountain scenery. Note that the eighteen-hole Oak Grove Disc Course (the first permanent disc golf course in the world!) is located in the upper Arroyo Seco, in Hahamongna Watershed Park which is north of the 210 freeway, off Oak Grove Drive. The course is played through mature oak trees, over rocks and throughout the Arroyo's natural elements.

Hours: Open daily, sunrise - sunset.
Price: Free
Ages: All

BURBANK SKATE / BMX PARK at VALLEY PARK

(818) 238-5390 / www.burbankca.gov
1625 N. Valley Street, Burbank

Skate one, skate all! This enclosed, good-size (over 10,000 square feet), concrete skatepark with a small bowl, pool, a street course, a small pyramid, rails and skating area is supervised and good, I understand, mostly for beginners to intermediate skaters. (It all looks hard to me.) There are separate sessions for skaters and for BMX riders, and lights for nighttime use. All participants must have a signed waiver and must wear a helmet and pads (yea!).

The rest of the park has a good, sand-based playground, plus picnic tables, grassy areas, shade trees, and paved pathways.

Hours: Open during the school year, Mon. - Thurs., 4pm - 8pm; Fri., 4pm - 9pm; Sat., 10am - 9pm; Sun.,
noon - 7pm. Open during the summer and on holidays, Mon., Wed., and Fri., 1pm - 10pm; Tues.
and Thurs., 11am - 5pm; Sat., noon - 9pm; Sun., noon - 5pm.
Price: There is a one-time fee for an ID card, then daily rates of $3 for Burbank residents; $5 for
non-residents.
Ages: 4 years and up.

CASTAIC LAKE RECREATION AREA

(661) 257-4050 - lake information; (661) 775-6232 - boat rentals / www.castaiclake.com;
www.rockymountainrec.com
32132 Ridgeroute Road and Lake Hughes, Castaic

There are so many ways to play in the great outdoors at the massive (8,000 acres) Castaic Lake Recreation Area! The gigantic, upper lake is mostly for motorized watercraft and fishing - both the lake and lagoon are stocked with rainbow trout and bass. A California state fishing license is needed for those who are over 16 years old. Boating activities are available in the Lower Lake (i.e. the lagoon), too, as is renting aluminum boats.

Life-guarded swimming at the lagoon, (i.e. swim beaches), with its small sandy beaches (which can get very crowded) is a great summertime activity. The "typical" park part is wonderfully huge and fun. There are acres and acres of rolling, grassy hills spotted with all kinds of shade and pine and other trees, plus paved pathways meandering and crisscrossing all over the park. Just beyond the dam are fire roads and dirt hiking/biking trails - up to seven miles of trails, with three access points. The trails range from an easy stroll to rugged hikes. Maps are available.

There are plenty of picnic tables and some great playgrounds which all differ from one another. At the northern end of the lagoon, one playground is kind of an abstract metal configuration with some ropes and hoops to climb on and through; another has the metal frame of a ship with a two-story cabin in middle with slides and steps and poles to play in and under; and another is comprised of big, flatish rocks to climb up that also have double ropes connecting them to tightrope walk on. The latter also has some fake logs and other scattered "rocks" - imaginative play! Another great playground is located at the southern end of the park - a big, multi-story one with all the newest and best amenities.

Come spend the night around the corner, up the road at one of sixty standard campsites, both tent and RV (no hook ups), with several sites that overlook the lagoon. However long you choose to visit, an escape to Castaic Lake fits all your recreational desires!

Hours: Open daily, sunrise - sunset. Closed Christmas. The swim lagoon is open Memorial Day - Labor Day, Thurs. - Sun., 10am - 5pm.

Price: $11 per vehicle; $5 for seniors on weekdays. Camping is $20 a night. A fourteen-foot aluminum, nine-horse-power boat rents for $35 for two hours and $55 for the day during the week; $35 for two hours and $78 for the day on the weekends. Seniors get a discount.

Ages: All

CASTRO CREST

(818) 880-0367 / www.nps.gov; www.lamountains.com; www.localhikes.com
Corral Canyon Road, Malibu

My kids jumped out of the almost-stopped car and made a bee-line for the rock formations directly in front of us, the tallest of which they dubbed Pride Rock. A variety of moderately difficult trails lead hikers past just a few more formations. The trails roller-coaster either along the ridgeline offering panoramic views, on fire roads, or on roads that cut through a gorge. Although the green, velvety-looking hills were covered with trees when we visited, we found relatively little shade along the trails we walked. Note that Backbone Trail, a trail that extends nearly seventy miles across and through the Santa Monica Mountains, is part of the Castro Crest trail system. For more information on Backbone, call the Santa Monica Mountains National Recreation Area at (805) 370-2301 or www.nps.gov/samo. Also note that there are no restroom facilities here. Tip: Bring your own water.

Hours: Open daily, 8am - sunset.

Price: Free

Ages: 6 years and up.

CERRITOS REGIONAL PARK and SPORTS COMPLEX

(562) 924-5144 - regional park; (562) 916-8590 - sports complex, (562) 403-7498 - pool / www.cerritos.us
19900 & 19700 Bloomfield Avenue, Cerritos

Fourteen lighted tennis courts; several baseball diamonds with stadium seating and lights; six soccer fields; basketball courts; playgrounds; two lakes (fishing is permitted); a swimming pool (open year round, to Cerritos residents and their guests, only); large open grassy areas; picnic tables and shelters; cement pathways throughout; and a large, outdoor skate park make this park a delight for the whole family. The gated, 10,000-square-foot concrete skate park has a grinding pole, pools, ramps, bowls, and a small fish bowl. The posted rules (enforced by patrolling policemen who <u>do</u> give out citations) state that skaters (no bikes allowed) must wear a helmet and elbow and knee pads. Aluminum benches are available for visitors and tired skaters. My kids love to skate and rollerblade here - I just don't like the foul language that is often prevalent.

Hours: The park is open daily, dawn - dusk. The skate park is open daily, 9am - dusk; closed on some holidays. The pool is open toward the end of June through August.

Price: Free. The pools is $2 for residents.

Ages: All

CHANTRY FLAT - STURTEVANT FALLS

(818) 899-1900 - park; (626) 447-7356 - pack station / www.bigsantaanitacanyon.com;
www.adamspackstation.com
Santa Anita Avenue, Los Angeles

Take the Gabrielino Trail about a mile-and-a-half into the tree-lined Big Santa Anita Canyon. Cross the Winter Creek Bridge up the trail and go straight through the three-way junction. Ford the creek, then re-cross it where it takes a sharp bend to the left, and scramble over boulders to reach the foot of Sturtevant Falls, a fifty-five-foot cascading waterfall. Caution: Climbing up the waterfall can be dangerous! The small rocky pool at the falls' end is just right for wading or even a dip. The canyon is beautiful - oak trees line the stream bed, along with maples and spruce trees. There are numerous other hiking trails to take in the immediate area (over forty miles), depending on how far you want to go. Note: The Adams' Pack Station is at Chantry Flat, offering a general store and a great historic place as this might be the last pack station of its kind in the U.S. The people at the station deliver supplies year-round to a community accessible only by footpath.

Hours: Open daily, 6am - 8pm. The pack station/general store is open Fri. - Sun., 8am - 5pm.

Price: $5 per vehicle for an Adventure Pass, available at the general store when they're open.

Ages: 5 years and up.

CHARLES WILSON PARK

(310) 328-4964 or (310) 328-5310 / www.torranceca.gov
2200 Crenshaw Boulevard, Torrance

   This large, elongated park has a delightful, sand-based playground for younger children with twisty slides, swings, and a small area for tots with animals on giant springs to ride back and forth on. The park also has a roller hockey rink that is available by reservation; four baseball diamonds; grassy "fields"; gently rolling hills lined with shade trees; stroller-friendly pathways that crisscross throughout; a horseshoe court in the northeast corner; several tennis courts; paddle tennis courts; basketball courts; sand volleyball courts; a fitness course; a fountain in the middle of the wading pond that ducks are very fond of; and a huge treehouse. The elevated treehouse is wheelchair accessible with wooden ramps going in every direction - what fun!

   On select weekends of each month, the Southern California Live Steamers Club offers free rides on their electric, steam, or diesel-powered scale trains. The train goes through a little wooded section which make is seem like more of an adventure. Contact www.southerncalifornialivesteamers.com for more info. Every Tuesday and Saturday a Farmer's Market is held in the main parking lot from 8am to 1pm.

Hours: The park is open daily, 6am - 10pm. Train rides are offered the first Sun., 11am - 3pm and the third Sat., noon - 3pm.
Price: Free
Ages: All

CHATSWORTH PARK

(818) 341-0377 / www.lamountains.com; www.laparks.org
22360 Devonshire (South) or 22300 Chatsworth (North), Chatsworth

   There are two Chatsworth parks; a north and a south. The north park has gigantic, sprawling, and climbable old oak trees; a lot of picnic tables under the trees; a rundown baseball diamond; a play area with some equipment (I like the play cannon); a basketball court; a volleyball court; some pathways to explore; and a small hill with a group of boulders to climb around on. Note: Don't go up on the rocks on the northern hills of rocks - it's not safe.

   Chatsworth Park South offers two tennis courts, a basketball court, a playground, open grassy areas, a community center building that offers lots of activities (including a wheelchair hockey league), a small natural stream running throughout, and picnic tables. There are some trails around the perimeter of the park and some lead into to the surrounding rocks. At the southern end of the south park, at 10385 Shadow Oak Drive, is the historic Hill-Palmer House. Take a tour through the old house while visiting the park. It is open the first Sunday of every month from 1pm to 4pm. Admission is free.

Hours: The parks are open daily, sunrise - 10pm.
Price: Free
Ages: All

CHEESEBORO CANYON

(818) 597-9192 / www.nps.gov/samo; www.localhikes.com
5792 Chesebro Road, Agoura Hills

   Hike or bike on the numerous dirt trails here that go through canyons, grasslands, and riparian areas. The road most traveled is the one immediately accessible, the Cheeseboro Canyon Trail. The hike starts off moderately easy along a streambed and through a valley of oak trees. A picnic area is about a mile-and-a-half from the parking lot. Stop here, or continue on to more strenuous hiking. Bring your own water! You'll reach Sulphur Springs (almost another two miles), where the smell of rotten eggs lets you know you've arrived. This particular trail goes on for another mile through a variety of terrain. Several trails branch off and connect to the Cheeseboro Trail. Note that on weekends mountain bikers tend to take over the trails. Pick up a trail map at the SANTA MONICA MOUNTAINS NATIONAL PARK HEADQUARTERS (pg. 84), which is down the road a bit.

Hours: Open daily, 8am - sunset.
Price: Free
Ages: 6 years (for shorter hikes) and up.

CHEVIOT HILLS RECREATION AREA

(310) 837-5186 - park; (310) 837-5186 - rec center; (310) 202-2844 - pool; (310) 836-8879 - tennis /
www.laparks.org

2551 Motor Avenue, Los Angeles

This large park really fits the bill of a recreation area with its basketball courts (indoor and outdoor), volleyball courts (indoor), archery range, baseball diamonds, tennis courts, and nice playground. During the hot summer months, when kids have played hard and need to cool off, they can take a dip in the municipal swimming pool.

Hours: The park is open Mon. - Fri., 9am - 10:30pm; Sat. - Sun., 9am - 7pm. The rec center is open Mon. - Fri., 9am - 10pm; Sat., 9am - 5pm., Sun., 10am - 4pm. Summer sessions for the pool are Mon. - Fri., 10am - 1pm and 2pm - 5pm; Sat. - Sun., 1pm - 5pm.

Price: The park is free. Each swim session costs $2 for adults; ages 17 and under are free.

Ages: All

CLAREMONT SKATE PARK and CAHUILLA PARK

(909) 399-5460 / www.ci.claremont.ca.us; www.socalskateparks.com

1717 N. Indian Hill Boulevard, Claremont

This medium-sized, concrete skate park has a bowl, grinding poles, grinding boxes, and some flat area to skate and gain momentum. Lights make it one of the few skate parks available at nighttime (although they don't always work). Wearing a helmet and knee and elbow pads is required. The rest of the park offers shade trees, lots of grassy space, picnic areas, and eight tennis courts, baseball fields, a basketball court, and a playground.

Hours: Open daily, 6am - 10pm.

Price: Free

Ages: 7 years and up.

COLDWATER CANYON PARK / TREEPEOPLE

(818) 753-4600 or (818) 623-4879 / www.treepeople.org; www.lamountains.com

12601 Mulholland Drive, Los Angeles

Coldwater Canyon Park is beautiful, with large oak and California bay laurel trees shading the meandering trails, making this a sanctuary for nature. Some of the five miles of hiking trails are covered with sawdust and small broken twigs - great for walking, though bumpy for strollers - and some are hard-packed dirt. Most of the trails, and two immediately branch off in opposite directions, eventually lead up along hillsides, affording hikers great vistas of the valley and mountains beyond. A very short hike from the main building leads up to a shaded overlook that has picnic tables, too.

If you and your kids are concerned about environmental issues, come visit the TreePeople, whose headquarters are in the park. This organization is dedicated to replenishing the diminishing number of trees and to encouraging recycling. Visit the greenhouse and walk through a part of a drainage tube to a watershed garden with a small scale river that flows and shows how modifications to it can help rain have a healthy impact our immediate environment. Check out the educational resource center and sign up for a guided eco-tour and hike to learn about conservation and sustainable living, as well as the importance of planting trees in areas damaged by pollution. Interactive games are sometimes offered to children as they explore and hike the trails.

Hours: The park is open daily, sunrise - sunset. Call to make a reservation for a TreePeople tour.

Price: The park and parking is free. Tours usually cost $5 per person for nonmembers; some activities are free.

Ages: 6 years and up.

CULVER CITY PARK

(310) 253-6650 or (310) 253-6470 / www.culvercity.org

9700 Jefferson Boulevard, Culver City

This is one fine city park! The playground is the newer style with free-thinking play apparatus and several independent units. It has polygon spheres with rock-climbing holds; poles that spin; cargo netting and metal bars in assorted shapes to climb; a few slides; rides on huge springs; elevated sand containers (wheelchair friendly) attached to a water pipe; and a few swings. Adjacent to the playground are two spots of green lawn with big shade trees, picnic tables, barbeque pits, two half-court basketball courts, and a great skate park.

The enclosed 1,300-square foot skate park features a Trog Bowl, Waterfall, Hubba Ledge, Ramp, Pier 7 Block,

Wall Ride, 90 degree banked hip (all terminology that will mean something to your pro-skater wanna-be), and more street features making this place a hit for skaters. Although unsupervised, we saw all the skaters wearing helmets and pads - yea! - as the posted sign states is required.

Across Duquesne Avenue the park continues with an ADA accessible interpretative trail that zig zags through trees and ground to baseball diamonds and a soccer field. Note that just down the street is The Boneyard, a good-sized dog park with all the accouterments a canine could want. Really close by is BALDWIN HILLS SCENIC OVERLOOK (pg. 49) and STAR ECO STATION (pg. 227).

Hours: The park is open daily, sunrise - sunset. The skate park is open Mon. - Fri., noon - 7pm or sunset, whichever comes first; Sat. - Sun., 9:30am - 4:30pm.

Price: Free

Ages: All

DESCANSO GARDENS

(818) 949-4200 - garden; (818) 949-0120 - tour info; (818) 790-3663 - cafe / www.descansogardens.org $$$
1418 Descanso Drive, La Canada

Descanso Gardens is over 150-acres of incredible beauty. It's not just a bed of roses here as there are acres of lilacs, camellias, tulips, dogwood, California poppies, and other flowers, that also bloom. Although flowers bloom here year round, you can call for a specific bloom schedule. A network of stroller-friendly trails wind through the grounds and around the pond, which is always an enchanting destination. One trail that is particularly delightful goes through a forest of mature California oaks. The edible garden looks good enough to eat, but don't. The fruit trees (such as apples, orange, and pomegranates) and seasonal vegetables (including pumpkins, corn, and squash), along with herbs and edible flowers, are enclosed by vines trellises, arches, bushes, and other greenery. There are also open grassy areas to run around, chaparrals to explore, and a bird observatory station overlooking a lake.

The tranquil Japanese garden is intriguing because of its unique, maze-like layout. It also has ponds and a stream. Be on the lookout for squirrels, and for more than 150 species of land and water birds, as this is their haven. (You don't have to find all 150.)

Hop aboard a five-minute model train ride - the Enchanted Railroad - for a kid-oriented trip. Ask about summer camps for kids and the numerous educational programs offered throughout the year - there is even one for toddlers. Hour-and-a-half guided tours are offered for school, and other, groups with advance registration.

Sandwiches, wraps, salads, fruit and other lunch options, including homemade desserts and ice cream, are available at the cafe daily, 9am to 4:30pm, with lovely outside seating. The Japanese Tea Garden in the Full Moon Teahouse is open in the summer only. Call (818) 790-3663 for more info. Or, bring your own food and use the picnic grounds outside the garden, adjacent to the parking lot.

Hours: The gardens are open daily, 9am - 5pm. Closed Christmas. Train rides are available Tues. and Fri., 10am - noon; Sat. - Sun., 10am - 4pm.

Price: $9 for adults; $6 for seniors and students; $4 for ages 5 - 12; children 4 and under are free. On the third Tuesday of each month, admission is half price. The train ride is $3 per person. See page x for info on AHS reciprocal memberships.

Ages: 2½ years and up.

DEVIL'S PUNCHBOWL

(661) 944-2743 / www.devils-punchbowl.com; www.localhikes.com   !
28000 Devil's Punchbowl Road, Pearblossom

The "punchbowl" is a spectacular geological formation that looks like a huge, jagged bowl created from rocks. The 1,310-acre park consists of rugged wilderness rock formations along the San Andreas Fault, plus a seasonal stream. The hiking trails vary in degree of difficulty. We hiked down into the punchbowl and back up along the one-mile Loop Trail in about half an hour. The seven mile (round-trip) hike to Devil's Chair and back is obviously tougher. The terrain is diverse, ranging from desert plants to pine trees, as the elevation changes from 4,200 feet to 6,500 feet. Rock climbing is a popular sport here, whether you prefer climbing on boulders or scaling sheer rock walls.

The nature center museum contains a small number of taxidermied animals and displays that pertain to this region, as well as a few rattlesnake, boas, scorpions, ant colonies, bees, and some insects. Outside, the center houses a few live birds, such as barn and great-horned owls. The park also offers picnic areas and equestrian trails, and is host to many special events throughout the year. School field trips are welcome.

Hours: The park is open daily, sunrise - sunset. The nature center is open Tues. - Sun., 9am - 5pm. Closed Mon. and Christmas.
Price: Free
Ages: 5 years and up.

DOUGLAS PARK

(310) 458-8310 or (310) 458-8300 / www.smgov.net
2439 Wilshire Boulevard and 25th Street, Santa Monica

This pleasant respite is just off a busy street. At the northern end is a wonderful playground for young children with a tennis court on either side. In the center of the park is a little nature area with a pond (and ducks, of course) and a cluster of trees. An expanse of lawn, a smaller pond, shaded concrete pathways throughout, and bridges add to the specialness of this park. One wooden picnic table is built around a mature, shade tree and another is built around, and almost into, a large boulder. Another unique feature is a very shallow concrete "pool" used for trikes and skaters, although not at the same time. In the summer, a few fountains shoot water up here at unexpected intervals, providing a refreshing way to cool off and eliciting giggles.

Hours: Open daily, sunrise - sunset.
Price: Free
Ages: 1 - 10 years old.

DRY TOWN WATER PARK AND MINING CO. - PALMDALE OASIS PARK AND RECREATION CENTER

3850-B East Avenue S, Palmdale

See DRY TOWN WATER PARK AND MINING CO. / PALMDALE OASIS PARK AND RECREATION CENTER, on page 2, for details about the park.

EARL BURNS MILLER JAPANESE GARDENS

(562) 985-8885 / www.csulb.edu/~jgarden
1250 Bellflower Boulevard at Earl Warren Drive on the campus of California State University Long Beach, Long Beach

This beautiful, one-acre Japanese garden has two waterfalls, a meditation rock garden, a quaint teahouse (to look in), and a koi pond. Kids can help feed the koi, so bring a quarter for the food dispenser. As you cross over the zigzag bridge into the gardens, share with your kids that it was built in this shape to sidestep spirits because, according to Japanese tradition, spirits can only travel in straight lines! Free guided tours are provided for school and community groups. The garden is ADA accessible.

Hours: Open Tues - Fri., 8am - 3:30pm; Sun., noon - 4pm. Closed Mon., Sat., spring break, Thanksgiving, winter break, and state furlough days (check the website calendar).
Price: Free. Park on the street or use metered parking (to your right) in Student Lot 16.
Ages: 3 years and up.

EAST AND RICE CANYONS

(310) 589-3200 or (310) 858-7272 / www.lamountains.com; www.localhikes.com
24255 The Old Road, Newhall

A year-round stream and a wide variety of plants and trees line trails that lead hikers away from city life and straight into nature. The Rice Canyon Loop Trail is a round trip of a little over two miles. It is a moderate walk that gets harder toward the end as it goes uphill. The trail follows along the stream and crosses over it a few times. If you smell petroleum, it's not coming from cars, but from natural oil seeping near the creek. This area was once part of an oil boom town. The East Canyon trail is almost four miles round trip. As you go steadily up in elevation, you'll pant harder, but you'll also see big-cone Douglas-fir trees and vistas of the Santa Clarita Valley. Be on the lookout for wildlife such as deer, foxes, skunks, and an abundance of birds. This trail doesn't loop, so I hope you like the way you came, because you get the opportunity to see it all again! Also look up ED DAVIS PARK IN TOWSLEY CANYON (pg. 56).

Hours: Open daily, sunrise - sunset.
Price: Free
Ages: 3 years and up.

EATON CANYON COUNTY PARK

(626) 398-5420 / www.ecnca.org; www.lamountains.com
1750 N. Altadena Drive, Pasadena

Located in the foothills of the mountains, this 190-acre wilderness park has several rugged dirt trails leading up into the mountains. One of the most popular hikes starts at the nature center and continues a little over a mile on an easy trail through oak and sycamore trees to the Mt. Wilson toll bridge. If you feel like pushing it a bit, take the ½-mile stretch past the bridge up to Eaton Falls. Hardy hikers can take a trail up to Mt. Wilson, a "mere" ten-mile hike. Approximately two-thirds of this park was burned in a 1993 brush fire. As the slopes and flats continue (still!) to recover from the fire, new plant growth continues to restore the park's beauty and this is marked along the Fire Ecology Trail. There are shorter trails in the immediate vicinity of the nature center. One such trail is only a quarter of a mile and has a self-guiding pamphlet (pick it up from the nature center) that helps identify the plants. The first (and most important) plant to recognize is poison oak.

The Eaton Canyon Wash (river bed) is filled with rocks and is fun to explore - when it's dry, of course. Eaton Creek usually flows through the canyon, except during the summer months. Pretty, shaded, and almost hidden picnic areas are found just off the parking lot. Remember to B.Y.O.W. - Bring Your Own Water.

The nicely laid-out nature center contains display cases that hold rocks and animal skulls, mounted insects, and several stuffed birds such as a great horned owl, quail, and a hummingbird. A diorama of the area is complete with a (stuffed) crouching mountain lion peering down. There are also several cases of live critters - snakes, including a rattlesnake, plus lizards, tree frogs, scorpions, and more. A few cubicles contain books, animal puppets, and some games. A 3-D map of the park shows the area's trails. Outside, a 150-seat amphitheater is the setting for environmental programs. The park offers many special events, such as free family nature walks which are given every Saturday from 9am to 11am, and tours for school children.

Hours: The park is open daily, sunrise - sunset. The nature center is open Tues. - Sun., 9am - 5pm; closed Mon., New Year's Day, Thanksgiving, and Christmas.
Price: Free
Ages: 3 years and up.

ECHO PARK

(213) 250-3578; (213) 485-1310; (213) 847-3281 / www.laparks.org
1632 Bellevue Avenue, Los Angeles

This long lake, which is occasionally stocked with trout, is between the freeway and an older, lower income Los Angeles neighborhood. Beside the cement pathway all around Echo Lake, there are some shade trees, a few palm trees, a small playground, picnic tables, and some run-around space. The north end also has a bridge with Chinese-looking decorations on it that reaches over to a small island. The real reason I'm writing about this park is that this end also holds huge seasonal lotus plants that are contained in this area by a rope. Every July, Echo Lake, actually one of the largest lotus ponds in the United States, undergoes a spectacular transformation as the lotus flowers explode into blossom.

Across the street and right next to the freeway is the Echo Park Recreation Center and a park. The park boasts a large sand box, a playground, an old basketball court, six lighted tennis courts, and a few picnic tables with shade trees. Note: Just down the street at 1419 Colton Street is an indoor swimming pool that is open year round for lap and recreational swim. The cost is $2.50 for adults per session; seniors and ages 17 and under are free. Call (213) 481-2640 for more info.

Hours: The park is open daily, sunrise - sunset. Call for hours for a specific activity.
Price: Free.
Ages: All

ED DAVIS PARK IN TOWSLEY CANYON

(661) 255-2974 / www.lamountains.com
24255 The Old Road, Newhall

This beautiful mountain wilderness park contains some spectacular geological structures. First, visit the nature center located at Canyon View trailhead, which contains displays on the history of the park. These include old photographs, taxidermied animals, and artifacts from the days when this area was an oil boom town. A picnic area and restrooms are here, too. Hiking trails range from easy to difficult. The two-mile Canyon View loop trail is a mostly moderate hike with a few short, steep grades. The five-and-a-half-mile Towsley View loop trail has more strenuous grades. This trail, which hooks up to Wiley Canyon, parallels the creek as it goes past grassy areas, the Narrows (where there are unique rock formations), and old oil drilling grounds. Be on the lookout for seasonal wildflowers, plus valley and coastal live oak trees, and animals that share this habitat. The Wiley Canyon trail is two miles round trip and a fairly easy walk. Also see EAST AND RICE CANYONS (pg. 55), as that park is just down the road.

Hours: Open daily, sunrise - sunset.
Price: Free
Ages: 3 years and up.

EL DORADO EAST REGIONAL PARK

(562) 570-1773 / www.longbeach.gov/park
7550 E. Spring Street, Long Beach

El Dorado has 450 acres of lush green park with lots for kids to do! There are three stocked fishing lakes that also have ducks clamoring for handouts. The park has a model glider field, several playgrounds, and four-and-a-half miles of biking trails, including access to the San Gabriel River cement embankment. Pedal boat rentals, (562) 824-7717, are available on Thursdays through Sundays, 11am to sunset, most of the year (closed November through January) at $8 per half hour. The archery range provides targets, but you must bring your own equipment. Note that free archery instruction, for all levels, is available on Saturday mornings. A one-mile, gasoline-powered, scale train ride, the El Dorado Express, runs Saturdays and Sundays, March through October from 10:30am to 4pm. The cost is $3 per person. Call (562) 824-7725 / www.caboosecorners.com for more information. Organized youth groups (which is an oxymoron) are invited to camp at the park overnight. You can be as active or relaxed as you want (or as the kids let you!) at El Dorado Park. Also see the following entries for EL DORADO NATURE CENTER and EL DORADO PARK WEST.

Hours: Open daily, 7am - dusk. Closed Christmas.
Price: $5 per vehicle Mon. - Thurs.; $6 on Fri.; $7 on Sat. - Sun.; $8 on holidays. Entrance fee is good for a same-day visit to the Nature Center located across the street.
Ages: All

EL DORADO NATURE CENTER

(562) 570-1745 / www.longbeach.gov/park
7550 E. Spring Street, Long Beach

The eighty-five-acre El Dorado Nature Center is part of the El Dorado East Regional Park. When crossing over the wooden bridge leading to the museum and trail-heads, look down to see the many ducks and turtles swimming and sunbathing in the water below.

The Nature Center Museum has skulls, antlers, and other artifacts to touch; bugs to look at under a magnifier; a few cases of live insects and reptiles; a display of feathers and wings; and a huge book depicting various animal habitats. Contact the center for information on their many terrific special programs such as educational field trips for schools, the Turtle and Reptile Show, and summer camps.

Walk on a short, quarter-mile paved trail (good for strollers and wheelchairs), or hike a two-mile, mostly stroller-friendly dirt trail that immerses you in nature as it goes under and through pine, oak and other trees; wildflowers; over bridges; and winds around two ponds and alongside a stream. This trail is very popular with walkers (no jogging allowed) and parents with strollers. I know the freeway is close by, but I don't hear it here: I love being in God's beautiful creation! Picnicking is not allowed inside the Nature Center, but picnic tables and shade trees can be found outside the gates at the end of the parking lot. The Nature Center is truly "an oasis of greenery and woodland in the middle of Long Beach." Also see EL DORADO EAST REGIONAL PARK and EL DORADO PARK WEST.

Hours: The trails and park are open Tues. - Sun., 8am - 5pm. The museum is open Tues. - Fri., 10am - 4pm; Sat. - Sun., 8:30am - 4pm. The trails and museum are closed Mon., New Year's Day, 4th of July, Thanksgiving and Christmas.
Price: $5 per vehicle Mon. - Thurs.; $6 on Fri.; $7 on Sat. - Sun.; $8 on holidays. Walk in or bicyclists are free. Entrance fee is good for a same-day visit to El Dorado Regional Park located across the street. Annual passes are $60.
Ages: All

EL DORADO PARK WEST

(562) 570-3225 - park; (562) 425-0553 - tennis courts / www.longbeach.gov/park; www.longbeachtennis.com

2800 Studebaker Road, Long Beach

This city park is just around the corner from its neighbors, EL DORADO EAST REGIONAL PARK and EL DORADO NATURE CENTER. (See above entries.) Sprawling across both sides of Willow Street, this park features lots of grassy areas; picnic tables under shade trees; a popular Frisbee golf course; a couple of ponds with ducks; baseball diamonds; playgrounds (some old-school ones with metal vehicle frames); a large library; fifteen tennis courts; and an outdoor skate park. The concrete skate park offers street-type skating with ramps, bowls, grinding boxes, and more. Wearing safety equipment - a helmet and elbow and knee pads - is enforced.

    Hours: Open daily, sunrise - sunset. The tennis courts are open Mon. - Fri., 7am - 9:30pm; Sat. - Sun., 7am - 8pm.

    Price: Free to the park and skate park. Tennis courts are $8 per hour most daylight hours; $13 per hour after 4pm during the week, on weekends and on holidays. (No additional fee if lights are used.)

    Ages: All

ERNEST E. DEBS REGIONAL PARK / AUDUBON CENTER

(213) 847-3989- park; (323) 221-2255 - Audubon Center / www.lamountains.com; www.ca.audubon.org

4235 Monterey Road, Highland Park - park; 4700 North Griffin Avenue, Los Angeles - audubon center

Nearly 300 acres of nature - California black walnut and oak woodland, hilly grassland, and coastal sage scrub - comprise this park in otherwise asphalt-covered Los Angeles. The inner-city park features a fairly well-manicured area near the main entrance off Monterey Road. This section has a playground, baseball fields, 100 picnic tables, and twenty barbecue pits. The majority of the park, however, is untamed open space, with some hiking trails, and an abundance of wildlife, such as snakes, lizards, rabbit, raccoons, and coyotes. Families can participate in docent-led hikes or walk the almost nine miles of hilly dirt paths and fire roads at their leisure. Atop the hill is a pond/lake where locals often fish. (Look for dragonflies around here.)

The Audubon Center, located in the western side of the park, is a "green" center that hosts workshops, children's bird counts (there are about 138 species of birds within the park - can you find them all?), nighttime astronomy hikes, and a myriad of other educational programs. Inside are interactive displays such as listening to bird calls via the touch of a button and touching a hummingbird's nest. The center also loans out backpacks that contain activities for the great outdoors. Outside is a ¼-acre Woodland Play Area with a courtyard, a pond, a children's garden, a playhouse, climbing trees, a water and sand play area, and picnic tables under shade. School tours are welcome.

    Hours: The park is open daily, dawn - dusk. The Audubon Center is open Tues. - Sat., 9am - 5pm; closed Sun. and Mon.

    Price: Free

    Ages: All

EXPOSITION PARK

(213) 744-7458 / www.expositionpark.org; www.laparks.org

700 Exposition Boulevard and S. Figueroa Street at Exposition Park, Los Angeles

The expansive Exposition Park encompasses the AIR AND SPACE EXHIBITS (pg. 98), CALIFORNIA AFRICAN AMERICAN MUSEUM (pg. 102), CALIFORNIA SCIENCE CENTER (pg. 103), IMAX THEATER (pg. 184), NATURAL HISTORY MUSEUM OF LOS ANGELES (pg. 139), and Los Angeles Memorial Coliseum. Most of the park is simply grassy areas, with trees, surrounding these attractions. More developed landscaping is just outside of the Natural History museum.

Enjoy the sunken Rose Garden, adjacent to the California Science Center, which has always been a *scent*ral part of the park. Its seven acres of beauty cultivates 16,000 specimens of 190 varieties of roses. (I bet your kids didn't know there are so many different varieties.) The gardens are wonderful for walking, smelling the perfumed air, and picture taking, plus it's stroller accessible. There is also a huge fountain in the middle of this park. Often on weekends, people of various nationalities have their wedding ceremonies in the garden. (We like looking at the different types of wedding attire.)

    Hours: Open daily, 9am - sunset. Closed January through mid-March for maintenance.

    Price: Free. Parking in the lots is $10.

    Ages: 3 years and up.

FORT TEJON STATE HISTORIC PARK

(661) 248-6692 / www.forttejon.org

Fort Tejon Road, Lebec

A long time ago, when battles were fought here, the U.S. Dragoons were garrisoned at this fort. Near the entrance is a very small museum with several informational panels and a few military uniforms. Come and explore the long barracks building, walk through the officers' quarters that display war-time memorabilia, and pretend to shoot the cannons at unseen enemies. Portions of the fort are still intact, such as a few foundational remains of buildings and a small cemetery. There are plenty of picnic tables and wide-open grass areas, plus a few trails for hiking. Note: Primitive overnight camping is permitted here.

I highly recommend coming here when Frontier Army Days/Dragoon Living History Days are presented, or during Civil War Reenactments. Dragoon program activities, with a different focus every month, could include adobe brick making, playing old-fashioned games, participating in chores from days of yore, and more. Visitors could also see a blacksmith in action, open hearth cooking, military drills, and the everyday life of a soldier. During Civil War Reenactment days troops of the Union and Confederate armies are authentically uniformed and equipped. Meet soldiers and civilians, and tour their camps. See demonstrations of weapons and watch half-hour battle skirmishes at 10:30am, noon and at 1:30pm. Guided tours of the fort are given in between battles. Come see history in action.

Come <u>live</u> history in action by participating in a day and/or overnight program called Students Living History program. Kids will live life as it was in the 1800's and participate in activities at different stations. The price includes two meals and most program materials. Note: Teachers must attend a teacher training session first.

Hours: The grounds are open daily, sunrise - sunset. The buildings are open daily, 9am - 4pm. Closed New Year's Day, Thanksgiving, and Christmas. Dragoon Era Programs are the first Sat. of most months, 10am - 3pm. Civil War Reenactments are held a few times a year - check the website calendar. The student overnight program is usually offered March - June.

Price: Regular day use is $3 for adults; $1 for ages 7 - 17; children 6 and under are free. Frontier/Dragoon Days are $5 for adults; $2 for ages 7 - 17 and scouts in uniform; $14 for family (parents and all kids 17 and under). Civil War Reenactments and other events are $7 for adults; $3 for ages 7 - 17 and scouts in uniform. Tours are $7 for adults; $5 for students. The student overnight program is $25 for students; $15 for adults. Camping is usually $15 a vehicle.

Ages: 3 years and up.

FOX HILLS PARK

(310) 253-6650 or (310) 253-6470 / www.culvercity.org
6161 Buckingham Parkway, Culver City

This attractive little park, surrounded on the street level by office buildings and condos, is tucked away on a hill and offers a pleasant respite from city life. The hillside is landscaped with flowers, bushes, and trees and has a packed-dirt jogging/walking trail winding all around it. Like a gym at a park, the isometric and resistance exercise equipment allows visitors to get a real workout (if they actually use the machines!).

For kids, and for those who work nearby and have extended lunchtime, the top of the hill has a playground, sand volleyball court, a basketball court, several tennis courts, a large flat grassy area (baseball field!), climbing trees, and picnic tables. Replacing more traditional equipment, this playground sports poles, bars, slides, climbing structures, and other objects to encourage more creative play.

Hours: Open daily, 9am - 6pm.
Price: Free
Ages: All

FRANK G. BONELLI REGIONAL COUNTY PARK - PUDDINGSTONE LAKE

(909) 599-8411 / www.bonellipark.org; www.lacountyparks.org; www.sandimas.net
120 E. Via Verde Park Road, San Dimas

This sprawling park (almost 2,000 acres!) is centered around the huge, man-made Puddingstone Lake Reservoir, which is an ideal water hole for all your fishing and boating desires. A fishing license is required for those over 16 years old. If the fish are biting, catch bass, catfish, crappie, carp, and trout. There are two fishing piers that go out a bit over the water. Feed the plentiful ducks and observe the wildlife at the lake area. We saw a heron and a crane, which my kids thought was pretty cool, plus lots of other birds and ducks. You can also launch your own boat here, but it must pass an inspection first. Jet skiing, fast boating, and water skiing are allowed on alternate days from personal water craft.

A portion of the lake is sectioned off in the summer months for swimming with lifeguards on duty. There is a sandy beach here, as well, that gets very popular.

The park boasts a vast amount of open, grassy space with trees and lots of picnic tables and BBQs. There are some great playgrounds here, too. One has a three-level play structure with tall slides, platforms to play on and under, "rock" climbing walls, metal spiral structures to climb, and toys on big springs to move back and forth on. Another is circular and has fake logs and lots of boulders with holes to climb through and over, plus sturdy ropes that connect the boulders - wonderful for cowboy or explorer play. One more play area worth mentioning looks like abstract art. It's made of rope structures, twisted shapes, poles (confused yet?), and more, all excellent for imaginations to soar.

There are over fourteen miles of hiking trails here, or you can rein in your children with a horseback ride (if you have your own horse), or take a bike ride. The scenery along the trails changes and ranges from cacti to pine trees - only in California!

Just outside the park grounds, treat yourself and the kids to a relaxing time in a hot tub. (Or just indulge yourself after spending a day with the kids!) Choose from fifteen private, hilltop tubs. Tub rentals are available Sunday through Thursday, from noon to 1am for $48 an hour for two people; Friday and Saturday, it's $58 an hour, $5 for each additional person. Call Puddingstone Hot Tubs Resort at (909) 592-2222 / www.hottubsresort.com for reservations. To reach the hot tubs, exit the 10 freeway at Fairplex Drive, turn left on Via Verde Drive and right on Camper View Drive.

Hours: Open March through September daily, sunrise - 9pm. Open October through February daily, sunrise - 7pm. Closed Christmas. The swim beach is open the end of May through mid-June, weekends only; open mid-June through September, Thurs. - Sun., 10am - 6pm.

Price: $10 per vehicle daily, April through October. $10 on weekends and holidays, only, and $5 for seniors, November through March - thus, free during the week.

Ages: All

FRANKLIN CANYON   ☼

(310) 858-7272 / www.lamountains.com   !

2600 Franklin Canyon Drive, Beverly Hills

Franklin Canyon, almost 600 acres in size, proves that there is more to Los Angeles than just skyscrapers. The lower canyon is the site of an old ranch house, which is now an office. A big, green lawn and a few picnic tables are the only things down here. Follow the creek along the mile-and-a-half trail leading to the Upper Canyon and the Nature Center. The canyon has a variety of trees such as California live oaks, black walnuts, and sycamores. Wildlife here includes deer, bobcats, coyotes, rabbits, and lizards. A moderate 2.3-mile trail, the Hastain Trail, leads to an overlook of the reservoir and summit of west Los Angeles and the coast. You'll pass an active apiary (i.e., bee houses) along the way. The Upper Reservoir has reverted to a natural lake and is a wetland area for herons and other waterfowl, as well as frogs. There are a few other, easier trails to hike as well. Check out the "Heavenly Pond," a smaller nature section and pond accessible for persons with disabilities.

Inside the Sooky Goldman Nature Center are mounted displays of the type of animals that live in the canyon, such as mountain lions; a scale model of the Santa Monica Mountains; an interactive exhibit and dioramas on Native Americans; and an exhibit on the importance of water conservation. For your tactile child, there are fossils, antlers, furs, bones, and even a few bird's nests to touch.

This Center is also the headquarters of the William O. Douglas Outdoor Classroom, which is really the name for numerous, on-going, free nature programs. Docent-led tours are open for the general public daily. Tours are available for school groups, Wednesdays and Thursdays by reservation. There are several programs for all ages that range from a stroller-friendly walk on a paved trail and nature crafts, to Nearly Full Moon Hikes, geared for older kids to have a howling good time, to Family Campfires (in the summer) with singing, stories, and s'mores. Whatever you do, enjoy your day in the wilds of L.A.

Hours: The canyon entrance is open daily, sunrise - sunset. The Nature Center is open Wed. - Sun., 10am - 4pm. The center is closed on major holidays.

Price: Free.

Ages: All

FRED HESSE JR. COMMUNITY PARK   ☼

(310) 541-8114 / www.palosverdes.com   !

29301 Hawthorne Boulevard, Rancho Palos Verdes

Behind the very nice community center, just down the steps, are a few playground areas cut into the slope of the hill with huge shade trees "covering" them. One play area has cement creatures to ride - a tortoise and dolphin. Another, larger playground has twisty slides, metal spiral elements to climb, wind chimes and pipes to play, and a short rock climbing wall, all in a sand base. Picnic tables and BBQ grills are clustered under a tightly bunched grouping of trees. The view from up here of the coastline just beyond the houses is stunning. This pretty park is popular on weekends.

An S-shaped, ¼-mile-dirt trail leads down the hill (that is brown and kind of ugly in the winter and a lovely green in the spring) which is good for hiking or bike riding. At the level, base part of the trail and hill is a soccer field, baseball diamond, climbing trees, sand volleyball court, and more picnic tables.

Hours: Open Mon. - Fri., 9am - dusk; Sat. - Sun., 10am - dusk. Closed New Year's Day, Thanksgiving, and December 24 and 25.

Price: Free

Ages: All

GANESHA PARK

(909) 620-2321 - park; (909) 620-2304 - pool / www.ci.pomona.ca.us

1575 N. White Avenue, Pomona

Just down the street from the Pomona fairgrounds and the WALLY PARKS NHRA MOTORSPORTS MUSEUM (pg. 155) is this nice, neighborhood park. It has two half basketball courts (which doesn't make a whole), a good-sized playground with a tall lighthouse slide, other slides, swings, picnic tables, barbecue grills, two tennis courts, a picnic pavilion, and some grassy run-around area. The pool here is open seasonally and has a diving board, a shallow end (although not where the diving board is), and a twisty water slide. The snack bar is usually open the same hours as the pool.

Hours: Open daily, sunrise - sunset. The pool is open June - August for lap and recreational swim.

Price: Free. Pool admission is $2.50 per person.

Ages: All

GATES CANYON PARK

(818) 880-6461 / www.cityofcalabasas.com

25801 Thousand Oaks Boulevard, Calabasas

Gates Canyon Park is a seven-acre park with open grassy areas and mature trees surrounding and interspersed with a basketball court, tennis courts, fitness course, cement pathways, picnic tables, and BBQ pits. The featured attraction for youngsters is Brandon's Village, an expansive, boundless playground designed by the Shane's Inspiration organization. There are two main separate play areas, created for both younger kids (in a sand base) and bigger kids (in a rubber base), for kids with all abilities. Each play pavilion is shaded. There are long ramps, tubes, tunnels, slides, swings (some that accommodate wheelchairs), objects to ride on, short rock climbing walls, metal ladders (both horizontal and vertical) and poles, raised sand tables, sand digger tools, a big play ship that rocks back and forth, and a pretend horse stable that looks like it has forts on either side of it. I love the fact that kids can play on the equipment as well as under it in little houses and such - so creative, so safe, so fun! A misting pole gently refreshes visitors during hot summer months.

Hours: Open daily, sunrise - 10pm.

Price: Free

Ages: All

GEORGE F CANYON NATURE CENTER

(310) 547-0862 or (310) 541-7613 / www.pvplc.com

27305 Palos Verdes Drive East, Rolling Hills Estates

This nature center and trailhead don't look like they are going to be something special from the small parking lot. But get out of the car and start walking on some of the thirty-six acres, and the natural world begins to unfold. Take the lovely, one-mile hike on a hard-packed dirt trail, that has some signage and benches, to see riparian canyon plants - coastal scrub, wildflowers in the spring, and trees - plus a seasonal stream, numerous species of birds and other animals, and pristine peninsula wilderness. After first dipping down into and through the canyon, you hike upward and if you make it to the top (which you can!), there is a great panorama. A claim to fame is seeing schist, a rock that covers all of the Peninsula but is only visible here.

The nature center has a viewing deck and a small demonstration garden outside. Inside there are maps; books;

taxidermied animals - foxes, possum, hawks and more; microscopes with slides; an exhibit of pinned insects; and small live critters (in glass displays) that inhabit these lands - snakes, lizards, turtles and frogs. They do great eco-friendly birthday parties here with nature crafts, learning about the live animals, a short hike, and more. Look on the calendar for night hikes, guided family nature hikes, and more.

Hours: The trail is open daily, dawn - dusk. The nature center is open Fri., 1pm - 4pm; Sat. - Sun., 10am - 4pm.
Price: Free
Ages: 3 years and up.

GRAND PARK
(213) 972-8080 / www.grandparkla.org
227 N. Spring Street, Los Angeles
See DOWNTOWN LOS ANGELES / GRAND PARK (pg. 167) for information on Grand Park and all the other places to go within this fairly immediate area.

GREYSTONE MANSION AND PARK
(310) 285-6830 / www.beverlyhills.org
905 Loma Vista, Beverly Hills
Edward Doheny made an oil discovery that enabled him to become one of the world's largest oil producers. In 1927 he put a great deal of his wealth into constructing the fifty-five room Greystone mansion, designed in Gothic and neo-classical styles. It was built using mainly gray stones (hence the name), plus limestone facing, a slate roof, and seven magnificent brick chimneys. Opened, iron gates at the end of a stone driveway lead to an outside porch that's made of marble. The basement used to house a bowling alley and billiards room. This multi-story, castle-like mansion is the epitome of opulence and, although you may not go into it, you are welcome to peer through the windows. We looked and saw an elegant entry way with black-and-white-checkered tiles, a gorgeous chandelier, elaborately carved wooden banisters, and several archways that are followed by incredibly long hallways. There isn't any furniture inside. Quite a few shows have been filmed here, including episodes of *Murder She Wrote* and the movie, *Ghostbusters II*. Walk around to the front sundeck for a gorgeous view of Beverly Hills and the Los Angeles area.

Behind the mansion is a dungeon (according to my boys) built into the hillside. The adjacent, closed, control room has levers and a high voltage sign, which clinched the dungeon notion. Imagination definitely reigns here!

Tiered, lush gardens and extensive grounds lavishly landscaped into and around the hillside are immaculately maintained. Go up the stone steps or walk the pathways to see the acres of grassy areas, courtyards surrounded by trimmed hedges, shade trees, some koi and turtles in the ponds, several reflecting pools, fountains, and a few park benches. This is a great place for taking photographs! A highlight for my kids was simply running down the long, sloping stone driveway - then panting their way back up.

Hours: Open March through October, 10am - 6pm. Open November through February, 10am - 5pm. Closed New Year's Day and Christmas.
Price: Free
Ages: All

GRIFFITH PARK
(323) 913-4688 or (323) 644-6661 / www.laparks.org; www.ci.la.ca.us
4730 Crystal Springs Drive, Los Angeles
The vast 4,200 acres of the eastern Santa Monica Mountains, known as Griffith Park, is really several parks in one. One part consists of enormous stretches of grassy lawns with several picnic areas and children's attractions, such as the merry-go-round and playground equipment near Park Center. A particularly interesting picnic area is the Old Zoo Picnic area on Griffith Park Drive, kind of just west of the Shane's Playground. It has tables near obsolete caves and cages that were once part of the original zoo. The caves, or concrete and stone outcroppings, were very small "natural" settings for lions and tigers and bears. Kids can prowl and roar in front of them. At the back of the shallow caves are locked, steep, stony steps leading up to other cages. There are several barred cages, too, along the same row of enclosures as the caves. More cages, a large empty building, and hiking trails are just steps away on a pathway that hairpins back over the caves. Explore away, but be safe!

Another part of the park incorporates the zoo, observatory, museums, and scale model train rides. Look up LOS ANGELES ZOO (pg. 221), GRIFFITH OBSERVATORY AND PLANETARIUM (pg. 115), AUTRY (pg. 101),

LOS ANGELES LIVE STEAMERS RAILROAD MUSEUM (pg. 130) and TRAVEL TOWN (pg. 154) for more information. Note: The Greek Theater, a nationally renowned venue for concerts and other events, is just down the road.

The largest part of the park, two-thirds of it, is the wilderness area with fifty-three miles of trails for hiking and horseback riding. Be on the lookout for deer, red-tailed hawks, opossums, coyotes, and other critters. One of the most popular hikes is three miles round trip, beginning at the observatory and extending up to one of the highest points in the park - Mt. Hollywood. On a clear day the view is unbeatable. The famous Hollywood sign is easily seen from the observatory, too. At the southwest side of the park, at 3200 (or 2960) Canyon Drive, is Bronson Canyon or Bronson Caves. A quarter-mile walk up the drive leads to a cave, which looks more like a tunnel, that was used as the Bat Cave from the *Batman* TV series. Rugged wilderness trails, as well as easy walking trails, network throughout this gigantic park located in the middle of L.A. Call or visit the ranger station in the park for all trail information. Also check out the L.A. Orienteering Club which offers nature walks for all skill levels. They incorporate learning survival skills, such as map and compass reading, with their hikes.

Ride on the bike trail that runs along a portion of the L.A. River which passes by Griffith Park (see pg. 209), or just ride along the fairly level roads inside the park. Rentals are available at Spokes 'N Stuff at 4730 Crystal Spring Drive, in the park, for about $8 an hour. Bikes are available year round, Saturday and Sunday from 10am to sunset. From Memorial Day to Labor Day they are also available Monday through Friday from 2pm to 6pm. Call (323) 662-6573 for more information.

Other noteworthy attractions, from the northern end of the park to the southern end, include: 1) The two **train places** (mentioned above) - located west of the Victory Boulevard entrance to the park. 2) **Merry-go-round** - located off Griffith Park Drive, south of the Zoo. The antique carousel, with its sixty-eight carved horses, offers rides daily in the summer, and on weekends and holidays only, the rest of the year from 11am to 5pm. Rides are $2 for every rider over 11 months old. A snack stand is here, too. Call (323) 665-3051 for more information. Free **tennis courts** are nearby. 3) **Shane's Inspiration Playground**, a large boundless playground, is also located in this section. It was constructed for physically challenged children and has several age-appropriate play areas with paved pathways, lowered monkey bars, high-backed swings, rocket ship and airplane apparatus, signs in Braille, ramps to interconnect the play areas, raised sand tables to accommodate wheelchairs, courts with lowered basketball hoops, and stainless steel slides for hearing-impaired kids. At Shane's Inspiration, able-bodied and disabled children can play side-by-side as it's just a great playground. 4) **Pony rides** and **covered wagon rides** - located at the Los Feliz entrance to the park. Each ride is $3 for kids 1 year old to 100 pounds. The rides are available Tuesday through Sunday from 10am to 4pm (until 4:30 with daylight savings). Call (323) 664-3266 / www.griffithparkponyride.com for more information. 5) **Train rides** and **simulator** - located at the Los Feliz entrance to the park. The eight-minute, mini-train ride chugs past weathered Western town facades and costs $2.75 for ages 19 months and older; $2.25 for seniors; children 18 months and under are free. (During the Christmas season, the train makes a stop in the "North Pole" and kids can visit with Santa for $7 per passenger.) The simulator, which simulates bobsledding, riding a roller coaster, or being in an airplane, costs $3 per person. Both attractions are open daily from 10am to 4:15pm or 5pm (daylight savings). Call (323) 664-6903/www.griffithparktrainrides.com for more information on either attraction. 6) **Tennis courts, soccer fields, rugby fields**, a **swimming pool**, and **golf course** - located at the Los Feliz entrance to the park. (The cross street is Riverside.) The twelve tennis courts, at 3401 Riverside Drive, are open during the week, 5pm to 9pm, and weekends and holidays, 7am to 7pm. The cost is free during the week from November through March; $8 an hour to play on all weekends, holidays, and daily during spring/summer months. Call (323) 661-5318 / www.laparks.org for more information. The pool is open mid-June to September, Monday through Friday, 11am - 2pm and 3pm - 6pm; Saturday and Sunday, 1pm - 5pm. Adults are $2.50 per session; seniors and kids 17 years and under are free. Call (323) 644-6878 seasonally, for pool information. This area also has the well-used, Los Feliz par-three, nine-hole course, which is great for beginners. It's only $5.50 per round; $4 for seniors. Call (323) 663-7758 / www.golf.lacity.org for more information. 7) **Bird Sanctuary** - located on Vermont Canyon Road, northeast of the Observatory. This verdant area has a short, stroller-friendly nature trail that crosses over a creek and loops around. A wide variety of birds flock here and make it their home. It's open daily from 10am to 5pm. 8) **Ferndell** - located near the Western Avenue entrance. This is a pretty spot to rest and picnic. Ferns and flowers growing along the brook make it an attractive, cool haven on hot days, and nature trails take you into the heart of the park. Check out A FAERY HUNT (pg. 183) for information about an interactive "production" where kids are invited to go on fairy hunts and learn about nature, too. The Trails Cafe snack stand, open Tuesday through Sunday, 8am to 5pm, is also available at this area. Contact the cafe at (323) 871-2102. There are other refreshment stands located throughout the park, as well as restaurants at golf courses and at the Autry museum.

me of the equestrian centers around the park include: **Rocken P Outfitters**, (818) 242-8443 / w.rockenpoutfitters.com - located at 1850 Riverside Drive in Glendale. It's open daily, 8am to 5pm (6pm in spring and summer). Riding, available on a first come- first served basis, costs $20 per hour per person. There is also a half hour ride available for $15. Cash only. The minimum age is 7. Special evening rides usually begin at 5pm (4pm in the winter) and include ninety minutes of riding, followed by a dinner break at Viva Cantina (www.vivacantina.com), then riding "home." Offered Friday through Sunday, the cost is $60 per person with a minimum of two people. Dinner is not included in this price, and reservations are required. Two-hour twilight rides (no dinner) are also available for $50 per. **Circle K Horse Rentals**, (818) 843-9890 /www.circlekhorserentals.com is located at 914 Mariposa Street in Burbank. It's open daily, 7:30am to 5pm (6pm in the summer). Riding costs $25 for one hour; $45 for two hours. Cash only. The minimum age is 7 years old. Ask about their nighttime and dining rides. **Griffith Park Horse Rentals**, (818) 840-8401 / www.griffithparkhorserental.com or www.la-equestriancenter.com, is located at 480 W. Riverside Drive in Burbank in the L.A. Equestrian Center. It's open daily, 8am to 5pm; open an hour later in the summer. Riding costs $25 per hour ($45 if you weigh over 200 pounds) and the minimum age is 6 years old (and four feet tall). Cash only. Younger kids can take a twenty-minute lead ride on a trail for $25. Three-hour sunset rides that include a stop off at a Mexican restaurant for dinner start at $75 per person - dinner is not included in this price. These rides are open nightly, with a minimum of two riders. Ask about the summer day camps for kids. **Sunset Ranch Hollywood Stables**, (323) 464-9612 or (323) 469-5450/ www.sunsetranchhollywood.com, is located at 3400 N. Beachwood Drive in Los Angeles. It's open daily, 9am - 5pm. Riding is $40 an hour; $60 for two hours, with a minimum age limit of 8 years. The much-acclaimed sunset rides, for ages 16 and up, begin around 4:30pm. Ride over the hills for about two hours, then come back to the ranch for a dinner of barbecue chicken, beans, potato salad, and rolls, and music. Offered on Saturdays, these sunset rides and dinner are $95 per person. Ask about other sunset rides where you stop off at a mid-range restaurant, or ones where you just ride for a few hours. Other options are lunch rides, kids parties, Girl Scout programs, horse and carriage rides, and more. This people-friendly place invites families to just come and visit and pet the horses - no charge.

Hours: The park is open daily, 5:30am - 10:30pm.
Price: Free
Ages: All

HANSEN DAM RECREATION AREA

(818) 899-8087 or (818) 896-6215 - recreation; (818) 899-3779 - aquatics center / www.laparks.org
11770 Foothill Boulevard, Lake View Terrace

This large park offers a few hiking trails, a picnic area, ball fields, trees and shaded areas, and a few scattered playgrounds. The huge, boundless playground is terrific(!) and it features equipment for all abilities. Slides, ramps, swings for wheelchairs, and lots of activities at the connecting platforms and in between them offers hours of fun. Two of the park's other best features are the smallish, nine-acre, man-made lake and an adjacent, year-round swimming pool. The man-made recreation lake, with cement sides, offers kayaking classes. Kayakers must first take a safety class to be eligible to rent the boats. Catfish and trout fishing are also available and stocked in their proper season. A fishing license is needed for ages 16 years and up.

The non-heated, gated pool, which is referred to as the swimming lake, is four-feet deep all around, very large, and extremely long. It also has two twisty water slides - one is enclosed - for those 48" tall and 8 years and up. Lifeguards are on duty when it's open. Coarse sand all around the pool, a sand volleyball court, and no shade offers a quasi, beach-like atmosphere. A snack stand is open in the summertime and showers are here, too.

Hours: The park is open daily, 7am - sunset. The pool is open Memorial Day - mid-June and the month of September on weekends only, 11am - 7pm; open mid-June - Labor Day daily, 11am - 7pm.
Price: Park entrance is free. Pool admission is $2.50 for adults; free for seniors, and ages 17 and under. Youths 7 and under must be accompanied by an adult.
Ages: 3 years and up.

HARRY M. DOTSON PARK

(714) 379-9222 / www.ci.stanton.ca.us
10350 Fern Street, Stanton

This 1.3 acre park is packed with kid-friendly amenities that include a half basketball court, cement pathways, open grassy areas, climbing area, pirate ship for mateys to climb aboard and say "aarrrgh" a lot, and a water play area. The pirate ship is large, has three masts, porthole windows, and has play equipment attached to it, like climbing apparatus and a slide. Boulders, with hand holds, are placed around the ship to increase the fun of "let's pretend", and there is a partially buried treasure chest next to an X, which marks the spot. The small Western-themed Wet Saloon water play area has fountains that erupt water from the ground, water cannons, and a play structure that looks like a skeletal pioneer wagon. Picnic tables are in this immediate area, under shade trees, so parents can dryly watch their wet little darlings.

Hours: Open daily, sunrise - sunset. The water part is open seasonally.
Price: Free
Ages: 1 ½ years and up.

HAZARD PARK

(213) 485-6839 / www.laparks.org
2230 Norfolk Street, Los Angeles

Hazard Park features another great playground built by Shane's Inspiration! Created for able-body and disable-body children to play together, this playground features a large area with interconnecting ramps and learning activities along the way and at the covered mini platform areas; tunnels; slides; swings; a few rock-climbing structures; rope climbing; sand diggers toys; and much more. The surrounding park has mature trees, lighted tennis courts, indoor and outdoor basketball courts, handball courts, lighted baseball diamond, utility fields, BBQ pits, picnic tables, and lots of grassy, run-around space with a jogging trail crisscrossing throughout.

Hours: Open daily, sunrise - sunset.
Price: Free
Ages: All

HERITAGE PARK - Cerritos

(562) 916-8570 / www.cerritos.us
18600 Bloomfield Avenue, Cerritos

One if by land, two if by sea . . . . The most unique feature of this noteworthy park is an island with a kid-size version of Boston, circa 1770. Cross the covered bridge and be transported back in time. (Not literally; it's just the atmosphere of the island.) This multi-level "town" has a replica of Paul Revere's house and a North Church Tower, which has two slides and climbing chains. (Creative parents can reinforce a Paul Revere history lesson here. Check out the Paul statue and plaques to do with the *Midnight Ride of Paul Revere*.) The town is also composed of a series of little buildings - apothecary, saddler, printer, etc. - with play space, sliding poles, and more slides in them, as well as outside and inside bridges that connect them. There are also small cannons to sit on or "fire", and small replicas of British ships harbored in the water, which are designed for pint-sized sailors to climb aboard. The island has a rock-lined brook running through it with small waterfalls and plenty of shade trees, so it is refreshingly cool even on hot days.

The ducks swimming in the "moat" surrounding the island are always looking for a handout, and watch for the sun-bathing turtles. Across the water is a wonderful, expansive, play area with swings, slides, and climbing apparatus. The park also has picnic tables, a few barbecues, basketball courts, large grass areas, climbing trees, and a baseball diamond with stadium-type benches.

Hours: The main part of the park is open daily, sunrise - sunset. The island is open Mon., Wed - Sun., 10am - dusk; Tues., 2pm - dusk.
Price: Free
Ages: All

HIGGINBOTHAM PARK

(909) 399-5490 / www.ci.claremont.ca.us
625 Mt. Carmel Drive, Claremont

A small, train-car playground makes this park worth mentioning and stopping by to play if you are in the vicinity. The main car looks like a steam engine so kids can climb aboard. They can also climb on top and through the windows and down the short slide. Bring a picnic lunch, hike about as the rest of the park is in a natural setting, and dream about riding the (real) rails.

Hours: Open daily, sunrise - 10pm.
Price: Free
Ages: 3 - 8 years.

HOPKINS WILDERNESS PARK

(310) 318-0668 - park; (310) 318-0670 - reservations / www.redondo.org
1102 Camino Real, Redondo Beach

Escape to the wilderness of Redondo Beach. This gated, eleven-acre hilltop park has two streams running through it, two ponds, and a wonderful view of the city. Hike along the nature trail that takes you through California Redwood and pine trees; through a meadow - be on the lookout for butterflies and lizards; and to the small waterfall and pond where turtles, crayfish, and bullfrogs have made their homes. Wilderness Park also has several campgrounds and is a popular spot for local, overnight camping for groups. Reservations are required. Picnic tables and barbecue pits are available for campers.

Hours: Open Thurs. - Tues., 10am - 4:30pm. Closed Wed., New Year's Day, Thanksgiving, Christmas, and in bad weather.
Price: The park is free to walk through. Day camping is available. Fri. and Sat. overnight tent camping (no stakes allowed) is $5 a night for adults; $3 a night for ages 17 and under, plus a staffing fee of $240.
Ages: 3 years and up.

HOUGHTON PARK

(562) 570-1640 / www.longbeach.gov
6301 Mrytle Avenue, Long Beach

This corner park is marked by the army helicopter suspended on a pole. The park has three baseball diamonds with lights and stadium seating; a volleyball court; a basketball court; cement picnic tables; a small playground with swings and a few twisty and tube slides; and green, open spaces studded with both pine and palm trees.

The spacious cement skate park is composed of two adjoining sections. One part has three bowls; the other has grinding poles, several steps, pyramids, and spines. We saw skateboarders, skaters, and bikers all using the park at the same time. A helmet and pads are required and note that the police do cruise by. The park is free and unsupervised. Benches border the skating area so nonparticipants can enjoy watching.

David Starr Jordan High School, adjacent to the park, has tennis courts. A youth/community center is also on the premises.

Hours: Open daily, sunrise - 10pm.
Price: Free
Ages: All ages; 7 and up for the skate park.

HUNTINGTON LIBRARY, ART COLLECTIONS AND BOTANICAL GARDENS

1151 Oxford Road, San Marino

See the entry for HUNTINGTON LIBRARY, ART COLLECTIONS AND BOTANICAL GARDENS on page 121 for details.

JAMES IRVINE GARDEN

(213) 628-2725 / www.jaccc.org
244 South San Pedro Street, Los Angeles

Go through the doors of this community center, down the elevator, to the "basement" for a brief bit of serenity in the midst of bustling L.A. This small, hidden, lush oasis is filled with plants, boulders, wooden footbridges, short waterfalls, a small pond, and a rock-lined pathway and stream that meander throughout the flowers, bamboo, and willow, pine, and other trees. See DOWNTOWN LOS ANGELES / GRAND PARK (pg. 167) for information on Grand Park and all the other places to go within this fairly immediate area, especially Little Tokyo and the JAPANESE AMERICAN NATIONAL MUSEUM (pg. 124), which are both just outside the front doors.

Hours: Open Tues. - Sun., 10am - 5pm. Call for weekend availability as it is sometimes closed for special events. Closed Mon. and holidays.
Price: Free. Metered parking on the street.
Ages: 3 years and up.

THE JAPANESE GARDEN

(818) 756-8166 / www.thejapanesegarden.com
6100 Woodley Avenue, Van Nuys

Sharing the same address (and waters) as the Tillman Water Reclamation Plant, but worlds apart, is this hidden and tranquil Oriental gem. The 6.5-acre garden is based on designs of 18th- and 19th-century gardens that were created for Japanese feudal lords who used them for contemplation.

While you'll like the dry, Zen meditation garden that makes up a small portion of the grounds, you'll really enjoy a stroll on the paved pathway through the startlingly lovely main garden that gracefully curves in and around a lake and waterway. Interspersed throughout are small bamboo groves; manicured shrubbery; several bridges, including a zigzag one; a Shoin building, which was a traditional type of dwelling used by samurais and aristocrats; a weeping willow tree; a variety of stone lanterns; Ginko trees; and a three-tiered waterfall. A narrow pond with water lilies runs along an entire wall of the garden. Be on the lookout for herons, egrets, grebes, and diff swallows here. Peek into a formal tea house and tea garden also on the premises. Read the information on the website to gain a greater appreciation of all the symbolism used in the layout and elements in the garden, or listen to your docent on a one-hour-and-fifteen-minute guided tour. Note: You will smell an unpleasant odor at times - this is the downside of using reclaimed water.

From a viewing platform, you can see the adjacent reclamation plant. Learn how the plant water brought about the existence of the garden. Note that the garden is adjacent to the ANTHONY C. BEILENSON PARK, LAKE BALBOA, etc. (pg. 47) parks and recreation area.

Hours: Open Mon. - Thurs., 11am - 3:15pm (the garden closes at 4pm); Sun., 10am - 3:15pm (garden closes at 4pm). Closed Fri. and Sat. Always call the day of your visit as many special events are held here and the gardens may be closed then. Guided tours are offered Mon. - Thurs. with advanced reservations.

Price: $3 for adults; $2 for seniors and children 9 and under. Guided tours are free with admission. See page x for info on AHS reciprocal memberships.

Ages: 7 years and up.

JOHNNY CARSON PARK

(818) 238-5300 / www.burbank.com
400 Bob Hope Drive, Burbank

Despite the proximity of the freeway, this pleasant park offers a refuge, of sorts, in downtown Burbank. Kids enjoy the large grassy areas, small woods, climbing and shade trees, and stroller-friendly dirt pathways that run throughout the park. The Tonight Show Playground, for today's kids, has slides, swings, and climbing apparatus. Picturesque bridges go over what I first thought was a seasonal stream, but it is only a drainage "creek." Come enjoy a picnic here before or after you take the WARNER BROS. (pg. 206) studio tours.

Hours: Open daily, sunrise - 10pm.
Price: Free
Ages: All

KENNETH HAHN STATE RECREATION AREA

(323) 298-3660 / www.lacountyparks.org
4100 S. La Cienega Boulevard, Los Angeles

This spacious, 336-acre natural parkland in the heart of Baldwin Hills has hilly grasslands, forest areas (including the Olympic section, which has a tree representing each participant country from the 1984 Olympics), and several dirt hiking trails that extend up to seven miles. A favorite is the one-mile hike to the waterfall. The park also features a large lake that is stocked with trout in the winter, and catfish, bluegill, and bass in the summer. The fishing is free, but ages 16 and up need a license. Swimming in the water is not allowed. You may, however, feed the ducks who are always looking for a handout. Make sure to check out the Japanese garden with its koi and little bridge. There are seven picnic areas (which were a bit run down when we visited) complete with barbecue grills for families to enjoy, as well as a few scattered playgrounds and basketball and volleyball courts.

Hours: Open daily, sunrise - sunset. Closed Christmas.
Price: Free during the week; $6 per vehicle on weekends and county holidays.
Ages: All

KING GILLETTE RANCH

(805) 370-2301 / www.nps.gov/samo
26800 Mulholland Highway, Calabasas

At 588 acres, maybe this ranch is king! On the grounds are a twenty-five room mansion, a single-family resident's home, a few other buildings that you can see, but not go into, and one that you are welcome to go into - the current home of the SANTA MONICA MOUNTAINS NATIONAL PARK HEADQUARTERS (pg. 84). Stop off to get some information here first. Bring a picnic lunch to enjoy at the picnic tables outside.

The ranch also has a walking path leading to a California native plant nursery; a pond to walk around where great blue herons, mallards, cormorants, and other birds visit; and a one-mile trail to Inspiration Point which is a steep climb, but worth it for the rewarding view. The chaparral and mature trees are naturally beautiful. If you are so inclined, walk another 1.5 miles along the ridge. Note that PETER STRAUSS RANCH (pg. 78), TROUTDALE (pg. 88) and PARAMOUNT RANCH (pg. 77) are just around the corner.

Hours: Open daily, sunrise - sunset.
Price: Free for the first 2 hours; $7 per vehicle for the day.
Ages: 5 years and up.

KYOTO GARDENS

(213) 629-1200 / www.3.hilton.com
120 S. Los Angeles Street, Los Angeles

Amid the hustle and bustle of downtown Los Angeles, take a quick breather at the Kyoto Gardens at the DoubleTree by Hilton hotel. Ride the elevator up to the small, but beautiful, half-acre, Japanese garden located - on top of the roof! The garden's plants, green grass, boulders, pathway and waterfall all give it a sense of serenity and we loved its unique location. Enjoy your short break from the busy world not far below. See DOWNTOWN LOS ANGELES / GRAND PARK (pg. 167) for information on Grand Park and all the other places to go within this fairly immediate area.

Hours: Open daily, 10am - 10pm.
Price: Free; metered parking is available.
Ages: 2 years and up.

LACY PARK

(626) 300-0700 / www.cityofsanmarino.org
1485 Virginia Road, San Marino

This is one of the prettiest parks we've visited - it's so well maintained and beautifully landscaped. In the center is a large expanse of immaculately kept grass. Encircling it are several varieties of trees, including oak, pine, and palm. An outside dirt loop track, which is about a mile long, is designated for joggers and walkers. An inside paved loop trail is designated for cyclists and rollerskaters. The playground has the normal play equipment, plus talking tubes (i.e., where two people can talk to each other through a long tube) and some patches of trees to play hide and seek. There are also a few scattered benches and picnic tables. The west entrance has several rose arbors blooming seasonally.

Six tennis courts, operated by the San Marino Tennis Foundation, are on the grounds, open 7:30am to sunset, with lighted courts. The cost is $10 for non-members. Call (626) 793-1622 for more info.

Hours: Open year-round, Mon. - Fri., 6:30am - sunset. Open May through October on weekends, 8am - 8pm; November through April, 8am - 6pm. Closed New Year's Eve, New Year's Day, Thanksgiving, Christmas Eve, and Christmas Day.
Price: Free Mon. - Fri. for everyone. Entrance is $4 for ages 5 and up on Sat. - Sun. for nonresidents; free for residents.
Ages: All

LADERA LINDA COMMUNITY CENTER

(310) 541-7073 - park; (310) 544-5264 - hikes / www.palosverdes.com/rpv/recreationparks
32201 Forrestal Drive, Rancho Palos Verdes

This park features a wilderness area, a basketball court, a small playground, and, closer to where the additional parking lot is located, two paddle tennis courts and (up the wooden stairs) soccer and baseball fields. There are picnic tables and a few shade trees, too. The community center building is home to Montessori school classes, game rooms, and a Discovery Room. The small Discovery Room has a few live animals; displays of rocks, fossils, and animals skins to gently touch; skulls of a raccoon, coyote, fox and skunk; an ostrich egg and hummingbird egg; and stuffed raccoons and great horned owl. Another little playground is here as are two basketball courts.

Two-hour, docent-led hikes offered by the center enable groups of kids to explore the coastal habitat of the Palos Verdes Peninsula. Look out for and learn about coastal sage scrub, native trees, and wildflowers, as well as important critters such as lizards, butterflies, and birds. Hikes are moderately difficult, so bring a water bottle and wear sunscreen.

The hike/tours can focus on a topic of your choice, such as plants, animals, fossils, or the geology of the area, including a visit to a rock quarry. A visit to the Discovery Room, with explanations about the exhibits, is included in your time here. Note that scheduled public tours are also offered - call for dates and times.

Hours: The park and Discovery Room are open July - Labor Day, Mon. - Fri., 1pm - 5pm; Sat. - Sun., 10am - 5pm. It's open the rest of the year, Mon., Wed., and Fri. - Sun., 1pm - 5pm. Closed Tues., Thurs., New Year's Day, Thanksgiving, and Christmas. Tours are set up by reservation.

Price: Free to the park. Tours are $2 for adults; $1 for children 13 and under.

Ages: All for the park; 7 years and up for the tours.

LA MIRADA REGIONAL PARK

(562) 902-5645 or (562) 943-0131 / www.cityoflamirada.org

13701 Adelfa Drive, La Mirada

Green rolling hills and other grassy expanses, a plethora of mature trees (for shade and for climbing), picnic tables, an acclaimed disc golf course (for the seasoned and beginner player), twelve, lighted tennis courts, a lighted baseball field, a cement pathway that meanders throughout, a playground, and a lake with a tiny island in it, constitute this 100-acre, lovely park. Benches and trees line the lakeside, while the resident (and requisite) ducks look for handouts. Bring your fishing pole because the lake is stocked with rainbow trout in the winter and spring, and catfish in the summer and fall. Bass and carp can also be caught here.

Entrenched in a wood-chip base the covered play structure is elevated so not only can kids run around on its swinging bridges and fort-like outlooks, and slide down the short slides and crawl through tubes, but they can also engage their imaginations as they play under it. Toddler swings, a truck and plane on giant springs to rock back and forth on, a small rock climbing wall, and a little clubhouse nestled in the sand (bring bucket and shovel) round out this playground.

Near the playground is a fully-stocked pro shop selling discs for the golf course (they hold tournaments here) and snack items, and offering sign-ups for the twelve tennis courts. Call Lifetime Sports / La Mirada Tennis Center at (562) 902-6371 for more information. Note - they also have a tennis wall here so you can practice without a partner. Just around the corner is a water park and swimming pools - see BUCCANEER BAY / SPLASH! LA MIRADA AQUATICS CENTER (pg. 2) for details.

Hours: Open sunrise - sunset. The tennis courts are open from sunrise to 9pm (when the lights go off).

Price: Free. Tennis courts are free for unreserved courts; $5 for reserved courts, which must be made 2 hours before play time.

Ages: All

LA PINTORESCA PARK

(626) 744-4724 / www.ci.pasadena.ca.us/humanservices

45 E. Washington Boulevard, Pasadena

This mid-size, neighborhood park is located just behind the La Pintoresca Branch Library. The park offers huge, shady oak trees to climb and relax under; a few barbeque pits and picnic tables; a paved pathway for biking or strolling; a basketball court; and a lighted, portable skate park with wooden ramps, a funbox, a small, quarter-pipe, and a pyramid. Parental consent for minors, and helmets and pads are required for skaters. A playground with wood-chip ground cover has several slides and a variety of climbing apparatus, plus a swing-set and a merry-go-round.

In the summertime, kids enjoy water play in a section of the park that has colorful loops and poles which act as fountains as water squirts out through them.

Hours: The park and skate park are open daily, sunrise - sunset.

Price: Free

Ages: All

LIBERTY PARK - Cerritos

(562) 916-8565 / www.cerritos.us

19211 Studebaker Road, Cerritos

Experience the freedom at Liberty Park to do almost anything. The park offers long grassy areas to run around; three good playground areas (one is like a pirate ship with enclosed slides, swings, platforms, play areas, etc.); picnic tables; barbeque pits; picnic shelters; three sand volleyball courts; a 330-yard walking/jogging track; a softball field; a disc (Frisbee) golf course; outside exercise clusters equipped with pull up bars and more; and six lighted tennis courts.

Tennis is free for Cerritos residents (show a driver's license or utility bill for proof of residency) and $7 per hour for nonresidents, starting at 10am daily - no lights for nighttime play. A bike path runs along the Los Angeles River just outside the park gates. (See BIKE TRAIL: SAN GABRIEL RIVER TRAIL on page 209 for more information.)

Inside the community building are racquetball courts ($7 per hour for residents, $11 for nonresidents) and a weight room. A Discovery Depot room has computers, a reading area, and even a dress-up play area for youngsters.

Summertime offers the refreshing pleasures of a small water park with sprayers and other fun features. This area is open daily, 1pm to 4pm. (You can ask in the office to turn the water on, if it's not already.) During the summer, too, is Monday night family time at the movies ('G' rated) and Wednesday night family entertainment consisting of puppets, magicians, or storytellers.

Hours: The park is open daily, sunrise - sunset. The community center is open April through Oct., Mon. - Fri., 10am - 9:30pm; Sat. - Sun., 10 - 8pm. Open Oct. - March, daily 10am - 6:30pm. Call for times for special programs.

Price: Free to the park. Fees for activities are listed above.

Ages: All

LINCOLN PARK

(213) 847-1726 - park / www.angelfire.com/ca4/lincolnpark; www.laparks.org
3501 Valley Boulevard, Los Angeles

This older park in an older section of town boasts a terrific (and huge!) bound-less playground with a kind of zoo and carousel theme. The playground has numerous, hands-on activities and features on and throughout its platforms, ramps, and bridges, plus two "tree houses", slides (including a tactile one with raised fish and flowers on it), speaking tubes, accessible swings, and even a raised water play area. What fun!

The park also has rows of picnic tables under huge pine and oak trees; paved pathways that crisscross throughout; four nice tennis courts; another playground with a sand base for younger children; grassy expanses; and a community building. A big lake (with a large fountain in it) is stocked with fish and home to numerous ducks. A fishing license is needed for ages 15 and over. We also enjoyed the large, grass-covered hill - walking up it and running back down Kamikaze-style! For those who like even more action, try the plaza-style, big skate park which has ramps, quarter- and half-pipes, and other skateboarding elements.

Hours: The park and skate park are open daily, sunrise - sunset. The community center is open Mon. - Fri., 10am - 9pm; Sat., 8am - 5pm; closed Sun.

Price: Free

Ages: All

LINDBERG PARK

(310) 839-0127 / www.culvercity.org
5401 Rhoda Way, Culver City

If you're in the neighborhood, this tucked-away park is a good one to visit. There are ball fields on each end of the park, exercise stations, a basketball court, outside handball courts, a lighted tennis court, grassy areas, picnic tables, barbecues, a recreation building, and, most notably, a good-sized playground with lots of fun play equipment all built in a sand base. Besides the typical slides and swings, there is a small pile of tires to climb up, a short rope wall, a small railcar and boat structure, monkey bars, and a pulley system with a bucket for the sand.

Hours: Open daily, sunrise - sunset.

Price: Free

Ages: All

LIVE OAK PARK (Los Angeles County)

(310) 545-5621 or (310) 802-5000 / www.ci.manhattan-beach.ca.us
1601 Valley Drive N. and 21st Street, Manhattan Beach

This park is formed around a bend in the road and is divided into various park pockets with grassy sections. The northern section has baseball diamonds, picnic tables, and some short, bent, gnarled trees - so great for climbing. Other pockets have playground equipment (one has little play trains), a lighted basketball court, soccer fields, places just to run and play, and tennis courts. The six courts are open weekdays and holidays from 7am to 10pm ($7 per hour until 5pm; $9 per hour after 5pm - for lights), and weekends 7am to 8pm ($9 per hour). Call (310) 545-0888 to make reservations.

Hours: Open daily, dawn - dusk.
Price: Free
Ages: All

LOS ANGELES COUNTY ARBORETUM & BOTANIC GARDEN

(626) 821-3222 / www.arboretum.org; www.pasadenasymphony-pops.org
301 N. Baldwin Avenue, Arcadia

$$$

Do you have a budding horticulturalist in your family? Come visit this awesome arboretum and explore the more than 127 acres of plants and trees from around the world grouped mainly by geography. The blooming flowers and the variety of gardens are astounding. We walked along the southern (and most interesting) route first. There are numerous paved pathways as well as several dirt pathways leading through trees, bushes, and jungle-like landscape which makes the walk an adventure for kids. Ducks and geese loudly ask for handouts at Baldwin Lake. (Look for the turtles in the lake's water.)

For your history lesson for the day, peek into the spacious Hugo Reid Adobe House, where each room is furnished with period furniture. The adobe grounds are beautiful and reflective of the mid-1800's. Peer into the gracious Queen Anne "Cottage" for another glimpse of the past. You'll see mannequins dressed in old-fashioned clothes, elegantly furnished rooms, and a harp in the music room. The nearby immaculate Coach Barn has stalls ornately decorated with wood paneling and iron grillwork. Instead of horses, they now hold farm tools, blacksmith tools, and a coach. Also see the Santa Anita Depot with a train master's office and railroad paraphernalia, and a little farther away are the Tongva kis (huts).

The lush greenery around the fifty-foot waterfall makes it one of the most enchanting spots in the arboretum. Walk up the wooden stairs for a panoramic view and "discover" a lily pond. Back down on Waterfall Walk you'll see a serene woodland area and rock-lined stream. I was utterly content to sit while the kids let their imaginations kick into gear and play. Colorful koi are just around the "corner" at the Tule Pond.

The northern section has a few greenhouses with exotic flowers and plants. An African and Australian section at this end has an abundance of trees.

Peacocks are everywhere - strutting their stuff and calling out in plaintive-sounding wails. Note that peacock feathers are available at the gift shop for $1.50 each, although I don't think these two facts are related.

Picnicking is not allowed on the grounds, but there is a shaded, grassy area between the parking lots. Or, eat at the Peacock Cafe, which has reasonably priced food, though note that it is closed on Mondays. Tip one: Take a half-hour tram ride around and through the extensive arboretum, or get off at any one of the seven stops along the way and reboard at a later time. Trams run from on weekends only, noon to 3pm on the hour. Tickets are $5 per person. Tip two: It gets hot here during the summer, so bring water bottles (and look for the sprinklers to run through).

Wonderful, family geared events are held here several times throughout the year. Science Adventure Day Camps, which include classes on space and rocketry, magic, and more, are offered in the summer. The Pasadena Symphony POPS offers five Summer Concerts during the summer here. The Saturday concerts start at 7:30pm and the arboretum closes at 3:30pm on these days. See the June Calendar section for more details.

Hours: Open daily, 9am - 5pm. Closed Christmas.
Price: $9 for adults; $6 for seniors and students with ID; $4 for ages 5 - 12; children 4 and under are free. The third Tues. of every month is free. (There is no tram on these days.) Free parking. See page x for info on AHS reciprocal memberships.
Ages: 2 years and up.

LOS ARBOLES PARK

(310) 618-2930 / www.torranceca.gov
5101 Calle de Ricardo, Torrance

!

What a blast! One of the few parks left that has a classic, metal rocket ship play structure for kids, this is a launching place for imaginations. The four-story rocket ship is the main feature with a ladder going all the way up, and a tall slide with which to come back down to earth. Nearby, fittingly, is a metal lunar module model (say that five times fast!) based in sand, perfect to spy out alien life forms, like siblings. It has a short ladder, a fireman's pole and controls. This smallish playground has a few other elements such as grassy areas and trees, plus an incredible, almost astronaut's view of the world. Well, the Los Angeles basin world. Note that the playground is unfenced and there are no restrooms.

Hours: Open daily, sunrise - sunset.

Price: Free
Ages: 4 - 12 years

MADRONA MARSH

☼

(310) 32 MARSH (326-2774) or (310) 782-3989 / www.friendsofmadronamarsh.com   !/$$
3201 Plaza Del Amo, Torrance

Tucked away in a business and suburban area, is the ten-acre Madrona Marsh. It's a vernal marsh, meaning that it's a depression flooded by runoff water from surrounding upland slopes. It has a seasonal pond and four different plant habitats that are home to small mammals (namely squirrels); insects, such as dragonflies and butterflies; and numerous bird species. Educational nature walks for kids (and adults) of all ages are given throughout the year. During the hour, or so, guided tour you'll see and learn mostly about birds, plus ground animals, like tree frogs, and varieties of plant life. Ask about the numerous other programs offered, such as junior naturalist, astronomy, art classes, and habitat restoration. (It does my heart good to see kids pulling weeds.) Bring snacks and a water bottle.

Across the street from the marsh, the handicapped-accessible, mid-sized Nature Center contains a room with large information and picture panels that explain the plants and animals of the marsh and the marsh, itself; glass case displays with several stuffed birds and other animals depicted in their natural habitats; and some interactive displays. The hallways offers a book nook; a place to color and display kid's artwork; live animals, such as turtles and snakes; furs to touch; and a microscope and prepared slides to look at. A classroom, project lab and little gift shop are also on-site. As the Nature Center and marsh are somewhat hidden, even if they aren't big enough to make you feel like you've gotten away from all of city life, they are at least big enough to make you feel like you've gotten away from some of it.

Hours: Marsh and Nature Center are open Tues. - Sun., 10am - 5pm. Closed on Mon. and holidays. Guided walks of the marsh are given the fourth weekend of every month, 10am - noon, and field study tours are given at various times. Call for details or to schedule a field trip.
Price: Free; donations gladly accepted. Field trips are $5 per person.
Ages: 6 years and up.

MALIBU CREEK STATE PARK

☼

(818) 880-0367 - park; (800) 444-7275 - camping reservations / www.parks.ca.gov; www.localhikes.com $$$
1925 Las Virgenes Road, Calabasas

Of the many hiking, mountain bike, and horseback riding trails to choose from in the Santa Monica Mountains, one of our favorites is the Malibu Creek Trail. Starting at the broad fire road, veer to the right as the trail forks onto Cragg Road. The scenery keeps getting better the further in you hike. Oak trees shade part of the trail as you follow the high road along the creek. Man-made Century Lake is a great place to stop for a picnic, take in the beauty of your surroundings, fish, or even use the rope to swing over and in the water. This spot marks a four-mile round trip. Continue on an additional two miles (round trip) to the former M*A*S*H set, which contains just a few of the shows artifacts, such as the ambulance and other vehicles. Being here might not have any meaning for your kids, but they'll at least think the rock formation, named Goat Buttes and used in the opening scene of the show, is worth a "wow."

A mile in from the parking lot is the Visitor's Center, which also has a small museum. One contains taxidermied animals, rocks, shells, and other displays. There is also M*A*S*H memorabilia and a room for school groups to work on craft projects.

Feel like taking a dip in cool, refreshing water? About a half mile beyond the Visitor's Center, over the bridge to the left and over a short trail of rocks, is Rock Pool, a rock-lined swimming hole. (*Swiss Family Robinson* and some *Tarzan* movies were filmed here.) It's a drag to have to hike food and such in, but it's like a hidden oasis, that is crowded on the weekends, so it's worth it. My boys thought jumping off the boulders into the "pool" formed by the creek was the ultimate.

Take advantage of all that the park offers by spending a night or two here. Each of the sixty-two campsites, some of which are shaded, has a picnic table and charcoal-use fire pit. Eight people per campsite are allowed. No RV hook-ups.

Hours: The park is open daily, 8am - sunset. The Visitor's Center is open Sat. - Sun., noon - 4pm.
Price: $12 per vehicle. Camping prices, $35, are seasonal, plus a reservation fee of $8.
Ages: 3 years and up.

MARIE KERR PARK - MARIE KERR SKATE PARK

(661) 267- 5675 or (661) 267-5611 - park and skate park; (661) 267-6145 - pool / www.cityofpalmdale.org
39700 30th Street West, Palmdale

Airborne! At least my kids keep hoping for this state when they skate at this skate park. I just hope they land unharmed. This sometimes supervised, 8,500-square-foot skate park has all the necessary ramps, grinding boxes, and other street elements to make it fun. A helmet and knee and elbow pads are required. A parent or guardian must sign a waiver if the participant is under 18 years old. Also, kids must show a city-issued photo I.D. card (available at the parks and recreation office - 38260 10th St. East - during regular business hours) each time they enter the park.

The surrounding park has tennis courts, basketball courts, a playground, soccer field, a seven-field softball complex and sports play field, baseball diamonds, gymnasium (at the recreation center), and picnic areas. A well-used walking/jogging/biking trail (.9 miles long) circles the perimeter of the park. Enjoy a refreshing dip in the pool which is open for lap swim year round and open in the summer for recreational swim. For the free, summer Starlight concert series, B.Y.O.B. (Bring Your Own Blanket, or lawn chair) and bring a picnic dinner, or purchase something from the food vendors.

Hours: The park and skate park are open daily, sunrise - sunset.
Price: Free. The pool is $3 for residents; $4 for non-residents; $1.50 for seniors.
Ages: 7 years and up.

MARINE AVENUE PARK

(310) 802-5410 or (310) 802-5000 / www.ci.manhattan-beach.ca.us
1625 Marine Avenue, Manhattan Beach

The park has a soccer field, baseball diamond, basketball courts, cement picnic tables, and two playgrounds - a newer-style abstract playground with domes, metal hoops, and ropes to climb in various configurations, and the other with swings and a short rocket ship to climb up into and blast off to parts unknown, and then to slide down. Restrooms, an activity center, and indoor racquetball courts are available here, too. Note that ADVENTURE PLEX (pg. 26) is located just across the way.

Hours: Open daily, sunrise - sunset.
Price: Free
Ages: All

MASSARI PARK - CHRIS O'LEARY SKATE PARK

(661) 267-5593 or (661) 267-5611 / www.cityofpalmdale.org
37716 55th Street East, Palmdale

This large park boasts a good-sized, colorful, fantasy-themed playground (it resembles a castle) with slides, swings, ramps, bridges, peekholes, and more, on spongy ground cover. Other park amenities include soccer fields, baseball diamonds, basketball courts, tennis courts, a sand volleyball court, picnic areas, and a walking/jogging trail.

The 12,000-foot, lighted, cement skate park has all the "tight" street features that challenge kids - ramps, bowls, steps, and more. A helmet and knee and elbow pads are required.

Hours: The park and skate park are open daily, sunrise to sunset.
Price: Free
Ages: All

MATHIAS BOTANICAL GARDEN AT UCLA

(310) 825-1260 / www.botgard.uda.edu
UCLA Campus, Westwood

See the entry for UCLA on page 176 for details.

MAYFAIR PARK

(562) 866-4776 - park; (562) 804-4256 - pool (in season) / www.lakewoodcity.org
5720 Clark Street, Lakewood

Mayfair Park is a very fair park indeed! The sand-based boundless playground, accessible for all abilities, has ramps; metal monkey bars and other metal climbing apparatus; a tire swing; interactive panels; rock climbing walls and fake rocks to climb on with hand and foot holds; swings; slides; and other really fun elements. Open grassy fields are plentiful here, plus there are basketball courts, free tennis courts, baseball diamonds with lights and stadium seating, barbecue pits, a (very popular) swimming pool, a wading pool, and an Express McDonald's that's usually open in the summertime and during special events.

Hours: The park is open daily, sunrise - sunset. The pools are open mid-May through mid-June, weekends only; open daily in the summer. Swim sessions are 1pm - 2:30pm and 2:45pm - 4:15pm. Call for extended nighttime hours.

Price: Free to the park. Each pool session costs $1.50 for adults; $1 for children 17 and under for Lakewood residents; $3 for adults; $2 for kids for nonresidents. The wading pool is free.

Ages: All

MEMORIAL PARK - Claremont

(909) 399-5460 / www.ci.claremont.ca.us
840 N. Indian Hill Boulevard, Claremont

The site for many community events, this stately old park has delightful, huge, gnarled oak trees all around with plenty of grassy, run-around space. It also has a picnic grove, BBQ pits, a tennis court, a basketball court, a wading pool that's open in the summer, two sand volleyball courts, a bandshell for outdoor concerts, and a small playground. The play area has toddler and bigger kid's swings, plastic tunnels, slides, and chain ladders to climb.

Hours: Open daily, sunrise - sunset.
Price: Free
Ages: All

MEMORIAL PARK - Santa Monica / THE COVE SKATEPARK

(310) 458-2201, ext. 2020 / www.smgov.net
1401 Olympic Boulevard, Santa Monica

Several baseball fields, soccer fields, four lighted tennis courts, and a gated children's playground with slides, swings, animals on large springs, and other equipment, plus a gym with indoor volleyball and basketball make this a memorable park. In-line skaters and BMX bikers should check out the terrific, gated, lighted, 20,000 square feet skate park, complete with ramps, bowls, stairs, a pool, an over vert bowl, and rails. Park skaters (and bikers) must register annually, in person at the park office, and youths 17 and under must have a waiver signed, in person, by the parent/guardian. Helmets and knee and elbow pads are required and are not available for rent here.

Hours: The general park is open daily, 6am - 11pm. The skate park is open during the school year daily, noon - 10pm, with designated times for bikes only and for adult (18 years and over) skaters. Call or check the website for those specific days and times. The park is open extended hours in the summer and on holidays.

Price: Free to the general park. The registration fee for the skatepark is $10 (ages 6 - 17 years, non-residents) - $16.50 (adults, non-residents), which includes use of the park once, too. Daily passes are $3 (youth) - $5.50 (adult, non-residents).

Ages: All for the park; 7 years and up for the skatepark.

MENTRYVILLE / PICO CANYON

(310) 589-3200 / www.lacountyparks.org; www.santa-clarita.com; www.scvhistory.com; www.lamountains.com
27201 Pico Canyon Road, Newhall

Mentryville was once an oil boom town. Of the few old buildings that remain, the Felton schoolhouse, built in 1885, is the only one open to the public. Inside are wooden school desks, a potbellied stove, blackboards, and a very small library room that no longer contains books. A dual-seat outhouse is just outside. Other structures on the grounds include Mr. Mentry's house, a barn and chicken coop, and a jail that was built just a few years ago for a movie. Please note that the entire "town" is currently undergoing a restoration. Short, guided tours of the town, where visitors learn the history of it and the area, are given by appointment.

Picnic tables are set up under shade trees. A seasonal creek runs through this area. Take a short hike on a service road that is stroller/wheelchair accessible. The road leads to Johnson Park, a picnic spot featuring a replica of a wood oil derrick. Hike a bit further through the surrounding hills of Pico Canyon, past foundation remains and up to some overlooks. Head south for about three miles on the service road which has a gentle grade. After that, the trail changes and only experienced hikers should continue as there are several very steep and strenuous sections. Tip: Bring your own water.

Hours: The park is open daily, sunrise - sunset.
Price: $5 per vehicle
Ages: All

MILLARD CANYON FALLS

(818) 899-1900 / www.fs.usda.gov
W. Loma Alta Drive and Chaney Trail, Los Angeles

Past the picnic tables and camping area is a fire road. Follow it for about a half mile - the walk is fairly easy. There are some boulders to climb over, but that's part of the fun. The sixty-foot falls are beautiful, and really flowing after a rain. The pool at the bottom is not very deep, but it is refreshing in the summer.

Want s'more time here? Bring your own everything and camp in one of the five primitive sites along the creek. There are fire rings, a pit toilet, and a campground host, but little else except for canopies of oak trees, being away from the city, stars, and the calls of nature - crickets, owls, and more.

Hours: Open daily, 6am - 8pm.
Price: $5 for an Adventure Pass (prepurchase at sporting goods stores or close by at Webster's Pharmacy - 2450 N. Lake Ave. in Altadena.) The cost of camping is just the $5 Adventure Pass.
Ages: 5 years and up.

MONROVIA CANYON PARK

(626) 256-8282 / www.cityofmonrovia.org
1200 N. Canyon Boulevard, Monrovia

This canyon park, bordering on the Angeles National Forest, backs into the wildlife corridor. The twenty developed acres contain a lovely nature center and several grassy and wooded picnic areas. Note that there is a cabin to rent near the nature center that sleeps up to twenty-eight people in sleeping bags - no beds. It comes with a fireplace, kitchenette, and other amenities. The cabin rents for $30 an hour (up to four hours), up to $270 for overnight, which is 6pm to 7am.

The nature center contains taxidermied animals such as foxes, coyotes, two small black bears, raccoons, a mule deer, and more. There are live lizards and walking sticks here, as well as gopher snakes, rosy boas, and king snakes. A mural depicts animals in their natural habitat. A historical display features the story of the original settlers to this area, a reproduction of some of their tombstones, and remnants from Deer Park lodge, which was a supply cabin just up the road.

The sixty other acres are woodland nature at its best, supporting wildlife like deer, mountain lions, and bears, as well as small mammals and lizards and such. One of the most popular and beautiful trails, which is only one-and-a-half miles round trip from the nature center, leads to a year-round, thirty-foot-high waterfall that's fed by springs. For a longer hike, take the trail from the entrance station of the park, or go another route completely and hike the Ben Overturff Trail. Take the fire road a portion of the way on this trail or go all the way on the footpath. The trail is a moderate grade of seven miles that leads through virtually undisturbed wilderness, including an overlook, and ends at the Deer Park lodge site.

Hours: The park is open Wed. - Mon., 8am - 5pm. Closed Tues., July 4th weekend, and Christmas. The nature center is usually open (if staffing is available) Wed. - Sat., 11am - 1pm; Sun., 9am - 5pm.
Price: $5 per vehicle.
Ages: 4 years and up.

MONROVIA SKATE PARK - RECREATION PARK

(626) 256-8246 - park / www.cityofmonrovia.org
843 East Olive Avenue, Monrovia

This nice-sized park features a playground, picnic areas with shade trees, ball fields, tennis courts, basketball courts, a roller hockey rink, and a youth center. A skate park here offers over 10,000 square feet of skating fun! The concrete skate park has two sections; a street side, with rails, stairs, ramps, kickers, and ledges; and a bowl side, with a kidney-shaped pool with roll-overs. Areas to watch the skaters are available. All participants are required to wear safety protection. The MONROVIA HISTORICAL MUSEUM (pg. 136) is also located inside Recreation Park.

Hours: The park is open daily, sunrise - sunset. The skate park is open daily, sunrise - 10pm.
Price: Free
Ages: All for the park; 7 years and up for the skate park.

NORWALK PARK

(562) 929-5702 or (562) 929-5566 - park; (562) 929-5754 - museum and house; (562) 929-5622 - pool /
www.ci.norwalk.ca.us
13000 Clarkdale Avenue, Norwalk

The park has a spacious grassy area, plus a playground for younger kids, picnic tables, a basketball court, a pool, and skate park. The enclosed skate park has several ramps, a pyramid, and a few other street elements. Skaters and bikers (as there are set times for bike riders) must wear a helmet and pads. The lovely pool is open in the summer for recreation swim.

The Sproul Museum and Hargitt House are also on the park grounds. They contain artifacts from early Norwalk, including pictures, a few articles of clothing, and some furniture. They are usually open to tour on the third weekend of the month from 1pm - 4pm - call for more specifics.

Hours: The park and skate park are open daily, sunrise - dusk.
Price: Free. Swim sessions are $4 for adults; $3 for seniors and ages 17 and under.
Ages: All

ORANGEWOOD PARK - SKATE PARK

(626) 939-8430 / www.westcovina.org
1615 W. Merced Avenue, West Covina

Orangewood Park has a playground, basketball court, baseball field, plenty of picnic tables and barbecues, and two covered roller rinks for open play most days, but used by leagues in the evenings. The unsupervised 12,000-square-foot skate park welcomes in-line bladers and skaters to get some big air. Participants must wear safety gear.

Hours: Open daily, dawn - dusk.
Price: Free
Ages: All

ORCUTT RANCH HORTICULTURE CENTER

(818) 346-7449 / www.laparks.org
23600 Roscoe Boulevard, West Hills

This horticultural center was originally created in the early 1900's. A stroll through these nostalgic gardens is a delightful way to pass a half an hour, or so. A short, wide, stroller-friendly, dirt trail leads into a grove of shady oak trees and through grounds that are lush with greenery and wildflowers. The adjacent pathway along Dayton Creek, which borders one side of the ranch's perimeter, is not for strollers. The path does have stone benches for resting and leads to a few bridges that extend over the water. On the other side of the creek is a cozy picnic area. Look for ancient live oaks throughout the ranch; one is over 700 years old (and still growing)! Also on the grounds are a picnic table in the small bamboo grove, and more formal gardens consisting of maze-like hedges around the rose gardens. Note: Visitors may not walk through the adjacent acres of citrus trees.

The adobe building, once the Orcutt's home, is now used for park offices and group rental functions. A quick walk around and through the mostly unfurnished building allows you to see the Mexican-influence architecture and hand-painted, South-of-the-Border tiles.

Hours: The grounds are open daily, sunrise - sunset. Many private functions are held here, however, so call first. (But you would do that anyhow, right?)
Price: Free
Ages: All

PALOS VERDES PENINSULA LAND CONSERVANCY

(310) 541-7613 / www.pvplc.org
Various locations throughout the Palos Verdes and San Pedro areas.

Once-a-month guided Nature Walks, most of them family oriented and suitable for children, are given by naturalists, historians, and geologists. Tour guides share information about the history of the area, wildlife, plants, and more. It's a great time and way to learn, enjoy fresh air, and spend time together. The walks range from one- to three-hours, and from easy to more difficult. All are on dirt paths. Starting points include Abalone Cove/Portuguese Bend, Madrona Marsh, and George F. Canyon Preserve, which are each listed separately in this section. Call or check the website for a calendar of events as there are also night hikes, special events, volunteer workdays on the trails, and more.

Hours: Public nature walks are usually given on the second Sat. of each month.
Price: Free, but donations are often requested.
Ages: 4 years and up.

PAN PACIFIC PARK / RENEE'S PLACE

(323) 939-8874 / www.laparks.org
7600 Beverly Boulevard, Los Angeles
        The train-themed, all-abilities playground has train cars (about the size of small cars) in a semi circle around one of the playgrounds. Kids can climb aboard, use the steering wheels, actually listen to sounds of the whistle blowing and trains chugging along the tracks, and poke their heads out the windows to go full steam ahead. An elevated play structure has slides, a short rock-climbing wall, bridges, tactile learning panels, space to play underneath, swings (some that are wheelchair accessible), monkey bars, climbing apparatus, and more fun and imaginative elements all on rubberized flooring. Another play structure, lower to the ground for the younger set, has a textured slide, ramps, tunnel, slides, and speaking tubes. The park also boasts a little sprayground for wet, summertime fun; two basketball courts; yet another playground on the lower level the tiered grassy lawn with a castle, a ship, and play houses; an exercise area with some legitimate workout equipment; a lighted baseball diamond; a soccer field; an amphitheater; plenty of picnic tables and BBQs under shade trees; a pavement for jogging, strolling, etc., that crisscrosses throughout the park; and a massive amount of grass to play on.
        This multi-ethnic park is a good park in and of itself and it's surrounded by more fun and educational places - the original FARMER'S MARKET (pg. 18); THE GROVE (pg. 94), an uptown, outdoor mall; and, sharing immediate park space, the LOS ANGELES MUSEUM OF THE HOLOCAUST (pg. 131). The park also shares space with a gym.

Hours: Open daily, 6am - 10pm.
Price: Free
Ages: All

PARAMOUNT RANCH

(805) 370-2300 or (805) 370-2301 / www.nps.gov/samo; www.lamountains.com
2903 Cornell Road, Agoura
        Howdy partners! Western Town, in Paramount Ranch, was once owned by Paramount Studios and used as a Western movie and TV set and it is still often used for filming. The "town" still stands. Walk the dusty roads and inspect the weathered town buildings from the outside. These buildings include V. Shank Undertaker; the two-story Hotel Mud Bug; a General Store (peer into the windows because it is stocked with clothing, canned good, supplies and more); a Saloon; a store "selling" mining equipment; a Blacksmith; Farmer's Exchange; a jail (again, peer into the windows to see the jail cell and sheriff's desk); and even a train depot. It all looks so real! Dress up your cowboy or cowgirl and bring your camera. Better yet, bring your video camera, props, and script and do your own Western mini-movie. Free, guided walking tours that describe the set and history of the area are usually given on the first and third Saturdays of each month at 9:30am.
        Meanwhile, back at the ranch. . . over the bridge, next to the main part of town, is a huge meadow with a few picnic tables and some gigantic, old trees. At the end of the meadow is a wonderful, wooded trail that follows along a creek. It's only one-eighth of a mile round trip. If the kids are in the mood for hiking into the mountains, go up Coyote Canyon Trail, just behind Western Town. This uphill, half-mile, round-trip trail goes through green chaparral-covered canyons overlooking the valley. The picnic spot up here has a view that is worth the effort. Ranger-led naturalist programs are also offered at the park. Call regarding the many special and seasonal events that the ranch hosts. Note that PETER STRAUSS RANCH (pg. 78), TROUTDALE (pg. 88), and KING GILLETTE RANCH (pg. 67), with the SANTA MONICA MOUNTAINS NATIONAL PARK HEADQUARTERS (pg. 84), are just around the corner.

Hours: The park is open daily, 8am - sunset. The visitors center is open daily, 9am - 5pm. Closed New Year's Day, Christmas, and some other federal holidays.
Price: Free
Ages: All

PETER STRAUSS RANCH   ☼

(805) 370-2300; (805) 370-2301 / www.nps.gov/samo; www.lamountains.com
3000 Mulholland Highway, Agoura Hills

This rarely-frequented, sprawling park, once owned by actor Peter Strauss, has an easy, about a mile, mostly shaded, hiking trail that weaves amongst the chaparral and oak trees. More ambitious walkers can take the Malibu Lake Connector Trail. Inspect the ranch house; huge grassy front lawn (good for picnicking); the waterless, fenced in swimming pool (once the biggest one in California); the remnants of the dam, aviary and some buildings; and other parts of this park, too. There are some funky stores and restaurants in this area. Note that TROUTDALE (pg. 88), PARAMOUNT RANCH (see above entry) and KING GILLETTE RANCH (pg. 67), with the SANTA MONICA MOUNTAINS NATIONAL PARK HEADQUARTERS (pg. 84), are just around the corner.

Hours: Open daily, 8am - sunset.
Price: Free
Ages: 4 years and up.

PIONEER PARK   ☼

(909) 394-6230 / www.cityofsandimas.com
225 S. Cataract Avenue, San Dimas

This park offers a playground in a sand base, two basketball courts, two tennis courts, picnic tables, and, most importantly for my boys, an 8,000 square-foot concrete skate park. It has all the elements of a good skate park - ramps, a grinding box, and more. A helmet and knee and elbow pads are required.

Hours: Open daily, dawn - dusk.
Price: Free
Ages: All

PIRATE PARK   ☼

(562) 804-1424 / www.bellflower.org
16559 Bellflower Boulevard, Bellflower

Shiver me timbers! This very small, gated, pirate-themed park has young mateys running, climbing, playing, swabbing the deck, and searching for pieces of eight. Go under the Spanish fort entrance and then cross the short suspension bridge to the fort's top, look out through its windows, and descend the ladder on the other side. Besides a large treasure chest, pint-sized slide (painted blue to look like water) cutting through rocks, small boat, and tiny island of boulders and palm trees, the main attraction is the pirate ship decorated with skulls on its side and two tall masts with netting for sails. Kids clamber aboard and play in and on the deck, sides, inset cannons, and gangplank. Another great feature of the park is the little cave where kids can crawl into and look up and out through barred rock windows. Parents appreciate the many flat-topped boulders that line the inside perimeter creating ample places to sit and watch their buccaneers, and the rubbery flooring of the park.

Just outside the gates is a courtyard with a fountain, eateries, and a wall mural of a pirate and his ship at dock, with the ocean behind him - great as a backdrop for pictures.

Hours: Open daily, usually about 9am - 5pm (hours vary a little monthly).
Price: Free
Ages: 2 - 12 years.

PLACERITA CANYON NATURE CENTER AND PARK   ☼

(661) 259-7721 / www.placerita.org; www.lacountyparks.org
19152 Placerita Canyon Road, Newhall

Placerita Canyon was the site of one of the first gold discoveries, small though it was, in California. In fact, the famed oak tree where gold was first discovered, Oak of the Golden Dream, is just a short walk from the parking lot. There is a wealth of history and wilderness to be found at this Nature Center and park.

The Center has a rescued live owl and hawk in cages outside. Inside are display cases with animal skulls, skins, and rocks; several taxidermied animals; some equipment that monitors weather conditions; and a few live spiders, snakes, and lizards.

An immediate large picnic area on the hillside of the park is nestled in a huge grove of oak trees. Play equipment is here, although the main attractions are the beauty of the area (I love this park!) and a few short hiking trails. Call to find out more about the Saturday nature hikes, the animal presentations from 1pm to 2pm, astronomy club, summer camps, and other special programs.

Extended hiking is great here, especially for slightly more experienced hikers. Canyon Trail, for instance, is a two-mile gradual climb, following along a stream and crossing over it several times, leading up to Walker Ranch, a cabin that has been refurnished and restored for a glimpse of yesteryear. The left fork leads to a Scout campground. The right fork leads to the Waterfall Trail, where, yes, about two-thirds of a mile back is a waterfall. Canyon Trail also hooks up to Los Pinetos Trail, which is a hardy, eight-mile hike.

Hours: The park is open daily, sunrise - sunset. The nature center is open Tues. - Sun. and holiday Mon., 9am - 5pm. Closed other Mon. and Christmas.

Price: Free

Ages: 2 years and up.

POLLIWOG PARK and BEGG POOL

(310) 545-5621 - park; (310) 374-7575 - museum; (310) 802-5428 or (310) 802-5448 - Begg pool / www.ci.manhattan-beach.ca.us

Corner of Manhattan Beach Boulevard and Redondo Avenue, Manhattan Beach

This expansive park is wonderfully deceptive. The part seen from the street is beautiful, with lots of grass and trees, a nine-hole disc golf course, and even a two-third-acre botanical garden with different, themed areas at the southwest corner of the park. There is also an exercise area with several pieces of equipment that offer a legit workout via lifting, running (gliding), pushing and pulling. The large, red and blue, all-abilities playground has long ramps, bridges, curvy tube slides, speaking tubes, mini zip line, climbing equipment, and towers to play on and under, plus traditional swings along with swings that are wheelchair accessible. A huge portion of the lawn is graded for free summer concerts. (Check the city's website calendar.) Some of the trees have low branches that beckon to climbers. An enclosed dog run is also here. The original, red, beach cottage in the park is a small historic museum. The rooms feature photos, old-fashioned bathing suits and other clothing, accessories, furniture and other artifacts of the olden days. Nearby is a rose garden.

As you take the stroller-friendly pathway leading down toward the interior of the park (there are pathways all around the park), you'll discover some "hidden" delights, such as a good-sized pond where marshy reeds and ducks abound. (Signs ask that you don't feed the ducks.) Tip: Watch your children around the water as there are no guard rails. Two other playgrounds are here - one is large and boat-themed with portholes, spiral tube slides coming out of the tall, multi-level structure, and lots of fun components, plus a good-sized cement lighthouse with misters, and a little cement play ship. Younger kids have another separate play area especially for them with swinging bridges, slides, and swings. This area also has grassy lawns, shade trees, cement picnic benches, and a small amphitheater.

Across the street from the main park are a baseball diamond and four lighted tennis courts. On the campus of Manhattan Beach Transition School, adjacent to the park, is Begg Pool. The pool is open during the summer for recreation swim, and at other times during the year for lap swim and lessons.

Hours: The park is open daily, dawn - dusk. The museum is open weekends, noon - 3pm; closed on major holidays. The pool is open for recreational swim mid-April through May, Sat., 1pm - 2:45pm and June through September, daily. Call for specific session times.

Price: Free to the park and museum. The pool is $4 per person.

Ages: All

PRIME DESERT WOODLAND PRESERVE

(661) 723-6000 - city/preserve; (661) 723-6234 - nature center; (661) 723-6257- tours / www.cityoflancasterca.org

43201 35th Street West, Lancaster

This stretch of desert preserve is carved out of the surrounding suburbia, which is within eyesight. Easy-walking, rope-lined, hard-packed dirt/sand trails meander through desert topography while interpretative signs allow visitors to learn about the plant and animal life they see. The longest trail is one mile, round trip.

The small nature center building displays a few taxidermied animals, pictures of old Lancaster, and a touch table with lots of great objects - fossils, feathers, an ostrich egg, and several replicas of dinosaur parts such as skin, claws, and a tooth. Check out the fairly extensive list of upcoming events on the website as well as information on guided tours for all ages.

Hours: The trails are open daily, dawn - dusk. The building is open Wed., Sat., and Sun., 10am - 4pm.

Price: Free

Ages: All

PYRAMID LAKE

(661) 295-7155 - lake/boat rental; (805) 434-1996 - campground / www.campone.com

Smokey Bear Road off Interstate 5, 20 miles N. of Santa Clarita Valley, Gorman

$$$

   This huge sparkling reservoir lake, surrounded by hills, offers a myriad of activities for families. Year-round boating, including waterskiing, canoeing, rowboating, and rubber rafting, is allowed. B.Y.O.B. (Bring Your Own Boat) or rent one here. 12' to 14' aluminum fishing boats, which seat up three adults, are $65 for four hours and usually available daily, year-round. Usually available year round, but not daily, are SUP or single kayaks - $30 for two hours; double kayaks - $40 for two hours; and pedal boats - $30 for four hours. Shaded picnic shelters and barbeques are near the docks. Some of the beach and picnic sites across and at the lake are reachable only by boat. Fish for seasonal bass, trout, catfish, crappie, and bluegill. A bait and tackle shop is on the grounds. A California state fishing license is required for those 16 years old or older. There are two waveless swim beaches open during the summer season at Emigrant Landing and Vaquero Day Use Area. They are patrolled by lifeguards on the weekends.

   Meander on trails along the lake, enjoy a picnic meal, visit the nearby VISTA DEL LAGO VISITOR CENTER (pg. 155), and/or camp at your choice of two campgrounds near the lake. Los Alamos Campground, two miles up the road, has room for ninety-three family units and three group units. Hard Luck Campground, on Piru Creek, has twenty-two family units.

Hours: The lake is open October through March daily, 7am - 5pm; April through September, 6am - 8pm. The swim beach is open the same hours in the summer. The lake shop is open most of the year, Fri. - Sun., 10am - 6pm; open longer in the summer. The park is closed New Year's Day, Thanksgiving, and Christmas.

Price: $11 per vehicle, which includes the swim beach. Call for fishing boat rentals prices. Camping is $20 per night.

Ages: All

RANCHO SANTA ANA BOTANIC GARDEN

(909) 625-8767 / www.rsabg.org

1500 N. College Avenue, Claremont

$$$

   This eighty-six-acre botanic garden is beautiful in scope and sequence, and abundant with plants native only to California. Thousands of different kinds of plants grow in our state, so this garden covers a lot of ground with its giant sequoias, fan palms, California live oak, manzanitas, cacti, wildflowers, and more. There is also a replica Tongva Village on site that visitors can walk through and even go into some of the buildings.

   The numerous trails, many of which are stroller friendly, afford good walking opportunities. Since the diverse vegetation attracts a wide variety of birds, bird lovers can pick up a bird check list at the gift shop, or join an organized bird walk on the first Sunday of each month. I don't know how much horticulture my kids take in when we visit botanic gardens, but it's a good introduction to the variety and importance of plant life, plus a beautiful walk is always enjoyable.

Hours: Open daily, 8am - 5pm. Closed New Year's Day, July 4th, Thanksgiving, and Christmas.

Price: $8 for adults; $6 for seniors and students, $4 for ages 3 -12; children 2 and under are free. See page x for info on AHS reciprocal memberships.

Ages: 3 years and up.

ROBERT E. RYAN PARK

(310) 377-2290 / www.palosverdes.com/rpv/recreationparks

30359 Hawthorne Boulevard, Rancho Palos Verdes

   From the parking lot of this nine-acre park, you get a glimpse of the California coastline and, on a clear day, Catalina Island. Steps lead down into the park itself. Note: Strollers and wheelchairs can take a ramp that leads all the way down to the playground. The play equipment is ADA approved and wheelchair accessible. Set sail on a large ship-like structure with slides and swings, or on a smaller ship with similar apparatus. Play in the tot area on a climbing structure shaped like a car, swing on swings, and ride on cement whales. Stroll under shade trees on cement pathways that go through a good portion of the park. Bring a sack lunch to enjoy at the picnic tables, or grill food at the barbeques. This is one of my favorite parks for the play equipment, view, and openness of it.

   The community center has some play equipment to check out, as long as you leave your driver's license in

exchange. Play a game of basketball or baseball, or just romp around on the large, open, grassy areas.

> **Hours:** Open July through Labor Day daily, and on holidays, 10am - dusk. Open the rest of the year daily, noon - dusk. Closed New Year's Day, Thanksgiving, Christmas Eve, and Christmas Day.
> **Price:** Free
> **Ages:** All

ROXBURY PARK

(310) 285-2537 - park; (310) 285-6840 - community center; (310) 550-4979 - tennis / www.beverlyhills.org
471 S. Roxbury Drive, Beverly Hills

This beautiful park fits right in with its surroundings of well-manicured lawns and stately homes. Although it is off a main street, it still seems somewhat removed from city life. The park offers a wealth of activities to choose from, such as tennis (four lighted courts, plus backboards), sand volleyball courts, and basketball. Along with a few picnic tables, barbecue pits, and some large shaded grassy areas, there is a good-sized playground. One of the areas is designed for slightly older kids with a big slide to go down, bridges to cross, and ropes to climb. The other is designed with younger kids in mind. It has swings and slides, too.

> **Hours:** The park is open daily, 6am - 10pm.
> **Price:** Free. Tennis courts before 5pm are $8 an hour for residents (with proof of residency); $11 an hour for nonresidents; after 5pm and on weekends, prices are $9 for residents; $12 for nonresidents.
> **Ages:** All

RUNYON CANYON PARK

(213) 485-5572 / www.laparks.org
2000 Fuller Street, Hollywood

Hike the hills of Hollywood in the popular Runyon Canyon. The dirt trail starts off at an upward slant, leading past ruins where house foundations and a few chunks of wall still remain. We walked the scenic, mostly woodland, main trail all the way up the mountain, as it affords a spectacular view of the famed city. The looping hike, which we walked counter-clockwise, is strenuous as it goes up steeply, then along the rim of the hills. The trail eventually levels off, then loops back down at a more gentle grade. The two-mile round-trip hike is not stroller/wheelchair accessible, nor is the slightly longer hike out to Mulholland. Bring water! Note: Look where you walk as this is a popular park for walking dogs. Inquire about periodic guided hikes.

> **Hours:** Open daily, dawn - dusk.
> **Price:** Free
> **Ages:** 5 years and up.

RUSTIC CANYON RECREATION CENTER

(310) 454-5734 / www.laparks.org
601 Latimer Road, Pacific Palisades

This pretty park is nestled in a somewhat secluded area of Pacific Palisades, but it's worth making the effort to visit here. Shade trees line the perimeter of a paved pathway that leads down into the park. A baseball field, basketball court, playground, grassy area, climbing trees (always a hit with my family), a wooden pyramid structure (to climb on and around), two picnic areas, and barbeque pits, make up the central part of the park. Several tennis courts are located in one corner. Up near the parking lot is an older-style recreation center which offers a variety of classes. An adjacent, medium-sized community swimming pool is open seasonally.

> **Hours:** The park is open daily, sunrise - sunset. The pool is open mid-June through Labor Day. Swim sessions are usually Mon. - Fri., 11am - 4pm; Sat. - Sun., 1pm - 5pm.
> **Price:** Free to the park. Swim sessions are $2.50 for adults; free for seniors and ages 17 and under.
> **Ages:** All

SADDLEBACK BUTTE STATE PARK

(661) 727-9899 or (661) 946-3055 / www.parks.ca.gov
17102 Avenue 'J' East, Lancaster

This state park is 3,000 acres of desert landscape, with Joshua trees scattered throughout and a huge granite mountain top, Saddleback Butte, jutting up almost a 1,000 feet above the valley. Be on the lookout for wildlife such as desert tortoises, rabbits, coyotes, kit foxes, kangaroo rats, and lots of reptiles and birds. Several hiking trails are

available here, including a two-and-a-half-mile trail that leads to the top of the Butte with a view that makes the hike worthwhile. Springtime is particularly beautiful at the park because the wildflowers are in bloom. Near the entrance and visitor center/park headquarters are several covered picnic areas, complete with barbecues. The visitor center features displays and some hands-on exhibits about the geology, history, plants, and animal life of the area. You can also pick up a trail map here. Please remember that desert weather is hot in the summer and cold in the winter, so dress accordingly. Overnight camping is available. Saddleback is located just a few miles down the road from the ANTELOPE VALLEY INDIAN MUSEUM (pg. 100).

> **Hours:** Open daily, sunrise - sunset.
> **Price:** Day use is $6 per vehicle; $5 for seniors; $3 for disabled. Camping is $20 per night and on a first come, first served basis.
> **Ages:** 5 years and up.

SALT LAKE MUNICIPAL PARK / HUNTINGTON SKATEBOARD PARK

(323) 584-6218 / www.huntingtonpark.org
3401 Florence Avenue, Huntington Park

This twenty-three-acre park comes fully equipped for a day of sports fun. It has four fenced-in baseball diamonds, plus basketball courts, a soccer field, tennis courts, a gym, picnic area with grills, a good-sized playground, and a 12,000-square-foot, gated skate park in the park's center. The lighted skate park has rails, pyramids, ledges, ramps, and a few smooth "open" sections for skating. Safety gear - a helmet and pads - is required.

> **Hours:** The park is open daily, sunrise - sunset. The skate park is open Mon. - Fri., noon - 9pm; Sat. - Sun., 10am - 6pm. It is open longer in the summer and during school holidays.
> **Price:** Free
> **Ages:** All

SAND DUNE PARK

(310) 545-5621 or (310) 802-5448 / www.ci.manhattan-beach.ca.us
At the corner of 33rd Street and Bell Avenue, Manhattan Beach

This little park has a big surprise. While there is a tiny playground for younger children, the park is really "beachy" and really popular because of its steep wall of sand (100 feet high) that is perfect for running, jumping, or rolling down. Take the 200 steps on the switchback that lead to the top of the hill, or just climb up the hill. Bring your own bucket and shovel to play with at the bottom. Here is a local's favorite tip: After it rains, take a snow sled down the hill! Look below for sand dune reservation information as it's the only way to access it, and only twenty people are allowed per hour.

Behind the playground is a green grassy stretch. Picnic tables and a few barbecue pits under a shelter are also available. Parking is limited.

> **Hours:** Use of the dune is by reservation only, one hour only, per day. Must submit printed online reservation to hand to dune attendant. $1 is due with your reservation form - no change is available. The dune is open at certain time slots, Mon. - Fri., 8am - 6pm; Sat., 8am - 4:30pm; closed Sun. The playground is open daily, 8am - 7pm and is free; no reservations needed.
> **Price:** $1 for the sand dunes. Monthly memberships are available, too.
> **Ages:** All

SAN DIMAS COUNTY PARK

(909) 599-7512 / www.lacountyparks.org
1628 N. Sycamore Canyon Road, San Dimas

Nestled in the foothills of the San Gabriel Mountains, adjacent to Angeles National Forest, is a wonderful county park/museum/wildlife sanctuary. The small nature museum contains a few live snakes, such as the California king and gopher snakes; taxidermied animals such as a mountain lion, fox, and birds; and several small collections including rocks, arrowheads, insects, and butterflies.

The outside wildlife sanctuary offers a caged home to several injured or nonreleasable native animals. Red-tailed hawks, heart-faced barn owls, and great-horned owls are part of the bird rehabilitation area - not part of the bird "rebellion" area as my son misread the sign. (Hmm - could be something to do with his childhood. . . .) Other live animals here include two deer, tortoises, and snakes, plus many squirrels running around freely.

An almost one-mile, self-guiding nature trail begins in the oak woodland just behind the nature center building

and loops around. There are plenty of picnic tables under the cover of shady oak trees. Some of the picnic areas have barbeques. The area below the museum has a baseball diamond, a few playgrounds, and large grassy areas. A portion of a long bike route goes through part of the park. Come visit the park on your own, take a guided tour, or come via a Jr. Ranger Program which is offered through the park system. A visit to the San Dimas County Park is great for temporarily escaping city life.

> **Hours:** The park is open daily, sunrise - sunset. The nature center and animal sanctuary are open Tues. - Sun., 9am - 4:15pm. Closed Mon. and Christmas.
> **Price:** Free
> **Ages:** All

SANTA CLARITA SPORTS COMPLEX - AQUATIC CENTER - SKATE PARK

(661) 250-3700 - sports complex; (661) 250-3747 - skatepark; (661) 250- 3766 or (661) 250-3761 - aquatics / www.santa-clarita.com; www.scskatepark.com
20850 Centre Pointe Parkway, Santa Clarita

Indoor, outdoor, year-round fun for the family is available at the nicely-landscaped Sports Complex. Those who got game can use the two, inside, full-sized basketball courts, badminton courts, and four racquetball/handball courts. A teen activity room is here, too. Outside, on the upper level, are two basketball courts and an exercise area with green, plastic, fun-looking, but serious equipment that appeals to kids and adults alike for training.

Take the cement pathway to the lower level (or park down here) to the unsupervised, massive (40,000 square feet!), lighted cement skate park for skaters and bmx riders - beginners to pros. It features large bowls, a street plaza, half-pipe tunnel, a bridge, snake runs, skate-able planters, rails, stairs, a perimeter path, and more. Skaters must wear a helmet and pads.

The adjacent Aquatic Center has three pools - a fifty-meter competition pool, a dive pool, and an activity pool. The activity pool is comprised of a 160-foot, twisty slide (must be 48" or taller to slide); a shallow splash pool; and a colorful, water play structure for young kids that has a small slide, water pipes with steering wheels and nozzles that squirt out water, and an umbrella that overflows with water. Proper swimwear must be worn. Lounge chairs are welcome and picnic tables are here as well. Kayaking and snorkeling classes are given in the competition pool at certain times.

> **Hours:** The skate park is open daily, 8am - 10pm. Lap swim is open year round. Rec swim is open Memorial Day - Labor Day, daily, noon - 5pm. The rest is open daily, sunrise - sunset.
> **Price:** Free to the gym and skate park. Recreational swim is $6 for adults; $4 for ages 3 - 17; children 2 and under are free. It's $4 for lap swim.
> **Ages:** 3 years and up, depending on the activity.

SANTA FE DAM RECREATIONAL AREA

(626) 334-1065 - park; (626) 334-6555 - boat, bike, bait and fishing poles rentals / www.lacountyparks.org; www.sgmrc.org; www.wheelfunrentals.com
15501 E. Arrow Highway, Irwindale

Though located in the middle of an industrial section, city sounds fade away while at this enormous recreational area that sports a mountainous backdrop. Our first stop was at the nature center trail, at the northern end of the park. The rock-lined, three-quarter-mile looping trail is paved, level, and a delight to walk. Desert is the predominant theme. We observed an abundance of cacti and other plant life, and animals such as jackrabbits, lizards, roadrunners, and hummingbirds.

The huge lake toward the entrance offers a nice-sized beach with a life guarded swimming area. A water play area for children 52" and under is located by the picnic area. It has a few slides, ramps, pipes, wheels that turn, and some colorful climbing and water squirting apparatus in shallow waters. This lakeside area, with its shade trees and acres of green grass, is vastly different from the northern desert area. Other attractions in the park include a playground; picnic facilities; a snack bar (usually open in the summer); unpaved walking trails; fishing - a California state license is required for those 16 years of age and older; and quiet boating activities (no gasoline powered boats allowed), with boat rentals of kayaks and pedal boats available on weekends and holidays year round.

Ready for a bike ride? Choose your route and go the distance all the way north to San Gabriel Canyon, or south to Long Beach and Seal Beach, using various trails that go through this park. Parts of the thirty-seven-mile bike trail are paved, while other parts are not. Bike rentals, for within the park, start at $20 for a surrey which seats three adults and two kids.

Hours: The park is open daily, 6:30am - sunset. The nature center is open daily, 10am - 1pm. The swim beach is open Memorial Day through Labor Day, Thurs. - Sun., 10am - 6pm. The water play area is open Memorial Day through Labor Day, Sat. - Sun., 10:30am - 6pm. Boat and bike rentals are usually available on weekends most of the year, and daily during the summer, 11am - 4:30pm.

Price: $10 per vehicle April through October; $10 on weekends and holidays, but free on weekdays November through March. There is no extra charge to use the swim beach. The water play area is $2 per person for each hour-and-a-half session. Rowboats are $20 an hour. Pedal boats start at $15 an hour for one person; $25 for a double. Kayaks are $10 an hour for one person; $15 for two.

Ages: All

SANTA MONICA MOUNTAINS NATIONAL PARK HEADQUARTERS - VISITORS CENTER (Anthony C. Beilenson Interagency Visitor Center)

(805) 370-2301; (805) 370-2300 / www.nps.gov/samo; www.lamountains.com; www.localhikes.com
26876 Mulholland Highway at King Gillette Ranch, Calabasas

From the thousands of acres of mountains, to the coastline beaches, to the inland grounds, the enormous Santa Monica Mountain National Park covers a major part of the wilderness and parkland in Southern California. This includes hiking, biking, and equestrian trails, plus camping, swimming, scenic drives, ranger-led programs, and more. One reason I'm writing about this place is because maps, for purchase and for free, and a calendar schedule of events for the numerous parks within the Santa Monica Mountains Park system can be found here. The parks, most of which can be found listed individually under the Great Outdoors Section, include Circle X Ranch, Coldwater Canyon Park, Franklin Canyon Ranch, Leo Carrillo State Park, Malibu Creek State Park, Malibu Lagoon State Beach, Paramount Ranch, Peter Strauss Ranch, Rancho Sierra Vista, Temescal Gateway Park, Topanga State Park, Will Rogers State Historical Park, and the UCLA Stunt Ranch. If you are a hiker extraordinaire, or want to just hike a fantastic trail, ask for information on the Backbone Trail, a trail that extends nearly seventy miles across and through the Santa Monica Mountains.

The center has a few interpretative displays; a gift shop containing hiking and nature books and other items; and a twenty-minute movie in the small theater about the history of the Santa Monica mountains. Outside are a few picnic tables, a CA native plant section and two hiking trails that begin from here, as it is located at the KING GILLETTE RANCH (pg. 67). See the Ranch to find out what else there is to see on the premises. You could spend some time just at the visitors center! Note that PETER STRAUSS RANCH (pg. 78), TROUTDALE (pg. 88) and PARAMOUNT RANCH (pg. 77) are just around the corner.

Hours: Open daily, 9am - 5pm. Closed on some federal holidays.

Price: Free

Ages: 5 years and up.

SCHABARUM REGIONAL COUNTY PARK

(626) 854-5560 / www.lacountyparks.org
17250 E. Colima Road, Rowland Heights

Looks can be deceiving. This park doesn't look like much from just driving by, but it goes deep. At 640 acres huge, this country has lots of green rolling hillsides and is seemingly removed from city life as ninety percent of it is left in its natural state. Toward the entrance are scattered picnic tables, barbeque pits, an exercise area with machines to use, a fun playground featuring a pirate ship, shade trees, and open space to run around. Take a quick stroll through the hummingbird and butterfly garden - you might see some! About a mile of paved trail follows along a creek as it winds through part of the park. There are twenty miles of mostly unshaded dirt hiking and equestrian trails (get a map!) that weave through the rest of the sprawling countryside, leading past shrub, a few groves of trees, wild flowers (in the spring), and cherry trees, which are beautiful in bloom. Come in the summertime and enjoy free Tuesday nights concerts in the park.

Hours: Open October - March, 7am - 6pm; April - September, 7am - 8pm. Closed on Christmas Day.

Price: The park is free during the week; $6 per vehicle on weekends and holidays.

Ages: All

SMITH PARK

(626) 308-2875 / www.sangabrielcity.com
232 W. Broadway, San Gabriel

A beautiful and intricate tile wall encompasses basketball courts, lighted tennis courts, handball courts, and youth and toddler playgrounds. A swimming pool, a wading pool, picnic areas, grassy run-around space, and more, are yours for coming to Smith Park. Another play area, based on Native American Tongva peoples, incorporates a picnic area, rolling green lawns, and a few concrete animals, such as dolphins. Take a look at the large concrete compass at this spot, too. Walkways crisscross throughout the park.

Hours: Open daily, 7:30am - 10pm. The swim pool is open mid-June through Labor Day for recreation swim.
Price: Free to the park. Swim sessions are $2 for adults; $1.50 for ages 17 and under. The wading pool is free.
Ages: All

SOLSTICE CANYON
(805) 370-2301 or (310) 457-8494 / www.nps.gov/samo
Corral Canyon Road, Malibu

This canyon offers a variety of trail lengths and terrain, from huge shady oak woodlands to shrubs to an intermittent stream. Short, easy trails include the 1.2-mile round trip on Dry Canyon Trail which ends near a seasonal waterfall, or the Solstice Canyon Trail, a 2.1-mile-round-trip paved road for bikers as well as hikers. Longer trails include the 3.9-mile Sostomo Trail/Deer Valley Loop. We found the canyon to be a peaceful and beautiful place to explore nature. A few picnic tables in a lovely grove are located near the parking lot. Note: There are restroom facilities. Tip: Bring your own water.

Hours: Open daily, 7am - sunset. Closed federal holidays.
Price: Free
Ages: 4 years and up.

SOUTH COAST BOTANICAL GARDENS
(310) 544-6815 or (310) 544-1948 / www.southcoastbotanicgarden.org
26300 S. Crenshaw Boulevard, Rolling Hills Estates

This attractive, eighty-seven-acre garden is a breath of fresh air for Southern Californians. Plants from around the world include exotic trees (redwoods, palms, and others), shrubs, and flowers from Africa and New Zealand. There are several different specialty areas here including a cactus garden, a rose garden (we love taking pictures of roses here - such color and variety), a woodland walk, and a Garden for the Senses. In the latter, vegetation with unique fragrances, textures, and color schemes flourish. Follow the yellow brick road to and through the Discovery Garden, a fanciful children's garden that features storybook figures and structures, as well as plants. Can your child spot Humpty Dumpty or the three little kittens who lost their mittens?

Stroll along the cement and dirt pathways through the gardens, under shade trees, and up and down the gently rolling hills and grassy areas. It feels good to be surrounded by such beauty! Feed ducks at the man-made lake and look for koi, turtles, and heron and other waterfowl who make their home here. Outside food can't be brought in, but a picnic area is just outside the gates.

Hours: Open daily, 9am - 5pm. Closed on Christmas.
Price: $9 for adults; $6 for seniors and students; $4 for ages 5 - 12; children 4 and under are free - cash only. Admission is free the third Tues. of every month. See page x for info on AHS reciprocal memberships.
Ages: 3 years and up.

STONER PARK
(310) 479-7200 / www.laparks.org
1831 Stoner Avenue, Los Angeles

This park rocks! (That's my take on its name.) It has a 20,000 foot skate park/plaza that has got all the latest and greatest elements - ledges, tables, room to actually skate, ramps, grinding rails, and lots, lots more.

Other facilities here include a basketball court; baseball diamonds; tennis courts; volleyball courts; picnic area with BBQs; a rec center; grassy, run-around space with lots of mature shade trees; and a long, narrow, all-abilities playground. The rubberized and sand-based playground has swings, raised sand basins, ramps, slides, misters (and a few missus), and places to play both on and under the play structures.

A tiny, shady, Japanese nature garden, complete with a few cherry trees and a wonderful, gnarly tree that's great

for sitting in, is located in front of the gated pool area. The pool has a graduated slope from the slightly deep waters (4.5 feet) into the more shallow end that sports a sprayground. This aquatics area has a tall "mushroom" that water flows off, pipes and tubes that squirts, spurts and rains down water. Note that the ratio is 1 adult to 1 child. A lifeguard is on duty. An adjacent, small, separate pool features a long and twisty waterslide. Proper swimwear must be worn in the pools by everyone coming inside the gates, even non-swimmers.

Hours: The park and skate park are open daily, sunrise - sunset. The pool and water play area are open mid-June - mid-September, usually for four-hour increments during the day, although they are open daily, 11am - 6pm the end of June through mid-August. Call or check the website for specific times.

Price: The park and skate park are free. The pool and water play area are $2.50 for adults; free for seniors, persons with disabilities, and ages 17 and under.

Ages: All

STONEY POINT

www.lamountains.com

11000 Topanga Canyon Boulevard, Chatsworth

Do you have a rock-climber wannabe in your household? Stoney Point, so named for the large boulder perched at the top of the sandstone hill, is a famous (at least locally) rock climbers' delight. Practice repelling on this small mountain of stone, or just hike the trail up to the top. Either way, it can be an exhilarating way to spend part of the day. Be on the lookout for the numerous alcoves and caves to crawl into, but use caution, too. There is a dirt path toward the "back" of the hill that visitors can hike for a bit.

Hours: Open daily, sunrise - sunset.

Price: Free

Ages: 6 years and up to hike; your discretion about rock climbing.

STOUGH CANYON NATURE CENTER - WILDWOOD CANYON PARK

(818) 238-5440 / www.burbank.com

2300 Walnut Avenue, Burbank

Snuggled right into the mountains, this nature center offers a variety of displays around the perimeter and some in the center, as well as in a few classrooms. The exhibits include taxidermied animals, such as bobcat, raccoons, deer, quail, and an owl; a few live tarantulas and snakes (which visitors can touch), and a few nonliving ones; a touch table with animal skins and bones; a beekeeping display; and several colorful information panels. Ask about the numerous educational programs and recreational opportunities, ranging from organized nature hikes to astronomy workshops. Tip: Pick up a trail map here.

The fire road behind the nature center winds its way up the mountain and leads to a main trail, the Verdugo Mountainway Trail, which traverses the Verdugo Mountains. Taken in the other direction, where the road branches, the path eventually leads to Brand fire road and BRAND PARK (pg. 49).

Just down the street from the nature center is Wildwood Canyon Park, at 1701 Wildwood Canyon Drive. A two-mile trail system here snakes around on the Burbank side of the Verdugo Mountains and a steep, three-plus-mile Vital Link Trail hooks up with the Verdugo Mountainway. There are a few places at Wildwood to park, picnic, and play, with some grassy areas to run around.

Hours: The nature center is open September - June, Tues. - Fri., 11am - 5pm; Sat., 9am - 5pm; Sun., 11am - 5pm. Closed Mon. It is open July - August, Mon. - Fri., 10am - 5pm; Sat., 9am - 5pm; Sun., 11am - 5pm. Closed most holidays. The trails are open daily, dawn - dusk.

Price: Free

Ages: 3 years and up.

SWITZER FALLS

(626) 574-5200 or (626) 574-1613 / www.fs.usda.gov; www.localhikes.com

Angeles Crest Highway, Los Angeles

Ah - the rewards of a hike! Follow the moderately graded Gabrielino Trail on the west end of the picnic area about a mile to the remnants of Switzer's Camp, which is a backpacker's campground, to reach the top of the falls, a fifty-foot chute. To reach the bottom, and your destination of a refreshing (i.e., cold!), rock-lined swimming hole surrounded by rock walls, continue hiking on the Gabrielino Trail, along the right-hand side (or west) of the canyon wall and over some boulders. Note: Please use caution around any waterfall - wet rocks are slippery rocks, and watch

out for poison oak. If you don't like heights, this is not the hike for you.

Another alternative is to take the three-mile-or-so hike to Bear Canyon. Once you've hiked down the initial trail and reached Switzer's Camp, go up the canyon to Bear Canyon trail. A primitive campsite, a seasonal stream, and careful boulder hopping await. Bring a water bottle.

The small parking lot fills up early on the weekends. Many families stay near the entrance to picnic and wade in the Arroyo Seco Creek.

Hours: Open daily, 8am - dusk.
Price: $5 per vehicle for an Adventure Pass.
Ages: 7 years and up.

TEMESCAL GATEWAY PARK

(310) 454-1395 or (310) 589-3200 / www.lamountains.com
15601 W. Sunset Boulevard, Pacific Palisades

This 140-acre, comely wilderness park is particularly pretty in the spring when the wildflowers are blooming profusely, though anytime is a good time to visit. Dirt trails meander throughout that are often shaded by large oak, sycamore and other trees. Follow the one-and-a-half-mile trail that winds uphill, back through the canyon along the seasonal creek to a bridge and waterfall. Other trails allow access to Topanga State Park and Will Rogers State Historic Park.

Picnic tables are scattered throughout the park, so bring a sack lunch. Ask about the Outdoor Education Program - a hands-on outdoor experience for urban youth.

Hours: Open daily, sunrise - sunset.
Price: $7 per vehicle. There is some free parking on the street, with lots of extra walking involved to get to the park, though.
Ages: All

TONGVA PARK

(310) 458-8310 / tongvapark.squarespace.com
1685 Main Street, #200, Santa Monica

This architecturally unusual, 6.2-acre park in the midst of Santa Monica offers a place of respite as plants flow around fountains and a spiral pathway leads up to a viewpoint of the ocean that's encased in an oval grid (lovelier than it sounds). Other features include nice landscaping, tiered cement and grass seating, a lawn, alcoves, some palms and shade trees, and forty-nine stainless steel poles in a grid that alternate in height and have a weather vane, or anemometer, on the ends - collectively, it's a sculpture. A stone stairs cascading waterfall spills into a small, zero depth splash walkway.

Discovery Hill is a section just for kids. One play structure is kind of in the shape of the frame of a hut that kids can climb on. They can also climb the rope ladders inside it. One area has slides that go down a covered surface hill. A rock climbing element is adjacent to it and to a boulder-enclosed water play area (i.e. fountains shooting up). Check out the music wall, sculpturers that double as play equipment, and more in this aesthetically-pleasing and fun park. It is located across from Ken Genser Square, a one-acre park.

Hours: Open daily, 6am - 11pm.
Price: Free
Ages: 3 years and up.

TOPANGA STATE PARK

(310) 455-2465 / www.lamountains.com; www.parks.ca.gov
20825 Entrada Road, Topanga

Believe it or not, this massive state park, actually a huge natural preserve, is all contained within the Los Angeles city limits. Forty-five miles of hiking, biking, and equestrian trails go through canyons, hills, and cliffs of the Santa Monica Mountains. One of the main access for the trails is Trippet Ranch. Which trail you choose depends on how long you want to hike. A two-mile hike to Eagle Junction leads to the looping Eagle Springs trail. We like this one because of the boulders. Or, choose the broad Topanga Fire Road, or various other routes. Another popular trailhead is at WILL ROGERS STATE HISTORIC PARK (pg. 158). Regardless of where you start (or finish), bring your own water and wear sunscreen. Note: No dogs allowed on the trails.

Hours: Open daily, 8am - sunset.

Price: $10 per vehide. (Parking at Will Rogers is $12.)
Ages: 5 years and up.

TROUTDALE
(818) 889-9993 / www.allyoucanfish.com
2468 Troutdale Drive, Agoura Hills

$$$$

"Fishy, fishy in a brook/ Daddy caught him with a hook / Mammy fried him in a pan / And baby ate him like a man." (Childcraft, Poems and Rhymes, 1966)

Troutdale is in a cute, woodsy setting with two small ponds to fish from - perfect for beginners, and those who want a sure thing. There are logs to sit on around the perimeter of the ponds, plus picnic tables and benches and even a separate picnic area for parties. The entrance price includes a bamboo fishing pole and bait. For an extra $1.50, you can get your fish cleaned. Munch at the snack bar or bring a picnic lunch to eat while you're catching dinner. Be sure to pick up a flyer that has recipe ideas. Note that PETER STRAUSS RANCH (pg. 78) is across the way, and KING GILLETTE RANCH (pg. 67), with the SANTA MONICA MOUNTAINS NATIONAL PARK HEADQUARTERS (pg. 84), are just around the corner.

Hours: Open most of the year, Wed. - Fri., 10am - 6pm; Sat., 9am - 6pm. Open in the summer daily, 9am - 7pm.
Price: $7 per person, fishing or not. Fish prices vary depending on their length. Usually fish cost between $6 - $11 each.
Ages: 3 years and up.

VASQUEZ ROCKS
(661) 268-0840 / www.lacountyparks.org
10700 W. Escondido Canyon Road, Agua Dulce

This park became an instant favorite with my boys with its 932 acres of eye-catching, spectacular and unusual rock formations, many of which are sandstone and almost triangular in shape, jutting practically straight up from the ground. They have ridges along their sides making them moderately easy to climb, although my kids also climbed much higher (to the tops!) than my heart could take. For those who don't like heights, there are several smaller rocks to conquer, and plenty of walking trails, plus Tataviam Indian sites and a seasonal stream.

If you experience "deja vu" while here, it's probably because this park has been used in numerous commercials and films, such as *The Flintstones* (the stones do look prehistoric), as well as several westerns and science fiction thrillers. Tip: Call before you come because sections of the park are closed when filming is taking place.

The Ranger Station, housed in a barn with corralled horses outside, enhances the mood for this all-natural, rustic park. Be forewarned - drinking water is not available in the park. Camping for organized youth groups is allowed.

Hours: Open daily, sunrise - sunset.
Price: Free
Ages: 3 years and up.

VERDUGO PARK AND SKATE PARK
(818) 548-2786 or (818) 548-6420 / parks.ci.glendale.ca.us
1621 Canada Boulevard, Glendale

This lighted, 15,000-square-foot skate park has two bowls, a kidney-shaped pool, ramps, slide rails, and more, all on a concrete surface. The park is fenced-in and staff is on hand at all times. Skaters under 17 years must have a parent or legal guardian sign a waiver. Wearing a helmet and knee and elbow pads is a requirement. No rentals are available.

The surrounding, forty-acre park has mature oak trees providing lots of shade and places to climb, picnic tables, a good-sized playground, baseball diamond, basketball court, horseshoe court, and more.

Hours: Open during the school year, Mon. - Fri., 4pm - 10pm; Sat., 10am - noon (for ages 14 and under) and noon - 10pm (all ages); Sun., 10am - 10pm. Open school holidays and summer daily, 10am - 10pm.
Price: $4 a day for adult nonresidents; $3 for ages 17 and under.
Ages: 7 years and up.

VINCENT LUGO PARK
(626) 308-2875 / www.sangabrielcity.com

300 W. Wells Street, San Gabriel

There are three great play areas immediately visible here: A small enclosed one for toddlers, one with a rocket structure to climb up and slide down, and another that is just fun. A sand pit, lots of grassy running space, and picnic tables help classify this park as a good one.

According to my "park-smart" kids, however, the best part of the park is across the service road and to the south, almost hidden from sight, near the bike path and bridge that goes over a dry creek bed. Children can play on the oversized cement sea creatures that have surfaced here, such as an octopus, seals, snail, and a whale, all based in sand (of course). Shouts of "This is the best!" came from my kids as they slid down the sea serpent that is wrapped around a lighthouse. Another giant sea serpent is curled around a short, rocky hill which has a huge shade tree growing from it and a slide to go down. The huge treasure chest and sunken pirate ship add to the ambiance and kid's imaginative play here. Created in the 1960's, this nautical park was a treasure of a modern-day find!

>   **Hours:**   Open daily, 7am - 10pm.
>   **Price:**   Free
>   **Ages:**   2 - 11 years old.

VIRGINIA ROBINSON GARDENS

(310) 276-5367 or (310) 550-2065 / www.robinsongardens.org

$$$

1008 Elden Way, Beverly Hills

Once the estate of the department store magnate, Robinsons (of Robinsons-May), this house has the distinction of being one of the first homes built in Beverly Hills. A ninety-minute- guided tour of the grounds includes a brief guided tour through the house, showing off the furnishings and other collections gathered from around the world. Visitors walk through the living rooms, bedroom, kitchen, and other rooms.

Probably of more interest to older kids is the bulk of the tour through the six acres of botanic gardens. The hilly gardens, which are not stroller or wheelchair friendly as there are numerous stairs, feature lush tropical and subtropical plants, roses, and more. Brick pathways connect the diverse areas of foliage that are also landscaped with ponds, fountains, and an Olympic-size pool. The grounds are a gardener's delight!

>   **Hours:**   Open by reservation only, Tues. - Fri. at 10am and at 1pm.
>   **Price:** $11 for adults; $6 for seniors and students; $4 for ages 5 - 12; children 4 years and under are free.
>   **Ages:**   9 years and up.

WILDERNESS PARK

(626) 355-5309 / www.ci.arcadia.ca.us

2240 Highland Oaks Drive, Arcadia

This 120-acre wilderness park/preserve is in the foothills of the mountains, on the same street as residential housing. A short dirt trail through the shade trees loops around a large grassy area. Plenty of picnic tables are scattered among the woods. A picnic shelter with enough picnic tables for a busload, or two, is on the grounds, next to the kitchen facility that has two sinks, a freezer, a refrigerator, and an oven. This shelter area is available for group rental and also has a fire ring with amphitheater-type seating. Call before you come to ask if the Santa Anita Creek, kept in check by controlling the water from the Santa Ana Dam, is flowing. If so, get at least your feet wet - so refreshing on a hot summer's day. A swimming hole at the north end of the creek usually has three or four feet of water, regardless if the dam is flowing or not.

The nature center contains quite a few glass-encased, taxidermied animals. We looked at barn owls, ravens, a gold eagle, black bear, mountain lion, coyote, raccoon, and lots more. The building also has a mounted insect collection, a few live snakes, and small waterfall and "pond." Ask about the many classes that the park offers, including merit badge classes.

>   **Hours:**   Open October through April, Mon. - Fri., 8:30am - 4:30pm. Open May through September, Mon. - Fri., 8:30am - 7pm. Weekend admission is by advanced reservation only.
>   **Price:**   Free
>   **Ages:**   All

WILLIAM S. HART MUSEUM AND PARK

24151 Newhall Avenue, Newhall

See the entry for WILLIAM S. HART MUSEUM AND PARK on page 157 for details.

—MALLS—

THE AMERICANA AT BRAND - KIDS CLUB

(818) 637-8900 or (818) 637-8982 / www.americanaatbrand.com
889 Americana Way, Glendale

Glitz and glamour don't just belong to Hollywood anymore. This fifteen-acre, upscale shopping (over seventy-five shops), dining (from Jamba Juice, Pinkberry, CrepeMaker, Cheesecake Factory, and Granville Cafe), entertainment (including Pacific Theatres), and residential center offers a luxurious experience. It includes rolling green lawns (not usually associated with a mall experience); awesome fountains that shoot water really high in the air (eighty-feet) and "dance" to music; live music on the quad on weekends; trolley rides along the mini streets; uniformed elevator men; and concierge personnel who offer an incredible range of services, for a fee. Lights at nighttime are especially pretty at the fountain.

Kids have their own entertainment event every Tuesday on the green, or in the Community Room on rainy days. Singers, comedians, magic, storytime, cultural performances, crafts, or animal presentations - every week is something different.

  Hours: The Kids Club is every Tues., 11am - 1pm.
  Price: Free. Parking is free the first hour, $3 the second hour, on up with a max of $18, although it can be less with merchant validation.
  Ages: Geared for ages 2 - 7

ANTELOPE VALLEY MALL - ANTELOPE ADVENTURES KID'S CLUB

(661) 266-9150 / www.av-mall.com
1233 Rancho Vista Boulevard, Palmdale

Kids, 3 to 11 years, can galvanize their artistic side monthly near the food court by participating in a seasonal craft. Paint an umbrella. Have fun with shamrocks. Ring in the holidays with a Christmas craft. Whatever the craft, it is fun (and free!). This mall also has PAINT A DREAM Ceramics (pg. 8); BUILD-A-BEAR WORKSHOP (pg. 162); High Desert Strollers (walking the mall and learning healthy living tips) at 7:30am the fourth Wednesday of the month; special events; a soft play area for younger ones; stroller rentals with a basket ($5); and of course, lots of shops and restaurants.

  Hours: Kid's Club is the second Wed. of every month, 4pm - 7pm.
  Price: Free
  Ages   3 - 11 years

DEL AMO FASHION CENTER - KIDGITS CLUB

(310) 542-8525 / www.delamofashioncenter.com; www.simon.com
3 Del Amo Fashion Center at Carson Street at Hawthorne Boulevard, Torrance

Join in the fun and frivolity on selected Saturday mornings near Jo-anns. The activities vary so it could be kids' entertainers encouraging your children to laugh, sing, and dance along with them as they tell stories, sing songs, and more, or an art and craft project to make and take. There are free drawings after every show. Annual membership to Kidgits is $5 per child, which includes a t-shirt, birthday gift, free goodies at the club events, and spinning the wheel for a prize any time you visit the mall.

The Fashion Center also hosts seasonal events and programs. This mall, by the way, is the largest one in the western U.S. - one mile of shopping! There are over 200 stores, including the DISNEY STORE (pg. 167), BUILD-A-BEAR WORKSHOP (see pg. 162 for more info), plus three food courts - talk about choices!, and an IMAX and 3-D movie theater.

  Hours: Kidgits is one Sat. a month, usually at 10am.
  Price: Free
  Ages: 1½ - 8 years.

GLENDALE GALLERIA

(818) 246-6737 / www.glendalegalleria.com
100 West Broadway, Glendale

Besides great shopping, a centerpiece for children is the carpeted Tot Lot, near JC Penney. Climbable,

soft-sculptured letters and numbers in this enclosed area add up to fun, as do other alphabet activities. Musical accompaniment is triggered as kids go down the slide and crawl under the arches and other shapes. There is also a little, kid's clubhouse, and a small area for them to sit and watch kids TV, plus soft benches for parental units.

Check out the interactive and magical DISNEY STORE (see pg. 314 for details), as well as the Lego store (pg. 36). Visit GIGGLES N' HUGS (see pg. 29 for details) - a great kid restaurant and indoor play place.

Hours: The mall is open Mon. - Sat., 10am - 9pm; Sun., 11am - 7pm.
Price: Free
Ages: 42" and under for the Tot Lot.

KIDS CLUB
(818) 637- 8921 / www.shopwaterside.com
4700 Admiralty Way at the Waterside Marina Del Rey shopping center, Marina del Rey
Conveniently located in front of Starbucks (so adults can indulge and get some energy first!), once a week entertainment for the kids at the outside Waterside Marina Del Rey shopping center can include magic shows; animals to pet and learn about; puppet and marionette shows; storytelling; songs and games; and more. And of course there are plenty of shops and restaurants to peruse, plus MARINA BEACH / MOTHER'S BEACH (pg. 11), MARINA DEL REY WATERBUS (pg. 213) and FISHERMAN'S VILLAGE (pg. 159) are just around the corner.

Hours: Every Tuesday, March - October, 11:15am - 12:15pm.
Price: Free
Ages: 2 - 8 years

KID'S CLUB AT 7+FIG
(213) 955-7150 / www.7fig.com/kids-club.html
735 S. Figueroa Street at the 7 + Fig shopping center, Los Angeles
In partnership with the Children's Museum of Los Angeles all sorts of wonderful crafts are created at these free workshops. Paper collages, animal murals, flower bouquets out of colorful tissue paper, paper kites, Mardi Gras masks, wands, weathervanes, cornucopias, and seasonal projects are made and treasured. The club meets at the lower level food court. Enjoy the club, shops, and dining here. If you're around on Thursdays from 11:30am to 2:30pm, buy something fresh at the Farmer's Market..

Hours: Every third Sat., noon - 2pm.
Price: Free. Parking, with validation, is $1 for the first hour, $2 for the second, etc.
Ages: 3 - 11 years

KID'S CLUB AT THE COMMONS
(818) 222-3444 or (818) 637-8922 / www.shopcommons.com
4799 Commons Way, Calabasas
Weekly entertainment at The Commons, usually about an hour, can include magic shows, mime, puppetry, storytelling, science demonstrations, animal presentations, or music. The Kid's Club meets at the community stage, which is between Mi Piace and Marmalade Cafe. Prizes are raffled off every week and some stores offer Kid's Club members discounts.

The Commons occasionally offers other events such as cooking classes, live music, pet adoption, Stroller Strides classes, holiday special events, and more. This lovely, upscale, outdoor mall also has several shops and restaurants to entice you, plus an Edwards cinema. Or, just come for the somewhat peaceful ambiance with rock-lined, small connecting ponds with real turtles, koi and ducks (and really neat, playful statues) at one end, and a waterfall and more nice landscaping at the other.

Hours: Every Tues., 6pm - 7pm.
Price: Free
Ages: 3 - 10 years.

LAKEWOOD CENTER KIDS CLUB
(562) 531-6707 / www.shoplakewoodcenter.com
200 Lakewood Center Mall, Lakewood
Teaming up with National Geographic Kids, the Kids Club features one hour of thematic activities and games once a month for young ones by Center Court. Themes have included castles, dinosaurs, under the sea, winter fun, big

cats, and more. The mall other special events throughout the year, too, so check the events section on the website.

Near Target is a small, semi-enclosed, soft-play area designed for younger ones. Against a colorful background mural, they can play on giant, padded, foam pieces representing picnic food, including a spilled soda, hot dog, and fruit. A mini train runs on a small oval track at the other end of the mall, near Penneys. Rides are about $2. Also see ROUND1 BOWLING AND AMUSEMENT (pg. 39) for more fun and games. Two of my favorite stores here are the Disney Store and $1 Bookstore!

Hours: Kids Club is the fourth Fri. at 11am.
Price: Free
Ages: 1 - 9 years.

LOS CERRITOS CENTER'S NATIONAL GEOGRAPHIC KIDS CLUB
(562) 402-SHOP (7467) / www.shoploscerritos.com
239 Los Cerritos Center, Cerritos

In partnering with National Geographic Kids, children are invited to engage via music and interactive games and then make a craft related to the focus of the day, whether it's baby animals, big cats, dinosaurs, marine dwellers, etc. The club meets in front of Forever 21.

Note that just north of the food court, near Sears, is a somewhat enclosed play area for young children. The large, padded, foam objects - like small trucks and cars - are perfect for kids to climb on and under, while parents rest on the surrounding padded benches.

Hours: The Kids Club is held one Sat. a month, 11am - noon.
Price: Free
Ages: 2 - 10

MANHATTAN VILLAGE KIDS CLUB
(310) 546 5555 / www.shopmanhattanvillage.com
3200 Sepulveda Avenue, Manhattan Beach

This Village plays host to a fun kid event every second and fourth Thursday near Center Court, sponsored by different organizations. On the second Thursday from 11am to noon, Wondertree Kids and Birdies Playhouse offers musical mornings to get kids clapping, singing, and moving to rhythms. The fourth Thursday, from 10am to noon, Superkids Gym offers physical fun of exercising to music, tumbling and gymnastics. Manhattan Village also does family-friendly special events throughout the year, as well as Stroller Strides, which is a free fitness class for moms to work out with babies in strollers. A slew of shops and restaurants are also available here.

Hours: Kids Club days and hours are mentioned above.
Price: Free
Ages: 1½ - 10 years.

MOMMY & ME KIDS CLUB
(310) 414-5280 or (408) 551-2249 / www.plazaelsegundo.com
760 South Sepulveda Boulevard at Plaza El Segundo, El Segundo

Mommy & Me (and daddies, too!) Kids Club meets in front of The Counter Restaurant once a month for live performances of music, storytelling, and puppetry, plus other activities such as crafts, making balloon animals, face paintings and more. Come join in the fun and join in free membership to receive discounts and rewards. Note that Stroller Strides classes are also held at this mall.

Hours: The third Thurs. of every month, April - December, 10am - noon.
Price: Free
Ages: 1½ to 8 years old.

NORTHRIDGE FASHION CENTER - KID'S CLUB
(818) 885-9700 / www.northridgefashioncenter.com
9301 Tampa Avenue, Northridge

Become an NFC kid and get in on all the fun! Forty-five minutes of storytelling, singing, dancing, craft making, circus acts, or puppet shows are on the morning's agenda on the upper level at the food court.

This mall features a large, free, soft-play area with a hard padded giant starfish, surfboards, and dolphins, plus play sports cars and a backdrop scene of the Hollywood Hills. It's located on the lower level, near Macy's. There is also a

train ride that choo choos around the lower level, and not on tracks. A *beary* fun store for kids here is BUILD-A-BEAR WORKSHOP. See page 162 for information on this store. Note that on Wednesdays, from 5pm to 9pm, April through October, the mall parking lot hosts a Farmer's Market with fresh fruit and vegetables, as well as a bounce house, pony rides, crafts to make, and a petting zoo for kids.

Hours: Kid's Club is the first and third Thurs. of each month at 10:30am.
Price: The Kid's Club is free. The train ride is $4 per person, per ride.
Ages: 1 - 8 years.

NORWALK TOWN SQUARE - KIDS FUN ZONE

(562) 868-2291 / www.norwalk-townsquare.com
11633 The Plaza, at the corner of Pioneer Boulevard and Rosecrans Avenue, Norwalk

Have you got crafty kids? They are invited to make free, seasonal crafts once a month at this outdoor mall. Tables are set up with supplies and staffed with volunteers willing to show and help out with the chosen craft - decorating aprons, creating gift boxes, making a Christmas ornament, etc. The Town Square also hosts special events throughout the year such as an Easter Eggstravaganza, Trick or Treating, Santa Claus, and a snow play area.

Hours: Kids Fun Zone is held the last Sat. of every month, noon - 3pm.
Price: Free
Ages: 2 - 12 years.

PLAZA WEST COVINA - KIDS CLUB

(626) 960-8032 / www.shoppingplazawestcovina.com
112 Plaza Drive, West Covina

The mall features a semi-enclosed, colorful, carpeted PlaySpace for kids with soft play objects to climb on and a few mini slides, plus comfortable bench seating for adults. A Family Lounge features a screen showing children's movies, plus it has private nursing stations and bottle warmers. If you want to rent a cool stroller, inquire here about a Smarte Carte Stroller ($5), which is a stroller in the shape of a colorful car. The mall also has a Tilt Arcade and Xtreme XD Theater, which is simulator rides on steroids!

Kids Clubs are geared for families with young children. These times can incorporate storytelling, crafts (like kite-making or creating flower pots), singing and dancing, and a myriad of other activities which are sometimes seasonally-based.

Hours: Kids Clubs are the 2nd Tues. from 3pm - 5pm in the center court, lower level.
Price: Free
Ages: 2 - 7 years.

SANTA MONICA PLACE - SAMOS KIDS CLUB

(310) 260-8333 / www.santamonicaplace.com
395 Santa Monica Place, Santa Monica

This upscale, mostly outdoor mall, located at the end of the Third Street Promenade which is lined with shops and restaurants, offers more shops and restaurants! Disney Store (see pg. 314 for details about this interactive store); Johnny Rockets, a 50's dining experience; rooftop dining, where you can see the ocean and (maybe) beyond; Crepe Maker; and Marbles: The Brain Store are just a very few favorites here.

Samos Kids Club takes place the first Wednesday of every month in the Food Court (level 3). Bring the kids to enjoy puppet shows (which includes puppets for the kids to use, too), music with interactive songs, and story time. Adjacent to the food court is Samo's Clubhouse, a play area for kids. They'll have a whale of a time climbing in and through the frame of a full-size humpback whale made of steel, netting and wood. Play panels, stairs, a slide, a balance beam, a short tight-rope, talking tubes, a periscope and other creative elements complete the nautical fun.

Just some of the events at the mall include a Nike Training Club every Tuesday at 6:30pm outside of the Nike store for a free, hour-long workout (call Nike at [310] 393-7384); the Nike Run Club for group runs; free Zumba classes on Saturday mornings at 9am; family game nights at Marbles: The Brain Store - (310) 260-8333; live music; and more.

Hours: Samos Kids Club is the first Wed., 11am - noon.
Price: Parking is available in 8 public parking structures, including Structure 7 and 8, immediately adjacent to Santa Monica Place. The first 90 min. are free; $1 the next hour; $1.50 for each 30 min.; $14 max. Library parking at 601 Santa Monica Blvd. is discounted on weekends.

Ages: 2 - 6 for the Samos Kids Club

SOUTH BAY GALLERIA - KIDS CLUB

(310) 371-7546 / www.southbaygalleria.com
1815 Hawthorne Boulevard, Redondo Beach

Twice a month, kids can come to the Galleria and enjoy an hour of free entertainment such as stories, puppets, animal presentations, magic shows, sing-alongs, or seasonally-oriented arts and crafts activities presented on the third level near the food court. After each show, raffles or drawings are held for mall certificates. Make new friends as you and your child become regulars! Make sure you sign up to become a Kids Club member (membership is free) because a postcard is mailed out once a month listing a schedule of events and the giveaways from retailers.

Hours: The first Tues. of each month at 6:30pm and the last Wed. at 10:30am.
Price: Free
Ages: 2 - 10 years.

THE GROVE - KIDS' THURSDAYS

(888) 315-8883 or (323) 900-8080 / www.thegrovela.com
189 The Grove Drive, Los Angeles

What a contrast in malls! The definitely upscale Grove is located just across the way from the down-to-earth, original FARMERS MARKET (pg. 18). The Grove is an outdoor complex with walking streets that boasts of beautiful landscaping, including a large pond (or small lake); a choreographed "dancing" fountain that moves every half hour to a variety of musical selections; a free ride on the double-decker trolley with a bell-ringing conductor who conveys patrons from one end to the other; eateries and restaurants; and special activities offered throughout the year. On Thursdays, kids are invited to listen to storytellers, make crafts, hear and join in on songs, watch a marionette show, or enjoy something else equally entertaining. Story time is shared every Tuesday at 11am at Pottery Barn Kids with rewards given along the way. Often there is entertainment on Saturdays as well - music, book signings by famous authors, and more. Check The Grove calendar website for more info.

The name retail shops here include Gap Kids, J. Crew, Nordstrom, Wentworth Gallery, Barnes & Noble, and many more. Pacific Theaters has fourteen screens here and, in keeping with the posh atmosphere, the theater has an elegant lobby, stadium seating (with some reclining seats!), and loge seating for private parties. The theater also offers Monday Morning Mommy Movies at 11am where infants and younger children are welcome. Dining opportunities abound, including the hands-down winner for young girls, AMERICAN GIRL PLACE (pg. 161).

Note that PAN PACIFIC PARK (pg. 77) with great playgrounds and picnic areas and more, and the LOS ANGELES MUSEUM OF THE HOLOCAUST (pg. 131) are just around the corner.

Hours: Kid's Thursdays are Thurs, 11am - 1pm, with other activities throughout the week. Call or check the website for a schedule. The stores are open Mon. - Thurs., 10am - 9pm; Fri. - Sat., 10am - 10pm; Sun., 11am - 7pm - restaurants and the movie theater are open later.
Price: Free, but bring spending money. Kids' Thursdays are free. Parking in the structure is free for the first hour, $4 for the second hour, etc.
Ages: 2 years and up.

THIRD STREET PROMENADE

(310) 393-8355 / www.downtownsm.com
3rd Street, Santa Monica

This three-block pedestrian walkway is a fascinating, outdoor mall experience. It rates an A+ for people-watching as the international mix of people, converging here from the nearby Los Angeles International Airport, make it a cultural adventure. Nighttime and weekends bring out performers who want to show off their talents, however glorious or dubious they might be. We've seen and heard African drum playing, tap dancing, folk songs, acrobatics, men acting like robots, clowns making balloon animals, and an organ grinder monkey begging - all within the span of an hour. Benches are plentiful, so if you really enjoy some of the entertainment, sit down and watch. A plethora of artsy and unique stores and boutiques, plus movie theaters, line the "street." Vendor carts are along the sidewalks. Choose from a multitude of restaurants of numerous ethnicities that range from upscale to grab-a-bite, or snack at a bakery or ice cream shop. See page 14 for an interesting Italian eatery at BUCA DI BEPPO. A few fountains, featuring dinosaurs spouting water, complete the eclectic ambiance at the promenade. Farmer's Market is nearby on Arizona Avenue between Second and Fourth streets on Wednesdays and Saturdays from 8:30am to 1pm. Check the November

Calendar section in the book for information about the ice-skating rink that's just down the street here during winter months.

Note: The Big Blue Bus, (310) 451-5444 / www.bigbluebus.com, runs a loop from Main Street to Third Street Promenade every fifteen minutes, from 6am to midnight at a cost of $1 per person; 50¢ for seniors; children 4 and under are free.

Hours: Most stores and restaurants are open daily, 10am - 9pm.
Price: Free, but bring spending money.
Ages: All

WESTFIELD CENTURY CITY - ART REBEL

(310) 277-3898 / www.westfield.com
10250 Santa Monica Boulevard, Century City

This posh mall features creative crafts for kids under the collective title of Art Rebel. Past creations include a mosaic heart, an accordion box, a wish jar, a popside bracelet, a spoon catapult, a paint your own Shakra, and more. Join in on the fun and take home a new treasure for free. GIGGLES N' HUGS (pg. 29) is here and, just outside Giggles N' Hugs is a great, outdoor, innovative playground with tables and chairs nearby. The playground has large, flat, cactus-looking pads (without the spikes) that are steps to climb up and down, enmeshed in netting that interconnect with other groupings of the pads - very fun! The mall also offers Smarte Cartes to rent for $5; a colorful stroller in the shape of a vehicle.

Hours: The mall is open Mon. - Sat., 10am - 9pm; Sun., 11am - 7pm. Art Rebel is held the second Thurs. of most months from 3pm - 5pm.
Price: Free. Parking is $1 per hour up to 3 hours; $1 every 15 minutes up to 5 hours. AMC validates up to 3 hours for free, $4 for up to 5 hours. Gelson's Market and Brighton Collectibles also validate.
Ages: 4 - 11 years.

WESTFIELD CULVER CITY - WFAMILY PLAY DAYS

(310) 390-5073 or (310) 390-7833 / www.westfield.com
294 Fox Hills Mall, Culver City

WFamily Play Days is a free, hour-long program and/or activity for kids such as puppetry, singing and dancing, clown acts, and more, along with prizes and games sponsored by the Children's Hospital of Los Angeles on level 1 at the JC Penney Court. There are other activities at the mall throughout the year. The toy store, Three Cheeky Monkeys, often hosts face painting, storytelling, and crafts. Check the mall website calendar or call for a listing of events. Another great store here is the interactive and magical DISNEY STORE (see pg. 167) for details.

Kids will enjoy PlaySpace, too, which is a small, free, semi-enclosed play area (which is open the same hours as the mall) that has colorful characters, soft play objects, and some activities to engage your young children, plus comfortable bench seating for adults. Lunch and shopping seem like a natural follow up! Ask at the concierge for a free balloon for your child and, if you want to stroll in style, rent a Kiddie Kruzzer ($5), which is a stroller in the shape of a car.

Hours: WFamily Play Days are the 3rd Tues. of the month at 10:30am
Price: Free
Ages: 2 - 8 years.

WESTFIELD FASHION SQUARE

(818) 501-1447 or (818) 783-0550 / www.westfield.com
13780 Riverside Drive, Sherman Oaks

This large, two-story indoor shopping center occasionally hosts performances or concerts for kids. Other mall accouterments include a food court; an interactive and magical DISNEY STORE - (818) 907-5094 (see pg. 314 for details); Karen's Toys; and a semi-enclosed, aquatic-themed PlaySpace for kids with soft play objects, like a whale mini slide, to climb on, over and through, keeping them happy and occupied, while adults can sit comfortably on the surrounding benches. Inside PlaySpace is a long, triangularly-shaped piece of plexiglass that pops up from the ground. It in is a fish tank. Just outside this area are a few kiddie rides.

A Family Lounge features a screen showing children's movies and a private nursing station. If you want to stroll your child in style, rent a Kiddie Kruzzer ($5), which is a stroller in the shape of a car. Note that a Farmer's Market is held here every Tuesday from 3pm to 8pm. Check out LOLLIPOP DREAM (pg. 36), that adjoins the mall, for

wonderful children's events.

Hours: The mall is open Mon. - Sat., 10am - 9pm; Sun., 11am - 7pm.
          Price: Free

WESTFIELD SANTA ANITA - WFAMILY FUN DAYS

(626) 445-3116 / www.westfield.com

400 S. Baldwin Avenue, Arcadia

Inside, the mall features a semi-enclosed PlaySpace for kids with soft play objects to climb, slide, and ride on (like critters and cars) to keep them occupied, plus comfortable seating for adults. A coin-operated rocket and motorcycle are here, as are carousel rides, for $3 per ride. A Family Lounge features a screen showing children's movies and private nursing stations. If you want to rent a cool stroller, get a Kiddie Kruzzer ($5), which is a stroller in the shape of a car. Check out the great indoor play area here called JUMP 'N JAMMIN (pg. 33) and the Disney Store.

Outside the mall, on the promenade, is a small play area where a friendly dragon is partly hidden in the ground, but his wide face, eyes, and body bumps are on the surface to play on. A rope climbing structure, and spiral objects to twirl around on, plus benches complete this playground.

On the last Tuesday of every month, for about an hour, WFamily Fun Days offer free entertainment for kids (and adults). With a different theme each month, there could be music, storytelling, crafts, games, snacks and more. Check the mall's website calendar or call for a complete schedule.

          Hours: WFamily Fun Days are the last Tues. at 11am.
          Price: Free
          Ages: 2 - 7 years.

WESTFIELD TOPANGA and STORY TIME

(818) 594-8740 / www.westfield.com

6600 Topanga Canyon Boulevard, Canoga Park

After shopping at this massive mall, parents can rest their weary bodies on padded benches (or on chairs at the outer counter tops) that encircle the enclosed, free Playtown area called The Canyon, while their younger kids enjoy climbing on the hard foam play figures. They can climb on, around, and in fake rocks, a huge snake, mountain lions and other critters. The Canyon plays host to storytelling one Tuesday a month at 11am where a book is read followed by an applicable art and craft, sing-a-long, or another form of entertainment. The free storytelling is put on by the mall's partnership with GIGGLES N' HUGS (see pg. 29), a fantastic restaurant with an imaginative play area for kids that is located just above this play spot, on the second floor.

Adjacent to the Canyon, located in the Target Court, is the unique, two-story (!) carousel with a dinosaur, bunny, tigers, hummingbird, zebras and other wondrous animals to ride. The cost is $3 for a child; free for an adult to stand with the child. My Gym Express is another play section that looks like a small train but has tunnels, cargo nets, and foam obstacle course for little kids to run around. The cost is about $4 a child.

One more noteworthy place here for kids is the Lego Store; see pg. 36 for details about making a free mini model.

          Hours: Storytelling is the first Tues. of each month at 11am. The mall is open Mon. - Sat., 10am - 9pm;
                        Sun., 11am - 7pm.
          Price: Free
          Ages: 1 - 8

WESTFIELD VALENCIA TOWN CENTER - WFAMILY FUN DAYS

(661) 287-9050 / www.westfield.com

24201 W. Valencia Boulevard, Valencia

This mall features a carousel and PlaySpace, a soft-play area for young kids. It has slides, tunnels, and short, climbing apparatus, plus animal characters and large puzzles. Come rest your weary feet, parents, and let the kids play.

Family Fun Day storytelling and crafts are a big hit for little kids. Past days have included stories about dancing, then decorating a guitar craft and kite, and finishing up with a dance party; and reading about Olympic games, designing a medal and participating in a mini obstacle course. Also be sure to check out the interactive and magical DISNEY STORE (see pg. 167 for details) and paint a wonderful keepsake at PAINT A DREAM (see pg. 8).

          Hours: Family Fun Days are the second Wed. at 11am.
          Price: Free
          Ages: 1½ - 6 years.

WESTSIDE PAVILION - KIDS CLUB ☀

(310) 470-8752 or (310) 474-6255 / www.westsidepavilion.com
10800 W. Pico Boulevard, Los Angeles

    Parents and kids can enjoy an hour-long presentation/show together once a month at Westside Pavilion. Shows can consist of puppetry, magicians, bubbles, silly science, ventriloquist comedy, musicians, and more. Free membership to the club allows kids to receive a monthly postcard promoting special offers from Pavilion retailers. Note that this mall has a BUILD-A-BEAR WORKSHOP (pg. 162), and a baby boot camp for mommies (i.e. a stroller fitness program) from 9am - 10am, before the mall officially opens. See www.babybootcamp.com for more info.

    Hours: Kids Club is the fourth Wed. from 6pm - 7pm.
    Price: Free
    Ages: 2 - 13

—MUSEUMS—

ADAMSON HOUSE AND MALIBU LAGOON MUSEUM ☀

(310) 456-8432 - museum; (310) 456-1770 - docent during museum hours; (818) 880-0363 - lagoon tour / $$$
www.adamsonhouse.org; www.parks.ca.gov
23200 Pacific Coast Highway, Malibu

    The Adamson House and its adjacent museum are on beautifully landscaped grounds just a few feet away from the Malibu Surfrider Beach and lifeguard station, and the Malibu Lagoon - definitely beach-front property. The outside of the house and the fountains integrate the colorful Malibu tiles in their design. We wandered around the grounds on flagstone walkways that wove through grassy lawns, beneath shade trees, along several gardens (including a rose garden), past a pool that was once filled with salt water from the ocean, and to the chain-link fence which marks the house boundaries. Here, just a short distance from the pier, we watched surfers do their thing.

    The small museum features exhibits pertaining to the history of Malibu, including cattle brands, arrowheads, maps, fossilized shells, and numerous photographs. I liked the Malibu Colony of Stars' pictures of Robert Redford, Bing Crosby, Clara Bow, Joan Crawford, and others. Ask for a tour or for explanations regarding the history of the railroad, the dam, and the movie colony.

    The two-story house was built in 1929. The rooms and grounds can only be seen on a ninety-minute, guided tour. Adults and older children will appreciate the bottle-glass windows, hand-painted murals, additional tile work (especially in the kitchen), furnishings, and unique decor.

    There isn't any direct access to the lagoon (i.e., the parcel of water and land that is a haven for various bird species) from the house. You can get to this area by walking or driving over the bridge and down Cross Creek Road. We observed pelicans, herons, sandpipers, and other birds coming in for a landing before taking to the skies once again. Visit here on your own or make tour reservations to educate your kids (and yourself) about the waterfowl, ecology, the area's Chumash Indian past, and more. The lagoon programs are given by a state park ranger. Note: Although the beach is accessible by going through the museum parking lot, the waters are for surfers only. If your kids want to go swimming, head toward Malibu Pier, just east up the street.

    Hours: The house and museum are open Wed. - Sat., 11am - 3pm. The last house tour begins at 2pm. Closed New Year's Day, July 4th, Thanksgiving, and Christmas Day, plus rainy days. Call for information on lagoon tours and programs.
    Price: The house and museum tour is $7 for adults; $2 for ages 6 - 16; children 5 and under are free. A tour of the garden is included every Fri. at 10am. Parking in the county lot adjacent to the museum costs $8 per vehicle. Some free street parking is available. Lagoon tours cost $6 per vehicle for parking Mon. - Fri., $8 on Sat.
    Ages: 7 years and up for the house tour and museum; 4 years and up for the lagoon tour.

ADOBE DE PALOMARES ☀

(909) 620-0264 or (909) 623-2198 / www.pomonahistorical.org $
491 E. Arrow Highway, Pomona

    This thirteen-room restored adobe was originally built in 1854, during the California Gold Rush. A guided tour of the house includes seeing the courtyard, with its horno (i.e. outdoor oven); the simple, but lovely, authentic period furniture; cooking utensils (how did they live without so many technical doohickeys?!); tools; antique clothing; canopy

beds; and children's toys. The rooms look quite livable, even by today's standards. The landscaped grounds are very pleasant. A blacksmith shop is also on site and features saddles, ranching tools, branding irons, and a horse-drawn carriage, circa 1880's.

Adjacent to the adobe is Palomare Park, so bring a picnic lunch and enjoy some running around space.

Hours: Open Sun., 2pm - 5pm. Closed Easter, Memorial Day weekend, Labor Day weekend, and
Thanksgiving weekend. Special tours are given by appointment.

Price: Donations of $2 for adults; $1 for ages 18 and under are suggested.

Ages: 6 years and up.

AFRICAN AMERICAN FIREFIGHTER MUSEUM   ☀

(213) 744-1730 / www.aaffmuseum.org   !

1401 S. Central Avenue, Los Angeles

This small, beautiful, two-story museum is in a Los Angeles neighborhood. It chronicles the history of black firefighters by honoring them and their white colleagues who pushed for integration. The walls and reference books contain photographs and stories that tell of the once-segregated station. For instance, although black and white men battled fires and fought side-by-side to save lives, they couldn't cook or eat together. African Americans even slept in beds designated "black beds." Exhibits include a fire engine, vintage fire apparatus, uniforms, boots, fire extinguishers, badges, helmets, and other mementos.

Hours: Open Tues. and Thurs., 10am - 2pm; Sun., 1pm - 4pm. Special tours can be arranged by
appointment. Closed Mon., Wed., Fri., Sat., and major holidays.

Price: Free, donations are suggested. Groups over 10 people pay a tour fee.

Ages: 5 years and up.

AIR AND SPACE EXHIBITS   ◐

(213) 744-7400 / www.californiasciencecenter.org $$$

Exposition Park, Los Angeles

This multi-story building is actually part of the CALIFORNIA SCIENCE CENTER. It's hard to miss with a United Airlines plane out front and a jet fighter perched precariously on its side!

The historic space shuttle Endeavour is a big draw and has its own display pavilion. Enter to see it and learn Endeavour's story with its twenty-five completed missions, including the first service mission to the Hubble Space Telescope and a trip to the International Space Station. Besides the Endeavour, the pavilion houses an SSME rocket engine; a Spacehab module, a kind of astronauts' workshop/extra *space* (haha!) area; a space potty with explanations (to answer the age-old questions); and the galley (i.e. kitchen) with food trays and food packages; plus videos, info panels, and items from the shuttle and more related to space and space travel. Walk-up or advanced reservations, with a specific entry time, are required to see the Endeavour and are $2 per person. Advanced reservations are required for weekends, holidays, special events and high attendance seasons.

The atmosphere inside the main building is uplifting with planes, such as a replica of the 1902 Wright Glider, a real Air Force jet, and an F-20 Tigershark, all suspended from the ceiling in mock flight. On the second floor, climb into a real police helicopter and man (or woman) the controls. To feel air lift, put on a pair of foam wings, stand in front of the wind machine, and fly. (I guess I was too heavy to get off the ground.) Press a button to launch small parachutes. On the upper level, press a button to hear the difference in heartbeats on earth and after just returning from orbit. Which beats faster? (Come to the museum and find out.) Look at your face in a mirror and see how it looks on earth. Then, look at a special mirror to see how you look in orbit, when fluids shift toward the upper body - it's not a pretty sight. Trace a pattern while looking in a mirror (it's harder than it looks) and work your muscles on an exercise bike to test the effects of muscle atrophy from prolonged space flight.

See a full-scale model of the Cassini (the real one was sent to orbit Saturn); a full-scale engineering model of the Viking Lander; three actual space capsules, including the Gemini 11 and Mercury-Redstone 2; a J47 turbo engine; a full-scale model of the Sputnik 1; a real Apollo spacesuit; and more. Look at the telescopes used to see the stars and enjoy the photos and information gathered from them.

Downstairs the Discovery Room is like a small mission control room for astronauts 7 years and under to pretend to be pilots on a shuttle or airplane, and learn about the planets and the moon. Sit at a table to read about space, put together puzzles, or "check out" (for free) a variety of discovery boxes filled with different kinds of toys and activities. One box holds packages of prepacked astronaut food to look at (not appetizing); one has astronaut-type clothes to try on; and another shows why planes have wings and it includes a glider plane. Another favorite activity is putting

together different types of small model planes and flying them in a specified area to determine which wing types and body shapes fly the fastest, or most on course. Look at the pieces of meteorites here, too. School tours are offered to enable kids to glean even more information about our universe.

A wonderful way to round out your day is to have a picnic and visit one of the other attractions in this complex - CALIFORNIA AFRICAN AMERICAN MUSEUM (pg. 102), CALIFORNIA SCIENCE CENTER (pg. 103), EXPOSITION PARK (pg. 58), IMAX THEATER (pg. 184), and NATURAL HISTORY MUSEUM OF LOS ANGELES (pg. 139).

Hours: Open daily, 10am - 5pm. Closed New Year's Day, Thanksgiving, and Christmas.
Price: Entrance to the museum is free. $2 reservation fee per person for the Endeavour. Parking is $10.
Ages: 3 years and up.

AMERICAN MILITARY MUSEUM

(626) 442-1776 / www.tankland.com
1918 N. Rosemead Boulevard, South El Monte

Attention! Over 170 pieces of equipment, representing all branches of the United States military, can be found at this outside museum. The collection contains vehicles and weapons from World War I through Desert Storm. It includes Jeeps, amphibious trucks, ambulances, helicopters, cannons, gun turrets, and thirty-ton Sherman tanks. The vehicles can be looked at, but not sat in or touched.

To the untrained eye it looks like a random compilation of old military equipment. And it is. However, some pieces are in the process of being restored, and some have been used in movies and T.V. shows. The volunteers are knowledgeable and know many of the "inside" stories about the vehicles. Pick up a booklet to learn more about the pieces of equipment here. Tip: This is an ideal setting if your kids are studying any of the wars and want to make a video, or to have a birthday party here and play Army (or Navy, or Marine, etc). Picnic tables are here, too.

Hours: Open Fri. - Sun., 10am - 4:30pm. Open at other times for group tours by appointment only. Closed on rainy days.
Price: $5 for adults; $4 for seniors and military; $3 for ages 10 - 16; $1 for ages 5 - 9; children 4 and under, and weekday groups, are free. Fridays are free to educational non-profit organizations.
Ages: 4 years and up.

ANGELS ATTIC

(310) 394-8331 / www.angelsattic.com
516 Colorado Avenue, Santa Monica

This quaint, two-story, 1895 Victorian-style house/museum is packed with collectable doll houses - over 60! The beautiful and exquisite doll houses, a lost art and playtime activity in this age of technology, are complete with wallpaper, dolls dressed in period costumes, and furnishings that fit the time period of the house. Chandeliers, tiny pieces of silverware and plates, miniature toys, and so more - such detail! Many of the houses are open or have exteriors that can be opened to be able to peer inside. For an educational slant, coming here is a fascinating way to learn social history - how architecture, interior design, clothing, and lifestyles have changed over the years.

Two of my favorites are the house designed like a shoe and one that contains intricate ivory furniture. Can't get to France? See the Versailles here in (large!) miniature. There are also several one-room, themed dioramas that hold miniatures, too, such as a bakery that's filled with tiny pastries that look good enough to eat (almost!). Although little hands may not touch, little eyes will enjoy looking, especially since most exhibits are at eye level. Upstairs are a few small rooms with doll collections and other antique toys.

If all this makes you long for a Lilliputian lifestyle, check out the small (of course) gift shop. Purchase doll house accessories, books and magazines related to collecting miniatures and dolls. Tea time, with homemade cake, cookies, and lemonade, is available here on the enclosed porch with advance reservations and an additional $8.50 per person. At Christmas time, the outside of Angels Attic is decorated and so is every doll house - truly a mini extravaganza. Don't miss Santa's Workshop in miniature, with reindeer, Santa and Mrs. Claus, and over 100 elves completing the festive scene.

Hours: Open Thurs. - Sat., 12pm - 4pm. Closed most major holidays.
Price: $8 for adults; $7 for seniors; $5 for children 11 years and under - no credit cards accepted.
Ages: 5 years and up.

ANTELOPE VALLEY INDIAN MUSEUM

(661) 946-3055 / www.avim.parks.ca.gov $
15701 Avenue 'M', Lancaster

Built into and around rock formations of the Mojave Desert, the outside of this Indian museum looks incongruously like a Swiss chalet. The inside is just as unique. Once the home of artist Howard Edward, portions of the interior (i.e., walls, ceilings, and flooring) are composed of boulders. My kids' reaction was simply "WOW!"

The first small rooms contain stone and mortar pestles, old photos, and info about the Native Americans that once lived in this area. A hallway room contains beautiful rugs; several glass-cased displays of pottery shards that were once used for money and jewelry; cradle-boards; baskets; and various items made from plants, such as yucca fiber sandals. The large main, Swiss Chalet and boulder room is lined with Kachina dolls on the upper shelves and colorfully-painted panels of the dolls on the ceiling. (The Hopi people believed that Kachina dolls brought rain.) The unusual furniture and the support beams are made from Joshua trees. Rugs, woven plates and baskets, paintings, and more pottery are also in here.

Kids love climbing up the narrow stony steps into another exhibit room, which is also carved out of rock. There are numerous glass displays cases in the walls, and several items not in cases. These collections include arrowheads, whale bone tools, shells, whale ribs, necklaces, more cradleboards, harpoons, pottery, and weapons. Read the descriptions because although most items are authentic, the designer of the exhibits made up some stories to go along with some of the artifacts - creative license! Go back down a few of the steps. Stop. Look up. You'll see Indian dioramas and recreated cave paintings.

Outside, you'll pass by a series of small cottages that were once used as guest houses. On guided tours, or at special events, there are hands-on activities for kids such as grinding corn with stone mortars and pestles, trying their hand at using a pump drill to drill holes, "sawing" with a bow drill to create smoke, and learning how to make a pine needle whisk broom. (The brooms may not have much practical use nowadays, but it's a fun and educational project.) Docents gladly explain the use of various seeds and other plant parts.

The museum is part of the California Department of Parks and Recreation. Enjoy an easy, but unshaded, quarter-mile loop trail just behind the Indian Museum. You'll walk through some desert, surrounded by mountains, and get a fantastic view of the valley below. A guidebook ($1) explains the fourteen Native American symbols on the posts along the trail.

Hours: Open Sat. - Sun., 11am - 4pm. Call about summer hours. Tours are available Thurs. by appointment.
Price: $3 for adults; ages 12 and under are free. (Cash or checks only.)
Ages: 5 years and up.

AUTOMOBILE DRIVING MUSEUM

(310) 909-0950 / www.automobiledrivingmuseum.org $
610 Lairport Street, El Segundo

The cars are the stars at this unique automobile museum. Some of the over 140 restored, rotating classic and vintage automobiles on display include Eleanor Roosevelt's limo; Joseph Stalin's Packard; the convertible Howard Hughes gave his wife (valued at 1.2 million dollars!); muscle cars; 1886 Benz Motowagon; 1999 350Z concept car; 1931 Ford Model A Roadster; 1929 Durant; 1909 Model T; 1936 red and roaring Packard Roadster; 1948 DeSoto; 1982 DeLorean DMC 12; lots of Packards; and many more. Is it *driving* you crazy to just look at cars? Here, you can see the cars up close, touch some of them, and even get inside one of them. Take a guided tour offered on the weekends if you'd like to hear their history. The docents are friendly, knowledgeable and enthusiastic.

What really makes this museum an *auto*matic favorite is that guests 10 years and older can actually take a two-mile joyride back through time in museum cars - what a classic (and classy) way to see L.A.! Check the website to see which three will be going out for a spin on any given Sunday, weather permitting. As you ride, you'll hear the back story of the cars - about the owners, how to start the car, its horsepower and what makes it so special.

There a small snack shop on-site, too, so enjoy an ice cream dessert. Tip: The L.A. Kings training center is on Nash Street, just two blocks away, where the Kings can often be found practicing during weekday mornings.

Hours: Open Tues. - Sun., 10am - 4pm. Close Mon. and holidays. Automobile rides are offered on Sun., only, with the last ride given at 3:30pm.
Price: $5 donation for adults is requested.
Ages: 5 years and up; 10 years for Sunday automobile ride.

AUTRY

(323) 667-2000 / www.theautry.org
4700 Western Heritage Way, in Griffith Park, Los Angeles

The cowboy lifestyle lassos our imagination. Bryce, my middle son, wanted to become a cowboy missionary (yes, he is special) and this museum really *spurred* on his interest, at least regarding the cowboy part of his career choice. It will also delight fans of the Old West with its complete array of paintings, clothing, tools, weapons (one of Annie Oakley's guns!), and interesting artifacts. Movie clips, videos, and movie posters throughout the museum highlight specific areas of this romanticized period. In the Spirit of Imagination Hall, a big hit is sitting on a saddle and making riding motions to become part of an old western movie showing on a screen behind the rider. My kids particularly enjoyed the hands-on children's Discovery Gallery, set up like the home and workplace of the Sees, a Chinese American family. Visit their parlor and read some books, or listen to an old-fashioned radio. Pretend to prepare a meal in the realistic mini kitchen. Visit the Sees' antique store; "cook" up some Chinese food at a recreated portion of a real restaurant, Dragon's Den; and try on Chinese clothing. The entire museum is interesting and wheelchair/stroller-friendly, but you do have to keep your kids corralled, as most of the exhibits are not touchable ones.

Don't be a fool - try your hand at gold panning at the outdoor, recreated miner's panning area. It's available every weekend, weather permitting, from 11am to 3pm and is free with museum admission. It's available daily in the summer. Monthly craft programs and two tours a month geared specifically for families that are interactive with storytelling, games, and even sing alongs, are also offered. Ask about the museum's weekly summer camps for kids and the National Day of the Cowboy and Cowgirl on the last Saturday in July with lots of Old West activities. The Autry also offers numerous outstanding programs throughout the year, even sleepovers. A plethora of age-appropriate, guided tours for school groups (and scout groups) are a bargain for the insider information dispensed and the price - $2 per person! Tour topics include role playing of Plains Indians, cowboys, and cowgirls; the CA Gold Rush with gold panning; animals of the West; exploring western lands and cultures; and more. Teachers - download lesson plans before your visit.

At the on-site Crossroads West cafe try frybread tacos, buffalo burgers, or red corn chicken tortilla soup, or a variety of salads and sandwiches. A children's menu is available. It is open Tues. - Fri., 9am - 4pm; Sat. - Sun., 9am - 5pm. There is also a wonderful, large, grassy area for picnicking, too. Note that this museum is part of the Autry National Center. See GRIFFITH PARK (pg. 62) for more things to do and see in the immediate area.

Hours: Open Tues. - Fri., (and certain Mon. holidays), 10am - 4pm; Sat. - Sun., 10am - 5pm. On Thurs. in July and August the museum is open until 8pm. Closed most Mon., 4th of July, Labor Day, Thanksgiving, and Christmas.

Price: $10 for adults; $6 for seniors and ages 13 - 18; $4 for ages 3 - 12; children 2 and under are free. Prices may vary for special events and theatrical programs. Admission is free for active military, veterans, peace officers, and park rangers with ID. Certain discounts available through AAA. Admission is free on the second Tues. of each month, plus New Year's Day, Martin Luther King, Jr. Day and Presidents' Day. See page xi for info on the Bank of America free weekend program.

Ages: 4 years and up.

BANNING MUSEUM

(310) 548-7777 / www.banningmuseum.org
401 E. M Street, Wilmington

This huge Victorian museum, where the founder of Wilmington once lived, is reflective of the Banning family lifestyle in the 1800's. The one-hour guided tours are best suited for older children as there is much to see, but not to touch. First, walk through the photo gallery, past a display of brilliant cut glass, and into the house where each of the seventeen rooms are beautifully decorated with period furniture and eclectic art work. (Note: The house is completely decked out at Christmas time and looks particularly splendid.) Check out the hoof inkwell in the General's office. Get the kids involved with the tour by asking them questions like, "What's missing from this office that modern offices have?" (Answer - a computer, a fax machine, etc. Surprisingly, a copy machine *is* here.) The parlor doubled as a music room and contains a piano, violin, and small organ as well as an unusual-looking chair made out of buffalo hide and horns. Other rooms of interest are the children's nursery; the bedrooms - one has a unique hat rack made of antlers, while another has a stepping stool that is actually a commode; and the kitchen with its potbellied stove and all of its gadgets. (Obviously some things never change.) Request to see the Stagecoach Barn, a fully outfitted, nineteenth-century working barn with real stagecoaches. Ask your children if they can figure out how some of the

tools were used.

School groups are given two-plus-hour tours, one geared for third graders and one for fourth, that include attending class in the one-room schoolhouse which has old-fashioned desks, slates, and McGuffy primers. Kids don an apron or ascot, get a math or English lesson from that time period, learn about family living from this era, and go out for recess to play games of yesteryear. Ask about Heritage Week in May, when special school programs and a free public weekend event encourage visitors to partake in activities from the 1880's. Also see the Calendar section in the back of this book for the variety of seasonal events hosted here throughout the year.

The museum is situated in the middle of a pretty, twenty-acre park that has a small playground, a few picnic tables, a rose garden, eucalyptus trees, giant bamboo trees, and grassy areas.

Hours: Tours are given Tues. - Thurs. at 12:30pm, 1:30pm, and 2:30pm; Sat. - Sun. at 12:30pm, 1:30pm, 2:30pm, and 3:30pm. Closed on national holidays.
Price: $5 per adult; $1 for children 11 and under.
Ages: 7 years and up.

BORAX VISITOR CENTER

(760) 762-7588 or (760) 762-7432 / www.borax.com
Borax Road, Boron

Borax isn't something that my family normally spends a lot of time thinking about. However, visiting this center made us realize how widely this mineral is used. As you drive past the active mine (and past the sign that states the speed limit is 37½ mph, which is a little tricky to actually do), you'll see what appears to be a little city, complete with buildings, trucks, and Goliath-type machines used to extract and process the borax. This area supplies nearly half the global need for the mineral!

Up the hill is a state-of-the-art visitors center. Outside are original twenty mule team wagons, with harnessed mule statues, that were once used to haul the ore over 165 miles through desert and rocky terrain. Inside is a large sample of kernite, a type of borate ore, plus a pictorial time line of the Borax Company, and an exhibit that shows the process of ore being transformed (crushed, actually) into fine dust. The Borax at Home display shows the mining and geology processing of raw ore into everyday finished products such as glass, ceramic glazes, detergent, shaving creams, and plant fertilizer. For products closer to a child's heart, the display features footballs, Play Doh™, and nail polish. Borax is also added to commodities to make them sparkle, including toothpaste and fireworks.

An adjacent room shows continuously running videos of Borax commercials starring Ronald Reagan, Dale Robertson, Clint Eastwood, and others. A ten-minute video titled *The World of Borax* gives a history of the mining process. An all-glass wall shows an unobstructed panorama of the entire open pit mine. High-powered microscopes are available for closer inspection of borax and other in-house crystals. Free, organized school tours of the center are given, and fun supplemental materials are available to aid learning. Don't forget to stop off at the TWENTY MULE TEAM MUSEUM (pg. 154) and the adjacent SAXON AEROSPACE MUSEUM (pg. 150), which are just down the road.

Hours: Open daily, 9am - 5pm, excluding major holidays and during inclement weather.
Price: $3 per vehicle.
Ages: 4 years and up.

CALIFORNIA AFRICAN AMERICAN MUSEUM

(213) 744-7432 / www.caamuseum.org
600 State Drive, at Exposition Park, Los Angeles

This museum portrays the works of African-American artists documenting the African-American experience in this country. The two large, permanent galleries contain an array of wood-carved masks and headdresses (one looks like a baby crocodile), plus statues, a room showcasing famous African Americans, and more works of art. We particularly enjoyed the lenticular pictures in the heritage section which change images as you walk by. The exhibits in the rotating galleries, which could be painting, sculptures, etc., are equally interesting to people of all races. See the nearby AIR AND SPACE EXHIBITS (pg. 98), CALIFORNIA SCIENCE CENTER (pg. 103), EXPOSITION PARK (pg. 58), IMAX THEATER (pg. 184), and NATURAL HISTORY MUSEUM OF LOS ANGELES (pg. 139).

Hours: Open Tues., - Sat., 10am - 5pm; Sun., 11am - 5pm. Closed Mon., New Year's Day, Memorial Day, Thanksgiving, and Christmas.
Price: Free. Parking costs $10.
Ages: 5 years and up.

CALIFORNIA HERITAGE MUSEUM

(310) 392-8537 / www.californiaheritagemuseum.org

2612 Main Street, Santa Monica

Inside this two-story house/museum, originally built in 1894, the downstairs living room is cozy and rustic-looking. The dining room atmosphere fluctuates, depending on the current exhibit, so it could be set with fine china, or pottery, etc. The restored kitchen is the one Merle Norman originally used to cook-up her cosmetic recipes. (From such humble beginnings . . .) Both the downstairs and upstairs are redecorated each time a new exhibit is installed. The guided tour illuminates the heritage and nuances in the exhibit pieces. Often the exhibitions are aimed at appealing to the younger generation. Past themes have focused on cowboys; guitars from all over the world; children's books and illustrations; and model trains. Call for information on the current display.

Outside, a grassy lawn welcomes picnickers. Note that several gourmet food trucks gather here on Tuesday from 5:30pm to 9:30pm (the museum is not open then) for outdoor family dinner time and that a Farmer's Market is held on the grounds on Sundays.

Hours: Open Wed. - Sun., 11am - 4pm. Closed major holidays.

Price: $8 for adults; $5 for seniors and students; children 11 and under are free.

Ages: 5 years and up.

CALIFORNIA SCIENCE CENTER

(323) SCIENCE (724-3623) or (213) 744-7400 / www.californiasciencecenter.org

700 State Drive, Exposition Park, Los Angeles

Hanging from a very high ceiling that connects the IMAX Theater to the Science Center are hundreds of various-sized gold balls dangling on wires: it's an intriguing mobile. The first floor contains the museum store, which has an extensive selection of science experiments, kits, books, and lots more. It also has a McDonald's (which gets extremely busy during lunch hours), and the less-crowded Rose Garden Cafe, with a Taco Bell Express, eatery.

The second floor is a favorite. The west wing, titled World of Life, is packed with exhibits that pertain to human and animal lives. Look closely at cells via a microscope and a video. Crank a knob to watch how a model's digestive system unravels to stretch over eighteen feet and listen to the sounds we make when digesting food. Watch a movie of an actual heart transplant as it is laser-beamed onto a statue patient. Drive a simulator car to experience the difference in driving sober and driving drunk. See preserved fetuses in jars ranging from a few weeks old to nine months. View a movie on conception (suitable for older children). Sit on a dear, no-butts-about-it chair filled with over 200 cigarettes and watch a film clip on lung cancer. Press buttons to match recorded heartbeats to real hearts that are on display, from the huge elephant's to the medium-sized cow's to the tiny mouse's. Look at the real brains of a human, monkey, and a rat. Learn about the basic needs of plants and animals through other interactive displays. Look at the chick hatchery and maybe you'll get to see chicks break out of their eggs. Tess, the reclining, fifty-foot human figure, comes to "life" in a well-done, fifteen-minute presentation in the BodyWorks room. A large movie screen above her head stars a cartoon character who helps Tess explain how her body parts work together to keep her system in balance (i.e., homeostasis). Periodically, her muscles, organs, and circulatory system are illuminated by fiber optics. An adjacent Discovery Room allows younger children to put on puppet shows and look at small live animals such as frogs, spiders, lizard, and a boa constrictor. Use the Discovery Boxes that are filled with creative and educational toys, games, musical instruments, and more.

Another exhibit hall here is the massive Ecosystems, with eight different recreated environments or zones, each one containing several hands-on experiments that pertain to that particular zone. The following are some highlights: First walk through a long room with a video screen on the walls that immerse you in different environments - under the sea, in a city, etc. In the Island Zone room shoot a ping pong ball toward the small center "island" to show how birds, insects, and the wind carry plant and animal life to populate islands. The room also contains live fish native only to Hawaii; a display case with skulls, insects, and more items native to islands; and an interactive exhibit to see how different kinds of beaks enable birds to eat various foods. In Extreme Zone go outside to Rocky Shore where a machine creates coastal waves, a touch tank has sea stars and anemones, and you can behave like a barnacle by reaching your gloved hand into a large glass box and trying to grab food. Extreme Zone also features Poles with a wall of real ice, polar bear fur, and a time line for visitors to create using wood's growth rings. The actually hot Desert room has dioramas with rocks and cactus, an infrared camera to find endothermic animals, mini flash floods, and bats in the small caves. Test an ROV at Deep Sea Vents and learn about the animals that survive here. The Global Zone stars a giant globe with various projections on it that show how climate and temperature affect conditions all over the

world. I know decay is a part of life (and death), but the Rot Room is gross with its live maggots, a wheel to spin to see decomposition (of strawberries, a rabbit, and more), and log with live bugs (in display cases). The cartoonishly-decorated Family Discovery Room is ideal for ages 7 and under (and I think its apropo that kids have their own zone!) with its living room, kitchen, and bedroom (geared for toddlers) filled with furniture, toys, books, and games that are educationally oriented (and fun). There is also an outdoor area here with picnic tables and a gardening plot for kids to work. The adjacent River Zone has interactive water/river elements, river fish, and a whole wall made of silver discs that flow and ripple like water when air from the fan you turn on hits them. My favorite room is the Kelp Forest with several tanks of live sea animals, a walk-through tunnel of fish (that swim overhead), and a capacious kelp forest tank with a school of fish, leopard sharks, Garibaldi, and bat rays. I also like watching the moon jellies.

The east wing, or Creative World, features communication exhibits. Inside the large, Creative World room, visitors can play virtual volleyball; whisper into a parabolic dish and have someone across the room hear them; type in telephone or television messages that are then relayed by satellite; play air drums and digitize the sound; construct buildings using scale model parts and then subject them to the shake, rattle, and roll of an earthquake via a shake table; build archways using Styrofoam blocks to learn about the strength of compression; look through a periscope; and more. There are several large and small screen videos in both the east and west wings that offer enticing and entertaining visual bits of information, although they are often not accompanied by written or verbal data.

Part of the third floor is a continuation of Creative World, focusing on transportation. Direct fans to blow wind to move model sailboats, and to race solar-paneled cars in the exhibits here. The Discovery Room has a play house that resembles a city street with several rooms such as the Hardware Store so kids can "purchase" supplies and build structures using tools and gadgets, and - "Quiet on the set!" - a TV Studio with costumes, puppets and a camera. The Discovery Boxes have more games and toys to use. Computers for younger kids incorporate more learning in the Tech Lab.

The west room, the Weingart Gallery, features wonderful, usually hands-on, special rotating exhibits. One exhibit focused on geography, so kids learned about people, customs, plants, and unique geological formations from all over the world, via interactive displays. Another was simply *Marvel*ous - it was the Marvel Super Heroes exhibit with artwork, hands-on attempts at super hero powers (such as testing the strength of spider webs against a strong, man-made material), and lots to do with heroes and villains. More geared for adults was Pompeii: The Exhibition which features over 150 excavated artifacts from this ancient Roman city, including marble statues, Gladiator helmets and shin guards, coins, and more, and a shaking reenactment of the volcano that covered the city and its inhabitants.

Ever want to join the circus and try the high-wire act? Here's your chance. Pedal a weighted bike across a cable wire that is forty feet above the ground. Although you're strapped in and safety netting is in place, it is still a slightly scary venture, especially when the staff person tilts the bike before pushing it across the cable wire! ($2) Other interactive exhibits in the science court are a motion simulator ride with themes from the Air and Space Exhibits ($4.50), and "Cliff Climb," a twenty-three-feet high rock climbing wall. ($3.50) Height requirements apply. An attraction pass is $7 for all three activities.

Ask about the numerous special classes and programs offered for children and adults. For instance, audience-participatory shows, including *Science Comes Alive*, are presented for various age groups. Call the education department at (213) 744-7444 for a schedule of other programs and for more information. Check the museum's calendar for special exhibits that might have a cost. The Titanic and Goose Bumps: The Science of Fear exhibits were outstanding!

Tips: 1) School kids come in busloads on weekday mornings, so several exhibits require waiting in line to view or use during these peak hours. Therefore, consider either arriving early to watch an IMAX movie and explore the grounds and other nearby museums first, or come here in the early afternoon. 2) Avoid restaurant lunch lines by packing a lunch. There are several shaded grassy areas for picnicking. 3) Locker rentals are available on the first floor. Note: The center is stroller/wheelchair accessible. Check out the nearby AIR AND SPACE EXHIBITS (pg. 98), which is actually part of the Science Center, CALIFORNIA AFRICAN AMERICAN MUSEUM (pg. 102), IMAX THEATER (pg. 184), and NATURAL HISTORY MUSEUM OF LOS ANGELES (pg. 139).

Hours: Open daily, 10am - 5pm. Closed New Year's Day, Thanksgiving, and Christmas.
Price: Free. Note that some special exhibits have a fee. For instance, Pompeii was $19.75 for adults; $12.75 for ages 4 - 12. Parking is $10 per vehicle. Membership here is a great deal for $65 as it includes four IMAX tickets, two parking vouchers, four high-wire bike rides or diff climbs, discounts to on-site activities and shopping, and free admission to more than 300 other science centers and museums nationwide. See page xi for info on ASTC reciprocal museum memberships.
Ages: 3 years and up.

COLUMBIA MEMORIAL SPACE CENTER

(562) 231-1200 / www.columbiaspacescience.org
12400 Clark Avenue, Downey

Ignite a desire to reach for the stars within your child by visiting this unique space center. Rich in aerospace history, including the site of the development of the first cruise missile in the 50's and the engineering and building of the Apollo space capsules, this former Boeing/NASA development site is now, fittingly, the home of an official national memorial to the Space Shuttle *Columbia* with an emphasis on engaging kid's hands and minds in the present and future of space exploration.

Outside is the Apollo Boiler Plate 12, an unmanned test vehicle. In the lobby, an 18' by 18' photo mosaic of the crew and shuttle of the *Columbia* moves visitors to learn about their lives, the mission, and the tragedy. Another wall shows a visual and informational time line of the history of Downey and the city's relationship with the aerospace industry. The rotating display in the storyteller's showcase contains photos and artifacts regarding astronauts and other people in the field, as well as space-related technology, instruments, and perhaps a model rocket. The orbital velocity exhibit is a fancy name for an exhibit where kids gently throw marbles, which represent planets and space debris, and watch as they spin around a vortex (demonstrating orbit) and drop into the center hole. The downstairs gallery also has a real space capsule, a flight simulator with real controls, a full mock up of the shuttle, a paper airplane make and launch station, an area for traveling exhibits, and a model plane in a cage that visitors can fly and steer using the wheel and the throttle.

Sign up to use the robotics lab where fourteen computers interface with fourteen, nine inch high, or so, robots in the Lego Mindstorm "game". Participants program their robot to walk on a tabletop that represents the surface of Mars and to rescue items, research a project, or whatever else they program it to do - both challenging and fun.

The upstairs gallery wall murals depict the space station, views from the Hubble telescope, our solar system, people involved in the space program, and more. A small area for ages 6 and under has a crawl tunnel, a (fake) Mars rock to play on, and a mini flight simulator to sit at the controls and blast away to parts unknown. An earth exhibit is a spherical video projector with touch screen panels that shows the view of the earth from the moon, planets, or other points in space. Step on a scale to find out how much you would weigh on certain planets or the moon. Try on a spacesuit. Use a touch screen to illuminate and animate planets and moons. At another exhibit match and piece together large photo cubes to form a from-space view of the earth - or is it Mars? The drop tower here allows guests to drop objects, at specified times, to the landing pad below, then reengineer the object so it won't break.

The apogee of the center is the Challenger Learning Center with three mission simulations, set up for field trips and school classes for 5th graders and up, for $3 per person with a minimum of fifteen students. Enter the Mission Control room, which looks like the real deal, and become immediately immersed in space travel, made more real with interactive screens. The situation room has medical, research, and scientific elements. Participants in both rooms interact with each other via camera and computer collaboration, working together to solve problems and deal with situations that arise on the space station and during space travel. In this two-hour program students, who switch rooms midway through their session so all have the opportunity to be mission controllers and spacecraft astronauts, learn teamwork and practical math and science applications in an unforgettable, interactive way.

Columbia Memorial Space Center also offers a stellar array of day camps and programs for all ages regarding potential careers in aerospace, geographic information systems, principles of flight, understanding our solar system, and so much more.

Hours: Open Tues. - Sat., 10am - 5pm. Closed Sun., Mon. and all major holidays.
Price: $5 per person; children 3 and under are free. Groups, with reservations, of 10 or more are $3 per person. See page xi for info on ASTC reciprocal museum memberships.
Ages: 5 years and up.

THE DOCTORS' HOUSE MUSEUM

(818) 548-2147 / www.glendalehistorical.org/doctors.html
1601 W. Mountain Street, Glendale

Tour through this delightfully restored, Queen Anne Eastlake-style home that was once owned by four doctors, in succession. (Hence the name.) Docents point out and discuss the doctors' office with its instruments and vials, period furniture from the early 1900's, clothing, and other artifacts from the Victorian time period. One-hour, free, school tours, for third graders and above, are given during the week. In addition to the house tour, students also play outdoor Victorian games. Ask about special functions throughout the year, such as the candlelight tour in December.

Just outside the house is an expansive green lawn and a gazebo. A Japanese tea garden, complete with a waterfall, koi, and a Japanese tea house to peek into is also on the grounds. The Doctors' House Museum and the adjacent beautiful Glendale Library are located in BRAND PARK (pg. 49).

Hours: Open Sun., 2pm - 4pm, except major holidays, inclement weather, and the month of July.
Price: The museum is $2 for adults; ages 16 and under are free.
Ages: 6 years and up.

DOMINGUEZ RANCHO ADOBE MUSEUM

(310) 603-0088 / www.dominguezrancho.org
18127 S. Alameda Street, Compton

Site of the First Spanish land grant in California by King Carlos III in 1784, of a skirmish in the Mexican-American War, and of an oil discovery in 1921, this site and rancho have a rich history. Walk through the sprawling and beautifully-restored adobe to see the family dining room, with the table set for a meal; the simply furnished yet stylish bedrooms - make sure to look at the wood bed frame that uses rawhide to hold the straw mattress and Manuel Dominguez's more elegant bed with a canopy; the parlour with a piano and phonograph; the living room with its elegant furniture; the display room exhibiting photographs in glass and wood cabinets; the room containing intricately-carved wood furniture; and the outside kitchen with big vats. Other artifacts around the Rancho include hides, saddles, branding irons, a spinning wheel, and a replica of an ox-driven carreta used during the rancho period.

The spacious grounds are lovely with rose gardens and pathways in the front and lots of grass areas with mature trees and picnic tables. On the guided tour you'll learn, among other interesting facts, about the cattle once raised here for hide, beef, and tallow, as well as how tallow was processed. School tours incorporate many hands-on activities to allow students to really experience history and what they experience, they remember. Call or look online for all of the special events and programs such as Living History Night, Adobe Brick Making, arts and craft days, and garden tours.

Hours: Guided tours are offered Wed., Sat., and Sun. and the first Thurs. and Fri. at 1pm, 2pm, and 3pm. Call to arrange a school or group tour for at least ten people or more.
Price: Free
Ages: 6 years and up.

THE DRUM BARRACKS CIVIL WAR MUSEUM

(310) 548-7509 / www.drumbarracks.org
1052 Banning Boulevard, Wilmington

The year is 1861 and the Civil War has broken out. Although most of the fighting was done in the east, troops from Camp Drum, California, fought on the Union side. Your forty-five-minute tour of the medium-sized barracks/house/museum starts in the library research room. (This is the last remaining original Civil War era military facility in the L.A. area.) A six-minute video tells the history of Camp Drum through reenactments, with a costumed character narrating. Apparently, a few good ghosts from the Civil War still hang out here. Needless to say, my kids heard "ghostly" noises throughout the rest of our visit.

The parlor room is where the officers entertained. Besides period furniture and a few pianos, it also has a stereoscope, which is an early Viewmaster™, to look through. Q: Why didn't people smile for photographs back then? A: Many people had bad teeth, plus it took a long time to actually take a picture.

The hallway shows a picture of the Camel Corps. which was a regiment that actually rode camels. It also has a flag from an 1863 battlefield - have your kids count the stars (states). Upstairs, the armory room has a few original weapons, like a musket and some swords. A room with rotating exhibits has displayed a hospital room with beds, old medical instruments, and a lifelike mannequin of a wounded soldier; a quarter master's quarters; and more. The officer's bedroom has furniture, a pump organ, personal effects, and old-fashioned clothing. Q: Why did women usually wear brown wedding dresses? A: You'll have to take the tour to find out!

Hours: Tours are given Tues. - Thurs. at 10am and 11:30am; Sat. - Sun, 11:30am and 1pm.
Price: $5 for adults; students and children 11 and under are free.
Ages: 5 years and up.

EL MONTE HISTORICAL MUSEUM

(626) 580-2232 / www.ci.el-monte.ca.us
3150 N. Tyler Avenue, El Monte

A visit to this adobe-style museum offers fascinating glimpses into the history of the United States, as well as the

history of the pioneers of El Monte. There is plenty to see and learn to keep young people's interest peaked, even though no touching is allowed. Items in the numerous glass displays are labeled, making it easy to self-tour. However, I highly recommend taking a guided tour, given for groups of ten or more people, so your family, or school group, doesn't miss out on the many details and explanations of the exhibits.

My kids were captivated by the hallway showcasing Gay's Lion Farm, which was a local training ground in the 1920's for lions used in motion pictures. The photos depict the large cats interacting with people in various circus-type acts. There are also several adorable shots of lion cubs. A lion's tail and teeth are on display, too. The Heritage Room, toward the back, looks like an old-fashioned living room with antique furniture and a piano, plus cases of glassware, ladies' boots, and clothing. The walls are lined with pictures of walnut growers and other first-residents of El Monte.

The Pioneer Room has wonderful collections of typewriters, lamps/lanterns, dolls, toys, books, bells, quilts, army medals, and Bibles. It also contains ornate swords, a flag (with two bullet holes in it) from the battlefield at Gettysburg, a piece of the Berlin wall, George Washington's lantern, and an actual letter written by the Father of our Country who, by the way, had nice handwriting! The Frontier Room is equally interesting with early-day policeman and fireman hats, police badges and guns, a 1911 Model T, a wall of old tools, early Native American artifacts, and a recreated old-time law enforcement office.

The huge Lexington Room is subdivided into smaller, themed "rooms" such as a turn-of-the-century schoolroom with desks, maps, and schoolwork; an old-time general store filled with shelves of merchandise; a barber shop with a chair; a music shop with ukuleles, violins, a Victrola, and more; and a dressmaker's shop with beautiful dresses, sewing machines, elegant hair combs, and beaded handbags. Most of the rooms also have period-dressed mannequins. This section of the museum also contains recreated rooms, the type that would have been found in a house of the early 1900's - a parlor, bedroom, kitchen, and library. Each room is fully furnished and complete to the smallest detail. The El Monte Historic Museum, with a plaque that commemorates it as "the end of the Santa Fe Trail," offers a window to the world!

For further study, or just for the joy of reading, the El Monte Public Library is only a few buildings down. Directly across the street from the museum is a park. This pleasant corner park offers plenty of picnic tables and shady oak trees, plus a few slides and some metal transportation vehicles to climb on.

Hours: Open Tues. - Fri., 10am - 4pm. Open on Sat. by appointment and during the week for school tours. Closed Sun., Mon., Sat., and holidays.
Price: Free
Ages: 5 years and up.

EL PUEBLO DE LOS ANGELES HISTORICAL MONUMENT / CHINESE AMERICAN MUSEUM / OLVERA STREET
125 Paseo de la Plaza #400, Los Angeles $$$
See this entry in the Potpourri section of the book (pg. 168) for details about the museums here.

FASHION INSTITUTE OF DESIGN & MERCHANDISING MUSEUM & GALLERIES
(213) 632-5821or (213) 624-1200 / www.fidm.edu $$
919 S. Grand Avenue, Los Angeles

Project Runway and other shows have helped promote the world of fashion and design to the average person. You will definitely notice a difference in the very trendy way the students on this campus dress versus other downtowners! The museum here showcases two major (and popular) exhibits a year that are particularly interesting to kids - The Art of Motion Picture Costume Design (usually mid-February through mid-April) and The Outstanding Art of Television Costume Design. These exhibits feature over 120 costumes (headdresses and all) from current Academy Award-nominated films (about twenty-five films are represented) and Emmy Award-nominated television shows, respectively. Do you recognize the costumes? Which ones do you think are winners? The galleries also include traveling exhibits (a past one was a tribute to Barbie), FIDM's student's work, and costumes from the thousands of pieces from the permanent collection from international couture, theater, and film. The galleries are closed in between exhibits. Upstairs is a tiny exhibit gallery with rotating exhibits - perfume bottles, period shoes and accessories, etc.

Look into the museum gift store that offers unique accessories and gifts for sale, and especially check out the adjacent Scholarship Store. That small store sells a great array (and often only one-of-a-kind) of new clothing (from evening dresses to t-shirts and jeans), jewelry, fabric and accessories all donated by top fashion companies and by students for sale at a fraction of the "real" cost - really.

In front of the campus is Grand Hope Park, a lovely sprawl of green grass and trees, benches, statues, a pavilion, and a playground with slides, bridges, swing, poles and extra large animals to sit and rock back and forth on. See DOWNTOWN LOS ANGELES / GRAND PARK (pg. 167) for information on Grand Park (a different Grand Park) and all the other places to go within this fairly immediate area.

Hours: Open Tues. - Sat., 10am - 5pm. Closed Sun., Mon., and holidays.
Price: Free. Parking costs about $6.
Ages: 7 years and up.

FLIGHT PATH LEARNING CENTER

(424) 646-7284 / www.flightpath.us

6661 West Imperial Highway, Los Angeles

Located right next to LAX, this commodious and unique museum displays the history (and future) Los Angeles Airport has played regarding flight, airlines, and even movies. The ample rooms hold pictures, murals, information panels, and memorabilia regarding flying, pilots, and airplanes.

Walk into the museum past a display of old luggage and the front end of a plane. Windows take up most of the central room which looks out onto the terminals and airspace so visitors can watch planes take off. You can even sit in airplane seats to do so. You can also listen to the radio control tower being transmitted in here. Exhibits in this room include the bright blue, eight-foot Stinson Model U used in the movie *Indiana Jones*; hanging model airplanes; goggles and a leather flying cap worn during WWI; flight schedules; navigational aids; and a glass display of cups, plates, and other items used on board a plane.

One room is devoted to the changing styles of flight attendant uniforms from the short skirts of the sixties to polyester to Hawaiian-themed ones - how styles have changed! In the hallways and in the corner of rooms, several airlines, such as Pan Am and TWA, are represented with a grouping of uniforms, model planes, and commemorative items. Be sure to check out the Flying Tigers gallery. The large conference room has several flight simulators - computers, foot pedals, and cockpit wheels - used for teaching and education. There is a research library available, too.

Visitors can board a 1935 DC-3 Spirit of Seventy Six plane and go up (walking at a tilt) to the cockpit area and take control, so to speak.

Groups are offered guided tours of the facility often given by retired pilots. Included in the school tours is a police dog demonstration (the kennel is right next door) where the dogs show how they sniff for drugs and bombs, and a fire truck demonstration where the highlight is having the kids come outside and watch the water cannon blast into the air. Ask about the numerous special programs offered here, too.

Hours: Open Tues. - Sat., 10am - 3pm. Closed Mon., Sun., and major holidays.
Price: Free
Ages: 6 years and up.

FOLK MUSIC CENTER AND MUSEUM

(909) 624-2928 / www.folkmusiccenter.com

220 Yale Avenue, Claremont

"We pluck dulcimers, not chickens" is the true, but quirky motto for the Folk Music Center. The shop, here since the 1950's, has an incredible variety of instruments - hundreds of them - from around the world for sale and in its small museum. Browse the store for banjos, guitars (there's a wall full of them), chimes, drums, gongs, sitars, percussion instruments, musical toys, and an assortment of ethnic instruments. The adjacent museum room has shelves and shelves of rare and antique musical instruments and artifacts from various cultures across the globe.

Informal, but informative, hour-long tours/field trips are tailored for whatever age group visits - kids or adults. The folk music educator shares the history of specific instruments and the culture of the people playing them, and then demonstrates their sounds. Listen to the call of the Tibetan Temple Horn (which is a very long instrument!). Hear the call of the sea via a conch shell. And check out the size of the giant harmonica. Then, a mini jam session takes place and visitors are encouraged to clap and sing along. So, take *note:* This museum and tour can help fine *tune* your kids' musical appreciation. The minimum number of people for a tour is ten; the maximum is about seventy.

Hours: The store is open Tues. - Sat., 10am - 6pm; Sun., 11am - 4pm. Closed Mon. and major holidays. Tours are offered, by reservation only, on Wed. at 10:15am.
Price: Free. Tours are free as well.
Ages: 5 years and up.

FORT MACARTHUR MUSEUM - ANGEL'S GATE PARK

(310) 548-2631- museum; (310) 548-7705 - Angels Gate Park / www.ftmac.org

3601 S. Gaffey Street, San Pedro

This concrete World War II coastal defense battery building really fires up kids' imaginations as they walk the grounds and tour the few open concrete rooms that contain mines, gun casings, uniforms, pictures, newspaper clippings, a gun tube, a twenty-two-foot-long rammer, a missile, GM-12 generator set, and other war memorabilia. Another set of rooms includes one filled with World War II information and the mess hall. The communication display room holds numerous restored radio equipment including WWII radio sets used on B-17 and B-24 Bombers, squad radios, transmitters, a Lane Victory radio room, and more. A sixteen-minute video shows recoil guns shooting, as well as the history of this museum. Peek into the small soldier's barracks displaying typical army articles.

Talking through the speaking tube system can keep kids busy for a time, as one person speaks through one end while someone else tries to find the receiving end. Don't forget to take the steps up to the top of the defense building used by lookouts with guns to watch for incoming, attacking ships. Note: Check the Calendar entry for Old Fort MacArthur Days war reenactments (pg.) and ask about other events, such as "living history" days. Ask to take a guided tour if you're interested in learning more about this site and about WWII and / or take a school group here on a fascinating trip through time.

Just east of the museum, on a hill in Angels Gate Park, sits the seventeen-ton Korean Friendship Bell set in a traditional, Korean-style pagoda. Let the kids run loose to enjoy the grassy knolls. There is a small playground here and a basketball court, and since it's a fairly treeless area, it's also ideal for kite flying. On a clear day the coastal view is gorgeous, and you can see Catalina Island. Note that the MARINE MAMMAL CARE CENTER (pg. 222) is just around the corner.

Hours: Open Tues, Thurs., Sat. - Sun., and holidays, noon - 5pm. Docent tours are offered by appointment. The park is open daily, sunrise - 6pm.

Price: Free. Suggested donations are $3 for adults; $1 for ages 12 and under.

Ages: 3 years and up.

THE GAMBLE HOUSE

(626) 793-3334 / www.gamblehouse.org

4 Westmoreland Place, Pasadena

Wood, and the way various types are crafted and blended, is the primary focus of the Gamble House. Teak, maple, cedar, redwood, and oak were used in the furniture, cabinetry, paneling, carvings, and exterior walls in a way that represents the best of the Arts and Crafts movement from the turn-of-the-century. Not that kids care about these details, but they are impressed by the natural beauty of the rooms, original furnishings, and terraces. A one-hour guided tour explains the history of the house, the era in which it was built, and the architecture's harmonious use of wood and natural light in the home in accord with its environmental surroundings. Highlights, besides the use of wood, include the appealing open porches (used as sleeping porches), and the Tiffany glass throughout. Note: Only the first floor of the house is stroller/wheelchair accessible. If you don't feel like you've seen it all, you haven't, but you can on a more leisurely, two-hour+ tour called Behind the Velvet Ropes. There are other special focus tours available, as well.

The outside grounds are classy looking, with beautiful landscaping, rolling green lawns, and a brick walkway and driveway. It's so nice here that mini-tours, called Brown-Bag, are offered on Tuesdays. This consists of a twenty-minute tour and the opportunity to just enjoy the grounds while enjoying a picnic lunch (that you supply) for a few hours.

Hours: Open Tues. for Brown-Bag from 11:30am - 1:30pm; mini-tours given at 12:15pm and 12:45pm. Open for regular tours, which leave every 15 min., Thurs. - Sun., noon - 3pm (last tour), although ticket sales begin at 10am Thur. - Sat. and at 11:30am on Sun. It's closed on national holidays.

Price: Brown-Bag Tues. tours are $8 per person in advance; $7 in person. Regular tours are $13.75 in advance for adults, $12.50 on the day-of; $11 - $10 for seniors and students with ID; children 12 and under are free.

Ages: 6 years and up.

GEORGE C. PAGE MUSEUM / LA BREA TAR PITS

(323) 934-PAGE (7243); (323) 857-6300 / www.tarpits.org

5801 Wilshire Boulevard, Los Angeles

Kids boning up on becoming paleontologists will really dig this place. First, take them to see the fifteen-minute movie, *Treasures of the Tar Pits*. It gives an interesting overview and explains that the fossils they'll see in the museum have been excavated from the pits, just outside. Another theater shows a continuously playing video called *Behind the Scenes*, highlighting the work that the public generally doesn't have access to see. Forewarn your kids that dinosaurs had been extinct for many years before the tar pit entrapments occurred, so there isn't anything here regarding dinosaurs.

The George C. Page Museum has over thirty different exhibits including several skeletons in life-like poses of sabertooths (what fangs!), a giant ground sloth, mastodons, extinct birds, and a Columbian mammoth (these animals were absolutely gigantic). Besides murals and dioramas, the walls are filled with fossils behind glass - skulls, jaws, femurs, claws, and more - of bison, deer, condors and other birds, etc. One wall contains over 400 dire wolf skulls found on the grounds. An animated model of a young mammoth startled me. Visitors can pit their strength against the force of asphalt by pulling on glass enclosed cylinders stuck in the sticky stuff. The futility of this effort makes it easier to understand why animals, of any size, couldn't escape the tar pits. And check out the sabertooth hologram, which changes from skeleton to "fleshed out" creature, and back.

 Observe through the huge, semicircle of windows a working paleontologist's laboratory, fittingly called the Fishbowl Lab, and the on-going process of cleaning, studying, and cataloging newly excavated fossils. When Kellan, my oldest son, was younger, he wanted to become a *bone*afide paleontologist until he saw how tedious the work can be. Toward the exit is a room with a pictoral and informational time line regarding the theory of evolution for animals. Walk through the lovely atrium in the center of the museum filled with plants and a pond with koi. Pick up a pencil scavenger hunt at the front desk to get the kids more involved with the exhibits and/or check online before your visit for information and a scavenger hunt. Forty-five minute guided tours, of the inside and outside, are offered weekdays at 1pm and 3pm, and on weekends at noon, 2pm and 3pm.

Ice Age Encounter is a fifteen-minute live and film presentation that also incorporates a life-size (and life-like) saber-tooth cat puppet that "comes to life" as it roars and stalk the museum floor, and visitors. The Encounter is $3 per person (ages 2 and under are free) and is usually offered only on weekends, though sometimes on Wednesdays, too.

Outside, enjoy a walk around the twenty-three acres of beautifully landscaped Hancock Park, otherwise known as the La Brea Tar Pits. The pits are composed of asphalt that has seeped to the surface to form sticky pools in which the animals got trapped and died. There are several active tar pits in the park, with hundreds more having been dug out and filled in. One gated pit out front has several, "stuck" mastodons statues. Look into the Pit 91 excavation site, open 10am to 4pm, to see undisturbed fossils. Project 23, open 6am to 10pm, is a live excavation site with people working there. The park, with its outdoor amphitheater and picnic facilities, is also a backyard, and has connecting walkways, to the LOS ANGELES COUNTY MUSEUM OF ART (pg. 129). Note: If all else fails, kids will have a great time rolling down the hills outside the museum and climbing on the statues!

Hours: Open daily, 9:30am - 5pm. Closed New Year's Day, July 4th, Thanksgiving, and Christmas.

Price: $12 for adults; $9 for seniors and students with ID; $5 for ages 3 - 12; children 2 and under are free. Admission is free on the first Tues. of the month, except July and August. Parking in the lot behind the museum is $9 (get $2 back with validation), or use the meter parking on 6th St. directly behind the museum - read parking sign carefully. Parking Sat., Sun., and holidays is $7.

Ages: 3½ years and up.

THE GETTY CENTER   ☼

(310) 440-7300 / www.getty.edu $$$
1200 Getty Center Drive, Los Angeles

Everything wonderful you've heard about the Getty Center is true! Your adventure begins with a four-and-a-half-minute tram ride up a winding track that seemingly hugs the edge of the road. You may also hike up the 1.9-mile road, but you'll get enough exercise walking around the Getty.

The architecture of the museum is stunning - it elicited several exclamations of admiration from my kids. The all-white travertine (i.e., marble-like) structures can also be blinding, so bring sunglasses. Once inside the lobby, make your first stop at one of two theaters that show a ten-minute orientation movie regarding the center. Next, use an app or borrow a free ipod touch GettyGuide that offers several types of tours in several languages, such as suggestions of special stops for families; descriptions, commentary, and interviews of more than 300 works in a total of nine hours (which is longer than you'll be here, I know); animals speaking about the artwork they star in; how food and wine connect to works of art in An Art Tasting tour; a tour - Demons, Angels, and Monsters - where listeners hear those aforementioned voice their perspectives; and more. Specific guided tours are available almost each day that cover an

exhibition, the Getty architecture, the gardens, and 17th and 18th century art as is a Collection Highlights tour. Tours and classes for school and other groups are available by reservation.

Stroll down the courtyard toward the boulder fountain as you aim for your next destination, the Family Room. This room is subdivided into five discovery "coves," each one highlighting a different form of art - photography, painting, sculpture, decorative arts, and manuscript and drawings. Each cove also contains a hands-on activity, such as making a mask, experimenting with mirrors and photographic lenses, reading books on an 18th century-style bed, designing and coloring a portion of an illuminated manuscript, and, most fun of all, rearranging foam tubes into a grid of holes on the wall to recreate a metal tubular sculpture. A treasure hunt wall containing about seventy peepholes at various heights allows guests to peer in and see detailed portions of art on display throughout the museum. (Can you match the portion with the whole piece of art?) You can get Art Detective Cards at the entrance or the Family Room that enables your kids to go from mere observers to interactive participants in the galleries as they look for certain pieces of art. Make up your own activities, too, such as having your children imitate portrait poses, or encourage them to be on the lookout for paintings with bridges or dogs or the color red. Note: The museum offers several kid-oriented tours and family workshops that include looking at kid-intriguing artwork and perhaps doing a related art activity. One more room/activity - for all ages - is the drawing room with easels, paper, colored pencils, and still life objects for aspiring artists to use for drawing their own masterpiece.

Now it's time to actually see the world-renown art. Forgive me for not going into detail here about the works - they are too numerous and grand. Suffice to say that the five magnificent, multi-level galleries feature paintings, sculptures, drawings, photography, and decorative arts (e.g., elegant, gold-gilded furniture, tapestries, vases, and more) in natural-light conditions, which enhance the beauty of the work. My boys were fascinated with the overhead sun panels that automatically adjust to let in the right amount of light. Many of the works have stories about the pieces printed alongside them, making them more interesting than just another pretty picture. A separate, darkened room features medieval, illuminated (i.e., hand-painted) manuscripts with still-vivid colors painted on vellum (i.e., sheep skin). From Van Gogh to Rembrandt to Renoir, the spectacular Getty it a "must see" and it has something to please every *palette*.

Hardwood floors and elevators make the Center stroller/wheelchair accessible, although the doors that connect the galleries are heavy to push and pull open. As the Getty is on a hill, the several terraces offer magnificent vistas from Mt. Baldy to Catalina to the surrounding Beverly Hills area. We particularly liked the cactus garden on top of a building outside the South Pavilion. Another outside attraction is the tiered, maze-like, central garden which you may walk in and around. In fact, garden tours, specifically, are offered because they are so remarkable

Hungry visitors have several options. Two cafeterias have both indoor and outdoor seating, and serve a variety of prepacked cold or hot lunch and dinner items for an average of $9. The on-site restaurant is an elegant, sit-down dining experience, and entrees range from $14 to $38. You may also bring a lunch to enjoy at the large picnic area by the base of the tram ride. It has grassy green lawns and numerous covered picnic tables. This last choice entails taking the electric tram down to the parking lot and then back up to the museum.

Here are a few tips to make your day more memorable: 1) Consider prepurchasing (through the Getty bookstore or elsewhere) *A is for Artist*, a Getty museum pictural alphabet book that inspires children to be on the lookout for certain works of art. (Familiarity, in this case, breeds pleasurable recognition.) Or, buy *Going to the Getty* by J. otto Seibold and Vivian Walsh, a book that gives a solid and fun overview of the museum, as well as a look at a few pieces in particular. 2) Look for fossils embedded in the Getty walls, particularly at the plaza where the tram arrives. 3) Pre-warn your children to stand 6" to 12" away from the art. There are no ropes in front of the pieces, and while the security guards are friendly, they are also insistent. 4) A free coat/bag check is available in the entrance hall. 5) Going outside, just to another building, is almost unavoidable, so if it's raining bring an umbrella. 6) Wear comfortable walking shoes! Our eyes were glazed over when we left the Getty, but our minds and hearts were filled with wondrous works of art.

Hours: Open Tues. - Fri. and Sun., 10am - 5:30pm; Sat., 10am - 9pm. Closed Mon., New Year's Day, 4th of July, Thanksgiving and Christmas.
Price: The museum is free. Parking is $15 per vehicle; $10 after 5pm. Visit the Getty Villa on the same day and pay just one parking fee.
Ages: 4 years and up.

THE GETTY VILLA   ☼
(310) 440-7300 / www.getty.edu $$$
17985 Pacific Coast Highway, Pacific Palisades

In a setting that would please the ancient gods, this utterly magnificent "villa," integrated into a terraced hillside, showcases antiquated works of art from Greece, Rome, and Etruria (i.e., part of Italy). The architecture blends elements inspired from first-century Rome and from the modern world, with columns, skylights, marble staircases, and a 450-seat outdoor, classical, coliseum-style-seating theater. The theater is host to year-round, classical dramas, concerts, and presentations. The four gardens are an intrinsic part of the villa experience, comprised of over 300 varieties of plants known to have grown in the bygone Mediterranean world, plus statues, fountains, and decorative columns. The large, formal, Outer Peristyle garden is most impressive with its 225-foot-long reflecting pool. And do take a look at the astounding beauty of the surrounding vistas.

Begin your visit by viewing a twelve-minute film that gives an overview of J. Paul Getty's vast collection, the architecture of the villa, and how antiquities are preserved. "Rent" a free GettyGuide audio guide which features commentary on over 150 works of art. Book/pamphlet guides are available as are various free tours throughout the day that spotlight different segments of the Villa. Forty-five minute Art Odyssey tours, geared for kids, are offered on weekends year round and during the week, additionally, in the summer. When kids are involved with art their visit has more of an impact.

Dating from 6,500 B.C. to 400 A.D., select objects d'art are elegantly exhibited in twenty-three permanent galleries and five rotating galleries that flow from one into another. Depictions of gods and goddesses, and renderings of the Trojan War, plus vases, glass, pottery, mosaics, gems, coins, jewelry, and sculptures are presented in galleries organized by theme and context, making your visit a walk through history. Kids are especially intrigued by the sculptures. (Note that there are many nude statues here.) Make sure to look where you walk as the floors are made of bronze, marble, and terrazzo pieces designed and inlaid in intricate, geometric patterns.

Just a few exhibit highlights: On the first floor, the Temple of Herakles room, featuring a stunning statue of Herakles; the resplendent Basilica with statues of divinities (don't *myth* this one); Dionysus, near the inside theater; and two interactive rooms - the TimeScape Room and Family Forum. The TimeScape Room features a colorful, visual time line incorporating audio commentary, sculptures, and rock strata for archeology buffs. In the hands-on Family Forum draw on urn replicas, use props and a shadow screen to imitate poses of famous works of art (or whatever) for an audience, and peek inside a simulated kiln to see how ceramics are fired. Upstairs, are bronzed animals of old; a real mummy; statues of athletes in various poses, including the bronze Statue of a Victorious Youth (i.e., an Olympian); funerary sculpture; and renderings of women and children in one room, men in another. The GettyGuide Room is here, as well, where you can view videos of art-making techniques and interact with a time line of the collection.

The Villa is host to numerous special events and cultural functions. Educators may obtain curriculum aids. A cafe on the grounds serves, fittingly enough, Mediterranean fare, and beyond, such as salads ($14.95), soups ($7), pizza ($11.95), Greek chicken wrap ($12.95), and beef brisket ($16.95). Bambini (i.e. children's) menu averages $5.95 for pastas or grilled chicken and mashed potatoes. Sit at the cafe or order a boxed lunch to go to enjoy on the grounds. A full-on tea is also served with scones, smoked duck breast panini, burnt cinnamon truffle and so much more - $36 per person. One thing is certain - this Getty isn't resting on its laurels.

Hours: Open Wed. - Mon, 10am - 5pm. Closed Tues., Jan. 1, July 4, Thanksgiving, and Dec. 25. A timed ticket, obtained in advance, is required.

Price: Free. Parking is $15; $10 after 5pm. Visit the Getty Center on the same day and pay just one parking fee.

Ages: 7 years and up.

GORDON R. HOWARD MUSEUM - MENTZER HOUSE   ☼

(818) 841-6333 / www.burbankhistoricalsoc.org   !
115 Lomita Street in the George Izay Park, Burbank

Make sure to save a weekend afternoon to come and explore the Gordon Howard Museum and other immediate buildings. The hallway has old toys and dishes on display, plus a drawing room and a music room. The salon contains wedding dresses, old dresses (that are now back in style), including a stunning 1898 dress with beads and lace, plus ladies boots, jeweled hat pins, and dolls.

The Historical Room is large and filled with interesting slices from Burbank's past. Along one wall are glass-enclosed rooms, each one complete with furniture and period-dressed mannequins. As you look into the rooms, pick up an old-fashioned telephone receiver, press a button that corresponds to the room, and listen to stories about Dr. Burbank (does that name ring a bell?), a family-owned winery, a 1920's hotel lobby (when $1 paid for a room!), a country store, and the *Jazz Singer*, Al Jolson. Other exhibits in this room include military uniforms, flags, and other war memorabilia; an ornate desk used by Spanish noblemen; a mannequin of world heavyweight champ James J. Jeffries in

a ring and his old boxing gloves; and a display devoted to Lockheed, composed of numerous pictures and model airplanes. A tribute to Walt Disney features animation techniques and cells, audio animatronics, photographs, posters, and a wall collage of every Disney movie made (up to a certain date). Use the zoetrope to see how early animation worked. A Warner Brothers Studio exhibit displays costumes from a *Batman* movie and from an old Errol Flynn movie. You can watch continuously running oldie cartoons.

Another room is packed with lots of antique "stuff," such as an old switchboard, tools, parking meters, a huge Gramophone, a hotel telephone booth, and fire hats. It also showcases classic cars in mint condition, and several vintage vehicles including a 1922 Moreland Bus, a 1909 Ford horseless carriage with a crank, a spring wagon, and a 1949 fire engine with a huge target net that my kids thought was a trampoline. The small upstairs gallery has pictures and paintings as well as a complete collection of old cameras. A video on the history of Lockheed is shown at 1:10pm and again at 2:30pm.

Follow the walkway from the museum courtyard to the reconstructed Mentzer House, which was originally built in 1887. On your walk-through tour you'll see two bedrooms, a dining room, and a living room containing period furniture, plus old-fashioned items such as a phonograph, an old telephone, and a vacuum cleaner. The kitchen has a beautiful coal-burning stove, plus china dishes, and cooking gadgets. Adult and children tours are given during the week for groups of ten or more by reservation.

A farm house holds a fully-equipped spring wagon and other farm equipment. Note that right next door is the Olive Recreation Center, easily identified by the model F-104 Starfighter in the front. The park has picnic tables and a playground, plus tennis and basketball courts.

Hours: Open Sat. - Sun., 1pm - 4pm.
Price: Free; donations gladly accepted.
Ages: 5 years and up.

GRAMMY MUSEUM

(213) 765-6800 / www.grammymuseum.org $$$$
800 W. Olympic Boulevard, Los Angeles

And the Grammy goes to . . . the Grammy Museum for most relevant music museum in L.A. There are a considerable amount of artifacts here, but really, it's all about the music. Ride the elevator to the fourth floor of this state-of-the-art, contemporary museum to start your time here at the top. The wall videos in the hallway are popping with images and sounds of Grammy winners singing. You become immediately engaged with the music, which is one of the purposes of the museum. The others include learning the history, the creative process, the art and technology, and the celebration of music from song writing to recording. This is accomplished mostly through multimedia displays that encourage interaction with the music and those who create it.

The next huge room features Crossroads, which is a long touch screen table with headphones at different stations for numerous users. Touch a photo, song, or story on the tabletop and listen to learn about the almost 160 genres of music, their history and how they are interconnected - pop, blues, jazz, hip hop, barbershop, folk, ambient, opera, disco, Southern gospel, and so much more. Explore the roots of key traditional music inside four pods that contain videos, interviews, and music regarding sacred, folk, pop, classical, and jazz genres. The outside of the pods contain personal memorabilia such as hand-written lyrics from artists, signed album covers, personal photographs, hand-written letters (e.g. from Elvis to a fan), and instruments. What is your musical heritage? At Music Epicenters a wall-size map of the U.S. connects with touch screens so visitors can see and hear who and/or what type of music states, cities, and time periods have contributed. Music generates passion. Culture Shock is an audio/video time line that features singers whose songs and/or styles have created controversy, including Elvis Presley, Bob Dylan, Kurt Cobain, and 50 Cent. The Grammy Archives and Hall of Fame showcases the history of the awards and nominations, as well as clothing donated from some of the winners. Sit and listen to any of the Grammy shows and songs. The display case of Influential Instruments contains, on a rotating basis, incredibly rare instruments from legendary musicians. It Starts With a Song is the kiosk area where significant songwriters describe their creative process and share the stories behind their songs.

Revolutions of Recorded Sound, on the third floor, focuses on the behind the scenes processes; the technology behind the recorded song. In this, the Roland Live exhibit contains electronic instruments for you to play and participate in the music-making process. It's fascinating to see and hear the impact the technological leaps have made on songs - from records to tapes to CDs and digital. Eight glass-enclosed, self-contained pods, like real recording rooms, offer more individual interaction with the touch screen and footage of top professionals in their specific area of expertise in the recording industry - engineering, producing with Eddie Kramer, mastering with Bob Ludwig, rapping

with Jermaine Dupri, and more. You have input to how the sound, track, and song turns out with your creative and technical choices. Can you make great music? There is also personal memorabilia displayed here, on a rotating basis. We saw eight of Michael Jackson's beaded and bejeweled jackets (one was worn on his Victory tour), and two of his gloves. Another rotating display area shows dresses, suits, and outfits worn on the red carpet for the Grammys, including Jennifer Lopez's almost dress from the 2000 Grammys. Behind the glamour, literally behind the showcase of outfits, is a small gallery that shows and describes how the nomination and award's process works and how it all comes together looking so polished (most times). Current winners are honored here and the Latin Grammys are highlighted here, too. Then, sit, relax and watch some of Grammys most memorable moments on the big screen.

The second, and last floor of exhibits, is set aside primarily for premiere, traveling exhibits. We saw Songs of Conscience, Sounds of Freedom which featured multimedia kiosks, footage, music, photographs, and personal items from private collections that aided in exploring the impact and connection between music and politics; music as a political force. Very powerful. It covered and displayed everything from an abolitionist songbook, J. Edgar Hoover's FBI summary of the MC5, Civil War memorabilia, Woody Guthrie's guitar, to the Dixie Chicks. This floor also has a 200-seat theater that shows the twenty-minute film *Making of a Grammy Moment* two times each hour. The theater is used for concerts, chat time with famous artists and producers, career panels, Civil War Reenactments, and much more.

Music is an effective tool to capture the attention of youth and bring history, sociology, and technology to life. The Grammy Museum has an assemblage (over fifty annually!) of public, family, and school educational programs. Guest speakers from all walks of the music industry and world renown performing artists offer the public uncommon opportunities to hear and see them. The school educational programs, geared for K through high school students, are equally all-encompassing with just some of the selections including Analyzing Lyrics; Careers in Music: The Grammy Museum; the Music of War; and Behind the Scenes: Building Exhibits. Monthly workshops change and have included Learning the History of Music; Connecting Music, Politics and Social Change; Celebrating Hispanic Heritage Month through Music; and more. Each field trip, which meets California state standards, includes a self guided tour of the museum and/or a workshop or performance. - $8 per student for tour only or tour plus a workshop. Tour only visits require a minimum of ten students; workshops are for a minimum group of twenty-five up to 200. Note that the museum is in the middle of the L.A. LIVE complex, which also has Staples Center, Nokia Theater, a Regal Cineplex, Lucky Strike Lanes, and plenty of restaurants. See DOWNTOWN LOS ANGELES / GRAND PARK (pg. 167) for information on Grand Park and all the other places to go within this fairly immediate area.

Hours: Open Mon. - Fri., 11:30am - 7:30pm; Sat. - Sun., 10am - 7:30pm.
Price: $12.95 for adults; $11.95 for seniors and students; $10.95 for ages 6 - 17; children 5 and under are free. Parking in the lots on Olympic start at $8 for the day.
Ages: 9 years and up.

GRIER MUSSER MUSEUM   ☼

(213) 413-1814 / www.griermussermuseum.org $$$
403 S. Bonnie Brae Street, Los Angeles

This thirteen-room, two-story, green and rust-colored Queen Anne-style house/museum was built in 1898. It was the Grier Musser family home. Since most of the tour guides are family relatives, they know and share the history and interesting stories of the memorabilia. The house is literally packed with personal ~~stuff~~ treasures accumulated over the years. The front parlor contains an original chandelier, Delph plates, a grandfather's clock, and other antiques. The family room has a 1950's television set, a piano, and a fainting couch for women who did just that. The dining room's fireplace is decorated with ornate tiles and beautifully carved wood work. The kitchen has a wood-burning stove, a gas stove, a beaded chandelier from the 1915 Exposition Fair, dishes from the Depression era, a collection of cookie jars, kitchen gadgets, and china cabinets filled with original boxes of Ivory Soap, Morton's Salt, and more. At the foot of the stairs is a red velvet chaperone's seat. While a gentleman courted his lady love, a chaperone would sit out of the way, but within eyesight.

An upstairs study contains a desk, grandma's diploma from high school, and a pictorial history of the Red Cross, plus a closet full of nursing uniforms from WWII. The master bedroom and adjoining bedroom have maple furniture, and closets full of hats, dresses, and boots. The children's bedroom is filled with toys, stuffed animals, dolls, and dollhouses. The dresser displays old bottles and hairbrushes as well as a more unique sign of the past - a container of leg makeup from WWII. Women would put this makeup on their legs to make it look like they were wearing nylons - seams and all. The sundeck is a favorite room for kids because of the numerous games and toys, and extensive Disney collection. Open the printer drawers to see even more treasures, such as jewelry.

Using the maid's stairway, go down to the basement to see pictures of the family and the Los Angeles area, and an extensive postcard collection from around the world. A visit here makes you wonder if maybe you should have kept that bottle cap collection, or at least your great grandfather's fishing pole as a potential museum piece.

Hours: Open Wed. - Sat., noon - 4pm. Call for a reservation for any size group.

Price: $10 for adults; $7 for seniors and students; $5 for ages 5 - 12; children 4 and under are free. Cash only.

Ages: 5 years and up.

GRIFFITH OBSERVATORY AND PLANETARIUM   ☼

(213) 473-0890 / www.griffithobservatory.org   !/$$

2800 E. Observatory Road, in Griffith Park, Los Angeles

The landmark copper domes and architecture of this world-famous observatory beckon star trackers. On a cloudless day the terraces around the building allow it be one of the best places to view the sprawling city of Los Angeles, and beyond, including a fairly close-up view of the iconic Hollywood sign. On a clear night, a magnificent view of the city lights and the stars await. Zeiss, the largest public telescope in California, is available to use (for free) every clear evening in the summer from dusk to 9:45pm, as are other "lesser" telescopes. It is available the rest of the year Tuesday to Sunday from 7pm to 9:45pm. Call the Sky Report, (213) 473-0880, for twenty-four-hour recorded information.

On the front lawn of the observatory is an almost forty-foot-tall statue featuring Copernicus, Hipparchus, Galileo, Kepler, Newton, and Herschel. Inside the lobby is the large Foucault pendulum which knocks over pegs, illustrating the rotation of the earth. Look up at the rotunda ceiling to see heavenly murals. The two exhibit hallways contain niches with displays of models, orbiting planets (always look overhead), photographs, pictures, videos, and buttons to press for cause and effect. The Hall of the Sky features displays of the moon phases; day and night; sun and stars pathway; tides - rising and falling; seasons; and eclipses. At the end of this corridor is a small, semi-circular room that offers real time images of the sun viewed via a filter on a solar telescope, as well as videos of eruptions on the sun, pictures of sun spots, and super nova explosions. The periodic table is shown in small, individual cases with its elements in their mineral forms. Press buttons to see which elements light up, accordingly, that comprise super novas, stars, humans, gases, and more.

The Hall of the Eye holds a model of the Hale telescope, observatory instruments, a replica of Galileo's telescope, information on astronomy and the history of it in California, a Tesla coil (watch the sparks jump as lightening is created!), and a camera obscura.

35,000-square-feet of underground space focuses on the exploration of space. The mezzanine showcases real meteorites, including a 395-pound fragment, and information on their origins and impact (literally). One video allows visitors to design their own velocity and density of a meteorite, and its destination. At another interactive display you answer questions either meteorite or meteorwrong! A corner exhibit has a huge, spinning model of the moon, information panels regarding where Apollo missions have landed, and a moon rock. The steeply graded, 200-seat Leonard Nimoy (yes, the Vulcan) Event Horizon Theater is used for special programs and free presentations, such as the twenty-four minute film about the observatory's history. A gift shop and cafeteria-style cafe are in this area, too.

The walls of the lower level are decorated like the night sky, full of constellations and our Milky Way. Each planet is represented along one wall in its own model and kiosk that promotes pictures; facts - temperature, days per year, and more; rotating models of the planet; and videos. Watch out - each one also has a scale that, when stepped on, allows all the other visitors to see how much you weigh on Earth, Venus, Mars, Saturn, etc. (Pluto rules!) Behind the Earth kiosk is an old planetarium projector; an enormous model of the earth, rotating and showing the changing surface; and a seismograph - jump on the floor to simulate an earthquake and see what it registers.

For a truly stellar experience, don't miss the planetarium shows as the seamless, seventy-seven feet across projection dome and the fiber optics make the stars appear incredibly realistic and vibrant. (Enjoy the plush seats that recline!) There are four live shows with eight half-hour+ presentations (with a variety of show titles to choose from) offered each weekday and ten shows each weekend day. Children 4 and under are admitted ONLY to the first show each day - 12:45pm on weekdays; 10:45am on weekends.

Call for information on school tours, which are usually geared for fifth graders. For other close-by attractions look up GRIFFITH PARK (pg. 62). Note: The Greek Theater, a nationally renown venue for concerts and other events, is also just down the road.

Hours: Open Tues. - Fri., noon - 10pm; Sat. - Sun., 10am - 10pm. Closed Mon., and most major holidays.

Price: Admission to the observatory is free. The planetarium shows are $7 for adults; $5 for seniors; $3 for ages 5 - 12; children 4 and under are free and they must sit on parent's lap.

Ages: 4 years and up.

GUINNESS WORLD OF RECORDS MUSEUM   ☼
(323) 463-6433 / www.guinnessmuseumhollywood.com $$$$
6764 Hollywood Boulevard, Hollywood

There are over 3,000 facts, feats, and world records told about and shown at this Hollywood museum, which has almost carnival-like atmosphere. There is something to astound all ages. See colorful, life-size models of people recreated in their record-breaking moments, plus pictures, videos, and special effects of the tallest, smallest, most tattooed, most anything and everything. (The kids should be great at Trivial Pursuit after this visit.) We were enthralled with the domino exhibit, which shows a video of an incredible domino run. Be prepared to read a lot of placards to your younger children.

Prep your children before their visit: Q: Do you know who holds a record for the most fan mail in one day? A: Mickey Mouse. He received 800,000 letters one day in 1933. Q: What animal had the smallest brain in proportion to his body? A: Stegosaurus. Q: What was the longest length a human neck was stretched using copper coils? And why? A: Fifteen and three-quarter inches. I don't know why, though. Watch some fascinating footage of intriguing and bizarre facts about our world and the people and animals in it: *The Human World*, *The Animal World*, *Planet Earth*, *Structures and Machines*, *Sports World*, and a salute to *The World of Hollywood*. Look up HOLLYWOOD (pg. 171) for details on other close-by Hollywood museums and attractions.

Hours: Open daily, 10am - midnight.
Price: $16.99 for adults; $14.99 for seniors; $8.99 for ages 5 - 12; children 4 and under are free. Combo tickets for Guinness, HOLLYWOOD WAX MUSEUM (pg. 119) and RIPLEY'S BELIEVE IT OR NOT! MUSEUM (pg. 149) are $29.99 for adults; $16.99 for ages 5 - 12.
Ages: 4½ years and up.

HACIENDA HEIGHTS YOUTH SCIENCE LEARNING CENTER   ☀
(626) 854-9825 / www.youthsciencecenter.org   !
16949 Wedgeworth Drive at Wedgeworth Elementary School, Hacienda Heights

The Youth Science Center functions as a museum and a classroom. Actually, the museum is in a classroom that's decorated with colorful, informative posters, at Wedgeworth Elementary School. Although it's not state-of-the-art, a lot of science is contained in this room. A sand pendulum creates patterns depending on how you swing it; a heat-sensitive, liquid crystal display leaves colored impressions when touched; a Jacob's ladder of electricity is on display; a case of fossils and drawers of butterflies and other insects can be examined; and there are a few live critters like a bearded dragon lizard and snakes. Also here are computer stations with educational games, including robotics programs, plus puzzles, books, construction toys, and numerous scientific films to borrow. The retail store area is a small space packed with rocks, shells, science books, and experiments.

For a minimal fee, children can attend classes like Fantastic Flight (a paper airplane race), where they'll learn about aerodynamics and wind, while making and flying paper airplanes. A terrific array of science-related classes, from model rocket-building to robotics to hands-on, physical science, are available during the summer as are an array of great field trips in August, such as tours to museums and of energy-efficient plants. Call for a schedule. The Center also offers a digital Starlab, an inflatable planetarium, for up to forty students, that comes to your site. The program includes hand-outs regarding constellations. Other outreach classes include model rocketry, Lego robotics, basic electronics, and chemistry.

Hours: Open September - mid-June, Tues. and Fri., noon - 3:45pm; Sat., 11:15am - 3pm. Open the end of June - July, Mon. - Fri., 8:30am - noon.
Price: Free
Ages: 4 years and up.

HAMMER MUSEUM   ☀
(310) 443-7000 / www.hammer.ucla.edu $
10899 Wilshire Boulevard, Westwood

The fairly large Hammer art museum features an interesting array of paintings, sculpture, photographs, lithography, and graphic arts in both its permanent and rotating exhibits. Impressionist and Post-Impressionist works

include paintings by Monet, Pissarro, Cassatt, and Van Gogh. Samples from European old masters to more modern American artists are creatively displayed on the walls and sometimes, on the floors. Modern art is definitely intriguing, if somewhat baffling, to kids. Ask about guided tours, lectures, classes, readings, screenings, and variety of educational programs. Check out the free Family Flicks of classic and new animated and kid-friendly movies usually shown on Sundays at 11pm.

Hours: Open Tues. - Fri., 11am - 8pm; Sat. - Sun., 11am - 5pm. Closed Mon., New Year's Day, 4th of July, Thanksgiving and Christmas.
Price: Free. Parking is $3 for the first three hours.
Ages: 8 years and up.

HERITAGE JUNCTION HISTORIC PARK

(661) 254-1275 / www.scvhs.org
24101 Newhall Avenue, Santa Clarita

A steam locomotive is on the tracks out in front of this restored, late 1800's train station/museum. Inside the museum are photographs, information, and artifacts that show and tell the history of this valley, including the Spanish era, the petroleum and mining areas, and its rich film history. Five building that have been restored and several other buildings, in various stages of restoration, such as a jail, comprise the rest of the junction. You can walk back and peek in through the windows of the little (very little!) red school house, the Ramona chapel, and the Edison house. On the first Sunday of the month, you may take a tour through the small Kingsbury house that contains nineteenth-century furniture. We weren't here long, but it was an interesting, historical, and photogenic stop. Note: The junction park is right next to the WILLIAM S. HART MUSEUM AND PARK (pg. 157).

Hours: Open daily, 9am - 5pm, just to walk the grounds. The buildings are open Sat. - Sun., 1pm - 4pm. Open for school tours during the week by appointment.
Price: Free
Ages: 6 years and up.

HERITAGE PARK - Santa Fe Springs

(562) 946-6476 / www.santafesprings.org
12100 Mora Drive, Santa Fe Springs

Heritage Park is like a breath of fresh air among the historical parks. Its six acres of beautifully landscaped grounds make any length visit here a pleasure. The high-ceiling, two-story, wood Carriage Barn, which holds turn-of-the-century exhibits, is a must-see. Two carriages from horse and buggy days take the center floor. Behind glass is a large display of period clothing, including a wedding dress, plus dolls, toys, and books. The small touch and play area has clothing to try on, an old telephone to dial (it's not a touch tone or cell phone), and a few other articles to play with. Inventing a Better Life display features old phonographs, typewriters, bikes, roller skates (not in-line skates), plus cameras and other equipment. It's interesting to see how the inventions of yesteryear benefit us today.

Walk down a short pathway to a thirty-two-foot dome-shaped dwelling that is the centerpiece of a recreated Native American village of the Tongva tribe. You can go into it. A small creek, a granary, a sweatlodge, and a canoe (that you can sit in) are also featured. This area often showcases storytellers, a craft time, demonstrations, and Journeys to the Past presentations.

Grab a bite to eat at Heritage Park Cafe, an outside, full-service snack bar. It's open Monday through Friday from 11am to 3pm, but closed on rainy days. The average cost of a sandwich, wrap or salad is about $5.50. Or, bring your own lunch, and enjoy the garden setting with beautiful old shade trees and plenty of tables and chairs.

Walk around the outside of an aviary that houses parakeets, canaries, and a few other birds. A small window to an archeological pit shows excavated trash such as cattle bones and pottery. There are remain sites marking original fireplace and basement foundations, but kids cannot go in them to explore. A hedge around the beautiful formal gardens gives way to an old fig tree with huge roots that are almost irresistible for kids to climb on. Walk through the greenhouse. An immaculate, wood-paneled tank house, once used to store water, is at the far end of the park. On a school tour, kids can go inside the windmill building and walk up the crisscross stairs to the top, then go outside, and take in the view.

I can't emphasize the beauty of this park enough. It's clean, green, and the walkways throughout make every area accessible. Ask about the park's special programs throughout the year.

Just outside the park gates are three restored railroad cars on a piece of track. Climb into the cab of the classic-looking locomotive and ring the bell, then look to see where coal was stored. Look at the caboose, the colorful

refrigerated boxcar and go inside the depot. There is a small picnic area, here, too.

Exceptional, two-hour, school tours of Heritage Park include lots of historical information, presented in a kid-friendly way, plus hands-on activities. These are offered on Wednesdays and Thursdays for ages 8 and up. The tours are free. Just a short walk away, near the pedestrian bridge on Norwalk and Telegraph, is an outdoor sculpture garden with artwork, fountains, and grassy areas - a nice reprieve.

Hours: The park is open daily, November - mid-March, 7:30am - 5pm; open daily, mid-March - October, 7:30am - 8pm. The Railroad cars area is open daily, noon - 4pm. The Carriage Barn hours are Tues. - Sat., noon - 4pm. Closed major holidays.

Price: Free

Ages: All

HERITAGE SQUARE MUSEUM

(323) 225-2700 / www.heritagesquare.org

3800 Homer Street, Montecito Heights

This little "town" behind a gate at the end of a residential street has nine historic structures, including five houses, plus a carriage barn (used for storage), a church building, and a train depot. The elegant Victorian homes, originally built between 1865 and 1914, have been relocated here and are in various stages of restoration. Each one has a different architectural style and coloring. One is white with columns, almost colonial-looking, while another is green and pink, gingerbreadish in style, and has brick chimneys. The octagon-shaped house is the most unique-looking house here. Its unusual configuration makes it interesting to look at as well as walk through.

Only on the one-hour guided tours can you go through some of the homes. The Queen Anne house on the tour is the only one completely furnished and restored. The grassy grounds are ideal for picnicking. Hour-long group and school tours are offered Monday through Thursday, starting at 10am for $2 for K through 6 and $3 for 7 through 12 graders. These living history school programs fit with California state standards. One several-day program, called Golden Vision, involves having a costumed docent come to the classroom to teach a lesson, followed by students doing assignments and activities, and culminates with coming to the museum and participating in real life living of 100 years ago. There are also many functions open to the general public throughout the year such as the Vintage Fashion Show and Tea, and the Holiday Lamplight Celebration, where lamp lights give a warm glow to the houses and area.

Hours: Open April through October, Fri. - Sun., noon - 5pm. Open November through March, Fri. - Sun., 11:30am - 4:30pm. Open in the summer, Fri. - Sun., noon - 5pm. Also open some holiday Mon. Guided tours are available from noon - 3pm (last tour), on the hour. Closed New Year's Day, Thanksgiving, and Christmas.

Price: Admission is $10 for adults; $8 for seniors; $5 for ages 6 - 12; children 5 and under are free. Discounts are available through AAA. Group tours are a minimum of $75.

Ages: 6 years and up.

HOLLYWOOD BOWL MUSEUM

(323) 850-2058 / www.hollywoodbowl.org

2301 N. Highland, Hollywood

While at the Hollywood Bowl for a concert, or if you're in the area, stop by the Hollywood Bowl Museum. This 3,000 square-foot museum displays musical instruments, memorabilia, photographs of performers (from opera to rock to Native American dancers) and conductors, and hall of fame. Videos show concerts featured at the Bowl and other film footage (even cartoons). The second story has rotating exhibits; the history of the Bowl displayed via photographs and audio and video kiosks; computer stations (for research); and some past museum exhibits. The Soundscape exhibit is all about how we hear music, using visual aids of talking (or singing) into a sound spectrogram and watching a moving picture of your voice; talking into an echo tube that encircles 100 feet around the museum's walls; play a musical wall of strings and percussion; and participating in a computer simulation that demonstrates the speed of sound.

Adults are welcome on a walking tour of the bowl and a museum visit. A music education program is offered for school groups where kids learn about music, try their hands at playing some instruments, and do a related arts and craft project. The program specifics change from season to season. Picnic areas are available so pack a lunch. Groups may also attend rehearsals of the Los Angeles Philharmonic and Hollywood Bowl Orchestra during the summer when available.

Hours: Open mid-June through mid-September, Tues. - Sat., 10am - showtime; Sun., 4pm - showtime.
Open mid-September - mid-June, Tues. - Fri., 10am - 5pm; open Sat. by appt. Closed New Year's
Day, Thanksgiving and Christmas.
Price: Free. Parking is free until 4:30pm.
Ages: 7 years and up.

THE HOLLYWOOD MUSEUM   ☀

(323) 464-7776 / www.thehollywoodmuseum.com $$$$
1660 N. Highland Avenue, Hollywood

Do you know who coined the phrase "makeup"? The cosmetic king, Max Factor. Located inside this landmark
Max Factor building, originally constructed in 1914, is a tribute to Hollywood, old and new. Most of the first floor
retains the essence of "old" Hollywood, with architectural elegance and several small rooms dedicated and denoted by
the color of one's hair. The "redheads" room has pale green walls, photographs of red-headed stars, and a case of
makeup and accessories that harmonize with a redhead's hair and skin tones. Blondes, brunettes, and brownettes each
have different, colored rooms with similar, specialized exhibits. Several hundred of Joe Ackerman's 6,000-piece
autograph collection, often accompanied by pictures, are on view throughout the hallways. The photo library room
displays 1,000 black-and-white photos of the changing Hollywood community, as well as head shots and "casual"
pictures of stars and their homes. An eclectic mix of props are also on display on this floor, including gigantic bunny
legs from the movie *Along Came Polly*, the space capsule and costumes in a re-created setting from *Planet of the Apes*, and
a Rolls Royce that belonged to Cary Grant. A small screening room shows classics throughout the day.

Take a ride in the freight (or fright) elevator that was once used to transport stars' cars to storage below. The
elevator is decorated with movie posters and a continuously playing silent movie. It takes you down to the basement,
to the Chamber of Horrors, which is comprised mainly of the original set of Hannibal Lector's jail. The brick walls,
pipes, and four cells are realistically creepy looking. Enter into the padded cell and look into the one that holds
Hannibal's mask, reading materials, and other props. Other exhibits down here include blood-splattered costumes
from *Sweeny Todd*, Jason's mask, costumes and props worn by Elvira, a guillotine with a severed head, an Iron Maiden,
torture beds, mummies, and more gory memorabilia.

The ample second and third floors contain a multitude of well-labeled permanent and rotating exhibits, many
behind floor-to-ceiling glass displays. A majority of the displays contain costumes, such as gowns worn by Mae West,
Lucille Ball, and Joan Crawford. Other costumes that we saw were used on the set of *Moulin Rouge*, *Master and
Commander*, *Star Trek*, *Flintstones*, and *Gladiator*. Often props from the corresponding movie are exhibited alongside the
costumes, such as cannons from *Master and Commander* and the bed from *Gladiator*. We also saw signed boxing gloves
from *Rocky*; Roddy McDowall's powder room (moved from his house); masks and molds; Pee Wee Herman's bike;
torture equipment from *Quills*; large, stuffed creatures from *Monster's Inc.*; vintage lighting and camera equipment; lots
of movie posters; a tribute to Bob Hope composed of letters, photos, and personal artifacts; a section devoted to silent
movies; and more. *Harry Potter* fans will love seeing Harry's ultimate broom, his robe, and his quill and ink bottle, plus
blueprints of Hogwarts, a collection of wands and their boxes, the actors' shoes, photos, and posters. The museum also
has an extensive collection of the ultimate movie icon - Marilyn Monroe. Memorabilia such as gowns, documents
regarding her death, personal accessories, dolls in her image, and a wall display of photographs of her in the nude are
on the second floor.

Take a guided tour to learn more about the displays and the people and props behind the scenes of movie- and
television-making. "Fame is fickle, and I know it. It has its compensations, but it also has its drawbacks, and I have
experienced both." - Marilyn Monroe. Note that the museum is adjacent to Mels Drive-In, which is a 50's hamburger
diner that is no longer a drive-in. Look up HOLLYWOOD (see pg. 171) for details on other close-by Hollywood
museums and attractions.

Hours: Open Wed. - Sun., 10am - 5pm. Close Mon. and Tues. and certain holidays.
Price: $15 for adults; $12 for seniors and students; $5 for children 5 and under.
Ages: 10 years and up.

HOLLYWOOD WAX MUSEUM   ◐☀

(323) 462-5991 / www.hollywoodwax.com $$$$
6767 Hollywood Boulevard, Hollywood

Hundreds of celebrities from the world of television and movies are presented in waxy, kind of lifelikeness,
immersed in settings appropriate to a favorite character that they've played, or just being themselves (which might be a

character they're playing). You can be a part of the movie-making magic as you interact with them (and take lots of photographs!) - practice a karate kick with the cast from Charlie's Angels; grab a mic and sing in front of renown singers like Celine Dion and Madonna; follow the yellow brick road with Judy Garland as Dorothy from *The Wizard of Oz*; have a chocolate (bring your own) with Tom Hanks as Forest Gump; and get up close and personal with Johnny Dep, Julia Roberts, Elvis, Robin Williams, Sylvester Stallone (dressed as Rambo), Clint Eastwood in his "make my day" attire, and so many more. We enjoyed debating how realistic the statue depictions were. New icons are being added on a regular basis. A word of caution: There are also recreated sets and characters from horror flicks which might frighten younger children.

Learn facts about your favorite stars by taking multiple choice quizzes on your self-guided tour in the museum. Look up HOLLYWOOD (pg. 171) for details on other close-by Hollywood museums and attractions.

Hours: Open daily, 10am - midnight.
Price: $16.99 for adults; $14.99 for seniors; $8.99 for ages 5 - 12; children 4 and under are free. Combo tickets for the Wax Museum, GUINNESS WORLD OF RECORDS MUSEUM (pg. 116) and RIPLEY'S BELIEVE IT OR NOT! MUSEUM (pg. 149) are $29.99 for adults; $16.99 for ages 5 - 12.
Ages: 4 years and up.

HOLYLAND EXHIBITION

(323) 664-3162

2215 Lake View Avenue, Los Angeles

I could take this tour at least three more times and still not see and learn everything this museum has to offer! The Holyland Exhibition is an inconspicuous two-story corner house that was built in the late 1920's. It contains an incredible collection of priceless Egyptian and biblical items. Most of the two-hour tour is not hands on. It does involve a lot of listening and learning. An incredibly well-informed costumed docent will take you first to the tapestry-rich Bethlehem/Egyptian room which, like all the rooms, is not large, but packed with artifacts. You'll feel transported to a different time and country. Some of the items explained in depth are the 2,600-year-old mummy case; the hand-made brass art pieces and plates; papyrus; shoes made of camel hide and ram skin; headdresses; and a lunch bag made of goat skin. Each item is presented with its history and its biblical connection. You'll also see jewelry, engraved leather goods, a 2,000-year-old lamp, and much more.

The Bible Art and Archaeology Room has stones, shells, pottery, spices, and more from Nazareth, Bethlehem, the Jordan River, and surrounding areas. You'll view the type of large thorns used in Christ's crown of thorns; a big chunk of salt called Madame Lot; a very comprehensive family tree detailing lineage from Adam to Jesus; the kind of stones crushed and used for pitch on Noah's ark; a picture of Mt. Ararat where *ark*eologists believe the ark landed; and a recreated Ark of the Covenant. Make sure your tour guide explains how Mr. Futterer, the museum founder, went on an expedition to find the ark and how this was the basis for the movie *Raiders of the Lost Ark*. (This will definitely spark your children's interest.) Again, amazing amounts of Bible references are given with the presentation of each article.

The Damascus Room has an intricate game table inlaid with mother-of-pearl that took fifty man-years to make - kids may not play games on it! The room also contains beaded lamps, musical instruments, a camel saddle, animal skin (to write on), and many unique pieces of furniture. In another room, enjoy a taste of Israel while sitting on oriental rugs around low tables, as you're served small samples of Holy Land refreshments. The Jerusalem Bazaar is a gift shop with souvenirs (and great teaching aids) made of olive wood, mother-of-pearl, and other materials, at bargain prices. Come, take a trip to the middle east, via the Holyland Exhibition, and learn about its peoples and customs. The interdenominational museum is frequented by Christians, Jews, Muslims, and people of various other faiths.

Hours: The museum is open to tour seven days a week, including holidays and evenings. Call at least a week ahead of time, and choose the most convenient time for your family or group.
Price: $2.50 for adults; $2 for ages 3 - 15; children 2 and under are free.
Ages: 6 years and up.

THE HOMESTEAD MUSEUM

(626) 968-8492 / www.homesteadmuseum.org

15415 E. Don Julian Road, City of Industry

The Homestead Museum resides on six acres of land. A major portion of the property is an open, grassy area between the main group of buildings and the old mausoleum. A shady picnic area is here, too, plus fish pond, gazebo, and some pretty landscaping. A one-hour guided tour, starting at the water tower, will take you behind the gates. Kids

will see and learn about the history of the United States, and about California in particular. They'll learn, for instance, that our state was once Mexican territory, and how that influence has factored in the development of our culture. They will also learn about the art and architecture of the 1830's through the 1930's.

The tour goes into the two residences on the premises. The Workman adobe home has no furniture inside, but outside are a few artifacts that kids can touch. La Casa Nueva house is spacious with twenty-six rooms, mostly furnished in 1920's decor. Kids will also get information about the on-site pump house, tepee, mausoleum, and cemetery, where Pio Pico, the last Mexican governor of California, is buried. Ask about the many events that go on year round.

Hours: The historic houses and grounds are open for guided tours, only, Wed. - Sun., 1pm - 4pm, on the hour. Open for tour groups, minimum ten people, at other times throughout the week. Call for a reservation. Closed major holidays and special tour weekends.

Price: Free

Ages: 6 years and up.

HUNTINGTON LIBRARY, ART COLLECTIONS AND BOTANICAL GARDENS ☼

(626) 405-2141; (626) 405-2100 / www.huntington.org $$$$

1151 Oxford Road, San Marino

The Library houses one of the world's greatest collections of rare books, manuscripts, and documents including a Gutenberg Bible; Ellesmere Chaucer's *The Canterbury Tales*; Benjamin Franklin's autobiography, in his own handwriting; original works by Whitman and Dickens; and letters written by George Washington, Thomas Jefferson, and Abraham Lincoln. In the west wing of the library is the permanent, five gallery exhibit titled, Beautiful Science: Ideas That Change the World. One gallery is a reading room with reference copies. Each of the other four focus on a specific area: astronomy, natural history, medicine, and light. Original books are the core of the exhibit including *Origins of Species* (in several languages), Louis Pasteur's personal diaries, and Isaac Newton's own copy of *Opticks*, plus Robert Hooke's 1665 incredibly detailed drawings of insects viewed under a microscope and more. Listen to an audio excerpt from written works at fourteen stations. The mural in the astronomy room portrays a supernova explosion in 1605. There are interactive components in each gallery such as computer terminals, a prism experiment, a camera obscura, and a replica of a 17th century microscope and of Galileo's telescope to look through.

The Huntington Art Gallery is the epitome of opulence. This mansion contains the collection's European art of sculptures (including the life-size bronze of the Roman goddess of the hunt, *Diana the Huntress*), rare tapestries, miniatures, period furniture, and famous paintings, including Gainsborough's *The Blue Boy*. Get kids involved with observing the paintings by pointing out the ones with children in them and ones with different styles of dress than theirs. Read to them the accompanying information (stories) about the subjects. For instance, sweet-faced *Pinkie*, which hangs opposite *The Blue Boy* by Sir Thomas Lawrence, died soon after her portrait was finished, and the boy in *Lavina, Countess Spencer and her son Viscount Althorp* was one of Princess Diana's great great (great, etc.,) grandparents. This is a gentle way to introduce children to some truly great works of art. Pick up a free Family Guide at the entrance that encourages kids to participate in certain artworks by striking similar poses, drawing a particular element, or listing objects in a painting. The Huntington has a world class collection of art so I'm thankful the atmosphere is not off-putting for kids.

The breathtaking Virginia Steele Scott Gallery and the Erburu Gallery display over 500 pieces of American art (all of which I won't all list here!); paintings (by John Singleton Copley, Mary Cassatt, and Sam Francis, to name just a few); and other media such as glass, ceramic, silver (by Paul Revere and others), sculpture, and furniture (some designed by Frank Lloyd Wright). The Boone building showcases stunning, changing exhibits; some from the Library's collection and others from around the world.

The Botanical Gardens are composed of twelve, separate, themed, massive, amazing gardens that cover 120 acres of the 200-acre estate. As Lisa Blackburn, a museum associate says, "The gardens . . . have wide-open spaces and vast rolling lawns; great for running, somersaulting, cartwheeling, shrieking, and releasing all that boundless energy that is sometimes stifled in traditional museum settings." There are waterfalls, lily ponds, koi, ducks, turtles, and frogs to capture kids' attention - almost more than can be seen in one day. The Desert Garden has, again to quote Lisa, "twelve acres of some of the most bizarre, colorful, creepy-crawly plants that a child could imagine." The Shakespeare Garden features plants mentioned in the bards' plays, accompanied by placards of pertinent poetry phrases. My Tarzans said one of the best part of coming to the Huntington, though, is hiding in the bamboo groves in the Jungle Garden. Another favorite garden is the nine-acre Japanese garden, which is a quarter-mile west of the main entrance. This has a traditionally-furnished Japanese teahouse (that overlooks so much of the Huntington below from its high vantage

point); stone ornaments; an old temple bell; a much-photographed, arching bridge; and a bonsai court. The tranquility and beauty of this garden is aided by the waterfall and stream, as well as the lawns and picturesque trees and plants. The three-acre Rose Garden, with its incredible varieties of roses, by any other name would smell as sweet (a paraphrase).

Think Ming Dynasty and you'll get a picture of the four-acre (in the process of expanding to twelve acres), authentic Chinese Garden, also called Garden of Flowing Fragrance. With a glimpse into the Chinese culture, it classically displays a 1.5-acre man-made lake with seasonally blooming lotus plants, and rocks imported from China that line its edge. It invokes a sense of serenity with lush landscaping of pine, bamboo, lotus, plum, and mature California oak trees; five stone bridges; several pavilions (most in Pagoda-style); a tea house and tea shop; pebble-embedded-in-cement pathways; and streams, waterfalls, and other waterways.

A one-acre Children's Garden, aimed toward younger children, is an absolute delight. Each of the four ancient elements - air, earth, fire, and water - has a section. In Air, a grotto surrounded by plants fills with fog every few minutes, then dissipates. Kids run around, temporarily "lost" in the mist. At Earth, create shapes with magnetic sand and, near the globe, drop pebbles through a maze of metal posts to compose a cacophony of sound. Crawl through a prism tunnel with rainbow arches in the front. See a topiary volcano. Watch for rainbows as you walk through the mist surrounding the rainbow room in Fire. In Water, this liquid reacts to sound vibrations and dances in response, so you can "feel" the sound waves. Jets make water jump from one pot of water to another, and just a touch changes the shape of small, dome-shaped waterfalls at the vortex and water bells exhibit. Interspersed throughout this magical garden are fragrant and colorful plants, tunnels, bridges, stepping stones, and a little playhouse formed mostly by vines and other plants. An adjacent Teaching Greenhouse offers youngsters an opportunity to get their hands dirty at the potting benches and provides a place for horticultural and botany programs for young people and adults.

The Conservancy, which looks like a huge greenhouse, is also located in this area. It has four different environments (most are somewhat hot and humid), each incorporating fascinating hands-on experiments and learning stations of some sort that appeal equally to kids and adults. The Tropical Forest, in the central rotunda, showcases giant palm fronds and huge water lilies. The Cloud Forest is lush with orchids, bromeliads, and pitcher plants. The Bog has carnivorous plants, such as the Venus flytraps. The large Plant Lab holds the widest variety of plant exhibits. Look through microscopes, use a refractometer to measure the amount of sugar in nectar samples, and smell fragrances to match them with a photo of their pollinator.

Choose from a wide selection of tours - free garden tours, audio and podcast tours, and tours geared for adults or specifically for kids or for the family. Take advantage of Kid's Crafts, which is offered the first Saturday of every month and the interactive, bi-monthly Family Workshops. Ask about the numerous educational classes and programs. Just one of the great programs involves the Ranch, a fifteen-acre fruit tree and vegetable garden where participants get their hands dirty as they learn about agriculture.

Picnicking is not allowed on the grounds at the Huntington. However, a special treat for you and your daughter, as it's not really a boy's cup of tea, is to dress up and sip English tea in the Rose Garden Tea Room, which overlooks three acres of roses. The all-you-can-eat buffet includes a variety of finger sandwiches (egg salad, white albacore, watercress, chicken-tarragon, and more), tea; scones served with dotted cream and jam (apricot, blueberry-rosemary, candied ginger, and more); cheese and crackers; tea breads (cranberry, chocolate chip, apple-spice, and more); salad; seasonal fruit; and delightful English desserts and miniature pastries (lemon bars, iced chocolate brownies, fruit tartlets, and more). The cost is $29.50 for adults; $14.99 for ages 4 to 8; $7.50 for ages 2 to 3. Reservations are recommended; walk ins are accepted by availability. Call (626) 683-8131 for more info. A cafe, overlooking the Shakespeare Garden, serves hamburgers, hot dogs, salads, fish tacos, sandwiches, and quesadillas (average $10 to $12), and offers a children's menu. The restaurant in the Chinese Garden section serves garlic shrimp spring rolls ($6.95), chicken chow mein ($9.50), Cantonese short ribs soup with rice noodles ($11.95) and more.

The Huntington is one of the top five "don't miss" destinations in Southern California - it's that fantastic.

Hours: Open most of the year, Mon., noon - 4:30pm (open holiday Mon. at 10:30am); Wed. - Fri., noon - 4:30pm; Sat. - Sun., 10:30am - 4:30pm. Open extended hours the week between Christmas and New Year's. Open Memorial Day - Labor Day, Wed. - Mon., 10:30am - 4:30pm (closed Tues.). Huntington is open at 10:30am on its free Thurs., the first one of each month. You can reserve a morning entry, 10:30am - noon or afternoon, 1:30pm - 3pm. Closed Tues., New Year's Day, 4th of July, Thanksgiving, Christmas Eve, and Christmas Day.

Price: Mon. - Fri., $20 for adults; $15 for seniors; $12 for ages 12 - 18; $8 for ages 5 - 11; children 4 years and under are free. Sat. - Sun. and holiday Mon., $23 for adults; $18 for seniors; $13 for ages 12 - 18; $8 for ages 5 - 11. Admission is free the first Thurs. of every month with advanced ticket reservations by phone or online. Tickets are available the first day of the month prior to your visit at 9am and they go fast (i.e. July 1 for an August visit). You may not purchase regular admission tickets on the free day.

Ages: 4 years and up.

INTERNATIONAL PRINTING MUSEUM

(310) 515-7166 or (714) 529-1832 / www.printmuseum.org $$$
315 Torrance Boulevard, Carson

With the smell of ink in the air and the ambiance of an old-fashioned printing press office (albeit a really large one), the printed page comes to life with a visit to this museum. The general, guided tour is informative, interactive, and presented in a fun, even spellbinding, manner. You'll walk around the museum and see and learn about several rare and working antique presses, including a wooden one from 1750, the ornate Columbian hand press from 1838, and a replica of Gutenberg's first press, plus numerous printing artifacts. General tours are offered for the public and specific tours are offered for groups of up to seventy people. A separate room, across the parking lot, contains an incredible array of typeset letters (drawers and drawers of them), more presses, and storage equipment. This museum is always a work in progress.

The two-hour Book Arts Tour includes components of the Ben Franklin Gallery Tour (see below) in learning, seeing, and understanding the history and importance of paper and the printed word. After printing their own pages of the Gutenberg Bible, students help set metal type and print pages for a book. Then, they sew and bind this book. They will also make paper (from "scratch"), learn about color and design, and gain knowledge regarding lithography and typography. Check out the day-long Book Arts Institute classes (starting at $120) to learn papermaking, fine printmaking, and more - print is truly a work of art. The library here houses over 7,000 books on all the facets of printing history.

There are two other outstanding, two-hour tours for students, which include a general museum tour. The first one is the Ben Franklin Gallery Tour, geared for 3rd graders and up, where the fascinating journey of the printed word began thousands of years ago when the Chinese first invented paper and "wrote" on it using carved blocks of wood. Children continue traveling to the period when Egyptian scrolls were written on papyrus, then on to the time of Gutenberg's invaluable contribution. Students learn about the tools of the trade while listening to anecdotes and information on writing, printing, and bookbinding. They also learn how long it took to make a hand-written book (three to five years); the price of a book; the increase in availability of books to the common people because of the press; and a lot more. The next stop on the tour is the Heritage Theater where a costumed appearance by Benjamin Franklin - not the real one, but a marvelous reenactor who looks and speaks just like him - then follows. Utilizing slides and equipment, Ben explains his numerous inventions and discoveries, such as electricity, an unsteady chair (i.e., rocking chair), markers called milestones, bifocals, swim fins, and more. Eager audience members participate in experiments that demonstrate static electricity and electricity generated through a replica 1750 electro static generator. He regales listeners about his life in Colonial America and encourages children to get educated by reading.

The Constitutional Convention Tour, geared for 5th graders and above, is a reenactment of the Constitutional Convention. Divided into thirteen groups (colonies), students use pre-written cards to debate foundational issues, such as representation taxation, election of the president, and slavery. Ben Franklin presides over the meeting which ends with the colony deputies signing the Constitution. This is an exceptional, experiential history lesson/tour!

Other options include an hour-long school assembly titled The Inventive Benjamin Franklin, where Ben takes students from inception to finished product of several of his scientific inventions, or an outstanding, almost two-hour, Museum on Wheels tour where a component of the museum, similar to the Ben Franklin Gallery Tour, comes to your site. Geared for 3rd graders and up, the show consists of a traveling van carrying a working Colonial printing press and many other visuals. Kids are enthralled as they learn and experience the history of print and books, and "help" Ben Franklin with his experiments and discoveries as they hear about his life from a master storyteller

There are several family days where touring the museum and making a print craft of some sort is offered as well as classes for older students and adults, such as making mini books, screenprinting, and letterpress printing. Also note that the museum hosts Boy Scout Merit Badge Days and annual standouts such as the Kids Krazy Krafts Day in April and the Dickens Holiday Celebration in December. (See the Calendar section for more details.) I can't recommend this museum and its tours highly enough.

Hours: Open Sat., 10am - 4pm. Open for groups and other individuals by appointment Tues. - Fri. Closed Sun. and Mon.

Price: $8 for adults; $7 for seniors and ages 5 - 18; children 4 and under are free. The Book Arts Tour is $225 for up to 25 people, then $9 per person up to 50. In-house group educational tours are $175 for up to 25 people, then $7 per person, up to 70. The school assembly is $400 for the first show; $200 for an additional show for the same day, for up to 120 students. Museum on Wheels is $600 for up to 150 students.

Ages: 6 years and up for the tours; 3rd graders and up for the school assemblies or Museum on Wheels tours.

JAPANESE AMERICAN NATIONAL MUSEUM ☼

(213) 625-0414 / www.janm.org $$$
100 N. Central Avenue, Los Angeles

During World War II more than 120,000 people of Japanese ancestry, most of whom were American citizens, were incarcerated in American relocation/concentration camps from 1941 to 1946. This museum is dedicated to preserving the memory of that time period, and learning from it. The glass building is nicely laid out and has seven gallery rooms, plus a research library, classrooms, and a theater room. The exhibit rooms holds rotating displays, varying from art exhibits, to the history of Japanese Americans, to athletes of Japanese ancestry. Permanent displays include authentic wooden barracks from an internment camp in Wyoming, plus videos of people's personal stories, and a gallery reminiscent of an Ellis Island tribute with suitcases and immigrants' belongings, such as clothing (e.g., wedding dresses, uniforms, and everyday clothing), personal articles, board games, and numerous photographs. Articles on discrimination in the 1920's and on the loss of citizens' rights during WWII offer both shameful and fascinating information. Videos in several galleries complete the museums' offerings.

Numerous tours are offered here with various emphasis, such as Taiko Drumming, Storytime, Origami Art, Object Analysis (showcasing some artifacts), and more for $4 per student. Many times throughout the year the second Saturday of the month is Target Free Family Day where admission is free, and crafts, workshops, and performances throughout the whole day are included.

The adjacent building, the National Center for the Preservation of Democracy, is another part of the museum and is essentially an auditorium and center for presentations and classes.

The museum also anchors the east end of Little Tokyo Historic District which is composed of ethnic shops and restaurants. Try mochi, a Japanese rice cake made of short-grain glutinous rice that is pounded into paste - it's better than it sounds. Small balls of ice cream wrapped in mochi come in unusual flavors, such as green tea, red bean, and mango. Check out Fugetso-Do or a concoction at Mikawaya Mochi. Also check out the nearby JAMES IRVINE GARDEN (pg. 66). See DOWNTOWN LOS ANGELES / GRAND PARK (pg. 167) for information on Grand Park and all the other places to go within this fairly immediate area.

Hours: Open Tues., Wed., Fri. - Sun., 11am - 5pm; Thurs., noon - 8pm. Closed Mon., New Year's Day, 4th of July, Thanksgiving, and Christmas.

Price: $9 for adults; $5 for seniors and ages 6 - 17; children 5 and under are free. Admission is free every Thurs. from 5pm - 8pm, and all day on the third Thurs. of every month. Check the website for the free Sat. Parking is about $6.

Ages: 7 years and up.

JOE DAVIES HERITAGE AIRPARK AT PALMDALE PLANT 42 / BLACKBIRD ☀ AIRPARK !

(661) 267-5100 - City of Palmdale; (661) 267-5345 - Joe Davies - tours; (661) 274-0884 - Blackbird Airpark / www.cityofpalmdale.org/airpark; www.afftcmuseum.org
2001 Avenue P at the Flight Test Installation at Plant 42, Palmdale

Plant 42 took the aeronautics industry soaring to new heights and now features two collections of vintage aircraft. The Joe Davies airpark pays tribute to those contributions and its heritage of aircraft flown, tested, designed, and produced here by displaying seventeen retired restored, military, important planes, with room (and plans) for more. The collection currently includes an F-104 Starfighter, F-86 Sabre, C-140 Jetstar, F-4 Phantom II, and F-105 Thunderchief, plus a scale model of the B-2 Spirit and a AGM-28 Hound Dog Missile. Walk around the planes to read the placards to understand their importance. Call to schedule a guided tour, offered Wednesdays and Thursdays from 7am to 11am.

Beside the planes, aviation buffs (and others) see salvaged aircraft parts used creatively as "decoration" elements. Plans for this acreage include buildings to house aerospace memorabilia and a visitors center.

Blackbird Airpark, at 2503 E. Avenue P, is just a building over from Joe Davies. Three historic, sleek-looking planes are on display here - the Lockheed SR-71A, the A-12, the spy plane U-2D, and the once-top-secret, D-21 drone. The A-12 is perhaps the best known because it is the first Blackbird ever built and flown. The inscribed, inlaid tiles recognize record setters and program participants. A gift shop is on the premises, as well. This park is not connected with Joe Davies, but they are too close to not see both in one day. Blackbird is an annex of, and maintained by, the Air Force Flight Test Center Museum at Edwards Air Force Base.

Hours: Both are open Fri. - Sun., 11am - 4pm. Closed federal holidays.
Price: Free
Ages: 7 years and up.

JOHN FERRARO BUILDING - LOS ANGELES DEPARTMENT OF WATER AND POWER - HEADQUARTERS

(800) 821-5278 / www.ladwp.com
111 North Hope Street, Los Angeles

This sixteen-story building is completely surrounded by a moat! Well, technically it's a water fountain that circumscribes the building, but it looks as cool as a moat. Part of the fountain is on top of a parking garage, too. Walk around the building because it all looks neat, especially as the fountains shoot upward.

Inside the light and airy lobby are surprisingly interesting displays regarding the history of the department of water and power. They consist of huge murals, an old switchboard, models, a replica of part of an aqueduct, pipes, tools and equipment used, historic artifacts, and some informational panels. As this building is near so many other attractions in DOWNTOWN LOS ANGELES (see pg. 167 for details), it's definitely worth a stop, look, and visit.

Hours: Open Mon. - Fri., 9am - 5pm. Closed weekends and holidays.
Price: Free, except for parking.
Ages: 7 years and up, as there are no guard rails around the water.

JUSTICE BROTHERS RACING CAR MUSEUM

(626) 359-9174 / www.justicebrothers.com
2734 E. Huntington Drive, Duarte

Justice Brothers is an established name in car care products. In the main lobby of their headquarters office building is a slick exhibit of their collection containing thirteen-plus cars and a few motorcycles. Featured models include gleaming and colorful vintage Kurtis midget and sprint cars dating back to the 1930's, a 1968 Ford GT-40 LeMans, a Ford Model T, and a classic Corvette and Thunderbird. Other memorabilia include numerous gasoline pumps, a great display of lights from the top of old gasoline pumps, models, photographs, engines, and even a biplane "flying" overhead. The winner for most unique motorcycle goes to an ice motorcycle, or "icycle," with its steel spikes on the tires to grip ice in Russia and a few other cold countries. There are two other, smaller display areas in adjacent buildings that showcase a few more race cars and a Chevy truck.

Hours: Open Mon. - Fri., 8am - 5pm. Closed Sat. and Sun.
Price: Free
Ages: 6 years and up. Visitors under 18 must be accompanied by an adult.

KIDSPACE CHILDREN'S MUSEUM

(626) 449-9144 / www.kidspacemuseum.org
480 N. Arroyo Boulevard at Brookside Park, Pasadena

Welcome to Kidspace - one of the best children's museum around! Go through the park and walk through a short tunnel that looks like the inside of a kaleidoscope with colorful pieces of odd-shaped tile and mirrors on the walls and ceiling. The large courtyard has picnic tables (purchase food at the cafe or bring your own), huge rubber balls, and splash dance - sections of ground fountains that spurt up water at irregular intervals. (Tip: Bring a change of clothing.) The early childhood learning center, geared for ages 4 and under, has padded floors. It contains soft foam blocks and shapes, short climbing apparatus, and entertainment such as story time and music, plus seats for parents to relax and watch. There is also an outdoor section just for little ones. The play equipment (think IKEA) is colorful and with it's small buildings, tables, slides, and more stimulates for imaginative play. There are also raised water basins for H2O fun. (Remember that change of clothing?)

Enter the main building and grab a bug to "eat" at Bugsy's Diner; perhaps a Poo-Poo Platter? (Don't ask.) The realistic-looking diner offers plastic and rubber bug cuisine while showing videos about bugs - their habits, habitats, anatomy, and even recipes such as roasted cricket pizza. (Dieting here is easy.) The Bug Inn is furnished with everyday objects that are disproportionately large so that things are seen from a bug's eye perspective, such as a wall made of pencils and tables made of bottle caps. An adjacent room has several live, caged insects, scorpions, and millipedes, as well as a live bee house. Gently move the table-top maze and see if you can roll the ball through the town, waterways, and around the nature trails without it falling into a trap. In the nature art center, paint an oversized leaf (using water colors) and play with push pins that make up the large flower heads.

The climbing towers are highlights for agile kids, and for parents who think they can keep up. Big, bluish-clear circles (that represent gigantic raindrops) spiral around and up forty feet to the top. Very cool. (Parents, duck your heads.) The second structure is shaped like a wisteria vine. Climb the large leaves, surrounded by netting, to the top for a view of the museum and surroundings. I let my kids do this one on their own as the zigzag leaf pathway is more narrow than the raindrop tower.

Another section of the pavilion has a paleontologist dig (i.e., a sand pit) where kids can don hats, vests, and gloves to uncover fossils using brushes. Learn about earthquakes and earthquake preparedness by viewing survival kits, interacting with retrofitted wooden model houses, and push large tectonic plates against each other to cause quakes. Get a bug's perspective and try the Ant Climber, a small climbing structure of curved leaves surrounded by netting. Go down the staircase to a trench to experience a dig site where trash is embedded in the walls as are insect burrows. Visitors can climb back via a short tunnel (or use the stairs).

The Nature Exchange is an information center housing books, shells, and numerous containers of rocks, such as quartz, amethyst, sodalite, coal, and garnet. Bring your rocks, plant life, and other natural finds to show to and discuss with the staff. In exchange, you'll earn points used to trade for the collections in the containers in order to build your personal collection.

The Imagination Workshop is for kids to repurpose old radios, gears, electronics, toys, and more into whatever they design. Staff is on hand to help design and create projects, too.

If you can't see the forest for the trees, look at a different forest, such as the Galvin Physics Forest. Instead of trees there are thirteen oversized exhibits outdoors for kids to interact with as they learn about launching bottle rockets; a cool fan that transforms energy into wind power; centripetal force and momentum by constructing a roller coaster; a giant lever; and so much more. Another great element to this area are the huge and numerous soft play blocks in all sorts of shaped and sizes. Kids create marvelous buildings, animals, robots - wherever their imaginations can think of.

All this and there is still the 2.4 acre "backyard," with crisscrossing paved trails, to explore! The back patio is paved like a road, complete with street signs, and kids can use Kidspace's sturdy trikes to ride the course. An outdoor amphitheater, with tiered seating, is put to good use for presentations and shows. Walk underneath an arbor to reach a sand pit and climb on a spider's "web" made from rope. (I'd rather be the spider than the fly.) Other exhibits here include the bee and butterfly garden, an interactive garden (learn about, make, and take home garden-related projects), a wildlife pond (with frogs, turtles, and fish), and a redwood bridge over a stream. Kids will get wet playing in and around this stream. A main attraction is the short, but wide, rock climbing wall designed with strata formations. Kids must place their feet and hands in strategic crevasses and footholds to get across. Younger children will also enjoy climbing a huge inverted tree root. Kirby's Kids Corner has padded flooring and a colorful play structure - including a playhouse, slide and water element - that make it an ideal place for little ones.

Ask about the thirty- to forty-five-minute educational programs and field trip options aimed at kids pre-K to fourth grade. Participants learn about the rocks, water, bugs, gardening, and more, via an array of arts, sciences, games, and activities. Tip/ be aware: Many school groups come here for field trips on weekdays mornings, so you might want to visit in the afternoons!

The on-site Spot Gourmet offers food selections such as a hamburger ($5); turkey or tuna sandwich ($6.50); Chinese chicken salad ($7.75); cheese cubes and grapes ($4); grilled cheese sandwich ($4); cheese pizza ($8); PB&J ($3); oatmeal ($2.95); bagel with cream cheese ($2); and three piece chicken tenders ($4); plus cookies and beverages.

Just outside the museum grounds is BROOKSIDE PARK / REESE'S RETREAT (pg. 49), another place for kids to run around and play. The park has a baseball diamond, lots of open, grassy areas, and playground equipment and Reese's Retreat, an all-accessible, pirate-ship themed playground.

Hours: Open September through May, Tues. - Fri., 9:30am - 5pm; Sat. - Sun., 10am - 5pm. Closed Mon., except for holiday Mon. Open in the summer, Mon. - Fri., 9:30am - 5pm; Sat. - Sun., 10am - 5pm. Closed New Year's Day, 4th of July, Thanksgiving, Christmas Eve, and Christmas, plus certain Saturdays because of football games at the Rosebowl.

Price: $11 per person; children under 1 year are free. Admission is free on the first Tues. of every month from 4pm - 8pm (but not in September). Educational programs are about $9 per person. See page xi for info on ASTC reciprocal museum memberships.

Ages: 1½ - 12 years old.

LANCASTER MUSEUM OF ART AND HISTORY ☀

(661) 723-6250 / www.lancastermoah.com !/$

665 W. Lancaster Boulevard, Lancaster

This three-story, modern museum has rotating exhibits featuring art interests that include paintings, sculptures, drawings, and photography. Artwork created by local artists and pertaining to the Antelope Valley is one focus, as is preserving the history of the area represented by furniture, musical instruments, antique clothing, mining tools, and more. There is also a display on prehistoric fossils - *really* early history! Some of the eclectic, historical objects are permanent, while some are rotated according to theme. The collection includes Egyptian mummies, space suits, Native American relics, military artifacts, historic clothing, and more. Note that the museum might close for a few weeks between exhibitions, so call first. School tours, art classes, and traveling trunk programs (where trunks are filled with hands-on educational and historical items) are offered here.

There are lots of restaurants and eateries nearby including the 50's style Katz N' Jammers on 44801 Beech Ave. Open for breakfast and lunch it has black and white checkered flooring, red vinyl booths, 50's memorabilia on the walls - records, posters, murals, and Coca Cola items, plus that-decade music playing in the background, all of which equals a fun extension of your outing. Also check out the little Five and Dime Candy Store, just down the street, that sells nostalgic candies and more modern brands, and its next door neighbor, Rainbow Ceramic Paint Studio, (661) 949-1010, at 709 W. Lancaster Blvd.

Hours: Open Tues. - Wed., 11am - 6pm; Thurs., 11am - 8pm., Fri. - Sun., 11am - 6pm. Closed Mon. and some holidays.

Price: Free; suggested donation is $2 per person.

Ages: 5 years and up, depending on the current exhibit.

THE LEONIS ADOBE ☀

(818) 222-6511 / www.leonisadobemuseum.org $

23537 Calabasas Road, Calabasas

Step back over 100 years in time when you visit the Leonis Adobe. The restored buildings help kids to picture the wealthy ranchero as it once was. The rustic grounds, complete with grape arbors, old farm equipment, windmills, and a corral containing longhorn cattle, horses, sheep, and goats, enhance the yesteryear atmosphere. Officially Los Angeles' Historic Cultural Monument No. 1, the adobe was once owned by Miguel Leonis, a Basque who led a very colorful life, and Espiritu, his Native American wife. Both the museum and its owners have a rich and fascinating history that kids will enjoy hearing.

The visitor's center is actually the relocated Victorian-style Plummer House, the oldest house "in" Hollywood. It contains a few glass-cased displays of mannequins dressed in period clothing and a gift shop. Outside, a huge, 600-year-old oak tree dominates the grounds. You are welcome to explore the barn, complete with wagons and buggies; a blacksmith's shop that is outfitted with saddles and tools; and the adobe. The bottom story of the adobe has a kitchen with a wood-burning stove and other old-fashioned kitchen implements; a pantry for preserving and drying food (kids like the hanging cow with fake blood); and a dining room with adobe floors. Upstairs is the Leonis' elegant bedroom that has a red velvet bedspread over the canopy bed, plus ladies' boots, and leather trunks. You'll notice that the hallway floor tilts at a downward angle, slanting away from the house. It was built like that to ensure that rains would run away from the walls, not seep into them. The Juan Menendez (bed) Room has a ghost story associated with it. (Every good historical home has at least one such story!) Also up here is an office, complete with desk, ledger, and guitar.

Elsewhere on the ranch grounds are penned sheep, goats, turkeys, ducks, chickens, horses, and a few longhorns; a covered beehive oven which was used for baking bread; and steps leading up to the tank house, or worker's bedroom. The Leonis Adobe is a classy reminder of the relatively brief, but pivotal Mexican/California era. Ask about the terrific

year-round school programs offered here, where kids immerse themselves in this time period with docents dressing the part. Note that there is a Farmer's Market here every Saturday morning.

Just a short walk eastward, past the Sagebrush Cantina restaurant, is the small, but beautiful Calabasas Creek Park. It offers a pleasant picnic area and respite with a rose garden out front, wrought-iron benches throughout, massive shade trees, re-created Chumash village, and bridges over the duck pond. The only drawback to this serene scene is the ever-present freeway noise.

Hours: The Leonis Adobe is open Wed. - Fri. and Sun., 1pm - 4pm; Sat., 10am - 4pm. Half-hour guided tours are given on the weekends at 1:15pm, 2:15, and 3:15pm. Closed Mon., Tues. and main holidays.
Price: $4 for adults; $3 for seniors and students; $1 for children 11 and under.
Ages: 4 years and up.

LOMITA RAILROAD MUSEUM

(310) 326-6255 / www.lomita-rr.org
2137 W. 250th Street, Lomita

Stop, look, and listen! This small, recreated, turn-of-the century train depot is as charming to look at - with its decorative wrought iron, gingerbread molding, and brick patio - as it is to tour. Inside the depot museum/souvenir shop, visitors will see various train memorabilia, such as an old-time station agent ticket office, scale model train cars, telegraph equipment, locomotive whistles, marker lights, an exhibit of railroad ties, and glass cases filled with photographs, and more artifacts. Hanging from the ceiling and the walls is a collection of hand-lanterns.

Outside, on real train tracks, are two railcars: An all-wood, 1910 Union Pacific "bobber" (i.e., caboose) to look in, and a 1902 Southern Pacific Steam locomotive with a cab that the kids can climb in and let their imaginations go full steam ahead. Note that the valves and handles are labeled with explanations for their use, but they are not for touching.

The museum annex park is just across the street. This pretty little grassy spot, with a picnic table under shade trees, boasts a real wood box car and a 1923 Union Oil tank car that are for display purposes only.

Hours: Open Thurs. - Sun., 10am - 5pm. Closed all major holidays.
Price: $4 for adults; $2 for children 11 and under.
Ages: 1½ years and up.

LONG BEACH FIREFIGHTERS MUSEUM

(562) 599-3985 or (562) 570-8628 / www.lbfdmuseum.org
1445 Peterson Avenue, Long Beach

This historic museum, housed in a fire station, holds a wonderful conglomeration of old equipment and numerous old engines. Throughout the main hallway and large rooms and into the crew room and captain's room are displays of breathing apparatus, nozzles, hats, alarm bells, hoses, ladders, a life net, basket stretcher, helmets, uniforms, medals, and even a horse hitching post. The vehicle collection includes an 1890 Rumsey ladder wagon, 1907 Amoskeg steam fire engine, 1897 hand pumper, 1901 hose cart, 1935 squad wagon, 1965 Mack fire truck and several Arhens Fox pumpers. Visitors are allowed to climb into some of the vehicles. The docents are knowledgeable and love to share information and stories, so ask away and listen.

Hours: Open Wed., 8am - noon; the second Sat., 10am - 3pm.
Price: Free
Ages: 4 years and up.

LONG BEACH MUSEUM OF ART

(562) 439-2119 / www.lbma.org
2300 E. Ocean Boulevard, Long Beach

This small, two-story art venue by the beach contains a permanent collection of paintings, drawings, sculptures, decorative furnishings, ceramics, and more. The rotating exhibits vary in medium and content, so call to see what's currently showing to see if it has kid-appeal. Note that on the third Sunday of every month, from 1pm to 4pm, a family art-making workshop is hosted for ages 5 and up. The museum also offers Summer Art Adventures (i.e., day camps) for kids to learn how to draw and paint, as well as education programs, music programs, and other special events.

Grab a bite to eat next door at Claire's at the Museum Restaurant. The food is good - soups, salads, sandwiches, pastas, and more. Eat outside on the patio, by the cool-looking water sculpture, for an incredible view of the beach and

Catalina!

Hours: Open Thurs, 11am - 8pm; Fri. - Sun., 11am - 5pm. Closed Mon. - Wed., New Year's Day, July 4, Thanksgiving, and Christmas.

Price: $7 for adults; $6 for seniors and students; children 11 and under are free. Free admission Thurs., 3pm - 8pm and all day Fri.

Ages: 7 years and up.

LOS ANGELES COUNTY MUSEUM OF ART   ☀

(323) 857-6000 / www.lacma.org $$$$
5905 Wilshire Boulevard, Los Angeles

Art, according to Webster, is: "The use of the imagination to make things of aesthetic significance; the technique involved; the theory involved." This leaves the interpretation of what constitutes art wide open! The world-class Los Angeles County Museum of Art campus is composed of a grouping of several, multi-story buildings each featuring a different style and/or country of origin of art, plus the Bing Center of theater and movies for older audiences.

The Art of the Americas building showcases art from the United States, as well as art from Latin America. Ancient and contemporary furniture, clothing, paintings, sculptures, and various other mediums are presented here on a rotating basis.

The Ahmanson Building contains both modern and contemporary art and more traditional works from Medieval European, the Romantic, and the Renaissance periods. Classic paintings and portraits by Picasso, Giovanni Bellini, Desportes, Koninck, and so many more hang in various galleries throughout the stately, three-story building. Gilbert gold and silver pieces, such as elaborate bowls and candelabras, are on display here, as are incredibly detailed, inlaid stone pictures. Other works of art on view include Islamic, African, and Oceanic art. Contemporary art appeals to kids in that they are attracted and puzzled by the larger-than-life sculptures, abstract paintings on gigantic canvases (that sometimes, to my untrained eye, just look like blotches of color), and common objects that express artistic creativity, like a kitchen sink, or an arrangement of cereal boxes.

The Hammer building features Chinese and Korean Art. The permanent and temporary exhibits here portray other mediums of artistic endeavor as they also specialize in photography, impressionism, drawings, textiles, and prints. This building also houses the Boone Children's Gallery, the most interesting gallery for kids as family members enjoy rotating, hands-on, themed exhibits and activities, and, in particular learn about brush painting and art from Korea and China by trying their hand at it. Enjoy storytelling in Boone's every Monday and Friday at 2 pm.

The adjacent Pavilion for Japanese Art is architecturally unique, inside and out. It houses mostly paintings and a few sculptures in a serene, natural-light setting. The Samurai warrior statue, dressed in eighteenth-century black chain mail armor, gets our vote for the most interesting piece here. The ramp spirals downward, toward the small waterfall and pond on the lowest level.

Under a covered walkway, go outside to the neighboring Broad Contemporary with 60,000 square feet of exhibition space. Take the long ride up the open-air escalator and check out the view of the surrounding city and mountains from the top. This building has three galleries focusing on always the interesting contemporary art, which translates as "anything goes", with some extraordinarily large pieces.

Don't miss *Metropolis II*. This amazing exhibit is like a Hot Wheels racetrack on steroids. It looks like a futuristic city and freeway system, during rush hour. The massive little city, which takes up the space of a small room, is comprised of small skyscrapers, single family homes, and other buildings all surrounded by a miniature commuter rail line, several roads, and a freeway that kind of resembles a roller coaster. Watch, and listen - then feel stressed out - as 1,100 mini cars and other vehicles race along these roads Fridays every hour on the half hour, starting at 11:30am until 6:30pm; and Saturdays and Sundays, 10:30am until 5:30pm. View this electrically-run metropolis from the ground or, better yet, from the balcony.

Between the Broad Contemporary and the Ahmanson, in the front plaza, is Urban Light - a variety of over 200 antique lampposts, which are great for picture taking, day or night. By the Resnick, on the north lawn, is Levitated Mass, a downward tunnel that runs underneath a 340-ton granite megalith - kind of cool! These exhibits are free and open to the public. Urban Light is available 24/7 and Levitated Mass is open 7am - sundown (but not when it's raining).

Behind the Broad Contemporary, the glass and stone, single story, spacious Resnick Exhibition Pavilion houses special exhibitions showcased in natural lighting. These have included massive sculptures, such as stone heads of ancient Mexican warriors (weighing up to 24 tons); a collection of over seventy European and royal court clothing items from the 1700's, and accessories; paintings; art deco furniture; and more.

Although many docents are on hand to insure that nothing is touched in the LACMA buildings, the atmosphere is not stifling. Contact the museum about their numerous and wonderful art classes, school tours, and family programs offered throughout the year. For instance, our school group took the free sculpture tour where we went on a guided tour of the sculptures and then went to the on-site classroom to make sculptures out of the provided clay. Andell Family Sundays are held for the general public almost every Sunday from 12:30pm to 3:30pm with different themes each month. These free days include a family gallery tour (which is also given in Spanish) and learning about a particular exhibit followed by art workshops and sometimes live performances. A cafe serving reasonably priced food and an eating area, plus a more formal sit-down restaurant are part of the outdoor, central courtyard.

Enjoy walking around the museum's spacious backyard, Hancock Park. The parks hosts concerts and presentations at the amphitheater; has picnic tables, grassy areas, and trees; is home to the La Brea Tar Pits; and is adjacent to the GEORGE C. PAGE MUSEUM (pg. 109). Note: Sign up (in person or on-line) for the free NexGen Arts program that gives free museum membership (which translates to free museum admission year round!) to youths 17 and under and to one adult.

Hours: Open Mon. - Tues., and Thurs., 11am - 5pm; Fri., 11am - 8pm; Sat. - Sun., 10am - 7pm. Select galleries are open Fridays in July and August until 11pm. Closed Wed., Thanksgiving, and Christmas. Note that the Boone Children's Gallery closes at 5pm. School tours are often given in the morning hours.

Price: $15 for adults; $10 for seniors and students; ages 17 and under are free. Admission is free on the second Tues. of each month, except for ticketed events; free to the permanent exhibits and non-ticketed exhibitions Mon. - Fri. after 3pm for L.A. County residents; often free (except for ticketed events) on holiday Mondays; and free to NexGen members. Parking costs $10. Metered parking is free on 6th St. on Sundays. See page xi for info on the Bank of America free weekend program.

Ages: 6 years and up.

LOS ANGELES HARBOR FIRE MUSEUM - OLD FIRE STATION 36

(323) 464 - 2727 / www.lafdmuseum.org   !/$
638 Beacon Street, San Pedro

This small museum is housed in the original fire station 36 - on the ground floor of city hall, built in 1928. Come inside to see four fire engines/apparatus - some old and some slightly more modern - plus a fireboat and diver display, hoses, fire extinguishers, photos, and a variety of tools related to the field of fire fighting and rescue.

Hours: Open Sat., 10am - 3pm.
Price: Free. Metered parking (.50¢ an hour) is available.
Ages: 4 years and up.

LOS ANGELES LIVE STEAMERS RAILROAD MUSEUM

(323) 662-8030 / www.lals.org; www.carolwood.com   !/$
5202 Zoo Drive, Los Angeles

Right next to TRAVEL TOWN (pg. 154) this park-like museum features a stationary steam plant, which is fired up on the third Sunday. It has seven working steam engines, three cabooses, a Union Pacific baggage dorm car and sleeper car. Most of the cars now serve as museum offices, *training* rooms (really!), and workshop rooms.

Walt Disney was a railroad aficionado and his actual backyard barn/workshop where he built and ran railcars and layouts, is here at this museum. Some say that inside this small barn was the genesis of Disneyland. Open to tour through on the third Sunday of the month, see several scale locomotives, photographs, an antique phone, Walt's control board, tools, some of his hats, drawings of the Main Street Station, toys, books, railroad paraphernalia, and Disney memorabilia. (And unlike anything else Disney, this is free!) Enjoy a lunch at the picnic tables here and maybe become inspired.

One of the best features of this museum is the large-scale train ride visitors can take over 1.5 miles (about twelve-minutes) through this part of Griffith Park. You'll pass by three miniature towns, plus water towers, bridges, train stations, and other buildings and scenery. See GRIFFITH PARK (pg. 62) for more things to do in this immediate area. Check the October Calendar section for info on their annual Ghost Train Ride.

Hours: Open most Sun. (weather permitting), except the Sunday before Memorial Day and the first Sun. in October, 10:45am - 3pm.

Price: Free. Suggested donations are $3 per person, per train ride.
Ages: 1 ½ years and up; at least 34" for the train ride.

LOS ANGELES MARITIME MUSEUM

(310) 548-7618 / www.lamaritimemuseum.org; www.portoflosangeles.org
600 Sampson Way, Berth 84, San Pedro

If you have older children who dream of sailing the oceans blue, they will enjoy walking through the two-story, nicely-laid-out galleries of changing exhibits in this maritime museum, which is housed in an old ferry terminal. Arranged in the rooms and up and down the hallways, there are hundreds of ship models to look at, many glass-enclosed, ranging from several real boats to scale sized to ones inside a bottle. (How do they do that?) An impressive twenty-one-foot scale model of the *Queen Mary* (made for and renamed *Poseidon* for the same-name movie) and two cut-away models, of the *Titanic* and *Lusitania*, give your kids the inside scoop on ocean liners. Other exhibits put the spotlight on the fishing industry in San Pedro and commercial diving. Check out the ship figureheads and maritime crafts. A highlight is the Amateur Radio Station where your child might be able to talk to someone on the other side of the world. It's *knot* impossible to practice tying any of the sixty-four types of seaman's knots on display. Play captain at the wheel of a 19th-century sailing ship.

Free, guided tours for all ages are also offered. Classes for the public include scrimshaw, celestial navigation, and ship model building. Check out the gift shop for nautical finds.

A ship's anchor (which is gigantic), a propeller, torpedo, mast, bow peak, and bell are out in front of the museum. There is a cannon on the small back deck where you can also watch the ships in the harbor.

Just next "door" is Fire Station #112 which shelters a classic behind glass - fireboat #2. The boat, commissioned in 1925, sports pumps and just looks really neat. A history of Los Angeles fireboats, and this one in particular, are on panels in front of the boat. There is no charge for viewing the fireboat. Note: You can catch the replica and vintage RED CAR TROLLEY just outside the museum for a fun excursion. See page 214 for more details. See PORTS O' CALL VILLAGE (pg. 159) for information about other attractions in the immediate area.

Hours: Open Tues. - Sun., 10am - 5pm. (Last admission is at 4:30pm) Closed Mon., New Year's Day, Thanksgiving, and Christmas.
Price: $3 for adults; $1 for seniors; ages 17 and under are free.
Ages: 5 years and up.

LOS ANGELES MUSEUM OF THE HOLOCAUST

(323) 651-3704 / www.lamoth.org
100 S. The Grove Drive, adjacent to Pan Pacific Park, Los Angeles

Enter through a long, narrow tunnel/hallway that goes at a slant, kind of underground. Get a free printed and/or audio tour which describes the exhibits and behind-the-scenes in more detail, making the personal stories around the museum hit the heart and mind. A video featuring a U.S. soldier who helped with the liberation of a concentration camp is the first stop. Several rooms then flow into the next, each containing necessarily graphic (i.e., piles of naked bodies) photos and informational panels, plus numerous artifacts. In the first room is a large and long, touch-screen table with images and videos that reveal the lives of Jewish people - education, family, culture, sports, etc. - before the Holocaust. In another room video terminals show actual footage from and of, and locations of, eighteen concentration camps, plus newsreels from WWII Germany that depict life in the camps. A seventy-screen video testimonial wall, called the Tree of Testimony, features powerful interviews with Holocaust survivors that interconnects each one just as leaves and branches from a single tree are connected. Other displays throughout the museum include a model layout of the Sobibor death camp; family belongings; religious antiques (including an old Torah once stolen by the Nazis); music of that era; artwork by Jewish artisans; and a walk through a recreated (human) cargo train car.

One-hour guided tours for school or other groups, tailored to meet the need of the given age group for fifteen to fifty people, are also offered. Allow another hour, or so, if you will, to incorporate into your tour the opportunity to meet and hear the powerful, first-hand testimony of a Holocaust survivor, when offered.

At the north end of the adjacent PAN PACIFIC PARK (pg. 77) is a martyr's memorial monument with its six black granite, triangular columns - please read the website for all of its symbolism. Note that the museum is also close to THE GROVE (pg. 94) and FARMER'S MARKET (pg. 18).

Hours: Open Mon. - Thurs., 10m - 5pm; Fri., 10am - 2pm, Sat. - Sun., 10am - 5pm. Closed some major holidays.
Price: Free. A $100 donation is suggested for group tours.

Ages: 4th graders and up.

LOS ANGELES POLICE MUSEUM   ☼

(877) 714-LAPD (5273) or (323) 344-9445 / www.laphs.org $$
6045 York Boulevard, Los Angeles

Here's an APB - this police museum offers arresting pieces of history while capturing the impact of the LAPD from its inception in 1869 through modern day. Take an audio tour, which is great, or take a one-hour, or so, guided tour, often given by an ex-law enforcement officer, through the building which looks like a classic police station from a Hollywood set. Actually, Clint Eastwood did much to restore and renovate it when he filmed *Blood Work* here.

The first floor contains a pictorial history of the city's changing styles and people, plus crime scene pictures. A display case contains blackjacks, batons, and handcuffs from various eras. Down the passageway, enter a cell block of five jail cells, once used to hold those who committed misdemeanor crimes. You may go in the cells (and leave them) of your own free will. Take pictures as you emphasize to your kids that this will be the only time they will ever be inside a jail cell. You can also take mug shots with your camera, here. The three display cases in this section hold foreign and American handcuffs and thumbcuffs, leg irons, and old jail locks.

The backyard has a helicopter you can climb into, a military armored personnel carrier (that looks like a small tank), and a few bullet-ridden and some vintage police cars and emergency vehicles. A suspects' car, from a robbery, is also here - check out its shattered windshield. Put on a helmet and sit on a police motorcycle.

Back inside, another room contains old communications equipment - radios, radars, car computers, and bull horns, plus light bars and helmets. Pass by the felony jail cells to see various hand-held radios and an exhibit of items that came from the New York 911 site, including a piece of the towers, some helmets, and newspaper clippings.

Upstairs, visitors can try on body armor (which is really heavy), helmets, an equipment belt, and a gas mask. Other displays are of the SLA (i.e., posters and a pipe bomb); part of a bomb shield on wheels; mannequins wearing uniforms from different time periods; a Jack Webb display case; and cases of various weapons, mostly firearms. Watch the almost twenty-five minute, riveting video of mostly real footage (and some reenactment) from a 1997 bank robbery involving two suspects and over thirty officers. There are some graphic scenes of people getting shot, and even killed. Then, walk into the next room which contains mannequins of these robbers dressed in gear and toting their AK-47s, plus other real weapons and bullet casings used in the shootout. Note that the suspects' getaway car you saw outside earlier belonged to these robbers.

A visit here increased our knowledge about the police force and elevated our understanding and respect for them. If you want to bring home something more tangible, stop off at the gift store - it would be almost criminal not to.

Hours: Open Mon. - Fri., 10am - 4pm; and on the third Sat., 9am - 3pm.
Price: $9 for adults; $8 for seniors; children 12 and under are free.
Ages: 5 years and up.

LOS ANGELES SHERIFFS DEPARTMENT MUSEUM   ☼

(562) 946-7081   !
11515 S. Colima Road, Whittier

Dispatch yourself to this 5,000-square-foot museum that depicts the history of the Los Angeles County Sheriffs Department from 1850 through the present day. A classic 1938 Studebaker police car cannot be touched, but kids can "ride" on the police motorcycle next to it and push a button to make the red lights flash. (I hope this won't bring back any bad memories!)

A western-style jail has a replica of a nineteenth-century sheriff's office, complete with a model sheriff and a prisoner behind bars. This room also contains a Western wall with photos, a mannequin, and saddles and spurs that were used on the horses in the early days of law enforcement. The Vice Exhibit showcases how different carnival-type games can be rip-offs, as well as illegal. The back room contains a gun case, handcuffs, a display of gang weapons and emblems, drug paraphernalia, and some scenes of some infamous cases. Other displays include items regarding riot squads and the reserve forces, and articles regarding women in the sheriff's department. There are also a lot of old photographs, badges, awards, model police cars, and mannequins dressed in various sheriff's uniforms spanning the decades.

Another room contains an entire helicopter. It also has the side of a Search and Rescue helicopter mounted on a wall, with a dangling child mannequin being airlifted in a basket. The live-video footage shows the awesome job that Search and Rescue teams perform. The gift shop has some interesting items to purchase! School tours are given for third graders and up.

Outside, a wall too filled with plaques, memorializes officers killed in the line of duty. For your information, every May a memorial ceremony is held here that commemorates the lives of peace officers who have died in the line of duty in L.A. County in the past year. This moving ceremony, attended by numerous officers, families of slain officers, and government officials, is also open to the public.

Hours: Open Mon. - Fri., 9am - 4pm. Closed on major holidays.
Price: Free
Ages: 5 years and up.

LOS ENCINOS STATE HISTORIC PARK

(818) 784-4849 / www.historicparks.org; www.parks.ca.gov
16756 Moorpark Street, Encino

Just off the very busy Ventura Boulevard is a little oasis. With a good-sized gated pond and plenty of ducks (purchase duck food for 25¢), expanses of grassy lawn under mature shade trees, and picnic tables, this park is delightful to visit in and of itself. Other reasons to visit include taking a tour of the De La Ossa Adobe, originally built in 1849. Walk through the rooms to see a writing desk, an antique wedding dress and shoes, pictures of families that once owned the adobe, and the simply-furnished rancho office and kitchen. Guests can also peer into the working blacksmith's shop, made of stone, to see the furnace and all the tools of the trade. The small visitors center holds displays of photographs, branding irons, and other artifacts.

Guided tours are offered to the public and to school groups. A docent dressed in historical costume usually tours the school groups who play 19th-century games, use the water pump outside, and do a few other old-fashioned chores while learning about the time period.

Hours: The park is open Wed. - Sun., 10am - 5pm. Free tours of the adobe are offered by appointment only.
Price: Free
Ages: 2 years and up for the park; 7 years and up for the adobe.

MADAME TUSSAUD'S HOLLYWOOD

(323) 798-1670 / www.madametussauds.com/hollywood $$$$$
6933 Hollywood Boulevard, Hollywood

I had my picture taken with President Obama, and then with Jennifer Lopez, Brad Pitt, Michael Jackson, Simon Cowell, Spiderman and many other famous people - all in the same day! Madame Tussaud's wax museum offers the opportunity to get more up close and personal with television, movie, sports, singing, and even political celebrities than you'll probably ever have a chance to do in real life, and new figures are added regularly.

This multi-level wax museum is unique from others of this genre in two ways in particular: One is that the over 120 wax figures, for the most part, look amazingly lifelike and truly like the person they are modeled after. (My top pick for realistic lookalike is the Steven Spielberg figure.) You can see this for yourself because of the second distinction - you can get close enough to touch the figures and to interact with them because there aren't any barriers.

There are several genres, or sections, of the museum - A-list Party, Crime, Action Heroes, Sports, Modern Classics and more. Many of the wax statues are set in famous scenes, backdrops and all, along with props that you can use so you can pose with them or even imitate them. Make sure to bring your camera! It was fun, for instance, to put on a robe and boxing gloves, get into the ring, and pretend to box next to Sylvester Stallone; sit on a camel next to Peter O'Toole in a setting from *Lawrence of Arabia;* pull up a chair at the table and join Audrey Hepburn in a replicated scene from *Breakfast at Tiffany's;* hop on a motorcycle and join Hugh Jackman as Wolverine; yell "hi ya" while chopping a wooden block in two near Jackie Chan; put on a jacket and twirl a cane around while standing alongside Charlie Chaplin; set a cowboy hat on your head and hang out with John Wayne, or with Robert Redford and Paul Newman from *Butch Cassidy and the Sundance Kid;* sit in the captain's chair onboard the deck of the *Star Trek Enterprise* alongside Captain Kirk and the rest of the waxy crew; and in an office room setting with Spiderman, pretend to be hanging upside down on the furniture and then reverse the picture on your computer at home - perfect! Many of the settings have sound effects to go along with them, such as the sound of swords clashing. Kiosks are interspersed throughout the attractions, too, where you can test your knowledge of the stars, movie terminology, trivia, and more.

From David Beckham to Clark Gable to Quentin Tarantino to Beyonce to Lady Gaga and Madame Tussaud herself (kind of) - there is someone here for everyone to get excited about seeing and posing with.

On the last floor you mingle with a bevy of stars (who are wearing clothing worn by the actual celebrities) at the Oscars as paparazzi camera lights flash. The final room in the museum allows visitors to see the intricate details of how

a wax model is made (over 800 hours of work per statue) and the painstaking details and measurements (of everything!) taken on a person being immortalized (unless there is a heat wave). You'll see the diagrams, models in various stages of being created, colorful locks of hair (which are inserted in the figure's head one strand at a time) and color and sizes of eyeballs to choose from. For an additional $12 you can dip your hand in a vat of wax to make a mold of your hand to give to someone special.

Day campers and students have additional options in viewing the wax museum. They can participate a forty-five minute, educational scavenger hunt and/or a field trip that incorporates subjects such as Hollywood History where students follow script notes throughout the museum to learn about Hollywood's influence on people and communities; World History where historical figures that shaped our world are studied; Modern-Day Superheroes which looks at real superheroes and fictional ones; and Special Effects where students study visual and technical special effects. There are also specialty themes such as Black History and Hispanic Heritage. The field trips also offer pre- and post-lesson plans and are for groups of fifteen or more students.

Note: Check out the Hollywood section in the Cities Index in the back of this book for an abundance of other things to see and do in the immediate area, such as the adjacent, historic TCL Chinese Theatre (used to be called Grauman's).

Hours: The hours fluctuate a lot! It is open every day, except Oscar day, and usually at 10am (9am in the summer). Closing times vary from 7pm on weekdays and 8pm on weekends most of the year, to 10pm daily in the summer.

Price: $26.95 for ages 13 and up; $19.95 for ages 4 - 12; children 3 and under are free. Do purchase tickets online and save $$! Parking is available at Madame Tussaud's garage, accessible off Orange Dr. at $2.50 every 15 min., $10 max., or park at the Hollywood and Highland Center with similar rates. At this center you can also park for $2 for first four hours with validation from a business inside the Hollywood and Highland Center. (Do lunch!) Madame Tussaud's does not validate parking. The metro red line stop is close-by.

Ages: 5 years and up

MARTIAL ARTS HISTORY MUSEUM

(818) 478-1722 / www.martialartsmuseum.com
2319 W. Magnolia Boulevard, Burbank

Small, but mighty, this unique museum artistically and creatively visually portrays the history of martial arts while dispensing a wealth of readable information. It was designed with the aid of Disney and other artists and animators. Enter under the long, paper dragon through the faux stone castle archway (and guard) and begin your journey. In chronological order, each country with a history of martial arts is represented in separate sections showcased by colorful picture panels, stories, memorabilia, and three-minute videos with tie-ins of the arts (opera, dance, and more.). Note that overhead is a pictural timeline of important events and people in martial arts history. Many martial arts pioneers, including Funakoshi, Kano, and Ueshiba, are honored in photos. Kids - ask for a paper scavenger hunt.

The Chinese section tells of how Kung Fu began and features a wonderful, huge lion "puppet" used for lion dancing, plus a wall of weapons and uniforms. The Art of the Samurai in the Japanese section shows and tells that story with three pieces of incredible armor from the style of the late 1500's (poised to look like three scary men) and over fifteen swords against a mural of Japanese warriors. Big pictures display the art of Sumo. Kabuki features more uniforms, weapons, and photos of masters, plus explanatory information such as sickles were originally farming tools, then modified. Ninjas are next with a life-sized torso of a hidden-faced Ninja, plus climbing claws weapons and a video that includes the introduction of Judo in the Olympics. After Korea, and its uniforms, is the tiki-hut-themed Hawaiian arts with a large tiki figure and shark teeth on the edges of several of its weapons. This is followed by Kali, and then the U.S. with its intro of mixed martial arts and UFC. Huge photos of champions line the walls here.

The last section is devoted to the influence of martial arts on comic books, film, televison, print, and other media. Cartoon-style panels and some movie memorabilia are in the last room, which is a theater that shows a three-part documentary called *Martial Arts in Film, TV and Print*. It also shows other films. Some of the movie props are the shield used in *Mortal Combat*, Billy Jack's hat from *Billy Jack*, the headband worn by Ralph Macchio in *The Karate Kid*, and Kato's mask from the *Green Hornet*.

The museum hosts a variety of events and seminars including special screenings, Samurai history, language workshops, sushi seminars, animation drawings, craft displays, martial art demonstrations (sometimes featuring celebrities), sword cutting performances, and more. Adult and kid groups can take educational tours; just call to make a reservation. Is it wrong that I still have these song lyrics running through my brain? - "Everybody was Kung Fu

Fighting, those kicks were fast as lightning. . . "

Hours: Open Thurs. - Sun., 11am - 6pm.
Price: $10 for adults; $5 for ages 6 - 15; children 5 and under are free.
Ages: 5 years and up.

MISSION SAN FERNANDO REY DE ESPAÑA

(818) 361-0186 / www.missionscalifornia.com
15151 San Fernando Mission Boulevard, Mission Hills

$$

What was life like in the early days of California? Take a self-guided tour of one of my family's favorite missions to find out. Mission San Fernando Rey, founded in 1797, was the seventeenth mission in the chain of outposts along the coast of California. It has a beautiful, large courtyard, with a small sundial at the north entrance, and west gardens that are surrounded by numerous rooms. These rooms lead to small, alcove rooms - what delightful exploration! The Museum Room is a good place to begin as it's filled with old photos (including one of a bathroom that looks like a small indoor pool), statues, bows and arrows, peace pipes, a bell collection, and several more artifacts. The Madonna Room is fascinating as it contains over 100 representations of the Madonna, each depicted by different nationalities and cultures. From simplistic versions to ornate ones, there are Chinese, African, and Indian Madonnas, plus one that looks like a prairie woman, another like an Eskimo, and more.

Other rooms and items of interest we saw include a hospice that held beds made with rope supports (before box springs); simply furnished bedrooms; plain wooden tables and chairs; the Convent, where meat was hung to dry; mission vestments; a library containing shelves of very old books including a colorful, hand-illuminated liturgical book with large Gothic lettering; brick ovens; and pipe organs. The workshop and weaving rooms are interesting because they hold, respectively, blacksmith tools, saddles, and scythes, and a large wooden loom with cowhide chairs. The church, which still holds regular worship services, has adobe walls and an ornately decorated altar with gold-leaf overlay. A small cemetery behind the church opens into a huge, neighboring cemetery. In the midst of all this history, my boys loved seeing the many peacocks that wandered the grounds. They even "discovered" a few roosters that were tame enough to pet.

Brand Park, once a part of the mission, is just across the street. This grassy park has a lot of shade trees, plenty of picnic tables and running around space, but no playground. It also has vats where mission wines were once produced.

Hours: Open daily, 9am - 4:30pm. Closed Thanksgiving and Christmas.
Price: $5 for adults; $4 for seniors; $3 for ages 7 - 15; children 6 and under are free. Admission to Brand Park is free.
Ages: 5 years and up.

MISSION SAN GABRIEL ARCHANGEL

(626) 457-3035 / www.sangabrielmission.org
428 S. Mission Drive, San Gabriel

$$

Located in the Mission District, California's fourth mission is aptly nicknamed "Queen of the Missions." The graceful buildings and pleasant grounds transport you back to 1771, when the mission was founded. They also offer a wonderfully visual way to learn about California's Spanish/Mexican heritage.

In the midst of the cactus garden are tanning vats, with a placard describing the tanning process. Walk up a few stone steps to see four large holes in the ground, which were once the soap and tallow vats. The San Gabriel Mission supplied soap and candles to most of the other missions. There is one fountain and several statues distributed throughout the mission gardens. In the cemetery, for instance, is a life-size crucifix - a memorial to the 6,000 Indians buried on the grounds.

The Mission Church is still in use. The wall behind the altar is eye-catching as it is ornately decorated. The small baptismal room is equally impressive. Next to the church, the small and somewhat dark museum contains only a few articles that were of interest to my kids - big, old books covered in sheepskin dating from 1489 and 1588, and a Spanish bedroom set. Knowing that the museum was once a series of rooms, such as sleeping quarters, weaving rooms, and carpenter shops, made it a bit more interesting.

Located in the center of the mission is the Court of the Missions. Models of each of California's twenty-one missions, varying in size and layout, but similar in style, are on display here. Vaya con Dios! (Go with God!)

Hours: Open Mon. - Sat., 9am - 4:30pm; Sun., 10am - 4pm. Closed New Year's Day, Easter, July 4th, Thanksgiving, and Christmas.
Price: $5 for adults; $3 for ages 6 - 17; children 5 and under are free.

Ages: 5 years and up.

MONROVIA HISTORICAL MUSEUM
(909) 297-6356 / www.monroviahistoricalmuseum.com
742 E. Lemon Avenue, Monrovia

One room of this small, local museum features artifacts and photos of the early city, including a police motorcycle and uniforms, along with other displays. Another features memorabilia of early Native Americans, such as pottery and arrowheads. The 1907 classroom has desks, blackboard, and even a teacher (i.e. a mannequin dressed in clothing from that time period). I love the display of telephones from the ages - some of those styles are making a comeback. The turn-of-the-century parlour holds a piano, furniture, and other items from this era. There is a courtyard and garden area out back. Call to book a tour for a school group. See MONROVIA SKATE PARK - RECREATION PARK (pg. 75) for details about the surrounding park.

> **Hours:**   Open Thurs. and Sun., 1pm - 4pm.
> **Price:**   Free
> **Ages:**   8 years old and up.

MONTEREY PARK HISTORICAL MUSEUM and GARVEY RANCH PARK
(626) 307-1267 / www.ci.monterey-park.ca.us; www.laas.org
781 S. Orange Avenue, Monterey Park

This small museum's claim to fame is its twenty-one scale models of the California missions. The adobe-like museum has three reconstructed rooms that also house Indian artifacts, household items (such as toys and a phonograph), tools, period clothing, photographs, and a corner dedicated to Laura Scudder (who lived in Monterey Park) - of the potato chip fame.

Adjacent to the museum is a small observatory, operated by the L.A. Astronomical Society, that is open for public viewing on Wednesdays from about 7:45pm - 10pm. The next-door Garvey Ranch Park is a nice park with grassy areas, trees, a few covered picnic areas, paved pathways, two lighted baseball diamonds with stadium seating, basketball courts, nice playgrounds, and two tennis courts, just up the hill.

> **Hours:**   The museum is open Sat. - Sun., 2pm - 4pm. Closed the 5th Sat. of the month, holidays and bad
>   weather. The park is open daily, sunrise - sunset.
> **Price:**   Free
> **Ages:**   5 years and up.

MUSEUM OF CONTEMPORARY ART / GEFFEN CONTEMPORARY / PACIFIC DESIGN CENTER
$$$$
(213) 626-6222 or (213) 621-1741 / www.moca.org
250 S. Grand Avenue, Los Angeles

The elegant Museum of Contemporary Art (MOCA), located on top of a plaza, presents rotating exhibits of eclectic art work - paintings, sculptures, photos, and more. This type of museum is a fun one to bring kids to as an introduction to art because the pieces are unusual, imaginative, and sometimes puzzling. Idea: After visiting the museum, have the kids come home and create their own contemporary or abstract piece of art. As we looked at the huge paintings on canvas, my boys and I took the liberty of renaming several pieces. (I think some of their title choices were more apropos than the ones the artists chose.) This involved the kids in studying the art and therefore enhanced our visit here. Downstairs in the museum is a reading room with several books, many geared for children, that pertain to the art and artists currently featured at the MOCA. On the first Sunday of every month free tours are offered for ages 7 to 18 years, followed by a workshop where participants paint, sculpt, or create a work of art pertaining to the tour focus. The plaza just outside has tables and chairs, a few trees and reflection pools.

One satellite building of MOCA, the Geffen Contemporary, is located one mile away at 152 N. Central Avenue in Little Tokyo, across the plaza from the JAPANESE AMERICAN NATIONAL MUSEUM (pg. 124). Another satellite is the Pacific Design Center (PDC) at 8687 Melrose Avenue in West Hollywood. The Center features rotating exhibits of architecture, design, and selections from MOCA's permanent collection. The Museum of Contemporary Art, then, is actually one museum in three buildings! See DOWNTOWN LOS ANGELES / GRAND PARK (pg. 167) for information on Grand Park and all the other places to go within this fairly immediate area.

> **Hours:**   Open Mon., 11am - 5pm; Thurs., 11am - 8pm; Fri., 11am - 5pm; Sat. - Sun., 11am - 6pm. Closed
>   Tues., Wed., New Year's Day, July 4th, Thanksgiving, and Christmas.

Price: $12 for adults; $7 for seniors and students with ID; ages 11 and under are free. Admission is free every Thurs., 5pm - 8pm. Admission to one of the MOCA museums is valid for all 3 if visited on the same day. Parking is $9 flat rate with MOCA validation ($20 deposit and $11 refund when exiting).

Ages: 6 years and up.

MUSEUM OF FLYING and AIRPORT PARK   ☀

(310) 398-2500 / www.museumofflying.com $$$
3100 Airport Avenue, Santa Monica

Consider this entry your boarding call to make a direct flight to the Museum of Flying. A Douglas DC-3 aircraft outside the museum hanger lets you know you've arrived. There are several other aircraft outside, too, including a Douglas A-4 Skyhawk, Blue Angels Naval plane, and the nose of a Fed Ex. plane.

Enter the mid-sized museum to gawk at planes suspended overhead such as a BD-5 Microjet, Cassutt III Formula One Air Racer, and Monerai Sailplane, and some that are grounded such as a replica of the Wright Flyer, a hot air balloon, a replica of a Lockheed Vega, a Douglas World Cruiser, and more - there are almost two dozen planes of all sizes. Some are undergoing restoration. Airplane seats, video kiosks, aviation artwork, model planes, airplane parts (engines, flight computer, etc.), and artifacts from aviators are also important components of the museum.

Play pilot and adjust the instruments in the cockpit of a Convair CV-240; sit inside a T-33 Jet Trainer; and go inside the cockpit of the Fed Ex. Boeing 727 (the one belonging to the nose you see outside) to listen to the live feed from the Santa Monica air traffic control tower. To experience flight, go on the full-motion simulator ride that allows 360 degree pitches and rolls, stunt flying and can even go upside down, though hopefully you won't experience that on a real flight! Participants, who must be at least 4 feet tall, can choose from a variety of aircraft such as air combat in a P-38 or cruising in a CD-3 over L.A. Non-participants can view what is showing on the screen, as well.

The Mezzanine features a replica of the Douglas Aircraft Company executive boardroom and office of its founder, Donald Douglas. The theater on this level features various aviation films.

The museum offers guided tours for all ages, as well as birthday parties for kids that include use of a party space, a guided tour, viewing of a Charlie Brown aviation movie in the theater and exploring the museum after the party.

Note that just down the street from the museum is the restaurant, TYPHOON (see pg. 25), and Airport Park. This park has a small, gated tot lot in the sand with swings; toys on huge springs to sit and ride on; and a fun, artsy-shaped object to climb on and play. There are also picnic tables, a few bbq pits, a block of grass with huge trees, an enclosed dog run area, and best of all, perhaps, is that it is close to the airport so you can watch planes land and take off.

Hours: Open Wed. - Sun., 10am - 5pm. Simulator rides are available Fri. - Sun. The park is open daily, 6am - 11pm.

Price: The museum is $10 for adults; $8 for seniors and students; $6 for ages 6 - 12; children 5 years and younger are free. The Maxflight Simulator is $8. The park is free.

Ages: 4 years and up.

MUSEUM OF LATIN AMERICAN ART   ☀

(562) 437-1689 / www.molaa.com $$
628 Alamitos Avenue, Long Beach

A nicely laid out main gallery and surrounding gallery rooms create a welcoming ambiance for exploring Latin American culture and heritage while experiencing its art. Rotating exhibits feature sculpture, paintings, and mixed media art by Latin American artists. Take a stroll through the outdoor sculpture garden to look at unique pieces set amongst cacti, palm trees, and other plants. The museum regularly hosts hands-on art workshops and even live performances on Sundays for children, usually geared for ages 6 and up, that tie-in with the present exhibit. Note: The gift shop is filled with wonderful selection of cultural items to purchase.

Hours: Open Wed. - Thurs., 11am - 5pm; Fri., 11am - 9pm; Sat. - Sun., 11am - 5pm. Closed Mon.,Tues., New Year's Day, 4th of July, Thanksgiving, Christmas Eve and Christmas.

Price: $9 for adults; $6 for seniors and students; children 11 and under are free. Admission is free every Sun. and the 4th Fri. of every month from 5pm - 9pm. See page xi for info on the Bank of America free weekend program.

Ages: 6 years and up.

MUSEUM OF TOLERANCE / SIMON WIESENTHAL CENTER ☼

(310) 553-8403 or (800) 900-9036 or (310) 772-2505 / www.museumoftolerance.com $$$$$

9786 W. Pico Boulevard, Los Angeles

Simon Wiesenthal was a Holocaust survivor who became a famed Nazi hunter that unearthed over 1,100 war criminals. The Museum of Tolerance, an educational component of the center, is unique in its format of numerous technologically advanced and interactive major exhibits, and in its focus on personal prejudice, group intolerance, the struggle for civil rights in America, and the Holocaust. Begin your journey on the lower level as you enter through the door marked Prejudice. A video wall exhibit (which changes) currently called the Power of Words shows famous politicians speaking - Joseph Stalin, President Kennedy, and several others; history has told us the effect of their words. In a mock 50's diner, called Point of View, visitors use jukebox monitors to watch various scenarios and answer a menu of questions about personal responsibility regarding drinking, drugs, hate speeches, and other issues. Enter the Millennium Machine where participants add their input by answering questions about global crimes, human rights abuse, and the threat of terrorism. You'll be riveted and affected by the sixteen-screen video Civil Rights Wall; an interactive U.S. map that discloses 250 hate groups in America called GlobalHate.com; and *We The People*, a timeline on a very long wall with photos and information from 1565 to the present day regarding the diversity of Americans and the struggles and intolerance that the people and country has and continues to overcome. An intense film called *In Our Time* focuses on Bosnia, Darfur, Rwanda, genocides, and contemporary hate groups that have violated human rights throughout the world.

The Holocaust section starts as you take a passport photo card of a person who was sent to the concentration camps, making the experience more personal. On a semi, self-guided tour you then walk along a series of chronological stylized vignettes, starting in the late 1920's, that light up when you stand in front of them, while listening to narration that explains the events leading up to the Holocaust. This factual and emotional one-hour tour is one of the most informative and visual ways to witness what happened. You then walk through a replica of the gates of Auschwitz into a recreated gas chamber to watch more detailed film clips regarding what happened to people at the camps; their stories and testimonies. Powerful. Your time here culminates when you receive a printout of the fate of the person whose passport you hold. The next area contains Simon Wiesenthal's actual office from Vienna with all of his papers, SS directories, books, videos, and more.

The second floor of the museum contains rotating exhibits and a multimedia learning center with work stations. Numerous films - on Anne Frank, Harriet Tubman, Helen Keller, and others - are available for viewing. Also housed here are copies of letters from Anne Frank. One of the most compelling experiences at the museum is hearing Holocaust survivors share their testimonies. They usually speak here for an hour every day, yet call to make sure.

Don't miss the one-hour Anne Frank exhibit/experience. Walk down a corridor with panels decorated to look like a Frankfort streetscape, then turn around to see Anne's profound words printed on the other side. Enter a hidden room, her Secret Annex, to immerse yourself in her story in so many different ways. Playing on the expanse of walls is a riveting film that re-creates what it felt like to live as Anne Frank, from being locked up in the attic to exploring her feelings and hopes and dreams to the nightly attacks of war just outside. Real footage is also shown in the exhibit, including a shot of Anne, as well as displays of prison uniforms, yellow felt Stars of David, copies of handwritten letters, photographs, and many more artifacts. The displays are interspersed on and with a wall of tightly folded shirts that wraps around and progress in color from pinkish pastels and colors to dingy grays and blacks as Anne's life progresses from childhood towards her untimely death. Kiosks in the Interactive Action Lab encourage visitors to become more involved with Anne's world and the Holocaust by responding to issues she brings up, ones that still need thought and action today. The words from her world-famous and poignant diary are printed around walls and pillars, as well as heard from a continually-playing audio narration hauntingly read by actress Hailee Steinfeld. An evocative exhibit/experience.

The third floor main exhibit is titled Finding Our Families, Finding Ourselves that aims at encouraging visitors to seek their own history and recognize commonalities between all peoples. The first display is a collection of personal belongings - all stuff actually left behind at Ellis Island. Bon voyage as you walk the gangplank onto a realistic-looking part of a boat, bypassing luggage and other artifacts. Walk past the ships's exam rooms while listening to Billy Crystal narrating what immigrants experienced. Through a hall of celebrities, such as Michelle Kwan and Kareem Abdul-Jabbar, who share how their heritage has affected them, you then enter a series of four rooms. Each room was decorated and chosen as a pivotal place to four famous Americans who also tell their story and influence of their family via videos: Dr. Maya Angelou and her grandmother's general store in Arkansas; Joe Torre and his family's Italian-influenced family room; Billy Crystal and his cartoonish-styled kitchen and living room; and Carlos Santana and his recording studio. There is a nook of computer monitors to assist visitors on how to research their own genealogy.

The fourth floor has a cafeteria that serves light snacks and refreshments. Notes: Each of the three main exhibit places take about an hour. Going through the Anne Frank exhibit takes another hour. Cameras are not allowed in the museum. The educational programs offered are wonderful - for school groups, and for adults and professionals, including Tools For Tolerance, From Hate to Hope (a former White Supremacist and one of his victims share their story), hearing survivors of human trafficking, and much more.

Hours: The museum hours, except for the Anne exhibit, are Mon. - Fri., 10am - 5pm (closes at 3:30pm on Fri., Nov. - March); Sun., 11am - 5pm. The last ticket is sold at 3:30pm, or at 1pm on the Fridays when the museum closes earlier. The Anne exhibit is open Sun. - Fri., 10am - 6:30pm, with the last entrance at 5:30pm. It is also open Thurs. until 9:30pm, with the last entrance at 8:30pm. Everything is closed Sat., national holidays, and Jewish holidays. School tours for twenty or more students are offered as early as 8:30am.

Price: Admission to all the exhibits, except Anne, are $15.50 for adults; $12.50 for seniors; $11.50 for students with I.D., active military, and ages 5 - 18; children 4 and under are free. Admission to Anne is an additional $15.50 for adults; $13.50 for seniors; $12.50 for students, active military, and ages 5 - 18. Advanced reservations are highly suggested for your visit to the museum. Teacher Appreciation Days (i.e. free admission for teachers with current school ID) are held on the 3rd Sundays, every other month, and RSVP's are mandatory. Free parking is available underground, under the museum, on Pico Blvd.

Ages: 10 years and up - it's too intense for most younger children.

NATURAL HISTORY MUSEUM OF LOS ANGELES COUNTY

(213) 763-3466 / www.nhm.org.

$$$$

900 Exposition Boulevard, Los Angeles

Your natural history experience begins (for free) before you enter the museum, while outside in the extensive North Campus, in urban nature. This Nature Garden features a pond with plant and animal pond inhabitants, like turtles and dragonflies, plus a variety of garden zones and microclimates. Groves of native trees, fruit trees, and plants beautify the park while butterflies, lizards, birds, and people enjoy it. I especially like the pollinator garden planted to attract hummingbirds, bees (not my favorite), and butterflies. See what is living in and on the Living Wall. A cafe is outside here, too, as are benches, picnic tables under shade trees, and walkways all around.

This extensive museum has a lot of a little bit of just about everything. In the foyer complete skeletons of a Tyrannosaurus rex and triceratops engage in battle with each other. A few enormous, long halls showcase numerous North American, African, and exotic mammals mounted in a backdrop of their natural habitat (i.e., huge dioramas). The gigantic walrus, buffalo, and elephant are the most impressive. Take a walk through time in the American history room (1st level) and California history room (basement). They contain early vehicles, such as tractors, stagecoaches, and a streetcar; mannequins dressed in period clothing; early weapons; and numerous other pioneer artifacts. The lower level also features the Nature Lab, a place to learn about the plants and animals that dwell in L.A. It also houses live rats, snakes, frogs, turtles, ants, geckos, tarantulas, spiders and more.

Back on the first floor is the Gem and Mineral Hall, with over 2,000 outstanding rocks and minerals, including fluorescent minerals (which shine neon colors under black light); spectacular rock pieces from all over the world that are so brilliant in color, or so oddly shaped that they look unreal; a touch area with a meteorite, a giant slab of jadeite, and more; 300 pounds of natural gold, plus mining artifacts; and a vault to walk through which contains cut rubies, emeralds, sapphires, and topaz. (I'm not coveting here; just admiring.) Other exhibits on this floor include a real mummy; a preserved, unusually long, and flat-looking fish - the oarfish; and the rare Megamouth shark. Walk around and be amazed at the colossal skeleton of a fin whale in this long gallery leading to some of the most popular exhibits - dinosaurs and mammals.

The two-story, two room Dinosaur Mysteries Hall, guarded by a triceratops, contains dinosaurs in life-like poses. Visitors can walk around and even view them up close; some even face-to-face. One of the massive animals is the thirty-foot skeletal form of Thomas the T.rex, who shares the limelight with two other, smaller rexes near the remains of a duckbill dinosaur. An allosaurus is locked in mortal combat with a stegosaurus. Some of the other twenty full-body, ancient creatures and 300 fossils include the head of a horned dinosaur, and a Mosasaur and a 68-foot-long-necked Mamenchisaurus (dinosaur speak is like learning a foreign language) - giant sea reptiles. There are also videos, illustrations, and interactive components speculating how dinosaurs may have looked and acted with the acknowledgment that science is always evolving and learning.

Under the beautiful stained glass sky light rotunda are rotating exhibits from the museum's vast collection - one

currently features a platypus egg and an ancient Peruvian gold feather, among other objects; another exhibit has incredible paintings of extinct animals (and places).

In stage-like settings, under natural lighting, the two-story Age of Mammals room showcases skeletons of animals - a mastodon, ancient horse, saber-tooth cat, thunder beast (great name!), giant jaguar, walking whale, and others. It also features fleshed-out animals - a zebra, tiger, polar bear, alpaca, and more, in action poses. The flow of the room represents the evolution of animals, especially in regards to climate change. Marine mammals skeletons - a sperm whale, sea lion, and more - are suspended overhead. Interact here by using multimedia technology to learn how movement of land masses affected temperature and weather changes. Be a palaeontologist and use the bones here to rebuild a Paleoparadoxiid skeleton.

The city of Los Angeles might not seem "natural", but four galleries are devoted to its history - how nature and culture and habitation have grown and changed it. A scale model of downtown L.A., circa 1940, a 1902 wooden automobile (the first manufactured in L.A.), a sword from the Mexican War of Independence, an animation stand used by Walt Disney for the first Mickey Mouse cartoon, a costume donated by Charlie Chaplin, Native American artifacts, cattle displays, WWII exhibits and much more comprise this eclectic collection that celebrates our city.

Upstairs more wonders await. An entire wing is devoted to our fine feathered friends. There are taxidermied penguins, vultures, ostriches, ducks, turquoise cotingas (guess what color they are?), and more. Pull out the drawers of the cabinets in the hallway to see a variety of feathers and bird eggs. A large part of the ornithology (study of birds) exhibit is interactive. Turn a disk to get a magnified view of wings, feathers, and bones. Step on a scale to see how much just your bones weigh - they make up 17% of your body weight. (Although I'm sure my bones weigh more than that.) Walk over the bridge of recreated marshlands to reach a dark, two-story rainforest habitat that resounds with bird noises and has a waterfall. Another room here presents an in-depth look at marine life via murals, mounted animals, and information.

Look into the Dino Lab through huge windows to watch real paleontologists unearthing and working meticulously on fossilized dinosaur bones and casts. Touch a real T.rex toebone and dinosaur footprint here.

"Hands-on" is the motto at the wonderful Discovery Center where visitors are greeted by a nine-foot tall, stuffed polar bear. Mounted animal heads, including moose, warthogs, a variety of deer, and more, plus models of large fish, decorate the walls and ceiling. Smaller taxidermied animals, as well as skulls and bones, are in display cases that guests are encouraged to rearrange; to play museum curator. Kids can touch (or wrap themselves in) skins of deer, fox, skunk, opossum, sheep, and other animals. Touch tables have rocks, minerals, horns, and shells to sort, and a saber-toothed cat to assemble. There are also stuffed animals, microscopes with slides, and more hands-on items and activities in this room.

The adjacent Insect Zoo room is a buzz with activity, too, because of the cases swarming with live insects! Show no fear (or disgust) in front of your kids - some of the little buggers are quite interesting. You'll see scorpions, millipedes, tarantulas, beetles, and more (than you've ever wanted!). Gorgeous photos of insects grace the walls. A small room, next door, in a vault, is devoted to pre-Columbian archaeology. Just some of the extensive Native American artifacts on display include baskets, beadwork, pottery, statues, and jewelry.

Inquire regarding the usually daily live animal presentations and the don't-miss Dinosaur Encounters. The latter, twenty-minute presentation uses juvenile, life-size (and life-like) puppets of a fourteen-foot T.rex and nine-foot Triceratops that "come to life" as they roar and stalk the museum floor, and visitors. Cool and just a little scary for younger ones (and some older ones). Check the schedule for show times. Ask about the museum's numerous, in-depth field trips for various age groups, as well as their special events held on site - there is always something good going on. One such event is the once-a-month, Family Fun Days where thematic activities, science experiments, and/or crafts are included in museum admission. You can also have a "night at the museum" experience (kind of) by having an overnight adventure here. Look at the May Calendar entry, too, for details about the Bug Fair (pg. 720). If you visit here late September through mid-November go into and look and learn and interact with all kinds of spiders at the Spider Pavilion. From mid-April through September walk into The Butterfly Pavilion, which is an enclosed, outdoor butterfly garden, and be enthralled as butterflies of every color of the rainbow alight on the plants and on you.

Picnic tables and lots of grassy areas surround the museum. Also see the nearby AIR AND SPACE EXHIBITS (pg. 98), CALIFORNIA AFRICAN AMERICAN MUSEUM (pg. 102), CALIFORNIA SCIENCE CENTER (pg. 103), EXPOSITION PARK (pg. 58), and IMAX THEATER (pg. 184).

Hours: Open daily, 9:30am - 5pm. Closed New Year's Day, 4th of July, Thanksgiving, and Christmas.

Price: $12 for adults; $9 for seniors and students; $5 for ages 3 - 12; children 2 and under are free. Certain discounts are available through AAA. Special exhibits raise the admission price a few dollars. Admission is free the first Tues. of the month, except July and August. Entrance to each the butterfly and spider pavilion is the entrance fee plus an additional fee of $3 for adults; $2 for seniors; $1 for ages 3 - 12; children 2 and under are free. Parking in the lot costs $10 (cash only). See page xi for info on ASTC reciprocal museum memberships.

Ages: 2½ years and up.

NETHERCUTT COLLECTION and NETHERCUTT MUSEUM

(818) 364-6464 / www.nethercuttcollection.org

15200 Bledsoe Street, Sylmar

There are two buildings that hold an impressive array of vintage automobiles - over 250 - as well as hood ornaments, mechanical musical instruments, and time pieces collected by J. B. Nethercutt, the cofounder of Merle Norman Cosmetics. The Nethercutt Collection, housed in a five-story box-like building, offers two-hour guided tours. The inside is opulently decorated with marble floors and columns in the Grand Salon room, plus chandeliers, elegant wood paneling, and spiral staircases elsewhere. The Lower Salon features more than two dozen classic American and European luxury cars in pristine condition, including a 1934 Packard Dietrich Convertible Sedan, a one-of-a-kind 1933 Dusenberg Arlington Torpedo Sedan, and a few Rolls Royces and Cadillacs. There are also dolls, coins, nickelodeons, and music boxes on display. The third floor mezzanine showcases over 1,000 "mascots" (i.e., hood ornaments), including some made out of crystal, and ornate, eighteenth-century French furniture (both originals and reproductions). The spacious fourth floor, known as the the Music Room, displays rare and elegant mechanical musical instruments such as music boxes, reproducing (i.e., player) pianos, nickelodeons, and the crown jewel - the Mighty Wurlitzer Theater Pipe Organ. The tour guide describes the mechanical system of each instrument and also plays a few of them. Check the website for the calendar of free organ concerts and silent movie showings. The Louis XV-style dining room has a chandelier similar to the one in Versailles, a stunning grandfather clock, and a collection of musical pocket watches

The Nethercutt Museum is another huge building, across the street, that displays over 130 more antique and immaculate automobiles, described as "rolling works of art." Let me whet your appetite for this stunning collection by mentioning just a few makes and models on display here from antiques to post-war: a 1913 Mercedes Dusenberg, Packard, Pierce Arrow, Rolls Royce, an 1898 Eisenach Runabout, a 1967 Ferrari 365, and a classic 1913 steam pumper fire truck. Again, the cars are displayed in beautiful surroundings. A fully-staffed automotive restoration facility, where classic cars are striped to the bare "bone" and then painstakingly rebuilt according to original specifications, is also on the premises. Outside are an immaculately restored 1937 Royal Hudson steam locomotive and a 1912 Pullman private rail car on tracks. Fifteen-minute tours of the railcars are available Tuesday through Saturday at 12:30pm and 3:45pm.

Hours: The Collection is open for guided tours only, Thurs., Fri., and Sat. at 10am and 1:30pm. Reservations are required and usually well in advance. The Museum is open Tues. - Sat., 9am - 4:30pm - peruse at will. Both are closed Sun., Mon., and most major holidays.

Price: Free

Ages: Must be at least 10 years old for a tour of the Collection; ages 8 years and up will enjoy the Museum.

NORTON SIMON MUSEUM

(626) 449-6840 / www.nortonsimon.org

$$$

411 W. Colorado Boulevard, Pasadena

The museum brochure describes some of the masterpieces as "highly important works" and "glorious compositions," which lets astute readers know that this is not a hands-on museum for younger children. A visit to the museum and observing the numerous museum employees/security guards confirm this impression.

The Norton Simon is, however, a treasure for art connoisseurs as the pieces are truly outstanding and tastefully displayed in an atmosphere of quiet elegance. The permanent collection of this thirty-eight gallery, two-story, fine arts museum consists of seven centuries of European art, from the Renaissance to the twentieth century. A sampling of the featured artists includes Raphael, Botticelli, Rembrandt, Renoir, Monet, van Gogh, Goya, Picasso, and Matisse. Western art and South and Southeast Asian art and sculpture are also well represented. A special exhibits section presents more of the permanent collection on a rotating basis. Do check out the sculpture garden outside. Tip: Ask for a free family guide to get the kids more involved with the paintings and sculptures. Another way to get children (and other family members) interested in the pieces is to rent one of two, self-guided audio tours. One is geared for adults,

covering eighty works; the other, for children and families, covers thirty-six works. The audio guides are $3 each.

Beginning at 12:30pm and running alternately throughout the day, the museum theater presents two films: A thirty-minute orientation documentary movie on the life and collections of Norton Simon called *Art of Norton Simon*, and an hour-long film hosted by the "art nun," called *Sister Wendy at the Norton Simon*. The theater room is also a venue for concerts and lectures.

Educational tours, and accompanying study guides with activity sheets, are available by reservation for students. Personally, I benefit greatly from the "insider" information and explanations. Note that there is a cafe on the grounds. Check out the Saturday family day projects, story time, and kids' workshops in the summer.

Hours: Open Wed. - Mon., noon - 5pm (open Fri. until 8pm.) Closed Tues., New Year's Day, Thanksgiving, and Christmas.

Price: $12 for adults; $9 for seniors; free for ages 18 and under. Admission is free on the first Fri. from 5pm - 8pm.

Ages: 10 years and up.

THE PALEY CENTER FOR MEDIA

(310) 786-1000 or (310) 786-1091 / www.paleycenter.org

465 N. Beverly Drive, Beverly Hills

Tune into The Paley Center for Media, which houses the ultimate collection of broadcasting programs - almost 150,000 programs covering almost 100 years. Inside the upscale, contemporary-looking building are various rooms to watch and listen to shows, with just the touch of a button. The lobby has rotating exhibits of costumes, set pieces, props (photo ops!), scripts, artwork, mementos, video clips, storyboards, and more from your favorite TV shows. I saw Warner Brothers feature items from *The Bugs Bunny Show, Big Bang Theory, Kung Fu, The Closer, Murphy Brown, Fringe, The Mentalist, Friends, Seinfeld, Smallville*, and many more shows.

The Radio Listening Room is just what its name implies. The room is quiet as visitors use headphones to choose from five preset radio channels. A sampling of the rotating selections can include comedy, rock 'n roll, history of radio, witness to history (e.g., historic speeches), etc. There is also a fully-equipped radio station in here to do live broadcasts. Next door, watch a preselected show in the fifty-seat Screening Room, or watch a film or program in the 150-seat Theater Room. Call or check the website to see what or who is playing as there are numerous special events such as appearances, interviews, and panel discussions with cast members of television shows, movie celebrities, and creative teams from the news and entertainment fields.

Use the upstairs computer library to select your choice of radio or television shows. For example, key your television selection into the computer, then view it in the adjacent Console Room. This room has individual monitors as well as family consoles, which accommodate up to four people. Your child is in couch potato heaven here, able to choose his own television programs from literally thousands of titles available.

Some of the other benefits of this center include viewing (and listening to) historic shows both for school-aged children and for researchers. Ready access to programs is also great if you just want to choose a favorite show. Call for information on special children's events.

Hours: Open Wed. - Sun., noon - 5pm. Closed Mon., Tues., New Year's Day, July 4th, Thanksgiving, and Christmas.

Price: Admission is $10 for adults; $8 for seniors and students; $5 for children 12 and under. The first two hours of parking are free.

Ages: 6 years and up.

PASADENA MUSEUM OF HISTORY

(626) 577-1660 / www.pasadenahistory.org

470 W. Walnut Street, Pasadena

Pasadena's stately heritage landmark Fenyes mansion showcases turn-of-the-century gracious living. A one-hour guided tour through the house allows visitors to see original (now antique) furnishings which came from all over the world. The stories about the artifacts are intriguing, especially the legend of flying carpets, which is thought to come from prayer rugs supposedly endowed with magical powers. A prayer rug is located in the studio. Some of the highlights include the wood-paneled study; the elegant living room with its exquisite furniture and period-dressed mannequins; a grandfather clock in the foyer that has rotating, colored-glass slides of early Pasadena; old-fashioned utensils in the kitchen (my boys needed an explanation about the rug beater); china in the butler's pantry; numerous volumes of books in the hallway and office; the solarium; fine wooden tables and chairs; and chests in the living room

and studio ornately finished with tortoise shell, ivory, and mother-of-pearl. The elegantly decorated master bedroom and a child's bedroom are upstairs. A few small rooms downstairs hold old tools, a piano, a collection of old cameras, and several military uniforms.

Another component of the Pasadena Museum of History is the two galleries that display changing exhibits. A past exhibit was of children's toys, quilts, and clothing from 1850 to 1950. It showed how life was before video games (was there life before video games?) and how things change over time, at least in design, with displays of dolls, trucks, stuffed animals, books, games, clothing, and more. Educational tours are offered for groups of all ages, as are special programs.

The well-stocked gift shop carries some unique items. The grounds are beautifully landscaped with plants, trees, a pond, and a rose garden. The Finnish Folk Art Museum, just next door, is a homey, three-room replica of a Finnish farmhouse that contains handmade furniture, plus utensils and folk costumes. Pasadena is a city steeped in rich cultural history that is well represented by this mansion and museum.

Hours: Mansion tours, which includes entrance to the Finnish Folk Art Museum, are offered Fri. - Sun. at 12:15. The galleries are open Wed. - Sun., noon - 5pm. The gardens are open daily, 9am - 5pm.

Price: Mansion tours are $15 for adults. Gallery admission is $7 for adults; $6 for seniors and students. Admission is free for children 11 and under in all of the buildings.

Ages: 6 years and up.

PETERSEN AUTOMOTIVE MUSEUM

(323) 930-CARS (2277) / www.petersen.org
6060 Wilshire Boulevard, Los Angeles

$$$$

The driving force behind this 300,000-square-foot, state-of-the-art museum is dedication to the art, culture, and history of the automobile. Cars on the first floor are chronologically displayed in their own walk-through, diorama-like setting, complete with asphalt, manholes, sidewalks, fake plants - whatever cultural and time period surroundings fit the car - as well as mannequins dressed in period outfits. Sounds, like birds chirping where a Model T exhibit is titled "Stuck in the Mud", help children enter into the spirit of the lifestyles represented here. Other exhibits include horse and buggy; beautiful vintage automobiles in front of an old-fashioned grocery store and fish market; a few DeLoreans; a 50's drive-in diner with a red-hot convertible; a huge, iconic, pipe-smoking dog advertising tamales and ice cream; an exhibit of gas pumps; a garage containing a car that's in desperate need of work; Indy cars (I like the Gurney Eagle with an eagle face); and prototypes, solar-powered, and other, futuristic-type cars. Kids can climb aboard the trolley car used in old Laurel and Hardy movies (with models of the comedians on a wrecked auto behind it), although other cars on this floor are not hands-on.

The second floor has six galleries, including a terrific collection of hot rods, roadsters, race cars, and classics in prime condition. A glitzy Hollywood gallery stars cars that were featured in movies and television shows, and/or that were owned by celebrities. Check out the changing exhibits here because they are consistently fabulous and always appeal to car aficionados, although the 1963 Volkswagen Beetle used in *Herbie the Love Bug*, John Travolta's car Greased Lightning, and the black pop-up car used in *The Great Race* have been here for a while. Biking enthusiasts will appreciate the adjacent Otis Chandler Motorcycle Gallery, including the 2006 Skeleton Bike, which has a skeleton attached to the motorcycle. As you enter the small room of Hot Wheels Hall of Fame through a giant tire, lights inside the tire flash on and race around inside it. There are a few full-size versions of the most famous Hot Wheels models, as well as cases of the die-cast miniatures and drawings and renderings of the cars at the developmental stages. The Alternative Power cars range from 1897 battery electric Anthony to 1909 White (steam operated) to 1957 Studebaker-Packard (atomic) to 2005 Nissan X-Terra FCV (fuel cell).

The third floor, the Discovery Center, will really get kids revved up with its 6,500 square feet of motor vehicle interaction! They can ride on a real Highway Patrol motorcycle, complete with sirens blaring and flashing lights. Learn about the Doppler Effect and how sound travels. Trigger infra red detectors to hear various sounds such as dogs barking or tires squealing. Have your children dress up in a motoring duster, cap, and scarves and "drive" a Model T against a woodland backdrop. (Bring your camera.) A Sparklett's water truck contains numerous plastic jugs filled with a variety of games, puzzles, costumes, and construction toys, all pertaining to the car motif. A play area is set up for toddlers to race mini-cars around on tracks and play mats. There is a dress-up area in here, too. However, the ultimate in kid-cool is getting behind the wheel of a real Indianapolis 500 race car! In the hallway, turn wheels to see how gears shift.

Another large, hands-on room is for the mechanically minded. It has a giant dashboard; a display that traces the route an engine takes to come to life from ignition to the voltage regulator; photos, information panels, and gear shifts

that coordinate together to teach about fuel and conservation; and other learning stations. Our favorite "feet-on" exhibit consists of sitting on a car seat, that's really part of a giant combustion engine on huge wheels, and becoming a human spark plug. Move the engine across the room when you (and some strong-legged friends) push down on oversized pistons that pop up at regular intervals. (Fun, but tiring.) A few other highlights include holding a spinning bicycle wheel at a tilt while sitting on a chair to feel angular motion; watching billiard balls clack their way down a giant maze of tracks to explore motion and gravity; and racing wheels down a track to learn about inertia (or just to see who wins). The temporary exhibits here are always geared to spark kid's imagination. The Discovery Center hosts fun activities the first Saturday of every month from 1pm to 4pm.

One-hour tours of The Vault allows visitors to see rotating premium, prize cars, such as a 1925/34 "Round Door" Rolls-Royce Phantom I Aerodynamic Coupe; a Ferrari given to Henry Ford II by Enzo Ferrari; a Jaguar XKSS once owned by Steve McQueen; a Mercedes used by Sadam Hussein; and a 1939 Bugatti given to the Shah of Iran as a wedding present; plus hot rods, muscle cars, Hollywood vehicles, vehicles used by heads of state, motorcycles, and even a Popemobile. Photography is not permitted and guests must be at least 12 years old.

Have kids take a pencil Treasure Hunt throughout the museum and/or ask about the other special activities and classes. A variety of wonderful, ninety-minute, guided school tours are offered during the week for all ages at $2 per person with a minimum of ten students and a maximum of sixty. A visit to this museum will definitely accelerate your child's interest in cars! Note that Johnny Rockets, an all-American, 50's-ish diner, is adjacent to the lobby.

Hours: Open Tues. - Sun., 10am - 6pm. The Discovery Center closes Tues. - Fri. at 4pm; Sat. - Sun. at 5pm. The Vault is open weekdays at 11am, 1pm and 3pm; weekends at the same times, plus 5pm. The museum is closed Mon. (except some holiday Mon.), plus New Year's Day, Thanksgiving, and Christmas.

Price: $15 for adults; $10 for seniors and students with I.D.; $5 ages 3 - 12; children 2 and under are free. The Vault is an additional $20 per person. Enter the museum parking structure from Fairfax - $12 for all-day parking, or use metered parking along the side streets for 50¢ per half hour.

Ages: 5 years and up.

PETTERSON MUSEUM   ☀

(909) 399-5544 / www.pilgrimplace.org   !
730 Plymouth Road, Claremont

This small, intra-cultural museum is housed on the grounds where a community of retired pastors, missionaries, and other church professionals live. Those who shared the gospel in far corners of the globe often return with significant mementos of their host culture and crafts, covering many centuries of human history. The museum consists of three galleries filled with these mementos. Some of the exotic artifacts in display cases include costumes, textiles, masks, statues, dolls, shells, and pottery. Exhibits do rotate, bringing in unusual displays from all over. The docent-guided tours give insight into the exhibits. Note: Check the Calendar entry for the annual Pilgrim Place Festival (pg. 760).

Hours: Open to the public, Fri. - Sun., 2pm - 4pm. Call to make a reservation to take a tour at another time.
Price: Free
Ages: 6 years and up.

PIO PICO STATE HISTORIC PARK   ☀

(562) 695-1217 / www.piopico.org   !
6003 Pioneer Boulevard, Whittier

Pio Pico was the last governor of Mexican California. His once-sprawling ranch is now a three-acre state park and house/museum. The restored adobe home, made from large, sun-dried bricks, is sparsely furnished, yet interesting to tour. You walk into and past bedrooms, a living room, dining room, and kitchen. Photos of Pio Pico, clothing that belonged to his wife and him, ranch tools, wine barrels, and personal items are on exhibit throughout. Some parts of the wall were purposely left unpatched and exposed, so that visitors can view the adobe underneath.

The garden and beehive oven outside are worth learning about and seeing. After your tour, enjoy a lunch at the picnic tables surrounded by the expansive green lawn. School and other groups are welcome to take a guided tour by making a reservation. Ask about the public Living History days, usually scheduled once a month on a Saturday. This is when costumed docents lead tours and incorporate extra activities, such as playing old-fashioned games and conducting demonstrations - blacksmith, panning for gold, rope making, adobe brick making and more - while teaching the history of the adobe, old California, and the Pico family. Check out the summer programs for kids, too.

Hours: The park is open Sat. - Sun., 9:30am - 4pm. The adobe is open Sat. - Sun., 10am - 3;30pm for
self-guided tours. Call to make a reservation for a guided tour.

Price: Free

Ages: 8 years and up.

POINT FERMIN PARK AND LIGHTHOUSE

(310) 548-7705 - park; (310) 241-0684 - lighthouse / www.sanpedro.com; www.pointferminlighthouse.org

807 W. Paseo del Mar, San Pedro

This good-sized corner park has lots of green grassy areas, shade trees and huge climbing trees, and a few, good
play structures. I love the diff-side picnic tables tucked in several nooks that overlook the coastline and the ocean -
what a great view!!

One of the park's best features is the charming, Stick Style (i.e., early Victorian) lighthouse, built in 1874. The
white picket fence and variety of flowers and other plants in the garden surrounding it make it very picturesque. There
is even a small vegetable garden. Best of all, the lighthouse is open for one-hour guided tours for individuals or groups
of no more than twelve. (Lighthouses aren't large buildings.) Use your imagination as you tour the unfurnished rooms
and learn the history of this lighthouse, its inhabitants, and the area. There is a small room for kids where they can try
on lighthouse keeper uniforms and hats, look through a spyglass, read books, play the push button activities, and do
some paper and crayon crafts. Children under 40" may not climb the winding tower steps to the top which lead to an
incredible 360-degree view. The lantern up here has been removed. All in all, though, it is an enlightening experience.

Hours: The park is open daily, sunrise - sunset. Lighthouse tours are offered Tues. - Sun. at 1pm, 2pm, and
3pm. Closed Mon., major holidays, and some holiday weekends.

Price: Free; donations gladly accepted.

Ages: All

POINT VICENTE INTERPRETIVE CENTER, PARK and LIGHTHOUSE

(310) 377-5370 - interpretive center; (310) 541-0334 - lighthouse / www.palosverdes.com;
www.vicentelight.org

31501 Palos Verdes Drive West, Rancho Palos Verdes

Just inside this 10,000 square feet interpretative center/museum is a large corner exhibit of underwater rocks and
tidepools, with animals underneath, that begin to immerse you in the sights and sounds of being under the sea. A
life-size baby gray whale "swims" overhead. The 3-D kelp forest, the mural in bright ocean blue, and the walk through
underwater cave with tunnels that have ocean sounds, like waves crashing overhead, add to the effect.

The hallway is filled with exhibits including a natural and cultural time line of the peninsula. This includes a shark
mural; fossils, starring a large shark fossil; and viewing holes to peer into to see a saber tooth cat and a ground sloth.
Press the corresponding button to view the animal's habitat. A full-size diorama showcases a recreated tule hut of the
Tongva, plus related artifacts such as arrowheads and soapstone bowls. Whale baleen is in the next display case. An
adjoining room contains shells, pictorial history of the ranchos and models and an ode to Marineland, Bubbles (the
pilot whale), and Shamu. This area has feeding buckets from Marineland, pictures, uniforms, and gift shop items.

Next, lift the flaps on the model whale to see pictures of a whale's insides. See how different whales measure up
when compared side to side. The adjacent room contains models of dolphins and porpoises, part of a gray whale's
cranium, and a huge try pot for rendering blubber. Objects made from whales include a piece of Eskimo armor (made
of baleen), an umbrella with a baleen handle, a bracelet, Eskimo goggles, wolf whirlers, candles from sperm whale
blubber, whale oil soap, and a whale's eye (made out of a whale's eye).

Enjoy a walk on the beautiful grounds. This gorgeous viewpoint of the ocean, the sailboats, and beyond is also a
premier whale watching site during the annual migration of the Pacific gray whale from late December through
mid-April. Enjoy a picnic lunch in the grassy grove surrounded by palm, pine, and other trees. Kids will like the
waist-high rock wall encircling the south end of the park. Walk a paved pathway to the lighthouse. And yes, you'll hear
the foghorn blow about every thirty seconds. (I timed it.)

To shed a little light on the subject of what the inside of a lighthouse looks like, take a tour of the adjoining
landmark Point Vicente Lighthouse. There isn't a lot to actually see in it, as it is sparsely furnished, but walk up the
somewhat steep steps for a view atop the cliffs overlooking the ocean. On a clear day, this is spectacular. The light still
sends out its beacon, albeit automatically, and the foghorn still blows. At the base of the sixty-seven-foot tower is a
very small museum that displays signal flags, photos, lights, and other lighthouse memorabilia.

Hours: The interpretive center is open daily, 10am - 5pm. Closed Jan. 1, Thanksgiving, Dec. 24 - 25. Adjacent park grounds are open daily, dawn - dusk. The lighthouse is open the second Sat., 10am - 3pm, except for March when it is open the first Sat. in conjunction with the annual Whale of a Day Festival.

Price: All are free.

Ages: 3 years and up for the center; 7 years old and up only for tours of the lighthouse.

QUEEN MARY   ☾

(877) 342-0738 or (562) 435-3511 / www.queenmary.com $$$$$

1126 Queens Highway, Pier J, Long Beach

Cruise over to Long Beach Harbor to see the Queen, *Queen Mary* I mean - one of the largest luxury passenger liners ever built. Take a one-hour, guided tour, called The Glory Days, which is a behind-the-scenes tour with fact and stories explaining the ship's fascinating history, her time serving as a troopship during WWII, and her glory days as once the world's most extravagant ocean liner. Only on this tour can you see the dining room/ballroom, an original first class suite, and much of the elegant interior decor materials and artwork. Younger children might get antsy. For understanding beyond school books and even good history movies, sign up for the forty-five-minute tour called Her Finest Hour: A WWII Tour Explore the Grey Ghost, which focuses on the role the ship played in bringing victory to the Allied Forces during the war. This, and other, specialty tours are only offered at certain times, so if you are interested in taking one, check the website for a current schedule. The *Queen Mary* also hosts temporary (two to five years), outstanding exhibits such as *Titanic*, which featured numerous artifacts, facts and stories about the ship and people on board. Get the inside scoop on royalty with the current exhibit of Diana: Legacy of a Princess that elegantly showcases nine of her evening gowns and dresses, plus personal accessories, photographs, writings, and more intimate memorabilia.

Capitalizing on the numerous ghost reports, the half-hour guided Ghosts and Legends "show" takes visitors through very dark hallways and rooms (with occasional apparition sightings and things hanging down from the ceilings) to the lower decks of the forward work areas, into the six-story boiler room (which I would like to see in the light), and the swimming pool filled with fog. Other special effects designed to make the paranormal experiences come alive, so to speak, include changes in temperature in certain rooms and the finale - a shudder like two ships colliding and a deluge of water that seemingly bursts through the hull of the *Queen Mary*. This is way too scary for younger kids. Haunted Encounters is a one-hour walking tour that shows where reported apparitions and the paranormal have been sighted and tells stories about the ship's purported hauntings. Nighttime tours with an emphasis on the paranormal are also offered.

We also thoroughly enjoyed walking through the enormous ship on our own self-guided tour, using the audio headsets and listening to history and stories that added a lot to our experience. The step-by-step audio guide, available in several different languages, covers everything in and about the ship, from bow to stern. On the lower deck, watch a video called *The Queen Mary Story* about its construction, maiden voyage, and service during WWII. The Hall of Maritime Heritage, a small museum, displays navigating instruments, ship models, and pictures and stories of famous doomed ships, including the *Titanic*. Everything in the engine room is clearly marked, making it easy to explain the machinery's function to youngsters. The last remaining propeller on the ship is in an open-top, propellor box in water. It looks like a shark fin at first. Tell your kids that the life-size diver in the water is just a model. We toured the bridge, the wheel house where officers were quartered, and the state room exhibits. A highlight for my boys was playing on the gun turrets on the bow of the ship, as they fought off invisible enemies. The view from the top deck of the shoreline and beyond is fairly amazing. The long, wooden upper decks are great for strolling around. Note: As an older ship, there are many narrow staircases, but not many ramps on board. Elevators enable those using strollers or wheelchairs to get from deck to deck.

There are also several fine shops and restaurants on the ship that run the gamut from the very fine and expensive at Sir Winston's (entrees average $40); to Chelsea Chowder House & Bar (average $26); to a more family-style and family-priced eatery, Promenade Cafe (French toast - $10, build your own CA omelet - $12; hamburger, club sandwich or bbq chicken salad - $14; spaghetti and meatballs - $17). The Cafe is open daily, 6:30am to 10pm or 11pm. The Tea Room elegantly offers authentic British afternoon tea. For instance, Windsor Tea includes tea; a variety of tasty and unique tea sandwiches; freshly-baked scones with dotted cream and homemade jam; and a sweet array of petit fours for $32 per person. An array of other menu selections include shrimp salad, $16, egg salad sandwich, $12, and creme brulee, $10.

One-hour educational (and other group) tours are available, with a minimum of fifteen students, and are a great

deal - kids are impressed by the size and history of this ship as they focus mostly on the WWII aspects. Tours are $10 per person, which includes general admission onto the ship after the tour. The audio tour can be added for only $2.50 more. Another "tour" offered to students and groups is a one-hour, interactive and fun Scavenger Hunt. Call for details.

Tips: 1) For a ~~cheap~~ inexpensive family date, come on board after 6pm when there isn't an admission charge, only a parking fee. Although some stores and many parts of the ship are not open then, some restaurants are open, so you can indulge in dinner, or just a dessert. And if you eat at a restaurant on board, bring the $17 parking voucher that will then go towards your food purchase. Plus, it's fun for kids to walk around, and the sunsets are beautiful. Don't miss the ship on this one! 2) Remember, that you can sleep on board the *Queen Mary*, as it functions as a floating hotel, too, with 314 rooms. 3) Look up SCORPION (pg. 150), a Russian submarine adjacent to the *Queen Mary*; SHORELINE VILLAGE (pg. 161); and AQUARIUM OF THE PACIFIC (pg. 216) for information on these nearby attractions. Also, catch the AQUALINK (pg. 208) for a cruise around the harbor.

Hours: Open most of the year daily, 10am - 6pm.

Price: There are several admission options and I've included just some: General admission is the Queen Mary Passport, which includes the self-guided audio tour, exhibits, and Ghosts and Legends Show - $25.95 for adults; $20.76 for seniors; $14.95 for ages 4 - 11; children 4 and under are free. (Ask about AAA discounts.) The First Class Passport incorporates the Queen Mary Passport, plus a tour of the Scorpion Submarine and either The Glory Days tour or Her Finest Hour: A WWII tour for a total of $30.95 for adults; $24.76 for seniors; $20.95 for kids. Parking for up to 1 hour is $3; $17 per vehicle all day. If you eat at a restaurant on board, there is a discount for parking. Beat parking prices by catching the free Passport shuttle that runs from downtown Long Beach, or from Shoreline Village (where parking is $8 for the day), to the *Queen Mary*. Check out www.lbtransit.com for more info.

Ages: 3 years and up.

RANCHO LOS ALAMITOS

(562) 431-3541 / www.rancholosalamitos.com

6400 E. Bixby Hill Road, Long Beach

This beautiful, historic ranch appeals to kids of all ages. The barn has several horse stalls, a few of which have been converted into small rooms, or self-contained history lessons. They display photographs, animal pelts, branding irons, and a suspended horse harness (which is a favorite because it looks like a horse just escaped and left that behind), showing how a horse was hooked up to help plow. Other buildings of particular interest, in this area, contain a blacksmith shop filled with old tools, and a room with lots of saddles and branding irons. A ranch is not complete without animals, so goats, sheep, chickens, ducks, and Shire horses are in outside pens.

A ninety-minute, guided tour includes going inside the adobe ranch house. It's always fun to try to guess the name and use of gadgets in old kitchens. The bedroom, library, music, and billiards rooms are interesting to older children and hold period furniture, clothing, photographs, and other objects. An Artifacts Room is open at certain times so kids can touch - that's right - artifacts! Most of the site is wheelchair/stroller accessible. Ask about the rancho's terrific school tours and their slew of seasonal events. Check the Calendar section at the back of the book.

The front (and side) of the house has five acres of truly lovely botanic gardens with dirt pathways that meander through them including two, 150-year-old Moreton Bay fig trees with huge roots; a bamboo section (listen to them when the wind blows); and picnic tables under weeping willow trees.

Hours: Open Wed. - Sun., 1pm - 5pm. Tours are offered on the half hour. School tours are given at various times throughout the week. Call to make reservations. The rancho is closed on holidays.

Price: Free; donations appreciated.

Ages: 3 years and up for the outside grounds; 6 years and up for a tour of the house.

RANCHO LOS CERRITOS

(562) 570-1755 / www.rancholoscerritos.org

4600 Virginia Road, Long Beach

This picturesque historic adobe rancho, originally built in 1844, is situated almost at the end of Virginia Road. The perimeter gardens are beautifully landscaped around a grassy center area. There is also a huge old Moreton Bay fig tree with tremendous roots. A one-hour tour takes you through the house which is furnished as it was in the late 1870's. You'll walk through the study, dining room, simply furnished bedroom, and other rooms to see furniture, clothing, hair

wreaths (yes, wreaths made from hair), oil portraits, and a velocipede (an early bicyde). This is a terrific way to see and learn about our Mexican-California heritage.

Kids can more easily relate to the bigger picture of state history when they explore a small part of it. Ask for a Kids' Activity Treasure Hunt, where young visitors use pencil and paper as they look for particular items throughout the museum - it makes a visit here that much more interesting. Bring a sack lunch as there are picnic tables on the grounds. Ask for a schedule of the Rancho's special family events - they are great. See the Calendar entry for Mud Mania (pg. 739).

School group tours include hands-on fun, such as candle-dipping and playing old-fashioned games. Students also have the opportunity to do chores, such as butter churning and washing clothes, the way they were done years ago.

Hours: Open Wed. - Sun., 1pm - 5pm. Guided tours are given on the weekends only, on the hour. School tours are given on Wed. and Thurs., 9:30am - noon.

Price: Free; donations appreciated.

Ages: 7 years and up.

RAY CHARLES MEMORIAL LIBRARY

(323) 737-8000 / www.theraycharlesmemoriallibrary.org; www.theraycharlesfoundation.org

2107 West Washington Boulevard, Los Angeles

This historic RPM building, originally built in 1964, is where Ray Charles had his office and his recording studio, which visitors can see on the guided tour. These were also used in the movie, *Ray*. Huge photos of Ray Charles, fellow musicians, and celebrities don the walls. B.B. King, Quincy Jones, and other luminaries welcome visitors via video to each of the seven galleries of this library/museum on the first floor. You'll see flashy and classy suits, and stage costumes worn by Ray, in display cases; a selection of his dark glasses; gold records; seventeen Grammy awards; his contracts; one of his customized chess boards; his personal piano and saxophone; his collection of microphones; letters he received from Bill Clinton, George W. Bush, Johnny Cash, and others; film footage of Ray; and more. Touch screens allow visitors to listen to his recordings and learn the background of why he wrote certain songs.

Feeling inspired? The library also includes a mixing station, where creative guests can compose their own mixes incorporating Charles' music - rhythms and melodies. In a karaoke room, sing along with Charles and the Raelettes. His tour bus and Mercedes 500 car are also on the grounds.

The second floor holds his wardrobe and current administrative offices of the foundation, which was created to give underprivileged children, and especially those with hearing difficulties, an opportunity to experience music and gain confidence in their abilities. *Let the Good Times Roll.*

Hours: Open by appointment for small groups to a maximum of forty-nine people.

Price: Free

Ages: 7 years and up.

RAYMOND M. ALF MUSEUM

(909) 624-2798 / www.alfmuseum.org; www.dinosaurjoe.com

1175 W. Baseline Road, Claremont

Make no bones about it, this unique, circular museum displays dinosaur skeletons, trackways, fossils, and archaeological finds from all over the world. See the complete (and very large) skeletal cast of the Allosaurus fragilis (how do you measure up?), the skull of a Tyrannosaurus rex, a giant fossil alligator skull, dinosaur eggs, saber toothed cats, three-toed horses, and more. A kid's area has computer games, books, dinosaur puzzles, and a small sandpit for archaeologists-in-training to "dig" for fossils (and they are guaranteed to find them - not quite like being out in the field). The touch table has mastodon tusks, vertebrae, rocks, and a fossilized turtle shell, which is surprisingly heavy.

The downstairs room consists mainly of trackways, which are rock slabs with castings of dinosaur, camel, horse, and bear-dog footprints, plus extinct spiders and scorpions. The trackways are displayed on the walls, around the room, and under glass-encased coffee tables (albeit, priceless ones). Footprints in the Sands of Time is an unusually large rock slab containing numerous reptile footprints that is reportedly 250 million years old. Video and exhibits describe how trackways are formed and studied, including field research and curation. Visitors can also view behind-the-scenes via windows cut into the fossil preparation lab and through to the center storage area where students work on specimens.

Good-sized rock and mineral specimens, like geodes and petrified wood, abound, as do fossils such as mammoth molars and fern imbedded in rock. Have your kids look at the rocks and ask them if they know the difference between a fossil and a mineral.

This museum is great for older kids who are interested in paleontology, or for younger ones to just see the sheer size of some of the animals from long ago. Ninety-minute school/group tours are offered Monday through Thursday at 9:30am, with reservations, for second graders and up. Travel presentations are also available. Second through fourth graders can attend after-school, junior paleontology classes. Enjoy day-long family fossil digs that enable participants to prospect and collect fossils. Shorter, half-day digs are also offered on select days for Family Science Discovery Days. Month-long research expeditions, which combine fossil collecting and camping, are available for high school students during summertime.

Hours: The museum is open Mon. - Fri., 8am - 4pm. It is open Sat., also, from September through May, 1pm - 4pm. It's closed Sun., during school breaks, July 4th, Thanksgiving weekend, and between Christmas Eve and New Year's day.

Price: $6 for ages 5 and up; children 4 and under are free. Cash or checks, only. Tours are $20 for up to 35 students.

Ages: 4 years and up.

RIPLEY'S BELIEVE IT OR NOT! MUSEUM

(323) 466-6335 / www.ripleys.com

6780 Hollywood Boulevard, Hollywood

$$$$

As a reporter, Robert Ripley traveled all over the globe visiting over 200 countries and meeting with kings and queens, cannibal chieftains, and tribesmen to collect interesting, humorous, and bizarre items and facts. This two-story museum displays nearly 300 unusual and amazing items and facts collected from around the world - pictures, life-size models, special effects, statues, and assorted odd artifacts. Just to mention a few: a portrait of Michael Jackson made out of candy; bowls made from skulls; a two-trunk elephant; a Bigfoot (perhaps) footprint; Marilyn Monroe made from a quarter million shredded dollars (and other Marilyn items, such as a portrait made of nail polish and one of her sweaters); Duct tape "art"; a two-headed goat; an 8-foot tall Transformer model from the movies; a 1950's prop Ray Gun from a sci-fi movie; a genuine shrunken head; and the world's largest tire (nearly 12 feet tall). Whew! My son, Bryce, summed up the exhibits best by saying, "They're kind of cool and kind of gross."

There are also videos throughout the museum that show amazing feats such as unusual body contortions, swallowing razor blades, and more. (Don't try these activities at home.) There is a small optical illusion room that also contains old-time, coin-operated machines featuring fortune tellers, bars to squeeze to test your strength, and more. Another warning - If you take an inquisitive child who can't read the explanations, be prepared to read a lot of information and answer a lot of questions! Note: Look up HOLLYWOOD (pg. 171) for details on other close-by Hollywood museums and attractions.

Hours: Open daily, 10am - midnight.

Price: $16.99 for adults; $8.99 for ages 5- 12; children 4 and under are free. Order tickets online and save. Combo tickets for Ripley's, HOLLYWOOD WAX MUSEUM (pg. 119) and GUINNESS WORLD OF RECORDS MUSEUM (pg. 116) are $29.99 for adults; $16.99 for ages 5 - 12.

Ages: 5 years and up.

RUTH AND CHARLES GLIB ARCADIA HISTORICAL MUSEUM

(626) 574-5440 / www.museum.ci.arcadia.ca.us

380 West Huntington Drive, Arcadia

!

This small museum is well laid out, chronicling the history of Arcadia in a timeline format with newspaper articles, photographs, documents, and plenty of memorabilia from various time periods. The artifacts include an old fire hose cart, coppering tools, military uniforms from several wars, a man's fur coat and mittens, pianos, a school desk, old cameras, tiaras from past Rose Queens, and even an alcove set up like a dining room with table, chairs, china, and a cupboard of kitchen implements. A hands-on table holds military helmets, phones, a typewriter, and cameras. School and other guided tour groups are welcome. Check out the free, Hands on History for Families events on select Saturdays.

Hours: Open Tues. - Sat., 10am - noon and 1pm - 4pm. Closed Sun. and Mon. and most holidays.

Price: Free

Ages: 7 years and up.

SANTA MONICA HISTORY MUSEUM

(310) 395-2290 / www.santamonicahistory.org

$$

1350 7th Street next to the Santa Monica Public Library, Santa Monica

This museum is small, but interesting to explore. The first room features rotating exhibits. The main room has a few sides rooms that, along with several information panels, contain old dolls and vintage dresses; an old movie camera and some props; bathing suits from yesterday in front of photographs from that time period; the Pacific Ocean Park wheel; very old barbells used on the original Muscle Beach; a player piano; a huge fiberglass seahorse (from the Park, too); a replicated section of a Douglas C-47 aircraft to walk into; skateboards from Z-Boys; "stylish" Hotdog on a Stick outfits; and a room dedicated to the local Outlook Newspaper (1875 to 1998), detailing the history of the area and beyond. In this room, you can use a green screen and camera to take a picture of yourself in a scene from Santa Monica's past. With the "Then & Now" exhibit use a touchscreen to bring up various locations to see the landscape change from then to now. This room also has an old school desk and typewriter. The last small room is a Research Library.

Docent-led school tours are free. Adult group tours are available for $5 per person. Free Craft and Story workshops for kids are held on the second Saturday of each month from 10:30am to 11:30am. Note that this museum is adjacent to the Santa Monica Public Library. The complex also has a small, but lovely courtyard and a cafe.

Hours: Open Tues., Thurs., 12pm – 8pm; Wed., Fri., Sat., 10am – 5pm. Closed Sun., Mon. and holidays.
Price: $5 for adults; children 12 and under and veterans with ID are free. Metered parking on the street, or park underground near the Santa Monica Public Library for $1 for the first hour.
Ages: 7 years and up.

SAXON AEROSPACE MUSEUM

(760) 762-6600 or (760) 762-5810 / www.saxonaerospacemuseum.com
26922 Twenty Mule Team Road, Boron

The F-4 fighter outside lets you know you've reached the right destination. The museum was built to look like a hangar and the artifacts inside all reflect aviation interests. There are several models, some experimental aircraft, a replica of the Voyager, a few computers with aeronautic programs, uniforms, lots of pictures, a rocket engine, missiles, and other interesting exhibits to look at and learn about. Come for a tour or explore it on your own. Just across the street is a small park with a roadside display that includes an antique fire engine. Make sure to visit the adjacent TWENTY MULE TEAM MUSEUM (pg. 154) and the nearby BORAX VISITOR CENTER (pg. 102).

Hours: Open daily, 10am - 4pm. Closed New Year's Day, Thanksgiving, and Christmas.
Price: Free; donations appreciated.
Ages: 4 years and up.

SCORPION

(562) 435-3511 / www.queenmary.com
1126 Queens Highway, Long Beach

$$$$

Do your kids like to play spy? The 300-foot-long *Scorpion*, technically known as the Povodnaya Lodka B-427, is a Soviet-built, Foxtrot-class submarine that is docked here. In service for twenty-two years, it was once equipped with low-yield nuclear torpedoes. (That information alone makes it interesting to kids.) It was assigned mainly to gather intelligence on Allied naval activities. Now a tourist attraction, the *Scorpion* inspires spy game ideas, at least with my kids, as well as being a vessel of education and intrigue. Note: You may view the submarine, topside, without going on a tour.

Before you board, go into a holding room that contains labeled artifacts from the sub, such as an emergency escape suit, flags, pressure gauges, manuals in Russian, and more. Get your feet wet, so to speak, by watching a thirteen-minute reenactment video on the history of the submarine and its "warriors beneath the waves."

Your actual tour inside the *Scorpion* is self-guiding, with a Russian-accented narration piped into each compartment. Begin by going down a narrow staircase to the forward torpedo room. The room contains six torpedo tubes and replicas of the warheads once loaded inside them. Then, think thin and squeeze through several porthole-style hatches, walk down narrow hallways, and look into (through glass-covered doorways) very small sleeping quarters, a control room, a dining room, the galley, and various other rooms. The tour has its own momentum as there is not a lot of room for the people behind you to pass. Visitors can peer through a periscope to the outside world, push the numerous buttons, and turn the wheels on board. My boys would have liked to stay down here for hours. Down another staircase is the engine room filled with gadgets that helped churn the water to power the sub. The last stop on your tour is the aft torpedo room which held four torpedoes. It is a relatively short tour for your money, but it is historic and fascinating.

Note that strollers aren't allowed on the *Scorpion*, nor may you carry children on the tour. If you get claustrophobic, this isn't the place to be. Ladies, stepping up through hatch openings and down narrow ladders doesn't lend itself to wearing dresses or heels.

See the entry for AQUARIUM OF THE PACIFIC (pg. 216), QUEEN MARY (pg. 146), SHORELINE VILLAGE (pg. 161), and AQUALINK (pg. 208) for attractions in the immediate vicinity.

Hours: Open daily, 10am - 6pm, with the last entry at 5:30pm.

Price: $12.95 for adults; $10.95 for seniors, military personnel, and ages 4 - 11; children 4 and under are free. Ask about combo packages for the *Scorpion* and the *Queen Mary*. Parking is $17 for the day. Take a free Passport shuttle from downtown Long Beach, or Shoreline Village (where all-day parking is $8), to save on parking fees. Check out www.lbtransit.com for more info.

Ages: 4 years and up and must be 48" or taller to tour.

SKIRBALL CULTURAL CENTER ☼

(310) 440-4500 / www.skirball.org $$$
2701 N. Sepulveda Boulevard, Los Angeles

This architectural gem of a cultural center tells the story of the Jewish people, from post-biblical days and journeys, to present day life in America. The core exhibit, Visions and Values, features objects from the museum's permanent collection and traces the history, accomplishments, and values of the Jewish people over 4,000 years. Exhibits include ancient and modern artifacts, photographs, art, film, a recreation of an immigrant's kitchen, and video screenings all housed in a building beautifully designed with archways and high-ceilings. The variety of the unique Torah mantles and Hanukkah lamps on display is outstanding. One of our favorite menorahs has each of its eight branches fashioned like the Statue of Liberty.

The Liberty Gallery features a reproduction of the hand and torch of the Statue of Liberty at seventy percent of full scale. It's huge! This room also contains documents from past United States Presidents that supported nondiscrimination, including a display paying homage to President Lincoln. This section contains cases filled with personal belongings of Jewish immigrants, too - clothing, shoes, mugs, toiletries, and more.

Rotating exhibits have featured Jewish holidays and the memorabilia that aids the rich traditions; Einstein - the Man and His Science; Jewish Life in Ancient Egypt; a room set for the Sabbath; and the altar and front portion of a beautiful temple. The third floor of Winnick Hall is also a venue for major traveling exhibitions.

The stairway heading down to the Archaeology Discovery Center is lined with ancient, palm-sized oil lamps. The centerpiece of this small room is a tomb in a rock with ledges that contain pottery. Surrounding the rock tomb are displays that show what objects remain intact over centuries; a table to see the Hebrew alphabet and do some rubbings; and a computer game called Dig It! Check out a free gallery kit, geared for ages 4 to 8, which contains games, books, related objects, and activity cards that motivate children to investigate the items in the galleries.

The much acclaimed (and rightly so!) main destination for kids (and adults) is the area adjacent to the archaeology room - Noah's Ark. WOW! FANTASTIC! I can try to describe it to you, but this truly is a must-see. A metal-framed Asian elephant, also comprised of Thai rain drums and vegetable steamers, stands just inside this gallery alongside zebras with piano keyboards for manes and black and white wind turbines for bodies. The whimsical, hand-crafted, life-size animals in this incredible menagerie were created from recycled and found materials and put together in the most innovative manner. Before you enter the wooden ark, made of almost Biblical proportions, interact with some of the animals outside by tugging on the pulley to make the coyote throw back his head and howl; manipulating bars to make the gigantic giraffe's neck move; sitting on the wooden camels; and loading small foam animals on a conveyor belt and turning a wheel so they go up to the ark, two by two. Also, help recreate (kind of) the epic storm and flood by pushing a button to watch torrential rain fall upon a mini ark in a glass display and spinning a wheel to watch leaves in a tube swirl around from the wind. Note the striking animal and plant life silhouettes on the walls and how several animals are peering and hanging out of the ark openings.

Inside the ark are numerous more animals to see and things to do. See kiwi birds made of oil cans; a chicken with a red cowboy boot body; a turtle with basketball skins for his shell; plus crocodiles (accompanied by rubber poop), aardvarks, owls, penguins, walruses, sheep, lions, and just about every other animal God created - 350 in all, although God may have created more than that. Guests are invited to look at, touch, sit on, and play with the animals, including all the stuffed animals and puppets. They can also climb up and down cargo ladders, crawl in and through rope tunnels in the ark rafters, and explore nooks and crannies, while hopefully gaining a sense of taking care of the animals while playing house (or playing ark, as the case may be). Don't forget to peer into the small room with corn on its walls and slide open the ceiling - it reveals tiers of fake food for storage.

Once through the ark, the adjacent large room has a real rainbow prism on the wall and a (fake) dove with an olive branch hanging from the ceiling. Storytelling, puppetry, and making crafts are offered here. There is also a small play area on the carpet for younger kids.

Outside, in the arroyo garden over a wooden bridge, is a short pathway leading to and around an arched metal sculpture that is reminiscent of a rainbow (that's laying down) which emits mist on hot days - look for the rainbows formed from the water (and get just a little wet).

There are numerous educational opportunities available at the Skirball, such as Immigration Journeys, performing arts programs, teen open mic night, specialty tours/programs, concerts, family musical matinees, and an archaeology study where students go outside and excavate roads, walls, an altar, and more, at a small mock dig site. Make sure you ask if a film is playing on the day of your visit as many classics are shown. Weekends during the summer, check out the family programs at the amphitheater - storytelling, magic acts, live animals, and more.

Zeidler's Cafe is a full-service restaurant within the center that offers reasonable prices for lunch or afternoon coffee. Menu choices include pizza, pasta, sandwiches, omelettes, salads, fish, house-baked breads, and chocolate desserts. The lovely courtyard just outside the cafe is a pleasant place to take a break and to gaze at the reflecting pool.

As you enter and exit the Skirball Center you'll see, etched in stone, words fit for everyone - "Go forth . . . and be a blessing to the world." (Genesis 12: 1 - 3)

Hours: Open Tues. - Fri., noon - 5pm; Sat. - Sun., 10am -5pm. Closed Mon., some national holidays, and on Jewish holidays. Noah's Ark has ticketed, timed entry, for up to two hours. While walk-up tickets can be available, getting advance tickets is highly recommended on weekends, school holidays, and Thursdays.

Price: $10 for adults; $7 for seniors and students; $5 for ages 2 - 12; ages under 2 are free. Admission is free on Thurs. See page xi for info on the Bank of America free weekend program.

Ages: 2 years and up.

S. S. LANE VICTORY

(310) 519-9545 / www.lanevictory.org $$

At the end of Miner Street at Berth 49, San Pedro

This seventy-year-old ship served as a cargo ship during World War II, the Korean War, and the Vietnam War. The large Victory ship is a seaworthy museum that you may explore unaccompanied. You and your kids will get shipshape by climbing up and down ladders and walking the hallways through the crew's quarters, past the radio room and kitchen, and on deck where there are guns and superstructures to investigate. (Tell your kids that they are on a poop deck - it will make your outing a big hit!) One-hour guided tours are given by retired merchant marines (advanced notice is usually needed) and this is the only way to see the bridge and the huge, multi-level engine room with its noises and bulk machinery.

Below deck, there are two museum rooms. One features memorabilia such as flags, whistles, photographs, newspaper clippings, lanterns, numerous model ships, uniforms, and navigational tools. The Gift Shoppe here sells wonderful nautical items from clothing to medals to model ship kits. The museum room, on the other "side" of the ship, contains an anti-ship mine, riveting gun, rivets, three jeeps from the Vietnam War (one with a bullet hole in the windshield), a torpedo, a degaussing control unit, and a wall display of knots. Visitors can lift block and tackles (i.e., a pulley system) to see which ones are easier and why, and push buttons on a board that has a hand-held (non-working) radio. Batten down the hatches and be sure to wear tennis shoes for your ship-to-shore adventure. Note that the ship is not stroller/wheelchair friendly.

Three times a year, July through September, the S.S. Lane Victory hosts an all-day cruise to Catalina where a "Nazi spy" is discovered on board. Nazi fighters are soon attacking the ship, but American aircraft come to the rescue. The mock aerial dogfight uses blanks, but the World War II planes are real. This is more exciting than any Hollywood movie! The cruise also includes continental breakfast, live music, and a buffet luncheon. The cost is $135 for adults; $80 for kids 12 years and under. See PORTS O' CALL VILLAGE (pg. 159) for information about other attractions in the immediate area.

Hours: Open daily, 11am - 4pm. Closed most holidays.

Price: $5 for adults; $2 for ages 5 - 15; children 4 and under are free.

Ages: 5 years and up.

THE BROAD

(310) 399-4004 / www.broadartfoundation.org   !/$

221 S. Grand Avenue, Los Angeles

Scheduled to open in 2015, this incredible contemporary art museum will house the vastly *broad* collection of more than 2,000 works and 200 artists; about a tenth of which will be on exhibit at any one time. From 1950's until current day, including Andy Warhol and Roy Lichtenstein, prominent artists' works will be on display in classy and artistic arrangements with purposed lighting. Most of the museum is located on the gigantic third floor - an acre of art - as well as the second floor, while the rest is in the storage vault/archives. Riding the escalator allows you to glimpse into sections of this vault. The Broad is all about experiencing art, and that extends even to the composition of the lobby.

Located next to the uniquely-designed Walt Disney Concert Hall, this building has stand-out architecture, as well, with its honeycomb-like diamond shapes forming the outside structure that allows filtered natural light in. See DOWNTOWN LOS ANGELES / GRAND PARK (pg. 167) for information on Grand Park and all the other places to go within this fairly immediate area.

Price: General admission is free; a nominal fee is charged for temporary special exhibitions.
Ages: 7 years and up.

TOURNAMENT HOUSE and THE WRIGLEY GARDENS

(626) 449-4100 / www.tournamentofroses.com
391 S. Orange Grove Boulevard, Pasadena

The Tournament House, more aptly referred to as a mansion, is used throughout the year as the meeting headquarters for committees, float sponsors, and practically everything else associated with the annual Tournament of Roses Parade. Once owned by Wrigley, of the chewing gum fame, each room is elegantly furnished. The downstairs contains a spacious living room, a library, meeting rooms, and the Eisenhower bathroom - so named because when the president was Grand Marshall, he got stuck in here and no one knew where he was, not even the Secret Service agents.

The second floor is interesting to kids who have some knowledge and interest in the Rose parade and Rose Bowl games. Each former bedroom is dedicated to various elements of Tournament of Roses' traditions. The Rose Bowl Room showcases pennants and football helmets from Rose Bowl teams, plus photographs, trophies, and other memorabilia dating back to the first game in 1902. The Queen and Court Room is femininely decorated to allow the reigning Queen and her Court, who attend over 100 events a year, a place to recuperate. A display case in here features past winners' crowns, tiaras, and jewelry. The Grand Marshall's Room shows photographs of past Grand Marshals like Bob Hope, Shirley Temple Black (do your kids know who she was?), Hank Aaron, Walt Disney, Charles Schultz, and others. Out in the hallway is an impressive 240-pound sterling silver saddle - heigh ho, Silver, away! The President's Room has pictures and other mementos of past presidents of the Rose Parade, plus models of the current year's winning floats. You are also invited to watch an interesting fifteen-minute behind-the-scenes film on how the floats and parade are put together.

The beautifully-landscaped grounds, with over four acres of flowers (over 1,500 varieties of roses!) have a fountain surrounded by one of the rose gardens.

Hours: Tours of the house are given February through August on Thurs. at 2pm and 3pm.
Price: Free
Ages: 7 years and up.

TOYOTA USA AUTOMOTIVE MUSEUM

(310) 468-4728 / www.toyotausamuseum.com
19600 Van Ness Avenue, Torrance

I get the feeling (which is Toyota's tag line) this museum is a huge hit for Toyota car lovers. Over 100 automobiles are on display, including Toyota Motorsports race cars. A favorite is the 1967 Toyota 2000GT featured in the James Bond movie, *You Only Live Twice*. Other cars include those that represent important milestones for the car company such as 1936 Model AA, a replica of the first car Toyota sold; 1958 Toyota Crown, the first Toyota sold in America; 1961 Land Cruiser; 1990 Lexus LS 400, Toyota's first luxury car; and numerous others. Surrounding the cars are photographs, memorabilia, and video kiosks that show the history of Toyota and information about its founding family. Note that the museum is open by appointment only for tours, to host dinners, and other functions.

Hours: Open by appointment only.
Price: Free to tour.
Ages: 5 years and up.

TRAVEL TOWN

(323) 662-5874 - Travel Town; (323) 662- 9678 / www.griffithparktrainrides.com - train rides / www.traveltown.org; www.griffithparktrainrides.com; www.laparks.org
5200 W. Zoo Drive, Los Angeles

"All aboarrrrrd!" This wonderful outdoor "town" has a "trainriffic" atmosphere. There are real boxcars, a few cabooses, and some steam locomotives to climb into (but not on top of). A few of the trains, still on tracks, are located in an open pavilion for preservation purposes. Grassy areas invite you to rest (one can always hope), play, and/or picnic. A scaled model train takes you for a ride around the small town - $2.75 for adults; $2.25 for seniors; free for ages 18 months and under.

Inside the buildings are old-fashioned carriages, wagons, and some period automobiles. It's tempting to touch the vehicles, but don't give in to temptation. For a listing of other things to do in this area see a neighbor train museum, the LOS ANGELES LIVE STEAMERS RAILROAD MUSEUM (pg. 130) and GRIFFITH PARK (pg. 62).

Hours: Open most of the year, Mon. - Fri., 10am - 4pm (last ride at 3:15pm); Sat. - Sun. and holidays, 10am - 5pm (last ride at 4:15pm). It closes at 5:30pm in the summer on weekends. Closed Christmas.
Price: Free; donations appreciated. Trains prices listed above.
Ages: 2 years and up.

TWENTY MULE TEAM MUSEUM

(760) 762-5810 / www.20muleteammuseum.com
26962 Twenty Mule Team Road, Boron

This small-town museum is built around its claim to fame - the Twenty Mule Team wagons. Beginning in 1883, these wagons were used for five years to haul borate ore 165 miles through the desert and rocky outcroppings, from Death Valley to the Mojave railhead. The museum displays the history of the surrounding area from the late nineteenth century up to the present day via enlarged photographs, a continuously running video, and four small rooms that contain artifacts. Some of the items on exhibit include samples of kernite and borate ore (components of Borax); mining equipment, such as replica scale mine cars, and caps that held candlesticks and lamps; models of planes tested at Edwards Air Force Base; clothing worn during the turn-of-the-century; a man-pulled fire wagon, and handcuffs and prison garb from the nearby federal prison. A small kitchen displays household items, and a beauty shop, circa 1930, which has tools of the trade and period-dressed mannequins. A big hit is the animated mule team.

Stroll around outside to see more exhibits, such as rusty agricultural and mining equipment, a large granite boulder with holes (it was used for drilling contests), water pumps, an ore bucket, a surrey, and a miner's shack. There is also a shade area with a few picnic tables. Just across the street is a small park with a roadside display that includes an antique fire engine. Make sure to visit the adjacent SAXON AEROSPACE MUSEUM (pg. 150) and the nearby BORAX VISITOR CENTER (pg. 102) listed in the previous entry.

Hours: Open daily, 10am - 4pm. Closed New Year's Day, Thanksgiving, and Christmas.
Price: Free; donations appreciated.
Ages: 4 years and up.

USS IOWA

(877) 446-9261 / www.pacificbattleship.com
250 S. Harbor Boulevard, San Pedro

Built in 1940, this Goliath battleship, once home to over 2,700 military personnel, served in WWII, the Korean War and Cold War. Her nickname was the "World's Greatest Naval Ship" because of her heavy armor, fast speed, longevity, and because of her big guns: Nine, 16 in (in diameter) Mark 7 guns/turrets; twelve, 5 in. Mark 12 guns; thirty-two Tomahawk cruise missile launchers; sixteen harpoon anti-ship missile launchers; and four, 20 mm/76 cruise missile defense phalanx guns. With its more than fifty years of service, including hosting three U.S. Presidents, when you tour the ship, you tour history.

Board the gangway to the wooden decks of the ship to begin your adventure where you'll see the guns and all other parts of the five-levels of ship up close. Although you explore the ship on a self-guided tour, there are explanatory placards everywhere and former shipmates stationed throughout to answer questions and dispense intriguing, behind-the-scenes information.

Much of the ship is outdoor exploration, so dress accordingly, and enjoy views of the harbor. You will climb up and down several narrow and steep ladders (the ship is in process of becoming more stroller and ADA accessible); step up and go through hatch doors; stroll past (unarmed) missiles and launchers; walk through the Captain's room (where

FDR once stayed) which boasts the only bathtub at sea; walk through the enlisted men's very tight quarters (may your kids never again bemoan the size of their bedrooms!); go onto the bridge (armored with 18" of steel - very safe for the captain and others to be stationed); meander down hallways; go through the crew's gallery and mess deck; and enter the ship's museum area.

This latter area contains information and photographic panels about the *USS Iowa*; a tribute to Pearl Harbor including a naval uniform, newspaper headlines, and other artifacts from that era; and a theater showing Iowa's history and its tows into L.A. And do check out the great gift shop! Look up San Pedro in the Index by City in the back of the book to see numerous other close-by attractions.

Hours: Open daily, 10am - 5pm. Closed Thanksgiving and Christmas Day.
Price: $18 for adults; $15 for active military and seniors; $10 for ages 6 - 17 years; children 5 and under are free. Parking is $1 an hour.
Ages: 5 years and up.

VISTA DEL LAGO VISITORS CENTER

(661) 294-0219 / www.water.ca.gov/recreation
Vista del Lago Road, Gorman

Overlooking Pyramid Lake via a view from the balcony, is a hexagon-shaped building showcasing California's liquid gold - water. This surprisingly interesting museum features many educational and interactive exhibits that show the State Water Project's water supply and delivery systems throughout California. Audio tours are available at no cost. Step on special scales in the first room and find out how much of your body is composed of water (60%), and how much you actually weigh. (Or, skip this exhibit.) Visual displays show the amount of water needed daily to grow and process food, manufacture household items, do laundry, and so on. Video presentations, projected on a giant map of California, and information panels point out that although water is abundant in the north, most of the population is in the south, so we need ways to transport it down. Learn how water is treated before it is delivered to homes and how it is tested for quality. Thirsty yet? Streamline your interest by playing the computer games and using the touch screens in each of the three display rooms.

The theater room shows several short films, ranging from five to seventeen minutes, that present various aspects of water, for instance *Wings Over Water, Water for Farming*, and *A Visit to the Feather River Fish Hatchery*. Educators take note: Not only can the videos be rented, but there is a lot of information given here on a field trip. Pamphlets, comic book-style booklets, teacher's guides, and lots more add to a guided tour of the facility.

The Visitors Center is a great place to quench your child's desire to learn about irrigation, flood control, and water conservation. Tip: After your visit here, enjoy the rest of the day at PYRAMID LAKE (pg. 80), where you can boat, fish, swim, picnic, hike, and even camp.

Hours: Open daily, 9am - 5pm. Closed New Year's Day, Thanksgiving, and Christmas.
Price: Free
Ages: 4 years and up.

WALLY PARKS NHRA MOTORSPORTS MUSEUM

(909) 622-2133 / museum.nhra.com
1101 W. McKinley Avenue #3A, Pomona

To see some really hot wheels, visit this stylish hot rod museum that showcases over eighty very cool cars in mint condition. The cars chronicle the colorful history of drag racing, from its days as an illegal street activity to its current status as a major spectator event. Some of the legendary cars on display include Kenny Bernstein's 1992 Budweiser King Top Fuel Dragster, the first car to break the 300 mph barrier in NHRA competition; Warren Johnson's 1997 GM Goodwrench Pontiac Firebird, the first Pro Stock machine to break the 200 mph barrier; and John Athans '29 Highboy, once driven by Elvis Presley; plus Indy roadsters, midgets, and much more. With all of this inspiration, what kid (or man) wouldn't dream of being behind the wheel of any one of these cars and racing toward the finish line?! Glass cases that run almost the length of the museum contain trophies, photographs, helmets, driving uniforms, and more. Murals and paintings decorate the other walls. School tours, group tours, and participating in the L.A. Fairkids program are just a few of the way the museum reaches out to educate the community.

Want to do some cruising of your own? The first Wednesday of each month, April through December, from 4pm to 8pm, join in on the Twilight Cruise. Over 300 of the finest early rods, customs, muscle cars, and classics fill the parking lot outside the museum. Cruise around on your own two legs to check out the autos and/or purchase some food and drink. This event is free and allows free entrance to the museum, too. So, don't be a drag; race to this

museum. Note: GANESHA PARK (pg. 61) is just east, on McKinley Avenue. It offers picnic tables, grassy areas to run around, basketball courts, and a community swimming pool.

Hours: Open Wed. - Sun., 10am - 5pm. Closed Mon. and Tues., and most major holidays. The hours change during the L.A. County Fair.

Price: $10 for adults; $8 for seniors and ages 6 - 15; children 5 and under are free. AAA discounts given.

Ages: 3 years and up.

WELLS FARGO HISTORY MUSEUM   ☀

(213) 253-7166 / www.wellsfargohistory.com $$

333 S. Grand Avenue at the Wells Fargo Center, Los Angeles

Discover the Old West in the middle of downtown Los Angeles. The history and development of the West (and of Wells Fargo) are laid out like booty in this small and interesting museum. Highlights include a 110-year-old stagecoach, which kids may not climb on; a replica stagecoach, that they are welcome to climb in; a replica of an 1850's agent's office; a mining display with yes, real gold; a gold miner's rocker; a telegraph machine to try out; photographs; murals; and a fifteen-minute film that depicts the hardships of a journey taken in 1852 from Omaha to San Francisco. Buy a pan (and some gold) here so kids can try their hand at working a claim in their own backyard! "Rent" a free audio guide for the exhibits. On free field trips here students will learn about the Gold Rush, and touch gold nuggets and coins; imagine travel conditions while riding on a stagecoach; see and hear about life and work in the 19th century; understand the importance of the invention of the telegraph, plus try using one; and more golden opportunities. Curriculum support materials are provided to teachers.

Note that there is a picnic spot with tables and chairs and eateries just outside the museum. See DOWNTOWN LOS ANGELES / GRAND PARK (pg. 167) for information on Grand Park and all the other places to go within this fairly immediate area.

Hours: Open Mon. - Fri., 9am - 5pm. Closed bank holidays. Tours are available with advanced reservations and a minimum of fifteen people.

Price: Free. Both metered parking and the lots can be $3 for 15 min.

Ages: 4 years and up.

THE WESTERN HOTEL MUSEUM   ☀

(661) 723-6250 / www.lancastermoah.org   !

557 W. Lancaster Boulevard, Lancaster

This small, quaint Western Hotel/Museum has been restored to look like it did when it was originally built in the late 1800's, when room rentals were only $1 a day. The downstairs has a few bedrooms and a parlor that contain old furniture, a wheelchair, and a phonograph that belonged to the last owner, Myrtie Webber. Kids are interested in hearing some of the stories about her, and are impressed that she lived until she was 110 years old! (She doesn't look a day over 70 in her photographs.)

Upstairs is a room with antique clothing; one with a recreated, turn-of-the-century schoolroom; another featuring Native American artifacts; and one that was Myrtie's bedroom, which displays some of her clothing and hats, along with her bedroom furniture. The highlight for my boys was seeing the vivid black-and-white pictures of jack rabbit hunts. The rabbits were hunted, corralled, and then clubbed to death. Although it is not a pretty sight, it is an interesting slice of Lancaster history.

Hours: Open the second and fourth Fri. and Sat., 11am - 4pm.

Price: Free

Ages: 4 years and up.

WESTERN MUSEUM OF FLIGHT   ☀

(310) 326-9544 / www.wmof.com $

3315 Airport Drive, Red Baron #3, at the Torrance Airport, Torrance

A rendition of "Off we go, into the wild blue yonder, flying high into the sky . . ." goes through one's mind when visiting this museum. The Western Museum of Flight "houses" plenty of model planes and about sixteen rare planes, like the YF23A Black Widow II, YF17 Cobra, a F-5A Freedom Fighter, JB-1Bat glider prototype from 1944, plus target drones from WWII and an exact replica of the first controlled aircraft, an 1883 glider. Some planes inside the hangar are in the process of being restored, so kids have the opportunity to see this process. Also in the hangar, which overall somewhat resembles a workshop, are displays of engines, an extensive model plane collection, medals, leather

helmets and jackets, and other memorabilia from WWI and WWII, as well as a nook that is dedicated to space flight. This museum is ideal for school fields trips, too. For those interested in doing aeronautical research, a library is available. Call for more details.

Hours: Open Tues. - Sun., 10am - 3pm. Closed Mon. and most major holidays.
Price: $5 for adults; children 11 and under are free.
Ages: 6 years and up.

THE WHITTIER MUSEUM

(562) 945-3871 / www.whittiermuseum.org
6755 Newlin Avenue, Whittier

Journey back in time to the early days of Whittier, circa 1900. Stroll along a wonderfully recreated, full-size Main Street. The Victorian style is predominate in both the store and home fronts, and in the fully furnished, walk-through rooms. A stereoscope and an old-fashioned stove and bathtub are some of our favorite items. Authentically dressed mannequins all around make the visitors feel a part of this era.

The next few rooms feature an outhouse; a water pump that kids can actually try; photos; murals depicting early Whittier as a farming community; a tractor; old farm tools; and a model of an oil derrick. Sitting on old church pews, kids can watch a video that shows the history of Whittier. The transportation room has photos and an encased display of old medical instruments and medicine vials, plus a doctor's buggy, a racing plane, and a replicated front end of the historic Red Car. Walk up through the Red Car into the children's room filled with hands-on delights, such as old typewriters, adding machines, telephones, and a switchboard. There are also old-fashioned toys to play with and clothes for dressing up. The Library Room is an archival room housing documents on the history of Whittier. Upstairs is a large gallery room with changing exhibits. Call to see what's currently showing. Kids enjoy walking through history at this museum.

Hours: Open Fri. - Sat., 1pm - 4pm. Group tours are also given by appointment.
Price: Free
Ages: 4 years and up.

WILLIAM S. HART MUSEUM AND PARK

(661) 254-4584 - museum; (661) 259-0855 - park and camping / www.hartmuseum.org
24151 Newhall Avenue, Newhall

William S. Hart was a famous western star of the silent films - a bit before my time. (Just a bit.) His Spanish, colonial-style home is now a museum. It is a short, but tough uphill hike to reach the house/museum on the hill. Note: Seniors and physically disabled people can get a pass from the park ranger to drive up the side street to the house. The half-hour guided tour of his home is quite interesting, as the house is filled with Western and Native American art and furnishings. Kids can look at, but not touch, the saddles, guns and other weapons, forty-pound buffalo coat, bear skin rug, stuffed buffalo head, paintings, and Western movie memorabilia.

The park covers over 265 acres, with almost 110 acres set aside for wilderness area. A herd of American bison roam the grounds (which definitely adds to the Old West ambiance), within an enormous fenced-in enclosure. Their feeding area is just down the road from the house museum. Many deer consider this area home, too. Hiking and nature trails through a chaparral and woodland start behind the museum, and loop back around. Camping is available for organized youth groups here, too.

At the bottom of the hill, a large picnic area, with tables and lots of grassy lawn, is located next to a grouping of bunk houses which contain period artifacts. A smaller picnic area is behind the on-site "farm." Purchase some animal feed to entice the barnyard animals - sheep, ducks, horses, and burros - to come within petting distance. Note: See the adjacent HERITAGE JUNCTION HISTORIC PARK (pg. 117). Also note that just down the street on Main Street in old town Newhall is the Western Walk of Stars. Kind of like the Hollywood Walk of Fame with its stars on the sidewalk, Western stars - cowboys and cowgirls - are commemorated with their name and a brass saddle embedded in the sidewalk here. Look for the stars of William S. Hart, John Wayne, Melissa Gilbert and more.

Hours: Hart park is open daily, 7am - 5pm; open in the summer until 7pm. The museum is open mid-June - Labor Day, Wed. - Sun., 11am - 4pm (last tour at 3:30). It's open the rest of the year, Wed. - Fri., 10am - 1pm; Sat. - Sun., 11am - 4pm. Docent-led tours are given every half hour. The museum is closed Mon., Tues., New Year's Day, July 4th, Thanksgiving, and Christmas.
Price: Free
Ages: All

WILL ROGERS STATE HISTORIC PARK   ☼

(310) 454-8212 / www.parks.ca.gov; www.willrogerspolo.org $$$
1501 Will Rogers State Park Road, Pacific Palisades

"I never met a man I didn't like." These famous words were spoken by the "cowboy philosopher," actor, columnist, humorist, and philanthropist - Will Rogers. His ranch house was deeded to the state, and is now a museum. It has been left virtually unchanged (except for maintenance) from when he lived here in the late 1920's. The rustic, wood-beamed living room features many Indian blankets and rugs, saddles, animal skins, a longhorn steer head over the fireplace, a wagon wheel "chandelier," Western statues, Will's boots, and furniture. On the guided tour you'll also see his library/drawing room, upstairs bedrooms, and an office, which are all simply and comfortably furnished, and decorated with a western flair, of course. The Visitors Center shows a free, continuously playing twelve-minute film on Will Rogers, featuring some of his rope tricks. An audio tour of the grounds is also available.

Picnic tables are plentiful at the park. The huge grassy area is actually a polo field. Games are held on Saturdays from 2pm to 5pm and Sundays from 10am to 1pm, mid-April through September. So come, have fun, learn a little history about a fascinating man, and if you feel like horsing around, watch a polo match. There is also a roping and training area for horses so you can watch them being put through their paces. You can even take riding lessons or take a guided trail ride. Fifty-minute horse rides through the park are available Tuesday through Sunday, 9am to 5pm, for $65; kids must be at least 8 years old. Contact (310) 662-3707 / www.willrogerstrailrides.com for more information.

There are several trails leading from the park that connect with its "backyard" neighbor, the massive TOPANGA STATE PARK (pg. 87). One of the most popular hikes is the almost three-mile loop trail to Inspiration Point which, on a clear day, gives an inspirational, breathtaking view. Note that Backbone Trail, a trail that extends nearly seventy miles across and through the Santa Monica Mountains to Point Mugu, has a trailhead here. For more information on Backbone, contact the Santa Monica Mountains National Recreation Area at (805) 370-2301/www.nps.gov/samo.

Hours: The park is open daily, 8am - sunset. Guided tours of the house are offered Thurs. - Fri., 11am - 3pm (last tour), on the hour; and Sat. - Sun., 11am - 4pm. School and special group tours are offered Thurs. and Fri., 10am.

Price: $12 per vehicle; $11 for seniors. House tours and polo matches are included in the price of admission. (There is very limited, free street parking before Villa View Rd., just before you enter the park.)

Ages: 5 years and up.

ZIMMER CHILDREN'S MUSEUM   ☼

(323) 761-8984 / www.zimmermuseum.org $$$
6505 Wilshire Boulevard, suite #100, Los Angeles

Shalom and welcome to this colorful, two-story, completely hands-on museum, developed for kids to have fun and learn about Jewish history and customs, while developing an appreciation of and for the community at large. Oy - what an undertaking, but it works!

The first floor has a nook that contains the front end of a real airplane, with cockpit controls, flight simulation, and headsets where passengers can watch a video of a flight to and around Israel and other countries. The theater encourages imaginations to reign with its dressing area, a great array of costumes, makeup tables, and props. The blue screen backdrop allows the video camera to superimpose children over a variety of locales, while showing the action on the monitor, which is just a few feet away. The ticket booth adds another element of creative play.

Downstairs (and peeking through to the upstairs) is a giant, neo-lit Tzedakah pinball game. Children inset disks to symbolize giving money, time, or of oneself (the latter disk is mirrored). Flick the puck up to the second floor and watch it come down pinball style. A majority of the large, bottom level is set up like a main street. No need for reservations at the bagel cafe which has a bar and stools, plastic food, kitchen, and clocks set in time zones all over the world. Next, enter a kid-size home with murals, table and chairs, and a kitchenette. Shop for fruit or veggies at the adjacent market. The synagogue has prayer shawls, a real Torah, and a dollhouse synagogue. Next door is a bookstore with a puppet theater, books, and toys. Make or sell pretend lemonade at the lemonade stand. Your little ones will tumble around on the foam in the toddler play area, which is complete with fun wall mirrors.

Tuck your own notes between stones (imported from Israel) at a mini version of the Western Wall. Play doctor, so to speak, in the mini emergency room that's complete with medical uniforms, a wheelchair, and X-ray machines, plus a full-size ambulance parked "outside" that's stocked with crutches and bandage wrapping. Become a wordsmith at the media room by using magnetic words on a huge wall, or doing a rubbing over letters. Build a dam at the water table, or

just splash around a bit. Using virtual technology, kids can compose their own music, play drums, and engage in a musical matching game.

A variety of family programs and workshops are offered throughout the year, including art projects that are messily designed in a separate art room. School and group tours are welcome.

Hours: Open Tues. - Thurs., 10am - 5pm; Fri., 10am - 4pm; Sun., 12:30pm - 5pm. Closed Mon., Sat., national and Jewish holidays.

Price: $8 for adults; $5 for ages 1 - 17; children under 1 are free. Grandparents are free on Thurs. when accompanied by a grandchild. Free parking is available on the west side of the building.

Ages: 2 - 11 years.

—PIERS AND SEAPORTS—

FISHERMAN'S VILLAGE

(310) 305-9545 / www.visitmarina.com   !/$
13755 Fiji Way, Marina Del Rey

This small, turn-of-the-century, restaurant and boating complex is located on the main channel of the Marina Del Rey harbor. It offers pier fishing and boat rentals. See the Los Angeles County Transportation section in this book for kayak rentals, harbor cruises, gondola rides, and more.

Some of the best things in life are free, or at least relatively inexpensive. It's fun just walking along the pier, looking at the boats, maybe grabbing a snack, checking out the souvenir shop, and feeling the ocean breeze. If you want more activity, then walk, bike, or skate along the twenty-six-mile SOUTH BAY BICYCLE TRAIL (pg. 210) that runs through the Marina along the coast. (It runs from Malibu to Palos Verdes.) Bring your own bikes or skates or rent them at Daniel's Bicycle Rental and Sales, located in Fisherman's Village. Call (310) 980-4045 / www.danielsbikerentals.com for more information. See MARINA DEL REY WATERBUS (pg. 213) for an inexpensive and fun summertime water excursion. Visit MARINA BEACH / MOTHER'S BEACH (pg. 11) for a place for little ones to swim in a lagoon.

Hours: The Village is open Sun. - Thurs., 9am - 9pm; Fri. - Sat., 9am - 10pm.

Price: Free. Two-hours of free parking with validation.

Ages: All

PORTS O' CALL VILLAGE

(310) 548-8076; (310) 548-8080 / www.portoflosangeles.org; www.sanpedro.com   !/$
Off Harbor Boulevard at Berth 77, San Pedro

This "village" has numerous shops and restaurants; something to please everyone. The majority of the restaurants are clustered together and several of these are fish restaurants containing tanks of live lobsters and crabs. Almost all of the eateries have outside only, waterfront seating, albeit waterfront that looks over the cargo and cranes - the port of Los Angeles. Stores sell unique gift items, clothing, and art pieces. And don't overlook the candy and ice cream shops! If you are interested in taking a narrated tour of the L.A. Harbor, the busiest cargo terminal in the U.S., see the Transportation section for cruises and also for whale-watching excursions that depart from Ports O' Call. Note that tall ships are docked here for cruises seasonally, as well.

Just down the street is FANFARE FOUNTAINS (see pg. 169), a huge reflection pool with fountains and a park. Other nearby attractions include the LOS ANGELES MARITIME MUSEUM (pg. 131), the S.S. LANE VICTORY (pg. 152), and USS IOWA (pg. 154). Tip: An old-time, mini adventure can be had by taking the replicated and restored RED CAR TROLLEY (pg. 214) up and down the boulevard, all day, for only $1 for adult; free for children 6 years and under.

Hours: Most shops are open daily, 11am - 6pm. Restaurants are open later in the evenings. Shops and restaurants are open longer in the summer. Closed Christmas.

Price: Free (parking is free, too), but bring spending money.

Ages: All

REDONDO BEACH INTERNATIONAL BOARDWALK / REDONDO BEACH PIER and KING HARBOR

$$

(310) 374-3481 - marina; (310) 376-6911 - visitor's center / www.rbmarina.com; www.redondopier.com
100 W. Torrance Boulevard, where Torrance Boulevard meets the sea, Redondo Beach

This is no ordinary pier, but a fascinating place to explore with your family! Starting at the north end of the harbor, come hungry because enticing food smells waft through the air. Choose from egg rolls, gyros, hamburgers, or pizza as the international restaurants run the gamut from grab-a-bite to elegant. We munched as we watched the ducks and boats in the water, and soaked up the ambiance. Stop off at Quality Seafood - it's like a mini sea-zoo with tanks of live crabs, lobsters, shrimp, and shellfish, as is the Fun Fish Market next to the Fun Factory.

You cannot entirely avoid the Fun Factory, which is a huge, under-the-boardwalk, amusement center. It is open daily and has over 200 video, arcade, and carnival-style games, plus kiddie rides, tilt-a-whirl, and other rides for all ages. All this adds up to a lot of noisy stimulus. Call (310) 379-8510 for more information. Come up for a breather and take a boat ride.

Back on the cement, horseshoe-shaped pier, have your kids look down at the various sea etchings, including blue whales and sting rays. Try your luck at fishing off the pier - no license needed. The gift shops on the older, wooden part of the boardwalk offer a variety of merchandise for sale.

This boardwalk and harbor area really extends outside of this immediate area. For instance, there are numerous restaurants to choose from, both in the marina confines and next "door" or within walking distance. Check out RUBY'S, a 40's diner (pg. 252), Polly's On the Pier, "Old Tony's" On the Pier, or Captain Kidd's, a fresh seafood waterfront restaurant with a "kidd's menu" and more. Look at the Transportation section and/or the city index in this book for information on cruises and watercraft rentals, including a semi-submersible sub with a viewing window, and for more attractions in the immediate vicinity, such as THE SEA LABORATORY (pg. 226).

Last, but not least, there are rock jetties here. Deeming them fairly safe for the kids to walk on, my husband and I won the coveted, "You guys are the greatest!" award from our children. Ah, the simple pleasures. A two-mile stretch of beach, with fine sand, is adjacent to the pier and harbor.

Veteran's Park, located just south of the pier on Catalina Avenue and Torrance Boulevard is a large, grassy park with plenty of trees, some picnic tables, and a great view of the ocean. Look for the nearby Whaling Wall. This incredible mural of the California gray whale, painted by marine artist, Wyland, decorates the massive wall of the Redondo Generating Station building located on Harbor Drive at Herondo Street. It's worth a drive by, or a stop and stare.

Hours: Most restaurants are open daily for breakfast, lunch, dinner, and after dinner. Most of the stores and attractions are open daily, 10am - 6pm; open later in the summer. The Fun Factory is open Sun. - Thurs., noon - 10pm; Fri. - Sat., noon - midnight.

Price: Parking, mid-May - mid-September is $2 each hour, .50¢ for the first hour weekdays, 8am - 6pm; mid-September - mid-May, $1.50 per hour, 50¢ for the first hour weekdays, 8am - 6pm.

Ages: All

SANTA MONICA PIER / SANTA MONICA BEACH

(310) 458-8900 / www.santamonicapier.org; parking.smgov.net
at the foot of Colorado Boulevard, Santa Monica

This renowned wooden pier offers a lot to do, including just soaking up the beach atmosphere. There are food stands, restaurants (including Bubba Gump Shrimp Company, and Soda Jerks with its numerous specialty sundaes, shakes, phosphates, and other drinks), and great shops that carry a little bit of everything. Peek in the fresh fish store as it has tanks of live lobsters, crabs, and other shellfish. Or, go fishing off the pier to catch your own fresh meal; no license needed. Rent a pole for about $4 an hour at the bait and tackle shop at the end of the pier.

A major kid-attraction on the pier is PACIFIC PARK (pg. 3). A food court is near the amusement park to service your tummy. A beautiful, vintage carousel is usually open Monday, Wednesday through Friday, 2pm to 7pm; Saturday and Sunday, 11am to 7pm. Open extended hours in the summer. Rides are $2 for adults; $1 for children. Call (310) 394-8042 for more info. The Playland Arcade draws kids like a magnet with its video and arcade games. It's open most of the year, Monday through Thursday, 10am to 10pm; Friday through Sunday, 10am to midnight, with extended hours in the summer. A friendly warning: Weekends in the summer can be almost overwhelmingly crowded here. Note that free concerts are given on certain nights at 7pm during the summer.

Do you believe you can fly? The Trapeze School New York on the pier gives you a chance to practice doing just that with two-hour flying trapeze classes at a cost of $47 to $65, plus a one-time $22 registration fee. Other classes include silks, trampoline, static trapeze (i.e. a bar hung from ropes), lyra/aerial hoop, and more. Contact (310) 394-5800 / www.trapezeschool.com for more information.

An attraction found under the boardwalk, down by the sea, is the SANTA MONICA PIER AQUARIUM (pg. 225), a place to discover teeming, touchable tidepool life.

The popular Santa Monica Beach offers plenty of long stretches of beach (three-and-a-half miles), great surf, and several playgrounds. On the south side of the pier is the original location of Muscle Beach. (The more famous one is in Venice Beach.) The beach gym is great for athletes (future Olympians?) to train with parallel bars of various heights, uneven metal bars, and ten, high-hanging single rings and several double rings. It's also great for kids who simply want to work out or just have some fun. Across this workout park is the International Chess Park, where numerous picnic tables with chess boards attached to them invite you to watch players of all levels play the traditional game or speed chess. Bring your own pieces (and a partner?) and try your skills. If you're feeling bold, play on the gigantic chess set with two-foot tall (or so) plastic chess pieces. The pieces are kept locked up; just ask to use them.

Feel like going for a ride? A twenty-six-mile bike path goes through Santa Monica; from the north at Wills Rogers State Beach to the south at Torrance Beach. If you forget your wheels, a little snack shop in front of Muscle Beach doubles as a bike and skate rental agency. Or, call Blazing Saddles at (310) 393-9778 as they have in-line skates, bicycles, and boogie boards for rent.

Hours: The pier is open 24 hours a day. The stores are usually open year round, 10am - 6pm and open extended hours in the summer.

Price: Free to the pier. Parking on or right next to the pier is $8 during the week; $12 on weekends. There is very limited metered parking nearby.

Ages: 2 years and up.

SHORELINE VILLAGE

(562) 435-2668 / www.shorelinevillage.com; www.visitlongbeach.com

419 Shoreline Village Drive, Long Beach

Shoreline Village is a turn-of-the-century coastal "village" with specialty shops, like Pirates Cove for all your piratey needs, and places to eat such as Parkers' Lighthouse Restaurant, a multi-story landmark lighthouse building on the water's edge with a great harbor view. Check out the all-important candy store, funnel cake, and ice cream shops. The Pelican Pier Pavilion offers an old-fashioned style carousel with horse, lights and music ($2 per person, per ride), as well as seventy video games and skee-ball, air hockey and more. Collect tickets and redeem them for prizes here. Call (562) 980-1415 / www.funfactorygames.com for more info.

Weekday mornings are a great time to enjoy serenity here. Stroll along the walkways and/or amble the cement pathway that winds along the waterfront with its various attractions. Catch a narrated harbor cruise via SPIRIT CRUISES (pg. 214). Take a water taxi or AQUALINK (pg. 208) to the Aquarium, the QUEEN MARY (pg. 146), or SCORPION (pg. 150). Rent your own type of boat at LONG BEACH BOAT RENTALS (pg. 212). Rent a surrey, beach cruiser, or skates at Wheel Fun Rentals. Call (562) 951-3857 / www.wheelfunrentals.com for more information.

Walk along the shoreline to the other end of the pathway, to the AQUARIUM OF THE PACIFIC (pg. 216). Continue on around to a grassy park with a small lighthouse and a view of the *Queen Mary*. Toward the aquarium, near the Bubba Gump's restaurant, is a pedestrian bridge with sides that looks like a roller coaster ride. Take this bridge over the street to THE PIKE AT RAINBOW HARBOR (pg. 175), which is a retail and entertainment venue.

Hours: The stores and restaurants are open daily, usually 10am - 9pm. The Pelican Pier Pavilion is open Mon. - Thurs., noon - 10pm; Fri. - Sat., 10am - midnight; Sun., noon - 8pm. Most places are open extended hours in the summer.

Price: Free for the Village. Parking is $1 for up to two hours with validation and purchase at any store or restaurant; $2 for every 20 minutes thereafter; $8 maximum.

Ages: 2 years and up.

—POTPOURRI—

AMERICAN GIRL PLACE

(877) AG PLACE (247-5223) / www.americangirlplace.com

189 The Grove Drive at The Grove, Los Angeles

Playing with dolls has been a favorite past time of girls since time began. The American Girl phenomenon now has a place of its own in L.A. It is a combination of retail boutique, cafe, and meeting place for American Girl enthusiasts. Come visit whether you are a fan, or are unfamiliar with this line of books; of eighteen-inch dolls and accessories based on nine-year old fictional heroines from America's past, as well as contemporary culturally diverse models; and of other products that foster celebrating girlhood.

The main floor is a bookstore and boutique that sells everything related to past and present American Girl dolls,

including outfits and furniture, and Bitty Baby dolls for preschool children as well. Several unique features add to the experience: One is a Doll Hair Salon, where your doll can get a new 'do for $10 to $25. Ask about classes to learn how to braid or create fancy hairstyles, too. Doll piercings and earrings run $14. Another, located upstairs, is a Peek into the Past which is a series of nooks decorated as scenes or rooms from the homes of American Girl characters from the past. See how they lived. There is more boutique merchandise upstairs, too. At the Photo Studio, pose and take home a photo or keepsake *American Girl* magazine featuring your daughter and her doll. Photo shoots start at $22.95. If your doll needs fixing, take her to the Doll Hospital. Ask about special events such as cooking classes, author book signings, and more.

The adjacent Cafe is the ideal location to treat your daughter to lunch, afternoon tea, or dinner. The decor lends a casual, but upscale ambiance with linen table cloths, fresh flowers, and nice table settings. All meals come with warm cinnamon buns. A charming dessert standard is the chocolate mousse flowerpot with a piece of cake and a cookie. Lunch is served with appetizers of mini pretzel baguettes, fruit, and veggies. Your choice of several entrees includes a burger; grilled vegetable sandwich; pastas; salmon; pizza; or chicken tenders. Dessert and a beverage accompany your meal. The cost is $23 per person. Afternoon Tea, at $20 per person, comes with appetizers of a fresh fruit kabob, rainbow of jello, and petite fruit muffin; a variety of finger sandwiches, such as soy nut butter and jelly, turkey and cheese, mini hot dog, and cucumber and cream cheese; and desserts and beverage. Dinner appetizers of hummus and artichoke-spinach dip with pita bread and baby carrots for dipping are followed by options similar to lunch. Dessert and a beverage round out the meal. The cost is $24 per person. Note that menu items are subject to change. And yes, dolls are welcome to dine - in fact, the cafe even has special chairs just for the dolls. Outdoor dining is available on the terraces.

For more information about The Grove, see page 94.

Hours: The boutique is open Sun. - Thurs., 10am - 7pm; Fri. - Sat., 10am - 9pm. The Cafe is open for specific seating times only: Lunch is served daily at 11am, 12:30pm, and 2:30pm; tea at 4pm; dinner at 5:30pm.

Price: The boutique is free to walk through the doors. Prices are listed above for the special attractions, including Cafe costs.

Ages: 3 years and up for the boutique; 5 years and up for the Cafe.

BLUES SCHOOLHOUSE (Los Angeles County)   ☼

(323)-769-4622 - schoolhouse; (323) 848-5100 - general # / www.ihobf.org   !/$$$
8430 Sunset Boulevard at the House of Blues, Hollywood

During the week this renown House of Blues music clubhouse is transformed into a Blues Schoolhouse. (For a description of the building, see HOUSE OF BLUES GOSPEL BRUNCH (Los Angeles County) on page 21.) The engaging ninety-minute "class" covers the history and evolution of the blues in a unique manner. The session sometimes begins on the third floor, with a description and look at the paintings out of mud, sculptures, stained glass, ceiling from a castle in England, carvings, collages using beads, murals, and other folk art that decorates the inside of this "house."

The focus is on the live performance of the band as they play samples of all the music that has been influenced by the blues including jazz, rock 'n roll, rap, hip-hop, call and response, rhythm and blues, and even country. Narration, educational dialogue, and dramatic presentations are given regarding the influence of African music from past to present day; events covering slavery and emancipation; the Civil Rights movement; and more as the role music has played on cultural impact (and vice versa) is also demonstrated. We were immersed in the performances. Toe-tapping, hip-hopping, interactive, sometimes deep and always educational - what a great way to learn!

Notes: Call in the spring to book for the fall; call in the fall to book for the following spring. 120-page curriculum guides are available. You may bring a sack lunch to consume down the street at West Hollywood Park, 647 N. San Vincente Boulevard. Note: Other Blues Schoolhouse/House of Blues locations are in Anaheim and San Diego.

Hours: Offered October through May (not during the summer), on select weekdays at 10am.

Price: Free to public school students and nonprofit youth organizations. The cost for a private group is $10 per person for up to 100 students; no more than $800.

Ages: 5th through 12th graders.

BUILD-A-BEAR WORKSHOP (Los Angeles County)

Headquarters - (877) 789-BEAR (2327); Los Angeles - (310) 446-3290; Montebello - (323) 720-9424; $$$
Northridge - (818) 772-5587; Palmdale - (661) 538-1096; Torrance - (310) 921-2327 / www.buildabear.com

Los Angeles -10800 W. Pico Blvd. at Westside Pavilion; Montebello - 2134 Montebello Town Center at Shops at Montebello; Northridge - 9301 Tampa Ave. at the Northridge Fashion Center; Palmdale - 1233 Rancho Vista Blvd. in Antelope Valley Mall; Torrance - 3525 Carson St. in the Del Amo Fashion Center

See the entry for BUILD-A-BEAR WORKSHOP (Orange County) on page 314 for details.

Hours: Most of the stores are open Mon. - Sat., 10am - 9pm; Sun., 11am - 7pm.

CAMERA OBSCURA

(310) 458-2239

1450 Ocean Avenue at Palisades Park inside the senior center, Santa Monica

A visit to the Camera Obscura takes just a little longer than it takes to snap a picture, but not much. The Camera's building design involves a revolving metal turret that pokes through the roof of the building with a mirror inside the turret angled at forty-five degrees. The outside surrounding city street and beach scene is reflected through a convex lens down onto a large circular table screen. Artists and drafts people have used this type of camera in years past to sketch landscapes. The bottom line is that kids can see a 360-degree view of the outside world and learn how a camera operates by (kind of) being inside one. Tips: 1) Come on a sunny day as the Camera Obscura depends on sunlight to work effectively, and 2) turn off the light in the small viewing room!

Palisades Park is a long, grassy park above the beach, with a paved pathway that parallels the beach. The park is popular with both joggers and transients.

Hours: Open Mon. - Fri., 9am - 3pm; Sat., 9am - 4pm. Closed Sun.
Price: Free
Ages: 6 years and up.

CATALINA ISLAND

(310) 510-1520 - Visitors Bureau; (310) 510-7410 / www.catalinachamber.com

$$$$$

Across the water!

Catalina Island is a resort in the truest sense of the word. It's twenty-one miles long, eight miles wide, 85% natural (meaning development is only allowed on 15% of the land), only twenty-two miles from the mainland, and packed with all sorts of things to see and do, or not - just relax. The city of Avalon has an abundance of shops and restaurants along the beach and harbor, and all within walking distance of each other. (It's only one-square mile and there is no traffic light.) Come to Catalina to fish in the deep blue sea; take a glass bottom boat ride; go horse-back riding, hiking, or camping on the untamed side of the island; take an Island safari, where kids thrill at seeing real buffalo; or just enjoy the beach and all the water activities, such as swimming, snorkeling, and canoeing in its crystal clear blue waters. Catalina has a quaint ambiance and is a wonderful family day trip, weekend, or even week excursion. The following information covers most of the main attractions and a few of the minor ones.

Walk parts of the island, bike it (pedal or electric), rent a golf cart around Avalon, or take the Avalon Trolley around town, which is like a mini tour - it also has a few stops at fun places. It runs mid-September through mid-June on weekends from 9am to 5pm and open mid-June through mid-September on Sunday through Thursday, 9am to 6pm and on Friday and Saturday from 9am to 10pm. The cost is $4 per person round trip or $7 for an all-day pass. Call (310) 510-0342 for more information or check out www.catalinatransportationservices.com for this and other means of transportation around the island.

There are two main, waveless beaches in Avalon - the very long, very narrow strip in front of the main harbor, and the more secluded Descanso Beach, which is a short walk away around the harbor on the other side of the Casino. Descanso is a beach cove, abutting at the rocky hillside, which costs $2 per person admission and is only open mid-April through mid-October. It has a resort feel, with cabana rentals (starting at $275, with some complimentary services) and chaise lounge rentals ($80 for 2 chairs), palm trees, and a restaurant/bar on the beach ($9 for salad; $13 for shrimp; $15 for a burger; $8 for a kid's meal). Kayak and snorkel rentals are also available here. (See below paragraphs.)

How much time you have in Catalina will dictate what you should do. I highly recommend ordering or downloading the Visitors Guide (at the above website) as it has all the information you need. Consider taking a tour or two as you'll see more of the island. Both Catalina Adventure Tours, (877) 510-2888 / www.catalinaadventuretours.com and Santa Catalina Island Company, (800) 322-3434 or 310-510-TOUR (8687) / www.visitcatalinaisland.com, offer numerous and diverse tours at comparable prices. The following prices are quoted from Santa Catalina Island Company, unless otherwise stated. They do not include tax or tip. Note: Children's admission prices are for ages 3 to 11, unless otherwise stated. Get acquainted with Catalina by taking a fifty-minute,

narrated **Avalon Scenic Drive tour** to see the Wrigley estate, the city streets, and an unparalleled view of the picturesque harbor while hearing about Catalina's history - $15 for adults; $13 for seniors and children. Catalina Adventure offers a ninety-minute **City Botanical Garden tour** that includes much of the above Avalon Scenic Drive tour, plus a stop at the Botanical Garden and Wrigley Memorial - a nice spot to walk along the pathways - $26 for adults; $24 for seniors and children. You can also visit the lovely, thirty-eight acre **Wrigley Memorial & Botanic Garden** on your own (a twenty+ minute walk, uphill, from town) and walk the flowers and plants native to California. One of the many island trails, the four-mile looping Garden to Sky Hike, begins here. The garden is open daily 8am to 5pm and the cost is $7 for adults; $5 for seniors and Vets; $3 for students and children 5 to 12; free for active military (with ID) and children 4 and under. See page x for info on AHS reciprocal memberships. Call (310) 510-2897 / www.catalinaconservancy.org for more information. During the narrated, two-hour+, kind of bumpy (but fun!) bus ride on the **Skyline Drive tour** with the Island Company tour, you'll go ten miles into the surrounding wilderness area and see breathtaking views of the ocean and coastlines from mountain ridge tops and canyons, plus maybe wild bison, turkeys and foxes. The information about the history of the island and its inhabitants from the tour guide/bus driver is really interesting. A stop at Airport-in-the-Sky is good for stretching your legs, watching small planes land and takeoff and trying a buffalo burger at the on-site cafe. This tour costs $43 for adults; $35.50 for seniors and children. A similar tour, but in a open-air Hummer so half the fun is in the ride, is the two-hour **East End Adventure** - $76 for adults; $68 for seniors and children. One of my favorite Island Company options is the almost four-hour **Inland Motor tour**, which includes all of the above two-hour tour listings, but going thirty-one miles into the inner island, plus a stop at the Pacific side of Catalina (a rugged beach overlook), then through Middle Ranch for more plant and animal nature. It also follows the 1800's stagecoach route - $76 for all ages. For more of an adventure, take the **Cape Canyon** tour, a four+-hour, off-road excursion in an open-air Hummer where the ride is as wild as the scenery, really. You can purchase lunch (a buffalo burger and other options) at Airport in the Sky - $110 for adults; $98.50 for seniors and children. Or, take an open **jeep tour** of the rugged inland with Jeep Eco-Tours, (310) 510-2595 ext. 108 / www.catalinaconservancy.org, starting at $70 per person for a two-hour tour, with a minimum of two people.

There are several cruise and water taxi options, at about $5 per person, if you want to see Catalina from the water. The two tour companies also offer forty-minute, narrated **glass-bottom boat rides**, which are *clearly* one of the best ways to see the many varieties of fish and underwater gardens just around the "corner" at Lover's Cove, a protected undersea area. Prices are $15 for adults; $13 for seniors and children. The Nautilus is a forty-five-minute **semi-submersible sub** ride offered by Adventure tours where visitors use specially designed tubes to feed the fish food, so you get to watch the feeding frenzy. (It's just like the dinner table at home!) A sub ride is $31 for adults; $27 for seniors; and $24 for children. Ask about nighttime excursions. Island Company's semi-submersible tours are $28.75 for adults; $24 for seniors and children. Adventure tours has an hour boat ride out (and back) to **Seal Rock**, where seals sunbathe, bark, and are just plain fun to watch. Admission is $18 for adults; $16.50 for seniors; $14 for children. The hour-long **Dolphin Quest** is a thrilling ride on a twelve-seater, high-speed, RIB (rigid inflatable boat) that heads straight into waves so riders are airborne at times, then land with a thud, and then airborne again; a little hard on the body, but what a thrill - I loved it! Dolphin sightings are of course not guaranteed (hence the "quest" in the name), but if they are spotted, the captain stops and drifts alongside them. Great info about them and about the island is dispensed. You will also see sea lions up close at their buoy hang out. Don't miss the amazing the Island Company tour's **nighttime Flying Fish Boat Trip**, where yes, the fish really do "fly" across the water, as far as a couple hundred feet. This movement is brought about by a bright searchlight from the boats that hits and excites (i.e., scares) the fish. Hour-long excursions cost $28 for adults; $26 for seniors and children. Our absolute favorite combo is the **Sundown Isthmus Cruise** with the Island Company. The almost five hour trip combines a cruise out to Two Harbors and the flying fish tour. Two Harbors is on the other side of the island. An hour stop over at this beach can include taking a walk on the beach and/or enjoying dinner at the Harbor Reef Restaurant, which you must purchase separately. The Flying Fish "tour" happens on the way back. This cruise is $54 per person.

There are a myriad of other water activities to choose from, too, besides the obvious choice of **swimming**. Rent a SUP (Stand Up Paddle board) or Jet Ski. Take a **guided kayak excursion** with Ocean Sports, (310) 510-1226 / www.kayakcatalinaisland.com. Two-hour guided tours, for instance, are really natural history field trips because of the all the knowledge imparted. These include two miles of kayaking for about $48 for adults; $36 for children 11 years and under. A four-hour **kayaking and snorkeling trip**, which includes all the gear and wetsuits, lunch, snacks, bottled water, and dolphin-watching on the way back, is $96 for adults; $72 for children 11 years and under. There is an abundance of other options, including classes for kids; just **kayaking**, starting at $22 an hour for single and $30 an hour for a double; and **snorkeling** - rentals are about $10 an hour for mask, snorkel and fins. Or, bring your own snorkeling gear! Tip: Great snorkeling is found at Lover's Cove, too - a protected marine sanctuary just a few minutes

walk south of town. The clear waters, with visibility ranging from 40 to 100 feet, is home to undersea kelp gardens and hundreds of fish. Contact Wet Spot rentals, (310) 510-2229 / www.catalinakayaks.com for snorkeling equipment ($10), kayaks ($15 for a single for one hour, $22 for a double), and glass bottom kayaks ($25 for a single, tho a child under 50 lbs can join in on this ride, too, for free). Walking on land is good, but walking underwater is way cool! **Sea Trek tours** allows even non-swimmers to walk under the water, wearing a special helmet attached to air hoses, plus a wetsuit and booties. Walk among the kelp forest, as schools of fish surround you. See the bright orange garibaldi, perhaps a bat ray, and observe sea lions in their element. The actual underwater time with this unique, ninety-minute aquatic adventure is about half an hour. The trek is $79 per person. Contact Scuba Luv at (310) 510-2350 / www.scubaluv.com for more info about this and **snuba** (a cross between scuba and snorkeling) tours.

Parasailing: Via Catalina Parasail, (310) 510-1777 / www.parasailcatalina.com, offers the thrill of flying - about ten minutes air time - for $65 to $75 per person, depending on the height. The flying and boat ride take about an hour total. You fly off and land on the boat, with an optional toe dip in the water. Additional, non-flying passengers are $20, if there is room in the boat. Tandem parasailing is available, too. Island Water Charters (310) 510-9280 / www.islandwatercharters.com is about the same prices. This company also offers tubing (being pulled on inner tubes behind a boat), snorkeling, and other fun rentals.

Dryer, land activities are fun, too! One of the most exciting tours in Catalina is the **Catalina Zip Line Eco Tour** offered by Santa Catalina Island Company. This two-hour walking and zipping journey consists of five consecutive zip lines up to 300 feet above the canyon floor. All of the lines are more than 500 feet long and one of the lines is over a 1000 feet long. At nighttime, the heights and lengths sure seem amplified! Ziplines during the day are $99 per person weekdays; $110 on weekends; nighttime excursions are $109 per person. Climb a 32-foot **rock climbing wall/tower,** with eight routes, located near Descanso Beach. The cost is $5 per climb; $10 for three climbs. Get it in gear and rent a **bike** at Brown's Bikes, (310) 510-0986 / www.catalinabiking.com, to explore the island - $8 an hour for a beach cruiser; $15 an hour for an electric bike. In the center of town, play a beautifully-landscaped **miniature golf** course with some really challenging holes at Golf Gardens, (800) 322-3434 - $10 for adults; $7 for seniors and children 8 years and under. Just down the street is **Three Palms Avalon Arcade,** (310) 510-0967 / www.threepalmsavalonarcade.com, with four lanes of mini or duckpin bowling (no special shoes needed), plus a small Pirate-themed laser shooting gallery, and some video and arcade games. There are two other noteworthy short stops: The small **Catalina Island Interpretive Center**, (310) 510-2745 / www.catalina.com/center, which has mostly pictorial and informational displays, plus rocks that were found on the island. A marine mural contains buttons to push to listen to whale sounds and a large kelp mural has text. Open seven days a week during peak season, 10am to 4pm, and admission is free. The **Catalina Island Museum**, (310) 510-2414 / www.catalinamuseum.org, is located in the famous Casino building (which isn't a casino as in a Las Vegas casino, but as in "social gathering place", which is what the word means in Italian). The museum has a wall with some trophy fish such as Marlin, a few models of ships, old switchboards, lots of ceramic pieces, a theater, and informational and photographic displays, plus lots of archaeological material of the island's history. It's open daily, 10am to 5pm. Admission is $5 for adults; $4 for seniors; free for ages 15 and under.

To really get away from it all, explore Catalina by **camping** and/or **hiking**. Reservations are always recommended, and are necessary in July and August. For more information regarding campgrounds, for reservations, to inquire about equipment rental (e.g., tents and such), and for bus/transportation information, call Santa Catalina Island Company at (888) 510-7979 / www.visitcatalinaisland.com. **Hermit Gulch**, the only camping site in Avalon, has forty campsites and nine tent cabins, all surrounded by trees. This is getting-away-from-it-all camping, but not too far away. Camp in your tent or rent a tent cabin that sleeps up to six people for $50 a night; fabric cots, a two-burner stove, and lantern are provided. A two- to three-night stay is required on certain weekends and holidays. **Two Harbors Campground** has forty-two sites and tent cabins, too, though the cabins are only available April through October. Four-man tents, sleeping bags, firewood, and other equipment rentals are available here. Camping at Two Harbors and Hermit Gulch is $21 for adults; $12 for children per night; sometimes more on weekends. Two Harbors Campground is a quarter-mile from the small town of Two Harbors, which is at an isthmus, down the coast quite a bit from Avalon. The seaside camping feels like being in another part of the world. The site is also popular because of its accessibility and water activities, such as kayaking and snorkeling. Two Harbors also has a snack bar, general store, and restaurant, as well as a twelve-room B&B (Banning House Lodge) in an historic building. Call (800) 626-1496 for more info. The **Wrigley Marine Science Center**, (310) 510-0811 / www.dornsife.usc.edu/wrigley, is an easy two mile hike away. The center is a marine lab and a teaching facility and laboratory for researchers, but it is open to the public Memorial Day through Labor Day on Saturdays from 2pm to 4pm. Admission is free. Touch tanks, demonstrations of the staff feeding moray eels, a science lecture and a tour of a hyperbaric chamber (unless it's in use) are offered to visitors. Ask about their other education outreach programs or book a private tour with a minimum of fifty people at

about $5 per. F.Y.I. - a two-hour bus drive from Avalon to Two Harbors is $32 one way for adults; $26 for children. **Parson's Landing Campground** is remote, located at the complete opposite end of the island from Avalon. A mandatory $14 additional fee is charged for firewood and water. It is beautiful, and suitable for older kids who like to backpack. **Little Harbor Campground** is on the east side of the island from Avalon. The campground is near two sandy beaches under small, but somewhat shady, palm trees, so it is great for kayaking, snorkeling and lazing about in the water. It is accessible by taking a shuttle bus ($32 for adults and $26 for kids) or an intense hike (16 miles from Avalon). **Blackjack Campground** is situated among a grove of pine trees, away from the water, toward the interior of the island. It's for hardy campers. The surrounding area is great for hiking. The latter three campgrounds cost $18 for adults; $9 for children in the summer; $16 for adults and $8 for children other seasons. Various length hiking trails intersect mainly through the campgrounds, or experienced hikers can do the Trans-Catalina Trail - 37.2 miles, one way.

Note: Catalina's busiest season is the summer. September and October, however, provide balmy weather and travel discounts.

Channel crossing time takes about an hour. Prices quoted are round trip. Some numbers to call for cruise information, with various points of departure, are: *Catalina Express*, (800) 481-3470 / www.catalinaexpress.com - departs from Dana Point for an hour-and-a-half cruise for the price of $74.50 for adults; $68 for seniors; $59 for ages 2 to 11; $5 for infants under 2. Departing from Long Beach or San Pedro Harbor for an hour cruise, prices are $72.50 for adults; $66 for seniors; $57 for ages 2 to 11; $5 for infants under 2. (Tip: Sit on the right-hand side of the boat, or starboard, to get better views of the *Queen Mary* and of Catalina island, especially of the iconic casino.) This company also leaves from San Pedro and cruises to Two Harbors (same prices as above from San Pedro). Bikes and surfboards are an additional $7 on any voyage. All-day parking is $12 at Dana Point and San Pedro; $15 at Long Beach. Note: See if *Catalina Express* is still offering free travel to Catalina on your birthday. *Catalina Flyer*, (800) 830-7744 / www.catalinainfo.com, departs from Balboa in Newport Beach at 9am and returns at 5:45pm daily. The hour-and-fifteen-minute cruise costs $70 for adults; $65 for seniors; $53 for ages 3 to 12; $6 for children 2 years and under. All-day parking is $15; $25 on holidays. If time is of the essence, take a fifteen-minute helicopter ride with *Island Express Helicopter Service*, (800) 2-AVALON (228-2566) / www.islandexpress.com, which departs from Long Beach (or San Pedro or Santa Ana, for more money) - $125, plus tax, one way for all ages; children under 2 ride free on a parent's lap. Once on the island, you'll need to walk fifteen minutes to get to town, or take a taxi which costs about $15 for two people.

Price: Prices given above. Note: See if *Catalina Express* is still offering free travel to Catalina on your birthday.

Ages: All

CERRITOS LIBRARY

(562) 916-1350 / www.menu.ci.cerritos.ca.us; www.cerritos.us
18025 Bloomfield Avenue, Cerritos

This is one of the coolest libraries in Southern California. From the titanium exterior to the fanciful fountains outside - enhanced by oversized fake flowers and a dolphin that looks ready to swim away - to the "extras" inside, this is the place to read, learn, and let imaginations soar.

Inside the library is a large, wall aquarium - ten feet high by twenty-one feet wide - filled with colorful tropical saltwater fish, and sharks! There is a short educational aquarium program offered here for all ages at 3:30 on the second Wednesday of each month - call to double check on the times, first.

Enter into the amazing children's library through enormous model books placed over the archway. There are over 80,000 kids' books and rows of computer cubicles. Special reading nooks are decorated with large fake rocks and plants. One nook has a lighthouse and a little wooden pier. Other intriguing elements in this huge room include constellations on a dome-shaped ceiling; a life-sized Tyrannosaurus rex skeleton on a rock, watching over a puzzle table (ever feel like someone is looking over your shoulder?); a scale model of a NASA space shuttle; and a large (fake) Banyan tree that's accompanied by piped in rain-forest sounds. Toward the back is an art area that has ready-to-do art projects and a geology wall with 3-D layers of rock formations. A corner theater has walls that contain three portholes showing fish videos. Learning should always be this entertaining! Stand in front of the green screen and act out what is showing on the screen in front of you. Pick up a brochure or ask about the numerous programs that the library offers including reading programs, performances, storytelling, puppet shows, magic workshops, arts and crafts classes, and tours.

The rest of the multi-story library is almost equally exciting. There is a multimedia presentation room; a circulation desk built to resemble a time machine; a small, elegant/vintage reading room across from the children's library with a

holographic fire; a very small, local and multi-cultural history museum; and a gift shop - and that's just the first floor. Upstairs are computer stations, reading rooms, and more books.

Hours: Open Mon. - Fri., 10am - 9pm; Sat., 9am - 5pm; Sun., 1pm - 5pm. Closed most major holidays.
Price: Free. Residents can check out books for free; nonresidents must pay $100 for a library card.
Ages: 3 years and up.

CHINATOWN

(213) 680-0243 / www.chinatownla.com
N. Broadway Street, Los Angeles

Instead of digging a hole to China, hop in the car and drive to Chinatown. Walk along North Broadway to meander through the red and gold decorated stores - I love the faux palace architecture. A few of our favorite shopping areas include the plaza around 737 Broadway. The two-story market is amazing (to me) with its grocery goods downstairs of shark fin, snail, reindeer antlers, and a variety of fish products, as well as the upstairs household items. I judge it to be authentic as Chinese is spoken here and by the number of Chinese people shopping here. Across the street, next to Bank of America, is a shopping mecca. It looks small from the sidewalk, but walk back and you'll discover a plethora of stores, with more that branch off from the main pathway.

You can also immerse yourself in this Far East experience by entering the pedestrian plaza through the large Chinese-style gate, West Gate, with a sign that announces "Chinatown." (This entrance is just past College Street.) Take along a few coins to toss at the wishing well inside that has signs directing you to throw your money at appropriate desires: love, health, wealth, etc. (And may all your wishes come true!)

Among the open air booths, small stores tucked away, and stores with neon signs, your kids will see touristy stuff as well as authentic Chinese items. You'll find Chinese-style silk dresses, fortune cookies (which did not originate in China), whole barbecued ducks hanging in windows, robes with beautiful embroidery, chopsticks, jewelry, dragon statues, toys, weapons, and lots, lots more. The herb shops are fascinating, and many people swear by the concoctions. The bakeries are tantalizing. Hungry for something more substantial? Give your taste buds (and stomach) a surprise by trying ostrich, fried large intestines, or other unusual fare.

Another cultural adventure here is CHINATOWN TOURS (pg. 197).

Hours: Most stores are open daily, 10am - 6pm, or so.
Price: Free, but bring spending money. Metered parking is available on the street or in lots.
Ages: 4 years and up.

DISNEY STORE (Los Angeles County)

Culver City - (310) 390-8014; Glendale - (818) 247-0222; Montebello - (323) 720-1055; Santa Monica - (310) 395-4365; Sherman Oaks - (818) 907-5094; Torrance - (310) 370-8686; Valencia - (661) 222-9132 / www.disneystore.com
Culver City - 6000 Sepulveda Blvd. in the Westfield Culver City Mall; Glendale - 1152 Glendale Galleria in the Galleria; Montebello - 2134 Montebello Town Center Drive in the Shops at Montebello; Santa Monica - 395 Santa Monica Place at the Santa Monica Place mall; Sherman Oaks - 14006 Riverside Dr. in Westfield Fashion Square; Torrance - 3525 W. Carson St. in Del Amo Fashion Center; Valencia - 24201 West Valencia Blvd. in Westfield Valencia Town Center.

See DISNEY STORE (pg. 314) for details about this interactive, Disney store - it's a whole new world! See pg. 95 for details about what else there is to do in the Culver City mall location, including the WFamily Play Days. The Montebello store is located in The Shops at Montebello mall. The mall also features BUILD-A-BEAR (pg. 162), a children's play area, Xtreme Toys, and lots of restaurants and a food court. The Santa Monica Disney Store is located in the upscale, open-air SANTA MONICA PLACE mall, just off the Third Street Promenade (pg. 93). The Sherman Oaks location, WESTFIELD FASHION SQUARE (pg. 95) has a kid's club and other great attractions at that mall. The Torrance location is inside the humongous DEL AMO FASHION CENTER (see pg. 90) with a kid's club and much more. See pg. 96 for other things to do in the WESTFIELD VALENCIA TOWN CENTER.

Hours: Call for individual store hours. Most are open Mon. - Sat., 10am - 9pm; Sun., 11am - 7pm. Closed Thanksgiving and Christmas.
Price: Free
Ages: 1 - 10 years.

DOWNTOWN LOS ANGELES / GRAND PARK

(213) 972-8080 / www.grandparkla.org

227 N. Spring Street, Los Angeles

The above address is just one of the many for the twelve-acre long, no-playground, Grand Park. I chose the park because it's fun (see the last paragraph) and as a point of reference. This Downtown Los Angeles entry is mostly a listing of a conglomeration of fairly immediate places to go in downtown Los Angeles, either within walking distance from one another, or very short drives. The attractions are listed alphabetically and most are found under that name elsewhere in the book, so look in the Alphabetical Index or Index by City in the back.

Here goes: Angels Flight, Cathedral of Our Lady of Angels, China Town, Chinese American Museum, Dodger Stadium, El Pueblo De Los Angeles Historic Monument, Fashion Institute of Design and Merchandising, Federal Reserve Bank, Grammy Museum, Grand Central Market, James Irvine Garden, Japanese American National Museum, John Ferraro Building, Kyoto Gardens, LA Boulders, L.A. Live, Little Tokyo, Los Angeles Central Library, Los Angeles Times, Music Center, Museum of Contemporary Art, Nokia Theater, Olvera Street, Staples Center, The Broad, Union Station, and Wells Fargo History Museum. Whew!

A word about GRAND PARK; well, a few of them. This park stretches from City Hall, where there is a Farmer's Market and food vendors on Tuesdays, all the way to the Music Center, crossing over several streets. Entrances are at the 200s of N. Grand Ave., N. Hill St., N. Broadway and N. Spring St. It is mostly lawn and a few shades trees, dotted with startling pink tables, chairs, and benches. I love the Little Libraries concept - freestanding, pink (of course) bookcases where people are encouraged to leave a book and/or take a book. The Flags of the U.S. Court flies the different flags flown by our nation, along with explanations. One of the park's best features, besides creating lovely respites, are the fountains. The one on the lowest level, called California Plaza, is enormous and, here's the best part - it is allowable for kids (and adults) to splash around in its ankle-deep waters with jets that shoot up. Other notable features - the perimeter, or edge, of the fountain disappears by your feet; there are more tables and chairs here, some food stands, a Starbucks, and a restroom; and the fountains look beautiful at nighttime, when they light up and change colors. Check the website for special events held at the park such as concerts, free yoga classes, community celebrations, food truck days, and more.

Hours: Grand Park is open daily, 5:30am - 10pm.

Price: Free, except for parking. Parking can be $3.50 per 15 min. or $20 for the day. A flat fee of $10 after 4:30pm is on weekends and for special events.

Ages: All

EL PUEBLO DE LOS ANGELES HISTORICAL MONUMENT / OLVERA STREET / CHINESE AMERICAN MUSEUM

$$$

(213) 485-6855 or (213) 628-1274 or (213) 625-3800 / www.elpueblo.lacity.org; www.lamountains.com

125 Paseo de la Plaza #400, Los Angeles

This attraction is not a single monument, but the oldest part of the city of Los Angeles. It contains twenty-seven historic buildings, eleven of which are open to the public, and four of those are restored as museums. A traditional Mexican-style plaza and Olvera Street are also here. Tip: Read up a little on the history of this area, as it will make your visit here more meaningful.

One of the museums is the **Chinese American Museum**, located at 425 North Los Angeles Street, across from Union Station. Follow the hanging red lanterns to the restored building to see art, history, and other exhibits on both ancient and contemporary Chinese culture. The museum is open Tuesday through Sunday from 10am to 3pm. Admission is $3 for adults; $2 for seniors and students; children 12 and under are free. Contact (213) 485-8567 / www.camla.org for more information.

The circular plaza is the central hub and has some interesting statues to look at. Usually a docent is on hand giving out maps and other information. Across the way is the **Firehouse Museum**. Inside is a restored, old fire engine that was once hooked up to a horse and a few other pieces of fire-fighting paraphernalia. The walls are decorated with different fire hats.

Olvera Street is one of the oldest streets in Los Angeles. In 1930 it was closed to through traffic and reborn as a Mexican marketplace. It is very commercial and a definite tourist attraction for shopping, but it still conveys the flavor of old Mexico and bonus - you don't need a passport. Enjoy a walk down the brick-paved/cobblestone "street" to look at the eye-catching displays, watch a glassblower at work, see candles being dipped, hear strolling mariachi bands, and munch on bakery goods. There are inexpensive and expensive Mexican handicrafts to purchase both inside the stores and at the center stalls, such as little guitars, leather purses, ceramic banks, colorful clothing, Mexican pottery, toys, and so much more. Note: Kids love the variety of candy that is conveniently placed at their grabbing level.

Olvera Street offers several full-service restaurants. A favorite one is La Luz del Dia, located toward the entrance,

because the food is good and kids can climb the ornately tiled steps and peer into the kitchen to see tortillas being made by hand.

The Sepulveda House is a few doors down from the entrance on the west side of Olvera Street. You can also enter it from Main Street. It has an encased display of Mrs. Sepulveda's bedroom, and her kitchen as it appeared in the late 1800's. It contains books, a small gallery around the corner with some interesting artifacts from the area, and a mural by a renown Latino artist.

The Avila Adobe is located almost directly across from the Sepulveda House. This is the city's oldest building, constructed in 1818. It has rooms to walk through that reflect the style of a wealthy ranch owner in the 1840's. Some of the more interesting items include a child's bed that used rope and cowhide instead of box springs, a wooden bathtub, and a Chinese shawl that was used as a bedspread. The Courtyard, which is really a packed-dirt patio, was used as a kitchen because most of the cooking was done outside. We enjoyed the side trip here, and learned a little along the way. It also houses a visitor's center with maps and gift items. Inside, watch an eighteen-minute film, *Pueblo of Promise* about the early history of Los Angeles. (My kids actually watched and enjoyed the movie.)

The Visitors Center offers a free, one-hour guided walking tour of the highlights of El Pueblo Monument. Best suited for ages 10 years and up, it is offered Tuesday through Saturday at 10am, 11am, and noon. Reservations are required for groups, but not for individuals. There is even a curriculum guide available online. As you walk around this historic area, either with a guide or on your own, enjoy soaking up the atmosphere of a different country while so close to home! Tip: Consider taking the train from your area to Union Station, which isn't too far away from Olvera Street. See DOWNTOWN LOS ANGELES / GRAND PARK (pg. 167) for information on Grand Park and all the other places to go within this fairly immediate area.

Hours: Olvera Street is open daily in the summer, 10am - 10pm. Open the rest of the year, 10am - 7pm. The Sepulveda House and Firehouse Museum are open Tues. - Sun., 10am - 3pm. The Avila Adobe is open daily, 9am - 4pm.

Price: The entrance to everything is free. Parking is available at a number of lots that charge about $8 for the day. The one on Main St., between Hope and Arcadia, charges $9 for the day.

Ages: 3 years and up.

FAIRPLEX GARDEN RAILROAD

(909) 623-3111 / www.fgrr.org
1101 W. McKinley Avenue at the Pomona Fairgrounds, Pomona

"I've been workin' on the railroad, All the live long day. I've been workin' on the railroad, Just to pass the time away. Don't you hear the whistle blowing?. . ." You don't have to work on this railroad; just come and enjoy one of the oldest (since 1927) and perhaps the largest miniature (which is ironic phrasing) railroads in the U.S. This outdoor, 100 x 300 foot model town has numerous ponds and rivers, mountains, deserts, residential buildings, bridges, tunnels, mining, a circus, a section of the Old West, missions, oil fields, farms, and everything else that a town (or state) might have, and then some. And because it's a garden railroad, the landscaping is exquisite. In fact, school groups are welcome to take a tour as they can learn about California history by seeing the varied terrain and the role the railroads have played. Over thirty G gauge trains can run at one time on the over 9,800 feet of track - that's a lot of train!

Hours: Open March - mid-August the second Sun. of the month from 11am - 4pm; open the end of August - September daily (during the L.A. County Fair), 1pm- 8pm. Call as hours fluctuate.

Price: Free

Ages: All

FANFARE FOUNTAINS AT GATEWAY PLAZA

(310) SEA-PORT (723-7778) / www.portoflosangeles.org
Harbor Boulevard and Swinford Street, San Pedro

If you are in the area, the fountain, encircled by tall palm trees with the iconic Vincent Thomas Bridge in the background, is worth seeing, especially when the "show" is on. Covering a total of ¾ of an acre, the two main fountains, 250 by 100 feet, are accompanied by programmable jets shooting as high as 100 feet, choreographed with music for three-minute presentations that go on periodically throughout the day. In the evening, lights add a little color and flare to the show. Kiosks usually abound in the summer time.

Even without the music and jets shooting, it's worth a visit. Feel like you're walking through water on the walkway that divides the twin fountains because the black granite infinity edge spills over the rim, over the basin ledge. (You can get all wet here, too, when the fountains dance, or just your feet by the continuous water flowing.) Just north of the

fountains is a reflection pool and south of the fountains, on Harbor Boulevard at 2nd Street, is a small, interactive fountain where waters jet up from the pavement at random intervals and kids can play and get wet (if mom and dad say it's OK). The pools are all connected by a nice, tree-lined, wide walking pathway.

Visit the fountains by taking a RED CAR TROLLEY (see pg. 214) and be sure to visit PORTS O' CALL VILLAGE (pg. 159) and other attractions which are just down the street.

Hours: "Shows" are daily 10am to 9pm - one song plays every 30 min.; from noon to 1pm and 7pm to 8pm one song plays every 10 minutes.
Price: Free. Some free parking on Swinford or in the lot for $1 an hour.
Ages: All

FOREST LAWN MEMORIAL PARK

(323) 340-4742 or (800) 204-3131 / www.forestlawn.com
Glendale - 1712 S. Glendale Ave.; Los Angeles - 6300 Forest Lawn Dr. in Hollywood Hills

A cemetery might seem like an odd addition to this book, but most of the Forest Lawn Memorial parks have outstanding works of art, including beautiful works of stained glass. Tip: Pick up a map at the entrance. The next few paragraphs reference the Glendale location: The Great Mausoleum at this park contains Leonardo da Vinci's Last Supper recreated in gorgeous stained glass, as well as replicas of Michelangelo's La Pieta and Moses. Please note that many of the statues are naked. A larger-than-life replica of David is on the grounds, as are several other statues and a huge mosaic titled Signing of the Declaration of Independence. You can also walk the labyrinth here.

Make sure to visit the Hall of Crucifixion/Resurrection. A twenty-two-minute "show" features an audio presentation of Christ's last days on earth, complete with various voices, sound effects, and a narrator. As the dramatic story is told, a spot light shines on parts of one of the largest religious oil paintings ever created, a 45-foot by 190-foot painting titled *Crucifixion*. At the end, the picture is seen in its entirety. The *Resurrection* painting, a close runner up in size and impact at 51-foot by 70-foot, is also highlighted in the same manner during the retelling. Did you ever think there could be so much history and art at a mortuary?

Next door, the on-site museum contains stained glass pictures, coins mentioned in the Bible, statues, medieval armor, and an art gallery with exhibits that rotate every three months. Take an audio tour using your cell phone by calling (323) 209-4143. A variety of educational and artistic, hands-on activities are offered here throughout the year, particularly for each of the holidays. Past activities included making a chocolate rose for Valentine's Day, creating a work of "stained glass", making a Father's Day bookmark, enjoying a pumpkin patch, and lots more.

The Hollywood Hills Forest Lawn in Los Angeles has several impressive art pieces and tributes to American history. There is a huge memorial and statue of George Washington, as well as larger-than-life commemorations of Abraham Lincoln and Thomas Jefferson. A 30-foot by 165-foot tiled mosaic graces the outside of the Hall of Liberty building. The colorful, chronological, mosaic scenes of freedom depict the surrender of General Cornwallis, the crossing of the Delaware, Betsy Ross making the flag, and the signing of the Declaration of Independence. Inside the hall is a replica of the Liberty Bell.

Note: See the Calendar entry for a Visit with Michelangelo and Leonardo da Vinci (pg. 713) and a Visit with Montezuma (pg. 713) - Forest Lawn's terrific, free, History Comes Alive programs.

Hours: The museum is open Tues. - Sun., 10am - 5pm; closed Mon. The Crucifixion/Resurrection paintings and "show" can be seen Tues. - Sun., on the hour, 10am - noon and 2pm - 4pm. The Last Supper can be seen daily, 9:30am - 4pm.
Price: Free
Ages: 7 years and up.

FRY'S ELECTRONICS (Los Angeles County)

Burbank - (818) 526-8100; City of Industry - (562) 463-2400; Manhattan Beach - (310) 364-3797; Woodland Hills - (818) 227-1000 / www.frys.com
Burbank - 2311 North Hollywood Way; City of Industry - 13401 Crossroads Parkway North; Manhattan Beach - 3600 Sepulveda Blvd.; Woodland Hills - 6100 Canoga Ave.

I know this is an odd addition (another one!) to the book, but some of these stores are so fancifully themed in their decor that I had to at least mention them. My husband and boys love to look around in here, and as much as I love to shop, electronics (over 50,000 per store!) doesn't do it for me. I do, however, like looking at the imaginative "decorations." The store in **Woodland Hills**, for instance, is themed after Lewis Carroll's *Alice in Wonderland*. Rose bushes, with white and red roses, and other huge topiaries, as well as gigantic cards "flying" overhead comprise an

eye-catching entryway. Other objects throughout the store include a flying dragon, a large "thatched" roof house, and oversized (ten- to fifteen-foot high) figures representing characters from the book. Very fun.

The other stores are equally well done: **Anaheim**: This one features a replica of the NASA flight deck for the Endeavor Space Shuttle, complete with launches on big screen TV's, and other space ships in flight. It also has a cafe that's open the same as store hours. **Burbank**: An alien space ship apparently crash landed into the entrance over this store. Inside, travel back in time to the 1950's with a retro space theme from Hollywood, complete with a Martian-style robot, army figures fighting aliens, spaceships overhead, and a giant octopus holding up a computer display. A cafe here, serving sandwiches, salads, and beverages, is designed to look like a drive-in movie, complete with three booths made from convertibles so you can eat and watch black and white movies on a big screen. **City of Industry**: This location has a factory setting that is a salute to the Industrial Revolution, complete with oversized gears and cogs. **Fountain Valley**: It hails the ruins of ancient Rome, complete with a flowing aqueduct. **Manhattan Beach**: Tahiti is recreated with sculpted lava Tiki heads and its own rainforest. **Oxnard**: Wood decor and wall murals depicting the coastal community, such as Hollywood Beach, and agriculture of this area pay tribute to this town. **San Marcos**: This store is one of my favorites! It is reminiscent of the lost city of Atlantis, with its huge aquarium and exotic fish, statues of gigantic seahorses, marine-oriented murals, and submarine windows (complete with rising bubbles in them) in the customer service section. This store has a sit-down cafe in its center that offers sandwiches, salads, pizzas, shakes, coffee, and smoothies. The cafe's corners are composed of more fish tanks. Any of the stores are worth a stop and peek if you're in the neighborhood.

Hours: Call for store hours.
Price: Technically, free.
Ages: 5 years and up.

HOLLYWOOD - the downtown tourist mecca

(323) 467-6412 - Hollywood & Highland Center; (323) 469-8311 - Hollywood Chamber of Commerce and visitors center / www.hollywoodandhighland.com; www.hollywoodchamber.net; www.discoverlosangeles.com

Hollywood and Highland, Hollywood

Lights! Camera! Action! Get ready for your closeup of the heart of Hollywood (at least the family-friendly part) that is glorified on screen and in the media, and embedded in the minds of moviegoers. Glamorous? No. But it's an interesting tourist mecca to see in real life. Look down and walk (and walk) to see **Hollywood's Walk of Fame**, which is actually hundreds of stars' names, each adorning a star on the sidewalk. Bring a pink strip of paper (to blend in with the pink terrazzo of the star) with your child's name on it and place it on a blank star. Take a picture of your child next to that star - he or she is now famous! (It's just that easy!) Find out when the next celebrity will be honored with a ceremony dedicating his/her star along this famous "walk" by contacting the chamber. All kinds of shops line Hollywood Boulevard - many of them offering kitschy and touristy souvenirs. This is a great place to people watch.

Take the palatial-like steps up to the **entertainment complex of Hollywood & Highland**. Hmm - notice how the facade looks like an old-time movie set? It, and the center's Babylon Court, which incorporates giant, rearing elephants atop columns, were inspired by D.W. Griffith's silent film, *Intolerance*. Look through the archway to see the famed Hollywood sign on the hill. The tiered complex has sixty, mostly brand-name, retail shops; numerous eateries and restaurants, including HARD ROCK CAFE (see pg. 21); TCL Chinese 6 Theatres movie theaters (of course); and an upscale bowling lounge, called Lucky Strike, which has twelve lanes, video screens, retro decor, American bistro food fare, and a bar. The DOLBY THEATRE (see pg. 182) is located here, as well. Little ones will enjoying running through the water fountain, too, where water spurts up seemingly randomly - bring a change of clothing.

If you want to see stars' homes or go sightseeing in the city on a double decker bus, contact Starline Tours, (800) 959-3131 / www.starlinetours.com, or another such company.

Look up these nearby attractions, most of which are within walking distance, in the back of the book: BUILD-A-BEAR WORKSHOP, EGYPTIAN THEATRE - AMERICAN CINEMATHEQUE, EL CAPITAN THEATER, TCL CHINESE 6 THEATRE (a must - it used to be called Grauman's), GUINNESS WORLD OF RECORDS MUSEUM, THE HOLLYWOOD MUSEUM, HOLLYWOOD WAX MUSEUM, MADAME TUSSAUDS HOLLYWOOD, PANTAGES THEATER, and RIPLEY'S BELIEVE IT OR NOT! MUSEUM. For about $3 per person for an all-day pass, have more of an adventure by catching the Metro Red Line subway for a twenty-minute ride from Union Station in Los Angeles to Hollywood Boulevard and Highland Avenue.

Hours: The mall is open Mon. - Sat., 10am - 10pm; Sun., 10am - 7pm. Some restaurants are open later.
Price: Free, technically.

Ages: 8 years and up.

HOLLYWOOD FOREVER CEMETERY

(323) 469-1181 / www.hollywoodforever.com   !
6000 Santa Monica Boulevard, Hollywood

"That's all folks". This saying is engraved on Mel Blanc's tombstone, the "man of 1000 voices", who spoke Bugs Bunny, Porky Pig, Tweety Bird and 997 other voices into existence. Hollywood Forever doesn't quite give the legendary actors, producers, musicians, and others buried here immortality, but it does give the public a place to see their tombstones and other memorials, and remember them. Other celebrities buried here include Charlie Chaplin, Jr., Don Adams, Vampira, Fay Wray, Rudolph Valentino, Cecil B. De Mille, John Huston, and many more.

This cemetery has also become a popular gathering place to watch movies, shown on the side of a mausoleum, and even attend concerts and other special events. Who knew?! Note: Another resting place for the famous (i.e. Marilyn Monroe, Natalie Wood, Ray Bradbury, etc.) is down the road a bit at PIERCE BROTHERS WESTWOOD VILLAGE MEMORIAL PARK AND MORTUARY (pg. 175).

Hours: Open daily, 8:30am - 5pm.
Price: Free
Ages: 8 years and up.

IFLY HOLLYWOOD

(818) 985-4359 / www.iflyhollywood.com $$$$$
100 Universal City Plaza at Universal Studios CityWalk, Universal City

What an adrenaline rush! This indoor skydiving/vertical wind tunnel allows you to fly safely and relatively inexpensively (for flying, that is). A single flight lasts only a minute, so I recommend the double flight (two minutes). This facility has its glass-encased tower right on the main strip of the entertainment mecca, UNIVERSAL CITYWALK, so you can watch people flying around inside it and people can watch you. (See page 175 for more details.) Enjoy shopping and eating before or after your flight. See PERRIS SKYVENTURE (pg. 345) for more of a description on what you'll be doing. Participants under 17 must have a signed parental waiver.

Hours: Open Sun. - Thurs., 10:30am - 9pm; Fri. - Sat., 10:30am - 11pm
Price: Double flight, first time flyers is $59.95. General parking is $16 before 3pm; $10 after 3pm.
Ages: 3 years and up.

LONG BEACH MARINE INSTITUTE

(562) 431-7156 or (714) 540-5751 / www.longbeachmarine.org $$$$
6475 East Pacific Coast Highway, #281, Long Beach

"The Long Beach Marine Institute is an association of researchers and educators dedicated to bringing marine field research into the classroom and the classroom into the field." (A quote from the institute's brochure.) L.B.M.I. offers over twenty different programs to encourage hands-on learning about marine life and their habitats. Most programs are offered for groups of twenty-five or more. If your group number is smaller, the L.B.M.I. workers will hook you up with another group. Besides going on the guided kayak tours, snorkeling excursions, and guided tidepool tours, being on board the *Challenger* is a main attraction. This 118-foot, shipshape vessel is the host and means of transportation for several field trips.

The ninety-minute Sea Creature Safari, $25 per student, is a popular expedition. After a boat orientation, set sail for adventure on this floating laboratory. Organisms from the sea are gathered in two ways, at two stops: One is mud from the harbor floor gathered on board to be inspected and sorted through. Kids love being able to put their hands in this fascinating pile of gunk to find "treasures." The second is the otter trawl, a net thrown into the waters and dragged for about ten minutes to see what is collected, then sifted through as well. Kids can also examine their findings under a microscope. The Oceanographer for a Day, $35 per student, is the above Safari with the add-on of a self-guided tour through the aquarium to enhance your time and learning. Summer camps are held here, too. Overnight camps - the Catalina Island Marine Science Camp - are offered in the fall and spring. One camp session is worth at least a semester of school (my opinion!) with all that you get to see and do and explore and study. L.B.M.I. will also come to your school or group for a presentation.

Hours: Call for times for various excursions.
Price: Some prices are listed above. Prices are $7 per person for a tidepool tour; $34 per person for whale watching; $16 for kayaking (must be at least 10 years old).

Ages: 4 years and up, depending on the activity.

LOS ANGELES CENTRAL LIBRARY

(213) 228-7000 - library; (213) 228-7250 - children's literary info; (213) 228-7025 - cultural and educational
activities; (213) 228-7168 - public tours / www.lapl.org

630 W. 5th Street, Los Angeles

This 125-year-old library is an absolute classic. From the unique architecture to the millions of books to the areas
and exhibitions that focus on special interests (such as Forty Years of Sesame Street Illustrations), it is an oasis to
researchers and readers of all ages who can easily spend hours here. The Language Learning Center offers audio aid
and instruction manuals in twenty-eight languages. What a unique adventure for your children's ears! Over 250
newspapers and periodicals are offered in numerous languages. The children's section is a haven for young book lovers
with its Old World library atmosphere, comfy furniture and shelves of books that open their imagination to new
worlds.

One-hour free tours are given of the library that allow visitors to see, know and appreciate its rich history.
Walk-ins are welcome. If you don't take the tour, at least walk around to see the beautiful rotunda, old library card
boxes, the eight-story atrium with its funky chandeliers, murals, and much more. Just outside are some small, park-like
areas with grassy spots, trees, a walkway and a fountain. One-hour school tours are given Thursdays and Fridays for
kindergarten to fifth graders at 10am and 11am. Tours consist of a half-hour tour of the library and a half hour of
story time, making a craft, or book reading. Call (213) 228-7055 or (213) 228-7250 to make a reservation.

Besides storytimes, the Children's Literacy Department and the KLOS Story Theater offers puppet shows, crafts
and other programs throughout the week. Various past shows have featured magic tricks, instructions on how to make
a book (followed by actually making one), and storytelling with puppets. At least once a month, on the first floor of the
library, at the Mark Taper Auditorium ALOUD presentations are given for teens and up. These are free, dramatic
readings of a favorite story by the author, or a discussion by an artist or scientist, or whomever, usually followed by a
Q & A. Also note that the Mark Taper contains galleries of rotating exhibits. (The one on pop-up books was
wonderful!) Look at the library calendar events for more details. See DOWNTOWN LOS ANGELES / GRAND
PARK (pg. 167) for information on Grand Park and all the other places to go within this fairly immediate area.

Hours: The library is open Mon. - Thurs., 10am -8pm; Fri. - Sat., 10am - 5:30pm; and some Sun., 1pm -
5pm. Closed most major holidays. Library tours are offered Mon. - Fri. at 12:30pm; Sat., 11am and
2pm; Sun. at 2pm.

Price: Free. Enter the parking structure under the library on 524 S. Flower St. - $1 for the first hour, $4 for
the second hour - with validation for library card holders at the times the library is open. For cars
entering after 3pm, until the library closing, and on Sat., 10am - 6pm - $1 flat rate.

Ages: 3 years and up.

MOUNT WILSON OBSERVATORY and SKYLINE PARK

(626) 793-3100 or (626) 793-3065 - observatory; (818) 899-1900 - ranger station; (213) 897-3656 - Caltrans
road closures / www.mtwilson.edu

Angeles Crest Highway, Los Angeles

Observant kids will enjoy the incredible view from atop the world, above the clouds, and also seeing the
observatory, which was founded in 1904. Hike around the grounds on your own on the aptly named Skyline Park
and/or come for a free, two-hour, guided tour. Besides walking the area, the tour takes visitors to the UCLA 150-foot
solar tower within a tower telescope where oftentimes access is allowed inside to see current images of the sun. You
also see the visitor's gallery with the 100-inch Hooker telescope, where you can gawk at the large instrument through a
big window, and you go to the astronomical museum. Inside the museum are numerous photographs taken of the skies
accompanied by information about the photographed objects, a scale model of the observatory, and a few star
searching tools. Special guided tours, where visitors go inside more of the Observatory facilities, are available upon
request, and so is viewing time through the historic 60-inch telescope.

If you come to visit this area during the week, or when guided tours are usually available, take a free copy of the
Self Guided Tour Brochure available at the museum. The Cosmic Cafe, offering sandwiches, hot dogs, snack,
beverages, and even souvenirs, is open on weekends from 10am to 5pm, April through November. Note the elevation
of Mt. Wilson is 5,800 feet and it is often cold, or at least cool, up here. There is frequently snow on the ground in the
winter.

Hours: The grounds, park gate, and museum are usually open April through November, weather permitting, daily, 10am - 5pm. Closed December through March. Guided tours are usually offered April through October, Sat. and Sun. at 1pm, weather permitting; call to make special arrangements during the winter.

Price: The tour and admission is free. To park, however, you must first purchase a $5 Adventure Pass at the Clear Creek Ranger Station half way up the road to Mt. Wilson or at a sporting goods store. Carpool as space is limited.

Ages: 6 years and up.

NATURALIZATION CEREMONY ☾

www.cacd.uscourts.gov $$$

Naturalized citizens must meet three requirements: be lawful permanent residents of the United States; have lived here for at least five years; and pass a written citizenship test. Many applicants study our history so intensely that they know it better than those of us who have lived here all our lives.

The naturalization ceremony takes place a few times a month at different locations - District Court in downtown Los Angeles, L.A. County Fairgrounds (Fairplex) in Pomona, L.A. Convention Center, and Quiet Cannon in Montebello - and as several hundred people (even 3,500 at Fairplex in Pomona!) can be inducted at one time, it can take a few hours. After green cards are turned in and the applicants seated, each one is given a congratulatory letter from the White House and a small American flag to wave after the swearing in. A district judge pounds the gavel and administers the Oath of Citizenship in which the almost-new citizens renounce any foreign allegiance and promise to uphold the Constitution. Next on the agenda, an INS representative gives a short speech, a patriotic song is sung (with not many dry eyes in the audience), and a short video shows a sweeping overview of America. Ta da - new American citizens have been born! Finally, Certificates of Citizenship are handed out.

I mention this ceremony as an outing because I think older kids who are studying the Constitution or immigration might be interested in seeing this process and perhaps even catch a little national fever. Note that the public is welcome, but they must sit or stand near the back of the huge hall.

Hours: Call for dates.

Price: Admission is free. $12 - $15 for parking.

Ages: 10 years and up.

OLVERA STREET

See EL PUEBLO DE LOS ANGELES HISTORICAL MONUMENT / OLVERA STREET on pg. 168 for details about this historic, Mexican street full of restaurant and shopping opportunities.

OXMAN'S SURPLUS, INC. ☀

(562) 921-1106 / www.oxmans-surplus.com   !

14128 East Rosecrans Avenue, Santa Fe Springs

Outside is a replica nose of the Columbia, as well as an array of military flags. Inside, the front section of this unique army surplus store is a small museum filled with an eclectic mix of items, mostly from WWII. These include ejection seats, uniforms, a gun collection, a whale harpoon, a periscope, a B-17 cockpit (which visitors may sit in), a 15th century suit of armor, a few surface-to-air missiles, a WWII oxygen breathing tank, Hitler's bayonet, helmets, patches, a Devil fish skeleton, a corner set up with sandbags, gas masks, a display of rations, a B-29 engine, a Dog Tag machine, grenades, field equipment, a Choctaw helicopter tails section (from the Korean War), and more. Many of the articles are labeled so a self-guided "tour" works. Hint - Boy Scouts love this sort of place!

Grab a bite to eat at the Mess Tent Cafe inside the museum space - there is seating and you can watch a military-oriented video. Each $6 meal comes with a drink and chips. Entrees include hot dogs, a sandwich (turkey, roast beef, etc.), or chicken nuggets. Or go authentic and have an MRE.

The surplus store part carries everything camouflage, plus camping gear, knives, boots, tarps, tools, swords, clothing, and lots more.

Hours: The store and museum are open Mon. - Sat., 9am - 6pm. The Mess Tent Cafe is open Mon. - Sat., 11am - 4pm. Both are closed Sun. Tours are given by appointment.

Price: Free

Ages: 6 years and up.

PIERCE BROTHERS WESTWOOD VILLAGE MEMORIAL PARK AND MORTUARY

(310) 474-1579 / www.dignitymemorial.com/pierce-brothers-westwood-village-memorial-park
1218 Glendon Avenue, Los Angeles

This hard-to-find, and very small, cemetery is worth a visit if you are interested in where some big name stars are laid to rest. Some of the celebrities here include Marilyn Monroe, Natalie Wood, Rodney Dangerfield ("There Goes the Neighborhood" is on his tombstone), Farrah Fawcett, Ray Bradbury, Don Knotts, Truman Capote, Donna Reed, Frank Zappa, Dean Martin, and many more. There are numerous other people buried, here, as well and some are from other fields that you may recognize. A few of the graves are from the the early 1900's. Another well-known cemetery is HOLLYWOOD FOREVER CEMETERY (pg. 172) where you can pay respects to Mel Blanc, Charlie Chaplin, Cecil B. De Mille, and many others.

Hours: Open daily, 8am - 5pm.
Price: Free
Ages: 7 years and up.

THE PIKE AT RAINBOW HARBOR

(562) 432-8325 - general info; (562) 668-4030 - Ferris wheel and carousel / www.thepikeatlongbeach.com
95 Pine Street and Shoreline Drive, Long Beach

A pedestrian bridge, with sides that looks like a roller coaster ride, crosses and connects the street by the marina near Bubba Gump's restaurant, to the Pike, which is a retail and entertainment venue. The venue features KDB, which is a higher-end arcade center with a restaurant and bowling alley inside. See page 33 for more details. There is also P.F. Changs restaurant, Gladstones, Cold Stone Creamery, CineMark Theater, clothes stores, gift shops, and Sgt. Pepper's Dueling Piano Cafe. The Cafe is appropriate for kids once a month at the sing-a-long Sunday brunch where the dueling piano show features songs that range from TV and cartoon themes to Jonas Brothers. The cost is $20.95 for adults and $9.95 for ages 5 to 13. Contact (562) 499-4600 / www.pepperspiano.com for more info. My favorite store here is the One Dollar Bookstore at 101 S. Pine Avenue (across from the convention center) because the books in this huge store are truly only $1. Call (562) 432-2665 for more info. Kids enjoy riding the carousel ($2 per person; 11 months and under is free), and the giant Ferris wheel ($3 per person). See AQUARIUM OF THE PACIFIC (pg. 216) and page 161 for details about SHORELINE VILLAGE and other close-by attractions.

Hours: Most stores are open daily at 11am. Closing times vary. The Ferris wheel and carousel open at 2pm most of the year and at 10am in the summer.
Price: Free to stroll around, but bring spending money.
Ages: 4 years and up.

SKELETONS IN THE CLOSET

(323) 343-0760 / www.lacoroner.com
1104 N. Mission Road, Los Angeles

Maybe it's morbid, but my kids thought coming to this tiny gift shop located inside the Los Angeles County Department of Coroners building was cool, in a weird sort of way. (Maybe it's a guy thing?) Park next to a coroner's car, walk into the building, ride up the elevator, and walk down the hallway past offices into the gift shop where an unusual selection of items are for sale. You may purchase, for instance, a welcome mat with a body outline ($30), toe tag key chains (and other ones) ($5 each), t-shirts ($20 and up), plastic skulls ($18), crime scene party tape ($6.50), BBQ aprons that read "spare hands, spare ribs" ($18), water bottles ($12), mugs (starting at $12), and mouse pads with a body outline and a phrase proclaiming "We're dying for your business." The proceeds from the gift shop support the Youthful Drunk Driving Visitation Program.

Hours: Open Mon. - Fri., 8:30am - 4pm. Closed holidays.
Price: Free
Ages: 8 years and up.

UNIVERSAL CITYWALK

(818) 622-4455 or (818) 622-9841 / www.citywalkhollywood.com
100 Universal City Plaza by Universal Studios, Universal City

CityWalk is an outdoor, multi-level mall built in theme-park style with stores, unique restaurants, and unusual entertainment. Everything here, from the larger-than-life neon signs (including a giant, neon gorilla - think King-Kong)

to the oversized, Disneylandish-decorated storefronts is done with spectacular Hollywood flair, and that's just the outside of the buildings! On weekend nights, live entertainment, such as jugglers, magicians, and musicians add to the carnival-like atmosphere. The crowds, activities, music piped in everywhere, and rock videos playing on a large screen outside the movie theaters, however, might be a bit too stimulating for younger children (and sometimes adults!).

Here are just a few of the major attractions along the walkway: **Jillian's Hi Life Lanes** has a games room downstairs featuring video games and virtual bowling using real balls. Upstairs, ten real bowling lanes have monitors above, showing mostly rock videos. Glow-in-the-dark balls and pins are standard equipment at nighttime and weekends during Cosmic Bowl. **Stop & Play** offers a good selection of games, toys, and novelty products for sale. Movie entertainment is available at AMC's nineteen-screen movie theater, (818) 508-0711 / www.fandango.com, and a **3-D IMAX** theater that shows both 3-D and 2-D movies on a screen six stories high. 3-D tickets, on average, are $17 for adults; $14.50 ages 2 to 12. **IFLY Hollywood**, an indoor skydiving venue, will literally blow you away. (See page 172 for more details on this thrilling experience.) Look out for the **water fountain** in the center circle of CityWalk, where water spouts up at unexpected times in hot weather. An unusual bookstore is **Upstart Crow Bookstore and Coffee House.** On the storefront of **Things From Another World** the back half of a spaceship, which is still emitting smoke, is all that remains from a crash landing. Look at the Calendar for concerts and other special events offered.

Restaurants and eateries on the walk, including a food court with all the usual fast food places, aim to please any tastebud and wallet, as the wide-ranging food selections indicate. Eat Chinese (including Dim Sun), Mexican, Italian (see BUCA DI BEPPO on page 14 for details), seafood (featuring Bubba Gump Shrimp Co.), sushi, hamburgers (at Tommy's World Famous), steaks, crepes, deli, and ice cream (at Ben and Jerry's). Outside the **Hard Rock Cafe** is a huge, neon guitar. Inside this restaurant, dedicated to the preservation of rock 'n roll, personal items from famed musicians decorate the walls as do their guitars, costumes, and posters. (See HARD ROCK CAFE on page 21 for details.) UNIVERSAL STUDIOS HOLLYWOOD (pg. 5) is at one end this pedestrian thoroughfare. You can experience practically all of Hollywood at CityWalk - all at one time!

Hours: Most stores and restaurants are open Sun. - Thurs., 11am - 9pm or 10 (until 11pm in the summer); Fri. - Sat., 11am - 11pm (until midnight in the summer).

Price: Free. Parking is $16 before 3pm; $10 after 3pm. End up paying only $2, with validation, if you see a movie here as you receive a rebate. Valet parking is $2 for the first 2 hours, Mon. - Fri., 11am - 3pm with validation from a participating restaurant, retail, or entertainment venue, then $15 for the next two hours.

Ages: 2 years and up.

UNIVERSITY OF CALIFORNIA, LOS ANGELES / UCLA   ☀
(310) 825-4321 / www.ucla.edu $$$
off Westwood Blvd. at UCLA Campus, Westwood

University of California at Los Angeles is a classic campus with huge old brick buildings and stately trees. I know our visit here planted some dreams in my children's mind of going to college. If, in fact, you have a college-bound high schooler, take the free, two-hour walking tour of the campus which highlights housing, academics, financial aid, and, most importantly, social activities. Tours are usually given Monday through Friday at 10:15am and 2:15pm, and Saturday at 10:15am - check the holiday schedule, though, and reserve online. The following are some of our "discoveries" as we simply walked the campus on our own.

For information on the **planetarium,** look up UCLA PLANETARIUM (pg. 193). Tip: There are several places on campus to eat lunch or grab a snack, and since you've paid for parking, you might as well make a day of it!

Mathias Botanical Garden, located on the lower part of the campus, gave us the feeling of being in a secret garden, with its stony pathways through a lush "forest" and a hidden dirt path along a small creek. Trails crisscross through cactus and various other plant sections, all of which are as interesting to study as they are beautiful. The gardens are open Monday through Friday, 8am to 5pm; Saturday and Sundays, 8am to 4pm; closed school holidays. Admission is free. Call (310) 825-1260 / www.botgard.ucla.edu for more information.

We took a free shuttle to the north end of the campus to the Murphy Sculpture Garden, which has over seventy sculptures by masters of the nineteenth and twentieth centuries scattered around an open grassy area. My middle one summed it up best from a kid's perspective; "I thought this was supposed to be great art. How come it's just a bunch of naked people?"

The **UCLA Fowler Museum of Cultural History**, (310) 825-4361 / www.fowler.ucla.edu is also on the north end of campus. The majority of the exhibits are sophisticated, with a focus on anthropology. Older kids might enjoy

them. Call for a current schedule of exhibits showing in the gallery rooms. Inquire about their children's programs and family workshops. The museum is open Wednesday through Sunday, noon to 5pm; open Thursday until 8pm. Admission is free.

The **Athletic Hall of Fame**, (310) 206-6662/ www.udabruins.com, is a showplace for UCLA athletes. It houses numerous displays of photos, trophies, memorabilia, Olympic mementos (including an Olympic torch), and equipment used by Bruin athletes who have excelled at tennis, basketball, football, volleyball, and other sports. Walk through Coach John Wooden's Den where he wrote, entertained guests, and watched TV. Sit in a stadium seat in the small theater to watch highlight clips of Bruin athletes in action. The hall is open Monday through Friday from 8am to 5pm and every 1st Saturday of the month from 10am to 4pm. Admission is free.

Visit a 357-pound chunk of a meteorite in the center of the **Meteorite Gallery** in the small Room 3697 of the Geology Building, along with 999 other space rock specimens in glass display cases lining the walls. Posters and other explanatory signs aid visitors in learning the composition of meteors, where these were found and more. It's open on weekdays from 9am to 4pm. Admission is free. Check www.meteorites/ucla.edu for more info.

UCLA abounds with other forms of entertainment, too. Check out the **Center for the Art of Performance at UCLA** (pg. 180) for first-rate theater productions.

Hours: The campus is usually open daily, 8am - 5pm. Attractions are usually closed on university holidays.
Price: Parking is $6 for two hours; $12 for the day.

VENICE CANALS

www.westland.net/Venice
In a grid between Washington Blvd. and Venice Blvd., and Pacific Ave. and Ocean Ave., Venice

Not quite Venice, Italy, but this town, originally founded after its namesake in 1900 with a network of twenty miles of canals, has a remnant of canals that still afford a lovely and unusual neighborhood to stroll around. Waterfront homes, most with huge glass windows, border the narrow, cement walkways that hug the shallow canals. Note that some houses really decorate for the holidays. Set in an enclosed, square grid the canals sport rowboats moored to the homeowner's parcels, numerous bridges that arch over the water, lots of ducks, and a multitude of plants, making the area very picturesque. One-way streets and no parking make this a walk-around attraction. A very small, gated park is located on Linnie Canal that has play equipment - slides, twisty apparatus to climb, and swings - in a sand base, plus a tiny patch of grass. Remember, the beach is just down the street!

Hours: Open daily, sunrise - sunset.
Price: Free
Ages: All

WAYFARERS CHAPEL

(310) 377-1650 / www.wayfarerschapel.org
5755 Palos Verdes Drive South, Palos Verdes

This unique, small church, is nicknamed the Glass Church because it's built almost entirely of glass (and some stone). It's nestled in a few overgrown trees so it looks to be almost a part of them - very picturesque. You can go inside of it when it's not being used. It was designed by Lloyd Wright, son of Frank Lloyd Wright. The church is built on a bluff overlooking the Pacific Ocean, surrounded by redwoods and gardens. The chapel is unique and charming, and the landscaping is beautiful. This is a short stop off, so look up ABALONE COVE (pg. 45), REDONDO BEACH INTERNATIONAL BOARDWALK (pg. 159), or SOUTH COAST BOTANICAL GARDENS (pg. 85) for other things to do in this area.

Hours: The church and grounds are open daily, 8am - 5pm. The visitor's center is open daily, 10am - 5pm. Church functions take precedence over public accessibility.
Price: Free
Ages: 5 years and up.

WHIMSIC ALLEY

(310) 453-2370 / www.whimsicalley.com
5464 Wilshire Boulevard, Los Angeles

Merlin's beard! Calling all *Harry Potter*, *Dr. Who*, *Game of Thrones*, wizard, steampunk, and fantasy fans - this is the store/experience for you. The captivating window displays draw you in, so enter the store designed to look like an old alley, with different tall buildings (i.e. rooms) on either side. Merchandise includes all kinds of hand-carved wands,

dothing, books, feather quill pens, pillows, hats, posters, jewelry, candy (including chocolate frogs and other Pilcher & Bott's confections), and all other items and specialty accessories associated with your favorite characters.

Make sure to walk down the long, medievalish hallway towards the back of the store that ends at a fake-brick wall with signage that says Platform 9 ¾. Old trunks, an owl's cage and a mural of a castle surrounded by woods complete the ambiance. And do turn on a light in the bathroom to see the "endless" hand and wand in the mirrors. Whimsic also holds special events and birthday parties in its great hall room for all kinds of magical beings.

Hours: Open Mon. - Fri., 11am - 6pm; Sat. - Sun., 10am - 6pm. Closed early New Year's Eve; closed Thanksgiving and Christmas Day.

Price: Technically free.

Ages: 6 years and up.

—SHOWS AND THEATERS—

AHMANSON THEATER

(213) 628-2772 or (213) 972-7211 / www.musiccenter.org

135 N. Grand Avenue at the Music Center of Los Angeles, Los Angeles

See the MUSIC CENTER OF LOS ANGELES entry on page 188 for details.

$$$$

ALEX THEATRE

(818) 243-ALEX (2539) - box office; (818) 243-7700 x216 - tours / www.alextheatre.org

216 N. Brand Boulevard, Glendale

$$$$

The gorgeous Alex Theatre seats 1,450 and offers a wide variety of performances and programs, for both professional and community performing arts groups. These include Peking Acrobats; dance ensembles; holiday shows; musical theater, with shows such as *The Music Man* and *Ain't Misbehavin'*; concerts starring the L.A. Chamber Orchestra; Shakespearean school performances; and family oriented and classic feature films and cartoons. (Look up www.alexfilmsociety.org for more information on the films.) Special kid's presentations that are given occasionally on Sunday afternoons at 2pm and 5pm have featured Parachute Express, Beakman's World, Gizmo Guys, and more. Ask about educational outreach programs for students including special school presentations, matinees, open rehearsals, and pre-performance lectures.

Free, ninety-minute "backstage" public tours are given so visitors can learn the history of the seventy-five-year-old theater, including regarding its architecture and artwork. Seeing the dressing rooms, green room, lobby, and backstage are all part of the tour, too. This walking tour includes climbing many stairs. Call to make a reservation.

Hours: Call or check the website for a complete schedule. Tours are offered on select Sat. at 10am.

Price: Prices vary depending on the show. Sun. afternoon kid's shows are $10 - $16 per person.

Ages: 4 years and up, depending on the show.

BOB BAKER MARIONETTE THEATER

(213) 250-9995 / www.bobbakermarionettes.com

1345 W. 1st Street, Los Angeles

$$$$

The Bob Baker Marionette Theater has been around since 1961, proving its staying power in this ever-changing world. Interactive marionette performances are given while children sit on a horseshoe-shaped carpet around the stage, and parents sit in chairs behind them.

The musical revues feature marionettes, and some stuffed animals, that range in size from very small to the size of a two-year-old. They "sing" and "dance" their way right into your child's heart. The puppeteers, dressed in black, become invisible to the audience as the kids get swept away in the magic of the show. The performance is done within touching distance of the kids, and sometimes the marionettes even sit in their laps! This is a great way to keep short attention spans riveted. If the story line seems a little thin to you and your attention drifts, watch the puppeteers manipulate the strings - it's a good show in itself. If it's your child's birthday, for an additional $10, he/she will get special recognition with a crown, a song just for him/her, and a little present.

After the hour-long show, chat with the puppeteers and enjoy a sack lunch (that you supply) at the picnic tables in the lobby - no strings attached. Note that there are puppets and marionettes for sale here, too. Reservations are required for all shows. Ask about touring puppet shows that come to you.

Hours: Performances are given Wed. - Fri. at 10:30am; Sat. - Sun. at 2:30pm. There are additional shows given during the month of December.

Price: $15 - $20 (depending on the show) for ages 2 and up; children under 2 (lap sitters) are free. Free parking next to the theater.

Ages: 2½ - 11 years.

CALTECH PRESENTS - SCIENCE SATURDAYS

(626) 395-4652; (626) 395-6059 / www.events.caltech.edu
332 S. Michigan Avenue at Beckman Auditorium at California Institute of Technology, Pasadena

Science Saturdays are just one of the numerous series and special events, including performing arts, held at Caltech. Check their website for the full listing. On selected Saturdays, come watch a screening of a variety of science movies. Titles have included *Weird Nature - Marvelous Motion*; *Planet Earth - Seasonal Forests*; *The Roachmobile*, and more. After the film a Caltech scientist leads a discussion on the science behind nature and space. School groups are invited to come on select Fridays at 10am for Reel Science - a movie and time of discussion, too, or for a performing arts event such as *Sounds of Korea*, *Lakota Sioux Dance Theatre*, or *The Iliad*.

Hours: Science Saturdays are at 2pm. School group science or performing arts presentations are Fri. at 10am.

Price: $5 per person. Parking is free.

Ages: 8 years and up.

CANDLELIGHT PAVILION DINNER THEATER

(909) 626-1254 / www.candlelightpavilion.com
455 W. Foothill Boulevard, Claremont

This family-owned, elegant dinner theater serves gourmet cuisine along with its ninety-minute, professional musical productions. Families dress up in their Sunday best, and sit down in padded booths with linen tablecloths. Larger groups may sit at equally nice, long tables. Tiered seating is available on the main floor, or choose terrace seats. Candlelight wall chandeliers and candles on the table add to the ambiance. (My sons liked the draped stage curtains, too.)

Dinner is served for almost two hours before the show begins. (If kids get antsy, wander outside on the cement pathways, near the fish pond.) Entrees differ with each show but usually include variations of tri tip, chicken, fish (we had grilled salmon with shrimp mousse strudel), or a vegetarian dish. Meals come with vegetables and delicious hot rolls. The children's menu changes, offering macaroni and cheese, spaghetti and meatballs, chicken strips with french fries, or something equally tasty. Full waiter service makes dining here a real treat. The dessert selection varies and can include cheesecake, lemon raspberry martini trifle, and (my personal favorite) chocolate strawberry euphoria - brownies topped with ice cream, fresh strawberries, chocolate mousse, and chocolate. Champagne brunches are served Sundays at the matinee seating. A performance is included with the brunch. Note: The show and dinner/brunch are included in the admission price, but appetizers, beverages, and desserts are extra.

The eight yearly musical productions are first-rate, and most of them are suitable for children. Past shows have included *My Fair Lady*, *Joseph and the Amazing Technicolor Dreamcoat*, *Big River*, *Shrek: The Musical*, and the annual *A Candlelight Christmas*. Reservations are required for all shows. Appropriate attire (i.e., no jeans or tennis shoes; jackets for gentlemen) is requested. The theater also hosts other events, such as bands that play classic rock, folk, and other music.

Hours: Dinner seatings are Thurs. - Sat. at 6pm; Sun. at 5pm. Enjoy brunch on Sat. and Sun. at 11am. Shows begin at 8pm, 7pm, and 12:45pm, respectively.

Price: Prices range from $53 for a weekend matinee to $68 for an evening terrace seat. Children's rates for Fri. evenings and Sat. matinees (excluding the holiday performance) are $25 in section A and on the main floor; $30 in the terrace. Children must be 12 or under to order a children's entree. (If a child's entree is desired at another show time, you must call ahead of time.)

Ages: 6 years and up.

CANYON THEATRE GUILD

(661) 799-2702 / www.canyontheatre.org
24242 Main Street, Newhall

Come see live performances in this 280-seat theater with mostly family-friendly shows that have included *Willy Wonka*, *Damn Yankees*, *Little Women*, and *A Christmas Carol*, plus concerts. Kids and school groups should check out the youth workshops and school field trips with productions of *The Lion, The Witch and the Wardrobe* and *Once Upon a*

Leprechaun. Be in a play, not just the audience - check out the website for information about auditions.

> **Hours:** Call for evening and matinee show times.
> **Price:** $15 - $19 for adults; $12 - $17 for seniors and children depending on the show, date, and time.
> **Ages:** 5 and up, depending on the show.

CARPENTER PERFORMING ARTS CENTER

(562) 985-7000 / www.carpenterarts.org

6200 Atherton Street, on the campus of California State University Long Beach, Long Beach

$$$$

Lovers of musical theater, dance, dramatic theater, juggling, concerts, and children's performances will enjoy shows given at this center. One-hour-plus family matinees, called Sunday Afternoon Concert Series, are also given on select Sundays at 2pm. Troupes have entertained youngsters with magic, comedy, circus-type acts, dance, storytelling, ballet, and more. Also see MUSICAL THEATRE WEST (on page 188) for Broadway musicals performed at the Carpenter center. Come join the fun!

> **Hours:** Call for show dates and times.
> **Price:** Prices range in price depending on your seat location, the date, and show.
> **Ages:** Some shows are for ages 5 and up; some shows are recommended for older kids.

CENTER FOR THE ART OF PERFORMANCE AT UCLA

(310) 825-2101 / www.cap.uda.edu; www.tickets.uda.edu

off Westwood Blvd. at University of California in Los Angeles / UCLA, Los Angeles

$$$$$

Name it, and it plays at UCLA There are several different concert and theater venues here - the huge, 1,800-seat Royce Hall, the 580-seat Freud Playhouse, the 500-seat Schoenberg Hall, and a smaller theater that seats 200. Over 200 performances, combined in all the theaters, are featured here annually including a wide variety of musicals, classical music, chamber music, ballet, dance, circus-type of performances, Broadway's best, theater, concerts, and for-the-family shows, including family film festivals. If UCLA doesn't have it - does it exist? One of our favorites was *Stomp,* a high-energy show where performers created rhythm and music using brooms, trash can lids, and other unusual "instruments."

> **Hours:** Call or check the website for a schedule of current shows.
> **Price:** Prices vary depending on the show, date, and time. Parking is $12 - cash only.
> **Ages:** It depends on the show.

CENTER FOR THE ARTS, PEPPERDINE UNIVERSITY

(310) 506-4522 / www.arts.pepperdine.edu

24255 Pacific Coast Highway at Pepperdine University, Malibu

$$$$

Pepperdine offers a wide variety of programs including orchestral, choral concerts, guitar competitions, musicals, comedies, and plays. Family shows at the theater, sometimes under the title of Weekend Wonders, include magic, acrobatics, puppetry, song, dance and other entertaining shows for kids. Show titles have included *Mermaid, The Very Hungry Caterpillar and Other Eric Carle Favorites, The Flying Karamazov Brothers, Recycled Percussion, Story Pirates, Golden Dragon Acrobats,* and *Rhythmic Circus.* Some of the performances allow talk-back sessions, a chance to meet the performers, or a hands-on art activity. Educators - check out the free peformances specifically for students!

The Weisman Museum of Art, adjacent to the theater, is open one hour prior to most performances and through intermission, besides its regular operating hours. The museum features rotating temporary exhibits of historic and contemporary art. Call (310) 506-4851 for more details.

> **Hours:** Weekend Wonders are on select Sat. or Sun. at 11am or 2pm. Call or check the website for other show dates and times.
> **Price:** Weekend Wonders show prices are $20 - $40 for adults; $20 for ages 17 and under. Call or check the website regarding prices for other shows. Parking in the lot is about $5, cash only, and a free shuttle is available at the Theme Tower parking lot.
> **Ages:** 3 years and up.

CERRITOS CENTER FOR THE PERFORMING ARTS

(800) 300-4345 or (562) 916-8500; (562) 467-8844 - shows for students / www.cerritoscenter.com

12700 Center Court Drive, Cerritos

$$$$$

Every season this absolutely beautiful Center (with grounds that are equally lovely) features four or five top-rate

performances specifically for families, such as puppetry, dance, circus acts, or dramatic theater. The packed calendar at Cerritos also features classical music series, Broadway musicals, the Moscow Circus, and star-studded headliners such as Bill Cosby, and Peter, Paul, and Mary, and numerous others. Educators, ask about the free or minimal cost professional performances given especially for students throughout the year - fantastic shows at a fantastic price.

Hours: Call for a schedule.
Price: Show prices vary.
Ages: 5 years and up.

COMEDYSPORTZLA at the NATIONAL COMEDY THEATRE

(323) 856-4796 / www.comedysportzla.com
733 Seward Street, Hollywood

This theater is the home of the nationally acclaimed ComedySportz, a ninety-minute, audience-participatory, improvisational comedy "show." Played like a sport in the sense that there are team competitions with a referee, uniforms, fans (i.e., the spectators), and even a rendition of the National Anthem, the audience yells suggestions (when asked) to the six players on stage and the games begin.

Each scene in a series has a time limit, so the quips are fast and the musical bits snappy and clever, usually. Of course no two shows are alike because the players, the audience, the input, and the witticism of the lines blurted out are different on any given evening. Fouls are given for poor taste (being unclean), being boring, and bad jokes. Not only is ComedySportz interactive and funny, it is also clean, musical, and all-round entertaining.

Special shows include college night, where the players are trained and talented college "kids"; and themes, such as U-sical where audience members are brought up on stage and briefly interviewed (be careful how you answer), followed by a song sung about their life. Celebrate a birthday party here using the back patio to serve pizza, cake, and party bags. The birthday person gets a starring segment in a show. Note that the theatre also provides workshops and high-school improv leagues.

Hours: Shows are performed on Thurs. at 8pm (this night the college team performs); Fri., 8pm; Sat., 8pm and 10:30pm, Sun., 7pm. Call or check the website for specific show titles and for shows performed at other times.
Price: Thurs. shows are $12 per person; $10 in advance. Fri. and Sat. evening shows are $19 per person at the door; $17 at least one hour in advance. Sun. show is $15 at door; $13 in advance.
Ages: 7 years and up.

CREATING ARTS COMPANY

(310) 804-0223 / www.creatingarts.org
1404 3rd Street Promenade, Santa Monica. Note: Creating Arts plays at numerous venues - check the website for a listing of performances.

This musical theater company was formed to perform for kids - to engage them in classic Broadway shows at a level that they understand and enjoy. They offer four different "styles" of shows: Twinkle Theater - thirty-minute, upbeat (i.e. no scary villains) musical shows for ages 5 and under; Mini Musicals - one-hour musical theater for ages 3 and up that is interactive as the audience is encouraged to sing and dance with the characters, cheer, boo (the villain), clap, and the play the musical instrument they are given when entering the theater; Pint Size Plays - a play version of the Mini Musicals; and Jr. Broadway - ninety-minute versions of Broadway plays and musicals for ages 7 and up. After many of the performances, the kids get to meet the actors and take pictures with them. Past shows include *School House Rock, Cinderella, Babes in Toyland, The Wizard of Oz, Thumbelina,* and *Peter Pan.*

I remember taking my oldest son to a live Broadway-style show when he was 4 years old - he was mesmerized! Check the website for the educational outreaches and numerous classes that the Company offers to get your child really involved in loving theater.

Hours: Most of the shows are on weekends. Check the website for specific dates and times.
Price: General seating (not reserved): $12 for ages 1 - 16; $20 for adults; 11 months and under are free - lap sitting only. VIP (reserved seating): $20 for kids; $30 for adults.
Ages: 3 - 16 years, depending on the show.

DEAF WEST THEATER

(818) 762-2773 - voice; (818) 508-8389 - TTY / www.deafwest.org
5112 Lankershim Boulevard, Hollywood

This unique theater puts on adaptations of classic, contemporary, children's, and original plays featuring deaf and/or hard of hearing actors, directors, costume designers, and others. A children's play is performed at least once a season. Hour-and-a-half shows are performed in American Sign Language, while a spoken version can be heard through headsets. Under-the-seat subwoofers enable deaf patrons to actually feel the music and the sound effects. Past shows include *Cinderella*, *A Christmas Carol*, and *Aladdin and the Wonderful Lamp*. Older patrons have enjoyed *Romeo and Juliet*, *Oliver*, and *Saint Joan*, among other productions. What a great opportunity for both hearing-impaired and hearing guests to enjoy a show together! Inquire about intermittent, one-hour children's workshops that are free and open to the public, where children hear a story and then help create characters on stage.

Hours: Call for show times.
Price: Prices range, depending on the show.
Ages: 6 years and up.

DOLBY THEATRE

(323) 308-6300 / www.dolbytheatre.com $$$$
6801 Hollywood Boulevard, #180, in the Hollywood & Highland Center, Hollywood

And the Oscar goes to . . . . the elegant 3,332-seat Dolby Theatre, which is host to the Academy Awards telecast. Although the theater was built for the awards, it is also used throughout the year for numerous Broadway plays and musicals, headlining concerts, opera, ballet, comedy acts, classic music events, motivational speakers, *American Idol*, and family events. The marvelous theater offers tiered levels, opera boxes, and a special media pit.

You are invited to take a thirty-minute guided tour of the theater - it might be the only time you'll stand behind the velvet rope. Touch and discover how the "silver screen" got that name; see an actual Oscar statuette; find out how Oscar got its name; visit the Dolby Lounge with its intriguing glass windows that alternate between foggy and clear; look at photographs of stars accepting their awards; learn where nominees sit and why; get a feel for what goes on behind the curtains; and walk where winners do after their Oscar acceptance speech. Depending on what's currently playing at the theater, you might also get to step onto the stage. Although this walking tour includes several flights of stairs, disabled guests are accommodated as well. (No strollers, however.) Check the plaques outside, honoring the Best Picture winners from past years. Look up HOLLYWOOD (see pg. 171) for details on other close-by Hollywood museums and attractions.

Hours: Call for a schedule of shows. Tours are offered every half hour, daily, from 10:30am - 4pm, when a show is not in progress. Call for tour schedule updates as tours are also not given on holidays, special event days, or mid-February through mid-March to prepare for the Academy Awards.
Price: Call for show prices. Tours are $17 for adults; $12 for seniors, students with I.D., and ages 3 - 17; children 2 and under are free.
Ages: 6 years and up for shows, depending on what's playing; 7 years and up for the tour.

DONALD E. BIANCHI PLANETARIUM

(818) 677-2488 - office or 818 677-5601 - info / www.csun.edu/phys $$$
1811 Nordhoff Street at California State University Northridge, Northridge

It's written in the stars, or so it seems when you visit this 105-seat planetarium. The show titles might change, but all explore different aspects of our universe. Show titles have included *The Mystery of Dusty Extrasolar Planetary Systems*, highlighting planets outside our solar system; *Magellan: Report from Venus*, a narrated program about the recent Magellan Mission to Venus; and *Total Solar Eclipse at the Navel of the World*, which combines travel, science and history as a 2010 solar eclipse in the Easter Islands is showcased. Two shows are given each night with a price discount for viewing both shows. Be on time as latecomers will not be admitted. Weather permitting, come look through the telescopes after the shows.

Hours: Shows are usually given every other Fri. at 7:30pm and 8:30pm, the end of January - mid-March; and select Thurs. and Fri., the end of March - mid-May. Check the website for the schedule during the traditional school year.
Price: $6 for one show for adults, $10 for two shows; $4 students for one show, $7 for two. Parking is $6 per car.
Ages: 8 years and up.

DOROTHY CHANDLER PAVILION / LOS ANGELES OPERA

(213) 972-7211 / www.musiccenter.org $$$$

135 N. Grand Avenue at the Music Center of Los Angeles, Los Angeles
See the MUSIC CENTER OF LOS ANGELES entry on page 188 for details.

EL CAPITAN THEATER

(323) 467-7674 / www.elcapitan.go.com
6838 Hollywood Boulevard, Hollywood

This Disney-owned, tiered theater is lavishly decorated, reminiscent of the late 1920's, with ornate edifices and a sense of grandeur. Besides regular Disney movies and those shown in 3-D, this theater also holds premiers of new Disney movies which are often accompanied by special, live, stage shows. *Planes*, for instance, was shown in 3-D and had a wildlife bird presentation before the movie and an exhibit of planes and model planes after the show. *The Pirate Fairy* had a dance party to favorite Disney Junior songs, Tinker Bell live on stage, and a special breakfast with Tinker Bell was offered, too. Note that Tiny Tot Tuesday is at 10am during the run of most movies.

If you need more Disney in your day, check out the mini Disney store/Ghiradelli shop next door. Also, look up HOLLYWOOD (pg. 171) for details on other close-by Hollywood museums and attractions.

Hours: Call for show dates.
Price: Ticket prices sometime vary according what is playing. Regular movies are $13 - $15 for adults; $10 - $12 for seniors and ages 3 - 11. Ask about VIP admission.
Ages: 4 years and up.

FAERY HUNT

(818) 324-6802 / www.afaeryhunt.com

With or without pixie dust, you can join A Faery Hunt as cast members of this interactive theater production, dressed as fairies, hide amongst the trees and bushes of various parks mostly throughout Los Angeles County on select weekends. Locations include Cheviot Hills Recreation Center, Corriganville Park, Crestwood Hills Park, Griffith Park, South Coast Botanic Garden, Sunset Theatre Company (the only indoor venue), and more. Visitors are invited to sing, dance, play games, and go on a fairy hunt, romping into and through the forest, looking for fairies (and squealing as they find them) and other fantastic creatures, while learning fairy lore. Strollers are welcome on this gentle hike, as participants also learn about respect for nature and kindness. What imaginative and delightful outdoor fun!

Hours: Usually at 10:30am. Arrive at 10am, though, for the pre-show.
Price: The cost is usually $12.50 per person. Ages 23 months and under are free. It's $15 per person at Ferndell in Griffith Park. Check the website for specific locations and calendar information, and to make reservations.
Ages: 2 - 9 years.

GLENDALE CENTRE THEATRE

(818) 244-8481 / www.glendalecentretheatre.com
324 N. Orange Street, Glendale

Many block-buster musicals and comedies suitable for the family are performed here throughout the year. This theater puts on at least two terrific, one-and-a-half-hour shows for children. Past productions have included *The Little Mermaid, Sleeping Beauty, Hansel and Gretel,* and *Jack and the Beanstalk.* The season begins in March and ends in November.

Check out the theater's Shakespearience outreach school programs for junior and senior high. It includes select interactive performances from the Bard, workshops, and study materials.

Hours: Children's shows are usually performed Sat. at 11am. Call for other show times.
Price: Children's show prices are usually $12.50 per person. Other show prices usually range from $26 (for adults) - $18 (for kids). The Christmas show is more expensive.
Ages: Depends on the show.

HARRIET AND CHARLES LUCKMAN FINE ARTS COMPLEX

(323) 343-6600 / www.luckmanarts.org
5151 State University Drive, on the California State Los Angeles campus, Los Angeles

The modern-looking buildings of the Luckman Fine Arts Complex consist of a 1,125-seat theater, which is the main presentation arena for modern dance, ballet, opera, and other musical performances; a modular 250-seat theater, which is a more intimate setting for solo artists; a contemporary art exhibits gallery, where an interactive workshop is

offered for kids to intertwine a hands-on art experience with a specific performance; and a small amphitheater for concerts and Street of the Arts presentations.

Hours: Call or check the website for show dates and times.
Price: Prices range from $15 - $75, depending on the show. Parking is $1 per hour.
Ages: Depends on the show.

HAUGH PERFORMING ARTS CENTER

(626) 963-9411 / www.haughpac.com
1000 W. Foothill Boulevard at Citrus College, Glendora

The Saturday Series for Kids (Kidtastic) is the ideal way to introduce live theater to children. There are usually six one-hour shows in the season, which runs from November through April. The wide variety of past performances have included *Stuart Little, Beauty and the Beast, Curious George, Gizmo Guys,* and *Golden Dragon Acrobat Circus.*

The center also hosts numerous headliner artists, dancers, comedians, acrobats, Christmas performers, and musicians - jazz, big band, pop, and more.

Hours: The Saturday Series is offered on select Sat. at 1:30pm and 3:30pm. Call for a schedule of other performances.
Price: Saturday Series shows are $8 per person. Call for prices for other shows.
Ages: 4 - 13 years, depending on the show.

HOLLYWOOD BOWL

(323) 850-2000 / www.hollywoodbowl.com
2301 N. Highland, Hollywood

Jazz, world music, classical, and every genre you can think of - that's what the historic Hollywood Bowl has to offer. With a seating capacity of just under 18,000, this outdoor amphitheater offers over seventy-five programs in the summer alone! Check the schedule because there is something here (almost) year-round to entertain everyone in your family. A few past programs that kids can relate to in particular include *Video Games Live,* featuring orchestra and choir music from some of the most popular video games; *Toyota Symphonies for Youth* series; and *Sing-A-Long Sound of Music.*

The hills surrounding the bowl are alive with music and offer the perfect spot for picnicking. So, pull up a piece of lawn, bring your own chairs, or snag a picnic table if you get here early enough. You are welcome to bring your cooler to your seat to enjoy, as well, while watching the concert. Some areas open four hours before the show begins. If you forgot to pack a meal, or just didn't want to, enjoy tasty options from the Rooftop Grill, Marketplace, a gourmet boxed dinner, or the refreshment stands. Coming to the Bowl is not just coming to a concert, but enjoying an event.

Make sure you check out the Calendar section for SUMMER SOUNDS (pg. 731), a fantastic program put on by the bowl. Also see page 118 for information about the HOLLYWOOD BOWL MUSEUM. Note about parking: It's painful. On-site parking is very limited and you can wait for hours (literally) to get in and especially out. Take the Metro Red Line and walk or take the Bowl Shuttle bus (free with Metro Red Line ticket) or park at one of three lots close by and take the Bowl Shuttle for $5 - cash only. Parking is free at two of the lots. My favorite? Taking a Park & Ride bus. The cost is $6 (prepaid online) or $10, cash only at the lot, round trip per person, is offered from several venues (up to fourteen for philharmonic performances) around L.A., and you don't have to drive in the traffic. Check the website for specifics.

Hours: Call or check the website for a schedule.
Price: Prices vary according to the show, date, and time.
Ages: 7 years and up, depending on the show.

IMAX THEATER

(213) 744-2014 or (213) 744-7400 / www.casciencectr.org
700 State Drive, Exposition Park, Los Angeles

Moviegoers can enjoy 3-D film format at this large screen IMAX Theater. In the 3-D format, the use of polarized glasses, a surround sound system, and the seven-story high, ninety-foot-wide screen takes you and your child on wonderful adventures. You'll explore the depths of the ocean and swim with fish (watch out for the sharks!); river raft through the Grand Canyon; enter the world of outer space; and more. In other words, you'll feel like you actually experience whatever is on the screen, without ever leaving your seat. "Edutainment" is what this theater is all about! Look up the following attractions as they are all in the same complex: AIR AND SPACE EXHIBITS (pg. 98), CALIFORNIA AFRICAN AMERICAN MUSEUM (pg. 102), CALIFORNIA SCIENCE CENTER (pg. 103),

EXPOSITION PARK (pg. 58), and NATURAL HISTORY MUSEUM OF LOS ANGELES COUNTY (pg. 139).

Hours: Call for show titles and show times. Shows run every hour, Mon. - Fri., 10:30am - 4:30pm; Sat. - Sun., 9:30am - 5:30pm.

Price: Most movies are $8.25 for adults; $6 for seniors and students; $5 for ages 4 - 12; children 3 years and under are free. Prices might fluctuate depending on the film. Parking is $10.

Ages: 3 years and up.

INTERNATIONAL CITY THEATRE

(562) 436-4610; (562) 495-4595 / www.ictlongbeach.org

!/$$$$$

300 E. Ocean Boulevard at the Long Beach Performing Arts Center, Long Beach

The five-play season offers some Broadway-type musicals, a little cabaret, dramatic and comedic plays, and other good theater for older kids. Past shows have included *Three Penny Opera*, *Is He Dead* (by Mark Twain), and *Songs for a New World*. The theater also offers a holiday shows and seven community and education outreach programs. One of the best deals in town is the Free Saturday Family Theatre Series with two to three performances a year. Some shows are funny and some are thought provoking. Although these shows are free, reservations are required. The Staged Play Reading series is also free. Be sure to check out the summer youth conservatory performance.

Hours: Call for a list of dates and times. The Free Saturday performances start at 11am.

Price: The plays are between $32 - $52, depending on the date and play. Parking at the garage is $10.

Ages: 4 and up for the Free Saturdays; 10 and up for the plays.

JOHN DRESCHER PLANETARIUM

(310) 434-3005 - ticket office; (310) 434-4767 - school tours / www.smc.edu/planetarium

$$$

1900 Pico Boulevard on the campus of Santa Monica City College in room 223 of Drescher Hall, Santa Monica

Do your kids have stars in their eyes? Bring them to the planetarium, then lean back, look up at the nighttime sky, and watch some of the mysteries of the heavens unfold. The first presentation, titled *Night Sky Show* is a fifty-minute, weekly interactive update on the night sky, highlighting the latest news in space exploration and astronomy. There is a time to ask questions at this show. The second show, a lecture and changing fifty-minute presentation, has titles such as *Alien Skies*, *Cataloguing the Sky*, *Starbirth in Orion's Sword*, or *Visualizing the Earth in 3-D*. These shows focus on different aspects of astronomy. The December show, *A Winter's Solstice*, discuses the various observances of the Winter Solstice and looks at a scientific explanation of the Star of Bethlehem as the astronomer/lecturer incorporates Bible passages and the research known to astronomers from that time period.

The planetarium is available for special showings for school or other groups during the week. The cost is $100 for up to twenty people, and $5 per person after the minimum is met, with a maximum of fifty.

Hours: Shows are on select Fri. nights at 7pm and 8pm. (The latter time is the feature presentation.)

Price: $6 for adults for a single show, $11 for both shows; $5 for seniors and ages 12 and under for a single show, $9 for the double feature.

Ages: 6 years and up.

JOY THEATRE

(818) 505-9355 / www.joytheatre.com

$$

5233 Lankershim Boulevard at the Raven Playhouse, North Hollywood

Giggle along with kid performers who, after attending classes and doing auditions, are performing standup comedy - improv out of scenarios suggested to them by the audience, plus character bits, and more in the Giggle Gaggle troop. Your kids will laugh and after watching them, may aspire to the stage, themselves. This playhouse is also home to Detention Span who target the slightly older kid crowd (and adults) while performing standup, improv, and sketch comedy.

Hours: Giggle Gaggle - Sat. and Sun., 2pm. Detention Span - Sat. and Sun., 4:30pm. Check the website for all the shows and dates.

Price: $5 per person for each above performance.

Ages: 5 years and up.

L. A. CONNECTION COMEDY THEATER

(818) 710-1320 / www.laconnectioncomedy.com

$$$

13442 Ventura Boulevard, Sherman Oaks

The Comedy Theater produces numerous shows appropriate for adults, however, you can also tickle your children's funnybones by bringing them here for special comedy improv performances by kids, for kids. The almost hour-long improvisational show is given in a small room with tiered, theater-type seating. There are two casts for the kids improv shows - one consisting of teenagers and another of one adult and usually six kids that are 5 to 15 years old. The kids are members of the Comedy Improv for Teens/Kids and are trained in the L.A. Connection's Improv Workshops.

Audience participation is mandatory as the actors ask for help in creating characters, or supplying ideas to use in a skit. Your children love to see their suggestions acted out. Remember, the performers are kids, so there is a lot of kid-type humor. As with any improv show, the success of a skit depends on the improvisationalists and the audience. The L.A. Connection really connected with my kids! If your child thinks the whole world is a stage, then maybe he should be on it. Sign him up for comedy improv classes and the next performance you see could be his.

Hours: Kids performances are Sun. at 3:30pm, teens are Sat. at 5:30pm.
Price: $7 per person for kids performances; other performance tickets are $10.
Ages: 5 years and up - younger ones won't get the humor.

LA MIRADA THEATER FOR THE PERFORMING ARTS

(562) 944-9801 / www.lamiradatheater.com
14900 La Mirada Boulevard, La Mirada

Symphony concerts, Broadway productions, youth presentations, and education programs are some of the offerings that this 1,250 seat theater hosts. Enjoy comedies, musical, dramas, and concerts. Just a few of the productions have included Moscow's Ballet *Great Russian Nutcracker, Vicki Lawrence and Mama, Happy Days*, and the *Smothers Brothers Show.*

Under the name of Phantom Projects (www.phantomprojects.com), teens have their own plays dealing with issues for their age, as well as plays that they study in school, such as *The Diary of Anne Frank, No Way to Treat a Lady*, and *The Crucible.* Ages 5 and up are enthralled with one-hour Programs for Young Audiences which have included *James and the Giant Peach, Sid the Science Kid Live, Pippi Longstocking,* and *Seussical the Musical.*

Hours: Programs for Young Audiences are offered about five times a year on Sundays at 1pm and 3:30pm. Call or check the website for a schedule of other shows.
Price: Tickets for Phantom Projects are usually $7 for all ages for field trip performances; 7pm shows are $20 for adults; $10 for high schoolers. Tickets for Programs for Young Audiences are $20 for adults; $13.50 for children. Tickets for Broadway and other shows range from $20 - $70; prices are higher for special shows and concerts.
Ages: 5 years and up.

LANCASTER PERFORMING ARTS CENTER

(661) 723-5950 / www.lpac.org
750 W. Lancaster Boulevard, Lancaster

The theater productions here run the gamut of Broadway musicals; classical ballet and other dance; jazz or big band music; comedies; and dramas. Past performers and shows include Earth, Wind and Fire; B.B. King; *The Music Man*; Cirque Eloize; Barry Manilow, and *Jack and the Beanstalk*. The Arts for Youth program is geared for schools to bring kids to see live theater, so performances are held weekdays, usually at 11am. Past productions have included *Rumpelstiltskin, Nutcracker, Sleeping Beauty*, and *Revenge of the Space Pandas*. If you're interested in taking a behind-the-scenes tour of the theater, call (661) 723-5876 for information.

Hours: Call for show dates and times.
Price: The Arts for Youth program are usually $5 per person. Other performances range from $15 - $75 per person, depending on the show, date, and time.
Ages: 3 years and up, depending on the production.

LONG BEACH SHAKESPEARE COMPANY

(562) 997-1494 / www.lbshakespeare.org
4250 Atlantic Avenue at the Richard Goad Theatre, Long Beach

Who wrote - "This above all; to thine own self be true." and "What's in a name? That which we call a rose by any other name would smell as sweet."? Maybe the title of the company gave it away, but yes, Shakespeare. This classical theatre company presents several Shakespeare plays throughout the year with traditional performances in period

costumes, accompanied by music, dancing, and fencing. It also presents Shakespeare farces, guest speakers, specials programs, and reading performances of old-time radio shows aided by Foley-type sound effects. With great prices and even several free events, the theatre troupe is advancing its mission of promoting literacy to all ages in engaging and creative ways.

Hours: Call for show dates and times.
Price: Tickets are usually $10 per person. Some performances are free.
Ages: 9 years and up.

LOS ANGELES CENTRAL LIBRARY
630 W. 5th Street, Los Angeles
See the entry for LOS ANGELES CENTRAL LIBRARY on page 173 for details.

MAGICOPOLIS
(310) 451-2241 / www.magicopolis.com
1418 4ᵗʰ Street, Santa Monica
Abracadabra - make a magical place appear. Poof! Magicopolis, meaning "City of Magic," was actually created by veteran magician, Steve Spill, to make first-class magic shows available for the whole family. He has succeeded wonderfully. Penn and Teller have even given their blessings to Magicopolis by having their hands and feet cast in cement inside the lobby. While waiting for the show to begin, watch what a resident magician might have up his sleeve.

Professional magicians execute ninety-minute shows in a 150-seat theater with a comfortable and intimate atmosphere. The performances entertain and mystify visitors with larger-scale illusions and Houdini-like escapes, as well as comedy and sleight-of-hand acts. My kids and I sat watching with mouths opened and asked, "How did he do that?" Each show incorporates some audience participation, adding to the overall enjoyment. For those who want to try a little magic of their own, check out the in-house retail shop.

At 10pm guests 21 or over are invited to the bar to watch more "up close" magic, integrating quicker-than-the-eye and "mind-reading" acts featuring two comedians and one magician. Note that there is no cover charge or drink minimum. Being close-up to the performers, however, does not insure that audience members will "get" the trick; at least it usually doesn't in my case. Note that school field trips are offered during the week and Summer Magic Camps in the summer.

Hours: Shows are given Fri. at 8pm; Sat. at 2pm and 8pm; Sun. at 2pm.
Price: $34 per person for an evening performance; $24 for a matinee. Parking is free for 2 hours before 6pm; and a flat rate of $5 after 6pm.
Ages: 6 years and up.

MARK TAPER FORUM
(213) 628-2772 or (213) 972-7211 / www.musiccenter.org
135 N. Grand Avenue at the Music Center of Los Angeles, Los Angeles
See the MUSIC CENTER OF LOS ANGELES entry on page 188 for details.

MORGAN-WIXSON THEATRE
(310) 828-7519 / www.morgan-wixson.org
2627 Pico Boulevard, Santa Monica
Home of the Santa Monica Theatre Guild, this community theater produces several productions a year and also has Y.E.S. (i.e., Youth Education/Entertainment Series) which helps develop talent in children 7 through 17 as they audition and perform five productions every year. Past shows have included *Frog Prince*, *A Wrinkle in Time*, *Midsummer Night's Dream*, and *Rumpelstiltskin*.

Hours: Y.E.S. shows are performed Sat. and Sun., usually at 11am.
Price: Y.E.S. show tickets are $10 for adults; $8 for ages 12 and under. Y.E.S. musicals are $20 for adults; $15 for ages 12 and under. Other prices fluctuate according to show, date, and time.
Ages: Depends on the show.

MOUNT SAN ANTIONIO COLLEGE PLANETARIUM
(909) 468-4050 - box office; (909) 594-5611, ext. 4774 - show info / www.mtsacplanetarium.com
1100 N. Grand Avenue at Mount San Antonio College, Walnut

Star gazers can take an almost one-hour journey through the solar system to learn about constellations in the night sky, our moon, comets, meteors, and about our sun via a state-of-the-art, Zeiss Skymaster projector. Check the website calendar for shows that also include a "tonight's sky" talk. The 75-seat planetarium holds shows for the general public, as well as shows for first graders through twelfth graders, boy scouts, girl scouts, etc. Rocket building and launching can be add-ons to the field trips.

Hours: Shows to the general public are offered on Fri. and Sat. at 4:30pm, 6pm and 7:30pm. They are offered for school and other groups Thurs. - Sat. at 10am and noon. Reservations are necessary and show spots fill up fast!

Price: Shows for the general public in the evening are $6 for adults; $4 for seniors, students, and ages 13 and under. Matinee shows are $3 for ages 6 and up; $1 for ages 5 and under. School and group tours are $3 per person, plus $1.50 for each student for the rocketry. Parking is $3 per vehicle.

Ages: 1st graders and up.

MUSICAL THEATRE WEST   ☼

(562) 856-1999 / www.musical.org $$$$$

6200 Atherton Street at the Carpenter Performing Arts Center on the campus of California State University Long Beach, Long Beach

Broadway's top musicals are performed locally, incorporating lavish sets and costumes, a live orchestra, and professional casts. Each production runs for three weeks and includes special performances for schools. Past shows include *Annie, The King and I, Young Frankenstein, The Music Man, West Side Story*, and many more. The Reading Series Program consists of five Broadway dusty musical's performed throughout the year with full script and score yet minimal sets and costumes - concert style. Teachers, inquire about the outstanding special matinee programs for classrooms.

Hours: Call or check the website for show schedules.

Price: Regular show prices range from $17 to $85 per person. The Reading Series is $27 in advance; $32 at the door. Ask about teacher discounts. (If you are a teacher.)

Ages: 7 years and up, depending on the show.

MUSIC CENTER OF LOS ANGELES   ☼

(213) 972-7211 or (213) 628-2772; (213) 972-8030 - shows for students / www.musiccenter.org $$$$$

135 N. Grand Avenue, Los Angeles

The Music Center is one of the crown jewels of the Los Angeles cultural scene. This sprawling, two-city block Los Angeles complex features four powerhouse entertainment venues, each with a resident company. The **Ahmanson Theater** seats about 1,700 and puts on world-class, big-name, mainstream and Tony-award winning musical productions, many of which are terrific for the whole family. Past productions have included *Phantom of the Opera* and *Les Miserables*. It is home to the Center Theatre Group. The **Dorothy Chandler Pavilion**, which seats almost 3,200, is home to the Los Angeles Opera. Kids who can read can now be drawn into the story as supertitles, the English translation of the words being sung, are projected above the stage at the performances. This Pavilion is also home to numerous kid-friendly programs. School programs offer low-cost to free, professional shows! The fabulous **Walt Disney Concert Hall** is home to the Los Angeles Philharmonic and the Los Angeles Master Chorale. There are several other performance and education facilities associated with the Disney Hall, too. Wow! The 2,265-seat, acoustically sophisticated, state-of-the-art, wheel-chair friendly concert hall is gorgeous. The fantastic-looking pipe organ in the back is particularly eye-catching. The hall also has two outdoor amphitheaters; the 350-seat W.M. Keck Foundation Children's Amphitheatre, located on the rooftop of the Disney Concert Hall, and a 120-seat venue for preconcert events. See WORLD CITY (pg. 195) for information on free Saturday performances. The 750-seat **Mark Taper Forum**, also a base for the Center Theatre Group, produces spectacular theater such as *Big River* and *Bring in 'Da Noise, Bring in Da' Funk*.

Call, or check the website, for the numerous family and educational events, some of which are free. Join in the Active Arts program which incorporates dance, drumming outdoors, sing-alongs, joining in playing music at different venues, and more throughout the year. Check the website for specific information. See MUSIC CENTER (pg. 202) for information on tours of the Music Center.

Notes: 1) Just down the road at 2nd and Hope streets is the Roy and Edna Disney/CalArts Theater (REDCAT) that seats up to 266 patrons. 2) Walk around the various buildings at the Music Center as there are hidden pleasures such walkways, views of L.A., and the pocket Blue Ribbon Garden on the rooftop of the Disney Concert Hall which is

a delight of trees, tables and chairs, and a huge rose statue fountain made of Delft porcelain mosaic pieces. 3) The twelve-acre Grand Park, kind of broken into variously landscaped chunks, begins here and extends to City Hall. The fountains, a performance lawn, hot pink benches and tables, and grassy areas make it a pleasant place to gather and relax in the outdoors and enjoy some special events such as concerts, dance performances, movie nights, farmer's markets, and more. See DOWNTOWN LOS ANGELES / GRAND PARK (pg. 167) for information on Grand Park and all the other places to go within this fairly immediate area.

Hours: Call for show dates and times.
Price: Varies, depending on the show. Parking in the Music Center and Disney Concert Hall garages is $9 on event weekdays, starting at 4:30pm, and all day Sat. and Sun. Parking is $20 max on non-event weekdays.
Ages: 5 years and up, depending on the show.

NOKIA THEATRE

(213) 763-6020 / www.nokiatheatrelalive.com
777 Chick Hearn Court and Figueroa Street, Los Angeles

$$$$$

Hosting an amazing array of over 100 premiere events a year, this 7,100-seat venue offers some of the hottest tickets in town. Awards shows, headlining concerts, dance performances, boxing matches, family shows - Neil Young, Mary J. Blige, So You Think You Can Dance? tour, Sesame Street - just to name a few. Note that the theater is in the middle of the L.A. LIVE complex, which also has Staples Center, a Regal Cineplex, GRAMMY MUSEUM (pg. 113), Lucky Strike Lanes, and plenty of restaurants. See DOWNTOWN LOS ANGELES / GRAND PARK (pg. 167) for information on Grand Park and all the other places to go within this fairly immediate area.

Hours: Call for show times or check the website.
Price: Call for show prices or check the website. Parking adjacent to the theater is $10 - $30. There are plenty of lots on Olympic Blvd. and around the (big) block ranging from $5 for 2 hours to $25 for all day.
Ages: 4 years and up, depending on the show.

NORRIS CENTER

(310) 544-0403 / www.norristheatre.org
27570 Crossfield Drive, Rolling Hills Estates

$$$$

Ballet, big band, off-Broadway shows, Chinese acrobats, storytelling, puppetry, and comedy are just a few examples of the assortment of programs and shows put on at the Norris theater. Past kid-friendly productions have included *Carnival of the Animals, Much Ado About Nothing, Dora the Explorer, Flat Stanley, Ugly Duckling*, and the *Nutcracker*.

Hours: Call for show dates and times
Price: Various shows cost different prices, usually $25 for adults; $15 for ages 18 and under.
Ages: 3 years and up, depending on the show.

OLD TOWN MUSIC HALL, INC.

(310) 322-2592 / www.oldtownmusichall.org
140 Richmond Street, El Segundo

$$$

Step back in time, to the golden era of film where silent movies and "talkies" dominated the screens. The rich red drapes, chandeliers, intimate seating, and the sound of the mighty Wurlitzer pipe organ, which is like a one-man band, create an atmosphere of yesteryear. The proprietors, two older gentlemen who have been in business together here for over thirty years, share organ duty and run the movies. The audience gets warmed up with four or five sing-alongs while on-screen slides provide lyrics and hokey cartoons. The Wurlitzer is played at every showing and accompanies silent epic and comedy films. Past films have included *The General, Wings, Phantom of the Opera*, and the original *Ben Hur*. Talkies have included *The Firefly* with Jeanette MacDonald; *Donkey Serenade*; *Roaring Twenties* starring James Cagney and Humphrey Bogart; and *The Little Princess* with Shirley Temple. Grand pianos are on hand for ragtime and jazz concerts. What a great this-is-the-way-it-was experience for kids (and adults!).

Hours: Show times are Fri., 8:15pm; Sat., 2:30pm and 8:15pm; Sun., 2:30pm. Most concerts start at 7:30pm.
Price: $10 per person; $8 for seniors. Concerts are $20 per person. Cash or check only.
Ages: 5 years and up.

PALMDALE PLAYHOUSE

(661) 267-5684 - playhouse; (661) 267-ARTS (2787) - recorded info; (661) 267-5685 - box office / www.cityofpalmdale.org/departments/playhouse

38334 10th Street East at the Antelope Valley Community Arts Center, Palmdale

$$$$

Comedy, drama, country music, jazz, magic, improv, ballet, community theater, and more is yours to experience throughout the year at the 350-seat Playhouse. Past performances have included a smorgasbord of shows from *A Victorian Holiday* to *1776* to *The Lion, the Witch, and the Wardrobe*. Annual festivals include the Children's Spring Fest which is a day of arts, crafts, pony rides, and fun zone.

> **Hours:** Call for show hours.
> **Price:** Prices vary according to the show.
> **Ages:** It depends on the show.

PANTAGES THEATER

(800) 982-2787; (323) 468-1770 / www.hollywoodpantages.com

6233 Hollywood Boulevard, Hollywood

$$$$$

The finest in Broadway musicals, as well as dramas and hot comedies, are performed at this classic venue. Theater doesn't get much better than this. A few of our favorite past productions include *Peter Pan*, which starred Cathy Rigby, and Disney's *Beauty and the Beast*. Call for a current schedule. Look up HOLLYWOOD (pg. 171) for details on other close-by Hollywood museums and attractions.

> **Hours:** Call for show dates and times.
> **Price:** Varies, depending on the show, but ranges from $25 - $215. Parking is $10 - $15, depending on the lot.
> **Ages:** 5 years and up.

PASADENA PLAYHOUSE

(626) 356-7529 / www.pasadenaplayhouse.org

39 S. El Molino Avenue, Pasadena

$$$$

The Playhouse offers two arenas of interest for kids. The first is the plays themselves. The Playhouse does not have a family series, but often the plays are appropriate for middle-school-aged children and older. The second area of interest is a one-hour tour. See PASADENA PLAYHOUSE, on page 203, for details.

> **Hours:** Call for dates and times of shows.
> **Price:** Show prices vary according to show, date, and time. Rush (discount) tickets are available at the theater on the day of the performance, one hour before the show, if available.
> **Ages:** 4th graders and up.

RAVE CINEMAS 18 + IMAX

(310) 568-9950 or (310) 568-3394 / www.cinemark.com

6081 Center Drive, in the Promenade at Howard Hughes Center, Los Angeles

$$$$

Rave is a classy movie theater located in an upscale, outdoor mall. It features a cafe and bar, and more importantly, a crazy soda machine with an incredible number of choices that you select via a touch screen. The cushy theater seats can be classified as a cut above as they recline and you reserve your seat when you purchase a ticket. A fun option is watching a movie in the IMAX theater here. This over-sized screen shows movies in both the 2-D and 3-D format. 3-D movies are a visual and sensory experience as the images seem to come out of the screen and right into the theater. The show titles change so there is always something new to see. Inquire about school field trips which, for a minimum of fifty people, cost $9.75 for a movie ($11 for a 3-D movie) that includes a small popcorn and beverage. Note that this theater is in the Promenade at Howard Hughes Center, so there are numerous restaurants, including the 50's era Johnny Rockets and DAVE & BUSTER'S (pg. 29), shops, and COLOR ME MINE (pg. 7).

> **Hours:** Call for show times.
> **Price:** Admission prices change depending on the movies being shown. 3-D tickets are usually $16.75 for adults; $12.75 for seniors and ages 3 - 11. IMAX tickets are usually $12.75 for all ages during the week; $15.75 on weekend evenings. Regular movies cost $11.75 for adults; $8.75 for seniors and kids. Tues. prices are $7 - all day. Parking is $3, cash only.
> **Ages:** 4 years and up.

REDONDO BEACH PERFORMING ARTS CENTER

(310) 937-6607 / www.redondo.org

1935 Manhattan Beach Boulevard, Redondo Beach

$$$$

This lovely theater, which seats about 1,450 patrons, puts on outstanding musicals that are often enthralling for the whole family. Past productions, via the 3-D THEATRICALS (pg. 317) troupe, have included *The Music Man*, *Ragtime*, *Damn Yankees*, *Forever Plaid*, and *Legally Blonde the Musical*. The center is also host to numerous other prestigious productions including ballets; dance troupes; folk ensembles, such as Aman; magicians; jazz musicians, such as David Benoit; country and rock and roll musicians; comedians; national athletic championships, such as California Bodybuilding Championship; and much more. The Distinguished Speakers Series has featured David McCullough, Ron Howard, Margaret Thatcher, Robert Kennedy Jr., and many others.

Hours: Call for a schedule of events.

Price: Prices range depending on the show, date, and seating.

Ages: 5 years and up, depending on the show.

ROSE CENTER THEATER

(714) 793-1150 / www.rosecentertheater.com

14140 All American Way, Westminster

$$$$

Four Broadway-style musicals are produced here every season. Past features have included *A Chorus Line*, *Phantom*, *Music Man*, *Gypsy*, *Nutcracker* and *1776*. Youth and cultural presentations are also offered here.

Hours: Check the website for show times.

Price: Tickets usually run between $15 - $25 for adults; $10 - $20 for seniors and students, depending on the show.

Ages: 6 years and up, depending on the show.

SANTA MONICA COLLEGE PERFORMING ARTS CENTER

(310) 434-3412; (310) 434-3412 - box office; (310) 434-3560 - education / www.thebroadstage.com

1310 11th Street, Santa Monica

$$$$

The acoustics are grand, yet the performing arts center theater is still intimate with 499 seats, each offering a clear view of the stage. See and hear first rate performances at the Broad Stage, which offers a broad range of categories. These include operas, symphonies, dance companies, musicals, plays, and films. For a really intimate experience see a show at the adjacent 99-seat theater, The Edye, which is just right for smaller audience shows, readings, and experimental theater. Note that there is an art gallery on the premises as well. Check the website or call the above phone number for more information on the free or low cost shows for students to see selected performances and/or participate in workshops.

Hours: Call for a schedule of shows.

Price: Prices depend on the show. Parking is usually $10.

Ages: 9 years and up.

SANTA MONICA PLAYHOUSE

(310) 394-9779 / www.santamonicaplayhouse.com

1211 4th Street, Santa Monica

$$$$

For over fifty years this ninety-two-seat Playhouse has offered original, one-hour, family-style musicals every weekend. Most of the productions are based on well-known characters and have titles like *Alice and the Wonderful Tea Party*, *Captain Jack and the Beanstalk*, and *Barnyard Madness with the Three Little Pigs*. There is a intermission with cookies and punch. Young and old will enjoy this theater experience. Ask about their much-acclaimed Theatre Field Trips for all age students. Younger kids come to the theater so see the play, then participate in a question and answer with the cast, take a backstage tour, and attend a workshop which encourages them to use and stretch their imaginations and critical thinking skills. Each participant also receives free tickets for a future production and an activity booklet. Sixth through twelfth graders have a similar program with the focus on Shakespeare, learning to understand and appreciate the language and seeing the modern relevance in his plays. Inquire about their special classes and workshops for acting, too, and come see international touring shows, concerts, and more.

Hours: Every Sat. at 2pm; Sun. at 12:30pm.

Price: $12.50 for adults; $10.50 for ages 12 and under. The school field trips are $695 for one show, $975 for two shows on the same day. Call for prices for other shows.

Ages: 3 years and up.

STORYBOOK THEATER AT THEATRE WEST

(818) 761-2203 / www.theatrewest.org $$$$
3333 Cahuenga Boulevard West, Los Angeles

Every Saturday, Storybook Theater presents a fun, musical, audience-participatory play geared for 3 to 9 year olds. Classics are redone to appeal even more to children (with all the violence eliminated), like *Little Red Riding Hood* and *Jack In The Beanstalk*. There is an apple juice intermission in this hour-long show. Afterward, the cast stays around to talk with the kids. What a wonderful "first theater" experience! Call or check the website to find out what's playing. Ask, too, about on-site school field trips.

Hours: Sat. at 1pm.
Price: $12 for adults; $10 for ages 12 and under. Cash or check only.
Ages: 3 - 9 years.

TCL CHINESE THEATRE

(323) 461-3331 or (323) 464-8111 / www.tclchinesetheatres.com   !/$$$$
6925 Hollywood Boulevard, Hollywood

The classic theater, built in 1927, used to be called Grauman's. It looks like a giant Chinese pagoda, with a huge dragon snaking across the front and two stone lion-dogs guarding the entrance. However, the big tourist draw is not just the architecture, but the *concrete* evidence of stars' shoe and hand sizes, and how well they write their name. Over 200 past and present stars have left their imprints - shoe prints, hand prints, and autographs - in the cement front courtyard. Step into and see if you can fill John Wayne's shoe prints, or Marilyn Monroe's. Harrison Ford, Tom Cruise, Jimmy Stewart, Jack Nicholson, Shirley Temple, Julie Andrews, Tom Hanks, Arnold Schwarzenegger and Darth Vader are just a few other immortalized stars. Celebrity lookalikes (some more so than others) and costumed cartoon characters are often outside the theater to entertain, take pictures with (and charge money for doing so), and just to be odd.

Inside the exotic theater, the lobby is rich with Asian motif murals. The actual theater continues along the same theme with more, although subtle, murals and friezes. The huge auditorium, under a Hollywood-esque, star-burst chandelier, faces the screen that plays first-run movies as well as IMAX movies (on an extra large IMAX screen).

Thirty-minute "Hard Hat" tours of the theater are given where visitors see the VIP Lounge and movie memorabilia, and hear the varied history of the theater and stories of the stars who left their imprints. In fact, you'll see some of the shoes worn by some of your favorites when they placed their feet into cement! Look up HOLLYWOOD (pg. 171) for details on other close-by Hollywood museums and attractions.

Hours: Tours are given daily, every 20 min. or so, starting at 10am with the last tour at 6:15pm. Call first as some hours fluctuate.
Price: Free to the front courtyard. Call for movie ticket information. The tour is $13.50 for adults; $11.50 for seniors; $6.50 for ages 12 and under. IMAX movies are $19 for adults; $18 for srs., $17 for children. Parking in the lots cost between $5 - $9.
Ages: 6 years and up.

TERRACE THEATER

(800) 776-7469; (562) 436-3661 - box office / www.longbeachcc.com $$$$
300 E. Ocean Boulevard at the Long Beach Convention and Entertainment Center, Long Beach

This beautiful and modern 3,051-seat theater is situated by the ocean and has a ocean view from the eastside of the facility. It play hosts a variety of performances from Broadway musicals (such as *Grease* and *Cats*) to celebrity headliners to the Long Beach Symphony to *Sesame Street Live* to local performing arts groups.

Hours: Call or check the website for show times.
Price: Call or check the website for ticket prices. Parking is $10.
Ages: 5 and up, depending on the show.

THE BROAD STAGE

(310) 434-3200 / www.thebroadstage.com $$$$
1310 11ᵗʰ Street at the Santa Monica College Performing Arts Center, Santa Monica

Come and see world-class performances of every kind - Broadway musical theater; dramatic theater; concerts

from the world of opera, pop, jazz and every other venue; dance; family performances; and so much more. Other offerings include free or low cost education and outreach activities; student matinees; student workshops; family events; master classes; and more.

Hours: Call for show dates and times.
Price: Prices vary depending on the show, date and time.
Ages: 5 years and up, depending on the show.

TORRANCE CULTURAL ARTS CENTER

(310) 781-7171 / www.torrancearts.org; www.tcac.torrnet.com
3330 Civic Center Drive at the Torrance Cultural Arts Center, Torrance

The center is composed of several buildings that serve the community in various capacities. The Armstrong Theatre has a 500-plus-seat theater with plush seats. It's host to a variety of professional and community productions, as well as film screenings and family friendly shows. The George Nakano Theatre is an intimate setting with only 180 seats for its productions.

The Torrance Art Museum has three galleries usually showcasing local artists' work. A music room; a performing arts studio, utilized mainly for classes and as a dance and exercise studio; and two outdoor plazas complete the complex. A small, traditional Japanese garden in the plaza area is a lovely way to connect all the buildings. It has a waterfall, koi pond, stone pathways, and something not so traditional - a redwood amphitheater.

Hours: Call for show times and dates.
Price: Prices vary for each show.
Ages: 3 years and up.

TOYOTA SYMPHONIES FOR YOUTH SERIES

(323) 850-2000 or (213) 972-0704 / www.laphil.com/tsfy
111 S. Grand Avenue at the Walt Disney Concert Hall, Los Angeles

At least five times a year the Los Angeles Philharmonic offers one-hour concerts under the collective title of Toyota Symphonies for Youth. They are designed to excite kids, particularly between the ages of 5 to 11, about the wonderful world of orchestral music. First, enjoy a variety of preconcert activities. Different stations can include arts and crafts, storytellers, dance, and/or meeting with musicians who will demonstrate their instruments. All the activities help to introduce (and reinforce) the morning's concert theme. Then, onto the concert. Past concerts include *Magical Melodies, Fun with Bach*, and *Peter and the Wolf*. See MUSIC CENTER, on page 202, for details about taking a tour of this gorgeous facility and page 188 for more about the facility and surroundings. See also DOWNTOWN LOS ANGELES / GRAND PARK (pg. 167) for information on Grand Park and all the other places to go within this fairly immediate area.

Hours: Preconcert workshop activities begin at 10am. Concerts begin at 11am on selected Sat., usually in the months of November, January, February, March, and April.
Price: $27.50 - $31.50 per person. Parking in the Disney Concert Hall garage is $9.
Ages: 5 to 12 years.

UCLA PLANETARIUM

(310) 825-4434 / www.astro.ucla.edu/planetarium
off Westwood Blvd. at UCLA Campus, Westwood

The planetarium offers a free, three-part presentation every Wednesday night during the traditional school year. The first part consists of a thirty - forty-minute talk and show about the current night sky in both hemispheres and the configuration of the galaxies in the night sky - covering stars, constellations, and other astronomical phenomena. A twenty-minute special-topic slide or video presentation follows. These shows are used as a teaching tool for astronomy students, but open to the public. Each program varies with the presenters. Afterward, view the real sky, weather permitting, through three rooftop telescopes.

Free private shows are given to educational and school groups for a maximum of thirty-five students and advanced reservations.

Hours: Public shows are Wed. at 8pm during the school year. Late arrivals will not be seated.
Price: Free - donations appreciated. Parking is $3 an hour.
Ages: 8 years and up.

VALLEY PERFORMING ARTS CENTER ☼

(818) 677-3300 - box office; (818) 677-8800 - tours / www.valleyperformingartscenter.org $$$$$
18111 Nordhoff Street on the campus of California State University Northridge, Northridge

The curtain rises on big-name talent at this 1,700-seat, very classy, glass-paneled, performing arts center. Performances have included Tyne Daly, the China Philharmonic Orchestra, Joel Grey and Marvin Hamlisch, Patti LuPone, Mandy Patinkin, the Russian National Ballet, Joan Rivers, Arianna Huffinton, and many more. The Arts Education program offers a Student Matinee Series for school groups with shows such as *The Stinky Cheeseman and Other Fairly Stupid Tales*, *A Midsummer's Night Dream*, *Beakman on the Brain*, and *Don't U Luv Me?* An art gallery is located on the loge level of the Center and is open one hour prior to performances and during intermission for ticket holders.

The Orange Grove Bistro, (818) 677-2076, offers prix-fixe dinners prior to the Friday, Saturday and Sunday evening performances. Reserve them in advance.

Tours are offered of the Center on the second Tuesday of each month for a behind-the-scenes look into the world of performing.

Hours: Call or check the website for a schedule.
Price: Tickets range from $15 - $150, depending on the show. Parking is $6 per vehicle.
Ages: 7 years and up.

WALLIS ANNENBERG CENTER FOR THE PERFORMING ARTS ☼

(310) 746-4000 / www.thewallis.org $$$
9390 N. Santa Monica Boulevard, Beverly Hills

The broad-reaching performing arts center has two theaters - one is the smaller, historic 1933 Italianate-style, 150-seat Lovelace Studio that was the Beverly Hills Post Office, and the other, connected by a grand staircase, is the contemporary, 500-seat Bram Goldsmith Theater. Both offer a variety of top-notch programs of theater, musicals, dance, music - classical, pop, opera, etc. - as well as children's theater and programs geared for the whole family. Classes for youth are also offered. A cafe and artwork are part of the Wallis experience, too.

Hours: Call for show dates and times.
Price: Prices vary depending on the show, date and time.
Ages: 5 years and up, depending on the show.

WALT DISNEY CONCERT HALL / LOS ANGELES PHILHARMONIC and LOS ANGELES MASTER CHORALE ☼

(213) 972-7211 / www.musiccenter.org $$$$
111 S. Grand Avenue at the Music Center of Los Angeles, Los Angeles

See the MUSIC CENTER OF LOS ANGELES entry on page 188 for details. For information on tours of the hall, look on page 202.

WILL GEER THEATRICUM BOTANICUM ☼

(310) 455-3723 - box office; (310) 455-2322 - more info / www.theatricum.com $$$$
1419 N. Topanga Canyon Boulevard, Topanga

Set in rural Topanga, a professional resident acting company uses repertory to perform mostly classical plays, with an emphasis on Shakespeare, along with some contemporary plays, at this 300-seat outdoor amphitheater. Past productions have included *Taming of the Shrew, Our Town, A Midsummer Night's Dream,* and *Harold and Maude.* June through October, Family Fundays Kid's Shows are also presented. (Check out Creative Playground, a company that performs literature-based theater here and at other venues - www.creativeplayground.org). They feature stories and plays such as the *Velveteen Rabbit* and *Legend of King Arthur*, or performers such as Justin Roberts & The Not Ready For Naptime Players ($12 per person). Dress warmly for evening shows, bring a blanket, and a seat cushion. If you arrive early enough before your production you can hike at the nearby Topanga State Park, enjoy some of the unique shops that line the Boulevard, and/or pack a picnic lunch or dinner to eat under the trees.

Besides the above performances, the Botanicum presents several other theater options for children including classes for (both children and adults); a summer youth drama camp; The Americana Series; in-school Shakespeare Assemblies or excerpts from great plays or novels (i.e., Mark Twain, Victor Hugo, or F. Scott Fitzgerald); and School Days educational programs. In the latter, students receive a resource packet and an in-class visit by an actor/teacher who explains the language and the story. Then, a visit to the theater. Once here, students meet costumed actors such as Queen Elizabeth I and William Shakespeare, J. R. R. Tolkien, or President and Mrs. Lincoln, depending on the time

period being studied. Some students rehearse for the play while others participate in workshops which include Stage Illusion, Mime, and Elizabethan Dance. After lunch, students watch the play.

Hours: Call or check the website for a schedule. The Fundays are usually performed on Sundays and the third Saturdays, June - October at 11am.

Price: Prices for the plays usually range from $20 - $28 for adults; $18 - $25 for seniors; $15 - $20 for students, depending on the seats; ages 7 - 12 are always $10; children 6 and under are free. The Fundays are usually $10 per person; children under 2 are free. Parking in the lot is $5; some free parking on the street is available. The School Days program is $14 per student for the full day and all the preliminaries; $9 per student for most of the program and the play. Call about other program offerings.

Ages: Plays - 8 years and up. Programs can be adapted for K - 12 graders.

WORLD CITY

(213) 972-7211 / www.musiccenter.org/events/worldcity.html
111 S. Grand Avenue at the Walt Disney Concert Hall, Los Angeles

Be a part of the music, storytelling, and dance seen and heard around the world at a World City performance. Professional tour ensembles have included the West African Dance Ensemble, Ballet Foldorico Do Brasil, and Navajo Storytelling, plus puppeteers, jazz musicians, Japanese drummers, and more that present family-friendly rhythmic shows at the 350-seat W.M. Keck Foundation Children's Amphitheatre, located on the rooftop of the Disney Concert Hall. Seating is first come, first served. Before and after the show a variety of workshops that tie into the ethnic presentations including art projects, music making, and storytelling sessions. These cultural performances are incredible as are the fun workshops.

See the MUSIC CENTER OF LOS ANGELES entry on page 188 for more details about the concert hall and its surroundings. See DOWNTOWN LOS ANGELES / GRAND PARK (pg. 167) for information on Grand Park and all the other places to go within this fairly immediate area.

Hours: Performances are offered one Sat. a month, January - June, and October - December. Show times are at 11am with a repeat show at 12:30pm. Ticket distribution begins at 10am and 11am, respectively.

Price: Free. Parking in the Concert Hall garage is $9.

Ages: 4 years and up.

—TOURS—

ALEX THEATRE (tour)

(818) 243-7700 / www.alextheatre.org
216 N. Brand Boulevard, Glendale

See ALEX THEATRE (pg. 178) for details about taking a tour.

Hours: Tours are offered on select Sat. at 10am.

Price: Free

Ages: 8 years and up, depending on the show.

BIOTREK

(909) 869-6701 / www.csupomona.edu/~biotrek
3801 W. Temple Avenue at California State Polytechnic University, Pomona

"It sure is hot in here!" is a comment from kids as they enter the humid jungle atmosphere of the rainforest. BioTrek is a three-building learning facility that features the rainforest, an ethnobotany area, and an aquatic biology center, all designed for visitors to learn about environmental preservation.

Enter the huge greenhouse - the rainforest environment, replete with 100 species of tropical plants. The tour guide explains the global impact and importance of the rainforest. He also talks about the different plants of the rainforest and their use - some are used to make spices, some for food, and some for other functions. The animals here representing this section of the world include a spectacled caiman, which is related to the crocodile; the odd-looking matamata "snorkeling" turtles; stick insects, which visitors can hold; and Madagascar hissing cockroaches. The building also houses a museum of sorts, showcasing the five biomes of Southern California in a diorama style; the impact man has had on the rainforest via mining and logging; and artifacts and exhibits that pertain to the Tongva and

Gabrielino Indian tribes.

Outside, adjacent to the rainforest green house, is the ethnobotany learning center garden. (Ethnobotany means the study of how different cultures use plants.) Native plants of indigenous people and other "wild" vegetation are landscaped around a pathway, running brook, and a pond. Visitors learn fascinating facts about the relationship between the Tongva and plants. They also can try their hand at grinding acorns with stones and a few other activities.

The aquatic biology component of this tour is in another adjacent building that holds a few large aquarium tanks, as well as several smaller ones. Set up by habitat, the facility includes a flood zone, representing when the Amazon River floods the rainforest and fish feed off treetops. One of the fish here is a lungfish, which adapts to search for food in muddy water. The mangrove habitat holds scat and puffer fish. Colorful, tropical fish can be seen in the coral reef tank, such as the downfish, foxface, and even an eel. The kelp forest contains bass, sting rays, a horned shark, and sculpin fish. Other intriguing creatures include fish that make loud sounds and ones that generate electricity. A table sink allows visitors to see tidal animals up close.

Group tours of BioTrek last about ninety minutes and require a minimum of sixteen people, and not more than ninety. At certain times the facility is open to the public and although the tours are not guided then, per se, staff members are available to answer questions. Note: There is a grassy area to enjoy a picnic lunch or go to the on-campus eateries, visit the Farm Store just around the corner at 4102 S. University Drive for farm-fresh produce, incredible chocolate milk, health foods and other products. Contact the store at (909) 869-4906.

Hours: Open September through mid-June. Call to schedule a tour. It is usually open to the public the third Sat. of the month from 11am - 3pm. Call first to confirm.

Price: Tours are $6 per person. Admission on the third Sat. is free.

Ages: 5 years and up.

BRAILLE INSTITUTE (Los Angeles County)

(323) 663-1111 / www.brailleinstitute.org

741 North Vermont Avenue, Los Angeles

See BRAILLE INSTITUTE (Santa Barbara County) on page 643 for details. Each campus has a slightly different feel, equipment and buildings to explore for their tours. Ask about speakers coming to your group, too.

Hours: Tours are available weekdays with appointments.

Price: Free

Ages: 8 years and up.

CALIFORNIA INSTITUTE OF TECHNOLOGY - SEISMOLOGY TOUR

(626) 395-3298, (626) 395-6327, or (626) 395-6811 / www.seismolab.caltech.edu

1200 E. California Boulevard on the Caltech campus in the South Mudd Building, Pasadena

Too often in Southern California there is a whole lot of shakin' going on. What causes this? Find out by taking a seismology tour. Much of the information is technical, but older children can appreciate it. The one-hour tour starts in the lobby, which has a timeline that shows how information comes into the lab. The lobby also has interactive displays and a computer that shows recent earthquake activity around the world and a computer with a touch screen that shows (with sound and animation) information on the Northridge quake and others. From here you go through the seismology lab, where researchers and scientists are at work, to see giant drums where seismic data are recorded, and learn how to read the seismographs. You also go through the media center, where press conferences are held after a quake. Note: This is not a hands-on tour and tours must be reserved one week in advance.

Tours for school, and other groups, must comprise of at least ten people, maximum twenty-five. If your group has less than ten, you will be assimilated in with another group, if possible. Students must be at least 12 years old or in the sixth grade. All school tours must book the date at least two months in advance so participants have time to receive and review the provided educational materials before coming. Note: It is a requirement that all tour participants be familiar with the materials prior to taking a tour as this outing is meant to supplement, not introduce, knowledge of seismology.

Hours: Just the lobby is open to the public Mon. - Fri., 8am - 5pm. Tours for the public and school tours are offered on the first Tues. and first Thurs. of the month at 10am, 11am, and 1:30pm. All tours are only offered October - December and February - June.

Price: Free

Ages: At least 12 years old or 6th grade and up.

CALIFORNIA PIZZA KITCHEN (Los Angeles County)

(800) 91-WE CARE (919-3227) / www.cpk.com

For curious kids who wonder what actually happens from the time they order something in a restaurant to the time it arrives on their table, take them on a tour of California Pizza Kitchen. They get to walk around the restaurant before it opens to the public, see behind-the-scenes, learn about the various positions that workers hold, and to top it all off, they get to make their own pizza! Each child also receives a free activity book and a coupon to come back for a free kid's meal. Such a deal! The tour is usually geared for children 6 to 9 years old. Call your local restaurant for more details, such as minimum number (which is usually twelve children) and maximum number of students, and to set up a tour.

Hours: Tours are usually offered, by appointment, at 9am or 10am - before the restaurant opens for lunch.
Price: Free for schools and non-profit organizations
Ages: 6 - 9 years.

CHINATOWN TOURS

(213) 680-0243 / www.chinatownla.com

near Broadway in Chinatown, Los Angeles

One option is to simply take a walking tour around Chinatown by yourself. (See the website for route ideas.) We opted for a two-and-a-half hour guided walking tour, "The Undiscovered Chinatown Tour". As we walked, our guide pointed out buildings of interest, so we learned the hows and whys of the colorful architecture throughout Chinatown, as well as a history of the Chinese people, particularly the ones in this vicinity, and a history of this area. It does depend on the tour guide as to exactly what you will see and learn about. We visited a local school, a bank, a temple, herb stores, and a few other places, plus we went shopping and found great bargains as we went through the maze of Chinatown through alleyways and shopping stalls. Shopping is definitely an emphasis on this excursion.

Hours: The walking tour is given the first Sat. of every month, 10:30am - 1pm.
Price: The two+ hour walking tour is $20 per person.
Ages: 8 years and up.

DOLBY THEATRE

6801 Hollywood Boulevard, #180, in the Hollywood & Highland Center complex, Hollywood

See DOLBY THEATRE (pg. 182) for details on the Academy Awards theatre tour.

EDWARDS AIR FORCE FLIGHT TEST CENTER MUSEUM

(661) 277-3510 - Edwards museum/tours; (661) 277-8050 - base / www.edwards.af.mil; www.afftcmuseum.org

Edwards Air Force Base

Your tour starts off at the parking lot where you'll board a bus that goes to the Air Force Flight Test Center Museum where you'll spend ninety-minutes listening to a talk about the history of the Air Force and Edwards, explanations of the items in the museum, and time to look around. The museum has over twenty aircraft on display outside such as a B-52D, T-33, F-104A, YA-10B, SH-34G helicopter, UC-45, SR-71A Blackbird, and F-86. Inside are several grounded airplanes while others are suspended in air. You'll see an F-16, F-22, NA-37, AQM-34 Firebee drone, the X-25B concept demonstrator, and a full-scale replica of the Bell X-1 and Orange X-1. The museum is packed with memorabilia fitting for the birthplace of supersonic flight. One section is dedicated to Mach Busters, the men who broke sound barriers, including, of course, Chuck Yeager. It shows and tells how planes (and men) were tested for this significant breakthrough. The First Flights Wall is a model display of the more than 100 aircraft that completed their first flight at Edwards AFB. Other items on exhibit include aircraft propulsion systems, rocket engines, life support equipment, photographs, fine art, flight jackets, personal memorabilia, and the geology, or history, of the formation of the lakebeds.

The second part of the tour consists of a ninety-minute windshield tour which includes a bus ride along the flightline to see test planes taking off, looking at several unmanned vehicles and more test planes, and seeing whatever else is going on the base that particular day as well as a drive through the community of Edwards to see how life there is lived. You'll continue to learn about the missions and the history of this center, too.

Some of the information on the tour is technical, so I was a little surprised how much my boys (as they range in ages) enjoyed it. Any and all questions (and my kids had a lot) are fully answered, and the knowledge that does sink in helps make this a memorable tour. Reservations for tours are necessary, so go to the website at least thirty days before

you'd like to visit. All visitors must provide place of birth, state I.D. or driver's license number (for those of age), last six digits of social security number, and other pertinent information. Drivers must show current registration and proof of vehicle insurance.

Hours: The museum is open only for tours to the general public. Tours are usually offered one Friday a month, except December, from 9am - 12:30pm. Large group tours can be given throughout the week for a minimum of 15 people. No tours are given on federal holidays, special engagements, or shuttle landing days. All tours are by reservation only.

Price: Free

Ages: 8 years and up.

EGYPTIAN THEATRE / AMERICAN CINEMATHEQUE

(323) 461-2020 or (323) 466-FILM (3456) /
www.americancinemathequecalendar.com/egyptian_theatre_events
6712 Hollywood Boulevard, Hollywood

Walk like an Egyptian or just come see a movie on a giant screen at the Egyptian Theatre. This restored, 616-seat theater, built in 1922 and originally managed by Sid Grauman, shows a variety of films offered by American Cinematheque, a film and cultural arts organization. Your children might be more interested in taking a one-hour walking tour of the building. You'll go behind the scenes and learn about the history and renovation of the theater, plus see the old dressing rooms, the projection room (and talk with the projectionist about the evolution of film technology), and more. Tours can include seeing the one-hour movie, *Forever Hollywood*, which was made exclusively to show at this theater. (This is worth the tour in and of itself!) It shows some of today's biggest stars narrating the history of movies and Hollywood by using numerous film clips and by being interviewed, themselves, in casual settings. The movie can also be seen by itself on select weekends at 11:40am. The theatre is handicap accessible. Also note that this theatre shows many classic films - look at the theatre website for a listing. Look up HOLLYWOOD (see pg. 171) for details on other dose by Hollywood museums and attractions.

Hours: Tours are given one Sat. a month at 10:30am. Check the website for a schedule. Groups of 10 or more can schedule a tour on other dates as well.

Price: Tours are $9 for adults, $7 for seniors and students. Or, do a tour and see a movie for $15 for adults; $12 for seniors and students.

Ages: 8 years and up.

FEDERAL RESERVE BANK OF SAN FRANCISCO

(213) 683-2900 / www.frbsf.org
950 S. Grand Avenue, Los Angeles

What actually happens to our money once it's deposited in a bank? Find out by taking a tour of the Los Angeles branch of the Federal Reserve Bank. The ninety-minute tour starts with a fifteen-minute video that describes the bank and the role of the Federal Reserve System in the U.S. economy. The rest of the tour focuses on the cash and check processing operations. You'll see how coin, currency, and checks are processed by high speed machines. You may also peruse the World of Economics exhibit in the lobby of the bank. The exhibit attempts to simplify the complex ideas of American economics by using a timeline, computer games, videotapes, colorful murals, and some samples of rare and historic bills. The best is the pachinko-like game where students rate the safety and soundness of a financial institution and the money wheel to identify counterfeit notes. Over 100 free publications are available to render further aid. High school students are invited to stay after the tour for a forty-five minute finance training session where they will learn the importance of saving and investing, how to develop a budget, and the relationship between risk and rate of return. (I need this.)

Rules are enforced at the bank as a matter of security. Visitors must wear badges at all times, pass through a metal detector, and stay with the tour. No cameras are allowed. Tours need a minimum of ten participants, a maximum of thirty, and must be arranged in advance. See DOWNTOWN LOS ANGELES / GRAND PARK (pg. 167) for information on Grand Park and all the other places to go within this fairly immediate area.

Hours: Group tours are by appointment only, Mon. - Thurs. at 10am and 1pm, excluding national holidays.

Price: Free. Parking costs about $8.

Ages: 9th graders and up only.

GOODWILL INDUSTRIES (Los Angeles County)

Long Beach - (562) 435-3411 - ask for community relations; Los Angeles - (323) 539-2185 - tour coordinator or (323) 223-1211 - ask for community relations; Panorama City - (818) 782-2520 / www.thinkgood.org; www.goodwillsolac.org

Long Beach - 800 W. Pacific Coast Highway; Los Angeles - 342 North San Fernando Road; Panorama City - 4565 Lanark Avenue

See the entry for GOODWILL INDUSTRIES (San Bernardino County) on page 437 for details. There are three campuses in the Los Angeles area and all three give tours. The facility on San Fernando Road is the biggest facility in the L.A. area and the main one for tours. The best tour time is usually between 10am and 11am, otherwise you might not see a lot of action going on. Purchase a lunch in the cafeteria for about $5, or bring a sack lunch and enjoy it on the patio. The Long Beach site requests a minimum of ten people for that half-hour tour. There is a donation center there and retail store, too.

Hours: Long Beach - Tours are offered Tues. - Fri., 10am - noon or 1pm - 3pm. Los Angeles - Tours are offered Mon. - Fri., 9am - 3pm. Panorama City - call to schedule a tour.

Price: Free

Ages: Preferably 5th graders and up.

GUIDE DOGS OF AMERICA

(818) 833-6437 - tours; (818) 362-5834 - general info / www.guidedogsofamerica.org

13445 Glenoaks Boulevard, Sylmar

Guide Dogs of America is a center that breeds, raises, and trains Labrador retrievers, golden retrievers, and German shepherds for the blind. It is also a school that teaches blind men and women how to use guide dogs. These services are offered free of charge. Free tours, which last about an hour and a half, are given of the facility.

First, you watch a twenty-minute video that shows puppies frolicking, and students getting to know their dogs and testimonies on their lives being changed by being mobile. The film tugs at your heart. You'll walk past the administrative offices and hallways lined with photos of graduates and tour the dormitories where students stay for a month while receiving training. Note: If students are in residence, this part of the tour is bypassed. The best part, according to kids, is seeing the kennels and whelping bays of future guide dogs. Tip: Call first to see if there is a puppy litter because seeing them makes the field trips extra special. Tours are offered for groups of fifteen to fifty people (if you have less than fifteen you can be added onto another group) with an advance registration of thirty days. Walk-in tours, or individuals, may join in on an on-going tour if one is scheduled.

Have you ever thought about being a foster parent - for a dog? Guide puppies, or future guide dogs, need temporary homes for the first eighteen months of their life. If you are willing to teach them basic obedience, love them, and encourage them to be well socialized (sort of like raising children), call for more information. The heartbreak of separation from your pup comes in the knowledge that your family enabled a blind person to be mobile and independent. You're invited to attend the graduation ceremony of your dog and the student you've helped.

Hours: Group tours are given Tues. - Thurs. at 10am and 1:30pm, by reservation only.

Price: Free

Ages: Kids must be at least 9 years old or in fourth grade.

JET PROPULSION LABORATORIES

(818) 354-9314 / www.jpl.nasa.gov

4800 Oak Grove Drive, Pasadena

"Space, the final frontier." JPL is a leading research and development center for NASA, with 160 buildings on 177 acres of land. Its mission is to observe earth, explore new worlds (via unmanned, robotic spacecraft), send back pictures, and ultimately, find the answer to the question, "Are we alone?" A twenty-minute film, *Journey to the Planets,* starts at the sun and then takes viewers through the solar system, to its outer limits. It made my family aware of the incomprehensible vastness of our universe. My boys were awed by this realization - I just felt very small and insignificant. (Did you know that one light year translates as six trillion miles?) The tour guide then dispenses information about JPL - its history and accomplishments.

The next stop is the museum, or visitors center. It contains vivid photographs of star fields and pillars of gas; replica models of the Voyagers; and a Voyager gold record made for other intelligent life forms to listen to and learn about planet earth. Press the display button and listen to a sampling of the recording. The actual recording contains greetings in fifty-five languages as well as photographs of our culture, and sounds of music, the rainforest, a heartbeat,

and much more. We watched a short "animated" movie about the Mars Rover, too. There are also replicas of early and modern space craft including the 1958 Explorer, the Mars Pathfinder, a full-scale model of the Galileo, and the Cassini. Our tour guide talked extensively about the models and their actual missions. Although some of it was a bit too technical for my kids (and me - I guess I'm no rocket scientist), we learned a lot.

Trekking over to another building, we watched Mission Control in action. The viewing room allows visitors to see the Operations Chief and others tracking and (maybe) communicating with spacecraft - it depends on what's going on. While here the docent explains all about the current space programs, hopeful future ones, and how transmission is accomplished. The last stop is the huge Spacecraft Assembly Facility (i.e. the assembly area, or clean area), where, again, depending on what is in process, you might see actual spacecraft being assembled. Maybe you'll see a piece of history in the making!

JPL facilities can only be seen on a two-plus-hour walking tour, which involves covering a bit of ground and going up and down several flights of stairs. You are welcome to take pictures. Note that special events could preclude the regular tour route. Reservations for tours are required, at least three weeks in advance, when the final roster of name must be submitted. Guests 18 and up must provide a photo i.d. Bring your space cadets here and have a blast!

Hours: Tours are offered for ten individuals or family members, on alternating Mon. or Wed., usually at 1pm. Tours are offered to groups comprising 20 - 40 people, Mon. - Fri. at 9:30am and at 1pm.

Price: Free

Ages: Must be 3rd grade or above.

LONG BEACH AIRPORT TOUR

(562) 570-2678 - tours; (562) 570-2600 / www.lgb.org
4100 Donald Douglas Drive at the Long Beach Airport, Long Beach

Take a pretend trip and a real visit to this great little historic airport for a sixty to ninety-minute, behind-the-scenes tour, tailored to your group's interests and age level. Depending on airport activity, kids and adults walk through the terminal and see model airplanes, photographs, and artifacts from early aviator, Earl Daugherty, while learning about aviation history and exactly what goes on at an airport. The facilities art, such as mosaic murals, and architecture (the terminal was built in 1940) is also viewed and discussed.

If the schedule permits, groups will be treated to a demonstration of the huge rescue vehicles, with all of its lights and sirens, by members of the airport's Fire and Rescue team. The tour concludes with a visit to the Observation Deck which is great for, well, observing planes landing and taking off. Flexibility is a key for this high-flying tour. Thirty is the maximum number of people for the tour and kids must be at least 8 years old.

Hours: Tours are available Mon. - Fri. from 10am - 4pm and the second Sat. of each month. Book your tour at least a month ahead of time. Extreme weather cancels all tours.

Price: Free

Ages: At least 8 years old.

LOS ANGELES SEWERS - HYPERION TREATMENT PLANT

(310) 648-5363 / www.lasewers.org
1200 Vista Del Mar, Playa Del Rey

Waste isn't wasted here, but processed, cleaned and reused. Four major sewer lines from the huge city of L.A., and other surrounding cities, carry wastewater (350 million gallons on an average day!) and converge at this massive Hyperion Treatment Plant. The sewers are over eight feet round. Take a ninety-minute tour and, after an intro video to get an overview of what this plant does and why, learn and see that one of the first and most important processes here is separating solids - plastic bags, branches, trash, sand, anything - from water. Preliminarily, this is done simply via screens and bars so you see big bins filled with just stuff at the headwaters. Take a big whiff! Sludge sinks to the bottom and the water and other elements go through a series of treatment systems and tremendous tanks (some look like gigantic eggs) where bacteria and liquid oxygen clean and clarify. This is done so the water can then be completely treated (i.e. cleaned) and pumped into Santa Monica Bay, used for irrigation, or reused in some other energy efficient matter. Solids are often reused as an energy resource and soil amendment-fertilizer. Guests learn that water doesn't just go down the drain and disappear!

Separately, or combined with the above tour, take an hour-long tour of the Environmental Learning Center where kids and adults not just learn about sustainable water and solid resource in our county, but see the principles demonstrated. Conservation, environmentally-friendly building materials and interactive exhibits allow this generation to know and make wise choices for clean water and wiser living for the future.

Hours: Tours are available for any size group or for an individual by appointment, Mon. - Thurs., with the last tour offered at 1pm. Closed all holidays.
Price: Free
Ages: 5th grade and up.

LOS ANGELES TIMES
(213) 237-5757 or (800) LATIMES (528-4637) ext. 75757 /
www.latimes.com/about/mediagroup/latimes/tour
202 W. 1ˢᵗ Street, Los Angeles

Children who are at least 10 years old with journalistic tendencies will enjoy seeing how a newspaper is put together. (So will adults.) The beautiful, historic building with marble flooring has a lobby that contains old printing artifacts, murals, a gorgeous globe, and an informational and visual timeline which chronicles the inception of the Times through present day. The one-hour Editorial Tour goes through the editorial offices, where news from all over the world is gathered, written, and edited; the composing room, where news stories, advertisements, and graphics are incorporated; the entertainment and features office; the sports area; and where TV spots are made incorporating newsworthy people. There are numerous empty desks and it might not look busy, but staff members are off getting, reporting and writing the news, nonetheless. Walk through the archives office where every article and every photograph is still kept on file! Look into the test kitchen, where recipes are tested and photographed for the Food Section. Along the way visitors learn the history of the company, how times have changed (pun intended!), and some of the how-to's of journalism and photojournalism.

One-hour Plant Tours are also given down the street, at 2000 E. 8ᵗʰ Street, through the aptly named Olympic plant - the enormous warehouse facility where over half a million copies of the newspaper are made each evening and temporarily stored. Pass through a pressroom, which is twice the size of a football field; the newsprint storage area, where robot-like automated vehicles carry rolls of newsprint weighing 2,500 pounds; the plate-making area, where newspaper pages go from photographic negatives to aluminum printing plates; and the mail room, where an automated distribution system takes newspapers from presses to the delivery trucks. Depending on the day of your visit, you might view the presses actually running, from the lobby. And yes, it can be loud.

Kids (and adults) rarely realize what it takes, on a daily basis, to put together the internationally acclaimed newspaper that gets read with a cup of coffee every morning. Individuals and groups (maximum of thirty for the Editorial Tour and forty-five for the Plant Tour) are welcome; just need to make reservations for either tour in advance. Tours are disabled accessible. Tip: Our group took both tours and found plenty to see and do in between tour times. See DOWNTOWN LOS ANGELES / GRAND PARK (pg. 167) for information on Grand Park and all the other places to go within this fairly immediate area.

Hours: Call for tour times of the Times; reservations are required.
Price: Free. Parking is free at the Times garage.
Ages: Children must be at least 10 years or older.

MELODY RANCH MOTION PICTURE STUDIO VIP TOURS
(661) 286-1188 - tours; (661) 259-9669 - studios / www.melodyranchstudio.com $$$$$
24715 Oak Creek Avenue, Newhall

Well, Pilgrim, if you're an Old West fan, you'll love taking a tour of this working studio built in 1915 specifically as a Western town for shooting films. Walk along the dusty main street and you'll be walking in the boot steps of John Wayne, Tom Mix, Gene Autry, Hopalong Cassidy, The Lone Ranger, and many others. You walk past and into the furnished buildings along here - the jailhouse, saloon, church, bank, hotel lobby, town hall, and more.

There are props galore around town and in the Prop Shop. Barrels, brooms, bottles, blankets, and other items that don't begin with the letter b. The museum, originally a house, contains over twenty-five mostly-military vehicles used in movies and television, plus a lot of photos from past and present shows filmed here - over 2,000 productions to date! Film fanatics favorite flicks are featured here, including *Django* and *The Last Stand*.

If you're interested in the film industry - acting, directing, camera work, etc. - you'll appreciate the behind-the-scenes and insider's knowledge dispensed throughout your two-hour walking tour. You'll also learn about the history of film-making and the history of the ranch. The information and tone of this casual tour adapts to the age group and interest level of the visitors.

The on-site sound stage is frequently in use, so tours are limited. When filming is being done here, and that could be for up to nine months at a time if a series is being shot, the ranch is not open for tours. Groups can comprise as

few as two and only up to ten people. It is imperative that you call before visiting.

Hours: Call to schedule a tour.
Price: $50 for adults; ages 17 and under are free with an adult.
Ages: 8 years and up.

MUSIC CENTER (tours)

(213) 972-4399 or (213) 972-7211 or (213) 972-3688 / www.musiccenter.org $$
135 N. Grand Avenue at the Music Center of Los Angeles, Los Angeles

This two-city block Los Angeles complex features powerhouse entertainment venues - the Ahmanson Theater, Dorothy Chandler Pavilion, Walt Disney Concert Hall, and Mark Taper Forum. For show information and knowing what else there is in the MUSIC CENTER, see (pg. 188). The free, ninety-minute, guided Symphonian Music Center Tour, meeting in the lobby of the Disney Concert Hall, goes into a portion of all four of the buildings, concentrating on their history, architecture, and resident companies. For more insight and knowledge specifically about the Disney Concert Hall take a free, hour-long guided tour that highlights the garden and architecture while going through parts of the interior as well. Another option is the free, sixty-minute self-guided audio tour, narrated by John Lithgow, for individuals or groups of fourteen or less. This tour focuses on the history and conception of the concert hall, as well as the final implementation. Note that tours include only the lobby of the Disney hall without going into the auditorium as it is almost constantly in use for rehearsals and productions. See DOWNTOWN LOS ANGELES / GRAND PARK (pg. 167) for information on Grand Park and all the other places to go within this fairly immediate area.

Hours: The Symphonian tours are usually given Tues. - Sat. at 10:30am and 12:30pm. Disney Concert Tours are usually offered Thurs. - Sun. at noon and 1pm, though sometimes Sun. at 10am. Check the schedule first as these days and times do fluctuate. Audio tours are usually available most days, 10am - 2pm.
Price: All tours, except ones booked privately, are free. Parking in the Music Center and Disney Concert Hall garages is $9 on event weekdays, starting at 4:30pm, and all day Sat. and Sun. Parking is $20 max on non-event weekdays.
Ages: 3rd graders and up.

NTC BOX TOURS

ntcboxtour@yahoo.com; (760) 386-4663 / www.irwin.army.mil/Visitors/Pages/TheNTCBoxTours.aspx   !/$$
Fort Irwin Road, past Barstow - you'll be on that road for about 30 min., Fort Irwin

Ever wonder how our soldiers get the on-site training they need to fight insurgents on their turf during war? Come see for yourself at Fort Irwin, home to the National Training Center (NTC). The NTC is renowned by all branches of the military for its tough and realistic training - a place to train for war just before overseas deployment.

This unique outing begins at 9am at Painted Rocks, a huge monument/hill of - yes, painted rocks. The boulders are colorfully painted with military insignias from various squadrons of the armed services. Quite a sight to behold!

The approximately forty-seater van/bus then takes visitors onto and through a portion of the absolutely massive base, while a military tour guide dispenses information about the base, the area, our armed forces, and much more. The entire tour is somewhat informal so questions are welcomed.

A short film at the visitor center introduces the history of Fort Irwin and its current status and goals. This is followed by a bus ride to one of the base cafeterias for an inexpensive lunch (that you must purchase - cash only). Then, on to the "Box", or training area, for the most intriguing part of the tour. You are driven, even more out into the desert, to a re-created village - complete with buildings of homes, cafes, and shops, plus mosques, statues, live goats, and roads - to look and feel like a village in Iraq or Afghanistan, depending on what is needed at the time of training. The scene is complete with actors dressed in appropriate cultural attire who speak the language and stay in character, mannerisms and all, as you walk down the main road, past street vendors who call out to you, wanting to sell you bread or other items. You are escorted to a roofless second story room of a building to safely stand and watch the action below.

For about an hour a real time battle unfolds. Tension builds as soldiers in full gear search the streets for the enemy. Tanks roll into the village. Shots are fired, from and at snipers and soldiers, and the citizen bystanders. People are "wounded". Body parts are blown off, portrayed by hired amputees whose limbs squirt "blood". "Bombs" explode, in cars or buildings. Sometime, it is intense and loud, with gunfire and bombs. Sometimes, it is very quiet and there is seemingly no action taking place. The Box is not a show, or for entertainment purposes. It is to prepare units for combat; to ultimately learn how to save lives. Soldiers are learning how to interact with and respond to

Afghan-speaking role players, terrorist cells, insurgents, civilian authorities and military forces.

After the battle, you might gather in an old hotel and debrief with several military personnel. The last stop before arriving back to the Painted Rocks at about 3:30pm is the 11th Armored Calvary Regiment Museum. Inside are displays of weapons, mannequins in uniforms (including one with a model camel), re-created war times scenarios, a helicopter, photographs, and more, plus a gift shop (cash only). Outside are several tanks to look at and touch, and even a playground.

Important notes: All participants must have a valid government ID, or drivers license. Closed toe shoes and eye protection (i.e. sunglasses or goggles) are required. Sunscreen and hats are recommended, especially in the summer when temperatures soar, because you are outside, without shade. Participants must be able to walk short distances and stand for approximately one hour, or more. To sign up for the tour email your name, date of tour, and driver license/ID number and expiration date to the above email address.

Hours: Tours are usually conducted twice a month, from 9am - 3:30pm. Check the website for dates.
Price: Free, excluding cost of lunch.
Ages: Must be at least 12 years old for the tour.

PARAMOUNT PICTURES

(323) 956-1777 / www.paramountstudiotour.com
5555 Melrose Avenue, Hollywood

$$$$$

Insider knowledge in Hollywood is of *paramount* importance, so take a two-hour, behind-the-scenes guided tour of this working movie and television studio. You will walk around this historic, Oscar-producing studio visiting several finished and furnished sets and seeing some still in the process of being built, depending on the current need. You'll see the daily operations of a studio; learn information about the shows, past and present, filmed here; and maybe see someone famous - it's all in a day's work! Free, reserved tickets are also available here to see a television show being filmed. This is a very fun, very Hollywood thing to experience. Call for a schedule of shows and show dates and times. You may also contact Audiences Unlimited, Inc. at (818) 260-0041 / www.tvtickets.com for more information about television shows.

Hours: Tours are available daily, by advance reservations only, every half hour from 9:30am - 2:30pm. Closed Thanksgiving and Christmas.
Price: $48 per person
Ages: 10 years and up only.

PASADENA PLAYHOUSE (tour)

(626) 792-8672 / www.pasadenaplayhouse.org
39 S. El Molino Avenue, Pasadena

$

The renowned and historic Playhouse offers tours that last a little over an hour that involved some walking and walking up and down steps. Visitors see first hand what the audience normally doesn't see - behind-the-scenes. The tour usually include seeing the green room, where the actors await their time on stage; dressing rooms; the shop where the scenes are designed and built; and other rooms and areas of interest, while hearing the history of the theater as well as this particular region. A minimum of five people is necessary. See PASADENA PLAYHOUSE (pg. 190) for details about the shows presented here.

Hours: Call to book a tour, as they are offered between shows.
Price: Free, but donations are customary and appreciated.
Ages: 4th graders and up.

PORT OF LOS ANGELES SCHOOL BOAT TOUR PROGRAM

(310) 732-3508 or (310) 732-3960 / www.portoflosangeles.org/education/sbtp.asp
600 Sampson Way, Berth 84 adjacent to the Los Angeles Maritime Museum, San Pedro

!

The Port of Los Angeles is America's busiest container port in the nation. It is incredibly impressive to see these massive container ships - that contain furniture, electronics, and anything and everything consumers use - up close. The facility itself, situated on the nearby manmade island, is almost 500 acres huge!

Free, one-hour educational boat tours are offered to school groups (fourth grade through college) so that as they visually experience what the port does, they also learn how it actually operates. They are also educated about the operations of world trade, environmental issues and initiatives, and security measures. Teachers, resource materials and information is provided for you on any area of focus - local history, international trade, or environmental awareness.

Combine a tour here with one at the LOS ANGELES MARITIME MUSEUM (pg. 131). Other programs offered by the port include scout programs; speakers for schools; the *Los Angeles Times* in Education series; and the TransPORTer, a mobile exhibit truck with interactive exhibits, displays, computer simulation games, "Sounds of the Port" listening center, and more. (The latter is for a minimum 400 students.) Note that one Saturday a year, in May, free, educational boat tours of the port are open to the public.

Hours: Go on the website to schedule a tour.
Price: Free
Ages: 4th grade - college

SANITATION DEPARTMENT OF PUBLIC WORKS - CITY OF LOS ANGELES

(800) 773-2489 / www.lacitysan.org; www.kids.lacity.org

How can you refuse to learn about refuse, especially if it's offered in such a "clean" manner? The city hosts several Open Houses at various refuse yards where Mr. Recycle and his mascot - Robo Blue (a kind of animated-looking trash can) make appearances. Your kids (and most males) will love all the big trucks here especially as they watch a demonstration of how they work and maybe get to sit in one and even operate one. A tour of the facility and learning about the importance of recycling, what gets recycled, and where the trash goes is all part of the day, too. They'll also get the chance to talk with truck operators about their job, see a trash truck engine, and do some recycling. Each Open House might offer something different - including food (not recycled), games, booths, a chance to use mulch and bring home a plant, and more. Recycling is good for the environment and can be fun.

Open Houses are held in the cities of Los Angeles (several locations), Northridge, San Pedro, and Sun Valley. Call or check the sanitation website for details. Note that tours can be given of the plants during the week for school and other groups - call for more information.

Hours: Open Houses are usually offered on select Sat., April - June, 9am - 2:30pm.
Price: Free
Ages: 2 years and up.

SANITATION DISTRICTS OF LOS ANGELES COUNTY TOURS

(562) 699-7411or (562) 908-4288 / www.lacsd.org
1955 Workman Mill Road, Whittier

Do your kids run after trash trucks? Mine did when they were little. Now it's a struggle to get them to take out the trash. The sanitation department offers two different tours regarding trash and sewage treatment. The ninety-minute landfill tour takes visitors into and kind of through one of the largest landfills in the country. (Don't breathe in too deeply.) There are several stops along the way including the station where trucks are weighed; the disposal yard where trash is sorted and separated by category such as recyclables, appliances, yard waste, etc; and an area where biogases, namely methane, are converted to electricity and clean-burning automobile fuel. Visitors learn about ecology and what happens when a landfill closes. Note that for this tour for students, only one vehicle (i.e., a bus) is allowed on the premises.

The one-hour walking tour of a water treatment plant can be taken in conjunction with the landfill tour, or separately. Students walk through the control room of the plant and see tanks of water where solids have settled. They'll learn how water is cycled, recycled for use like landscape irrigation, about water quality, conservation, and see pictures and samples of treated water. The minimum number of participants on each tour is ten; the maximum is thirtyish. If you can't come to the plant, staff members will come to your facility to talk about wastewater treatment, solid waste management, and even environmental careers. Various resources are available for teachers, such as a down loadable teacher's guide. Note that the facilities are open to the public a few Saturdays, too, and at these tours ages 7 and up are invited.

There are numerous water reclamation facilities in L.A. County - Carson, Cerritos, City of Industry, El Monte, La Canada Flintridge, Lancaster, Long Beach, Palmdale, Pomona, Saugus, Valencia, Whittier - and several Solid Waste facilities - Calabasas, Commerce, Long Beach, Los Angeles, Palos Verdes, Puente Hills, Walnut, and Whittier. Most of the facilities offer tours (although the main plants are in Carson and in Whittier) to schools and groups living within these communities.

Hours: Groups need to call to schedule a tour at least a month in advance. Tours are offered Mon. - Fri. from 8am - 3pm. Tours for the general public are offered at least once a quarter, on select Sat., 9am or 11am for a water reclamation plant; 10:30am - 12:30pm for a landfill.
Price: Free

Ages: Must be 10 years old and up.

SONY PICTURE STUDIOS TOUR   ☼

(310) 244-TOUR (8687) / www.sonypicturesstudios.com $$$$$
10202 W. Washington Boulevard, Culver City

Catch a glimpse of great moments in movie and television history that have been made on this forty-four-acre lot. The two-hour-plus walking tour begins in the lobby of the architecturally gorgeous Sony Plaza building. Some of the costumes we saw on display behind glass here included Captain Hook's pirate outfit, Tinkerbell's dress, and dresses (as well as furniture and a stagecoach) from the 1994 version of *Little Women*.

First watch a twenty-minute movie on the history of Columbia/Tristar/Sony, including some classic film footage. Then, walk across the street to the main cluster of buildings. In a park-like setting, visit the Thalberg building which houses two original Oscars, as well as several others made for the studios, for Best Picture awards. The tour continues past numerous buildings that were once dressing rooms to stars and are now less-glamorous editing or business offices. You'll hear a little bit about Louis B. Mayer, Judy Garland, Joan Crawford, and other famous alumni.

Because this is a real working studio, what you see next differs from tour to tour, depending on the day, the time of day, and what shows are being filmed. We saw the scoring stage, with chairs and microphones ready for musicians to record; the wardrobe department, where seamstresses were busy at work and where the clothes "closet" was almost as big as my house; and we walked through many of the sound stages, including the one housing the Jeopardy set. The huge sound stages, which have padded walls that block out 98% of sound, are in a constant state of flux - either under construction, being torn down, or containing sets of shows currently on the air. Not to take away from the magic of Hollywood, but we saw a lot of equipment, free-standing doorways, stairs that led nowhere, props of all kinds, and lots of stuff (e.g., nails, trash, and boards) just left around. Watch your step! Our tour guide pointed out the sound stage where the yellow brick road once wound through Munchkinland, the one where agents from *Men in Black* battled outlaw aliens from outer space, and another one that holds a pool (i.e., tank) where Ethel Merman swam. You also might be able to visit the sets of *Jeopardy* or *Wheel of Fortune*. If you want to see a taping of either of these shows on the day of your tour, call (800) 482-9840 for more info. Tip: Call ahead to get a schedule of other shows being filmed to combine a tour with the possibility of being part of their studio audience. Finish your time here by shopping on Main Street, which is the only place picture-taking is allowed. The "street" is composed of a row of stores, including an emporium stocked with Sony products, and a few places to grab a bite to eat such as the Commissary; The Museum Marketplace; Gower Cafe, with Wolfgang Puck's pizza and more (this restaurant interior features costumes and props direct from movies and shows); and cafes.

Hours: Tours depart Mon. - Fri., at 9:30am, 10:30am, 1:30pm, and 2:30pm. Purchase tickets online. Twilight Tours, offered Thursdays at 6pm from the end of June - September, are also available. Reservations are highly recommended for all tours. Government-issued photo IDs are required for all adults. Closed weekends and all holidays. Groups may schedule tours at other times.
Price: $38 per person.
Ages: 12 years and up only.

TOPSAIL YOUTH PROGRAM - KID'S DAYS   ☼

(310) 833-6055 / www.lamitopsail.org $$$$$
Berth 78 at Ports O'Call Village, San Pedro

Get ready to sail the ocean. The 111-foot tall ships, brigantines *Exy Johnson* and *Irving Johnson,* and the 70-foot *Swift of Ipswich,* a representation of a Revolutionary War privateer, are wonderful to behold, but a cruise, or tour, on them is even better.

Kid's Days, for kids and families, take place on specific dates, usually when traditional schools are on break. The sail times vary from three to five hours, allowing young sailors to experience the wind in their hair, the sun on their faces, and sea lions and dolphins (hopefully!) in the water. They will enjoy the high (well, medium) seas adventure while literally learning the ropes of sailing as the sea teaches kids about life. Check the website calendar for these special days.

Topsail is an educational program partnered with the Los Angeles Maritime Institute. It is geared for youth primarily between 6th to 12th grades, but flexible enough to accommodate almost any age and ability with school and organized youth groups. The ships don't feel like a classroom (which is good!), yet students learn seamanship, navigation (geometry and algebra), history, charts, piloting, marine biology, geology, sail training, team-building, problem-solving, planning, leadership and so much more, all in an adventuresome and participatory way on day sails

and overnight voyages.

Hours: Call or check the website for program dates.

Price: Kid's Days and other public events start at $25 per person. Topsail starts at $1700 per day for a five-hour day sail for up to 35 participants, which is $48.50 per person.

Ages: 70 lbs and up.

VAN NUYS AIRPORT TOUR

(818) 442-6526 / www.lawa.org

Roscoe Boulevard at Van Nuys Airport, Van Nuys

Here's a way to stay grounded while touring an airport - take the ninety-minute bus tour of the Van Nuys airport. Groups can provide their own bus, or, with a minimum of fifteen people, ask if the airport has one available for the tour. There are several stops along the way, depending on what's available on the day of your visit. You cruise along the service road and runway, and look inside hangars. Stops could include seeing the fire station and the radar facilities. You will definitely learn the history of the airport and importance of it in aviation and even in its use of Hollywood and TV shows. Visit Vinny, the airport's kid-friendly, hands-on, educational airplane. As the children watch planes land and take off, they'll learn the history of the airport and gain some high-flying knowledge. Bring a sack lunch and eat at the observation site while watching the planes in flight.

Hours: Tours are offered most of the year, Wed., Thurs. and select Sat. at 9:30am and 11am. Tours are offered in the summer only at 9:30am. Reservations are required.

Price: Free

Ages: Must be at least in the 1st grade.

WARNER BROS. VIP STUDIO TOUR

(818) 972-TOUR (8687) / vipstudiotour.warnerbros.com $$$$$

3400 Riverside Drive, Burbank

"What's up, doc?" A two-hour, behind-the-scenes tour of the world-renown Warner Bros. studio - that's what's up! First, watch a ten-minute film that shows a montage of highlights of shows created by Warner Bros., just to get you in the mood. Hop on board the twelve-passenger tram (such a small number allows the tour to be intimate) for a part-driving and part-walking tour around some of the 110-acre studio that incorporates thirty sound stages, a gas station, a multitude of outside sets, the four-story prop building, and much more.

The first stop is a few streets that look familiar as they have been, and continue to be, used in a multitude of movies, including the *Spiderman* films. You'll learn that doorknobs denote a time period; that the trees are potted in the ground and removable or ready to show foliage with fake leaves tied on; that many of the realistic looking buildings are merely facades; and so much more insider information and facts you never knew about movie-making. The tour will either take some of the romance out of picture-making, or make your child want to be involved in the process!

You'll see numerous backlots and exterior sets from classic to current movies and television shows, lots of equipment, and the inside of some sound stages (but not all thirty). See what you recognize from your favorite flicks. You might see a celebrity. The interior sets rotate, depending on what is currently being filmed here. We went onto the set of *Chuck* and saw where *Gilmore Girls*, *The Mentalist*, *Ellen DeGeneres Show*, and so many more shows were filmed. We saw sets being constructed at the craft/production shop and learned that Stage 16 is one of the tallest in the world and was used in the *Batman* trilogy and *Perfect Storm*. We drove past *ER*'s emergency room entrance and learned how movie "snow" is made. (They use instant mashed potato flakes - we can do this at home!) We walked into the immense prop building and saw rooms and rooms of just lamps, plus antique furniture, costumes used in *Last Samurai*, and everything else you could imagine (and some you can't), all rentable for a huge price tag. We also went into the *Friend's* Central Perk coffee shop here. Cars from *Scooby Doo*, *Batman*, and *Get Smart* are really fun to walk around and look at. In this car building, too, you stand in front of green screen and take a photo with a wand, and that picture you receive at the end of a tour now has a scene from *Harry Potter* starring you.

The last twenty-five minutes are a rare treat as you walk around the costume and prop museum on the grounds. The lower level has rotating costumes. We saw some from *Dark Knight* (and the down masks), *Inception*, *300*, *Watchmen*, *The Matrix*, *Where the Wild Things Are* (and the monsters), and more. The upper level, Privet Drive, is completely devoted to *Harry Potter* with costumes, props, and parts of sets - it's like living in parts of the movie. Fans love this place!

If you are hungry before or after your tour, enjoy a bite to eat at the adjacent Studio Plaza Cafe (open weekdays only). A small gift shop is stocked with movie and TV merchandise. No matter what you see and do, this tour affords

visitors a great opportunity to see what actually goes go on behind the scenes. Adults need photo I.D. No video or tape recording is allowed, but cameras are at many of the stops. The tour is partly outside, so dress warmly for the tram ride. Note: If you really want to experience all that the studio has to offer, take a deluxe, five-hour tour which includes lunch, available on weekdays at 10:15am for $250 per person.

Hours: Tours, for no more than 12 people at a time, leave every twenty minutes, Mon. - Sat., 8:15am - 4pm. Tours are also available some Sun. in the summer. Tours in Spanish are available Mon. - Fri. at 12:15pm and 3:15pm. Reservations can be made for the first three tour times of the day - all other times are first come, first served basis. You must arrive at least 20 minutes before your allotted tour time.

Price: $54 per person. Parking is $7 at gate 6.

Ages: Children must be at least 8 years old.

WILDLIFE SANCTUARY TOUR

(909) 274-4794 - tours; (909) 594-5611, ext. 4794 / elearn.mtsac.edu/biology/wildlife

1100 N. Grand Avenue at Mount San Antonio College, Walnut

A forty-five-minute guided tour of this ten-acre wildlife environment includes walking the dirt footpath, which is not stroller-friendly, to see and learn about the plants and animals and their eco systems. Look for the turtles in the pond and the variety of birds that visit. The sanctuary also has a lake, a swamp, a pond, and a stream. There aren't any caged animals here, but free-roaming lizards, squirrels, raccoons, insects, and a few other critters. A guide from the college explains why the plants and animals need protection and what visitors can do to help - check out the website for curriculum supplements. The minimum number of students is ten; the maximum, thirty. Also see FARM TOUR (pg. 219) for another tour given by Mount San Antonio College.

Hours: Tours are offered Tues. and Thurs. at 9am, 10am, 11am, 2pm, 3pm, and 4pm. Reservations are required.

Price: Free, but donations are appreciated.

Ages: Elementary-school age kids.

—TRANSPORTATION—

ALFREDO'S BEACH CLUB

(562) 477-6820 or (562) 434-1542 / www.alfredosbeachclub.com

Alfredo's has several concessions within Los Angeles County; along the beach and in many parks. They rent kayaks - $10 an hour for single, $20 an hour for double; pedal boats - $30 an hour; as well as bikes ($10 an hour), three-person surreys ($25 an hour), aqua cycles, stand-up boards, and boogie boards. Check the website for their locations and specific details.

AMERICAN PRIDE - CHILDREN'S MARITIME FOUNDATION

$$$$

(714) 970-8800 / www.americanpride.org

Rainbow Harbor Dock 3 off Shoreline Drive, Long Beach

Isn't she a beauty? *American Pride*, a three-mast tallship originally built in 1941, now serves as a historic nautical educational tool for students and adults. Several programs, both at dock and at sea, are offered throughout the year. For instance, Making of a Sailor is a four-hour at-dock program which includes getting the galley ready for a pretend voyage. Nautical chores like swabbing the decks, singing sea chanteys, and hoisting barrels await sailors and land lubbers alike. Participants also talk with the in-costume characters/sailors about their life and their duties on board the ship. The cost is $29 per student; $25 for adults. Sailors Ahoy is a six-hour program, three hours sailing and three hours at dock, which includes reliving the life of a 19th-century sailor; learning history by living it. The cost is $60 per student; $45 for adults. Other programs include Sunday brunch sails, overnight programs on the ship, sailing to Catalina, and even five-day journeys. What a fabulous time of teamwork and learning about marine biology, geology, environmental systems, and much more! Teachers note that there is a minimum of twenty-six students per program and that classroom prep resources arrive about a month before your excursion.

Adults, do not despair! Whale-watching tours are given in season - December through April - with a marine biologist on board. Participants look for whales as well as help raise the sails, dissect fish, and learn elementary navigation skills. Bring binoculars, a jacket, and sunscreen. The cost for whale watching starts at $19 per person.

Hours: Call for a schedule of events or to book a tour.

Price: Prices are listed above.
Ages: Most programs are geared for 3rd graders and up.

AMTRAK (Los Angeles County)

(800) USA RAIL (872-7245) / www.amtrakcalifornia.com $$$$$

Trains are a great alternative to driving. By incorporating a train trip into your day's excursion, it makes the journey almost as much fun as the destination, whether you're visiting a park, a special restaurant, or a major attraction.

The Amtrak phone number and website gives fares and other pertinent information. For example, from Union Station in Los Angeles to San Juan Capistrano, the round-trip fare is $21 for adults; $17.85 for seniors; $10.50 for children ages 2 through 15. (Kids ride for half price with each paid adult fare.) Ask about AAA discounts.

Check out the website for information on the Kids 'N Trains Program (at the bottom of the website). This program is offered mid-September through June, Monday through Thursday (except some blackout dates). It allows teachers, designated leaders, chaperones, and kids - students, scouts, church groups, and other community groups (minimum of twenty, ages 5 to 18) - to ride the rails from Los Angeles to Santa Barbara (and up to San Luis Obispo) for $10 per person round trip and from Los Angeles to San Diego, for $12, or somewhere in between. Reservations must be made online at least a month in advance of departure date.

Note that Union Station, at 800 N. Alameda Street in Los Angeles, is not only a hub for Amtrak and Metrolink, but a gorgeous, historic building. Starring in numerous movies, the station, which is open from 4am to 1am, is just across the street from OLVERA STREET (see pg. 168).

ANGELS FLIGHT RAILWAY   ☀

(213) MA6-1901 (626-1901) / www.angelsflight.org $
351 South Hill Street, Los Angeles

"The Shortest Railway in the World" may only be 298-foot, but the ride up (or down) the steep slope of Bunker Hill is memorable aboard the 113-year-old funicular. Wooden and rickety-sounding, the two cars connect the residential streets with the California Plaza and the Grand Central Market and other cultural attractions, plus they offer a great view. Note: You can also walk up and down the steep stairway on the side of Angels Flight. See DOWNTOWN LOS ANGELES / GRAND PARK (pg. 167) for information on Grand Park and all the other places to go within this fairly immediate area.

Hours: Open daily, 6:45am - 10pm.
Price: .50¢ per person, one way.
Ages: All

AQUALINK / AQUABUS   ☀

(562) 591-2301 / www.lbtransit.com $$
Shoreline Drive, Long Beach

"Taxi!" The AquaLink, or water taxi, is a fun and inexpensive way to see a part of the Long Beach Harbor. The seventy-five-seat catamaran cruises by the *Queen Mary*, past charter fishing boats, and past the working port in the fifth largest city in California. A snack shop is available on board. One-way fare covers departing from the QUEEN MARY (pg. 146), which is a wheelchair-accessible boarding area, to AQUARIUM OF THE PACIFIC (pg. 216), which is also wheelchair accessible, and arriving at Alamitos Bay Landing (toward Seal Beach), or vice versa. The *Queen Mary* leg to the Aquarium takes twenty minutes; to Alamitos Bay takes about an hour. If you de-board at the *Queen Mary*, you'll have to pay another fare if you want to resume your cruise.

The Aquabus is an open-air water shuttle, too, but its route is within the Queensway Bay; basically from the Aquarium to Shoreline Village to the Queen Mary and back.

Hours: Open daily in the summer; open the rest of the year, Sat. - Sun., 11am - 6pm. Call for a schedule of
              specific departure/arrival times.
Price: The Aqualink is $5 per person each way. The Aquabus is $1 per person.
Ages: All

BEVERLY HILLS TROLLEY TOUR   ☀

(310) 285-2500 / www.beverlyhills.org/exploring/trolleytours $$
Departs from the southwest corner of Rodeo Drive and Dayton Way, Beverly Hills

This is the best bargain in Beverly Hills! If you're in the area and want to give your kids a taste of the posh lifestyle, at an affordable price to you, hop on board an old-fashioned looking trolley (which is a fun mode of transportation) for a forty-minute, narrated tour and ride by some of the most famous sights in Beverly Hills (but no celebrity homes), including Rodeo Drive, film locations, some of the high-priced boutiques, and the elegant hotels. The tour guide points out some of the most significant art and architectural locations around town, including City Hall, galleries, Creative Artists Agency, The Paley Center for Media, and more. Note: Parking in the structure is free for the first two hours so you've got time to window shop on Rodeo Drive. Note also that there is a lovely and nicely-landscaped, outdoor courtyard /park with tables and chairs between buildings by the parking structure on Beverly Dr., so bring a picnic and enjoy.

Hours: Tours are offered year-round on weekends on the hour, 11am - 4pm. They are also offered July through Labor Day, and after Thanksgiving through December, Tues. - Sun., 11am - 4pm, on the hour. (Not available on Dec. 24 and Dec. 25.) Tours are usually canceled if it is raining.

Price: $5 for adults per tour; $1 for children 12 and under. Tickets are available from the trolley driver on a first come, first serve basis.

Ages: 5 years and up.

BIKE MAPS (Los Angeles County)

See BIKE MAPS (Orange County) on page 326 for information.

BIKE TRAIL: LONG BEACH SHORELINE

(562) 570-3100

Bay Shore Avenue to Shoreline Village, Long Beach

This 3.1-mile (one-way) easy, paved riding path follows along the Pacific Ocean. An ocean breeze and practically no hills makes it a delightful ride for the family. Stop and shop at SHORELINE VILLAGE (pg. 161) with its nice array of quaint-looking restaurants and stores. Also, check out other places nearby - AQUARIUM OF THE PACIFIC (pg. 216), QUEEN MARY (pg. 146), and SCORPION (pg. 150). At the other end, check out BELMONT SHORE BEACH (pg. 10).

Hours: Open daily, dawn - dusk.

Price: Free, although parking at Shoreline Village costs up to $8 maximum.

Ages: 5 years and up.

BIKE TRAIL: LOS ANGELES RIVER TRAIL

(323) 223-0585 - Friends of the L.A. River; (323) 913-7390 - Griffith Park / www.labikepaths.com; www.folar.org; www.thelariver.com

Griffith Park, Los Angeles

The first five miles of this urban bikeway are not always quiet, as some of it parallels the Golden State Freeway. The paved bike trail is, however, entirely off-road. Although the riverbed is up against concrete slopes, there are also trees, flocks of birds, and even a few ponds along the way with ducks and some fish, plus portions of it are lit at night. The next forty-seven miles are still in the planning and making-it-work stage, although the next three-mile stretch, which heads past the huge Elysian Park and through the neighboring, small Egret Park toward downtown L.A., has already begun. Eventually, the pathway will stretch from the mountains all the way to sea along the Los Angeles River. A good place to park is inside Griffith Park, near the bike trail entrance where Zoo Drive meets Riverside Dr./Victory Blvd.

Just across the river from Egret Park, which is also an entrance/exit point for the bike trail, on Riverside Drive, is the Los Angeles River Center. If you want more information about the river, the center is located at 570 W. Ave. 26. For now, the bike path goes along GRIFFITH PARK (pg. 62), so enjoy a side trip into the park. (See that entry for more details about the park, its zoo, and its museums.)

Hours: Open daily, sunrise - sunset.

Price: Free

Ages: 6 years and up.

BIKE TRAIL: SAN GABRIEL RIVER TRAIL

www.bicyclela.org; www.labikepaths.com

Lakewood, Long Beach, Seal Beach

This two-way, concrete river trail, a right-of-way for bicyclers and skaters, actually travels almost the whole length of the San Gabriel River (i.e., flood control waterway). It begins (or ends, depending on how you look at it) in Seal Beach at Marina Drive, just west of 1st Street, and ends (or begins) in Azusa at San Gabriel Canyon Road, north of Sierra Madre. The pathway has several access points along the way. The route sometimes follows along main streets, although it just as often veers completely away from them. Depending on where you catch the trail, it passes under bridges; goes through some scenic areas that are a delight to behold; past parks; past people's backyards; and even through sections that don't feel as safe as I'd like.

One of our favorite stretches starts at LIBERTY PARK (Cerritos) (pg. 69) and goes all the way to SEAL BEACH (pg. 243). Along the way, we sometimes stop off at Rynerson Park, which has playgrounds and paved pathways throughout; the Long Beach Town Center, which has restaurants, fast food places, a movie theater, Barnes & Noble, Sam's Club, and lots more stores; and EL DORADO NATURE CENTER (pg. 57) and EL DORADO PARK (pg. 57). The latter park is beautiful and there is no admission fee from the bike path. Sometimes we actually make it to Seal Beach! We then ride to the ocean's edge and go along Main Street into the quaint town of Seal Beach, where there are plenty of shops and restaurants. (We also cheat sometimes and invite my husband to meet us for lunch or dinner, and then have him drive us all home in the van!) Nonstop from Liberty Park to Seal Beach takes my older children and me about an hour. This section of the riverbank route is also great for birdwatching. We've seen numerous herons, egrets, and pelicans.

Hours: Open daily, dawn - dusk.
Price: Free
Ages: 4 years and up.

BIKE TRAIL: SOUTH BAY

www.bicyclela.org; www.labikepaths.com
Torrance County Beach to Pacific Palisades

Life's a beach and this twenty-six-mile, two-lane, relatively flat concrete bike trail emphasizes that by cruising mostly right along the sandy shores of California's beaches. From Malibu/Pacific Palisades to Torrance/Palos Verdes, it passes through Venice beach, the Santa Monica Pier, and other state treasures. There are many stores and eateries (and restrooms!) to stop off at along the strand. Of course weekends, especially in the summer, are very crowded. Don't forget your sunscreen. From Torrance, find an entrance near Esplanade Ave. From Pacific Palisades, you can start at Will Rogers State Beach, by the intersection of PCH and Sunset Blvd.

Hours: Open daily, sunrise - sunset.
Price: Free
Ages: 4 years and up.

GONDOLA AMORE

(310) 376-6977 / www.gondolaamore.com $$$$$
260 Portofino Way at the Portofino Hotel and Yacht Club, Redondo Beach

Now this is amore! This one-hour gondola cruise is a unique way to see the Redondo harbor and shoreline. During the day you'll also see Catalina Island (on a clear day), sailboats, waterfowl, and maybe a few seals. Nighttime rides bring about their own magic (and romance). The two gondolas, operated by the owner and by lifeguards, seat up to four people, have canopies for privacy, and small twinkling lights around the boat and canopies. Amore provides blankets, as the ocean air can get chilly even on a summer night, and cups for the drinks that you provide. Your other list of things to bring includes jackets, a music CD, and your camera. Champagne (or sparkling cider) rides, where your beverage, glasses, fresh fruit, chocolate, and bread and cheese are provided, are also offered. Tips: Before or after your cruise, take some time to walk around the pier. Look up REDONDO BEACH INTERNATIONAL BOARDWALK (pg. 159) for details.

Hours: Open daily, noon - 9pm. Reservations are required. Note: Holiday seasons book quickly.
Price: $95 for two people; $15 for each additional person. Champagne rides are $135 for two people.
             Note: AAA members can receive a discount.
Ages: 4 years and up.

GONDOLA GETAWAY

(562) 433-9595 / www.gondolagetawayinc.com $$$$$
5437 E. Ocean Boulevard, Long Beach

Long Beach, California is transformed into Venice, Italy when you go on this gondola ride. I know this attraction is thought of as a romantic excursion, and it is. It is also a wonderful treat for your child. Step into a Venetian gondola and for one hour, gently slip in and out through the waterways and canals of Naples. Your gondolier will serenade you with Italian music, regale you with interesting tales, or quietly leave you alone. After our kids plied my husband and me with questions about the possibility of sharks and whales, they settled down to enjoy the ride and look at the incredible homes along the waterfront. Christmas time is particularly spectacular, as many of the houses are decked out with lights, animated figures, etc. Make reservations for this time period far in advance.

A bucket of ice is provided, as is a blanket for the colder nights. Bring your own liquid refreshment. Your child will now be dreaming of visiting a tiny little town far away in a boot-shaped country. Ciao!

Hours: Open daily for cruises, 11am - 11pm. Suggested reservations are two weeks in advance.

Price: Gondolas carry two to six people - $85 for the first two passengers; $20 for each additional person. Gratuity not included. The Carolina carries seven to fourteen people - $250 for up to ten, $25 for each additional person. Fleet cruises carries twenty to fifty-six people - $20 per person. 18% gratuity is added. Check the website for special holiday and dinner cruises.

Ages: 4 years and up.

GONDOLAS D' AMORE

(310) 736-7301 / www.gondolasdamore.com

$$$$$

14045 Panay Way, Marina Del Rey

Glide through the becalming waters of Marina Del Rey, enjoying the scenery of yachts, houses, and even the sea life of seals and birds, and most of all, enjoying this peaceful ride with someone you care about in an Italian-style gondola with a small canopy on the top. Soft Italian music can be playing in the background and while your gondolier gently oars you through the waters, you can enjoy a picnic lunch or dinner (that you supply or it can be ordered) at the small table on board while snuggled under a warm blanket that's provided for you. Also provided are appetizers, chocolates, roses, and an ice bucket. Nighttimes are especially pretty with the lights on the houses and in the sky. Doesn't this make you want to go, right now?!

Hours: Call to make a reservation.

Price: Rates start at $140 for an hour for two people. Children 12 and under ride for free.

Ages: 5 years and up.

HARBOR BREEZE CRUISES

(562) 432-4900 / www.2seewhales.com; www.harbor-cruises.com; www.californiadolphincruises.com

$$$

100 Aquarium Way, dock #2, Long Beach

Enjoy a forty-five-minute cruise of the inner and outer harbor, past supertankers, cruise ships, a Coast Guard station, Terminal Island, a Federal Prison, and Angels Gate Lighthouse. Three-hour blue whale-watching cruises are available May through September. Two-hour gray whale-watching cruises are available November through April. Enjoy the same length dolphin and sea lion cruises where the playful creatures often come right up to the boats.

Hours: Forty-five-minute cruises depart from the Village Boat House Mon. - Fri. at 12:30pm, 1:45pm, 3:15pm, and 4:45pm. Sat. - Sun. they depart every 45 min. from 11:30am - 6:15pm. Call for summer and school break hours. Gray whale-watching cruises depart daily at noon and 3pm, with an additional time on weekends, at 9am. Check for hours for blue whale cruises during the summer. The dolphin and sea lion cruise departs at noon and 3pm on weekends only, most of the year and daily during school breaks and in the summer.

Price: Prices for the forty-five-minute cruises are $12 for adults; $10 for seniors; $6 for ages 3 - 11; children 2 and under are free. Dolphin/sea lion and gray whale-watching cruises are $35 for adults; $30 for seniors; $25 for kids. Blue whale-watching cruises are $45 for adults on weekdays and $50 on weekends; $40 for seniors; $30 for kids.

Ages: 4 years and up.

KAYAKS ON THE WATER - STAND UP PADDLEBOARDS

(562) 434-0999 / www.kayakrentals.net; www.standuprentals.net

$$$

5411 East Ocean Boulevard, Long Beach

Sometimes it's nice to lay on the beach. Sometimes we need to be more active. Kayaks launched here allow newbies at kayaking, and those more experienced, to get their feet wet, so to speak, around the harbor, the Naples

Island canals (which is a lovely and calm-water route in front of gorgeous, waterfront homes), to a restaurant or snack place, or to a cove where you'll see floating moon-jellies, in season. At high tide you can kayak to see birds at a small wildlife refuge. All kayakers <u>must</u> know how to swim. Afterward kayaking, go back and enjoy, again, the stretch of beach at Los Alamitos Bay.

Stand ups are at first challenging to stand up on! If you are qualified to use a stand up paddleboard (and you can take lessons here and/or join lifetime membership for $10), then rentals are $16 for the first hour, for members. If you are trying it out, it is $25 for an hour with an instructor. Also check out the dolphin adventures, which is taking a boat ride out to find a pod of dolphins, then paddleboard and interact with them as they swim around and under your stand up. This adventure is about $150; prices may vary.

Hours: Open April through September, daily, 9am - until an hour prior to sunset. Open October through March, Sat. - Sun., 9am - until an hour prior to sunset.

Price: $9 an hour per person for kayaks - prices are pro-rated. Groups of 20 or more are $6 per person per hour with a 2 hour minimum.

Ages: 5 years and up - all kayakers and paddleboarders must know how to swim.

LONG BEACH BOAT RENTALS

(562) 491-7400 / www.boats4rent.com
401 Shoreline Village Drive, Long Beach

Boat rentals here include Sea-Doos - $115 an hour; electric boats (that seat eight) - $75 an hour; and power boats - starting at $70 an hour. Before or after your boating excursion, stroll along SHORELINE VILLAGE (definitely see pg. 161 for info) and its environments for a myriad of great places to shop, eat and sightsee.

Hours: Open daily most of the year, 11am - 5pm (last rental at 3:45pm); Sat. - Sun., 10am - 5pm. Open one hour longer in the spring and summer.

Price: Prices listed above.

Ages: 5 years and up.

LONG BEACH HYDROBIKES

(562) 546-2493 / www.lbhydrobikes.com
110 North Marina Drive, Long Beach

Not quite like walking on the water, but maybe its the next best thing. Biking on water you won't/shouldn't get wet, unless you want to, as the bikes are very stable. There is so much to see along the way, besides the coastline and water - the homes along Naples Canal, shops, restaurants, a jellyfish cove, and more. If your kids legs can't reach the pedals, they can ride on the center platform of one of the side-by-side bikes, sandwiched between two riders.

One favorite excursion is to rent a bike a little before sunset. Another is to rent a decorated bike during the ninety-minute Holiday Lights (group) Tour between the day after Thanksgiving through the end of December to be a part of the celebration and to see the spectacular lights up close. These nights include a few extra surprises, too.

Hours: Call to reserve your bike which are available seasonally at 11am, 12:30pm, 2pm, 3:30pm and 5pm.

Price: $10 for ½ an hour. The Holiday Lights Tour is $60 per rider.

Ages: 4 years and up.

LOOKING GLASS TOURS

(310) 909-3179 or (310) 755-8359 / www.fastkayak.com; www.rbmarina.com
233 N. Harbor Drive, where Torrance Boulevard meets the sea at Redondo Beach Pier at the marina, Redondo Beach

Hourly rates for single kayaks are $15, double kayaks are $25; pedal boats are $10 for adults, $5 per child; stand up paddleboards are $15 an hour (ask about stand up tours). For a different point of view, try a ride on the *Looking Glass*, a bright yellow, semi-submersible underwater viewing boat with two, seven-foot long windows to see the fish, rays, and other harbor sea life, including sea lions. The forty-minute sub ride is $15 for adults; $10 for kids and is only open Friday through Monday. See REDONDO BEACH INTERNATIONAL BOARDWALK (pg. 159) for adjacent activities.

Hours: Open mid-March(ish) - mid-October(ish), daily, 9am - 6pm; open the rest of the year daily, 10am - 4pm. These are the same hours for the sub ride, too.

Price: Prices are listed above. Park in the lot (not the parking structure) for two free hours of parking with validation.

Ages: 4 years and up.

MARINA DEL REY BOAT RENTALS
☼

(310) 306-4444; (310) 306-2222 - parasailing / www.marinadelreyboatrentals.com
$$$
13717 Fiji Way, Marina Del Rey
    Located in FISHERMAN'S VILLAGE (pg. 159), Marina Boat Rentals rents kayaks - $15 per hour for a single, $25 an hour for a double; motorboats - beginning at $75 an hour for a four-passenger boat; $115 for waverunners; $25 an hour for a stand up paddleboard; and electric boats (which hold twelve people and are much quieter than motor boats) starting at $105 an hour. For an uplifting experience, go parasailing - go 500 feet up for $75 per person, or 800 feet for $85.
    Hours: Open year-round, daily - the hours vary greatly, but they are almost always open until sunset. Call for info and to make a reservation.
    Price: Prices listed above.
    Ages: 4 years and up.

MARINA DEL REY WATERBUS
☀

(310) 628-3219 / www.marinawaterbus.com
$
13717 Fiji Way in Fisherman's Village, Marina Del Rey
    The waterbus (i.e. boat) is one of the best deals in town! From eight different locations, including the above stop at Fisherman's Village, plus Burton Chace Park and Marina Beach / Mother's Beach, hop on board with the kids and take in the sights of the marina and coastline via a boat and/or stop for a while and reboard. (You will have to pay for another fare.)
    Hours: Open the end of June through Labor Day, Fri., 5pm - midnight; Sat., 11m - midnight; Sun., 11am-9pm, plus for Thursday night concert series until midnight.
    Price: $1 per person, one way.
    Ages: All

METROLINK (Los Angeles County)

(800) 371-LINK (5465) / www.metrolinktrains.com
$$$
    See the entry for METROLINK (Orange County) on page 329 for details.

METRO RAIL

(323) GO METRO (466-3876) / www.metro.net
$
Los Angeles
    This rail mode of transportation is terrific and also a work-in-progress as there are more miles to the tracks being added. That said, the rail lines that are complete make going to a destination an adventure. The advantages of riding the rails are numerous, such as it's inexpensive, you don't have to fight traffic, you don't have to try to find a parking spot, and kids consider it a treat. Pick up a map of the route at Union Station or ask for a copy to be mailed directly to you and/or check online for maps and park and ride lots of which there are over 100 in the county and most are free. Trains run every ten minutes.
    With numerous stops along the way (and the website makes the lines and where to pick up the buses very easy to understand), here are the basic lines: The Blue Line runs north/south, between 498 Pacific Avenue in Long Beach through Compton and San Pedro, just south of Pershing Square at 7th Street/Metro Center at 660 S. Figueroa St. in downtown Los Angeles. The Silver Line runs parallel to the Blue Line for a bit, starting from Artesia Transit Center in Long Beach (the next stop is Rosecrans Ave.) to 3501 Santa Anita Ave. in El Monte. The Green Line runs east and west, connecting at 12901 Hoxie Ave. in Norwalk to 2406 Marine Ave. in Redondo Beach. Trains run alongside, but separate from, the 105 freeway. The Red Line runs from 801 N. Vignes St. at Union Station in downtown Los Angeles through Hollywood and Highland and Universal City to Lankershim Blvd. in North Hollywood. The Orange Line picks up where the Red Line stops - North Hollywood to west through Van Nuys and Reseda to 6101 ½ Owensmouth at Warner Center. The Purple Line parallels the Red Line for a bit - going from Union Station through Pershing Square to 3775 Wilshire Blvd. near Western. The Gold Line runs from 149 N. Halstead at Sierra Madre Village in Pasadena through Chinatown in downtown L.A., Union Station, and Little Tokyo to end (or begin) at 5150 E. Pomona Blvd. in E. Los Angeles. Note that Union Station, at 800 N. Alameda Street in Los Angeles, is not only a hub for Amtrak and Metrolink, but a gorgeous, historic building. Starring in numerous movies, the station, which is open from 4am - 1am, is just across the street from OLVERA STREET (see pg. 168).

Hours: Trains usually run daily, 6am - 11pm; some lines run 24 hours.

Price: About $1.50 for adults, plus 35¢ for a transfer; 55¢ for seniors, 10¢ for transfers; two children 4 and under are free with each paid adult ticket. The Silver Line has a different fare structure, so check online for prices. A day pass is $5 for adults; $1.80 for seniors.

Ages: All

RED CAR TROLLEY   ☼

(310) 732-7678 / www.portoflosangeles.org; www.sanpedro.com $

Park at the north station, the Cruise Center Station at Gateway Plaza and Swinford Street or the south end at Marina Station at East 22nd Street and Miner Street. Or, park in the middle at Harbor and 6th St. at Ports O' Call Village.

Take a vintage, mini adventure by riding the replicated and the restored Red Cars, circa 1920 (although ADA compliant), 1.5 miles up and down Harbor Boulevard with unlimited boarding and reboarding throughout the day. The cool-looking railcars (riding them is part of the adventure) stop at several local attractions along the route. See PORTS O' CALL VILLAGE (pg. 159), which is also near FANFARE FOUNTAINS (pg. 169), for information on these and other local attractions.

Hours: The trolleys run Fri. - Sun., noon to 9pm. They run Mon. - Thurs. when cruise ships are in port, too.

Price: Unlimited rides for the day are $1 for adult; children 6 years and under are free. Park for free at the 6th St. station or Marina Station at 22nd St. Parking at the Cruise Center station is $1 an hour.

Ages: All

SPIRIT CRUISES - Long Beach   ☼

(562) 495-5884 / www.spiritdinnercruises.com $$$$

429 Shoreline Village Drive #100, Long Beach

Spirit Cruises offers one-hour (offered year-round), ninety-minute (offered select weekend during spring and summer), and two-hour cruises (offered select weekends in summer and on holidays). Each one is narrated and goes through Queen's Way Bay, past the QUEEN MARY (pg. 146), SCORPION (pg. 150), and AQUARIUM OF THE PACIFIC (pg. 216). The longer the tour, the more you'll see and learn. During the two-hour cruise you'll navigate past cargo ships and tankers, cross under four bridges, and much more. Adults enjoy the two-hour plus dinner cruise, with prime rib and chicken on the menu, dancing, and more. Reservations for all cruises are always recommended.

Hours: See above for cruise availability.

Price: The one-hour harbor cruise is $14 for adults; $7 for ages 5 - 12. The ninety-minute cruise is $18 for adults; $10 for kids. The two-hour cruise is $25 for adults; $15 for kids. Dinner cruises are $59.50 per person.

Ages: 5 years and up.

SPIRIT CRUISES - San Pedro   ☼

(310) 548-8080 / www.spiritdinnercruises.com $$$$

Berth 77, Ports O' Call Village, San Pedro

Cruise through the main channels and see the sights! Reservations are suggested. See the above SPIRIT CRUISES for a complete description. This location also hosts narrated whale-watching cruises, usually about two hours in length, available the end of December through March.

Hours: Along with the other cruises mentioned, whale-watching cruises leave Sat. at 2pm and Sun. at 12:30pm.

Price: Whale watching is $25 for adults; $15 for ages 5 - 12.

Ages: 5 years and up.

VOYAGER EXCURSIONS   ☼

(310) 944-1219 / www.voyagerexcursions.com $$$$

181 N. Harbor Drive at the International Boardwalk at Redondo Beach Marina, Redondo Beach

The *Voyager* is a double deck wooden boat ideal for those who like viewing the ocean at a slower pace. Be on the lookout for the colony of sea lions that usually hangs around. Three-hour whale-watching cruises are offered the day after Christmas through mid-April to look for migrating whales as well as common and bottlenose dolphins, plus maybe a shark and sea lions. A member of the Cetacean Society is aboard the cruise, sharing knowledge about what you see and why.

Cruise around the harbor and just beyond on forty-five minute, guided nature rides offered May through October - a great time of learning while experiencing.

Hours: Whale watching tours are offered daily at 10am and 1:30pm, with a minimum of 10 paying passengers - call first. Boat rides are offered Sat., Sun., and holidays, 1pm - sunset.
Price: Whale watching is $25 for adults; $15 for ages 5 - 12; children 4 and under ride free. Nature cruises are $10 for adults; $5 for ages 4 -11; children 3 and under ride free.
Ages: 4 years and up.

WILLOW SPRINGS INTERNATIONAL MOTORSPORTS PARK

(661) 256-6666 / www.willowspringsraceway.com $$$$

3500 75th Street West, Rosamond

This sprawling 600-acre complex has enough vrooooom for six very different race tracks, ranging from day oval, paved oval, a kart track, a lighted speedway, a road course, and the original 2.5 miles, nine-turn raceway built in 1953. Call or check the website for the complete schedule to make sure you're seeing the cars, karts, and motorcycle races that you want. General admission also allows you access to the pit area as long as kids are supervised by parents or other adults.

Hours: Races are usually held on Fri., Sat., and Sun. Call for a schedule.
Price: Usually $10 for adults; children 8 and under are free with a paying adult.
Ages: 5 years and up.

YOUNG EAGLES PROGRAM (Los Angeles County)

National number - (877) 806-8902; Compton, Hawthorne and Torrance - (310) 374-4812 - Glen, chapter #96; Long Beach - (877) 806-8902 - chapter #7; Pacoima - (818) 725-4AIR (4247) - chapter #40; Santa Monica - (310) 458-8591 - airport, chapter #11; / www.youngeagles.org

at the above airports

"They will soar on wings like eagles." (Isaiah 40:31) I think all kids (and adults) dream of flying, and the Young Eagles Program helps those dreams become a reality. Young Eagles is a national program sponsored by the EAA (Experimental Aircraft Association) that desires to introduce children to the joy of aviation. There are a multitude of Young Eagle chapters throughout Southern California that offer kids, between the ages of 8 and 17 years, the opportunity to actually fly, one time only, for free!, in a two- or four-seater airplane. Please remember that everyone here is volunteering their time, including pilots, so be patient with a process that will take at least two to three hours. Although the following information is fairly standard, call the particular program you're interested in for specific dates, times, and other details. Reservations are necessary at most of the airports. A signed consent form by a parent or legal guardian is required for each child.

At the airport, after your child registers, he/she will participate in a preflight inspection training, which means looking over an airplane to make sure it's mechanically sound while learning some technical aspects of how to fly a plane. Then, he/she will fly! The flight is usually twenty minutes round trip. What a thrill! If it becomes too thrilling for your child, airsick bags are provided. Two more wonderful freebies are a certificate upon completion of the flight, and a magazine called *Sport Aviation for Kids* that comes later in the mail. Plan on bringing something to munch on as many airports have picnic tables available. Kids who are grounded will enjoy watching the planes take off and land. Blue skies and tail winds to you!

Some locations offer a tour of the control tower, if available. Kids will need to keep their voices low so they don't disturb the tower operators. Most chapters have an education program of some sort. Notes: Compton, Hawthorne, Torrance - Most pilots at this program try to let the kids have a turn at the controls, for just a short period of time. Pacoima - Kids fly over Magic Mountain, which makes their flight extra special. Santa Monica - Check the website for a phone number to call for this chapter.

Hours: Compton, Hawthorne, Torrance - Offered about eight times a year on selected Sat., starting at 11:30am. Long Beach - call the national number for more info. Pacoima - The fourth Sat. of every month, usually, starting at 10am. Santa Monica - Three or four select Sat. a year, starting at noon.
Price: Free
Ages: 8 - 17 years old.

—ZOOS AND ANIMALS—

ANIMAL ACRES   ☼

(661) 269-5404 / www.animalacres.org $$
5200 Escondido Canyon Road, Acton

This lovely, twenty-six acre ranch is sanctuary to hundreds of barn animals - horses, cows, pigs (some weigh up to 1100 pounds!), goats, turkeys, chicken, ducks, and sheep - that have been rescued from slaughter houses and animal cruelty. A four-minute video at the beginning of the guided tour emphasizes the sanctuary's stand on not eating animals and caring for all creatures equally. The casual, one-hour tour allows visitors to ask lots of questions, hear the animal's rescue stories, and walk around interacting with the mostly free-roaming animals by petting them, feeding them, and giving them love, thus educating and maybe changing minds and diets when people "meet what they eat."

Hours: Open Sun. for one-hour guided tours at 11am and 1pm. School and other groups may call to make an appointment at other times.
Price: $5 for adults; $3 for ages 4 - 11; children 3 and under are free.
Ages: 2 years and up.

ANIMAL ADVENTURES - EXOTIC ANIMAL TRAINING SCHOOL   ☼

(323) 665-9500 / www.animalschool.net $$$$$
Canyon Country, Santa Clarita

Eighteen lions, seven Bengal tigers, an elephant (who paints and exhibits over 300 other behaviors), a zebra, a few grizzly bears, a black bear, and monkeys and chimps consider this compound home. The school's primary objectives are to educate the public on animal preservation, and to give formal training to people who are interested in careers as animal caretakers and trainers - mostly for film and TV. The owner is a veteran Hollywood animal trainer and many of the animals here have been featured in movies and on television. The school is not a zoo, park, or college, but a working professional studio animal company. However, even if intensive training is not what you are looking for, the school does offer a few other options for those who might want some exposure to animal training. Note that there is no direct physical (i.e. hands on) contact with any of the animals.

Animal Encounters, for instance, allows two hours of one-on-one time between you and the animal, or animals, of your choice. Get to know the animals by working with them, learning the training methods, giving commands, giving rewards, and even photographing them. What a wild opportunity! Be a Trainer for a Day, minimum age of 16, as you get to assist the real trainers and see what it really takes to do this type of a job.

Hours: Call or check the website for a list of schedules.
Price: Animal Encounters are $595 per person for the encounter or $1095 for a couple. Trainer for a Day is $775 per person.
Ages: 15 years and up only.

AQUARIUM OF THE PACIFIC   ☼

(562) 590-3100 / www.aquariumofpacific.org $$$$$
100 Aquarium Way, Long Beach

Something fishy's going on at one of the largest aquariums in the United States. The first stop in this multi-level aquarium is the spacious entryway where your attention is immediately riveted by a life-size, eighty-eight-foot blue whale (no way can a creature be so large!) hanging overhead with her calf "swimming" beside her. This hall also contains preview tanks of the main exhibit regions. Watch a sea-related film in the theater or even a 4-D special presentation movie for an additional $4. Information and breath-taking footage on the audio/video screens throughout the aquarium answer many of the questions visitors have about the animals here. Note that almost everything in the tanks, besides the fish, is man-made, although it is incredibly realistic looking. Note, too, that small Discovery Labs are located in each area of the main exhibits and are staffed with docents to answer questions, give demonstrations, and allow you to touch selected sea creatures. All exhibits are handicapped accessible. There are four main exhibit areas to view: California/Baja, Northern Pacific, Tropical Pacific, and Explorer's Cove.

The natural flow of the aquarium leads visitors toward the back of the building, to the **Southern California/Baja** area. Watch the mesmerizing moon jellies' milky white bodies and other exotic drifters float gracefully around in their tanks. Peek at the Swell Shark egg cases where baby sharks are getting ready to be born. A kelp display shows those of us who aren't marine biologists that kelp is used as an ingredient in lipstick, Jell-O, toothpaste, and other household

items. Catch an underwater look at the seals and sea lions splashing around. (Ask about feeding times, when divers often interact with the animals.) Walk up the stairs and outside to see these mammals sun themselves on the surface of the rocky "shoreline." Tiered cement seating allows good viewing for everyone. This outdoor plaza also features sea turtles, shore birds (that are unable to fly away), and a touch tank that holds stingrays and batrays, which feel like rubber. You can feed them ($5). It's a weird sensation and worth it. The Discovery Lab here contains sea urchins, anemones, sea stars, and crabs to gently touch. A favorite is the penguin habitat that holds more a dozen Magellanic penguins, which are native to South America. You can see them swimming around from above and below, and even at eye level at a crawl-in space. Back inside, on the second floor of the gallery, you'll see aptly named garden eels and a rocky reef that holds unusual looking fish, particularly the Lookdowns, which are a vertically-flattened fish.

For a change in venue and temperature, enter the **Northern Pacific** gallery. The most popular attractions here are the playful sea otters in a tank with underwater and above-water viewing. Ample information is given about their fur (for which they've been voraciously hunted), their food, their habitats, and more. Other draws include the tank of anchovies (no pizza!), diving puffins (seabirds), monstrous-looking Giant Japanese Spider Crabs, and a Giant Pacific Octopus, which is not menacing, but so shy that you might not even see him.

Ocean on the Edge Gallery explores the top ten ocean issues. This hallway, with small nooks, showcases great visuals of wall-sized photos, maps, videos, 3-D models of the earth and parts of the ocean, wheels to turn to uncover facts, and animal exhibits on rays, coral reefs, and jellies. The information presented deals with global warming, destructive fishing, ocean pollution, and more.

The Ocean Science Center offers a unique and visual way to view and understand the effects of climate change and rising sea levels, and maritime trade and ports via "science on a sphere". Both stories are told through the medium of satellite images and videos projected onto a rotating, six-foot diameter globe.

The **Tropical Pacific** is one of the most colorful sections here. It's set up so you'll "travel" through the reef and into deeper waters as you venture deeper into this gallery. The coral lagoon showcases brilliantly colored fish - electric blue, canary yellow, jade green, and vivid purple. The largest tank, containing a tropical reef and its 1,000 inhabitants, offers various levels of viewing which is interesting because of the diversity of life shown in here. You'll see clown fish, zebra sharks, giant groupers, puffer fish, Picasso Triggerfish, and more. At feeding time the divers are equipped with aquaphones to answer any questions. A partial water tunnel allows visitors to see sharks, and every parent knows that an aquarium visit is not complete without seeing sharks. Other outstanding exhibits in this gallery include deadly sea snakes; sea horses; the strange-looking leafy sea dragons and weedy sea dragons; upside-down jellies, who were created to live like this; orange-spined unicorn fish; sex reversal fish (mainly wrasses) who change from females to males as they mature or undergo stress - go figure; and beautiful, but venomous or poisonous fish, such as the lionfish. The lower level has an array of colorful jellies including the Leidy's comb jelly with iridescent pink and green flashing lights, and sea nettles with their long, stringy tentacles. Also on display here are Flashlight fishes, which live in the dark depths of the sea. These truly odd, but practical, creatures have headlights located under their eyes that they can switch on and off.

Outside is a favorite area - the shark lagoon. It contains 150 sharks, many of which swim right up to the glass partition so you can clearly see and count all three rows of their teeth. A favorite of ours is the sawshark with a nose that looks like a saw. Try to come by at feeding time, usually at 11am and 2pm, to see a frenzy of activity. At a nearby shallow "petting" tank, roll up your sleeves and touch a variety of sharks (which feel like sandpaper) and rays. Ask about Shark Lagoon Nights, when the public is invited to see these predators up close, touch them, and enjoy live music. Behind the shark exhibit is Molina Animal Care Center which provides onsite healthcare for animals. Visitors can come in and see veterinarians at work.

Also out this way is a walk-through lorikeet aviary. Purchase a small cup of nectar to feed these colorful birds. Take pictures of your astonished kids as the birds land on their head and arms. The canopied-covered Marine Life Theater has fifteen-minute presentations of an animal or storytelling time.

The outdoors, and covered, classroom **- Our Watershed: Pathway to the Pacific** - is strongly educational in teaching what happens to water once it rains or flows down from the mountains; water conservation; and drought-resistant plants. It has an interactive, 3-D watershed model where visitors can manipulate a map, "make" it rain, learn about conserving water, and more.

Cafe Scuba has good food and indoor tables, plus outdoor tables that overlook the seal and sea lion exhibit and Rainbow Harbor. And yes, fish is on the menu.

There are "shows" every day for visitors such as the feeding times for the animals, learning how certain animals are cared for, and more. Ask about the multitude of special events and programs offered to families and school groups including sleep-overs, which are so fun to do with your child ($70); two-hour animal encounters with sharks, otters,

penguins, or seals and sea lions ($109 each - aquarium admission included); one-hour, behind-the-scenes tours, which incorporate feeding the fish at Tropical Reef ($42.95 - aquarium admission included); whale watching tours; and studies of a particular animal or species. Check their calendar online for more annual events. Two classrooms in the educational wing are fully stocked with lab equipment, live systems (touch-tank animals), terrestrial aquariums, craft projects, and other good stuff. An educator's room, available for teachers, contains computers, books, arts and crafts resources, and more.

Note: Weekend and holidays are peak attendance times, which translates as lots of people and waiting in line to get in. Prepurchase tickets at a discount online and avoiding waiting in line.

The aquarium is adjacent to Rainbow Harbor. In between the aquarium and harbor are an esplanade and a large green lawn. Feel free to bring a blanket and a picnic lunch. Head out on the esplanade (i.e., cement walkway) to the colorful-looking buildings of SHORELINE VILLAGE (pg. 161), a shopping and eating complex. Head the other way around the harbor toward a quasi park (i.e., an expanse of green lawn with a few picnic tables) where you can view the QUEEN MARY (pg. 146) and SCORPION (pg. 150) just across the waters. Take an aquabus around - see AQUALINK (pg. 208) for details. Catch a free ride to the aquarium on a bright red Long Beach Passport shuttle bus that cruises Pine Ave., Shoreline Dr., and Ocean Blvd. in the downtown area, and connects to the Metro Blue Line at the Transit Mall on First Street. Passport buses will also deliver you to the *Queen Mary* and *Scorpion*.

Hours: Open daily, 9am - 6pm. It is open on select nights throughout the year and Sunday nights in the summer, 5pm - 8:30. Closed Christmas and the Fri. - Sun. of the Grand Prix in April.

Price: $28.95 for adults; $25.95 for seniors; $14.95 for ages 3 - 11; children 2 and under are free. Save $ by pre-purchasing tickets online. The 5pm - 8:30pm nighttime only tickets are only $14.95. AAA members receive a discount. Parking is $8 with validation.

Ages: All

CABRILLO MARINE AQUARIUM

(310) 548-7562 / www.cabrillomarineaquarium.org
3720 Stephen M White Drive, San Pedro

Explore the underwater treasures of Los Angeles Harbor without ever getting wet! Cabrillo Marine Aquarium specializes in the marine life of Southern California. Originally built in 1935, it doesn't have the polished look or feel of more modern aquariums, but that is absolutely part of its charm. It features quite a few smallish tanks, mostly at kids' eye-level, filled with a wide variety of sea life.

The front courtyard has full-size killer whale, shark, and dolphin models, plus a full-grown gray whale outlined on the cement. Kids are welcome to touch the whale bones in the adjacent Whale Graveyard.

The exhibit halls and rooms have tanks filled with several kinds of live jellies (usually referred to as jellyfish), crustaceans, octopuses, fish, leopard sharks, seahorses, moray eels, the kelp forest and inhabitants, and other sea animals. Some of the animals - the sea stars, some of the fish, and a lobster - are huge, having lived here for a long time. There are numerous displays of preserved animals, such as seals and sea lions; bones, skeletons, jaws, and teeth of sharks and whales; shells; pictures; and other models of sea life. My boys liked pushing the button to hear the recording of a whale singing, although their renditions of it were more grating than musical. We also watched a shark blend into the sandy ocean floor; touched a sample of shark skin and compared it to a sample of sandpaper; and saw a video presentation at the auditorium. Call to see what's currently showing.

As most kids have this inherent need to explore the world with their hands and not just their eyes, a definite favorite is the tidepool touch tank. Here kids can gently touch sea anemones, sea stars, and sea slugs.

The adjacent buildings feature an Exploration Center and an Aquatic Nursery. The educational-oriented Center has a tank that allows kids to crawl up into the middle so it looks like they are surrounded by fish. (And they are!) It also contains touch screens; a puppet theater with puppet sea creatures and a monitor so actors can watch themselves; a craft station; microscopes with lots of slides; a no-touch tank of sea slugs and fish; a short tunnel of a recreated mud flat with hinged informational panels on the outside; and a touch table of fossils, shells, and jarred specimens. The Nursery looks like a scientist's lab with large, bubbling tubes that contain sea monkeys (i.e., brine shrimp) and phytoplankton, along with other equipment. See the breeding area for baby seahorses and other sea animals, and look at live abalone. Lift the panels for more information, learn about salmon farming and abalone, and listen as staffers explain about the inhabitants and the function of the nursery.

The Cabrillo Aquarium offers seasonal events such as whale watching (January through April) and grunion hunting (March through July), plus various workshops and programs, such as Sleep With the Fishes. At low tide - call for particular times and seasons - tidepool tours are given at the beach in an area called Point Fermin Marine Life

Refuge. A paved, wheelchair-accessible trail runs from the parking lot to the aquarium, across the beach, and to the water's edge at the tidepools. You are welcome to explore this area on your own, too.

Don't forget to pack your swimsuits and beach towels as CABRILLO BEACH (pg. 10) is right outside the aquarium. Wonderful sandy stretches and a play area await your children. There are also some rock jetties to explore and a fishing pier. Enjoy your day playing by the ocean, and learning more about it.

Hours: The Aquarium is open Tues. - Fri., noon - 5pm; Sat. - Sun., 10am - 5pm. Closed Mon., Thanksgiving, and Christmas. The touch tank doors open for twenty minutes at a time Tues. - Fri. at 1:30pm, 2:30pm, and 3:30pm; Sat. - Sun. at 11:30am, 1:30pm, 2:30pm, and 3:30pm. Slide shows are presented Tues. - Sun. at 11am and 2pm. The beach is open daily, 6am - 10pm.

Price: $5 (suggested donation) for adults, $1 for seniors and ages 12 and under. Parking is $1 an hour, $9 max. If you get here early enough, you can park on the street and just walk through the beach/aquarium entrance gate.

Ages: All

DANNY'S FARM

(909) 869-2216 - Danny's Farm; (909) 869-4906 - store / www.csupomona.edu/~farmstore
4102 S. University Drive at California State Polytechnic University, Pomona

Farm fresh animals in this case means a petting zoo, located in the AG area of Cal Poly Pomona. Enter the pens to gently stroke and even feed miniature horses, goats, sheep, rabbits and a pot-bellied pig. Bring your camera! Picnic tables are available here, too. If you didn't bring food, grab a snack (and something to take home for dinner) at the adjacent Farm Store which offers farm-fresh produce, pork, and beef; incredible chocolate milk; health foods; plants; and other products.

Hours: Open March - November, Sat., 10am - 2pm, weather permitting.
Price: $3 per child; one adult free with each paying child. Food cups are $1 each.
Ages: 1 - 12 years.

EFBC'S FELINE CONSERVATION CENTER

(661) 256-3332 - recorded info; (661) 256-3793 - live person / www.cathouse-fcc.org
Rhyolite Avenue, Rosamond

This place is the cat's meow! In the middle of desert and dirt, this nicely-landscaped, mid-sized compound has fifty exotic wild cats living here, representing over fifteen different species. Since it is a breeding compound, you're almost guaranteed to see a few kittens, too. Unlike traditional zoos, the safety fences keep you only a few feet (not yards) away from the caged animals. This allows for plenty of up-close viewing and photo opportunities.

Stroll along the cement pathways to see jaguars, panthers, pumas, lynxes, fluffy Amur leopards, regal-looking servals, weasel-like jaguarundi, and lots of Chinese leopards. Read the information plaques at the enclosures or ask for a guided tour to learn about the animals - what they eat, how much they weigh, their life span, and more - and about the importance of this breeding compound.

In the center of the grounds is nice, green and shady spot and some tables. You can enjoy a picnic lunch here; just don't feed the animals. The gift shop has a few displays showing some of the reasons these cats are facing extinction - one fur coat was made from fifteen bobcats, and another was made from over fifty leopards. Tip: Late afternoon and cooler months are the best times to visit the compound as this is when the felines are more active. Special Twilight Tours are offered three times a year for ages 18 and older. See areas not open to the daytime public, like the Siberian tigers, and have your picture taken with a cat (if one is cooperating). Please call if you want to schedule a tour for ten or more people. Educational outreach programs are also available.

Hours: Open Thurs. - Tues., 10am - 4pm. Closed Wed., Thanksgiving, and Christmas.
Price: $7 for adults; $6 for seniors; $5 ages 3 - 12; children 2 and under are free. Twilight tours are $20 per person.
Ages: 4 years and up.

FARM TOUR

(909) 274-4794; (909) 594-5611, ext. 4794 / www.mtsac.edu
1100 N. Grand Avenue at Mount San Antonio College, Walnut

Take a forty-five-minute guided tour of the farm animals on this college campus. You'll see cows, horses, goats, and sheep, and depending on your guide, learn about what the animals eat, how to take care of them, and more. The

tour is geared for younger children and is simply a fun introduction to farm animals. Note that it is not a petting zoo. Pack a sack lunch to enjoy at a picnic area under nearby shade trees, adjacent to a hilly, grassy field. The minimum number of students is ten; the maximum is seventy. Check out WILDLIFE SANCTUARY TOUR (on pg. 207) for another tour offered by the college.

Hours: Tours are given Tues. - Thurs., 9am, 10am, and 11am. Reservations are required.
Price: Free, but donations are appreciated.
Ages: 3 - 10 years.

GENTLE BARN

(661) 252-2440 / www.gentlebarn.org
15825 Sierra Highway, Santa Clarita

The over 120 animals at the farm-like Gentle Barn sanctuary have been rescued from abusive situations and have found a new home here where people lovingly connect with them. Watch and stroke horses playing in the grassy field and go to their stalls to feed them carrots ($5 a bag). Brush the cows and give them a hug. Go into the pen to pet llamas, sheep, goats, an emu, chickens, and turkeys, and give the big pigs a belly rub. Hands on, your own leisure timing, education about where the animals (and each one has a name) came from and why, and many volunteers to assist you and answer your questions make Gentle Barn a warm, welcoming, and therapeutic animal encounter. There is a picnic area here, too, plus snacks and a little gift shop for purchases. Special needs groups, at-risk kids, school field trips, and other groups are invited during the week.

Hours: Open to the public Sun., 10am - 2pm.
Price: $10 donation per person.
Ages: All

INTERNATIONAL CENTER FOR GIBBON STUDIES

(661) 296-2737 / www.gibboncenter.org
19100 Esguerra Road, Santa Clarita

What's the difference between a monkey and an ape? If you answered, "Monkeys have tails," you are correct. Next question: Are gibbons monkeys or apes? Hint - they have no tails. A one-hour, or so, guided tour of this outdoor facility takes you past sixteen enclosures that hold over forty gibbons in their natural family groupings. The enclosures are sizable chain-link cages, scattered over the hard-packed dirt grounds and under shade trees. The tours are informative, entertaining, and vary according to the interests and ages of the participants in the group, from elementary-age kids to anthropology professors. Note: To ensure the safety of the gibbons, visitors must be in good health, not have had any recent contact with a person or animal with an infectious disease, and stay a minimum of five feet away from all enclosures.

Gibbons are arboreal apes - they swing from tree to tree - and are found in the rainforests of Southeast Asia. This research facility, which has five out of the nineteen existing species, studies their behavior and helps to increase their endangered gene pool, which means you could see babies on your visit here. Gibbons are the only nonhuman primates to walk upright and they have earned the name of loudest land mammal. Every species has a different way of singing (that's the technical name - I call it screaming) to each other, usually in the morning hours. They can project their voices a distance of up to two miles. We heard them. I believe it. The kids loved it. Siamangs have vocal sacs that inflate to the size of a large grapefruit (reminiscent of a bullfrog) when they sing. This is fascinating to listen to and watch. Males and females in certain species are born one color and change colors as they mature. (Is this the same thing as humans "going gray"?) We also learned about gibbons' nutrition, why they are dying off, preventative medical care, and more. My boys went ape over this center!

Hours: Open to the public, Sat. - Sun., 9:30am - noon, except for rainy days and holidays. Guided tours are at 10am. Open by appointment at other times for groups of twenty or more people, or a minimum of $120 for 8 people. These tours preferably start between 8:30am and 10:30am, when gibbons are most active. Individuals may call to see if they can join an already scheduled tour.
Price: $15 for adults; $12 for teens and students; $10 for seniors; $5 for ages 6 - 12; children 5 and under are free.
Ages: 4 years and up.

KELLOGG ARABIAN HORSE CENTER

(909) 869-4988; (909) 869-2224 / www.wkkelloggarabianhorsecenter.com

3801 W. Temple Avenue at California State Polytechnic University, Pomona

The Kellogg Arabian Horse Center at Cal Poly houses over 130 purebred Arabian horses. The center's thirty-eight scenic acres are set in the hills and encompass a huge pasture, three barns, foaling stalls, a breeding area, a veterinary clinic, a farrier shop, an arena, and a covered grandstand that seats 900.

Staff members, and students of horse husbandry and equine sciences, present hour-long shows that put the horses through their various paces. Guests see demonstrations of English and western riding, with riders in appropriate costumes, as well as drill team and precision maneuvers, and horses jumping over small fences. Riders in silver and gold flowing Arabian dress are crowd pleasers as their horses, decorated in jewel-toned brocade and tassels, prance around the ring. Our favorite act was the horse that performed several tricks, including walking a baby carriage and rocking a cradle.

After the show children can ride a horse on a lead around a path for $4, walk around the stables where families can watch the beautiful horses being bathed and groomed, and simply enjoy the ambiance. Springtime is the best time to visit as there are newborn colts to see. Note that visitors are welcome to visit the horse center during the week from 8am to 5pm to just walk through the stables. Horse camps are usually held here for youth during the summer.

Be sure to visit the Farm Store just around the corner at 4102 S. University Drive for farm-fresh produce, pork, and beef; incredible chocolate milk; health foods; plants; and other products. It's open daily from 10am to 6pm. For more info contact the store at (909) 869-4906 / www.csupomona.edu/~farmstore.

Hours: Shows are offered October through May on the first Sun. of each month at 2pm. Shows are also offered several Thurs. in both the spring and fall at 10:30am for elementary students. Reservations are required for the school presentations.

Price: Sun. shows are $4 for adults; $3 for seniors and ages 6 - 17; children 5 and under are free. Sometimes the Thurs. shows are $1 per person. Parking on Sun. is $3.

Ages: 3 years and up.

LOS ANGELES ZOO

(323) 644-4200 / www.lazoo.org
5333 Zoo Drive, Los Angeles

All the big-name animals star at the Los Angeles Zoo - Asian elephants (in six acres of their own exhibit - see training demonstrations daily at 11am), tigers, African lions, giraffes, bears, okapi, kangaroos, alligators, jaguars, wolves, and rhinoceros. (You can touch and feed an Indian rhino on weekends for an additional $12.) Many of the animals live in the context of their natural environment with plants, rocks, etc., and yet plenty of viewing areas, too. Our favorites are the gorillas, apes, orangutans, chimps, and other primates - they provide entertainment that tops television any day - all in their own habitats that also immerses visitors because of the plants and other authentic setting props. An aquatic area features otters and seals splashing in the water, or posing or sleeping on rocks. You'll want to catch the sea lion training in the aquatics section and the animal encounters "show." The hippos have an underwater pool with glass walls so visitors can view their below the waterline activities. The darkened Koala House has koalas in their nighttime environment, since they are supposed to be more active at that time. Don't forget to sssstop by the two-building LAIR (Living Amphibians, Invertebrates and Reptiles) to see snakes and lizards from all over the world, and my favorites, the Komodo dragons and the Chinese alligators.

If your kids get tired of walking around this huge and hilly zoo (and it is a hilly zoo), or you get tired of pushing a stroller, purchase an all-day shuttle pass for $4 for adults, $1.50 for seniors and disabled, $2 for ages 2 to 12. The shuttle goes around the perimeter of the zoo, and will drop you off or pick you up at various stops along the way.

Enter the children's zoo (which closes daily at 4pm) to pet and even brush goats and sheep, and see miniature horses, rabbits, and potbellied pigs. Don't miss the fifteen-minute "Animals and You" presentations here to see, maybe touch, and definitely learn about an assortment of critters in an intimate setting on weekdays at 10:45am and 11:45am, with an additional show on weekends at 12:45pm. Spelunkers can explore a man-made cave, which offers tunnels to crawl through, exhibits on cave creature dwellers to look at, and (pretend) stalactites and stalagmites to see. One cave features Desert Trail, a tunnel exhibit showcasing tortoises, bearded lizards, scorpions, and tarantulas. At the prairie dog exhibit kids can pop their heads up from underneath the ground into a plexiglass dome while real prairie dogs are looking at them! This is a fun photo opportunity. The Animal Care Center (i.e., nursery) houses small mammals, birds, and newborns that need special care.

An animal-themed, boundless playground has climbing sculptures; slides, including a textured slide; a bridge; a toddler area; and larger play structure that are suitable for kids with and without disabilities. It also has water misters and a picnic area. Take a spin on the huge carousel ($3) featuring sixty-four animals including giraffes, bears, tigers, a

poison dart frog, and a dung beetle.

Look - it's a bird, it's a plane, it's Superman! No, it's a bird! The World of Birds show features about twenty, mostly free-flying birds that perform daily at 11:30am - a ~~flight~~, sight not to miss.

On select dates during warmer months, join in a Creature Camp Out ($85 per person) where your family (kids must be at least 5) can join numerous others and sleep in tents on the zoo grounds. Enjoy a campfire snack and continental breakfast, plus enjoy special nighttime and early morning behind-the-scenes tours of the animals and an animal encounter, plus a souvenir t-shirt. What a great experience! Ask about their numerous other special programs and events, such as forty-five-minute Toddler Totes classes ($18 plus zoo admission) with activities and animal encounters; Zoopendous Nights for groups and scout troops ($45 per person), which is an overnight adventure that includes working on badge-related activities; daytime patch programs for scouts; and free guided tours given to mid and upper elementary school-aged kids. Stroller and wheelchair rentals are available. A free audio tour regarding some of the weirdest animals is available by calling on your cell phone at the zoo. Look under GRIFFITH PARK (pg. 62) for other attractions in this immediate area.

> **Hours:**   Open daily, 10am - 5pm. Closed Christmas.
> **Price:** $18 for adults; $15 for seniors; $13 for ages 2 - 12. Certain discounts are available through AAA.
>   Parking is free.
> **Ages:**   All

MARINE MAMMAL CARE CENTER AT FORT MACARTHUR

(310) 548-5677 - center; (310) 547-9888 - tours / www.marinemammalcare.org

3601 S. Gaffey Street, San Pedro

Can you hear them barking? Injured or sick marine mammals, like sea lions and seals, are brought here, doctored, and taken care of until they can be released back into the wild. Rehabilitation can take one to three months, depending on the case. We saw one seal that was severely underweight and another that had numerous shark bites. This small facility houses from five to ninety marine mammals outside in chain-link fence pens, depending on the season. Stormy weather and pupping season (February through July) bring in more injured or abandoned animals. However, the staff has more time to spend with visitors during non-busy times. Your children have an opportunity to learn more about these animals as knowledgeable volunteers are on hand to answer any questions kids might ask. And they do ask! Try to visit at feeding time (for the seals and sea lions, not the kids) which are usually at noon and 4pm because this is when the animals are most active. Call first to make sure of the times.

A variety of educational tours and classes are offered for all ages that incorporate a visit with the animals, a video, reinforcement activities, and pre- and post-visit materials. Fourth graders and up may also utilize the laboratory inside the adjacent building, operating the microscopes and computers and looking at the aquarium. Tours are an hour for preschoolers through kindergartners, and two hours for older children, with an emphasis on the academics. Inquire about the MMCC Seal Day event in May.

Look up FORT MACARTHUR MUSEUM (pg. 109), as it is located just across the street. Check out the nearby Angels' Gate Park for picnicking, kite flying, basketball, and running around.

> **Hours:**   Open daily, 10am - 4pm.
> **Price:**   Free. The educational tours and classes cost about $30 for curriculum materials for up to 60 people.
> **Ages:**   All - younger ones will just enjoy seeing the animals, while older ones can learn about them and
>   appreciate what the Center does.

MONTEBELLO BARNYARD ZOO and GRANT REA PARK

(213) 718-5442; (323) 887-4595 / www.montebellobarnyardzoo.com

600 Rea Drive, Montebello

A small Barnyard Zoo is at one corner of the Grant Rea Park. It has a small pond for ducks, an aviary with doves and peacocks, and pens holding goats, pigs, a cow, llamas, alpacas, horses, and sheep that kids can pet through the fences. Visiting this "zoo" makes a stop at the park a little more special. The entrance fee to the zoo is $3 per person. Other activities include a short train ride around the "track" - $3 per person; a merry-go-round - $3 per person; and pony rides for younger children, twice around the walking track - $4. A snack bar is open here on the weekends with hot dogs, churros, beverages, and more. School groups, with a minimum of twenty kids, pay only $7 per child for one ride on each attraction and unlimited time at the zoo.

The surrounding, nice-sized park is pretty. It has baseball diamonds, batting cages (open at certain times), picnic tables under shade trees, barbeques, a playground, and bike trails along the river bed.

Hours: The park is open daily, 7am - dusk. The zoo is open during the winter, Wed. - Fri., 10am - 4pm; Sat. - Sun., 10am - 5pm. It is open in the summer daily, 10am - 5pm. The rides are usually available during zoo hours.

Price: Free to the park. Prices for the zoo and rides are listed above.

Ages: 1 - 10 years.

PASADENA HUMANE SOCIETY

(626) 792-7151 / www.phsspca.org

361 S. Raymond Avenue, Pasadena

This atypical animal shelter is quite lovely with open-air kennels and plants all around. Besides the numerous dogs and cats, there are rabbits in penned play yards, guinea pigs, birds, iguanas, turtles, peacocks, and other kinds of animals that need a home. (Sometimes even wildlife, such as deer, show up.) The permanent residents here include an alligator, some parakeets and cockatiels in the aviary, and a few snakes.

Free, forty-five-minute tours are offered for school children, scouts, and other groups. Note that the program will come to your facility as well. Kids learn about why the animals are here (i.e., homelessness or abuse), facts about pet care, animal safety, how animals communicate, careers with animals, and more. After a presentation with various animals such as reptiles, birds, a chinchilla, and others, the group takes a guided walk around the shelter. Smaller groups may go into the veterinary hospital, depending on the happenings there. Your kids come away with a better understanding of animals and of the humane society's resources. Ask about summer workshops and other programs.

Hours: Open to visit Mon. - Fri., 9am - 6pm; Sat., 9am - 5pm; Sun., 11am - 4pm. Open for tours Tues. - Fri., 9:30am - 4:30pm. Call to schedule a tour. Closed holidays.

Price: Free

Ages: 4 years and up.

POLO MATCH - WILL ROGERS STATE HISTORIC PARK

(310) 454-8212; (818) 509-9965 / www.willrogerspolo.org; www.parks.ca.gov

$$$

1501 Will Rogers State Park Road, Pacific Palisades

If you feel like horsing around, come watch a polo match on the beautiful grassy field at Will Rogers State Historic Park. To learn more about what a game entails, look up SANTA BARBARA POLO (pg. 652). Picnic tables are plentiful at the park. And if you want to incorporate a tour of Will's house and/or a hike through the adjacent Topanga State Park, look up page 158.

Hours: Games are held mid-April through mid-October, Sat., 2pm - 5pm; Sun., 10am - 1pm. The park is open daily, 8am - sunset.

Price: $12 per vehicle; $11 for seniors. House tours and polo matches are included in the price of admission.

Ages: 5 years and up.

PONY TIME

(951) 201-3928; (909) 297-176 / ponytimeatlakewood.weebly.com

$$

11369 E. Carson Street, Lakewood

In the midst of the Lakewood Equestrian Center is this short adventure for young children. They can ride a pony that's on a walking lead around a small, center ring, and/or go for a short walk and a trot on a pony in a more open walking area. Come inside the little farm to pet and feed several goats, rabbits, sheep, and chickens. An alpaca and a cow are in their own enclosures to see up close. Ask about the hour-long Mommy (Daddy) and Me classes where kids can brush, saddle and ride ponies, too. Picnic tables under shade trees are reservable for parties.

Hours: Open Wed. - Sun., 10am - 4pm., until 5pm at spring daylights savings time. Trot ponies are available on Sat. and Sun., only.

Price: $5 per ride, either walking or trotting. $1 for the petting zoo. $1 for food for the animals.

Ages: 1 ½ years - 100 pounds for the walking ring; 3 years - 100 pounds for a pony trot.

ROUNDHOUSE AQUARIUM

(310) 379-8117 / www.roundhouseaquarium.org

!/$

Manhattan Beach Boulevard at the end of Manhattan Beach Pier, Manhattan Beach

Come see the stars of Manhattan; sea stars that is. The Roundhouse Aquarium is a small marine learning center,

but packed with information and exhibits. The shark tank (always a favorite!) contains three species of sharks common to this area, plus moray eels, and some fish. Watch the sharks be fed on Saturdays at 12:30pm. A lobster and crab tank hold a California spiny lobster, giant spider crabs, and more. The nursery tank shows off just-hatched babies of the sea. A petting pool contains several types of rays to gently stroke. Rainbow stars, sunflower stars, and the sheephead are in the deep ocean habitat tank. You'll also see clownfish, Garibaldi (our state fish), an octopus, hermit crabs, and more. A tidepool touch tank containing mostly sea stars, a surge tank, and a few other aquariums with tropical fish and local invertebrates round out the collection at Roundhouse Aquarium. Note: It gets crowded quickly inside the aquarium. Upstairs is a play and study center that is complete with sea animal puppets, books, whale bones and shark's teeth to examine, more aquarium tanks, and videos.

The aquarium offers many marine science programs, field trips for students, and fun family activities. Sunday story times are at 11:30 and include making a craft. The one-hour Ocean Discovery class, for at least eight or more people of any age, includes learning about the marine environment and teaching time by the touch tanks. The cost is $5 per person with a minimum of $75. A three-hour class, given for kindergartners through twelfth graders, includes a lot of fascinating information, pollution awareness, beach exploration, animal anatomy, and hands-on fun such as touching sea stars and even petting a shark. The cost is $225 for thirty students. Sleeping with the Sharks is an overnight field trip that includes a pizza party (similar to a shark feeding frenzy), touching sharks and shark teeth, dissecting parts of a shark, and more. The cost is $75 per person. Join in free arts and crafts and/or storytelling on Sunday mornings.

On your way out to the aquarium, which is located at the end of a concrete pier, check out all the beach activity - lots of sand volleyball, surfing, swimming, and of course, sun bathing. You can also, ironically, fish from the pier. Sidewalk shops are just down the street.

Hours: Open Mon. - Fri., 3pm - sunset; Sat. - Sun., 10am - sunset. Call for hours, though, as they are often open earlier if staff is available. Call for tour and program times.

Price: Free entrance to the aquarium; donations of $2 per person or $5 per family are encouraged. Tour prices are given above. Metered parking ($1.25 an hour) is available on Manhattan Beach Blvd. by the stores, or wherever you can find it.

Ages: 2 years and up.

SANTA ANITA PARK   ☀

(626) 574-RACE (7223) - general info; (626) 574-6677 - tram tours; (626) 574-6362 - tram tour reservations / $$
www.santaanita.com
285 W. Huntington Drive, Arcadia

Hold your horses! One of the most famous thoroughbred horse racing parks in the United States is surprisingly family-friendly. Watch the horses being put through their paces during their morning workouts from 5am (this is a little too early for me!) to 9:30am, and while you're at it, grab a bite to eat at Clocker's Corner Cafe breakfast counter (open everyday, 7am to 10am). The Cafe offers inexpensive items that can be eaten at the outside patio area overlooking the track.

On most Saturdays and Sundays during the season and weather permitting, at 8:30am and 9:45am, take a free, fifteen-minute, behind-the-scenes, narrated Seabiscuit Tram Tour. Arrive fifteen minutes early. Reservations are highly suggested. You'll ride along dirt "roads," through a hub of horse activity, and past rows of stables where walkers, trainers, and jockeys are exercising, bathing, and grooming horses. The guides point out Barn 38 where Seabiscuit was stabled from 1937 to 1940 and the locations where the movie *Seabiscuit* was filmed. A forty-five-minute walking tour follows the tram tour where you can peek into a jockey's room and saddling paddock, see behind-the-scenes action, and much more. Tip: Call first as the tram ride is not offered on days of major races. Catch the tram near Clocker's Corner Cafe in the parking lot near the west side of the grandstands.

Walk in the beautifully landscaped Paddock Gardens, located just inside the admission gate, to look at the flowers, statues, and equine-themed topiary plants. In the gardens, twenty minutes prior to post time, there is a brief "show" as jockeys, in their colorful silks, walk and ride their mounts around the walking ring before going on to the race track. Note: The first race on Monday usually begins at 1pm while races Wednesday through Sunday begin at 12:30pm. Weekends bring special events such as mariachi bands and dancers, costumed park mascots strolling about, and more. Ask for a schedule of their numerous, family-oriented events, such as Family Fun Days and the annual Irish Faire.

Go through a paved tunnel from the gardens to the infield (i.e., interior of the racetrack) to reach a playground. Kids can horse around on the large play structure with slides, monkey bars, a merry-go-round, and swings. One end of the playground is best suited for toddlers and the other for slightly older kids. The infield, which is only open on

weekends and holidays, also features large grassy areas for running around and picnicking, so pack a lunch. Family Fun Days are held once a month on the infield which include a bounce house, face-painting, pony rides ($2 per), and other fun things to do. Note: You may stay in the infield during races.

From the time the starting gates (which are portable) and jockeys are in position, to the finish line, enthusiasm runs rampant through the crowd. The actual races, although over quickly, are thrilling, even for nonbetters. (The numerous manned windows and wagering machines receive a lot of frantic activity.) My boys "scientifically" deduced who to root for - according to the horse's name and/or the color of the jockey's silks. Tip: Sitting in grandstand seats is the best way to see the action as the slanted cement standing area in front of the seats fills up quickly with people who are always taller than you. Note: It is almost a half an hour between races.

Lunchtime food can be purchased at concession stands; the cafeteria; the casual, but nice Turf Club; or the posh Club House, where appropriate posh dress is required. Prices vary according to venue.

I wager your kids will have a good time watching the Sport of Kings.

Hours: The season runs the end of December through April. Racing is Wed. - Sun. and holiday Mon. Post time on weekdays is 1pm; weekends and holidays, 12:30pm.

Price: Sometimes there is free admission before the gates open at 10:30am, so watch the horse workouts and, on weekends, go on the tram ride. If you arrive after gates open, general admission is $5 for adults; free for kids 17 and under when accompanied by an adult. Clubhouse admission is $8.50. Parking is $4 after 9:30am.

Ages: 4 years and up.

SANTA MONICA PIER AQUARIUM

(310) 393-6149 / www.healthebay.org/smpa; parking.smgov.net
1600 Ocean Front Walk, at the foot of Santa Monica Pier, Santa Monica

$$$

Discover what really lives in the Santa Monica Bay at the aquarium, located under the Santa Monica Pier. This small, but fascinating center, part of the Heal the Bay community program, has several tanks of live sea creatures to look at and touch. One large aquarium holds crabs, sea stars, California sheepshead, halibut, and other fish. Other tanks include the octopus tank, kelp forest tank, rocky reef tank (which holds a moray eel and other sea life), and sandy bottom tank (look closely to see the ocean floor move with animals). Use the provided flashlight to see tiny swell sharks (which aren't necessarily wonderful sharks, it's just the name of that shark species) developing inside their hanging egg cases. Mature swell sharks, sand crabs, sand dollars, leopard sharks, and bat rays are too fragile for fingers to touch, but they are easily seen in shallow tanks placed at a child's eye level. In three touch tanks, however, kids can gently touch tidepool life such as sea stars, sea anemones, and sea slugs. A touch table displays a shark's jaw and individual teeth. It also has a microscope for a closeup look at scales, shells, etc.

Another prime attraction in the center is the Kid's Corner filled with age-appropriate activities, games, and/or books. A small puppet theater stars sea creatures that kid's make come to life. The microscope lab, with its array of microscopes, computers, and viewing screens offers a closer perspective of sea organisms. On Saturdays at 3:30pm join a naturalist presentation, which includes feeding the octopus and/or a few other animals. On Sundays at 3:30pm, a short, ocean-related film (usually about sharks) is shown, plus you can participate in a shark craft and watch the feeding of the horn and swell sharks. Help feed the sea stars at 2:30pm on Tuesdays and Fridays.

The beautiful, marine-muraled classroom was designed for the instructional use of the school programs that are offered here. These informative, wonderful, and interactive one and two-hour programs are offered year round. Some of the programs include a "field trip" to the adjacent Santa Monica Beach. Inquire about other classes and special events.

Make a day of your visit to the aquarium by taking a walk on the pier (see SANTA MONICA PIER on page 160), enjoying some rides at PACIFIC PARK (pg. 3), or just playing at the beach!

Hours: Open most of the year, Tues. - Fri., 2pm - 5pm; Sat. - Sun., 12:30pm - 5pm. Open in the summer until 6pm. Call first as hours sometimes fluctuate. Closed Mon. and weekday mornings for school programs. Closed most major holidays, including the week before Christmas.

Price: $5 suggested donation for adults; children 12 and under are free. $3 per person for groups of 10 or more. Parking on or right next to the pier is $8 during the week; $12 on weekends. There is very limited metered parking nearby.

Ages: 3 years and up.

THE SEA LABORATORY

(310) 318-7438 / www.lacorps.org/sealab.php

1021 N. Harbor Drive, Redondo Beach

Inside the small building of the Sea Laboratory are tanks containing a variety of sea creatures such as octopus, eels, Garibaldi, seahorses, coral, horn and swell sharks, moonjellies, and skates (not roller, but ones that look like rays, yet with funny looking faces). A small display on a storm drain vs. sewage, and the subsequent effects that trash has on the oceans and sea animals is here as is the ocean supermarket exhibit showcasing products on a shelf, like at a supermarket. When visitors use a scanner on a product, it reveals how much of what ocean element is used in that particular everyday item, such as seaweed in ice cream.

Outside is a good-sized tidepool touch tank with sea stars, sea anemones, and more. Beyond the gate, and open to the public on a guided "tour", are several large tanks, that look like small pools, containing an assortment of sea life. There are lobsters, large halibuts (sorry, no fishing allowed) that are part of the halibut hatchery, giant sea bass, bat rays, sea stars, and more. Most of these creatures arrive at this destination via saltwater intake systems from generating stations that suck in, and sometimes trap, even injure, the animals. Many of them are here only briefly before being released back to the ocean. Big "selling points" for a visit to the lab are that kids can ask as many questions as they want, and they can see and touch almost all of the animals here. The staff will even take the lobsters and sea stars out of the tanks for a closer look and touch. Saturdays at noon you can either watch the feeding of the fish or participate by purchasing a tray of food for $2 and then feeding it to them. A native plant nursery at the facility is also a butterfly habitat.

Coming here is a fun family outing. There are oceans of opportunity for school field trips, too. Three-hour, age-appropriate classes cover a gamut of topics that not only meet the state science standard, but are engaging. Time is spent at the lab, learning about the animals, and seeing and touching them. A portion of the time is also spent at the big lab, the beach. One project that the kids do is look at the water from a different perspective, through a microscope, and test for water quality. After expending some energy and gaining more knowledge about aquatic life, it's back to the building for a related craft or hands on activity. Can't come to the Sea Lab? Then they'll come to you. Note: If you have a teen who is 14 years or older inquire about the volunteer program.

Hours: Open Tues. - Fri., 9am - 3:30pm, with tours of the touch tank at 1pm, 2pm and 3pm; Sat., 10am - 4pm, with touch tanks open every hour on the hour. Closed Mon., Sun., and holidays.

Price: Free. A suggested donation is $2 per person; $4 per family. School field trips are about $5 per student.

Ages: 4 years and up.

SHAMBALA PRESERVE

(661) 268-0380 / www.shambala.org

6867 Soledad Canyon Road, Acton

The word Shambala means "a meeting place of peace and harmony for all beings, animal and human". This is a preserve for over sixty exotic big cats - African lions, Bengal and Siberian tigers, bobcats, servals, a lynx, a liger (a hybrid of tiger and lion), cougars, and black, spotted, and Asian leopards - all who have been rescued from people and/or agencies that owned them and often abused them. The three-hour planned program Safari tour, for those 18 years and older only, includes a one-hour guided walking tour that is often hosted by Tippi Hedren, actress and founder of The Roar Foundation, the supporting foundation of the preserve. While learning about the history of the preserve and stopping at most cages, visitors see the magnificent cats and learn their stories - some good and some horrible. They are also educated about legislation regarding illegally owning exotic felines and the unfortunate need for sanctuaries, while hopefully spurred on to become active in caring for these animals and others like them. The animal enclosures are natural and lovely with some run-around room, trees, plants, toys, and more creature comforts. The walking tour is mostly on hard-packed dirt trails, with some steps, on the beautiful, park-like grounds. There is even a lake with a picnic area and a wooden walkway, so bring a lunch to enjoy at the conclusion of your tour. A gift shop is also on the premises. Note that there are other opportunities, besides the Safari, to support the preserve, as well.

The one-hour, education program is the only way for students, 8 to 17 years old, to visit the animals at Shambala. While they are learning about and observing the animals (and the animals are likewise watching them!), they are also listening to the animal noises, like tigers chuffing and lions roaring. All this makes a power impact on the kids (and adults). Each child is also given an educational booklet and encouraged to support a particular animal, perhaps as a group project. Bottom line - a lion is not a pet!

Hours: Open one weekend a month (usually the second one), noon - 3pm (gates open at 11:30am), for a Safari by advance reservation only. Open for student educational tours usually on Tuesday mornings - you must call first to reserve.

Price: The safari tours are $50 per person. The educational programs are a minimum of $100 - $5 for students; $20 for adults.

Ages: 18 years and up for the Safari tour; 8 - 17 years for the educational tour.

STAR ECO STATION

(310) 842-8060 / www.ecostation.org
10101 W. Jefferson Boulevard, Culver City

The inside of the Eco Station is done in the style of a lost Mayan temple, complete with archways, wall friezes, floor tiles with "fossils," (fake) greenery all around, and murals so the ECO Station's message of teaching kids the importance of preserving the environment and protecting wildlife comes across in an inviting manner. This place is, in fact, a designated wildlife sanctuary and works with the Department of Fish and Game, as well as other organizations. Illegal articles and animals, seized from people trying to smuggle them into the country via airports, seaports, and over the border, are displayed here for show and tell.

One hour-plus guided tours, the only way to see the station, are given to see the rooms and their inhabitants. The tour guides continually share interesting stories of how and why the animals are here and emphasize why wild animals should not be kept as pets. Note: The critters at the Station vary at any given time because of newcomers.

Two aquarium rooms contain tanks with colorful angelfish, blue tangs, Picasso fish, coral that's been harvested, lionfish, seahorses, pufferfish, red-ear slider turtles, and other aquatic creatures taken from people attempting to bring them into the U.S. Walk through a room painted like a kelp forest that simulates scuba diving, while learning about the food chain and how to keep the ocean healthy and free from litter that comes through storm drains.

The reptile room houses chameleons, numerous iguanas, geckos, bearded dragons, Burmese and ball pythons, boas, several caimans, and some tortoises. There are also quite a few tarantulas here and other arachnids. Guests are invited to touch some of the chameleons and iguanas and/or wrap the pythons around themselves, or for the more squeamish, to merely stroke them (or not).

An adjacent Environmental Village room contains information about saving the environment and wildlife and it features Chumash and Hope artifacts, such as drums, tools, and headdresses. The mammal rescue center room provides temporary homes for various animals, depending on which creatures are in need of the Eco Station facilities. We saw bobcats and servals.

You'll be greeted with loud "caw"s inside the large bird room, filled with green-cheeked Amazons, toucans, cockatoos, African gray parrots, Macaws, and others. Some of them are practically bald as they pick at their feathers, habits they had previously that can't be undone.

Two-hour school or group tours are offered during the week. There is a park nearby for picnic lunches. If you can't come to the station, the station will come to you with mobile exhibits and workshops. Check the website for information about camps and special events, including the popular Dinofaire and Earth Day. Note that CULVER CITY PARK (pg. 53) is just down the street.

Hours: Open to the public most of the year, Fri., 1pm - 5pm (last tour is at 4pm); Sat. - Sun., 10am - 4pm (last tour is at 3om). It is also open July and August and certain holidays, Mon. - Fri., 1pm - 5pm (last tour is at 4pm); Sat. - Sun., 10am - 4pm (last tour is at 3pm). Tours leave every half hour. Open for school/group tours, minimum 20 students and maximum 120, Mon. - Fri. between 10am - 4pm.

Price: $8 for adults; $7 for seniors; $6 for ages 2 - 12; children under 2 are free. The cost for a school/group tour is $5 per person.

Ages: 2 years and up.

WHALE WATCHING

See the TRANSPORTATION section.

WILDLIFE LEARNING CENTER

(818) 362-8711 / www.wildlifelearningcenter.com
16027 Yarnell Street, Sylmar

This mid-size center, with rows of cages that hold over fifty species of animals, is prettified with lots of plants in, around, and on the enclosures, as well as huge shade trees all over, so it's an attractive place to visit. Of course the

reason to come is to see and learn about the unusual animals here - bobcats, lynxes, servals; Arctic, red, gray, and fennec foxes; porcupines; sloths; owls; coatimundis; squirrel monkeys; armadillos; alligators; woodchucks; tortoises; macaws; and kinkajous (which you might not have seen before). There is also a small reptile and amphibian room starring the blue poison dart frog, red-eyed tree frog, anaconda, tarantula, scorpion, lizard, and others. Catch a Trainer Talk every hour on the hour starting at noon to see, learn about and maybe even touch an animal.

Stroll the pathways to view the animals. If you'd like to really learn about particular critters and even have the opportunity to interact with some of them, sign up to take one or more of the Individual Animal Experiences, which take about ten minutes each. For instance, gently stroke a fennec fox (so soft!); hold an owl (with a gloved hand); go into the porcupine habitat and feed them (this was one of our favorites!); meet a prairie dog; touch an alligator; pet a lynx; hold a huge python; and more. Bring your camera for great photo ops! A ninety-minute Zoofari Tour combines several of the above interactions, which is what we did and it really added to our experience. The center also does school and scout programs, birthday parties, and assemblies, summer camps, and much more.

Hours: Open daily, 11am - 5pm. Closed Thanksgiving, and Christmas.

Price: $7 for adults; $6 for seniors and ages 3 - 13; children 2 and under are free. The Individual Animal Experiences range from $25 - $35 per animal for most of the animals, for 1 to 4 people, up to $100 for up to 4 people for the lynx. The Zoofari Tour is $190 for up to 4 people, $35 each additional person.

Ages: All

ORANGE COUNTY

Upwardly mobile urbanites live in this county designed to meet the needs of growing families. It boasts a great number of parks and playgrounds, including the most famous one of all - Disneyland. The intimate San Juan Capistrano, the upscale Laguna Beach, the natural preserves of Coto de Caza, the bustling Anaheim, the hills of Mission Viejo, and every city in between comprise a county that offers numerous places to sightsee. From Knott's Berry Farm to Huntington Beach to Medieval Times to Rainforest Café to Richard Nixon Library to Dana Harbor to Fullerton Arboretum - "orange" you glad you came to visit?

—AMUSEMENT PARKS—

ADVENTURE CITY

(714) 236-9300 / www.adventurecity.com $$$$

1238 S. Beach Boulevard, Anaheim

My family travels a lot and one of our favorite cities to visit when the kids were younger was Adventure City. This clean, two-acre little theme park is perfect for younger children. The colorful city scene facades throughout resemble storybook illustrations. The eighteen rides and attractions, many designed to accommodate parents, too, include a wonderful train ride around the "city," a few roller coasters, a carousel, an airplane ride, a hot-air balloon ride, a bus with wheels that go 'round and 'round, and Crank n' Roll, a kid-powered little car ride. Kids can have a really hot time dressing up in full fireman apparel before (or after) they "drive" around on the Rescue Ride 9-1-1 ambulance, police, and firemen vehicles.

Adventure City also offers do-it-yourself face painting, a few video and arcade games, plus interactive puppet, magic, and other shows at the theater. Thomas the Tank Engine play area has a huge wooden train set that encourages toddlers' imaginations to go full steam ahead. A small petting zoo has goats, sheep, an alpaca, and bunnies. At twenty-four-feet high the rock climbing tower is just the right size for kids (and adults) to scale. $3 per person to climb.

The food onsite is good and reasonably priced. Note: You may not bring your own food inside, but there is a small picnic area just outside the gates. Up a tree for a different place to have a birthday party? You can have one in the building adjacent to Adventure City which was created to look like a big trunk of a tree.

Hours: Open most of the year usually on Fri., 10am - 5pm; Sat., 11am - 8pm; Sun., 11am - 7pm. Open in the summer and during school breaks, Mon. - Thurs., 10am - 5pm; Fri., 10am - 7pm; Sat., 11am - 9pm; Sun., 11am - 8pm. Call for holiday hours and check the schedule before you come as hours fluctuate.

Price: $16.95 for ages 1 and up; $11.95 for seniors; children 12 months and under are free. Certain discounts are available through AAA.

Ages: 1 - 10 years.

CALIFORNIA ADVENTURE

(714) 781-4565 - recorded information; (714) 781-7290 - operator / www.disneyland.com $$$$$

1313 Harbor Boulevard, Anaheim

This is a Disney version of vintage California, so it's sometimes realistic, and always entertaining. Take a Red Car trolley from the entrance through and around the main street, to the Tower of Terror.

To the left of the entrance is **Hollywood Pictures Backlot** area, which describes exactly what it looks like. The main road looks like a real street with a huge backdrop of blue sky and a few white clouds at the end. Famous Hollywood movie facades line the streets. The ten-minute Muppet Vision 3-D show is great for Muppet fans. Watch out for objects that seemingly come flying right out of the screen. The Muppet preshow, shown on several large screens in a "dressing room" with lots of costumes and props, is equally entertaining. Take a ride with the monsters through scenes from the show, *Monsters Inc*. The Disney Animation building is a main attraction. Inside, you can interact, via questions and answers, with a computer-animated Crush (the turtle from *Finding Nemo*) - this is so cool. Or, learn how to draw a Disney character in fifteen minutes - an instructor and paper and pencils are provided. A small adjacent "museum" shows the creative process of animation - inception to the final product - via sketches and sculpture of several famous Disney characters. In the Sorcerer's Workshop, which is decorated in a dark, dungeon-style tone, draw your own Zoetrope (i.e., an early animation strip); enter the Beast's Library, which looks like a set from *Beauty and the Beast*, to match up your personality traits with a Disney character by having your picture taken and pressing buttons on a "magic" book; and, relive (as well as rewrite) Disney scenes in Ursula's Grotto by replacing the real voices with your speaking or singing voice, matched to an on-screen scene. Just next door is the Playhouse, where favorite Disney characters perform live. At the end of the street is the Hyperion Theater, which seats 2,000, that features a forty-five-minute, professional musical show, *Aladdin - A Musical Spectacular*. The sets, music, acting, special effects, humor, and more make this a musical spectacular not to be missed. In the adjacent haunted hotel ride of The Twilight Zone Tower of Terror, you'll take the dark elevator up to the top floor, get a blinding glimpse of the outdoors, and then hurtle down (then bounce up and then back down a few floors) free-fall-style to the hotel lobby.

Carthay Circle Restaurant is an upscale restaurant and bar in the center of "town" with dining inside and dining outside on the terrace overlooking Buena Vista Street. Elegantly and beautifully furnished with numerous, tasteful tributes to Walt Disney via photographs, this is the place to go for a fine dining experience while at the park, with

prices that reflect that.

To the right of the main entrance is **Condor Flats** and **Grizzly Peak**, which includes the highly touted, and rightly so, Soarin' Over California ride. Walk through its hangar (with great photos and stories of real aviators) and sit in a chair, with your feet dangling over the edge, in front of a giant screen that will immerse you in a virtual hang gliding adventure over California. Swoop over San Francisco, seemingly dip your feet into the Pacific Ocean, barely avoid treetops - watch riders lift their feet! - and literally smell orange blossoms and pine trees. You will get wet on the next ride, Grizzly River Run, which is an eight-passenger raft ride that goes down mountain sides, through caverns, under waterfalls, and down a river onto a spouting geyser. At the extra large, outdoor play area, Redwood Creek Challenge Trail, kids let off steam by running around, scaling a short rock climbing wall, going up fire towers, down slides, and across cargo nets, zip lines, and swaying bridges.

"a bug's land" is themed around the animated film, *A Bug's Life*. Walk back to Flik's Fun Fair where several kiddie rides, and the scenery, are oversized, supposedly reducing visitors to a bug's size. The rides include Heimlich's Chew Chew train, very slow bumper cars (with a minimum height requirement of 42" to ride; 48" to drive alone); spinning ladybugs (similar to the teacups ride); and pretend hot-air balloons. There is also a water play area with a few water fountains that spurt up at unexpected times. (Bring a change of clothing.) Bug's land also features *It's Tough to be a Bug* 3-D animation show - not for those with arachnophobia. The show features bugs of all kinds, such as termites, huge tarantulas that seemingly come out of the screen, stink bugs (with an olfactory emission), an angry hoard of hornets that buzz loudly in a blackened room as a "stinger" pokes through the back of your chair. Not my favorite attraction. Next door is a cluster of restaurants with outside seating only. This area also features a ten-minute walk through tour of a sourdough bread "factory", along with bread samples. The adjacent restaurant offers salad or soup in a very freshly-made bread bowl. And make sure you pick up your free Ghiradelli chocolate square (the flavor of the sample changes with the seasons) at the next door Ghiradelli Soda Fountain and Chocolate Shop. Just across the way watch a seven-minute film on the making of wine at Wine Terrace where wine and wine sampling is available for adults.

Walk back to a star attraction, the incredibly well-themed **Car's Land**. Besides Mater's Junkyard Jamboree where trailers are pulled by a tractors in a figure 8 configuration, and Luigi's Flying Tires ride, it is home to one of the most popular rides at the park - Radiator Spring Racers. The massive and eye-catching mountain scenery (look for the disguised tail fins of Cadillacs that create the mountain range) is reminiscent of the Grand Canyon, with colorful rock formations and a waterfall. Cars ride through parts of the movie, basically, and conclude with a very fast and fun race to the finish line, high banked turns and all. Eat at either the Crazy Cone Motel area, where ice cream and everything else is served in orange safety cones, or at Flo's V8 Cafe, refueling while eating comfort food by the kitschy gas tanks outside or inside with completely-themed 1950's and *Cars* decor. Ordering a kid's meal here allows little crew members to take home a sporty car-shaped container.

Enjoy a meal at Ariel's Grotto with the decor inspired by *The Little Mermaid*. Snow White, Belle, Sleeping Beauty, Ariel, or Cinderella come by the table to pose for pictures and bestow hugs to their loyal (and adoring) subjects. The cost for breakfast ranges from $28.99 (low season) to $34.99 (high season) for adults, and $16.99 to $18.99 for ages 3 to 9. Lunch is $32.99 to $36.99 for adults, and $18.99 to $20.99 for ages 3 to 9. Reservations are usually necessary - call (714) 781-DINE (3463). Just across the way from the Grotto is The Little Mermaid; Ariel's Undersea Adventure which wondrously steeps guests in an under-the-sea-like experience as passengers ride clam shells through scenes from the movie, aided by music, special effects, animation, and favorite, colorful characters.

On to **Paradise Pier**, which is a Disneyfied boardwalk carnival, filled with old-fashioned rides and carnival-type games. The "E-ticket" ride here is California Screamin', a colossus roller coaster that earns its name with steep hills, high speed drops, and a loop-de-loop around a blazing sun. The giant Ferris wheel, sporting a colorful Mickey's face, is another heart-stopper. Cages swing independently of each other, so passengers go around and around, <u>and</u> around and around! Other rides here include a King Triton's carousel; Silly Symphonies swing ride; Goofy's Sky School, a really goofy coaster ride; the Jumpin' Jellyfish parachute ride; and old-fashioned-looking rocket ships. In fitting with the classic midway games theme, guests wear 3-D glasses and take a ride and compete on a favorite - Toy Story Midway Mania!, shooting lasers at targets for points and interacting with other video-enhanced games while the movie's characters coach vocally from the sidelines. Good Mediterranean and Italian food are available back in this area, too, as well as some of the best corn dogs ever at Corn Dog Castle.

Live shows, including *Aladdin*, are performed throughout the day and evening. See the twenty-minute, Disney Junior - Live on Stage! for preschoolers; Pixar Play Parade with floats starring characters from favorite films, plus dancing and acrobatics; the interactive Phineas and Ferb's Rockin' Rollin' Dance Party; and more. For tweens and teens, the Mad T Party area offers live bands for singing and dancing to (think safe concert area) and a video/arcade area designed via Tim Burton's *Alice in Wonderland*, though with discoish lights and more of a club feel.

My favorite nighttime attraction is twenty-five-minute Disney's World of Color at the Pier lagoon where over 1,200 water fountains reach as high as 200 feet (!). Colors pulsate through the fountains as the waters dance and sway to the music, enhanced by other lighting and effects, and fire, to create a truly memorable and magical show. Scenes from *Finding Nemo*, *The Lion King*, *Pocahontas*, *Toy Story*, and other classics are projected during the show on the water screen that is 380 feet wide by 50 feet tall. Make sure you get a fast pass for the show/time of your choice to reserve a spot in the viewing area and then get to the show early to get a good place to stand and watch. It is standing room only, no sitting, and on a first-come, first-served basis. Other options that reserve you a spot in the preferred viewing section for this water extravaganza include: Pre-purchase (but at least a day ahead of time) a picnic meal online for $15.99; enjoy a full-service lunch ($29.99 for adults; $18.99 for ages 3 to 9) or dinner ($41.99 for adults; $21.99 for ages 3 to 9) at Wine Country Trattoria and receive a viewing ticket; make reservations to eat at the refined Carthay Circle Restaurant where a three-course prix fixe meal ($59 for adults; $24 for children) allows you a center stage viewing area ticket; or make dinner reservations at Ariel's Grotto ($41.99 for adults; $21.99 for children ages 3 to 9). Note that the princess characters do not appear at dinner times at the Grotto.

Tips: 1) Make use of the Fastpass system, which means that timed passes are dispensed from ticket machines, one ride at a time, to reserve a designated time for each ticket holder to be in line to board the ride - you bypass others in the "regular" line. Fastpasses are available for California Screamin', Goofy's Sky School, Grizzly River Run, Radiator Springs Racers, Soarin' Over California, The Twilight Zone Tower of Terror, and World of Color. 2) Single rider seats are for those willing to not ride with others in their party, but to fill in when a single rider is needed. You usually radically reduce your ride wait time and are only a departure or two away from others in your party. Single rider is available on California Screamin', Goofy's Sky School, Grizzly River Run, Radiator Springs Racers, and Soarin' Over California. 3) Parent swap system - Everyone waits in line. Then, show and tell the line attendant that one parent is going to wait and that waiting parent/person will receive a pass to then go to the front of the line, once the first parent is done. Almost every ride honors this. 4) For guests with disabilities and/or in wheelchairs, download the Guide for Guests With Disabilities to know which rides offer special, and usually faster, entrances. 5) Note that there are traditionally fewer crowds here on Mondays and Tuesdays. 6) We often pack a meal to save money by renting a locker for the day (about $15) that fits a small cooler and some jackets. 7) Download the free Disney app to check wait times for rides, where which Disney characters currently are, and more. See DISNEYLAND, on page 232, which is just across the walkway from California Adventure, and DOWNTOWN DISNEY, on page 314, a huge pedestrian "street" adjacent to both amusement parks that offers unique shopping and dining experiences.

Hours: Usually open daily in the summer, 8am - 1am. Open the rest of the year usually, Mon. - Thurs., 10am - 8pm; Fri. - Sun., 10am - 10pm. Hours fluctuate a lot, so check before you visit.

Price: $92 for adults; $86 for ages 3 - 9; children 2 and under are free. Parking is $16. A park-hopper pass (good for entrance and re-entrance to both Disneyland and California Adventure on the same day) is $137 for adults; $131 for kids (though you can't do both entirely in one day). Check out 2 to 5 day passes. Several times throughout the year Southern California residents are offered a discount on admission.

Ages: 2 years and up.

DISNEYLAND

(714) 781-4565 - recorded information; (714) 781-7290 - operator / www.disneyland.com

$$$$$

1313 Harbor Boulevard, Anaheim

The world-famous "happiest place on earth" amusement park has so many things to do, see, and ride on, that entire books are written about it. The following description is a brief overview along with some tips.

Orient yourself by taking a train ride, located just inside the Disneyland entrance at **Main Street, U.S.A.**, around the perimeter of the park. You'll see the whole park and go through some fun, old, and "hidden" attractions, like the dinosaur diorama and the mining cave. It stops at each main section of Disney. Main Street is perfect for all your mini (and Mickey) shopping needs. It also features restaurants and ice cream eateries. One of our favorite stops is the Candy Palace, where you can watch delicious confections being made before your eyes. (No free samples, though - sigh.) At Christmas, the candy makers create candy canes - a fascinating process. Also inside this palace are a few penny arcades to see short, old-time "movies." This street also has a cinema house that shows Disney cartoons, including the 1928 *Steamboat Willie,* and an opera house showcasing Disney history culture and a model of the White House. A very patriotic, almost documentary-style presentation of Great Moments With Mr. Lincoln in here has stirring film and music and gives and shows a condensed history of the Civil War. An animatronic President Lincoln appears and speaks towards the end.

The park is "divided" into different sections and each section favors a particular theme. The following attractions

are just *some* of the highlights in these various areas. **Fantasyland** is located mostly in the courtyard of the park's centerpiece - Sleeping Beauty's castle. Actually walk inside the castle walls (up and down several staircases) to see this classic story retold in film vignettes. The Bibbidi Bobbidi Boutique is to bring out the princess in young girls. Prices start at $55 for the Crown Package which includes a choice of hairstyle (plus a tiara or hairpiece), sparkly makeup, nail polish, a Princess sash, face gems and more, and go up to $200 for the Castle Package which includes all of the above, plus a Disney Princess costume, some accessories and photos. Your child can also meet a "real" Disney princess just outside the castle walls at Fantasy Faire and Royal Hall (bring your camera and autograph books) and even see a condensed show of *Rapunzel* and/or *Beauty and the Beast* at performances at the Royal Theatre in this same area. The rides in Fantasyland include Mr. Toad's Wild Ride (which has things popping out at riders, loud noises, and even a dark and fiery section of hell, complete with demons); Alice in Wonderland (where the ride vehicle is shaped liked a caterpillar); Mad Tea Party (a spinning tea cups ride); Casey Jr. Circus Train; King Arthur Carousel; Peter Pan's Flight - to Never Land and back (I like this gentle and flying-high ride); and more. Although this area is definitely geared for the younger set, some of the images on the rides may be scary for them. Storybook Land is a boat ride through canals lined with miniature buildings that are from Disney's classic tales. Fantasyland also features the jolting Matterhorn Bobsled roller coaster with a few roaring abominable snowmen, and "it's a small world," where a slow moving boat takes you past animated children figures from all over the world dressed in their culture's attire and singing the theme song in their native language. (If you didn't know the song at the beginning of the ride, you will never forget it afterward.) Look for characters from Disney and Pixar movies, too, situated in their country of origin. Just down the road is Pixie Hollow where visitors go down enchanted walkways to meet Tinker Bell and other fairies.

Mickey's Toontown, with town buildings put together at colorful, crazy, cartoonish angles. Walk through and meet Mickey and Minnie in "person" at each of their houses and get your picture taken with him/her. Kids enjoy playing in Goofy's Playhouse; riding on the scaled-down roller coaster; climbing all around the tree house and cargo nets at Chip n' Dale Treehouse; simply sitting in cars that look like they are straight out of a cartoon; and just running all around this toddler-friendly "town." Roger Rabbit is the most popular ride here as riders sit in a car that they can actually spin around. Catch the twenty-minute, great musical and dance production of Mickey's Magical Map just outside Toontown.

Frontierland features Big Thunder Mountain Railroad (a roller coaster); Big Thunder Ranch (a small petting farm with goats, sheep, pigs and more); Mark Twain River boat (which looks authentic); Sailing Ship Columbia (an intriguing fifteen-minute ride around Pirate's Lair on a replica, three-masted ship from the 18th century); and Pirate's Lair on Tom Sawyer's Island. Visitors are rafted to the island where they can climb up, on and under (fake) rocks; go through secret passages in caverns; go up in a treehouse; enter a spherical cage made of bones and skulls; cross a suspension bridge; and just run around. Back on the mainland, make a reservation (on busy days) to eat at the Golden Horseshoe revue where a fun hillbilly-type musical/comedy show accompanies your meal. You can also just come in to watch a show. Practice shooting skills at the shooting gallery with 100 interactive targets set up like the Tombstone, Arizona in the Old West.

The adjacent **New Orleans Square** continues the pirate theme in the classic ride, Pirates of the Caribbean. Yo ho, yo ho - with its catchy music, cannons "blasting, and piratey scenes all under a realistic-seeming nighttime setting, it's a pirate's life for me. Captain Jack Sparrow makes multiple appearances. A different place to eat here is at the Blue Bayou Restaurant, where a nighttime sky is always in effect and the seating overlooks a section of the Pirate's ride. The Haunted Mansion is a ride through, well, a haunted mansion, that showcases various ghosts.

Critter Country features everyone's favorite bear, Winnie the Pooh. Take a "hunny" of a ride through the Hundred Acre Wood, a very popular attraction with the younger set, and enjoy the rest of the similarly themed area, including a photo op with Pooh and Tigger. This country also has Splash Mountain, a wet roller coaster ride, with entertaining characters on the sidelines. For an early American experience, pick up a paddle and go on Davy Crockett's Explorer Canoes. These real, twenty-passenger canoes (no motors or tracks) go around Tom Sawyer's Island. They operate seasonally and close at dusk.

Adventureland has the thrilling (and bumpy) Indiana Jones roller coaster ride. You'll encounter snakes, skeletons, a huge boulder rolling toward your jeep, and other "dangers". Height restrictions apply as younger children will most likely be frightened by the content. Be sure to take the slow moving Jungle Cruise where the hysterical one-liners tossed off by the boat captains about the jungle animals and activities are the highlight. (Your kids will repeat these same lines for a long time to come.) Walk the narrow stairs up and through Tarzan's (giant) Treehouse to see how the ape man (and his family) lived. And who doesn't love the Enchanted Tiki Room where the birds and flowers talk and sing?

Tomorrowland, with its sixty-four-foot mobile of gold spinning planets at the entrance, ushers in a new era. Zoom through the darkness of outer space in Space Mountain, one of the fastest (and darkest) roller coaster rides at

Disneyland. Bump along through Star Tours, an exciting motion simulator ride that has riders battle with the Empire in over fifty possible scenarios portrayed on screen, making your experience different every time. A fun fact to share is that the retail store here sells make-your-own light sabers! Turn 360 degrees in your Star Cruiser pod as you blast DayGlo intergalactic enemy targets with hand-held laser guns in Buzz Lightyear Astro Blasters. (It's like a shooting gallery ride.) Check your score at the end. Look for Nemo and other friends in the Finding Nemo Submarine Voyage which plunges you into the ocean's depths, kind of. At the Autopia course, drivers 52" and taller can rev up the engines and drive. Bring a bathing suit (or change of clothing) in the summertime if you want to get wet running through the huge fountain in Tomorrowland. The water shoots up in some sort of pattern, but my kids usually just got wet, pretty much on purpose, I think. The two-story, rotating Innoventions building has both educational and entertaining components. Homes, cars, medical breakthroughs, health, energy management, and technology choices for the future are showcased here and interspersed with a lot of computer and virtual reality games. One of the rotating exhibits featured several of the Ironman suits from the movies. Next door, the interactive Jedi training academy stage is a fun place for knight wanna-bes. And yes, the monorail is still here to offer a (low flying) bird's eye view of the park as it meanders throughout.

For a breakfast buffet with Disney characters, join Minnie and Friends Breakfast in the Park at the Plaza Inn on Main Street. A delicious array of food - pancakes, made-to-order omelets, Mickey-shaped waffles, fresh fruit, and more - is served in old-fashioned, spacious rooms decorated in pink and white. Best of all, Minnie, and sometimes Daisy, Max, and other costumed friends, come around to dispense hugs and take pictures with your children. Bring your camera! The cost ranges from $23.99 (low season) to $27.99 (high season) for adults and $11.99 to $13.99 for ages 3 to 9. Reservations are usually necessary - call (714) 781-DINE (3463). Open until 11am.

The daily, nightly, and seasonally-themed parades and shows are memorable. They are often based on Disney's latest animated films. *Fantasmic* is usually shown daily in the summer, and on weekends only the rest of the year. This somewhat dark, twenty-five-minute show, presented near Tom Sawyer's Island, centers around Mickey Mouse's imagination battling forces of evil. Fountains of water create a misty "screen" for laser-projected images from *The Sorcerer's Apprentice, Dumbo,* and other films. Lighted boats cruise by with costumed characters on board acting out scenes from Disney movies. Fire flashes on the water, fireworks explode, and the finale is played with a thunderous symphony of music. Weekend evenings throughout most of the year and every night during the summer is an utterly fantastic, choreographed fireworks extravaganza accompanied by music and narration. Sleeping Beauty's castle magically changes color and even projects patterns according to the music. Call for a complete list of show information and times, and arrive early to get a good viewing spot for each show.

If you want to have more knowledge than the average tourist, take a guided tour of the park, such as "A Walk in Walt's Footsteps". This tour provides a deeper understanding of Walt's life and dreams, a peek into many places unaccessible to the average visitor, two rides, and lunch. "Discover the Magic" is part scavenger hunt looking for Mickey clues (two-and-a-half hours, $59) while "Welcome to Disney" is a tour where you can learn insiders tips about both parks and lots of Mickey trivia (two-and-a-half hours, $25). All tour prices are per person and in addition to admission prices. Note that discounts are offered for Auto Club members. The Youth Education Series is offered to students to incorporate a field trip to the park with learning about the world of physics, animation, history of California, and leadership strategies. Contact (877) WD-YOUTH (939-6884)/www.disneyyouth.com for more information.

Disney goes all out and is completely redecorated for Halloween (even some of the rides are switched up to include ghosts and monsters) and for Christmas. Another Halloween addition is Mickey's Halloween Party on select nights and usually extended hours, open only to special event ticket holders. For five hours (plus an optional, additional three hours before the event), visitors dress up in costume, go trick or treating at various stations, encounter Disney villians, go on rides, watch a special parade, join in a dance party, create a creepy craft, and more, for the whole family. The cost is $67 to $74 per person. Christmas brings two special offerings - the Candlelight Processional and the Holiday Tour. The Candlelight Processional is a one hour, riveting presentation of traditional Christmas carols and music rousingly and beautifully sung by hundreds of choir members who enter Main Street carrying candles, and some of whom configure into the shape of a Christmas tree. The choir is joined by an orchestra. The music is interspersed with the Christmas story read from the Bible by various celebrity narrators. It extends for twenty nights, usually twice a night, and is presented on Main Street. Seating for the show is available usually to VIPs, annual pass holders and sometimes via a dining package, but there is lots of standing room to see and hear it. The "Holiday Time at Disneyland" tour is a winner, providing the holiday history of Disneyland, as well as holiday legends and cultures throughout the world. It also allows express boarding for "its a small world" and the Haunted Mansion; a commemorative pin; reserved, front row seating for the Christmas Fantasy Parade; and some hot chocolate in a keepsake mug ($64).

Tips: 1) Your child's favorite Disney characters are strolling all around the park, so keep your eyes open and your camera ready. Quite a few of the characters are gathered at Town Square when Disneyland opens in the morning. The lines to see them are shorter then. 2) Make use of the Fastpass system, which means that timed passes are dispensed from ticket machines to reserve a designated time for each ticket holder to be in line to board the ride - you bypass others in the "regular" line. Fastpasses are available for Autopia, Big Thunder Mountain Railroad, Indiana Jones Adventure, Roger Rabbit's Car Toon Spin, Space Mountain, Splash Mountain, and Star Tours. 3) Single rider seats are for those willing to not ride with others in their party, but to fill in when a single rider is needed. You usually radically reduce your ride wait time and are only a departure or two away from others in your party. Single rider is available on Indiana Jones Adventure, Splash Mountain, and Matterhorn Bobsleds. 4) Parent swap system - Everyone waits in line. Then, show and tell the line attendant that one parent is going to wait and that waiting parent/person will receive a pass to then go to the front of the line, once the first parent is done. Almost every ride honors this. 5) For guests with disabilities and/or in wheelchairs, download the Guide for Guests With Disabilities to know which rides offer special, and usually faster, entrances. 6) Note that there are traditionally fewer crowds here on Mondays and Tuesdays. 7) We often pack a meal to save money by renting a locker for the day (about $15) that fits a small cooler and some jackets. 8) Download the free Disney app to check wait times for rides, where which Disney characters currently are, and more. 9) For a free Disney souvenir, go to City Hall and get a free button commemorating a first visit, birthday, wedding, just celebrating, and more. 10) For the fun of it: Check the website www.hiddenmickeys.org for fun facts and to find hidden mickeys throughout Disneyland. See CALIFORNIA ADVENTURE (pg. 230), which is the other Disney theme park adjacent to Disneyland, and DOWNTOWN DISNEY (pg. 314), a huge pedestrian "street" adjacent to both amusement parks that offers unique shopping and dining experiences.

Hours: Open daily in the summer, 8am - 1am. Open the rest of the year, Mon. - Thurs., 10am - 8pm; Fri. - Sun., 9am - 11pm or 8am - midnight, depending. Hours fluctuate a lot, so check before you visit.

Price: $92 for adults; $86 for ages 3 - 9; children 2 and under are free. Parking is $16. A park-hopper pass (good for entrance and re-entrance to both Disneyland and California Adventure on the same day) is $137 for adults; $131 for kids (though you can't do both entirely in one day). Check out 2 to 5 day passes. Several times throughout the year Southern California residents are offered a discount on admission.

Ages: All

KNOTT'S BERRY FARM

(714) 220-5200 / www.knotts.com $$$$$
8039 Beach Boulevard, Buena Park

The atmosphere of the Old West is recreated throughout a good portion of California's original theme park via authentic and vintage-looking period buildings - almost a town's worth of them. Almost all of the stores in the section of the park called **Ghost Town** have a Western motif, including a real working blacksmith shop, a wool spinning shop, and numerous arts and crafts stores. There is a surprisingly big rock store which has such a variety of rocks, gems, and fossils for sale, including mammoth fossils for $2,500, dinosaur poop for $12, and geodes that you purchase whole to be cut right there and see what's on the inside - some with amazing crystals. The Western Trails Museum here is an interesting and wonderful dusty museum - filled with items from that time period such as brands, saddles, a gun collection, buttons, toys, dolls, a wagon, knick knacks, and much more. There is small, fake cemetery here, too, with humourous headstones. Go inside the genuine Old School House and sit at a desk and chat with the docent schoolmarm, but you don't have to do homework. Find the small jail and go back to visit the criminal behind bars because this mannequin "talks" to visitors. (I won't tell the secret.)

A lot can actually be learned about the Old West and Native American life styles by talking to some of the costumed employees and using some of the stores and places as mini-museums in the Ghost Town and Indian Trails areas.

Enough about stores - onto the real reason kids visit. Ghost Town has a twenty-minute, slap-stick, western-themed stunt show with cowboys, gunfights, and stunts; a ride in an old-fashioned Butterfield Stagecoach around the park (with real horses) - a favorite; a very short ride in steam engine trains from the early 1900's; Calico Mine Ride - a fairly mild roller coaster ride through a mine; the log ride (on which you will get splashed, if not soaked); and one of the quickest rides, time-wise, I've ever been on - a modern-day Pony Express. Straddle your "horse coaster" and bank around tight turns and Old West features. The mail (and rider) must go through! A huge, relatively long, wooden-trestle roller coaster named Ghost Rider is a fast, bone-rattling, high-*spirited* thrill ride. (Part of the time I was lifted out of my seat!) Reputed to be the longest, tallest suspended (i.e., inverted) roller coaster in the West is the Silver Bullet: It climbs up to 146 feet, drops fast and furious, turns riders upside down several times and includes a vertical loop. This ride endears Knott's to thrill seekers. I think, however, that the bumper cars are more my kind of

style. Beware - the Bigfoot Rapids raft ride <u>will</u> get you completely drenched. There is even Laser Tag - $5 for seven minutes of play. The Mystery Lodge is a show that hosts a mystical Native American storyteller narrating his tales around a fire that produces images to his stories.

The adjacent **Indian Trails** section has tepees to go into, Indian crafts to see, and terrific outdoor small-stage shows featuring Native American storytellers and dancers. The energetic hoop dance is our favorite. We learn something new about the featured tribe every time.

Fiesta Village's rides and shops have a Mexican theme, for the most part. Enter Jaguar, a roller coaster, through a Mayan-styled pyramid temple and experience ancient wonders (and a fun ride!). A dragon, pendulum-type swing ride; a merry-go-round; the hat dance (similar to a spinning teacup ride, only with hats); and Montezuma's Revenge roller coaster are all here, as is La Revolucion with inward-facing passenger seats that rotate and spin, simultaneously.

The **Boardwalk** section has some of the most exciting rides. Go straight up about 250 feet and take a free fall, dropping at faster than 50 mph in the appropriately named Supreme Scream. And this is fun? My boys responded to that question with a resounding, "YES!" Go head over heals (literally) on Rip Tide. Your heart rate will accelerate on the Xcelerator, a 50's-themed roller coaster that both rocks and rolls. The Boomerang coaster zooms riders forward through six loops, and then does it all again, in reverse. Coast Rider has plenty of tracks that zig zag on the top before plunging downward, then up again. For a really great view of the area, go on Sky Cabin, a slowly spinning ride up the tower and gently back down. The Boardwalk also has an arcade and quite a few mid-way games. A favorite venue here is the Charles M. Schulz Theatre, where major entertainers, including Snoopy, perform in extravaganzas. (My favorite are the ice skating shows.)

Kids 2 to 8 years old can spend the whole day in **Camp Snoopy** with its numerous rides and attractions. Many of Snoopy's friends, such as Peppermint Patty, Lucy, and Charlie Brown, are on hand dispensing hugs, along with Snoopy himself. This "camp" has a kiddie roller coaster; a Huff and Puff (kid-powered); Red Baron airplane ride; Charlie Brown's kite flyer (a swing-type ride) with kites caught in trees, of course ; little trucks to ride; a mini-scrambler; Pig Pen's mud buggies (mini ATV's that give a bouncey fun ride); Linus' "blanket" that launches riders ten feet in the air, then around and around; a scaled-down steam train ride; hot-air balloon ride; a rocking tug boat ride; Ferris wheel; a camp bus (with wheels that go round and round); and several other attractions geared just for young Peanut's fans. The Camp Snoopy Theater features the Peanuts Gang in musical performances throughout the day.

There are also many truly terrific educational tours (for students and scouts) available through KNOTT'S ADVENTURES IN EDUCATION (pg. 324). Knott's goes all-out for major holidays in decor and special events, and offers a variety of shows, concerts, and dancing during the summer. Note: Mondays and Tuesdays are the best days to come here as it's usually less crowded. In addition to Knott's Berry Farm's rides, attractions, shops, and eateries, there are several shops and delicious restaurants, including the famous Mrs. Knott's Chicken Dinner Restaurant, directly adjacent to the amusement park. Across the street is a full-size reproduction of INDEPENDENCE HALL (pg. 316) and a water park, KNOTT'S SOAK CITY U.S.A. (See the next entry.)

Hours: It always opens at 10am. Closing times fluctuate between 5pm - 11pm, so call or check the website calendar before you go. Closed Christmas.

Price: $62 for adults; $33 for seniors and ages 3 - 11; children 2 and under are free. Certain discounts available through AAA. Knott's often offers discount tickets online, including some for Southern California residents only, and sometimes admission is discounted after 4pm. Fast Lane passes are an additional $55 - they allow purchasers to bypass the lines to the most popular rides, repeatedly, throughout the day. Parking is $15. The first 3 hours of parking are free, with validation, if you're eating at one of the restaurants, doing some shopping, or visiting Independence Hall.

Ages: All

KNOTT'S SOAK CITY   ☼

(714) 220-5200 / www.soakcityoc.com; www.knotts.com $$$$
8039 Beach Boulevard, across from Knott's Berry Farm, Buena Park

Hang ten at this thirteen-acre water park with a 1950's and early 1960's Southern California beach cities theme. Long boards and surf woodies dot the landscape and surf music plays in the background. Take a spin on Pacific Spin, the gigantic, funnel-looking ride. You'll twist and swirl around in your tube on the wide part as you circle ever closer to the narrow "escape" hole. Some of the other intense rides and attractions include six high-speed slides - lie on your back and let 'er rip; tube rides that range from a little thrilling to hair raising; a relaxing tube ride that circles around a portion of the park in two-and-a-half feet of water; Tidal Wave Bay, where a series of waves roll out into a good-sized "bay" every few minutes for body surfing or boogie boarding; a racing slide (six people side-by-side) that utilizes mats; and two activity areas for kids. The Beach "House" is four stories of hands-on water fun with big, stationary squirt

guns, slides, and a huge bucket that periodically unloads hundreds of gallons of water to deluge everyone below. For younger children, the colorful Gremmie (surfer lingo for "young surfer wannabe") Lagoon is a pint-sized playground with gadgets to squirt, sprinkle, and soak fellow playmates. Climb aboard a submarine in the middle of the lagoon which is covered by an octopus with slides for tentacles. Sit and play on sea turtles and crabs that spurt out water, too.

A few grassy areas and plenty of lounge chairs round out this way cool water park. Hot tip: Wear water shoes or sandals as the walkways get very hot. Note that swimsuits or boardshorts may not have plastic or metal rivets. Rent your own tube for $5. Locker rentals are available for about $5. Full-service food and snack stations abound, of course. Tip: Bring a picnic lunch to enjoy on the grounds of INDEPENDENCE HALL (pg. 316), located just outside the gates.

Hours: Open Memorial Day to mid-June, Mon. - Fri., 10am - 5pm; Sat. - Sun., 10am - 6pm. Open mid-June to mid-August daily, 10am - 7pm. Open mid-August to Labor Day and on weekends through mid-September, 10am - 6pm. Call or check the website first as hours fluctuate.

Price: $36 for adults; $26 for seniors and ages 3 - 11; children 2 and under are free. Admission is often reduced after 3pm. Parking is $15. With proof of residency, Southern Californians often receive a discount.

Ages: 1½ years and up.

—ARTS AND CRAFTS—

COLOR ME MINE (Orange County)

Brea - (714) 671-2808; Costa Mesa - (714) 241-8072; Mission Viejo - (949) 367-9757; Tustin - (714) 505-3975 / www.colormemine.com

Brea - 260 W. Birch St. #5; Costa Mesa - 949 South Coast Dr., suite 103 at Metro Pointe; Mission Viejo - 27741 Crown Valley Pkwy., suite 323 in the Kaleidoscope mall; Tustin - 2931 El Camino Rd. at the Tustin Marketplace

See the entry for COLOR ME MINE (Los Angeles County) on page 7 for details.

Hours: Hours vary at each location. Most open daily at 10am or 11am and close at 9pm - call first.

DRAGONFLY SHOPS AND GARDENS

(714) 289-4689 / www.dragonflyshopsandgardens.com

260 N. Glassell Street, Orange

Amidst the charming shops of Old Towne Orange is a stand out - Dragonfly Shops and Gardens. The shop is in an old Victorian home where each room showcases a different artisans' merchandise, including distinctive gifts for the home, clothing, accessories, gourmet food, jewelry, paintings, collectibles, and more. Outside is a garden bursting with colorful flowers and plants for sale, surrounded by charming and funky statuary, mosaics, and garden art.

Shopping here is gratifying, but for more satisfaction, take one of the many classes offered. For instance, have you ever needed (or wanted) a bracelet, necklace, earrings, or anklet to match an outfit, or just for the fun of it? Make it yourself at the Dragonfly. Need some help in design? The Bead Lady (aka Beth Davidson) holds jewelry workshops and classes for all ages including girl scouts, birthday parties, a get together with friends, etc. She has a plethora of beads to choose from - glass, vintage, seed, crystals, and so much more. From the simple to the elegant, you can make a memorable piece of wearable art and have a delightful time doing it. If you don't mind getting down and dirty, take a potting class with the on-site gardener who helps fashion attractive arrangements in a unique pot or container. A truly enchanting, one-hour class geared for ages 5 to 10 years, is the Fairy Garden workshop. Kids paint a pot and then create a fairy garden complete with plants, mini critters, and fairy dust. The Miniature Garden workshop is similar, just geared for preteens to adults. Decorate a pot, incorporate the plants you want and then add in miniature furniture, accessories, statues and more. I love mine! The Dragonfly also offers classes in making boxes, wire wrapping, mosaic tiling, watercolors, cooking, soap-making, scrapbooking, candles, stamping, designing and making cards (go home with a set of six to eight custom cards!), and so much more. Kids, especially, take note of the Arts & Crafts camps offered in the summer and on school breaks. Note that the Dragonfly is located next to Rutabegorz Restaurant, so combine a class with shopping and a great lunch.

Hours: The store is open Mon. - Sat., 10am - 5pm; Sun., 11am - 4pm(ish). Call or check the website for a schedule and description of classes and workshops.

Price: Fairy Gardens workshops are $25 per person. Miniature Garden workshops start at $10 (and go up, depending on the plants, mini items, etc.). Call about the several types of beading classes and workshops offered, as well as all the other ones.

Ages: 4 years and up.

FIRED UP

(949) 498-3929 / www.firedupsandemente.com $$$$
143 Avenida Granada, San Clemente

Get fired up to paint a unique ceramic piece to give as a gift or make for yourself. This inviting studio, with several round tables and chairs, has a wide selection of items to choose from including boxes, mugs, plates, (mini) surf boards, animals, and seasonal figurines. If you're not sure how to paint your hand-picked item there are books, stamps, stencils, and staff personnel to help ignite your creativity. Finished, glazed, and fired masterpieces may be picked up after a few days. Food and beverages may be brought in. Scouts can earn their ceramics badge here.

Hours: Open Mon. - Thurs., noon - 6pm; Fri., noon - 9pm; Sat. - Sun., noon - 6pm.
Price: There is no studio fee. Prices for your item start at about $15, which includes your time, paint, and glaze.
Ages: 4 years and up.

HIDDEN TALENTS CERAMIC STUDIO

(714) 840-6833 / www.hiddentalentsceramicstudio.com $$$$
16917 Algonquin Street, Suite E, Huntington Beach

Do you have a hidden talent? This small, but airy paint-it-yourself ceramic place could be just the venue to showcase that artistic flair. Walls are lined with shelves holding mugs, vases, figurines, plates, and more, that await your masterful brush strokes and clever designs, or at least some paint. Bring a child or bring a friend and share some time creating memories and a keepsake. Paints, firing, and glazing are included in your price.

One wall is covered with a mural of a mountain, a wizard, and a fairy. This area also has a tiny play area for young children with a dollhouse, toys, and books. Child-size tables are here, too. Ask about classes and summer camps.

Hours: Open most of the year, Tues. - Fri., 11am - 6pm; Sat. - Sun., 11am - 5pm. Closed most Mon., except school holidays and during the summer. Closed on major holidays.
Price: The price of a piece plus a flat studio fee of $8 for adults; $6 for ages 17 and under.
Ages: 4 years and up.

—BEACHES—

ALISO BEACH PARK

(949) 923-2280 or (949) 923-2283 / www.ocparks.com; www.lagunabeachinfo.com $
31131 Pacific Coast Highway, Laguna Beach

You can smell the ocean here! Surrounded by million dollar homes (some are perched on the cliffs overlooking the beach) this beautiful beach in a cove has a wide section of sand dotted with palm trees, tidepools among the rocky promontories that are just around the "corner", and a few fire pits. Part of Aliso Creek empties into a section of this beach, too. The nice, mid-size playground has swings; an elevated sand play area (accessible for wheelchairs); a structure with two towers that has slides, a chain ladder and a short, rock climbing wall. Another component (playship) dubbed Adventure Ship has portholes, talking tubes, climbing apparatus, and more. Note that Aliso Beach Park, one in a series of cove beaches in Laguna Beach, connects with the northern TREASURE ISLAND PARK, which is a walk around the bend over some difficult and rocky terrain. (See page 244.)

Hours: Open daily, 7am - 10pm.
Price: $1 an hour for parking, or catch a (free) ride - see LAGUNA BEACH TRANSIT (page 329).
Ages: All

BALBOA BEACH

(800) 94-COAST (942-6278) / www.visitnewportbeach.com; www.newportbeachca.gov $$
Main Street, Newport Beach

See BALBOA PIER on page 313 for details.

Hours: Open daily.
Price: Parking in the lot is $1.50 per hour; $15 max; $25 on Memorial Day, 4th of July and Labor Day.
Ages: All

BOLSA CHICA STATE BEACH

(714) 846-3460 - beach; (800) 444-7275 - camping reservations / www.parks.ca.gov;
www.beachcalifornia.com; www.stockteam.com

Pacific Coast Highway, between Golden West and Warner Ave., Huntington Beach

There are miles of beach here that are ideal for families because of the picnic areas, outdoor showers, five snack bars, volleyball courts, and beach rentals. The waves can be great (or not). This beach is popular year round because of the fire pits - bring your own wood and even your own barbecue. Tip: Arrive early to save one for a weekend or holiday evening. Dogs are allowed on certain portions of the beach. Camping in self-contained vehicles is allowed, but there are no hook ups. No tent camping is permitted. Check out the adjacent SUNSET BEACH (pg. 243), as well.

Hours: Open daily, 6am - 9pm.
Price: $15 per vehicle. Camping is $65 for a beach-front site, $50 for one in the "back" row.
Ages: All

CORONA DEL MAR STATE BEACH / PIRATES COVE - INSPIRATION POINT

(949) 644-3309 - beach; (949) 723-0798 - Rooster's / www.parks.ca.gov; www.newportbeachca.gov;
www.eatatrooster.com

Marguerite Avenue and Ocean Boulevard, Corona Del Mar

Beside a large, wide parcel of sand and water, the popular Big Corona (as it is known) provides fire rings, picnic tables, and volleyball courts, plus beach equipment rentals and Rooster's Cafe, both open seasonally. Rooster's, open Memorial Day through Labor day, offers two eggs with bacon and hash browns ($6.49); short stack ($5.49); breakfast burrito ($5.95); build-it sandwiches ($6.49); Cobb salad ($8.95); grilled chicken wrap ($7.95); Mexican hot chocolate ($3); and more. A rock jetty forms around one part of the beach and has a cement walkway that reaches out to it.

Avast! **Pirates Cove**, found at the the north end of beach, yields the treasure of waveless waters and some sandstone caves for mateys who climb over and around the rocky hill (which is part of the adventure in and of itself!). Walk around the rocks during low tide, or carefully climb over more of the stony hill, to reach another, very little cove. A small square lawn and picnic area, with BBQs, is almost hidden among the trees in front of Pirate's Cove.

Inspiration Point, located at the south end of the beach, has two worthwhile viewpoints - one along the bluff-top pathway, dotted with benches, that offers a stunning overview of the beach and ocean, and one beach level where you can see for miles. For free beach access from this point, head down to the beach by climbing down a short nature trail or take the steep, cement, ramp.

Check out the tidepools at LITTLE CORONA BEACH (page 241) at the very southern end of Big Corona.

Hours: Open daily, 6am - 10pm.
Price: Some free parking can be found on Ocean Blvd., just beware that you must hike down a bit (and then back up) on steep ramps to access the beach. The parking lot costs $15 a day; $25 on peak holidays.
Ages: All

CRYSTAL COVE STATE PARK

E. Coast Highway, between Laguna Beach and Newport Beach, Laguna Beach

See the entry for CRYSTAL COVE STATE PARK on page 274 for details.

DANA COVE PARK, "BABY BEACH" and TIDEPOOLS

(949) 248-3500 or (949) 923-2280 / www.danapoint.org

Dana Point Harbor Drive by Cove Rd., Dana Point

The protected harbor of "Baby Beach" (called so because of its waveless waters) offers picnic tables on the bluffs, plus barbecues, free parking, showers, and lifeguards. Check for water quality first, however, at (800) 432-5229 or www.healthebay.org or www.ocbeachinfo.com, as this beach has had a history of problems. A good tidepool area is just around the "corner." See DANA POINT HARBOR (pg. 313, 765), DOHENY STATE BEACH PARK (pg. 240), and the OCEAN INSTITUTE (pg. 309) for more details about the surrounding area.

Hours: Open daily, sunrise - sunset.
Price: Free
Ages: All

DOHENY STATE BEACH PARK

(949) 496-6172 - beach; (800) 444-7275 - camping reservations / www.dohenystatebeach.org;
www.beachcalifornia.com

25300 Dana Point Harbor Drive, Dana Point

Doheny State Beach Park is big and absolutely gorgeous. Towards the entrance is an Interpretative Center with a few interactive displays and a small aquarium with fish tanks and a tidepool, all with an underwater motif. The park is divided into three parts. The northern area, also accessible by metered parking off Puerto Place, is for day use. It is five acres of grassy, landscaped picnic area, with barbecue grills and fire rings along the beach. The adjacent butterfly garden is a delight. Walk through the wooden entrance frame with huge butterflies (additionally marked with a large sign) on a gravel trail. Each fall the Monarch butterflies roost and hibernate here, ultimately on their way to migrating south. A small picnic area is inside. The rocky area is ideal for tidepool exploration during low tide. Since DANA POINT HARBOR (pg. 313, 765) is right next door, this is also a perfect spot to watch the boats sail in and out.

The central section, south of the San Juan Creek, is a campground with 118 sites. Farther south is another day use area with fire rings, beach volleyball, and showers. Throughout the entire stretch of the park there are sandy beaches and beckoning ocean waves! Word of caution: Check for water quality first, at (800) 432-5229 or www.healthebay.org, as this beach has had a history of problems. Check out the nearby OCEAN INSTITUTE (pg. 309).

Hours: The park is open daily, 6am - 10pm.
Price: $15 per vehicle for day use; $14 for seniors. Admission to the Interpretative Center is free. Camping prices are $35 - $60, depending on campsite location. The camping reservation fee is $8.
Ages: All

HUNTINGTON CITY BEACH

(714) 536-9303 - recorded beach info; (714) 536-5281; (714) 733-3167 - Surf City Nights /
www.hbonline.com; www.ci.huntington-beach.ca.us; www.stockteam.com

Pacific Coast Highway at the end of Main St., Huntington Beach

The combined beaches of Huntington Beach (both the city and connecting state beach), known as Surf City USA, have waves; about eight miles total of long and wide sandy beach; thirty public volleyball nets (as competition games are played here, too) - bring your own ball or rent one; fire pits; and one of the longest concrete piers in California, with a RUBY'S restaurant (see pg. 252) at its end. The Kite Connection is a well-known kite shop located on the pier. You can also make use of the bait and tackle shop on the pier and fish off the pier's sides.

The Strand is a very popular, almost nine miles of paved biking, jogging, and blading pathway that hugs this same span of coastline, as it expands north from Warner Boulevard at Sunset Beach to south on Brookhurst Boulevard almost into Newport Beach. Several of the parking lot entrances have Beach Cafes that offer food, snacks, and beach rental equipment, including bikes, seasonally. Tip: Always check for the water quality before you visit. Top-rated surfing, skateboard, volleyball, and BMX competitions are held here in the summer. A plethora of funky and fun shops and restaurants await you just across the street on Main Street. Surf City Nights, a great weekly street fair, art fair, and Farmers Market, is held on Main Street every Tuesday night from 5pm to 9pm. A Farmer's Market is held here on Fridays, noon to 5pm.

This is a preferred beach, year round, for beach bonfires - bring your own wood and lighter. Arrive early to claim a pit on weekends and holidays, especially during the summer.

Hours: Usually open daily, 6am - 10pm. Winter hours can fluctuate.
Price: The lots near the pier are $1.50 per hour; $15 all day. Parking on the 4th of July is $27. The southern state beach lots are usually $10 per vehicle. There is some metered parking available, too.
Ages: All

HUNTINGTON STATE BEACH

(714) 536-1454 / www.parks.ca.gov; www.beachcalifornia.com; www.stockteam.com

Pacific Coast Highway, Huntington Beach

See the above entry for detailed information on this renown beach which is just south of the city beach. Note: We have found the Magnolia Street entrance to be one of the few open during "off" season.

Hours: Open daily, 6am - 9pm.
Price: $15 per vehicle. There are parking lots are off Brookhurst, Magnolia, Newland, and other streets.
Ages: All

LITTLE CORONA DEL MAR BEACH and TIDEPOOL TOURS   ☼

(949) 644-3151 - beach info; (949) 644-3038 - tidepool reservations / www.parks.ca.gov; $$$
www.city.newport-beach.ca.us

On Poppy Avenue and Ocean Avenue, Corona Del Mar

Come for a few hours to explore some of the best tidepools in Southern California, then spend the rest of the day playing at the adjacent beach. It's a great kids' hangout! Tidepools are a rich natural resource and a fascinating way to learn about marine life. You are welcome to investigate the tidepools on your own, or sign up for a two-and-a-half-hour guided tour. After giving a short lecture, tour guides are helpful in pointing out interesting animal and plant life. Age-appropriate curriculum is sent to classrooms beforehand. Tours are given to groups of up to thirty people. See CORONA DEL MAR STATE BEACH in this section (page 239) for more info on the big beach just a short drive away.

Hours: Open daily, 6am - 10pm. Guided tidepool tours are given by reservations only.
Price: $15 per vehicle. There is some free street parking if you just want to go tidepool exploring. Tidepool tours are $69 per group.
Ages: 3 years and up.

MAIN BEACH / HEISLER PARK   ☼

(949) 497-0706 / www.lagunabeachcity.net; www.lagunapages.com $
Cliff Drive and Myrtle Street at Pacific Coast Highway, Laguna Beach

I mention this park and beach together because they are on either side of Highway 133/Broadway Street. Both are incredibly popular (i.e., crowded) and noted for their unparalleled views of the ocean. The water is clear, and the horizon seems to go on forever.

Heisler Park offers a paved, picturesque (palm trees, flowers, etc.) walkway along the cliff top, plus benches, picnic tables, and a small grassy area with a few fun climbing trees all overlooking the beach and horizon. The cove beaches below, namely Diver's Beach, Picnic Beach, and Rockpile Beach, have stairs access at several points, as well as a ramp access. A few spots are more rock than beach, so there is some great tidepooling here, too.

The large and wide Main Beach, adjoining Sleep Hollow Beach, offers (besides the beach) a few, decent-sized grass expanses along with two, half basketball courts; several sand volleyball courts with nets; a few barbecues pits and picnic tables; and a short boardwalk that parallels the shoreline. A small, older-looking playground is at one end as is a colorful, cement and mosaic table inlaid with chess/checkers squares, and the same-style chairs. Rock jetties and tidepools add to a day of fun and exploration.

This nice stretch of sand is lined with houses and condos on one side, and is just across the street from the heart of Laguna Beach with its variety of restaurants and shops, including Main Beach Toy store that offers beach rentals. All in all, these are good places for beaching it and for swimming. Good luck finding a parking spot, though!

Hours: Both are open daily, sunrise - sunset.
Price: Free. Most parking is metered, at 25¢ per 15 minutes or catch a (free) ride - see LAGUNA BEACH TRANSIT (page 329).
Ages: All

NEWPORT DUNES WATERFRONT RESORT MARINA   ☼

(800) 765-7661 or (949) 729-3863 / www.newportdunes.com $$$
1131 Backbay Drive, Newport Beach

Toddlers to teens enjoy the enclosed acres of clean beach here, along with a waveless lagoon and a myriad of boating activities. There is a large fiberglass, stationary whale, nicknamed Moe B. Dunes, in the water for kids to swim out to, and another one on the beach. The playground equipment includes a pirate ship to climb aboard - ahoy mateys! Outdoor showers are also available.

Remember the joys of collecting seashells? Newport Dunes is one of the rare beaches around that still has shells. Note: Shellmaker Island and NEWPORT BAY CONSERVANCY (pg. 285) are adjacent to the resort marina.

Make sure you check out MOE B'S WATERSPORTS (pg. 330), located across the water in the park, for your kayaking, pedalboat, electric boat, and windsurfing needs, and for info on the Water Playground.

If you forget to bring food, have no fear of a growling tummy as a grocery store and the Back Bay Bistro, (949) 729-1144, are inside the gates, just around the corner from the beach. The Bistro offers California-style cuisine for breakfast, lunch, and dinner, with indoor or outdoor seating that overlooks the water.

Overnight camping is available and there are plenty of RV hookups; some on the waterfront. There are a few

spaces for free-standing (i.e., no stakes) tent camping, too. Cottages, with kitchens, are available as well. The surroundings are pretty; activities for campers, such as crafts, ice cream socials, and free, family-friendly movie showings on a large inflatable screen (May through September on weekend nights for campers and the public) are offered; and the Dunes has a swimming pool, indoor showers, and laundry facilities. What more could you want out of life? This local resort is my kind of "roughing it" vacation!

Hours: Open daily, 8am - 10pm.
Price: Day parking is $16. Camping prices/small RV sites start at $64 a night during the winter and $99 a night during the summer, depending on location and camping equipment. Studio "camping" cottages start at $90 in the winter; $175 in the summer.
Ages: All

NEWPORT MUNICIPAL BEACH

(800) 94-COAST (942-6278); (949) 644-3309 / www.visitnewportbeach.com; www.beachcalifornia.com
Balboa Boulevard at Oceanfront and 21st, Newport Beach

This fine, five-mile stretch of clean sandy beach offers plenty of summer fun for swimmers, surfers (near the jetty), and sunbathers. Walk out onto the pier and/or bring your fishing pole to catch a meal. If you don't have success, catch something fresh on weekends around 7am to 9am at Dory Fleet Market, located at the base of the pier. Fresh fish and crab are hauled in and sold by local fishermen at this open air market. Contact (949) 632-5939 / www.doryfleet.com for more details.

Tired of lying around? Walk or ride the bike path, which goes around most of the peninsula. Bike, skate, and board shop rentals are available, too, plus there quite a few retail shops and restaurants close by.

Hours: Open daily, 6am - 10pm.
Price: Parking in the lot is $1.50 per hour; $15 max; $25 on Memorial Day, 4th of July and Labor Day.
Ages: All

NORTH BEACH

(949) 361-8200 - beach; (949) 361-3811- Kahuna's Grill / www.san-clemente.org
Pacific Coast Highway and Avenida Pico, San Clemente

Cross over the train tracks to reach this not too large and sometimes pebbly stretch of beach, which is north (of course) of the city beach and pier. Amenities, besides the main attraction of sand and water, are a playground, a fire ring, Kahuna's Grill, a railroad, and the ending/beginning point of the 2.6 mile, one-way, flat, San Clemente Beach Trail that parallels the coastline down to the State Beach and Calafia Beach Park (see those separate entries).

Hours: Open 4am - midnight
Price: Free. Metered parking in the lot is $1.50 an hour from 9am - 6pm.
Ages: All

SALT CREEK BEACH

(949) 923-2280 / www.ocparks.com; www.beachcalifornia.com
33333 S. Pacific Coast Highway, Dana Point

Way cool beach! Walk along the street (good for strollers and wheelchairs) through the underpass to reach the park/beach. The grassy, seven acre hillside, called Bluff Park, is spotted with some shade trees and picnic tables with an amazing view from the top of the Pacific Ocean and beyond. This park area also boasts a half basketball court and fire pits. The seasonal snack stand sells cheeseburgers, chili, quesadillas, and Hawaiian shaved ice.

The wide and long expanse of beach is clean, has rocky promontories, a lifeguard in the summer, tidepools to the south, and a bike path to the north that runs parallel to the ocean. Surfing is good here (so I'm told).

Hours: The parking lot is open 5am - midnight.
Price: Parking is $1 an hour.
Ages: All

SAN CLEMENTE CITY BEACH and MUNICIPAL PIER

(949) 361-8200 or (949) 276-8866 / www.san-clemente.org; www.beachcalifornia.com
Avenida Del Mar and Avenida Victoria, San Clemente

This beach, itself, is a two-mile long, narrow strip of sand on either side of the pier, dotted with palm trees and a few, scattered picnic tables. It is bordered by the sea on one side and train tracks that run parallel to the water on the other. (An Amtrak station is here, too.) Amenities include a few pieces of play equipment, a restroom, fire pits,

volleyball courts, and the Fisherman's Restaurant, in case you don't catch any of your own lunch or dinner off the pier. This beach is also the center point for the 2.6 mile (one-way), hard-packed dirt, San Clemente Beach Trail - go south to the State Beach and Calafia Beach Park or head north to North Beach (see those separate entries). The scenic, flat trail follows the coastline. I have to admit I'm partial to the antique and other fun stores and restaurants that line Avenida Del Mar, too.

Hours: Open daily, 4am - midnight.
Price: Free. Parking is $1.50 an hour at metered spots.
Ages: All

SAN CLEMENTE STATE BEACH / CALAFIA BEACH PARK

(949) 492-3156 / www.parks.ca.gov; www.beachcalifornia.com
225 and 250 Avenida Calafia, San Clemente

This adjacent beaches, located mostly under steep cliffs, offers swimming and sand, in addition to the 2.6 mile (one-way), hard-packed dirt, San Clemente Beach Trail (the entrance is marked by the Calafia Park Trail head placard) that heads north to City Beach and North Beach (see those separate entries) while hugging the coast line, so it's a lovely trek. Each tent and RV camp site here, open year round, has a fire ring and picnic table. Railroad tracks parallel the beach. Carefully explore some of the water-carved caves and pathways along the beach, too. Ask about the educational programs offered and/or guided hikes.

Scheppy's at the Beach, which is opened seasonally, offers grilled food and beach rentals.

Hours: Open most of the year daily, 6am - 8pm; open in the summer daily, 6am - 10pm.
Price: $15 per vehicle. Camping is $35 for tent; $60 for hook-ups.
Ages: All

SEAL BEACH

(562) 430-2613 - lifeguard station / www.ci.seal-beach.ca.us; www.beachcalifornia.com
the end of Main Street, W. of PCH, Seal Beach

This beach is one of my local favorites. It has lifeguards, the second longest pier in California, great swimming, and a playground with swings and slides. My kids love to gather the crabs crawling along the pier wall and put them in buckets. (We let them go before we go home.) Take a walk on the pier as the coastline view is terrific. No license is required for fishing off the pier and bait is available to purchase.

Directly across the street from the beach is Main Street, which is lined with unique shops and restaurants from casual to upscale, plus a few ice cream stores.

Hours: Open daily, sunrise - sunset.
Price: Park along the street or in a nearby lot for $3 for two hours; or pay a $6 entrance fee for the day at the parking lot at the beach.
Ages: All

SUNSET BEACH

(949) 923-2290 or (949) 923-2295 / www.ocparks.com; www.beachcalifornia.com
Pacific Coast Highway at the intersection of Warner Avenue, Sunset Beach

Sandwiched between BOLSA CHICA STATE BEACH (pg. 239) and SEAL BEACH (pg. 243), is a great stretch of sand. We frequent this beach often as it offers (limited) free parking, it has lifeguard stations, restrooms, outdoor showers, generally decent waves for boogie boarding and surfing, and it's a short walk to the fire pits at Bolsa Chica. Although I'm usually good about bringing food to the beach, the Jack-in-the-Box is very convenient.

Hours: Open daily, 7am - 10pm
Price: Free
Ages: All

THOUSAND STEPS BEACH

(949) 661-7013 / www.lagunabeachcity.net
Pacific Coast Highway and 9th Street, Laguna Beach

Not sure if you're in or out of shape? Come find out! Although there is actually only 227 steep, cement steps down to the beach, it can feel like 1,000 coming up! The beach itself is scenic (and romantic), so you could just enjoy a day of water and sand and staring at the beauty. There is also a volleyball court here. Look up to see magnificent mansions on the bluffs - I love the ones with private elevators built into the hillside.

If you head to the left from the stairs, past the abandoned building, you'll reach rocks and tidepools, and the best thing - a good-sized sea cave. Exploring this, in low tide, is a fun and memorable adventure. We stayed for sunset and got awesome photos. Note that coastal access sign is easy to miss.

Hours: Open daily, 6am - 10pm.
Price: Free
Ages: 5 years and up - the stairs are tough.

TREASURE ISLAND PARK - BEACH

(949) 497-3311 - city hall; (866) 271-6953 - Montage resort / www.lagunabeachinfo.com
30801 South Coast Highway, Laguna Beach

Not buried, but a little hidden, the scenic and beautiful Treasure Beach is accessed and viewed from the utterly lovely landscaped cement pathway that gently winds around the cliff top in front of the gorgeous Montage resort. Enjoy the stroll, or sit on one of the numerous benches up top to gaze at unforgettable panoramas. Flowers, palm trees, cactus, and other plants cover the hillside and line the several stair access points leading down to the beach. A ramp is available, too. Go down to one of several coves and enjoy sweet stretches of beach, dotted with juts of rocks, where swimming and snorkeling are popular in the blue/green waters. A few tidepool areas are here, too. Note that this a marine reserve so look, but don't touch.

This beach is also accessed (although it's a difficult passage through water and over rocks) by the southern, adjoining ALISO BEACH PARK. (See page 238 for details.)

Hours: Open daily, 8am - 7pm.
Price: Parking at the Montage Resort off Wesley into very small underground lot is $1.50 an hour with a 3 hour limit. There is also metered street parking. Or, catch a (free) ride - see LAGUNA BEACH TRANSIT (page 329).
Ages: All

—EDIBLE ADVENTURES

ANGELO'S AND VINCI'S RISTORANTE

(714) 879-4022 / www.angelosandvincis.com
550 N. Harbor Boulevard, Fullerton

$$$

Attenzione - this ristorante and full bar not only bears the names of two of Italy's finest artists, but the cuisine and atmosphere are sure to please any *palette*. The dimly lit restaurant creates a cozy ambiance by its eclectic decor packed around a main square room and upstairs mezzanine. Look up to see recreated Italian marketplace stalls along the walls. The fruit store, meat market, wine shop, etc., display realistic-looking fruit, hanging sausages, jars of pasta, hanging grapes and grapevines, and more, all with toddler-sized dolls dressed as merchants. There are also small knights in shining armor, framed art work, angel mannequins, signs, posters of the Mona Lisa, banners, a doll-sized stage, and bottles of wine all around, as well as trapeze figures and white Christmas lights suspended from the ceiling - always something to keep one's attention. A chapel wall holds statues, including a replica of the David, and old family photographs. There are a few uniquely decorated banquet rooms at the restaurant, too. Take a quick peek, if you want, at the small basement/dungeon with its display of monsters, such as Dracula and Frankenstein.

Luncheon menu specialties include Old World-tasting pizza with a huge variety of toppings ($17.95 to $22.95 for a medium), extra large calzone ($17.25), spaghetti (average $8), ciccaglione ($8.50), and linguini and clams ($10.50), plus chicken, shrimp, salads, and more. There isn't a children's menu, but young ones can easily share a meal. The all-you-can-eat buffet lunch is $8.50 for adults and $4.95 for ages 9 and under during the week for chicken wings, pasta Alfredo, spaghetti, lasagna, salad, soup, breads, and more. The brunch buffet on Sunday is $13.95 and includes all the aforementioned food choices, plus an omelet bar, chocolate fondue station and champagne.

Hours: Open Sun. - Thurs., 11am - 9pm; Fri. - Sat., 11am - 10pm. Closed Thanksgiving and Christmas.
Price: See menu prices above.
Ages: All

BENIHANA OF TOKYO (Orange County)

Anaheim - (714) 774-4940; Newport Beach - (949) 955-0822 / www.benihana.com
Anaheim - 2100 E. Ball Road; Newport Beach - 4250 Birch Street

$$$$

See the entry for BENIHANA OF TOKYO (Los Angeles County) on page 14 for details.

BREWBAKERS - ROOT BEER BREWING AND PRETZEL PARTY

(714) 596-5506 / www.brewbakers1.com

7242 Heil Avenue, Huntington Beach

This small microbrewery and bread shop with a bar-like atmosphere knows what's brewing. Stop by for freshly-made yummy pretzels ($1.25 per), pizza ($17.50 for a large), and sandwiches ($4.75 for a bratwurst or cheeseburger wrapped in cooked pretzel dough), as well as a variety of fresh bread (sourdough, Irish soda, chocolate, and more), pretzel bun rolls, and even scones.

I think the real fun is in having a party here and brewing your own batch of root beer. (Yes, adults can brew their own "real" beer here, too.) The vats around the perimeter of the room with tubing make it look like a fun laboratory. Each person in the group of at least six and no more than thirty, first creates a customized group label. (This can be submitted to Brewbakers prior to your visit.) Then, you roll out, twist, and design your own pretzel, so it is baking while you make your root beer. After combining the root beer ingredients and rolling the cannister around on the ground for a while to mix them all together, while singing "roll out the barrels", you use a bottling machine to fill up the allotted two bottles per person. Cap and label your bottles. By this time, the pretzels are finished baking, so sit at a table and enjoy your scrumptious, doughy pretzel while sipping truly delicious root beer. The whole process takes about ninety minutes and is a fun, educational, and flavorful outing. You can order a pizza, or two, to make a meal out of your party.

You can also brew your own other kind of sodas, too (or even lemonade) - cola, orange creme, cream soda, or a customized flavor - for $65 for two cases, which makes twenty-four, twenty-two ounce bottles.

> **Hours:** Open Tues - Sat., 11am - 9pm (last brewing appointment at 7pm); Sun., noon - 6pm. Closed Mon. and holidays.
>
> **Price:** The root beer brewing parties (2 root beers and a pretzel) are $9.75 per person; $12.50 if including a pizza.
>
> **Ages:** 6 years and up.

BUCA DI BEPPO (Orange County)

(866) EAT BUCA (328-2822) for all locations; Brea - (714) 529-6262; Garden Grove - (714) 740-2822; Huntington Beach - (714) 891-4666; Irvine - (714) 665-0800 / www.bucadibeppo.com

Brea - 1609 East Imperial Hwy.; Garden Grove - 11757 Harbor Blvd.; Huntington Beach - 7979 Center Ave.; Irvine - 13390 Jamboree Rd.

See BUCA DI BEPPO (Los Angeles County) on page 14 for details.

CHIP 'N DALE BREAKFAST AT STORYTELLER'S CAFE

(714) 956-6755 or (714) 781-DINE (3463) / www.disneyland.com; www.wdinfo.com

1600 Disneyland Drive at Storytellers Cafe in the Grand Californian Hotel, Anaheim

Which one is Chip and which one is Dale? Only kids know for sure. The two chipmunks, often accompanied by Pluto or another Disney character, walk around to greet each guest at this special breakfast, sign autographs, lead in sing-alongs, and hug (or high five) little guests. Order the buffet, which consists of a variety of egg dishes, sausages, fresh bakery items, fruit, and juice, or order a la cart. Menu choices include two eggs any style, served with country potatoes, ham/sausage or bacon, fresh fruit and toast - $18.99; eggs Benedict - $17.99; and Mickey-shaped waffles - $17.59. A Farmer's Market buffet comes with fruit, omelets, home-style breakfast, and bakery goods for $27.99. From the kid's menu a scrambled egg with potatoes, fruit and yogurt is $7.49 and chicken nuggets with fruit is $12.99.

The restaurant is done up in turn-of-the-century style and decorated with storytelling murals. Ask your server to tell you a few of the stories. Visit the adjacent DOWNTOWN DISNEY (pg. 314) for more fun things to do and see. DISNEYLAND (pg. 232) and CALIFORNIA ADVENTURE (pg. 230) are just next door. Tip: You can park at Downtown Disney for 3 hours for free.

> **Hours:** Open Mon. - Fri., 7:30am - 11am; Sat. - Sun., 7am - 11am. Reservations are highly recommended.
>
> **Price:** The buffet is $27.99 for adults; $12.99 for ages 3 - 9; children 2 and under eat for free. Other menu items are available.
>
> **Ages:** All

CHUCK E. CHEESE'S (Orange County)

See the entry for CHUCK E. CHEESE'S (Los Angeles County) on page 16 for details.

ESPN ZONE
(714) 300-ESPN(3776) / www.espnzone.com; www.wdinfo.com   ☀
1545 Disneyland Drive at Downtown Disney, Anaheim $$$$

I took my kids to the ESPN Zone. Now, I got game! This place is a must for sports fans of all ages. Live radio broadcasts that visitors are welcome to watch (and maybe become part of) happen occasionally in the studio inside the entrance. This is one of the many features that makes ESPN Zone unique. The majority of the downstairs is a restaurant. One side features a sixteen-foot digital television screen that dominates a wall, surrounded by twelve other screens showing various sporting events. The booths in here have their own screen on the table with capabilities to change channels (sports channels only) and volume. The sound is heard through a system that wraps around the inside of the booth. Recliner chair occupants get front-row viewing with their own personal sound system. There is a full bar in this section. Check out the wall sculpture of an athlete made from sand.

The other restaurant side features more television screens, of course. Note: There are over sixty-five throughout the Zone, including in the bathrooms, so you don't miss a moment of action! This section also features slightly elevated newscasting areas, where actual broadcasts take place. You could be part of the local affiliate audience. Call about events. The food, which is very tasty American grill, got two thumbs up from my kids - they cleaned their plates. The menu includes buffalo wings ($10.99); cheese fries; grilled chicken Caesar salad ($14.99); baby back back back ribs ($25.99); salmon ($19.99); hamburgers ($10.99); pasta ($11.99); and New York strip ($27.99). The children's menu offers a choice of mac and cheese, burger, chicken breast nuggets, or grilled cheese sandwich, plus carrot sticks or apple wedges, and a beverage for $7.99. Ordering over the din of the televisions is a fun challenge - talk about kids getting distracted! But it's worth it. Note that it gets very crowded and lively here during any play off or major sporting event.

Upstairs is the sports arena, or games area, which you are welcome to visit without eating at the restaurant. Purchase a "credit card" in any monetary increment worth a certain amount of points. Slide it into whatever game you want to play and that game's point value will be deducted. For instance, air hockey "costs" eight points; bowling, sixteen points; wave runners are eight points, and so on. All the games are sports themed. Knock down pins at the two, forty-five-feet bowling lanes using heavy mini balls. The score is kept electronically for you. Test your slapshot in a small enclosed hockey area where you shoot pucks at a life-size metal goalie that moves back and forth. Another player (i.e., a friend) can pay and stand outside, behind you, and make the goalie move by pulling on a lever. Throw a football through metal receivers with holes for arms (which seems just like a real receiver's arms sometimes!) as they move back and forth. Use a pole and reel to land an on-screen marlin, or another big one, in a specially designed fishing chair. Shoot some hoops (ten points). Put up your dukes and MoCap Box with a virtual opponent by jabbing the air toward him and physically moving to dodge punches. A motion capture system guides you in your endeavors to become the champ. Other interactive games, and most incorporate "playing" against a screen, involve shooting at targets, becoming a jockey on a mechanical horse (this is funny to watch), skateboarding, swinging a golf club, Daytona racing, NFL 2 Minute Drill, and Stomper DLX - games to stomp around, including a dance contest. And once again, you are never far from the TV action in the sports center. Note that not all of the games are open in the daytime.

The Zone has an attached gift shop. After or before your visit, take some time to walk around DOWNTOWN DISNEY (pg. 314).

Hours: Open Sun. - Thurs., 11am - 11pm; Fri. - Sat., 11am - midnight.
Price: Menu prices for food are listed above. Cards for the sports arena cost, for instance, $20 for ninety points.
Ages: 5 years and up.

FARMER'S MARKETS (Orange County)
See the entry for FARMER'S MARKETS (Los Angeles County) on pg. 18 for details. I will have to mention three markets here because they are good, fun, and good and fun for kids. Admission is free to all of them. The **Fullerton Market** (www.cityoffullerton.com) offers farm-fresh produce, flowers, fresh-baked breads, and live entertainment, plus arts and crafts and other activities for children. The market is open on Thursdays, 4pm to 8:30pm, April thru October. It's located on Wilshire Ave., between Harbor Blvd. and Pomona Ave., right next to the Fullerton Museum Center, which offers $2 off admission during market hours on the first Thurs. of the month. **Farmer's Market at Orange County Great Park** (www.ocgp.org) is held every Sunday, 10am to 2pm with artesians bringing fresh bread, fruit, veggies and other goodies. To uninterruptedly enjoy everything else that the park has to offer (see pg. 287 for more details), purchase breakfast and/or lunch here. The Groves Antique Market is also held here on the first Sunday of every month, so the Farmers Market opens early then, at 8am. **Surf City Nights Street Fair and**

Farmers Market in Huntington Beach (www.hbdowntown.com) on Main St., between Orange and Pacific Coast Highway, is held every Tuesday night, 5pm to 9pm. Just down the street from the beach and pier are booths with fresh produce plus all kinds of street vendors with food, jewelry, art, clothing, and live music, plus bounce houses, and kiddie train.

FARRELL'S ICE CREAM PARLOUR RESTAURANTS (Orange County)

Brea - (714) 990-4FUN (4386); Buena Park - (714) 484-9700; Mission Viejo - (949) 364-5411 / www.farrellsusa.com

$$$

Brea - 215 S. Brea Blvd; Buena Park - 8650 Beach Blvd.; Mission Viejo - 799 The Shops at Mission Viejo Blvd.

This resurrected restaurant, with several other locations throughout Southern California, has a wholesome, fun, and patriotic atmosphere, just like the "old" Farrell's from the 70's and 80's. Actually, Farrell's is designed to be older than that as it recreates an ice cream parlour of 100 years ago with music from that era playing on a player piano, American flags all around, and servers dressed in pin-striped vests, old fashioned ties and cane hats. The menu is printed on newspaper type and features hamburgers (average $12); club, Philly cheese steak, buffalo chicken, and other sandwiches (average $12.50); 10" wood-fired pizzas (average $13); and a variety of salads (average $11). Kids' meals are $7.49 for a choice of grilled cheese, hot dog, hamburger, pizza, mac and cheese, or chicken nuggets accompanied by a beverage and fries or fresh fruit.

Farrell's real speciality, though, is desserts and they offer a slew of them. One favorite is the Trough ($13.99) which is two banana splits piled high with goodies, eaten from a trough as the waiter exclaims, "This person made a pig of himself at Farrell's." A Zoo ($59.99) feeds up to ten people with four flavors of ice cream, three scoops of sherbet, and four toppings like whipped cream, cherries, nuts and bananas. The Zoo is delivered to the table with a lot of fanfare, sometimes with musical accompaniment by the player piano. There are, of course, single-serving choices such as a Tin Roof ($7.89), shakes ($5.29), and the fake chicken dinner - ask your server for this without the kids around ($5.49). Child-sized desserts are $2.99 for a shake or float, and $3.49 for the special down sundae (with an upside down cone hat). This is a great place for a birthday party. If not for a party, then know that you get a special sundae for free on your birthday, with proof provided. Good luck getting the kids past the tempting candy counter towards the front!

The Brea location is extra big (with an extra big candy section) and it has a walk-up window along Birch Street to order Farrell's ice cream treats and food. The Mission Viejo location is in The Shops at Mission Viejo mall, so see page 297 for more to do here. The Buena Park location is down the street from Knott's Berry Farm and other attractions on Beach Blvd.

Hours: Hours vary from store to store. Most are open Sun. - Thurs., 11am - 10pm; Fri. - Sat., 11am -11pm. Closed at 7pm on Christmas Eve and closed all day Christmas.

Price: Prices are listed above, though some prices might fluctuate in different restaurants.

Ages: All

GOOFY'S KITCHEN

(714) 956-6755 or (714) 781-DINE (3463) / www.disneyland.com; www.wdinfo.com

$$$$$

1150 Magic Way at the Disneyland Hotel, Anaheim

This all-you-can-eat brunch or dinner buffet is described as "character dining." I'm still not sure if the "character" reference refers to Disney characters or to my children! Your kids favorites come by the tables for a hug. We were visited by Pluto, Minnie Mouse, Chip (or was it Dale?), John Smith, Miko and, of course, Goofy. Kids even eat a bite or two in between hopping up to touch the costumed characters. Remember to bring your camera (and your autograph book)!

The brunch buffet includes an array of delicious foods such as omelets made any way you like 'em (my boys considered watching the cook make omelets part of the entertainment), salads, fruit, vegetables, pastas, chicken, barbecue beef ribs, Mickey-shaped waffles, pancakes, home fries, cereal, oatmeal, yogurt with toppings, omelets, and peanut butter and jelly pizza.

We stuffed ourselves at the dinner buffet with prime rib, ham, chicken, seafood, fruit, salad, and scrumptious desserts. (The way my family suffers just to be able to share with you!) The kids have their own food bar that offers familiar favorites like macaroni and cheese, mini-hotdogs, spaghetti, breaded shrimp, and chicken strips.

Goofy's Kitchen offers good food in a fun, family atmosphere. Make your outing even more of a treat by coming early, or staying after mealtime, to walk around and enjoy the hotel grounds. Visit the adjacent DOWNTOWN DISNEY (pg. 314) for more fun things to do and see. DISNEYLAND (pg. 232) and CALIFORNIA ADVENTURE (pg. 230) are just next door.

Hours: Open Mon. - Fri., 7am - noon; Sat. - Sun., 7am - 1:30pm. Open daily for dinner, 5pm - 9pm.
Price: Brunch buffet is $31 for adults; the dinner buffet is $37 for adults. Each buffet is $16 for ages 3 - 9; children 2 and under eat for free. Parking is free for the first three hours, with validation.
Ages: 1½ years and up.

GYU-KAKU (Orange County)

Brea - (714) 671-9378; Huntington Beach - (714) 842-8333; Tustin - (714) 731-1719 / www.gyu-kaku.com $$$$
Brea - 120 S. Brea Blvd., #1; Huntington Beach - 7862 Warner Ave., #109; Tustin - 14181 Newport Ave.

See the entry for GYU-KAKU (Los Angeles County) on page 20 for information on this grill-it-yourself restaurant.
Hours: Brea is open Mon. - Thurs., 5pm - 10:30pm; Fri. - Sat., 5pm - 11:30pm; Sun., 5pm - 10pm. Huntington Beach and Tustin are open Mon. - Thurs., 11:30am - 10:30pm; Fri. - Sat., 11:30am - 11:30pm; Sun., 11:30am - 10:30pm (9:30pm for Tustin).

HOUSE OF BLUES GOSPEL BRUNCH (Orange County)

(714) 778-BLUE (2583) / www.houseofblues.com $$$$$
1530 S. Disneyland Drive at the House of Blues at Downtown Disney, Anaheim

See the entry for HOUSE OF BLUES GOSPEL BRUNCH (Los Angeles County) on page 21 for details. This location's menu selection is still tasty, just more limited than the one in Hollywood. Also, the Anaheim building doesn't resemble a shack and it is located in DOWNTOWN DISNEY. (See pg. 314.) Look up BLUES SCHOOLHOUSE (Orange County) on page 314 for information about a history of the blues presentation for students.
Hours: Gospel Brunch is every other Sunday (usually the second and fourth Sunday) at 11am. Get here earlier. Ask about holiday Sun., such as Easter and Mother's Day.
Price: $40 for ages 10 and up; $18.50 for ages 3 - 9; children 2 and under are free.
Ages: 5 years and up.

JOE'S CRAB SHACK (Orange County)

Garden Grove - (714) 703-0505; Newport Beach - (949) 650-1818 / www.joescrabshack.com $$$
Garden Grove - 12011 Harbor Blvd.; Newport Beach - 2607 W. Coast Hwy.

See the entry for JOE'S CRAB SHACK (Los Angeles County) on page 22 for details.

JOHNNY REBS' SOUTHERN ROADHOUSE (Orange County)

(714) 633-3369 / www.johnnyrebs.com $$$
2940 E. Chapman Avenue, Orange

See the entry for JOHNNY REBS' SOUTHERN ROADHOUSE (Los Angeles County) on page 22 for details. This location's building looks like an authentic ramshackle shack, complete with a corrugated tin roof. The enclosed patio's lampshades are tin buckets with holes, which just add to the down and out old Southern atmosphere.
Hours: Open Sun. - Thurs., 7am - 9pm; Fri. - Sat, 7am - 10pm.

JOHN'S INCREDIBLE PIZZA CO. (Orange County)

(714) 236-0000 / www.johnspizza.com $$$$
8601 On the Mall, Buena Park

Incredible is a good way to describe this pizza play place. The broad selection of all-you-can-eat buffet food offers pizza with toppings that include, besides the traditional standards, BBQ chicken, cheeseburger, spicy peanut butter, margherita, Hawaiian, design-your-own, and other specialties. Gluten free personal pizza is an additional 99¢. Other choices are the salad station, with lots of options and bread sticks; the pasta bar with mac and cheese, marinara sauce, chipotle, etc; chili; soup; baked potato with various toppings; and desserts of soft serve ice cream, cinnamon rolls, fudge cake, donuts fresh from the donut machine, and more. Yum!

Enjoy your meal in any one of several themed rooms such as Fusion, which has optical illusion framed images on the walls and magic tricks showing on the screen; Hall of Fame, showcasing baseball and other sports; Toon Time Theater that shows cartoon films and poster art; Cabin Fever with stone and timber decor, plus a fireplace and antler chandelier; and Vertical, the surfer and skateboard themed room with thatched roofs and beach umbrellas.

John's is more than just fun food. The game center, laid out on colorful star carpet, has rides for big and little kids, and games to play, including arcade and redemption games. (Tickets and prizes are always fun.) Rides, which are different at different locations, can include bumper cars, twister, little rockets, frog hopper, little roller coaster, and

others. Play skee ball, UFO stomper, feel-like-you're-really-the-driver car games, Deal or No Deal, jumping jackpot, Guitar Hero, basketball, six-lane mini bowling, air hockey, and more. A toddler play room has Little Tyke slides, playhouse, and small rocking rides.

One hit here is Dance Heads Recording where for $5 per CD you (and a friend or two) enter a small photo booth, choose a song to sing along with while your head is superimposed on an animated dancing body. Song choices include Barbie Girl, Jailhouse Rock, Car Wash, Wild Thing, Achy Breaky Heart, and more.

School group packages, for twelve students or more, are available on weekdays for $9.99 for dinner and $7.99 for lunch for adults, and $6.99 for kids 12 and under. They include the buffet, beverages, and 20 credits per person. An almost two-hour, behind-the-scenes tour, for twelve or more students who are 12 and under (plus chaperones), includes participating in creating pizza - from making dough to eating their own finished product. That cost is $8.99 per person which includes the individual sized pizza, buffet, beverages, 20 credits, a certificate, and a ride of their choice. A pizza chef's patch is an additional $1.50. This tour is offered Monday through Friday, from 8am to 3pm. Check out John's other group and party options, too, as well as their kid's reward cards, VIP awards cards ($5 to join and you get a free buffet during the month of your birthday plus other great deals!), and exchanging credits for good grades. Note that different locations may differ on what they offer.

Hours: Open Mon. - Thurs., 11am -10pm; Fri., 11am - 11pm; Sat., 10am - 11pm; Sun., 10am - 10pm
Price: Everyone must pay for the buffet: $9.99 for adults; $8.99 for seniors; $6.29 for ages 7 - 12; $4.99 for ages 3 - 6; children 2 and under are free with a paying adult. Prices Mon. - Fri. from 11am - 3pm, only, are $7.29 for adults; $6.29 for seniors; kids' prices are the same. Unlimited fountain or coffee beverages are $1.89 per person. Video and redemption games and rides operate on a credit system - 75 credits for $14.99; 100 credit + 1 ride for $19.99; 112 credits + 2 rides for $24.99. Games take between 1 - 4 credits; rides and attractions take 6 - 10 credits: bowling is 6 credits, lazer maze is 8, bumper cars are 10, etc.
Ages: 2 years and up.

KOBE JAPANESE STEAKHOUSE (Orange County)

(562) 596-9969 / www.kobebistro.com
3001 Old Ranch Parkway, Seal Beach

See KOBE JAPANESE STEAKHOUSE (Rancho Mirage) (pg. 385) for details. They also offer monthly Sunday brunches.

Hours: Open for lunch Mon. - Fri., 11:30am - 2pm. Open for dinner Sun. - Thurs., 4:30pm - 9:30pm; Fri. - Sat., 4:30pm - 11pm.
Ages: 4 years and up.

MCDONALD'S (with a train theme)

(714) 521-2303 / www.mcdonalds.com
7861 Beach Boulevard, Buena Park

We've nicknamed this "Train McDonald's" because the center of the eating area has an enclosed, extra large model train exhibit with seating available all around it. Kids (and adults) are enthralled as the train goes around the mountains, through the tunnels, and past villages. Tracks and a train also run overhead. There is also a small arcade room here. And yes, there are all the regular McDonald's foods.

Hours: Open daily, 5am - midnight.
Ages: All

MCKENNA'S TEA COTTAGE

(562) 431-0200 or (714) 655-1456 / www.mckennasteacottage.com
810 Electric Avenue, Seal Beach

This comfortable, dressed-up cottage tea room has lace tablecloths under glass; chandeliers with beads hanging from them, and wood and glass curios and wood dressers filled with plates, teapots, bric-a-brac, candles, teas, tea paraphernalia, and gift items for sale.

Just a sampling from the liberal menu follows: Queen Mums Tea is tea, scone with Devonshire cream and jam, soup of the day or salad, assorted sandwiches, seasonal fruit, and dessert for $27. Lady Hamilton Tea is tea, scone with cream and jam, and sandwiches for $20.50. Little Duchess Tea is a pot of tea and two scones with cream and jam for $11.50. Lady Price Tea is tea, crumpets with butter and jam or cheddar cheese and scallions for $10.50. Prince and Princess Tea, for 10 years and under, is a pot of lemonade (or decaf tea); miniature scone with cream and jam; a choice

of peanut butter and jelly, turkey or cheese sandwich; and petite dessert for $16. Meal choices include a variety of quiches served with salad or soup for $14.50; tuna, chicken, roast beef or turkey sandwich served with soup or salad for $14; and a selection of salads that start at $10.50. Sides and desserts are also available. Both adult and themed children's parties (Snow White, Little Mermaid or other characters can even come and visit) can be enjoyed inside, or out in the private garden surrounded with plants and lattice work. Parties of twenty or more can make reservations for evening parties.

Hours: Open Mon. - Fri., 11am - 4pm, with seatings at 11am and 1pm; Sat., 11am - 5pm, with seatings at 11am, 1pm, and 3pm; Sun., noon - 6pm, with seatings at noon, 2pm and 4pm. Closed most major holidays.

Price: Tea and menu prices are listed above.

Ages: 4 years and up.

MEDIEVAL TIMES

7662 Beach Boulevard, Buena Park

    See the entry for MEDIEVAL TIMES on page 319 for details.

$$$$$

THE OLD SPAGHETTI FACTORY (Orange County)

Fullerton - (714) 526-6801; Newport Beach - (949) 675-8654 / www.osf.com

Fullerton - 110 E. Santa Fe Ave.; Newport Beach - 2110 Newport Blvd.

    See the entry for THE OLD SPAGHETTI FACTORY (Los Angeles County) on page 23 for details.

$$$

OLIVIA'S DOLL HOUSE TEA ROOM (Orange County)

(714) 669-0435 or (916) 481-3655 / www.oliviasdollhousetearoom.com

13011 Newport Avenue, suite 100a, Tustin

    See the entry for OLIVIA'S DOLL HOUSE TEA ROOM (Los Angeles County) on page 23 for details.

$$$$$

PARIS IN A CUP

(714) 538-9411 / www.parisinacup.com

119 South Glassell Street, Orange

    If you can't meet at the Eiffel Tower, the next best thing might be to meet for tea at Paris in a Cup. (It does have a photo mural featuring the Eiffel tower.) Located in the heart of Old Town Orange, this intimate tea salon, with padded wrought iron chairs and lanterns, oozes chic, French charm and elegance.

    The front part of the restaurant has shelves stocked with French gourmet chocolates, teas, jellies, other food gift items, plus teapots, books, music, and a selection of fragrances.

    A sample from le menu, served with tea or coffee, includes Claudette - baked potato soupe in croc and breads for $16; Maurice - soupe du jour in croc and chicken salad on croissant for $16; Marie Antoinette - scones with creme and confit, soup, assorted tea sandwiches, petite salad, and petit fours for $36; and Madame de Pompadour - baked potato soupe in tasse and assorted tea sandwiches for $15. Afternoon faire choices served with tea or coffee, offered from 2pm until closing, include lemon tart with fresh berries for $12; white chocolate cheesecake for $12; creme brulee for $12; and scones with cream and jam for $11. Tantalize your tastebuds, too, with French drinking chocolate served with creme Chantilly or flavored lemonade for $4 each.

    Paris in a Cup also hosts special*tea* teas and special events.

Hours: Seatings are Wed. - Fri., 11am - 2:30pm; Sat. - Sun., 11am - 3:30pm. Closed Mon. and Tues.

Price: Prices are listed above.

Ages: 5 years and up.

PIRATE'S DINNER ADVENTURE

7600 Beach Boulevard, Buena Park

    See PIRATE'S DINNER ADVENTURE on page 320 for all the swashbuckling details.

$$$$$

POWELL'S SWEET SHOPPE (Orange County)

(949) 831-9652 / www.powellslagunaniguel.com; www.powellssweetshoppe.com

27000 Alicia Parkway in Pacific Park shopping center, Laguna Niguel

    How sweet it is! It's like being a kid in a candy store - really. But this is no ordinary candy store - this is a candy experience. Powell's is devoted to and filled with nostalgic candy and sweet treats such as Mary Janes, Necco Wafers,

Candy Cigarettes, Bit o' Honey, Beemans, Atomic Fireballs, Moonpies, huge Sweet Tarts, dots, bubblegum cigars, Pez candy (and a large selection of Pez candy dispensers), and so much more, all in baskets and barrels and on shelves. It also has today's candy crazes, even themed areas featuring *Harry Potter* candy and products, and *Willy Wonka* candy and products. In fact, there are three theater seats (from a 1929 movie theater) toward the back that face a screen that continuously shows the original *Willy Wonka and the Chocolate Factory*, just to get you in the mood.

Powell's stocks over 5,000 products, specializing in hard-to-find, imported, and I-remember-this. There are also collectible tins with both traditional and unusual array of mints (try garlic mint or nacho cheese mint); unique and trick items (how about Wasabi lip balm or French Toast dental floss); weird candy, like insect in a sucker, gummy band aids, or Shakespeare insulting gum; t-shirts; games; toys; chocolates from all over the world; and much more. One wall is dedicated to jelly belly candy dispensers. Another area has create-your-own candy sand art. One center display case offers a tempting array of truffles and another offers gelato in flavors such as chocolate-dipped banana, blackberry Cabernet sorbet, coconut macadamia nut, creme brulee, and white chocolate raspberry. (Scoops are $3.29 for child-size and $5.29 for a regular.) The decor here also includes stuff from the past - a 1955 fire hydrant from Main Street in Disneyland; 1940's Coca Cola cooler packed with antique bottle caps; a 1939 gasoline pump from the mid-West; and more. Note that gingerbread house decorating parties are held here at Christmas time.

Parties, and even the party room, are a confectioner's delight. The candy castle wall mural, the stools that look like suckers, the table covering that looks like candy wrappers, and the game-board floor designed with candy boxes make a party here all the sweeter. Parties consist of cotton candy, gelato, retro soda, a scavenger hunt throughout the store for thirty kinds of candy, making candy leis, and each child becoming a game piece on the game board floor and rolling huge fuzzy dice to move. There are other activities to add on, as well. Sweet sixteen, or any age party, would be sweet to have here! They also have incentive rewards for kids with free candy bars and candy events - check their web calendar.

Hours: Open Sun. - Thurs., 10am - 9pm; Fri. - Sat., 10am - 10pm.
Price: Technically, free (but not a chance!)
Ages: 2 years and up.

RAINFOREST CAFE (Orange County)   ☀

(714) 772-0413 / www.rainforestcafe.com $$$$
1515 S. Disney Drive at Downtown Disney, Anaheim   ♨

You'll enter the Cafe under a 6,000 gallon fish tank archway that holds a colorful array of saltwater fish. Two more aquariums are inside the cafe and one contains beautiful, but poisonous, lionfish. Deep in the heart of the Rainforest Cafe, realistic-looking animatronic beasts come to life - gorillas beat their chests, elephants trumpet, and parrots squawk. Periodic thunder and lightning "storms" explode through the restaurant. This is not a quiet place to eat. Cascading waterfalls, fake dense foliage, and "rock" walls add to the atmosphere, as do the jaguars and cheetahs that are partially hidden in the banyan trees. Rain drizzles down from the ceiling around the perimeter of the cafe, ending in troughs of misty waters. There is always something to grab your attention here!

Savor your meal at a table, or on a bar stool that is painted to look like a giraffe, zebra, frog, or another animal. The delectable menu offers everything from salmon, flatbread pizza, coconut shrimp, rotisserie chicken, Oriental chicken salad, and Jamaica Me Crazy! porkchops to hamburgers, meatloaf, and lasagna. Prices start at $13.99 for hamburgers and go up to $25.99 for steak and fish. Portions are large. Children's meals average $5.99 for a choice of a grilled cheese sandwich, hot dog, Jurassic chicken nuggets, popcorn shrimp, mac and cheese, or pizza and a beverage. Desserts are deliciously unique, especially the sparkling volcano overflowing with chocolate. Tip: Join the Select Club. For $25, in which you receive $25 towards the purchase of food or retail items, you also save money whenever you eat here (or at 400 other Landry-owned restaurants), are given a $25 credit to be redeemed in your birthday month, and you get priority seating.

The adjacent Rainforest Cafe Retail Village (i.e., store) is themed with equal attention to detail. There is also a short bird presentation outside (weather permitting) every hour from noon until 4pm. Ask about educational programs that take students on a half-hour safari through the restaurant to learn about endangered species, conservation, and the environment. Tours include lunch and a lesson plan. Catch jungle fever and experience the Rainforest Cafe! Note: This location is multi-level and it is located in DOWNTOWN DISNEY (pg. 314). There is another location in ONTARIO MILLS MALL (pg. 421).

Hours: Open Sun. - Thurs., 8am - 10:30pm; Fri. - Sat., 8am - midnight.
Price: Menu prices are listed above.
Ages: All

ROCKET FIZZ SODA POPS AND CANDY SHOP (Orange County)

Irvine - (949) 453-0992; Laguna Beach - (949) 715-5200; San Clemente - (949) 492-0099 /
www.rocketfizz.com

Irvine - 95 Fortune Dr. at the Irvine Spectrum Center; Laguna Beach - 243 Broadway St.; San Clemente - 107 Avenida Del Mar, San Clemente

    See ROCKET FIZZ SODA POPS AND CANDY SHOP (Los Angeles County) on page 24 for details on this shop with an incredible array of unusual sodas and candy and more.

    Price: Technically, free.
    Ages: 3 years and up.

RUBY'S (Anaheim)

(714) 635-7829 / www.rubys.com

1128 W. Lincoln Avenue, Anaheim

    This is a RUBY'S (see the below entry for more information), but deserves a special entry because this one is a drive-in (not a drive-thru) that sometimes has skateresses. These talented carhop roller skating servers bring you your meal, to your car, while skating. (Sometimes I have a problem walking and chewing gum at the same time.) Watch old TV shows and movies of the 1940's and 1950's while waiting for your food. There are also outside patio tables here.

    Inside, this Ruby's is authentic in its details of that time period with historical architecture, photos, posters (themed around Southern California), gumball machines, and other vintage decor, plus an early model Indian motorcycle. Note: Kids love the sturdy and retro-looking paper cars (and stickers to decorate them) that they get with their meals! What a great blast from the past!

    Hours: Open Sun. - Thurs., 7am - 10pm; Fri. - Sat., 7am - 11pm.
    Price: Kid's 11 and under eat free Tues., 4pm - close, with a paid adult meal.

RUBY'S (Orange County)

(800) HEY RUBY (439-7829) - for all locations. Note that all the phone numbers end in RUBY (7829):
Balboa - (949) 675-RUBY; Corona Del Mar - (949) 673-RUBY; Costa Mesa - (714) 662-RUBY; Costa Mesa - (949) 646-RUBY; Fullerton - (714) 871-RUBY; Huntington Beach - (714) 969-RUBY; Irvine - (949) 552-RUBY; Irvine - (949) 753-RUBY; Laguna Beach - (949) 497-RUBY; Laguna Hills - (949) 588-RUBY; Mission Viejo - (949) 481-RUBY; Newport Coast - (949) 464-0100; San Juan Capistrano - (949) 496-RUBY; Tustin - (714) 838-RUBY; Yorba Linda - (714) 779-RUBY / www.rubys.com

Balboa - #1 Balboa Pier on the pier; Corona Del Mar - 2305 E. Coast Hwy.; Costa Mesa - 3333 Bear St., suite 120 at South Coast Plaza West; Costa Mesa - 428 E. 17th St. (this one has vintage pedal cars); Fullerton - 1301 S. Harbor Blvd. at Metrocenter; Huntington Beach - #1 Main Street on the pier; Irvine - 4602 Barranca Pkwy. (this one has a lake view); Irvine - 57 Fortune Dr., suite 240 at Irvine Spectrum; Laguna Beach - 30622 S. Pacific Coast Highway (this one has vintage cars); Laguna Hills - 24155 Laguna Hills Mall, suite 1636, at the mall (this one has airplanes "flying" overhead on tracks); Mission Viejo - 27000 Crown Valley Pkwy., suite B258 at the Shops mall; Newport Coast - 7703 E. Coast Highway; San Juan Capistrano - 31781 Camino Capistrano (this one has trains running on tracks overhead); Tustin - 13102 Newport Ave.; Yorba Linda - 21450 Yorba Linda Blvd.

    These 1940's-style diners offer good food and have a terrific atmosphere for kids. They've readily become one of our favorite places to eat. Old-fashioned-looking jukeboxes that play favorite oldies; red vinyl booths and bar stools; decorations that match the time period ambiance; and the kind of attentive service that all but disappeared years ago, are some of Ruby's trademarks. Since the restaurants are franchised, each one is slightly different in decor (some have trains going around on tracks overhead), and in their choice of menu items. Most breakfast choices include omelettes (about $8.99), waffles (about $10), etc. Lunch and dinner foods include a wide selection of burgers (beef, turkey, veggie, or chicken), or a sandwich for an average cost of $10. Salads and and soups are available, too. The delicious concoctions from the soda fountain, including flavored sodas and old-fashioned ice cream desserts, keep us coming back for more. Kids' meals average $5 to $6 for a choice of a grilled cheese sandwich, corn dog, hamburger, or chicken fingers. Their meals come with fries, a beverage, and a toy. Note: You'll often find Ruby's at the end of several Southern California piers, kind of like a pot of gold at the end of a rainbow.

    Hours: Most locations are open Sun. - Thurs., 7am - 10pm; Fri. - Sat., 7am - 11pm. Call for hours to the specific restaurant you're going to.
    Price: Menu prices are listed above. Kids 11 and under eat free Tues., 4pm - close, with the purchase of an adult meal.
    Ages: All

SURF'S UP CAFE

(714) 842-1111 / www.boomersparks.com
16800 Magnolia Street, Fountain Valley

Adjacent to the BOOMERS! (pg. 256), this separate cafe is colorfully Surf City-themed with surfboards, beach scenes, wooden planks, surf photos and signs, and fake palm trees on the walls, plus real boards hanging overhead, netting with sea stars, and a small boat to sit in with a surfboard as a table and part of the mast. This tri-level room doesn't have games, but the smallish adjoining room does. Themed with a city-scape mural, there are token-taking video and arcade games here and a prize redemption center at the cafe entrance.

Along with Pizza Hut food, with a personal pan cheese pizza and drink for $9.99, menu choices include nachos and drink, $5.99; wings, $9.99; Caesar salad, $6.99; and a grilled cheese sandwich, $5.99. Combo meals are $8.99 for a cheeseburger, fries, and soda, or for chicken tenders, fries, and soda. Kid's meals include two mini burgers or chicken nuggets or mac and cheese, plus fries and a drink for $5.99.

Hours: Open Mon. - Thurs., noon - 9pm; Fri. noon- 11pm; Sat., 11am - 11pm; Sun., 11am - 9pm.
Price: Prices are listed above.
Ages: All

SURF'S UP! BREAKFAST WITH MICKEY AND FRIENDS

(714) 781-DINE (781-3463) / www.disneyland.com; www.wdinfo.com
1717 S. Disney Drive at Paradise Pier Hotel, Anaheim

Hang ten with Mickey and four or five of his friends that come by to give guests high fives! Mickey leads the way in fun, too, as he invites kids to be a part of singing, dancing, hula hooping, or other activities intermittently throughout the morning. Decor and music from the California beach scene, hugs, photo ops, and signing autographs enhance the aloha ambiance.

In between dances and laughs, enjoy a variety of food selections. The all-you-can-eat buffet includes fresh fruits, Mickey Mouse-shaped waffles; French toast topped with berries and maple syrup; omelettes and eggs fixed any way you like 'em; breakfast burritos; bakery goods; bacon; sausage; fruit; yogurt; and more. Make sure to check out the adjacent DOWNTOWN DISNEY (pg. 314) and, of course, DISNEYLAND (pg. 232) for more places to go and things to do.

Hours: Open Mon. - Fri., 7:30am - 11am; Sat. - Sun., 7am - 11am.
Price: $30.99 for adults; $15.99 for ages 3 - 9; children 2 and under are free.
Ages: 2 years and up.

TEA AND TEACUPS

(714) 572-9825 / www.teaandteacups.com
18154 Imperial Highway, Yorba Linda

Even though Tea and Teacups is located in a good-sized strip mall, once you walk inside, it is a quintessential tea room. The back room is decorated in forest green, burgundy, and mauve colors with matching rose wallpaper. China plates, pictures, and some hats adorn the walls. The dimly lit wall lamps and soft music playing in the background add nice touches. The tables are grouped together in intimate settings. The front room is a retail shop with lots of goodies such as teapots, teacups and saucers, cozies, jewelry, British food imports, and gift items.

Now for the food: High Tea includes a pot of tea, a scone with strawberry jam and Devonshire cream, quiche, soup du jour, an assortment of finger sandwiches, and a dessert for $25.95. Elegant Tea comes with a pot of tea, soup du jour, an assortment of ham and chicken sandwiches, and a dessert, or scone with jam and cream for $18.50. Traditional Tea is served with a pot of tea, finger sandwiches, and a dessert or scone for $16.95. For slightly more filling items, for $13.50 each, choose a House salad; Cornish pasty with a house salad; or tea, scone and a house salad. All of the above include a pot of tea.

There are several selections for kids. Children's tea, for ages 10 and under, comes with tea, lemonade or milk; assorted sandwiches, such as peanut butter and jelly; chicken nuggets; fruit garnish; a mini scone; and a dessert for $10.95. Princess Tea includes the above tea, plus a head dress, wand, and necklace for $14.95. Boys aren't left out. Order a Dinosaur Tea (did they serve tea back then?) that is a Children's Tea plus a dinosaur stamp, spacey eyeglasses, grabber, book, or a few other fun goodies for $19.95. A Pirate's Tea costs the same but includes hat, gold coins, compass, tattoo, and eye patch.

Hours: The gift shop is open Wed. - Sat., 10am - 5:30pm; Sun., noon - 4pm. Closed Mon. and Tues. Tea is served Wed. - Sat., 11am - 4pm; Sun., noon - 4pm. Reservations are required for tea.

Price: Menu prices are listed above.
Ages: 4 years and up.

TEA HOUSE ON LOS RIOS

(949) 443-3914 / www.theteahouseonlosrios.com
31731 Los Rios Street, San Juan Capistrano

$$$$

Take a sip of tea and just relax. The ambiance of this historic district flows with Old World charm, as does this tea house which is in a restored, 1911 cottage. The rustic garden has a profusion of flowering plants growing every which way. The white picket fence, trellis, and covered veranda, with plenty of outdoor seating on an enclosed patio that wraps around the house, and some stained glass windows, add to the atmosphere. Inside are three intimate rooms decorated with flowered wall paper, plates, tea cups, other tea time paraphernalia, and fresh flowers. Fine china and linens are used at the tables.

A wide variety of teas are offered here, ranging from Cottage Tea, with scones, cream, and preserves, and a selection of tea for $16.95 to Victorian Tea, with scones et. al, and tea, plus soup and salad, assorted finger sandwiches, fruit with heavy cream, dessert, and champagne for $37.95. Children 9 years and under will especially enjoy the Tree House Tea which consists of a peanut butter and jam sandwich, fruit, scones, and a soft drink or juice for $13.95, or $15.95, with a grilled cheese sandwich. A la carte lunch entrees include a cup of soup, ($4.50), petite salad ($6.95), Mediterranean salad ($15.95), Shepherd's Pie ($16.95), island-style rice with chicken breast ($17.95), and prime rib ($31.95). Weekend brunch, served from 9:30am to noon, includes salmon benedict with a poached egg and a crumpet, home fries and seasonal fruit for $16.95, and prime rib and eggs with a crumpet and preserves for $19.95, as well as other items.

Before or after your tea time, take a stroll around the Los Rios district and the streets of San Juan Capistrano to enjoy the rest of what this quaint city has to offer. Watch out for younger children around the nearby train tracks. Look up ZOOMARS PETTING ZOO (pg. 336) and MISSION SAN JUAN CAPISTRANO (pg. 307) for more to do in this immediate area.

Hours: Open Wed. - Fri., 11am - 5pm; Sat. - Sun., 9:30am - 5pm. Closed Mon., Tues., Easter, Thanksgiving and Christmas.
Price: Prices are listed above. Note: There is a $7.95 per person minimum.
Ages: 4 years and up.

WATSON DRUGS AND SODA FOUNTAIN

(714) 633-1050 - restaurant; (714) 532-6315 - pharmacy / www.watsonsdrugs.com
116 E. Chapman Avenue, Orange

$$$

Watson Drugs and Soda Fountain, built in 1899, has the distinction of being the oldest drugstore in Orange County. Located in the wonderful shopping center of Old Town, it is a great place to stop for a meal, or just a treat. Part of Watson Drugs is a pharmacy/gift shop. Look up at the eclectic, old-fashioned items on the overhead shelves. The old-fashioned candy selection is fun, too.

The other half is a small, retro 50's diner, with a big jukebox, red vinyl seats, and lots of memorabilia, including old license plates that decorate the walls. Breakfast, such as omelets, pancakes, or French toast, costs about $8.50. Lunch, like chicken salad, roast beef, burgers, or tuna melts, costs about $8.50. Dinner, such as steak, fish, or chicken, costs, on the average, $13 - $15. The kids' menu includes a choice of a hot dog or a grilled cheese sandwich for $6. Fries and drink are included in the kids' meals. Let's not forget the most important food item - dessert! Ice cream floats, sundaes, shakes, and more, are yours for the asking (and the paying). Eat inside and enjoy the ambiance, or choose one of the tables outside, and watch the world go by.

Hours: Open Mon. - Thurs., 7am - 8pm; Fri., 7am - 10pm; Sat., 6:30am - 10pm; Sun., 8am - 8pm. Closed Christmas.
Price: Menu prices are listed above.
Ages: 2 years and up.

—FAMILY PAY AND PLAY—

AESTHETIC CLIMBING GYM

(949) 716-7116 / www.aestheticclimbinggym.com
26794 Vista Terrace, Lake Forest

$$$$

This indoor rock climbing gym was designed by climbers for climbers and for those who want to give the sport a try. It has 8,500 square feet - about half is bouldering and the other half is lead climbing and top roping. The ambiance is a little hipper than some other gyms as there is artistic graffiti painted on the walls; the top rope walls (and some are just seemingly unattached walls) are red and not the more typical granite-like textured ones; and the party rooms are nice, having outdoorsy murals and beautiful wood tables and benches.

Scale the rocks using various hand and foot holds that incorporate different routes; some with sharper angles and some just vertical. Climbing is a great alternative to more traditional physical activities! A variety of both indoor and outdoor classes are available, as well as deals and special events.

Hours: Open Mon - Fri., noon - 10pm; Sat. - Sun., 10am - 6pm.
Price: $15 for a day pass, which includes all the equipment needed. $10 for military day pass.
Ages: 5 years and up.

ALISO VIEJO AQUATIC CENTER

(949) 425-2559 / www.alisoviejoaquaticscenter.com; www.cityofalisoviejo.com
29 Santa Barbara Drive, Aliso Viejo

This gated, nice aquatic center is set on a hilltop, next to a golf course, with a breathtaking view of the surrounding mountains. It has a junior Olympic five-lane lap pool, a recreational swimming pool, an adult whirl pool, a children's wading pool, a small sprayground on recycled rubber ground in between the pools, and a shower area. There is also a picnic area inside the gates with an outdoor fireplace, a full-service snack bar called the Oasis Cafe, and locker facilities. No outside food is allowed in. Just outside the center is a small playground with slides, a little rock climbing wall, and some climbing apparatus.

Hours: Open May and September, Mon. - Fri., 2pm - 6pm; Sat. - Sun., 10am - 6pm. Open Memorial Day - Labor Day, daily, 10am - 6pm. The Cafe is open May and September, weekends only, 11am - 4pm; open in the summer daily, 11am - 4pm.
Price: $7 for non-resident adults; $5 for residents; $5 for non-resident seniors and ages 2 - 13; $3 for residents.
Ages: Toddler and up.

BALBOA FUN ZONE

(949) 673-0408 / www.thebalboafunzone.com; www.balboaislandferry.com
600 E Bay Avenue, Newport Beach

This strip, called the Fun Zone, is across the road from the pier. (See BALBOA PIER on page 313 for details on the pier.) Rides and attractions include the Ferris wheel, $3; Ocean Motion - trampoline bungee jump, $10; a mechanical bucking bull shark (not a bull), with eyes that light up at night and a snapping jaw, $10; and a Fish Pipe, a water-coated plastic sphere that rotates as "riders" slip and slide around inside, $10; plus a host of arcade games at Bay Arcade (www.thebayarcade.com). Note that the EXPLOROCEAN (museum) (pg. 302) is also located in this immediate area.

Kids also enjoy walking the short pedestrian street, shopping, or eating a famous Balboa Bar, which is an ice-cream bar topped with chocolate, sprinkles, and nuts. If you're looking for physical activity, bike rentals are available in the immediate area at Easy Rides, (949) 566-9850. See the Transportation section for information on the numerous boat rentals and harbor cruises launched from the Fun Zone.

Take the historic Balboa ferry which runs Sunday through Thursday from 6:30am to midnight, Friday and Saturday from 6:30am to 2am (starts at 6am everyday in the summer), across the water to Balboa Island. At only $1 for adults, 50¢ for ages 5 - 11, and free for children 4 years and under, or $2 for car and driver - the ferry is a fun, affordable way to get to the island and kids love this mini-adventure. (You can even bring your bike for $1.50 for adults; .75¢ for kids.) Once on the man-made island, there is not a lot for kids to do. Enjoy a walk or ride on the paved pathway along the beach, or perhaps head east toward the main shopping street. Note: The Island can also be reached by exiting Pacific Coast Highway [1] S. on Jamboree Road, where it turns into Marine Ave.

Hours: Stores and attractions along the Balboa Fun Zone are open most of the year, Mon. - Thurs., 11am - 6pm; Fri., 11am - 9pm; Sat., 11am - 10pm; Sun., 11am - 7pm. Summer hours are Mon. - Thurs., 11am - 11pm; Fri., 11am - 11pm; Sat., 10am - 11pm; Sun., 10am - 10pm. Most parking along the street is metered.
Price: Attractions are individually priced above.
Ages: All

BIG AIR TRAMPOLINE PARK   ☀

(949) 305-9788 / www.bigairoc.com $$$$
23251 Avenida De La Carlota, Laguna Hills

The term "big air" means "a high jump in an extreme sport" - and that's exactly what this place is! The huge, main room with a floor of trampolines (and some up on the walls, too) is perfect for working off all the excess energy, and then some. Other rooms, divided by netting, include two dodgeball courts; two basketball courts; a foam pit area for jumping and spinning and trying tricks; and a room, called Lil' Air, just for younger jumpers who are ages 8 and under. And a resting room - different than a restroom! - with couches and TV.

This facility also offers some unusual and fun features such as good-sized rock climbing areas for bouldering, with overhangs, that have foam pits under the climbers for them to fall into, and a Battle Beam. The latter is a padded beam over a foam pit that contestants joust on using large, hard-foam "lances". Cosmic nights (with lights down and music up, plus lasers and strobes), Toddler Time, Special Needs Days, cardio workouts and more give Big Air a leg up on similar parks. Purchase pizza, corn dogs, and other snacks and beverages at the snack bar inside, or bring your own food to enjoy on the picnic tables outside. Notes: All jumpers must wear non-skid socks (sold here for $1). Signed waivers are required.

Hours: Open Mon. - Tues., 3pm - 9pm; Wed. - Thurs., 1pm - 9pm; Fri., 3pm - 11pm; Sat., 10am - 11pm; Sun., 10am - 8pm. Open during school holidays and summer, Mon. - Fri. at 11am. Cosmic Nights are Fri. - Sat., 8:30pm - 11pm. Toddler Time is Wed. - Thurs., 10am - 1pm, except during school holidays and summer when it is 8am - 11am.

Price: $12 an hour Mon. - Thurs., $14 an hour Fri. - Sun. Subsequent hours are 50% off. $17 for the entirety of Cosmic Nights. $7 per jumper for Toddler Time. Military discounts are given. Spectators are always free. Check on-line for specials and deals.

Ages: 3 years and up.

BOOMERS! - Fountain Valley   ☼

(714) 842-1111 / www.boomersparks.com $$$
16800 Magnolia Street, Fountain Valley

Boomers is fun for the whole family. The attractions here include **two miniature golf courses** with hazards of a schoolhouse, pagoda, mini Eiffel Tower, windmill, fountain, and pond, plus lots of (real) palm trees for landscaping attractiveness - $9 for ages 5 and up; children 4 and under are free with a paid adult; **bumper boats** - $6 for a six-minute ride, and drivers must be at least 44" tall to ride by themselves (passengers under 40" can ride with an adult for $1.99); **batting cages** - twenty-five pitches for $2; **go karts** - $7 for a five-minute ride, and drivers must be at least 54" tall to drive by themselves, $2 for additional passengers who must be at least 40" tall; a **rock wall** - $6 for two climbs up the thirty-two-foot wall; and a game room with ticket redemption center. The **Kiddie Big Top** has carnival rides, geared for ages 7 and under, such as a Ferris wheel, a roller coaster, train ride, whirly bird, and balloon ride - each ride is $3. Picnic tables are here as well. A full-service SURF'S UP CAFE (pg. 253) is on-site, too.

Hours: Open Mon. - Thurs., noon - 9pm; Fri., noon - 11pm; Sat., 10am - 11pm; Sun., 10am - 9pm. Open extended hours during holidays and the summer.

Price: Attractions are individually priced above, or purchase an all day pass wristband, $29.99, which includes $5 of video play, or another package deal.

Ages: 2 years and up.

BOOMERS! - Irvine   ☼

(949) 559-8341 / www.boomersparks.com $$$
3405 Michelson Drive, Irvine

This palace, which can be seen from the freeway, is definitely a kids' kingdom. There is an almost overwhelming amount of video and arcade games, or, to quote my boys, "Yes!" There is also a ticket redemption center and a Surfer's Sunset Grill offering chicken strips, pizza, burgers, and more.

Outside, are two terrific, themed **miniature golf** courses with windmills, castles, houses, and other mini buildings - $9 for ages 5 and up; children 4 years and under are free. **Rock climbing** is $7 for two climbs up the wall. Splash Island **bumper boats** are $7 a ride and drivers must be 44" tall; $2 for additional riders who must be over 40" tall. I allowed my youngest to steer the boat and he did so gleefully - right under the fountain's waters. Oh, the joy of spending time together! **Go-carts,** where drivers must be a minimum of 58" tall, are $7 per ride; $2 for additional riders who must be at least 40" tall. Younger speedsters, at least 42" tall, can drive their own cars at **Kiddie Go-karts**

for $4 a ride. **Flame Thrower** is $4 ride; riders must be 52" tall (but not over 76" tall). **Batting cages** are here, too. In **Laser Tag**, you and your at least 5-year-old child (personal recommendation) enter a darkened, maze-like room with walls that are three-feet high and lit by fluorescent markings. For about five minutes you'll engage in laser tag, which entails alternately safeguarding your base while shooting at the players on the opposing team. It's a blast. The cost is $7 per game. King Arthur's Carnival has **five kiddie rides** and each ride is $3.

Get splash happy at **Bucaneer Cove Waterpark**. The pirate themed, main play structure is five stories of at least six enclosed and open twisty slides (the blue one is in the shape of a figure 8); tunnels; bridges; burst pipes that squirt water every which way; steps; water cannons to shoot at people (and be shot at); an aqua dome; buckets that fill up and splash down; and lots more wet fun. There is also a partial boat to get into and shoot water, wheels and other configurations spraying out water, and good clean fun. If wet isn't for you, watch those playing from a lounge chair on the perimeter.

If the urge strikes, next door is the Irvine Recreation Center with plenty of bowling lanes.

Hours: Open Mon. - Thurs., noon - 9pm; Fri., noon - 11pm; Sat., 10am - 11pm; Sun., 10am - 9pm. Hours may fluctuate. Bucaneer Cove Waterpark is open mid- April - Memorial Day and Labor Day - mid-September Sat. - Sun., 11am - 6pm; open Memorial Day - Labor Day, daily, 11am - 6pm.

Price: Prices are listed above. $29.99 equals four hours of unlimited attraction and $5 of video play. Entrance to the waterpark is $19.99 per person; dry spectator adults are $5..

Ages: 2 years and up.

BOUNCEU

Huntington Beach - (714) 892-4842; Orange - (714) 744-JUMP (5867) / www.bounceu.com
Huntington Beach - 5445 Oceanus Dr., #115; Orange - 428A W. Katella Ave.

Jumping, hopping, sliding, bouncing, laughing, running, playing - this is what happens at BounceU. Kids can knock themselves out (not really!) in the inflatable boxing ring where participants wear oversized, inflatable boxing gloves and protective helmets. The huge interactive inflatables include obstacle courses, basketball, and bounce houses. One really cool element in one of the bounces is a tiered, web-like rope climbing structure that kids love. The red, white, and blue theme lends itself a fun place for younger kids and older kids, too, as it's not too cutesy for them. Remember that all participants must wear socks and that reservations, even for open play, are recommended and necessary for certain programs.

Celebrate birthday parties, team parties, fundraisers, field trips, or anything you can think of here. Family Bounce is for everyone to get in on the action. Pay a little extra for dinner. Be the light of the party by having a Cosmic Bounce party where the black lights, disco lights, and glow-in-the-dark accessories are especially a hit with teens. Parent's Night Out is a popular drop-off program as kids get to play and eat dinner for over three hours while parents go out somewhere else to play and eat dinner. Check out the variety of camps offered for kids as one incorporates art and another engineering with Legos.

Hours: Orange - Open play for all ages is Tues. and Thurs., 4pm - 6pm; Sat., 9am - 10:30am. Family bounce night is Wed., 6pm - 8pm. Preschool Playdates, for ages 7 and under, are Wed. and Fri., 9:30am - 11:30am. Huntington Beach - Check the calendar for open play dates, cosmic bounce, parent's night, camps, and all other events as they frequently change. Both locations are open special hours on school holidays.

Price: $8 per session for open play and family nights. Parents and non-walking infants are free. Preschool Playdates are $7 per child. Cosmic Bounce is $10 per child. Parent's Night out is $20 (at Orange) $25 (at Huntington Beach) for the first child; $15 for siblings.

Ages: 3 years and up.

BUENA PARK RACEWAY

(714) 827-9979 / www.bpraceway.com
6161 Lincoln Avenue, Buena Park

Slot cars are four to eight inches long, look like real cars (i.e. race cars, hot rods or muscle cars), run on a slot in a track, and are powered electrically with speeds manipulated by a hand-held controller operated mostly by the male gender! This store not only has all the supplies one needs to build, own and run slot cars, but several tracks to race competitively, and even rental cars for those who want to test drive the sport first. Race you to the finish line!

Hours: Open Wed. - Fri., 3pm - 9:30pm; Sat., 8am - 10pm; Sun., 11am - 7pm. Racing is usually held on Thursday nights and on the weekends.

Price: Free to watch. Track time is $5 per 30 minutes with your own car and controller. Or, $2.50 for a rental car, $2.50 for a controller, $5 for 30 min. of track time = $10 total.

Ages: 6 years and up.

CAMELOT GOLFLAND   ☀
(714) 630-3340 / www.golfland.com/anaheim $$$
3200 Carpenter Avenue, Anaheim   🎂

In short, there's simply not a more congenial spot for happy ever aftering than here in Camelot! This huge castle has dragons, knights in shining armor, and anything else your prince or princess might consider fun decor. Choose from four, exciting **miniature golf** courses with obstacles and "decorations" to putt through- $8.45 for adults, $7.95 for ages 4 - 11 and under; free for ages 3 and under with paid adult admission. One additional replay is $4. **Lazer Knights** is an exciting game of tag using laser guns - $6.75 for the first game, with a replay game for $4.50. Get your engines running as you race around the **Fast Car Raceway** - $6 for the six-minute ride; drivers must be at least 58". The five-story **water slides** (usually open from mid-June to September) are $8.50 for an all-day rides pass or $5.50 after 3pm. There are over 200 video and arcade games (ask about arcade-mania pricing - if you want) and a full-service snack bar serving fresh pizza, sandwiches, and Dryer's ice cream.

Hours: Most of Camelot is open Mon. - Thurs., 10am - 10pm; Fri., 10am - midnight; Sat., 9am - midnight; Sun., noon- 10pm. Note that the race track opens at 5pm during the week, most of the year. Call first as hours might fluctuate. The water slide is open Memorial Day - mid-June on weekends only from noon - 5pm; mid-June - Labor Day, Mon. - Sat., noon - 5pm. Closed Sun.

Price: Attractions are individually priced above.

Ages: 2½ years and up.

CHUCK E. CHEESE'S (Orange County)
See the entry for CHUCK E. CHEESE'S on page 16 for details.

CLIMBX   ☀
(714) 843-9919 / www.climbxhb.com $$$$
18411 Gothard Street, Unit I, Huntington Beach   🎂

This indoor rock climbing facility is not as large as others we've found, but it has all the essential ingredients - several contoured wall structures built at angles that look and climb like real rock; colorful hand and foot holds that mark a variety of "trails"; a small bouldering cave; twenty-six top ropes; and enough challenges for seasoned climbers, along with lots of encouragement and easier routes for beginners. It's encouraging to know that athletic prowess is not necessary when learning how to climb. This is a sport that teaches balance and thinking while instilling a sense of confidence. Climbers are in a safety harness which is attached to a belayer, so even if one should misjudge a hand or foot hold (which my kids sometimes did on purpose), the climber will not fall, but merely swing in the air. ClimbX marks the spot for indoor fun! Note: This facility has a separate party room. Signed waivers are required for all participants.

Hours: Open Mon. and Fri., 11am - 8pm; Tues. - Thurs., 11am - 10pm; Sat. - Sun., 11am - 6pm.

Price: An all-day pass is $15 per person. Shoe and harness rentals are $3 each, per person, or $5 for both. Introductory classes are $70 for two hours.

Ages: 5 years and up.

DAVE & BUSTER'S (Orange County)   ☀
Irvine - (949) 727-0555; Orange - (714) 769-1515 / www.daveandbusters.com $$$
Irvine - 71 Fortune Drive at Irvine Spectrum; Orange - 20 City Boulevard West at The Outlets   🎂

Sometimes, adults just want to play. Dave & Buster's is mainly geared for adults as it has a full bar in the restaurant area and another centrally located in the massive arcade room, plus there are some more mature/intense video games, but kids are welcome here, too. There are over 200 games to play, both classics and the newest of motion simulator rides, plus arcade, video and virtual reality games such as Mario Kart Arcade Grand Prix Deluxe, Monopoly, Simpson's Soccer, Snow Down, Typhoon, Temple Run, Dizzy Chicken, Milk Jug Toss, Harpoon Lagoon, and Dark Escape 4-D. On top of a ticket redemption area with prizes, table shuffleboard, billiards, sports games, several big screen HDTV's (up to 180"), and more attractions, is the restaurant feature. Menu choices include, for appetizers - four mini-cheeseburgers, buffalo wings and fries ($13.99), potato skins, and calamari; main meals (between $10 to $30) - bacon-wrapped sirloin medallions and grilled shrimp, Black Jack bbq chicken, sweet apple pecan salad, chicken and

waffles, peppercorn New York strip steak, burgers, pastas, sandwiches, and more; and decadent desserts like Belgian chocolate fondue. The kid's menu, ranging from $4 to $7, offers linguine pasta with sauces, grilled chicken with rice, cheeseburger, grilled cheese sandwich, pretzel dog, or salad.

Guests under the age of 18 or 21 (it varies by location) must be accompanied by a parent or guardian 25 or 30 years of age, or older. One parent or guardian can accompany up to a maximum of six underage guests who, in turn, must remain with their authority. Check the website for specials, such as the Eat & Play Combo - one entree (from a choice of eight) and a $10 game card for $16.99, and Power Hour - play an hour of video games for just $10. See IRVINE SPECTRUM CENTER (pg. 297) and VANS SKATE PARK (pg. 268) for more details about the respective mall attractions.

Hours: Open Sun. - Wed., 11am - midnight; Thurs. - Sat., 11am - 1am.
Price: Some prices are listed above.
Ages: 7 years and up.

ESPN ZONE
1545 Disneyland Drive at Downtown Disney, Anaheim
See the entry for ESPN ZONE on page 246 for details.

FLIGHTDECK AIR COMBAT CENTER
(714) 937-1511 / www.flightdeck1.com
1650 South Sinclair Street, Anaheim

For older kids (and adults) aiming to be Top Guns, these eight authentic, military flight simulators are the next best thing to actually being airborne. The simulators, which are lined up side-by-side in this small room, have single-seat cockpits. After suiting up in flight gear, you'll receive a twenty-minute briefing and in-flight instruction on the basics of flying (for novices) and the particulars of your "plane". The pilot (that's you!) flies in a cockpit replica of an F-16 jet fighter interacting with the screen in front of you. Cockpits are realistic with fully functional avionic control panels, heads-up display, and hands-on stick and throttle controls. Learning take offs, aerial maneuvers, landings, and more are part of your experience. During your forty-minute flight you are in constant contact with the control tower instructors while competing in dog fights against computer-generated opponents or against a buddy in the next plane. Either way, you get so completely immersed in your experience, that it doesn't feel like *virtual* reality - it feels like the real thing (only safer). Being a part of a military combat squadron is another option. Squadron members also learn advance piloting skills such as air combat maneuvering, precision bombing, and navigation. Fly with the big birds by piloting the Boeing 737-700 commercial jetliner simulator for thirty minutes ($89), an hour ($149), or ninety minutes ($199). Ask about the education programs that are offered here, too.

For those who remain grounded, go upstairs to the small room called the Officer's Club, or watch the action on monitors from the observation deck that show exactly what each pilot is experiencing.

Hours: Usually open Tues. - Sun. 11:30am - 8:30pm yet by reservation only, so call to schedule a flight.
Price: Forty-minute missions on the F-16 are $59. Special programs have different fees.
Ages: Must be at least 11 years old with a minimum height of 4'11".

FROGG'S BOUNCE HOUSE
(714) 418-0442 / www.froggsbouncehouse.com
16121 Brookhurst Street, Fountain Valley

With a welcoming and almost a jungly feel, this 9,000 square foot, big, long room, decorated with primary colors on the walls, is filled with six inflatables on each side of a center isle. The isle, with its clustering of comfy couches and tables and chairs, and even large-screen TV in one area, is a great place for parents to chat, relax, and watch their kids bounce around. The inflatables include a giant double slide; an island-themed jumper combo with slide and bounce; a mega obstacle course with "hills" and slides and tunnels; a bounce for ages 5 and under only; and a round, birthday cake bounce.

Frogg's also has a train table, bean bag chairs, Little Tykes cars, air hockey, karaoke and a play treehouse There is an eating area too, so bring a lunch so you can stay and play longer. The party room in the back has murals featuring sunshine, mountains, trees, and happy frogs. Love those kids, but drop them off here so you and yours can go out for date night - offered every Friday. It includes pizza for the kids. Note that socks are required for everyone and liability waivers must be signed for all ages. The fun is here, just waiting for you, so hop to it!

Hours: Open Sun. - Thurs., 10am - 7pm; Fri. - Sat., 10am - 8pm. Closed all major holidays. Date night every Fri., 5pm - 8pm.

Price: $3 for adults; $10 for ages 4 - 17; $6 for ages 3 and under; $8 per person for a group of 10 or more
kids. The last two hours of every day admission is $8 for ages 4 and up. Check the website or call
for specials.

Ages: 2 years and up.

GET AIR SURF CITY (Orange County)

(714) 916-5815 / www.getairsurfcity.com
5142 Argosy Avenue, Huntington Beach

What does a kangaroo, a rope, a frog, and Get Air have in common? They all have to do with jumping! This
10,000 square foot indoor trampoline park literally has wall-to-wall trampolines in several different rooms including a
room just for jumping around, one to play dodgeball (on trampolines!), one to play basketball, and one with a foam pit
(to practice tricks, safely). Giant flat screen monitors allow everyone to see everyone else's moves in the pit and with
delayed playback, allow jumpers to review their style and technique. The separate Kids Court is a jump zone and foam
pit area for youngsters only.

If you are looking to exercise in a whole new way, take a fitness class here and bounce back to health. Get Air also
has private rooms for parties. Signed waivers are required as are non-skid socks.

Hours: Open Mon. - Thurs., 2pm - 10pm; Fri., 2pm - midnight; Sat., 10am - midnight; Sun., noon - 8pm.

Price: $12 for the first hour; $8 for the second hour and for kids 45" and under if they stay in the Kids
Court area; kids under 2 jump for free with a paying adult.

Ages: 3 years and up, depending on the time/day.

HANGAR 18 (Orange County)

(949) 454-8043 / www.climbhangar18.com
23812 Via Fabricante, suite A4, Mission Viejo

This Hangar 18 facility is different from the other Hangar 18s in that it is a bouldering-only gym. That said, with
4,200 square feet, it is a bouldering paradise with walls jutting out at various angles that prove a fitting challenge for
your young athletes, and for those who are not so athletically inclined. Both seasoned climbers and those new to the
sport will experience a sense of accomplishment as they conquer the rocky obstacles and terrain. The routes are
changed to continually stimulate your mind and body. So, if you're feeling caught between a rock and a hard place,
come to Hangar 18 for safe, challenging, fun exercise for the whole family!

Hours: Open Mon. - Thurs., 10am - 10pm; Fri., 10am - 9pm; Sat. - Sun., 10am - 8pm.

Price: $16 for adults for a day pass; $11 for ages 13 and under. Shoe rentals are $3.

Ages: 5 years and up.

JOHN'S INCREDIBLE PIZZA CO. (Orange County)

8601 On the Mall, Buena Park

See JOHN'S INCREDIBLE PIZZA CO. (Orange County) (pg. 248) for details.

JUMP 'N JAMMIN (Orange County)

(949)582-5890 / www.jumpnjammin.com
27741 Crown Valley Parkway in the Kaleidoscope mall, Mission Viejo

Truly, this children's entertainment center is jumpin' and jammin! The gigantic, multi-story play structure is the
main draw and it can keep kids (and adults) busy for hours. It has large plastic tubes to crawl through on all levels,
slides to zip down, bridges to cross, nets to climb up, inflatable and foam obstacle courses to power through, zip lines,
large balls to roll around on, and a totally fun feature - guns to shoot out foam balls at other guests. A fountain in the
center, on the floor, gushes out more colorful foam balls. This is an ideal play place to let off some steam and have a
blast doing it. Adults are invited to join in the fun, too.

Other activities include a bounce house, a short rock climbing wall, and virtual jump rope. Toddlers have a
separate, enclosed space just for them with soft foam objects to play on. Each child has a wristband that corresponds
to the adult that brought them. Socks must be worn at all times.

No outside food may be brought in, but since you're in a mall, there are plenty of places to grab lunch or just a
snack before or after your visit. Try Islands for burgers, El Torito Grill, or the pizzeria, and top it off with a visit to
Yogurtland. The mall also features COLOR ME MINE (pg. 237 and and LASER QUEST (pg. 261).

Hours: Open Sun. - Thurs., 10am - 6pm; Fri. - Sat., 10am - 8pm. Closed New Year's Day, Easter, July 4th,
Thanksgiving, and Christmas. Jump closes at 4pm on several other holidays.

Price: $12.95 for ages 2 and up; $5.95 for children under 2 years or free with a full-price paid sibling; one adult is free with each paid child admission, additional adults are $3. Ages 13 - 18 are $12.95 and only admitted with a younger sibling.

Ages: 2 - 12 years.

K1 SPEED (Orange County)

Anaheim - (888) K1-KARTS (515-2787); Irvine - (949) 250-0242 / www.K1speed.com
Anaheim - 1000 East Edward Court; Irvine - 17221 Von Karman Avenue
$$$$$

See K1 SPEED (San Diego County) on page 486 for details. The Irvine location is huge at 100,000 square feet and three tracks.

LASER QUEST (Orange County)

Fullerton - (714) 449-0555; Mission Viejo - (949) 367-1421 / www.laserquest.com;
www.shopkaleidoscope.com
$$$

Fullerton - 229 E. Orangethorpe Ave.; Mission Viejo - 27741 Crown Valley Pkwy., suite 315 Kaleidoscope Courtyards

This large arena, with fantasy decor, sets the stage for an exciting game of laser tag. Armed with laser guns, and vests with target lights, enter the multi-level maze with mirrors on the walls, lots of corners, columns, and obstacles to hide behind. Amid the strobe lights, black lights, ramps, catwalks, partitions, fog, and pulse-pounding music (which covered up my heavy breathing from being out of shape), race against the clock to "tag" the opposing team members with laser shots, and score. The twenty-minute games are fast-paced, and leave you either tired or fired up to play another round! The lounge has video games and three separate party rooms. Ask about their special events, such as themed overnight events from 11:45pm to 6am for $35 (in advance) and field trips for fourth through tenth graders. There are even school field trips where students learn about optics and reflection or how lasers work, lasers as a form of light, and the history of mazes and how they are a part of everyday life. These programs include watching a short video and actually playing two games of laser tag, with an educational perspective, of course. That two-hour program is $16 per students with a minimum of twenty students.

The Mission Viejo location is in the Kaleidoscope Courtyards (mall) which also boasts COLOR ME MINE ceramic place (PG. 237) and JUMP 'N JAMMIN (pg. 260) indoor play center, plus shops and restaurants.

Hours: Fullerton - Open Tues. - Thurs., 6pm - 9pm; Fri., 4pm - 11pm; Sat., noon - 11pm; Sun., noon - 8pm. Open on holiday Mon. Mission Viejo - Open Mon. - Thurs., 4pm - 9pm; Fri., 4pm - 11pm; Sat., noon - 11pm; Sun., noon - 7pm. Both locations are open extended hours in the summer and on holidays.

Price: $9.50 per game.

Ages: 6 years and up.

LEGO - MINI MODEL BUILD (Orange County)

Anaheim - (714) 991-6512; Costa Mesa - (714) 668-9017; Mission Viejo - (949) 347-6867 /
shop.lego.com/en-US/MiniBuilds;
!

Anaheim - 1585 Disneyland Dr. at Downtown Disney; Costa Mesa - 3333 Bristol St. at South Coast Plaza; Mission Viejo - 555 The Shops at Mission Viejo

See LEGO - MINI MODEL BUILD (San Diego County) on page 488 for info on this great, free LEGO mini model build. The Downtown Disney location usually has models for the first 200 kids. The Costa Mesa store gives out raffle tickets to kids who are there before 4pm to participate in a mini model speed build competition where they can win LEGO mini prizes. Then, they get to make the featured model, too. At Mission Viejo, the kids can get a timed entry card, at about 4:30pm so they don't have to wait in line the entire time.

Hours: The first Tues. of each month, 5pm - 7pm.

Price: Free

Ages: 6 - 14 years old, only.

NICKEL! NICKEL!

(714) 847-2191 / www.nickelnickelhb.com
$$

7454 Edinger Avenue, Huntington Beach

Arcade and video games abound in our culture and there are numerous places to play them. I think Nickel! Nickel! is different enough to warrant mention, however. It's affordable in that a majority of the over 180 games in this 7,000 square feet arcade can be played using one to four nickels, and some games are actually free. Games include skee

ball, air hockey, dance steps, boxing, skiing, basketball throws, pinball, and the latest in video. Every time we visit there is the gamut of ages - lots of young kids, as well as older teens and even adults. Many of the games give tickets - prize redemption is an important part of any visit. The facility has a party room, too. So, ante up and play.

Hours: Open Mon. - Thurs., 1pm - 11pm; Fri., 1pm - midnight; Sat., 11am - midnight; Sun., 11am - 11pm. Open in the summer and on school breaks at 11am.

Price: $2 per person; parties of six or more, $1.25 per person. Check online for specials, like Mon. - Thurs., students with I.D. are only $1.

Ages: 5 years and up.

OC_RC RACEWAY AND HOBBIES

(714) 892-6699 / www.ocrcraceway.com

15282 Jason Circle, Huntington Beach

Remote-controlled off-road racing is a fun sport to watch, and a funner one to participate in. Come race your car or truck at this indoor high-bite clay track with plenty of turns and bumps to maneuver around. Spectators are welcome, as are racers. The adjacent hobby shop is fully stocked with everything you need to get started, or for repairs.

Hours: Open for practice Mon. - Tues., noon - 11pm; Wed., noon - 6:30pm; Thurs., noon - 11pm; Fri., noon - 7pm; Sat., 11am - 9pm; Sun., noon - 2:30pm. Open for racing Wed. at 7pm; Fri. at 7:30pm; Sun. at 3pm.

Price: The practice fee is $15 for members; $20 for non-members. The racing fee is $20 for members; $25 for non-members. Membership is $40 a year. All day rentals are $35.

Ages: 7 years and up.

ON TARGET AIM 4 FUN

(949) 367-2950 / www.ontargetaim4fun.com

27696 Camino Capistrano, Laguna Nigel

Ready? Aim. Fire. Located next door to a regular shooting range, Aim 4 Fun's aim is for kids (of all ages) to enjoy this small, shooting gallery room using provided low-powered airsoft guns and bbs. There are two themed bays to choose from with six stations each - Forest, with colorful grass and trees with moving targets all over, and Space, with a cartoonish alien spaceship and planets that also has moving targets that rotate and spin and fall over when hit. There isn't any scoring - it's just for the fun of it and to practice. Wearing safety goggles, even little ones can load their bbs and shoot away at the targets. A signed waiver is mandatory. Note that On Target Aim 4 Fun is located next to a "real" indoor shooting range.

Hours: Open Fri., Sat., and school holidays, 10am - 6pm; open in the summer, Mon. - Sat., 11am - 7pm. Call first.

Price: $3 per person who is going to shoot; $5 for ammo and gun rental.

Ages: 3 years and up.

PRETEND CITY CHILDREN'S MUSEUM

(949) 428-3900 / www.pretendcity.org

29 Hubble, Irvine

Kids (and parents) will have real fun at this Pretend City. Much more than just an indoor play place this large "city" has fifteen different, interconnected stores, offices, and areas that motivate kids to interact and to expand their understanding of how a healthy community can work together.

Citizens walk down main "street," complete with streetlights and a park centerpiece, and go into the buildings around its perimeter and linking roads. Here are some of the city components: Ralph's grocery market is a spacious mini mart fully stocked with groceries, plus shopping baskets and cash registers. The farm has a wonderful mural with fake apples to pick from trees imbedded in the walls, as well as carrots and cabbage and other produce to harvest, plus an elevated gardening box. It also has fertilized eggs and live baby chicks in the incubator. Kids can use wood pieces and PVC pipes at the construction site to create (small) buildings. Acting out is encouraged on the amphitheater stage which is complete with lighting and music and costumes. Storytellers ply their trade here often, too. A complete little house has all of its rooms redecorated every few months with furniture and accessories pertaining to various ethnicities and the family room TV shows films starring a family explaining their culture. The beach section has ocean and whale murals, as well as beach chairs and a play area with buckets, shovels, and real sand. Learn about the environment by looking down at the transparent street drain to see pollution travel from trash to the sea. Adjacent to the beach is the marina with raised tables of water to create waterways using wind and water machines. Make your own sailboats, here,

too. Dress the part with uniforms and get into the appropriate child-size vehicles at the tiny fire, police, and gas stations. The dispatch desk has buttons and a real siren. Is your child a chef? She can try her hand at the restaurant (which changes the ethnicity of its food and ambiance every few months) by working in the real-size kitchen. Customers are welcome at the tables. The health center is fully equipped with X-rays, charts, models of body parts, a doctor's table, sink, uniforms, and even crutches, all designed to ease kids' fears in going to visit a real doctor's office. A good-sized room toward the back of the city features special traveling exhibits. And these are just some of the city's structures and elements!

Other important areas include the Real Cafe, where outside food can be eaten (note that food, such as packaged sandwiches, snacks, and beverages, can be purchased here, too); the Art Studio where lots of supplies (and some instruction) for arts and crafts masterpieces are provided; and two, padded, infant play spaces. An educational ingredient is the time cards which can be stamped at certain offices and stores here to be turned in for play cash from the ATM or bank, to be used at other stores. And be sure to call (or answer) the phones located at several stations throughout the city. One more feature worth mentioning - the bathrooms. Behind each toilet is a glass panel, revealing pipes, titled "Where does the poop go?"

Parents are helped in leaving with joyful (not tearful) kids at closing time as the staff head a parade involving all the kids that leads them around and out of the city to the front door. Hmm, wonder if I can get keys to this city? Ask about the numerous events and programs, including those for kids specifically with autism.

Hours: Open Mon., 10am - 1pm; Tues. - Sun., 10am - 5pm. Closed all major holidays.
Price: $12.50 per person; $9.50 for active military (and their family); 12 months and under are free. Admission after 4pm is $6.25 per person; $4.75 for military.
Ages: Infants - 9 years

PUMP IT UP (Orange County)

Anaheim Hills - (714) 693-9663; Huntington Beach - (714) 847-9663; Irvine - (949) 261-7867; Lake Forest - (949) 951-9663 / www.pumpitupparty.com
Anaheim Hills - 5397 E. Hunter Ave.; Huntington Beach - 16351 Gothard St.; Irvine - 16871 Noyes Ave.; Lake Forest - 26242 Dimension Dr., suite 100

See PUMP IT UP (San Diego County) on page 491 for details.
Hours: Check your locations website calendar for details on Open Jump and other specialty jump times as the times vary even within a particular month.
Price: Open Jump is $8 per child; adults are free.
Ages: 3 years and up.

ROCK CITY CLIMBING CENTER

(714) 777-4884 / www.rockcityclimbing.com
5100 E. La Palma, suite 108, Anaheim Hills

I'm gonna rock 'n roll all night! Well, I'll at least rock for a good portion of the day at one of my favorite indoor rock climbing facilities. This large gym is very family oriented and particularly kid-friendly, including a wall specifically for younger climbers. Rock City has thirteen top ropes, numerous lead routes on variously angled walls, a bouldering wall, a bouldering cave, and a tunnel to crawl through. Take glow stick through the latter (because it is pitch black!) and crawl through the tunnel which is angled, has ladders, a short fire pole, and other elements to make it an extra-ordinary venture.

Each climb here is a unique experience because of the different colored-coded routes. Rock climbing is not just a physical challenge, but a mental one as well. Done on a regular basis, it builds confidence and discipline. Perfect for first time climbers and still very challenging for experts, Rock City offers the best of both worlds. Parents, learn to belay your kids (which is so easy to do!) so it's something you can do with them.

A huge variety of classes are available for all skill levels. Inquire about climbing programs for kids including camps, joining the climbing team, and more. Note that Boy Scouts can earn merit badges here. A separate party room is available, too. I've had numerous parties and team-building gatherings here. A two-hour party for any age, for 7+ climbers, includes two hours of rock climbing, rental equipment, use of the party room, and the staff teaches parents or ages 16 and up to belay kids and each other (or use a staffer as the belayer for an additional $35) - all for just $15 a person; $100 minimum. A signed waiver and liability form, available online, is required for all rock climbers. Note that Rock City also owns and operates the HIGH ROPES COURSE CHALLENGE (pg. 279).
Hours: Open Mon. - Fri., noon - 10pm; Sat., 10am - 8pm; Sun., 10am - 6pm.

Price: $14 for an adult day pass; $10 for a day pass for 7 years and under. A bouldering day pass is $12. The harness and shoe rentals are an additional $6 per person.

Ages: 5 years and up.

ROCKREATION (Orange County)

(714) 556-ROCK (7625) / www.rockreation.com
1300 Logan Avenue, Costa Mesa

$$$$

Get the kids geared up - it's time to *rock* out at Rockreation! This huge (12,000 square feet) indoor warehouse/rock climbing gym is devoted mostly to Top Roping, where belayers (i.e. those who hold the rope so if you slip you don't fall) are needed. It's a great place for beginners to learn climbing techniques in a safe and controlled environment and it provides lots of rocky terrain for serious climbers to train. The multi-colored rocks of various shapes and sizes jut out from the twenty-seven-foot geometrical walls for handholds and footholds, offering over 150 different climbing routes. Some of the walls are straight up and down, others have slight inclines, while still others have very challenging angles and overhangs. Even if you were to hit rock bottom (which you won't), it's "carpeted" with black foam padding. A bouldering cave here offers another type of challenge for using climbing technique and strength without ropes.

Belayers are provided when you reserve an hour, or two, of Climb Time, which is for those who want to try climbing but might be unsure, or who need a belayer; for ages 6 and up. Kids Climb, specifically for kids, is available, too; also for ages 6 and up. Kids warm up using a short practice wall and then go for it. Although when my boys were younger they were a bit intimidated at first, by the end of our time here, they were really climbing the walls - all the way to the top.

Enroll your child in a summer camp, a climbing league, or one of the year-round classes offered for various levels and ages. A separate party room is available. Waivers are needed for all climbers. Hang out with your kids here, or better yet, tell them to go climb a rock!

Hours: The gym is open Mon. - Thurs., noon - 10pm; Fri., noon - 9pm; Sat. - Sun., 10am - 6pm. Closed major holidays. Call to reserve Climb Time which is usually offered Fri., 4pm - 6pm; Sat. - Sun., 1pm - 3pm. Kids Climb is usually offered Wed., 4pm - 6pm.

Price: Day passes, for experienced climbers who must pass a test, are $16 for adults; $11 for 11 and under. Equipment rental - shoes and harness - is an additional $7. Climb Time is $12 per hour; Kids Climb is $25 for two hours - all equipment is provided for both. Reservations are needed.

Ages: 6 years and up.

ROCK WALL

(657) 278-PLAY (7529) / www.asi.fullerton.edu/src/rockwall.asp
800 N. State College Boulevard at California State University Fullerton

$$$

Climb your way to the top - the top of this 30' tall, 27' wide, 1,100 square foot rock wall, that is. With nine top rope stations and a bouldering area, it's a decent size to practice and enjoy climbing. All participants must first either test out by appointment ($10) or take a Climb I class to pass a top rope safety belay test. The class is $32 for two hours of instruction and climbing - what a great way to start your climbing "career", especially because subsequent visits are only $5! During Open Climb the staff provides the necessary supervision and all equipment. Come for other classes or just for the climb of it. Note that the FULLERTON ARBORETUM (pg. 278) is also on this campus.

Hours: Open during the school year Mon. - Thurs., 5pm - 9pm; Tues., Wed., Fri., Sat., noon - 3pm. Open during the summer daily, 11am - 8pm.

Price: $5 per person for Open Climb. Parking is about $8.

Ages: 7 years and up.

SAN CLEMENTE AQUATICS CENTER

(949) 429-8797 / www.san-clemente.org
987 Avenida Vista Hermosa, San Clemente

$$

Located right next to COURTNEY'S SANDCASTLE (pg. 273), this aquatic center sports a competition and recreation pool, as well as a very small, but fun water play structure for little ones in almost zero depth. The colorful structure has a few slides, steps, pipes, and buckets that squirt out water. Lounge chairs on the ample deck are available.

Hours: The rec pool and playground pool are open year round, Mon. - Fri., 12:30pm - 2:30pm; Sat. - Sun., noon - 4pm. In the summer, the hours are Mon. - Fri., 1pm - 3pm; Sat. - Sun., noon - 4pm (still).

Price: $4 a day for resident adults, $8 for non-residents; $2 for resident seniors and ages 17 and under, $6 for non-residents.

Ages: 2 years and up.

SCOOTER'S JUNGLE (Orange County)

Aliso Viejo - (949) 349-9090; Placentia - (714) 223-5730 / www.scootersjungle.com
Aliso Viejo - 25 Journey; Placentia - 921 S. Via Rodeo

Grab a vine and swing on over to Scooter's Jungle. The small lobby has a few toys and some fun-house mirrors to keep kids occupied before they enter the main play room. Palm tree murals in the large play room add to the tropical theme ambiance. Your little monkeys will go bananas! There is a huge inflatable bounce structure that is a twenty-foot-high slide; a sport's inflatable for playing basketball, soccer, and volleyball, as well as boxing (with oversized, inflatable gloves) and jousting - very fun!; and a third bounce with a zip-line and place to just play. Each of these bounces rate off the charts with kids. There is also a multi-story play structure with a slide, cargo nets, tunnels and more - for all ages to play. Free air hockey, foosball, and ping pong just make a fun outing funner. Socks are always required.

An adjacent party room has long tables and chairs and a throne for the birthday child. Although Scooter's is mostly open for private parties, there are three ways for the public to come play: 1) ninety-minute, open play for young kids, called Toddler Time as it's for ages 6 and under, are offered several times during the week; 2) three-hour Family Fun Events, where everyone plays and pizza by the slice may be purchased for an additional $2 per slice; 3) All Ages Open Play (exactly what it says) which gives two hours of fun for everyone. Call or check the website for day camp information. Catch jungle fever and visit Scooter's Jungle!

Hours: Most locations have such varied calendars, so check the websites. A few have regular times: Aliso Viejo - Toddler Playtime is every Wed. and Thurs., 10:30am - noon.

Price: Toddler Playtime is $7 per child, which includes one adult free per paying child, $2 for additional adults. Family Fun nights are $10 per child, which includes one adult. All Ages is $8 per child which includes one adult; additional adults are $3.

Ages: 2 years and up, depending on the activity.

SEASCAPE KIDS FUN

(714) 970-7100 / www.seascapekidsfun.com
4771 E. Hunter Avenue, Anaheim

Escape to Seascape, an indoor play area for younger children. With cutely animated sea creature murals in the lobby and actually throughout, the underwater theme carries into the different rooms. The Aquarium Room has fish, shark, and sea turtles swimming on the walls (mostly in various shades of soothing and fun blues) and a super large bounce with obstacle courses, inflatable palm trees, inflatable logs to roll on and over, and areas to bounce. The Beach Ball room is the bomb. Enter the play space, enclosed with netting, and get bombarded by soft foam balls erupting from a fountain in the middle and by being shot at from kids manning the ball guns up above. There is a fun game with balls to play in here, too. Kids can also go up and down this multi-level jungle gym to shoot at someone below, go down the wavy slides, run around, blitz through an obstacle course, cross over a bridge, and more. Foosball and air hockey are free table games offered here. Seascape also has a place for parents to sit in a room that has a playhouse and other toys for younger children. *Sea* you here!

Hours: Usually open Mon. - Fri., 10am - 5pm; sometimes on Sat. Call, or check the calender, on the website as open play hours sometimes fluctuate.

Price: $8 for ages 1 and up; children under 1 are free with one paid admission; adults are free.

Ages: 1 - 14 years

SENDER ONE

(714) 881- 3456 - rock climbing; (714) 881-3FUN (3386) - Funtopia / www.senderoneclimbing.com
1441 S. Village Way, Santa Ana

Scale new heights, literally, at one of the best, biggest and most innovative climbing gyms I've had the pleasure to "play" at. Sender One, meaning "one who ascends" plus the number one, is creative, clean, colorful and wonderfully designed to encourage the beginner and challenge the more experienced climber. The massive rock climbing room is 25,000 square feet with 108 top ropes and walls that are up to fifty feet high! The central wall sports a huge vertical wave in it while other cavernous walls are built at various angles in and around pillars, arches, cracks, and other inclines. There is a lounge area in the pit, the center of the room, with couches and chairs, etc, and a very relaxed vibe.

Walk up the stairs for an overlook of the gym, or to use the exercise bikes up here. Tip: If a parent doesn't want to belay or climb, or doesn't have a buddy who will do so, rent a staff belayer for $25 an hour.

An archway and tunnel connect the top roping side of the gym to the other side, an extensive bouldering element which boasts eighteen-foot high walls and a topout boulder. There is a lot of space and problems to move around and to clamber the walls both vertically and horizontally. The central lounge area works here well, too.

A fantastic and unique feature at Sender One is a separate Funtopia room, geared for kids, but so much fun for all ages. Using the auto-belay system there are at least ten distinct walls that present different challenges. For instance, one wall has hand and foot holds that are gears so they turn as you climb and a fire escape wall has a backdrop that looks like windows and ladders so as you touch particular holds (ladder rungs), the background fire lights up. Another wall has a brick facade. Its jutting bricks are the climbing holds, thereby incorporating the Spiderman effect. One very easy route/wall just has smiley cut outs and another is inside a tower with black light holds. Two walls, positioned side-by-side, have rocks on the end of flat levers that pop out. These walls offer three challenges. One is called Chase, where the levers with rocks slap back into the wall behind you as you go up the wall - the knowledge that the holds are disappearing faster and faster and the loud clacking sound they make puts a little motivation in the climb. Another is called Random, where the levers disappear randomly, maybe even while you're stepping or pulling up on them. The last takes teamwork as each person, climbing side-by-side, at each level must push a button for the other person's levers to pop out.

Just a few more great activities to do in Funtopia include attaching yourself to a velcro wall (and peeling yourself off); climbing a tower and taking a leap of faith off (while in a harness) to a rope bar or to a padded pole ($5 extra); and holding onto a bar to be lifted up, then let go to go down a long, curved slide ($5 extra). One more that was scary and fun was stepping onto the tops of a series of padded pillars (while harnessed) that gradually get higher and higher, and then jumping off! The entire floor is thickly padded. There are also big padded blocks to play and learn with, as well as bean bags chairs to just hang and relax in. Party rooms are right off this main room. All sessions in Funtopia are one hour long, starting on the hour. All participants must weigh at least 40 pounds and those under 11 years old must be accompanied by an adult. Call to make a reservation, although drop ins are welcome if there is space.

Sender One also has a separate room for strength training and working out with free weights, weight machines and cardio equipment; a training wall and area to learn belaying using GriGri belay devices; several specific training walls for serious climbers; yoga classes; and a myriad of classes (only $30 for an intro to climbing class), clinics, and opportunities. Waivers are required for all climbers. Come to this gym and begin to reach your summit.

Hours: Open Mon. - Fri., 6am - 11pm; Sat., 8am - 10pm; Sun., 8am - 8pm. Funtopia is open Mon. - Fri., 2pm - 8pm (last session at 7pm); Sat. - Sun., 10am - 6pm (last session at 5pm).

Price: A day pass, which includes climbing, yoga classes and use of the fitness room, is $20 for adults, $16 for student and military; $12 for ages 12 and under with a paying adult. A package rental of shoes, harness and chalk is $5. An hour-long session in Funtopia is $17 per person.

Ages: 4 years and up.

SKY HIGH SPORTS (Orange County)   ☀

(714) 437-JUMP (5867) / ocy.jumpskyhigh.com $$$$
2970 Airway Avenue, Costa Mesa   ♨

The sky's the limit! Well, almost at this indoor trampoline place that is veritably wall-to-wall trampolines because, yes, they are on the walls, too. Inside, up the ramp and to the right is the main jumping arena which has a network of over fifty trampolines that line the floor like a grid - you can't fall off. Parents, note that all pads and springs are covered by two inch thick safety pads and that there are staff supervisors. Tricks, flips, or just jumping around prove that cardio can be fun.

Up the ramp and to the left are three separate areas or rooms - one is for little one who can walk up to age 8 only, with over twenty trampolines; one has trampolines lined up in front of a huge foam pit so people (of all ages) can safely try out flips and tricks by landing in the foam; and one is for those who like extreme sports - it is a dodgeball trampoline court. Players in this arena rotate into games that are continuously in play as a staff member keeps order and aids those who might not know or acknowledge that they were hit so they are out of that game. Sky High also hosts dodgeball tournaments.

Lockers, a few video games, free Wi-Fi, a couch, a big screen TV, and a snack shop that offers inexpensive pizza, hot dogs, chicken tenders, nachos, soft pretzels, beverages, and more make this an up-lifting destination. Ages 17 and under must have a parent-signed waiver. All jumpers must be in bare feet or wear grip socks ($2 a pair here). A separate party room of trampolines and an eating area is also available to reserve for any age group and any celebration. Check the website for Special Needs Days, Airobics classes, Munchkin Mondays, Home School Days,

Family Night, Wild Wednesdays, Cosmic Jumping (jumping with music on and lights off - except for black lights; even play with glow-in-the-dark dodgeballs and hoola hoops!), and other specials and deals. Knowing how much my kids love this place, so I'm confident yours will literally flip for Sky High!

Hours: Open most of the year Sun. - Mon., 11am - 10pm; Tues. - Thurs., 2pm - 10pm; Fri., 11am - midnight; Sat., 10am - midnight. Open during school breaks and holidays Mon. - Sat., 10am - midnight; Sun., 11am - 10pm. Note that you can call ahead of time and book your time as there are a limited number of participants allowed.

Price: $14 for the first hour; usually $6 for the second hour, Mon. - Thurs. (Holiday rates may be higher.) Children under 2 are free with a paying adult. Military and dependents discount is $2 per hour. Spectators are free and can watch the action from viewing platforms.

Ages: 4 years and up.

SKY ZONE (Orange County)

(714) 693-0250 / www.skyzone.com
1301 N. Kellogg Drive, Anaheim.
   See SKY ZONE (Los Angeles) on pg. 41 for details.

Hours: Open Mon. - Thurs., 2pm - 9pm; Fri. - Sat., 10am - midnight; Sun., 11am - 10pm. Open extended hours in the summer and on holidays.

Price: $10 for 30 min.; $15 for 60 min.; $20 for 90 min. Check the website for specials.

Ages: 3 years and up.

TAC CITY AIRSOFT(Orange County)

(657) 888-6111 / www.taccityairsoft.com
2430 Artesia Avenue, Fullerton

   Tac City is in a 30,000 square foot large warehouse. It's nothing fancy or pretty, but who cares? This indoor airsoft battle field is part obstacle course and part maze, with ladders and window cutouts in particle-board walls and buildings which are in various configurations - dumped together and standing separate - to hide behind and tactically maneuver around in order to shoot members of the opposing team. There is also a ladder leading to an overhead walkway. Does it hurt to get hit? I think so, but wearing protective clothing helps and facial protective gear is mandatory, plus the thrill is in the hunting. Join in open games or get a team together to come play. Waivers must be signed by a parent or guardian for players 17 years and under. There is an upstairs parent's lounge with chairs and free WiFi.

Hours: Open Mon. - Fri., 5pm - 11pm; Sat. - Sun., 1pm - 11pm. Closed New Year's Eve, New Year's Day, Christmas Eve and Christmas Day.

Price: $15 on weekdays for 1 player or $20 for 2; $25 on weekends, but $15 on weekends after 7pm. There are lots of specials offered. Bring your own gear or rent it here: full auto M4, $15; full face mask, $5; body armor vest, $5.

Ages: Minimum 10 years old.

THE FACTORY BOULDERING

(714) 639-ROCK (7625) / www.thefactorybouldering.com
1547 W. Struck Avenue, Suite A, Orange

   The phrase "you rock" takes on a whole different meaning here with over 4,500 square feet of just bouldering terrain for beginning to advanced climbers. Don't be deceived just because the walls aren't as tall as other rock climbing gyms: it's all in the angles, overhangs, and color-coded routes. There are no ropes or belaying - it's navigation, problem solving, technique, and strength. The three walls, with thick padding underneath, are descriptive - the Wave Wall, Slab Wall and Steep Wall, which practically runs the length of the gym, is just that - steep. It also has a small cave. The staff is not only helpful, but they make everyone feel invited, like being part of a community.

   A lounge area is centrally placed with couches, benches, free Wi-Fi and a pool table for non-climbers or those needing a break. The Factory also has a fitness area with a treadmill, rower, and weights, plus a campus board and system wall for dedicated climbers seeking to advance in technique. Inquire regarding classes, specials, and events.

Hours: Open Mon. - Fri., 11am - 11pm; Sat. - Sun., 10am - 9pm.

Price: $14 for adults for a day pass; $12 for students (24 years or younger with college ID) or students (18 or younger). 10 visits (on a prepaid punch card) are $100. Shoe rentals are $3.

Ages: 6 years and up

THRILL IT FUN CENTER

(714) 937-1600 / www.thrillit.com

20 City Boulevard W. at The Outlets at Orange, Orange

In the midst of this outdoor shopping mall, this center for kids has a little bit of everything for a thrill including a mechanical bull ride. Apparently I thought more highly of my hanging-on skills than I ought and of course people are watching! P.S. No skirts or dresses as you will be thrown off at one point or another. The ride is $5 for three minutes. A twenty-one-foot rock climbing wall with auto belay and three levels of difficulty is $5 for five minutes. Look up! Several short, safe yet adventurous, high ropes challenges are right above patrons' heads. Participants wear harnesses as they start from platforms then walk on and across multiple ropes courses - $8 for ten minutes. The Area 51-themed, two-story, laser tag arena has black lights, numerous partitions to hide behind, and murals of planets on the walls - $7 for ten minutes. Ballocity is a large, colorful, three-level, interactive play area. Its centerpiece is a plethora of foam balls that kids shoot out of several cannons and ball blasters, located on all the levels, at other kids. Ballocity also has padded obstacle courses, cargo nets, tunnels, huge balls, fast slides, and lots of other fun elements - $10 for all day play. Thrill It also has a few arcade games, tables and chairs in the center of all the activity stations for easy viewing (and to relax), and private party rooms.

The mall has lots of other fun things to do, see, shop and eat. See VANS SKATE PARK (pg. 268) for more details regarding The Outlets.

> **Hours:** Open Mon. - Thurs., 1pm - 9pm; Fri., 1pm - 11pm; Sat., 10am - 11pm; Sun., 11am - 9pm. Open longer on school holidays and summer. Closed Christmas.
> **Price:** Prices listed above.
> **Ages:** 4 years and up, depending on the activity.

VANS SKATE PARK

(714) 769-3800 / www.vans.com/skateparks-orange.html

20 City Boulevard West, Orange

Wow! Awesome! Incredible! And these were just the first few words out of my boys' mouths. This part-indoor, part-outdoor skate park at this outdoor mall has 46,000 square feet of wooden ramps, concrete bowls, a Combi pool, half-pipes, pro and outdoor street courses, mini and vert ramps, and more, all at a mega mall. Rollerbladers and skateboarders, and cyclists can all use the park at various times. It is a training "camp" for competitors as well as a practice place for enthusiasts of all levels. Beginners and Pee Wee skaters have certain areas that have scaled-down elements just for them. Observers can sit anywhere on the multi-level stadium seats that semisurround the main skate area. Our first few times here we just watched before my older boys actually ventured out on the ramps, and then they were off! Participants under 18 must have a waiver signed by a parent or legal guardian, in front of a Vans staff member. Waivers are available online. An attached pro-shop hawks Vans brand merchandise and everything that a skateboarder needs and wants. It also provides rentals of helmets, knee pads, and elbow pads, all of which are mandatory. There is also a small arcade inside.

The over 120 stores and fun restaurants at The Outlets include THRILL IT FUN CENTER (see pg. 268); DAVE & BUSTER'S (see pg. 258); Cafe Tu Tu Tango (an art-themed restaurant, often with artists painting here); Johnny Rockets (a 50's themed diner); and an AMC Theaters, with an IMAX and 3-D theater.

> **Hours:** Open Mon. - Sun., 10am - 10pm. It is open for BMX Tues., Thurs., 6pm - 10pm; Sun., 5pm - 9pm. Closed Christmas.
> **Price:** Free to observers. Day passes are $7 for members, $10 for non-members ($12 for BMX non-members), Mon. - Fri.; $10 for members, $15 for non-members, Sat., Sun., and holidays. Membership is $25 a year. Gear rentals are $2 - $3 per item or $5 for all of it, per day.
> **Ages:** 3 years and up to watch; 7 years and up to participate.

—GREAT OUTDOORS—

ALISO AND WOOD CANYONS WILDERNESS PARK

(949) 923-2200; (949) 923-2201 / www.ocparks.com

28373 Alicia Parkway, Laguna Niguel

This regional park has about 4,000 acres of wilderness sanctuary and thirty miles of trails to explore by hiking or biking. You and your child will see everything that patience allows - coastal sage, chaparral, oak woodlands, open

grassland meadows, canyons, and creeks, plus wildlife such as deer, possums, coyotes, bobcats, and lizards.

    This huge park is like life, offering many paths to choose from. Take a trail from here into the adjacent Laguna Niguel Regional Park; ride the twelve-mile Aliso Creek Bikeway, which basically follows along Alicia Parkway; or choose from several other hiking trails inside the park. We walked the Aliso Trail. Note that there is also a small picnic area at the trailhead. The first part is wide, paved and rather bland, scenically speaking. As we reached the dirt pathway and went into the hills, the terrain and scenery became much more interesting. (Strollers and bikes can go here, but it does get a bit bumpy. Cyclists under 18 must wear helmets.) Note that this trail can be very busy on weekends.

    There are numerous caves, or overhangs, throughout the park. A few are open to the public. Past the Nature Center, or Gate 2, is Cave Rock. Kids enjoy climbing up into Cave Rock, and sliding back down. Further back on the trail, is Dripping Cave, also called - and this has much more kid-appeal - Robbers Cave. Legend has it that bandits used this cave as a hideout after a robbery! At one time the holes inside supposedly had wooden pegs to hold their saddle bags, and bags of booty. Tell this to your kids and let their imaginations take over. Now, it's a resting place. If you have the time and energy, keep on going to Coyote Run, deeper into the heart of the park, with more hills to climb. Tip: Bring water!

        Hours: The park is open daily, 7am - sunset.
        Price: $3 per vehicle, or park across the street for free.
        Ages: 2 years and up.

AROVISTA PARK / BREA SKATE PARK

(714) 990-7100 / www.ci.brea.ca.us
500 West Imperial Highway at Berry Street, Brea

    The park has baseball diamonds, two lighted basketball courts, sand volleyball courts, an amphitheater, a playground, soccer and football fields, and open grassy areas with picnic tables and barbecues. The 10,000-square-foot cement skate park has a kidney pool, pyramid, table top, quarter-pipes, rails, and street section. Skateboarders and rollerbladers only - no bikes allowed. Spectators are welcome to gather 'round and watch the show. Wearing a helmet and knee and elbow pads is strictly enforced.

        Hours: The skate park is open daily, 7am - dusk. The park is open daily, 7am - 10pm.
        Price: Free
        Ages: All

ATLANTIS PLAY CENTER

(714) 892-6015 / www.ci.garden-grove.ca.us; www.ggparksandrec.com
13630 Atlantis Way, Garden Grove

    This "lost island" park is quite a find. Atlantis Play Center is a wonderful, large, enclosed play area for kids of all ages that has been around for over 50 years! Several different playgrounds are scattered around the park that feature slides, tubes, swings, sand pits, grassy expanses, and big, concrete aquatic creatures to play on. The sea serpent slide is a favorite. The green rolling hills are perfect for picnicking. Numerous shade trees make the park surprisingly cool, even in the heat of the summer. One of my boys' favorite things to do when they were younger was to play in and amongst the bushes that go around the perimeter of the park. The bushes become hideouts, forts, a pirate's landing, or whatever - a little imagination goes a long way!

    To keep even cooler, run around in the wonderful water-play area with colorful aquatic creatures that squirt out water and fountains that shoot up at random times encased by a sitting area that gets wet. The surrounding walkway has other fun water elements, like an extremely long pelican head and shorter sea dragons that spew out water, plus more ground fountains and artsy-looking bars with water coming out.

    Check the city webiste calendar for the several events held here throughout the year. Note that a full-service snack bar is open here daily during the summer, only. Also note that just outside Atlantis is Garden Grove Park, with more play equipment and wide open grassy areas.

        Hours: Open in the summer, Tues. - Sat., 10am - 4pm; Sun., noon - 4pm. Open the rest of the year, Tues. - Fri., 10am - 2pm; Sat., 10am - 4pm; Sun., noon - 4pm. Closed Mon. and most major holidays. The water park element is open summer hours only.
        Price: $2 for ages 3 and older (cash only); children 2 and under are free. Adults are not admitted without a child.
        Ages: 1½ - 12 years.

BEEBE PARK / MISSION VIEJO SKATE PARK

(949) 470-3061 / www.cityofmissionviejo.org
24190 Olympiad Road, Mission Viejo

This 9.8-acre sports park also sports the "latest" in sports - a skateboard (and in-line skates') park. The 9,000-square-foot unsupervised concrete park has bowls, a vert wall, bauer box, rails, spine, pyramid, hips, steps, and ramps. Helmet and elbow and knee pads are required. Other park amenities include a lighted soccer/football field, lighted baseball diamond, a sand volleyball court, playgrounds, short walking trails, and picnic tables.

Hours: Open daily, 7am - dusk.
Price: Free
Ages: All

BLUEBIRD PARK

(949) 497-0716 / www.lagunabeachcity.net; www.funorangecountyparks.com
798 Bluebird Canyon Blvd. / (730ish) Cress Street, Laguna Beach

Walk through the decorated gates to see for yourself that the bluebird of (park) happiness has landed on this nicely-landscaped park with imaginative play equipment. One structure is comprised of ropes, knobs, poles, rock-climbing walls and artistic-looking structures - they can be whatever you want them to be. Blast off in an adjacent, multi-story, rocket ship with an enclosed metal slide. Climb over, under, and on a good-sized, metal, half-spherical object.

Another sand-based, younger-kids-oriented playground is just up the steps that has slides, swings (and toddler swings), and more colorful, fun apparatus. Two short tunnels (through rocks) and a little wooden bridge are located in this area, too.

A spacious grassy lawn has trees and benches around its perimeter, plus an older, half basketball court. The southern end features a large, brilliantly-colored mosaic turtle to ride, plus picnic tables and BBQ grills. One side of the lawn also has steps up it that connect kids to several slides that whoosh down the short hillside.

The bathroom, which looks like a stone cottage, has a Boys and Girls Club perched above it. Every element of this park adds up to a welcoming atmosphere and fun play times.

Hours: Open daily, sunrise - sunset.
Price: Free
Ages: All

BOLSA CHICA ECOLOGICAL RESERVE

(714) 846-1114 - interpretative center; (714) 840-1575 - tour info / www.bolsachica.org
17851 Pacific Coast Highway, Huntington Beach

This 300-acre, saltwater wetland reserve is home to a variety of plant and waterfowl such as avocets, egrets, plovers, sand pipers, ducks, and terns. We also saw herons, and a few brown pelicans that swooped down to scoop up fish. Bird lovers should bring binoculars. The nesting and breeding islands are protected by a chain-link fence. You may, however, cross over the wooden bridge to walk along an easy and stroller-friendly, mile-and-a-half trail that loops through the reserve, and partially along the highway. No bikes or dogs are allowed. My little explorers especially liked walking down to inspect the water and its inhabitants, a little closer than I felt comfortable with. Free, guided tours are given the second Saturday of every month from 10am - noon.

A small Interpretative Center is housed in a trailer on the corner of the reserve, at 3842 Warner Avenue and Pacific Coast Highway. Inside are local ecology displays such as pictures of birds in the area, and a rattlesnake skin, plus live snakes and spiders, a touch table, a salt water fish tank with native species, and information panels on the value of wetlands. Interested in helping take care of this area? Clean-up Saturday, where volunteers pick up trash and remove nonnative plants, is held the last Saturday of each month. Note: For more fun in the sun, BOLSA CHICA STATE BEACH (pg. 239) is directly across the street from the reserve.

Hours: The Reserve is open daily, 6am - 8pm. The Center is open daily, 9am - 4pm.
Price: Free
Ages: All

BOYSEN PARK and ANAHEIM TENNIS CENTER

(714) 991-9090 - tennis center / www.anaheimtenniscenter.com
975 S. State College Boulevard, Anaheim

Take off to this park whose main attraction at the small playground is a large red, white, and blue cement airplane. The wings are tipped just enough so kids can climb up on them (wingwalkers!) and into the instrumentless cockpit. Other park amenities include picnic tables, baseball fields, and sand volleyball courts. The adjacent schoolyard, available to use when school is not in session, has basketball courts, a few scattered playgrounds, and more baseball diamonds. The park wraps around the Anaheim Tennis Center. Get in the swing of things by playing on one of the Center's twelve lighted courts and/or the ball-machine court.

Hours: The park is open daily, sunrise - sunset. The Tennis Center is open Mon. - Fri., 7am - 10pm; Sat. - Sun., 7am - 6pm.
Price: The park is free. Tennis costs vary from $5 - $8 an hour per individual, depending on the time of day.
Ages: All for the park.

BROOKHURST COMMUNITY PARK / ANAHEIM WEST SKATEPARK

(714) 765-5263 or (714) 765-3373 or (714) 765-5155 / www.anaheim.net; www.socalskateparks.com
2271 W. Crescent Avenue, Anaheim

Baseball diamonds, a basketball court, a few picnic tables, mature shade trees, and barbecue pits are here, but more importantly, your kids can come to this park and walk on the moon! Crater Park, our nickname for it, resembles the surface of the moon with crater-shaped areas that contain play equipment such as swings, a small rock climbing wall, and several older-style metal climbing structures. Wood chips cover the play area ground. Alien-looking white shapes are plopped in clusters, while a few long, curvy, white, raised cement walkways (which look like open-top tunnels) - complete with arches and holes - interconnect the play areas. This is a great area for tag and hide-and-go-seek! Being here almost eclipses playing at other parks.

The enclosed, 10,000 square-foot skatepark that is in the park has a six-foot deep concrete pool, steps, grinding rails, planters, and other street elements. Although it is not supervised, wearing protective gear - helmet, knee pads, and elbow pads - is required in the skate park and is often enforced (and ticketed if riders aren't doing so) by local police and security.

Hours: The park is open daily, sunrise - sunset. The skate park is open daily, 10am - dusk.
Price: Free
Ages: 2 years and up

CARBON CANYON REGIONAL PARK

(714) 973-3160 or (714) 973-3162 / www.ocparks.com
4442 Carbon Canyon Road, Brea

Talk about recreational opportunities! Carbon Canyon is 124 acres big and offers everything for the sports-minded and fun-loving family. There are eight lighted tennis courts, three sand volleyball courts, horseshoe pits, softball fields, a huge open field for whatever other sport you feel like playing, plenty of picnic areas scattered throughout the park, tons of run-around space with huge shade trees in abundance, and five great playgrounds that are kind of grouped together. The playgrounds alone are worth visiting the park. Based in sand, a few of them are huge and offer lot of slides, covered platforms, animals on large springs, intricate climbing apparatus, swings, learning stations, bridges, and a series of metal and chain ladders.

A good-sized butterfly garden with lots and lots of birdhouses (have the kids count them) among a shady grove of trees, is located just by the trail head. Hikers and cyclists can take this hard-packed dirt nature trail (very wilderness-like), which is not good for strollers, 1.1 miles to the ten-acre Redwood Grove. Equestrians can ride here or even take a trail that accesses the adjoining Chino Hills State Park. The beautiful four-acre lake in the middle of the park has two, short fishing piers. A license is required for ages 16 and up. Bring suntan lotion and food, and have a great day.

Hours: Open November through March daily, 7am - 6pm. Open April through October, 7am - 9pm.
Price: $3 vehicle entrance Mon. - Fri.; $5 on Sat. - Sun.; $7 - $10 on holidays.
Ages: All

CARL THORNTON PARK

(714) 571-4200 / www.ci.santa-ana.ca.us
1801 W. Segerstrom Avenue, Santa Ana

The front part of this park is a huge open area, great for kite flying because the trees are short (at least right now). A small creek runs through this area, ending in a big pond that attracts a lot of ducks, geese, and sea gulls. (Don't get

272 ORANGE COUNTY - GREAT OUTDOORS

goosed by the geese!) For your sporting pleasure, there are also two baseball diamonds.

At the northeast corner of the park, accessible by paved pathways, is an enclosed "barrier free" playground. This means that it has special apparatus designed for disabled children. One of the swings can hold a wheelchair-bound child. A sand play area, with water fountains to make sand castles, is elevated for kids in wheelchairs. Other play areas are great for all-ability kids, as there are slides, tunnels, and things to climb. Stone turrets give the playground a castle-like setting. A large grassy area is inside the enclosure for safe, run-around play.

Hours: Open daily, 10am - 10pm.
Price: Free
Ages: All

CEDAR GROVE PARK

(714) 573-3326 / www.tustinca.org
11385 Pioneer Road, Tustin

This park has play equipment for all ages, including two half-basketball courts (which don't equal a whole) and two grassy, volleyball courts. Starting at the parking lot, follow the winding pathway past the large cement frog and snake back to the playgrounds. One large playground has some shaded, elevated platforms and tunnels that connect to platforms, plus slides, interactive play boards and short rock climbing walls. Slightly older kids have their own play area with several colorful, metal ladders and geometric shapes and spheres for kids to climb on or across. (Being practical minded, I wondered if the shapes had a particular function or purpose, but my imaginative kids had a great time just playing on them.) Other fun things here include trying to climb the rope ladder, twisting on poles, and traversing between boulders on ropes that connect them. Plenty of picnic tables line the playground's pathway. Towards the back is a fitness area with man-powered machines that can offer a genuine workout.

The huge, adjacent grassy area has numerous cedar trees around its perimeter, and a pathway all the way around. Next to this is a grove of shady pine trees with picnic tables nestled underneath. The park also has a trail that connects to PETERS CANYON REGIONAL PARK (pg. 289).

Hours: Open daily, sunrise - sunset.
Price: Free
Ages: All

CENTENNIAL REGIONAL PARK

(714) 571-4200 / www.ci.santa-ana.ca.us
3000 W. Edinger Avenue, Santa Ana

Good-sized lakes stocked with carp and other fish, plus ducks, scattered large rocks, shade trees, barbeques, picnic tables, gently rolling green hills, and two play structures - one in ship-shape (or the shape of a ship) and the other with slides, bridges, swings, metal climbing structures, and talking tubes - make this park a fun family destination. At more than seventy acres, Centennial also boasts a skatepark with all the street elements, baseball diamonds, basketball court, fields for soccer or football, and paved hiking/biking trails within the park's boundaries.

Hours: Open daily, 8am - 10pm.
Price: Free
Ages: All

COASTAL PEAK PARK / LAGUNA COAST WILDERNESS PARK - PACIFIC RIDGE TRAILHEAD

(949) 644-3151 - Coastal Peak Park; (714) 508-4757 - Irvine Ranch Conservancy / www.newportbeachca.gov; www.irlandmarks.org; www.ocparks.com
20403 East Coastal Peak, Newport Beach

This park is a winner on so many levels. One of the playground's best feature is the big, Spiderman-like rope web/climbing structure - way fun. Other elements include fairly tall slides on a raised platform that leaves play space underneath; two huge fake rocks for climbing and imaginative play; poles with disc to sit and spin; other climbing components; seats (or whatever) that lend themselves to creative play on the sea-blue recycled rubber flooring; swings; little vehicles; diggers in the sand; and attached short walls with interactive dials and games. The park also features a basketball court, baseball fields, cement picnic tables and benches, shade trees, and plenty of grassy areas for running around and to use as soccer fields.

This is also a major access point for the 7,000 acres and forty miles of Laguna Coast Wilderness Park via the

Pacific Ridge Trailhead. Take in the incredible on-top-of-the-world scenery - on a clear day you can see forever. Several trails lead off in different directions - two go opposite ways on ridges along the mountaintop and another leads directly down the mountain surrounded by oak, sycamore, coast scrub, flowers, and other vegetation and mountain vistas, with wooden railings along one side. Some of the trails/fire roads are hard-packed dirt so they are popular for hikers, bikers, and parents with strollers. The trail system is extensive and while some trails lead down to the beach and hiking area at Cove State Beach, others lead further and deeper into the mountains and canyons. See the websites for trail maps.

Hours: Open daily, 7am - sunset.
Price: Free for the playground. Parking is $3 for the Wilderness Park.
Ages: All

COLONEL BILL BARBER MARINE CORPS MEMORIAL PARK

(949) 724-6714 / www.cityofirvine.org; www.funorangecountyparks.com
4 Civic Center Plaza, Irvine

I salute the outstanding, patriotic-themed, huge playground at this forty-two acre park. Ramps connect most of the three separate play areas with their numerous platforms and play structures, make them accessible for everyone. Equipment includes slides, metal climbing apparatus, tunnels, raised sand (or water) basins, little play houses, and swings, plus places to play on, through and under the playgrounds. Nearby are walkways and a garden area that surrounds a fountain where city celebrations are held.

Besides the playgrounds, other huge draws to the park include a main baseball stadium, three lighted softball diamonds (and three soccer overlay fields), two concession stands, batting cages, six lighted tennis courts, open run-around areas, and lots of picnic tables and barbecue pits.

Hours: Open daily, sunrise - 9pm.
Price: Free
Ages: All

COURTNEY'S SANDCASTLE

(949) 361-8264 / www.courtneyssandcastle.com
987 Avenida Vista Hermosa, San Clemente

The central, multi-story, universally-accessible, castle-themed play structure is huge! It features so many fun and unique components: ramps; bridges; towers and turrets; multiple slides; several rock climbing-type walls; poles; gears; play space under the castle; educational activity boards (one with music keys so you can actually play songs); rope ladders; and more. A smaller play area here is ship themed with masts, low portholes, speaking tubes, slides, ramps and activity panels. The playground also features several swing sets; a sand play area with raised sand basins, digger toys, and a dragon to sit on; free-standing tall and wide rocks to climb on and climb through its holes; run-around space; boulders just plunked around; and shaded picnic tables in the center of it all. All of it is enclosed.

A ¼ mile trail loops around an adjacent park. Just next door is the SAN CLEMENTE AQUATICS CENTER (pg. 264) with a water playground for kids.

Hours: Open daily, 6am - 10pm.
Price: Free
Ages: 1 - 12

CRAIG REGIONAL PARK

(714) 973-3180 / www.ocparks.com
3300 N. State College Boulevard, Fullerton

Much of these 124 acres are hilly and woodsy, blessed with lots of mature pine, oak, alder, and sycamore trees, lending it a peaceful ambiance. Holidays, however, can be extremely busy here, so it's not so peaceful. The playground in the upper area, near one parking area, has slides and animals on oversized springs to ride on. A cement pathway - great for walking and biking - meanders all throughout the park, leading down and through much of the park's rolling hills and alongside the year-round creeks (water play time - whether or not you want your kids to!). Besides other playgrounds, including one for older kids with steeper slides, there are picnic gazebos, baseball diamonds, volleyball courts, horseshoe pits, basketball courts, racquetball courts, and a lake. Fishing is allowed in the lake, but it isn't stocked so bring your wiggliest worms. Ages 16 and up must have a fishing license.

Hours: Open April through October daily, 7am - 9pm. Open November through March daily, 7am - 6pm.
Price: $3 per vehicle Mon. - Fri., $5 Sat. - Sun.; $7 - $10 on holidays.

Ages: All

CREEKSIDE PARK   ☼

(949) 248-3500 / www.danapoint.org   !
25743 Stonehill Drive, Dana Point

 A favorite! This attractive park has several reasons that make it so great. A large wooden (so, rustic-looking) playground has separate, spread out, components all based in wood chips. These include monkey "bars" (that are rings); a small, shaded wooden seat that glides horizontally across a pole; a chain bridge (on the ground) with curvy metal hand railings; a tire swing; other swings; a balance beam; and a legit, really good-sized curved, bouldering wall with hand and foot holds and a little cave, plus a sign that explains exactly how to climb effectively. A multi-story play structure has slides, steps, twisty poles, a rope ladder, a small tunnel and three short, side-by-side racing slides. There are a few other, smaller, play structures, too, with vehicles to ride on; assorted shapes to simply play on; mini play houses in sand and a digger toy; a seesaw; a train-shaped play structure for littler ones; a wooden fort; and more. All around are benches, a few picnic tables, mature shade trees, landscaping, and grassy areas.

 Walk further into the park as it narrows to reach the half basketball court, then along the paved trail that leads pretty far back to the end, over bridges, through several more grassy spots, and picnic tables. A paved walking/bike trail - the San Juan Creek Trail - parallels the San Juan "creek" and passes by the park.

  Hours: Open daily, 6am - 10pm
  Price: Free.
  Ages: 1 - 12 years.

CROWN VALLEY COMMUNITY PARK   ☼

(949) 425-5100 / www.ci.laguna-niguel.ca.us   !/$
29751 Crown Valley Parkway, Laguna Niguel

 This prince of a park is worthy of a crown as it has something that will appeal to each member of your family. A network of trails wind through the eighteen-acre hillside botanical garden. Some of the trails are cement, and therefore stroller-friendly (although uphill), and some are dirt paths with wooden steps. Enjoy beautiful landscaping, shade trees, evergreen forest, children's garden with a small maze and a fort, and benches along the hike up to the picturesque viewpoint, small butterfly garden, and cactus garden at the top. A sizable, castle-themed playground at the base of the hill has swings, slides, climbing apparatus, and a wooden ship to climb aboard. Picnic tables are scattered throughout the park. Summer concerts are given on an outdoor stage with tiered seating on a grassy hill. At the top of another hill is a soccer field and baseball field.

 Between the park office and the adjacent Y.M.C.A. is a regulation-size swimming pool that is open year round to the public and for swim meets. Diving competitions also take place on the two low diving boards, two high dives, and a (really high) diving platform. Cement stadium seats are on one side of the pool. The canopy-covered wading pool is great for your little tadpoles. Finally, a three-quarter-mile bike path here connects to Laguna Niguel Regional Park. This park is a crown jewel in Laguna Niguel.

  Hours: The park is open daily, dawn to dusk. The pool is open for public swim sessions year round, Mon. -
      Fri., 9am - noon and 1pm - 4pm; Sat. - Sun., noon - 4pm. It's open in the summer Mon. - Fri., 1pm
      - 4pm; Sat. - Sun., noon   5pm. The park is closed on city holidays.
  Price: Free to the park. Swim sessions are $4 for adults; $3 for seniors and children 2 - 13.
  Ages: All

CRYSTAL COVE STATE PARK   ☼

(949) 494-3539 - beach; (800) 444-7275 - camping reservations / www.crystalcovestatepark.com; $$$
www.parks.ca.gov; www.reserveamerica.com; www.crystalcovecottages.com
8471 N. Coast Highway, Laguna Beach

 This expansive state park is a combination of 2,400-acres of largely undeveloped park land that encompasses everything from coastal and canyon areas on one side of the freeway, and three-and-a-half miles of beach on the other side.

 The backcountry, mountain side of the park has numerous, and fairly strenuous, hilly, multi-use trails - hiking, mountain biking, and equestrian. One such trail is the Moro Canyon Trail, with various offshoots making it anywhere from five to almost twenty miles, which is especially pretty in the spring time when the wildflowers are blooming. Reference COASTAL PEAK PARK (272) for more trail info and free parking. Bring water!! Environmental camping - meaning whatever you backpack in, you take out - is a rugged three-mile hiking adventure to reach the two

campgrounds at Moro Ridge or the one at Deer Canyon. No open fires are allowed. There are also sixty campsites at the southern end of the park. Parking is at Moro Canyon behind El Morro School at 8681 N. Coast Highway. Maps are available at the ranger station here.

The 3.5 miles of rocky and sandy shoreline has seven small coves, numerous tidepools, an underwater park in the offshore waters that is popular with scuba and skin divers, plus surf, sand, and a paved, moderate hiking/biking trail that goes along the eighty-foot bluff top and through the coastal sage scrub and dunes. There are restrooms and playgrounds along the way. Activity and relaxation - both are opportunities to commune with nature.

From the Los Trancos parking lot there is a pedestrian tunnel under the highway that leads to the Beachcomber restaurant and to the beach. The twenty-one cottages down here, originally built in the 1920's to 1930's, are available for rent. If interested, go to the cottages website at 8am on the first of each month for seven months in advance - they fill up quickly.

Hungry? The oceanfront Beachcomber, open daily from 7am to 9:30pm, serves upscale meals - breakfast, lunch, and dinner. The indoor/outdoor restaurant, with a train set and station displayed in the dining room, can be reached at (949) 376-6900 / www.thebeachcombercafe.com. Parking validation, thus entry to the beach, with a purchase of $15 or more, is included. Walk from Los Trancos parking lot or pay $1 for a shuttle ride. (Kids 12 and under are free.) You can also grab a bite at Ruby's Crystal Cove Shake Shack, which serves sandwiches, hamburgers, hot dogs and fries, across the way at 7703 E. Coast Highway, (949) 464-0100. This little "shack" also offers up a tasty selection of shakes including monkey flip, oreo, and date. There are a few benches and tables here, too, overlooking the ocean for a vista of the shoreline and beyond. It's open daily, 7am to 9pm.

Hours: The park is open daily, 6am - sunset. Closed Thanksgiving and Christmas.
Price: $15 per vehicle. Primitive camp sites are $25 a night; other camping is $50; and RV's are $75 - all require an $8 reservation fee.
Ages: All

DEERFIELD COMMUNITY PARK
(949) 724-6725 / www.cityofirvine.org
55 Deerwood West, Irvine
A good-sized park with lots of fun things to do is what works for parents with kids. The smaller playground, designed for younger kids, has climbing chains, slides, and swings in a sand base. The slightly bigger playground has a rock climbing wall, twisty slides, and fun metal shapes to climb and play on. The park also has open grassy areas, two sand volleyball courts, a nine-hole disc golf course, four lighted tennis courts, two racquetball courts, a fitness course, bicycle trails, picnic tables, and BBQ pits.

Hours: Open Mon. - Fri., 9am - 9pm; Sat., 9am - 10pm; Sun., 12pm - 6pm.
Price: Free
Ages: All

EDISON COMMUNITY CENTER
(714) 960-8870 or (714) 536-5486 / www.huntingtonbeachca.gov; www.stockteam.com
21377 Magnolia Street, Huntington Beach
Although the park is not outstandingly pretty to look at, it is packed with fun things to do. Within its forty acres it has four lighted tennis courts, open to play on a first-come, first-*served* basis; six racquetball courts; four full basketball courts and several half courts, with lights; two baseball diamonds; lots of open space; a paved trail throughout; a covered picnic area with barbeque pits; a community center building; sand and grass volleyball courts; horseshoes pits (bring your own horseshoes); and a large, sand-based play area complete with slides, swings, tot swings, climbing apparatus, and a section boasting a ship motif.

Hours: The park is open daily, 5am - 10pm. The community center is open Mon. - Thurs., 9am - 9pm; Fri., 9am - 8pm; Sat., 9am - 12:30pm. It is closed Sun. and on holidays.
Price: Free. Tennis costs only if you make a reservation; $4 an hour.
Ages: All

EISENHOWER PARK
(714) 744-7272 / www.cityoforange.org
2864 N. Tustin Avenue, Orange
Driving down Lincoln Boulevard, it's easy to miss Eisenhower Park, but it's worth finding. At the south end of the park is a good-sized lake with a paved pathway all the way around it. Fishing is allowed, although it is only stocked

annually. Ages 16 and up need a license. No license needed to watch the ducks, though!

This big park has a stream running through a good portion of it, with almost irresistible stepping stones. There are two small play areas for slightly older kids. Plenty of green rolling hills and a wide variety of mature shade trees (oak, willow, and pine), plus a few scattered picnic tables and barbecue pits make your day picnic perfect. Cement pathways make the entire park stroller accessible.

Hours: Open daily, sunrise - 11pm.
Price: Free
Ages: All

ENVIRONMENTAL NATURE CENTER

(949) 645-8489 - center; (949) 645-8489 - butterfly house / www.encenter.org
1601 16th Street, Newport Beach

This small, three-and-a-half acre nature center is an almost hidden gem that has been here for more than forty years! Walking back to the trailhead, notice the rocks along the path containing imbedded fossilized shells. Although buildings are around the perimeter of this wooded area, you'll still feel like you're in the midst of nature while walking along the various crisscrossing trails. You'll see a cactus garden, pine trees, woodland trees, and a small rock-lined stream. You can purchase a pamphlet at the center to help identify the various plants and animals found here.

During warmer weather, make sure you walk through the small butterfly house - a greenhouse that is home at various times to chrysalises and Painted Ladies, Red Admirals, Mourning Cloaks, and several other species. Someone once said that butterflies are like flying flowers; what a lovely description!

The eco-friendly green learning center has shelves and tables that contain rocks, shells, animals' skins, turtle shells, taxidermied animals, skulls, feathers, and bird's nests, plus many nature-inspired craft ideas and interactive exhibits. My boys also liked seeing the live snakes, crickets, and lizards in here. Note: The center hosts programs for Boy Scouts and Girl Scouts, school kids, and summer camps.

Hours: Open Mon. - Fri., 8am - 5pm; Sat. - Sun., 8am - 4pm. The butterfly house is open May through September, daily, 10am - 3pm, weather permitting. Both are closed on major holidays.
Price: Free
Ages: 2½ years and up.

ETNIES SKATE PARK OF LAKE FOREST

(949) 916-5870 / www.etniesskatepark.com
20028 Lake Forest Drive, Lake Forest

At 62,000 square feet, this lighted cement park designed by several pro skaters is a skater's paradise! The park is composed of a plaza that features open space with ledges and rails; a street course with a street run features fun boxes, more ledges, a vert wall, and rollers; and bowls, a pool, pyramids, and other exciting elements. Safety gear for skaters - a helmet and pads - is required and enforced. A signed waiver is necessary for all skaters 17 years and under. This is a great place for birthday parties. Skating camps are also offered here.

Hours: Open the school year, Mon. - Thurs., 11am - 9pm; Fri., 11am - 10pm; Sat. - 10am - 10pm; Sun., 12:30pm - 9pm. Open daily in the summer, 10am - 10pm.
Price: Free for residents. A one-time fee of $5 is charged for non-residents.
Ages: 7 years and up.

FAIRVIEW PARK

(949) 54TRAIN (548-7246) - engineers; (714) 754-5009 or (714) 754-5300 - park / www.ci.costa-mesa.ca.us; www.ocmetrains.org
2501 Placentia Avenue, Costa Mesa

Fairview Park has two main attractions - dirt trails and model train rides. There are miles and miles of dirt trails, which are great for jogging, but kid-wise, they are ideal for riding dirt bikes. Up and down, over hill and dale, and to the outer edge of the park, which is lined with coastal shrubs, the trails are just plain fun. There is also a wetlands area. The large size of the park, slight wind factor, and layout also lends itself to flying kites and model glider airplanes.

Just across the road is a station that hosts one of the largest scale model layouts of its kind in Southern California. The Orange County Model Engineers run five miles of track and offer rides, about fifteen minutes long, for free, to park-goers. Bring a picnic, a bike, a kite, and make a day of it.

Hours: The park is open daily, dawn - dusk. The train is here on the third weekend of each month, 10am - 3:30pm, weather permitting.

Price: Free
Ages: All

FLORENCE JOYNER OLYMPIAD PARK

(949) 470-3061; (949) 470-3095 / www.cityofmissionviejo.org; www.funorangecountyparks.com
22761 Olympiad Road, Mission Viejo

Named for the Olympiad athlete, this popular, pretty, and colorful park has tons of fun elements. The big pirate ship, with its slides, poles, talking tubes, and portholes, encourages little ones to yo ho ho. Based in both recycled rubber and sand, there are two other covered major play structures that have several twisty and straight slides, metal bars and poles to climb, monkey bars with steps to go across, tunnels, bridges, a climbing configuration, rocks, and much more. There are also swings, smiley face free-standing walls, and several separate, kid-sized buildings with cut outs in the walls, windows, steering wheels, tables, and hands-on imaginative elements. A covered area with picnic tables and BBQ grills, expansive grassy lawn, plenty of mature trees and landscaped perimeter, and an adjacent sports field round out this winning park.

Hours: Open daily, 7am - 11pm.
Price: Free
Ages: All

FORSTER RANCH COMMUNITY PARK

(949) 361-8264 / www.san-clemente.org; www.funorangecountyparks.com
3207 Camino Vera Cruz & 1291 Sarmentoso, San Clemente

Land ho! Play areas shaped like ships (making them shipshape!) with portholes, treasure maps, slides, and more; big alligators "swimming" through the sand; fake palm trees; and a large playground in a sand surface make this island-themed park the perfect getaway for kids. The large, central play structure has steps, plus wooden and chain bridges; tunnels; several slides; monkey bars; climbing apparatuses made of ropes, chains, metal and plastic; a zip line; a short tunnel through an open lion's mouth; and climbing ropes. Two stationary jeeps to "drive" around in, a low and fairly wide balance beam, and swings, including toddler and wheelchair accessible swings, make the enclosed island park seem not so deserted. Ball parks and grassy areas are adjacent.

Hours: Open daily, 6am - 10pm
Price: Free
Ages: All

FOUNDERS PARK

(714) 990-7100 / www.ci.brea.ca.us
777 Skyler Way, Brea

We found a great playground at Founders! It has a dynamite rock climbing wall - wider and taller than most other parks, like part of one that you'd find at a rock climbing gym, but not too high. The playground has lots of fun elements within its two play structures including slides, overhead wheels to hang on (like monkey bars), and a favorite - a raised sand play area that's kind of inset into fake rocks - bring sand toys. The park also has a basketball court, two tennis courts, grassy areas, and picnic tables.

Hours: Open daily, sunrise - sunset.
Price: Free
Ages: All

FRONTIER PARK

(714) 573-3325 or (714) 573-3000 / www.tustinca.org
1400 Mitchell Avenue, Tustin

This nice corner park features a plastic playground in sand with a fort-like theme. It has many slides, some bridges, and a rope wall to climb. Other key components are a short frisbee golf course with chain baskets, fitness stations with exercise equipment, plus picnic tables, barbecue pits, shade trees, and a grassy area to run around.

Hours: Open daily, dawn - dusk.
Price: Free
Ages: All

FULLERTON ARBORETUM

(657) 278-3407 / www.fullertonarboretum.org   !/$
1900 Associated Road, Fullerton

This comely, twenty-six-acre botanical garden, with more than 4,000 plants, is a delight to wander around. Divided into four main sections, the cultivated garden section is a favorite because it is a verdant refuge, with flower-lined pathways, a pond, a stream, and a few bridges. It's also big enough to let the kids run loose, a little. Take a whiff - the air is perfumed with the scent of roses, mint, and citrus, from the rose garden, herb garden, fruit grove, and deciduous orchard, respectively. Garden benches here (and everywhere, actually) offer a picturesque resting spot, underneath shade trees in the midst of the plants and flowers. Bring your camera for some potentially great shots in a garden setting.

The woodland section features redwoods, pines, bamboo grove, rainforest plants, a meadow, and a colorful subtropical garden with a small pool. The Mediterranean area showcases chaparral and shrubs, while the desert section grows a variety of cactus. The delightful Children's Garden is created particularly for kids to enjoy. There are fanciful supersized garden tools; a small hay bale maze; a short building made out of soil; a Weird and Wonderful Do-Touch Garden with fuzzy and odd plants; and a Sniff N' Seek Garden so kids can make *scents* of gardening!

An 1894 Victorian Heritage House, once the home and office of the first physician in Orange County, is also on the grounds. Older kids will appreciate a tour through the house that has turn-of-the-century furnishings. The visitor's center/museum contains displays that reflect the birth of freedom from the Civil War to Civil Rights in California.

There are many special events going on at the Fullerton Arboretum throughout the year, including Science Adventure programs, volunteering opportunities, Victorian teas (with tableau scenes featuring Queen Victoria), planting how-to's for all ages, and much more. Call or check the website for details. Note that picnicking is not allowed on the grounds.

Hours: The Arboretum is open daily, 8am - 4:30pm. Closed New Year's Day, Thanksgiving, and Christmas. The house is open for tours Sat. and Sun., 2pm - 4pm. Call to make an appointment for other days and hours. The house is closed for tours in January and August.

Price: The Arboretum has a donation box by the entrance gate - $3 suggested. The house tour is a $3 for adults; $1 per child. See page x for info on AHS reciprocal memberships.

Ages: All

HARRIETT M. WIEDER REGIONAL PARK   ☼

(949) 923-2290 or (949) 923-2295 / www.ocparks.com   !
19251 Seapoint Avenue, Huntington Beach   🎂

What a crazy fun park this is! The play equipment looks like abstract art, albeit sturdy and colorful, and lets unrestrained imaginations invent ways to play on the circular, cylindrical, straight up, and twisted shapes. Kids can climb, swing, spin, slide, and even zip on the good-sized playground that offers a view of the Bolsa Chica Wetlands. One area is designed for ages 6 to twelve years; the other for toddlers. Both have rubberized surfaces and play components comprised of recycled materials. Several picnic tables are here as well. The few short walking trails will be maintained and expanded in the future.

Hours: Open daily, 7am - sunset.
Price: Free
Ages: 2 - 14 years

HART PARK   ☼

(714) 744-7274 or (714) 733-5599 - park; (714) 744-7266 - pool / www.cityoforange.org   !/$
701 S. Glassell Street, Orange   🎂

Stone walls add to the beauty of this spacious park. The northern section has <u>lots</u> of picnic tables and barbecue pits, a playground, trees to climb, a few tennis courts (although kids were roller skating on them when we visited), horseshoe pits, a sand volleyball court (or, for younger kids, a sandbox with a net), and a swimming pool. Come for a concert at the ampitheatre on Wednesday nights in the summer.

The southern section has a large open grassy area lined with trees, plus soccer fields and a few baseball diamonds. One of the diamonds has stadium seating and lights.

Hours: The park is open daily, 5am - 11pm. The pool is open mid-June - Labor Day daily, with one-hour-and-fifteen-minute swim sessions, Mon. - Tues., 1:30pm - 4:15pm, Wed., 1:30pm - 4:15pm and 7:15pm - 8:30pm; Thurs. - Fri., 1:30pm - 4:15pm; Sat. - Sun., 1pm - 5:15pm.

Price: The park is free. Each swim session costs $2.50 per person.
Ages: All

HARVARD COMMUNITY ATHLETIC PARK

(949) 724-6821 - park; (949) 337-6577 or (949) 724-6830 - skate park / www.cityofirvine.org
14701 Harvard Avenue, Irvine

    This expansive park has four soccer fields, seven lighted baseball/softball fields, picnic tables, barbecue grills, and open play areas. The big attraction for skateboarders is the concrete corner skate park which has a pool, ramps, verts, grind boxes, grinding poles, and other standard skate street equipment. Safety equipment - helmet and knee and elbow pads - is required.

Hours: The park is open daily, dawn - dusk. The skate park is open during school hours, Mon. - Fri., 2pm - 8pm; Sat., 10am - 9pm; Sun., noon - 8pm. During the summer and on school breaks, it is open Mon. - Sat., 10am - 9pm; Sun., noon - 8pm. Closed major holidays.
Price: Free
Ages: All

HAWES PARK

(714) 536-5486 / www.huntingtonbeachca.gov; www.stockteam.com
9731 Verdant Drive and Everglades Drive, Huntington Beach

    The large and colorful play structure has some great features such as two, short rock climbing walls; twisty slides; swaying bridges; a domed, metal climbing apparatus with cross bars; monkey bars; and more. A separate play area has swings, enclosed slides, and a long curvy slide stationed in a sand pit. Other amenities include picnic tables, basketball courts, shade trees, expanse of lawn, and ball fields. Note that since this park is adjacent to an elementary school the playground is often in use during school hours.

Hours: Open daily, 5am - sunset.
Price: Free
Ages: All

HERITAGE PARK - Irvine

(949) 724-6750 - youth services center; (949) 724-6717 - Aquatics Complex; (949) 724-6824 - athletic field / www.cityofirvine.org
14301 Yale Avenue, Irvine

    Heritage Park is an extensive community park with the emphasis on community. The park has a terrific and large, low-to-the-ground playground with several, interconnected play areas in ship and castle configurations and motif. They incorporate lots of slides; talking tubes; ramps; rope and metal climbing structures; a rock climbing wall; play panels; a boat-shaped teeter-totter with plastic mini couches on each side; other teeter totters; several sand pits with fine sand; wheels to spin around on; raised sand tables; swings; animals on large springs; and more - all to stimulate creative play and all surrounded by small, grassy hills, shade trees, and benches. A small water play area is here, too, with a few fountains that shoot water up from the ground.

    The centerpiece of the park is a beautiful small lake with numerous ducks and a fountain in the middle. Skate or stroller around the paved pathway, play on the boulders that also ring it, and run around on more of the grassy, gently rolling hills. There are also basketball courts, twelve lighted tennis courts, three soccer fields, and four fields for organized sports play at the park.

    Several buildings line the perimeter of the park, such as the community services center, which has a few billiard tables and other games; the library; and the Irvine Fine Art Center, which has a small art gallery and offers art classes. The William Woollett Junior Aquatics Complex is just around the corner at 4601 Walnut Avenue. Two of their pools are open for recreational swim in the summer.

Hours: The park is open daily. The pools are open daily in the summer, Mon. - Fri., 1:15pm - 3:15pm; Sat. - Sun., 1pm - 2:30pm.
Price: The park is free. Swimming costs $4 for adults; $2 for seniors and ages 17 and under.
Ages: All

HIGH ROPES COURSE CHALLENGE

(714) 777-4884 - ropes course; (714) 637-0210 - Canyon RV Park / www.rockcityclimbing.com
24001 Santa Ana Canyon Road at the Canyon RV Park in Featherly Regional Park, Anaheim

Are you up for a challenge? Up at least sixty feet off the ground, that is? Constructed with telephone poles, steel cables, and ropes, there are several elements (over twenty different challenges) to mentally and physically test participants in this ropes course. The emphasis here is not on speed, but on attempting and doing. (Just don't look down!)

The course consists of a rock climbing wall, Burma bridge, cargo net traverse, cat walk, rope bridges, and two zip lines extending up to 277 feet each in length. On some of the elements you stand and walk the ropes, while on others you might move from one swing (made from two ropes with a bar between them) to another in the series. (Did I mention to not look down?) Every phase is supervised and each person wears a safety harness.

The park also offers lots of picnic tables and hundreds of shade trees, a playground, grassy areas, and the beginning (or end) of a bike path, plus youth group camping, cabin rentals ($75 a night), and 140 RV hookup sites. (The park does not offer day use.) Campers have use of the pool (open seasonally) and other amenities. Located within a wildlife preserve, the long and somewhat narrow Featherly Park is bordered by the Santa Ana River. The river adds another scenic element to the park as well as another place to explore, which when done safely, is fun for kids.

The three-hour ropes course challenge is designed for groups only - birthday parties, scout outings, youth group gatherings, team building, etc., although individuals may sign up for seasonal camps. A signed waiver and liability form, available online, is required by all participants. Note that ROCK CITY CLIMBING CENTER (pg. 263) owns and operates this ropes course.

Hours: Call to schedule an outing.
Price: Minimum $400 for the group.
Ages: 8 years and up.

HILLCREST PARK / LEMON PARK

(714) 738 - 6575 / www.cityoffullerton.com
1200 N. Harbor Boulevard, Fullerton

For some Fullerton fun, try Hillcrest Park. This huge, hilly park has a winding road throughout, with parking lots in several different spots along the way. Originally opened in 1922, some of that older ambiance shows in a classic way with graded, grassy areas, dotted with numerous mature trees, and stone steps leading to various levels. We saw some creative kids using cardboard to slide down a hill, which probably isn't great for the grass, but it looked like fun. Hillcrest has a few woodland areas with dirt paths for hiking. There are also some play areas, picnic tables, and barbecue pits.

Lemon Park, at 701 S. Lemon Street, is at the base of the Hillcrest hill. The wooden play here is in the shape of a ship. It has cargo nets to climb, a mini zip line, twisty metal climbing structures, slides, a short tunnel, and other innovative elements. A rec center is located here, too, as are basketball courts, more picnic tables, and, a rejuvenating feature on a hot day, a spray pool. Run and play in the water spurting up from the fountains. Note that kids must wear swimwear to play in this area.

Hours: Both parks are open daily, sunrise - sunset. The spray park in Lemon Park is open mid-June - September daily, noon - 5pm.
Price: Free
Ages: All

HUNTINGTON CENTRAL PARK / SHIPLEY NATURE CENTER

(714) 536-5486 - park; (714) 842-4772 - Shipley / www.huntingtonbeachca.gov.org; www.shipleynature.org; www.stockteam.com
18000 Goldenwest Street, Huntington Beach

This gigantic park offers many options for all kinds of fun. Fish at the stocked lake, which is tucked in the corner. Let the kids go wild on the five different playgrounds. Ride bikes along the six miles of cement pathways that crisscross all over. Walk on the several other miles of dirt trails. Romp on the expansive green lawns. Retreat under shade trees. Enjoy lunch using the picnic tables or barbeque grills. Work it out on the exercise stations located throughout. The equipment, such as pull up bars and rings, is provided as are how-to instructions. Score on the disc golf course located on the west side of Goldenwest Street, which offers instructions, maps, and an opportunity to purchase your own disc. It's much more fun than golf (personal opinion!) as the discs are thrown into above ground metal baskets (if you're good). If you can throw a frisbee, or disc, you can play. Call (714) 425-9931 for more information. See a weekend horse show at the Equestrian Center. Riders 7 years and up can also rent a horse here to go on a trail ride. Call (714) 848-6565 for details.

Check out books from the huge library off Talbert Street (see HUNTINGTON BEACH PUBLIC LIBRARY on

page 315). Get dirty at Adventure Playground (pg. 725) for summertime fun. Play at the adjoining Huntington Beach Central Sports Complex with its eight baseball and soccer fields, batting cages, concession stand, and imaginative children's play area. The latter has a short rock climbing wall, lots of slides, monkey bars, and metal climbing structures.

The tiny Park Bench Cafe, located at 17732 Goldenwest Street, serves up breakfast and lunch with tables inside and outdoors. They also have a Doggie Diner section where you can eat with (and order for) your pooch. Contact (714) 842-0775 / www.parkbenchcafe.com for more information.

Shipley Nature Center is a fenced-in, eighteen-acre preserve with a very family friendly walking trail, a pond, and an interpretive building with animal skins, rocks, and other exhibits on wildlife and ecology. Tip: Come on the second Saturday of every month from 11am to 2pm for children's activities. Maintenance is done during the week so contact them to help clean up the center by weeding, planting and clearing trails. Come on Thursday nights (6pm to 7pm) in the summer to enjoy free presentations of raptors and other animals, to learn about plants, and more.

> **Hours:** The park is open daily, 5am - 10pm. The disc course is open Mon. - Fri., 9am - 5pm; Sat. - Sun., 8am - 5pm. Shipley is open Mon. - Sat., 9am to 1pm. Closed Sun. and major holidays.
>
> **Price:** Free to the park and Shipley. The disc course is $2 for adults to play on weekdays; $3 on weekends; ages 15 and under are free. Disc rentals are $2.
>
> **Ages:** All

INDEPENDENCE SKATE PARK

(714) 738-5369 / www.ci.fullerton.ca.us

801 W. Valencia Drive, Fullerton

12,000 square feet of cement bowls, rails, ledges, and mini ramps are great for practicing. Although self-supervised, helmet and pads are required. The adjacent recreation building houses a basketball court, racquetball court, and an aquatic facility.

> **Hours:** Open daily, sunrise - sunset.
>
> **Price:** Free
>
> **Ages:** 7 years and up.

IRVINE LAKE

(714) 649-9111 / www.irvinelake.net

4621 Santiago Canyon Road, Orange

Casting around for fun places to go with your little fisherman? Irvine Lake is a large lake off a main road, yet surrounded by hillsides, too. It's stocked seasonally with a variety of fish such as bass, trout, catfish, crappie, and bluegill. There is a five-fish limit per person. (I wish I had this problem!) Fish from the lake's edge, or rent a boat to navigate into one of the numerous inlets. Motorboats rentals are $55. Pontoons, for up to eight people, are $150.

A five-acre kid's lagoon is cordoned off just for ages 12 and under to fish. If there are dryer areas of the lake bed, depending on the season, it's a terrific place to bird watch. We saw herons, pelicans, cranes, and at least a half dozen other birds I feel like I should be able to identify. We also hiked a bit on some of the trails around the lake and through the grounds.

Toward the entrance is a small playground, a grassy area, a horseshoe pit, a volleyball court, and a few picnic tables under shade trees. Conveniently, a bait and tackle shop, and even a breakfast and sandwich cafe counter, are also on the grounds. No fishing license is needed.

Overnight tent or RV camp sites (for up to six people) are not necessarily scenic, but a place to stay in order to fish more.

> **Hours:** Open November - May, Sun. - Thurs., 6am - 4pm; Fri. - Sat., 6am - 5pm. Open June - October, Sun. - Mon. and Wed., 6am - 4pm, Thurs., 6am - 11pm, Fri. and Sat., 6am - midnight. Closed in the summer on Tues.
>
> **Price:** Fishing is $24 for ages 12 and up; $21 for seniors Mon. - Thurs.; $19 for ages 4 - 11; children 3 and under are free; $5 for dogs. Rates include the entrance fee and up to five fish. If you get this far and catch more, ask about a second limit pass. Rental rods are $10. Campsites are $25 a night.
>
> **Ages:** 4 years and up.

IRVINE OPEN SPACE NATURE TRAIL / TURTLE ROCK PARK

(949) 854-8144 - park; (949) 724-6738 - nature trail / www.cityofirvine.org

1 Sunnyhill Drive, Irvine

Irvine Open Space operates a nature center building that is the entrance way to a small, five-acre nature preserve. The preserve has both a desert habitat and pine trees, so that the stroller-friendly trail is partially in the sun and partially in the shade. A ranger here said that going around a little pond, over a few bridges, and looping back around takes "ten minutes if you don't see anything, thirty minutes if you follow the trail guide. The longer you're here, the more you'll learn." Guided tours of the trail are offered by reservation, as are tours for scouts earning badges, with a minimum of ten people.

The surrounding Turtle Rock Park has lighted tennis courts, a basketball court, sand volleyball courts, and a nice playground, plus a nature trail that goes over a creek.

Hours: The park is open Mon. - Fri., 9am - 9pm; Sat., 9am - 10pm; Sun., noon - 6pm. The nature center is open Mon. - Fri., 9am - 5pm; Sat., 9am - 4pm.

Price: Free to the park and to walk the nature trail on your own. Guided tours are $2 per person; scout tours are $5 per scout.

Ages: 2 - 13 years.

IRVINE REGIONAL PARK

(714) 973-6835; (714) 973-3173 / www.ocparks.com

1 Irvine Park Road, Orange

Spend entire days exploring all there is to see and do at this 477-acre regional park, which is one of my favorites. A multitude of huge, old oak (and other) trees spread their large branches and roots, so enjoy some back-to-nature time. The middle area is "carved out," with lots of grass for picnic areas, several great playgrounds, and baseball diamonds.

Toddlers through about 8 years old can ride ponies around a track that is open Tuesday through Friday 11am to 4pm. Rides are $5 each. Call (714) 403-7914 for more details. Kids 8 years and older can take a guided horseback ride inside the park past coastal live oaks, sycamore trees, and chaparral. Rides are available Tuesday through Sunday for $45 an hour by reservation only. Call Country Trails at (714) 538-5860 / www.ctriding.com for further horseback riding rental information. More fun can be had with pedal boat rentals for $15 per half hour, and bike rentals, for $12 an hour for a chopper. Both pedal boat and bike rentals are available Monday through Friday, 10am to 4pm, and on weekends and holidays, 10am to 5pm. Irvine Park Railroad offers ten-minute, one-third-scale model train rides around the park daily (closed major holidays), 10am to 4pm at $5 per person; children 12 months and younger ride free. This is a fun little trip! Call (714) 997-3968 or (714) 997-3636 / www.irvineparkrailroad.com for more information. The railroad also offers school field trips for 4th graders, incorporating panning for gold, miner's camp, and more, that corresponds with the California history curriculum. The train's website is good for all the above-listed attractions.

The Interpretive Center, (714) 973-3187, has taxidermied animals to look at; skulls, furs, and animal pelts to touch; a grinding rock to try out; plus displays and information about the wilderness part of the park. Biking, hiking, and equestrian trails are plentiful in Irvine Regional Park with creeks, sagebrush, and animals throughout. Rangers are available for school and scout tours for park trails. Note that the twenty-two-mile Mountains to Sea Trail, accessed from this park, begins at Weir Canyon in Anaheim Hills and reaches to the Bay in Newport Beach. Hikers and mountain bikers follow the trail system that encompasses all of Irvine Ranch and passes through some of the most scenic topography of parkland and open spaces that Orange County has to offer. Check www.IrvineRanchLandReserve.com for more information. Also, look up ORANGE COUNTY ZOO (pg. 333), as the zoo is located inside the park.

Hours: Irvine Park is open April through October daily, 6am - 9pm. It's open the rest of the year daily, 6am - 6pm. The Nature Center is usually open Sat. - Sun., 11:30am - 3:30pm, providing a volunteer is available.

Price: $3 per vehicle, Mon. - Fri., $5 on Sat. - Sun; $7 - 10 on holidays.

Ages: All

IRVINE TERRACE PARK

(949) 644-3151 / www.newportbeachca.gov

721 Evita Drive, Newport Beach

Up a hill, via grass or the cement pathway, is a delightful playground with a two-story play structure with enclosed slides shooting out, metal climbing apparatus, steps, platforms with steering wheels and games, monkey "bar" rings, and metal wheels to hang from. Underneath is a plenty of space for pretending. A shorter play structure, partly in the sand, is just as much fun with slides, tunnels, wide plastic climbing "rocks", and raised sand basins, plus a little house underneath. A four-sided, free-standing rock climbing wall; a play ship on large springs; talking tube; diggers;

four-person teeter-totter; and swings complete this section.

The park also sports a basketball court, two tennis courts, wide open grassy areas, pine and other mature trees, and a view of the bay via a very small Zen garden with plants and statues.

Hours: Open daily, sunrise - sunset.
Price: Free
Ages: 1 - 10

LAGUNA COAST WILDERNESS PARK TRAILS / LITTLE SYCAMORE CANYON STAGING AREA / NIX NATURE CENTER

(949) 923-2235 or (949) 923-3702 / www.lagunacanyon.org; www.ocparks.com
18751 Laguna Canyon Road, Laguna Beach

The headquarters for the massive Laguna Coast Wilderness Park is this small nature center which has a wall mural, corn and stone pestle, and informational panels about the Native Americans, as well as a phone to pick up and hear a recording about spirit animals. Pick up trail maps here and enjoy the use of the picnic tables. An easy, half-mile loop trail just outside the nature center is a fun starting point. We opted to take another, about five-mile, dirt trail that looped around after it went up and up (and up) a hill, got steep and rocky at times, rewarded us with a fantastic view of the entire area as we walked along the perimeter amongst a few trees, sage, etc., and left us with a feeling of accomplishment and joy at seeing such beautiful creation as we headed back down to the center. Bring water and know there is not a lot of shade at the top!

Just down the road are other parts of this 6,400-acre park, which is part of the 17,000-acre South Coast Wilderness Park system, including Willow Canyon Staging Area, on 20101 Laguna Canyon Road which is just south of the El Toro Road intersection and James Dilley Preserve, and just north of the 73 Toll Road.

Hours: Open daily, 8am - 4pm.
Price: Parking is $3.
Ages: All

LAGUNA HILLS SKATE PARK

(949) 707-2608 / www.ci.laguna-hills.ca.us
25555 Alicia Parkway, Laguna Hills

The skate park is part of a community parks and sports center. Skateboarders and bladers can skate at the lighted, 10,000-square-foot cement park that features a pyramid, cones, steps, grinding rails, volcano, and ramps. All participants must wear a helmet and knee and elbow pads.

Hours: Open Mon. - Sat., 8am - 10pm; Sun., 8am - 6pm.
Price: Free
Ages: 7 years and up.

LAGUNA LAKE PARK

(714) 738-6575 / www.cityoffullerton.com; www.dfg.ca.gov/
3120 Lakeview Drive, Fullerton

In contrast to my earlier thinking, I now know that parks don't require a playground to make them "good." They simply must have kid-appeal, and this one does. The dirt path around the long lake, seasonally stocked with trout, is bike and stroller friendly. The marshy reeds are a great place for dragonfly hunting. Bring bread for the ducks, bait for your fishing pole (over 16 needs a fishing license), and enjoy this unusual park. Barbecue pits and picnic tables are here, too. There is a longer Fullerton loop to hike or bike on, too.

Hours: Open daily, sunrise - sunset.
Price: Free
Ages: All

LAGUNA NIGUEL REGIONAL PARK

(949) 923-2240 - park; (949) 362-9227 - fishing / www.ocparks.com; www.lagunaniguellake.com
28241 La Paz Road, Laguna Niguel

This park is 236 acres of adventures waiting to be had. It offers volleyball courts, horseshoe pits, tennis courts, bike trails, an area for flying remote-controlled airplanes, several toddler-friendly playgrounds, open grass areas, barbecue pits, and picnic shelters, plus a forty-four-acre lake for fishing and boating. No fishing license is required, but

day use permits are. The lake is seasonally stocked with catfish and bluegill, with a limit of five fish per permit. Bass are strictly catch and release. Fish from the floating docks or rent a boat at $15 an hour. A bait and tackle shop are conveniently located on the park grounds. The shop offers pole and net rentals for $10 a day; float tube rentals for $5; and snacks and beverages to purchase. The park tends to get crowded on weekends and holidays, so get an early start!

Hours: Open daily, 6am - 6pm. Fishing closes at 5pm.
Price: $3 per vehicle Mon. - Fri.; $5 on Sat. - Sun.; $7 - 10 on holidays. Fishing permits are $28 for adults; $18 for ages 4 -11.
Ages: All

LAGUNA NIGUEL SKATE & SOCCER PARK
(949) 916-7766 or (949) 916-7755 / www.ci.laguna-niguel.ca.us
27745 Alicia Parkway, Laguna Niguel

The 22,000 square-foot concrete lighted skate park has all the features both intermediate and advanced skaters look for; bowls, rails, funbox, a street course, and more. It is a supervised park and requires a parental waiver on file for ages 17 and under. Skaters must wear a helmet and pads. The adjacent soccer park's playing field is synthetic grass. The field has lights for night play.

Hours: The skate park is open during the school year, Mon. - Fri., noon - 9:30pm; Sat. - Sun., 9am - 9:30pm. Holidays, school breaks, and summer time hours are daily, 9am - 9:30pm. BMX bikers can utilize the park Tues., 7pm - 9:30pm, Fri., noon - 4:30pm and Sun., 4:30pm - 9:30pm.
Price: $10 per person for the skate park per day, or purchase an annual pass for $40 for residents; $80 for nonresidents.
Ages: 7 years and up.

LANTERN BAY COUNTY PARK
(949) 248-3530 / www.danapoint.org
25111 Park Lantern Road, Dana Point

This bluff top park offers spectacular vistas of the ocean and features a large, grassy, run-around area, barbecues, picnic tables under pine trees, a full basketball court, physical fitness cluster, a playground with short slides and other play equipment, and a paved pathway that winds throughout and around the park.

Hours: Open daily sunrise - sunset.
Price: Free
Ages: All

LIBERTY PARK & SKATE PARK - Westminster
(714) 895-2860 / www.westminster-ca.gov
13900 Monroe Street, Westminster

The park is a typical, medium-sized park with open grassy areas, a few trees, a few picnic tables, a basketball court, and a playground. The real draw, I think, is for skateboarders and bladers. Their play area is a mid-size cement skate park which has a mini-pool, kidney pool, stair-rail plaza, funbox, and a street course. Wearing safety gear - a helmet and knee and elbow pads - is enforced.

Hours: The park and skate park are open daily, 8am - dusk.
Price: Free
Ages: 7 years and up for the skate park.

MILE SQUARE REGIONAL PARK
(714) 973-6600 or (714) 973-3197 - park; (805) 895-8480 - Wheel Fun Rentals / www.ocparks.com; www.wheelfunrentals.com
16801 Euclid Avenue, Fountain Valley

Have a full day of family fun at Mile Square Park; be there or be *square*. Enjoy picnic areas with lots and lots of tables and barbecue grills; cement bike/stroller pathways that crisscross throughout and that go around the park perimeter; an archery range (bring your own equipment); two playgrounds (with several short slides; both curvy and enclosed, swings, and a short climbing wall); a nature area; two soccer fields; baseball fields; a good-size, boulder-lined lake (with a bridge and small island of palm trees) toward the north end and another (smaller) one in the south; a stream; and sand volleyball courts. You may fish in the two man-made lakes - no license is needed unless your child is over 16 years old. Ask about the fishing derby. There are plenty of lovely shade trees interspersed throughout the park

with some open grass areas.

The Fountain Valley Recreation Center is on Brookhurst Avenue, sandwiched between golf courses. This center has several basketball courts, twelve tennis courts, outdoor racquetball courts, two sand volleyball courts, numerous baseball diamonds, and a playground.

Get physical on the weekends with various pleasure rentals by the hour - surrey bikes (seating three adults and two children) are $30; quad sport (similar to a go-cart) are $10; and single pedal boats are $15 for half an hour. All rentals are available on weekends only, mid-September through April, noon - 5:30pm; May to mid-September, 11am to dusk.

Hours: Open March - October daily, 7am - 9pm. Open November - February daily, 7am - 6:30pm.

Price: $3 per vehicle Mon. - Fri; $5 on Sat. - Sun.; $7 on holidays. Some free street parking is available on Euclid and Edinger Ave.

Ages: All

MOULTON MEADOWS PARK

(949) 497-0716 / www.lagunabeachcity.net; www.funorangecountyparks.com

Balboa Avenue at the intersection of Capistrano Avenue, Laguna Beach

For kids who like to climb, this great little park's main attraction is the section dedicated to thick, crisscrossing ropes in different configurations to climb up and on. What fun! More climbing apparatus includes a short rock climbing wall and several tall, big, fake boulders. The sand-floor playground also offers shade-covered platforms with several slides, monkey bars, twisting metal structures, toy animals to rock back and forth on, swings (including toddler swings), and flat, inverted triangle seats (some with poles through them) to incorporate with creative play.

The park also has two, half basketball courts; two tennis courts (with parking meters to keep track of court time); a soccer field in the upper area; a fitness course along the pathway to the field; and small portions of grassy green lawn with trees and a few picnic tables and BBQ grills. There is a short, dirt, nature trail leading through some of the landscaping and around parts of the park, too.

One of the most inviting elements of Moulton Meadows is the breathtaking view driving up (and up!) to this hilltop park - wow! Laguna Beach and the ocean is laid out before you and on a clear day you can see Catalina.

Hours: Open daily, sunrise - sunset.

Price: Free

Ages: All

NEWPORT BAY CONSERVANCY / PETER AND MARY MUTH INTERPRETIVE CENTER

(714) 973-6820 - interpretive center; (949) 640-9956 - Back Bay Science Center; (949) 923-2269 - Back Bay tour / www.newportbay.org; www.ocparks.com

2301 University Drive, Newport Beach

The impressive-looking Peter and Mary Muth Interpretive Center, which is not visible from above as it's tucked under the observation bluff overlooking the northern portion of the reserve, offers several hands-on activities for kids. Lift panels to find answers to questions such as "Why does mud stink?". Walk through a short tunnel of (fake) mud to see what lives there. The center also has numerous information panels and displays around the inside perimeter; an exhibit on what comprises an estuary, accompanied by a real fish tank; taxidermied animals; a cut away to show life above and below the waterline; a theater room with several TV screens to view films; and classrooms filled with fun and educational equipment. Look for butterflies in the butterfly garden planted just outside the building.

A short, somewhat stroller-friendly dirt hiking trail in this immediate area takes visitors to vistas overlooking the bay and reserve. A three-and-a-half-mile paved biking/walking trail goes around the reserve, mostly along the one-way street, Backbay Drive, where cars can only go fifteen miles an hour. This is a great way to explore the estuary. Note: You will frequently hear planes flying overhead from the nearby John Wayne Airport.

This ecological reserve, a remnant of a once-extensive wetland, is part of an endeavor to conserve wildlife in the Upper Bay. Although surrounded by urban development and ringed by roads, the bay and small islands are home to sea critters, a variety of plants, and hundreds of waterfowl as it's a stopover for migrating birds on the Pacific Flyway. Introduce your children to the valuable natural resources that God originally put on the earth by involving kids in the wide variety of interactive and interpretive programs offered at the interpretive center, at the Back Bay Science Center (www.backbaysciencecenter.org), and at the California Department of Fish and Game next to Shellmaker. Curriculum aids are available. Join in on a free walking tour, or participate in youth fishing programs, clean-up day, or shark study - mere samplings of what is offered here. Special tours are offered for students, scouts, and interested adults.

A knowledgeable Newport Bay Naturalist is the guide for a two-hour kayak tour of the Back Bay, the wildlife estuary reserve, every Saturday and Sunday at 10am. In the estuary, you can see crabs, blue herons, snowy egrets, and other birds and animals in their natural habitat. We took this tour and learned why this reserve is becoming endangered, as well as some of the clean up projects that we can get involved with. What a workout of paddling for those of us not physically fit! But it is also a fun and educational way to spend some family time together. The cost is $25 for ages 8 and up, which is the minimum age. Call (949) 923-2269 / www.newportbay.org for more info.

For swimming, camping, and more water-sport fun, look under the NEWPORT DUNES WATERFRONT RESORT MARINA (pg. 241) and MOE B'S WATER SPORTS (pg. 330), which are at the southern end of the bay.

Hours: The center is open Tues. - Sun., 10am - 4pm. Closed Mon. and major holidays. The reserve is open daily, sunrise - sunset.
Price: Free to the center. Program prices vary.
Ages: 5 years and up.

NORTHWOOD COMMUNITY PARK (aka Castle Park)
(949) 724-6728 - park; (949) 724-6620 - community center / www.ci.irvine.ca.us
4531 Bryan Avenue, Irvine

The focal point of this park is the big, fortress-like structure which is great for climbing on and around. It has a slide, steps, a fireman's pole, and castle-like walls built into the rocky side, completing the fortress image. The wonderful, all-abilities playground also has tire swings, ramps, a balance beam, slides, bridges, animals on large springs to ride, a wooden and cement pirate ship, and sand boxes.

The surrounding park has soccer fields, large grass areas, tennis courts, fitness course, a basketball court, shuffleboard, a handball court, and baseball diamonds, plus a paved pathway all around the fields. You can check out play equipment, free of charge, at the community center building, which also has an exercise room and classroom space.

Hours: The park is open daily 8am - 9pm. The community center building is open Mon - Fri., 9am - 9pm; Sat. 9am - 10pm; Sun 9am - 6pm.
Price: Free
Ages: All

OAK CANYON NATURE CENTER
(714) 998-8380 / www.anaheim.net
6700 Walnut Canyon Road, Anaheim

This rustic Nature Center is a fifty-eight-acre natural park nestled in Anaheim Hills. Surrounded by such beauty, it doesn't seem possible that there is a city nearby. Take a delightful, easy hike along the wide pathways along the creek and through the woods that boast of huge oak and other shade trees. Or, opt for more strenuous hiking on the six miles of trails offered here. No bikes or picnicking is allowed, so that the animals and plants that consider this canyon their home can continue to live here unharmed.

The good-sized, interpretative center building houses live critters, plus several trays of mounted butterflies and other insects. The small stage area is great for putting on shows using the animal puppets.

The Nature Center offers many different programs, including a family hike every Saturday morning. On Wednesday evenings throughout the summer, Nature Nights for families begin at 7pm with a twilight walk through the canyon followed up by a presentation at 7:30pm at the outdoor amphitheater ($5 per family donation). Ask about their summer day camps.

Hours: The park is open daily, sunrise - sunset. The interpretive center is open Sat., 10am - 4pm.
Price: Free to the park. The nature center asks for a $2 donation per family.
Ages: All

OLINDA RANCH PARK
(714) 990-7600 / www.ci.brea.ca.us
4055 Carbon Canyon Road, Brea

This beautifully landscaped and maintained park has a long paved pathway that runs along Lambert. It also has stretches of green grass, a baseball field, picnic tables, lighted basketball courts, a mini skate park, and a small, but good playground with swings, slides, some play panels (a favorite is one that is like a mini piano where you can strike the keys to play songs) and climbing appartus all in a sand base. The park is across the street from CARBON CANYON REGIONAL PARK.

Hours: Open daily, sunrise to sunset.
Price: Free
Ages: All

O'NEILL REGIONAL PARK and ARROYO TRABUCO

(949) 923-2260 or (949) 923-2256 / www.ocparks.com
30892 Trabuco Canyon Road, Trabuco Canyon

As we explored parts of this over 2,000 acre park, I kept thinking of how absolutely gorgeous it is. O'Neill Park is a canyon bottom and so filled with trees, it's like being in a forest. A creek runs throughout, creating lush greenery. The abundant nature trails (about eighteen miles!) are mostly hilly dirt trails, though a few are paved "roads".

The playground has a log cabin-like building with slides and swings and such around it. Inside the small Nature Center are taxidermied animals around the perimeter of the room. A few tables in the middle display skulls, furs, and rocks to touch. Join in a morning, ranger-led hike to learn how to identify animal tracks and find out other facts about the park's inhabitants.

Arroyo Trabuco is a more than 900-acre parcel of pristine wilderness preserve adjacent to O'Neill park area. Hiking, mountain biking, and wildlife observation are the main recreational activities available here. The park also has beautiful campgrounds. This entire park is nature at its finest.

Hours: The park is open daily, 7am - sunset. The Nature Center is usually open Sat. - Sun., 8am - 4pm.
Price: $3 per vehicle on Mon. - Fri.; $5 on Sat. - Sun; $7 on holidays. Camping starts at $20 per night.
Ages: All

ORANGE COUNTY GREAT PARK

(866) 829-3829 - Visitor's Center; (714) 733-3167 - Farmer's Market / www.ocgp.org
Trabuco Road, Irvine

Still in the process of being built (for years and years to come) on the former Marine Corps Air Station at El Toro this absolutely gigantic park (1,347 acres) has and will have a lot to offer.

The runway has a walkable historical time line painted on it that commemorates 162 significant historical events from around the globe - a kind of interactive educational tool. The Museum of Heritage and Aviation at this site will feature military artifacts, exhibits, and interactive experiences that incorporate music and film.

Here are the current attractions, which are all grouped together on site, surrounded by a whole lot of space: The big, orange, tethered, **hot air balloon** is hard to miss, especially as it rises up, up, and away - 400 feet up in the air, overlooking the park and surrounding neighborhoods. The gondola (i.e. passenger basket) can hold up to twenty-five adults, depending on wind conditions. All ages are invited to go airborne, as there are safety nets in place surrounding the basket area. "Flyers" can walk around the basket for different panoramic viewpoints during the seven-minute ride. Note that a waiver must be signed for all riders and children 12 and under must be accompanied by an adult. Visitors can also ride the thirty+-animal **carousel** which was moved here from Fashion Island. A small, but fun **Kids Rock Playground** features a few fake boulders to climb on and through, with a kid-size cave thrown in, all on cushy, recycled rubber. Misters operate during the hotter months. There are plenty of picnic tables and chairs scattered throughout, so bring a lunch. **Palm Courts Arts Complex** is a huge courtyard, lined by extra large palm trees, that hosts two buildings. One is called **Makers Depot**, an artists studio and innovention center where the public is invited to create and learn about inventing alongside more experienced artists and engineers in workshops and just by stopping by. 3-D design workstations and 3-D printers and other new tools are available. Workshops can include learning how to make underwater robots, SUP paddle boards, smart phone covers and lots more. Makers Depot is usually open Saturday, 10am to 4pm. The other building is **Great Park Gallery**, featuring free, rotating art exhibits. It's open Thursdays through Sundays until 4m. For a hands-on gardening experience, the adjacent **Farm & Food Lab** has a conglomeration of garden beds and a variety of plants and flowers with activities and information. We saw strawberries, oranges, and lemons growing; and a butterfly garden. Some plaques show and tell visitors ingredients and toppings that go into meals, such as the Pizza and Spaghetti Garden, which grows ingredients for sauces. There is information to learn about and do composting, planting, fertilizing and more. The **Farmer's Market** offers fresh seasonal fruits and produce, plus flowers and bread every Sunday from 10am to 2pm. Breakfast and lunch are available to purchase here then, too.

The massive North Lawn features reflecting fountains/ponds and a **multi-purpose recreation field** - an open play area with grassy spots for picnics and to run, run, run around. You can even check out soccer balls, footballs, jump ropes, Bocce ball sets and frisbees for free at the Visitors Center. Use the frisbees, or bring your own disc, to use on the disc golf course. The 4.5 acre **Incredible Edible Farm** grows vegetables that are harvested by Second Harvest

Food Bank volunteers (and that could be you!) who pick the food to help feed the hungry in Orange County. See www.FeedOC.org for more info. A lot of special events are held here throughout the year, so check the website calendar, and/or just come to hang out, play and relax any time.

Hours: The park is open Mon. - Wed., 10am - dusk; Thurs. - Fri., 10am - 10pm; Sat. - Sun., 9am - 10pm. The hot air balloon ride is open Thurs. - Fri., 10am - 3pm and 7pm- 10pm; Sat. - Sun., 9am - 3pm and 7pm - 10pm. Note that registraton begins thirty minutes before morning operating hours and an hour before nighttime operating hours. Always call first as wind conditions effect flights. The carousel and Visitors Center are open Thurs. - Fri., 10am - 10pm; Sat. - Sun., 9am - 10pm. The Farmer's Market is open Sun., 10am - 2pm. Farm and Food Lab is open daily, 10am - 3pm. The balloon and carousel are open on certain Monday holidays. The whole park is closed on New Year's Day, Veteran's Day, Thanksgiving, Christmas Eve, and Christmas Day.

Price: The carousel is $2 per person a ride or $3 for all day. Balloon flights are $10 for ages 18 and up; $5 for ages 12 - 18 without a paid, accompanying adult; free for ages 17 and under with a paid adult. Parking is usually free, except for special events, such as the Great Park Pumpkin Harvest, and Flights and Sounds Summer Festival, when the fee is $10 per car.

Ages: All

OSO VIEJO PARK - OSO CREEK TRAIL

(949) 470-3095 / www.cityofmissionviejo.org; www.funorangecountyparks.com

24931 Veterans Way, Mission Viejo

Oso (which means "bear" in Spanish) Viejo Park features a playground, sports park, nature hiking trail, and intergenerational community center at its center. The Norman P. Murray Community Center has a lovely outside patio to sit at and enjoy the nature of the park and/or have a picnic. Behind the center is a sand-based playground that boasts a three-story-high play tower with two, very long, enclosed slides jutting from the top, plus a few shorter slides, rock-climbing walls, metal climbing apparatus, and platforms. The playground also includes another, less-imposing play structure, plus a rope climbing wall, talking tubes, a swing set surrounded by a large rainbow imbedded in the ground, a teeter-totter, and more.

To walk the Oso Creek Trail, head south of the Community Center, down past the playground and baseball diamonds. The stroller-friendly trail, often shaded, parallels the creek and an upper walking trail. Be on the lookout for ducks, turtle, bunnies, lizards, birds and other wildlife. Across a short wooden bridge is a butterfly garden and a plant maze created from bushes. Head north of the center, over 1.5 miles, and you'll eventually reach PAVION PARK (pg. 288), which has a good-sized playground with a huge funnel and play equipment. The upper cement pathway at Osos also features some neat stopping points along the way, such as mosaic wall murals, garden spots, animal statues, picnic tables, and benches to rest. There is a multi-purpose field up here, too.

Hours: Open daily, 7am - 11pm.
Price: Free
Ages: All

PAVION PARK

(949) 470-3093 or (949) 470-3061 / www.orangecounty.net/html/park-missionviejo.html

24051 Pavion Road, Mission Viejo

The five-acre Pavion Park can be the starting or ending point for your walk along the long, paved walking/biking pathway along Jeronimo Road. You'll stroll alongside a rocky creek, with a small seasonal waterfall, amongst the trees and other foliage, making for a pleasant excursion. There are even a few benches to stop and rest. See OSO VIEJO PARK / OSO CREEK TRAIL (pg. 288) for details about a park on the other end.

The park itself has a playground that is wheelchair accessible with ramps and bridges. There are also tunnels, short slides, twisty slides, a zig zag rope climbing structure, circular sand tables, picnic tables, barbecues, and a soccer/football field.

Hours: Open daily, sunrise - sunset.
Price: Free
Ages: All

PEARSON PARK

(714) 765-5274 - amphitheater; (714) 765-5191 - park; (714) 635-9622 - pool / www.anaheim.net

400 N. Harbor Boulevard, Anaheim

At the north end of this attractive, nineteen-acre park is a series of small, interconnecting, rock-edged ponds with

a few bubbly fountains and lots of friendly ducks. Besides an abundance of palm trees and a variety of mature shade trees (which make good climbing trees!), there is plenty of green lawn, some scattered picnic tables and barbecue pits, and cement pathways throughout which allow the whole park to be accessible. The sports oriented will enjoy the six tennis courts, sand volleyball courts, baseball diamond with stadium seating and the swimming pool with a small, adjacent, two-and-a-half-feet pool.

The playground, with wood chip flooring, has a swing set, slides, a short "rock" climbing wall attached to a good-size play structure with steering wheels in place of monkey bars, and a giant plastic climbing thing that it looks like an oversized leaf.

A large, enclosed amphitheater, located on the east side of the park, is the hot spot for terrific family entertainment during the summer months, such as Friday night Family Series ($3 for ages 8 and up; children 7 and under are free) and movie nights. This venue, with flower-lined walkways, has a box office and a refreshment stand in the courtyard.

Hours: The park is open daily. The pool is open mid-June - mid-August, Sat., 1pm - 4pm.
Price: The park is free. Swimming is free, too.
Ages: All

PETER GREEN PARK

(714) 536-5486 / www.ci.huntington-beach.ca.us
7421 Seagate Drive, Huntington Beach

Up a gently sloping hill covered with grass and sprinkled with shade trees is a great playground for young'uns on recycled rubber flooring. A large, multi-level play structure, with plenty of room for imaginative play underneath, has several slides sprouting from it, including two twisty enclosed ones, and circular and twisty metal climbing shapes. The tall platforms and ramps are lined with protective bars. A shorter play structure has more slides, including side-by-side slides, plus a bridge, steps, talking tubes, and climby things. Kids can also climb in and on a play fire truck and dump truck (?), ride on large cement turtles, play giant tic-tac-toe, swing, and climb a free-standing rock wall. (Seems like the word "climb" comes up a lot for this park.) The park also features a tennis court, sand volleyball court, basketball court, and picnic tables in and out of the shade. Alas, there are no restrooms here.

Hours: Open daily, sunrise to sunset.
Price: Free
Ages: All

PETERS CANYON REGIONAL PARK

(714) 973-6611; (714) 834-2400; (714) 973-6612 / www.ocparks.com
8548 E. Canyon View Avenue, Orange

My boys and I have decided that this huge, 354-acre undeveloped park, bordered by occasional housing developments, is best geared for at least somewhat hardy hikers and bikers. The seven miles of narrow dirt trails are sometimes barren and sometimes lined with sage scrub, grassland areas, and willow and sycamore trees, as they traverse up and down and through the hills and canyon. (Bring drinking water and know that it is hot during the summer!) The 2.5 mile upper Lake View Trail loops around the reservoir, while the lower East Ridge Trail and Peters Canyon Trail provide a panoramic view of the canyon and the surrounding area. Be on the lookout for lots of wildlife.

The reservoir by the parking lot offers one of the most scenic spots, as it overlooks the water often teeming with diverse waterfowl - bird watchers flock here. Picnic tables under a few shade trees are also here. Another scenic area is along the Creek Trail as it goes along a creek. Note that the park is closed for two or three days after a rain.

Hours: Open daily, 7am - sunset.
Price: Parking is $3 per vehicle.
Ages: 5 years and up.

PIONEER ROAD PARK

(714) 573-3000 / www.tustinca.org
10250 Pioneer Road, Tustin

Round up your young uns and bring 'em to this Western-themed park. Its most unique feature is the several, hardy, wooden-sided, wire-meshed and open-topped stagecoaches with wagon wheels and short ladders to climb aboard. The wagons are arranged in a semi-circle, just like the old days. The park also has wonderful, covered, multi-story play structures that have enclosed tube slides, open slides, ropes and chains to climb, twisty metal apparatus to climb, lots of swings, a zip line, a dear tunnel connector, bridges, and nooks and crannies to play in and on. There is

even room underneath one of the towers with a little table and chairs. Other amenities include a basketball half court, grass volleyball court, walking trail encircling the park, grassy areas, and a seasonal water spray area. In this area, water spurts up from the ground and feels good on our hot summer days. An open-sided log cabin eating area has numerous picnic tables under its roof, as well as barbecue pits. The facilities here are nice, not rustic.

Hours: Open daily, sunrise - sunset. The water play area is open Memorial Day - Labor Day daily, 10am - 4pm.

Price: Free

Ages: All

PREHISTORIC PLAYGROUND

(949) 707-2680 / www.ci.laguna-hills.ca.us

25555 Alicia Parkway, Laguna Hills

See LAGUNA HILLS COMMUNITY CENTER AND SPORTS COMPLEX (pg. 306) for details about this great, primordial playground. The sports complex also has ball fields, a roller hockey rink, and a huge skate park. The Community Center features a museum, of sorts, showcasing locally found fossils.

RALPH B. CLARK REGIONAL PARK

(714) 973-3170 / www.ocparks.com

8800 Rosecrans Avenue, Buena Park

This 100-acre park is one of the most aesthetically pleasing parks we've seen. It has all the things that make a park great - a lake to fish in, short waterfalls, ducks to feed, tennis courts, horseshoe pits, three softball fields, a baseball diamond, volleyball courts, and a few small playgrounds. Take a short hike around Camel Hill, or let the kids climb on the small, therefore ironically named, Elephant Hill. A paved bicycle trail goes all around the perimeter of the park. The playgrounds are wonderfully rustic-looking. One has duel slides, swings, climbing structures, and shaped, fake rocks plopped around to climb on and pretend with, all in a big area of sand.

The Interpretative Center has a working paleontology lab where kids can look through a big window and observe the detailed work being done. The Center also houses a twenty-six-foot Baleen whale fossil; a skeletal sabertooth "attacking" a skeletal horse; fossils of a ground sloth and a mammoth; shells; and more.

Kids really dig the marine fossil site across the street where a *bone*afide paleontologist conducts Family Fossil Day four times a year, usually in February, May, September, and December. This three-hour class is geared for youngsters 6 years and up. They can practice their fossil-finding skills by looking for fossilized shells at the marine site, then study and classify them back at the lab at the Interpretive Center. They may also make a craft, play a game, or enjoy another activity related to that day's theme. The price for the field trip is simply the price of admission to the park.

Hours: The park is open November through March daily, 7am - 6pm; April through October daily, 7am - 9pm. The Interpretative Center is usually open Tues. - Fri., 12:30pm - 5pm; Sat. - Sun., 9:30am - 4:30pm. Call first to make sure staff is available.

Price: $3 vehicle entrance Mon. - Fri.; $5 on Sat. - Sun.; $7 - $10 on holidays.

Ages: All

RANCHO MISSION VIEJO LAND CONSERVANCY

(949) 489-9778 / www.rmvreserve.org

Off Ortega Highway, San Juan Capistrano

The Land Conservancy manages a 1,200 acre wilderness reserve in the coastal foothills. They offer an incredible array of special programs to the general public and to school groups that give intimate glimpses into the wilderness of Orange County. Programs include guided nature walks, bird watching (and finding), wildlife workshops, astronomy nights, owl outings, bat walks, butterfly classes, butterfly counting (for research purposes), trail maintenance, and much more. The programs are given by trained docents, or professionals in that field of study. What a wonderful opportunity for kids to become aware of wildlife, and what they can do to help protect it. Also see RONALD W. CASPERS WILDERNESS PARK (pg. 291) which is just down the road.

Hours: Check the website for program hours and to look at the calendar of events. Visitors are not allowed on property without a conservancy staff member.

Price: Depending on the program, the fees range from free to $10 for adults; $5 for ages 16 and under.

Ages: Varies, depending on the program.

RICHARD T. STEED MEMORIAL PARK / RALPH'S SKATE PARK

(949) 361-8264 or (949) 361-8200 / www.san-demente.org

247 Avenida La Pata, San Clemente

The memorial park has several ball fields and is home to many tournaments - it even has a concession stand. There are also batting cages, a playground (with twisty slides and cargo nets), picnic areas, volleyball courts, and a skate park. This great, unsupervised 14,000-square-foot, concrete skate park features bowls, ramps, stairs, rails, and pyramids. It has lights, too. A helmet and knee and elbows pads must be worn for safety's sake and because the patrolling police will cite offenders.

Hours: The park is open daily, 6am - 10pm. The skate park is open daily, dawn - dusk. Note that the skate park is closed Fri., 8am - 10am for maintenance.

Price: Free

Ages: All

RONALD W. CASPERS WILDERNESS PARK

(949) 923-2210 - park; (800) 600-1600 - camping reservations / www.ocparks.com

33401 Ortega Highway, San Juan Capistrano

Orange County's largest park is massive, and consists mostly of canyon wilderness such as seasonally verdant valleys, groves of live oak and sycamore trees, meadows, and running streams. We saw mule deer and jackrabbits scampering through the woods and quail walking/running alongside the dirt road. The over thirty miles of hiking trails range from easy walks to strenuous, mountain-man hikes. The moderate, four-mile Bell Canyon loop is a nice jaunt. Start on the nature trail loop, go through oak trees, left on the Oak Trail cutoff that heads north along a streambed then onto a fire road. Your best bet is to pick up a trail map at the front entrance. Give kids the freedom to hike, but beware that mountain lions sometimes roam this area, too. Mountain bike usage is permitted on designated roads only. Visitors can also enjoy a barbecue under shade trees and playing on the large wooden playground with swings and slides, surrounded by trees. Check out the Nature Center that has a few taxidermied animals and hands-on activities.

The numerous camp sites are picturesque, wonderful for enjoying nature. Campsites have picnic tables, charcoal-burning stoves, fire rings, and a nearby water source. Also see RANCHO MISSION VIEJO LAND CONSERVANCY (pg. 290) which is just down the road.

Hours: Open daily, 7am - sunset. Call for extended hours. The nature center is open Sat. - Sun, 9am - 3pm.

Price: $3 per vehicle Mon. - Fri.; $5 Sat. - Sun; $7 - 10 on holidays. Camping is $20 a night.

Ages: All

SAN JOAQUIN WILDLIFE SANCTUARY / SEA & SAGE AUDUBON

(949) 261-7963 / www.seaandsageaudubon.org

5 Riparian View, Irvine

Who would have imagined that there would be this beautiful, peaceful bird sanctuary smack in the midst of the Irvine business district? Park at the grouping of six buildings, one of which is the Audubon center. The center contains a collection of taxidermy birds and is a great place to pick up information and maps, and perhaps even purchase something from the small gift shop. Binoculars and birding guides are available for loan here, too. The nicely landscaped grounds have an open green lawn, a few picnic tables, and restroom facilities. Note: Across the road from the center is the San Diego Creek, which offers more diverse wildlife (and a walking trail alongside).

There are twelve miles of fairly level, dirt, walking trails through the almost 300 acres of the sanctuary, as well as five large ponds (and several smaller ones), nesting islands, and riparian habitat. What a delight! This area is home to 223 species of birds, as well as rabbits (we saw several), raccoons, coyotes, lizards, dragonflies (by the marshy areas), and bats. Come to look for Canada geese, snowy egrets, peregrine falcons, great blue herons, black-necked stilts, and more birds, or just come to enjoy being in nature.

Explore the sanctuary on your own or join in any number of programs, such as the free monthly bird walks offered on the first Saturday of the month at 9am; workshops for teachers and students, including classroom kits on owls, songbirds, butterflies, and more; nature camps; and two-hour hands-on field trips for schools on wetland birds and pond life. If you're *pond*ering what to do, come here and let your imagination take flight!

Hours: Trails are open daily, dawn - dusk. The center is open daily, 8am - 4pm. Closed major holidays.

Price: Free

Ages: All

SANTA ANA RIVER LAKES

(714) 632-7830 / www.fishinglakes.com
4060 E. La Palma Avenue, Anaheim

$$$$

Not incredibly scenic and just off the main road, the reason to come here is for the fishing. Stocked twice a week in the winter with rainbow trout and lightning trout (you gotta be quick as a flash to catch these!) and catfish in the summer, plus bass and crappie, the lakes are great for fishermen of all ages. The lakes are also known for the large size fish that are often caught. A fishing license is not required. There is a five fish limit for adults and a three fish limit for children. The area is handicap accessible as you can drive right up to the lake's edge to fish. Motor boat rentals ($50 a day), rowboats ($25 a day), and pontoons ($100 a day) are available.

The park also offers picnic tables, a grassy area, and some large shade trees. Kids are almost guaranteed to catch a fish, or two, at the enclosed, small, rock-lined Huckleberry Pond, which is a nice-looking spot. There are chairs, a big shade tree, ducks, and picnic tables. Rod rentals are available for $6. Kids can also pan for minerals, gemstones and fossils here, too, via the Huckleberry Mining Company so they'll catch something - fish and/or rocks!

Other amenities include an on-site tackle shop that carries bait, as well as snacks and sandwiches to satisfy humans. There are lots of birds - I saw storks, kingfisher, herons, and ducks. Camping here is free and pretty much on the dirt, but for those who like to get an early start in the morning, it's ideal.

Hours: Open daily, 6am - 4pm for the day session; 12:30pm - 11pm for midday; and 5pm - 11pm for the evening session. Mining is open Wed. - Sun., 9am - 4pm.

Price: $25 for ages 13 and up, $15 for additional adults in the same vehicle (this includes fishermen and spectators); $10 for ages 4 - 12; children 3 and under are free. Midday session are $5 more with a fish limit of seven for adults; five for kids. Ask or check the website for specials. Huckleberry Pond costs $3 per person and fish from there costs $6.50 a pound.

Ages: 3 years and up.

SANTIAGO OAKS REGIONAL PARK

(714) 973-6620 or (714) 973-6622 / www.ocparks.com
2145 N. Windes Drive, Orange

$

Get back to nature at this 350-acre park that has beautiful hiking and equestrian trails that connect to the Anaheim Hills trail system. Take a short path along the creek leading to a waterfall at the dam, or travel more rugged terrain into the heart of the park. Be on the lookout for animals such as lizards, squirrels, deer, and birds. Mountain lions have been seen on rare occasion, too.

A favorite activity here is cooking breakfast over the charcoal barbecues early in the morning, while it's still quiet and cool. A small playground and a few horseshoe pits round out the facilities under a canopy of oak trees. The small Nature Center has taxidermied animals, pictures, and a few hands-on activities. Free, ranger-led tours are given on the first Sunday of the month at 10am, by reservation only.

Hours: The park is open daily, 7am - sunset. The nature center is open the first Sun., 10am - 2pm.

Price: $3 per vehicle Mon. - Fri., $5 Sat. - Sun.; $7 - 10 on holidays.

Ages: All

SANTIAGO PARK NATURE RESERVE

(714) 571-4200 / www.ci.santa-ana.ca.us
2535 N. Main Street, Santa Ana

You can literally stroll along Memory Lane here, simply because that's the name of the street adjacent to the park. This long park, located directly across the street from the DISCOVERY SCIENCE CENTER (pg. 301), has several areas with play equipment, plus scattered picnic tables, shade trees, grassy patches, and barbecue pits. We usually spend most of our time at the first play area, with its slides, swings, sand area, wooden bridges, tunnels, and a green, wooden fort-like structure. A little further east is a slightly sunken grassy area (perfect for a group party), a lawn bowling center, a baseball diamond, an archery range, tennis courts, and more play equipment. A rocky riverbed path follows along one side of the park. The pathway actually leads all the way to HART PARK (pg. 278), although it is a half hour, nonstroller friendly walk to get there.

Hours: Open daily, sunrise - sunset.

Price: Free

Ages: All

SIGLER PARK SPLASH PAD

(714) 895-2860 / www.westminster-ca.gov
7200 Plaza Street, Westminster

This long park has various components including three and a half basketball courts, two racquetball/handball courts, BBQ pits, a multipurpose field at one end, and a small playground at the other. The colorful playground has twisty slides, a slide shaped like a fish, swings (including toddler swings), a short rock-climbing wall, some rope climbing walls, play areas under platforms, and metal configurations to climb.

What really makes this park stand out, though, is the enclosed water playground with lots of fun elements. Palm trees dot the area. Poles with pelican heads squirt out water, as do sea dragons, and kids can run under arches and whales tales that shoot out water. H2O also shoots up from the ground at certain points. There are cement benches for parents to sit and watch. The splash pad may be rented out for private parties.

Hours: The park is open daily, sunrise to sunset. The water park/splash pad is open Memorial Day - mid-June, weekends, noon - 5pm; open daily mid-June through Labor Day, noon - 5pm.
Price: Free
Ages: All for the park; toddler - 8 year old for the water park.

TEWINKLE MEMORIAL PARK / VOLCOM SKATE PARK

(714) 754-5300 - park; (714) 754-5326 - skate park / www.ci.costa-mesa.ca.us
970 Arlington Drive, Costa Mesa

The fifty-acre Tewinkle Memorial Park is another one of my favorite parks. The huge and colorful and shaded Angel's Playground is a barrier-free playground, meaning it's accessible for those in wheelchairs, as well as those who aren't. Several ramps adjoin the various play elements like the many slides, tunnels, and platforms, plus tic-tac-toe, chimes, metal spiral climby things, short climbing walls, spinning wheels, and monkey bars and monkey bars with handles. There is also lots of play space and components underneath the platforms with little houses, portholes, and more.

Other parts of the play area are sand based (so bring your bucket and shovel) and incorporate diggers; swings; and raised sand basins. There are also plus pedals on poles, green stools (or seats), and a large plastic vehicle to sit in and move back and forth propelled by kid motion. Picnic tables and barbecue pits are interspersed along the cement pathways that flow throughout and the plenty of wide open grassy areas and big shade trees. The trees help make the park cool, even on a hot day.

Nature-loving kids will also enjoy this park (just ignore the planes flying overhead from the nearby airport) as at least half of the park is dedicated to three separate lakes connected by streams and short waterfalls, with wooden bridges and a walking path around them. There are numerous (!) ducks of all varieties here having a swimmingly good time. A large hill, with hefty rocks imbedded in and around it, divides the playground from the lakes. A short hike up the hill, dotted with pine trees, yields the treasure of a pond in a small, forest-like setting at the top.

For the sports-minded, there are also volleyball courts and baseball fields, and across the street are tennis courts at the Costa Mesa Tennis Center and a skate park. The popular and nicely-laid out Volcom Skate Park is 15,000 square feet of free skate fun with all the necessary street elements of ramps, rails, bowls, and steps. Helmet, knee and elbow pads are required.

Hours: The park is open daily, dawn - dusk. The skate park is open Mon., Wed. - Sun., 9am - 9pm; Tues., 3pm - 9pm.
Price: Free
Ages: All

THOMAS F. RILEY WILDERNESS PARK

(949) 923-2265 / www.ocparks.com
30952 Oso Parkway, Coto De Caza

This hilly, 523-acre wilderness preserve is a sanctuary for native wildlife - coyotes, mountain lions, raccoons, mule deer, a multitude of birds, and lots more. It's composed of hills with protected sagebrush, oak trees, and other plant life, plus a pond and two seasonal creeks. Five miles of rugged dirt trails (stroller occupants would have a bumpy ride) loop throughout the park and visitors are asked not to stray from them. Although housing developments border part of the park, miles of undeveloped canyons, tree groves, and Santa Ana Mountain peaks can still be seen from the viewpoints.

Take a self-guiding nature hike, or sign up for a guided walk or program. The park makes a wonderful outdoor

"dassroom" and offers students of all ages firsthand knowledge about the environment. Some of the programs offered indude merit badge dasses, which could indude a topical game and craft; Critter Talk, which emphasizes learning about animal life styles and their habits and habitats, and indudes animal presentations; Star Watch, designed for viewing and learning about the stars and moon; Jr. Rangers, which is a six-week, springtime dass; special dasses for toddlers; and more. Most of the programs have a minimal fee.

The small nature center contains a few taxidermy animals and a game that kids can take on the trail to help them identify objects they find along the way. A few picnic tables are under shade trees in front of the nature center. A butterfly garden is here, too. Note: The rangers are very friendly and dedicated to enabling children to learn more about the wilds of Orange County.

Hours: Open daily, 7am - sunset. Call for seasonal hours. Usually dosed for 3 days after rain.
Price: $3 parking fee.
Ages: 4 years and up.

TIERRA GRANDE PARK

(949) 361-8264 / www.san-demente.org; www.funorangecountyparks.com
399 Camino Tierra Grande, San Clemente

Old McDonald might have had a farm, but kids can invite all their barnyard friends to Tierra Grande Park (also known as Red Barn Park) - a farm-theme park without the smell and mess of a real farm! The main, multi-level, interconnected, large structures are comprised of platforms and red poles and bars that sport barn facades, along with short bridges, mesh-like roofs, several slides, a large tic tac toe game, wheels, speaking tubes, metal spiral elements, tubes to crawl through, fireman poles, and more fun. Based in sand and recycled rubber, kids can play on, in, through and under the "barn."

Other components of the playground indude a corral with animals on large springs to ride on; a hay and milk tractor cut outs with play equipment behind them; a big circle to sit on and spin around and around; swings, induding toddler swings and a wheelchair-accessible swing; and sandy areas for digging and building. The park also features a large expanse of open grass with trees and a paved pathway around the perimeter; softball/multipurpose fields; two lighted basketball courts; horseshoe pits; and a large area with picnic tables, sinks, and barbecue pits. Come cock-a-doodle-do and more at this playground.

Hours: Open daily, 6am - 10pm
Price: Free
Ages: All

TRI-CITY PARK

(714) 834-5400 or (714) 973-3180 / www.ocparks.com
2301 N. Kraemer Boulevard, Placentia

Named for being in dose proximity to Brea, Fullerton, and Placentia, the centerpiece of this established park is a large lake for fishing, feeding ducks, and gazing at. Benches are placed around the lake's perimeter. Picnic benches overlook the park giving it an air of restfulness. There are a multitude of old trees, a considerable amount of grassy areas, paved pathways that meander throughout, a sand volleyball court, bicycle trails, and a playground toward the south end of Tri-City.

Hours: Open April through October daily, 7am - 9pm. Open November through March daily, 7am - 6pm.
Price: Free
Ages: All

TUCKER WILDLIFE SANCTUARY

(714) 649-2760 / www.tuckerwildlife.org
29322 Modjeska Canyon Road, Silverado

At the end of a windy, tree-lined country road is this twelve-acre wilderness destination that's adjacent to the Cleveland National Forest. It's owned by Cal State Fullerton and used for research purposes. The small, welcoming, natural history/interpretative center contains taxidermied wildlife such as a cougar, bobcat, eagle, squirrel, owl, grizzly bear, and lots of local birds. Live animals indude some snakes, frogs, lizards, and a millipede. Look under microscopes at insects, butterfly wings, cat hair, vacuum cleaner lint, and more. One wall mural has the foodweb; others are equally informative and colorful. Play with animal puppets; look at X-rays of animals; dissect owl pellets; and study and touch animal skins and bones, fossils, and rocks, that are on display and in drawers to pull out. A small gift shop and snack shop is here, too.

Just outside is a patio with a picnic area under the canopy of large oak trees. A little, children's garden has interesting plants to look at, touch, and smell. Seasonally, you'll see butterflies fluttering around, attracted to the garden's plants.

Across the road are several easy walking trails that take visitors in and amongst the trees and chaparral. A looping trail, partially paved, is 1.5 miles around the sanctuary. Along the scenic and well-maintained trail you'll encounter a creek that runs through the property; two ponds that contain mosquito fish, turtles, and water lilies; desert tortoises in an open air enclosure; lots of benches; trees, sage plants, cactus, and more; squirrels and lizards; and a bird observation porch. Sit quietly inside the porch area and watch hummingbirds and other species fly in and fill up at the feeders hanging just outside. Identify the birds by using the pictures and info on the porch wall. I think this tranquil place is a human sanctuary as much as a bird sanctuary.

Other popular trails include the Harding Truck Trail, which is a fire road from the sanctuary that goes uphill (at least one way!) and extends twenty miles into the forest (although you can stop and turn around whenever you want), and the Laurel Springs Trail, which is about a 5.5 miles round-trip and leads up to natural streams and even little waterfalls that appear after a rain.

Guided tours are offered for grades K through 12, Tuesdays through Fridays, that include hiking part of a trail, and insight and education regarding native plants and animals.

Note that the ARDEN - THE HELENA MODJESKA HISTORIC HOUSE AND GARDENS (pg. 298) is nearby.

Hours: Open Tues. - Sun., 9am - 4pm. Closed Mon. and major holidays.
Price: Free. $2 donation per person is recommended. Guided tours are $6 per participant, or a minimum of $80 and must be scheduled in advance.
Ages: 4 years and up.

WHITING RANCH WILDERNESS PARK

(949) 923-2245 / www.whitingranch.com; www.ocparks.com
Santiago Canyon Road, Portola Hills

"Real" hikers can explore the hills of Trabuco Canyon via the 4,300 acres and eighteen miles of trails of Whiting Ranch Wilderness Park. Follow the trails through forested canyons with huge oak trees, along streams, and past huge boulders. A moderate hike starts at the Borrego Trail and leads to the Red Rock Canyon trail, which is about five miles round trip and loops back around. Note: This trail is more easily reached from the Market Street entrance. The scenery is outstanding. The size and beauty of this park offers the opportunity to enjoy some good, back-to-nature time with your kids. I'm not trying to give contrary information, but also remember that this is a wilderness area and wild animals, including mountain lions and rattlesnakes, inhabit this place. The on-site ranger station has some taxidermied animals and historical info about the region.

Hours: Open daily, 7am - sunset. The park is closed for several days after rain.
Price: $3 per vehicle.
Ages: 5 years and up.

WILDCATTERS PARK

(714) 990-7100 / www.ci.brea.ca.us
3301 E. Santa Fe Road, Brea

The two playgrounds here, built on recycled rubber, are really fun as they feature some usual elements - slides and swings and places to climb, plus some unusual ones such as a little log tunnel; a tree trunk with "cut" branches and steps; a good-size fake boulder to climb on; a quirky-shape that has drums and a piano-like panel to create music (or just noise); and play horses on big springs to ride.

The rest of the nicely-landscaped park is part of a sports complex with a baseball field; a football/soccer field; concession stand; and basketball court, plus picnic tables (and lots of benches), bbq, and a .6 mile paved, looping walking trail.

Hours: Open daily, sunrise - sunset.
Price: Free
Ages: 2 ½ years and up.

WILLIAM R. MASON REGIONAL PARK

(949) 923-2223; (949) 923-2220 / www.ocparks.com
18712 University Drive, Irvine

This 345-acre park is serene (even with kids!) and beautiful. The picturesque lake is a central feature. Fishing, with a license, is allowed, but be forewarned - the lake isn't stocked. Honking gaggles of geese will vie for your attention (and bread crumbs). You can also bring your model boat for sailing on it. There are three different playgrounds with modular plastic equipment such as tunnels, slides, swings, forts, etc. The park also boasts of volleyball courts, a ball field, a fitness course, horseshoe pits, picnic shelters, open grassy expanses, large shade trees, and two miles of lovely paved walking/biking trails that crisscross throughout and a butterfly habitat.

Hours: Open November through March daily, 7am - 6pm. Open April through October daily, 7am - 9pm.
Price: $3 per vehicle Mon. - Fri.; $5 Sat. - Sun.; $7 on holidays.
Ages: All

YORBA REGIONAL PARK

(714) 973-6615 - park; (714) 461-1652 - Wheel Fun rentals / www.ocparks.com; www.wheelfunrentals.com
7600 E. La Palma Avenue, Anaheim

This pleasant, 175-acre elongated park follows along the Santa Ana River. It offers a myriad of activities such as nice, flat, paved and unpaved trails for healthy distances for family hiking, horseback riding biking, and biking, including going the distance on the twenty-mile Santa Ana River Trail which leads all the way to the ocean! (See pg. 370 for bike route information.) Other amenities include four softball fields and a lighted baseball diamond; an exercise course; horseshoe pits; several volleyball courts; and a few noteworthy playgrounds. The playgrounds are colorful and have fun, twisty tunnels to go through, plus some good, metal, climbing apparatus. One of the playgrounds has a whimsical fish ladder, poles with seats to move and spin on, swings, and more.

A wonderful urban get away to nature (though the freeway is right there), this park is flush with a variety of trees including wooded areas, shade trees, and great climbing trees, plus lots and lots of grassy run-around space, barbecue pits and numerous (over 400!) picnic tables. Water is always a draw. (I think of this from Psalm 23 - "He leads me beside quiet waters, He refreshes my soul.") The lakes here are really scenic, with bridges to connect them and some short piers for fishing. Note that a valid fishing license is necessary for fishermen over 16 years. One of the lakes allows operating model boats and another is great for kayaking and paddle boating. Streams also weave their way throughout the park. Note that bikes and boats are available to rent here: Hourly rentals include $20 for a surrey; $10 for a cruiser bike; $6 for a kid's bike; $20 for a pedal boat; $15 for a single kayak; $20 for a double.

Hours: The park is open April through October daily, 7am - 9pm; November through March daily, 7am - 6pm. Rentals are available September - mid-June, Sat., Sun. and holidays, 10am - sunset; mid-June - August, Wed. - Fri., noon - 7pm; Sat., Sun., and holidays, 10am - sunset.
Price: $3 per vehicle during the week; $5 on weekends; $7 - $10 on holidays.
Ages: All

—MALLS—

ANAHEIM TOWN SQUARE - KIDS FUN ZONE

(714) 956-3411 / www.anaheimtownsquare.com
Lincoln Avenue and State College Boulevard, Anaheim

You can shop at the K Mart, 99¢ Only Store, and Ralphs and eat at the restaurants here any day, but only on the last Saturday of each month can kids gather together at the long tables set up then to make a free, seasonal craft such as heart art for Valentine's Day or painting a tote bag (for the fun of it). Kids are offered merchant discounts on those days, too. The Square also hosts events throughout the year, so check the online calender.

Hours: The last Sat. of the month, 11am - 3pm.
Price: Free
Ages: 3 - 12 years

BELLA TERRA - KIDS CLUB

(714) 897-2534 / www.bellaterra-hb.com
7777 Edinger Avenue, Huntington Beach

This lovely outdoor mall features a Kid's Club at the amphitheater outside the Century Theaters that can include magicians, jugglers, puppet shows, storytellers, and/or musicians. The performances are often interactive, so kids become part of the show. Wholesome entertainment in the California sunshine surrounded by shops and restaurants, including BUCA DI BEPPO (pg. 14) and the movie theater that has 3-D capability - this is the place to be. During the

summer, sign up for the Summer Movie Clubhouse where children's movies are shown for $1 a movie on select days at 10am.

Bella Terra also offers live music on most weekend evenings ranging from alternative rock to Latin contemporary to jazz. Check the website for more info.

Hours: Kids Club is April - October, every Mon., 10:30am - 11am. From October - April, the club is the first Mon. of every month. No Kids Club on holidays.

Price: Free

Ages: 2 - 10 years

IRVINE SPECTRUM CENTER

(949) 789-9180 or (949) 753-5180 / www.shopirvinespectrumcenter.com

71 Fortune Drive, Irvine

How can I choose favorites from a choice of over 120 shops, restaurants, and entertainment venues? I vote for Barnes & Noble Bookstore, ROCKET FIZZ SODA POP AND CANDY SHOPS (pg. 24), and the Edwards with an IMAX and 3-D theater. Kid favorites include playing (and getting wet) on the turtle statues in the fountain outside the food court, or in the small, shaded playground towards the Target. They also enjoy riding the 108-foot Giant Wheel ($5), found at one end of the spectrum; the carousel ($3) with its three rows of animals to ride on such as bears, deer, a rabbit, tigers and more; and/or the kiddie train ride ($3).

Hungry? This outside mall includes a gigantic a DAVE & BUSTER'S (pg. 258); a food court; and restaurants such as California Pizza Kitchen, Cheesecake Factory, RUBYS (pg. 252), and more. The Cold Stone Creamery can help you (or hurt you) in the dessert area.

Note that there is an Improv Comedy Theater here, too - for adults. Call (949) 854-5455 / www.improv.com for dinner and show information. Check the November Calendar, under Holiday on Ice Irvine Spectrum (pg. 758), for details about the seasonal ice-skating rink.

Hours: Most shops are open Sun. - Thurs., 10am - 9pm; Fri. - Sat., 10am - 11pm.

Price: Technically, free.

Ages: All

SOUTH COAST PLAZA

(714) 435-2034 or (800) 782-8888 / www.southcoastplaza.com

3333 Bristol Street, Costa Mesa

With 250 stores restaurants, this upscale mall is REALLY big! Of particular kid interest are Pottery Barn for Kids, because it hosts storytelling every Tuesday at 11am; the interactive and magical DISNEY STORE (see pg. 314 for more details); a Lego Store (see pg. 261); RUBY'S restaurant (see pg. 252); and a carousel on the lower level between Sears and Bloomingdales. The mall also hosts seasonal and special events.

Hours: The mall is open Mon. - Fri., 10am - 9pm; Sat., 10am - 8pm; Sun., 11am - 6:30pm.

Price: Free

Ages: All

THE SHOPS AT MISSION VIEJO - KIDGITS CLUB

(949) 364-1832; (949) 364-1771 / www.simon.com

555 The Shops at Mission Viejo Boulevard, Mission Viejo

The Shops offers fun places to shop as well as great places to eat and play. *Extra* fun stores and eateries here include BUILD-A-BEAR WORKSHOP (pg. 314), the interactive and magical DISNEY STORE (pg. 314), Optimus Toys, FARRELL'S ICE CREAM PARLOUR RESTAURANTS (pg. 247), P.F. Chang's China Bistro, RUBYS (pg. 252), and the food court (try Crepes de Paris). The food court has free Wi-fi and plays music videos of your choosing (unless someone else chooses first) via your cell phone. There is also a free, semi-enclosed kid's soft play area here (near the Disney Store) with a small building and a short tunnel to crawl and climb through, plus a hard-foam car, caterpillar, and a few other objects to play on. The mall also offers Kiddie Kruzzers (i.e. strollers that look like cars) to rent for $5; a small Lullaby Lounge for moms and infants to rest on comfy couches and chairs and to even watch toddler-friendly shows on TV; and daily opening times (of the doors, not the stores) of 7am for mall walkers.

On certain days the mall hosts the free Kidgits Club, usually near the play area. Club times can include crafts, storytelling, singing, dancing, entertainment by Radio Disney, and more. Annual membership is $5 per child which includes a t-shirt, goodie bags at events, a chance to spin the prize wheel whenever you visit the mall, and special discounts.

Hours: The mall is open Mon. - Fri., 10am - 9pm; Sat., 10am - 8pm; Sun., 11am - 6pm. Closed on Christmas. Restaurant and store hours may vary. Call for hours for Kidgits Club, though it is usually on a Sat., 10am - noon.

Price: Free, but bring spending money.

Ages: All

WESTFIELD MAIN PLACE - WFAMILY FUN DAYS

(714) 547-7000 / www.westfield.com

2800 N. Main Street, Santa Ana

Not all malls are designed with kids in mind, but it helps when they have a free PlaySpace play area that caters to them! This semi-enclosed, carpeted space has an area just for younger ones to play on the colorful, hard-foam objects, surrounded by comfy benches for parents to rest.

Selected Thursdays at 5pm on the first level by the kids play area are free Family Fun Days with interactive story time, snacks (like string cheese and dried apple slices), and crafts for little ones (ages 2 to 5), plus crafts and other activities and games for bigger kids (ages 6 to 12). Past make it and take it crafts have included making a kite; decorating an apron with paint, gems, pictures, etc; and more.

Fun places at the mall, especially, include a Disney store, Optimus Toys, CrepeMaker, and Picture Show Theaters, which presents second-run movies for only $2; $1 on Tuesdays. 3-D movies are an additional $2. Call (714) 836-7469 for movie information.

Hours: Family Fun Days are the first and third Thurs. from 5pm - 6pm.

Price: Free

Ages: 2 - 12 years

—MUSEUMS—

ARDEN - THE HELENA MODJESKA HISTORIC HOUSE AND GARDENS

(949) 923-2230 / www.helenamodjeska.net; www.ocparks.com

Modjeska Canyon Road, Modjeska Canyon

Waaaaay off the beaten path is the fourteen-acre, wooded parklands and picturesque old cottage and surrounding gardens that have withstood the test of time in a gracious manner. Once owned by a renowned Shakespearean actress, Madame Modjeska, the public is now invited to tour through the residence to admire the furnishings and the architecture. The porches and gables are reminiscent of a more romantic era. Besides the main attraction of the white cottage home, there is a cabin, guest cottages, a hexagonal building (once a music room), reflection ponds, lily ponds, a well, and two stages extending into the gardens. The wooded area around the house is alive with oak trees, a grove of redwoods, palms, and other plants. Walk along the rock-lined pathway through the Forest of Arden, so named from Shakespeare's play *As You Like It*. On the guided tour, which is the only way to see Modjeska, the docent explains the history of the home and the theatrical lifestyle of the original owners. Note that the Tucker Wildlife Sanctuary is close by. (See page 294.)

Hours: Guided tours are offered the first and third Tues. and the second and fourth Sat. at 10am by advanced reservations only - no walk-ins allowed.

Price: $5 per person.

Ages: 10 years and up.

BEALL CENTER FOR ART AND TECHNOLOGY

(949) 824-6206 / beallcenter.uci.edu

712 Arts Plaza at Claire Trevor School of the Arts at University of California, Irvine

"The mission of the Beall Center is to support research and exhibitions that explore new relationships between the arts, sciences, and engineering, and thus, promote new forms of creation and expression using digital technologies." So, the rotating, technologically-based exhibitions are really intriguing. For instance "Sight and Sound" was a varied group of artists who presented beautiful footage along with a cacophony of sounds and music. Virtual reality images, along with sound sculptures, were featured in the accompanying exhibit "Wall of Sound". Past exhibit titles include "Information as Art" and "Morphonano", which were interactive works through space and time created by an artist and nanoscientist. Intriguing, right? Call if you'd like a tour. Definitely check out their Family Day events, offered in the fall and in the spring, because of the hands-on art and science activities and demonstrations. Note

robotics camps are offered during the summer.

Hours: Open Tues. - Wed., noon - 5pm; Thurs. - Sat., noon - 8pm. Closed Sun. and Mon.
Price: Free. Parking is $2 an hour.
Ages: 8 years and up.

BLAKEY HISTORICAL PARK AND MUSEUM

(714) 893-0134 or (714) 891-2597 / www.westminsterhistorical.wordpress.com; www.westminster-ca.gov
8612 Westminster Boulevard, Westminster

Like many other cities that want to preserve their roots for future generations, the city of Westminster has a historical museum. It houses displays from its founding in 1870 to the present day. The museum building, which looks like a converted auditorium, has exhibits, mostly in glass cases, set up in chronological groups. Each grouping has a number that corresponds to an information sheet which explains the memorabilia, thus making for an easy self-guided tour. If you prefer, a docent will explain articles more fully and allow children to touch just a few items - this is a mostly "eyes-on" (as opposed to hands-on) museum. Some of the more interesting items to see include a very small 1897 child's bed; an old stove, washboard, butter churn and other kitchen implements; an antique, wind-up phonograph that still works; old-fashioned ladies' hats and clothing; a collection of dolls from around the world; war posters; and the head of a water buffalo.

Four other small buildings are on the park's grounds. A California Crazy, or Shutter Shack, is a little, picture-perfect "store" that looks like a camera. (It was once used for dropping off and picking up film.) A docent will take you through the other buildings: The small, restored McCoy-Hare House was the community's first drugstore, as well as a home. The front room contains a pump organ, plus shelves filled with jars of medicine, bolts of fabric, and sundries. The adjacent living room has some period furniture and clothing. Next, walk through the Warne Family Farmhouse to see the parlor, which holds a 1749 grandfather's clock and a piano; a dining room, with its table set with china; the bedroom that contains a bed (people were much shorter back then!) and a ceramic pot (i.e., port-a-potty); and the kitchen with its stove and old-time telephone. A sink wasn't necessary as water and garbage were simply thrown out the back door to feed the plants and the chickens, respectively. The adjacent large barn contains saddles, large farm equipment, a wooden sugar beet wagon, and tools. Everything is well-labeled. Walk into the the barn and discover two fire engines and an antique paramedic "van." Kids may climb into the cab of the 1959 white fire engine and "drive" around.

A few grassy areas and a picnic table on the premise complete this park.

Hours: Open to the public the first Sun. of each month, 1pm - 4pm. School groups may call to book a tour during the week.
Price: Free
Ages: 5 years and up.

BODIES, THE EXHIBITION

(657) 529-7224; (888) 647-2789 / www.bodiestheexhibition.com/buenapark/ $$$$
7711 Beach Boulevard, Buena Park

What does your body look like on the inside, really? One incredible way to find out is by going through the numerous rooms in Bodies, The Exhibition. Each room focuses on a particular body part and/or system and features those real body parts; technical, yet readable, information about them; posters; and massive photos and/or wall murals. The highlight is the eleven complete, real, preserved human bodies, sans skin. The permanently Polymer-preserved bodies, and body parts, captured via liquid silicone rubber, allow people to see and study the skeletal, muscular, nervous, respiratory, digestive, urinary, reproductive, endocrine and circulatory systems in unparalleled detail.

The first room features a full skeleton and separate bones, identified by their parts and functions. Walk into the next room with its emphasis on muscles. A central model has a skeleton leaning back with its hands almost holding onto its other real-life, full- body counterpart of just muscles, tendons, ligaments, etc. Another body, with its rib cage and intestines particularly on view, is playing basketball. Another man body is in mid-stride, running, with his muscles and tendons cut away from him, so they kind of looking like feathers. The nervous system room has a (I will say) kind of creepy-looking display of a brain and eyes attached to just a complete nervous system - reminds me of a moon jelly with its floating tentacles. The next bodies show insight into how a conductor conducts and what brain and other functions are utilized in the creative process of drawing. You can also see and learn about the thyroid and slices of the brain that shows hemorrhages. The circulatory system room has, fittingly, red walls and close-up photos of blood cells. Real arms and hands, and a leg and foot, showcase the red, complicated artery system, as does a full prone body on a table. Smaller display cases reveal the bronchial tree and pulmonary arteries, hearts and lungs. One wall shows several

video screens of a heart beating as blood is pumped through its 100,000 miles of vessels. Continue on with respiration and circulation in another room, with more bodies cut away to expose relevant parts; a smoker's lung vs. a healthy one; the stomach; intestines; and cancerated body parts. One body is holding the top layer of her upper body open, like a door, to reveal the compact state of many of the internal organs. The reproductive and urinary systems, with more cutaway male and female bodies and all of the individual body parts, is next. The following room can be bypassed if desired: It contains several jars containing fetuses that died in utero during different stages of development, along with videos of ultrasounds. Amazing (and sad - because they didn't live) to see a baby three weeks after conception develop into looking like a little alien, then to a recognizable baby. The last room has a body that has been sliced into sections that simulate what an MRI of the body looks like, as well as a body that has parts that have had surgery.

The entire exhibit presents such valuable and integral insights and visuals as to how our fantastic bodies work; it's like taking anatomy 101 all the way through 401. There are docents in lab coats on hand to answer any questions who are qualified to do so as each one has "at least" a college degree in the sciences.

Notes: Most of the bodies on display are males, with all their parts. Some people will find the displays creepy. Rent an audio for an additional $7 that goes more in depth with all that you see. Give yourself at the *very* least an hour to go through this exhibit. No photography is permitted. Group tours and school tours are given and enhance the experience and understanding. The school tours have many hands-on components, too. The adjacent exhibit, sharing the same building, is TITANIC - THE EXPERIENCE (pg. 312) - another awesome attraction to walk through and see.

Hours: Open Sun. - Thurs., 10am - 7pm; Fri. - Sat., 10am - 8pm.
Price: $19.75 for adults; $17.75 for seniors; $15.75 for ages 5 - 11; children 4 and under are free. Prepurchase tickets on line to save $. A combo ticket for Titanic and Bodies is $34.50 for adults; $30.50 for seniors; $26.50 for kids.
Ages: 8 years and up.

BOWERS MUSEUM   ☼

(714) 567-3600 / www.bowers.org $$$$
2002 N. Main Street, Santa Ana

This culturally rich museum contains permanent exhibits showcasing art from pre-Columbian, Art of the Pacific, Art of Africa, Art of Asia, First Californians (Native Americans), and early California history, with a focus on ranchos and missions in the Segerstrom gallery. This collection includes baskets, statues, body adornment pieces, clothing, spurs, a huge copper brandy still from early 1800's, murals, and paintings. Another permanent gallery is the Ancient Arts of China: A 5,000 Year Legacy. Bronze vessels, ivory carvings, robes, sculptures, porcelains paintings, and more are on display here. All the art in the galleries and in the hallway are classically displayed.

The first-class, temporary exhibits have included treasures from Tibet; portions of the Dead Sea Scrolls; gemstones; and Beethoven: The Late Great with drafts of scores, a personal letter, locks of his hair and more. Just a few of the blockbuster exhibits have included Egyptian mummies and funerary objects on loan from the British Museum and the Terra Cota Warriors. Wow - these have been incredible!!

An audio guide, available for rent, aids in interpreting the various artifacts. One-hour guided tours are available for all ages as are one-hour cultural art classes. School groups also receive a curriculum guide for select galleries. Enjoy the outdoor courtyard before or after your visit. For fine dining on the museum grounds, indulge in Tangata, a restaurant that serves salmon Cobb salad ($18), blue crab cakes ($14), grilled flat iron steak ($22), spinach and ricotta ravioli ($17), and burgers ($14). A market menu changes frequently but starts at $22 for two courses.

KIDSEUM (pg. 305) is located just down the street, is geared specifically for kids (obviously), and is associated with Bowers. In fact, ages 6 and up are admitted free into Kidseum with a same day ticket stub from the Bowers Museum.

Hours: Open Tues. - Sun., 10am - 4pm. Closed Mon., New Year's Day, 4th of July, Thanksgiving, and Christmas Day.
Price: $13 for adults Tues. - Fri., $15 on Sat. - Sun.; $10 for seniors and students, Tues. - Fri., $12 on Sat. - Sun.; children 11 and under are free with a paying adult. Note that special exhibits may cost extra. Admission is free to the permanent exhibits on the 1st Sun. for all visitors and every Tues. for Santa Ana residents, only. Audio headphones rentals are $5. Parking at the lot is $6. There is some free parking on the streets and 2 blocks down the street at Kidseum, as well as some metered parking.
Ages: 8 years and up.

CHILDREN'S MUSEUM AT LA HABRA

(562) 905-9793 / www.lahabracity.com

301 S. Euclid Street, La Habra

$$$

This great museum, housed in a renovated Union Pacific Railroad Depot, has a child's interest at heart. Out front are (fake) dinosaur print trackways of a Tyrannosaurus rex, sauropod, and theropod, and a replica nest containing unhatched "dino" eggs.

Inside, a Science Station room encourages hands-on exploration with a Dino Dig (i.e., digging in sand for "fossils") and a huge T.rex skull that hangs from the ceiling, watching you. The room also features a cut-away of a bathroom and kitchen that partners with an exhibit (with fake rocks and clouds) on evaporation; a shadow wall that takes a temporary picture; and a gas pump to fill 'er up. The adjoining room has a carousel to ride, a mini-market for kids to shop like grownups (without the grownup bills), and the front end of an Orange County Transit bus to get in an dpractice driving skills. The next room has wonderful, interactive, changing exhibits. Past themes have included Cowboys and the Wild West, which featured western gear to try on, a wooden horse with a saddle, and a guitar to strum on the range; and Would You Look At That?, which featured fun with lenses, light, and optical equipment. This room is always enlightening! Just outside this room is a train caboose, filled with train memorabilia, that is open to walk through at certain times. See how tiny the bathroom is and look at the seats perched up high for good viewing.

Do you hear trains chugging, clanging, and whistling as they come around the mountain? A connecting room contains a large model train layout. The train room then leads to Nannies Travels, a living room-like setting that features a collection of cultural artifacts - masks, costumes, games, artwork, furniture, and more - from all over the world. The next connecting room is the nature room. Listen to the sounds of nature (e.g., birds chirping) as you go through a little cave and look at the taxidermied wildlife, such as bears, mountain lions, a raccoon, a wart hog, and birds "flying" overhead. Real critters are here, too - snakes, lizards and other reptiles. Hanging on the wall are stuffed animal heads of deer, moose, and buffalo. A touch table holds furs, bird's nests, and skulls.

Quiet on the set! The large dress-up area, with a stage, piano, numerous and varied costumes (including several fireman uniforms), and even prepared scripts, inspires future actors and actresses. The lighting booth, with all of its working buttons, is perfect for aspiring directors. The adjoining playroom, for children 5 years and under only, has a fake tree to climb, a little puppet theater, toys, building blocks, books, a stuffed cow that kids can milk, and a play castle.

The museum often hosts special programs such as craft projects in the Family Art room, storytelling, or shows for kids to enjoy and participate in. Call or check the website for a schedule of events.

Portola Park, the museum's backyard, is open daily and features a playground, baseball fields, tennis courts, picnic tables, and barbecue grills.

Hours: Open Tues. - Fri., 10am - 4pm; Sat., 10am - 5pm; Sun., 1pm - 5pm. Closed Mon., Mother's Day, Father's Day, and major holidays.

Price: $7 for ages 2 and up; children under 2 are free. See page xi for info on ASTC reciprocal museum memberships.

Ages: 1½ - 10 years.

DISCOVERY SCIENCE CENTER

(714) 542-CUBE (2823) / www.discoverycube.org

2500 N. Main Street., Santa Ana

$$$$

This two-story, high-caliber science center, with full-size mock up of the space shuttle outside, has over 100 hands-on exhibits, plus live science demonstrations, 4-D movies (with wind and fog effects that you can feel!) in the theater, and special programs. Lie down on a real bed of nails, over 3,500 of them, and not get hurt due to the equal distribution of body mass. (May your kids never complain about an uncomfortable mattress again!) Press your flesh against a wall of pinheads to create a 3-D impression (and some mighty odd poses). See yourself in a "new light" inside a room with a camera that takes real time pictures of your movements. Watch your image reflected on a screen in vivid colors and lights. If you can't get enough of the real California quakes, enter the Shake Shack, a room with a platform that simulates major and minor quakes. Or, use a seismograph and construct a model building to see if it's up to earthquake code. Walk through an eight-foot-tall artificially-generated tornado and even redirect its pattern. Speak through a tube that changes your voice from normal to sound like you're underwater, in an opera, inhabiting an alien, and more. Use wind to blow sand into dunes or other formations. Form dams or create erosion, or just get your hands dirty, at the stream and silt table. Create a cloudy day (inside!) by pushing on large rings around a cloud machine which then form various-sized clouds. Fly a model airplane into the wind using a throttle. Experience what you would weigh

on the moon or on Mars by hoisting yourself up on a properly weighted pulley system. See what speed you get docked at when you pitch a ball. Balance yourself on a board resembling a seesaw. (This is much harder than it looks!) Duck underneath to go into a giant kaleidoscope. Play virtual volleyball and learn about green screen technology used in movies. Participate in live science shows. Climb a rock wall. Play a laser beam harp. Log on to computers to play educational games and/or take a computer class at the Digital Lab. Stare at the ginormous globe in the center of the room and see a hurricane swirling around, rain pouring down, and all other kinds of weather all around the world, in real time from satellites. Learn about the planets from the interactive stations.

One reason kids stick to it at the fabulous and very hands-on Science of Hockey exhibit is they can "drive" the almost life-size model of a Zamboni machine stationed on the ice-like flooring of the room. Wannabe sportscasters can try out their chosen career in the broadcast booth. Players can try their skating skills with an interactive video game. Compare surfaces as you see whose puck goes the fastest at the ice and friction table. Be the goalie, or at least hear the game from his perspective in the goalie sound room. Your kids will actually want a time out in the Penalty Box as it has hockey-oriented ways to learn math equations, statistics, physics, and more sports applications.

In the underwater-themed KidStation, designed for children five years and younger, kids dress up and act out a scene in front of a background screen that can change from a shark, to a school of fish, to other nautical images. Youngsters can climb in a submarine and slide down it, fingerpaint electronically (a lot less messy than the real thing), play with puzzles, and read books.

The eighty-five-foot tall Delta III rocket and gigantic cube aren't the only outside museum attractions you see from the freeway; you can't miss the 120-foot long, almost friendly-looking Argentinosaurus and the skeletal, life-size T.rex. Walk inside the partly-fleshed and partly-exposed Argentinosaurus to see its innards. Young kids can slide down its tail, put together dino bone puzzles, and ride on small dinosaurs. Visitors become paleontologist assistants in Dino Quest where they embark on up to seven different missions, or scavenger hunts. Players hunt for clues among bones, among pretend dino scat, and throughout the outside exhibit and then flick their electronic wand at their findings to see if they made a correct discovery. The video screen scientists tell them if they are on track or not. Participants learn classification, identification, habitats, and more.

3... 2...1... blast off! You can go up inside the cube and experience a rocket blasting off, kind of. Enter a real Delta Rocket RS-68 booster engine, press the launch button, and with sound effects, smoke (i.e. fog), and video screens that simulate a rocket taking off, it feels almost like the real thing. Three interactive stations enable visitors to work the buttons and screen while seeing the real life enactment of fueling a rocket, launching one (and if you don't get the right ratio of water to air, you might get wet), and the gasses a rocket leaves behind as it thrusts and takes off.

Uniting education with entertainment in an appealing format for all generations, the Discovery Science Center also hosts terrific traveling exhibits, such as *Sesame Street Presents: The Body*, plus workshops, science camps, scout programs, and a packed calendar of events including a favorite - the BubbleFest, held in April. Note that an on-site eatery has an indoor and outdoor eating area. Also, see SANTIAGO PARK (pg. 292), which is across the road, but accessible by an underpass. Parking at the park is free.

Hours: Open Mon. - Sat., 10am - 5pm; Sun., 11am - 5pm. Closed Thanksgiving and Christmas.
Price: $15 for adults; $12.95 for seniors and ages 3 - 14; children 2 and under are free. Free admission for Santa Ana residents (bring a valid photo ID with your Santa Ana address) is offered on the first Tues. of every month. Shows at the 4-D Theater are an additional $3 per person. Playing Dino Quest is an additional $5 per player. Parking is $4 per vehicle. See page xi for info on ASTC reciprocal museum memberships. See page xi for info on the Bank of America free weekend program, but note that this museum offers it only on that Sunday.
Ages: 2 years and up.

EXPLOROCEAN   ☀

(949) 675-8915 or (949) 673-3377 / www.explorocean.org $$
600 East Bay Avenue, Newport Beach

This waterfront destination (the museum called ExplorOcean) within a destination (the Balboa Fun Zone) gives *berth* to an attraction for nautical lovers. The museum's three wings offer lots of interactive fun, starting with the lobby of the Ocean Literacy Center. It has two table-top tidepool touch tanks (what a tongue twister!) containing sea stars, sea slugs, limpets, and more. Feed and watch them eat (sea stars eat mussels, etc.) at 2pm on Wednesdays and Saturdays. This section also boasts a world record giant black bass, weighing in at 450 lbs., in its own tank. Another interactive exhibit in this wing is a ship's wooden wheel to steer. Marvel at the detail and workmanship of the several model ships on display, such as the fourteen-foot *S.S. Willochra* passenger steamship/troop carrier, and the ships-in-a-bottle. This wing also showcases outboard motors, scrimshaw art, a gray whale vertebra, a changing art

gallery, and a classroom. The Ocean Literacy Center encourages visitors to be physically engaged, via visuals and tools (i.e., microscopes, buckets of building/modeling supplies, and learning boards), with the learning process of its ocean-oriented displays and artifacts. The Science Courtyard invites visitors to "play" at Sand Slam, Gravity Defying Water, and Erosion Engineers.

The other museum building, the Steele Model Pavilion, contains many more model ships (I like the wooden outrigger and carved people manning the oars); wall-sized, continuous playing videos of extreme sailing and sports fishing; a Liberty ship bridge telegraph and binnacle compass; cannon balls and a small cannon; historical video of Balboa Pavilion; and an actual *Snowbird* and dinghy.

Ahoy mateys! One of the fun and educational classes offered via the museum is Sea Life Storytelling for mini buccaneers (ages 2 to 5) with stories, sea chanteys, and crafts. Another is Innovation Labs, for ages 10 and up. The various labs allow and encourage explorers to also be creators as they experiment with 3-D printers, laser engravers, electronic invention kits, and other advanced tools and supplies. For more to do in this immediate area see BALBOA FUN ZONE (pg. 255) and BALBOA PIER (pg. 313).

Hours: Open September - mid-June, Mon. - Thurs., 11am - 3:30pm; Fri. - Sat., 11am - 6pm; Sun., 11am - 5pm. Open in the summer and on school holidays daily, 11am - 6pm. Closed major holidays.
Price: The Steele Model Pavilion is free. The Ocean Literacy Center is $5 for ages 13 and up; $4 for seniors; $3 for ages 4 - 12; children 3 and under are free. All active military personnel are free.
Ages: 4 years and up.

FULLERTON MUSEUM CENTER

(714) 738-6545 - museum; (714) 738-3136 - tour info / www.ci.fullerton.ca.us
301 N. Pomona Avenue, Fullerton

This small cultural museum has two galleries with rotating exhibits that often have kid-appeal, plus a video that explains more about what is currently showing. Past exhibits have included The Nature of Collecting, which featured different collections ranging from *I Love Lucy* paraphernalia to pencil sharpeners and old radios; Touchable Sculptures, with over seventy touchable, lifecast sculptures of contemporary and historic figures such as George Bush, Clint Eastwood, and Dizzy Gillespie; Anne Frank, a recreation of the life and times of Anne Frank through photographs and facsimiles of her diary, plus commentary; and Prehistory of North Orange County with hands-on arts and crafts for the whole family, a simulated fossil dig, a guided tours of the exhibit and more.

A gallery honoring Leo Fender, the man who revolutionized guitars with Telecaster, Stratocaster, and Precision Bass Fender guitars, is towards the back. It exhibits several of his classic guitars such as a 1962 fiesta red custom color Telecast guitar, a (wild looking) paisley Telecast from 1968, and a 1990 Celtic guitar inlaid with rich, Celtic symbols. A continuously running film shows Fender being interviewed, as well as celebrities and more of the history of his guitars. A visual time line with more guitars and old amps are also on display.

Ninety-minute school tours are given that include an in-depth tour of the museum and a hands-on activity that correlates to the current exhibit. Also inquire about Family Days; Wednesday Art Studios; after-school programs; summer art camps; Stroller Brigade for docent-led stories, crafts and games - for free; and other special programs and events.

Just across the street is the fun Plaza Park. It has fountains that squirt to life at random intervals (great for cooling off), benches under shade trees, grassy spots, a few picnic tables, and a funky playground. The playground has a wall for rock climbing and metal objects (think modern art) to motivate the imagination - saucer shapes to swing, play and climb on; bars that spin; and more.

Hours: The museum is open Tues. - Sun., noon - 4pm; open Thurs. until 8pm. Closed Mon., 4th of July, Thanksgiving and Christmas. The park is open daily.
Price: $4 for adults; $3 for seniors and students; $1 for ages 6 - 12; children 5 and under are free. The first Thurs. of every month from 4pm - 8pm admission is $2.
Ages: 5 years and up.

GEORGE KEY RANCH HISTORIC SITE

(714) 973-3190 or (714) 973-3191 / www.ocparks.com
625 W. Bastanchury Road, Placentia

Orange groves, originally planted in 1893, once covered most of the George Key Ranch. On your guided tour here you can still see (and smell!) the remaining acre of producing orange trees and the verse garden. Tours of the beautiful grounds begin with a brief history about the Key family. The stately, two-story house contains furnishings dating from the 1800's that came from local ranch houses; old photographs; the kitchen with a 1908 wood-burning

stove and a gas stove; one of Mrs. Key's dresses dating from 1866; and artifacts related to ranch life. These include a squirrel and gopher smoker, an avocado picker, an alfalfa/grass chopper, and implements used in picking and packaging oranges, plus carpentry and blacksmith tools. Walk the Old Farm Trail among the fruit trees - apricot, peach, orange and tangerine - and you'll also see old, rusted farm equipment and machinery scattered about, such as plows, harrows, spreaders, seeders, orchard heaters, a citrus spray rig, and even wagons from the early 1900's.

Guided tours for groups are given by advanced reservation. Come during public hours to see the first story of the house and enjoy a stroll along the brick-lined garden and grounds. Bring a sack lunch to enjoy at the picnic tables under gigantic, shady trees. Ask about the ranch's special programs.

Hours: Open Tues. - Fri., 12:30pm - 4:30pm; and the first Sat. of every month, 2pm - 4pm. Call to reserve a spot.

Price: Free to walk the grounds. A guided tour is $2 per person; a free tour is given the first Sat. of each month at 2pm.

Ages: 6 years and up.

HERITAGE HILL HISTORICAL PARK

(949) 923-2230/2232 / www.ocparks.com

25151 Serrano Road, Lake Forest

Heritage Hill consists of several restored historical buildings in a beautiful gated setting. Four buildings that reflect part of Orange County's heritage are open to tour. The Serrano Adobe dates from 1863 and has furniture from the late nineteenth century. The Bennet Ranch House, built in 1908, reflects a ranching family's lifestyle from the early twentieth century. St. George's Episcopal Mission, built in 1891, has many of its original interior furnishings. El Toro Grammar School was built in 1890. The school is a favorite with kids because it has school books from that era, as well as desks and other school-related items. The Historical Park has a few picnic tables on the grounds.

Three school tours are offered. The third grade tour is called "Hands On". It is ninety-minutes long, costs $2 per person, and is designed for ten to sixty students. Groups go through the houses and do an activity in each one, such as grinding corn in the adobe. In the school house, they participate in a mini school session. The fourth grade tour is called "Living History". It is two hours long and cost $2 per person. Seventeen to thirty-five students participate in hands-on lessons in the school house. The Native American Tour incorporates knowledge of native inhabitants with activities. Learning was never so interesting! Reservations for tours are required.

If your kids need more running around space, visit Serrano Creek Park, just behind Heritage Hill. Serrano is a long, narrow, wooded park with a paved walkway and a creek running through it. The big wooden play structure, which looks like a clubhouse, has a bridge, slides, and some huge tires to climb on.

Hours: Heritage Hill is open Wed. - Sun., 9am - 5pm. Guided tours are the only way to see the interior of the buildings. Tours for the general public are given Wed. - Fri. at 2pm; Sat. - Sun. at 11am and 2pm. School groups must make reservations for tours at other times throughout the week. Closed major holidays.

Price: Free to the public. Groups of 8 or more are $2 per person.

Ages: 6 years and up.

HERITAGE MUSEUM OF ORANGE COUNTY

(714) 540-0404 / www.heritagemuseumoc.org

3101 W. Harvard Street, Santa Ana

Travel back to Victorian times as you visit the Kellogg House (i.e., the Heritage Museum), built in 1898. Take a few moments to walk around the truly lovely grounds. Tours begin in the parlor where kids can play a pump organ, crank an old telephone, listen to music played on an Edison talking machine, and look through a stereoscope - an early version of the modern-day View Master™. The kitchen has wonderful gadgets that kids can learn about as well as touch. The wood dining room is oval-shaped with cabinets specially made to bend with the curves, like the inside of a ship. The twisted, wooden staircase got "cool" raves from all the kids. Upstairs, children play a game that teaches them the parts of a Victorian house. The master bedroom is now a room to dress up in Victorian-style clothing, with beautiful dresses for the girls and dapper coats and vests for the boys. The children's room has old-fashioned toys to play with.

Outside, on the back porch, children can practice *real* chores like "washing" clothes on a scrub board and drying them with the clothes wringer. Sometimes visitors are invited to make their own butter or learn how to play Victorian-era games. Make sure you take a look into the working blacksmith's shop. After the official tour, kids are welcome to go back and explore their favorite rooms, with parental supervision, of course.

Enjoy a picnic lunch in the gazebo area. Throughout the year the museum offers special events, such as themed teas where kids are invited to make crafts and participate in topical projects; and family activities, such as storytelling, a craft, blacksmith demonstrations, or a nature hike. Call for a schedule and for pricing. School groups, with a minimum of ten students, should inquire about their wide array of programs, such as Journey in Time, Great Grandpa's House, and Gold Rush. Two-hour classes start at $10 per student.

Of all the historical homes we've toured, and we've been through quite a few, this one has earned one of the highest ratings from my boys. Most houses, while beautiful and worthy of a tour, are understandably hands off. The Heritage Museum has hands-on activities, plus the docents gear the tour toward whatever age group is taking the tour, both in the tour length and the way the information is presented. Come here and let your kids touch history!

Hours: Open to the public Fri., 1pm - 5pm; Sat., 9am - 2pm; Sun., 11am - 3pm. Open to tour groups of ten or more by appt. only, Mon. - Thurs., 1pm - 5pm. Closed most holidays.

Price: $5 for adults; $4 for seniors and ages 17 and under. Santa Ana residents are free on the first Sun. of the month.

Ages: 3 years and up.

HUNTINGTON BEACH INTERNATIONAL SURFING MUSEUM

(714) 960-3483 / www.surfingmuseum.org

411 Olive Avenue, Huntington Beach

Surf's up at this small museum that celebrates surfing and surf culture, from its roots in Hawaii to the present day. Get in the mood with beach music playing in the background. Feel like catching a wave? Check out some of the famous and unique surfboards here. Look at early examples of slalom and vertical to current long boards and motorized boards. There are also trophies, clothes, and photographs. Past rotating exhibits have included a wall completely covered with skateboards, with clothing, posters and movies featuring skateboards completing the display. Another included a skin-diving exhibit featuring early face masks, fins, spear guns, and other diving gear, as well as photos and information panels. Surfing movies play continuously, and there is a gift shop. Note that the Surfing Walk of Fame, honoring thirty-six people, is just down the street. Summertime brings free surf-music concerts in the parking lot on Sunday afternoons.

Hours: Open Tues., noon - 9pm; Wed. - Sun., noon - 7pm. Closed Mon. and holidays.

Price: Free, donations appreciated.

Ages: 6 years and up.

KIDSEUM

(714) 480-1520 - museum; (714) 567-3680 - tours / www.bowers.org

1802 N. Main Street, Santa Ana

Kidseum is a hands-on, cultural museum designed to assist kids, preschoolers to 12 years old, develop an appreciation of art and the ways of life in cultures from around the world. Cross over the short (symbolic) rainbow bridge (from a Chumas legend) from the lobby into the main gallery.

The main room has wonderful, changing, interactive exhibits always geared towards the above-stated, central goals. Check the website to see what is currently "showing" here. The side Archaeology Room is done in an Egyptian motif with vivid paintings of gods and animals. It holds a small (fake) sarcophagus; an Egyptian vessel; rubbings (of world symbols, the Aztec calendar, and more); a large Languages of the World map to press buttons and hear phrases in languages from all over the globe (my Swahili is rusty!); and puzzles. Elsewhere in the museum, play games from foreign lands; learn through discovery box projects; dress up in a variety of ethnic costumes; work in the computer lab that is in the original bank's safe; participate in an archaeological dig; and do other engaging activities. Your kids will love the small, colorful music room. It has mostly drums, but they can also play unique musical instruments, like deer hoof shakers and some string instruments.

Stop by the Art Lab, where kids can paint, color, experiment with sand art, and more at different times throughout the year. Most activities are included in the price of admission. School tours here are my favorite combination of hands-on fun and learning and ask about their after-school programs. The museum also has kits available to classrooms for rent; cultural and arts Scouts' badge requirements with special art projects and presentations; summer art camp adventures; and more. Kidseum proves that learning about other cultures can be exciting!

Note: The BOWERS MUSEUM (pg. 300), located just down the street at 2002 N. Main Street, is the parent museum of Kidseum. It contains carvings, pictures, and other art work from African, Asian, and Native American cultures. Older kids might appreciate a walk through the galleries. Admission to Kidseum is free with a same day ticket

stub from Bowers Museum - so why not visit both?!

Hours: Open most of the year, Fri. - Sun., 10am - 4pm; open in the summer, Tues. - Sun., 10am - 4pm. Call to make a reservation to take a group tour during the week.

Price: $6 for ages 2 and up. Admission to Kidseum is free with a same day ticket stub from the Bowers Museum. Admission is free on the 1st Sun. of each month, when there are usually fun events/crafts going on, too.

Ages: 3 - 11 years.

LAGUNA HILLS COMMUNITY CENTER AND SPORTS COMPLEX

(949) 707-2680 - center; (949) 707-2692 - school tours / www.ci.laguna-hills.ca.us
25555 Alicia Parkway, Laguna Hills

This huge community center is more than just a beautiful building filled with great activities for families to enjoy. Built on a rich fossil site, it's a museum, of sorts, that showcases prehistoric fossils and bones unearthed during its construction. Various display cases, highlighted by murals that illustrate the paleo-environments and changing landscape of this site, are situated in the lobby and throughout the building. You'll see teeth from Great White sharks, seashell fossils, whale vertebrae, Mammoth tusks, bison and mastodon bones, and skulls of a bottlenose dolphin, extinct sea lion, and sabertooth. The displays have descriptive placards, or you can rent (for free) headphones and CD, available in English and Spanish, that auditorily explains each item, along with scientist's recordings. To enhance the educational value of your self-guided tour, ask for a paleopack, which is a folder that contains age-appropriate worksheets. School tours for elementary-aged kids are also available, Tuesdays through Thursdays. There is a wagon with dirt and fossils to find and match to a chart, too.

The adjoining sports complex features baseball fields, a soccer field, a roller hockey rink, and, behind the center and next to the high school, a really big (20,000 square feet!) cement skate park with a bowl, rails, stairs, pyramid, and other street elements. Pads and helmet are mandatory when using the skate park.

For more primordial-style fun, walk up the stone-line pathway past the ball fields and covered picnic areas, to the extra large, adjacent, dinosaur-related, Prehistoric Playground with its several nooks and crannies. A jeep is parked toward the entrance to get visitors in the exploring mode. A shallow cave here is embedded with numerous real fossils! Under a bridge is a short tunnel with more shell fossils and a fossil of a duck-billed dinosaur. At the two-level play area, kids can play on and under the whale skeleton and cement turtles; splash in a stone-tiered fountain; climb up a chain ladder; slide down a long, enclosed slide and other slides; swing on swings, including a tire swing; and engage in play using apparatus on the good-sized playground. The flooring is sometimes padded recycled rubber and sometimes sand-based, depending on the section. There is a small parcel just for toddlers. Shade awnings cover certain portions of the play area. Modern-day kids of all ages will delight in this excellent "primitive" playground.

Hours: The Community Center is open Mon. - Sat., 8am - 10pm; Sun., noon - 6pm. The playground is open daily, sunrise -sunset. The skate park is open Mon. - Sat., 8am - 10pm; Sun., 8am - 6pm.

Price: Free

Ages: All

LOCK MUSEUM OF ORANGE COUNTY

(714) 993-4300 / www.keedex.com/Main_Pages/about_us/about_us.html
510 Cameron Street, Placentia

Contained in a warehouse, I just can't keep this unique little museum under lock and key! The locksmith owner, who began avidly accumulating keys and locks when he was a kid, has an amazing and varied collection. He has the keys to many cities from all over the U.S. and the world, including ones made from steel, glass, and ivory. He also has amassed ten locks and keys that belonged to Houdini; ensembles that have been used in movies; manacles dating back to days of slavery; time locks used to thwart bank robbers; leg irons and neck cuffs with spikes; over 175 handcuffs (and some thumbcuffs); and keys and locks to jails and to a castle. Feeling all keyed up? Half-hour, interactive tours are offered to school groups, adults, Boy Scouts (who can earn a patch), or any group.

Hours: Open Mon. - Thurs., 8:30am - 5pm by appointment only. Closed Fri. - Sun.

Price: Free

Ages: 6 years and up.

LYON AIR MUSEUM

(714) 210-4585 / www.lyonairmuseum.org
19300 Ike Jones Road, Santa Ana

With a view through huge glass windows of the John Wayne Airport runway, this clean and well laid out aviation museum specializes in beautifully restored and operational WWII aircraft and vehicles. A centerpiece is the gleaming American Airlines DC-3. Kids are most intrigued by the Douglas A-26 Invader - perhaps because it has a face with sharp teeth painted on the front. One highlight is the B-17 Flying Fortress, complete with machine guns, that you can actually look into. It once transported generals Dwight Eisenhower and Douglas MacArthur. Other planes include a Cessna O-1E Bird Dog, Douglas C-47 Skytrain, B-25 Mitchell, WWII trainer plane - AT+6F/SNJ6, and more.

The vehicles include a 1941 Dodge Command Truck; 1940s Helms Bakery Truck; a shining, like-new 1947 Lincoln Continental; military jeeps; and motorcycles such as BMW R-75 sidecars, a 1945 Indian Chief, and a 1943 Japanese Rikuo. The most intriguing automobile is the Mercedes Benz G4 touring wagon, which has bullet-proof glass - it was once used by Adolph Hitler. The history of each vehicle and plane is told with signage and also by the knowledgeable docents, many of whom are WWII veterans.

A few display cases exhibit helmets, documents, and other memorabilia. Large maps on the walls show USAF deployments. Enter through the realistic-looking theater (because it is one) to watch continuously running aviation-themed movies. Individuals, tour groups, and school groups are welcome to walk around, and even under, some vehicles to get close up. Some of the planes might not be here at all times are they are flown for special events.

Hours: Open daily, 10am - 4pm Closed Thanksgiving and Christmas.
Price: $12 for adults; $6 for seniors, vets, and ages 5 - 17; children 4 and under are free. School groups are free.
Ages: 7 years and up.

MARCONI AUTOMOTIVE MUSEUM

(714) 258-3001 / www.marconimuseum.org

1302 Industrial Drive, Tustin

The museum's main purpose is to raise money for children's charities by showing automobiles from Dick Marconi's private collection, and renting out the facility. That said, the public, too, can come and look. The front hallway of this classy museum is lined with gleaming motorcycles. Inside are over fifty cars (specific ones sometimes rotate) that are housed here and kept in mint condition. They vary in style, shape, and color. His collection includes a 1929 Ford Model 'A' Cabriolet, 1937 Ahrens-Fox Fire Engine, 1954 green Chevrolet, 1973 canary-yellow convertible Ferrari Daytona Spider (once owned by Cher), restored 1964 Corvette Sting Ray, and a jet-black 1989 Lamborghini Countach, plus seventeen racing Ferraris, an assortment of motorcycles, and a few kid-size cars. Marconi's prized possession is the last car Mario Andretti drove to victory at the 1993 Phoenix International Raceway. It is signed by Andretti. My boys' favorite was the rather colorful car completely decoupaged with magazine covers featuring boxing champions. Racing flags, trophies, drivers' jumpsuits and helmets, and a huge, shining silver horse constructed out of old car bumpers complete this museum.

Hours: Open Mon. - Fri., 9am - 4:30pm by appointment only. You may call as little as a few hours before you would like to visit. Closed for special events and on most major holidays.
Price: $5 for adults; children 12 and under are free.
Ages: 8 years and up.

MISSION SAN JUAN CAPISTRANO

(949) 234-1300 - mission; (949) 234-132 - program coordinator / www.missionsjc.com

26801 Ortega Highway, San Juan Capistrano

The Mission, founded in 1776, is the oldest building in California. It is ten acres of historic stone buildings and beautifully landscaped gardens, courtyards, and walkways. It's easy to see why the San Juan Mission was considered the "Jewel of the Missions." There are many parts to the Mission, so there is something to interest almost any age child. It's a history treat for school kids as they visit and "experience" the early Native American, Spanish, and Mexican lifestyles, depicted in separate rooms. Walk through rooms that contain murals such as Indians hunting, and artifacts such as bone weapons. The Soldiers' Barracks room looks lived in, just as it did many years ago. It contains life-size models of soldiers and their (few) possessions. Note: Outside, behind the barracks, are some picnic tables. Kids will especially enjoy the brick Mission Clubhouse room with colorful informational posters all over and the activities offered. They can practice weaving a basket in the traditional way, using an extra large model basket; be a mission architect and build a Roman archway with blocks; and spin a wheel to find out their chore/ job could have been back then.

The extensive grounds are a maze of pathways. The Central Courtyard, the cemetery, the areas of archaeological excavation, and the industrial center are all interesting. For instance, tanning vats in the industrial center were used to

turn animal skin into sellable leather, while the ovens were used to turn animal fat into candles, soap, and ointments.

The Mission has two churches. One is the Serra Chapel, the oldest building in California, where mass is still regularly performed. The glittery baroque altar, made of gold leaf overlay, is eye-catching. The other church, the Great Stone Church, was once a magnificent cathedral. Some of it was destroyed by an earthquake in 1812. Today, the ruins have been handsomely preserved and stabilized.

Mission San Juan Capistrano offers many special, educational activities such craft days, storytelling, playing games, making old-fashioned toys, panning for gold, adobe brick making, and more. Guided school and group tours are also available that offer historic insight into the mission and this area.

If you're looking for somewhere fun to eat, RUBY'S (pg. 252) is across the street and up the stairs at the shopping district. This 1940's diner has a train going around overhead, red vinyl seats, and kids' meals that are served in a forties-style, cardboard car. Or, have tea at TEA HOUSE ON LOS RIOS (pg. 254). Afterwards, take a walk around Camino Capistrano, which is a street with many interesting stores with truly unique merchandise. Idea: Take a train into town and really make a day of your visit here! The train depot is only two blocks away from the Mission. Definitely look up ZOOMARS PETTING ZOO, on page 336, for a fun, close-by, petting zoo adventure and other ideas of what else to do in the immediate area. Check the Calendar entry for the Fiesta de Las Golondrinas (pg. 710) held at the mission.

Hours: Open daily, 9am - 5pm. Closed Good Friday at noon, Thanksgiving, Christmas Eve at noon, and Christmas. Sometimes closed due to rainy days; call first.

Price: $9 for adults (includes audio tour); $6 for seniors; $5 for ages 4 - 11; children 3 and under are free. Discount coupons are available online.

Ages: 5 years and up.

MUZEO   ☼
(714) 95-MUZEO (956-8936) / www.muzeo.org $$$
241 S. Anaheim Boulevard, Anaheim

This urban cultural museum showcases three outstanding traveling exhibits each year. Vastly diverse in theme, past titles have included Chicano Art and Soul; The Color of Rock (about rock legends); Bizarre Beasts Past and Present; Imperial Rome: Discovering the Ancient Civilization; How to Make a Monster (the process of designing and molding life-size finished monsters for major films); and Treasures of Napoleon. The high quality, integrity, and feeling of immersion is consistent in all the exhibits.

In the exhibit Under African Skies, for instance, the rooms were transformed into an African veldt, a village, and even a slice of America. African maps depicting various peoples and languages lined the entryway. Videos of jelis (i.e. singing historians), cultural dances, a sheep herder, and more people and places played against the backdrop of pictures, costumes, weapons, and even jewelry. Piped-in African music and chants filled the air adding to the "you are there" experience. Plaster-cast faces of gorillas were available to touch and feel their patterned wrinkles and I listened to the sounds of gorillas. Doors on a camel opened to see and learn about what the hump consists of (fat). I also learned that fine camels are a sign of wealth to the Tuarey, as sports car are to Americans. One room contained a tribal dwelling. I also walked down a hallway that was like the inside of a slave-carrying ship, with silhouettes on the wall and a voice speaking about the hardships of sailing. It opened to a platform and when I stood on the small balcony portion inside designated footprints, a slave auctioneer's voice was selling me. Timelines, pictures, a recreated cabin, and artifacts told the story of the cost of slavery in America.

A second, smaller building, just across the way, continues with the main exhibit. This building also holds a one-room, permanent exhibit regarding the history of Anaheim. Displays include clothing, fine jewelry, boots, irons, a hair wreath, a rabbit skin cape, shell and bone necklaces, a (replica) saber tooth cat skull, items from the grape/wine industry and the citrus industry, an homage to Disneyland, and uniforms and news headlines from WWI and WWII.

Educational field trips at the museum meet the California State standards and lesson plans are available. Ask about special programs, lectures, and events. Note that the museum gift store sells rotating merchandise that is pertinent to the current exhibit. Surrounding the museum are courtyards and a few retail stores and eateries. Catch a (small) farmer's market here on Thursdays.

Hours: Open January - mid-March, Tues. - Sun., 10am - 5pm; open the rest of the year, Tues. - Sun., 10am - 7pm. Closed Thanksgiving and Christmas Day.

Price: $10 for adults; $6 for ages 4 - 12; children 3 and under are free. Educators, check the website and download a form for a free pass.

Ages: 5 years and up, depending on the exhibit.

NEWLAND HOUSE MUSEUM

(714) 962-5777 / www.hbnews.us/nwhouse.html

19820 Beach Boulevard, Huntington Beach

$

Once the only building on acres of land, the restored, two-story Queen Anne Victorian house, originally built in 1898, is now next door to a shopping complex. It does, however, retain its elegance with its upkeep and well-manicured lawn, and it makes an interesting slice of history to learn about and explore.

A half-hour tour includes walking through the various rooms of the house that are furnished not only from that time period, but with many items that belonged to the original owners. See an old-fashioned kitchen with a stove, wall telephone, and cupboard of glass containers; a sunroom with wicker and Mission oak furniture; a dining room with a table all set for a meal; a patterned-wallpapered parlour with a grand piano and 1924 Victrola, and; several bedrooms with mannequins wearing clothing from that era (check out the wool bathing suits!), wash basins, and ¾ size beds; a nursery with a rack of children's clothing and rocking chair; a playroom that contains christening gowns, a few toys, and a cabinet of old dolls; a sleeping porch with brass beds; and a boy's room where three young boys slept on the one bed (until they got too big).

> **Hours:** Open the first and third weekends of each month, Sat. - Sun., noon - 4pm. The museum is closed on major holidays and rainy days.
>
> **Price:** $2 for adults; $1 for ages 12 and under.
>
> **Ages:** 8 years and up.

NEWPORT SPORTS MUSEUM

(949) 721-9333 / www.newportsportsmuseum.org

100 Newport Center Drive, suite 100, Newport Beach

Name a sport, any sport. Almost any one that you can think of is represented in this over 8,000 square-foot sports museum filled with signed memorabilia. The hundreds of game-used and game-worn equipment and clothing on display include jerseys, shoes, helmets, rows and rows of hockey sticks, basketballs, golf clubs, a multitude of footballs, skateboards, snowboards, baseballs, bats, and more. Included in this collection is the ball Babe Ruth hit for his last home-run, George Kelly's 1920 first baseman's mitt, and other baseball items signed by Cal Ripken, Joe DiMaggio, Nolan Ryan, Jackie Robinson, and lots more. The downstairs room contains numerous baseball keepsakes and has stadium seats facing a mural of a baseball field. One room upstairs is devoted to baseball, especially Angels' memorabilia from 1940 to present day, including a ball signed by the entire winning team. Several other small rooms display boxing gloves honoring Mohammad Ali, hockey items that belonged to Wayne Gretzsky, a football signed by John Elway, and pictures of/or equipment used in water polo, tennis, horse racing, etc. An Olympic section contains Olympic memorabilia and paraphernalia. Every living baseball hall of fame inductee, every Heisman trophy winner, and every Cy Young award winner is represented at the museum.

> **Hours:** Open Mon. - Fri., 10am - 5pm. Closed Sat., Sun. and major holidays.
>
> **Price:** Free
>
> **Ages:** 6 years and up.

OCEAN INSTITUTE

(949) 496-2274 / www.ocean-institute.org

24200 Dana Point Harbor Drive, Dana Point

$$$

The Ocean Institute's series of buildings consist of a research center and classroom setting designed to teach maritime history and facts about the marine environment to kindergartners through highschoolers, and beyond. Students and teachers are here in force during the week, while the public can enjoy the facilities on the weekends.

The lecture hall is interesting to peek into because of the whale skeleton hanging from the ceiling. The ecology learning center contains several learning stations complete with wet tables, hydrophones, microscopes, and magnification cameras for up-close viewing. Some of the tanks in here have large bubbles where kids can stick their heads up "inside" and get a fish-eye view. The tanks hold an octopus, crabs, squid, flatfish, and perch. The adjoining theater is used for virtual underwater experiences, interactive shows, puppet shows, or other presentations.

The two-story surf science building has a wave tank downstairs, a small skate and ray pool, and a research station to study the physical sciences of the surf zone. Upstairs, with a balcony and a great view of the surf, is a room decorated with netting, surfboards, and surfboard sleeping mats. Students can spend the night and learn what makes a perfect wave while they track storms at sea in the National Weather Service-certified observation station.

A favorite stop is the last one because of the tank farms which contain moon jellies, small sharks, huge lobsters,

sea bass, sea stars, and bottom-dwelling creatures. A forty-five-minute, behind-the-scenes tour of the facility is offered on Thursdays and Fridays at 3:30pm, with advanced reservations, for $2 per person.

A 130-square-foot replica of the historic Tallship *Pilgrim,* rigging and all, is moored in front of the building and open to walk through most Sundays. (See the Calendar entry, pg. 746, for details on the terrific annual Toshiba Tallships Festival.) *Pilgrim* offers one- to eighteen-hour on-board programs which recreate the austere life of a sailor in the early nineteenth century. Students learn sea chanteys, how to raise the sails, load cargo, and other period-related activities.

Just one of the many cruises the Institute offers is the Bio-Luminescence cruise. This two-and-a-half-hour night cruise highlights glowing worms, glow fish, and plankton. Children must be at least 4 years old for this cruise. Check out the Marine Wildlife Cruise where nets are hauled in filled with sea life. Sort through the creatures (and sediment) to study certain specimens via microscopes. Of course, you'll get the bigger picture by looking at the waters, too, for dolphins and whales, in season. The cost for each cruise is $35 for adults; $22 for ages 4 to 12. Want to swab the decks, matey? You can with a two-and-a-half-hour Pirate Adventure Sail on board the *Spirit of Dana Point* replica clipper schooner. Carrying swords, sporting eye patches, and wearing hats with skull and crossbones are part of the costume when raising the sail, taking the helm, and playing lookout. This outing is a real treasure. The cost is $40 for adults; $23 for ages 4 through 12.

The Institute offers a full range of outstanding classes for school kids of all ages - check out the extensive field trip list! that incorporates literature, social sciences, and history with the maritime theme. Ask about guided tidepool hikes, too. Behind the Institute is a small park overlooking the harbor, with rock jetties, a few picnic tables, and tidepools. See DANA POINT HARBOR on page 313, 765 for details.

> **Hours:**   The Institute is open to the public, Sat - Sun., 10am - 3pm. (It is open during the week for classes, only.) The *Pilgrim* is open most Sun., 11am - 3:30pm. Call for school group tours. Everything is closed on major holidays.
>
> **Price:**   Call for class fees. Weekend admission, which includes boarding the *Pilgrim* on Sundays, is $6.50 for ages 13 and up; $4.50 for ages 3 - 12; children 2 and under are free.
>
> **Ages:**   3 years and up.

OLD COURTHOUSE MUSEUM

(714) 973-6605 - courthouse; (714) 973-6607 - tours / www.ocparks.com
211 W. Santa Ana Boulevard, Santa Ana

Order in the court! Older kids interested in the history of our legal system, or in seeing what an actual courtroom looks like, will enjoy visiting the oldest courtroom in Southern California. Built in 1901, this huge, red sandstone building contains three floors of Orange County history. The bottom floor has a few glass cases of archaeological artifacts, such as fossils and bones. The second floor, which is the entrance, has two displays containing information about the museum, the history of the courthouse, and the court of law.

The third floor is the most interesting destination. It features a turn-of-the-century courtroom, jury room, and judge's chambers, plus a court reporter's room that has original transcribing machines, a candlestick telephone, and an old roll-top desk. My boys and I role-played a bit here so they could get a feel for how the court system is set up. The museum, which is a room of changing exhibits, is across the way from the Superior Courtroom. Past exhibits have included displays of sheriff's badges, war posters, a mock-up of a 1940's living room, and World War II artifacts from Orange County. A visit to the Old Courthouse Museum is a good beginning for future lawyers. I rest my case.

> **Hours:**   Open Mon. - Fri., 9am - 4:30pm. Closed on holidays. Forty-five-minute guided tours are available by appointment.
>
> **Price:**   Free
>
> **Ages:**   6 years and up.

OLINDA OIL MUSEUM AND TRAIL

(714) 671-4447 / www.ci.brea.ca.us
4025 Santa Fe Road, Brea

Still pumping out about two barrels a day, Olinda's first oil well (dug in 1897) keeps on giving. Located in a residential area this twelve-acre historical site is wonderfully maintained. The building holds artifacts regarding oil, such as a safe, photos, and even small warehouse, yet I think the outside holds a kid's interest more. On the grounds is a pump, the original oil well #1, a records vault, a steam boiler (from 1910), a rusted 1924 Model T, and a few picnic tables on the grass under shade trees. School and group tours are welcome.

Just behind the office building is a moderate, two-mile, looping hiking dirt trail which actually retraces the

footsteps of oil pioneers. Going to the top rewards hikers with panoramic views of Orange County.

Hours: Open Wed., 10am - 2pm and Sun., noon - 4pm. Hiking trails are open daily, sunrise - sunset.
Price: Free
Ages: 7 years and up.

ORANGE COUNTY DENTAL SOCIETY MUSEUM

(714) 634-8944 / www.ocds.org
295 S. Flower Street, Orange

This small museum doesn't floss over America's early dental period. It contains several old dental chairs, including an 1855 wooden chair with a straight back and a spittoon - no running water on this device; an 1876 velvet, rose-colored chair with fringe and a spittoon; and a modern-day chair with all the amenities. The glass-enclosed display shelves are lined with old dental tools that made me wince just to look at them, such as extraction forceps, clamps for separating teeth, and small saws. My youngest son commented, "I'm going to brush my teeth ten times a day from now on!" We also saw a lot of false teeth, porcelain shade guides (used to match teeth for bridge work or capping), metal swagging sets (for making gold crowns), a buffalo horn mallet (used before plastic), and numerous steel instruments - some made with ivory and some with mother-of-pearl handles. The crowning jewel here is in a silver trinket box - a partial denture of four of George Washington's ivory teeth! You are welcome to explore the museum on your own, as everything is labeled, or ask for further explanations across the hall at the Dental Society. This museum is something you can really sink your teeth into!

Hours: Open Mon. - Thurs., 7am - 4:30pm - please call at least one hour in advance.
Price: Free
Ages: 9 years and up.

RICHARD NIXON PRESIDENTIAL LIBRARY AND BIRTHPLACE

(714) 993-3393 / www.nixonlibrary.gov; www.nixonfoundation.org
18001 Yorba Linda Boulevard, Yorba Linda

This museum/library/grave site/rose garden features nine acres of galleries and gardens, plus the restored birthplace of - here's a quiz - what number president? (The answer is at the end of this description.) Bring a pencil and request a Children's Scavenger Hunt to encourage your kids to become more involved with the exhibits in the museum. They'll search for objects like the Presidential Seal, the Woody Station Wagon Nixon used for campaigning, and the piano he practiced on in his younger years.

The theater presents a half-hour film, documenting Richard Nixon's political career with vintage news footage, campaign clips and more. It's a great introduction to who he was, both personally and presidentially. There are several videos and touch screens throughout the museum showing different aspects of his life, including the Kennedy/Nixon debates, footage from his speeches, a tribute to Pat Nixon, and a presidential forum with over 300 questions to choose from. I was pleasantly surprised at how interested kids were in all of this. The Road to Presidency starts from Nixon's beginnings and takes visitors through his growing up years, on the campaign trails, and into the White House.

The exhibit of ten, life-size statues of world leaders (some of whom were very short) is impressive. Touch screens offer comments and biographical summaries on the leaders. Gifts of State - jewelry, carved ivory, statues, and more - and gifts from the people are unique treasures to view. My oldest son thought the pistol from Elvis Presley was the coolest present. The Structure of Peace gallery features presentations about Nixon's strategy for peace regarding Peoples Republic of China, the Soviet Union, and Vietnam which includes a replica of a South Vietnamese house and uniforms belonging to former POWs. A twelve-foot high chunk of the Berlin Wall is also in this gallery. Other pieces of history include the presidential limo that at various times held Johnson, Ford, Carter, and Nixon; a fully furnished recreation of the White House's Lincoln Sitting Room (which is quite small); numerous photographs; Nixon's daughters' wedding dresses and some of Pat's dresses; and Nixon's private study from his New Jersey home, complete with hand-written letters and speech notes. A small room dedicated to the space program contains an astronaut suit, a piece of moon rock, photographs, and the recording between the president and Apollo 11 astronauts when they landed on the moon. The Domestic Affairs Gallery contains info and touch screens regarding Nixon's achievements in many reforms - space, health, environment, crime, etc. Listen to the "smoking gun" tape in the Watergate exhibit, as well as hundreds of other Watergate tapes and interviews. Use the interactive screens, watch videos, and read the section called "Dirty Tricks and Political Espionage". The comprehensive, really well-done, bipartisan pictorial and descriptive timeline of this historic scandal takes up an entire room. Tip: At the very least, know how to explain the term "impeach" to your kids. Docents are available in most rooms to give some brief, interesting, and helpful background on the exhibits and to answer questions.

On the other side of the U-shaped building is a room with rotating exhibits and a full-size replica of the White House East Room. This large room has beautiful crystal chandeliers, an ornate ceiling and wall carvings, and some information panels. It is often used for private functions or museum events. Kids usually make just a brief visit here.

Walk outside, through the First Lady's beautiful rose gardens (which look pretty when they're in bloom), past the large reflecting pool, to the home where Nixon was born. A tour of the small house only takes fifteen minutes. A million dollar, restored Sea King helicopter used by this elected official, as well as Kennedy, Johnson, and Ford, is stationed near the house. Walk through it and get a feel for being presidential. Richard Nixon was, by the way, our thirty-seventh President.

Ask about the numerous special programs offered here including Sunday Family Concerts, war reenactments, a myraid of political speakers, and much more. Two-hour, free, guided tours are given Monday through Friday for fifth through twelfth graders, with advanced reservations. First through fourth graders are welcome on a self-guided tour, using a scavenger hunt worksheet.

Hours: Open Mon. - Sat., 10am - 5pm; Sun., 11am - 5pm. Closed New Year's Day, Thanksgiving, and Christmas.

Price: $11.95 for adults; $8.50 for seniors; $6.95 for students; $4.75 for ages 7 - 11; children 6 and under are free. Certain discounts are available through AAA. President's Day is usually free and there are special activities going on.

Ages: 6 years and up.

TITANIC - THE EXPERIENCE   ☼

(657) 529-7224; (888) 647-2789 / www.titanictheexperience.com/buenapark/ $$$$
7711 Beach Boulevard, Buena Park

On April 15, 1912 when the unsinkable sank, 1517 people died. Only 706 survived. Walk through each of the rooms in this unique "museum" that recreates - with mood lighting, period music and sounds, decor, murals, huge black and white photographs, signage, costumed docents, and glass-enclosed cases that contain original artifacts (over 250) from the *Titanic* - the step-by-step process of the building the ship, the excitement around it, the passengers who sailed on her, the unseen iceberg, and the tragedy that ensued. Experience the *Titanic*.

A costumed docent/actor welcomes you aboard and after giving a brief verbal history of the time period and the ocean liner, invites you to choose a card with a photo and history of one of the passengers, a boarding pass, for you to "be". You'll see what happens to "you" (i.e., that person) at the end. The first room has dark red walls, wood flooring, photos and explanations of the ship being built and, among other items, huge whistles from the *Titanic*. The next room is similar. It has a large model of the ship in the center and photos of the finished cruise liner and of launch day with a placard of the ship line's director quote, "The *Titanic* is now about complete and will, I think, do the old firm credit tomorrow when we sail." Set sail via walking up a gangplank here, surrounded by old trunks, crates, barrels, bags of food, and newspaper articles that proclaim the wonder of the *Titanic*. The gangplank leads into a carpeted hallway of stateroom doors on board the ship, which then leads to the next series of rooms. These hold more photos and information about the passengers, plus items like drinking glasses, soap dishes, jewelry, time pieces and other personal effects. Walk into the elegant grand stairway entrance on tiled floor, with a real chandelier overhead and burnished wooden pillars. The staircase is depicted realistically on a wall mural photograph. The next room has a full-size replica of a luxurious first class cabin that is fully furnished with a bed, dresser, clothing, and a table set for tea. (A first class ticket cost, in today's terms, $57,200!) An assortment of plates and bowls and other original items are in the display cases. The third class passengers slept in tighter quarters which you'll see next - pretty much just two bunkbeds. Listen to the throbbing sounds of the engines here.

Go down a ramp to enter the boiler room with walls marked black and red to look like dancing flames. There are some open doors at the bottom of a huge steel door to show the coal, as well as photos of some of the engineers and pieces of equipment from this section of the *Titanic*. Walk through another steel door to see the words reported from another ship "Ice Warning" and "Ice Reports: Passed two large icebergs" and then, from the *Titanic* "Iceberg Right Ahead!". The latter is on the wall just before you enter a room with black walls and a spotlight on a real iceberg! Well, it is a ten feet wide by four feet high chunk of ice that visitors are encouraged to touch. The ocean was colder than that, so most people didn't die from drowning, but from hypothermia. In this darkened room is also a brass steering stand (from the *Titanic*), a video showing how the *Titanic* sunk, and a fragment of its hull that visitors can touch. (That's kind of cool!)

Go into the next room and sit on the seats inside the frame of a lifeboat. As footage shows in the background, listen as a docent describes that fateful night and how it felt, using actual words from passenger's accountings. The next ramp and room contains more photos and passenger information, plus a full list of who died and who survived.

Find out what happened to "you" here.

The final room is really special, too. It is like walking on the bottom of the ocean as the glass floor reveals the real sand underneath and the lighting is flickering blues and greens. The showcase artifact is the massive rusted steel gangway door used by Titanic's first class passengers. On the walls are footage of the wreck of the *Titanic* and photos of some of the objects found. Below the photos are the actual recovered dishes, pots, and side of a bench on display in cases imbedded in sand. Walk through a replica of the rusted ship, back into modern-day life. And actually, into the gift shop. What an immersive experience through time!

Notes: Give yourself at the *very* least an hour to go through this exhibit. Rent an audio for an additional $7 that goes more in depth with all that you see. No photography is permitted. Group tours and school tours are given that enhance the experience and understanding. The rooms are wheelchair accessible. The lighting in the rooms is kept low so it is fairly dark for the most part, as the artifacts would be damaged by light. The adjacent exhibit, sharing the same building, is BODIES, THE EXHIBITION (pg. 299) - another awesome attraction to walk through and see.

Hours: Open Sun. - Thurs., 10am - 7pm; Fri. - Sat., 10am - 8pm.
Price: $19.75 for adults; $17.75 for seniors; $15.75 for ages 5 - 11; children 4 and under are free. Prepurchase tickets online to save $. A combo ticket for Titanic and Bodies is $34.50 for adults; $30.50 for seniors; $26.50 for kids.
Ages: 6 years and up.

—PIERS AND SEAPORTS—

BALBOA PIER

(949) 644-3309 or (800) 94-COAST (942-6278) / www.newportbeachca.gov; www.visitnewportbeach.com
Main Street by E. Oceanfront, Newport Beach

Enjoy the miles of sandy beach for sunning and surfing; fish from the pier just for the fun of it; or grab a bite to eat at the small RUBY'S Diner (pg. 252) at the end of the pier. Peninsula Park is on the east side of the pier. This decent-size, grassy park, shaded only by palm trees, has barbecues, picnic tables, and even a small playground with a fun, triangular, rope-climbing structure. Note that there are many trendy cafes and equipment rental places in the area. Combine BALBOA FUN ZONE (pg. 255) and EXPLOROCEAN (pg. 302) attractions, located just across the road, for a full day of fun.

Hours: Open daily, 6am - 10pm.
Price: Free. Parking in the lot is $1.50 per hour; $15 max. $25 for Memorial Day, 4th of July, and Labor Day.
Ages: All

DANA POINT HARBOR

(949) 923-2255 / www.danapointharbor.com
34675 Street of the Golden Lantern, Dana Point

Dana Point Harbor has beaches, tidepools, a seaside shopping village, boat rentals, picnic areas, and more. The shopping village offers many specialty stores, from Indian jewelry to seafaring items. Food choices range from the elegant to the quick bite, plus ice cream and candy shops, of course. Your young sailor can watch boats of all sizes, shapes, and colors sail in and out of the harbor and up and down the coast. See the Transportation section for details about cruises and whale watching.

At the western end of the harbor, next to the Ocean Institute, is Dana Cove Park, or "Baby Beach." There are a few picnic tables here overlooking the bluffs, a long rock jetty to climb out on, a waveless beach, and a youth group facility which holds classes for water sports. On the other side of the Institute is a rocky patch of beach and the tidepools of the marine preserve, which you can explore on your own or call for a guided tour. Tip: Wear shoes with good tread.

Enjoy the day with your family at Dana Point, whatever you choose to do! (See DOHENY STATE BEACH PARK, on page 240, and OCEAN INSTITUTE, on page 309, for other things to do here.)

Hours: Most shops are open daily, 10am - 8 or 9pm.
Price: Parking is free.
Ages: All

—POTPOURRI—

BLUES SCHOOLHOUSE (Orange County)

(714) 520-2388 / www.ihobf.org

!/$$

1530 S. Disneyland Drive at the House of Blues in Downtown Disney, Anaheim

See the entry for BLUES SCHOOLHOUSE (Los Angeles County) on page 162 for details about this educational program. Go on the website for direct contact information. Note that this House of Blues is in DOWNTOWN DISNEY, so see this entry on page 314 for details.

Ages: 5th - 12th grade

BUILD-A-BEAR WORKSHOP (Orange County)

Anaheim - (714) 776-5980; Mission Viejo - (949) 347-6992 / www.buildabear.com

$$$

Anaheim - 1540 S. Disneyland Drive, suite 104, in Downtown Disney; Mission Viejo - 555 The Shops at The Shops Mission Viejo

Make your own new best friend at Build-A-Bear stores. First, choose a furry bear, frog, cow, monkey, kitty, or dog body. Add a sound or record your own message to put inside the critter. Then, help stuff it by pressing on a pedal that (gently!) shoots stuffing into your animal, fluffing him/her until he/she is just right. After putting a little heart inside your new buddy, have the last few stitches sewn up, and choose a name to put on a personalized birth certificate or inside of a storybook. The stores also offer over 200 outfits and accessories to dress up your furry friend. What a fun excursion or *bear*thday party idea! Note that there are several workshops throughout Southern California; many of them located inside malls.

For other things to do at the Anaheim location, see the entry for DOWNTOWN DISNEY (pg. 314) and for the one in Mission Viejo, see the entry for THE SHOPS AT MISSION VIEJO (pg. 297).

Hours: Anaheim is open Sun. - Thurs., 10am - 10:30pm; Fri. - Sat., 10am - 11:30pm. Mission Viejo is open Mon. - Fri., 10am - 9pm; Sat., 10am - 7pm; Sun., 11am - 6pm.

Price: The "bear" minimum prices are $10 - $25, depending on the size of the bear. Clothing, accessories, and storybooks are extra.

Ages: 2 years and up.

DISNEY STORE (Orange County)

Costa Mesa: (714) 751-8080; Mission Viejo: (949) 364-2107 / www.disneystore.com

!/$$

Costa Mesa - 3333 Bristol Street at South Coast Plaza; Mission Viejo - 555 The Shops at Mission Viejo Boulevard;

These Disney stores have a few extra magical components, besides the world of Disney merchandise here. The glittery walkway (sprinkled with pixie dust, I presume) leads to a kid-sized bejeweled castle door. Walk through and come face-to-face with a set of mirrors. Wave special wands in front of the main one (employees will show you which wands) and it becomes animated, showing scenes starring Disney princesses. Look up at the enchanted trees - they periodically come to life with changing colors and Disney images and footage.

The last special feature is a small theater that continuously shows favorite Disney trailers, music videos, cartoons, and movie clips - you can even select which ones you want to view. This area is where teas and mini parades (both events encourage kids to come dressed as their favorite Disney character), storytelling, and other celebrations are held. There are also crayons and coloring pages here, too, to use any time. Parents shop leisurely (or rest a bit), kids are mesmerized and happy - a fairy tale ending. Note that Disney is in the process of transforming most of their retail stores to this immersive and interactive format. See THE SHOPS AT MISSION VIEJO (pg. 297) for more info about what else there is to see and do at this mall. See SOUTH COAST PLAZA (pg. 297) for more details about this massive mall.

Hours: Costa Mesa store is open Mon. - Fri., 10am - 9pm; Sat., 10am - 8pm; Sun., 11am - 6:30pm. Mission Viejo store is open Mon. - Fri., 10am - 9pm; Sat., 10am - 7pm; Sun., 11am - 6pm. Closed most major holidays.

Price: Free, but bring spending money.

Ages: 1 - 10 years.

DOWNTOWN DISNEY

(714) 300-7800; (714) 635-2300 - Grand California Hotel / disneyparks.disney.go.com

!/$

Disneyland Drive/Disneyland Way, Anaheim

Downtown Disney has an uptown feel. It is a wide, non-gated, beautifully-landscaped pedestrian walkway, lined with unique restaurants, shops, nightclubs, and a movie theater.

Top restaurant picks include the Inca temple-styled, multi-level RAINFOREST CAFE (see pg. 251 for details); Ralph Brennan's Jazz Kitchen, an upscale French Quarter-look building with Cajun cuisine, a kid's menu, and live New Orleans jazz at night (usually); Naples Ristorante e Pizzeria, serving Italian cuisine, using a wood burning oven, in an elegant, Mediterranean atmosphere; and the ESPN ZONE (see pg. 246 for details), done in a red-bricked, brewery architectural design, that combines American grill food, live sports telecasts from around the world shown on numerous monitors all around, and competitive sports games. Of course, sometimes it's just as much fun to come downtown for a scoop (or two) of ice cream at Haagen-Dazs. Nighttime brings a (clean) party atmosphere with street entertainers, live music, and fun kiosks.

Favorite stores in this eclectic mixture, include the massive World of Disney, which is one of the world's largest collections of exclusive Disney merchandise. If you can't find it here, they don't make it! Lego Imagination Center carries a huge variety of Lego products. See BUILD-A-BEAR WORKSHOP (pg. 314) for a *beary* good treat for kids. RIDEMAKERZ (pg. 316 is the place to make a customized toy car or truck. An independent book store, candle shop, surfer's shop, traveler's aide stores, AMC Theaters, and more round out this area.

Downtown Disney is located in between DISNEYLAND (pg. 232) and CALIFORNIA ADVENTURE (pg. 230), and connects with the Disneyland Hotel and the Grand Californian Hotel. The latter gigantic (and expensive) hotel is done in the Arts and Crafts design with a woodsy yet understated elegant theme. Take a walk through and gawk at the high, high beam ceiling, at the lobby fireplace that dominates the room because of its size, and at the timber trusses that look like a castle gate door. The lobby actually feels like an inviting living room / family room. You can just relax in the plush chairs here for a bit. The hotel does offer free, hour-long tours a few times a week, by reservation, and free storytelling in the lobby, usually nightly at 530pm and 7:30pm, by reservation. For a usually quiet nook or picnic area, go through the hotel onto its grounds' walkway where you'll be surrounded by trees. There you'll find a few cafe-style tables and chairs. This hotel also has two, on-site restaurants; the comfortable, Storyteller's Cafe (see CHIP 'N DALE BREAKFAST AT STORYTELLER'S CAFE on page 245) and the more refined Napa Rose, which has three hosts for every table, incredible food fixed in a theater-type kitchen (the "show" makes it great "eatertainment"), and even a children's menu. Other fun places to eat that are just around the corner are SURF'S UP! BREAKFAST WITH MICKEY AND FRIENDS (pg. 253) and GOOFY'S KITCHEN (see page 247).

Hours: The "street" is open daily, 7am - 2am. Most of the stores and restaurants open at 9am. Closing times vary.

Price: Free. Parking is free for the first 3 hours. Validate an additional 2 hours from a full-service restaurant or the movie theaters.

Ages: All

FRY'S ELECTRONICS (Orange County)

Anaheim - (714) 688-3000; Fountain Valley - (714) 378-4400 / www.frys.com
Anaheim - 3370 East La Palma Ave.; Fountain Valley - 10800 Kalama River Ave.

See the entry for FRY'S ELECTRONICS (Los Angeles County) on page 170 for details.

HUNTINGTON BEACH PUBLIC LIBRARY and CULTURAL CENTER

(714) 842-4481 / www.hbpl.org
7111 Talbert Avenue, Huntington Beach

When is a library more than just a place to peruse books? When it is the Huntington Beach Public Library! This multi-level facility is a delight to visit. Kids are captivated by the huge center fountain inside and the spiraling paved walkway that encircles it. The fountain is loud, especially on the lower level, in contrast to the normal quiet tones associated with a library. On the bottom floor is a cafe stand that sells sandwiches, salads, corn dogs, muffins, and a range of coffees. Use the adjacent tables and chairs for enjoying a snack, reading, and/or studying. Look up and see returned books being transferred to be reshelved via a metal conveyor belt. (Only kids notice this sort of thing.)

The Huntington Beach Playhouse is located on the lower level. Several, mostly adult-oriented performances, are given throughout the year. Children's productions are occasionally offered here, although usually given in the upstairs theater room. These can include marionette and puppet shows, musicals, and so on.

One side of the main floor has an incredible number of books organized on several levels within the library. A map is available to help you find your topic of interest. There are even a few small art galleries in this wing. Adjacent to this room is a large section with used books and videos for sale. The library also has a small gift shop.

Just outside the Children's Room is a circular aquarium - look for the eel. The Children's Room has a large

selection of books. It also contains a reading area, a toddlers' section, and a wooden frame of a boat for tots to play in. The adjacent Tabby Storytime Theater, which is used for storytelling events, and a media/computer room make this library complete. Pick up a calendar listing of children's events, or call (714) 375-5107 for children's programing information.

HUNTINGTON CENTRAL PARK (pg. 280) surrounds the library. Directly behind the library is a trail leading down to a pond. Acres of trails, rolling green hills, shade trees, and picnic areas are all here to enhance your visit. For summertime fun, check out Adventure Playground (pg. 725), just up the hill from the library.

Hours: The library is open Mon., 1pm - 9pm; Tues. - Thurs., 9am - 9pm; Fri - Sat., 9am - 5pm. Closed Sun. and on certain holidays. Call for hours for special events, and for the shows.

Price: Free to the library, although it is $25 a year if you are a nonresident and want to check books out and/or $5 an hour to use the computers.

Ages: All

INDEPENDENCE HALL

(714) 220-5244 / www.knotts.com
8039 Beach Boulevard, Buena Park

This full-size reproduction of Independence Hall houses, among other things, a replica of the Liberty Bell. Press a button to hear a prerecorded history message about the bell. See the recreated room where the Declaration of Independence was signed. Every half hour, a twenty-minute "show," called *Storm in Philadelphia*, is presented. It consists of sitting in the darkened room while candle lights flicker and a "storm" rages outside, and listening to voices debate the ratification of the Declaration of Independence. It is very well done and stirs up patriotism in an American's heart. The gift shop here has patriotic memorabilia to purchase at good prices. Tip: Bring a dime to put in the machine to watch the miniaturized Spirit of '76 army march around. It also has period-dressed mannequins and artifacts, such as a cannon. Tip: Pick up a copy of the self-guided tour brochure before you bring a group here, just to acquaint yourself with all the hall has to offer. Before you visit Independence Hall, you might want to call first and see if a school tour will be in progress. Check Knott's Berry Farm for a list of outstanding educational programs offered.

The surrounding, lush park area has a pond with ducks, shade trees, and grass - perfect for picnicking.

Hours: Open daily, 10am - 5pm. Closed Christmas.

Price: Free. The first hour of parking is complimentary; an additional 2 hours of parking (so 3, total) are free with proof of purchase if you're eating at one of the restaurants or doing some shopping. Or, pay $15 for parking for the day in the Knott's Berry Farm lot (not the Marketplace where all-day parking is $25).

Ages: 5 years and up.

IRVINE RANCH OUTDOOR EDUCATION CENTER

(714) 923-3191 / www.iroec.webs.com
2 Irvine Park Road, Orange

$$$

Being a big advocate of "the world is our classroom" learning makes me appreciate all the programs that Irvine Ranch has to offer groups for half-day, full day, and overnight school field trips, scouting excursions, team building and more. Programs can include really cool science experiments (like firing rockets) and astronomy; going into a mine to dig and learn about rocks, earthquakes, panning for gold, geology and mining; experiencing a day at the rancho at the citrus grove, seasonal vegetable garden, windmill, and solar-powered well to learn about compost, plants, the water cycle and more; archery; shooting BB guns; zip lining; obstacle courses; high ropes courses; hiking; swimming; and much more. Tent and cabin camping, plus nighttime activities are also available.

Hours: Call for a schedule or to create a schedule for your own group.

Price: Depends on the activities and time.

Ages: Depends on the activity.

RIDEMAKERZ

(714) 776-0216 / www.ridemakerz.com
Disneyland Drive/Disneyland Way - it's in Downtown Disney, Anaheim

$$$$

Red? Blue? With flames on the sides? How about some chrome? At Ridemakerz you create the (toy) car or truck of your dreams. Going through seven different zones in the store, you first choose a body style - Ford Mustang, Dodge Viper, Chevy Corvette, Hot Rod, Pick-up truck, Concept car, or something else - in your color preference, then add to it (or not) - the chassis, wheels, tires, spoiler, tail pipe, engine, decals, lights, paint details (ink it yourself and

make stripes, etc.), radio controller, sound effects (like screeching around a corner, horns, engines revving, music, etc. - way cool!), etc. Assemble everything at the store workstation that has all the tools you need, plus a pit crew (i.e. store staff member) to help you if you need it. Take your tricked out ride for a spin. Vvvrooom - "start your enginuity"! Ridemakerz is in DOWNTOWN DISNEY (pg. 314).

Hours: Open Mon. - Thurs., 10am - 10pm; Fri. - Sun., 10am - 11pm (open until midnight when school is out).

Price: Basic cars and trucks, with stock wheels, etc., range from $18- $38. Upgrade to a monster truck for $5. Add remote control feature for $25. Each accessory costs "extra".

Ages: 3 years and up.

ROGER'S GARDENS

(800) 647-2356 or (949) 640-5800 / www.rogersgardens.com
2301 San Joaquin Hills Road, Corona Del Mar

Enter the world of gardening fantasy; a fantasy for me as I have a black thumb. Roger's Gardens sells an enormous variety of plants and shrubs in a beautifully landscaped, garden-like setting. Walk the two-tiered paved trails and fill your eyes with an explosion of color. My kids loved the unusual plants as well as seeing ones that could supposedly bloom in our garden, too. There are a few good-sized gift shop rooms that sell gardening tools, books, dried flower arrangements, specialty soaps, cards, and other paraphernalia.

The kid-draw happens from the end of October through the middle of January when a large patch of elevated grass on the grounds has an extensive model train layout set up and completely decked out. The train, smoke and whistles and all, runs over hill and dale, around miniature cities and scenery. There is also a section at the gardens adorned with decorated Christmas trees.

Hours: Open January - February, 9am - 5pm; March - September, 9am - 6pm; October - December, 9am - 8pm. Closed New Year's Day, Easter, Thanksgiving, and Christmas..

Price: Free

Ages: All

—SHOWS AND THEATERS—

3-D THEATRICALS

(714) 589-2770 - box office / www.3dtshows.com
201 E. Chapman Avenue at Plummer Auditorium, Fullerton

This professional company has had terrific seasons and productions with shows such as *Wizard of Oz, All Shook Up, Always Patsy Cline,* and *Peter Pan.* Check the website, or call, to see what is playing next. They also perform at REDONDO BEACH PERFORMING ARTS CENTER (pg. 191).

Hours: Call or check the website for the schedule.

Price: Tickets range in Fullerton from $28 - $60 per person; in Redondo Beach from $35 - $65.

Ages: 7 years and up.

BROADWAY ON TOUR FAMILY THEATER

(714) 542-6939 / www.broadwayontour.org
625 French Street at the Ebell Theater, Santa Ana

At this 300-seat theater, kids 8 to 20 years old put on presentations for younger children who delight in seeing just slightly older versions of themselves on stage. The one-hour musicals are usually based on classic fairytales, and they run for six weeks. Past performances include *Sleeping Beauty, Snoopy, Aladdin Jr.,* and *Twelve Dancing Princesses.* Come early for cookies, tea, and pink lemonade with the cast before the show. Reservations are required for the tea.

Longer (usually about two hours), full-length Broadway musicals, still performed by kids, are offered for the whole family. Past productions have included *Peter Pan* and *The Princess and The Pea.* Broadway on Tour's motto is, "Children bringing theatre to children." Call for show information and to find out how your child could become a performer.

Hours: Show times are usually Sat. and Sun. at 2pm. "Tea" is served an hour before the show. Some shows are also given on Sat. at 4:30pm. Full-length musicals are usually performed on Fri. evening, and Sat. - Sun. afternoons. Call for hours.[

Price: $12 per person; $17 for the tea and show - ages 1 and older need their own ticket. Save $2 per by preordering tickets on line.Cash or check only. Full-length musicals are more expensive.

Ages: 4 - 12 years.

COSTA MESA CIVIC PLAYHOUSE

(949) 650-5269 / www.costamesaplayhouse.org

661 Hamilton Street, Costa Mesa

School House Rock Live!, *The Diary of Anne Frank*, and *Seussical - the Musical* are just three of the shows produced at this seventy-three-seat community theater. Of the four productions put on each year, at least one of them is geared specifically for family and kids.

Hours: Showtimes are generally Fri. and Sat. at 8pm; Sun. at 2pm. Call for a schedule.

Price: Tickets are generally $20 for adults; $18 for seniors and students.

Ages: 7 years and up, depending on what's playing.

CURTIS THEATER - CITY OF BREA GALLERY

(714) 990-7722 - theater; (714) 990-7731 or (714) 990-7730 - gallery / www.ci.brea.ca.us; www.breagallery.com

1 Civic Center Circle, Brea

The 199-seat Curtis Theater and Brea's Youth Theater boast a variety of plays and productions, musicals and comedies, that are family friendly. The theater's regular season has put on shows such as *West Side Story*, *Peter and the Wolf*, *The Alley Cats* (singing group), and *4 Stand Up Dads* (comedians). The Youth Theater is made up of a talented cast of young actors and actresses (i.e., kids) who put on two musical extravaganzas a year; one in the summer and one in the winter. Past productions include *Peter Pan*, *Aladdin*, and *Bye-Bye Birdie*. Call for information about signing your kids up to be in a future production.

Across from the theater, the Civic Center has a small gallery called City of Brea Gallery where painting, photography, sculpture and other exhibits change periodically. The gallery hosts workshops for adults and also a Children's Art Workshop where young visitors, ages 5 to 13, may create their own masterpiece related to the current exhibits on select Sundays from 1pm to 3:30pm. The cost is $75 for each multi-week session. The Brea Gallery is usually open on performance nights and allows kids to peruse art while waiting for the theater doors to open.

Hours: Call for a schedule of performances. Youth Theater productions are usually in July and January. The gallery is open Wed. - Sun., noon - 5pm.

Price: Tickets usually range from $21 - $30, depending on the show. Tickets for the Youth Theater usually run $12 per person. The gallery is $2 for adults; free to youth 11 and under and Brea residents.

Ages: 5 years and up.

IRVINE BARCLAY THEATER

(949) 854-4646 / www.thebarclay.org

4242 Campus Drive, Irvine

This theater offers four to five family-oriented shows a year, plus several touring shows geared for kids, and for adults. The various types of shows include circus acts, folk singers, Indian dancers, ballet, chorus music, modern dance, ensembles, youth orchestras, acrobats, and specifically, the *Nutcracker Suite*. Applause, applause - not a seat in the house is more than sixty feet away from the stage.

Hours: Call for show dates and times. Even children sitting on your lap must have a ticket.

Price: Tickets range from $20 - $150. Parking is $10 at the UCI parking structure.

Ages: 5 years and up.

THE LAGUNA PLAYHOUSE

(800) 946-5556 or (949) 497-9244; (949) 497-2787 - box office / www.lagunaplayhouse.com

606 Laguna Canyon Road, Laguna Beach

"Orange County's Award-Winning Theater for Young People and the Young at Heart!" The playhouse offers a main stage season, a youth theater showcase where youth acting companies perform, and Theatrereach - an ensemble that comes to schools for on-site performances. Four great-for-the-kids plays are presented here each year. Past productions include *Charlotte's Web*, *Treasure Island*, *Wizard of Oz*, and *The Best Christmas Pageant Ever*.

Hours: Call for show dates and times.

Price: Tickets by the youth companies are usually $18 - $25, depending on the show. Other tickets usually run from $30 - $70, depending on the show. Parking is $7.

Ages: 5 years and up.

MEDIEVAL TIMES

(800) 899-6600 or (714) 521-4740; (714) 521-2342 - student field trips / www.medievaltimes.com; educators.medievaltimes.com

7662 Beach Boulevard, Buena Park

Joust the sight of this eleventh-century-style castle sets the mood for a *knight* to remember. Upon entering the castle hall, wear the crowns given ye, good Lords and Ladies, as the color designates which one of the six knights you'll cheer for. The Lord of the castle and his daughter-in-law, the princess, have invited you and hundreds of your closest friends, neighbors, and foes to a two-hour royal tournament. Bring your camera to take pictures with the knights in shining armor all around the castle. Note: The Museum of Torture is open before the show. This unusual museum displays over thirty reproductions of instruments of torture and ridicule used during the Middle Ages, like the Rack, and the Stock and Pillories. Each instrument is explicitly labeled as to its use. Personally, I wouldn't go through the museum again. Admission is $2 per person.

Tiered spectator seating encircles the dirt floor arena where fog starts to rise up and the music swells - the story and show begin. Hear and become part of the tale where the king, the princess, a master of arms, and six knights and their squires first celebrate a victory, and then discover a treachery.

As dinner commences, the invited guests (that's you and your family) are first entertained by silky-maned horses that prance, high-step, and even jump. These elegant displays of horsemanship delight horse fans young and old. The royal falconer then commands his trained birds of prey as they swoop around the arena. As the story continues to unfold (and you continue to eat) the main event is held - an authentic jousting tournament over which the castle Lord presides. Six knights on horseback compete against one another as they perform feats of real skill in several medieval games before the king and his daughter, and a wildly cheering crowd. (Yelling is encouraged!) After every game, the winning knight throws flowers out to his rooting section. As the show progresses, the knights engage in choreographed battle by pairs, with their swords actually sparking as they strike each other. The knights fight on horseback and on foot until there is just one victor. The traitor is subsequently revealed, beaten in battle, and vanquished to the dungeon.

Throughout the evening serfs and wenches serve a four-course feast, eaten without utensils, of course. The finger-licking delicious meal consists of half a roasted chicken, bread, spare ribs, potatoes, vegetable soup, a pastry, and beverage. We enjoyed the food and were riveted by the action. After the show, the gift shop selling medieval memorabilia is open. Sometimes there is dancing at the in-house Knight Club. Note: If you have a birthday or anniversary or some sort of celebration to celebrate, let your server know immediately so that person(s) can be given a shout out by the king in front of everyone.

Student Field trips/matinees are offered several times a month, year round, during the week, on selected dates from 11:30am to 1pm for kindergartners through twelfth graders. In place of some of the pageantry of the nighttime show, a medieval history lesson is presented in an engaging, storytelling style, delivered while on horseback, by a Master of Ceremonies. The topics covered include knighthood, feudalism, weaponry and combat, and even geography. Kids still see, though, the knights engaging in period games, sword fights, and all the good stuff. This educational outing includes a lunch of chicken, potato, corn cobette, garlic bread, a cookie, and soda. Teachers take note: The matinee also includes an educational resource packet which meets the California state standards. The packet emphasizes reading, writing, and social studies in a story that revolves around the famous Spanish knight, El Cid.

Hours: Knightly performances are usually Mon. - Thurs., 7pm (6pm during July and August); Fri., 6:30pm and 8:45pm; Sat., 3:30pm, 6pm and 8:15pm; Sun., 3:30pm and 6pm. Call first as the times fluctuate greatly.

Price: The price, for the dinner and show, is $59.95 for adults; $36.95 for ages 12 and under. Note that children 2 and under are free if they sit on your lap and share your food. Reservations are required. Certain discounts available through AAA, but not on Sat. Note: A person gets in free during the month of his/her birthday, with proof that it really is his/her birthday, as long as there is another adult in the party paying the full amount. Advance registration is required. Student matinees are $24.70 per person.

Ages: 3 years and up.

MERLIN'S MAGIC DINNER SHOW

(714) 744-9288 / www.merlinshow.com; www.ribtrader.com

2710 E. Chapman Avenue at the Rib Trader (restaurant), Orange

It's no illusion, Merlin's Magic Dinner Show is very entertaining. Located in a room that seats about 100 people, guests are invited to sit at long tables for two-hours of down-home magic, comedy, and food. Medieval music plays in the background. Homemade soup is served as Merlin opens with jokes and sleight of hand tricks. Then, comes more delicious food, served by wenches. The adults are given baby back ribs, barbecued chicken, honey-baked corn bread, beans, and coleslaw. Kids receive chicken strips, fries, and fresh fruit. Appetizers, beverages, and desserts are extra. Merlin periodically appears on stage for interludes of more magic and comedy.

After dinner, he performs the bulk of his show, which includes a lot of audience participation. He confounds guests with his cards, ropes, and rings tricks, as well as numerous other magical feats. There were several times after he finished a trick that no one clapped immediately, only because we were trying to figure out how he did it. (In fact, we're *still* trying to figure out how he did it!) Most of the comedy is kid appropriate. Reservations are required. Sidenote: The adjacent, small Rib Trader restaurant is jungle-themed with bamboo decor and (fake) animal heads on the walls, such as zebra, rhino, lion, and more. The food is great.

Hours: Shows are performed Thurs. - Fri., 7:30pm; Sat., 5pm and 8pm; Sun., 5pm. Seating is half-hour before the show.

Price: Admission includes the show and dinner, but not tax and tip: $29.95 for adults; $18.95 for ages 12 and under.

Ages: 4 years and up.

OBSERVATORY AT THE UNIVERSITY OF CALIFORNIA, IRVINE

(949) 824-7773 / www.physics.uci.edu $$

Campus Drive, University of California, Irvine

Are the stars out tonight? Can you tell if it's cloudy or bright? Six times a year UCI hosts two-hour-long Visitor Nights where the public is invited to attend the outside lectures, which are about thirty minutes long, and to use the university's telescopes to view the stars and planets. You can also bring your own telescope. Night sky maps are distributed to help those, like me, who are constellation-challenged. Dress warmly as you will be outside, and bring flashlights to help you walk up the short, gravel road leading to the observatory. You might also want to bring your own lawn chair as there are often up to 400 people that attend. Free shuttle buses transport visitors from the parking lot to the entrance of the observatory road. You also tour the inside of the Observatory dome to learn how the main, 24-inch, computer-controlled telescope works.

UCI's astronomy outreach program gives tours to school and scout groups by reservation. During the daytime, ninety-minute presentations are given to students who receive a guided tour of the dome, look through telescopes at solar flares and sunspots, listen to a lecture, and participate in some hands-on activities such as building a scale model solar system and using dry ice to help create a comet. The nighttime programs are similar to the Visitor Nights. The program is also portable in the sense that it can come to schools or parks as well.

Hours: Visitor Nights are usually on Sat. from either 7pm - 9pm or 8pm - 10pm (daylights savings time). Call or check the website for exact dates and times. Call to schedule a tour.

Price: Free for Visitor Nights, though donations of $5 per family are encouraged and an RSVP to say you'll be attending is requested. Parking is $2 per hour, $14 max. Group tours: Afternoon tours are $300 for up to 100 students; evening tours are $140 for 50 people.

Ages: 5 years and up.

PIRATE'S DINNER ADVENTURE

(866) 439-2469 or (714) 690-1497 / www.piratesdinneradventure.com $$$$$

7600 Beach Boulevard, Buena Park

Pillaging, plundering, rifling, and looting aside, pirate's have an un*arrrr*guable appeal. Arrive before show time to enjoy some appetizers of meatballs, cheese and crackers, and chips (buy your own drinks); purchase souvenirs at the gift shop; and witness a preshow. The slapstick preshow involves audience participation and introduces some of the main characters in the featured production.

The audience, up to 750 people, then enters the main room and, on tiered seats, surrounds a replicated 18th-century Spanish galleon with a flying skull and crossbones flag and forty-foot masts anchored in an actual indoor lagoon. Guests are separated into six different groups and assigned a color. That color represents the pirate that you cheer for throughout the ninety-minute dinner and over-the-top show and musical performance. The storyline is classic - a princess is kidnapped and her life is saved when the pirate Captain's son falls in love with her. The dasterdly Captain's crew consists of his shrewish wife and the pirates who are sometimes funny, sometimes silly, and often loud

as they taunt each other, interact with the audience, encourage the audience to drink beer and rum (and drink and drink), and engage in stunts. The pirates sing, fistfight (accompanied by cheesy sound effects), perform acrobatics, fire cannons, duel with swords, and fight a sea dragon who rises out of the water. The sea dragon has been guarding treasure. They also use audience members to aid them in competitive games. Guests throw balls to their team's pirates, help raise flags, toss around money bags, and more. A captured gypsy woman (the princess' friend) entertains the crew (and audience) by performing acts of balance and gymnastics on a pole using ropes and silks, and on a trapeze-like swing. A battle to save the princess breaks out and there is more fistfighting, swordplay, and choreographed stunts.

Food is served along with the swashbuckling action. The fare consists of soup or salad; roasted chicken or BBQ beef; rice or mashed potatoes; and vegetables. Vegetarian and Captain Kid's meals are available upon request. Brownie a la mode is your just dessert. After the dinner and show, you're invited to meet the pirates and take pictures with them and, on Friday and Saturday evenings after the last show, get your booty together and join the dancing.

Hours: Shows are Mon. - Thur., 7pm; Fri., 7:30pm; Sat., 2:30pm (sometimes), 5:30pm and 8:30pm; Sun., 3:30pm and 6:30pm, although sometimes there is just one show at 5pm. Call first. The doors open ninety minutes before showtime for appetizers and the preshow.

Price: $56.95 for adults; $36.95 for ages 3 - 11; children 2 and under are free. Tax and gratuity are not included. Discounts available online.

Ages: 3 years and up.

SADDLEBACK COLLEGE PERFORMING & VISUAL ARTS

(949) 582-4656 / www.saddleback.edu/arts
28000 Marguerite Parkway, Mission Viejo

Saddleback College attracts local and featured guest talent from all over and the shows here - music, dance, theater, concerts, art galleries, and more - represent that. Past performances, from all genres, include The New Shanghai Circus (acrobats of China), An Evening of Comedy and Magic, jazz concerts, Beatles music, Dance Collective, Big Band music, *Seussical Jr. The Musical*, orchestra music, and much more. The Broadway-style past Civic Light Opera shows have included *Footloose, The Musical*, *Damn Yankees*, *Phantom of the Opera*, and more.

Hours: Call for performance hours. Civic Light Opera performances are usually given on select evenings in July at 7:30pm and on certain weekends at 3pm.

Price: Call for performance admissions. Civic Light Opera tickets are $24 for adults; $22 for seniors; $18 for students; $12 for ages 12 and under. Parking is $2.

Ages: 7 years and up.

SEGERSTROM CENTER FOR THE ARTS / FAMILY MUSICAL MORNINGS

(714) 556-2787 - performing arts center; (714) 755-5799 - Pacific Symphony / www.scfta.org; www.pacificsymphony.org
600 Town Center Drive, Costa Mesa

This world class Center offers top-rate performances that include Broadway plays and musicals, cabaret, jazz, ballet, concerts, opera, symphony performances, dance, and much much more. Past productions have included National Acrobats of China, *Oklahoma*, *Lord of the Dance*, Cirque Du Solei, *Blues Clues! Live*, *Forever Plaid*, a sing-a-long of *Sound of Music*, headlining entertainers, etc. The complex is comprised of Segerstrom Center Hall, 3,000 seats; Segerstrom Concert Hall, 1,700 seats; and Samueli Theater, 500 seats. Note: One hour prior to most performances in the Dance, Jazz, and Chamber Music Series, a noted expert gives a free, informative talk, open to all ticket holders, to share insights about the performance. Call to verify there will be a lecture if you are interested in this. See SEGERSTROM CENTER FOR THE ARTS (tour), on page 325, for information on taking a tour of this center.

Several Saturdays a year Family Musical Mornings are offered. Designed especially for kids ages 5 to 11, they are more than just concerts. Fun for kids, as well as interactive, the forty-five-minute performances vary in content, but aim to be pieces and stories that children are familiar with, such as music from *Nutcracker Suite* or *Peter and the Wolf*, from cartoons, or a famous fairytale.

Hours: Call for a show schedule. Family Musical Mornings are on select Sat. at 10am and 11:30am.

Price: Performance prices vary according to show, date, and time. Family Musical Mornings, depending on your seat, range from $19 - $41. Parking is $10 - cash only.

Ages: 4 years and up, depending on the show.

SOUTH COAST REPERTORY

(714) 708-5555 or (714) 708-5577 / www.scr.org

655 Town Center Drive, Costa Mesa

Come to this acclaimed theater for year-round professional productions. Note that most plays are geared for older children and adults. There is a series of three family productions a year, titled Theatre for Young Audiences . . . and Their Families, that run for about three weeks. Productions have included *The Emperor's New Clothes*, *James and the Giant Peach*, *The Stinky Cheese Man*, and *Wind in the Willows*. These shows range from $20 to $33. Kids, ages 4 to 18, can also sign up to be in a production that, after months of rehearsals, culminate in performances given for the public, such as *Jack and the Giant Bean Stalk*. These productions are usually $12 per person.

Or, invite the theater to come to your child's school as the repertory has fantastic educational outreach programs. Musicals and dramatic presentations correlate with school curriculum on a variety of subjects, including multi-cultural themes, dealing with relationships, and even Shakespeare. Call for a schedule and pricing information.

Hours: Call for show dates and times.

Price: Varies, depending on the show. Parking is $10.

Ages: 10 years and up, depending on the show.

TESSMANN PLANETARIUM AT SANTA ANA COLLEGE

(714) 564-6356 or (714) 564-6600 / www.sac.edu $$$

1530 W. 17th Street, Santa Ana

Twinkle, twinkle little star, how I wonder what you are? Your kids can begin to find the answers to this question, and many more, at shows in the ninety-seat planetarium. Several hour-long programs, such as *How Rare is Earth?*, *Where are You?*, *How Far is Up?*, *What is a Black Hole?*, or *America in Space*, are wonderful trips around the galaxy, as you see and learn about planets, constellations, our solar system, comets, and more. There is also a shorter show, written by a former preschool teacher, geared for kindergartners and first graders called, *Can You See in the Dark?* This show is only $3. All the shows have live narrations given by an astronomer. Various programs appeal to guests 5 to 95 years old. There is time after the presentation for questions and answers. If you have a group of thirty-five or more, ask about reserving the auditorium for your group. Dates depend on availability and reservations are required. See the Calendar entry for more information on the wonderful Christmas show, *The Star of Bethlehem* (pg. 760).

Hours: Shows are presented on selected dates year round, Mon. - Fri. at 9:30am and 11am; Sat. at 11am. Reservations are needed. School, or other groups, are welcome to make reservations, too, and large groups, of 35 or more, can book the planetarium at other times.

Price: $6 per person weekdays; $7 on Sat. Parking is $2.

Ages: Must be at least 5 years old, except for the shorter show mentioned above.

TRINITY CHRISTIAN CITY INTERNATIONAL

(714) 708-5405 - recorded info; (714) 708-5410 - gift shop/theater info; (714) 708-5476 - taping of shows /   !
www.tbn.org

3150 Bear Street, Costa Mesa

A lavish fountain outside, surrounded by beautiful landscaping and white archways, enhances the serene garden setting. The lobby of T.C.C.I.'s international headquarters is opulently decorated in whites and golds, along with beveled mirrors on the walls and around the columns. (I kept wishing for my own bottle of Windex™, so my children's visit here wouldn't be *so* obvious, although they were never looked at disparagingly. I've rarely encountered friendlier staff.) A powerful-looking angel at the top of the ornate central staircase immediately draws your attention. He is made out of white marble, brandishes a real sword, and is stepping upon a representation of Satan. The ceiling of the rotunda, just over his head, depicts heavenly scenes painted in a Victorian style.

Take the stairs, or a glass-enclosed elevator, to the second floor where you'll see a nontraditional church setting and a broadcasting room. Check out all the lighting and camera equipment! You are invited to attend free broadcasts and tapings of the Trinity Broadcast Network programs that air from either room. Call for dates and times.

After my boys and I stopped gaping, we went back downstairs into a small theater room. Tip: Just before you enter, note the "mirror room" where you look through several sets of beveled mirrors, seemingly into infinity. A fifteen-minute preview, hosted by Paul Crouch, founder of T.B.N., presents the history and Christian heritage of Orange County and T.B.N. Afterward, as the screen and curtain rise, you are invited to walk along an excellent recreation of Via Dolorosa, the cobblestone street in the city of old Jerusalem where Jesus carried his cross to Calvary. The street ends at the entrance of another theater.

Five, one-hour-long movies (and *Megiddo*, which is almost two hours) are shown in this forty-nine-seat Virtual Reality Theater. (Virtual Reality, or "surround" sound, means that you literally feel the rumblings of earthquakes and thunder, and that the loud noises and music are amplified.) Three of the movies are outstanding reenactments that

vividly bring Biblical events to life. Note that the films, mostly shot on location in Israel, powerfully and realistically portray their subject, so certain scenes are necessarily graphic and thereby intense for younger children. *The Revolutionary* shows the life of Christ, from His birth to His resurrection. Graphic scenes include a demon being cast out and Christ being nailed on the cross. It shows Mon. through Sat. at 11am, and Fri. and Sat. at 6pm. *The Revolutionary II* is about the miracles of Jesus' ministry. Graphic scenes include a demon being cast out and Christ being nailed to the cross. (I know that last part sounded familiar.) It shows daily at 1pm. *The Emissary* depicts the Apostle Paul's life, his conversion, his subsequent new life of faith, and his struggles. Graphic scenes include the stoning of Stephen, beatings, and a shipwreck. It shows Mon. through Sat. at 5pm, and Sun. at 3pm. *One Night With the King* is the story of Esther. It shows daily at 2pm. *The Omega Code* is more modern. It deals with Bible prophecy and end times. It's definitely geared for older kids as the storyline is somewhat complex and there is on-screen violence. It shows Mon. through Sat. at noon, and Sun. at 4pm. *The Megiddo* is part two of the *Omega Code* and shows the destruction of the devil. It shows Mon. through Sat. at 3pm. Note: You can usually request a certain movie to be shown at any time, especially if no one else is here. Call for groups of twenty or more as the theater only has forty-nine seats.

A beautiful, fully stocked gift shop is also on the premises. Tip: Pack a sack lunch because Shiffer Park is just across the street. The park has a few playgrounds, large grassy areas, shade trees, and picnic tables.

Hours: The building is open Mon. - Thurs., 11am - 6pm; Fri. - Sat., 11am - 7pm; Sun., 1pm - 6pm.
Price: Free
Ages: 6 years and up.

ULTRASTAR GARDEN WALK 14 (Orange County)

(714) 399-0300/0305 / www.ultrastarmovies.com; www.anaheimgardenwalk.com
321 W. Katella Avenue, Anaheim

Fourteen screens show films inside this beautiful theater, including an IMAX, Star Class, DBox, and 3-D screens. See movies on the big, big, BIG IMAX screen for an incredible movie experience. (Most living rooms still aren't big enough to hold this size screen!) Check the website for show times. The cafe inside the theater has a coffee bar and serves panini sandwiches, specialty popcorn and some other slightly upscale options.

This theater also caters to parents when it's not a crying shame to bring a baby to the movies at either Parent Movie Morning, with changing facilities in the auditorium and movies that adults want to see - Wednesday at 10am, or at Baby's Night Out, on select nights at 7pm. The surrounding GardenWalk is a lively outdoor mall with numerous restaurants to choose from.

Hours: Call for show times.
Price: Prices range from $6 for early bird matinees and discount days to $15 for adults for 3-D films at night. Check the online deals for buying tickets online and other specials.
Ages: Infants and up, depending on the movie! Free parking for 4 hours with validation.

—TOURS—

ANGEL STADIUM

(714) 940-2070; (714) 940-2045 / losangeles.angels.mlb.com
2000 Gene Autry Way, Anaheim

"Let me root, root, root for the home team . . ." . Take this behind-the-scenes, seventy-five-minute tour to see areas that you don't normally see during a ball game. You'll visit the press box, press conference room, stadium clubhouse, dugout (not onto the playing field) and more. The walking tours, which can have parts that are wheelchair accessible, are a must-do for fans! Tours are not offered on dates when the Angels have a home game. Reservations are highly suggested. Note that the team store is open for groups after the tour.

Hours: Tours are offered April - September, Tues., Wed., and Fri. at 10:30am, 12:30am, and 2:30pm, when the team is out of town. Tours are not offered when the Angels have a home game. Tours are offered October through March on Tues. at 9:30am, 11:30am and 1:30pm. No tours are given on major holidays, or when there is a special event at the stadium.
Price: $7 for adults; $5 for seniors, active military, and ages 3 - 17. Parking is free.
Ages: 5 years and up.

CALIFORNIA PIZZA KITCHEN (Orange County)

See the entry for CALIFORNIA PIZZA KITCHEN (Los Angeles County) (pg. 197) for more information.

FULLERTON MUNICIPAL AIRPORT

(714) 738-6323 / www.cityoffullerton.com
4011 W. Commonwealth, Fullerton

Educators - Does your kindergartner or older child have lofty ambitions? If so, then they'll enjoy this one-hour, walking tour on the airfield led by a docent who is a member of the Fullerton's Pilot Association. Tours are modified to fit your particular school group's interests, and covers topics such as airport operations, types of airplanes, how airplanes fly, airport businesses, and more. The tour ends on a high note as souvenirs, like plastic wings for future pilots, are given out. Tours are offered for a minimum of five people and will be broken into groups of ten to fifteen. Wings Cafe is located just inside the airport terminal and is open daily, to the public, from 7am - 2pm.

Fullerton hosts the Antique Aircraft Display Days every second Sunday of the month from 9am to 2pm. Join the owners and admirers to look at warbirds and homebuilts, and perhaps a few antique cars, and more. Free admission.

   Hours: Tours are given for school groups only, Mon. and Tues., between 10am - 2pm, and by reservation
                 only. Two weeks advance notice is needed for small groups and one month for a larger group.
   Price: Free
   Ages: 5 years and up.

GOODWILL INDUSTRIES (Orange County)

(714) 480-3355; (714) 547-6308 - ask for public relations / www.ocgoodwill.org
410 N. Fairview Street, Santa Ana

See the entry for GOODWILL INDUSTRIES (San Bernardino County) on page 437 for details.

   Hours: Tours are usually given twice a month - call for specific information.
   Price: Free
   Ages: At least 8 years old

JOHN WAYNE AIRPORT THOMAS F. RILEY TERMINAL TOUR

(949) 252-5168 / www.ocair.com
3151 Airway Avenue, Costa Mesa

This terrific, ninety-minute tour is tailored toward the participants' ages and interests, showing all aspects of the airport. Guests see the public access places while learning about the history of the airport and some basic information on aviation, such as the answer to what makes a plane fly. The tour starts at the statue of John Wayne and goes all around the terminal, on both arrival and departure levels, to see the various activities. There are huge windows all along the field, and a V-shape one jutting into it that offers a wonderful view of the planes taxiing, landing and taking off, being serviced, and baggage being loaded and unloaded. A fun remembrance, such as an airplane activity guide, is given out at the end of the tour. Happy landings! The docents are knowledgeable and some are even retired pilots. A minimum of two people and maximum of twenty-five are needed for a tour. Note that high school and college tours may be arranged with aviation career speakers provided.

   Hours: Tours are available Mon. - Fri. at 10:30am and 2:30; call for other times. Sat. tours can be
                 accommodated. Reservations are required at least 2 weeks in advance.
   Price: Free; parking is $2 per hour.
   Ages: Must be at least 5 years old.

KNOTT'S ADVENTURES IN EDUCATION

(714) 220-5244 or (714) 220-5166 / www.knotts.com
8039 Beach Boulevard, Buena Park

The education department with Knott's Berry Farm provides over twenty, outstanding, guided tours for all grade levels and for scouts, as well. The tours incorporate aspects of the amusement park, and sometimes a few rides, such as Ghost Town - a very real Western part of Knott's Berry Farm; a visit with a re-enactor, like Benjamin Franklin; and/or a visit to Independence Hall (see pg. 316). The programs are offered year round and range from ninety-minutes to five hours. Some of the programs are: Geologist - Panning for Gold (gold panning can actually be added to any tour for an additional $8 per person); Indian Trails; Transportation - Past and Present (which includes a ride on the Knott's stagecoach); Early American Heritage; Early California (this incorporates a 1830's trapper re-enactor, blacksmith demonstration, and candlemaking demonstration); Energy in Motion - Physics (one physics program taught by a physics teacher is for jr. and sr. highers, and another is geared for younger kids); Classic Christmas; and Natural Science.

Adults (40 years and older) and with a minimum group of fifteen - you are not left out! For $20 per person, choose either two-hour tour: 1) Early American Heritage tour, which highlights significant moments in Early American history including a tour of Independence Hall, meeting Benjamin Franklin, Abigail Adams, or Patrick Henry and more, or 2) Pathways to the Past, which focuses on the Old West throughout Ghost Town, including the blacksmith shop, the school house, a ride on restored train cars from the 1880's, and more. Each tour also includes a complete, set menu for lunch at the Chicken Dinner Restaurant. Admission to the park for the day is extra.

Hours: All tours are offered by reservation only.
Price: The first 3 hours of parking are free. Or, $15 for parking for the day.
Ages: K - 12th grade; or adults.

ORANGE COUNTY SANITATION DISTRICT

(714) 962-2411 / www.ocsd.com
10844 Ellis Avenue, Fountain Valley

The seventy-five-minute education program is geared for high schoolers and up. A fifteen-minute video explains how water is treated. The rest of the program is spent hearing about and seeing the different levels of water treatment. Students learning about microbiology, for example, will look at various water particles under a microscope and identify what they see. Visitors also learn why it's important to conserve. The minimum number for a tour is ten, the maximum, twenty-five, although there are tours for groups under ten people at select times - check the website.

Hours: Tours can be scheduled Mon. - Fri. from 9am - 3pm.
Price: Free
Ages: Geared for 10 years and up.

O'S AMERICAN KITCHEN (Orange County)

(714) 836-5500 / www.osamericankitchen.com
763 S. Main St., Orange

See O'S AMERICAN KITCHEN (San Diego County) on page 576 for details about this pizza-making tour for kids.

SEGERSTROM CENTER FOR THE ARTS (tour)

(714) 556-2122 / www.scfta.org
600 Town Center Drive, Costa Mesa

All the world's a stage! Get a behind-the-scenes look at the hall that comprises the Center, especially the 3,000-seat Segerstrom Hall. This grand facility is where major symphony concerts, operas, ballets, and Broadway musicals are presented. Take an hour-and-fifteen-minute tour, beginning at the ticket box office, then through the theater, to the star's dressing rooms and wardrobe area, and finishing up backstage. Tour routes may vary due to rehearsal and performance schedules, and backstage set construction. Visitors will also see and learn about the architecture, sculptures, and other art objects that grace the interior and exterior of the Center. For show information, please see SEGERSTROM CENTER FOR THE ARTS (pg. 321, 782).

Hours: Guided tours are offered Wed. and Sat. at 10:30am. Tours of the Renée and Henry Segerstrom Concert Hall and Samueli Theater are offered on Sat., also at 10:30 a.m. Reservations are required for a group of 10 or more people. Closed on some holidays.
Price: Free. Parking in the lot is $1.50 for each 20 minutes.
Ages: 10 years and up.

—TRANSPORTATION—

AIR COMBAT USA, INC.

$$$$$

(800) 522-7590 / www.aircombat.com
3815 W. Commonwealth Avenue, Fullerton

If being a Top Gun is your top dream, here's the opportunity to make it a reality. You, perhaps being an unlicensed pilot and leading an otherwise normal life, will actually fly and fight air-to-air combat. "The SIAI Marchetti SF260 is a current production, Italian-built, fighter aircraft. It has 260 horsepower, can fly at 270 MPH, FAA certified to +6 to -3 G's and can perform unlimited aerobatics. It was originally designed to transition student pilots to jet fighters. It is maneuvered by the stick grip complete with gun trigger, identical to the F4 Phantom. The pilot and guest

pilot sit side-by-side with dual controls." (Excerpted from Air Combat's brochure.) If all this has your adrenaline pumping, go for it!

You'll be prepped for your flight in a one-hour ground school which covers the basics, with emphasis on tactical maneuvers. After being fitted with a flight suit, helmet, and parachute, you'll soar for one hour with the birds over Catalina waters, which in itself is exciting. You're actually in control of the aircraft 90% of the time, while receiving constant instruction on how to get the "enemy." More excitement! After practicing maneuvers, you'll engage in six "g-pulling" (i.e., gut wrenching) dogfights against a real opponent (e.g., friend, spouse, etc). A direct hit registers through an electronic tracking system, complete with sound effects and smoke trailing from the other aircraft. What a sensational experience! It's as close to the real thing as you can possibly get without being in the military. I will confess that after a few high/low yo-yos and roll overs, I used that special white bag and became part of the 10% that share in this ritual. Too much excitement for me.

After you've landed, and come down from your high, you can view the videos that were simultaneously recorded from each aircraft. Relive your flight and your "hits" again and again on the copy you receive to take home. This is an unforgettable experience! Note that SKYTHRILLS (pg. 331), offering thrilling aerobatic airplane rides, shares the same location.

Hours: Several classes/flights that accommodate two people each are offered almost every day. Check the website for flight schedules.

Price: $1395 a flight. Ask about specials, such as discounts for two people at $1295 per.

Ages: 8 years old and up - large enough to wear a parachute and in good health.

AMTRAK (Orange County)

(800) USA RAIL (872-7245) / www.amtrakcalifornia.com

Ride the rails! See AMTRAK (Los Angeles County) on page 208 for more information.

BALBOA BOAT RENTALS AND PARASAILING   ☀

(949) 673-7200 / www.boats4rent.com $$$$

510 E. Edgewater, Balboa

Rentals include kayaks - $15 per hour for a single, $25 an hour for a double; pedal boats - $25 an hour; stand up paddleboards - $25 an hour; sailboats - $45 an hour for a fourteen footer; motorboats - $70 an hour for a six-passenger boat that doesn't leave the harbor, and $90 an hour for a six-passenger boat that does; pontoon boats (in harbor) that seat up to ten - $95 an hour; and electric boats (which are much quieter than motor boats, hold eight to twelve people, and some are enclosed) start at $75 an hour. See BALBOA FUN ZONE on page 255 for more things to do in this immediate area.

Parasail and fly with the birds, kind of. You take a short boat ride out into the water and, attached to a harness, you'll soar 800 feet, or higher, above Newport Beach - what a view! This exhilarating experience lasts about ten minutes, but the thrill of it last much longer. The whole trip takes about ninety minutes, as each rider (maximum six) take turns flying. You may go single or tandem. Parasailing starts at $70 per person per hour; there are different rates for different heights. It is $20 for observers to just ride along in the boat, if there is space available.

Something to keep in mind when Christmas lights are turned on: Tour the harbor to see all the houses and boats that are decorated magnificently - before, during or after the wonderful parade of lights - by either renting a Duffy electric boat or a pontoon, or take a narrated tour of the waterfront homes in a "private" boat that seats twelve. Each of the above is about $30 per person. Make your reservation early.

Hours: Open daily in the summer, 10am - 8pm. Open the rest of the year daily, 10am - 5pm. Call first. Parasailing is open daily March through November. Reservations are highly recommended for all rentals.

Price: Prices listed above. Parking validation is $5 for the first two hours; $12 for the day. There is some metered street parking available.

Ages: 6 years and up.

BIKE MAPS (Orange County)

These websites - www.bicyclela.org and www.labikepaths.com - are fantastic resources. They actually cover all of Southern California, not just L.A., with links to specific counties for maps, bikeways, and other cycling information. They can be your two-stop shopping sites for maps and info. Other great websites are www.traillink.com and www.trails.com for mountain bike trails. Caltrans Office of Bicycle Facilities: (916) 653-0036 / www.dot.ca.gov/hq/tpp/offices/bike gives you tons of options all over.

Also contact the Orange County Transportation Authority at (800) 636-RIDE (7433) or (714) 560-OCTA (6282) / www.octa.net for (paved and unpaved) maps and more information. For the city of Irvine, check out www.cityofirvine.org/bikeways. Many Orange County buses are equipped with bike racks. To inquire about trail closures and detours on county-operated off-road trails (i.e., mountain biking), call the EMA - Harbors, Beaches, and Parks Operation at (714) 834-2400 or County of Orange RDMD/Harbors Beaches & Parks at (866) -OCPARKS (627-2757) or (714) 973-6865 / www.ocparks.com.

BIKE TRAIL: HUNTINGTON BEACH ☼

www.ci.huntington-beach.ca.us; www.bicydela.org; www.labikepaths.com
Pacific Coast Hwy between Warner Ave. and Brookhurst St.

Huntington Beach is known not only for its great roads but also for the well-maintained, 8.5 mile cement bike path that runs parallel to Pacific Coast Highway. Located on the ocean side of the highway, this path sees thousands of bicydists, joggers and walkers on a daily basis. The scenic paved path (which some prefer to call a promenade, boardwalk or road) stretches from Sunset Beach (1 mile in length), through Huntington Beach (8.5 miles) and through Newport Peninsula (nearly 3 miles). It is possible to get a twelve-mile workout one direction or twenty-four miles total. For the distance workouts, you can take the underpass that connects to the Santa Ana River Trail near the bridge beyond Brookhurst Street. That trail goes all the way through Orange County, via Yorba Linda and Featherly Park, for an estimated additional thirty-two miles one direction.

Bicydists and roller bladers share the paved Huntington Beach path with pedestrian traffic. Be aware and ride defensively as you will find people and pets crossing the path. State law requires children riding bicycles in public to wear helmets for protection. Bicycle lanes are often provided on city streets; cydists must travel the same direction as traffic, obeying vehicle rules and regulations. Speed limits along beachfront paths in Huntington Beach are enforced. Orange County Transportation Authority (OCTA) buses are public buses connecting this section of Huntington Beach with all of Orange County, and even Long Beach to the north and San Diego to the south. There are several bus stops along the paved path route in Huntington Beach with buses that have bicycle racks. For OCTA routes and times, there are posted signs at bus locations that include the Warner Avenue and Pacific Coast Highway turn around area near Jack in the Box restaurant. You can also call OCTA at 714.636.RIDE (7433).

BIKE TRAIL: SANTA ANA RIVER (Orange County) ☼ $

(714) 973-6615 / www.ocparks.com; www.bicydela.org; www.labikepaths.com
7600 E. La Palma Avenue in Yorba Regional Park, Anaheim

See BIKE TRAIL: SANTA ANA RIVER (Riverside County) on page 370 for information.

Hours: The trail is open daily. The park is open April through October daily, 7am - 9pm; November through March daily, 7am - 6pm.
Price: $3 per vehicle during the week; $5 on weekends; $7 - $10 on holidays.
Ages: 5 years and up.

CAPTAIN DAVE'S DOLPHIN SAFARI ☼ $$$$$

(949) 488-2828 / www.dolphinsafari.com
24440 Dana Point Harbor Drive, Dana Point

Captain Dave is a marine naturalist who is passionate about dolphins and whales. On board his fifty-foot catamaran is an underwater viewing compartment and camera, speakers, and a hydrophone for listening to the mammals and playing music to them. The two-and-a-half hour safaris are a time of learning about and observing the dolphins, whales (in season), sea lions, and other sea life in the wild aquarium (i.e., the ocean). Models of dolphins and whales, plus whale vertebrae and baleen are also on the vessel for teaching aids. Bring some munchies and a jacket or windbreaker, and set sail.

Hours: Open year round - cruises usually depart at 9am and noon, but also at other times. Call first.
Price: $59 for adults; $39 for ages 2 - 12; children 1 and under are free, but still need a ticket.
Ages: 6 years and up.

DANA WHARF SPORTFISHING, CHARTERS, AND WHALE WATCHING ☼ $$$$$

(949) 496-5794 / www.danawharf.com
34675 Golden Lantern, Dana Point

Cruise the coastal waters in the lovely ninety-five-foot vessel, *Dana Pride*. Two-hour whale-watching cruises are offered November through April for the gray whale and May through October for the blue whale. Sunset cruises and

sportfishing are available as well.

Hours: Whale watching cruises depart daily in season at 10am, noon, and 2:30pm. Check the website for other cruise hours and options.

Price: Whale watching cruises are $45 for adults; $35 for seniors; $25 for ages 3 - 12; children 2 years and under are free. See the website for info about parking.

Ages: 6 years and up.

DAVEY'S LOCKER

(949) 673-1435 - whale watching; (949) 673-1434 - fishing / www.daveyslocker.com $$$$$
400 Main Street, Newport Beach

Skiff rentals, fishing, and two-and-a-half-hour whale-watching cruises are offered here. See BALBOA FUN ZONE on page 255 for more things to do in this immediate area.

Hours: Cruises are offered November - April, Mon. - Fri. at 10am and 2pm; Sat. - Sun. at 10am, 1pm and 3:30pm. May - October, daily at 10am, 1pm, 3:30pm and 6pm.

Price: $32 for adults for whale-watching on weekdays, $36 on weekends; $26 for seniors and ages 3 - 12 on weekdays, $30 on weekends; ages 2 and under are free. $105 for a half day for skiffs.

Ages: 7 years and up.

DUFFY ELECTRIC BOAT COMPANY

(949) 645-6812 / www.duffyofnewportbeach.com $$$$$
2001 W. Coast Highway, Newport Beach

Be your own captain as you pilot the canopy-topped electric boat around the harbor and through the channels of Newport Beach. The boat, which seats up to twelve people (ten comfortably), is an ideal way to see the multimillion-dollar homes on the waterfront and enjoy a relaxed time on the water with family and friends. Note that several restaurants offer dock side service, or bring your own food on board. See page 255 for information on the nearby BALBOA FUN ZONE.

Hours: Open daily, 10am - 8pm. Reservations are highly recommended, especially during weekends and holidays.

Price: Rentals Mon. - Thurs. are $85 an hour, Fri. - Sun., $99. Note that there is a two-hour minimum rental on weekends and holidays, and after 4pm on weekdays. Closed major holidays and in inclement weather.

Ages: 3 years and up.

FUN ZONE BOAT COMPANY

(949) 673-0240 / www.funzoneboats.com $$$$
600 E. Edgewater Place, Balboa

Board the *Pavilion Queen* for a forty-five-minute narrated cruise that is perfect for kids as they'll go around Balboa Island and, hopefully, see some sea lions. On the other forty-five-minute cruise see several stars' homes and hear the history of Balboa Island Peninsula. The ninety-minute cruise is a combination of both cruises - the best of both worlds. One-hour sunset cruises are also available mid-May through September. You are welcome to bring your own food on board. Special sightseeing tours are available in December during the Parade of Lights - what a view! See BALBOA FUN ZONE on page 255 for more things to do in this immediate area.

Hours: Summer tours depart daily every half hour from 11am - 6pm. Sunset cruises leave at 6pm or 7pm, depending on the time of sunset. The rest of the year, tours depart every hour from 11am - 4pm.

Price: $14 for adults for a forty-five-minute cruise; $11 for seniors; $7 for ages 5 - 11; children 4 and under are free. $19 for adults for the ninety-minute cruise; $17 for seniors; $7 for ages 5 - 11; children 4 and under are free. Closed Thanksgiving and December 24 - 25.

Ages: 4 years and up.

GONDOLA ADVENTURES, INC.

(855) 436-3652 or (949) 200-8037; (888) 480-9472 - educational tours / www.gondola.com $$$$$
3101 W. Coast Highway, suite 110, Newport Beach

O sole mio! These authentic Italian gondolas are made out of mahogany, have leather seats and a canopy, and are operated by gondoliers either dressed in the traditional Venetian outfit, or a tuxedo, depending on the occasion. Yes, of course it's romantic to take this peaceful cruise along the waterways of Newport Beach Harbor and Newport isle,

viewing the boats and waterfront homes, and kissing under bridges (mandatory). But a gondola ride can also be a family-friendly excursion. It's a time to relax and enjoy down time together, soaking in the sights and ambiance. We enjoyed learning a little about the area, seeing the variety of birds, a gentle breeze over the harbor, and gliding through the waterways.

The gondoliers begin your cruise from the harbor office, or pick you up at one of several harbor-side restaurants. Gondola Adventures provides a chilled bottle of Martinellis and Godiva chocolates, or it can provide a completely catered dinner served on china - definitely an upscale adventure! If interested, ask about taking an educational tour.

Hours: Open daily, call for reservations.
Price: Prices begin at $135 for two people, $25 each additional person, for a one-hour classic cruise.
Ages: 4 years and up.

LAGUNA BEACH TRANSIT AND FREE TROLLEY

(949) 715-4405; (949) 497-9229; (949) 497-0766 / www.lagunabeachinfo.com

!/$

The transfer point between the North, South and Canyon routes is at the Transit Center/Bus Depot on Broadway (where Laguna Canyon/the 133 ends), Laguna Beach

Consider taking a bus around Laguna Beach, where parking is usually at a premium, especially in the summer months. During the summer, take a trolley ride for free. The route includes twenty-one stops along Pacific Coast Highway, south of Broadway/133, plus nine stops north of Broadway/133 - so all of the major beaches are covered. It also includes a few stops actually on Broadway/133. It runs every twenty minutes. Check the website's map to see where you can park your car for the day. The regular transit shuttle runs the rest of the year.

Hours: The trolley runs mid-June - August, daily 9:30am - 11:30pm (July 4th - 9:30am - 7pm). The shuttle runs the rest of the year, Mon. - Fri., 6:30am - 6:30pm; Sat., 9:20am - 6:30pm. Closed daily from 12:30pm - 1:30pm and on Sun.
Price: Free trolley, mid-June - August. The rest of the year shuttle rides are 75¢ for adult riders, 30¢ for seniors, and free for ages 6 and under with a paying adult.
Ages: All

MARINA BOAT RENTALS

(949) 673-3372 / www.newportbeachboatrentals.com

$$$$$

600 E. Edgewater Place, Balboa

What kind of boat would you like to captain in Newport Bay? Marina Boat Rentals can make much of that happen with their fleet of rental boats. For instance, 16 foot runabouts (seats four) are $69 an hour; 16 foot deckboats are $79 an hour; eight passenger electric bay cruisers are $89 an hour; single kayaks are $18 an hour; and tandem kayaks are $25 an hour. Stand Up Paddle boards are $25 an hour.

What can you do while on the water? Take a self-guided tour past the homes along the waterfront; zip amongst the seven islands; get a good workout on the kayak; bring your own lunch or dinner to enjoy on a pontoon; or stop off at one of the several restaurants on the way. See BALBOA FUN ZONE on page 255 for more things to do in this immediate area.

Hours: Open Sun. - Thurs., 10am - 6pm, Fri. - Sat., 10am - 7pm.
Price: Prices are listed above.
Ages: 5 years and up.

METROLINK (Orange County)

(800) 371-LINK (5465) / www.metrolinktrains.com

$$$

Metrolink offers a fairly hassle-free mode of transportation that links the counties of Ventura, Los Angeles (mostly in the Antelope Valley), San Bernardino, Riverside, and Orange. Teachers, ask about traveling with students at great discount rates, such as $3 per student, round-trip, for groups of fifteen or more students, ages 5 - 18 years. Reservations are mandatory six weeks prior to travel date. Ask about taking a rail safety program for school, organization, or community groups.

Forget the hassle of driving in traffic and parking fees on weekends, and take the MetroLink Weekends, where unlimited rides to the beach, amusement parks and beyond are only $10 per person! Other prices include weekday ride prices for a round trip from Rialto to Oceanside, for instance, at $33 for adults; $16.50 for seniors; $25 for ages 6 - 18; up to three children 5 and under ride free with a paid adult.

Hours: Trains run daily and offer limited service on most major holidays.

Price: One-way tickets start at about $5.75; round trip, $11.50 - depending on the origin and destination. Senior rate is 50% discounted off regular rate. Kids 5 and under ride for free with a paying adult. Weekend prices for unlimited riding are $10.

Ages: All.

MOE B'S WATERSPORTS

(800)765-7661; (949) 729-3863; (949) 729-1150 - marina during summer months; (949) 999-3180 - marina/market during the rest of the year / www.newportdunes.com

1131 Backbay Drive, Newport Dunes Resort, Newport Beach

Located in NEWPORT DUNES WATERFRONT RESORT MARINA (see pg. 241 for all that this resort has to offer to day visitors and campers), this rental facility has everything you need to make your day at the beach even more exciting. Going rates are: $24 an hour for a two-person pedal boat; $90 for electric-powered boats; $25 an hour for stand up paddleboards; $20 an hour for surreys; $35 an hour for 14' catamarans; $25 an hour for single kayaks; and $29 an hour for double kayaks. Bike rentals are also available.

The Water Playground, available only during the summer, June to Labor Day, 11am to 5pm, has huge inflatable objects to climb up and on, such as "rock" climbing walls (that resemble icebergs) with hand and foot holds and a slide on one side; a water version of a teeter-totter that can help launch participants into the water; a climbing dome; a water trampoline; a twelve-foot slide; and colorful oversized floating "lily pads". The Water Playground is $10 an hour, $20 for half day, or $35 for all day usage for RV guests; $15 an hour, $30 for half day, or $45 for all day usage for day visitors.

Hours: Open mid-September - May, Fri. - Sun., 11am - 5pm (Go to the marketplace, not the marina in the "winter"). Open June - mid-September daily, 11am - 5pm. (Go to the marina).

Price: Prices are stated above, plus a day- use vehicle entrance fee of $16.

Ages: 5 years and up.

NEWPORT AQUATIC CENTER

(949) 646-7725; (949) 923-2269 / www.newportaquaticcenter.com

1 Whitecliffs Drive, Newport Beach

Enjoy a serene kayak ride in the calm harbor waters. Single kayak rentals are $15 an hour; doubles and stand up paddle boards are $20. Two-hour naturalist tours of the Upper Newport Bay Ecological Reserve are given so as you paddle, you'll learn about the many birds you encounter and the history of the bay and native plants you see along the way. These tours are offered every weekend at 10am for $25 per person. The minimum age is 8.

Hours: Rental hours are Mon. - Fri., 7am - 3:45pm; Sat. - Sun., 7am - 3:15pm. The center closes early on holidays.

Price: Prices are listed above.

Ages: 8 years and up.

NEWPORT LANDING SPORTFISHING

(949) 675-0550 or (949) 647-0551 / www.newportwhales.com

309 Palm, suite A, Newport Beach

Two-and-a-half hour whale-watching cruises are available here November through April for the California gray whale, and May through October for giant blue whales and finback whales. Full-service snack bars are on all vessels. See BALBOA FUN ZONE on page 255 for more things to do in this immediate area.

Hours: The boats depart November - April, Mon. - Fri. at 10am and 1pm; Sat. - Sun. at 9:30am, noon, and 2;30pm. They depart May - October, daily at 10am, 1pm, and 3:30pm.

Price: Weekday prices are $32 for adults; $26.50 for seniors and children 12 and under. Weekend prices are $36 for adults; $30 for seniors and kids.

Ages: 7 years and up.

OCEAN INSTITUTE

24200 Dana Point Harbor Drive, Dana Point

See the entry for OCEAN INSTITUTE, on page 309, for details about boat outings.

PADDLE POWER

(949) 675-1215 / www.paddlepowerh2o.com

1500 W. Balboa Boulevard, Newport Beach

Kayak rentals are available here, at a store dedicated to ocean sports, particularly kayaking. Single kayaks are $14 an hour; $20 for a double. Stand up paddle boards are also available for $20 an hour. See BALBOA FUN ZONE on page 255 for more things to do in this immediate area.

Hours: Open Thurs. - Tues. and Sun., 10am - 4pm, with the last rental at 2:30pm. Closed Wed. Usually open an hour later in the summer.

Price: Prices are listed above.

Ages: 5 years and up.

SKYTHRILLS

(866) 4-THRILL (484-7455) or (714) 402-4888 / www.skythrills.com $$$$$

3815 W. Commonwealth Avenue, Fullerton

Be a stunt pilot for a day, or for at least five minutes or more! The son of the owner of AIR COMBAT (pg. 325) and who shares the same building space, also shares a passion for something equally thrilling at SkyThrills - encouraging people to experience the joy of high-performance flying.

There are different styles of rides to choose from. One is a more mild ride called an Adventure Thrill Ride - thrilling in what you'll see and because of flying in the Citabria Adventure plane, yet it's more like sightseeing. It includes aerial tours of Catalina Island and the stunning California coastlines, and even over some landmarks like Knott's Berry Farm. Then, there is the more extreme wild ride of performing aerobatics in a Pitts S-2C, Extra 300L, Marchetti SF-260, or a Waco YMF-5, which is a modern version of the 1930's open cockpit biplane. And G-forces? Oh yes. Up to 250 mph and 6 Gs. Pure power. What a rush! (Think of a dog in a car on the freeway, with the window rolled down, only much more so. This visual is for the feel of the force as well as the dog's/your look of pure enjoyment.) You can also choose an in-between option because your ride is customized as to how you, the passenger and co-pilot, want to fly. And you are a co-pilot because you can fly as much as 90% of the time - a real hands-on (please be hands-on!) experience with no prior flying experience necessary.

The first part of your time is spent in a fairly comprehensive ground school briefing that covers what you need to know about flying and performing aerobatics in an aircraft - the loop, the roll, the hammerhead, the spin and the intricacies of more advanced manueuvers, if that's your choice. Gear up by changing into your flight suit, putting on your parachute, and away you go! Experience of a lifetime? Yes. All rides are recorded onto a DVD for you to take home (and ironically, relive the experience of a lifetime more than once). Note that aerobatic and formation flight training are also available here.

Hours: Flight times are usually daily, at 8am, 10:30am, 1pm, and (June - October), 3:30pm, but call to work around your desired timeframe. There are also sunset pleasure flights available. All flights are by reservation only. Closed on some holidays.

Price: 45 min. sightseeing tours start at $395 per person. A 30 min. flight time of you flying and practicing turning and such, but no tricks, is $149. An 35 min. flight with 10 min. of aerobatics starts at $465. There are numerous options to choose from with full explanations - check the website.

Ages: 8 years and up.

SOUTHWIND KAYAK CENTER

(949) 261-0200 / www.southwindkayaks.com $$$

near 100 N. Bayside Drive at East Coast Highway and Bayside Drive, Newport Beach

This company knows kayaks. Around since 1987 with a retail store in Irvine, rentals are available on the waterfront - $14 an hour for single sit-on-top kayaks; $20 for tandems kayaks, stand up paddle boards, single Hobie Mirage kayak, or pedal boats; $25 for a double Hobie Mirage kayak.

Southwind is also known for their guided kayak tours. The Harbor Highlights Tour, for instance, allows one or two adults and a child per kayak to paddle for two hours around the harbor, learning the basic strokes and safety for $55 per person. The Kayak Back to Nature is a two-hour, outstanding, educational kayak "tour" with a naturalist. You'll paddle along the Upper Newport Bay Ecological Reserve where you'll see and learn about herons, egrets, and numerous other birds and animals, as well as the geology of the area for $55 per person - kids must be at least 9 years old. A day of learning and fresh air - an unbeatable combination.

Hours: Open most of the year, Fri. - Mon., 9am - 4pm; open in the summer daily, 9am - 5pm.

Price: Some prices are listed above.

Ages: 3 years and up, depending on where you go.

SUNSET GONDOLA

(562) 592-3295 - gondola; (800) 979-3370 - reservations / www.sunsetgondola.com

$$$$$

16370 Pacific Coast Highway, Huntington Beach

That's amore! Steeped in the tradition associated with an authentic gondola ride, such as the gondolier wearing a nautical-looking outfit and singing an Italian song, and kissing under bridges (for the passengers, not the gondolier!), riders enjoy a serene cruise around islands, gliding in and out of channels and inlets, past estates and mansions of Huntington Harbor. Time of day and year help create a variety of moods - a daytime jaunt; a romantic, moonlit evening out; a sunset reverie; or a Christmas-time ride to see all the decorated houses and brightly lit boats. Bring your own beverage and/or snack. Note that there are several restaurants in the immediate area.

> **Hours:** Open daily, 11am - midnight. Reservations are required.
> **Price:** Prices range from $83 for a forty-minute ride for two people to $173 for a two-hour ride for two people, plus a $3 handling fee. (Holiday prices can be higher.)
> **Ages:** 4 years and up.

YOUNG EAGLES PROGRAM (Orange County)

National number - (877) 806-8902 / www.eaa92.org; www.youngeagles.org

$$$

4011 W. Commonwealth Avenue at Fullerton Airport, Fullerton

See both the entry for YOUNG EAGLES PROGRAM (Los Angeles County) on page 215 and, more specifically, YOUNG EAGLES PROGRAM (San Bernardino County) on page YOUNGEAGLESSANBERN for details.

> **Hours:** The program is offered once a year through this airport, usually in June, but the chapter also flies out of the Chino airport.
> **Price:** A $20 donation is asked per youth that is flying - it covers lunch, fuel costs, materials, and more.
> **Ages:** 8 - 17 years old.

—ZOOS AND ANIMALS—

CENTENNIAL FARM

(714) 708-1619 / www.ocfair.com/farm

88 Fair Drive, Costa Mesa

This outdoor working farm has pigs, chickens, sheep, bunnies, llamas, and cows. During the springtime, in particular, be on the lookout for the many animal babies that are born here, like squealing piglets that are so ugly they're cute. Walk around the grounds to learn about other aspects of farming. Younger kids will probably be amazed to see vegetables such as carrots, zucchini, lettuce, and corn being grown, not already picked and packaged, as in the grocery stores. (Please do not pick the vegetables or feed the animals.) The Millennium Barn has animal stalls, a tack room, a small museum area, and a milking parlor. A few picnic tables are here at the farm too, so pack a sack lunch. The huge parking lot is usually empty at this time, so bring skates or bikes. Note that on Thursdays there is a Farmer's Market just next door from 8am to 1pm.

A ninety-minute tour of the farm is available for kindergarten through third gradeers for groups of ten or more students. One day a month is reserved for preschoolers. The tour includes walking all around the farm; milking a cow (this is fun to watch); going into the main building and petting or holding baby chicks; planting a seed (and then taking it home); and learning about the food groups. Reservations are required.

> **Hours:** The farm is open to the public August - June, Mon. - Fri., 1pm - 4pm; Sat. - Sun., 9am - 4pm. Tours for kindergartners and up are given October - May, Mon. - Fri. at 9am and 11am. The farm is open in July only with paid admission to the Orange County Fair (pg. 734). Access may be limited on some weekends due to special events. Closed on state holidays. Call for hours.
> **Price:** Free. All tours are also free.
> **Ages:** 2 years and up during public hours; K - 3rd graders for most tours.

LAGUNA KOI PONDS

(949) 494-5107 / www.lagunakoi.com

20452 Laguna Canyon Road, Laguna Beach

This fun little stop off has several cement tanks filled with koi and a store carrying fish supplies. We enjoy just looking at these colorful fish with their beautiful patterns. Who knows, you may want to purchase a few to raise at home. You may also feed them at certain times with a handful of pellets. It's fun to watch their large mouths open

quickly and bite at the food. Combine a trip here with a visit to the PACIFIC MARINE MAMMAL CENTER (pg. 334), which is located just south of the ponds.

Hours: Open Mon. - Sat., 9am - 5pm; Sun., 10am - 5pm
Price: Free
Ages: All

LOS ALAMITOS RACE COURSE

(714) 995-1234 / www.losalamitos.com
4961 E. Katella Avenue, Los Alamitos

Thoroughbreds and quarter horses are the attractions here. Have your child cheer for his favorites! Call for schedule information.

Hours: Open year round - call for specific races and hours.
Price: $3 for adults for grandstand seats, $5 for the clubhouse, $10 for Vessels Club; ages 17 and under are free. Parking is free for general; $5 for preferred.
Ages: 4 years and up.

MAGNOLIA BIRD FARM (Orange County)

(714) 527-3387 / www.magnoliabirdfarms.com
8990 Cerritos, Anaheim

Take your flock of kids to visit their fine feathered friends at the Magnolia Bird Farm pet shop. Birds here range from common doves and canaries to more exotic cockatoos and macaws. A small-bird aviary is located just outside the main building.

The Bird Farm has bird accessories, including a wide assortment of bird cages. Here's a craft idea: Buy a simple wooden cage for your kids to paint and decorate, then fill it with bird seed, and hang it up in your backyard. While you're here, have your kids take the bird challenge - see if they can get one of the talking birds to actually speak to them! Short, free tours are offered for groups of ten to fifteen people during the week. (Also see MAGNOLIA BIRD FARM (Riverside County) on page 372.)

Hours: Open Tues. - Sat., 9am - 4:30pm. Closed Mon., Sun. and holidays.
Price: Free
Ages: All

ORANGE COUNTY POLO CLUB

(714) 791-8369 / www.ocpolo.com
23401 Via Pajaro at the Coto Valley Equestrian Center, Coto de Caza

To find out the "how tos" of a polo game, see SANTA BARBARA POLO (pg. 652). The public is welcome to watch year-round practices/games and tournaments at this O.C. club. If you're interested in picking up the sport, lessons are offered here. Come watch! Come play!

Hours: Practices/games are usually held Thurs. at 6pm; Sat. and Sun. at 11am, but not usually in December. Check the website for tournaments.
Price: Free to all the events.
Ages: 3 years and up.

ORANGE COUNTY ZOO

(714) 973-6847 - zoo; (714) 973-6846 - tours / www.ocparks.com/oczoo
1 Irvine Park Road, Orange

Take a trip to the zoo while you're in the park! Tucked away in the massive IRVINE REGIONAL PARK (pg. 282) is the eight-acre Orange County Zoo. The zoo has barnyard animals such as sheep, goats, and potbellied pigs to pet through fence pens. Food dispensers are here, too. The main section of the small zoo features primarily animals native to the southwestern United States, such as mountain lions, bobcats, deer, beaver, coyotes, a coati, an Island fox, a black bear, burro, porcupines, and a variety of birds, including a bald eagle, golden eagle, and several types of owls. Look for Discovery Carts scattered around in the zoo with hands-on artifacts.

Toddler programs ($5 per person) and scout programs ($3 per person) are offered, as are ninety-minute school tours for any grade level for $3 per person. These all include a zoo guide and animal presentation. Topics covered may include habitats, adaptations, feeding habits, and general information about animals native to the southwestern United States. A train ride at Irvine Park Railroad may be added to any tour for an additional fee of $3 per student. Check the

website or call about special events.

Hours: Open daily, 10am - 4pm. Closed New Year's Day and Christmas.
Price: $2 for ages 3 and up; children 2 and under are free. This admission is in addition to the vehicle entrance fee to the park which is $3 per vehicle, Mon. - Fri., $5 on Sat. - Sun; $7 - 10 on holidays.
Ages: All

PACIFIC MARINE MAMMAL CENTER

(949) 494-3050 / www.pacificmmc.org
20612 Laguna Canyon Road, Laguna Beach

This Center is a small, safe haven and rehabilitation hospital for pinnipeds - more commonly known as sea lions, elephant seals, and harbor seals. When these animals are abandoned, injured, or in need of medical attention they are temporarily housed in the facility's small outdoor pools until they are ready to be released back into the wild. This is a good opportunity for kids to see these animals up-close, while learning more about them and the effects that we have on our ocean environment. The volunteers are great at answering the numerous (and sometimes off-the-wall) questions kids ask.

Feeding time, usually around 10:30am and 3pm, is lively as the sea lions go wild, barking in anticipation of a meal. (It sounds like mealtime at our house.) There are anywhere from ten to 100 mammals here, as many of them arrive when pups are weaned from their mothers - January through July. One-hour educational programs that feature a slide presentation and a guided tour are $25 plus $7 per person; with a minimum of six people. Ask about summer day camp, after-school programs, and Girl Scout troop workshops. (Also see LAGUNA KOI PONDS, on page 332, located just north of the center.)

Hours: Open daily, 10am - 4pm.
Price: Free; donations gladly accepted.
Ages: 2 years and up.

PREHISTORIC PETS / THE REPTILE ZOO

(714) 964-3525 / www.thereptilezoo.com; www.jurassicparties.com
18822 Brookhurst Street, Fountain Valley

The word "prehistoric" evokes imagery of a reptilian world where creatures roam and forage under canopies of trees. This huge, 10,000-square-foot pet store and zoo does a good job of fleshing out this concept.

A large, rock-rimmed pond with lots of greenery is near the entrance of the retail store. It is filled with a multitude of turtles, giant tortoises, and giant catfish, while a large monitor lizard, or two, usually basks on a rock in the middle. You may purchase food to feed the always hungry critters for $3. Jungle-theme music through the speakers and tiki-style decor add to the atmosphere.

The glass cages lining the store are filled with exotic animals such as skinks (not skunks), chameleons, frogs, scorpions, tarantulas, iguanas, lots of monitor lizards, rattlesnakes, other snakes and more to purchase (and stare at).

There is an entrance fee to go into the adjoining area, The Reptile Zoo. This zoo contains reptiles that you will gawk at such as Thelma and Louise, a two-headed snake (doubly creepy!); American alligators (which eat raw chicken); an albino iguana; anacondas; several different types of pythons; a cobra; water monitors (one weighs about 60 pounds!); bearded lizards; and the star - Twinkie (an albino reticulated python), reputed to be the world's largest snake at over twenty-feet long and weighing in at 350 pounds!

Brave visitors are invited to pet and even hold a rotating variety of ball pythons (grab a hug from one of these and don't forget your camera), bearded dragons, leopard and crested geckos, and others at the Hands-On Learning Zone in the Zoo. Another section houses the husbandry facility, egg incubators, life cycle learning zone, and more.

Schedule a hands-on, educational tour, or a unique birthday party in a Jurassic party room. A two-hour party allows up to thirty guests (adults and children) an hour in a private party room and an hour presentation with twelve to fifteen animals - snakes, frogs, lizards, bugs, etc, that guests get to touch, hold and learn about. Visitors of all ages will enjoy the animals as they come out to play, crawl, coil, and slither. The cost is $250. A one-hour Reptile Zoo Tour includes the presentation and interaction of the above party, just not the room usage. That cost is $175 for up to thirty people. Other options are available. Prehistoric Pets will also bring the critters to you for a party or function of some sort.

What makes this pet store/zoo so spectacular is not just the variety, rareness, and number of reptiles and such, but the greatness of size of so many of them. I would not want to meet some of them outside their cages!

Hours: Open Mon. - Sat., 11am - 8-pm; Sun., 11am - 6pm. Closed Thanksgiving and Christmas, and early on other holidays.

Price: Free for Prehistoric Pets, the retail store. The Reptile Zoo admission is $5; children 3 and under are free.

Ages: 3 years and up.

SANTA ANA ZOO

(714) 835-7484 or (714) 836-4000 - zoo; (714) 647-6568 - education coordinator; (714) 569-0779 - cafe / www.santaanazoo.org

1801 E. Chestnut Avenue at Prentice Park, Santa Ana

Lions and tigers and bears - not here! This small zoo, however, is perfect for young children. They can easily walk around it, see all the animals, and still have of time to play on the playground, all within just a few hours. The zoo houses llamas; wallabies; a dromedary camel; hedgehogs; cavies; emus; anteaters, rheas, porcupines; a sloth; birds, including a bald eagle, toucans, macaws (who squawk loudly!), and scarlet ibises; and a wide variety of monkeys, our personal favorites. In fact, the zoo is mandated to have at least fifty monkeys living on its premises at all times so you'll see golden-headed lion tamarins, emperor tamarins, capuchins, black howlers, spider monkeys, gibbons (which are technically apes), and others, most living on Monkey Row. The cages and animals are not far off in the distance, but right along the pathways so you can see (and hear) all the antics. Walk through the wonderful aviary where you can observe beautiful and exotic birds close up. The Santa Ana Zoo abounds in all kinds of green plants, too.

The Crean Family Farm area has several small, farm-looking buildings each home to a particular barnyard animal such as pigs, bunnies, goats (no kidding!), cows, and sheep which you can pet through pens. A few owls are here, as well. A hatchery holds newborn chicks at certain times. Catch a six-minute ride on a scale model electric locomotive that circles around this enclosure and northern part of the zoo for $3 per person. Ride on the thirty-three animal conservation carousel for $3. Ages 2 and under are free for both.

Come for a presentation near the stage to see and learn about Macaws, snakes, and other inhabitants. Stop by the jungle-like, large room called Jaguar Exploration Outpost, modeled after a real outpost, to learn research techniques regarding the Amazon rainforest animals, plus weather patterns and conservation efforts via hands-on experiments. And look at the insects here, including a bird-eating tarantula - the Amazon grows them all bigger! Open at certain times, go through the not-scary Rainforest Adventure maze with four interactive learning stations. If you answer questions correctly regarding the rainforest, you venture deeper into the maze; if you don't, the info panels shows diffs and dangerous animals and you're at a dead end.

The on-site playground has two play structures with a rope tower, slides, rings, and other fun elements. The Knollwoods Cafe, with an adjacent covered eating area, offers hot dogs (average $3.15), hamburger (average $4.50), chicken sandwich ($5), tacos ($3), Chinese chicken salad ($7.95) and kids meals ($4.50). Or, enjoy a sack lunch right outside the zoo gates at the adjoining Prentice Park which offers picnic tables, grassy areas, and shade trees.

A variety of educational and interactive programs are offered throughout the year. Note that membership at Santa Ana Zoo is reciprocal for free or discounted admission at 150 other zoos throughout the United States.

Hours: Open daily, 10am - 4pm. (The grounds close at 5pm.) Closed rainy days, New Year's Day, Thanksgiving, and Christmas Day. Train and carousel rides are available daily from 11am - 2pm.

Price: $10 for adults; $7 for seniors and ages 3 - 12; children 2 and under are free. Admission Mon. - Fri. after 2pm is $6 for adults; $4 for seniors and kids. Admission is free the third Sun. of each month for Santa Ana residents. AAA discounts are available.

Ages: All

SHANGRILLAMA WALK

(661) 221-5813 / www.shangrillama.com

El Cajon Trail, Yorba Linda

Anyone can take their dog for a walk, but how about walking a llama?! Get to know the five llamas, one per person (or double team), as you take turns walking them for about three hours through a neighborhood, across a few streets, on a trail, to a park, past the Richard Nixon Library & Birthplace, and then back. What fun!

Each llama has a unique personality (and names - Pajama Llama, Barack Llama, Como T. Llama, etc.) as well as being distinctive in size, coloring, and age. They make strange noises that sound like moaning, although it's officially called humming. Hmm. We stroked them and walked them with a lead rope while learning that llamas have three stomachs, rectangular pupils and a split lip; are born during the day while mothers stand up to give birth (which sounds rather painful!); are mostly from South America; are social creatures; poop in pellets that don't smell and which are good fertilizer for roses; make great pets; and more. OK, yes - I kind of want a llama now! Amazing how much you can bond with a llama during this brief time together.

We stopped at a park and tied the llamas to trees so they could munched on leaves and we could snacks on snacks. (Bring your own!) Then, we continued on our journey, crossing a few streets (I love the look people driving by gave us!), and eventually on a trail that led toward home.

Hours: October - April, Sat. - Sun., 9am - noon; May - September, Sat. - Sun. 5pm - 8pm. Walks are available at almost anytime with a group of at least 5 people.

Price: $50 per person.

Ages: 12 years and up, only.

WHALE WATCHING
See the TRANSPORTATION section.

ZOOMARS PETTING ZOO and LOS RIOS PARK

(949) 831-6550 / www.zoomars.com

$$$

31791 Los Rios Street, San Juan Capistrano

This animal park will become a favorite stopping place and/or destination whenever you visit San Juan Capistrano with the kids. Pass through the gates into this spacious and clean petting zoo with separate enclosures for each of the animals. There are two pens with over 100 guinea pigs - so cute and curious as you sit on the ground and they crawl all over you! (Especially if you have food for them.) The bunnies (and there are a multitude of them, of course) are irresistibly soft. Gently stroke goats and sheep, as well as other animals through fence pens - llamas, alpacas, emus, and a few horses. You can purchase a basket of food - carrot sticks, lettuce, etc., to lure the animals closer, feed them, and pet them. There are also two rare zonkeys (a cross between a zebra and a donkey) to just look at, and a few cows.

Starting at 12 months old, kids up to eighty pounds can take a hand-led pony ride around a dirt track. Scale model train rides around a short track are also available (and fun). An a*maize*ingly interesting place for kids to play is the covered corn box (ie. like a sand box) filled with unpopped kernels of corn. Buckets and toys are provided. Kids are happy and not sandy. Parents are happy and not sandy. A little playground here has a slide and raised, wooden forts to play in. Parents can rest on some of the picnic tables and stone benches scattered around. Against a nicely-done backdrop of Old West building facades, miners-in-training can pan for rocks, minerals, and other treasures at Miner's Gulch. As water comes down the sluice young prospectors take their chosen bag, which is filled with sand and minerals, and sift it over a screened pan. We got some great rocks, an arrowhead, and even a shark's tooth - felt like we struck gold.

Field trippers and birthday party goers are welcome as Zoomars has several separate areas to accommodate each group.

There is a lot to do in this immediate area because this area, in fact San Juan Capistrano, is not large. In front of the farm is the 100-year-old Olivares Home. Next door is the O'Neill Historic Museum. A short stroll down the quaint street is the TEA HOUSE ON LOS RIOS (pg. 254). Fun and funky places to eat include the Hummingbird House Cafe with Mediterranean appetizers and desserts; sandwiches, wraps, gyros and salads at $8.50 each; and a kids' menu - average $3.50. It is located directly next to the railroad tracks, so you have front row seats to the rumbling trains! The vintage, beautiful, bricked old depot of Sarducci's Capistrano Depot (restaurant) has window seats and outside seating next to the tracks, too (and elsewhere).

Behind Zoomars is a lovely area with a butterfly garden, stone and wood picnic tables under shade trees, and a paved path leading to **Los Rios Park**. The well-landscaped, good-sized park has some great features - raised, fort-like, wooden play structures with steps, a swinging connecting bridge, slides, a fireman's pole, and swings; a separate section with boulders to climb on, under and through; a wading pool filled in with sand; plenty of trees; and lots and lots of benches all over, plus a grouping of picnic tables under a trellis of grape vines. Note that MISSION SAN JUAN CAPISTRANO (pg. 307) is only a block, or so, away. If you don't live in the immediate area, consider traveling here by train as that adds a whole other adventure element to your outing. (The train station is located right next to the parking garage.)

Hours: Open Mon. - Fri., 10am - 4pm; Sat. - Sun., 10am - 5pm

Price: $9 for ages 14 and up; $7 for children 12 months - 13 years. Pony rides are $5 for one lap around the track. Train rides are $3 per person. A basket of food for the animals is $4. Miner's Gulch bags are $8 - $10 per.

Ages: 2 - 10 years.

RIVERSIDE COUNTY

   Once a grove of orange trees that spawned a thriving citrus industry, the southern Inland Empire is now very diverse. It claims the city of Temecula, a fast-growing community that still maintains its small-town feel; historic downtown Riverside with its famous Mission Inn; and Palm Springs (and the surrounding desert cities) - an oasis that's no mirage. With all of the county's attractions and small cities, Riverside still has plenty of open spaces left to explore.

   Note: Since the Palm Springs area is often a multi-day destination, its attractions are listed in a separate section in the back of this county.

—AMUSEMENT PARKS—

CASTLE PARK / BUCCANEER COVE

(951) 785-3000 / www.castlepark.com
3500 Polk Street, Riverside

The family-fun amusement park, **Castle Park**, has a lot of action packed into its twenty-five acres. The compactness of the park makes it easy to walk all around. It has four scenically-landscaped and challenging eighteen-hole, miniature golf courses complete with waterfalls, bridges, a miniature Big Ben, Dutch windmill, Chinese pagoda, castle, and western fort. The huge, multi-level arcade has over 200 video games and games of skill including virtual boxing, Dance Dance Revolution, bass fishing, and Daytona race car simulations, plus a prize redemption center. Check out the fun and kind of hokey Ghost Blaster ride, within the arcade, where riders go into a haunted house and shoot moving ghosts with their laser "Boo Blaster" to receive redemption points.

The rest of the park contains over thirty-five rides and attractions. There are many classic Midway rides and other rides, including the short log ride (which *will* get you wet); a huge carousel with all sorts of interesting animals; roller coasters; swing rides; a scrambler; bumper cars; an airplane ride; a free fall; a sea dragon ride; a Ferris wheel; two train rides; and lots more. Besides the "big kids" rides, there are plenty of kiddie rides - tea cups that spin, small coasters, antique car rides, train rides, mini motorcycles, and more.

The atmosphere at Castle Park reminds me of Coney Island in that the flashy rides are interspersed with carnival-type games. There are also kind of unusual features for an amusement park, such as the reproduction of the Liberty Bell, proclaiming liberty throughout the park, and an authentic gypsy wagon.

Summer is funner (and wetter) at **Buccaneer Cove** here. This small, piratey-themed water park, next to the castle building, has a main, colorful, multi-level play structure in zero depth water. Attached to it are five water slides; water tunnels; interactive aqua domes; spray cannons; colorful loops and cylinders with spray fountains shooting everywhere; a huge bucket that fills up with water and pours out intermittently; and several other interactive water elements, including water spurting up from the cement ground. Lounge chairs and and some shade are around the perimeters for those who need a break. Bring a change of clothing to enjoy the drier rides and attractions.

For big time fun, come eat at Big Top Restaurant. The good-sized restaurant resembles a circus big top, complete with a lifelike statue of a circus elephant outside. The inside feels like a circus, too. (Then again, meal times at our house always felt like a circus what with balancing plates of food, kids acting clownish, etc.) The food is good, with pizza being the featured item - $7.99 for a personal one. A salad bar; burgers ($8.99, which includes fries and a drink); corn dogs ($3.49); chicken tenders ($8.99); and sandwiches are also available. Children's meals are $5.99. The Big Top bear mascot occasionally appears on stage for a short show. There are a few kiddie rides, a small arcade room with G-rated games, and a redemption center inside here, too.

The restaurant and Castle Park are good places for a birthday party. Special events and package deals are on-going at the park, including scout programs, so call for a schedule and more information. Motivate your kids because good grades and school attendance are rewarded here with free tokens!

Hours: Most of the year, miniature golf and the arcade area are open Mon. - Thurs., 1pm - 8pm; Fri., 1pm - 10pm; Sat., 11am - 10pm; Sun., 11am - 9pm. Rides are open Fri., 5pm - 9pm; Sat., noon - 9pm; Sun., noon - 8pm. During the summer and on holidays, golf and arcades are open Mon. - Thurs., 11am -8pm; Fri. - Sat., 11am - 11pm.; Sun., 11am - 10pm. Rides are usually closed on Mon. Call first as the hours fluctuate a lot. Buccaneer Cove is usually open from Memorial Day - Labor Day, Mon. - Fri., noon - 6pm; Sat. - Sun., noon - 7pm. It is sometimes open on weekends in May and September, too. Big Top Restaurant is open Sat., noon - 5pm, and usually Sun., noon - 3pm. Call for other hours.

Price: Duke's Deal: Choose either unlimited rides, unlimited mini golf, or entrance to Buccaneer Cove - $9.99; Duke's Duo: Choose two unlimited attractions from the previous list - $15.99; Dukes's Deluxe: All three unlimited choices - $19.99. Everything includes admission to Castle Park video games. Check online for discounts and promotions. AAA members receive a discount. Parking is $6.

Ages: All

THE COVE WATERPARK - JURUPA AQUATIC CENTER

(951) 360-1974 / www.covewaterpark.com

4310 Camino Real, Riverside

'ey mon! This smallish, Caribbean-themed water park has huge (fake) parrots, plus overturned ships, cargo netting, treasure chests, and tiki "umbrellas" with lounge chairs underneath, decorating the deck. The suitably-named Crow's Nest is a tower with three twisty slides (one is totally enclosed) that plummet, plunge and plop. Catch a gnarlatious wave while surfing at the double-sized Flowrider at Riptide Reef. Take it easy in an inner tube and float along the Ne'er Endin' River that encircles part of the park as it goes under bridges and waterfalls. A colorful activity pool for younger kid is the pirate-themed, Lil' Mates' Lagoon. It has several slides, even enclosed curvy ones; huge barrels of water that tip over periodically; squirting water elements; and plenty of room for splashing around, all in very shallow waters. An adjacent pool for older kids (and adults) is fun to just play around in.

Landlubbers can play on a ship that is torn apart enough to let mateys board it and pretend they are adventuring on the high seas.

The snack bar serves made-to-order grilled food - hotdogs ($3.50), cheeseburgers ($4.50), and grilled chicken sandwiches ($6.95), plus smoothies ($3.95), snacks of soft pretzels ($3.95) and funnel cakes ($4.95), and beverages. Kids meals are $5.95. No outside food is allowed in. Locker rentals are $4. Traditional swimwear is required.

The adjacent competition pool, 25-yard by 35-meter, has a diving board and spectator seating. It is open for lap and recreational swim year-round.

Hours: The water park is open daily, Memorial Day weekend - mid-August, 11am - 6pm. Open mid-August - Labor Day weekend on weekends only (and that Monday), 11am - 6pm. Check the website calendar for discount days, especially for Jurupa residents, special events and extended hours. The pool is open for recreational swim daily, 12:15pm - 3:15pm.

Price: The water park is $18 for 48" and taller; $14 for seniors and 37" - 47"; $9 for tots 30" - 36"; children 29" and under are free. Entrance to the waterpark includes use of the pool. The pool is $3 for adults; $2 for ages 13 and under. Parking is free.

Ages: 2 years and up.

—ARTS AND CRAFTS—

CERAMIC CUPBOARD

(951) 737-3521 / www.ceramiccupboard.com

1660 Hamner Avenue, Norco

This full-service, ceramic art studio holds more items than a normal cupboard! There is a wide selection of ready-to-paint objects to make the perfect gift for someone special. All the paints you want and need, stencils, and instruction, plus firing, are included in your studio price. Other services offered include day-works, mosaics, glass painting, and pottery wheel workshops and rentals. Another bonus feature is that the studio store carries the supplies and mechanisms for finishing particular projects, such as clock workings, music boxes, trivets, and more. Ask about kids' club and classes, as there are a variety of them available.

Hours: Open Sun. - Thurs., 11am - 6pm; Fri. - Sat., 11am- 8pm.

Price: $6 per person per day, plus the price of your item.

Ages: 4 years and up.

COLOR ME MINE (Riverside County)

Redlands - (909) 792-2622; Riverside - (951) 687-1630 / www.colormemine.com

Redlands - 9900 Alabama Street, suite D in the Redland Town Center / Palm Grove Marketplace; Riverside - 1299 Galleria at Tyler in the Galleria at Tyler mall

See the entry for COLOR ME MINE (Los Angeles County) on page 7 for details.

CRAFTY U TOO!

(951) 684-2645 / www.craftyutoo.com

5225 Canyon Crest Drive, #3, Riverside

Feeling crafty (and not in a devious way)? Come in a pick out a mug, dish, figurine, bank, or any of the other numerous objects that you then paint into a one-of-a-kind keepsake. All the materials - paint, brushes, ideas, and space to work on your design - are provided.

Hours: Open Mon. - Thurs., 11am - 9pm; Fri. - Sat., 11am - 10pm; Sun., noon - 6pm.

Price: The studio fee is $10 for adults; $6 for ages 12 and under; plus the price of your piece.

Ages: 4 years and up.

PAINTED EARTH

Menifee - (951) 679-6800; Temecula - (951) 676-2447 / www.paintedearthpottery.com
Menifee - 30010 Haun Road; Temecula - 27507 Ynez Road at Tower Plaza

Paint your own ceramic masterpiece at Painted Earth. Choose from decorative figurines to microwavable plates and mugs. All the paints, brushes, and glazes are included in the studio fee, so feel free to express yourself and enjoy a lasting, hand-crafted treasure.

Hours: Open Mon. - Thurs., 10am - 9pm; Fri. - Sat., 10am - 10pm; Sun., 11am - 7pm. Closed Christmas.

Price: $7 per person, all-day studio fee, which includes the price of glazing and firing. The price of the item is an additional fee. For example, a figurine is $5, a bowl or coffee mug is $10, and a dish is $12.

Ages: 4 years and up.

—EDIBLE ADVENTURES—

BOMBSHELTER SPORTS BAR AND GRILL

(951) 943-4863 / www.skydiveperris.com
2091 Goetz Road, Perris

Drop in for a bite to eat at Bombshelter, a restaurant adjacent to one of the best drop zones for sky divers in the United States. The two rooms in here are decorated wall-to-wall with photos and posters of skydivers. Flags, jumpsuits, and even two painted, real bombs hang from the ceiling. A large-screen TV shows the flyers from the neighboring, indoor wind tunnel on live-feed camera. See PERRIS SKYVENTURE (pg. 345) for more information on this thrilling adventure.

Look out the huge picture windows to view the mountains, and watch skydivers floating down. A pool table ($1 a game) and two computers (with airplane-related games) are also here.

Breakfast items include two eggs with bacon or sausage ($6.49); breakfast burrito ($6.54); four pancakes ($4.99); or two biscuits and gravy ($3.49). For lunch, order cheeseburger and fries ($7.49); chicken strips and fries ($6.49); Philly cheese steak ($8.99); Reuben ($7.99); Cobb salad ($7.99); chili dog ($3.29); roast turkey wrap ($7.49); or a deli sandwich (from $5.75 to $7.99). Dinner selections consist of appetizers - mozzarella sticks ($6.99); buffalo chicken wings ($7.99) and sliders ($6.49); and real meals of NY steak with baked potato ($12.99); lasagna ($7.95); linguini and clams ($7.25); blackened strip steak ($11.99); lemon rosemary chicken ($10.99); grilled pork chops ($10.99); or grilled steak and shrimp ($14.99).

Hours: Open Mon. - Fri., 8am - 8:30pm; Sat. - Sun., 7am - 7pm.

Price: Menu prices are listed above.

Ages: All

CHINESE BISTRO

(951) 928-3837
28490 Highway 74, Romoland

Located just before the city border of Hemet, this isn't a slow train to China; it is a parked train restaurant serving Chinese cuisine. Inside the railcars, which are actually on a track, each small table has flowers, padded chairs, and a window seat. Hanging lanterns overheard and plenty of red and gold decor add to the Chinese ambiance.

A huge selection of food includes crispy spicy shrimp ($11.75); pineapple shrimp ($11.50); Kung Pao beef ($9.75); orange peel beef ($11.50); oyster beef ($11); lemon chicken nuggets ($9.50); Sesame chicken ($9.75); sweet and sour pork ($9.50); and vegetable egg fu yong ($8.25); plus a wide variety of soups, appetizers, and lunch and dinner combinations. You're guaranteed to find something (or some things!) to please your palate.

Hours: Open Mon. - Thurs., 11am - 9pm; Fri. - Sat., 11am - 9:30pm; Sun., 11am - 9pm.

Price: Menu prices are listed above.

Ages: 4 years and up.

CHUCK E. CHEESE'S (Riverside County)

See the entry for CHUCK E. CHEESE'S (Los Angeles County) on page 16 for details.

FARMER'S MARKETS (Riverside County)

See the entry for FARMER'S MARKETS (Los Angeles County) on pg. 18 for details.

FARRELL'S ICE CREAM PARLOUR RESTAURANTS (Riverside County)

(951) 351-1200 / www.farrellsusa.com
3610 Park Sierra Dr., Riverside

See FARRELL'S ICE CREAM PARLOUR RESTAURANTS (Orange County) on pg. 247 for details on this terrifically fun restaurant. This location is the biggest one of all (so far) and is near CASTLE PARK (pg. 338).

JOHN'S INCREDIBLE PIZZA CO. (Riverside County)

(951) 656-5555 / www.johnspizza.com
6187 Valley Springs Parkway, Riverside

See JOHN'S INCREDIBLE PIZZA CO. (Orange County) on page 248 for details.

Hours: Open Mon. - Thurs., 11am - 9:30pm; Fri., 11am - 11pm; Sat., 10am - 11pm; Sun., 10am - 9:30pm.

THE OLD SPAGHETTI FACTORY (Riverside County)

(951) 784-4417 / www.osf.com
3191 Mission Inn Avenue, Riverside

See the entry for THE OLD SPAGHETTI FACTORY (Los Angeles County) on page 23 for details.

Hours: Open for weekday lunch, Mon. - Fri., 11:30am - 2pm; weekday dinner, Mon. - Thurs., 5pm - 10pm; Fri., 5pm - 11pm. Open on weekends, Sat., 11:30am - 11pm; Sun., 11:30am - 10pm.

SHOGUN - (Riverside County)

Corona - (951) 737-3888; Temecula - (951) 296-9133 / www.restaurantshogun.com
Corona - 275 Teller Street #130; Temecula - 41501 Margarita Road

See the entry for SHOGUN (Los Angeles County) on page 25 for details.

Corona - Open Mon. - Thurs., 11:30am - 9:30pm; Fri., 11:30am - 10pm; Sat., noon - 10pm; Sun., noon - 9pm.
Temecula - Open Sun. - Thurs., 11:30am - 9pm; Fri. - Sat., 11:30am - 10pm.

TIOS TACOS #1 MARISCOS

(951) 788-0230 / www.tiostacos.com
3948 Mission Inn Avenue, Riverside

Eclectic. Odd. Unusual. Cool! These are the first words I can think of to describe this restaurant's fairly extensive (one acre) ground and decor. Not really stroller friendly, but you can walk around outside to see folk art at its finest, or is it at its weirdest?! There are several groupings of outdoor eating areas with patio chairs, and multicolor tiled tables and benches. But you'll first notice the odd statues and unusual things all around, all made from recycled products. One long walkway is imbedded with beer bottles, shells, and rocks as wells as a bike, dolls, dishes, computer components, fishing rod, curling iron, and just about anything else you can possibly think of. Some of the colorful plaster statues here have masks; some don't. One is holding a sword while astride a horse statue. Many of the creations are shaped using chicken wire and stuffed with a variety of objects - Barbie dolls, little plastic toys, coconuts, junk, etc. A few, shaped like humans, have plants growing out of them with plaster heads wearing wigs. One section has a stone slab with a cascading fountain. Water shoots over (and onto) the cobblestone circular pathway under trees, while busts, a waterfall made out of shovels, a tree with circular saws sticking out, lamps, ant statues, and other bizarre items surround it. On the rooftop of the old house are little kid figures riding trikes and scooters, and one riding a bike E.T. style, with its front wheel suspended in air. There is a small chapel made out of white, green, and brown beer bottles, forming various designs, plus mosaics, all held together by cement. Angel statuary and even windows complete the chapel. Inside, with its vividly-painted ceiling of a Bible scene, are benches, an altar, Jesus and Mary statues, and the lip of the bottles. You have to see this whole outside place to believe it.

The inside of the adjoining small restaurant is decorated with sea-themed mosaic floors, a ceiling painted like blue sky with clouds, and a large wall collage of sea stars, shells, sea anemones, coral, and more creating a 3-D effect. Fanciful. Unique. Cool. The authentic Mexican food, all served with complementary fresh chips and salsa, is delicious and reasonably-priced. Bring your appetite because the restaurant has a huge variety of foods, juices, and smoothies. Try a steak taco, $2.50; huevos rancheros, $6.99; breakfast burrito with ham and eggs, $5.99; BBQ pork burrito, $5.99; tongue burrito, $5.99; beef tostada, $4.99; nachos (the works), $9.99; taco salad, $8.99; twenty shrimp, $12.99; whole,

deep fried catfish, $12.99; half a dozen oysters, $9.99; and a fish filet meal, $12.99, plus lots of combo plates and a la carte items. Desserts include flan, $2.75; frozen bananas; and a delicious Hawaiian-Bionic which is an apple, strawberry, banana, papaya, and mango fruit salad topped with yogurt and condensed milk, $3.99.

Hours: Open Sun. - Thurs., 8am - 10pm; Fri. - Sat., 8am - midnight.
Price: Prices are listed above.
Ages: 2 years and up.

TOM'S FARMS

(951) 277- 4422 / www.tomsfarms.com
23900 Temescal Canyon Road, Corona

    Tom's Farms consists of several separate buildings, each one selling different products. The front building has a terrific selection of farm fresh produce, dried fruit, nuts, and candies. This is a delicious stop. Señor Tom's Mexican Restaurant (open 10am to 8pm) offers breakfast, lunch, and dinner - the whole enchilada. Menu items include burritos ($5.69 to $6.99), and chimichangas ($5.99), plus tacos, salads, quesadillas, and more, either in a combo plate or a la carte. Kid's meals are $4.99 for a choice of burrito, quesadilla, enchilada, or taquitos. If you prefer American-style food, the small restaurant, Tom's Hamburgers (notice a reocouring theme?), offers large portions of food. Tasty hamburgers start at $3.99 or order a pastrami sandwich ($5.95), Chinese chicken salad ($6.95), or jumbo chili cheese fries ($4.95). Kids have their choice of a corn dog, grilled cheese sandwich, chicken strips, or a burger, plus fries and a drink, for $4.89. Shakes and malts are $3.95. This restaurant is open at 7am for breakfast, too. A wine and cheese store also offers baked goods and a gourmet deli, as well as pizza ($9.99 for a 14" cheese), sub sandwiches and more. A lovely outside eating area is set up around a series of small ponds and bridges.

    Just beyond the pond, open on weekends only, the farm takes on the feel of a small "old tyme" country fair with craft booths, face painting, and shaved ice, as well as a carousel ride ($2 per person); tractor ride around a small dirt track ($2); pony ride around a small ring ($5); tiny petting zoo ($3); shooting gallery ($1); a chance to play with the mini-tractor digger in the dirt ($1); and a train ride ($2) through a portion of the ten acres of countryside and under a bridge. The train is a reproduction of an 1800's steamer. Enter Tom's Mining Company to pan for gold, or work a sluice and unearth fossils and gems ($4 to $8, depending on your bag of rock treasures). Live music and a magic show are free, added attractions. (Some of the rides might be open during the week, too - call first.) There is also a koi pond in this back area and a large spread of lawn with picnic tables. Ask about the seasonal activities, such as the Pumpkin Patch in October and Festival of Lights at nighttime in November and December. Come grab a snack, or eat a meal at this "farm" with a folksy ambiance.

Hours: Open daily, 8am - 8pm. The country fair happens every Sat. - Sun., 10am - 6pm.
Price: Free entrance.
Ages: All

—FAMILY PAY AND PLAY—

ADAMS MOTORSPORTS PARK

(800) 350-3826 or (951) 686-3826 / www.adamsmotorsportspark.com
5292 24th Street, Riverside

    Kart racing, drifting, time attack, pocket bikes/mini-moto, motorcycles, or supermoto racing can all be had at Adams Motorsports Park. The main track, which is six-tenths of a mile long with fourteen turns and twists and a long straight-away, is a great introduction to real racing. Junior karts and "full-size" karts are available. This race track school offers classes for kart racing, available for kids 5 to 7 years, and 8 years and up. Call for a class schedule.

Hours: The track is open Mon. - Fri., 10am - 5pm and Sat. - Sun., 8am - 5pm for practices, classes, and events. Call or check online for the nighttime events. Closed New Year's Day, Thanksgiving, and Christmas.
Price: Standard race track is $25 a race, which includes the kart, racing suit, helmet, etc. Bring your own kart for the main track - $45 a day for nonmembers; $30 for members; $30 for an extra passenger; $10 for pit person/spectator. Classes start at $179 for two hours of instruction and racing.
Ages: 5 years and up for class; 18 years and up (or 56" and with a legal guardian) to race.

CHILD'S PLAY

(951) 699-7696 / www.childsplaytemecula.com

28860 Old Town Front Street, Suite A2, Temecula

One big room, brightly decorated in primary colors, filled with toys and activities in a clean and safe environment make this an ideal destination for younger children. Child's Play has a small ball pit; a treehouse with two slides; little go karts; Little Tyke cars; a caterpillar tube to crawl through; mini-trampolines; soft play blocks; dress-up areas; short slides; an infant area; and more. Note that every participant must wear socks. You are welcome to enjoy outside food and drinks in the lobby/eating area.

Hours: Open play is Mon. - Tues., 9:30am - 7pm; Wed., 9:30am - 3pm; Thurs., 9:30am - 7pm; Fri. 9:30am - 3pm. Open Sat. and Sun. for private parties only. Closed major holidays.
Price: $9 for the first child; $7 for a sibling; $5 for 10 months - 1 year. Parents are free.
Ages: 6 months - 6 years. (Older children are invited to be in the lobby/eating area only.)

CHUCK E. CHEESE'S (Riverside County)

See the entry for CHUCK E. CHEESE'S (Los Angeles County) on page 16 for details.

FAST LAP INDOOR KAR RACING

(951) 681-3601 / www.fastlaplv.com
3215 Corridor Drive, Mira Loma

Feel like you're really racing as the karts, equipped with gas-powered Honda 200cc engines, can reach speeds up to 50 mph. Helmets on, buckle up and drive - you are going for a fast ride!

Hours: Sun. - Thurs., 10am - 10pm; Fri. - Sat., 10am - 11pm.
Price: $25 for ten minutes (about 18 - 24 laps). Membership is $10 per year, then races are $18 per.
Ages: Must be 4'10" tall.

GET AIR TEMECULA (Riverside County)

(951) 239-4247 / www.getairtemecula.com
26201 Ynez Road, Ste 101, Temecula

Put a bounce in your step (a big one!) by coming to play at this 20,000 square foot indoor trampoline park. The open jumping area is fun by itself, especially with trampolines curved up on the walls and even some platforms to leap from (reminiscent of a skate park or parkour). For more of a challenge try the dodgeball court, or Air Jam Basketball, and practice new tricks by landing in the foam pit, which also has flat screen monitors with delayed playback to see how good, or not, you really are. There is also a small, separate room just for younger jumpers that contains trampoline slides and their own foam pit (and a couch for parents to simply watch). Participate in AIRobics for a different way to exercise. This facility also has private rooms for parties and other gatherings. Signed waivers and non-skid socks are required.

Hours: Open Mon. - Thurs., 10am - 10pm; Fri. - Sat., 10am - midnight; Sun., 11am - 9pm.
Price: $12 per hour; $6 for 45" and under who use the kid's room only.
Ages: 3 years and up.

HANGAR 18 (Riverside County)

(951) 359-5040 / www.climbhangar18.com
6935 Arlington Avenue, Riverside

Stick it. That's rock climbing terminology for having a sure grip in a climbing move. This indoor rock climbing location has one of the largest freestanding bouldering walls in the U.S., plus 12,000 square feet of textured climbing terrain. For more info, see HANGAR 18 (San Bernardino County) on page 407.

Hours: Open Mon. - Thurs., 10am - 10pm; Fri., 10am - 9pm; Sat. - Sun., 10am - 8pm

JERICHO AIRSOFT

(805) 807-6850 / www.jerichoairsoft.com
14881 Temescal Canyon Road at Jungle Island Paintball Park, Lake Elsinore

Sharing the acreage with JUNGLE ISLAND PAINTBALL PARK (pg. 344) the airsoft games are played like military simulation scenarios and players are sometimes treated like soldiers. Players are required to dress in military attire - at least a military-style jacket, which you can rent here for $5. Know that teams are divided by color of clothing so if you want to be on the same team with others that you come with, dress in similar clothing. Zombie games are also played at times and so are other team-type competitions. There are four fields for players to crawl through trenches,

splash in creeks, hide behind boulders or vehides, run through buildings, and other realistic settings. Very important: Read the rules posted on the website before you come so you come prepared because rules are strictly adhered to! Waivers must be signed.

Hours: Open Sat. - Sun., 8am - 4pm. Night games are offered during daylight savings time on Sat., 5pm - 10pm. Group of 15 or more can book games during the week.
Price: $25 for self-equipped walk ons. $55 for all-day admission, rifle, bbs, a mask and BDU jacket.
Ages: 8 years and up.

JOHN'S INCREDIBLE PIZZA CO. (Riverside County)

(951) 656-5555 / www.johnspizza.com
6187 Valley Springs Parkway, Riverside
      See JOHN'S INCREDIBLE PIZZA CO. (Orange County) on page 248 for details.
Hours: Open Mon. - Thurs., 11am - 9:30pm; Fri., 11am - 11pm; Sat., 10am - 11pm; Sun., 10am - 9:30pm.

JUNGLE ISLAND PAINTBALL PARK

(800) 5JUNGLE (558-6453) or (877) 303-7914 / www.jungle-island.com
14881 Temescal Canyon Road, Lake Elsinore
      It's a jungle out there! Actually, there are fourteen themed, paintball-playing fields on fifty-six acres and the Jungle is only one of them. The Castle field has cement fortresses, archways, and steps galore to hide and seek. Valley field has a mock battle field with a camouflage truck, ambulance, defensive hill, foxholes, and more. Pipes field has countless cylindrical cement pipes. Volcano field looks like there were several eruptions. City field looks like an inner city with vehides and eighteen buildings. There is also Trenches field (go into the trenches, but watch out above), Congo (with monster tire truck bunkers), and more. Games last about twenty minutes. 6 to 12 year olds have their own arena called Little Warriors where they play a version of Paintball called Splatmaster. The markers (i.e., paintballs) have a softer hit and lighter equipment is used. Adults are welcome to play here, too, with a private group. There are also four fields here exclusively for airsoft. See JERICHO AIRSOFT (pg. 343) for more information on them.
      A snack bar serving pizza and beverages is on the premises. A picnic table is out front. Wear appropriate attire - old, long sleeve shirts, jeans, and running boots. A parental waiver, available online, is necessary for ages 17 and under.
Hours: Open Sat. - Sun., 8am - 4pm. Open in the spring and summer on Fri. nights, too, 5pm - 10pm. Call first. Open most school holidays; dosed Thanksgiving and Christmas. Little Warriors Arena is open Sat. - Sun., 9am - noon and 1pm - 4pm.
Price: $25 for walk ons with their own equipment. Package deals, which indude all the necessary gear, start at $55. Little Warriors arena is $20 with their own equipment; $30 for admission and rental gear.
Ages: Must be 10 years or older for paintball.

MULLIGAN FAMILY FUN CENTER (Riverside County)

(951) 696-9696 / www.mulliganmurrieta.com
24950 Madison Avenue, Murrieta
      Calling all ranch hands: Git 'long to Mulligan Family Fun Center for some family fun! Take a look at all the fun props outside, like cowboy mannequins literally hanging around. This western-themed miniature golf center has two impressive **miniature golf** courses, with water hazards and sand traps. (Note: You can see the red rock boulders, small western buildings, and stagecoaches from the freeway when you're heading southbound on the I-15.) A round of golf costs $7.50 for ages 11 and up; $5.99 for seniors and children 10 and under; replays are $3. Other attractions indude **batting cages**; **go-karts** - $6.50 for drivers, $3 for passengers (height restrictions apply); **rookie go-karts** in a police and fire engine cart for guests 40" to 56" and at least 5 years old, $5; **lazer tag** in a 3,500 square-foot arena, which is a lot of running around and shooting space, that's decorated with neon bright colors lighting up some obstades - $6.50; a twenty-one-foot-high **rock climbing wall** - $5.50 for two dimbs; and **Waterworks, a water slides play area**. The hot summers have met their match with this water play structure with several slides; pipes bursting with water; a huge bucket that dumps over water by the, well, bucketloads; stairs; and places to play under the structure where water pours out everywhere, and almost all in zero water depth. At the Kiddie Korral there are four **kiddie rides** - tea cups, train ride, frog hopper, and a carousel - $3 per ride. Complete your day (or night) on the town by coming into the spacious "town hall," which is done up right fine with a jail and kids' saloon (cafe). The cafe serves salads ($6.99 for grilled chicken); pizza ($13.99 for a large cheese); hot dogs ($2.79); chicken strips ($14.99 for an eight-piece); grilled

chicken sandwich ($6.99); and other food essentials. Kids' meals are $4.99 for a choice of chicken nuggets, hot dog, or grilled cheese. There are also plenty of modern-day, shoot-out games (i.e., arcade and video games), including two mini bowling lanes with bumper rails and smaller-than-usual balls. A prize redemption station is here, too. Inside, too, younger kids will enjoy the small Fort Mulligan play area with a multi-level, wooden play structure that looks like, yes, a fort. It also has slides, steps, and room to play underneath.

Hours: Open Mon. - Thurs., 1pm - 8pm; Fri., noon - 10pm; Sat., 11am - 10pm; Sun., 11am - 8pm. Open in the summer, Sun. - Thurs., 11am - 9pm; Fri. - Sat., 11am - 10pm. Closed Thanksgiving and Christmas. The water play areas is open mid-May - summer, Sat., 11am - 6pm; Sun., noon - 5pm.

Price: Attractions are individually priced above. Unlimited all-day passes are available Fri. - Sun. and holidays most of the year, as well as daily during the summer for $21.99. Kiddie Korral all-day passes are $11. Water slides, only, are $14.99. Ask about or check their website for other specials.

Ages: 3 years and up.

PERRIS SKYVENTURE

(800) 832-8818 or (951) 940-4290 / www.skydiveperris.com
2093 Goetz Road, Perris

$$$$$

Have you ever dreamt you could fly? Me, too. Skydiving is one way to get as close as you can to actually flying. This indoor skydiving facility offers both a safe and utterly exhilarating experience. The tall tower houses a wind tunnel that is a skydiving simulator. Walk up stairs to a small classroom to watch a video, learn the hand signals of a flyer, and practice correct body position - back arched, arms and legs slightly bent upward, and chin up. (So natural - not!) Put on a jumpsuit, earplugs, elbow and knee pads, and helmet, and get ready. Participants enter the doorway of a small, glass-enclosed room (i.e., flight chamber) where wind speeds of up to 120 mph blast through the grids on the floor and air gets sucked up from overhead fans. At first, the wind makes it difficult to breath, but then - lift off. As you go horizontal, for a few minutes you experience the sensation of free falling. An instructor is standing by your side, aiding you at all times. First-time flyers generally don't fly higher than about five feet above the ground, but oh - what a feeling!!

Family and friends can watch through the flight chamber windows, or at home via the live-feed web cam. Just tell them your flight time. Souvenir t-shirts (starting at $10) and hats and a DVD of your flight ($35) are available for purchase. Ask about the other flying options, such as group flying, camps, and even aerobatic shows.

Adults, 18 years and up, can go one step further and actually sky dive onto the huge field adjacent to the tower. Classes, instructors, gear, and encouragement are all part of the package. If you opt out of skydiving, sit on the lawn under shade trees and watch the colorful show as the divers jump from the planes and float down onto the landing field. Some of the formations are thrilling. Listen to the parachutes open - they sound like firecrackers. This is a premiere facility to see skydivers from all over the world.

If all of this sounds like more than you want, or can afford to do for now, grab a meal at the onsite BOMBSHELTER SPORTS BAR AND GRILL (pg. 340) and just watch the action. The restaurant offers good food and the opportunity to watch skydiving via the huge picture windows. A small, outdoor, gated pool with lounge chairs is available for skydiving customers and families to use free of charge. How cool is that! Children under 18 years must be supervised by an adult and have a signed waiver to use the pool.

Hours: Indoor skydiving is open most of the year, Mon. - Fri., 9am - 5pm; Sat. - Sun., 8am - 6pm. Open less hours in the summer. Reservations are highly recommended. Closed Thanksgiving and Christmas. The drop zone is open most of the year, Mon. - Fri., 9am - sunset; open daily in the summer, Mon. - Fri., 8am - sunset; Sat. - Sun., 8am - 10pm.

Price: Indoor Skydiving: For first time flyers - about thirty minutes in the staging area and two minutes of flight time is $55 per person. An extra two minutes of flight time is an additional $20 (and worth it!). Block rates are available, starting at $195 for ten minutes of flight time. This can be split among multiple flyers. Ask about skydiving rates.

Ages: 3 and up for the indoor skydiving; 18 and up for real skydiving.

POLE POSITION RACEWAY

Corona - (951) 817-5032; Murrieta - (951) 461-1600 / www.polepositionraceway.com
Corona - 1594 E. Bentley Drive; Murrieta - 41810 McAlby Court

$$$$

Not quite ready for the Grand Prix? This clean, spacious, indoor kart racing facility is the place to race. You will zoom around the state-of-the-art track, wearing provided helmets, in fast electric karts that look like the real thing.

Junior karts are also available. The intensity, adrenaline rush, and competition (against opponents or the clock) are all part of the experience. Check the event calendar for tournaments. Before or after your race, take a look at the collection of racing memorabilia, watch major sporting events on big screen TVs, play some video games or air hockey or pool, or grab a bite to eat at the snack bar. Kids must be at least 48" tall and able to safely operate the kart in order to drive. Minors must have a signed waiver.

Hours: Corona - Open Mon. - Thurs., 11am - 9pm; Fri. 11am - 11pm; Sat., 10am - 11pm; Sun., 10am - 8pm. Murrieta weekend hours are different - Sat., 11am - 11pm; Sun., 11am - 7pm. Both are closed Christmas. Call for holidays hours.

Price: For non-members, the price is $19.95 for adults, 56" and taller, for a 14-lap race; $16.95 for kids, 48" - 55", for a 10-lap race.

Ages: 48" and taller.

PUMP IT UP (Riverside County)

(951) 677-1933 / www.pumpitupparty.com
41785 Elm Street, Murrieta

See PUMP IT UP (San Diego County) on page 491 for details.

Hours: Open Jump hours are Tues. - Thurs. from 10am - noon. There are more Open Jump hours on holiday breaks and during the summer, as well as special events throughout the year.

Price: Open Jump is $8 per child; adults are free.

Ages: 3 years and up.

ROUND1 BOWLING AND AMUSEMENT (Riverside County)

(951) 697-0260 / www.round1usa.com
22500 Town Circle, Suite 2030, Moreno Valley in the Moreno Valley Mall

See ROUND1 BOWLING AND AMUSEMENT (Los Angeles County) on page 39 for details. Bowling at this location starts at $4 a game. See MORENO VALLEY MALL / KIDS CLUB on page 356 for more goings-on at this mall.

Ages: 5 years and up.

S.C. VILLAGE PAINTBALL PARK

(949) 489-9000 or (562) 867-9600 / www.scvillage.com
8900 McCarty Road, Corona

Rambos, Terminators, Xenas, and people from all other walks of life are invited to play paintball on this massive, sixty-acre premiere playing field with twenty different settings. Battle it out in desert terrain, jungle tracts, or even in the city of Beirut. Each field has special props which may include a downed helicopter, ambulance, tents, tanks, radar towers, huts, bridges, tunnels, swamp, camouflage netting, and acres of woods or brush. In this updated version of Capture the Flag, paintball guns and nontoxic gelatin capsules (i.e., paintballs) are used. Two teams compete against each other using the props to run around and hide behind. The object of the game is to somehow capture your opponent's flag and return it to your team's flag station. However, if you are hit with a paintball (which can sting), you are out of the game. Games last twenty to thirty minutes. All games have referees to insure safe and fair play. There are two levels of play - beginner and advanced. Come by yourself or with a group of friends. All amenities, including a food concession, equipment rentals, and supplies are on-site. Participants under 18 must have a waiver signed by a parent or guardian. Note that there is also an airsoft field here.

Hours: Open to the public, Fri., 5pm - 10pm; Sat., 9:30am - 4:30pm and 5pm - 10pm; Sun., 9:30am - 4:30pm. Weekday games are by appointment only for groups of twenty or more.

Price: General admission is $27 for all day paintball - $28 for airsoft - if you come with your own equipment, plus $11 for air. Rental equipment varies in price according to what you want. Goggles/face masks (mandatory) are $6; jumpsuits are $10; guns are about $24; and paintballs start at $19 for 200 rounds. Package deals are available. For instance, a $59 starter package includes all-day admission, full mask, pump rifle, 200 rounds of paintball, and initial tank of CO_2 air. For an additional $5, play all day.

Ages: At least 10 years old.

SKY HIGH PARTY ZONE

(951) 304-9727 / www.skyhighpartyzone.com
26015 Jefferson Avenue, suite D, Murrieta

This indoor play zone is essentially one humongous, carpeted room, done in primary colors, filled with several wonderful inflatables - giant slides; a jousting ring with headgear and lances with large foam tips (jousting is harder than it looks!) and boxing gloves; an Rush Express slide and obstacle course; a basketball court (airball, for some); a cannon bouncer where you launch foam balls; and a African safari where you walk through incredibly large, inflatable tusks, "rock" climb up, and encounter wild animals. Other entertainment includes a few arcade games, air hockey, Dance Dance Revolution, and a ping pong table. Comfy couches create a relaxing place to watch the action. A small tot play area with Little Tyke cars, miniature houses, and other play stuff is in this area, too. A music system (for listening and for karaoke); a snack area (with reasonably-priced chips, sodas, and ice cream for sale); and parent's or private room round out this fun facility. The parent's room has a wide-screen TV, Play Station, dart board, pool table, and couches.

One thing I really appreciate about Sky High is that not only is it open for open play, field trips, team parties, and other private parties, but the facility rents out for almost any age group, including teens and adults. Socks and signed waivers are mandatory for all participants. Ask about Sky High's hours just for special needs kids.

Hours: Open play is Tues. and Wed., 11am - 1:30pm and 5:30pm - 8pm. Family Night, where adults are welcome to stay and play with the kids, is Sat., 6pm - 8:30pm. Closed Mon. and major holidays.
Price: Open play and Family Night are $8 per child; one adult is free with every paid child, additional adults are $5. Parties start at $205 for up to 10 kids.
Ages: 3 years and up.

SKY HIGH SPORTS (Riverside County)

(951) 681-5867 (JUMP) / ont.jumpskyhigh.com
3230 Cornerstone Drive, Mira Loma

See SKY HIGH SPORTS (pg. 266) for details about this fantastic, indoor trampoline place.

Hours: Open Mon., 11am - 9pm; Tues. - Thurs., 2pm - 9pm; Fri., 2pm - midnight; Sat., 10am - midnight; Sun., 10am - 9pm. Open in the summer and on holidays, Mon. - Thurs., 10am - 10pm; Fri - Sat., 10am - midnight; Sun., 10am - 10pm.
Price: $13 an hour; the second hour is $6, Mon. - Thurs. Check for specials.
Ages: 4 years and up.

SKY ZONE (Riverside County)

Ontario - coming!; Riverside - (800) 933-1247; (951) 354-0001 / www.skyzone.com
Ontario - coming!; Riverside - 4031 Flat Rock Dr.

See SKY ZONE (Los Angeles) on pg. 41 for details.

Hours: Open Tues. - Thurs., 3pm - 9pm; Fri., 3pm - 11pm; Sat., 10am - midnight; Sun., 10am - 9pm. Open during the summer and holidays extended hours.
Price: $9 for 30 min., $14 for 60 min., $19 for 90 min.
Ages: 3 years and up.

THRESH HOLD CLIMBING AND FITNESS

(951) 742-8479 / www.climbth.com
2111 Iowa Avenue, unit A, Riverside

The word threshold means a point of beginning, or the point at which a stimulus is of sufficient intensity to begin to produce an effect. Rock climbing fits both of these meanings. This 9,000 square feet of climbing terrain offer top roping routes for both the beginner and expert to conquer and utilize to improve their skills. Bring your own belayer, or come with a "party" of five people for $20 each, and a belayer will be provided.

There are also great bouldering areas with crash pads; upper level observation decks; a full work-out gym with weights, treadmills, ropes, and more; and a WiFi lounge with couches, a large screen TV, and tables and chairs. Ages 17 and under must have a waiver signed by a parent or legal guardian. Ask about the youth programs, summer camps, and joining their competitive climbing team.

Hours: Open Mon. - Fri., 10am - 10pm; Sat., 10am - 8pm; Sun., noon - 7pm. Closed New Years Day, 4th of July, Thanksgiving, and Christmas. The gym closes early on some holidays.

Price:	A day pass is $14 per person, which allows the participant to work out in the gym, too. Ask about specials as they sometimes have a $5 rate available. Shoe rentals are $4, a harness is $3, and chalk bag, $2.
Ages:	5 years and up.

VITAL CLIMBING GYM (Riverside County)

(951) 251-4814 / www.vitalclimbinggym.com

29990 Technology Drive, suite 22, Murrieta

See VITAL CLIMBING GYM (San Diego County) (pg. 495) for details.

Hours:	Open daily, 11am - 9pm. (Open 24-hours for members.) Holiday hours fluctuate.
Price:	The first visit is free for adults; $10 for ages 15 and under. Thereafter, $10 for all ages for a day pass. Optional shoe rentals are $2.
Ages:	At least 5 years, and up.

—GREAT OUTDOORS—

ARLINGTON PARK

(951) 826-2000 / www.riversideca.gov/park_rec

3860 Van Buren Boulevard, Riverside

This nice corner park has a playground and well-used shuffleboard courts. It also has basketball courts, tennis courts, barbecue pits, and a swimming pool.

Hours:	The park is open daily. The pool is open June - August, Mon. - Thurs. and Sat., 1pm - 4pm, and Tues. and Thurs., 6:30pm - 8:30pm. Closed Fri. and Sun.
Price:	Free to the park. Swim sessions for residents are $2.50 for adults; $1 for ages 17 and under; non-residents are $3.75 for adults; $1.50 for ages 17 and under.
Ages:	All

CALIFORNIA CITRUS STATE HISTORIC PARK

(951) 780-6222 - park; (951) 637-8045 - visitors center / www.parks.ca.gov

Van Buren Boulevard and Dufferin Avenue, Riverside

Take a whiff - the park, with its acres of citrus groves, captures the spirit of Riverside's slogan, "The land of citrus and sunshine." The main section is attractively landscaped with plenty of shade trees and has a big, grassy area for running around and for picnicking. Around the corner is a small visitor's center/gift shop/museum in a restored home. The center, which resembles a citrus packinghouse, features mostly historical photographs with narrative regarding the citrus industry. Two-hour school tours, for third and fourth graders, include a guided tour of the museum, the grove, and citrus tasting. Yum!

A good short (1.25 miles round trip) nature hike starts at the gazebo (where interpretative pamphlets are usually available), goes through the groves and to the canal. Don't forget to stop and smell the oranges along the way!

Hours:	The park is open daily, 8am - 5pm; open April - September, Sat. and Sun until 7pm. The visitor center is open Fri - Sun., 10am - 4pm.
Price:	$5 per vehicle. If you just want to visit the visitor center, you can get a pass for free.
Ages:	2 years and up.

CEDAR CREEK

(951) 685-7434 / www.jcsd.us

6709 Cedar Creek Road, Eastvale

This little park is great for the little ones. It has a tot lot and play area, grassy lawn, a cement pathway, picnic tables, BBQs, and a small water play area that is self activating. Turn the green cone on to start the water running. The water play area/splash pad just has fountains that shoot up, but sometimes that's all you need to cool off. The park is also the temporary home of the fire station.

Hours:	The park is open daily, sunrise - sunset. The water feature is available April - October daily, sunrise - sunset.
Price:	Free
Ages:	1 year - 10 years old.

CITRUS PARK

(951) 736-2241 / www.incorona.com/parks.asp
1250 Santana Way, Corona

The twenty-acre Citrus Park is like a park within a park. The park itself has two great playgrounds side-by-side, with slides, speaking tubes, several small towers, ramps, swings, and more. There are also softball fields, picnic tables, and lots and lots of grassy areas to run around.

The park within is a waterpark/splash pad, the base of which looks like an orange slice, with leaves on poles sprouting up (3-D) out from the center. It has several interactive features, such as fountains spurting up from the ground, large rings to walk through that spray, and water cannons to shoot. It's all a slice of refreshment on hot summer days.

Hours: The park is open daily, 5:30am - 10pm. The waterpark is open May - September daily, 10am - 7pm. (Hours may fluctuate.)
Price: Free
Ages: 1 year and up.

CORONA LAKE

(951) 277-4489 / www.fishinglakes.com
12510 Temescal Canyon Road, Corona

See the entry for SANTA ANA RIVER LAKES on page 292 for details.

DAIRYLAND PARK

(951) 685-7434 / www.jcsd.us
14520 San Remo, Eastvale

Some of the best features of this park are the water features on the splash pad. It is self-activating in that when you pass your hand over the yellow rod, the water features turn on. Fountains jet water up from the ground rather randomly, boulders dot the area, and fake palm trees not only decorate the circular wet area, but water rain down from them, too. Benches, with shade, are around the perimeter so parents can dryly watch their kids run, play, and get wet. The rest of this neighborhood park has picnic tables, a nice and enclosed dog park, and plenty of wide open space.

Hours: Open daily, sunrise - sunset. The water park is open April - October, daily, sunrise - sunset.
Price: Free
Ages: 1 year - 10 years old.

DIAMOND VALLEY LAKE

(877) DVL-LAKE (385-5253) - recorded info; (800) 590-LAKE (5253) / (951) 926-7201 - marina / www.dvmarina.com; www.dvlake.com
Domenigoni Parkway, Hemet

This enormous, man-made lake (i.e., reservoir) holds 260 billion gallons of water - enough to secure a six-month supply in case of an earthquake emergency. (I knew you wanted to know that!) With its twenty-six miles of shoreline, you can fish from designated areas at the water's edge, seasonally, for perch, catfish, bass, and trout, or try your luck from a boat. Sailing and other boating opportunities are available - check the website for boating regulations. There are also two large dams (and one smaller one) to contain the water - one on the west end of the lake, and one on the east.

Drive westward on Domenigoni Parkway (to a security check point), park, and then walk up a short paved road to the viewpoint, which offers a panoramic vista of the lake, surrounding mountains, the dam, and the open space/wild animal corridor. You won't be here long, but it's an interesting stop and see. Feeling in good physical shape? Hike the six-mile pedestrian/equestrian trail that starts near the viewpoint (parking, picnic tables, and water for horses is available here), and stretches to just north of the visitor's center, on Searl Parkway. Bring water. Feeling in great shape? Hike or bike the 21.8-mile pedestrian/bicycle trail (or a portion of it) that circumnavigates the lake. Restrooms, and some shade, are found along the hilly Lakeview Trail. You'll also get great views of the lake, the dams, and the quarry where rocks were mined for the dams.

Just up the road is the WESTERN SCIENCE CENTER (pg. 365), the DIAMOND VALLEY LAKE VISITOR'S CENTER (pg. 358), and the DIAMOND VALLEY LAKE COMMUNITY PARK / AQUATIC CENTER (pg. 350).

Hours: The lake is open daily, sunrise - sunset. The viewpoint is open Mon. - Fri., 8:30am - 4pm; Sat. - Sun., 9am - 4:30pm.

Price: The lake is $7 for parking; $3 per person for a fishing access permit. All fishermen/fisherwomen must have a valid fishing license. Boat rentals are $30 an hour; $60 a half day for a basic fishing boat; $50 an hour for an eight-person pontoon. Hiking is $2 for adults (trail fee); free for ages 12 and under; $5 for equestrians (all ages).

Ages: 4 years and up.

DIAMOND VALLEY LAKE COMMUNITY PARK AND AQUATIC CENTER

(951) 929-0047 - aquatic center; (951) 926-5917 - park / www.vwrpd.org
1801 Angler Avenue, Hemet

This park's best summertime feature is the heated 25-meter pool that has a long, twisty water slide. Riders must be at least 48" tall. Younger ones can splash around in the connected, but kind of separate, colorful, water playground which has a few short slides, an enclosed slide, tunnels to crawl through, a cargo net bridge, and water equipment that sprays, squirts, drips, and waterfalls, all in an ankle-deep wading area. Lots of lounge chairs make it a nice place for mom and dad to hang out, too. No coolers or outside food are allowed in. Dive in movie night and ice cream socials are offered on special nights during the summer.

The park also features eight lighted baseball diamonds, soccer fields, two pickleball courts, picnic areas, a fitness trail, and play areas. What a fun place to spend the day! Just up the road is the WESTERN SCIENCE CENTER (pg. 365), the DIAMOND VALLEY LAKE VISITOR'S CENTER (pg. 358), and the DIAMOND VALLEY LAKE (pg. 349).

Hours: The park is open daily, sunrise - sunset. The pool is open weekends only, May through mid-June. Open in the summer, Mon. - Fri., 12:30pm - 4:30pm; Sat. - Sun., 12pm - 5pm.

Price: The park is free. The pool is $6 for ages 3 and up, $5 for seniors Mon. - Fri.; $7 for ages 3 and up, $6 for seniors Sat. - Sun. Children 2 and under are $2 every day.

Ages: 1 and up.

FAIRMOUNT PARK

(951) 826-2000 - park / www.riversideca.gov/park_rec
2601 Fairmount Boulevard, Riverside

This lush park has a lot to offer. The huge, all-access and very fun circus and carousel-themed playground has swings, slides, bridges, metal climbing apparatus, interactive panels, places underneath the raised platforms to imagine and play, a mini Ferris wheel, and an entire section that is covered by the big top. A zero-depth splashpad offer a fun and welcome reprieve during the summer months. The surrounding grassy area is large, with plenty of shade trees and picnic tables. With all this, plus tennis courts, basketball courts, and horseshoe pits, kids can play here all day. Pedal boats are available to rent in the summer time, too. The park's rose garden is located at the corner of Redwood and Dexter drives.

Take a winding drive around the lakes, and watch out for the ducks - they're everywhere. Don't forget your fishing poles as you can stop almost anywhere to fish, including from a small, horseshoe-shaped pier. A fishing permit is required.

The Information Center is open Monday through Friday, 8am to 5pm, and on the weekends, 10am to 5pm. It has exhibits of local history and environmental projects. You'll have a better than fair day at Fairmount Park!

Hours: The park is open daily, sunrise - 7pm.
Price: Free.
Ages: All

HIDDEN VALLEY WILDLIFE AREA

(951) 785-7452 / www.rivcoparks.org
11401 Arlington Avenue, Riverside

Aptly named, this 1,500-acre wildlife area is indeed off the beaten path. There are several options to see at least parts of this "park": Drive along the ridge to see vast expanses of treeless stretches that are close to the road, and wooded areas that are further back into the park; hike along the numerous trails (twenty-five miles!) and view the wildlife closer up; or horseback ride, which is obviously a popular option judging from the number of horse trailers we observed.

As Hidden Valley is located along the Santa Ana River, much of the wildlife encouraged and seen here are migratory birds. There are many ponds, too, as you'll discover if you hike into this sprawling park. A small Nature Center is up the road a bit.

Hours: Open most of the year daily, 7am - 4:30pm; open Memorial Day - Labor Day daily, 7am - 7pm. The Nature Center is open Sat., 10am - 4pm; other days by appointment.

Price: $6 per vehicle

Ages: 4 years and up.

HUNTER PARK

(951) 826-2000 - park; (951) 779-9024 - Live Steamers train rides / www.riversideca.gov/park_rec

1400 Iowa Avenue, Riverside

Hunter Park is composed mostly of grassy playing fields. Its best feature occurs on the second and fourth Sunday of each month when scale model train rides are offered. Kids love taking a ride on the track that encircles the park.

Hours: Steam train rides are on the second and fourth Sun., 10am - 2pm.

Price: Free

Ages: All

HUNT PARK

(951) 826-2000 or (951) 351-6132 / www.riversideca.gov

4015 Jackson Street, Riverside

This park has several family-fun amenities such as a softball field (with lights); basketball court (with lights); volleyball court; playground; run around space; picnic facilities; soccer field; swimming pool; a community center; and a 17,000 square-foot, lighted, cement skate park that has street course elements such as ledges, stairs and rails, as well as a cement bowl and other features. A helmet and pads are required for skateboarding.

Hours: The park is open daily, sunrise - sunset. The skate park is open daily, 10am - dusk. The pool is open mid- June - Labor Day, Mon. - Thurs., 1pm - 4pm and 7pm - 8:30pm; Sat., 1pm - 4pm.

Price: The park and skate park are free. Admission to the pool is $2.50 for adults; $1.75 for ages 17 and under for residents; non-residents are .75¢ more.

Ages: All

JEAN'S CHANNEL CATS

(951) 679-6562

28393 Somers Road, Murrieta

Ironically, Jean's Channel Cats is a fishing spot! Just off a dirt road, this enclosed, quite lovely, old-fashioned, nice-sized, stocked, fishing pond is a relaxing place to take in the scenery of the distant mountains while fishing for catfish during the warmer months, and rainbow trout during the cooler months. Picnic tables, some shade trees, a bait and tackle/snack shop, fish-cleaning area, and outhouse complete the amenities here. Fishing poles are available to purchase for $20 per, so bring your own. Hopefully, you'll bring some dinner home.

Hours: Open Fri. - Sun. and holiday Mon., 8am - 5pm.

Price: $10 per fisherman; $5 per non-fisherman. The fish (no throwbacks allowed) cost $7 per pound. Cash only.

Ages: 3 years and up.

LAKE PERRIS STATE RECREATION AREA

(951) 940-5600 or (951) 940-5603 - general info; (951) 657-2179 - marina; (951) 657-0676 - Indian Museum; (800) 444-7275 - camping reservations; (951) 940-5656 - school tours. / www.parks.ca.gov

17801 Lake Perris Drive, Perris

Come for at least a day of play at the popular Lake Perris. This gigantic (8,800 acres!), man-made lake supports a multitude of water activities. (It's hot out here in the summer, so you'll need them.) There are two swim beaches with placid waters along sandy shores, plus adjacent grassy areas, a small playground, and barbecue pits. For your boating pleasure choose a four passenger boat for $30 for the first two hours (two hour minimum), and $8 an hour after that, or a pontoon boat for $85 for the first three hours. Waterskiing is available, if you bring your own boat. A cove is here for nonmotorized boats, such as sail boats and kayaks. Fish at the lake and catch a big one, or at least try to. A license and day permit is required for those 16 years and over. Licenses and bait are available at the Lake Perris Store.

Drier activities include geocaching; listening to a concert at the amphitheater; picnicking; rock climbing (just around on the boulders or, specifically at Big Rock, which has 110 bolts, so you must bring your own equipment); and biking or hiking on the fairly-level, nine-mile, mostly-paved trail that goes around the lake. What more could nature-loving kids want?! Camping! There is so much to do at Lake Perris that you'll want to spend a night, or two, here. Ask about their summer programs, such as campfire times held on Saturday evenings and the Jr. Ranger program for ages 7 to 12. Also check out the Ya' Heki' Regional Indian Museum, which is free with paid park admission. The museum highlights this area's Native Americans via photos, dioramas, and artifacts.

Hours: Mid-November - mid-March, the lake is open daily, 6am - 6:30pm; the rest of the park is open daily, 6am - 8pm. Mid-March - mid-November the lake is open daily. 6am - 8:30pm; the rest of the park, daily, 6am - 10pm. The Ya' Heki' Indian Museum is open Fri., 10am - 2pm; Sat. - Sun., 10am - 4pm. School tours can call to make an appointment for other times.

Price: $10 per vehicle; $9 for seniors; $8 per vessel/watercraft. Tent camping is $30 a night March - November; $25 during off season. Seniors are $2 less. RV camping is $45. Prices include vehicle admission, but not the $8 camping reservation fee.

Ages: All

LAKE SKINNER COUNTY PARK   ☼

(951) 926-1505 or (951) 926-1541 - park; (800) 234-7275 -camping reservations. / www.rivcoparks.org $$
37701 Warren Road, Winchester

Here's the skinny on Lake Skinner. The main attraction is fishing, either from a boat (a four-passenger motorboat is $28 for the first two hours, which is the minimum), or from the shore. A California state license is required for ages 16 and up. Day permits for fishing are $4 for adults; $2 for children 12 years and under. Ten passenger pontoon boats are $60 for two hours, which is the minimum. It's a $100 deposit for motorboats and $250 deposit for pontoon boats. The well-equipped marina offers all sorts of fishing supplies as well as a cafe/restaurant for those who didn't have much luck catching their own meal.

Other activities include hiking, picnicking, and playing on the modern, two-story playground with its twisty slides, chain climbing "walls", and other fun elements. Cool off at the good-size garden - a splash pad that has oversized "flowers", leaves and plant stalks that spout water along with water that shoots up from the ground. Boulders are inter-sprinkled. A smaller, separate, water play area has a giant faucet - that pours out water - and handles, and more water shooting up from the padded ground. Overnight camping is available here as well.

Hours: The park is open daily, 6am - dusk. Fishing is available daily, 6am - dark. The splash pad is open April - October, Mon., noon - 6pm (holidays Mon. at 10am); Tues. - Sun., 10am - 6pm.

Price: $6 per vehicle, Mon. - Fri.; $8 - $15 on weekends, holidays and special events. Walk-ins are $2 per person; dogs and horses are $1. Tent camping is $23 a night. RV camping is $30 with full hook ups. The camping reservation fee is $8.

Ages: All

LOUIS ROBIDOUX NATURE CENTER   ☼

(951) 683-4880 / www.rivcoparks.org   !/$
5370 Riverview Drive, Riverside

This nature park is wonderful for kids who have an adventuresome spirit. A grouping of big rocks in front of the nature center is fun for climbers. A pond is at the trailhead of Willow Creek Trail, which is an easy half-mile loop to walk around. Other pathways veer off in all directions, allowing some real hiking excursions. Walk along a tree-lined creek; explore the woodlands and water wildlife along the Santa Ana River; or go farther into the Regional Park system along the horse trail that has extensive chaparral. No biking is allowed, and only off-road strollers will make it. Pick up a self-guided trail map, which also has nature questions for kids to answer.

The main building, or Interpretive Center, houses live animals such as snakes, plus taxidermied animals, and an extensive butterfly and insect collection. Kids are welcome to touch the various animals pelts; use the discovery boxes that contain skulls, seeds, or feathers; or just play with the puzzles. As with most nature centers, special programs are offered throughout the year, such as night hikes, summer camps, and Butterfly Day in April. Note: The trail by the parking lot leads into RANCHO JURUPA PARK (pg. 353).

Hours: The park and trails are open daily, sunrise - sunset. The Interpretive Center is open to the public on Sat., 10am - 4pm. With advanced reservations, it's open Tues. - Fri. for school groups and other large groups.

Price: Usually free, $3 per person during special events.
Ages: All

MCVICKER SKATE PARK - CANYON PARK

(951) 674-9000 / www.lake-elsinore.org
29355 Grand Avenue, Lake Elsinore

A focal point of this entire park is the large (18,000 square feet!), lighted, supervised skate park on a concrete slab with ramps made of skatelite surface. The street course has grind rails, a mini half-pipe, a half pyramid, and several planters and ledges. All the elements are spaced out so there is plenty of room to skate, maneuver, and gain speed. BMX riders and scooter riders are allowed on the course at certain times. Sessions are two hours long and all participants must wear safety gear (rentals are available) and have a signed parental waiver, if 17 or younger. Ages 10 and under must have a parent supervising here. The rest of the park consists of two baseball fields, a small playground, and some picnic tables.

Hours: The skate park is open Wed. - Sat., 3pm - 9pm; Sun., 2pm - 6pm. Call for specific sessions.
Price: All sessions are free for residents; $5 a day for non-residents. A rental pack is $5. Exact cash or check only.
Ages: 6 years and up, only, for the skate park.

MOUNT RUBIDOUX

(951) 826-2000 / www.riversideca.gov/park_rec
Mount Rubidoux Drive and 9th Street, Riverside

For kids who enjoy a somewhat rugged hike, climbing Mount Rubidoux is a great adventure. The steep, almost three-mile (roundtrip) trail winds around the hill that is barren except for boulders and cacti. "The trail is two miles up and one mile down." Reaching the top is a climax. At the top is a cross and a flag. There are also rocks to climb. On a clear day, the panoramic view of the San Gabriel and San Bernardino Mountains is beautiful. On the western slope of the hill, watch vintage planes take off and land at Rubidoux's Flabob Airport. (A paved trail is down this side of the hill.) Hiking here in the summer gets hot, so bring a water bottle. Plan on about an hour-and-a-half round trip. Next door, along the river, is the Mount Rubidoux Park. The bike trail at the base of the mountain goes a few miles back to Martha McClean/Anza Narrow Park and beyond.

Hours: Open daily, sunrise - sunset.
Price: Free
Ages: It depends how far up you want to hike!

RANCHO JURUPA PARK

(951) 684-7032 - park; (800) 234-PARK (7275) - camping and cabin reservations / www.rivcoparks.org
4800 Crestmore Road, Riverside

This huge (200-acre) mountain-wilderness park, which is part of the even bigger Santa Ana River Regional Park system, provides a delightful escape from the city. Where to start? The three-acre lake is stocked with trout in the cooler months and catfish in the summertime. Fishermen (and women) 16 years and older must have a state fishing license. Near the lake is a big play structure with slides, swings, monkey bars, towers, twisty-metal climbing apparatus, and more. Horseshoe pits are located over here, too.

Enjoy a day (or two or three) here by camping in one of the 140 camp sites that are slotted in a big open space near one end of the lake. Coin-operated showers (be quick!), a general store, and laundry facility are available. If camping isn't your thing, rent a cabin. The six cabins sleep up to four people and have bunk beds, a room with a queen-size bed, a bathroom, and a room with full kitchen facilities, an eating area with table and chairs, and a couch. Each cabin has a front porch, too, and a picnic table in the small front yard.

On the other side of the main lake are a few smaller lakes; big, grassy open spaces for baseball or whatever; plenty of picnic tables; and barbecue pits. The boulder play area is great for kids to use their unlimited imaginations to hide, play cowboy, or whatever else they pretend. The good-size splash pad for kids (or anyone who wants to get wet) is open usually March through September. It features poles that hold buckets of water that spill over onto waiting kids below, pipes bursting with water from their seams, water cannons, and a water play structure with steps, ropes, poles, and other fun elements. A pretty, rustically-landscaped with lots of boulders, eighteen-hole miniature golf course, surrounded by waterfalls, adds to the fun here. The cost to play is $5 per person. Flip your wrist with just the right amount of twist to make the disc fly and land in the holes at the disc golf course, which is free to play with entrance

into the park. Bike rentals are available and help you enjoy your time here that much more.

Hike trails throughout the wooded landscape and meadows, and enjoy an easy hike along the river trail to the adjoining LOUIS ROBIDOUX NATURE CENTER (pg. 352) where more trails, an Interpretive Center, and more rocks to climb on await your kids.

Hours: Open Sun . - Thurs., 7am - sunset; Fri. - Sat., 7am - 10pm.

Price: $5 for adults; $2 for ages 16 and under. Dogs and horses are $1 each. Fishing is $8 for ages 16 and older; $5 for ages 6 - 15; children 5 and under fish for free with a paid adult. A campsite is $25; with full hook-ups, it's $30. Group rates are available. Cabins are $80 a night, Sun. - Thurs.; $100 a night, Fri. - Sat. with a two-night minimum. Holidays are extra.

Ages: All

ROCK VISTA PARK

(951) 736-2241 / www.incorona.com
2481 Steven Drive, Corona

Climbing on rocks makes kids happy - it just does. And that's pretty much what this park has to offer. An enormous grassy area has a looping dirt trail, interspersed with groupings of trees and boulders, that leads up to the surrounding hills. Some of the hills have houses on top, but one in particular just has a cluster of rocks and boulders that are high enough, but not too high. This might not sound like fun, but imaginations are given reign here. I also like the "stream" of rocks that wind down a portion of the park.

Hours: Open daily, sunrise - sunset.

Price: Free

Ages: 2 years and up.

RONALD REAGAN SPORTS PARK AND COMMUNITY RECREATION CENTER / TEMECULA SKATE PARK

(951) 694-6410 - park; (951) 695-1409 - skate park / www.cityoftemecula.org
30875 Rancho Vista, Temecula

Have a ball at this terrific sports park! It has twelve ball fields, seven soccer fields, lots of open grassy areas for running around, two great playgrounds, shade trees, picnic shelters, and barbecue grills. The roller hockey rink has some open time, although it is used mostly by leagues. Bring your Tony Hawk wannabes to practice at the gated, one-acre, staffed, outdoor cement skate park which is equipped with all the "necessary" features. The sixty-foot-diameter bowl has ramp entry which also leads to an upper bowl with a street plaza that consists of a pyramid, fun box, curbs, ramps, stairs, and a hand rail. All participants must have a signed waiver form prior to park entry. Proper safety equipment is mandatory - helmet, elbow pads, and knee pads - and may be rented on site.

The indoor gym offers basketball, but it can be set up for volleyball, too. Keep your cool in the twenty-five-meter outdoor swimming pool that has a diving board and a water slide. There is also a shallow pool just for tots. The Teen Center is a great place for 12 to 18 year olds to hang out. It offers pool, air hockey, ping pong, Carom, Nintendo, and more. This park offers everything active kids need - my boys would be very happy living there!

Hours: The park is open daily, sunrise - 10pm. The skate park is open Mon. - Fri., 4pm - 8pm; Sat., 3:15pm - 8pm; Sun., 1:15pm - 6pm. The sessions vary for scooters or skateboards - check the website calendar. The skate park is open in the summer Mon., Wed., Fri., Sat., 2pm - 8pm; Tues., Thurs., 9am - 3pm; Sun., 1pm - 6pm. The roller hockey rink is usually available for open play Mon. - Fri. before 3:30pm and Sun. until 3:30pm. After 4pm and on most weekends it's booked for league play. Call for pool hours, as they fluctuate.

Price: The park is free. Skateboard sessions are free for residents; $5 for nonresidents. Pool sessions are $2.50 for adults; $1 for seniors and ages 12 and under for residents; $5 for nonresidents of any age. The Teen Center asks that a resident card be purchased - $1 for a year's membership.

Ages: All ages for the park. Skateboarders under 7 years must be accompanied by an adult. Kids must be from 12 to 18 years to hang out inside the Teen Center.

SANTANA REGIONAL PARK

(951) 736-2241 / www.discovercorona.com; www.incorona.com
598 Santana Way, Corona

One of the park's best features is the nice cement skate park with a pool, fun boxes, steps, grinding rails, and

pyramids. Lighted ball fields, soccer fields, cement pathways, grassy areas, a playground (with a zip line), and more round out this twenty-one-acre park.

> **Hours:** Open daily, 5:30am - 10pm.
> **Price:** Free
> **Ages:** 6 years and up.

SANTA ROSA PLATEAU ECOLOGICAL RESERVE

(951) 677-6951 / www.santarosaplateau.org
39400 Clinton Keith Road, Murrieta

From riparian stream sides to basalt-capped mesas, this gigantic 9,000-acre reserve covers the gamut of topography. The thirty-plus trails range from easy, one-mile hikes to hardier five-mile round-trip hikes. Depending on which trail you choose, you'll hike through oak woodlands, acres of grasslands, chaparral, up the Santa Ana mountains, and down to creek beds. Look for tree frogs and turtles in the water, and ground squirrels, woodpeckers, hawks, and horned lizards along the wooded pathways. There is a picnic spot at the vernal pools, which is a four-mile round-trip hike. Pick up a trail map from the visitors center where there are also a few displays to look at. Guided hikes are offered some Saturdays at 10am and other interpretive programs are offered at various times by reservation. A plethora of school, scouting, and other programs and tours are offered.

> **Hours:** Open daily, sunrise - sunset. The visitor's center is open Tues. - Sun., 9am - 5pm. Closed Mon.
> **Price:** $3 for adults; $2 for children 2 - 12.
> **Ages:** 3 years and up.

SKULL CANYON ZIPLINE

(951) 471-0999 / www.skullcanyon.com
13540 Temescal Canyon Boulevard, Corona

Skull Canyon is a great local place to go for a combination of good hiking and ziplining. Get geared up in this shaded outdoor facility nestled into the 160 acres of canyons and hillsides. One choice is the Original Course, which incorporates a ten-minute hike uphill and has six different ziplines varying between 200 and 660 feet long. The weight limits are 60 lbs up to 250 lbs and the cost is $85 per person. The other choice is for those who are a little more daring - the Extreme Course. The thirty-minute hike is followed by five ziplines with a total length of more than double that of the Original Course. It is higher, longer and faster, and not for those with a fear of heights. The weight limits are 100 lbs up to 250 lbs and the cost is $115 per person. No more than ten people go on either of the two-hour excursions, so the attention from the guide is personal. Ziplining is a thrilling adventure! The guides here not only make it a fun and educational excursion, as you learn about the eco-systems, but a memorable one as well. This is a great group bonding activity.

For those who are impatient, or want a quick adrenaline fix, do the Speed Run. It's actually the last run of the Extreme Course, a 1,600 foot, side-by-side, racing zipline. All yours for $40. Spectators for any of the outings can hang in the shade and enjoy a picnic here.

> **Hours:** Open daily. Call to make a reservation.
> **Price:** Prices are listed above.
> **Ages:** 60 lbs to 250 lbs.

STAGECOACH PARK

(951) 736-2241 / www.incorona.com
2125 Stagecoach Road, Corona

Seems like this town <u>is</u> big enough for the both of us, or even more than that! This little playground is set up like an Old Western town, with smaller buildings and funner things to play on. The two-story Post Office and connected General Store have stairs, slides, balconies, short rock climbing walls, wagon wheel climbing walls, ladders, and poles. There are a few other free-standing play apparatus with bridges, climbing structures, and slides, including one that is a stagecoach. Climb aboard to ride it, looking out the little side windows, and whoosh down the attached slide. There are also speaking tubes, swings, a decent-sized rock climbing rock, monkey bars (rings), chin up bars, and black ponies on huge springs to ride back and forth on, plus benches with wagon wheels on the sides of them, a covered picnic area with bbqs, grassy spaces, and a .4 miles paved pathway.

> **Hours:** Open daily, sunrise - sunset.
> **Price:** Free

Ages: 2 - 9 years.

STONEY MOUNTAIN PARK

(951) 658-3211 / www.sanjacintovalley.info/parks.html
Inglestone Drive and Cinnabar Avenue, Hemet

This small playground has colorful equipment with a short tower, slides, and other equipment. There is also a basketball court here and, best of all, a short trail dotted with trees and surrounded by grass, that leads to a good-sized hill of boulders and rocks. I love climbing and scrambling around on rocks and my kids share this passion, so we think this park is "boulderdacious."

Hours: Open daily, sunrise - sunset
Price: Free
Ages: 2 - 13 years old.

UNIVERSITY OF CALIFORNIA AT RIVERSIDE BOTANIC GARDENS

(951) 784-6962 or (951) 827- 4650 / www.gardens.ucr.edu
Campus Drive, at the University of California, Riverside

Riverside's climate ranges from subtropical to desert to mountains, all within forty acres and four miles of hilly trails. A gently-sloping walkway provides access to the gardens' main areas for wheelchairs and strollers. Explore the botanic gardens to see rose gardens, fruit orchards, an herb garden, saguaros, barrel cacti, pine trees, giant sequoias, and more.

Besides the diverse plant life, numerous animals share this habitat. Be on the lookout for bunnies, lizards, squirrels, snakes, coyotes, and numerous bird species. A main trail loops around and is walkable in forty-five minutes. At the far end of the trail is a pond supporting more wildlife such as frogs, turtles, dragonflies, and koi. A dome-shaped building made of cedar that houses a "living fossils" collection and a greenhouse are more discoveries you'll make along the way. Come with your kids to enjoy the beauty of the gardens, and/or come for an educational field trip.

Hours: Open daily, 8am - 5pm. Closed New Year's Day, Primavera Day (sometime in mid-May), July 4th, Thanksgiving, and Christmas.
Price: Free, but $5 donation is suggested. Parking is .25¢ an hour. See page x for info on AHS reciprocal memberships.
Ages: All

—MALLS—

KIDS OUTLET at LAKE ELSINORE OUTLETS

(951) 245-0087 / www.lakeelsinoreoutlet.com
17600 Collier Avenue, suite 106 at Lake Elsinore Outlets, Lake Elsinore

Twice a week kids have a special time of entertainment, learning, and creating at the Outlet. The one-hour event has featured a drum circle workshop where kids (and adults) were taught how to play the drums; a puppet show; storytelling; making and decorating a picture frame; making a flip book; decorating an umbrella (♪ ella, ella); doing science experiments; and a presentation of tidepool animals to learn about and then gently touch. Call or check the website to see what's coming next.

The Outlet has about fifty name-brand stores and restaurants for your shopping and dining pleasure.

Hours: Kids Outlet meets every Wed. and Fri. at 11am.
Price: Free
Ages: 3 years and up.

MORENO VALLEY MALL - KIDS CLUB

(951) 653-1177 / www.morenovalleymall.com
22500 Town Circle, Suite 2030, Moreno Valley in the Moreno Valley Mall

Kids gather together and have club time here for about an hour, once a month. Each month's activity looks different depending on what holiday or season is being celebrated. It could be a storytelling event, or craft, or entertainment of some sort - come by and see. Parent tip: Want to go see a movie but don't have a babysitter? The Harkins Multiplex theatre offers an on-site supervised play center with crafts, games, books, complimentary popcorn

and even a movie area for your potty-train kids ages 3 to 8 years for only $6 per child! Call (951) 653-6161 for more info. The mall also features a free play area by the food court. See ROUND1 BOWLING AND AMUSEMENT (Riverside County) on page 346 for another fun place to go.

> **Hours:** Kids Club is the first Wednesday of each month at 10am, near Round 1.
> **Price:** Free
> **Ages:** 2 - 10 years

THE PROMENADE IN TEMECULA - KIDS CLUB

(951) 296-0975 / www.promenadeintemecula.com
40820 Winchester Road, Temecula

This mall has a lot going on! Kids (and adults) can watch a movie at the Edwards Cinema during the summer on Tuesdays and Wednesdays at 10am for only $1 per person. The Kids Club program offers a free craft project, activity, or education program for ages 3 to 10, once a week near the JC Penney court, usually only in the summer. There are other Kids Club events on select Fridays throughout the year. Open all year round is Paradise Play Land, a soft-play area with cars to climb on and over, a few very short slides, and a resting area for parents. Other happenings can include live entertainment, such as a concert or Inland Idol competition; a Farmer's Market every Wednesday from 9am to 1pm with fresh fruits and veggies, and crafts for the kids; and seasonal festivities such as photos with the Easter Bunny, craft activity, and an Easter celebration with a continental breakfast while dressed in pj's. Circus Vargas is usually here the end of March and the first few weeks of April. Get tickets and more information at (877) 468-3861 / www.circusvargas.com.

A few stores to take note of here include BUILD-A-BEAR WORKSHOP (see pg. 366) and an interactive and magical DISNEY STORE (see pg. 367 for details).

> **Hours:** Call or check the website for a listing of events. The Kids Club is usually held Thurs., 11am - 1pm during the summer; check for other times throughout the year.
> **Price:** Free
> **Ages:** 3 - 10 years.

—MUSEUMS—

CALIFORNIA MUSEUM OF PHOTOGRAPHY

(951) 784-FOTO (3686) or (951) 827-4787 / www.artsblock.ucr.edu
3824 Main Street, Riverside

Expose your kids to the photographic arts at the unique, three-story California Museum of Photography. The main level has rotating photo exhibits, with an emphasis on various photography styles or photographers, such as Ansel Adams. The back area houses a part of the museum's vast collection of vintage cameras, including working miniature cameras (my boys refer to them as "spy" cameras), old-fashioned cameras with the drape cloth, a Spiderman camera, and one that is part of a radio-controlled car!

Take the spiral stairs up to the mezzanine terrace, which is a catwalk-like hallway gallery. The top floor often focuses on kids with its small, interactive gallery with rotating exhibits. When we visited, children used the Zoetropes to draw pictures and spin them around in a drum, creating moving images - early animation! We also learned that not all shadows are black as the images shadowed here produced a rainbow of colors. The next display visually explained how the aperture of a camera is similar to the pupils in eyes. We looked into a light and watched in the mirror as our pupils enlarged or contracted, according to the amount of light entering in. The Shadows Room temporarily imprinted body outlines on the photosensitive wall when a light flashed. Use computers in the Digital Studio to see some of the wonders that can be performed with digital photography.

Camera Obscura is a small, dark room with a tiny hole of light that projects an upside-down image of the outside scene on its wall. This is a visual demonstration of how a camera lens works. Kids will get a wide angle view of photography at this Museum! Note: Guided school tours are available for 7th through 12th graders. This museum, and several others in the area plus galleries, are open for free, October through May for community events: the first Sunday of each month for First Sundays, with crafts and activities for families, 1pm to 4pm, and on the first Thursday, 6pm to 9pm, for Riverside Artswalk. Adjacent to the museum, and part of the Artblock, is the Sweeney Art Gallery, a cafe, a seventy-five seat film screening room, and a natural light atrium gallery and performance space.

> **Hours:** The museum is open Tues. - Sat., noon - 5pm. Open the first Thurs. from 6pm - 9pm and the first Sun. from 1pm - 4pm. Closed most Sun., Mon., New Year's Day, Thanksgiving, and Christmas.

Price: $3 for adults; seniors, students and children 11 and under are free. Entrance is free on the first Thurs., 6pm - 9pm and the first Sun., 1pm - 4pm.

Ages: 3 years and up just to look at things; ages 5 and up will begin to really appreciate it.

DIAMOND VALLEY LAKE VISITOR'S CENTER

(951) 765-2612

2325 Searl Parkway, Hemet

Where does our water come from? That question and many more are answered by exploring this unique visitor's center, which is more like a museum and educational facility featuring several exhibit galleries - just go with the flow. Above the reception desk is an enclosed waterfall. A small alcove here holds computers with games to play, plus pamphlets about Diamond Valley Lake and hiking trails. Look up over the hallway entrance to see a huge mermaid and merman.

Dive into the room on the left by first looking at the pictorial timeline showing the history of water in California, incorporating Spanish armor and some picks used by Gold Rush Forty-niners. This room seems like it's underwater because towards the blue-hued ceiling the underside of a rock-lined lake is depicted. Lily pads "float" on it while fish, sea turtles, frogs, and other creatures "swim" in the suspended water. Very cool. Watch educational and entertaining films regarding water properties, qualities, and uses hosted by an animated, smart alec water drop (think Robin Williams in *Aladdin*) called Hydro. The screens are in an aquarium-like setting. Yank (hard!) on levers to light up areas on the large globe that have fresh, salt, or frozen water. Look through large microscopes to get a close-up look at photosynthesis at work. Note that an adjacent Liquid Lifeline Theater shows films regarding various water topics on a small TV screen.

Across the way, go behind a curtain and peer into a well to see an animated movie on Roman aqueducts and dinosaurs. (They <u>do</u> go together.)

The next room tracks the journey water takes from reservoirs and aqueducts to a home in California. This is done via oversized maps, a power station with hydroelectric turbines and pumps, a display featuring dam construction, sedimentation station, and even filters to open and touch the various rocks. To recreate pumping water, get on an exercise bike and pedal to pump water up to the top of the attached cylinder. Is the water heavier as it gets higher (or am I just out of shape)? Behind another curtain is a 4-D map of the story of California water, accompanied by lights and sounds. Be sure to look in all the nooks and crannies of this center, such as the display case holding artifacts they unearthed while digging the site which includes an ice age mastodon tusk.

Instruments on the wall at the end of the hall show real time temperature, wind speed, and solar intensity. There are also photographs of plants and animals found in the immediate area as well as a larger-than-life pictoral timeline of the history of the planners and builders of the aqueduct. Can you *fathom* all that your child can learn and experience at this facility, and for free? Outback are unshaded picnic tables and a water cycle table used for all the amazing school tours provided here. Note that a trailhead for the almost six-mile North Hills Trail is behind the center.

The acreage is shared with WESTERN SCIENCE CENTER (pg. 365). DIAMOND VALLEY LAKE COMMUNITY PARK / AQUATIC CENTER (pg. 350) is just around the corner, and DIAMOND VALLEY LAKE (pg. 349) is down the road.

Hours: Open Thurs. - Sun., 10am- 4pm.

Price: Free

Ages: 3 years and up.

FINGERPRINTS YOUTH MUSEUM

(951) 765-1223 / www.fingerprintsmuseum.com

123 S. Carmalita Street, Hemet

This place has kids' fingerprints all over it! The huge, rectangular room is divided into sections with various hands-on exhibits and activities. Each one emphasizes a particular educational aspect that visitors can touch, learn about, and test. Note: Some exhibits do rotate.

The first section allows open play with building supplies, puzzles, and bins of arts and crafts materials, plus colorful tables and chairs. The adjacent party room has a great undersea mural. Kids can uncover bones at a paleontology pit that uses recycled rubber instead of sand. To the right is a book nook to sit and read. Great animal and habitat murals are the backdrop against the enclosed Little Critters Kingdom (for your little critters) that has a wooden play boat; petite constructed army jeeps; really big blocks; short play structures; and a play kitchen with all the appliances.

Be green: A Waste Management truck is parked in a section on composting and recycling information. Storm the castle, or at least climb the wall designed to look like a castle as rocks jut out from it, providing hand and foot holds. Become a temporary member of law enforcement by wearing a helmet and hopping on one of the two real police motorcycles, complete with a radio and working lights, or climbing into a real police car. Practice rescuing techniques in a fully-equipped ambulance with gurney, lights, and a two-way radio that is connected to the police motorcycles. Respond to an emergency by dressing up in firemen outfits and boots, and using the hoses on board the mock fire engine.

Along the back and side walls are several city-themed, mini rooms. These include a post office with boxes and a desk; a bank with a teller's desk; and a Walmart with mini shopping carts, shelves stocked with fake food, and a check out stand, scanner, and cash register. The kid-size humane society has a fire hydrant out front, and inside, an examination table, stethoscope, lab coat and stuffed animals. The doctors office is equipped with white lab coats for visiting "doctors", as well as stethoscopes, crutches, an examination table, scales, and more. Work out in the small fitness center with a mini trampoline, some exercise machines, hula hoops and pretend weights. Helmets and a police desk await next door at the police station. Future anchormen and women can first get glamed up with some costumes before going on air in the next room, Kids TV Station. Sit behind a desk here with lights and buttons - action!

Ninety-minute school tours are offered that focus on a particular theme and include plenty of just play time. Special workshops and events are offered for families throughout the year. Tip: Just around the corner from the museum is the MINOR ZOO (pg. 372).

Hours: Open most of the year, Tues. - Fri., 11am - 5pm; Sat., 10am - 5pm. Open during the summer, Tues. - Sat., 9am - 5pm. Closed Sun., Mon., and most holidays.
Price: $5 per person; $4 for seniors; children under 2 are free.
Ages: 1 - 12 years.

GILMAN HISTORIC RANCH AND WAGON MUSEUM

(951) 922-9200 / www.rivcoparks.org
1901 West Wilson Street, Banning

Wagons, ho! Take the dirt road back to the Gilman Historic Ranch and Wagon Museum and explore life as it was over 150 years ago. The exhibits are set up in a chronological order. Over fifteen wagons from yesteryear are inside the museum including chuck wagons, stagecoaches, and prairie schooners. Some of the wagons are hitched to large wooden horses. Learn how our pioneer ancestors traveled across the country, and hear about the hardships that they endured. Also on exhibit are photographs, saddles, a bedroom set with a ladies' riding habit and surrey, a blacksmith's shop, and Indian artifacts.

The adjacent section of the ranch has a few historic buildings, including the beautifully-restored, furnished Ranch House, which looks like it did in the 1890's (but with a fresher coat of paint). It is open to tour. There are also shaded picnic grounds and some hiking trails. Some of the trails go across the creek and to the upper reservoir, while others go deeper into the canyons. Be on the lookout for rabbits, deer, and other wildlife.

School groups, geared for third and fourth graders, with a minimum of ten students and maximum of sixty, can take outstanding and informative two-hour tours which include a tour of the museum, grounds, and adobe ruins, plus a craft to make and take home. For instance, for $8 per person in the California Gold Rush program, students will also go on a nature hike, including walking on the wagon trail originally blazed here; pan for real gold flakes in sluices set in the woods (you may keep whatever you pan); use hand-powered drills and tools to drill holes in logs; and learn about ranch life by making rope, branding a piece of wood, and more. The Native Americans program, also $8 per person, incorporates the above tour, plus seeing and learning about indigenous plants for medicine and other purposes, grinding seeds with a mano and metate, demonstrations of primitive skills, and making a relevant craft. Scout groups may use the campfire sites and fire rings, and choose badge-earning activities. Whatever you choose to do here, enjoy your day reliving the past!

Hours: The museum and grounds are open to the public Fri. and the second and fourth Sat., 9am - 4:30pm. Crafts for kids are offered on Sat. from 10am - noon, for an additional fee. Tours for school and other groups are offered throughout the week by reservation.
Price: Admission/self-guided tours are $3 for adults; $2 for ages 12 and under; $1 for dogs. Guided tours are $5 per person.
Ages: 5 years and up.

HERITAGE HOUSE
(951) 689-1333 or (951) 826-5273 / www.riversideca.gov/museum/heritagehouse $$
8193 Magnolia Street, Riverside

Heritage House is a beautiful Victorian house built in 1892. It is fully restored and filled with elaborate, turn-of-the-century furniture. Adding to its charm is the wrought-iron fence in front, the well-kept grounds, the backyard windmill, and the barn complete with ducking chickens.

Given by a docent in period dress, your older children will appreciate the forty-minute guided tour as they see and learn about a different era and style of living. Downstairs is the formal dining room, elegant parlor, kitchen with a brick oven, and music room. Kids are invited to look through the stereo-optic, which is an early version of today's View Master™ and view a unique, old music box. Explaining the Edison phonograph is a lot harder now that record players are also a thing of the past! The formal oak stairway leads upstairs to bedrooms, the library with trophy animal heads and a bearskin rug, and the servant's quarters. Heritage House graciously displays the life of an affluent citrus grower. Select Sundays are "Living History" days where docents, dressed in Victorian attire, go about "their" daily lives throughout the house and grounds, remaining in character while interacting with visitors.

Forty-five-minute group tours, for a minimum of twenty people, are offered by appointment. Check out the free ice-cream social given in June, with Victorian games and musical entertainment, and garden teas.
>   **Hours:**   Open Fri. - Sun., noon - 3:30pm. Closed July through Labor Day.
>   **Price:** $5 per person.
>   **Ages:**   7 years old and up.

JENSEN-ALVARADO RANCH HISTORIC PARK
(951) 369-6055 / www.riversideca.gov $$
4307 Briggs Street, Riverside

This historic site brings the history of the 1880's to life. The front part of the park is a large area with picnic tables. Rusty old farm equipment lines the main pathway. The corral and animal pens, with a few horses, sheep, potbellied pig, chicken, and other ranch animals, are located next to the Jensen-Alvarado Ranch House. Behind the house was a winery; it's now a small museum. Inside is period furniture, plus wine-making presses, barrels, and other equipment.

A two-and-a-half-hour school tour includes seeing all of the above, plus hearing a living history presentation from a costumed docent; participating in hands-on demonstrations such as making ice cream, butter, or tortillas; and, maybe, feeding the animals. Reservations for the upcoming school year start in May. Ask about special events such as the 4th of July picnic, and the summer history camp.
>   **Hours:**   Open to the public Sat., 10am - 4pm. Open Mon. - Fri. for school and large groups only, by
>   reservation.
>   **Price:**   Sat. admission is $4 per person. School tours are $6 per person.
>   **Ages:**   6 years and up.

JURUPA MOUNTAINS DISCOVERY CENTER / EARTH SCIENCE MUSEUM
(951) 685-5818 / www.jmdc.org   !/$$$
7621 Granite Hill Drive, Riverside

This center is a rock hound's paradise where kids can either start or add to their rock collection. The main building is a gigantic warehouse/gift shop with an incredible array of rocks, minerals, dinosaur skeletons, and fossils of all sizes and quality, for display and purchase, at good prices. The store also sells jewelry and toys.

The adjacent Earth Science Museum has outstanding rocks, minerals, fossils, and Indian artifacts displayed according to classification. The large crystals, geodes, carbons, etc., are worthy of a few "oohs" and "aahs." A major hit with kids is the *egg*straordinary dinosaur egg collection. A camptosaurus, a plant-eating, bird-hipped dinosaur, awaits here, too. The assemblage of ancient and modern Native American artifacts includes tools, weapons, a wonderful arrowhead exhibit, an 1100-year-old corn cob, and costumes - in particular, a beautiful fringed and beaded wedding dress. Products, like Borax, are shown in their commercial form next to their original mineral form. Other unique exhibits are the florescent exhibit, which literally highlights rocks with luminescent characteristics; the space exhibit, which includes moon rocks; a mining display; and the ivory exhibit, which has examples of intricately carved scrimshaw. Watch the video, hosted by a talking mammoth, that discusses how the Jurupa Mountains were formed. Note: The outside of the building is made with petrified wood and fossils.

If your kids want to take home their own hand-picked treasures, go Rock Collecting at the Dinosaurs on Saturdays. This drop-in, hour-long(ish) family field trip starts at the magnetic rock, proceeds to the small, petrified

wood "forest," and has several other stops along the way, with kid-appropriate explanations about the fascinating plants and rocks you see. (I finally understand that fossil simply means, "something that was once living.") You'll go past botanic gardens, boasting lots of cactus and succulents; a nursery; and some dino statues hanging out in the gardens. You can't miss the seventy-foot brachiosaurus sculpture near the entrance to your destination, Dinosaur Mesa. This hilly area has several dinosaur statues including a pachyrhinosaurus, styrachosaurus, velociraptors, T.rex, and more. The highlight of the excursion is sorting through the huge spread of rocks and rock chips strewn at the dinos' feet, and picking out twelve to take home! Crystals, jasper, malachite, petrified wood, amethyst, chrysocolla, and sulphur are some examples of what can be found here. Egg cartons are provided to carry your rocks. Back at the warehouse/store, you can label each of your treasures, with a geologist's help if needed. Bring a picnic lunch to enjoy at the outside tables, as well.

Three onsite gardens are the Iris Garden (beautiful in full bloom); the Enabling Garden, where people in wheelchairs can work the raised garden beds; and the Biblical Garden, where once you've walked past a cedar of Lebanon and through a Middle-Eastern style arch, you enter grounds where all the plants are mentioned in the Bible and each one has a placard with a biblical reference. There is also a nursery here, with plants for sale.

The Jurupa Cultural Center offers a wide variety of terrific school group programs (with a minimum of twenty-five students) and a slew of scout programs, such as gold panning at sluices, adobe brick-making, lapidary workshops, creating an Indian pictograph, forestry, textile, first aid, insect study, environmental science, archaeology, nuclear science, weather, and lots more. A visit to the Earth Science Museum is usually included in the programs. The Center also comes to schools for on-site classes. Call for information on their periodic Pow Wows and Renaissance Fairs, as well as week-long classes of Nature School in the summer that range from hiking and survival to Indian lore to dinosaurs and fossils.

Hours: The gift shop and Earth Science Museum are open Tues. - Sat., 8am - 4pm; Sun., noon - 5pm. Both are closed on Mon. and national holidays. Rock Collecting at the Dinosaurs is held every Sat. at 9am, noon and 2pm, weather permitting. During inclement weather, inquire about other Sat. outings.

Price: Entrance to the warehouse/gift store, the gardens, and the museum is free. Rock Collecting at the Dinosaurs is $8 per person. School programs range from $8 - $12 per person, depending on the activity and materials; scout programs are $16 - $20. Call for specific information and a class schedule or check the site's website.

Ages: 3 years and up.

MARCH FIELD AIR MUSEUM

(951) 902-5949 / www.marchfield.org

16222 Interstate 215, March Air Force Base

March Field Museum is the proud home to one of the most extensive collections of military aircraft and aviation artifacts in the United States. The walkway is lined with airplane engines, plus a jeep that kids can get into and "drive" around. Outside, over sixty historic airplanes are on display, from the smaller F-84 to the massive B-52 to the sleek Blackbird SR-71. Half-hour narrated tram tour rides are offered that go around the perimeter of the airfield every hour on the hour. The cost is $3 per person. Kids are welcome to look at the planes, but they may only climb aboard them on open-cockpit days, the second Saturday of every month. At these times three, or so, airplanes are opened up to climb aboard and there are pilots and mechanics to speak with. Sometimes there are extra things to do and see, too.

Inside, the two huge hangars display everything possible pertaining to the Air Force, starting from 1918 to present day. Airplanes, such as a biplane trainer, have landed in here, plus there are exhibits of flight uniforms, a "war dog" memorial, photographs, model planes, engines, medals, weapons, control panels, aerial cameras, and equipment from both World Wars, Korea, Viet Nam, the Cold War, and Desert Storm. Other highlights include a mock German POW compound, a PT-13D Kaydet with bombs below, a gyro copter, a rare P-59 fighter, and Firebolt missile. (Exhibits do rotate.) In the simulated barracks from WWI a replica Nieuport 11 flies overhead while a documentary of the conflict appears through trench periscopes mounted on the trench wall. Space exploration is paid tribute in a room devoted to NASA with space artifacts and articles, and mission control. Three computers offer mission control programs of jet simulators. Planetarium shows are an additional $3 per person. Hanger 2 houses the library, several more planes and memorabilia and is used for educational programs and special events. Your pilots-in-training will also enjoy the interactive area in here with ejection seats, a little mock plane to board, and clothing, including flight suits, to get dressed up in with a biplane on a mural in the background. You can tour the restoration hangar on Saturdays at 1:30pm. This museum defines the word "comprehensive"!

Fire Base Romeo Charlie is a half-acre adjacent to the museum's education hanger. It replicates a Vietnam-era fire base complete with helicopters of the period including an AH-1 Cobra gunship, two UH-1 Iroquois, H-21 Shawnee, and others. Sandbags and other defensive walls; bunkers; a flight control tower; and vehicles add to the immersion experience and authenticity of the tough living conditions.

School and other group tours are offered for a minimum of twelve people. Birthday parties are offered here on board a Starlifter cargo plane. Call or check the website for air show dates. By the way, the museum has a great gift shop.

Hours: Open Tues. - Sun., 9am - 4pm. Closed Mon., New Year's Day, Thanksgiving, and Christmas.
Price: $10 for adults; $5 for ages 5 - 11; children 4 and under and active duty personnel in uniform are free.
Ages: 3 years and up.

MISSION INN and MISSION INN MUSEUM

(951) 784-0300 - Inn; (951) 788-9556 - museum; (951) 781-8241 - school tours / www.missioninnmuseum.com; www.missioninn.com
3696 Mission Inn Avenue, Riverside

$$$

Is it a European castle? Not quite, but this elegant, old, sprawling Inn is beautiful to look at and tour. The hour-plus tour shows much of its eclectic architecture and furnishings. Mediterranean style, emphasized in the colorful tiles, spiral columns, and bells, is fused with an Oriental influence. This combo is reflected in a hotel kitchen chimney which is in the shape of a pagoda, plus other unique touches. Only through the tour can you see all four wings of the hotel with highlights including the gilded eighteenth-century altar in the wedding chapel; the music room; the Court of Birds (there are no actual birds still here, but the stories about them give wings to the imagination); the Taft Chair, that seats up to five kids at one time; and the open-air, five-story spiral staircase in the rotunda, which is quite grand looking. If your kids are interested in architecture or hearing about the Inn's history, they will enjoy the tour. If not, at least take a quick walk through the grounds. Note that one-hour school tours are given that are aimed toward certain age groups.

A small museum is located on the pedestrian walkway, next to the Inn's gift shop. Frank Miller, the Inn's builder, had an international collection that reflected his tastes. Housed in the museum are a scale model of a pagoda, encased figurines, artifacts, and photos. The most appealing exhibit to kids has old-time barber shop chairs (not to sit in) with mirrors and hair-cutting instruments.

Hours: The Inn is a functioning Inn so it is open daily. Tours are given Mon. - Fri. at 10am, 11:30am, 2pm, and 4pm; Sat. - Sun. at 10am, 11:30am, 1:30pm, 2:30pm, and 4pm. Reservations are recommended. The museum is open daily, 9:30am - 4pm.
Price: You can walk around the hotel at no charge. The tour costs $13 for adults; children 12 and under are free, except during the Festival of Lights when the cost is $16 per person. The museum is $2 per person donation. Both are closed during all major holidays.
Ages: 8 years and up.

ORANGE EMPIRE RAILWAY MUSEUM

2201 S. 'A' Street, Perris

!/$$$

See the entry for ORANGE EMPIRE RAILWAY MUSEUM on page 371 for details.

PENNYPICKLE'S WORKSHOP - TEMECULA CHILDREN'S MUSEUM

(951) 308-6370 / www.pennypickles.org
42081 Main Street, Old Town Temecula

$$

This innovative children's museum, housed in a Victorian-style house, is supposed to be the home of Professor Phineas Pennypickle, a wacky and ingenious inventor. With this premise, each themed room in the house is tastefully crammed with gears, gizmos, and gadgets. Tip: Whenever you see an oversized pickle and penny, it is a sign that the exhibit is interactive.

The small center room in the hall (i.e., the flight and aviation room) has a hot air balloon basket to climb into where kids can ring a bell, tug on a rope to activate pretend flames, pull on knobs, and peer through a periscope and telescope. Experiment with the Bernoulli effect using a vacuum and ball, and "use" an old-fashioned switchboard, telephone, and adding machine. Peer into a doorway window in the hall to see an adjoining looooooong hallway - an optical illusion.

The library contains a time-travel chair (not really) that uses centrifugal force via modified bike wheels. This room is packed with books, maps, and clocks that tell the time all over the world. There are also clothes, hats, and costumes to dress up in. The best part of this room is the secret passageway. Walk through the fireplace into a maze with black lights that leads to the bedroom, or perception and illusion room. Try grabbing the springs in a broken clock (you can't); duck under a triangular-shaped fence to look at yourself through a kaleidoscope of mirrors; and walk into a wardrobe closet to look through a one-way mirror that hangs over a sink in an adjacent bathroom (not a real bathroom). The people on the bathroom side tend to make very funny faces in the mirror at what they think is just themselves.

The music room contains a grand piano that is hooked up to numerous other instruments that hang on the wall - drums, banjo, flute, trumpet, and more - that play when corresponding piano keys are pressed. Speak into an old-fashioned mike, which is really a voice modulator that delays speech and changes voices with a turn of a dial. A jukebox and records decorate this room. The kitchen, or chemistry and physics room, has a sink filled with very small magnet pieces that can be sculpted into various shapes. Open the frig, stove, microwave, and other appliances. Check out the fake cake hovering in a plastic container - it demonstrates how maglev (short for magnetic levitation) trains operate. I like the peanut butter and jelly maker invention on the wall with the ingredients going through all the coils and jars. The small room off the kitchen, the pantry, demonstrates earthquake safety via a seismograph, shake table (press the button), and proper food storage.

The dining room features an electrolight-o-later chandelier that uses disco lights, a bug zapper, and other unique items. Flip switches on and off to see the power usage of incandescent, fluorescent, and other wattage and redirect lines of current. Harness power by touching a static wall and see how your body acts as a conduit. Run a magnet across a TV screen to see all the colors change as beams of electrons move. (Don't do this at home.) Best of all, go through a secret passageway crawl space which leads to a recycling basement room. The recycling room shows how bottles can be transformed into t-shirts and how cans are crushed, recycled, repackaged, and reused. In the back of the house, a small toddler room has great murals plus stuffed animals, soft foam shapes to build with and crawl into and through, and a play cash register to purchase toys and food.

One more terrific feature to this museum is the gift shop. It offers one of the best selections of scientifically oriented toys and games that I've encountered. There are also tables available in a room off the gift shop to eat snacks and food. This is definitely a field trip and school outing destination. Ask about or peruse the website for information on the numerous special programs that explore topics from the science of jellybeans to knights to hot air balloons to dinosaurs. Since the museum is located in Old Town, take some time to shop around.

Hours: Open Tues. - Sat., 10am - noon, 12:30 - 2:30pm, 3pm - 5pm; (Fri. night, 5:30pm - 7:30pm for science adventures); Sun., 12:30 - 2:30pm and 3pm - 5pm. (The museum is closed for a half hour in between sessions for clean up.) Closed Mon. and major holidays.

Price: $5 per session for ages 3 and up; children 2 and under are free.

Ages: 1½ - 12 years.

PERRIS VALLEY HISTORICAL MUSEUM

(951) 657-0274 / www.perrismuseum.com
Fourth Street and D Street at the Santa Fe Depot, Perris

This 1892 renovated, Victorian red brick building, once the home of the historic Santa Fe Depot, now displays a restored survey wagon originally used by city founder, Fred. T. Perris. The museum also exhibits farming equipment, mining tools, vintage clothing, and artifacts regarding Native Americans, and from families from the surrounding area. Note that the ORANGE EMPIRE RAILROAD MUSEUM (pg. 371) is just down the street.

Hours: Open Thurs. - Sun., noon - 4pm.

Price: Free, donations appreciated.

Ages: 6 years and up.

RIVERSIDE ART MUSEUM

(951) 684-7111 / www.riversideartmuseum.org
3425 Mission Inn Avenue, Riverside

This beautiful and historic two-story art museum contains a printmaking center, classroom and youth gallery, library, atrium restaurant, rooftop courtyard, and over twenty rotating exhibits a year in four of the galleries. The galleries display traditional and contemporary paintings, photographs, and sculptures with a focus on American, Californian, and specifically, Inland Empire artists. Just outside the museum is an expanse of green lawn to walk or run

around. Down the street is the RIVERSIDE METROPOLITAN MUSEUM (pg. 364) and TIOS TACOS #1 MARISCOS (pg. 341), which is a folk art experience and great place to eat. This museum, and several others in the area plus galleries, are open for free, October through May for community events: the first Sunday of each month for First Sundays, with crafts and activities for familes, 1pm to 4pm, and on the first Thursday, 6pm to 9pm, for Riverside Arts Walk.

Hours: Open Tues. - Sat., 10am - 4pm; Sun., 1pm - 4pm. It is also open October through May on the first Thurs. during Riverside Artswalk from 6pm - 9pm. Closed Mon., and most holidays.

Price: $5 for adults; $3 for seniors, students with I.D. and educators; ages 11 and under are free. Entrance is free on the first Thurs., 6pm - 9pm and the first Sun., 1pm - 4pm. See page xi for info on the Bank of America free weekend program.

Ages: 7 years and up.

RIVERSIDE INTERNATIONAL AUTOMOTIVE MUSEUM

(951) 369-6966 / www.riversideinternational.org

815 Marlborough Avenue, suite 200, Riverside

Hot rodding, drag racing, and sports car racing are a vital part of Riverside's history. Some of the most exciting cars in racing history are inside this museum looking raring to go, and sometimes they are taken out and driven, if not raced, again. Rare sports and exotic automobiles are also on display; about forty-five cars in all. To name drop just a few: a red hot 1951 Maserati A6G 2000 Farina Coupe; 1969 AAR Eagle #42 USAC-Indy; 1974 Jaguar XKE Roadster; 1979 Penske PC-7 Indy-CART; 1984 Ferrari 512BBi; 427 Cobra; and 2005 MaseratiMC12. The museum holds the largest collection of production Maserati cars in the U.S., including the Quattroporte II of Juan Carlos, the King of Spain. Check out the restoration corner to see select cars being restored.

The museum's focus is two-fold: To present this unique collection of cars, and to preserve the history of Riverside racing - its racetracks, racers, cars, and more. The latter is done via the memorabilia throughout the museum such as original race programs, film footage, photographs, posters of races, stickers, trophies, and banners, plus a few motorcylces, like a Ducati championship bike.

Hours: Open Mon. - Fri., 10am - 4pm; Sat., 10am - 4pm by appointment, only.

Price: $5 adults; children 7 and under are free.

Ages: 5 years and up.

RIVERSIDE METROPOLITAN MUSEUM

(951) 826-5273 / www.riversideca.gov/museum

3580 Mission Inn Avenue, Riverside

This museum contains a wealth of information and fun for both kids and adults. The natural history exhibits are a natural place to start. Push a button and the taxidermied mountain lion crouched on the ledge "roars." Other stuffed animals are also posed in animated positions. For instance, a baby bobcat is batting at the air and a skunk is doing a handstand on its front paws. The geology area has a nice display of rocks and minerals, plus a section on earthquakes. The paleontology exhibits have a saber-toothed cat skeleton, some fossilized elephant tusks (they are huge!), and a few dinosaur bones, including an allosaurus reproduction. The anthropology section has displays of Indian clothing, baskets, musical instruments, hunting weapons, and a few dioramas. The local history display features missions, cowboys, tools, and guns, plus machinery, tools, equipment, and crate labels of citrus growers.

Upstairs we saw exhibits that emphasized Mexican heritage via ethnic costumes and artifacts. The hallway is lined with small botanical dioramas. A favorite room is the small Nature Laboratory. Kids can inspect shells and bugs under a microscope. They can also dissect owl pellets. There is a small sea display with preserved sea horses, and a few live reptiles - snakes, iguanas, lizards, and turtles - and insects, that you can touch and hold.

The entire museum rates high on kid-interest! Check out the free, hands-on, science program, Discovery Days, geared for ages 3 to 10 years old, on the third Wednesday of every month from 1:30pm to 4:30pm. This museum, and several others plus galleries, in the area, are also open for free, October through May for community events: the first Sunday of each month for First Sundays, with crafts and activities for familes, 1pm to 4pm, and on the first Thursday, 6pm to 9pm, for Riverside Artswalk. Inquire about the after-school science adventure programs - no presign-ups necessary. Note that just down the street is TIOS TACOS #1 MARISCOS (see page 341) which is a folk art experience and great place to eat.

Hours: The museum is open Tues. - Fri., 9am - 5pm (open until 9pm on the first Thurs.) Sat., 10am - 5pm; Sun., 11pm - 5pm. The Nature Laboratory is open Tues. - Sat., 1:30pm - 4:30pm. Both are closed on major holidays.
Price: Free
Ages: 2 years and up.

TEMECULA VALLEY MUSEUM / TEMECULA - OLD TOWN

(951) 694-6450 / www.temeculavalleymuseum.org   !/$
28314 Mercedes Street, Temecula

Mosey on over to Old Town Temecula and enjoy an hour or so shopping along Main Street. This western strip of town looks and feels authentic, right down to its wooden sidewalks. The over 100 antique and specialty shops offer many unique gift items for sale, making it an alluring place to shop, even with children.

The museum is located by a corner park - Sam Hicks Park, which has a small playground, and a large rock inscribed with the names of pioneers. The small museum is an interesting glimpse into Temecula's past. On the first floor a few tools, household goods, guns, saddles, and army equipment portray life on the local ranches and frontier towns. There are also some Native American artifacts, plus memorabilia from Erle Stanley Gardner, the author of the Perry Mason stories and a one-time resident of Temecula. At the more interactive second-floor room, there are rotating exhibits. When we visited, my boys became a part of the Old West mostly by dressing up in vintage clothing and sitting on a pretend horse (I brought my camera!), plus looking at facades that depicted a frontier town. Kids also sold or bought pretend items at the well-stocked mercantile store; put on a puppet show; cooked over a play 1880's stove; made imaginary s'mores over the pretend fire at the Mormon Battalion campsite; and more. Don't miss PENNYPICKLE'S WORKSHOP (pg. 362) which is a great children's museum located just down the street.

Hours: Open Tues. - Sat., 10am - 4pm; Sun., 1pm - 4pm. Closed Mon. and holidays. Main Street shopping is usually open daily, 10am - 6pm.
Price: Suggested donation of $2 for adults.
Ages: 5 years and up.

WESTERN SCIENCE CENTER

(951) 791-0033 / www.westerncentermuseum.org $$$
2345 Searl Parkway, Hemet

Kind of in the middle of nowhere (no insults intended) this small, yet terrific, state-of-the-art museum complex holds a fascinating array of history, such as ice age beast fossils unearthed while preparing for construction on the adjacent Diamond Valley Lake. The huge room to the right of the entrance holds three particularly eye-catching exhibits: Max, a colossal (i.e. ten-feet high) mastodon whose remains were discovered on the grounds; Xena, a behemoth mammoth; and an almost seven-foot tall composite of a giant ground sloth. Another mastodon has been somewhat reburied beneath the room's floor; it is visible via tempered glass. Visitors can actually walk on the glass and look down into the re-created dig site. Also on display are skulls of dire wolves and an extinct bison; the skull and leg bone of a sabertooth; the teeth and jawbone of mammoths and mastodons; and mammoth tusks.

This room, set up to look like a study lab, is very hands on. Supplies are given to do rubbings of a short-faced bear, sloth, saber-toothed cat, and more. Look through large magnifying glasses to view fossils of gophers, owls, kangaroo rats, and snakes. Rotate a knob that triggers a brush and blower (under glass) to sweep away sand and dirt from imbedded fossils. Become a critter-scene investigator and study case files to determine how victims die. Follow the tracks on the ground. And best of all, cast your own fossil mold to take home. Use the provided lump of clay and push it into molds of a saber-toothed cat tooth, a golden eagle talon, or mastodon tooth. Let it air dry while you explore the rest of the museum. This room also hosts rotating exhibits, such as Brain Teasers with twenty-one mind boggling puzzles, and Art meets Science where guests designed bridges, towers, and more using planks.

The central hallway is set up like a geological time line, with alcoves containing displays. The Big Dam Hole (you might want to rephrase that one when you mention it to the kids) answers the question - Where are the dinosaurs? It also visually and textually explains about the inhabitants (people and animals) that once lived in this area. Press a button to hear about hydrology, climate, native peoples, water, and the dam. See a cut-away adobe-style home in another section. Other alcoves host rotating exhibits such as heirlooms from families of this area and Remains of the Day, which has Native American baskets and scenes from years ago accompanied by sound effects.

Don't miss seeing a show in the 270-degree immersion theater which is set up like a cave, with boulders for seats, albeit comfortable ones with flat tops. Watch the seven-minute animated *Echoes of the Past* about how this valley looked

thousands of years ago, and the ten-minute *Discovery and Recovery* documentary regarding the excavation here. Both are excellent and kid and adult friendly. The very cool thing is that when the heavy-footed mammoths and mastodons thunder on the screen, you feel it - literally! The theater floor and seats vibrate and rumble along with the movies.

If fact-finding is your passion, incorporate the audio tour for an additional $2. You'll also appreciate the on-site curation unit, research lab, and education and learning center with several classrooms. Visitors, school groups, scouts, day campers, and others are invited to participate in various down-to-earth programs such as working a simulated dig site; workshops; and the monthly Science Saturdays, offered the first Saturday of every month for a time of learning, talking with scientists, and doing a craft. More than just a sandbox, the dig site excavations take place on site with elements such as heat, wind, and dust aiding in recreating an actual dig. Replicas of artifacts and fossils are buried to be exhumed through real-life scientific methods. Perhaps a future career of archaeology or paleontology will be discovered in the past!

See DIAMOND VALLEY LAKE VISITOR'S CENTER (pg. 358) for information on the adjoining facility. See page 350 for details on the neighboring DIAMOND VALLEY LAKE COMMUNITY PARK / AQUATIC CENTER, and page 349 for information about the nearby DIAMOND VALLEY LAKE.

Hours: Open Tues. - Sun., 10am - 5pm. Closed New Year's Day, Easter, Thanksgiving, Christmas Eve, Christmas Day, and New Year's Eve.
Price: $8 for ages 13 and up; $6.50 for seniors; $6 for ages 5 - 12 and students (13 - 22) with current ID; free for children 4 and under and military with current ID.
Ages: 4 years and up.

WORLD MUSEUM OF NATURAL HISTORY

(951) 785-2209 or (951) 785-2500 / www.lasierra.edu/wmnh
4700 Pierce Street in Cossentine Hall on the campus of La Sierra University, Riverside

This quality museum is tremendous in its comprehensive scope of minerals and unique (and several endangered), taxidermied animals. Full-grown and young animals are displayed according to species. The old and new world primates - or monkeys, gorillas, and chimps - all look so life like! The size and variety of the Crocodiles of the World is impressive. We had not heard of at least half the ones featured here. The Indian Gavial is especially unique with a snout that resembles a long, thin saw blade. The numerous types of turtles are similarly astounding. They range from the very small to the gigantic alligator snapping turtle. Snakes of the World boasts another record-breaking variety, ranging from boas, pythons, and common garters, to venomous snakes and even a two-headed snake. Other reptiles, including the world's largest Komodo dragon (365 pounds at time of death!), are also on display. Birds from all over the world are represented here, such as pelicans, flamingoes, penguins, an eagle blue-face, and a blue-hued hunting green magpie. Some of the more unusual animals on display are the flat-headed cat, bats (one is just the size of a pin), armadillos (one is rolled up into a ball), a bush dog, pangolin, linsang, Columbian little spotted cat, a kangaroo, and an Indian rhino.

An outstanding collection of rocks and minerals are grouped, in one section, according to color. (I loved the blue agate.) These include large specimens of amethyst, malachite, etc. Other groupings include meteorites, fluorescent minerals (look at them under black light), geodes, opals, and huge slabs of petrified wood. There is also a large display of sphere balls or, in kidspeak, "cool-looking bowling balls." Part of this display shows the progression of a chunk of raw rock to a cube and then to the finished, sphere product. A fine display of Indian artifacts, such as arrowheads and headdresses, is also noteworthy. Pick up a copy of the paper scavenger hunt to help kids partake in what they see. The World Museum of Natural History is a gem of a place!

Hours: Open Sat., 2pm - 5pm, or weekdays by appointment.
Price: Free; donations gladly accepted.
Ages: 2 years and up.

—POTPOURRI—

BUILD-A-BEAR WORKSHOP (Riverside County)

Riverside - (951) 688-8690; Temecula - (951) 719-1389 / www.buildabear.com
Riverside - 1299 Galleria at Tyler; Temecula - 40820 Winchester Rd. at the Promenade Mall

See the entry for BUILD-A-BEAR WORKSHOP (Orange County) on page 314 for details. The Temecula workshop is in THE PROMENADE IN TEMECULA, so see page 357 for mall details.

Hours: Most stores are open Mon. - Fri., 10am - 9pm; Sat., 10am - 8pm; Sun., 11am - 7pm.

DISNEY STORE (Riverside County)

(951) 296-0557 / www.disneystore.com

40820 Winchester Road in The Promenade, Temecula

See DISNEY STORE (pg. 314) for details about this interactive and magical store! See THE PROMENADE IN TEMECULA (pg. 357) for details on lots of other fun things offered at this mall.

Hours: Open Mon. - Fri., 10am - 9pm; Sat., 10am - 7pm; Sun., 11am - 6pm.
Price: Free
Ages: 1 - 10 years old.

—SHOWS AND THEATERS—

DOS LAGOS STADIUM 15 THEATRES

(877) 795-4410 - show times; (951) 603-0654 - other inquiries / www.doslagos15.com

2710 Lakeshore Drive, The Shops at Dos Lagos, Corona

Movie showings include: 3-D movies; classics on the big screen every weekend evening at 8pm and Saturday morning at 10:30am for only $4 per person; family-friendly movies every Saturday morning at 10:30am - for free for all ages!; ballet and opera in cinema; special presentations; free movies for kids during the week in the summer; and first-run films.

Hours: Call for show schedules.
Price: Check the website for show prices. The first shows of the day are $5. Shows all day and evening Tues. are only $5 (an additional $3.50 for 3-D movies).
Ages: 3 years and up, depending on the film.

LANDIS PERFORMING ARTS CENTER - PERFORMANCE RIVERSIDE

(951) 222-8100 / www.performanceriverside.org; www.inlandarts.com; www.landispac.com

4800 Magnolia Avenue at Riverside City College, Riverside

Performance Riverside is the resident troupe that performs Broadway-style musical theater at the Landis Performing Arts Center. Most of their productions are suitable for the family and all are professionally produced and presented. Past shows include *The Music Man*, *Ragtime the Musical*, and *Evita*. The Children's Series is the perfect introduction to theater for youngsters. Past shows have included *The Elves and the Shoemaker*, *Tom Sawyer*, and *Schoolhouse Rock Live!* Teachers note that school field trip performances, called Discovery Theatre, are usually given on a Friday morning at 10am and cost about $8 per student. Check the website for more information.

Hours: Call for a schedule.
Price: Prices can range from $15 - $49, depending on the seating and the type of show.
Ages: 5 years and up.

OLD TOWN TEMECULA COMMUNITY THEATER

(866) OLD TOWN (653-8696) / www.temeculatheater.org

42051 Main Street, Temecula

In the heart of Old Town is a contemporary theater. With over 350 seats, an orchestra pit, balcony, and box seats (even a courtyard outside), the theater accommodates all manner of shows - musicals, dramas, community presentations, concerts, plays, dances, and more. There are productions geared specifically for children, such as *Willy Wonka Junior*, as well as workshops where kids culminate their time by putting on a performance. The theater, and the quality and variety of its productions, is another jewel for the city of Temecula.

Make sure to spend some time, probably before your show, walking and shopping Old Town. Also see PENNYPICKLE'S WORKSHOP - TEMECULA CHILDREN'S MUSEUM (pg. 362) which is a great children's museum in the immediate vicinity.

Hours: Call for a schedule of shows.
Price: Prices vary, ranging from $15 - $25, depending on the show.
Ages: 4 years and up, depending on the show.

RIVERSIDE COMMUNITY COLLEGE PLANETARIUM

(951) 222-8090 / www.rccommunityed.com

4800 Magnolia Avenue at Riverside Community College, Riverside

Come see a truly star-studded show at the college planetarium! The theater seats fifty-five people and each presentation has a live narrator. Different shows study various aspects of astronomy such as constellations, revolutions (the earth's, not a country's), galaxies and measuring distances between them, lunar eclipses, and what makes the sun shine.

School groups, or other groups, of up to fifty-five people can schedule a time to rent out the theater for $75 to see fifty-minute shows such as *Sun's Family*, or *Finding Your Way in the Sky*, or others. These shows are geared specifically for elementary-aged kids. There are several shows and programs geared for secondary grade levels, too. *Christmas Star* is offered only in the month of December, to the public and for groups. It explores the possible origins of the Star of Bethlehem, utilizing biblical passages and astronomer's technology and understanding of the heavens.

Hours: Public shows are offered March - May and December, once or twice a month on Fri. nights at 7pm. Groups can call to make reservations at other times.

Price: Public shows are $5 for adults; $4 for students; $2.50 for children 12 and under. Cash or checks, only.

Ages: 7 years and up.

—TOURS—

CALIFORNIA PIZZA KITCHEN (Riverside County)

See the entry for CALIFORNIA PIZZA KITCHEN (Los Angeles County) (pg. 197) for more information.

DE JONGS DAIRY

(951) 674-2910
31910 Corydon Road, Wildomar

This thirty-two-acre, family-owned-and-operated dairy invites you to come and buy really fresh eggs and milk, as well as pre-packaged snacks, beverages, souvenirs, and animal feed from its little convenience store. You might come here just to pet and feed the enclosed animals including goats, ducks, geese, a pig, rabbits, sheep, peacocks, and a variety of birds.

With a minimum of eight people, take a ninety-minute tour and learn all about the daily dairy operations, from cow to bottled milk. See the over 100 cows, perhaps watch a baby calf get bottle-fed, walk through the barn where the cows are milked and then through the processing plant where milk is put into containers. Included in the tour are fun "extras" such as feed for the farm animals, and chocolate milk and cookies. (I brought a cooler to bring even more chocolate milk home - it is so rich and creamy!)

Hours: The dairy is open daily, 8am - 8pm. Tours are offered daily, by reservation.

Price: Tours are $3 per person.

Ages: 4 years and up.

FENDER VISITOR CENTER

(951) 898-4040 / www.fender.com
301 Cessna Circle, Corona

Tune in to the Fender Visitor Center and Factory Tour to see how these acclaimed guitars are made, step-by-step, and who plays them. Enter the really extensive Visitor Center which is like a museum and a store combined, but better. Hundreds of "celebrity" guitars (or guitars owned by celebrities and musicians) hang on several of the rooms' walls alongside their poster-sized autographed photos, album covers, and sometimes some personal items - it's like a who's who and walk of fame. Some of the famous featured are Steve Miller, Paul Rodgers, Eric Clapton, Jimi Hendrix, Phil Collen, Kurt Cobain, John Campbell, Buddy Holly, Jimmie Vaughan, Brad Paisley, and many more. The Beach Boys have their own wall showcasing their album covers, guitars, a surfboard, clothes, and lots of photos. There is also a wall with classic twelve-string Fender guitars and a video room with a really large screen to watch some of your favorite artists playing.

Go into the Jam Room and try out the dozens of guitars and amps waiting for visitors to strike a chord. Or, purchase a guitar that you "build" in the adjoining specialty room where you can hand-pick, from a huge variety, the color, style, wood, and design of the body, neck, face, and more. The Visitor Center is also a retail store with racks and racks of clothing, plus accessories, guitars, guitar accessories, amps, collectibles, and other items for sale.

Take the hour-long factory tour to observe the transformation from raw wood and other materials to the glossy finished product of a Fender guitar. As the guided walking tour goes through each section of the factory - the wood mills, metal shop and final assembly - you see and hear about every piece and step that goes into creating a guitar and amp, and you see and even meet many of the workers. The rows and rows of necks hanging are amazing as is the quantity (thousands) of wooden bodies which are sanded, painted (look overhead at one point and see hundreds of them drying), buffed, and polished and finally, assembled. It's a very up close, personal, informative and fun tour and it's interesting to see how much is truly hand crafted. For the "wow" factor, the last area of the tour is the "Dream Factory". This is the custom shop where you will see, and salivate over, some of the most unique and high-end custom guitars. And this is as close as I will ever get to owning one. Know that you must wear closed-toed shoes for the tour and there is a maximum of twenty-five people. Rock on.

Hours: The Visitor Center is open Mon. - Tues., Thurs. - Fri., 9am - 4pm. Factory Tours are given at 10am and 11:30am on those days. Both are closed Sat., Sun., and Wed.

Price: The Visitor Center is free. The factory tour is $10 for adults; $8 for seniors; $6 for students and ages 13 - 17; ages 9- 12 are free.

Ages: Must be 9 years and up for the factory tour.

QUALITY WEST WING   ☼

(951) 808-1676 / www.qualitywestwing.com $$

1705 W. 6th Street, Corona

"I, name, do solemnly swear (or affirm) that I will faithfully execute the office of the President of the United States . . ." If a trip to Washington D.C. is not in the foreseeable future, travel instead to Corona and see miniature replicas of important government institutions and a full-size recreation of the Oval Office, via a two-hour interactive tour.

Bud Gordon, president of this Quality Toyota dealership where the West Wing was built, has a vision - for people, and students in particular, to know their government by bringing America's history to life. He made an executive decision and created Quality West Wing. The tour begins with a twenty-minute Charlie Brown video called *Birth of the Constitution*, which recaps the delegates and founding fathers debating how to best establish our government. A scavenger hunt is next involving the documents and political pictures on the walls, then researching answers on the computer. Then, visitors can fill out the worksheets that include word searches and crossword puzzles. In the computer lab, use a terrific program to make weighty decisions as you become the president in *A Day in the Life Of*. Take the oath of office, write or veto bills, run a reelection campaign, and more. Next, walk down the halls and hear a short oral biography on the presidents whose portraits hang here, as well as lots of fascinating presidential facts and trivia. Q: How many consecutive years can a person serve as president? A: (Look at the bottom of this entry.)

"Tour" the detailed, authentic, scale model of Capitol Hill, which includes all the famous monuments. 3-D replicas also depict the interiors of the House, Senate, and Supreme Court buildings in session. The highlight is a visit to the full-size Oval Office. What an impressive office, even in replica, especially the Resolute desk which is truly a treasure. The tour guide explains how the decor in the real Oval Office changes with each president, what the emblems on the rug mean, how the president signs a bill into law, and other life-altering functions that take place here. (The somewhat western decor in this Oval Office is based on Ronald Reagan's terms.) Get your picture taken behind the desk and the current president will be digitally placed there for you to purchase for $1.

As an introduction to American government and as a reinforcement for those who have studied the topic more in depth, the Quality West Wing tour wins by a landslide. For group tours during the week, a minimum of ten students and maximum of sixty-two are allowed per visit. (Groups of more than sixteen will be split into multiple groups.) There is also a small gift store on the premises. This outstanding tour certainly has my vote! The answer to the above question, by the way, is ten years. Note that a tour of the adjacent UNCLE BUD'S CAR MUSEUM (the next entry) is often included in this tour, too.

Hours: Tours are offered Mon. - Fri., 8am - 3pm for school groups by reservation only. One Sat. a month the tour is open to the public at 9am, by reservation only, for up to thirty participants.

Price: Free for school tours; public tours are $5 per person, which allows visitors into the Uncle Bud's Car Museum, too.

Ages: 4th graders and up

UNCLE BUD'S CAR MUSEUM   ☾

(951) 808-1676 / www.unclebuds.org $$

1705 W. 6th Street

Bud Gordon, president of this Quality Toyota dealership where the museum and QUALITY WEST WING (see the above entry) is located, has a vision for kids in junior and senior high school, or older, who are interested in the automotive industry or in a future as an automotive technician: He wants to motivate them and enable them.

The mid-size car museum is incredibly well put together. Students, and other visitors, get their engines revved up as they enter and see the vehicles here displayed in chronological order, starting with horse and buggy. Behind each beautifully restored car is a colorful and realistic mural depicting that time period, bringing the settings to life. Most cars, and there is at least one per decade, are also accompanied by another piece of history from that era, as well as information panels. Some of the vehicles here include a per-1900 horseless carriage; a 1916 Ford Model T; a 1935 Packard; a few Mercedes Benz; a fintail convertible with propellers behind the wheels; and a 1963 Dodge Polara 500 (one of five built). Follow the carpet that looks like a road - yellow lines and all - around the curve to a complete 50's diner called Rosie's. Go into it and see the jukebox, red vinyl booths, and a soda fountain. Keep going around the horseshoe-shaped pathway to the race cars, motorcycles, and more modern vehicles. An important element of this museum is the hands-on activities, such as the cut away to a car engine to see how the engine works, crank the differential gears, check out the entire electrical system to a Lexus, and so much more. There is also a fake gas station, depicted by a gas pump, murals, and lots of traffic signs covering the walls.

Groups, minimum ten and maximum thirty, may call to book a ninety-minute-plus tour. The public is welcome once a month.

Hours: Tours are offered Mon. - Fri., 8am - 3pm for school groups by reservation only. One Sat. a month, at about 11am, after the tour of Quality West Wing, it is open to the public, by reservation only, for up to thirty participants.

Price: Free for students; donations appreciated. Public tours are $5 per person, which allows visitors into the Quaility West Wing, too.

Ages: 10 years and up.

—TRANSPORTATION—

AMTRAK (Riverside County)

(800) USA RAIL (872-7245) / www.amtrakcalifornia.com

Ride the rails! See AMTRAK (Los Angeles County) on page 208 for more information.

APEX GO KART TRACK

(951) 940-0701 or (888) FOR KART / www.apexracing.com
18700 Lake Perris Drive at the Lake Perris Fairgrounds, Perris

Zoom around this quarter-mile track, learning the finer elements of kart racing, or just drive for the thrill of it. If you bring your own kart, you may use the track all day for $25. Kids 13 years and older who are beginners, or who just want to try it out, can participate in the "arrive and drive," where they drive around the track for about eight minutes for $25. (Kart and safety equipment are included.) Half day classes are offered for children as young as 5 that start at $279.

Hours: Call for a schedule of events.
Price: Prices are quoted above.
Ages: 15 years and up.

BIKE MAPS (Riverside County)

See BIKE MAPS (Orange County) on page 326 for information.

BIKE TRAIL: SANTA ANA RIVER (Riverside County)

(714) 973-6615 - Yorba Regional Park / www.santaanarivertrail.org; www.bicyclela.org
Beginning point: 5215 Green River Road, Corona. Great entry point: 7600 E. La Palma Avenue in Yorba Regional Park, Anaheim. Ending points: Pacific Coast Highway, Sunset County Beach, Huntington Beach

This bike path is planned to eventually be 110 miles long - from the mountains to the sea. In the meantime, the continuous, almost twenty-nine mile, mostly easy-riding trail extends from Green River golf course in Riverside County through beautiful Yorba Linda Regional Park to a premiere beach, Huntington Beach. Some parts of the bike path are paved; some are packed dirt. Some sections go along a street, while others encounter more nature.

The first five miles from the golf course have moderate hills, while the rest of the trail is fairly flat. Starting from or continuing through Yorba Linda park, these few miles are park-scenic, then meander through an adjacent wilderness area with shade trees and flocks of birds, mostly waterfowl such as ducks and egrets. A good stopping point (and maybe turning around area?) is about the fifteen-mile mark, just before the Honda Center at 2695 E. Katella Avenue, where a pocket park has the necessary amenities. (Bring your own snacks, though.) Hearty bikers - bike on!

Hours: The regional park is open daily, 7am - 8:45pm.
Price: The regional park charges $3 per vehicle Mon. - Fri.; $5 on Sat. - Sun.
Ages: 5 years and up.

METROLINK (Riverside County)

(800) 371-LINK (5465) or (951) 222-7000 / www.metrolinktrains.com; www.takethebeachtrain.com $$$
See the entry for METROLINK (Orange County) on page 329 for details.

ORANGE EMPIRE RAILWAY MUSEUM

(951) 657-2605 or (951) 943-3020 / www.oerm.org   !/$$$
2201 S. 'A' Street, Perris

If you are a train aficionado, make tracks to the Orange Empire Railway Museum where you can really go full steam ahead! This sixty-five-acre, unique, outdoor museum is best described as a work in progress. Numerous railcars from all over the country, in various states of disrepair, find their way here. Some are being restored while others are just stationed at the yard and inside buildings. Walk around the massive property to see which railcars the volunteers are working on, take pictures, soak in ambiance from yesteryear, and/or learn more by taking a guided tour.

Walk through the several car houses (i.e., buildings that house railcars) to see historic Yellow Cars (which my kids thought looked like school buses), a San Francisco cable car, electric railway streetcars and locomotives dating from 1900, steam engines, and wood passenger cars. The car houses are open during the week whenever volunteer staff is available; they are almost always open on the weekends.

Check out the Middleton Collection that includes old toy and scale model railroad cars, and others. There is an ongoing video that shows how tracks are laid. We got derailed at the gift shop, which offers videos, books, and all sorts of train paraphernalia.

The museum is open daily, but weekends are the prime time to visit as this is the only time when train and trolley rides are available. Purchase an all-day ride ticket which is good for rides on a locomotive, electric trolley, streetcar, freight car, and/or passenger car. (Three types of cars are usually running.) Each ride lasts about fifteen minutes and a conductor explains the history of the vehicles and the museum, and the impact of train transportation in Southern California. The train's whistle, the clickety-clack of its wheels, and the clanging of streetcar bells add excitement to your adventure.

A real treat for an engineer wanna-be is to actually be one, for an hour, with a program called Run One. Up to four people can share the rental hour to ride with an engineer and actually operate the locomotive on the museum railway. You must be 18 years old to actually "drive," but ages 5 and up can ride along with an adult. This activity is available on Mondays, Wednesdays, Fridays, and weekends and ranges between $225 to $350, depending on the type of train. It includes a true fashion statement - an engineer's cap. Reservations are required. Another option is to simply ride with an engineer in the cab on regular operating day - ages 5 and up can do this for an additional $10 per person for a diesel-powered train and $20 per on a steam engine train.

A few picnic tables and grassy areas are also on site. Ask about the special events throughout the year, such as the bunny train, Rail Festival, pumpkin train (and pumpkin patch), Thomas the Tank Engine appearance and rides, Santa Christmas train, and Railroadiana Swap Meet. The museum also conducts school, scout, and several other acclaimed program and group tours throughout the week. Note that just up the street, at the corner of Ellis and A Street, is Rotary Park - you passed it on the way to the museum. The small, sand-based playground has swings, slides, a twisty metal climbing structure, picnic tables, and a few trees.

Hours: The grounds are open daily, 9am - 5pm. Train and trolley rides are available only on weekends and major holidays, 11am - 4pm. Closed Thanksgiving and Christmas.
Price: The museum is free. Weekend, all-day ride passes are $12 for adults; $8 for ages 5 - 11; children 4 and under ride free. A $40 family pass is good for 2 adults and all the kids in the family.
Ages: All

PERRIS AUTO SPEEDWAY

(951) 940-0134 / www.perrisautospeedway.com
18700 Lake Perris Drive at the Lake Perris Fairgrounds, Perris

Get up to speed and race to this premier half-mile oval dirt race track. Competitions include super stocks, street stocks, champ trucks, dwarfs, sprint cars, cruisers, and more. Join in on the dance contest (or not) that happens before the race begins. A sound system in the 8,000-seat grandstand is hooked up to speakers so the audience can hear, even over the roar of the engines.

Hours: Call for a schedule of events - often times Sat. at 5pm.
Price: Tickets start at $15 for adults; $5 for ages 6- 12; children 5 and under are free.
Ages: 6 years and up.

YOUNG EAGLES PROGRAM (Riverside County)

(877) 806-8902 - national number; (951) 683-2309 - chapter #1 / www.flabob.org; www.youngeagles.org
4130 Mennes Street at Flabob Airport, Riverside

See the entry for YOUNG EAGLES PROGRAM (Los Angeles County) on page 215 for details. This particular airport also features a half-hour ground school and preflight instructions, plus a snack bar and small souvenir store, and perhaps a chance at the controls while in the air. Reservations are required.

Hours: Usually the second Sat. of the month, except August and December, starting at 7:15am.
Price: Free
Ages: 8 - 17 years old.

—ZOOS AND ANIMALS—

MAGNOLIA BIRD FARM (Riverside County)

(951) 278-0878 / www.magnoliabirdfarms.com
12200 Magnolia Avenue, Riverside

See the entry for MAGNOLIA BIRD FARM (Orange County) on page 333 for details. The main difference between the two is size, with this location being almost three times as large. The aviary here includes parakeets, love birds, finches, and quail, as well as doves and pigeons.

As springtime brings the birth of new baby birds, kids can sometimes see them being hand fed through the glass walls. Tour groups, with a minimum of fifteen people, will learn about seed, such as which kind is best for what species; see and study a (live) white dove; and more.

Hours: Open Tues. - Sat., 9am - 5pm. Closed Sun., Mon., the first two weeks of August, and some holidays. Reservations are needed for the free, half-hour tour.
Price: Free
Ages: All

MINOR ZOO

www.sanjacintovalley.info/parks.html
4080/4090 Park Avenue, Hemet

This zoo is the personal collection of the Minor family. It is not a destination in and of itself, but a stop and stare. There are several domestic animals, such as horses and goats, and several exotic animals such as zebras, camels, gazelles, a buffalo, and peacocks. Just pull over to the side of the road and admire them all. At Christmas time, there is a nativity set up with the live animals as well. Tip: FINGERPRINTS YOUTH MUSEUM (pg. 358) is down the road a bit and a terrific "real" destination.

Hours: Open daily, sunrise - sunset.
Price: Free
Ages: All

—PALM SPRINGS—

PALM SPRINGS (and the surrounding desert cities)

I know that Palm Springs, and the surrounding desert communities, are officially part of both Riverside and San

Bernardino Counties. I've grouped them all together under "Palm Springs" because I think most people refer to this area as a destination in and of itself. Creative liberties? (Or just thinking like a tourist!)

A collage of words and images used to come to mind when I thought about Palm Springs and the other areas - desert, hot, resort, homes of the rich and famous, golf, and shopping mecca. Now that my family has thoroughly explored them, I can add to this list - kid-friendly, fun, beautiful, great hiking opportunities, and educational treasures. Note that the Palm Springs Bureau of Tourism publishes free guides that have up-to-the-moment happenings. Call (800) 347-7746 or (760) 778-8418 or check their website at www.visitpalmsprings.com. for information.

ADVENTURE HUMMER TOURS

(877) WE-HUMMER (934-8663); (760) 285-0876 / www.adventurehummer.com

$$$$$

74880 Country Club Drive, Palm Desert

The great outdoors is awesome, and sometimes it is wonderful to see it from inside a really cool car like an open-air Hummer H1 or more luxury, air-conditioned H2. (A little pampering doesn't hurt.) The all-terrain vehicles do quite a bit of climbing - up and down mountain sides, taking you into some incredible places.

One of the most popular tours is the Joshua Tree Adventure, an excursion that goes into Joshua Tree National Park, a place that boasts the highest bio diversity in the U.S. And the 360-degree view is spectacular! The open-air hummer (my preference for the Indiana Jones-style ride) is mostly backroads in and through parts of Joshua Tree not seen by regular tourists - along the Big Game Corridor and to and around incredible rock formations with opportunities to get out and walk around to explore. You'll see and learn about geology, Native American plants, earth's history and more as each of the tours are hosted by a learned and versatile naturalist who makes your time an outstanding and educational experience. This tours also goes through the canyons of the San Andreas Fault, which is marvellous to see and encounter first-hand. Take this daytime tour or see your surroundings in a new light and book this as a sunset tour.

Several other tours are offered, as well - one with a focus along the San Andreas Fault, one to the Salton Sea near bubbling mud holes, and another throughout the city of Palm Springs. Depending on your adventure, your tour will last between one to ten hours.

Hours: Open daily - call to schedule a tour.

Price: The four-hour Joshua Tree open-air tour is $169 for adults, $139 for ages 16 and under; the Joshua Tree luxury H2 tour is $229. The three-hour, open-air San Andreas Fault tour is $149. Check the website for discounts.

Ages: 7 years and up.

AGUA CALIENTE CULTURAL MUSEUM

(760) 323-0151 or (760) 778-1079 / www.accmuseum.org

!

219 S. Palm Canyon Drive, Palm Springs

This small, tribal museum relates the history and culture of the Agua Caliente Band of Cahuilla Indians via changing exhibits. Baskets and the meaning behind the street names in Palm Springs are included. School tours feature an explanation of the exhibits, demonstrations, and a video presentation. The museum also offers classroom visits and field trips.

Hours: Open Memorial Day - Labor Day, Fri. - Sat., 10am - 5pm; Sun., noon - 5pm. Open Labor Day - Memorial Day, Wed. - Sat., 10am - 5pm; Sun., noon - 5pm. Closed New Year's Day, Easter, Thanksgiving, and Christmas.

Price: Free

Ages: 7 years and up.

BAGDOUMA PARK

(760) 347-3484 or (760) 347-4263 / www.myrecreationdistrict.com

!/$

84-620 Bagdad Street, Coachella

This sprawling, thirty-four acre park has several baseball/softball fields (with stadium seating) and soccer/football fields, tennis courts, several basketball courts, three play areas, and a swimming pool. The gated swim center has a pool with two enclosed slides, a small grassy area with a picnic table, and a covered wading pool for younger ones. One playground has twisty and straight slides; colorful, metal climbing apparatus; a raised tube to crawl through; monkey rings (instead of monkey bars); and a play car. The other two play areas have similar equipment, although one is much smaller and one has a really big - tall, wide, and double-sided - rock climbing wall. A seasonal waterspray ground is

here, too, with water fountains shooting up from the ground on a somewhat covered, cement pad.

Hours: The park is open daily, sunrise - sunset. The pool is open seasonally, daily, 11am - 4pm and Mon. - Fri., 7pm - 9pm, as well. Call to verify pool hours.

Price: The park is free. The swim center is $2 for adults; $1 for ages 17 and under.

Ages: All

BIG MORONGO CANYON PRESERVE

(760) 363-7190 / www.blm.gov

11055 East Drive, Morongo Valley

This massive preserve is a favorite and a visual treat as it can be unexpectedly lush with a variety of trees and plants, and fresh water marshes and springs in contrast to the more traditional dry desert landscape. The quietness of this peaceful preserve was broken by shouts from my kids whenever they spotted a lizard, bunny, roadrunner, or other animals. Other wildlife here includes bighorn sheep, raccoons, coyotes, and so many species of birds that people come just to observe them. Bring binoculars!

The trails are relatively easy to walk, and many of them go in and through the canyon and trees, along the willow-lined seasonal creek. There are several short, looping trails on the boardwalk, making them stroller and wheelchair friendly, as well as a longer hike of almost ten miles (round trip) along the Canyon Trail, extending the length of the canyon. Note that the preserve's terrific website offers a great trail map and detailed description of the trails.

Several educational programs and tools, such as microscopes and field guides, are available to school groups.

Hours: Open daily, 7:30am - sunset. No dogs or pets allowed.

Price: Free

Ages: 3 years and up.

BOOMERS! - Cathedral City

(760) 770-7522 / www.boomersparks.com

67-700 E. Palm Canyon Drive [111], Cathedral City

This huge, family-fun center (the first castle off Highway 111), offers a variety of entertainment for everyone. Choose from three funtastically-themed **miniature golf** courses - $9 per round for adults, ages 4 and under are free with a paid adult admission; **go carts** - $7 a ride for drivers, $2 for passengers; **bumper boats** (avoid the shooting fountain waters or get refreshed) - $7 a ride for drivers, $2 for passengers; a thirty-foot tall **rock climbing wall** - $7 for a two climbs; **batting cages**; and over 200 video and sport games, plus a prize redemption center. Note that height restrictions apply on some rides. A snack bar serving pizza, corn dogs, nachos, and more is also on the premises.

Hours: Open most of the year, Mon. - Thurs., noon - 8pm; Fri., noon - 11pm; Sat., 11am -11pm; Sun., 11am - 8pm. Open later hours in the summer and on school holidays.

Price: Attractions are individually priced above, or purchase one of the super saver packages.

Ages: 4 years and up.

BRAILLE INSTITUTE (Rancho Mirage)

(760) 321-1111 or (800) 272-4553 / www.brailleinstitute.org

70-251 Ramon Road, Rancho Mirage

Kids, as well as adults, often have preconceived ideas on what visually impaired people can and cannot do. A forty-five-minute tour through this institute enables visitors to see, firsthand, how well blind people can function. A tour guide, who is legally blind, takes your family or group (up to thirty people) around the campus and classrooms to look at the computers, art room, cooking facility, garden, and any other area that teaches life skills. Visitors are encouraged to ask questions - it's the best way to learn! You can also arrange to watch a film on being visually impaired and/or to have a special speaker, and you may be able to stand on a talking scale, something I personally opted out of doing. Visitors receive a card with the Braille alphabet - try it and see if you can discern the difference in letters.

Hours: Tours are offered Tues. and Wed. at 10am when classes are in session, by reservation only.

Price: Free

Price: 8 years old and up only.

CABOTS PUEBLO MUSEUM

(760) 329-7610 / www.cabotsmuseum.org

67616 E. Desert View Avenue, Desert Hot Springs

This four-story, thirty-five-room, Hopi-style pueblo with sixty-five doors and 150 windows, was built out of the side of a mountain. Cabot, the owner and builder, believed in mysticism and an Indian belief that symmetry retains an evil spirit, so he constructed the abode with slanted doorways and floors, uneven walls, windows with odd shapes, and small, narrow doorframes and staircases. (It looks like our house before we remodeled.) The almost one-hour tour includes the fascinating history of Cabot and his pueblo.

On the first floor is a cave-like bedroom (raised off the floor to avoid rattlesnakes), a living room with a dirt floor, a Kiva (i.e., prayer room), a small art gallery, a smaller Alaskan room, and a kitchen. Some of the artifacts in these rooms include ceremonial Indian costumes, headdresses, drums, carvings, pottery, baskets, and a rock collection. The upstairs belonged to Cabot's second wife and contains a series of rooms - a tiny bathroom, bedroom, kitchen, and more - displaying "finds" from Cabot's travels. It also has a short and small (one to two people at a time can go up) meditation tower that oversees some of the grounds.

The outside grounds are almost as eclectic as the inside house, with an enormous (forty-three-foot tall) Indian statue carved from a giant Sequoia, old signs, and some rusted tools and equipment. There is also a small picnic facility, a multi-room gift shop and visitor's center. School tours offer a wide range of topics - call to schedule one.

Hours: Open October - May, Tues. - Sun., 9am - 4pm. Tours are offered 9:30am - 2:30pm (last tour) and limited to 12 people at a time. Open June - September, Wed. - Sat., 9am - 1pm. Closed Mon., Tues., (in the summer), and on major holidays.

Price: $11 for adults; $9 for seniors and ages 6 - 12; children 5 and under are free.

Ages: 7 years and up.

CAP HOMME / RALPH ADAMS PARK

(760) 346-0611 / www.cityofpalmdesert.org

72-500 Thrush Road, Palm Desert

The park offers twenty-seven acres of natural desert - hills and cactus - to hike through, plus a picnic table under a thatched roof near a few palm trees by the trailhead. The Homestead Trail winds up into the mountains (take a moment to soak in the sights of the sprawling desert and the valley below) and just before it connects with the much longer Hopalong Cassidy Trail, there is a shaded rest stop. Continue along the narrow dirt trail, up and down some steep grades, and keep right to the Gabby Hayes Loop. Follow the trail along the road for the final bit, making your hike about 2.5 miles in length. Cap Homme is just part of the Cahuilla Hills Trails System. Bring water and sunscreen.

Hours: Open daily, dawn - dusk.

Price: Free

Ages: 6 years and up.

CHILDREN'S DISCOVERY MUSEUM OF THE DESERT

(760) 321-0602 / www.cdmod.org

71-701 Gerald Ford Drive, Rancho Mirage

The desert, well known for golf and retirement living, boasts of a terrific museum for children. The building is deceptive. Its architectural style befits an art museum, and its high ceilings are complemented by numerous windows and tall, pastel, modular room dividers. Upon entering the lobby, my middle son whispered, "Are you sure this is a hands-on place for kids?" Most definitely!

The exhibits flow easily from one to another. Note that no strollers are permitted. Some of the scientific exhibits in the front include a music machine of sorts, where a touch on a metal sculpture produces a jazz or percussion musical sound, and a stroboscope, which is a display where kids can draw their own design, attach it to the fan, and watch it "dance" in the strobe light. Follow any one of three colored ropes through a kid-size, spider-web-looking rope maze. Get properly suited up with a safari hat, goggles, and gloves and use the tools provided to find faux artifacts in a simulated dig. Climb a (fake) rock wall, complete with hand and foot holds. Pull! Or at least pull yourself up on the pulley system and see how much weight you can pull. Try to follow light and sound patterns by tapping the icon. Design and implement a sort of tunnel/roller coaster using tubes and platforms that balls go through. The relatively large Make-It-Take-It work area is a real treat for kids who like to take apart radios, computer components, and other household gadgets. They can even use the screwdrivers, glue, pieces of wood, and recycled materials to make a new creation to take home. (Parents will be thrilled!) The magnetic wall promotes ingenuity by creating a sculpture from magnetized household objects. Painting a car is not normally allowed, at least at my house, but the VW Beetle here is a much-decorated canvas on wheels. Smocks, paints, and brushes are supplied. The Art Corner has paper, markers, a

computer with art programs, and even a giant loom for young weavers. Animation is harder than it seems as kids try to make their own short movie at this station. The Braille station and wheel chair racer enable kids to experience how those physically challenged have to maneuver differently to get around in the world. Toward the back of the museum is a well-stocked, pretend grocery store with mini-carts and a checkout counter. Pizza, every child's favorite food, can be made to order just next door. This pizzeria has all the ingredients (made from cloth) to make pizzas, as well as aprons, hats, and a pretend brick oven, plus tables and chairs for "customers." An enclosed toddlers' play area and a real CHP motorcycle are also located in this wing.

Walk up the snake-like, winding ramp to the second story to Grandma's Attic Room. This area is decorated with old trunks, hat boxes, fishing poles, pictures, and adding machines and telephones. One of the best features is the quality costumes in which to play dress up. They range from princess dresses with sequins to military uniforms to suits and everything in between. Lots of hats, an assortment of shoes and boots, plus boas and ties are some of the accessories.

The above merely lists the highlights of the museum! Parental supervision is required at all times but, as each activity was so much fun, I was delighted to participate, too. Both the adjacent Dinah Shore theater and the outdoor amphitheater put on a variety of performances year round. Note that there is a grassy play area between the buildings, along with a sand table, balls and other toys, plus a garden and small maze. Ask about plethora of special programs and classes offered for children, such as art classes, ballet lessons, manners classes, and lots, lots more.

Hours: Open January through April daily, 10am - 5pm. Open May through December, Tues. - Sun., 10am - 5pm. Closed Mon. School field trips here are offered Tues. - Fri. Closed New Year's Day, Easter, Labor Day, and Christmas.

Price: $8 per person; children under 2 are free. Yearly membership is a great deal at $25 per person. School groups, consisting of a minimum of ten students, are $3.50 per student (although the price is discounted during certain months); teachers and chaperones are free.

Ages: 2 - 11 years.

CHUCK E. CHEESE'S (Palm Springs area)

See the entry for CHUCK E. CHEESE'S (Los Angeles County) on page 16 for details.

CIVIC CENTER PARK AND AQUATIC CENTER

(760) 568-9697 or (760) 346-0611; (760) 565-7467 - aquatic center / www.cityofpalmdesert.org; www.palmdesertart.com; www.desertymca.org
73-510 Fred Waring Drive (and San Pablo Avenue), Palm Desert

The beautiful seventy-acre park, bordered by the civic center and the sheriff's station, encompasses a good portion of land and offers a wide variety of things to do and see. There are four baseball fields; six tennis courts; a dog park; four volleyball courts; three basketball courts; a YMCA building; a tot lot; a playground for older kids with great play equipment and imagination-inspiring apparatus; an amphitheater for concerts and special events; jogging paths; a beautiful lake with bridges and fountains; a rose garden; acres of wildflowers; artwork; and a skate park. There are about twenty-five works of art, mostly bronze sculptures and some memorials, scattered throughout the park land. Favorite pieces include the large abstract baseball catcher titled "Today"; "The Dreamer," a two-piece work of art depicting a young man reposed on the grass with his stomach being part of the lawn; and the figures of children. The Holocaust Memorial is powerful with the faces of the statues etched in pain, an eternal flame, and a place to repose and ponder.

15,000 square feet of the skate park are designed for the advanced skater. It has two connected bowls, one four feet in diameter and one six feet, plus boxes, pyramids, rails, drop ins, and stairs. The other 5,000 square feet are geared for beginners with a shorter pyramid, box, drop in, and rails. The skate park is lighted, fenced, and monitored. Skaters must wear a helmet and pads, have a signed parental waiver for ages 17 and under, and have a registration card which costs $5 a year.

Located at 73751 Magnesia Falls Drive, at the northeast corner of the park, the aquatic center has an Olympic-size pool, with competition diving platforms, and a recreation pool and a zero depth area, all of which are open year round. The splash pool, open seasonally, is ideal for kids to enjoy its wavy slides, fun fountains, and colorful water play structures. The center also features changing rooms, a multipurpose room, and a concession stand open to all pool and park users. Consider it your civic duty (and a lot of fun!) to visit the Civic Center Park.

Hours: The park is open daily, sunrise - sunset. The skate park is open during the school year, Mon. - Fri., 2pm - 9pm; Sat. - Sun., 8am - 9pm. It is open during the summer and on holidays daily, 8am - 9pm. The lap and rec pool in the aquatic center are open year round. The splash pool is open in warmer weather, daily, usually mid-March - September. Call for specific hours as they vary.

Price: Free. The skate park is $5 for per year. The aquatic center is $4 for adult Palm Desert residents, $6 for adult non-residents; $3 for senior and ages 6 - 12 residents, $4.50 for non-residents; $2.50 for ages 2 - 5 residents, $3.75 for non-residents.

Ages: All

COACHELLA VALLEY HISTORY MUSEUM ☀

(760) 342-6651 / www.cvhm.org

$$$

82-616 Miles Avenue, Indio

Each city desires to preserve its history and make it available for future generations. The Coachella Valley Museum does so through various collections inside the three buildings on the park-like grounds and gardens. Each room inside the Smiley-Tyler House is dedicated to a different aspect of the valley. The first room, fittingly, contain baskets, pottery, stone mortar and pestles and other artifacts from the first settlers, the Cahuilla Indians, as well as photos (not of the Cahuilla!) and diagrams. Visitors are encouraged to touch sandals made of plants, shell necklaces, baskets, and plants. Other rooms focus on water and agriculture, with an interactive exhibt where you can touch a button corresponding to a photo and hear about supply and demand; plus a railroad room with a desk, signs, lanterns and other railroad memorabilia; a fully-arrayed 1926 kitchen with cans, jars, pots and pans, a butter churner, very old toasters, icebox, stove and other appliances; and an homage to farming set up like a feed store with some old farm tools, a telephone, crates of food, and old-time photographs. Another room is a fully-equipped doctor's office with all the instruments and devices a physician would need.

85% of the nation's dates are exported from the Coachella Valley, so go inside the nicely-laid out Date Museum to see displays, videos and explanations of date farming and learn the date's non-romantic history. Go under the huge fake date palm leaf to see a video, then enjoy a pictoral timeline and glass displays containing equipment used to farm dates, colorful Middle Eastern costumes, packaging, and related date items.

If you ever wondered what school was like in the early 1900's, visit the handsomely restored, 1909 Indio Schoolhouse to answer that question. The one-room schoolhouse is set up with desks, blackboards, old books, crayons, and other implements - let the lessons begin! School groups, especially, enjoy hands-on learning in the schoolhouse - so different from modern-day ones.

Outside, on the beautiful grounds, are lots of old agricultural tools, machinery, and farm equipment, plus fire and railroad equipment, and even an outhouse. Peek inside the blacksmith shop to see forges, anvils, tongs, and other tools and look at the saw mill and adobe replica. Check out the desert submarine (a "hut" for rr workers to keep warm) and water tower. Stroll among the garden sections in the "back" of the museum which include a Japanese garden, rose garden, and a lovely desert garden growing native plants that the Cahuilla Indians used, interspersed with boulders. The working date garden is spacious and help connect the learning gained from the museum into real life. Take a guided tour of the entire museum to learn background information on the articles here and to get a rich, visual sampling of history.

Hours: Open Thurs. - Sat., 10am - 4pm; Sun., 1pm - 4pm. Closed Mon. - Wed., except for school tours, and all major holidays.

Price: $10 for adults; $8 for seniors and students; $5 for ages 6 - 12; $1 for ages 3 - 5; children 2 and under are free. Admission is free on the first weekend of the month.

Ages: 5 years and up.

COACHELLA VALLEY PRESERVE �

(760) 343-2733 - visitor's center; (760) 343-1234 - park / www.coachellavalleypreserve.org; www.cnlm.org

!

29200 Thousand Palms Canyon Road, Coachella

This 18,000-acre preserve, with its twenty-five miles of hiking trails, is not only immense, but diverse in topography and wildlife. The preserve straddles Indio Hills and the infamous San Andreas Fault. Thousand Palms Oasis (I'm not sure it contains quite this many palm trees) is at the heart of the Coachella Valley Preserve. The oasis is supported by water constantly seeping along the fault line.

Start at the rustic visitor center that has a few natural history exhibits behind glass. The displays include arrowheads, mounted insects, birds' nests, and eggs. Just outside the center is a small oasis with very large palm trees,

including "shaggy" ones, that have several picnic tables nestled among them. From here, first walk on planks that cover the swamp-like surrounding ground and then hike the one-mile trek to the most popular destination, the pond. Most parts of the path are not very stroller/wheelchair friendly.

Kids begin to appreciate the many faces of the desert as they hike through the preserve. It's sandy, dry, and rocky, and these elements create sand dunes, bluffs, and mesas. It is also mountainous and interspersed with dense palm trees, cacti, and various other vegetation. Some of the trails are as short as one-quarter mile, while others are longer at one-and-a-half miles, and more.

Bring a water bottle and/or a picnic lunch and have a delightful time exploring desert wilderness at its finest.

Hours: The preserve is open October - April, daily, 7am - 5pm; open May - September, daily, 7am - 6pm. The visitor's center is usually open daily, 8am - 4pm, but closed June - August.
Price: Free
Ages: 4 years and up.

COACHELLA VALLEY WILD BIRD CENTER

(760) 347-2647 / www.coachellavalleywildbirdcenter.org
46500 Van Buren Street, Indio

This center offers a wonderful opportunity to learn about native wild birds in a variety of ways. The small inside exhibit room has taxidermied animals, literature, and a few other displays, as well as several iguanas and live snakes such as rosy boas, racers, and king snakes. Outside are enclosures that hold birds that have been injured, imprinted, or abused. Some are releasable; some are not. The enclosures hold several owls, including great horned owls, plus hawks, geese, quail, and others. Knowledgeable volunteers are on hand to answer questions about the birds - why they are here, what they eat, why they are not good to have as pets, and lots more good information. Beyond this area are fenced-in wetlands with reeds, a few ponds, and more life-sustaining elements. Sandpipers, mallards, pelicans, and other waterfowl nest here, or at least drop in for a visit. Bring binoculars and/or take a look from the viewing towers. Bring a sack lunch to take advantage of the on-site picnic area.

Hours: The center and wetlands are open daily, 8am - noon. A guided birdwalk tour is offered the first Sat. of each month, October - May at 8am.
Price: Free; donations are appreciated.
Ages: 4 years and up.

COVERED WAGON TOURS

(800) 367-2161 or (760) 347-2161 / www.coveredwagontours.com
Washington Street, Thousand Palms

Travel in a mule-drawn, covered wagon for a two-hour narrated tour of the Coachella Valley Preserve. You travel along the San Andreas fault and see three oases and perhaps some wildlife as the naturalist shares information about the geology, plants (which ones were used for food and which ones for medicinal purposes), animals, and way of desert life, both past and present. Occasionally, you get out and walk a bit along the way. The wagons are not the primitive ones that pioneer ancestors used, as these have padded seats, springs, tires, and other amenities, although part of the fun is the bumpiness of the ride. This is a great family outing as the Old West appeals cross generationally. School groups guides will tailor the tour to include facts about Western expansion, and an emphasis on geology and earthquakes.

Take just the tour, or add on a chuck wagon cookout dinner and cowboy entertainment for the full western experience. The tasty barbeque dinner consists of chicken, tri-tip, beans, coleslaw, garlic bread, and pie with topping. The entertainment usually consists of a singer with a guitar, although sometimes it's cowboy poetry or Native American dancing. After dinner and the show, you are invited to grab a skewer and roast some marshmallows over the campfire. The whole evening takes about three-and-a-half hours. Note that group lunch tours are available by reservation, too.

Hours: Call for tour and dinner times. A minimum group of 12 adults is needed. If you are a family group, ask to add on to another group. Reservations are required.
Price: Tours only are $40 for adults; $20 for ages 7 - 16; children 6 and under are free. Tour and dinner costs $76 for adults; $38 for ages 7 - 16; children 6 and under are free. Ask about group rates.
Ages: 5 years and up.

DATELAND PARK

(760) 398-3502 / www.coachella.org
51-805 Shady Lane and Bagdad Avenue, Coachella

This terrific park equals fun. The spacious skate park (about 12,000 square feet) has the necessary street elements - ramps, rails, pyramids, boxes, and plenty of skating area and spectator seating enclosed in perimeter fencing. The small, seasonal water-play spray area has water that spurts up from the ground and down from fake palm trees. There are also grassy fields for open play; a covered picnic area; lots of pavement, and a kind of dirt trail for bikes, scooters, and strollers where one loop around the park equals one-quarter of a mile; and sizable, wonderful, covered playgrounds with wood chip flooring. One of the play areas has a giant, geo-shaped climbing structure with heavy duty ropes crisscrossing all over its inside and bars on the outside. A slide tower, with several curvy and straight slides emanating from it, also has a rock climbing wall attached. There are numerous slides, swings, bridges, large metal climbing coils, platforms, talking tubes, and plenty of places to play on and under the structures. Make a play date with your kids to come to Dateland Park.

Hours: The park is open daily, sunrise - 10pm. The skatepark is open daily, 6am- 10pm.
Price: Free
Ages: All

DEMUTH

(760) 323-8272 - city; (760) 320-6430 - community center / www.palmsprings-ca.gov
3601 E. Mesquite Avenue, Palm Springs

This long and large park has several amenities for families - a grass volleyball court; four tennis courts; lots of picnic tables with shade trees; plenty of run-around, grassy areas; two soccer fields; six baseball diamonds; walkways throughout the park; and several climbable, colorful, sculptured metal shapes. The two good-sized playgrounds have a few twisty slides and even enclosed slides, plus swings, and a rock climbing wall on what looks like a large sandwich board. A community center is open weekdays, 7am to 8pm and on Saturdays until noon.

Hours: Open daily, sunrise - 10pm.
Price: Free
Ages: All

DESERT ADVENTURES

(888) 440-JEEP (5337) or (760) 324-5337 / www.red-jeep.com
67555 E. Palm Canyon Drive, Cathedral City

Explore the natural wonders of the desert by choosing from several different excursions via a two- to five-hour, seven-passenger jeep ride. I almost feel like these adventures should be required for school kids and anyone else who has a desire to learn, as all the guides are wonderfully knowledgeable about history, geology, plants, animals, Native American heritage, and more.

The three-hour San Andreas Fault tour is a great combination of learning Native American culture and heritage, and seeing geography (hopefully not too much in action!). Guests go through archaeology sites; an authentically recreated Cahuilla Indian village; a hidden, lush oasis; and a stream, all the while learning about the history of the Palm Springs area and the Cahuilla Indians, plus how they used the local plants. Also on this tour, through no *fault* of their own, visitors may also straddle the San Andreas Fault line, as well as inspect a fossil bed and look at the great geography. Going at sunset and adding stargazing was a personal favorite. Besides seeing God's masterpiece sunsets on His original canvas, you also walk into the San Andreas Fault as the area is transformed by shadows and, eventually, the dark of night. Millions of stars appear in the sky (at least out here in the desert!) and you study them using telescopes and even laser light pointers.

Some of the tours involve hiking around the area, such as the Indian Canyons Jeep & Hiking tour and the Mecca Hills/Painted Canyon Jeep tour. Bighorn sheep, coyotes, and other wildlife are abundant along these back roads, so keep your eyes open. Bring your camera! Dress appropriately with closed-toed shoes and a hat, and bring sun block, sunglasses, and a water bottle. Be informed that restrooms are nonexistent, except for the bushes beyond the bend in the road. Check out the Desert Adventure website for additional excursions, such as the tour with the wind turbines and Whitewater Preserve. Find out which adventures are offered year round and which are offered seasonally.

Hours: Open year round, weather permitting. Call first to make a reservation.
Price: Three-hour tours are $135 for adults; $110 for ages 12 and under. Call for other tours and prices and check the website for specials.

Ages: 6 years and up.

EL DORADO POLO CLUB

(760) 342-2223 - games info; (760) 831-POLO (7656) - Clubhouse reservations / www.eldoradopolodub.com
50950 Madison Street, Indio

   This dub features ten polo fields (and just one is really big as it's the size of nine football fields!), a stick and ball field, an exercise track, and stabling for 400 horses. Visitors are invited to come and watch an exciting game of polo, where the thundering hooves and "whack" of the mallet keep eyes riveted on horses and riders. Practice matches are generally held during the week. View Saturday and Sunday matches from the Cantina restaurant and fieldside patio. View Sunday afternoon games from the Clubhouse, which offers a full-service menu and bar as well, or bring a picnic lunch to enjoy on the grass or a tailgate party in areas north and south of the Clubhouse. Make reservations at the restaurants or arrive early to grab a picnic/tailgate spot.

   Hours: Practices are Wed.. - Fri. and spectators are welcome. Games are played Sat. at noon and Sun. at 10am, noon and 2pm. The season runs (or gallops!) the end of December - March. Call or check the website for a schedule for specific practice and game times.
   Price: Watching the practices and games is free as is tailgating, unless it's a special event.
   Ages: 3 years and up.

FELLOW EARTHLINGS WILDLIFE CENTER

(760) 363-1344 / www.fellowearthlings.org
11427 West Drive, Morongo Valley

$$$$$

   "Awwww - so cute!" That's the first thing we exclaimed when we entered the enclosure with the small mob (i.e. group) of about seven meerkats at this unique center. We spent our allotted two hours sitting on the ground as the meerkats ran around (constantly!), dug holes (constantly!), climbed up the fence, climbed on us, fed out of our hands (we wore gloves), and entertained us by their constant antics. As we took pictures and played with them using paper bags, balls, stuffed animals, and other items, Pam, the proprietor, taught us so much about the cute little critters. We learned about their habits, their personalities, how to care for them, that they do not make good pets, and much more. Note that this center partnered with Animal Planet for *Meerkat Manor* and that Pam consulted for Disney for Timon's character in *Lion King*.

   The encompassing rustic grounds are beautiful with numerous huge old oak and pine trees, a quaint-looking cottage, and a rock-lined pond with a large paddlewheel and short waterfall. Don't *meer*ly read about Fellow Earthlings, come by for a visit! Each visit is considered an adoption and you are sent a portfolio for the meerkats and information on them. Each visit is for two hours, costs $100, and is for up to four people - no more. It is a private visit - your group is the only one on the grounds. Visitors must be in good health and be able to sit relatively quietly for two hours, on the ground. The facility and enclosure are not handicapped accessible.

   Hours: Visits are available May - September on select Fri., Sat., and Sun. You must call or email beforehand to schedule a visit.
   Price: $100 for up to 4 people.
   Ages: Must be at least 8 years old.

FORTYNINE PALMS OASIS

(760) 367-5500; (760) 367-5502 / www.nps.gov
Fortynine Palms Canyon Road, Twentynine Palms

   Part of Joshua Tree National Park, this moderate, delightful, three-mile (round trip) trail cuts through desert hillside and sparse vegetation and around red boulders leading to a cool, green oasis in the canyon. Depending on the season, the water trickles or streams into a smallish pool that provides a drinking hole for the wildlife and waters the numerous fan palm trees here. (The palm trees look like they're wearing shaggy coats.)

   The view from the hilltops is great - you can see all around the valley and Twentynine Palms area. You can also clearly see some of the surrounding fault lines. It's too hot to hike here in the summer, but its a great hike through rugged scenery at other seasons. Regardless of when you come, bring plenty of water!!!

   Hours: Open daily, sunrise - sunset.
   Price: Free.
   Ages: 6 years and up.

FREEDOM PARK

(760) 346-0611 / www.cityofpalmdesert.org
77-400 Country Club Drive, Palm Desert

Feel free to find something wonderful to do at the twenty-six acre Freedom Park. It has three baseball fields, with stadium seating and a concession stand; three basketball courts; two tennis courts, two sand volleyball courts; two huge fields for soccer or football; plenty of open, grassy areas; a small, narrow skating area with a few ramps and rails; a small and a large dog park; plenty of covered picnic tables; hard packed dirt/sand walking paths throughout; gardens (it's a usable and scenic park!); and three playgrounds. One play structure looks ready to set sail as it is designed like a ship with portholes, plus slides and ladders. Another area has swings, animals on big springs to ride and rock on back and forth, slides, and cargo rope to climb. The last playground captures the imagination as the apparatus looks like abstract art. There is a curved rock climbing wall; shapes to sit on and climb; cables with discs to climb up and on; a tilted trampoline ring (with no trampoline); a twisted metal pole with a small platform to twirl around on; and other unique elements.

> **Hours:** Open daily, dawn - 10pm.
> **Price:** Free
> **Ages:** All

GENERAL PATTON MEMORIAL MUSEUM

(760) 227-3483 / www.generalpattonmuseum.com
62-510 Chiriaco Road, Chiriaco Summit

Any study of World War II includes at least one lesson on war hero, General George Patton. Even if kids don't know who he is yet, they will like all the "war stuff" at the museum. Outside the memorial building are over a dozen tanks from WWII to Vietnam. Kids can't climb on them, but they can run around and play army. There are several Walls of Rememberance on the grounds with names engraved of honorees from all branches of the service and from all wars. There is a picnic area located by tanks and other vehicles.

Inside, the front room is dominated by a five-ton relief map depicting the Colorado River Aqueduct route and surrounding area. The large back room is filled with General Patton's personal effects, and lots of WWII memorabilia such as uniforms, weapons, flags, artillery, helmets, and more. Our favorite exhibits include a jeep, a lifelike statue of General Patton (who looks amazingly like George C. Scott), and rounds of machine gun bullets. Special displays showcase Nazi items taken from fallen Nazi soldiers; a small, but powerful pictorial Holocaust display; and items found on the battlefield of Gettysburg. There are also exhibits and items from WWI, the Afghanistan, Iraq and other wars, plus photographs, flags, guns, and more.

Over one million servicemen and women were trained at this huge Desert Training Center site during WWII. If your child is especially interested in this period of military history, take him to the remnants of the training camps, accessible by four-wheel vehicles. Call the museum for directions and more details. Note that the gift shop features a good selection of military-themed toys, clothing, and souvenirs.

> **Hours:** Open daily, 9:30am - 4:30pm. Closed Thanksgiving and Christmas.
> **Price:** $5 for adults; $4.50 for seniors; $1 for ages 7 - 12; children 6 and under are free.
> **Ages:** 3 years and up.

GUIDE DOGS OF THE DESERT

(760) 329-6257 / www.guidedogsofthedesert.com
60740 Dillon Road, Whitewater

Thirty, or so, dogs consider this place their temporary home as they are trained to become guide dogs for their blind owners. Visitors learn about the program which takes pups, places them in loving homes for eighteen months or so, then brings them back for serious training as guide dogs, and matches them with a new master or mistress. Explore the kennels where the puppies are raised (call first to see if any puppies are currently here); tour the dormitories (if they are unoccupied) where owners stay for their orientation; watch dogs being trained; learn how to treat guide dogs (i.e., when it's acceptable to touch them and when it's not); and learn how to put a harness on the dogs. Tours can last a half hour up to an hour and a half, depending on the interest of the visitors.

> **Hours:** Tours are given by reservation.
> **Price:** Free; donations appreciated.
> **Ages:** 3 years and up.

HI-DESERT NATURE MUSEUM / YUCCA VALLEY COMMUNITY CENTER ☼

(760) 369-7212 / www.hidesertnaturemuseum.org; www.yucca-valley.org

57116 Twentynine Palms Highway, Yucca Valley

    I *highly* recommend the Hi-Desert Nature Museum. It offers lots of activities and has fascinating exhibits on wildlife, geology, culture, and science. Just some of the rotating exhibits in the front room have included Wild on Wildflowers; Shake, Rattle & Roll - Living With Earthquakes; and Holiday Traditions from around the world. We saw one called Black Widow. Arachnophobia aside, the fantastic photographs, video, and information combined with live and dead specimens made learning about this feared insect interesting. The far wall in this room contains several encased displays of Indian baskets, arrowheads, pottery, and Kachina dolls.

    Another good-sized room has taxidermied waterfowl, plus animals that are unique to the desert such as mule deer, quail, roadrunners, jack rabbits, and coyotes. A touch corner in here has skulls and soft fur to match to the stuffed animals.

    Fossils, a sabertooth cat skull, and a wonderful rock and mineral collection comprise the earth science room. The petrified logs are unusual, as are the sphere balls. Rocks such as amethyst and malachite are shown in their rough, natural state, and also in a polished version. Raw minerals are shown next to their commercial counterparts such as fluorspar next to toothpaste and talc next to baby powder. This helps kids to make connections and understand that man-made products were first God-created resources.

    A mini-zoo has live lizards, Madagascar hissing cockroaches, snakes, a tarantula, and some furry little creatures, too. A docent is often on hand to assist your child in holding one of the animals. I'm proud to write that, after recovering from my cold sweat, I held the (large!) tarantula.

    The Kids' Corner is action packed. There is a small sand pit (I mean archaeological dig); animal puppets; a butterfly and insect collection; stone mortar and pestles with corn kernels to grind; animal tracks to match with animals; a touch table with whale bones, rocks, and shells; books; and containers of construction toys. The Hi-Desert Nature Museum also offers special events, kids craft programs, educational tours, and themed traveling classroom programs on insects, wildflowers, a particular animal, and more.

    The community center/park just behind the museum is equally fine. It has four basketball courts; a baseball field; a skateboard park with cement ramps and steps; a sand volleyball court; a covered picnic area; grassy areas; and three playgrounds complete with slides, climbing apparatus, and swings. All this and a few shade trees are against the backdrop of Joshua trees and the desert mountains.

    Opening an oyster and finding a pearl created by a grain of sand is comparable to opening the doors to this museum and finding a part of the sandy desert that has been transformed to a treasure of great worth.

       Hours: Open Thurs. - Sat., 10am - 5pm. Closed Sun. - Wed. and major holidays.

       Price: Free

       Ages: 1 year and up.

HISTORICAL SOCIETY PALM DESERT ☀

(760) 346-6588 / www.hspd.org

72-861 El Paseo Drive, Palm Desert

    This historical museum has four small rooms. The lobby holds numerous styles and models of cameras throughout the ages; a display case of marionettes used in TV shows, including the "mother" of Howdy Doody; an homage to Hopalong Cassidy; and photographs of Palm Desert as it was in the olden days. There are also photographs and some memorabilia from the famous people who have called Palm Springs home and some of the famous places in Palm Springs.

    The second room holds firefighting memorabilia as this museum is located in the old firehouse. (A fire truck out front advertises this fact.) There are helmets, axes on one wall, hose nozzles, copper and brass fire extinguishers, a leather fire bucket, little plastic fire coats for kids to try on, a Darth Vaderish smoke helmet from the 1900's, and an 1820 Molly Stark fire engine pump. The next room has a 3-D wall map tracking the Cahuilla Trail (Road) and exhibits regarding water - a precious commoditiy especially for the desert. The tiny room off here contains a collection near and dear to my heart - chamber pots. Some of the porcelain ones are quite decorative, like the one fit for royalty made in England in 1891, as well as some basic bed pans. Hmmm. An outhouse door is attached to the wood paneled wall in here - you can open it if you want. A Nolan organ is also in this room and a few other household items. Guided tours are offered as are several annual events, such as fire safety training to school children.

       Hours: Open October - May, Mon., Wed., Fri., Sat., 10am - 3pm. Closed Sun., Tues., Thurs., and June through September.

Price: Free
Ages: 6 years and up.

HOVLEY SOCCER PARK
(760) 346-0611 / www.cityofpalmdesert.org
74-735 Hovley Lane, Palm Desert
    This elongated park is mostly comprised of five full-size soccer fields. Around the perimeter of the fields is a disc golf course which is very technical because of the straight drives. Along the side of the fields, near the concession stand, are two small, covered playgrounds - one is ship-themed - with metal climbing apparatus, a short chain ladder, swings, and slides. Past the playgrounds are three horseshoe pits, which can see a lot of action, plus three shuffleboard courts, and a basketball court.
    Hours: Open daily, dawn - 11pm.
    Price: Free
    Ages: All

INDIAN CANYONS
(760) 323-6018 - canyons; (800) 790-3398 - officei / www.indian-canyons.com $$$
38529 S. Palm Canyon Drive, Palm Springs
    Vast, spectacular, and awesome are three words that come to mind when exploring Indian Canyons. Long ago, ancestors of the Agua Caliente Cahuilla Indians made their homes in these canyons and the surrounding area. Today, a large number of Indians still reside on the reservation here. The Tribal Council has opened the canyons for the public to explore.
    A mile or so past the entrance gate is the trading post. Kids enjoy looking at the trinkets, jewelry, and Indian art work. Beyond the store are picnic grounds and hiking and horse trails.
    Palm Canyon is fifteen miles long and abundant with palm trees - a stark contrast to the surrounding rocky hills. The moderately graded, paved walkway into this valley leads you along a stream and to a picnic oasis. The scenery almost makes you forget that you're hiking! Andreas Canyon is unexpectedly lush with fan palms and more than 150 species of plants, all within a half-mile radius. Walk along a stream and see unusual rock formations. Challenge your kids to look for shapes or people in the rocks. There are also Indian caves back in the canyon and old grinding stones.
    Hike to Murray Canyon from Andreas Canyon. Murray is smaller and less accessible, but no less beautiful. There are caves here also, which always sparks a child's imagination. Hiking in Indian Canyons is a wonderful opportunity to explore the desert wilderness surrounded by the stunning backdrop of the rocky mountains and there are several trails for all levels of difficulty. See TAHQUITZ CANYON (pg. 392) for information on another nearby canyon.
    Hours: Open October - June, daily, 8am - 5pm (last entrance at 4pm). Open July - September, Fri., Sat., Sun., 8am - 5pm.
    Price: $9 for adults; $7 for seniors, military, and students; $5 for ages 6 - 12; children 5 and under are free.
    Ages: All, but older kids for real hiking.

JOE MANN PARK
(760) 346-0611 / www.cityofpalmdesert.org
77-810 California Drive, Palm Desert
    This nice neighborhood park has a sand volleyball court; a basketball court; one large, gated, covered playground with plenty of space to play under the raised elements and lots of activity to play on them; an open grassy area; covered picnic tables; some BBQs; and a small waterplay area used seasonally. The waterplay is just one twisty piece of metal that shoots out water from its various holes, but sometimes that's all you need to cool off and have fun. The playground has slides, bridges, tic-tac-toe, swing, curvy metal pieces of equipment to climb on and up, ladders, and a stepping structure that looks like a small hillside.
    Adjacent to the park is a gated Rose Garden, promoted as a quiet area. It contains old shade trees, picnic tables, grass areas, and a rose garden.
    Hours: Open daily, 7am - 10pm. The rose garden is open daily, 7am - 4pm.
    Price: Free
    Ages: All

JOSHUA TREE AND SOUTHERN RAILROAD MUSEUM

(760) 366-8503 or (760) 366-8879 / www.jtsrr.org
8901 Willow Lane, Joshua Tree

Nestled into the rocky, desert hillside, this site is great for those who are *loco* about trains! The trains range from two-and-a-half-inch scale models to full-size rail cars. If it's running, you're invited to ride on a model train which covers about a mile of track, some of which is elevated over the ground, and some goes on bridges and through desert terrain. Take a tour of the full-size cars including a diner, with its old-fashioned stove and icebox; a mail car, with small pigeonholes that are labeled with city names; a Pullman sleeping car, which always makes sleeping on a train seem romantic; and the grand finale - a caboose. Both the Live Steam Club and the railroad museum are located here. Model railroad enthusiast members cannot only work on their hobby, but engineered it so that they and guests can camp here, too.

Inside the museum, a replicated railroad station, are model steam engines and lots of railroad memorabilia from Francis Moseley's collection. Ask to watch the video which shows how a model train operates.

Hours: Check the calendar to visit at an open event or call to make an appointment for a ride and tour.
Price: Free; donations of $2 per adult are asked for group visits.
Ages: 3 years and up.

JOSHUA TREE NATIONAL PARK

(760) 367-5500 - park; (760) 367-5522 - Keys Ranch tour / www.nps.gov/jotr
South entrance - on Pinto Basin Rd. at the Cottonwood Springs Visitor Center; North entrance - at 74485 National Park Dr. for the Oasis Visitor Cener in Twentynine Palms; West entrance - at 6554 Park Blvd. for Joshua Tree Visitor Center. This is the best way to reach Keys View and Hidden Valley. In Yucca Valley, Black Rock Nature Center is located at 9800 Black Rock Canyon Rd., Joshua Tree

This over 900,000-acre park gets its name from the unique Joshua trees that Mormon visitors likened to the biblical Joshua reaching up to God. Explore the riches of this national treasure by car, by foot, and/or by camping.

Entire books are written on Joshua Tree National Park, so consider the following information a very condensed version. Just a few phrases attributed to this enormous park are "wind-sculpted boulders"; "massive granite monoliths"; "five fan palm oases dotting the park"; "wildflowers and wildlife"; "mountainous"; and "rugged." Start your visit at the main headquarters/visitors center in Oasis of Mara, located off the north entrance. You can get a map here, look at the botanical displays, and watch a slide show that gives a good overview of the park. One destination worth mentioning in particular is Keys Ranch. Explore and learn about the ranch and its colorful owners and see the numerous vestiges of the people that once lived here, including the schoolhouse and workshop. Against a backdrop of boulders, the ranch grounds are strewn with old rusty equipment and half-buried cars, and vestiges of a Desert Queen Ranch, a gold mine turned into a ranch. Ninety-minute guided tours, the only way to see the ranch, are offered at 2pm on Fridays and Saturdays, and at 10am on Sunday. The cost, plus vehicle fee is $5 for ages 12 and over; $2.50 for ages 6 - 11.

If you are automobile adventurers, which is a good way to get a lay of the land, there are many roads to travel. Keys View is the most popular destination because of its breathtaking view of the valley, mountains, and deserts. (Bring a panoramic camera.) If you don't mind a few bumps along the way, and kids usually don't, there are many dirt roads accessible only by four-wheel drive. Particularly outstanding is the eighteen-mile Geology Tour Road, which showcases some of the most incredible landscape the park offers.

Hiking runs the gamut from easy, one-tenth-of-a-mile trails, to strenuous, over thirteen-mile long trails. Three of the trails that offer fascinating terrain also lead to special destinations. The first one is the one-mile loop, Hidden Valley, with trails winding through massive boulders. It leads to and through legendary cattle rustlers' hideouts and past petroglyphs. The second is Barker Dam, which was built almost 100 years ago and is now a reservoir that many desert animals frequent. Approach it in whispers, if possible, so as not to scare away any critters. Encourage your children to look for some of the "hidden" wildlife in the water. The third is Lost Horse Mine, which is a rugged one-and-a-half-mile hike. This mine was used for prospecting and gold mining. Maybe there still is gold in them thar hills! **Bring water** no matter which trail you take because it is not supplied in the park.

Rock climbing is a very popular sport here. Even if your kids are too young to participate, they'll get a vicarious thrill at watching more experienced climbers. Boulder hopping is also fun, and that can be done by kids of all ages. There are many groups and classes that come here to climb, including a locally-based school called Joshua Tree Rock Climbing School. Call (800) 890-4745 or (760) 366-4745 / www.joshuatreerockclimbing.com for more information.

Camping is primitive at most of the 500 sites of the nine campgrounds in Joshua Tree. Many campsites are located

in the shelter of rocks, while others, at higher elevations, offer spots of shade. It is hot during the day, much cooler at night (even cold), and at times quite windy, but kids revel in it all. Water is only provided at Cottonwood and Black Rock Canyon campgrounds, so other sites are really back to basics.

National parks are sometimes referred to as "universities of the outdoors." Joshua Tree National Park is an outstanding university to attend. Everyone will go home with a special memory, and a different reason for wanting to come back.

Hours: Open daily, 24/7. Joshua Tree visitors center is open daily, 8am - 5pm; Oasis is open daily, 9am - 5pm; Cottonwood is open daily, 9am - 4pm; Black Rock is open October - May daily, 8am - 4pm (noon - 8pm on Fri.)

Price: $15 per non-commercial vehicle, which is good for 7 days admittance. $5 per person if by foot, bike, horse, etc. Family campgrounds are $10 - $15 a night, depending on location.

Ages: All

KOBE JAPANESE STEAKHOUSE (Rancho Mirage)

(760) 324-1717 / www.koberanchomirage.com
69-838 Hwy. 111, Rancho Mirage

$$$$

Knives, flames, and food - it doesn't get any better than this for my boys. Go past the waterfall over the footbridge and the koi pond to enter the somewhat dark restaurant. Quality food - seafood, Angus (not Kobe) steak, chicken, and even Oriental vegetables - with sauces and such are sliced, diced, and prepared at communal Teppanyaki grill tables, so it's kind of like having your own personal chef. Some of the menu items are teriyaki chicken and prawns, $27.50; filet mignon, $31.50; scallop and tiger prawns, $29.90; Halibut steak, $25.50; teppan shrimp, $26.50. Dinners include shrimp appetizer, white rice, miso soup, vegetable blend, and hot green tea. Sherbet or green tea ice cream is dessert. Sashimi choices include maguro tuna, $12.25 and shake salmon, $11.50, while sushi choices include rainbow roll of snowcrab meat, cucumber and avocado topped with five kinds of sashimi, $14.90; California roll, $7.50; and several other selections. (The onion volcano is a fun thing to watch the chef cook.) Kids meals include the same appetizer, soup, veggie, and dessert as an adult. Choose from teriyaki chicken, $11.90; sirloin steak or steak and chicken, $13.90 each; or steak and shrimp, $14.90.

Hours: Open Sun. - Thurs., 5pm - 8:30pm; Fri. - Sat., 5pm - 9pm. Reservations are highly recommended.
Price: Prices are listed above. Check out the Early Bird specials.
Ages: 5 years and up.

LAKE CAHUILLA

(760) 564-4712 - lake; (800) 234-PARK (7275) - camping reservations / www.riversidecountyparks.org
58075 Jefferson, La Quinta

$$

Escape from the heat at Lake Cahuilla recreation park. The gigantic, stocked lake is a prime spot for fisherboys and girls to reel in the catch of the day. Kids 16 years and up need a state fishing license, which are not sold at the lake. Night fishing is open Friday and Saturday during the summer. Although swimming in the lake is prohibited, there is a pool available for your aquatic pleasure. (The pool is open for anyone to use, not just overnight campers.) A playground is located behind the pool - youngsters always have energy to play, no matter what temperature it is!

The park is not abundantly blessed with shade trees, but there are large grassy areas and palm trees to enhance its beauty. Hiking trails traverse the park, so make sure you've got plenty of sunscreen and water. Over 100 campsites are available here, complete with barbecues and other amenities. Come escape the city life, if just for a day or night.

Hours: The park is open mid-October - April daily, sunrise - sunset. It is open May - mid-October, Fri. - Mon., sunrise - sunset. The campground is open the same months and days. The pool is open mid-April - mid-October on weekends only, for two hour sessions starting at 11am, 1:30pm, and 4pm.

Price: Park entrance is $3 for adults; $2 for ages 2 - 12. The swimming pool is an extra $2 per person, per session. Primitive camping (space and a table - no shade trees) is $15 a site (reservations are not necessarily needed); a site with hookups is $23 a night. The camping reservation fee is $7. Fishing permits are $6 for ages 16 and up; $4 for ages 6 - 15; children 5 and under are free. Fishing licenses are an additional fee and not available here.

Ages: All

THE LIVING DESERT WILDLIFE AND BOTANICAL GARDEN PARK

(760) 346-5694 / www.livingdesert.org

$$$$

47900 Portola Avenue, Palm Desert

Kids can experience a lot of living in the 1,200-acre Living Desert! Choose one of three areas of interest - botanical gardens, wildlife, or hiking - or partake in some of each.

Start your visit at the good-sized children's Discovery Room with great murals and an eight-foot giant ground sloth skeleton. Replica bones and skulls are on the fossil wall. Children can get a real "feel" for desert life as they touch live snakes, turtles, and a big hairy tarantula, plus feathers, bones, rocks, and fur. They can also put together puzzles, do rubbings, look at a seismograph, and watch ants (10,000 of them) run here and there inside the ant lab. Stand in a darkened room here with a nighttime sky lit up by constellations, listening to sounds of the desert, seeing animal projections and glow in the dark animal tracks. Watch sand dunes reform as the sand blows around in an encased display.

The northern section of this "like a zoo, only better" park is mostly botanical. The pathways weave in and out amongst an incredible variety of desert floral including saguaros, yuccas, and towering palm trees. Caged bird life is abundant along the walkways, too. We took the time to really watch our feathered friends' activities and learned quite a bit.

Eagle Canyon houses twenty desert animal species living in their natural element. Powerful mountain lions, Mexican wolves, and the small fennec foxes dwell in their own craggy retreats that are easily viewed through glass. Don't miss the tree-climbing coyote! The three-acre African Village, WaTuTu has hyenas, camels, leopards, a petting zoo (but not with the aforementioned animals!), and a time for story telling. This section also houses the hospital where examinations and medical procedures occur. You can go in and see a part of this facility on your own, or take a docent-led tour. Fanciful Flyers is the name of the exhibit which showcases a variety of butterflies and hummingbirds from October through April - I love this attraction.

A trail system lies to the east, traversing through some of the 1,000-acre wilderness section of the park. Three loops offer something for every level hiker: An easy three-quarter-mile hike; a moderate one-and-a-half-mile hike; and a strenuous five-mile, round-trip hike to the base of Eisenhower Mountain, all of which is open in cooler months. Don't get me wrong, however, even the walk around "inside" the park is a hike in itself. If you get tired, take a shuttle ($6 for adults; $3 for ages 3 - 12) which you can hop on and off throughout the park, throughout the day.

Animals in the Living Desert dwell in outdoor enclosures that resemble their natural habitat. A rocky mountain is home to the Bighorn sheep. Look for them leaping among the boulders. Other exotic animals include Arabian oryx, aardwolves, zebras, cheetahs, small African mammals, giraffes, and birds. We saw several other animals in the wild, too, such as a snake slithering across our path and the ever-speedy roadrunner darting out of the bushes. Seeing them authenticated the unique setting of this park. Want to see more animals, more up close? See Wildlife Wonders, a live animal presentation at the outdoor theater, featuring your favorite desert critters, or see Animal Presentation, an intimate stage "show" with smaller residents - hedgehogs, foxes, snakes, owls and others. Also check the schedule for Keeper Chats, where the animal keepers visit the enclosures and talk about five different critters each day, such as cheetahs, hyenas, big horn sheep, and more. Help feed the giraffes at the Giraffe Feeding, usually at 10am. Go on a safari ride without going to Africa by taking a camel ride here for only $5 per person for a three-minute ride - open seasonally. Go inside the aviary and hand feed small budgies, a type of parakeet with a feeding stick ($2 - entrance fee and stick). Become a Gecko explorer - a member of a naturalist club to see more than meets the eye, for kids 6 to 12 years old, held on most Saturday mornings.

Kids will especially enjoy Gecko Gulch, a one-acre play area for youngsters. There are oversized reptile sculptures to climb on, a saguaro cactus slide (not a real saguaro), a tortoise shell to crawl into and hide, underground animal burrow tunnels, sand dune play area, a "gold" panning trough, and shade area for parents (thank goodness!). Ride the endangered species carousel for $2.

Train afficionados of all ages enjoy the acre-large, G-scale, model train exhibit with three loops and five distinct layouts. Trains make tracks past the Grand Canyon, Mount Rushmore, a California mining town, the Swiss Alps, and much more. The exhibit is usually shut down mid-June through September for maintenance and construction.

Inquire about the numerous programs offered during the year, such as family evening adventures; two-hour behind-the-scene safaries; summer zoo camp; and (a favorite) Starry Safaris (i.e., sleepovers), which include a wildlife presentation, dinner, walking through the park at dark, s'mores, breakfast, and a pass to stay at the zoo for the day. Visit here during the spring when the desert flowers and trees explode in a profusion of colors, or come in the winter to see Wildlights (pg. 761). Anytime you choose to visit the Living Desert will be a time of wonder, relaxation, and education.

Hours: Open October - May, daily, 9am - 5pm; open June - September, daily, 8am - 1:30pm. Closed Christmas. The weekend Wildlife Wonders show is usually given at 11am and 2pm most of the year; at 10am in the summer.

Price: $17.25 for adults; $15.75 for seniors and active military; $8.75 for ages 3 - 12; children 2 and under are free. School groups, with reservations, are $5 per person for admission, or $6 per person for admission plus a two-hour guided tour. See page xi for info on the Bank of America free weekend program.

Ages: All

LUCKIE PARK

(760) 367-7562 - park; (760) 367-5777 - pool / www.ci.twentynine-palms.ca.us
Two Mile Road and Utah Trail, Twentynine Palms

The best park in town, Luckie features a great playground with a twisty slide; swings; funky-shaped, metal climbing apparatus; a short rock climbing wall; and more, all on chipped wood flooring. Green grassy lawns (a rarity in the desert), three lighted basketball courts, baseball fields, a soccer field, indoor racquetball courts, horseshoe pits, a pool that's open seasonally, and a nice skate park complete this park. The mid-size skate park, which is just across the street from the park on Joe Davis Road, has a bowl, ramps, and other street elements. Helmet and pads are mandatory.

Hours: The park is open daily, sunrise - sunset. The pool is open Memorial Day - mid-June, Sat. - Sun., mid-June - August daily, 1pm - 5pm. Call for skate park hours.

Price: The park is free. The pool cost $3 per person.

Ages: All

MCCALLUM THEATRE

(760) 340-ARTS (2787) / www.mccallumtheatre.org
73000 Fred Waring Drive, Palm Desert

This beautiful theater seats over a thousand people and has three levels of seating, including box seats. First class productions include *Sound of Music*, *Riverdance*, *Cats*, and *The Nutcracker Suite*, as well as famous individual acts and artists. There are also several productions that are enjoyable for the entire family, such as the Peking Acrobats. Ask about the Field Trip Series in which slightly abbreviated dance and theater performances are given for free for students and educators - fantastic! Art is important! Tours often focus on the stage and technical aspects of the facility. Contact the McCallum for more information.

Hours: Call for a program schedule.

Price: Tickets range from $45 and up, depending on the show.

Ages: 4 years and up.

MOORTEN BOTANICAL GARDEN

(760) 327-6555 / www.palmsprings.com/moorten
1701 S. Palm Canyon Drive, Palm Springs

This place has plenty of prickly plants along pleasurable pathways. In other words, this compact botanical garden, specializing in cacti, is a delightful stroll and an interesting way to study desert plant life. There are over 3,000 varieties of cacti, trees, succulents, and flowers, plus lots of birds! You'll see giant saguaros, ocotillos, and grizzly bear cactus, and you may walk through a greenhouse (or cactarium). Toward the entrance are petrified logs, and a few, small desert animals in cages. Enjoy this spot of greenery in the midst of the sandy, brown desert.

Hours: Open Mon. - Tues., Thurs. - Sun., 10am - 4pm. Closed Wed., Thanksgiving, and Christmas.

Price: $4 for adults; $2 for ages 5 - 15; children 4 and under are free.

Ages: All

OASIS DATE GARDEN

(800) 827-8017 / www.oasisdategardens.com
59-111 Hwy. 111/Grapefruit Boulevard, Thermal

Is your date worth the drive? I think so. Take a twenty-minute tour first which includes watching an eight-minute movie about date growing. The video room also has date artifacts - palms, cultivating and harvesting tools, hats worn by harvesters, and the fruit. Although you can't walk through the date grove, you can go outside and hear more about date pollination and see male and female trees. Tour groups of all ages are welcome. The outside has a lovely picnic

grounds with a grassy area and plenty of picnic tables surrounded by towering date trees from the 175-acre ranch. Bring your own lunch, or purchase a meal in the small Oasis Date Gardens cafe inside. Meals average about $7 and include salads (try the spinach date salad), hamburger, deli sandwiches, and more, plus a wide variety of shakes from date to butterscotch to cactus and pineapple.

Back inside, choose from a variety of dates to sample and purchase, other souvenir merchandise, and a date shake. (Tip - the Palm Desert Visitor Center often has brochures regarding Oasis that include a coupon for a free, small date shake.)

Hours: Open daily, 9am - 4pm. Close some holidays.
Price: Free
Ages: 6 years and up.

OFFROAD RENTALS

(760) 325-0376 / www.offroadrentals.com
59511 US Highway 111, Palm Springs

Come ride the sand dunes in Palm Springs! After watching a ten-minute video on safety in a cave-like setting, put on a helmet and goggles (provided by Offroad), hop on your single-seater, four-wheel ATV, and go for an exhilarating ride. An expansive, flat area immediately in front of the rental facility is great for beginners, and it is the only place children may ride. The "course" has tire obstacles, too. More experienced riders (i.e., older) can venture out on the large sand hills beyond this area. Machines are suited to the age and size of the rider, and speed limits are built into the vehicles. (Yea!) For instance, children 6 to 10 years, or so, are assigned vehicles that can't exceed four mph The ride here was a highlight for all of us. A beverage is included in your admission price, but bring your own sun block. Riders must wear long pants and closed-toed shoes. Ask about their two-hour, educational dune buggy tours.

Hours: Open daily, 10am - sunset. Hours might vary during the summer.
Price: Forty-five-minute rides start at $40 per person (those who obey the rules get a little longer).
Ages: 6 years and up.

THE OLD SCHOOLHOUSE MUSEUM

(760) 367-2366 / www.29palmshistorical.com
6760 National Park Drive, Twentynine Palms

Originally built in 1927, the old schoolhouse museum looks like an old schoolhouse room, complete with wooden desks, a flag, phonograph, books, and a blackboard. The books on display are on Native Americans, gold miners, cowboys, and homesteaders. It also houses a small research library and historical exhibits of the early settlers, mostly via pictures and written information. The small gift shop carries pamphlets on the history of this area as well as cards and gift items. Call if you would like information on a school field trip.

Hours: Open September - May, Wed. - Sun., 1pm - 4pm; open June - August, Sat. - Sun., 1pm - 4pm.
Price: Free
Ages: 7 years and up.

O'S AMERICAN KITCHEN (Palm Desert)

(760) 674-8425 / www.osamericankitchen.com
72840 State Hwy. 111, suite W465, Palm Desert

See O'S AMERICAN KITCHEN (San Diego County) on page 576 for details about this pizza-making tour for kids.

PALM CANYON THEATRE

(760) 323-5123 / www.palmcanyontheatre.org
538 N. Palm Canyon Drive, Palm Springs

Palm Canyon Theatre specializes in light, musical theater so you'll enjoy such productions as *Oklahoma*, *The King and I*, *Noises Off*, and *Little Shop of Horrors*. Other productions include dramatic plays and Shakespeare.

Hours: Performances are usually given Thurs., 7pm; Fri. - Sat., 8pm; Sun., 2pm.
Price: Tickets usually range from $25 - $32 for adults; and can be $10 for students and children.
Ages: 6 years and up.

PALM SPRINGS AERIAL TRAMWAY

(888) 515-TRAM (8726) - tram info; (760) 325-4537 - Peaks Restaurant / www.pstramway.com
1 Tramway Road, Palm Springs

$$$$$

In only ten minutes, an eighty-passenger, rotating, enclosed car, carries you seemingly straight up the side of Mount San Jacinto. The scenery change in this short amount of time is almost unbelievable - from cactus and desert sand below, to evergreen trees and cool air up above. Call ahead to see if there is snow at the top because Mount San Jacinto State Park is at an altitude of 8,516 feet.

The Mountain Station at the top has a game room, a gift shop, restaurants, a snack bar, and observation areas where you can see a panoramic view of the entire valley, including the Salton Sea which is forty-five miles away. The bottom floor of the Station also has a few taxidermied animals and an interesting, twenty-minute film on the history of the tramway.

Outside, behind and down the Mountain Station building, is Mount San Jacinto Wilderness State Park, with fifty-four miles of great hiking trails, campgrounds, and a ranger station. Download a map from the website. The Desert View Trail is a delightful beginner trail at 1.5 miles, or, for younger kids the ¾ mile loop. The San Jacinto Peak is 5.5 miles, one way and leads you to the second highest point in Southern California for a spectacular view. Call (951) 659-2607/ www.parks.ca.gov for (primitive) camping information; permits are $5. Though we just walked along the easier trails, the mountain scenery anywhere up here is unbeatable! Just remember that the trail you go down from the peak Mountain Station, you must also go back up to catch the tram. During the summer on the weekends, free, forty-minute, guided nature walks are offered. In the winter you can rent cross-country skis ($21 for adults for the day) and snow shoes ($18 per person for the day) at the Adventure Center. These are available November 15 through April 15 (weather permitting), weekends only from 9am to 4pm. There are also plenty of areas to go sledding, snow-tubing, and, most importantly, snowman-making and snowball-throwing. Tip: Always bring a jacket and wear closed-toed shoes - it **really** does get cold up here, no matter the temperature down the mountain!

If you're hungry, inside the Mountain Station is the Pines Cafe, a cafeteria-style restaurant open from 11am to 3pm for lunch. Prices are between $9 to $18 per entree. It's open for dinner, too, from 4:30pm to 8:30pm. Entrees include vegetable lasagna, chicken, sliced tri tip, pasta, roasted potatoes, Caesar salad, and more. Fine dining is available at Peaks Restaurant for lunch - Greek salad, $9; pasta with Brie cheese, $13; steak and fries, $18; burger, $13; grilled salmon, $16; chicken club, $14; and dinner - N.Y. steak, $36; grilled salmon, $26; or brick chicken, $22. Children's meals are $10 for a choice of grilled shrimp, grilled cheese sandwich or grilled chicken. If you venture up the tramway after 4pm (and only after 4pm), you can purchase a Ride 'n' Dine ticket which includes a round trip tram ride plus dinner at Pines Cafe, which is served starting at 4:30pm.

Hours: Cars go up every half hour, Mon. - Fri., starting at 10am; Sat., Sun., and holidays starting at 8am. The last car goes up at 8pm, and the last car comes down at 9:45pm.

Price: $23.95 for adults; $21.95 for seniors; $16.95 for ages 3 - 12; children 2 and under are free. Tickets after 4pm are $20.95 for all adults; $13.95 for kids. Ride 'n' Dine tickets are $36 for adults; $23.50 for ages 3 - 12.

Ages: 3 years and up.

PALM SPRINGS AIR MUSEUM

(760) 778-6262 / www.palmspringsairmuseum.org
745 N. Gene Autry Trail, Palm Springs

$$$$

Enjoy happy landings at this classy air museum, conveniently located next to the Palm Springs Airport. Inside the three hangars and outside on the grounds are usually thirty vintage WWII aircraft; some come and go on a rotating basis. Most of the planes are in flight-ready condition and some are being restored. The collection can include a Grumman F4F Wildcat, Grumman 56F Hellcat, Grumman F7F Tigercat, Grumman A6 Intruder, P-40 Warhawk, B-17, and many more. The planes are not cordoned off, making it easier to look at them close up, although touching is not allowed. Walk under and look up into the belly of an A-26 Invader attack bomber. My kids were thrilled to see the places where it actually held real bombs!

The hangars are designated Army/European, Navy/Pacific, and B17. The planes are fascinating for the part they've played in history, and they are visually exciting for kids because most have decorative emblems painted on their sides. In the Navy/Pacific hangar, climb aboard a Grumman Goose and/or Nomad N22 cockpit and pretend to pilot it. Bunkers and displays around the perimeter of the airy hangars honor different eras of flight by featuring various uniforms, flight jackets, combat photographs, patches, model planes, combat cameras, murals, and more. Other exhibits include maps of missions, touch screens, documentaries showing on five TV screens throughout, and five,

ten-foot-long replicated warships. Tour the inside of a B-17 for a donation of $5 for adults, children 17 and under are free; or just admire it from the outside.

Starting at 11am, the Buddy Rogers Theater continuously shows military documentaries, combat videos, or interviews with war heroes - all with an emphasis on WWII. Kids always enjoy watching small planes land and take off at the adjacent runway. In the library use a computer and joystick to engage in a simulated dogfight for $3 per person. For more entertainment with an *altitude*, every other Saturday hear a special guest speaker in a program that can conclude with a flyover or flight demonstration. Or, take a twenty-five-minute ride in a Steerman open-cockpit bi-plane for $150 per person offered on most Saturdays. Call the museum to ask about their almost two-hour school and group tours (minimum age is 8) offered on weekdays. If you'd like to hear the complete history of all the planes at the museum, ask a docent as they gladly answer any and all questions. This museum also offers a plethora of other programs and events and all of them are exceptionally well done. And if all this travel has made you hungry, grab a bit to eat at the on-site cafe.

Hours: Open daily, 10am - 5pm. Closed Thanksgiving and Christmas.

Price: $15 for adults; $13 for seniors, military with ID, and ages 13 - 17; $8 for ages 6 - 12; children 5 and under are free. The family deal is $30 for 2 adults and 3 kids, ages 12 and under.

Ages: 4 years and up.

PALM SPRINGS ART MUSEUM ☀
(760) 325-7186 or (760) 322-4800 / www.psmuseum.org $$$
101 N. Museum Drive, Palm Springs

There are many facets of this mid-size, museum jewel that showcases modern and contemporary American works. Different components include paintings, some specifically California-oriented and some very modern; photography; classic western art (i.e., cowboy art); Native American pottery, basketry, and blankets; and sculptures - from abstract designs to Old Couple on the Beach, which looks exactly like an old couple just sitting on a bench (although the older I get, the more I think they look middle age).

The fine arts galleries are thematically grouped and some have rotating exhibits. The George Montgomery Collection features the western star's movie posters, plus furniture, paintings, and bronze sculptures of cowboys and Indians that Montgomery designed. The William Holden Collection offers some of Holden's prized art pieces. A small gallery contains art from ancient Latin American civilizations.

The upper level room and mezzanine level have over 100 rotating exhibits of twentieth century art, which means expect the unexpected. I love seeing what's new up here. Some favorite pieces from the glass studio include Virtual Waterfall, which is a bronze, blown-glass depiction of a waterfall, and End of Day, which is an explosion of colorful and funky glass pieces shooting in different directions. My middle son has an artistic temperament, so I'm hoping art exposure will develop his talents, too! Actually there are ample opportunities to do that at the museum as they often offer hands-on activities on the second Sunday of the month (when admission is free) with activities themed around a featured artist include, as well as KidStudio projects, camps, classes, and school tours.

The downstairs Annenberg Theater presents shows mostly for adult audiences, such as plays, ballets, operas, and concerts. Even if you don't eat at the gallery cafe, at least take a stroll through it to check out its colorful mobiles and art deco decor. Outside, all-age visitors will enjoy the small, twentieth-century sculpture garden. Inquire about the variety of guided tours offered for the public, and for school or other groups.

Hours: Open most of the year, Tues. - Wed., 10am - 5pm; Thurs., noon - 8pm; Fri. - Sun., 10am - 5pm. Closed Mon. and major holidays.

Price: $12.50 for adults; $10.50 for seniors; $5 for ages 6 - 17; children 5 and under are free. Admission is free on Thurs. from 4pm - 8pm (during the street fair VillageFest) and on the second Sun. of every month. See page xi for info on the Bank of America free weekend program.

Ages: 8 years and up.

PALM SPRINGS VILLAGEFEST ☀
(760) 320-3781 or (760) 325-1577 / www.villagefest.org; www.pschamber.org !/$
Palm Canyon Drive between Baristo and Amado, Palm Springs

It's Thursday night and you're in Palm Springs with the kids, wondering what to do. Then, you pick up this terrific book called *Fun and Educational Places to go With Kids and Adults* and read about VillageFest - problem solved! The VillageFest, or international old-time street fair, is held along several blocks on Palm Canyon Drive in the heart of Palm Springs where businesses stay open late and admission is free to the PALM SPRINGS ART MUSEUM - see

above entry. There is food, arts and crafts vendors, boutiques, cafes, and entertainment, such as live music. For kids, various attractions could include pony rides, magic shows, a bounce house, a gyroscope, school band competitions, or a stage for children's productions.

> **Hours:** Thurs. nights, October - May, 6pm - 10pm; June - September, 7pm - 10pm. Closed Thanksgiving.
> **Price:** Free entrance.
> **Ages:** 4 years and up.

PIONEERTOWN
(760) 365-5956 - Pappy and Harriet's; (760) 365-7001 - Pioneertown Motel / www.pappyandharriets.com   !/$$
Mane Street, Pioneertown

I enjoy the drive to Pioneertown, up a windy mountain road through hillsides dotted with desert boulders and funky-looking Joshua trees. Most of our "knowledge" of the Wild West comes from TV shows or movie screens. This very small town, about a half-hour drive north of Palm Springs, was used for numerous western films and looks like time has stood still. Although there are actual homes and businesses here, the Old West permeates the atmosphere and physical structures. Check out the real hitching posts and bullet holes on some of the signs.

Every Saturday from April through October the Mane Street Stampede, all dressed in period attire, performs mock gunfights and Old West Re-enactments. Shows commence about 2:30pm, staged along Mane Street.

Since you're in the area, eat at the honky tonk Pappy and Harriet's Pioneertown Palace, a restaurant and bar for locals and tourists where bands play almost every night. The menu includes a cheeseburger ($9.50); Santa Maria steak sandwich ($11.95); Southwest chicken salad ($13.95); chicken quesadilla ($10.95); and chili dog ($7.95); plus, with mesquite barbeque, rib eye steak ($28.95); half-rack of baby back pork ribs ($18.95); and one-half of a smoked chicken ($18.95). Kid's meals are $3.95 - $5.50 for a cheeseburger, chicken fingers, grilled cheese, hot dog, or cheese quesadilla.. The restaurant is open Monday, 5pm to midnight, and Thursday through Sunday, 11am to 2am, although the kitchen closes hours earlier. It is closed Tuesday and Wednesday.

If you like it so much you want to stay, the ranch-style, rustic and basic Pioneertown Motel has eighteen rooms furnished in Old West decor, starting at $80 a night during the week. There is also camping behind the motel, $10 a night, as well as a few other options

> **Price:** Free, for the most part.
> **Ages:** 4 years and up.

ROCKET FIZZ SODA POPS AND CANDY SHOP (Palm Desert)
(760) 568-9111 / www.rocketfizz.com $
72840 Highway 111, Suite F196

See ROCKET FIZZ SODA POPS AND CANDY SHOP (Los Angeles) on page 24 for details on this shop with an incredible array of unusual sodas and candy and more.

> **Price:** Technically, free
> **Ages:** 3 years and up.

RUBY'S (Palm Springs area)
(800) HEY RUBY (439-7829) - for all locations. Morongo/Cabazon - (951) 849-3850; Palm Springs - (760) $$$
406-RUBY (7829) / www.rubys.com
Morongo/Cabazon - 49000 Seminole Drive by the Morongo casinos; Palm Springs - 155 S. Palm Canyon Drive on the main shopping drag

See the entry for RUBY'S (Orange County) on page 252 for details.

SHIELDS DATE GARDEN
(760) 347-7768 - date store; (760) 775-0902 - cafe / www.shieldsdategarden.com   !/$$
80-225 Highway 111, Indio

Wanna date? Since 1925, this date garden has been a staple in the desert area, growing a variety of dates, some of which are exclusively sold here. And you can't miss the sign - a gigantic knight, pointing to the store holding a shield that says "Shields". The old theater, with 108 seats, shows the old, fifteen-minute movie with a catchy title, *The Romance & Sex Life of the Date*. The film is informative and tells the history of the date and how fruit is produced. (Forty-nine females to one male within one acre of land - that's not dating, that's a harem.) You can look at the huge trees outside, and even walk the grounds through a biblical garden that goes through the parts of the seventeen-acre date farm. The

garden, with a small lake, overlooks and bridges, has fourteen scenes and twenty-three statues that chronologically depict Christ's life. Listen to an audio narrative using your smart phone describing the scenarios.

The onsite Cafe offers breakfast - the works omelet ($12); French toast ($9.50); pancakes with dates ($12); a fruit plate with cottage cheese ($11); and lunch - Shields signature salad ($11); N.Y. steak sandwich ($12.95); chicken tacos ($10); date burger (bacon, cheese, and sauteed dates, $13); and chicken club ($10.50). Kid's meals are about $5.95. Get a date shake, purchase some dates or date crystals from the large gift shop, definitely sample the dates and other treats at the sampling counter, and enjoy this little, but not really romantic, excursion.

Hours: Open daily, 9am - 5pm. The Cafe is open daily, 7am - 2:30pm.
Price: Free
Ages: 7 years and up.

SUNRISE PARK / PALM SPRINGS SWIM CENTER AND SKATE PARK

(760) 323-8278 - swim center; (760) 323-8272 - park/skate park / www.palmsprings-ca.gov

!/$$

401 South Pavilion Way, Palm Springs

This park has activities that will keep your family busy and refreshed from sunrise to sunset. Besides the wonderful grassy areas and big playground with bridges, slides, and swings, there is an extra large (30,000 square feet!!) skate park. It has three bowls, ranging from features for entry-level skaters to an area in one of the bowls that is nine-and-a-half feet deep with three feet of vert wall. Street elements include rails, hips, pyramids, stairs, ramps, and quarter-pipes. Touted as one of the best skate parks in Southern California, participants relish skating here at night, too because of the unique, no-shadow, lighting. A helmet and pads are mandatory. There is an adjacent, lighted baseball stadium.

Another important attraction of the park is the Olympic-size swimming pool that has a shallow end for younger kids to cool off. Bring your own lawn chairs.

Hours: The park is open daily, sunrise - sunset. The skate park is open daily, 11am - 8pm. The pool is open year-round for recreational swim - Mon. - Fri., 11am - 5pm; Sat. - Sun., 11am - 3pm. Night swimming is available in the summer.
Price: The park and skate park are free. Swim sessions are $5 for non-resident adults; $4 for resident adults; $3 for ages 4 - 12; children 3 and under are free with a paid adult.
Ages: All

TAHQUITZ CANYON

(760) 416-7044 or (760) 323-6018 / www.tahquitzcanyon.com

$$$

500 W. Mesquite, Palm Springs

At the visitors center, watch the short video called *Legend of the Tahquitz Canyon* to get a feel for the history of this region. There are also a few indigenous displays here, as well. This gorgeous canyon doesn't have palm trees, so during the day it just gets hot without shade. It does, however, have other trees and plants along with the major reason to visit - a sixty-foot waterfall. The one looping, hiking trail goes to the base of the waterfall and is almost two miles long. It's rated easy to moderate, with some rock steps that vary in height, along the Tahquitz Creek. (The trail is not stroller friendly.) Be on the lookout for wildlife, caves, rock art, and impressive landscape.

A free, two-and-a-half-hour ranger-led interpretative hike goes along the same path that gives insight as to the topography, history, Cahuilla Indians, animal life, and plant life along the way. Such knowledge gives participants a deeper appreciation for what they see. Check out INDIAN CANYONS (pg. 383) for details about nearby canyons.

Hours: Open October - June daily, 7:30am - 5pm; open July - September, Fri., Sat., Sun., 7:30am - 5pm. Visitors must be inside the gate by 3:30pm as the canyon closes at 5pm. Free ranger hikes are offered when the canyon is open at 8am, 10am, noon, and 2pm.
Price: $12.50 for adults; $6 for ages 12 and under.
Ages: 6 years and up.

THE BEST OF THE BEST TOURS

(760) 320-1365 / www.thebestofthebesttours.com

$$$$$

490 S. Indian Canyon Drive, Palm Springs

This tour company offers several types of tours, most of them in an open-air jeep. We took the Windmill Tour and if you like learning about alternative energy sources and are fascinated by the power that wind can generate, you'll be (literally) blown away by this tour. To state the obvious, it is usually very windy out here. Why? Because cool coastal

air comes inland and pushes the hot air through the narrow mountainous San Gorgonio Pass. Driving around on the grounds of one of several wind farms in the world, you'll hear the thumping noise created by the huge pinwheels in motion. At selected stops you'll have the opportunity to inspect components (e.g., blades and nacelle [battery covers]) up close. Blades, by the way, can span more than half the length of a football field. You'll see the older-style wind turbines and new, sleeker, more efficient ones. And, yes, you'll finally find out if these wind mills are simply tax shelters or actually producing usable, affordable energy and other related environmental and economic issues. A lot of technical information is given during this two-hour tour, and though some of it might be long winded for kids, even I understand a bit more now about electricity, sources of clean energy, and what makes a kilowatt hour. The tour is $35 for adults; $30 for seniors; $10 for ages 12 and under. Other tours include the two-hour+Indian Canyon tour ($45 for adults; $40 for seniors and ages 12 and under); ninety-minute Rich and Famous tour ($35; $30); and the almost four-hour Bonanza tour - a combo of Windmill, Indian Canyon, and Rich and Famous ($89; $84).

Hours: Tours are offered daily. Reservations are suggested.
Price: Prices are listed above.
Ages: 9 years and up.

ULTRASTAR CINEMAS MARY PICKFORD THEATER - Cathedral City

(760) 328-7100 / www.ultrastarmovies.com
36-850 Pickfair Street, Cathedral City

See the ULTRASTAR CINEMAS website, then click the Kids & Family button to see the special offerings. Also see ULTRASTAR GARDEN WALK 14 (Orange County) (pg. 323) for more information on the programs these theaters offer. See below entry as the theaters are just down the street from each other.

ULTRASTAR DESERT IMAX-1- Cathedral City

(760) 324-7333 / www.ultrastarmovies.com; www.desertimax.org
68510 East Palm Canyon Drive, Cathedral City

Larger than life! That's the images shown on the huge IMAX screen, which features several films on any given day. Some of the films are entertaining and some are educational. I am personally partial to the 3-D format, also available here, as viewers get more involved with the on-screen action as things and people seemingly pop out. Nature films are especially fun viewed this way. Ask about double feature specials and school group discounts. See above entry as the theaters are just down the street from each other.

Hours: Call or check the website for movie time.
Price: 2-D (IMAX large screen) and 3-D movie tickets vary - evening shows are $14 for adults; $9 for seniors; $12.50 for students; $10 for ages 12 and under. Matinees are less expensive; first matinees even cheaper.
Ages: 4 years and up

WESTFIELD PALM DESERT - FAMILY FUN DAYS

(760) 346-2121 / www.westfield.com
72840 Highway 111, Palm Desert

Calling all young kids! A free PlaySpace area, near JCPenney, allows little ones to climb on hard foam animals and play on a big, tic-tac-toe wall hanging. The mall also offers Family Fun Days, monthly, on select Saturdays from 11am to 1pm. There is almost always a seasonal craft involved to make - cute ones!, and sometimes storytelling (with costumed characters), drawings, and snacks. The mall also hosts some special events such as an Easter carnival and more.

Hours: Family Fun Days area on select Sat., 11am - 1pm.
Price: Free
Ages: 2 - 9 years.

WET 'N' WILD

(760) 327-0499 / www.wetnwildpalmsprings.com
1500 Gene Autry Trail, Palm Springs

This twenty-two-acre waterpark is truly an oasis in the desert. Six water slides for big kids range from mild uncovered slides, to enclosed forty-mph slides, to a seventy-foot, free-fall slide. Cowabunga - the four-story interactive water playground is really rad with water squirting everyone, squirt guns, so visitors can tag other visitors, slides, a

bucket that dumps 1,000 gallons of water at regular intervals, several more slides and everything fun. Get carried away in the gentle, three-foot-deep, circular, Lazy River inner tube ride. Catch a wave, dude, in the large wave pool where kids can body or board surf. Hang ten on Surf Rider, a multi-person, open raft ride. Literally go for a spin as a two-to-four person ride spins rafters around and around and then through a funnel-shaped hole. Younger children can take the plunge in their own small water play area that has two slides and a large mushroom that showers water.

Wet 'n' Wild offers locker rentals (about $7), private cabana rentals, full-service snack bars, and an indoor restaurant for all your creature comforts. There is a video arcade here, too. Bring water shoes or flip flops because the cement gets really hot. Note: You cannot bring a cooler or your own food inside the park. Proper swimwear must be worn, meaning that anything with rivets is not allowed.

Hours: Open mid-March - mid-May, usually Fri. - Sun. (on some weekdays as well), 11am - 5pm (sometimes 10am - 6pm). Open Memorial Day - Labor Day daily, usually 10am - 6pm. Open September and the first weekend in October on weekends only, usually 10am - 6pm. Call or check the website first as hours fluctuate.

Price: $36.99 for adults; $26.99 for seniors and ages 3 - 11; children 2 and under are free. Parking is $14.

Ages: All

WORLD'S BIGGEST DINOSAURS

(951) 922-8700 or (951) 922-0076 / www.cabazondinosaurs.com   !/$$$
50800 Seminole Drive, Cabazon

Cruising down the desert highway, looking out the window, your kids see the usual things - big trucks, cactus, and dinosaurs. Screech go the brakes! The gigantic (150-feet long) apatosaurus is almost triple the size of the actual dinosaur that roamed the earth long ago. The same goes for the sixty-five-foot Tyrannosaurus rex behind him. Enter the steel and concrete apatosaurus through its tail, up the stairway and into the belly to the gift shop, looking at some of the fossils, info, and dioramas built into the walls along the sides. Bring food to enjoy a snack or meal on the picnic tables outside, under his belly. And yes, these are the same dinosaurs featured in *Pee-wee's Big Adventure* and *Wizard*, although a little more worn looking than they were back then. It's a great, cheesy, roadside attraction.

More fun starts when you head back to the World's Biggest Dinosaurs. Go through a cave-like entrance, with an inset of baby dinos in the cave wall, into a huge gift shop filled with everything dinosaur (and then some) - books, models, t-shirts, stuffed animals, stones, etc. There are two robotic dinosaurs in here that move and roar; two large dinos to actually ride ($2 a ride); and a big dino skeleton. Colorful posters and info panels abound sharing facts and fiction regarding the origins of dinosaurs and of man from a creationist perspective. In a separate video room the best seats are the dino eggs chairs where visitors can watch films and documentaries given from a creationist's view point.

Stroll through the outdoor dino garden (my term for it) on a gravel and hard-packed pathway lined with over forty dinosaurs of all sizes and species amidst palm trees and other plants with a backdrop of desert hills. There are stegosauruses, scary-looking velociraptors, T.rexes, brachiosauruses, and dimetrodons, as well as dinosaur families and a statue of a lion and lamb. Photo ops abound! This garden also boasts a good-sized, covered, hands-on dino dig (basically a place to play in the sand), plus a sluice where you can pan for gemstones for free, trying your luck with leftovers, or purchase a bag of dirt with gems planted in it - $5 to $10 per bag, depending on size and quality of gems.

A highlight (pun intended) is climbing the steps (that get narrow and steep towards the top), which are lined with greenery, logs, info posters, and models of dinosaurs, to the top of the extra large T.rex you saw from the parking lot (ie. this is the T-Rex Museum). You are now in his mouth, behind his rows of sharp teeth! Tip: Look up and see why his eyes glow red at nighttime.

School field trips, play groups, or any type of or age group are welcome, as are individuals and families. Note that there are some fast-food restaurants in the immediate vicinity as well as a sit-down restaurant. All in all, this is a *dino*-mite stop!

Hours: Open daily, 10m - 5pm (gates close at 4:30pm). It is open extended hours in the summer, usually until 6:30pm. Closed Thanksgiving and Christmas. The apatosaurus store is open on select weekdays and on weekends, 10am - 5pm.

Price: Free to look and just walk around the two dinosaurs out front. Entrance to the museum/dino garden is $7.95 for adults; $6 for seniors and military; $6.95 for children; ages 2 and under are free.

Ages: All

SAN BERNARDINO COUNTY

   Originally settled by the Serrano Indians, the land has changed hands many times over the years and today incorporates a flavor from all of its past inhabitants. Tour through a restored rancho in Rancho Cucamonga. See a once-working silver mine in the revitalized ghost town of Calico. Take a walk in the deserts of Barstow (but not in the summertime). Enjoy the mountainous woodlands of Big Bear Lake. Pick apples in Oak Glen. Shop at Ontario Mills Mall. Visit airplane museums in Chino. This Inland Empire has something to cater to every interest.

   Note: Since Big Bear is often considered a resort destination, you'll find its attractions listed in a separate section in the back of this county.

—AMUSEMENT PARKS—

SPLASH KINGDOM

☼

(909) 335-7275 / www.splashkingdom.net

$$$$$

1101 N. California Street, Redlands

Located in the first pyramid off the freeway, "mummies" (and daddies) looking for a place to keep kids royally entertained have found their answer at this Egyptian-themed play kingdom. Enter through the giant, sunglasses-wearing Sphinx into a modern (not ancient) world of **arcade** and virtual reality games (with a ticket redemption area); a large, indoor trampolining area called SKYTOWN (see pg. 412 for more info); restaurants; a water park; and more.

The outside **Fun Park** offers mini **go-kart racing** with a banked Indy speed track; some height and age restrictions apply. **Bumper boats** are another great (and usually wet) family attraction with controls to press that squirt water at the other boaters. Travel to ancient and exotic lands via the four, nine-hole, themed, **miniature golf** courses that are nicely landscaped and intriguingly embellished with either dinosaurs, space rockets, safari animals (like giraffes), or Egyptian idols and other artifacts. The holes aren't incredibly challenging and need some upkeep (at the time of this writing), but they are enjoyable to play.

At the Splash Kingdom **water park** walk up the central tower to go down the eight slides (with names like Wrath of Ra and Ramses Rocket) that range from enclosed and open body slides (the Anileator is aptly-named at ninety-feet tall and pretty much a sheer drop!), as well as twisty single and double tube rides that hurl riders down. My favorite is the yellow, double tube ride because the tubes get flung up high on the sides of the ride as water cascades down. Enjoy a blissful raft ride in three feet of water on the Nile River, a large circular river encompassing the water park, replete with some waterfalls and Egyptian markings along the way. See how long you can board surf via the wave machine at Riptide. Younger children have their own wading pool (one foot of water) with huge colorful butterfly, frog and fish slides; pipes and fountains spouting water; and short slides. Another activity pool, the Forgotten Lagoon, for slightly older kids, has a few short slides, a three-foot deep pool to lounge about in, a cargo net to climb on, an umbrella structure that rains down water, and a challenging ropes course over and on large, hard, foam squares. Castaway Cove is a good-size wave pool where waves are created for ten minutes, every ten minutes. There are plenty of lounge chairs in the shade (and sun) available, or rent a cabana. Tube usage is free. King Tut never had it so good!

Reasonably-priced food is available in the water park ($4.50 for a bacon-wrapped hot dog; $5.75 for chili cheese nachos) or upstairs in the pyramid at the Upper Deck Sports Lounge and bar. The Lounge has casual and comfy seating (either at tables or on couches) to view the several, huge TV/ projection screens (including a 35-foot screen and a 50-foot screen outside) specializing in showing sports programs, including pay-per-view specials and NFL football. There is also a section of the lounge that oversees part of SkyTown. The menu includes a 16" pizza for $14.99 or a personal (7") pizza for $5.75; chicken strips or sliders with fries for $7.75; and loaded tri-tip nachos for $8.25. Save room for a Skyzookie, a freshly baked, extra large, chocolate chip cookie served with vanilla ice cream (that melts all over it), chocolate sauce and whipped cream, all for $5.

Note that the facility also offers birthday parties and Summer Adventure Camps, with arts and crafts, jr. lifeguard programs, daily visits at the water park and Skytown, and more. There is also a large, private, elegant dining room called The Loft for business dinners, special events, etc. Concerts are often held at the outdoor amphitheater, too.

Hours: The **arcade and Fun Park** are open most of the year Fri., 4pm - 8pm; Sat. - Sun., 10am - 8pm. In summer they are open Mon. - Fri. 11am - 8pm; Sat. - Sun., 10am - 8pm. For the most part, the **waterpark** is open mid - May thru the end of May, and late August thru mid-September (plus Labor Day) on weekends only, 11am - 6pm. It is open during the summer daily, 11am - 8pm. The Lounge is open Mon. - Thurs., 3pm - 9pm; Fri., 3pm - 11pm; Sat., 11am - 11pm; Sun., 11am - 11pm.

Price: Unlimited admission to the waterpark and Fun Park (but not go-karts) is $29.99 for 48" and taller; $16.99 for 47" and under; $9.99 for srs. Entrance is $16.99 for ages 3 and up after 4pm. All-day play for mini golf and the bumper boats is $14.99 for 48" and taller; $10.99 for 47" and under. Go-karts are $5.99 a ride. Locker rentals are $8 for a small. Parking is $7.

Ages: 5 years and up.

—ARTS AND CRAFTS—

COLOR ME MINE (San Bernardino County)

(909) 628-7744 / www.colormemine.com
13865 City Center Drive, suite 3065 at the Promenade, Chino Hills
    See the entry for COLOR ME MINE (Los Angeles County) on page 7 for details.

THE SAWDUST FACTORY

(909) 946-0866 / www.thesawdustfactory.com
1525 Howard Access Road, Upland
    *Wood*n't your kids enjoy making a craft to take home? The aptly-named Sawdust Factory allows kids (and adults) to do just that. Gather inspiration from the many country crafts, toll-painted items, and practical products in the retail part of the store. Then, choose a project to paint and/or assemble to take home to do, or complete a project on-site and make it yours, through and through. Even if you are craft deficient, like me, you'll leave with a finished project that pleases you.
    The good-size workshop room towards the back of the store is set up with long tables. Choose from hundreds of precut items including picture frames, signs, notepad holders, treat boxes, bug boxes, bird feeders, toolboxes, holiday items, and much more. Customize your project by adding wood figures for a 3-D effect, or by painting and adding embellishments such as buttons, wire, raffia, bows, and wiggle eyes. If you can't decide what to do, sign up to take a special workshop with a predetermined craft which usually revolves around a particular theme. Come here on a walk-in basis, or come for a scheduled workshop. Birthday parties, scout outings, and school field trips are welcome. On field trip tours, kids won't *leaf* without learning about trees, the milling process, and wood tools on their twenty-minute guided tour, plus they see a demonstration of how a drill press and scroll saw work, and make a pre-selected woodcraft project.

Hours: Open Mon. - Fri., 9am - 4pm; Sat., 10am - 4pm. Open Sunday for special events and parties. Closed major holidays. Call or check the website for scheduled workshop dates and times.
Price: Walk in workshop fees are $4 per person, plus the cost of the project, which range from $3 to $20 - check the calendar for the no-workshop-fee days. Scheduled workshops are an all-inclusive fee, starting at $10, depending on the project.
Ages: 3 years and up.

—EDIBLE ADVENTURES—

BARSTOW STATION

(760) 256-0366 / www.barstowstation.net
1611 E. Main Street, Barstow
    Several retired railroad cars are grouped together to form a unique, albeit brief, shopping and eating experience. Eating McDonald's food in an old train car might taste the same as eating it elsewhere, but the atmosphere here makes it fun. Other rail cars offer Hollywood Subs, Panda Express, ice cream, candy, souvenirs, and knickknacks. The Station fulfills its goal of being an interesting, edible adventure.

Hours: Open Mon. - Thurs., 8am - 8pm; Fri., 8am - 10pm; Sat., 7am - 8pm; Sun., 8am - 10pm. McDonald's is open Sun. - Thurs., 6am - 10pm; Fri. - Sat., 6am - 11pm.
Price: Free to enter; bring spending money.
Ages: All

BENIHANA OF TOKYO (San Bernardino County)

(909) 483-0937 / www.benihana.com
3760 E. Inland Empire Boulevard, Ontario
    See the entry for BENIHANA OF TOKYO (Los Angeles County) on page 14 for details.

CENTER STAGE THEATER

8463 Sierra Avenue at Center Stage Theater, Fontana

See the entry for CENTER STAGE THEATER on page 435 for details on terrific dinner and stage shows.

CHUCK E. CHEESE'S (San Bernardino)

See the entry for CHUCK E. CHEESE'S (Los Angeles County) on page 16 for details.

THE EATING ROOM

(909) 792-5400 / www.allmarthagreen.com

107 E. Citrus, Redlands

$$$$

This contemporary, country restaurant with black laquer tables and chairs has barn-red painted walls filled with hens, roosters, citrus trees, and fruit motifs. In the back room a large, faux brick wall has a life-size (fake) citrus tree protruding from it. The popular eatery also has a flower shop inside of it and an adjoining gourmet bakery called Dough'Lectibles Bakery, which sells delectables such as breads, cookies, cakes, cupcakes, and other pastries.

A sampling of the breakfast fare includes a house blend of muselix, $5.50; eggs Benedict, $9.50; French toast with croissants, cream eggs, maple syrup, cream cheese, and vanilla combined, $8.75; and a breakfast burrito, $7.75. Appetizers include Thai chicken strips, sweet 'n' saucy, $7.75; potato skins, $7.50; and fried zucchini, $6.50. Lunch is served with choices of Cobb salad, $10.50; cheeseburger, $8.25; tuna melt, $9.50; pulled-pork sandwich, $9.50; chicken with grilled pineapple, $9.50; "My Big Fat Greek Sandwich", $9.95; and an assortment of wraps, $9.50. A casual, high tea offers a time to indulge, relax, and enjoy. A three-tiered rack comes with a selection of petite fours; small cookies; fruit tarts; scones with Devonshire cream and jam; tiny sandwiches of egg or chicken salad; and a brewed pot of tea. The cost is $20 per person.

Hours: Open Mon. - Fri., 7am - 2:50pm; Sat. - Sun., 8am - 2:50pm. Tea is served Thurs. - Sat., 4pm - 6pm, by reservation only.

Price: Prices are listed above.

Ages: 6 years and up.

THE ENCHANTED ROSE TEA PARLOUR

(909) 394-4588 / www.enchantedrosetea.com

120 W. Bonita Avenue, #G, San Dimas

$$$$

Surrounded by the ambiance of bygone days in Old Town, the Enchanted Rose blooms among a garden of antique shops. The vintage parlor setting is enhanced by hutches and shelves that hold tea sets, dolls, china plates, hats, bird houses, candles, frames, floral arrangements, and all sorts of tea embellishments. The various chandeliers add a charming touch, as does a faux fireplace with a lace mantel covering. If you want to play dress up (because we are never too old or too young for that), you may choose from an assortment of hats and/or feather boas.

Not only is the atmosphere inviting, but the food is good as well. The namesake Enchanted Tea, $17.75, includes a raspberry vinaigrette salad or cup of soup; a fresh-baked scone with Devonshire cream, jam and lemon curd; tea sandwiches; chocolate-dipped seasonal fruit; dessert; a pot of tea; and a signature pink chocolate rose. The Lady Sheila Tea, $14.75, offers a scone or dessert; chocolate-dipped seasonal fruit; tea sandwiches; a pot of tea; and chocolate rose. Little Prince or Princess Teas, for ages 5 to 11, $11.95, include a mini scone, petite sandwiches, dessert, tea or punch, and a chocolate rose. Ask about the special-occasion tea parties for adults and for children ages 5 and up.

Nice gift items and teas in tins available to purchase are interspersed throughout the tearoom. Take the time to stroll around and browse through the numerous shops of Old Town San Dimas. Of special interest to kids is a train store toward the west end of town. There are real trains that run by the town as well. A small park and a small historical museum are also in the immediate vicinity.

Hours: Open for tea Wed. - Sat., 11am - 3pm. The shop is open slightly longer hours. Reservations are suggested. Open Sun. - Tues. by special reservation, only.

Price: Menu prices are listed above.

Ages: 5 years and up.

FARMER'S MARKETS (San Bernardino County)

See the entry for FARMER'S MARKETS (Los Angeles County) on pg. 18 for details.

FARRELL'S ICE CREAM PARLOUR RESTAURANTS (San Bernardino County)

(909) 989-8777 / www.farrellsusa.com

10742 Foothill Boulevard at Terra Vista Town Center Shopping Center, Rancho Cucamonga

$$$

See FARRELL'S ICE CREAM PARLOUR RESTAURANTS (Orange County) on pg. 247 for details on this terrifically fun restaurant.

GAMEWORKS

4541 Mills Circle, Ontario

See the entry for GAMEWORKS on page 407 for details.

$$$

GRANLUNDS SWEET TEMPTATIONS

(909) 790-6266 or (909) 790-1876

$$$$

12164 California Street, Yucaipa

The inside of this restaurant reminds me of a floral store (not a florists). First, you walk through the oak and glass door through an archway full with fake greens twisted with vines of bright red berries into a room filled with greenery which is dripping from the ceiling, and deftly placed along the walls, on oak shelves, and on round tables topped with topiary wrapped with white lights. The greenery is also interspersed among other plants, statues, lamps, and picture frames, plus pitchers and vases in classic white, all artfully arranged and for sale. Wooden floors and wooden tables and chairs, touches of red, wood ceiling fans, and ornate gold ceiling (tin-plated) tiles that look like they've been hand tooled, plus Big Band music, all work together to create a classy, yet relaxing dining experience. There are seven tables, well spaced to give room to the diners, along with a semi-circular counter top imbedded with small red tiles with red vinyl stools to eat at. The room is kind of divided by wood and glass display cases. In the back area is a long display case holding tantalizing desserts. How hard is it to eat a meal back here while being tempted with dessert!

Food selections, with approximate prices, include soup in a sourdough bread bowl (a personal favorite), $7.99; chicken Caesar salad, $9.75; summer fruit salad with sherbet, surrounded by fruit served with cinnamon swirl bread, $9.75; brioche - sweet, egg bread stuffed with spinach or mushroom or tomato/basil, and topped with cheese, then toasted, $6.50; smoked turkey breast sandwich, $8.75; French dip, $7.99; cheese enchilada, $8.98; and lasagna, $9.50. Try some hand-churned ice cream, fresh pastries, or hand-made chocolates, truffles, and other sweet temptations from the dessert case. Note that there is some outdoor seating, as well.

Hours: Open Mon. - Fri., 11am - 4pm; Sat. - Sun., 9am - 4pm.

Price: Prices are listed above.

Ages: 5 years and up.

GYU-KAKU (San Bernardino County)

(909) 899-4748 / www.gyu-kaku.com

$$$$

7893 Monet Avenue in the Victorian Gardens Shopping Center, Rancho Cucamonga

See the entry for GYU-KAKU (Los Angeles County) on page 20 for information on this grill-it-yourself restaurant.

Hours: Open Mon. - Thurs., noon - 10pm; Fri., noon - 11pm; Sat., 11am - 11pm; Sun., 11am - 10pm.

ISLAMORADA FISH COMPANY

(909) 922-5400 / www.restaurants.basspro.com/FishCompany/RanchoCucamonga

$$$$

7777 Victoria Gardens Lane, in the Bass Pro Shops Outdoor World, Rancho Cucamonga

Located inside the fantastic, sportsman's dream, BASS PRO SHOPS OUTDOOR WORLD (pg. 431) and adjacent to VICTORIA GARDENS REGIONAL TOWN CENTER (pg. 422), this small, wood-paneled, nautically-themed restaurant offers the taste of the outdoors inside. With sword fish and other fish mounted on the wall and on the ceilings (check out the huge ray), and a large (13,000 gallon!) salt water fish tank, the mood is set for eating fresh fish. There is also a large fireplace in the center.

Served with most meals, the mini loaf of bread topped with sugar is delicious. Appetizers include breaded American alligator, which doesn't taste like chicken ($9.95); fried crawfish tails ($8.95); and venison-stuffed mushrooms ($8.95). Meal choices include Islamorada salad with candied cashews, bleu cheese, dried cranberries and greens ($6.95); fish tacos ($8.95); a bowl of clam chowder ($4.95); fish and chips ($11.95); five-piece coconut shrimp ($10.95); pulled BBQ pork sandwich ($8.95); burger ($8.95); creamy shrimp pasta ($14.95); grilled mahi mahi ($16.95); half rack of spare ribs ($13.95); and top sirloin ($13.95). Kid's meals range between $4.99 to $7.99 for a choice of mac and cheese, popcorn shrimp, pizza, mini corn dogs, and more. Drinks are included.

Hours: Open Mon. - Sat., 11am - 10pm; Sun., 11am - 9pm.

Price: Menu prices listed above.
Ages: 2 years and up.

JOE'S CRAB SHACK (San Bernardino County)

(909) 463-6599 / www.joescrabshack.com
12327 Foothill Boulevard, Rancho Cucamonga
    See the entry for JOE'S CRAB SHACK (Los Angeles County) on page 22 for details.
Hours: Open daily, 11am - midnight.

JOHN'S INCREDIBLE PIZZA CO. (San Bernardino County)

(760) 951-1111 / www.johnspizza.com
14766 Bear Valley Road, Victorville
    See JOHN'S INCREDIBLE PIZZA CO. (Orange County) on page 248 for details.
Hours: Open Mon. - Thurs., 11am - 9pm; Fri. - Sat., 11am - 10pm; Sun., 11am - 9pm.

LEGENDS BURGERS

Rancho Cucamonga - (909) 941-9555; Upland (College Park) - (909) 445-9400; Upland - (909) 949-6363 /
www.legends-burgers.com
Rancho Cucamonga - 8775 Baseline Rd.; Upland (College Park) - 2420 W. Arrow Rte.; Upland - 1645 N. Mountain Ave.
    A fun homage to the 50's, this restaurant's walls are completely filled with memorabilia from that era, such as old
movie posters, street signs, license plates, and record albums - even the blinds are decorated with movie star's portraits.
Vintage-type cars run on a track overhead, 50's music plays in the background, and the floor tiles are black and white
checkered.
    The food is good and prices decent. For instance, a cheeseburger is $4.20; steak sandwich, $9.71; chicken breast
club, $8.52; hotdog, $3.77; Greek salad, $7.33; chicken burrito, $7.55; and zucchini fries, $3.99. Complete kid's meals
are $6.47.
Hours: Open daily, 7am - 11pm.
Price: Menu prices are listed above.
Ages: All

MANIAC-MIKES CAFE AT CABLE AIRPORT

(909) 982-9886 / www.maniac-mikes.com; www.cableairport.com
1749 West 13th Street at the Cable Airport, Upland
    The planes might be up in the air, but the food here is down-to-earth. The cafe is located just off the airport
runway, so you can readily observe the small planes landing and taking off, whether you're eating inside or out on the
patio. The airport is snuggled next to the mountains, so the view is tremendous. Note that the YOUNG EAGLES
PROGRAM (pg. 441) flies from this airport.
    The retro cafe (vintage 1940's) has a few model airplanes on the ceiling and leather aviation jackets on hangers,
plus a speaker to listen to the radio control tower. Typical American breakfast menu choices include eggs (a three-egg,
cheese omelet served with hash browns or fries starts at $6.90); pancakes - short stack ($3.30); country-fried steak and
two eggs ($8.35); and French toast ($4.95). Lunch items are burgers ($5.55); BLT ($6.90); chef salad ($7.65); bowl of
chili ($5.50); or turkey or ham sandwich ($7). Kid's meals, served with chips, fries, or a cookie, include French toast
with bacon ($3.75); grilled cheese ($3.75); hot dog ($3.50); or peanut butter and jelly sandwich ($3.50).
Hours: The cafe is open daily, 7am - 3pm.
Price: See menu prices above.
Ages: 3 years and up.

MILL CREEK CATTLE CO. & DIAMOND JIM'S SALOON

(909) 389-0706 / www.millcreekcattlecompany.com
1874 Mentone Boulevard, Mentone
    From the outside, this very unique restaurant looks like building fronts along Main Street in an Old West town.
Wooden facades are labeled saloon, hotel (complete with balconies), barbershop, and U.S. Marshall's office, with a
painted silhouette of a cowboy marshal. Bales of hay, cactus, antlers, and travel trunks complete the ambiance.
    Enter through the restaurant doors for inside and inside/outside seating. The lobby continues the Old West

theme with saddles hanging on the walls, old lanterns, old-time photographs, steer skulls, and an old-fashioned furnace. Eat inside the bar area, decorated with bits, bridles, a fireplace, a bear head over the piano, swords, and a flag that is half Confederate and half Union, plus pictures of Robert E. Lee and Ulysses S. Grant.

The other dining area is really quirky. It is inside the restaurant walls, but the roof is only camouflage netting. (Tip: Find an alternative place to eat on a rainy day. Just kidding - the restaurant is big enough.) Two real, tall, palm trees shoot up through the "ceiling," surrounded at their base by an odd combination of more fake flowers and real cactus. The decor is an eclectic mix of more Old West building fronts, highlighted with neon signs, plus a corner waterfall enhanced by fake rocks and colorful fake flowers. The room also has heat lamps, old posters, and mounted deer and wild boar's heads.

Amid the unusual atmosphere of the Cattle Co., enjoy great food. Appetizers include jalapeno peppers stuffed with cream cheese ($8.95); spicy buffalo wings ($8.95); and quesadillas ($9.25). Meal menu items include chili ($5.95); Cobb salad ($12.95); liver and onions ($13.95); burgers (start at $6.95); smoked tri-tip sandwiches ($8.25); baby back ribs ($21.95 - full rack); spicy sausage links ($10.95); ham steaks ($13.95); smoke house chicken ($11.95); rib eye steak ($22.95); jumbo gulf shrimp ($17.95); and catfish ($15.95), plus a choice of pastas and seafood. Check out the website for the weekly specials! Kids' meals are $4.95 for either chicken tenders, grilled cheese, hamburger, barbecue ribs, barbecue chicken, or spaghetti. Drinks are extra. Breakfast, with cowboy beans, biscuits and gravy, and apple coffee cake, is also available.

While here, visit the adjacent MB's Gift Shop and General Store. It stocks all sorts of country store goodies, collectibles, antiques, dolls, and more.

Hours: Open Mon. - Thurs., 11am - 9pm; Fri., 11am - 1am; Sat. - Sun., 8am - 9pm.
Price: Menu prices are listed above.
Ages: 3 years and up.

MOUNT BALDY SCENIC LIFT RIDE

8401 Mount Baldy Road, Mount Baldy

See the entry for MOUNT BALDY SCENIC LIFT RIDE (pg.417) for more information.

MY ENCHANTED COTTAGE & TEA ROOM

(760) 264-4141 / www.myenchantedcottage.com
214 W. Ridgecrest Boulevard, Ridgecrest

High tea out in the desert? Is it proper? I don't know, but it is a delightful treat. This very small, old cottage has been freshened up and radiates charm. The first few rooms contain gift items and collectables such as jams, tea accessories, pillows, and hand-painted keepsakes. Tea is served in the last room, as well as outside near the garden.

All of the food is made on the premises, based on traditional recipes that have been tweaked and enhanced with fun flourishes. Enchanted Tea, $15.95, consists of freshly-made scones with cream and preserves; three tea sandwiches with unusual combinations; a petite salad; dessert; and choice of tea. (There are over fifty teas to choose from!) For ages 10 and under, Prince Ali Tea, $12.95, includes four tea sandwiches, fruit, marshmallow treat, and mini-scones, and tea or hot chocolate. Princess Camila Tea (for children 7 and under) is a cupcake and choice of cocoa or tea, $6. A la carte items are also available such as a pot of tea, $5; scone with cream and preserves or another dessert, $3.50; tea sandwiches, $4 to $5; and a small salad, $3.

Hours: Open Tues. - Sat., 11am - 3pm(ish) for tea; the tea room is open extended hours. Hours change so call first. Reservations are required for formal teas, but walk-ins are usually accommodated by the la carte selections.
Price: Menu prices are listed above.
Ages: 4 years and up.

OAK GLEN / APPLE PICKING

(909) 797-6833 / www.oakglen.net
Oak Glen Road, Oak Glen

Your *delicious* journey into Oak Glen takes you on a five-mile loop through a town that is *ripe* with fun things to do. Several orchards offer U-pic, which means you pick your own apples, raspberries, blackberries, pears, and pumpkins, all in season, of course. Apple varieties range from the exotic, such as Ida Red, Pearmain, Winesap, Cameo, and Cinnamon Spice, to the more familiar ones of Jonagold, Granny Smith, Pippin, Braeburn, Rome, and Red

Delicious. Most orchards also have wonderful country stores with all sorts of apple concoctions and apple-related items for sale. Even though berry-picking season starts in late July and apple season runs from September through the middle of November, there are many year-round reasons to visit Oak Glen. Tips: Although weekends in the fall (especially mid-September through mid-October) can be crowded, some orchards will only let you pick apples then, so get an early start on your day's adventure. Call the orchards to find out when your favorite type of apple will be ripe. Buy an apple-recipe book, as kids get a little carried away with the joy of picking apples! Here are a few of our favorites stops:

Parrish Pioneer Ranch, 38561 Oak Glen Road, (909) 797-1753 / www.parrishranch.com: The Ranch has a picnic area, prepicked apples for sale, a few gift shops, and a restaurant. Goats, emus, a donkey, miniature horse, sheep, peacocks, and a cow are in pens by the parking lot - to be looked at, not petted. Harvest season entertainment includes Yodeling Merle, who sings cowboy songs (May through December). In October, on Sundays, an over-the-top pirates stuntshow is performed in melodrama-style in a professional-looking set at the outside theater at 11am, 1pm, and 3pm, weather permitting. Call first. Admission is free; donations are appreciated. The barn and restaurant are open daily during apple season, 9am to 5pm; the store opens at 10am. Everything is open until 6pm. Out of season, the barn and restaurant are open Thurs. - Mon., 9am - 5pm; the store opens at 10am.

Oedekerk's Peddler's Pack, 39065 Oak Glen Rd., (909) 790-0774 / www.thepeddlerspack.com: Five acres of ranch are home to about forty-five alpacas, plus a few wild birds and an emu. The alpacas are for sale. The small gift shop sells a variety of alpaca products, such as clothing, blankets, and accessories, plus other items. Open weekends, 10am - 5pm.

Oak Tree Village, 38480 Oak Glen Rd., (909) 797-4420 / www.oaktreevillageoakglen.net: Located in the center of Oak Glen is the Village - a wonderful place to shop, play, and eat. See OAK TREE VILLAGE on page 434 to find out all of the fun things to do in this village including the Animal Park, pony rides, fishing, and so much more. Open daily, 10am - 5pm; closed Christmas.

Mountain Town, 38480 Oak Glen Rd., (909) 797-4420 / www.oaktreevillageoakglen.net: Just up the walkway from the Oak Tree Village is MOUNTAIN TOWN. See page 443 for details on this unusual, animal/reptile museum that has some live reptiles and some taxidermied animals inside in a recreated cave/mountain setting.

Snow-Line Orchard, 39400 Oak Glen Road, (909) 797-3415 / www.snow-line.com: This short drive up the road offers rows and rows of U-pic raspberries in season. (We pick basketfuls and freeze them.) In the store, purchase fresh apples and tasty blends of raspberry/apple cider and cherry/apple cider. Tip: Watch the doughnut machine at work providing sweet concoctions seven days a week - there is always a line with people waiting to purchase these. Also, taste samples of their thirty-eight kinds of apples (depending on what's available at the time) before you decide which ones you want to purchase. The orchard is open September through November, daily from 9am to 5pm.

One-hour tours are offered for a minimum of twenty-five students (or adults) and a maximum of 125 at $6 per person. The tours include learning about this orchard, which has been here for more than a century, and seeing how it operates, plus making cider and packing and grading fruit. For school tours, teachers receive a bag of apples and the children get an apple and a cup of cider (and a lot of knowledge). Tours are offered Wednesday through Friday mornings; call first to make a reservation. If you are interested in the history of Snow-Line orchard, or Oak Glen or apple farming, specifically, you'll enjoy the Orchard Walk tour. Call to make a reservation.

Riley's at Los Rios Rancho, 39611 Oak Glen Road, (909) 797-1005 / www.losriosrancho.com: This working apple ranch has acres of orchards that are ready to be picked, baked, sauced, and pressed in the fall; a large store selling everything apple, including up to twenty varieties of apples (depending upon the season), plus apple cider, apple butter, and gift items; a delicious deli and bakery (really fresh apple pie!); a BBQ open on weekends, only in season, serving up tri-tip sandwiches, roasted corn on the cob, Polish or chicken apple sausages, and more; wonderful nature walking trails (see Wildlands Conservancy below); and two picnic areas. One picnic area is the large, grassy front lawn that has picnic tables. The other is a pretty, wooded area with picnic tables, located behind the store.

Los Rios offers hour-long tours during harvest season (September through mid-November) for groups of twenty-five or more. This informative tour includes taste-testing and comparing the different types of apples; walking through the packing house/cider mill; packing apples; pressing cider; and going into the apple orchards to learn about agriculture, particularly the organic aspects of farming, often accompanied by Johnny Appleseed. Also included is a caramel apple and one extra activity, such as a hayride or candle dipping. Tours are $8 per person. Take a Little Seedling Tour where youngsters, twenty minimum, can taste apples with Johnny Appleseed; visit, pet, and feed barnyard animals; and go through a hay bale maze for $5 per person. For an additional $3.50 per person on any tour, you can go pumpkin picking in October. You can also add on a lunch of hot dogs, chips, and drink for $3.50 per

and/or caramel apple for another $2 per person. All tours are offered Tuesday through Friday only during the fall. A spring tour, offered April through June at $8 per person, offers groups of twenty-five, or more, a visit to a hand-built log cabin and a choice of four activities.

Ask or check the website regarding special events. Enjoy once-a-month, year-round, special entertainment such as hometown jamborees with dinner (the first Saturdays - $10 for all ages) and gospel nights (the third Fridays - free). Mark your calendar for the Apple Butter Festival in November, Currier & Ives Christmas in December, and Cowboy Chuckwagon Supper in August. U-pic raspberries are available mid-August through September, or so, and U-pic pumpkins are ready in October. The Rancho is open December through Labor Day daily, 10am to 5pm; Labor Day through Thanksgiving weekend, daily, 9am to 5pm.

Wildlands Conservancy, 39611 Oak Glen Road, (909) 797-8507 or (909) 790-3698 / www.wildlandsconservancy.org: The conservancy shares and operates the land with the above-mentioned Los Rios Rancho. An almost two-mile dirt nature trail, with several offshoots and dead-ends, loops around on one section of the ranch land. It leads alongside a stream, through chaparral, and past two ponds where ducks flock when the pond water is not being used to irrigate the apple orchard. One trail branch, the California tree trail, even has a few redwoods and Giant Sequoias along the route. The trails are open to the general public on weekends and holiday Mondays (except Christmas) from 8am to 5pm. Admission is free. It is open for tour groups, only, during the week. Sign up for a night hike, offered the 3rd Saturday, April through October, 7pm - 9pm and November through March, 5pm - 7pm - for ages 8 and up..

Oak Glen School House Museum (see separate entry on page 427 for details.)

Willowbrook Apple Farm, 12099 S. Oak Glen Road, (909) 797-9484 / willowbrookapple.tripod.com: Stop here briefly as this farm sells candied apples, preserves, and Winesap apples, exclusively. You can pick your own Winesaps (one of my favorite apples) and press your own cider. A tour is available for groups of twenty-five or more which includes cider pressing and a tractor ride The tour is $10 for children, $7 for adults. The farm is open August through mid-November, weekends only, 10am to 4pm.

Riley's Apple Farm, 12201 S. Oak Glen Road, (866) 585-6407 or (909) 797-4061 / www.rileysapplefarm.com. In the tradition of various Riley's farms up on the mountain, this original farm offers exceptional Colonial-era tours, activities (including archery, corn husk doll-making, and rope-making), and sweet treats. See RILEY'S APPLE FARM on page 438 for more details.

Riley's Farm, 12261 S. Oak Glen Road, (909) 797-7534 / www.rileysfarm.com: These members of the Riley's dynasty offer a variety of attractions, including outstanding school and group tours with an emphasis on early America, U-pic fruits, and a re-created Colonial restaurant which is open for breakfast and lunch. See page 439 for more information.

Ages: All ages for most activities; 5 years and up for the educational tours.

THE OLD SPAGHETTI FACTORY (San Bernardino County)

Rancho Cucamonga - (909) 980-3585; Redlands - (909) 798-7774 / www.osf.com
Rancho Cucamonga - 11896 Foothill Blvd.; Redlands - 1635 Industrial Park Ave.
$$$

See the entry for THE OLD SPAGHETTI FACTORY (Los Angeles County) on page 23 for details.

OLIVIA'S DOLL HOUSE TEA ROOM (San Bernardino County)

(661) 252-1404 / www.oliviasdollhousetearoom.com
569 N. Central Avenue, Upland
$$$$$

See the entry for OLIVIA'S DOLL HOUSE TEA ROOM (Los Angeles County) on page 23 for details.

PEGGY SUE'S 50's DINER

(760) 254-3370 / www.peggysuesdiner.com
35654 Yermo Road, Yermo
$$$

If your cruisin' for food served in a really happening place, head over to Peggy Sue's. (This is the "Peggy Sue" that Buddy Holly crooned about.) This original roadside diner has a few rooms, including small ones packed with booths and a larger room with chairs and tables. The walls are filled with an impressive and eclectic array of movie and television personality memorabilia, including Lucille Ball, Ricky Ricardo, Cary Grant, Marilyn Monroe, Elvis, James Dean, Buddy Holly, Laurel and Hardy, and the gang from the *Wizard of Oz*, all portrayed in pictures, posters, masks, dolls, and paintings. Gaudy decor (i.e., paintings on black velvet and cheesy trinkets) is interspersed with nicer

mementos (i.e., fine portraits of celebrities and expensive-looking paraphernalia). An occasional mannequin dressed in period clothing adds to the wonderful kitschyness. The jukebox plays 50's music every night except Friday nights, when live music is performed.

The diner also features a full pizza parlor toward the back and a small arcade. Outside is a small park with picnic tables, a pond for ducks, fountains, grass, a koi pond, a few shade trees, and some quirky statues on small dirt hill - dinosaurs, King Kong, and other creatures. Toward the front of the restaurant is a soda fountain for old-fashioned drinks and desserts, and an attached Five and Dime Store that sells touristy television and movie souvenirs, older-style toys from a simpler time, and collectors items. Look at the thirteen-foot Marlin here and life-size model of Betty Boop. Note that CALICO GHOST TOWN (pg. 433) is just down the road.

Breakfast options include three eggs any style with ham ($8.89) or pancakes ($5.99). Lunch fare includes a burger ($7.49); club sandwich ($8.79); or meatloaf ($7.99). For dinner, try a New York steak ($12.99); ham steak ($10.79); Southern fried chicken ($11.79); or chef salad ($8.79). Desserts include Green River or cherry phosphates ($2.49); malts or shakes ($3.99); Chuck Berry pie ($3.39); or pineapple cheesecake ($4.69). Kid's menu choices for breakfast include an egg with toast ($2.69); one egg, two strips of bacon or sausage and hash browns ($3.69); French toast and two strips of bacon or sausage ($3.99); and a hot cake with bacon or sausage ($3.99). Lunch and dinner selections, which all include french fries, range from grilled cheese sandwich or chicken nuggets to a hot dog or a hamburger. Each kid's meal is $3.99 and drinks are an additional $1.19. Note: The food is O.K., but the atmosphere gets top ratings.

Hours: Open daily, 6am - 10pm. Closed Christmas.
Price: Prices are listed above.
Ages: All

RAINFOREST CAFE (San Bernardino County)

(909) 941-7979 / www.rainforestcafe.com
4810 Mills Circle in Ontario Mills Mall, Ontario

See the entry for RAINFOREST CAFE (Orange County) on page 251 for details. This location doesn't have a live bird presentation, but it does have a (pretend) lifesize crocodile in the front of the store that resides in a small swamp. He moves around and roars every few minutes.

RILEY'S FARM

(909) 797-7534 / www.rileysfarm.com
12261 S. Oak Glen Road, Oak Glen

See RILEY'S FARM on page 439 for details.

SUMMIT INN CAFE

(760) 949-8688
5960 Mariposa Road, Oak Hills

Once part of the famous Route 66, this kitschy restaurant/gift store is a memorable place to stop and eat. From the outside of the building, with its old vehicles, to the inside, with its red vinyl booths and seats at the counter surrounded with memorabilia (i.e. a defunct gas pump, neon signs, movie star pictures, and road side signs and attractions), Summit Inn is like a page out of time.

Breakfast selections include egg dishes, and flapjacks. For lunch, you can order an all-American hamburger ($6.99) or a hot dog, or go for the exotic and try an ostrich burger ($12.95), or a buffalo burger ($10.95) - I like 'em. Kid's meals are $4.95 for a choice of burger, corn dog, quesadilla, or chicken fingers, or PB&J. While you're waiting for food, operate the jukebox, or better yet, the fortune-telling napkin holders on the tables. Just ask "yes" or "no" questions for the Swami to give you the right answer.

Hours: Open Mon. - Thurs., 6am - 7pm; Fri. - Sun., 6am - 9pm.
Price: Some prices listed above.
Ages: All

—FAMILY PAY AND PLAY—

BOOMERS! (San Bernardino County)

(909) 946-9555 / www.boomersparks.com
1500 W. 7th Street, Upland

Upland Boomers fun center offers fun for everyone in your family! This giant fun center has two, themed outdoor **miniature golf** courses with all the whimsical decorations such as waterfalls, windmills, and more obstacles that make each hole fun. Two other courses, the Old West and Storybook Land, are indoors so rainy days won't put a damper on your swing. The Old West is seen in a different light with **cosmic golf**, where holes glow neon colors in the dark under black lights. All golf prices are $9 a round per person; children 4 and under are free. Over 150 arcade and video games are also inside the building. Take a spin on a **go kart** at $7 a ride (no sandals allowed) - drivers must be over 58" tall. An additional passenger under this height is $2. **Bumperboats**, a seasonal attraction, are always fun - $5.25 for kids over 44" tall, $2 for riders under this height. There are a few **kiddie rides** here including a Ferris wheel, mini jets, and kidz karts. Each ride is $3. The **rock climbing wall** is $7 for two climbs, for participants who weigh at least forty pounds. Kids can also practice for the big league at the **batting cages.** And of course there are virtual reality games. If you've worked up an appetite, Be-Bop Cafe is right next door. Your choice of hamburgers, pizza, or chicken is served in a fun atmosphere, where there are more arcade games to play. (There is no escape from them.)

Hours: Open most of the year, Mon. - Thurs., noon - 8pm (arcade and golf); 3pm - 7pm (most other attractions); Fri. 11am - 11pm (arcade and golf), 3pm - 8pm (most other attractions); Sat., 11am - 11pm (arcade and golf), 11am - 8pm (most other attractions); Sun., 11am - 8pm (arcade and golf), 11am - 7pm (most other attractions). Attractions are open longer in the summer and during school breaks.

Price: Attractions are individually priced above, or purchase an all-day pass. Definitely check the website regarding specials.

Ages: 3 years and up.

THE BULLET HOLE TRAINING CENTER

(760) 245-3307 / www.thebullethole.net
15315 Cholame Road, Unit D, Victorville

2,200 square feet of climbing surface, sixteen top ropes, and over fifty routes (including bouldering) equals an ideal gym to practice and perfect climbing techniques for beginners and for more accomplished climbers. Hooked, harnessed, and belayed, you shimmy up the vertical and slanted rock walls using hand and foot holds. This sport teaches participants much about physical and mental agility, as well as teamwork. (It's also something active to do on a rainy day.) You can come here with someone else, so you can a belay each other. If you don't know how, learn to do so here, and then climb for the whole day. You can also come by yourself, or just have your child climb for ninety-minutes with a staff member belayer. Kids can first get comfortable climbing by using the twenty-five-foot sloped wall, learning to climb up and repel down.

Birthdays, scout trips, or any kind of parties are great here - mainly because it wears kids out! They also have a great time learning or brushing up on skills, and challenging themselves. As Bullet Hole is more of a typical gym and a training center than other climbing centers, the rock climbing area shares the room with boxing, kickboxing, and various styles of martial arts that are also offered here.

Hours: Open Mon. - Thurs., 4pm - 9pm; Fri., 4pm - 8pm; Sat., 10am - 2pm. Closed Sun.

Price: $20, which includes shoes, harness, and a belayer and instruction for ninety minutes. During this time a parent can learn how to belay, which then makes the time limit obsolete and you can stay for the day. There are several other options available, including membership.

Ages: 5 years and up.

CHINO SKATE PARK - AYALA PARK

(909) 591-9834 / www.skatepark.com
14225 Central Avenue, Chino

At almost 28,000 square feet, this huge, free-flowing, gated, cement skate park has received many well-deserved kudos. Street, vert, and pool riders rate this park as one of the best in the area - worth driving for, especially because of

its stairs, funboxes, rails, three-leaf dover bowl, nine-foot bowl, and several other bowls and banks. The adjacent park has some open grass areas, ball fields, and a playground.

Hours: Open daily, sunrise - 8pm.
Price: Free
Ages: 7 years and up.

CHUCK E. CHEESE'S (San Bernardino County)

See the entry for CHUCK E. CHEESE'S (Los Angeles County) on page 16 for details.

DAVE & BUSTER'S (San Bernardino County)

(909) 987-1557 / www.daveandbusters.com
4821 Mills Circle at Ontario Mills Mall, Ontario
See DAVE & BUSTER'S (Orange County) (pg. 258) for details. See ONTARIO MILLS MALL (pg. 421) for other things to do at the mall.

Hours: Open daily, 11am - midnight.
Ages: 7 years and up.

FIESTA VILLAGE

(909) 824-1111 / www.fiestavillage.com
1405 E. Washington Street, Colton
Just off the freeway, come party at Fiesta Village! The two, Western-motif **miniature golf** courses, are well kept up and have some crazy, fun holes complete with fountains, palm trees, and small structures such as a lighthouse, castle, windmill, mini Western town facade, and more. Unlimited use of the two courses is $8.95 for players 53" and taller, $6.95 for seniors and children 37" to 52", kids 36" and under are free (with a paying partner). The **go karts** in the raceway are a blast to zip around the track - drivers must be at least 53" tall and the cost is $6.95 for a five-minute ride. Five amusement **rides** include a Gear Jammer (i.e., swinging arm); Bizzy Bear (like a teacup ride); Tilt a Whirl; bounce house; and a giant, super slide. Six tickets are $6.95 and rides take one to three tickets per. The maze-like, **lazer tag** arena is really a fun one with numerous nooks and crannies to hide behind and shoot your opponents. The eight-minute games can have up to fifteen players and costs $6.95 for a single mission; $9.95 for two. The outdoor **roller blade and skate rink** is a great way to burn off some extra energy or try some fancy moves - $6.95 for unlimited skating, with rentals an additional $3. **Batting cages** are also on the grounds. During the summer enjoy wet refreshment at **Pyrite Rapids Waterpark** which consists of three water slides - a double tube, a body slide, and a high-speed plunge, with a lounging area for spectators - $12.95 for an all-day pass for 48" and taller; $9.95 for juniors - those under 48"; $1.95 for a spectator. Note: No swimming around in the landing pool.

Video arcades are in the main lobby with ticket redemption center. Picnic tables are located outside and a few are inside, as well. Eating places include Dairy Queen, with a full snack bar, and Nickelodeon Pizza restaurant, which has more video and arcade games like Dance Dance Revolution Extreme, Jumpin' Jackpot, and Deal or No Deal. Inside Dairy Queen is an AnimaLand kiosk machine - a place to stuff and fluff the stuffed animal of your choice for $19.95, which includes an outfit.

Hours: The Village is open most of the year, Mon. - Thurs., 11am - 10pm - for most attractions (lazer tag and the arcade open at 4pm, and the amusement rides aren't open at all); Fri., 11am - 11pm - most attractions (lazer tag, arcade and amusement rides open at 4pm); Sat., 10am - 10pm - all attractions; Sun., 11am - 9pm - all attractions. All attractions are open during the summer and school breaks, Mon. - Thurs., 11am - 10pm - (rides open at 4pm); Fri., 11am - 11pm - (rides open at 4pm); Sat., 10am - 11pm - all attractions; Sun., 11am - 10pm - all attractions. The water slides are open May and mid-September on weekends only, 11am - 5pm; daily in the summer, noon - 6pm.
Price: Attractions priced above. Ask about package deals. Note that good grades on a report card earns Fiesta Village tokens (and parental approval).
Ages: 4 years and up.

FONTANA PARK - SKATE PARK - AQUATIC CENTER

(909) 349-6900 - park; (909) 899-5320 - skate park; (909) 854-5111 - pool / www.fontana.org
15556 Summit Avenue (park); 15610 Summit Avenue (aquatic center), Fontana

Wahoo - this 25,000 square-foot mega skate park is fantastic for both beginners and advanced skaters. It has four cement bowls - from one- to three-feet, up to seven- to nine-feet, and one is a full capsule (skaters can go 360° around it inside); street elements with fun boxes, rails, and stairs; one sidewalk that meanders around the perimeter of the skate park and another that encircles an island of grass and shade trees; and a small pro shop and concession stand. Safety equipment - a helmet and pads - must be worn as police officers will cite offenders. Lights are here for nighttime fun. Lessons, summer camps, friendly competitions, and birthday parties are all available here.

The surrounding park has plenty of amenities including picnic tables, BBQ pits, a hockey rink, walking and biking pathways, health and fitness community center, dog park, sports pavilion, palm trees, and a playground. The huge playground inspires lots of creative play. It features a sunken ship play area with a whale and dolphin "swimming" alongside; big fake boulders to climb on and under; four tall, kinetic sculptures that have elements that twirl in the wind, adding to the cool factor of the park; and colorful sculptures of frogs, caterpillars, a snail, and ladybugs to climb on as they reside underneath wildly-oversized (metal) flowers and butterflies - all on recycled rubber flooring.

This large aquatics center has two heated pools open year-round; one for rec swim and the other for lap and competitive swim. Along with two diving boards, the center has three slides that swoosh down from a tower - one enclosed slide and two open ones that end in a catch pool. These are for guests 48" and taller only. The good-sized splash pad (zero depth water play area) for younger kids has large buckets on the end of tall poles that look like trees that fill up with water and tip over; fountains that squirt up from the ground; a rainbow arch to run under with misters that spray; and some other play elements - all fun and refreshing, especially on hot summer days. There are also lounge chairs and picnic tables.

Hours: The park is open daily, sunrise - sunset. The skate park is open most of the year, Mon. - Fri., 2pm - 9pm; Sat. - Sun., 9am - 9pm. It is open during school breaks and the summer starting at noon during the week. The rec pool, slides, and splash pad are open year round, Sat. - Sun., noon - 4:30pm. They are open Memorial Day - Labor Day, or so, daily, noon - 5pm, along with some nighttime sessions.

Price: The park is free. The skate park is $5 a month for residents; $7 for non-residents; or $2 a day. Yearly passes are available. Rec swim is $5 for adults for just the pool, $7 for the pool and slides; $3 for seniors and ages 3 - 17 for just the pool, $5 for the pool and slides; children 2 and under are free. Picnic tables cost $10 to rent.

Ages: 1½ years and up.

GAMEWORKS

(909) 987-4263 / www.gameworks.com
4541 Mills Circle, Ontario

GameWorks is a two-story, high-tech entertainment venue dedicated to the latest (and greatest) interactive virtual reality and video games, such as Primeval Hunt, Rambo, Deal or No Deal, Sega's Initial D-4, Terminator - Salvation, House of the Dead 4, and more. Many of the games are sports-oriented. There are also some motion simulator rides. The rides allow participants to be at the controls and interact with the screen to move all around. At the Indy 500, hop in a full-size race car and zoom around the curves shown on the screen (kind of). It's a lot of virtual fun. Play the "classic" games, too, such as Pac-Man, air hockey, and billiards.

The full-service grill serves appetizers (three Angus beef sliders - $8 or fried pickle and chips, $8); salads (Far East chicken - $12); Chicken Caesar wrap ($10); pizzas ($10 for an individual); Southwestern burgers ($11); sandwiches (Philly cheese steak or Santa Fe chicken - $10 each); fried chicken and waffle sandwich ($7); and desserts. Kid's meals are $4.99 for a choice of mac and cheese, two sliders, chicken tenders, spaghetti, or quesadilla and include a beverage. Note that there is a bar in the restaurant, too. See ONTARIO MILLS MALL (pg. 421) for details about the mall.

Hours: Open Sun. - Wed., 11am - 11pm; Thurs. - Sat., 11am - midnight. Only patrons 18 years and older are allowed inside after 10pm.

Price: Admission is free. A debit-style game card costs $5 for 20 credits; each game is 3 to 12 credits.

Ages: 7 years and up.

HANGAR 18 (San Bernardino County)

(909) 931-5991 / www.climbhangar18.com
256 Stowell Street, suite A, Upland

Love a good cliffhanger? This location of Hangar 18 boasts 12,000 square feet of overhangs; a forty-foot-long

roof climb across the ceiling; two huge top rope areas; textured climbing walls dotted with numerous multi-colored stones that represent different routes; and a gigantic bouldering wall with a large lead cave. Both lead climbing and the bouldering areas give seasoned climbers, as well as beginners, the opportunity to practice their bouldering technique. (Have you ever noticed how most rock climbers don't have an ounce of fat on their bodies? After attempting the sport - I know why!) Come with a friend (i.e. a fellow belayer) or call beforehand to see if a belayer will be at the gym. There is also a viewing platform and rails at the top for non-climbers to look down at the climbers.

The Adults Intro package and Kid's Intro package, for ages 12 and under, includes a belay lesson, for the attending adults; gear - shoes, harness and chalk; and a day pass. Hangar 18 also has youth climbing teams which compete all over the U.S. This fun and safe activity builds confidence and stamina. Groups with a minimum of six people can do a ropes course at this facility, only, where participants swing thirty feet in the air to dunk a really tall basket ball hoop, walk the high wire (all while safely harnessed), and other special activities. The cost for this two-hour event is $14 a climber, plus a $50 set-up fee. You can also choose to do half-ropes course, half-climbing for the same price. Notes: A party room is available. Waivers must be signed for all climbers at Hangar 18.

Hours: Open Mon. - Thurs., 10am - 10pm; Fri., 10am - 9pm; Sat. - Sun., 10am - 8pm.
Price: Day passes are $16 for adults; $11 for ages 12 and under. Rental equipment - shoes and a harness - is $5. Adults Intro package is $30; Kids Intro package is $25.
Ages: 5 years and up.

JOHN'S INCREDIBLE PIZZA CO. (San Bernardino County)

(760) 951-1111 / www.johnspizza.com
14766 Bear Valley Road, Victorville

See JOHN'S INCREDIBLE PIZZA CO. (Orange County) on page 248 for details.

Hours: Open Mon. - Thurs., 11am - 9pm; Fri. - Sat., 11am - 10pm; Sun., 11am - 9pm.

JUMPING JACKS (Riverside County)

(909) 989-6820 / www.jumpingjacksparty.com
11138 Elm Avenue, Rancho Cucamonga

Jumping Jacks makes me want to hop to it and play, slide, and bounce on these crazy fun and massive inflatables - some of the funnest ones I've seen under one roof. Working up a good sweat never hurt anyone! There are eight "jumps" in this 13,000-square-foot play place and some run-around space in the two rooms. One room is jungle themed and the other is marine themed via wall murals that are nicely done and not cartoonish. One enormous slide looks like a skateboarding half-pipe; one is like a pinball machine where you can throw balls or be the ball; one is a conglomeration of bounce, slide, climbing wall, and obstacle course; another is underwater themed. The jousting arena is great with it's inflatable pugil sticks as is the boxing ring where contestants use oversize, inflatable boxing gloves. Free game tables like foosball and air hockey are also part of the deal. If parents want a time out they can retreat to the Hideout, a small room with a couch, coffee bar, and wireless internet. Jumping Jacks is also carpeted, air conditioned, and has a sound system. Socks are mandatory. Note that there is a park next door to enjoy a picnic lunch.

Hours: Open play, family fun times are Tues. - Wed., 10:30am - 1pm; Wed. - Thurs., 6pm - 9pm. The rest of the time is for private parties.
Price: $7 per child for ages 2 and up; children under 2 with a paid sibling, and adults, are free.
Ages: 4 years and up.

K1 SPEED (Ontario)

(909) 980-0286 / www.k1speed.com
5350 East Ontario Mills Parkway, Ontario

See K1 SPEED (San Diego County) on page 486 for details.

LASER ISLAND

(909) 982-0044 / www.laserisland.com
207 E. Foothill Boulevard, Upland

Playing tag on a deserted island. Can it get any better than this? Yes, when it's laser tag - running around black-lit erupting volcanos and ducking behind an island temple into a jungle hut, or alongside and in the scattered parts of a

plane wreck that "crashed" here. Even the walls and partitions are painted and decorated with the theme - bamboo-looking forests, jungle plants, rocks, etc. Up to thirty-six players are divided into two teams that "tag" each other with lasers and try to score the most points, while strategically hiding to avoid getting "hit".

This island offers even more fun with a nine-hole, Tiki-themed miniature golf course, arcade games with tickets and redemption prizes, and Coco Climb. Climbers strap in and shimmy up the three, twenty-foot fake coconut trees. All this adventuring can build up an appetite so grab a pizza ($14 for a 16") in the tiki cafe/lobby, or a salad ($3.75 for a small), toasted sandwich (about $6.50), nachos ($3), buffalo wings ($7.50), or a root beer float with freshly-made ice cream ($3.35).

Hours: Open Mon. - Thurs., 3pm - 9pm; Fri., 3pm - midnight; Sat., 10am - midnight; Sun., noon - 9pm. Open in the summer and on holidays at noon - same closure times.

Price: Laser tag is $8. Mini golf is $5. CoCo Climb is $5. Additional games are less. Check out the numerous specials offered like after school specials of unlimited laser tag for $16 or, my favorite - Family Dinner Adventure for up to 6 people. This includes pizza, a pitcher of soda, garlic bread and 2 laser games each for only $45.

Ages: 6 years and up.

LASER QUEST (San Bernardino County)

(909) 591-2626 / www.laserquest.com
5479 Philadelphia Street, suite A, Chino

$$$

See LASER QUEST (Orange County) on page 261 for details about this laser game arena.

Hours: Open usually Mon. and Tues. for private parties; Wed. - Thurs., 6pm - 9pm; Fri., 4pm - 11pm; Sat., noon - 11pm; Sun., noon - 6pm. Open summer, school breaks, and holidays extended hours.

Price: $9 per person.

Ages: 6 years and up.

LEGO - MINI MODEL BUILD (San Bernardino County)

(909) 758-9303 / shop.lego.com/en-US/MiniBuilds
One Mills Circle, Space 631, at Ontario Mills mall, Ontario

!

See LEGO - MINI MODEL BUILD (San Diego County) on page 488 for info on this great, free LEGO mini model build. Timed tickets for entry to the store are given out at 4pm - so enjoy shopping at the mall in between.

Hours: The first Tues. of each month, 5pm - 7pm.

Price: Free

Ages: 6 - 14 years old, only.

NAVITAT CANOPY ADVENTURES

(855) 628-4828; (760) 249-9990 / www.navitat.com
6047 Park Drive, Wrightwood

$$$$$

Exhilarating! Ziplining through the treetops and over mountain terrain is literally quite breathtaking and simply Exhilarating!!! One of the two zipline adventures offered is called the Zipline Canopy Tour. For about three and half hours you trek into and through the forest; cross four sky bridges (i.e. suspended bridges that swing) that are high up in the air; rappel down trees (from as high as ninety feet); and whoosh across and down eight ziplines, some of which are up to 300 feet high and as long as 1,500 feet. There is even a side-by-side zipline so you can race someone to the finish line.

The two-and-a-half hour Mountain View Zipline Tour includes six ziplines up to 135 feet high and 1,100 feet long; leaping off tree platforms (free fall rappels) that can be sixty feet off the ground (while in a safety harness and gear and auto-belay); and hiking, because ground to air perspective is impactful. (No bridges on this tour.)

With no more than eight people per tour, you get a lot of personal attention from the two guides and a lot of information about conservation, geography, history, and safety, plus - what an adventure!

Come prepared by wearing layers (note that tours run, rain or shine); wearing pants or long shorts (these are more comfortable in the harness); and close-toed shoes (a must). Requirements include being in good health, weighing at least 90 pounds and no more than 250 (participants will be weighed), and being at least 10 years old. Waivers must be signed and kids under 14 must be accompanied by a parent or adult designated as his chaperone. Come and see and experience the mountains from the treetops!

Hours: Zipline Canopy Tours are available mid-March - November, Fri. - Tues; closed Wed. - Thurs. In the summer, they are also open on Thurs. Tours are offered December - mid-March, Fri. - Sun. Mountainview Tours are available mid-March - November, weekends only. Always call to make a reservation. The first tour starts around 9am and the last leaves about 2pm.

Price: The Zipline Canopy Tour is $109 on weekdays and $129 on weekends and holidays, March - November. It is $109 during the winter season. Mountainview tours are $99. Take both tours in one day for $195.

Ages: At least 10 years old, and up.

PARTY KINGDOM

(909) 628-9900 / www.inflatablepartykingdom.com
3937 Schaefer Avenue, Chino

The jungle-themed, indoor, nine-inflatable Party Kingdom is a wild place to play. In the enormous rooms with primary-painted walls and jungle-leaf carpeting, the giant slides are fun (for the kids and me), as is the huge, open-mouthed crocodile obstacle course with long inflatable teeth. The croc also has a climbing element to it. I loved the sixty-foot-long obstacle course because it was great fun and wore me out (I have to field test these things, you know), while the boys enjoyed the joust inflatable and the sports-themed one, where you can throw the basketball. There is an inflatable maze, an inflatable zip line, and foam pit (way fun), and bounce houses, with some geared just for younger children. A play area in the middle of the floor has toddler toys, and table and chairs for parents. The arenas are open so moms can sit and chat while keeping an eye on their little darlings. Free air hockey and ping pong are also here. Socks must be worn by all participants. The party rooms have junglish murals on the walls - monkeys and vines and all. Family Fun Nights include light snacks and lemonade, and you can preorder a mini pizza for an additional $3 per person.

Hours: Open playtimes are Wed. - Thurs., 9:30am - 1pm; Family Fun Night is Thurs., 5:30pm - 8:30pm.

Price: Open playtimes are $7 per child; free for children 11 months and under with a paying child, and for adults. Family Fun Nights are $8 per child; free for children 11 months and under with a paying child, and for adults.

Ages: 18 months - 8 years for open playtimes; all ages for Family Fun Night.

PUMP IT UP (San Bernardino County)

Chino Hills - (909) 949-3176; Rancho Cucamonga - (909) 466-0806 / www.pumpitupparty.com
Chino Hills - 4510 Eucalyptus Avenue; Rancho Cucamonga - 11966 Jack Benny Drive

See PUMP IT UP (San Diego County) on page 491 for details.

Hours: Chino Hills - Open Jump is Mon. - Thurs., 4:30pm - 8pm; Tues. and Wed., 10am - noon. Rancho Cucamonga - Open Jump is Tues. - Wed., 10am - noon and 4pm - 6pm. Toddler Time, for ages 6 and under, are Thurs., 10am - noon. There are more Open Jump hours on holiday breaks and during the summer (sometimes daily, 9:30am - 8pm!), and special events throughout the year.

Price: Open Jump time is $10 per child at Chino; $8 at Rancho Cucamonga; adults are always free.

Ages: 3 years and up.

REVELATION RACEWAY

(909) 628-9909 / www.revrace.com
4871 E. State Street, Ontario

Race your smaller, remote-controlled version of a real race car around this jumbo, dirt racetrack, over big bumps and around tight corners. 1/10 and ⅛ scale, electric and gas-powered - all are welcome. If you don't want to participate, just watch the cars, trucks, and buggies fly around the track (we saw some going 45mph), jumping, turning, and even tumbling. Spectators are welcome to sit at the bleachers or stand. Rows of tables are available for drivers to work on their cars, like a pit area.

The track is attached to the incredibly well-stocked Genesis Hobby Shop, which can take care of any car parts needs you might have.

Hours: Both the track and store are open Mon., Wed., Fri., 10am - 7pm, Tues. and Thurs., 10am - 11pm; Sat. - Sun., 8am - 6pm. Racing is usually on Sat. nights - for all levels. All-day racing is usually one Saturday a month.

Price: Free for spectators. Practice fees are $10 on Mon., Wed., and Fri., $15 the other days. The last hour is only $5.

Ages: 5 years and up.

SBR - SAN BERNARDINO RACEWAY

(909) 824-7804 / www.sbraceway.com
$$$$

217 E. Club Center Drive, San Bernardino

Indoor go karts zoom around the track at 35+ mph, with a maximum of twelve to fifteen cars on the track at any one time. Each race lasts ten minutes, which is about twelve to seventeen laps around. Participants without a valid driver's license or permit, can race, too, as at least once an hour unlicensed drivers start at half speed for two laps to demonstrate their ability to handle the karts. If they are good to go, they can compete full throttle and can then join in on other, regular races. Cosmic karting on Saturday nights takes races to whole new dimension.

Hours: Open Mon. - Thurs., 11am - 10pm; Fri., 11am - 11pm; Sat., 11am - midnight; Sun., 11am - 8pm.

Price: $17 for a race. Check the website for specials and membership prices.

Ages: 12 years and up.

SCANDIA AMUSEMENT PARK

(909) 390-3092 / www.scandiafun.com
$$$$

1155 S. Wanamaker Avenue, Ontario

Vikings might have come to this country just to play at this amusement park! Well, maybe not, but it is a lot of fun and very well kept up. Attractions include two Scandinavian-themed **miniature golf** courses with unlimited play at $10.95 for 48" and taller; $7.95 for 48" and under. The sixteen **amusement rides** include some for big kids, such as a roller coaster, bumper boats, Tilt-A-Whirl, go-karts, Thor's Hammer, free fall, and scrambler; and some for little kids, such as a small semi-truck ride around a track, a carousel, a mini coaster, train ride, and a slide. The rides have various height requirements. Tickets cost $1.25 each or $24.95 for twenty-five of them. Children's rides require one to three tickets; big kids' (or adult) rides require three to six tickets. There are also **batting cages**, arcade and video games with a prize redemption center, and a full-service snack bar here, too. Incorporate fun and education with a field trip to Scandia. Learn about gas and electric motors, hydroelectric energy, centrifugal force, gravity and friction, and more, and then experience it via rides. Call for times, prices and more info.

Hours: Open most of the year, Mon. - Thurs., noon - 10pm for most everything (rides are open 3pm - 7pm); Fri. - Sat., noon - 11pm for most everything (rides are open 12:30 - 10pm); Sun., noon - 10pm for most everything (rides are open 12:30pm - 8pm). During holidays and school break, Scandia is open the hours as Sun. above.

Price: Attractions are individually-priced above, or purchase an unlimited pass (excluding arcade games) - $24.95 for 48" and taller; $17.95 for 47" and under. Inquire about weekday specials.

Ages: 3 years and up.

SCANDIA FAMILY FUN CENTER

(760) 241-4007 / www.scandiafun.com
$$$$

12627 Mariposa Road, Victorville

Enjoy some high desert fun at this Scandia location. There are two Scandinavian-themed **miniature golf** courses, with castles, bridges, and other small buildings that add interest - $7.75 for unlimited play for 48" and taller; $6 for 47" and under. **Go-karts, bumper boats, Sky Screamer,** which earns its name by spinning riders in complete circles at 55mph at sixteen stories off the ground, and a few other rides are purchased via tickets that are $1 per. **Batting cages,** a full-service snack bar, arcade and video games, and prize redemption center are also here for your enjoyment. Incorporate fun and education with a field trip to Scandia. Learn about gas and electric motors, hydroelectric energy, centrifugal force, gravity and friction, and more, and then experience it via rides. Call for times, prices and more info.

Hours: Open most of the year, Mon. - Thurs., 3pm - 10pm; Fri., 3pm - 11pm; Sat., noon - 11pm; Sun., noon - 10pm. Open during the summer and school breaks, Sun. - Thurs., noon - 10pm; Fri. - Sat., noon - 11pm. Hours can fluctuate, so call first.

Price: Attractions are individually-priced above, or buy an unlimited pass for $17.50 for 48" and over; $8.75 for 47" and under, which includes some tokens, too.

Ages: 4 years and up.

SKYTOWN INDOOR TRAMPOLINE PARK

(909) 335-7275 / www.skytownredlands.com
\$\$\$

1101 N. California Street, located inside Splash Kingdom, Redlands

Enter through the pyramid and massive Sphinx head wearing sunglasses of the Eygptian-themed SPLASH KINGDOM which is an arcade, Fun Park and waterpark. (See page 396 for more details.) Inside, next to the arcades, is SkyTown - 12,000 square foot of indoor trampoline fun! One room has a patchwork of about twenty-four good-sized trampolines to jump and twist and freestyle on. (I can last only 10 minutes, but the kids go on and on!) SkyTown also features a trampoline dodgeball court (way fun); two courts to slam dunk a basketball (while trampolining); and a foam pit to try tricks and flips into. Other fun elements are the Wall and Battle Beam, where opponents walk out on a padded beam and joust with padded lances over a foam pit. There is a small play place just for younger children, too - not with a trampoline, but on carpet with huge soft blocks. Special events held here include Kosmic Kingdom, which is jumping to music highlighted by blacklights and lasers on Friday and Saturday nights; Bounce Fitness, a fitness class; Special Needs Days; Dodgeball Tournaments; and Toddler Time, which is a time open to all jumpers as long as they obey the rule of "gentle jumping" as it caters specifically to the younger crowd. There are also extra balls and toys for toddlers at this time. Note that a signed waiver (by a parent or guardian for those under 18 years) is necessary for all jumpers, at all times.

Hours: Open most of the year, Mon., Wed., Thurs., 3pm - 9pm (closed Tues.); Sat., 11am - 11pm; Sun., 11am - 9pm. Toddler Time is Mon. and Thurs., 9am - 1pm. It's open holidays and summer, Mon. - Thurs., 11am - 9pm; Fri. - Sat., 11am - 11pm; Sun., 11am - 9pm. Toddler Time is then Mon. and Thurs., 8am - 11pm.

Price: \$10 an hour Mon. - Thurs., \$12 an hour Fri. - Sun. Additional hours are 50% off. At Toddler Time, addtional kids are \$5 each. Check the website for specials. Parking is \$7.

Ages: 3 years and up.

—GREAT OUTDOORS—

AFTON CANYON

(760) 252-6000 / www.blm.gov
!

Afton Road off I-15, between the Afton Rd. and Basin Rd. exits, Afton

Referred to as the "Grand Canyon of the Mojave," the canyon is at the site where the river surfaces after being underground for more than fifty miles. Since this is one of the few places in the desert where water is available, several wildlife species consider the canyon home, including bighorn sheep, migratory birds, and birds of prey. There are a few established roads through the multi-colored canyon, as well as hiking and equestrian trails. Washes and dry stream beds make for good hiking trails, too, although not during a flash flood. Hobby rock collecting is permitted. Primitive camp sites are available with a picnic table and single tap. Bring your own firewood and water. Note that hunting is permitted here in season.

Hours: Open daily, sunrise - sunset.
Price: Free to the park. \$6 to camp.
Ages: 6 years and up.

AMBOY CRATER

(760) 326-7000 / www.blm.gov
!

National Trails Highway (Old Route 66), off Kelbaker Rd., Amboy

What do volcanoes look like? Well, instead of seeing one erupt (which would be thrilling, but potentially deadly), you can see the aftermath by hiking to and around this cinder cone. The surrounding lava flows surface is black with specks of green-colored, olivine crystals. The surface texture is alternately rough like jutting rocks or smooth like glass. There are twelve, bowl-shaped depressions that add even more variety to the volcanic features.

The Bureau of Land Management suggests a minimum of three hours hiking time to hike around the entire crater rim. The cone is about one mile from the parking lot and it is one mile in circumference. If you follow the trail to the right of the cinder cone, you'll head up to its wide opening where an eruption breached the crater wall. From here, the climb to the top is only an eighty-foot incline. There are a few, scattered picnic tables, some informational kiosks, and

even restrooms. A favorite time to visit is from March to May when the desert flowers are blooming, and the sunrises and sunsets are often pink and purple hued.

Tips: Carry water! Wear tough boots or tennis shoes as the lava rock can cut bottoms of shoes. Winters can be really cold here, and summer is blazing hot. If you drive east a few miles on National Trails Highway past the crater turn off, the "town" of Amboy, and Roy's (which is closed) you'll see the shoe tree, which has fallen over. This large shade tree is "decorated" with shoes of all sizes and styles that are still being tossed into its branches. But this is just a *foot*note for your trip.

> **Hours:** Open daily, 7:30am - 4pm. (In the summer it is waaaaay too hot!)
> **Price:** Free
> **Ages:** 7 years and up.

CALICO EARLY MAN ARCHAEOLOGICAL SITE ☀

(760) 254-2248 / www.blm.gov$$

Minneola Road, about 6 miles east of Calico Ghost Town, Calico

At this brief natural pit stop, visitors hike a half-mile to look into this "in-place museum" of Pleistocene archaeology. In other words, look down into excavated pits to see artifacts on the walls and floors made by early man. There are two master pits where most of the findings have been made, one training trench, and four test pits. On your guided tour, which is the only way to see the pit, you'll learn about the area's geography and history. A very small museum shows some of the pottery shards and other artifacts that have been excavated.

> **Hours:** Open Wed., 12:30 - 4:30pm, with tours at 1:30pm and 3:30pm; open Thurs. - Sun. at 9am - 4:30pm, with tours at 9:30am, 11:30am, 1:30pm, and 3:30pm. Close Mon. and Tues.
> **Price:** $5 for the first two adults in your group, $2.50 for each adult thereafter; $2 for seniors; $1 for ages 12 and under.
> **Ages:** 7 years and up.

CUCAMONGA-GUASTI REGIONAL PARK ☀

(909) 481-4205 or (909) 38 PARKS (387-2757) / cms.sbcounty.gov$$$

800 N. Archibald Avenue, Ontario

Guasti Regional Park offers seasonal catfish and trout fishing at its nice-sized lakes. In fact, it is host to the annual Huck Finn Jubilee in June (see pg. 728) and, indeed, it looks like it belongs in Huck Finn country. Pedal boat and aqua cycle rentals are available in the summer. The playground has a tire swing, monkey bars, and cement tubes with holes to climb through, plus open grassy areas for running around.

During the summer have some wet fun by going down the two water slides (must be 48" or taller) and/or swimming in the lagoon. You can also just beach it on the sandy area around the lagoon and grassy area beyond that. Lifeguards are on duty. A snack bar, open seasonally also, sells hot dogs, burritos, chips, and ice cream, and is located next to the bait shop - make sure you choose the right food place for yourself!

> **Hours:** The park is open most of the year daily, 7:30am - 5pm; open during the summer daily, 7:30am - 7pm. Fishing is usually closed on Thurs. for restocking. Water fun is available Memorial Day - Labor Day.
> **Price:** $8 per vehicle Mon. - Fri.; $10 on Sat. - Sun. and holidays. Pedestrians are $2; dogs are $1. Fishing permits are $8 per person. Pedal boat and aqua cycle rentals are $10 each a half hour. Swimming Wed. - Sun. is $5 for ages 4 and up, plus the entrance fee. Swimming and all day water slides is $10 per person, plus entrance fee.
> **Ages:** All

DANA PARK COMMUNITY CENTER / BARSTOW SKATE PARK ☀

(760) 256-5617 / www.barstowca.org

850 Barstow Road, Barstow

Dana Park has a community center, picnic shelters, some grassy hills to roll down, a playground, and a 12,000-square-foot cement skate park with elements for beginning and advanced skaters, including a bowl, pyramid, and grind rails. An adjacent ride shop/snack shop provides boards and equipment for purchase or rent, as well as food (for purchase - not for rent). Note that the park is just across the street from the MOJAVE RIVER VALLEY MUSEUM (pg. 426) and down the street from the DESERT DISCOVERY CENTER (pg. 423).

Hours: Open daily, 7am - dusk.
Price: Free
Ages: All

ENGLISH SPRINGS PARK

(909) 364-2700 / www.chinohills.org
2201 Grand Avenue, Chino Hills

   This picturesque park, located on the corner of Grand Avenue and Chino Hills Parkway, has a small playground, a few picnic tables, and grassy area with plenty of mature trees surrounding the centerpiece pond that has a short waterfall. The other end of the park has a volleyball court and two basketball half courts, and more run-around space.

Hours: Open daily, dawn - dusk.
Price: Free
Ages: All

GLEN HELEN REGIONAL PARK

(909) 887-7540 / cms.sbcounty.gov/parks
2555 Glen Helen Parkway, San Bernardino

   This scenic 1,340-acre park, nestled in the mountains, is worth the drive. It offers an assortment of year-round fun, such as catfish, bass and trout fishing in the stocked and sizeable lakes (a license is needed for those over 16 years old) - note that there is a bait shop, here, too; volleyball courts; a baseball diamond; eighteen holes of disc golf; horseshoe pits; wide open grassy areas; lots of trails for hiking up and down the mountain; and playgrounds. These atypical playgrounds, partly based in the sand, spark the imagination with metal configurations to climb on, under, and through; slides; talking tubes; hanging monkey bar rings; netting to climb on; gyro twister; and more.

   Favorite summer activities include sunbathing on the surrounding beach; swimming in the pool; playing in the a zero-depth water play area that has a huge "umbrella" with water pouring over it and more; and slip-sliding down the two water slides (minimum 48" tall) that end in a small pool. Replenish your energy at the nearby snack bar. Many special events occur at the massive outdoor pavilion including concerts and other programs, as well as at the Glen Helen Raceway. Camping is available for organized groups only.

Hours: Open daily in the summer, 7:30am - 8pm; open the rest of the year daily, 7:30am - 5pm. Fishing is usually closed on Thurs. for restocking. Water activities are open Memorial Day through Labor Day, Wed. - Sun., 10am - 5pm.
Price: $8 per vehicle Mon. - Fri.; $10 per vehicle Sat. - Sun. and holidays. $2 for pedestrians. Fishing permits are $8 per person. Swimming and water slides are $6 per person; $10 on holidays and holiday weekends. Group camping is $5 per person, with a twenty-person minimum, plus a $10 reservation fee.
Ages: All

HESPERIA LAKE PARK

(760) 244-5951 / www.hesperiaparks.com
7500 Arrowhead Lake Road, Hesperia

   This good-sized, enclosed lake park, surrounded by mountains, is mainly great for fishing and camping, although it's fun for day use, too. A rock-lined, seasonal creek runs throughout the park which is rich with large shade trees and picnic tables. Other facilities include barbeque pits, a soccer field, volleyball court, and sizable playground with a wood-chip base. The latter has swings, including toddler swings, a talking tube, and twisty slides.

   The picturesque lake, which has small marshy islands in the middle, is apparently home to numerous ducks and birds, all eager for a hand-out! We saw pelicans, herons, swans, wood ducks, and other ducks and birds I can't identify. The lake is stocked every week, October through April, with trout and sturgeon, while catfish are stocked May through September. No state fishing license is required. If you are so inclined, you can even walk around the lake - about a mile round trip.

   Tent, RV, and equestrian campers can stay here and get away from it all for a weekend or week. All sites have a picnic table and fire ring. The on-site store offers camping supplies, food, drinks, bait, and tackle.

Hours: The park is open daily, 6am - 10pm. Fishing is open Sun. - Thurs., 6am - 5pm; Fri. - Sat., 6am - 8pm. Hours could be longer in the summer.

Price: Day use is always free for residents. It is free for non-residents in the winter. Non-residents pay $2 for adults and $1 for ages 10 and under, March through October. Fishing sessions are $15 for adults for a 5 fish limit; (residents and seniors are $12 at certain times); $4 for ages 10 and under with a 2 fish limit (or pay the adult rate for a 5 fish limit). Camping starts at $35 per site, with a two-night minimum; dogs are $2 per dog, per night. Camping fees do not include fishing fees.

Ages: All

JACK BULIK PARK AND SKATE PARK

(909) 823-8751 - skate park; (909) 349-6900 - park / www.fontana.org
16581 Filbert, Fontana

The park offers plenty to do to keep everyone in the family happily busy. There are several ball fields, picnic facilities with BBQ pits, soccer fields, snack bar, covered basketball courts, tennis courts, a covered roller-hockey rink, a playground, teen center, and a skate park.

The massive and well-laid-out skate park (27,000 square feet) has rails, ledges, a three-bowl clover, a eight- to nine-foot round vert bowl, banks, steps, and more street elements. Again (and always) - skaters must wear safety equipment. The park is supervised. Lessons, summer camps, friendly competitions, and birthday parties are all available here.

Hours: The park is open daily, 9am - 9:30pm. The skate park is open Mon. - Wed. and Fri., noon - 9pm; Sat. - Sun., 9am - 9pm. (Closed Thurs. am for maintenance.)

Price: The park is free. The skate park is $5 a month for residents; $7 for non-residents. Yearly passes are available.

Ages: All

JESS RANCH LAKES

(760) 240-1107 / www.jessranchlakesnews.com
11495 Apple Valley Road, Apple Valley

Serious, and not so serious, fishermen and women will have a great time angling for their fish limit at the two large lakes here. The area around the lakes has dirt pathways, as well as trees and other plants, plus a view of the mountains beyond. The fishing limit is five trout and/or catfish, plus up to five bluegill for adults, for $20; and two fish for ages 12 and under for $10. No fishing license is needed. Each angler must have his/her own string or basket, and children 12 and under must be accompanied by and supervised by adults.

If lake fishing didn't pan out at all for you, you may catch one trout, instead, at the nice-sized angling pond. The pond, surrounded by shade trees, grass, a short protective wall around some of it, and benches, is also available for those who just want to fish from there. The entrance fee for the angling pond is $3 for adults; ages 12 and under are free with a paying adult. The trout cost $4 per and poles are available to rent for $5. The cleaning fee is $1 per fish. The fish hatchery on the grounds supplies trout for the weekly stocking. Lake One is for float tubers only, with a minimum of two tubers. The lake entrance fee is $25 for a half day, and bass are catch and release only.

There is a picnic area with BBQs for those who can't wait until they get home to eat their fish. You are also welcome to bring in a picnic meal and/or purchase something from the snack and bait shop. (Snack food for you; bait for the fish - just to be clear.) Be on the lookout for an amazing array of birds around here, too, such as woodpeckers, herons, road runners, quail, and egrets, plus ducks and geese, of course. Enjoy your day of fishing and fun in the great outdoors!

Hours: Open Fri. - Sun., 7am - 4pm.

Price: Day parking is free. Overnight RV parking is $10 a night. Other prices are listed above.

Ages: 3 years and up.

MARTIN TUDOR JURUPA HILLS REGIONAL PARK

(909) 349-6900 / www.fontana.org
11925 Sierra Avenue, Fontana

Jurupa Hills is another good park nestled into a rocky mountainside. It has a great wooden playground for slightly older kids, with wavy slides, a big spiral slide, swaying bridges, and swings. The lower level of the park has a grassy picnic area, along with a baseball diamond, horseshoe pits, volleyball courts, and a few swings. Look at the MARY VAGLE MUSEUM AND NATURE CENTER (listed below) because it is just around the corner. In fact, a

hiking/biking trail at the south end of the park goes around the base of the hill to the nature center. Another trail goes up and over the hill.

Hours: The park is open daily, 9am - sunset.
Price: Free
Ages: All

MARY VAGLE NATURE CENTER

(909) 349-6994 / www.nature.fontana.org
11501 Cypress Avenue, Fontana

This delightful nature center is at the foothills of a rock-covered hill, which is great for climbing and hiking on trails. One such trail leads up to petroglyphs. A winding bike trail goes around the base of the hill to connect to the MARTIN TUDOR JURUPA HILLS REGIONAL PARK (look at the above entry) on the other side.

The front of the nature center has a pond and acres of land for wildlife. Inside the building are live animals such as snakes, tarantulas, a rabbit, a chinchilla, lizards, and a tortoise. A small touch tidepool tank has sea stars and sea anemones. Microscopes, books and videos on nature, and touch tables are also available here. Join the staff of the center in an array of family programs and classes, critter crafts on Saturday afternoons, guided nature walks, and seasonal events. Teachers, inquire about the three-hour school field trips which incorporate a nature craft, tour of the center, and hands-on live animal experience. Field trips are $5 per student for grades K through 12th.

Hours: The center is open Wed. - Sun., noon - 5pm. Closed Mon., Tues., and major holidays. The grounds are open daily, sunrise - sunset.
Price: Free.
Ages: All

MITCHELL CAVERNS

(760) 928-2586 / www.parks.ca.gov
Exit I-40 N. on Essex Rd., drive 16 miles, in the Providence Mountains State Recreation Area in the Mojave National Preserve

If you feel like you're out in the middle of nowhere, you're right - you are. The panoramic view from the small visitors center at the top of the one-lane road offers a wonderful vista. Note that you may tent camp up here, if you're so inclined.

The ninety-minute, guided tour of the limestone caverns begins with about a .5 mile walk to the entrance, learning some history and geology of the area as you go. Inside, the branching, narrow passages open to a few large rooms containing stalactites, stalagmites (do you know the difference?), shelves, flows, curtains, and formations named according to what they look like (at least to someone). The casual pace and informal manner of the guide makes the excursion both relaxing and interesting.

Back at the visitor's center, hike the short Mary Beale Nature Trail; the mile-long trail leading to a spring above the building; or, for a more strenuous outing, any one of the trails that crisscross the back country through the peaks and valleys of the mountains.

The cavern tours often sell out during busy and holiday weekends, so phone ahead, and don't be late for your tour time.

Hours: Tours are offered Memorial Day - Labor Day daily at 1:30. They are offered Labor Day - Memorial Day, Mon. - Fri. at 1:30pm; Sat. - Sun. at 10am, 1:30pm, and 3pm. Tours are also offered on some state-recognized holidays. Closed New Year's Day, Thanksgiving, and Christmas.
Price: $6 for adults; $3 for ages 6 - 16; children 5 and under are free.
Ages: 6 years and up.

MOJAVE NARROWS REGIONAL PARK

(760) 245-2226 - park; (760) 955-1913 - horse and pony rentals / cms.sbcounty.gov/parks
18000 Yates Road, Victorville

This delightful, 840-acre park features two lakes. The larger one, Horseshoe Lake, is great for fishin' (no license needed for ages 15 years and under), has a bait shop near the entrance, and an island in the middle of it. The pond is stocked with trout, bass and catfish. A stream runs through part of the park which boasts of wide open grassy spaces; lots of trees, including willow thickets and patches of cottonwoods; some hiking and riding trails; and pasture land for the numerous horses boarded at the on-site stables. Seventy percent decent tent and full hookup RV camp sites (with

showers) are here, but be aware that trains run by this park frequently; day and night. An equestrian campground is also onsite.

Pedal and row boat rentals, an archery range, snack bar, hay rides (arranged through the stables), picnic shelters, a water play park for younger children with zero depth water, a Challenge Course, and a few dry-land playgrounds complete the park. Part of one good-sized playground is for all abilities with a ramp leading up to platforms and the slides. There is also twisty metal and plastic apparatus to climb, a tire swing, and other fun elements. The water play park has fountains and such that squirt up to drench kids running around the splash pad. The Challenge Course has a ropes course that is similar to military-style, and two, really tall, rock-climbing walls, plus climbing boulders.

Hours: Open mid-October - mid-April daily, 7:30am - 5pm; open mid-April - mid-October, Sun. - Thurs., 7:30am - 6pm; Fri. - Sat., 7:30am - 7pm. Horse rentals are available Sat., Sun, and holidays, 8am - 5pm. All boat rentals are available year round on weekends only.

Price: $8 per vehicle Mon. - Fri.; $10 on Sat. - Sun. and holidays. Pedestrians are $2. Tent camping (which includes park entry) is $25 a night ($35 during holidays); $35 with hookup ($45 during holidays). Youth group camping (minimum of 20) is $5 per person. Horseback riding is $35 an hour for ages 7 and up. Fishing permits are $8 per person.

Ages: All

MOUNT BALDY SCENIC LIFT RIDE

(909) 982-0800 / www.mtbaldyskilifts.com
8401 Mount Baldy Road, Mount Baldy

$$$$

Skiing, tubing and snow boarding at Mt. Baldy, with rentals available, are great winter sports. With four chair lifts and twenty-six runs, there is something for every level. See SKIING, SNOWBOARDING, SNOWSHOEING, and SNOW PLAY (pg. 456) for more info. The scenic lift ride is also open year round, therefore wonderful for non-skiers, too. Take the twenty-minute ride up to the top for a gorgeous panoramic view - almost 8,000 feet high. While up there, enjoy a meal at Top of the Notch restaurant. Breakfast options include a short stake of pancakes, $7.45 to an Awesome Burrito stuffed with scrumptious items, $11.95. Lunch menu includes salads and sandwiches and burgers, ranging from $9.95 for nachos, $7.25 for a personal cheese pizza to a double decker burger for $13.95.

You can also hike up to the restaurant - about 2.5 miles - to work up an appetite. More experienced hikers can take the direct, steep route; straight up under the lift. Slaloming on the fireroad takes longer, but it's easier. Hiking trails from Top of the Notch include Thunder Mountain, a few miles from the Notch; and Devil's Backbone Trail. Head left from the Notch to take the Devil's trail, also known as Old Baldy, which climbs 3.5 miles (one way) to San Gabriel's tallest peak, Mt San Antonio, at 10,064 feet! Hiking this trail during non-winter months is recommended, and even then it is recommended for advanced hikers as the altitude can cause altitude sickness and the trail hugs the backbone ridge of the mountain (so it's narrow with some drops on either side). Bring water - lots of it!! Mountain biking is suggested only for very experienced riders as the terrain is rough. Check the website for weekend Moonlight Hikes in which you can hike up to the restaurant (or not) and enjoy a bbq dinner and/or a lift ride up and down.

The adventure is in the lift chair ride, the view, and a meal at the top, and perhaps a hike, too.

Hours: Skiing, snowboarding and tubing are offered daily, seasonally, 8am - 5pm. Scenic lift rides are open Sat. - Sun. the rest of the year, 8am - 6pm. Breakfast is served Sat. - Sun., 8am - 11am. Lunch is served daily, 11am to 5pm. Dinner is served only in the summer, Fri. - Sun.; hours vary.

Price: Scenic lift tickets are $25 roundtrip for adults, $15 going up only (so hike down); $20 roundtrip for ages 13 - 18, $13 for going up only; $15 roundtrip for seniors and ages 12 and under, $10 for going up only; free for children 35" and under with a paying adult. Parking is $5.

Ages: 4 years and up for the ride; 10 years and up for the hike.

MOUNT BALDY TROUT POOLS

(909) 982-4246 / www.mtbaldytroutpools.com
6945 Mount Baldy Road, Mount Baldy Village

$$$

No waders (or fishing license) are needed to catch fish at this delightful fishing spot up in the mountains. The clear, spring water ponds are surrounded by shady oak trees. The first pond stocks fish 13" through 18"; the second holds smaller fish, 9" through 13". The fish are abundant here, so chances are your young fisherboy/girl will make at least one catch of the day! All fish caught must be kept and paid for. After you've caught your fill, or the kids need more action, take a hike through the woods on the surrounding trails.

During the summertime, enjoy a refreshing dip in the nearby stream. There are places to hike and bike here year-round, plus the MOUNT BALDY SCENIC LIFT RIDE (see the entry below) for rides up and down the mountain to biking and hiking trails (and skiing during the winter), or for a meal at the top, Top of the Notch restaurant, that is. And while you're in the area, check out Mount Baldy Village, which has a few shops and places to eat, and the MOUNT BALDY VISITOR CENTER (see two entries below), where you can pick up a map of the area hiking trails and a wilderness permit.

Hours: The ponds are open Sat., Sun., and holidays (including week-long school holiday breaks), 9am - 4pm. Additionally, they are open July through August, Fri. - Mon., 9am - 4pm. Note: You must be here at least a half hour before closing time. Closed Thanksgiving and Christmas.

Price: $1 if you bring your own pole; $2 to rent a pole. You may share poles. Fish prices range from $6 for 12" to $18.10 for 18". Price includes bait, cleaning, and packing fish in ice.

Ages: 3 years and up.

MOUNT BALDY VISITOR CENTER

(909) 982-2829 / www.sgmha.org; www.fs.fed.us

1113 Mount Baldy Road, Mount Baldy Village

This place is worth a stop off on your way up or down the mountain. Inside the pleasant center's building, which was originally a schoolhouse built in 1921, are taxidermied animals - great horned owl, eagle, gray fox, bighorn sheep, mountain lion, and more. Display panels and photographs show the history of the area and its inhabitants. You can also pick up hiking trail maps, your Adventure Pass ($5), and other information here for your day of fun at Mt. Baldy. (Also see the previous two entries regarding other things to do in the immediate vicinity, plus skiing and snowboarding in the winter.)

Explore the wooded grounds, and sneak in a history lesson, as you see and go into a small, re-created village of the Gabrielino/Tongva native inhabitants. Here you'll find a replica ceremonial enclosure, a mountain lodge made of poles, and a traditional, dome-shaped house made of tules. The gold mining camp here has a canvas, miner's wedge tent; a general store (not like our current-day ones); a gravesite; and sluice boxes. One of the oldest buildings in the Mt. Baldy area, built in 1912, is here and made out of river stones and mortar. Bring a picnic lunch to enjoy at the tables under the trees. Scouting programs and other educational programs are offered through the ranger's station.

Hours: Open to the public Fri., 9am - 2pm; Sat. - Sun., 7am - 3:30pm. Open Tues. - Thurs. for educational programs/tours only.

Price: Free. An Adventure Pass is $5, which is needed for hiking around.

Ages: 3 years and up.

PERRIS HILL PARK

(909) 384- 5233 - park; (909) 384-5419 - swim center/water park / www.ci.san-bernardino.ca.us

1135 E. Highland Avenue in Perris Hill Park, San Bernardino

Perris Hill Park has numerous amenities - a small playground with slides, swings, and a speaking tube; a large shady area packed with cement picnic tables; a few dirt trails up and around the hillside; an outdoor amphitheater with stadium-style seating built into the hillside; a tennis center with seven courts; horseshoe pits; a baseball diamond at one end; and a swim center with a splash playground. The enclosed, Jerry Lewis Swim Center, open seasonally, has a pool with a diving board and a good-sized water playground on cement. The latter has several rainbow-colored shapes that squirt out water; a large frog statue slide that ends in a wading pool; a long twisty water slide; an area where water fountains spurt up randomly; and umbrellas that drip water showers.

On Tuesday nights from 6pm to 9:30pm, May through October, enjoy a Farmer's Fair and Market at this park. There is fresh produce; vendors that sell leather products, jewelry, hats, glasses, baked goods and more; and entertainment throughout the evening of singing, bands, pony rides, bounce houses, kids rides, and more.

Hours: The park is open April - September daily, 6am - 8pm; open October - March daily, 6am - 6pm. The swim center is open Memorial Day - mid-June and August - September, weekends only, Sat. - Sun., 11am - 1:30pm, 2pm - 4:30pm, and 5pm - 7:30pm. It is open daily from mid-June - August, noon - 2:30pm and 3pm - 5:30pm.

Price: Free to the park. The swim center is $3 per 2½ hour session for adults; $1.50 for seniors and ages 8 - 17; $1 for ages 2 - 7. Family passes are available.

Ages: All

PRADO REGIONAL PARK

(909) 597-4260 - park information; (909) 597-5757 - horse rentals / www.sbcounty.gov
16700 S. Euclid Avenue, Chino

This is another, has-it-all regional park! Besides the three softball diamonds; two soccer fields for tournament games or family fun; a nice, eighteen-hole disc course; and several playground areas, there is year-round fishing at the massive, stocked lake - over 16 years old needs a license. Bait and tackle are available at the nearby snack bar and mini store by the dock, both of which are open on weekends. There is a special area for radio-controlled boats on the lake, too.

On top of a large slab of cement is a small water play park, open seasonally, that has a few shapes that squirt out water to run through and under. The extra large "Fun for All" playground (a Shane's Inspiration one) is divided into several sections, with one being shaped like a ship. The playground is absolutely wonderful and accessible for all children, regardless of physical ability or disability. There are several ramps; bridges; many slides; monkey bars; climbing steps; a rock climbing wall; and activities to play and learn (i.e. Braille alphabet, a musical section - press a key to play a note and then play a song, and tic-tac-toe); plus swings, stepping stones, talking tubes, and much more, with places to play on the apparatus, as well as under it. Note that when you touch the sea creatures imbedded in the water wall, they will splash, squirt, and/or make their animal noise.

For those of you with delicate noses, you have correctly detected the nearby presence of horses, cattle, and sheep, as this is farm country. There are herds and ranches all up and down Euclid Street. The Prado Equestrian Center is located at the northern end of the park. Children 7 years old and up can take a one-hour guided trail ride through the park and to the basin. Rides are $25 an hour. Kids 2 to 7 years can be led inside the arena for a minimal charge; a helmet is required.

The paved street that winds all around the park will have to suffice for most skating or hiking desires, although there is a dirt trail along the lake and Chino Creek about a mile and a half long. Just down the street is a radio-controlled model plane airport and flying facility. Across Euclid Street, the park also has trap and skeet fields, an Olympic shooting range and an archery range.

If you like it here so much that you don't want to go home, stay and camp. The campgrounds are at the far end of the park and are O.K. looking. A few of the seventy-five sites have shade trees and a majority of the campsites are near barren, gently sloping hills. This area does have laundry and shower facilities.

Hours: The park is open most of the year Mon. - Fri., 7:30am - 5pm; Sat. - Sun., 7:30am - 6pm. It is open Memorial Day - Labor Day daily, 7:30am - 8pm. Horseback riding is available Sat. - Sun., 9am - 5pm (last ride leaves at 3:30pm), or during the week with advanced reservations.

Price: $8 per vehicle, Mon. - Fri.; $10 on Sat. - Sun. and holidays. $2 for pedestrians; $1 for dogs. Fishing permits are $8 per person. Camping begins at about $35 a night; reservations are $5.

Ages: All

RAINBOW BASIN

(760) 252-6000 / www.blm.gov
Fossil Canyon Loop Road, 8 miles N. of Barstow

ROY G BIV (red, orange, yellow, green, blue, indigo, and violet) and all the in between, somewhat muted, colors of the rainbow are represented at the aptly-named Rainbow Basin. Note: Although the dirt roads are a bit bumpy, the destination is worth the jolting. (Four-wheel drive vehicles are highly recommended, but our mini van made it without too many problems.) Tip: Bring water! The colorful sedimentary rock formations are eye catching. We stopped the car several times to get out and look more closely at the variety of rocks, and to hike and climb the peaks, valleys, and cave formations, although there are no developed trails. We didn't find any, but we read that this area is rich with mammal fossil remains as mastodons, pronghorns, "dog-bears," and horses have been found here. Collecting fossils, however, is forbidden.

The adjacent Owl Canyon Campground has thirty-one fairly primitive sites. Facilities include fire rings, grills, and vault toilets. Bring your own firewood and water. Remember that, as with any desert area, extreme temperatures occur.

Hours: Open daily, dawn - dusk.
Price: Free. Camping is $6 a night.
Ages: 4 years and up.

SILVERWOOD LAKE STATE RECREATIONAL AREA

(760) 389-2281or (760) 389-2303 - park office; (760) 389-2299 - marina boat rentals and beach store; (760) 389-2288 - Fun2Go for kayak and other boat rentals / www.parks.ca.gov; www.fun2gomotorsports.com
14651 Cedar Circle, Hesperia

As we traveled north on Interstate 15, almost at the Highway 138 turnoff, we noticed trains on several different tracks, so we pulled off to watch them intersect and chug by below us.

The upper area of the huge lake, by Highway 173, is for waterskiing and boating activities. The overlook of the lower section reveals surprisingly blue waters that reach into the several nooks and inlets all around the lake. Three miles of maintained hiking trails branch off in various directions and two swim beaches are complete with sections of sand. Note that a portion of the colossal Pacific Crest Trail, the 2,650 mile trail which spans from Mexico to Canada, passes through Silverwood Lake. Fish from the shore for striped bass, crappie, catfish, largemouth bass, and trout (which are stocked during the cooler are months), or from fishing boats and float tubes. Fourteen-foot aluminum fishing boats ($30 for two hours) are available to rent year round, weather dependent. Summer rentals include kayaks and paddle boats ($15 to $20 an hour) and jet skis ($105 an hour). Note that there are a few picnic areas that can only be reached via boat. Bait, tackle, fishing licenses (a must for ages 16 and up), snacks, drinks and sundries are available past the main entrance at the marina/beach store.

Down near the waterside, the Cleghorn area has a big grassy spot, picnic tables, and barbecues under shade trees, plus a rock-lined brook, one of the swim beaches, and the stunning beauty of the surrounding mountains. A short drive down the road is Sawpit Beach, just in front of the store, the most popular spot (i.e., crowded) for swimming, sunbathing, and picnicking. The close-by Black Oak picnic area is just a short walk to Sawpit, but it boasts of fewer people, lots of grass, large oak trees, and picnic tables. Miller Canyon picnic area is a few miles past the main entrance east on Highway 138 and is more secluded. It's ideal for fishing, kayaking, hiking, and relaxing. Note: Cleghorn area is closed November through April.

If you like it so much that you want to stay here, do. Bring your camping gear. Note that there are no hook-ups. The 136 developed campsites for tents and RVs are decent and there are plenty of outdoor activities, including all the above-mentioned, plus eleven miles of biking trails. Ride around the relatively easy paved trails which loop around a part of the lake. For more summertime fun, join in on campfire talks, junior ranger and wild flower walks, bald eagle boat tours, and other park programs.

Hours: Open April - September daily, 6am - 9pm; open October - March daily, 7am - 7pm.
Price: $10 per vehicle; $9 for seniors. Camping starts at $45.
Ages: All

SKY HIGH DISC GOLF

(760) 249-5808; (888) 754-7878 / www.mthigh.com/discgolf
24510 Hwy. 2, Wrightwood

It's a bird, it's a plane - no, it's - a disc? Maybe your disc won't be flying that high, but the course is almost 8,000 feet above sea level, on the north side of the Mountain High Ski resort. Talk about a view! To complete the three nine-hole courses is a 2.5 mile hike (in thin mountain air) through the Angeles National forest. Players throw the discs around trees and wildlife - perhaps hawks and even deer - as well as up and down hills. (And then players must walk wherever they threw the disc.) If you don't have a disc, don't worry because you can purchase one (or more) from the full line of accessories at the onsite pro shop, which also sells food. A combo meal of a freshly grilled hamburger, plus chips and a soda is $6. You can also purchase a hot dog or pizza, or even bring your own food. There are picnic tables inside and outside for your dining pleasure. Special events and tournaments are hosted here, too, as Sky High is rated high on the list of the top courses to play in the country. Extreme disc golf; extremely fun.

Hours: Usually open May - the beginning of October, Fri. - Sun., 8am - 6pm. Hours fluctuate depending on if the there is snow for skiing, so call first.
Price: $7 per person for 27 holes.
Ages: 7 years and up - or able to throw a disc.

UPLAND SKATEBOARD PARK

(909) 931-4280 / www.uplandpl.lib.ca.us; www.socalskateparks.com
1100 E. Foothill Boulevard, Upland

Rated a top-notch skatepark by skaters, this 12,000 square foot cement park has a large half-pipe and, unusual for

parks in this area, a twenty-foot full pipe that ends in a large vert bowl. This section is very fast, therefore not for beginners. It also has all of the "required" street elements - funbox, rails, and pyramid - built in an aesthetically-pleasing and skater-approved fashion. Helmet and knee and elbow pads are required.

The surrounding park has lots of mature shade trees, a wonderful playground, baseball fields, a basketball court, and picnic tables with BBQ pits.

Hours: The skate park is open Sun. - Thurs., 10am - 9pm; Fri. - Sat., 10am - 10pm.
Price: Free
Ages: 7 years and up.

YUCAIPA REGIONAL PARK

(909) 790-3127 / cms.sbcounty.gov/parks
33900 Oak Glen Road, Yucaipa

$$$

Nestled in the rocky San Bernardino Mountains is this huge, beautiful oasis of a park offering year-round fun. Fish in any one of the three very large, picturesque, stocked lakes to catch seasonal bass, trout, or catfish. A fishing license is required. A bike rental shop is on the grounds so you can get physical any time of year and/or try your hand at the eighteen-hole disc golf course and horseshoes.

During the summer months, get in the swim of things in the one-acre swim lagoon, and/or go for the two long water slides. White sandy beaches frame the water's edge, with grassy areas just beyond them. A few steps away is a full-service snack bar, which also carries bait and tackle for your fishing needs, plus pedal boat and aqua cycle rentals. A wonderful playground is right outside the swim area. Another playground, designed specifically for disabled children, is across the way.

RV and tent camping is available for those who really want to get away from it all for a weekend or so. The grassy areas, trees, and mountains are a scenic setting for the camp sites. There are plenty of picnic tables and shelters, as well as barbecue pits. Hiking is encouraged on either paved trails or along the few dirt pathways. (See OAK GLEN and APPLE PICKING, on page 401, for nearby places to go.)

Hours: The park is open most of the year daily, 7:30am - 5pm; open in the summer daily, 7:30am - 6pm. Swimming is available Memorial Day - mid-June and mid-August - Labor Day, weekends only, 10am - 5pm; mid-June - mid-August, daily,10am - 5pm. The snack bar is open most of the year, Fri. - Sun. 8am - about 3pm.
Price: $8 per vehicle Mon. - Fri.; $10 on weekends and holidays. Pedestrians are $2; dogs are $1. Fishing permits are $8 per person. Entrance to the swim lagoon is park admission, plus $5 per person for ages 4 and up. An all-day water slide and swim pass is $10 per person, plus park admission. Pedal boat and aqua cycle rentals are $10 for a half hour per. Camping prices range from $25 (no hook-ups) to $40 (hook-ups) per night, for up to six people per site. Hot showers, grills, and fire rings are available.
Ages: All

—MALLS—

ONTARIO MILLS MALL

(909) 484-8300 / www.simon.com
One Mills Circle, Ontario

!/$

Ontario Mills is California's largest outlet mall with over 200 outlet, speciality, and name brand retail stores. Kids favorites include LEGO Factory Store (see pg. 409), The Disney Store Outlet, and Sweet Factory. The mall also offers various forms of "shoppertainment." Other entertainment offered at the mega mall includes GAMEWORKS (pg. 407); DAVE & BUSTER'S (pg. 406), a combination restaurant/bar and game/arcade center geared for adults; and Improv Comedy Theater for adults (909) 484-5411 / www.improv.com. Kids will love making their own teddy bears here at BUILD-A-BEAR WORKSHOP (pg. 432). Note that Circus Vargas is usually here the end of March. Get tickets and more information at (877) 468-3861 / www.circusvargas.com.

The food court is fancifully-decorated with large, colorful, inflatable foods. Other tantalizing eating experiences in unique surroundings are Wolfgang Puck's Cafe and RAINFOREST CAFE (pg. 404).

Hours: The mall and most attractions are open Mon. - Sat., 10am - 9pm; Sun., 11am - 8pm.
Price: Technically, free.

Ages: All

VICTORIA GARDENS REGIONAL TOWN CENTER - VG KIDZ club - CULTURAL CENTER

!/$$

(909) 463-2830 - guest services; (909) 477-2720 - library / www.victoriagardensie.com; www.vgculturalcenter.com
10500 Civic Center Drive, Rancho Cucamonga

The "mall", for lack of a better work, is a shopping complex of over 150 shops and restaurants (and places to indulge in dessert). Part of it is a typical mall, but the other part is a cohesive, classy, outdoor venue stretching several city blocks with pedestrian streets and a park-like ambiance of grassy areas and fountains interwoven between groupings of stores. Some of the draws for kids are the free rides up and down the streets on a vintage-style trolley; the AMC movie theater; a ride on the trackless scale model train ($3 for ages 3 and up); the fountains that spurt up at random intervals for them to play in and run through; horse-drawn carriage rides ($5 per person for about a fifteen-minute ride); all the lights at Christmas time; and the special events, especially those held at Chaffey Town Square. The latter includes family-oriented entertainment such as free summertime movies (bring your own blanket or lawn chair), and concerts. The free, VG Kidz club meets one Saturday a month from 11am to 1pm at Chaffey Town Square. Past activities have included a flower pot craft, summer luau, back to school event, tree craft, and other seasonal happenings. Buy something special at the Farmer's Market and Craft Fair that meets here every Friday from 10am to 2pm.

Check out BASS PRO SHOPS (pg. 431), for all (and I mean <u>all</u>) of your outdoors needs, and for the ambiance. You'll see what I mean. Other favorites include Fuzziwig's Candy Factory, GYU-KAKU (page 20) Japanese BBQ, Richie's Real American Diner, and lots more.

The Victoria Gardens Cultural Center is one of the anchors for the town center. One component is the stylish LEWIS FAMILY PLAYHOUSE PERFORMING ARTS CENTER (see pg. 436), which hosts a multitude of terrific shows and performances. Adjacent to the Playhouse is a state-of-the-art public library with a themed children's section, storytelling theater, and, of course, lots and lots of books. Enjoy the outdoor landscaped courtyards, interactive learning stations, wishing fountain, and the glass elevator. (Take a ride!) Just outside the center is a small playground and a food hall with several, express-food options.

Hours: Call or check this center's website for a schedule of events. The VG Kidz is the third Sat. of each month from 11am - 1pm. The shops, restaurants, and entertainment times vary. Little train rides are offered Sat., 10am - 9pm; Sun., 10am - 7pm. Trolley rides are usually offered Fri. - Sat., noon - 9pm; Sun., noon - 6pm. (Open extended hours during holidays.) Horse-drawn carriage rides are usually offered Fri., 7pm - 10pm; Sat., 8pm - 10pm; Sun., 5pm - 7pm. (Open extended hours during holidays.)
Price: Free; bring spending money.
Ages: All

—MUSEUMS—

BARSTOW ROUTE 66 "MOTHER ROAD" MUSEUM

!

(760) 255-1890 / www.route66museum.org
681 N. First Avenue, Barstow

The small Mother Road museum has a few mother lode exhibits. Some of the vehicles on exhibit here from the Route 66 heyday are a 1947 Police Servi-Car, a 1964 red Mustang convertible, a 1915 Model T, and an old, wooden, one-horse carriage. Other memorabilia includes gas station pumps; lots of roadway signs; old toys (anyone else remember trolls?); a camera collection; display of products and the minerals from whence they came; license plates; WWII paraphernalia (ration books, hair curlers, and more); toy cars; photographs of the local area from around the turn of the century; and lots of information on Route 66. The gift shop sells postcards, t-shirts, and other souvenirs. Note that the WESTERN AMERICA RAILROAD MUSEUM (see pg. 430) shares this same brick building, which is located in a working railroad depot, first reached by going over a trestle bridge.

Hours: Open Fri. - Sun., 10am - 4pm.
Price: Free
Ages: 7 years and up.

CALIFORNIA ROUTE 66 MUSEUM

(760) 951-0436 / www.califrt66museum.org
16825 D Street, Victorville

You can still get your kicks on Route 66! The more you know about the history and the culture of Route 66, the more you'll appreciate this terrific museum. Actually, the museum was once a Route 66 road house. The rooms are now packed with memorabilia and artifacts that encapsulate this era, such as Hula Ville art, roadway signs, gas pumps, neon signs, lots of photographs and information on local history, a Model-T, toy cars, and some decorative roadside art saved for posterity. (Exhibits do rotate.) The attached gift shop is filled with nostalgic-type items.

Hours: Open Mon., Thurs. - Sat., 10am - 4pm; Sun., 11am - 3pm. Closed Tues. and Wed.
Price: Free
Ages: 7 years and up.

CHINO YOUTH MUSEUM

(909) 334-3270 / www.chinoyouthmuseum.com
13191 6th Street, Chino

This compact children's museum has a main room with several smaller rooms that branch off from it. Each room is themed around a particular function, or career, found within a city. The themes are enhanced with a colorful mural or building facade, and a prop or two. For instance, kids can become a fireman for a day by putting on firemen uniforms, sliding down a short pole, and sitting on a wooden fire engine. They can "shop" in a market with play food; work at a bank behind the teller's window with cash registers; and be a newscaster behind the desk with the camera pointed on them. Ah, to be young again and just have to pretend at working a job! The museum also has a room just for arts and crafts, and an area to play with puzzles, Legos and other hands-on fun. Ask about monthly shows and activities, such as First Friday when the museum is open between 3pm and 5pm, for free, and offers a free craft project, entertainment, and snack; and Kid's Night Out, a Saturday night, when ages 3 to 12 can be dropped off for three hours of play, games, storytelling, and a light dinner.

Just outside the museum is a plaza with a fountain, cement picnic tables, and a grassy area with trees.

Hours: Open Wed. - Sun., 10am - 4pm. The museum closes at 2pm on the days of First Friday events to reopen at 3pm. Closed Mon. and Tues. and most major holidays.
Price: $3 for 1 - 12 years old; $2 for ages 13 and up, including adults. The first Fri. of each month is free admission from 3pm - 5pm. Kid's Night Out is $12 per child.
Ages: 2 - 8 years.

DESERT DISCOVERY CENTER

(760) 252-6060 / www.discoverytrails.org; www.desertdiscoverycenter.com
831 Barstow Road, Barstow

This center, in partnership with several other organizations, is the nucleus of a wide range of educational programs exploring the resources in association with the vast Mojave Desert. It is also a museum. The building houses the renown Old Woman Meteorite, weighing in at 5,000+ pounds. It is the second largest meteorite found in the U.S. Other displays include native plants and taxidermied animals indigenous to the area, such as big horn sheep, foxes, birds, snakes, and more. Animal tracks dating from prehistoric times include those of camels, other mammals, and even some dinosaurs. Fossils, skulls, rocks, replicas of petroglyphs, tools from the Calico mine site, and exhibits on the water cycle are also found here.

The garden outside consists of native plant species. The small pond out back hosts numerous turtles and quite a few dragonflies. And look for the several desert tortoises that consider the center home. (They hibernate, though, November through February.)

Area school kids benefit greatly from all the free programs offered, including plant and animal adaptation, recycling, geology, and the all-inclusive Jr. Naturalist certification program. The latter has requirements in nine categories - biology, botany, history, paleontology, archeology, and learning environmental stewardship. The hands-on approach makes it fascinating and fun for primarily elementary-school-aged kids. Ask about day camps.

Hours: Open Tues. - Sat., 11am - 4pm. Closed Sun., Mon., and holidays. Call for program information.
Price: Free
Ages: All

EDWARD-DEAN MUSEUM AND GARDENS

(951) 845-2626 / www.edward-deanmuseum.org

9401 Oak Glen Road, Cherry Valley

This elegant, medium-sized fine arts museum seems almost out of place in the rural town of Cherry Valley. It is situated on beautifully-landscaped grounds with formal gardens, accompanied by grassy lawns and a small pond with lily pads. Just outside the museum is a fountain surrounded by a rose garden.

The two-story museum has seven galleries that specialize in interior decorative art from the late 16th to early 18th centuries. The North wing gallery has rotating exhibits. We saw "Art in Miniature," which showcased buildings, artwork, and scenes in miniature. The permanent upstairs galleries are situated in a home-like atmosphere. They feature European and Oriental art which includes furniture; china; a Buddha exhibit in a room with ornate wood wall carvings; silk tapestries; portraits; a beautiful oriental robe; statues; and a music room with a piano and a harp. Downstairs is a small reference library, plus a wing displaying a pope's wooden traveling desk and few other items. The docents we encountered were friendly and readily explained many of the exhibit pieces. There are several group tours and free school programs offered. Note that the museum is just down the road from all the fun at OAK GLEN. (pg. 401.)

> **Hours:** Open Thurs. - Sat., 10am - 5pm. Call to make a reservation for a school tour.
> **Price:** $5 for adults; children 12 and under are free.
> **Ages:** 7 years and up.

GRABER OLIVE HOUSE

(800) 996-5483 or (909) 983-1761 / www.graberolives.com

315 E. Fourth Street, Ontario

This is an unusual pit stop for kids. On the lovely grounds are picnic tables, a grassy area with shade trees in the front, and old machinery, plus a small museum, an olive processing plant, a gift shop, and the owner's house. The one-room museum shows a pictorial history of olive processing. It also has an eclectic mix of antiques such as a big wooden olive grader, a Singer sewing machine, a sausage stuffer, and more.

Take a twenty-minute tour around the working olive plant. Harvesting, the "on-season", is mid-October through December, when the machinery and workers are in full production. This, then, is the best time to take a tour. Walk into the grading room, where olives are sorted by size and quality, and peer into the enormous olive vats. The boiler room, where olives are sterilized, the canning machine, and the labeling machine are all interesting to look at. A ten-minute video, that shows the history of the packing plant, is also available to watch.

One of the gift shops carries unique kitchen and cooking utensils. The other is very classy with etiquette videos, stationery, delicious jams, and elegant candies. (The chocolate-covered cherries are to die for!) Kids can sample Graber olives, and this brand might mean more to them after a tour.

> **Hours:** Open daily, 9:30am - 5:30pm. Closed major holidays.
> **Price:** Free
> **Ages:** 5 years and up.

INLAND EMPIRE MILITARY MUSEUM

(909) 885-6324 or (909) 888-0477 / www.juanpollo.com; www.inlandarts.com

1394 N. E Street, San Bernardino

Operated by a veteran, this relatively small museum holds a lot of great memorabilia from WWI, WWII, Korea, Vietnam, Gulf, Afghan, and Iraq wars. Divided into sections according to each branch of the military, on display are military dress uniforms, hats, helmets, medals, flags, a 1953 restored Willis Jeep, a model of an aircraft carrier, photographs, and more. Take a guided tour and/or take the time to read the information accompanying the artifacts and learn the stories and history behind the items. Note that this museum is right next door to the MCDONALDS MUSEUM. (pg. 426).

> **Hours:** Open Sat. - Sun., 11am - 5pm. Open during the week by appointment only.
> **Price:** Free
> **Ages:** 7 years and up.

JOHN RAINS HOUSE - CASA DE RANCHO CUCAMONGA

☽

$$

(909) 989-4970 / www.sbcounty.gov/museum

8810 Hemlock Street, Rancho Cucamonga

Built with bricks in 1860, this restored rancho residence is a lovely example of a house from this era. Tours are given through the historical home to see period furniture in the bedrooms, living rooms, and other rooms, and around the beautiful grounds, complete with green lawns, trees, picnic tables in the backyard, and the central courtyard. Docents recount stories about the people who once lived here. Their lives were like soap operas, complete with affairs, murders, buried treasure, and more sordid happenings - kids love this! (And they are learning history.) Ask about school and group tours and the special events that the Rancho hosts, such as Rancho Day, where each year the house is decorated according to a different theme, accompanied by costumed docents and activities for kids. Note: The house is exquisitely decked out at Christmas time.

Hours: Open Tues. - Sat., 10am - 3pm. Tours are given every forty-five minutes. Closed Sun., Mon., New Year's Day, Thanksgiving, and Christmas.

Price: $5 for adults; $4 for seniors; $2.50 for students and ages 6 and up; children 5 and under are free.

Ages: 6 years and up.

KIMBERLY CREST HOUSE AND GARDENS

☀

$$$

(909) 792-2111 / www.kimberlycrest.org

1325 Prospect Drive, Redlands

This exquisite-looking, three-story, rather large (7,000 square-foot!), light lime green and gray French chateau, with yellow trim, was originally built in 1897. The turrets add to its eye-catching appeal, as do the formal Italian-style gardens and grounds, complete with lotus blossoms and koi in the lily ponds under the stone steps and bridge, a series of cascading pools, and mature cypress, magnolia, palm, and orange trees.

The period (replicated) furniture and decor is as grand as the outside with gilt furniture, glass mosaics, and silk damask wall coverings. Tour the French parlor, library, living room, dining rooms (set with crystal), bedrooms, and other beautifully-accessorized rooms - the first two floors of the house and the Carriage House Museum. The gift shop is located in a one-hundred-year-old carriage house, as is a small picture gallery/museum with some memorabilia. Specialized tours include a two-hour Behind the Scenes Tour geared for older kids and for adults that includes seeing the house, including the third floor, the basement and Carriage House, with an emphasis on the architecture and preservation of it all, for $25 per person. See the April Calendar section for the wonderful Princess at the Castle event for younger ones.

The Crest House is nestled in one end of the lush, Prospect Park. After your tour, enjoy a walk on the dirt trails through the park.

Hours: Tours are given September through July, Thurs., Fri. and Sun., 1pm - 3:30pm, every 30 minutes, with the last tour at 3:30pm. Closed holidays and some of August. The surrounding park is open daily, 9am - 5pm.

Price: $10 for adults; $8 for seniors; children 5 and under are free.

Ages: 6 years and up.

LINCOLN MEMORIAL SHRINE

☀

!

(909) 798-7636 - Shrine; (909) 798-7632 - Heritage Room at the Smiley Public Library / www.lincolnshrine.org

125 W. Vine Street, Redlands

"Fourscore and seven years ago . . . " begins the Gettysburg Address. If your older children are studying our revered sixteenth president, but can't make it to Washington D.C., bring them to the Lincoln Memorial Shrine in Redlands. The central, octagon-shaped building also has two wings, all devoted to Abraham Lincoln and Civil War memorabilia. The building contains research books; surgical instruments; letters and documents written from and about Abraham Lincoln, Robert E. Lee, and Stonewall Jackson; Civil War photographs; bullets found on battlefields; officers' uniforms; medals; and a lifemask (i.e., an exact likeness of a person via a mold) and handcast of Abraham Lincoln. Mementos from his assassination include his cuff links, a strand of his hair, mourning bands, and the wreath that laid on his casket. The shrine also displays other Civil War artifacts such as swords, an 1863 Springfield rifle, hardtack, documents, models, and pictures of Abraham Lincoln, Robert E. Lee, and Ulysses S. Grant.

Come view the materials here on your own. Better yet, take a guided tour and benefit from knowledgeable

docents who explain the exhibits in more detail. Exhibits at the memorial rotate because the small shrine cannot contain the 3,000-plus manuscripts and other items in the archives. The outside of the building is inscribed with excerpts from Lincoln's inaugural addresses and various other speeches. Look in the Calendar section, page 707, for information on the annual Open House.

The shrine is located behind the Smiley Public Library, with a lovely expanse of green lawn, old shade trees, and benches in between. The multi-level library, established in 1894, is an architectural and book-lovers delight.

Hours: Open Tues. - Sun., 1pm - 5pm. Closed holidays, except for Lincoln's birthday. Small group tours can be arranged for morning hours.

Price: Free

Ages: 7 years and up.

MCDONALD'S MUSEUM (unofficial)

(909) 885-6324 / www.juanpollo.com

1398 North 'E' Street, San Bernardino

"We love to see you smile!" is just one McSlogan touted at this museum. The building is on the site of the first McDonald's Restaurant, which was established in 1948. Inside, half of the space is used for the administration offices of Juan Pollo Restaurants, the company that now owns the building. The other half is a tribute to McDonald's and a refuge for all of its merchandising paraphernalia throughout the years - that's a lot of Happy Meal toys! (Kind of makes you wish you hadn't thrown out all of those toys; kind of.) Besides the toys, games, and array of promotional products, display cases hold old menus; to-go bags; a 1940's milk shake machine; a 1950's potato press for making French fries (check out the old, moldy fry that is a eleven feet long); and lots of photographs and articles on McDonald's, including the ones detailing the feud between the McDonald's brothers and Ray Kroc. There are also a few pieces of Playland equipment and character costumes - lots of McMemories!

In the back of the museum are some artifacts, such as road signs, souvenir mugs, and posters, plus information panels from and about historic Route 66. Note that just next door to this museum is the INLAND EMPIRE MILITARY MUSEUM, see page 424 for details.

Hours: Open daily, 10am - 5pm.

Price: Free

Ages: 5 years and up.

MOJAVE RIVER VALLEY MUSEUM

(760) 256-5452 / www.mojaverivervalleymuseum.org

270 E. Virginia Way, Barstow

This little, and sometimes dusty, museum is full of interesting artifacts and displays. The rock and minerals on display include nice specimens of arrowheads, quartz, calcite, and black and gold forms of chalcopyrite, plus fluorescent minerals that glow neon colors under black light. Other glass-encased exhibits are an eclectic mixture, such as lanterns, irons, rug beaters, pottery, clothing, a collection of glass insulators used by telegraph companies, and more. Kids can try their hand at grinding corn with stone mortar and pestle. They can also touch various animal skins, a turtle shell, bones, pinecones, rocks, and cotton. Short nature films are available to watch upon request. Call to arrange a field trip, and students will not only learn a lot about local history, but they can pan for real gold (and keep it!). Classes are usually taught by Mr. Walker, an archaeology instructor at the college.

Outside of the museum is some large mining equipment - ore carts, picks, and other tools, as well as a jail cell. Across the street is the small Centennial Park, which is actually an extension of the museum. It has a caboose, an army tank, and a mining display, which are representative of the three industries that helped formed Barstow. Note that DANA PARK (pg. 413) is just across the street and the DESERT DISCOVERY CENTER (pg. 423) is just down the road.

Hours: The museum is open daily, 11am - 4pm. Closed Christmas.

Price: Free to the museum, though donations are appreciated.

Ages: 3 years and up.

MUSEUM OF HISTORY AND ART, ONTARIO

(909) 395-2510 / www.ci.ontario.ca.us

225 S. Euclid Avenue, Ontario

The Museum of History and Art captures the flavor of historic Ontario. The small museum's galleries feature artifacts regarding early inhabitants from Native Americans and California Rancheros to early twentieth century settlers and, in particular, the founder of Ontario. Displays represent home and community life, and exhibits from the agricultural heritage, citrus groves, and industry and social life. The artifacts consist of saddles, bikes, toys, irons, clothes, military uniforms, pictures, and a replicated assay office from the 1900's. Another section focuses on locally famous roads, such as Euclid Avenue and Route 66. I like the big neon eagle sign that lights up when you walk into that section. The north wing presents changing exhibits every two months or so. Ask about docent guided gallery tours and family workshops that include a hands-on, theme-related projects, or the classroom outreach programs. Set in a Mediterranean-style building with a big fountain out front, huge shade trees, and a grassy area, the museum is a pleasant way to learn more about local roots.

Hours: The museum is open Thurs. - Sun., noon - 4pm.
Price: Free
Ages: 6 years and up.

OAK GLEN SCHOOL HOUSE MUSEUM

(909) 797-1691 / www.oakglen.net
11911 S. Oak Glen Road, Yucaipa

The small, one-room school house museum was originally built in 1927. The stone exterior encompasses a room containing old-fashioned desks facing a black board, a potbelly stove, a phonograph, a stereoscope, newspaper clippings, apple crate labels from ranches, and old pictures. Tours are offered to the public upon request. School groups can take the basic fifteen-minute tour and then add on additional activities, such as making a candle by rolling up a sheet of beeswax, dipping pen in an ink bottle and writing, and taking a short nature walk. Teachers are welcome to bring their own curriculum to teach, too.

The adjacent, picturesque small park has grassy lawns, shade trees, picnic tables, and some play equipment. See OAK GLEN (pg. 401) for more attractions in this area.

Hours: Open most of the year, Sat. - Sun., noon - 4pm, weather permitting. Open in the fall (apple-picking season), Wed. - Sun., noon - 4pm. Closed the month of December. Call to make a reservation for a school tour and for extended hours during apple-picking season (September through November).
Price: Free. Suggested donations are $1 for adults; 50¢ for children. School tours cost 50¢ per student, per activity.
Ages: 4 years old and up.

PLANES OF FAME AIR MUSEUM

(909) 597-3722 / www.planesoffame.org
7000 Merrill Avenue, Chino

$$$

For some *plane* old fun, come see over 150 rare and vintage aircraft (about thirty of which are flyable) that have landed here, including the only original and air-worthy Japanese Zero in the world. Many of the planes are touchable without any formal barriers to keep visitors away, making it a comfortable place to take children. The model aircraft collection, displayed in numerous cases throughout the several hangers, is one of the largest we've seen in one place.

The two south hangars hold numerous colorful and historic airplanes. The adjacent USS Enterprise hangar, which currently has ten planes on display, is dedicated specifically to Navy and military planes that were on the carrier. Take the catwalk around the interior part of that building and look into the built-in exhibit windows that hold uniforms, artifacts, and the carrier's timeline, Just a few of the planes on display in these hangers (with the understanding that some aircraft are out flying or on loan) include the Cessna 0-1Bird Dog, Douglas A-4B Skyhawk, Formula One Racer "Mr. D", Lockheed P-38J Lightning, Grumman J2F-6 Duck, P-51D Mustang, Piper L-4, and Stearman PT-17 Kaydet. There is also an "office" display with posters and information about the B-17 Fortress (which is actually located out front), as well as some upper gun turrets, a replica of the Wright Brothers plane, and a mock up of an Apollo space capsule here.

Across the way is the restoration hangar, where planes in various stages of repair and restoration are being worked on. Planes, parts of planes, jet aircraft, and tanks and other military vehicles are stationed outside the north hangar. Read the history of the aircraft on the placards or ask a docent for their fascinating stories.

Inside the hangar are foreign planes; Japanese and German aircraft from WWII, some of which are "flying" around overhead, while others are grounded. My boys were drawn to the "Wild Grinning Face of the Green Dragon

Unit" - a nose of a plane that has machine guns and is decorated with a fire-breathing dragon painted on its side. A G4MI Hamaki (code named "Betty") bomber on display looks like it has crashed landed in a jungle, complete with an overgrowth of plants and camouflage covering, plus dirt and a background mural. Hitler's very rusted and bullet-holed jet fighter, the Heinkel HE-162A1 Volks Jager, is here, too. Watch a video interspersed with real footage that tells the story of what happened. This building also displays airplane engines and small models of Japanese army aircraft, plus news clippings regarding Pearl Harbor.

One smaller hanger contains the P-38 Lightning and 475th FG displays and another is devoted to a variety of colorful jets and air racers.

Kids who are aeronautically inclined will be in their element at the Aviation Discovery Center with interactive displays such as flight simulators, wind tunnels (don't get blown away!), a control tower simulator, an aviation movie theater, and educational programs such careers in aviation, historic and scientific significance of planes and more.

A B-17 Bomber is available on weekends, only, to walk through or sit down in and "fly." The first Saturday of every month features a particular plane, or type of planes, plus a seminar at 10am with panelists or veteran pilots who were directly associated with that plane. Whenever possible, this event concludes with a flight demonstration.

Planes of Fame is on the grounds of the Chino airport, so kids can experience the thrill of seeing planes take off and land. Don't miss the annual Air Show in May! (pg. 723.) If you get hungry, pilot your way to Flo's Cafe, which is also on airport grounds. Note that just three blocks west of this museum is another one - YANKS AIR MUSEUM. See page 430 for details.

Hours: Open Sun. - Fri., 10am - 5pm; Sat., 9am - 5pm. Closed Thanksgiving and Christmas. The Aviation Discovery Center for kids is open most Sat. only, 10am - 2pm, but also during the week for groups with reservations.

Price: $11 for adults; $10 for seniors; $4 for ages 5 - 11; children 4 and under are free. AAA discounts are available.

Ages: 3 years and up.

SAN BERNARDINO COUNTY MUSEUM   ☀

(909) 307-2669 / www.sbcounty.gov/museum $$$

2024 Orange Tree Lane, Redlands

The distinctive half-dome attached to the main building of the San Bernardino County Museum is the Fisk Gallery of Fine Arts, which features changing exhibits. The wonderful Crossroads in History room is down the ramp from the main level. Here you'll find a covered wagon, 1888 buggy, 1901 fire wagon, and a Wells Fargo stage coach, along with mannequins dressed in period clothing. You can even dress up in some of the clothing and take a photo in a stagecoach cutout, and play with some simple toys from yesteryear. The anthropology section has Indian artifacts, such as arrowheads, dolls, pottery, an Eagle feather dance kilt, and painted rock art. An Edison exhibit displays hydro-electric generators.

The hallway going to the upper level is lined with exhibits such as old-time medicine bottles, fossilized mammoth tusks, the bones of a ground sloth, and the skull of a sabertooth. The other side of the hallway is a wonderful prelude to the upper level, displaying taxidermied birds and bird eggs. The eggs in this substantial collection vary in size from extra large elephant bird eggs to very small hummingbird eggs.

If your kids show any interest in ornithology, which is the study of birds (and calling each other bird brain doesn't count), they will be fascinated by the entire upper level which contains hundreds of birds, and their eggs, on display in two, extra large rooms. There are many birds and types of birds flocked together including penguins, woodpeckers, swans, ostriches, hawks, geese, and so many more. The water and land birds here takes you on flights of fancy, although with taxidermied birds you won't get very far. Look for the "awww, so cute" hatchling display. Press a button at one exhibit to match the call of the bird to its picture on the wall. A large stuffed California Condor guards the entrance to the upper dome gallery which has rotating exhibits of art work.

Enter the gigantic room at the lower level, the Mammal Hall. The walls in here are lined with fossilized animal bones, horns, and teeth. Bug collectors will be bug-eyed at the comprehensive collection of mounted insects of all sizes, shapes, and colors. Also along the walls are dioramas of smaller taxidermied animals and reptiles, such as spotted skunks, possums, raccoons, beavers, and turtles. The hall is unique in that it also has exhibits of larger taxidermied animals, such as a polar bear, an Alaskan brown bear, a mountain lion, a bison, big horn sheep, wolf, and a gigantic moose. My kids and I were really impressed by the sheer size of some of the animals! A video here shows about and how to help save animals in the wild.

Outside, between the main building and the Exploration Station, is a patio area. One diorama has a mining car carrying "explosives" on track toward a tunnel. A find-a-fossil sand pit has "hidden" fossils and brushes with which to uncover the finds. There is also a full-size caboose and steam engine on tracks. Picnic tables are here for snack attacks - bring your own food. (Other picnic tables are located just outside the museum entrance.)

The Exploration Station is a learning center that has small, live critters such as bunnies, iguanas, boas, an alligator lizard, frogs, turtles, scorpions, tarantulas, giant cave cockroaches, and walking sticks. Kids can touch fossils, animal furs, antlers, snake skin, and casts of bones and dinosaur fossils, as well as look at a variety of animals skulls from kitty cat to an American (yes, American) lion. Taxidermied animals scattered around the room include birds, raccoon, and a cougar, plus a rhino head and hippo head. Often times there are free, nature-oriented crafts to do, too.

The Hall of Geological Wonders is a work in progress. It will have a dazzling display of rocks, minerals, and gemstones, from quality pieces (along with some very large ones) of petrified wood to quartz to geodes to everything else.

Check the calendar for Family Fun Days, designed to educate the entire family about a particular topic or animal in a fun, hands-on manner, as well as other special programs, and know that the museum's field trips, school tours, and scouting programs are wonderful.

Hours: Open Tues. - Sun. and holiday Mon., 9am - 5pm. The Exploration Station is open Tues. - Fri., 9:30am - 12:30pm; Sat. - Sun., 1pm - 4pm. The museum is closed most Mon. (except holiday Mon.), New Year's Day, Thanksgiving, and Christmas.
Price: $10 for adults; $8 for seniors and active military; $7 for students with ID; $5 for ages 5 - 12; children 4 and under are free.
Ages: 2 years and up.

SAN BERNARDINO HISTORY AND RAILROAD MUSEUM
(909) 888-3634 / www.sbdepotmuseum.com
1170 W. Third Street at the Santa Fe Depot, San Bernardino

Located at the restored Santa Fe Depot, originally built in 1918, the small museum is in the former baggage room and has brick flooring. It displays a collection of lanterns, railroad signs, horse-drawn fire wagon and hose reel, block signals, dining car memorabilia, china dishes, baggage-handling equipment, uniforms, and other artifacts, plus lots of historical photographs and a six-foot long model of a steam engine. The museum is adjacent to a working Metrolink station. The lobby is open for morning and evening Amtrak stops.

Hours: Open Sat., 10am - 3pm.
Price: Free
Ages: 5 years and up.

SAN BERNARDINO RANCHO ASISTENCIA
(909) 793-5402 / www.sbcounty.gov/museum
26930 Barton Road, Redlands

This lovely restored set of buildings was once an outpost as part of Mission San Gabriel's Rancho. A grassy courtyard, surrounded by a few small adobe buildings, a bell tower, a fountain, and a grist mill complete this picturesque asistencia. Explore a part of the ranchero history as you walk through the main structure. The tour guide helps bring the past to life, explaining the people that once lived here and their way of life. School groups are welcome; just call to make a reservation.

Hours: Open Tues. - Sat., 10am - 3pm. Closed Sun., Mon., New Year's Day, Thanksgiving, and Christmas.
Price: $5 for adults; $4 for seniors; $2.50 for students and kids; children 4 and under are free.
Ages: 6 years and up.

VICTOR VALLEY MUSEUM
(760) 240-2111 / www.sbcounty.gov/museum/
11873 Apple Valley Road, Apple Valley

This classy, off-the-beaten-track museum is like an oasis in the desert that stays true to its motto of "Discover Your Own Backyard". An art wing with rotating exhibits of local and regional art is to the left of the lobby.

The museum also contains taxidermied animals in life-like poses such as a cougar, buffalo, muskox, and grizzly bear. Old West artifacts include saddles, horseshoes, rope, bronze cowboy sculptures, a stagecoach, farm tools, and

great-great-grandma's kitchen and household utensils, such as a butter churn and candle mold. Items from a living room of long ago include a phonograph, pump organ, radio, an early TV, and various other items. There are also collections of telephones, cameras, pictures (people back then didn't smile because they had to hold absolutely still for an entire minute or so), and real monies from the Bible (e.g., thirty pieces of silver and a widow's mite). Baskets, arrowheads, and other Native American artifacts are here. A doctor's buggy circa 1890's and a replica of the Old Woman meteorite are also found here.

A self-guided tour is good, but a guided tour, as usual, is much better. We learned about heros, such as Indians - how they made and did so much with seemingly so little - and Earl Bascom, a local rodeo star. As we inspected Native American baskets we learned how the weaving was so tightly done that the baskets could hold water. And we gained more knowledge about the rocks, minerals, and numerous other artifacts on display. Pre- and post-visit lesson packets are available for classroom field trips. Check the website for special events as many are kid-oriented.

Hours: Open Wed. - Sun., 10am - 4 p.m. Closed New Year's Day, Thanksgiving, and Christmas.
Price: $5 for adults; $4 for seniors; $2.50 for students; children 5 and under are free.
Ages: 6 years and up.

WBC LEGENDS OF BOXING MUSEUM

(909) 889-5555 / www.americansportsuniversity.com
399 North D Street on the campus of American Sports University, San Bernardino

On the campus of American Sports University, which is the only four-year college dedicated to sports education in the nation, get a ring-side seat for this unique, small museum that honors boxing greats. Honorees include World's Boxing Council championship fighters such as Muhammad Ali, Julio Cesar Chavez, Sugar Ray Leonard, Roger Mayweather, Ken Norton, Lennox Lewis and many more. Learn their personal and boxing histories at the museum via newspaper articles, numerous photographs, and some of their personal memorabilia. This cache includes autographed boxing gloves from Ali and others; belts; Championship rings; books about the boxers; information on them; and signed collectibles. This museum is a knock out for boxing afficionados. It is available for school and other group tours, too.

Hours: Open Mon. - Fri., 8am - 6pm.
Price: $2 per person
Ages: 5 years and up.

WESTERN AMERICA RAILROAD MUSEUM

(760) 256-WARM (9276) / www.barstowrailmuseum.org
685 N. First Street, Barstow

Train enthusiasts are invited to get on track by visiting W.A.R.M. The museum is dedicated to preserving railroad history and to getting the public involved with train "culture." Outside the building are several railcars, locomotives, and rolling stock - specifically, the Santa Fe 95; cars used to ship horses and their trainers; a CE-8 and a CA-8 caboose; a flat car used for freight service, now carrying an old neon sign; and a General Electric 44 tonner.

Inside the nice-sized museum are a few rooms that hold an assortment of train-related paraphernalia: two small, track inspection cars - one hand pump and one gas engine; photographs; a huge collection of date and pole nails (i.e., nails with the date stamped on the head driven into railroad ties for record keeping purposes); uniforms; scale model steam engine; recording equipment; tools; china used on old train cars; locks and keys; timetables; artwork; switchlights; Harvey girl displays; and old signs. Visitors also enjoy the thirteen-foot model train layout with all its bells and whistles. Ask about their special events.

This beautiful brick building, reached by first going over a trestle bridge, is an authentic train depot, currently home to an Amtrak station and a welcome center, as well as the BARSTOW ROUTE 66 "MOTHER ROAD" MUSEUM. (See pg. 422.)

Hours: Open Fri. - Sun., 11am - 4pm.
Price: Free
Ages: 4 years and up.

YANKS AIR MUSEUM

(909) 597-1734 / www.yanksair.com
7000 Merrill Avenue, Chino

"The Yanks are coming!" That phrase was uttered in celebration as the Yanks brought liberation for the people throughout Europe and the Pacific during WWII. This museum, which encompasses three dean hangars, as well as some outside space, is dedicated to American aircraft and aviation with one of the largest collection of single-engine, WWII aircraft on display, with a focus on fighters and dive bombers. Many of the over 170 planes have been restored, maintained, and are air-worthy, while other planes are in process of, or awaiting, this same fate/hope. The signage in front of each plane lets visitors know why that plane, in particular, is special - whether it is vintage, one-of-a-kind, or it has a unique history. A very short list of some of their planes includes a Bell P-36C King Cobra; Grumman F-14 Tomcat; Curtiss JN-4D Jenny biplane (with exposed frame, no skin); Bell 47B1 medical evacuation helicopter; P-40E Warhawk (with a shark's mouth painted on it); a 1950's F-106B Delta Dart (a trainer and interceptor plane with supersonic and nuclear capabilities); Blue Angels; and Republic P-47M Thunderbolt. The museum also contains a replica Wright Brother's 1903 Wright Flyer and other history-making aircraft.

One of the hangers is a restoration warehouse where you'll see frames of helicopters and planes, siding, wings, engines, propellers, lots of shelves with dusty parts, and mechanics working on their projects. (Get a whiff of the lacquer!)

Just beyond the workroom is a room containing flight suits from Viet Nam, survival kits, gas masks, photos, newspaper articles, NASA space suits, military dress, hats, and an array of helmets and goggles. Other paraphernalia in the hangers include instruments, medals, and a large collection of scale models planes. Take a self-guided tour, or schedule a guided one to get all the information.

The third Saturday is Open Cockpit Day which could include cockpit access into a Blue Angels F-18 Hornet, WWII Bomber, E-2C Hawkeye, or other historic aircraft; touring the Super Constellation; riding in a bi-plane or aerobatic plane (an additional $50 per person); or joining WWII reenactors and jumping from a (grounded) C-47 Skytrain. Food, posters and, for little ones, a ride in the small planes amusement ride, are all included in admission.

Note that just down the road is the PLANES OF FAME AIR MUSEUM (pg. 427) and Flo's Cafe.

Hours: Open Tues. - Sun., 9am - 4pm; closed Mon. and holidays.

Price: $11 for adults; $10 for seniors; $5 for ages 5 - 11; children 4 and under are free. Open Cockpit Days are an additional $5 per person. Ask about AAA discounts.

Ages: 3 years and up.

YORBA & SLAUGHTER FAMILIES ADOBE

(909 597-8332 - adobe; (909) 307-2669 - San Bernardino County Museum / www.sbcounty.gov/museum/ $$
17127 Pomona Rincon Road, Chino

Just for the record, the name "Slaughter" refers to a family that once lived here - not the slaughtering of animals. The adobe was built in 1852 and therefore receives the distinction of being the oldest standing residence in San Bernardino. A tour through the adobe, which is fairly well kept up, allows visitors to see its low beam ceilings; a dining room, with a table set for company; a living room and music room with period furniture and artifacts that include a piano, sewing machine, and dolls; a kitchen; a potbellied stove; a bedroom; and a few, simply-furnished rooms upstairs.

There are a few other buildings on the grounds that are also original, and very weathered in appearance. Step inside the post office/general store which contains advertising from the 1890's, artifacts, and even exhibits of agricultural animal husbandry. A shed with a stone chimney, a winery building, a one-ton solid copper pot (used for tallow), a grist mill, and a few pieces of old farming equipment complete the homestead. Note: Group and school tours are given by appointment.

Hours: Open to the public Tues. - Sat., 10am - 3pm. Closed Sun., Mon., New Year's Day, Thanksgiving, and Christmas.

Price: $5 for adults; $4 for seniors; $2.50 for student and kids; children 4 and under are free.

Ages: 7 years and up.

—POTPOURRI—

BASS PRO SHOPS OUTDOOR WORLD

(909) 922-5500 / www.basspro.com   !
7777 Victoria Gardens Lane, Rancho Cucamonga

"Welcome fishermen, hunters, and other liars" reads the sign over the doorway. Saying that this wholly outdoor-themed store is massive is almost an understatement. Wood, boulders, antlers (more of those than I've ever

seen anywhere, collectively); taxidermied animals (such as bears, deer, moose, wild boar, buffalo, elk, rams, birds, and more) - more than 400 wildlife and trophy fish mounts; and murals of Joshua Tree National Monument, Big Bear Lake, and Silverwood Lake fills the walls and ceilings. *Anything* pertaining to the great outdoors dominates every inch of the building. I've never seen so much outdoors underneath one roof.

Downstairs, besides the large boat showroom section, is a marine and fishing area with schools (and schools) of fish hanging overhead and every piece of equipment I can imagine (and some I can't) that you'd need/want for fishing. Clothing, a kid's toy and games area, bikes, home decor, and a fudge shop selling homemade fudge and coffee are also downstairs. One fun thing to do is to drive the Nascar race car video game - $2 per game. There is a forty-foot-high rock climbing wall just for looks.

Last, but not least downstairs, near the lodge fireplace, is a cascading waterfall creating a mini retreat with benches and a boulder-lined stream at its base, replete with posed stuffed animals, model fishermen, and real fish - bass, catfish, stripper, and blue gill - in the indoor trout stream. View and help with the fish feeding every Saturday at noon. Free classes are offered to learn or improve an outdoor skill - fishing, first aid, hunting, camping, amateur radio, predator seminar, intro to archery, and a lot more. Scouting merit badges can also be earned here. A free, one-hour Wild Animal Tour is offered by reservation to learn about the animals here (stuffed and live), where they came from, why, and about conservation.

Upstairs, you'll find everything camouflage, plus camping gear, bows and arrows, guns, and a fine gun room (i.e. expensive guns) with even more stuffed animal heads. Use the indoor archery range (i.e. an enclosed long hallway) if you purchase a bow here, or bring in your own and use it for a half hour for free, if the department isn't busy. If you've got your sights on using the laser shooting gallery, the cost is only 50¢ to play.

If you're hungry and don't have time to hunt or fish immediately, eat at the small, nautically-decorated ISLAMORADA FISH COMPANY restaurant (pg. 399) which is inside the store. Theoretically, Pro Bass is a store, but it's so much more. Note that Pro Bass is adjacent to VICTORIA GARDENS REGIONAL TOWN CENTER (pg. 422).

     Hours: Open Mon. - Sat., 9am - 10pm; Sun., 9am - 9pm.
     Price: Free, technically.
     Ages: All

BUILD-A-BEAR WORKSHOP (San Bernardino County)

(909) 980-0520 / www.buildabear.com

One Mills Circle in Ontario Mills Mall, Ontario

     See the entry for BUILD-A-BEAR WORKSHOP (Orange County) on page 314 for details. See ONTARIO MILLS MALL (pg. 421) for more information on the mall.

     Hours: Open Mon. - Sat., 10am - 9pm; Sun., 11am - 8pm.

CAL-EARTH

(760) 956-7533 / www.calearth.org

10177 Baldy Lane, Hesperia

     Nestled among Joshua trees, the California Institute of Earth Art and Architecture (aka Cal-Earth) has an educational facility that emphasizes building structures utilizing the four basic elements - earth, water, air, and fire. Domed, igloo-like structures made out of superadobe bricks, which look like sand bags, are on the grounds; prototypes for future buildings. The structure uses archways instead of the typical, box-like corners and doorframes. Both the United Nations and NASA have expressed interest in the designs and environment-friendly building materials.

     The general public is invited to come, learn, and tour around one day a month. Bring a potluck dish, enough to feed four to five people, on this day, too, or contribute $7 if you want to share the meal. At other times, a minimum group of fifteen students is offered three-hour or full-day workshops. In the "class," they learn how (by hearing about and by physically working) to build homes with arches and vaults using the earth (i.e., dirt); how to build emergency housing that is flood and fire-proof; teamwork; and how to live in harmony with the environment, using solar energy for glazing buildings and for cooling them. Deforestation is examined as alternative choices are shown and worked with. Prepare the kids for some hard labor and for out-of-the-box thinking here. Note: Located a short drive away at the end of Main Street is HESPERIA LAKE PARK (pg. 414). This lake offers picnic tables, fishing, a children's play area, and camping.

Hours: Open the first Sat. (but closed in August), 10am - about 3pm. Call first. Tours are given by appointment or for school groups during the week at 1pm.

Price: Free on the first Sat. School tours cost from $10 - $35 per person, depending on the length of time and activities. For instance, a ninety-minute tour for up to 5 people is $50.

Ages: 8 years and up.

CALICO GHOST TOWN

(800) TO CALICO (862-2542) or (760) 254-2122 / cms.sbcounty.gov/parks/
36600 Ghost Town Road, Yermo

Once upon a time a rich vein of silver was found in a mine underneath some multi-colored mountains. Word about the strike spread like wildfire, and pretty soon there were 5,000 people, of twenty different nationalities, living in and around this mining town. The town was called Calico because the varied minerals that created the different colors of the mountains were "as purty as a gal's Calico skirt." Between 1882 and 1907, the 500 mine claims produced eighty-six million dollars worth of silver and forty-five million dollars worth of borax. Then, the price of silver dropped. And the boom town went bust. Thankfully, the story doesn't end here.

Nowadays, this small, authentic western town has over twenty unique shops and eateries on both sides of the wide, dirt, main road that snakes up the mountainside - put your walking shoes on. Some of the current shops are even housed in original buildings. Topping our list of favorite shops are the rock and fossil shop, the leather works, and an 1890's general store.

There are several other attractions here. Gun fights break out daily every hour on the half hour starting at 10:30am. Visit the recreated schoolhouse at the end of the road where an authentically-dressed schoolmarm will gladly teach your kids what going to school was like in the olden days. There is a sturdy wooden teeter-totter and swing outside the schoolhouse. Don't be a fool when you pan for gold 'cause it's only fool's gold. The Mystery Shack is a small house of optical illusions where water rolls uphill, a broom stands up at an angle without falling over, and more. Before you walk through Maggie Mine, a real silver mine, look at the mining tools on display, such as a stamp mill, ore cart, recreated assay office, and more. Just inside the mine is a display of a few rocks and minerals mined from these parts, including fluorescent ones that glow in neon colors when the lights are turned off. Take the short walk through the mine, which has mannequin miners in action and audio explanations of the mining process. The Odessa Railroad is simply an eight-minute train ride on a narrow-gauge railcar. It takes you around part of a mountain where you'll see small cave-like openings that were front doors to miners' homes. On your ride you'll learn that the huge pile of "tailing" from the Silver King Mine still contains six million dollars worth of silver ore, but it would cost nine million dollars to process. Oh well! Sharpshooters can test their skill at the shooting gallery. Look at and into the house made of bottles - it's the ultimate in recycling.

School tours are offered to educate students on the history of the town and this era. Tours include a free education packet and a discount on entrance and attraction fees. For instance, the two-hour Silver King Mine Tour lets students see and experience behind-the-scenes of the town and mine, with hands-on activities. Ask about the Off Road Tours which is off the property, exploring the surrounding landmarks and mining districts along the wagon train road. Call for a schedule of special events or check the Calendar section for information on a Civil War Days (pg. 706) on President's Day Weekend, Calico Days (pg. 742) on Columbus Day Weekend, and Holiday Fest (pg. 758) on Thanksgiving weekend. Oh, and do explain to your kids that the term, "ghost town" doesn't mean that there are ghosts here, but just that the town went from being inhabited to being deserted.

Tent, RV, or cabin "camping" is available just below the town, as is a bunkhouse, which sleeps from twelve to twenty people. The basic, dirt sites are small, but the surrounding area can make it attractive for kids because there are (small) caves all over. In fact, seeing and even going into a few caves, was one of the things my children liked best about Calico. If you have a four-wheel drive vehicle (trust me, a mini-van doesn't cut it), turn left after leaving Calico and head for the hills on Mule Canyon to explore some of the hiking trails and go rock hunting in this area.

Hours: Open daily, 9am - 5pm. The town is closed on Christmas.

Price: Entrance is $8 for adults; $5 for ages 6 - 15; children 5 and under are free. On special event days/weekends, prices are usually $10 for adults; $5 for ages 6 - 15. Train rides are $3 for adults; $2 for kids. Maggie's Mine, the Mystery Shack and Gold Panning is $2.50 each for ages 10 and above; $1.50 for ages 5 - 10; children 4 and under are free. The schoolhouse, shootouts, guided tours, and tram ride up the hill from the parking lot are free with admission. Tent camping is $30 a night; hookup sites are $35; the cabin is $45; the bunkhouse starts at $80 (for up to 12 people).

Ages: All

OAK TREE VILLAGE

(909) 797-4420; (909) 797-2311 - Apple Annies / www.oaktreevillageoakglen.net; www.oakglen.net
38480 Oak Glen Road, Oak Glen

☀
!/$$

Oak Tree Village is fittingly located in the heart of OAK GLEN. (See page 401 for information on the surrounding apple orchards and places to enjoy along Oak Glen Road.) This fourteen-acre village, with a Western motif, is a funky and wonderful conglomeration of family activities, animals, shopping, and eating. The row of shops and restaurants, with plenty of outdoor picnic tables under huge oak trees, beckons travelers to buy, eat, and visit. Craft booths are located throughout the village on weekends. Definitely indulge in a slice of apple pie or a caramel-dipped apple!

Walk up the road where on the weekends, year round, kids enjoy pony rides that are led around in a circle attached to a wheel ($4) and scale model train rides ($3). On the weekends during apple season, which is September through November, there are also several large bounces and slides ($3 to $5) in front of a Western town facade. Family-friendly gun fights take place at this location on weekends, too. (The bad guys aren't killed - they go to jail.) Other special activities include piglet races, fishing contests, and live entertainment.

Kids really enjoy walking on the hilly dirt trail through the good-sized **Animal Park**. Over 100 animals reside here including penned deer, zebra, alpacas, llamas, steer, Angora goats, ostriches, emus, kangaroos, wallabies, zebu, singing dogs, and birds, ducks, and swans, plus a lot of squirrels and peacocks that freely roaming the grounds. The petting zoo in the Animal Park contains long-haired (and long horned) goats, pot-bellied pigs, and big woolly sheep. Admission to the Animal Park is $5 per person; children 1 year and under are free.

Inside the Animal Park are three picturesque (with a short waterfall and stream), stocked rainbow trout ponds that are usually open weekends only, year round. Fishing fees are the $5 entrance fee to the Animal Park, plus $2 per fisherman to rent a pole (no license needed), plus a $1 per-inch fee for each fish. No catch and release. Fish can be cleaned and packed in ice, also.

Just up the walkway is MOUNTAIN TOWN. See page 443 for details on this unusual, animal/reptile museum that has some live reptiles and some taxidermied animals inside in a recreated cave/mountain setting.

Numerous group tours/field trips are offered year round via Mountain Town such as: Fishing Tour - Learn about fish and the importance of the ecosystem, plus you actually get to fish and keep what you catch in this two-and-a-half tour - $16 per person. (Fish will be packed in ice to take home.) Pioneer Farm Life - Learn what life was like on the farm as participants milk a goat, collect eggs, make butter, and learn the chores of an 1800's homesteader - $9.95 per person. California Gold Rush - A two-hour tour at $9 per person with the main activity of gold panning in an actual stream for real gold (which is a lot harder and not as much fun as it seems). Learn about the importance of the Gold Rush and keep whatever you find. Harvest Tours (this is great one for older folk, too) are offered in season. They include lunch, an entire apple pie (per person) to take home, and an informative talk on the history of Oak Glen and all about apples - $27 per person. All tours/field trips include entrance to the Animal Park, feed for the animals, admission to Mountain Town, a twenty-five-minute animal presentation (i.e. learning about them and touching them), and fun. The docent is very flexible, gearing tours around particular interests or studies. A minimum of twenty is needed per tour/field trip. Check the website for other tours. Note that picnic facilities are available here.

Hours: Open daily for shopping and food, depending on the weather.
Price: General admission is free. Other prices are listed above.
Ages: All

WIGWAM MOTEL

(909) 875-3005 / www.wigwammotel.com
2728 W. Foothill Boulevard, Rialto

$$$$$

Originally built in 1949 along the famous Route 66, this classic and kitschy motel consists of nineteen, wood-framed, cement and stucco tepees that are thirty-feet tall arranged in a kind of semi-circle around a grassy area and gated, kidney-shaped pool. The pool is open seasonally and has a few lounge chairs around it. There are a few picnic tables and benches on the grounds near the pool. Bring your camera and take some fun pictures of the Wigwams. The surrounding area is run down, but the motel itself feels safe and offers clean rooms; comfy beds with decorative, half-wagon-wheel headboards; a mini fridge; free internet; and TV. The bathrooms are very small and ours didn't have an electric outlet, but we didn't care - we were sleeping in a wigwam and that's a cool adventure! And for

being on a major street, we were pleasantly surprised not to hear traffic noises inside our room. This motel is also pet friendly.

Outside the office are great retro signs and inside are Route 66 souvenirs to purchase. I have no reservations about sleeping at the Wigwam Motel again. Note: Check the San Bernardino area in the back of this book for close-by places to explore.

Price: Rooms run from $70 (one queen bed on weeknights) to $85 (two queen beds weekends and holidays).

Ages: All

—SHOWS AND THEATERS—

AT THE GROVE
(909) 920-4343 / www.grovetheatre.com
276 E. 9ᵗʰ Street, Upland

Fine, professional, dramatic live theater is performed at the grove, along with comedies, concerts, six musicals per season, and children's workshops. Past shows have included *My Fair Lady, Fiddler on the Roof,* and *Barnum.*

Hours: Call for show dates and times.
Price: Varies, depending on the show.
Ages: Varies, depending on the show.

BEATTIE PLANETARIUM
(909) 384-8539 / www.valleycollege.edu
701 S. Mount Vernon Avenue at San Bernardino City College, San Bernardino

Join in a gathering of the stars, the celestial stars that is. The sixty-seat planetarium shows the night sky and a live narrator discusses what the heavens are up to. Shows titles have included *Star Tales, The Little Star That Could,* and *The Amateur Astronomer's Universe. The Christmas Star* shows in December with a presentation regarding the star of Bethlehem. Hour-long show topics change frequently so you can come back more than once.

Hours: Shows are presented September through April, twice a month on Fri. at 7pm; doors open at 6:30pm. No late seating.
Price: $3 for adults; $2 for seniors and students; $1 for ages 10 and under.
Ages: 6 years and up.

CALIFORNIA THEATER OF PERFORMING ARTS
(909) 885-5152 / www.theatricalarts.com
562 West 4th Street, San Bernardino

It's show time! This beautiful old theater, which originally opened in 1928, seats 1,700 patrons inside its classical Spanish colonial design with ornate moldings, elegant chandeliers, tapestries, inlays, and wide, sweeping staircases. Will Rogers is featured on the exterior in two huge murals. Home to musicals, Broadway shows, plays, the San Bernardino Symphony, the Inland Dance Theater, ballet, concerts, and even naturalization ceremonies, this historical building hosts some kind of entertainment for everyone. Past shows have included the Blue Man Group, *Hunchback of Notre Dame, Cats, Chronicles of Narnia,* and *Les Miserables.*

Hours: Performances are usually given on Fri., 8pm; Sat., 2pm and 8pm; Sun., 2pm and 7pm.
Price: Tickets for plays and musicals range from $38.50 for the rear balcony to $77.50 for orchestra. Contact the theater for ticket prices as they vary depending on date, time, and performance.
Ages: 6 years and up, depending on the show.

CENTER STAGE THEATER
(909) 429-SHOW (7469) / www.centerstagefontana.com
8463 Sierra Avenue at Center Stage Theater, Fontana

Center Stage is both an historic and contemporary, gorgeously renovated "theater" that showcases and hosts several performance series - Tibbies Center Stage Dinner Theater; Broadway; Cabaret; Celebrity; and special events.

Tibbies offers more than just dinner, and more than just a show - it is a wonderful, two-hour dinner and musical song and dance revue in an upscale, classy atmosphere that is not off-putting for kids. The eight waiters and waitresses

also serve up the entertainment as the shows's performers. They start the show by singing as they bring in the Caesar salad, and they entertain all the way through dessert. They perform on the stage, as well as all around you. Their high energy, beautiful voices, numerous costumes changes, and well-choreographed dance moves make any show here a delight. Past show titles have included *From Stage to Screen* (favorite Broadway show tunes and movie music), *Forever Fifties* (songs from the 50's), and the fantastic, annual Christmas show, *Holiday Follies*. Audience participation and other surprises throughout the evening add to your family's enjoyment.

The delicious dinner selections for adults can include salmon, a chicken entree, chef's pasta special, or prime rib roast. All meals come with oven roasted potatoes, fresh bread, veggies, and an ice cream dessert. Children are offered creamy mac and cheese or chicken strips, with a salad, bread, garlic mashed potatoes, and veggies, plus a beverage and the special dessert. If your child or another member of your party is celebrating a birthday, graduation, or other special occasion, be sure you tell Tibbies beforehand so they will mention it sometime during the show. Various Tibbies shows are presented throughout the year, so call for particular show titles.

Center Stage is also home to excellent Broadway productions, such as *Five Guys Named Moe, Dream Girls,* and *You're a Good Man, Charlie Brown*, with a menu similar to Tibbies, although the adult main selections are top sirloin, almond crusted mahi, roasted garlic chicken, or vegetable pasta. The Cabaret and Celebrity series, such as *Barbara and Frank The Concert That Never Was, The Platters Live!,* and *Ticket to Ride* offer similar menus and equally choice talent. Special events can include murder/mystery shows, dazzling magic performances, Latin music and dancing, and a variety of other shows or community involvement.

Enjoy your night out on the town at either Tibbies, Broadway or another Center Stage production, where the food is good and the entertainment is clean and fun. One to two week reservations are suggested.

Hours: Tibbie and Broadway dinner shows are usually Fri. at 7:30pm; Sat. at 7pm (tho sometimes there is a matinee show at 2pm and then nighttime show at 7:30pm); Sun. at 2pm. Arrival time for Tibbies and Broadway shows only (no dinner) are Fri., 8:15pm; Sat., 7:45pm (or Sat., 2:45pm and 8:15pm); Sun., 2:45pm. Ask about their expanded holiday hours.

Price: Tibbies and Broadway shows, dinner, and dessert are usually $39.95 - $59.95, depending on the meal and show time; $29.95 for children 12 and under. Prices for the show only (no dinner) are usually $18 per person. Cabaret and Celebrity series dinner and show, or show only, tickets are usually more expensive. Prices can change according to the show in any of the series, so call or check the website first.

Ages: 6 years and up.

LEWIS FAMILY PLAYHOUSE PERFORMING ARTS CENTER

(909) 477-2752 / www.lewisfamilyplayhouse.com
12505 Cultural Center Drive at the Victoria Gardens Cultural Center, Rancho Cucamonga

The 540-seat Lewis Family Playhouse Performing Arts Center brings a plethora of top-notch talent and productions such as popular children's literary pieces (that come to life via stage productions), Broadway musicals, marionette shows, world renown guest artists, opera, dance, concerts, and authors. Past shows include *Aesop's Fables, Willy Wonka, Sid the Science Kid - Live, Ferdinand the Bull, Noises Off*, Riders in the Sky, Diavolo, Art Garfunkel, Rockapella Holiday, and more. Ask about school field trips, workshops, and educational programs because they offer an amazing array for students and teachers. See VICTORIA GARDENS REGIONAL TOWN CENTER on page 422 for details about the upscale mega mall surrounding the Playhouse.

Hours: Call for performance times.
Price: Prices vary depending on the show.
Ages: 3 years and up - depending on the performance and activity.

—TOURS—

CALIFORNIA PIZZA KITCHEN (San Bernardino County)

See the entry for CALIFORNIA PIZZA KITCHEN (Los Angeles County) (pg.197) for more information.

GOLDSTONE DEEP SPACE COMMUNICATIONS COMPLEX

(760) 255-8688 / www.deepspace.jpl.nasa.gov/dsn/features/goldstonetours.html

Off Fort Irwin Road, Fort Irwin

Who knew that you can't really learn all about deep space from *Star Trek* and *Star Wars*?! Goldstone, working alongside NASA and JPL, is only one of three facilities in the world where a network of antennas receive ALL the information transmitted from ALL the interplanetary spacecraft missions, as well as radio and radar astronomy observations, for processing. Wow! This includes signals and pictures from the over thirty-year-old Voyager I to the more current Mars Exploration Rover and Earth-orbiting missions.

The tour guide car escorts you as you drive your own vehicle during this two-hour, part-driving and part-walking tour around the fifty-three acre complex. The first stop is an up-close viewing of a gigantic, decommissioned antennae and satellite dish which acted as a backup to the Apollo flights. We gawked. Note: You are welcome to take as many photographs as you want.

The adjacent Goldstone museum, partly set up like a (visually stimulating) classroom, has numerous colorful posters, models, photos from space telescopes of exploding supernovas, and more. The guide's presentation was part lecture (very interesting!) and part questions and answers. Just a few things we learned - the 10th planet Eris, was discovered years ago; Pluto has three moons, not one; signals from our moon come back in 2 ½ seconds, while they return from Voyager 1 in over twenty-nine hours; and there is definite proof that liquid once flowed on Mars. The other small museum room contains history timelines via information panels and pictures; a dichroic plate with holes that allow frequencies to pass through; tools; an astronaut's uniform; a huge gear box for antennas; an orb to spin that shows the turbulence in flowing water; and more.

Next, drive about fifteen minutes, past wild burros and dry lake beds, to see the working Mars antennae/dish, that stands 210-feet tall and whose surface is more than one acre across. Here you'll learn more about how antennas work, why the desert is a perfect location for deep space communication, and some human interest stories about the facility. Walk through the "engine" room (filled with computers and such) to the Mission Control room. Look in to see consoles and radio frequency technicians that provide links between tracking stations and messages, while learning the importance of schedules, as equipment must match up to the tracking time when spacecraft "check in". This stellar tour makes exploring our vast solar system and universe relevant, important, and down to earth, so to speak.

Hours: Tours, which must be scheduled in advance, are available Mon. - Fri., at 9am and 1pm.
Price: Free
Ages: 7 years and up.

GOODWILL INDUSTRIES (San Bernardino County)

(909) 885-3831 / www.goodwillsocal.org
8120 Palm Lane, San Bernardino

Learn how to spread goodwill as you accompany your kids on a forty-minute tour of this facility. This location is a main donation center, where goods get consolidated and processed. It also has manual production lines and a work activity area. You'll get an overview of what Goodwill Industries does by observing people, including many disabled people, being trained to work in several different areas. Watching assembly lines are interesting, as things are put together and packages are shrink wrapped. Kids will also see recycling in action, as old stuffed animals and toys get fixed up for someone else to play with and love. Check out the receiving dock where the donations are piled. Idea: Clean out your closets and have your kids bring their old toys and clothes to Goodwill on your tour date. Tip: Next door to this facility is a thrift store. (I think we bought as much as we brought!) There is no minimum number of people required for a tour, but a week's notice is requested. There are other GOODWILL INDUSTRIES in Los Angeles County.

Hours: Tours are offered Mon. - Fri., 8am - 4pm by reservation.
Price: Free
Ages: 7 years and up.

LIVE OAK CANYON

(909) 795-8733 / www.liveoakcanyon.com
32335 Live Oak Canyon Road, Yucaipa

This 450-acre working farm offers seasonal tours that correspond with the seasons. Each ninety-minute tour costs $8 per person and includes a tractor pulled ride into the fields (you'll see Indian corn, gourds, hay, and more) and around the farm, while learning about the plants, farming, insects, and local history; a time of petting and feeding the barnyard animals, which include goats, sheep, donkeys, chickens, peacocks, horses, ducks, and a llama; a lesson and

hands-on learning in the Discovery Area; and something to take home. Spring/summer tour participants plant and take home a sunflower. Take home a pumpkin with the fall tour and hay, just for the fun of it, play on the giant hay castle where hundreds of bales of hay are stacked on top of each other creating a fortress. During the winter tour take home a Christmas tree seedling and play on the hay castle. Other seasonal tour options, which can be taken singularly or combined, include a t-shirt to color and take home ($13), corn maze tour ($11), nature hike ($10), and a gourd tour ($13). With the gourd tour participants learn all about gourds and their past and present uses, and then select one to drill holes in it for doing a project back at the classroom - a unique birdhouse, or other craft. Add-ons to your tours can also include a quad train ride through the farm ($3), a visit and feeding of the birds at the bird aviary ($2), time in a bounce house ($3), and zipping down a giant, inflatable slide ($3).

The farm is open to just come and visit in the fall and walk around its twenty-five-acre pumpkin "patch" where guests can go out into the fields and help pick their own pumpkins off the vine. The bordering sunflowers make for some great photo ops, too. Each weekend brings a special event. You can also visit Thanksgiving Friday through December when there are Christmas trees in abundance. During both of these seasons the general public can pet the barnyard animals; play on the hay castle (free); play on the several huge bounces, slides, and other rides; take a tractor drawn ride around the farm (free); take a quad train ride around the farm; enjoy a pony ride; eat a picnic at the tables under shade trees (there are several food venues open on weekends); partake in the special weekend activities of music, character appearances, animal presentations, and more; and peruse the Gift Tent with it's huge selection of fall and winter crafts and decorations, as well as fresh produce. And I've never seen a bigger and more varied selection of pumpkins! I love walking around Live Oak - it's close to the city, but rural, plus there just aren't a lot of real farms left in Southern California.

See the October Calendar section (pg. 750) and the November Calendar section (pg. 759) for more details of activities involving the pumpkin farm and Christmas tree farm.

    Hours: All tour are offered Mon. - Fri. Spring/summer tours run April - June. Fall tours, September - October. Winter tours, Thanksgiving Friday - end of December. The gourd tour is offered most seasons by appointment. Open to visit and play mid-September - beginning of October, daily 9am - 6pm; open October - beginning of November daily, 9am - 9pm. Amusements are open weekday at 3pm; weekends at 9am. The Christmas Tree Farm is open the Friday after Thanksgiving to just before Christmas, daily, 9am - 8pm.

    Price: Entrance to the farm is free in September and weekdays in October. On weekends in October, admission is $2 per person - pay once and it's good for the season. Tour prices are listed above. Check the website for specials.

    Ages: 4 years and up.

OAK GLEN / APPLE PICKING   ☼

Oak Glen Road, Oak Glen $$
    See the entry for OAK GLEN and APPLE PICKING on page 401 for details.

RILEY'S APPLE FARM   ☼

(866) 585-6407 or (909) 797-4061 / www.rileysapplefarm.com $$$
12201 S. Oak Glen Road, Oak Glen
    This orchard looks like it is set in the same time period as *Little House on the Prairie*. It has a delightful store that offers colonial-times toys and games, books, hand-made soaps, candles, and more modern purchases. On weekends in July and August come pick berries, some apples, and a few other types of fruit. In the fall, thirteen different varieties of apples, plus pumpkins, are ripe for visitors to harvest.

    A bountiful crop of fall tours includes a colonial or farm Bible study; participating in frontier skills such as chopping wood, washing clothes through a wringer, writing with a quill pen, starting a fire with flint and steel, pumping water, and gardening and harvesting crops; building a log cabin; learning old-fashioned dances such as the minuet and/or square dancing; grinding corn and baking Johnny cakes; taking an etiquette class; listening to a cowboy explain life on the range; archery; tomahawk throwing; and pressing apple cider. Tour options range from two to four hours and cost from $10 to $15 per person, with a minimum of twenty and maximum of eighty people. Tours begin Labor Day weekend until the end of November and are offered Tuesday through Thursday, usually from 10am to 4pm. Rope making, kazoo making, a nature walk, crafting a corn husk doll, and creating a water carrier are the other activities offered. You can order lunch for $3.95 to $6.50, or bring a sack lunch to enjoy by the pond picnic area. Two-hour

weekend tours are offered to groups, families, scouts, etc., of at least twenty people for $10 per person and include some of the above activities. Advanced reservations are needed for all tours. Parking mid-September through October is $5 on weekends.

Riley's is also open on weekends during the fall from 10am to 4pm for individuals and families to stop by. Visitors are welcome to pick their own apples or partake in some activities such as pressing cider at $20 a gallon; practicing archery for $2 for four shots; tomahawk throwing for $2 for six throws; knife throwing for $2 for five throws; and eating hot-dipped caramel apples for $3.75. (Winner!) Saturday entertainment includes fiddle and banjo playing. The farm also hosts occasional musical programs and hoedowns at Los Rios.

Spring tours are given in May and June that are similar to the fall tours, with the added bonus of apple tree planting.

Hours: See tour info above.
Price: Prices are listed above. Parking is $5 per car on weekends in the fall.
Ages: 5 years and up, depending on the tour.

RILEY'S AT LOS RIOS RANCHO

(909) 797-1005 / www.losriosrancho.com
39611 Oak Glen Road, Oak Glen

See the entry for RILEY'S AT LOS RIOS RANCHO under the OAK GLEN AND APPLE PICKING entry on page 401 for details about this place to eat and to take apple-related tours.

Ages: 4 years and up, depending on the tour.

RILEY'S FARM

(909) 797-7534 or (909) 790-TIME (8463) / www.rileysfarm.com
12261 S. Oak Glen Road, Oak Glen

Enjoy a meal at Hawk's Head Public House, a re-creation of an 18th-century Colonial restaurant with simple wood floor and tables and chairs, brick fireplace, pewter mugs, etc., and where servers are dressed in period clothing. Breakfast choices fit for a country squire include homemade bread for French toast with apples; scrambled egg with bacon or sausage; or biscuits and gravy at an average cost of $9. Lunch and dinner fare includes roast beef, ham, or turkey sandwich, $8.95; chicken pot pie or cider-baked ham, $12.95 each; and apple walnut salad, $10.75. The restaurant is open Tuesday through Friday, 10am to 4pm; Sat., 9am to 4pm. Special Living History dinner events are offered throughout the year on select Saturdays and they might incorporate a barn dance, an evening in the colonies with Patrick Henry, Sleepy Hollow, and more.

Pluck, pick, press, squeeze, and savor a myriad of fruit here from the end of May through November. Crops include strawberries, watermelon, raspberries, pears, peaches, and apples. Call to find out when the fruit is ripe. You can pick twenty different varieties of pumpkins here in the fall, too. Some picking is done by appointment only. U-pic hours, in season, are usually Mon. - Fri., 10am to 4pm; Sat., 9am to 4pm.

The year is 1775. The Revolutionary War is imminent. Students can learn first hand how it felt to be involved with this radical war by participating in a four-hour reenactment. Upon arrival, students are broken into "townships" and each group then visits various stations to experience life in this era. Some of the activities they participate in include visiting a blacksmith; witnessing Colonel Fenton's attempt to bribe Sam Adams; encountering British soldiers; learning about the Stamp Act; going through a court trial; grinding wheat; churning butter; learning etiquette of the times; and in a grand finale - marching across the orchard lands with arms (i.e., sticks and fake gun stocks) in a battle recreation. Kids become a part of the history - living it and learning it. A typical fare of a lunch ration is handed out: cornbread, slice of cheese, piece of fruit, and beef jerky. Tip: Bring some of your own food for lunch! The tour begins at 10am and cost $13 - $17 per person, depending on the season, with a minimum of fifteen people; $19 for groups under fifteen people. This tour was a favorite for my troops! The Revolutionary War Overnight combines the above reenactment with more of the same - sentry duty against the redcoats, period dancing, skirmishes, sleeping on rope bunk beds, and eating. The cost is $120 per person with a thirty-five person minimum.

If kids are studying the Civil War, Riley's also has a reenactment for this pivotal time period that is almost as engrossing (no shooting, though) and just as authentic. The Civil War requires prep work as students have drama assignments, costume guides, vocabulary helps, etiquette information, and more for this recreation. A similar, learn-it-by-living-it two-hour Colonial Farm Life tour offers a choice of activities including playing 18th-century games, making cheese and butter, pressing cider, weaving, baking bread, learning etiquette, making candles, stamping, and

eating a hot-dipped caramel apple. This tour is $10 per person with a fifteen-person minimum; $11.50 per for groups under that number. The four-hour Gold Rush field trip, 10am to 2pm, offers gold panning in a sluice box, panning for gold, dry mining, digging in a mine shaft, looking inside a miner's cabin, etiquette and manners "class," a rope climbing challenge, and tomahawk throwing, as well as a lesson in California economics and a drama involving a gold theft. The price is $10 per person for a minimum of fifteen guests; $17 per person for individuals or families that want to join a tour. A period lunch, a ration, is served. Bring your own lunch here, too. Ask or check the website for other tours. If your group is too small to meet the minimum number needed for a tour, ask about joining up with another group.

Riley's Farm, set in the hills of Oak Glen, has a naturally rural ambiance with running streams, apple orchards, and dirt trails. See OAK GLEN and APPLE PICKING (pg. 401) for more on fruit picking at this farm and for other things to do in this immediate area.

Hours: Tours are offered by reservation.
Price: See above for prices.
Ages: 3rd graders through high schoolers, depending on the tour.

RILEY'S FRONTIER EVENTS

(909) 790-2364 / www.losriosrancho.com

$$$$

12211 S. Oak Glen Road, Oak Glen

The Riley's name is big up here in apple country. In fact, these Riley's also operate Riley's at Los Rios Rancho (see pg. 401). This orchard is only open for tours so gather around the Conestoga pioneer wagon to start your two-hour, Living History tour. The tours are offered September through November, Tuesday through Friday at 9am and 11:30am, and on weekends at 9am, for a minimum of twenty-five people. The fall tour activities include a visiting an authentic log cabin; taking a horse-drawn hayride; making cider (a fascinating process); drinking cider (an even better process); eating hot-dipped caramel apples (a personal favorite); walking the Johnny Appleseed through the orchards; and your choice of butter churning, candlemaking, leather craft, seed planting, tin smithing, making a small wooden toy, or gaining access to the petting farm. You can buy a hotdog lunch for $3.50 (with advance notice), or bring a lunch to enjoy at the picnic area. The farm also has U-pic apples and berries.

Living History tours are also given April through June, Tuesday through Fridays. These tours consist of the log cabin visit and four of the optional activities. Reservations are required for all tours.

Hours: Hours are listed above.
Price: $8 per person (a great deal!)
Ages: 6 years and up.

—TRANSPORTATION—

AMTRAK (San Bernardino County)

(800) USA RAIL (872-7245) / www.amtrakcalifornia.com

Ride the rails! See AMTRAK (Los Angeles County) on page 208 for more information.

BIKE MAPS (San Bernardino County)

See BIKE MAPS (Orange County) on page 326 for information.

CALIFORNIA SPEEDWAY

(800) 944-RACE (7223) / www.autoclubspeedway.com

$$$$$

9300 N. Cherry Avenue, Fontana

The best in NASCAR racing roars to life in Southern California! Located on over 525 acres, this state-of-the-art speedway features a two-mile, D-shaped oval super speedway with a 1.3-mile infield road course. The track can accommodate three to four cars side-by-side. (Racers clock average speeds of up to 200mph!) The stadium seats allow great views of the races. Gigantic screens and hundreds of smaller monitors show the action to spectators, too. Thirteen huge message boards, an incredible speaker system, a car-themed children's play area, sometimes live entertainment, and "real" food (including lobster), as well as standby's of hot dogs and hamburgers, all aid in making this a very fan-friendly speedway. Check out the website for information on the Lefty's Kids Club for more offerings, including going to select races for free. The street festival atmosphere is enhanced by a concert stage, town center, retail store, and cuisine by Wolfgang Puck. RV camping (no hookups) is available at certain times, too. Note there are

many special happenings, including motorcycle racing, driving a NASCAR race car yourself, exotics racing, racing schools, and more.

Hours: Call or check the website for a race schedule.

Price: Prices vary greatly according to the race. Fri. practices are $20 for adults; ages 12 and under are free; Sat. assigned seating is usually $50 for adults while general seating is $30 for adults; ages 12 and under free; Sun. assigned seating starts at $50 - $105; $15 for kids. Pay an additional $55, in addition to a grandstand pass, for a pit pass.

Ages: 5 years and up.

METROLINK (San Bernardino County)

(800) 371-LINK (5465) / www.metrolinktrains.com

See the entry for METROLINK (Orange County) on page 329 for details.

YOUNG EAGLES PROGRAM - Chino

National number - (877) 806-8902; Planes of Fame Museum - (909) 597-3722; Yanks Air Museum - (909) 597-1734 / www.eaa92.org; www.youngeagles.org

7000 Merrill Avenue at Chino Airport, Chino

See the entry for YOUNG EAGLES PROGRAM (Los Angeles County) on page 215 for details. This program is run by the Orange County chapter, #92, and has an educational emphasis and a lot of excitement about the program. The ground school first covers what makes an airplane fly, special instruments in the plane, how pilots navigate using charts and maps, careers, pre-flight checks, and making and testing a model glider. Then, they fly! Afterward, they get a certificate and a bag that contains a few treasures for them. The whole program takes about 3.5 hours. Young Eagles aids Boy Scouts in getting their aviation merit badge. Since you are here, check out the adjacent PLANES OF FAME AIR MUSEUM (pg. 427) and YANKS AIR MUSEUM (pg. 430).

Hours: Twice in the spring and twice in the fall on select Sat., starting at 10am (registration starts at 9:30am). The website is very up-to-date.

Price: A $20 donation is asked per youth that is flying - it covers lunch, fuel costs, materials, and more.

Ages: 8 - 17 years old.

YOUNG EAGLES PROGRAM - Redlands

(877) 806-8902 - national number; (909) 798-7655 - city of Redlands / www.youngeagles.org

1745 Sessums Drive, Redlands Airport, Redlands

See the entry for YOUNG EAGLES PROGRAM (Los Angeles County) on page 215 for details. Reservations are needed.

Hours: Offered four or five times a year on selected Sat., starting at 9am.

Price: Free

Ages: 8 - 17 years.

YOUNG EAGLES PROGRAM - Upland

(877) 806-8902 - national number / www.youngeagles.org

1749 W. 13th Street, Cable Airport, Upland

See the entry for YOUNG EAGLES PROGRAM (Los Angeles County) on page 215 for details. At this location, a forty-minute video is viewed that shows the history and goals of EAA (Experimental Aircraft Association). This chapter also offers follow-up programs and activities for young flyers.

Hours: Offered periodically throughout the year. Check the website for specific information.

Price: Free

Ages: 8 - 17 years.

—ZOOS AND ANIMALS—

AMY'S FARM TOURS

(909) 393-2936 / www.amysfarm.com

7698 Eucalyptus Avenue, Chino

Breath in the country smell (i.e. cows); breath out the city. For a really mooooving tour, visit Amy's Farm, which is really a family-run, working ten-acre cow ranch and crop farm. Other animals that consider the farm home, besides the over 100 cows, include penned ducks, bunnies, geese, a water buffalo, sheep, goats, pigs, and horses, plus chickens that are roaming all over the place. A tour, with a minimum of ten paying guests and maximum of sixty, is the only way to visit the farm and reservations are required. If you have a smaller group, you can be added on to another, larger one. Tours are age-appropriate. For $8 per person, tours for elementary-aged children last about an hour and include learning all about the animals; the story of milk - from cow to grocery store; petting goats and sheep; grooming mini horses; feeding the pigs; perhaps harvesting crops from the vegetable garden; perhaps petting newborns (depending on the season); and milking a cow - this is a highlight! In October, the pumpkin tour includes taking home a pumpkin for an additional $2 per person. One hour plus tours for middle and high schoolers, at $10 per person, have more of an emphasis on ecological and sustainable farming incorporating composting, crop rotation, seasonal planting and more. A visit here is an awesome way to gain first-hand introductory knowledge and experience with and on a farm.

Although the tours involves walking around, it is also set up for special needs groups. A picnic area, with attached grassy area, is on the grounds, as is a farm stand with fresh produce for sale. Check the website regarding other seasonal events, such as summer camps, and for information about specialty classes such as Fun on the Farm and the Science of Farming. See the Calendar entry for information about the pumpkin tours (pg. 747). Note that PLANES OF FAME AIR MUSEUM (pg. 427) and YANKS AIR MUSEUM (pg. 430) are just down the street at the airport.

Hours: Tours are offered in the morning, Mon. - Fri. starting at 9am. Tours on select Sat. start at 10:30am. Call to book a specific date and time.
Price: Prices listed above.
Ages: 2 years and up.

BRACKEN BIRD FARM

(909) 792-5735 / www.brackenbird.com
10797 New Jersey Street, Redlands

This store is for the birds, and for people, too. The wide variety of birds for sale here include canaries, doves, parrots, finches of all kinds, cockatoos, macaws, and even toucans. Their colors range from drab brown to a rainbow of hues. We walked by the cages indoors and strolled by more in the outside aviary.

Adjacent to the bird farm, along a dirt pathway, are some animals in enclosures. We saw a longhorn steer, a camel, a donkey, a few potbelly pigs, goats, turkeys, and farther off (harder to see) ostriches and emus. Ducks were swimming in the small pond, also behind a fence.

Hours: Open daily, 9am - 5pm. Closed New Year's Day, July 4th, Thanksgiving, and Christmas.
Price: Free
Ages: All

HESPERIA ZOO

(760) 948-9430 / www.thehesperiazoo.com
19038 Willow Street, Hesperia

The animals at this small, ten-acre zoo (which is surrounded by a housing development), who have either been rescued or purchased, spent time in the spotlight as they have been featured in movies, TV commercials, and print ads. Do you recognize any of them? See the animals close up in their hard-packed-dirt floor pens and learn more about them because the guided tour (which is the only way allowed to experience the zoo) is given by an animal trainer. On the hour tour, you hear stories about the animals - where they came from, their traits, habitats, and some of their personality quirks. You see a black bear, ostriches, llama, tiger, lion, camel, baboon, prairie dogs, monkeys, birds, hoofed animals, porcupine, alligator, reindeer, and other exotic animals. Some domestic animals are here as well.

Your tour usually finishes with a presentation of some sort, like watching certain animals be led through paces to show how they use their instincts in the wild. Kids, especially, enjoy the petting zoo, also, which has llamas; Australian sheep (who have hair, not wool); goats; pigs; and more. You may purchase animal feed for $1. There are also boas, scorpions, tarantulas, and other such critters at this zoo.

For an additional $20 per person, visitors can help feed spider monkeys, lemurs, reindeer, tigers and more animals at 4pm on Saturdays. Private guided tours and educational programs are offered during the week by reservation. Off-site programs are available as well.

Hours: Open in the fall and winter, Sat. - Sun., 10am - 3pm, with guided tours leaving every hour on the hour; the last tour leaves at 2pm. Open in the spring and summer, Sat. - Sun., 10am - 5pm; the last tour leaves at 4pm. Closed New Year's Day, Easter, 4th of July, Thanksgiving, and Christmas.
Price: $7 for adults; $5 for seniors and ages 2 - 12; children under 2 are free.
Ages: 2 years and up.

MOJAVE STATE FISH HATCHERY

(760) 245-9981 or (909) 484-0167 / www.dfg.ca.gov
12550 Jacaranda Avenue, Victorville

This facility is the largest trout-producing hatchery in California. Six raceways (i.e., holding tanks for the fish) at 1,000 feet long each, hold six strains of rainbow trout that supplies seven counties. You won't be here long, but come see them at feeding time, if possible, as the fish practically leap in the air to snatch their food. And note that tempting though it may be, you may not bring your fishing pole. Tours are offered upon request. There is a picnic table under a shade tree on a small patch of grass here, too.

Hours: Open daily, 7am - 3:30pm.
Price: Free
Ages: 2 years and up.

MOUNTAIN TOWN REPTILE MUSEUM

(909) 797-4420 / www.oaktreevillageoakglen.net
38480 Oak Glen Road, Oak Glen

Inside, just beyond the gift shop/lobby is a huge, long, funky room with a "mountain" built in its middle, niches inset into its sides, and dioramas along the perimeter walls. Perched on the mountain and in the mountainside, along with a number of fake trees (which add ambiance) and mannequins (one of which "talks" about one of the snakes below it), are taxidermied animals. These include bear, big horn sheep, ostriches, deer, raccoons, a mountain lion, birds in flight, ducks, and a wolverine, all in life-like poses. The niches inset into the mountain hold small, live animals such as a variety of snakes, frogs, lizards, and insects. Some of the dioramas along the walls display taxidermied animals. One collection, in a cave-like setting, has a polar bear, a family of Emperor penguins, seals, and an Arctic fox. The next diorama is a one-room log cabin with a period-dressed mannequin, a stove, and animal furs. Another room along the wall contains several live snakes (in glass enclosures) including boas, pythons, corn snakes, and milk snakes, plus a skink, a legless lizard (which is somehow not a snake), and tortoises. Other live animals in Mountain Town include Nile monitors, Flemish giant rabbits (about 20 lbs. each) and other rabbits, plus chinchillas, salamanders, Madagascar hissing cockroaches, African grey parrots, macaws, and more. In the fall, animal and reptile presentations are given at 1:30pm and 3:30pm.

In the Mountain Town lobby is a souvenir shop; a few more taxidermied animals, such as a bear and deer heads; and Animaland, a machine you can use to purchase and fill a soft, stuffed animal to bring home. You can also purchase food for the animals at $1 a cup here. Just outside the shop are fallow deer in enclosures. In the fall, gold pan here at the sluice on weekends for $10 which gets you a bag with gold flecks and semi-precious stones. See the entry for OAK GLEN and APPLE PICKING (pg. 401) and OAK TREE VILLAGE (pg. 434) for more things to do in this immediate area and for information on great school and group tours that explore the area and allows participants to interact with the animals in the adjacent Animal Park.

Hours: Open daily, 10am to 5pm, weather permitting.
Price: $3 per person.
Ages: 3 years and up.

OAK TREE VILLAGE

38480 Oak Glen Road, Oak Glen

See OAK TREE VILLAGE (pg. 434) for information on the Animal Park and other fun things to do here.

—BIG BEAR—

BIG BEAR LAKE / LAKE ARROWHEAD (and the surrounding area)

Instead of categorizing Big Bear Lake and Lake Arrowhead attractions in my usual way throughout San Bernardino county pages, I've grouped them together in their own section because I think most people think of these areas as destinations in and of themselves.

These four-season mountain resorts are close enough to escape to for a day or a weekend, although they offer enough activities for at least a week's vacation. The pine trees and fresh air that beckon city-weary folks, plus all the things to do, make them ideal family get-aways. November through March (or so) the mountains become a winter wonderland with lot of opportunities for snow play and skiing. This section, however, also covers a broader base of activities because Big Bear Lake and Lake Arrowhead are great any time of year!

For specific information on events held during the time you plan to visit Big Bear Lake, call (909) 866-4607 / www.bigbearchamber.com - chamber of commerce, or www.BigBeartodaymag.com. I appreciate www.bigbearlake.net for general information, as well. For lodging information and visitor's guide, call (800) 4BIG BEAR (424-4232) / www.bigbearinfo.com. For similar information about Lake Arrowhead, call (909) 337-3715 / www.lakearrowhead.net or www.lakearrowhead.com. Camping information can be found by contacting the Forest Service at (877) 444-6777 / www.recreation.gov. The website www.mountaininfo.com is a popular site for information for all of the San Bernardino Mountains. Note: Fishing in Big Bear Lake is available to the public; those 16 years and older must have a valid license. Fishing in the lake in Lake Arrowhead is open only for Arrowhead Lake Association members and their guests.

General directions to Big Bear Lake are as follows: From San Bernardino Fwy [10], head N. on Hwy. 30, which turns into Hwy. 330, E. (or R.) on Hwy. 18. To Lake Arrowhead: You may go the same route as above, except head W. (or L.) on Hwy. 18 - follow signs to Lake Arrowhead. Or, you may exit the 10 Fwy N. on the 215, N. on 259, E. on the 30, L. on Waterman Ave., which becomes Hwy. 18 (which is also known as Rim of the World Hwy.), for about 20 miles, and L. on Hwy. 173 toward Lake Arrowhead. Check road conditions first in the winter time before heading up - (800) 427-ROAD (7623).

ACTION ZIPLINE TOURS

(909) 866-0390 / www.actionziplinetours.com

41647 Big Bear Boulevard, Big Bear Lake

Literally zipping through forest tree tops is an incredible adrenaline rush! And you get to do this nine times! The three-hour Action Zipline Tour even starts off exciting, in a Pinzgauer (safari-type jeep) that rides and climbs the mountainous terrain, incorporating several stops along the way. Hiking is part of the trip as is walking across a suspension bridge (the bouncing always gets to me!) all the while learning the history of the area. There are nine zip lines to zoom across, ranging from the baby step one at 120 feet all the way to 860 feet. Zip lines are cables suspended really high up. Riders wear a harness with a carabineer attached to a pulley to let 'er rip from one side of the cable to the other. Coming back from your adventure, you might just be ready to do it again as the experience is different in the cold and snow, than in the warmth of spring or summer. Add to your adventure by going off-roading on a Segway! Take this additional two-hour tour and learn and see the area while zipping along in another fashion.

Hours: Open daily, weather permitting, with a minimum of 4 people, maximum of 16. Zipline tour times are 9am, 11am and 2pm. An additional tour is added in the spring and summer. Call for other tour times.

Price: Zipline tours are $120 per person. Zipline and Segway tours are $169.

Ages: Riders must be at least 8 years old.

ALPINE SLIDE at MAGIC MOUNTAIN

(909) 866-4626 or (909) 866-4627 / www.alpineslidebigbear.com

800 Wildrose Lane, Big Bear Lake

Alpine Slide lifts family fun to new heights! Take the chairlift up the mountain. Then, you and your child sit on heavy-duty plastic toboggans and rip down the quarter-mile, cement, contoured slide that resembles a bobsled track. Control your speed by pushing or pulling on the lever. We were cautious only on our first ride. Your child can go

$$$$$

down by himself if he's at least 7 years old.

The compact, eighteen-hole miniature golf course, Putt 'N Around, has just a few frills, but kids still enjoy puttin' around on it. Single and double go karts are available for drivers at least 57" tall. Inside the main building are a few video games, of course, and a snack bar. That delicious food you smell is a burger (about $4) or hot dog (about $3) being barbecued right outside, or it may be a bowl of soup or chili (but not being barbecued).

Summer play is enhanced by two zippy water slides. You'll end with a splash in the three-and-a-half-feet deep pool, but it's not for swimming in. Winter allows you and the kids a chance to inner tube down the snowplay hill on four side-by-side runs that resemble a snake's trail. Instead of trudging back up the hill with tube in hand (which you're not allowed to do), ride the covered Magic Carpet which is similar to a moving conveyor belt covered in plexiglass. Nighttime runs add an extra touch of magic. You'll have mountains of fun any season you come to Alpine Slide at Magic Mountain.

Hours: The Alpine Slide, miniature golf, and go karts are open mid-June - mid-September, Sun. - Thurs., 10am - 6pm; Fri. - Sat., 10am - 9pm. Open weekends only in the spring and fall, 10am - 5pm or 6pm; open in the winter, daily (weather permitting), 10am - dusk. The water slide is open Memorial Day weekend to mid-September daily, 10am - 6pm. The snow play area is usually open November - Easter (they make their own snow here) daily, 10am - 4pm. Night sessions are Fri., Sat., and holidays, 5pm - 9pm.

Price: Alpine ride - $5 for one ride; $20 for a five-ride book. Miniature golf - $5 a round for adults; $4 for ages 12 and under. Go karts - $5 a single car; $7 a double car. Water slide - $2 for one ride; $10 for a ten-ride book; $15 for an unlimited day pass. Snow play - $25 for an unlimited day-pass which includes a tube as you may not bring your own. Nighttime tubing sessions are $20 per person. Children 2 to 6 are free on the Alpine slide, water slide, and snow play area, as long as they are accompanied by a paying adult.

Ages: 3 years and up.

BALDWIN LAKE STABLES AND PETTING ZOO

(909) 585-6482 / www.baldwinlakestables.com

E. Shay Road, Big Bear Lake

Leave the city behind and horseback ride through the scenic national forest. The breathtaking mountain views, and sore bottoms for those unused to trotting, are all included in your ride price. Enjoy a one- to- four-hour ride along the Pacific Crest Trail, or see things in a different light by taking a sunset ride! (The latter ride is only available during the summer.)

Hand-led pony rides for young bronchos are $10 per child that last about fifteen minutes - a few laps around the track. A petting zoo here has bales of hay all around and a barn-like small building. For $3 per person, enter the pen to pet and/or feed llamas, bunnies, goats, sheep, potbellied pigs, a chinchilla, guinea pigs, and ducks.

Hours: The stables are open daily most of the year, weather permitting, 10am - 5pm, although hours fluctuate. Call before you come. Pony rides and the petting zoo are open most of the year on weekends only, 10am - 5pm; open daily in the summer the same hours.

Price: $45 an hour per person. Sunset rides are $60 per person - no children allowed.

Ages: At least 7 years old and 4' tall for horseback riding.

BIG BEAR DISCOVERY CENTER

(909) 866-3437 or (909) 382-2790 / www.mountainsfoundation.org

40971 N. Shore Drive, Highway 38, Fawnskin

This classy-looking ranger station is the best place to visit (or call) for hiking and biking trail maps and camp sites. Exhibits at the center include informational and pictorial panels, animal pelts, and stuffed animals such as a black bear, bobcat, gold eagle, barn owl, and raven. A seventeen-minute film about the history of Big Bear Lake runs continuously. An hands-on exhibit hall includes an explanation and visual of the formation of mountains, plus touchable rocks. Activities in here include mining limestone, building dams, climbing through a hollow log, and building a log cabin. You may buy a bite to eat at the snack bar to enjoy at the outside patio tables and chairs. Outside, too, is a huge, 370-year old pine slab displaying a time line, of sorts, via its rings that indicate the year Mickey Mouse was created; the year the Dodo bird became extinct; the War of 1812 (guess which year?); and more.

The center, which boasts a 300-seat, outside amphitheater, is also host for a variety of special programs, held

mostly in the summer, such as weekend campfires. Another program focuses on Native American lifestyles and includes arts, crafts, and demonstrations such as drum making, working with clay, and gourd painting. Hour-long Nature Nights presentations, held every Thursday night during the summer and every other Friday in other seasons, cover various topics. Half-hour guided nature walks are offered every weekend, twice a day. Ask about Jr. Forest Ranger programs for kids, too.

During the summer, as well, join in on a three-hour, Holcomb Valley Off-Road, naturalist-led, mountain mining adventure tour where participants travel in a van to a limestone quarry to see equipment blasting; sit on a giant tractor; learn the history of the Gold Rush in this area; and visit the site of the Gold Mountain Mine. On two-hour guided canoe tours of Grout Bay, for ages 6 and up, you'll paddle along the bay while learning about gold mining and the history of the lake, plus looking for beavers, great blue herons, and ducklings. Bottled water and snacks are included. Two-hour guided kayaks tours, for ages 10 and up, are also available.

One of the winter jaunts is a three-hour, guided snowshoe excursion (based on snow availability). The trip is ideal for both beginners an experienced snowshoers.

Pick up an Adventure Pass at the center. This Pass is required for all vehicles parking on national forest property for recreational purposes.

Hours: Open mid-April - mid-September daily, 8:30am - 4:30pm. Open in the winter, Mon. - Tues., Fri. - Sun., 8:30am - 4:30pm. Closed Tues., Wed., New Year's Day, Thanksgiving, and Christmas. Snowshoe trips are offered in January, February, and March on Sat., if there is enough snow. The Holcomb Valley Off-Road tour is offered March - Labor Day, Thurs. - Sun. Canoe tours are available mid-May - August, Fri. at 4pm and Sun. at 1pm. Kayak tours are offered mid-May - August on Sat. at 1pm and 4pm; Sun. at 9am. Reservations are required for all tours.
Price: The Adventure pass is $5 per day or $30 for an annual pass. The snowshoe excursion is $30 for adults; $20 for ages 8 - 12. The canoe tour is $22 for adults; $11.50 for ages 6 - 12 (must be at least 6 years old). Kayak tours are $32 per person.
Ages: All

BIG BEAR HISTORICAL MUSEUM

(909) 585-8100 / www.bigbearhistory.org; www.bigbearinfo.com/mpcspmuseum.html
600 Greenway Drive, Big Bear Lake

The past is definitely present at the Big Bear Valley Historical Museum. The buildings that comprise the museum are very old (and old looking). The small main building contains a good assortment of taxidermied animals such as a golden eagle, skunk, red fox, badger, and others, displayed mostly behind glass in "natural" settings. Other exhibits include birds' nests, eggs, arrowheads, rocks, fossils, unique leather carvings, old photographs of old Big Bear, Native American artifacts, and old-fashioned toys. Outside on the porch are turn-of-the-century post office boxes, plus mining equipment and mining artifacts.

An on-site, furnished, 1875 one-room log cabin offers a real look into the pioneer lifestyle. The docents in here are wonderful at explaining to kids how pioneer families lived, and the uses of some of the household items. My boys couldn't believe that chamber pots were really used as portable potties. It finally dawned on them that entire families lived together in this one room; sleeping, cooking, eating, and playing together. I hope they'll be more thankful about their own living arrangements!

One log structure here is actually a mule barn used to house mules. A stamp mill used to crush gold bearing ore and hard rock to recover gold, and lots of old, rusted agriculture equipment are also on the grounds.

An adjacent park has a few pieces of play equipment and some old tennis courts. The park is good mostly for visitors to just run around in its fields. Shade is scarce, but there are a few picnic tables here.

Hours: Open Memorial Day to the second Sun. in October on Wed., Sat., and Sun. (and holiday Mon.), 10am - 4pm.
Price: Free; donations gladly accepted.
Ages: 3 years and up.

BIG BEAR LAKE PERFORMING ARTS CENTER

(909) 866-4970 or (909) 866-5831 / www.citybigbearlake.com
39707 Big Bear Boulevard, Big Bear Lake

This 400-seat center is a catch-all for almost any kind of stage performance in the Big Bear area. Shows run the

gamut from professional productions of *Oklahoma*, comedy acts, magicians from the Magic Castle in Hollywood, Barbershop Sweet Adelines, and master chorale groups, to high school and middle school performances, dance recitals, and dog shows. Check the schedule to see who or what is playing.

Hours: Depends on performance.
Price: Depends on performance.
Ages: Depends on performance.

BIG BEAR MARINA BOAT RENTALS / BIG BEAR QUEEN CRUISE

(909) 866-3218 / www.bigbearmarina.com
500 Paine Road, Big Bear Lake

The Marina offers a boatload of fun for the family. Five-passenger motorized fishing boats start at $45 for two hours. Kayaks, stand up paddleboards, and canoes rent for $20 an hour per. Two-seater wave runners are $125 an hour (early bird special is $100). Rent a small pontoon, a flat-bottomed boat that is almost seasick proof, for $65 an hour, plus $20 fuel, so $85 an hour. It seats up to six people. A larger pontoon, which seats up to twelve people, is $90 an hour, plus $20 for fuel, so $110 an hour.

Take an hour-and-a-half, narrated tour around Big Bear Lake on the *Big Bear Queen*. You'll learn the history of the marina, and the town of Big Bear, plus the happenings of the area. Tours are given daily, in season, always at 2pm, and sometimes at 10am, noon, and 4pm, if at least fifteen people are signed up. Prices are $19 for adults; $17 for seniors; $13 for ages 3 to 12; children 2 years and under are free. Bring your own food and beverage to enjoy a sunset cruises at $20 per person, although this cruise isn't recommended for kids. Sunset cruises are offered Wednesday and Saturday, July through Labor Day.

Hours: Open daily, seasonally, usually spring through October, 7am - 7pm.
Price: Prices are listed above.
Ages: 3 years and up.

BIG BEAR OFF-ROAD ADVENTURES

(909) 585-1036 / www.offroadadventure.com

Up to thirteen people can ride in the convertible, four-wheel drive Pinzgauers used on these off-road adventures. A myriad of tours are available from easy, ninety-minute rides on forest roads to three-hour serious twists and turns on rugged canyon roads, as well as two-hour moderate excursions, which offer a little of everything.

The trips are not just about riding in a cool-looking vehicle (although that counts) or gaping at the spectacular mountain scenery of forest, lakes, streams, canyons, and more (although that really counts). The trips also incorporate learning about the environment and the history the land and people - Native American, old pioneers, and miners. Note that a minimum of four adults (or the price for four adults) are needed for a tour, although the owner will try to find other passengers if your numbers are too few. You will be picked up at your place of lodging or at BIG BEAR DISCOVERY CENTER.

Hours: Call to schedule a tour.
Price: $20 per person per hour for adults; $10 per hour for ages 4 - 12; children 3 and under are free.
Ages: 4 years and up, depending on the excursion.

BIG BEAR PARASAIL AND WATERSPORTS

(909) 866-IFLY (4359) / www.bigbearparasail.net
439 Pine Knot Boulevard, Big Bear Lake

Ever had dreams where you can fly? Parasailing is the next best thing. Start off (and end) on the boat's landing platform, attached by a harness to the parasail and by a tow rope to the boat. As the boat pulls away, you are lifted into the air for ten minutes of flight. You can stay dry if you want, and if all goes well, or take a quick dip (more like a toe touch) in the lake before being airborne again. This is a thrill-seeking experience for kids and adults.

You may also rent wave runners here at $109 an hour (for three people) and/or take an exhilarating (i.e. really fast!) jet boat ride here - $29 for adults; $19 for children 12 and under. See PINE KNOT LANDING BOAT RENTALS (pg. 456) for details about other activities offered in this marina.

Hours: Seasonal only - late spring through early fall - Mon. - Fri., 9am - 5pm; Sat. - Sun., 8am - 6pm.
Price: Parasailing is $79 for single; $129 for tandem (go with your child!); $20 for an observer just riding on the boat.

Ages: 90 pounds and up.

BIG BEAR SOLAR OBSERVATORY   ☀

(909) 866-5791 / www.bbso.njit.edu $

40386 North Shore Lane, Big Bear Lake

The world's largest solar telescope, 1.6 meters, is housed in the dome-shaped observatory located on a strip of land that juts into Big Bear Lake. The observatory offers a unique way to study the often sunny skies (300 days on average) in Big Bear. Opening the shutter allows sunlight in, at almost any angle, to strike the central mirror of the telescope. Other observatory instruments also monitor and record often dramatic images of the sun, which are then displayed on video monitors. Cameras can show sharper details than the unaided eye can see. Take a forty-five-minute tour to get the hot facts about the sun. School groups may call to schedule an appointment.

Hours: Open July 4th through Labor Day, Sat., 4pm - 6pm.

Price: $2 for adults; $1 for children.

Ages: 8 years and up.

BIKING

www.bigbearinfo.com/bike.html; www.mybikesite.com; www.bigbearhostel.com

There are several places to rent mountain bikes and helmets; most include a free bike map of the area. Pedal your way across town, down a mountain, or along forest trails. Some of the rental shops also offer guided tours. This list is not exhaustive by any means, but includes several favorite trails.

BIKE TRAILS

BIG BEAR LAKE:

Alpine Pedal Path

A five-mile (round trip), very easy, asphalt path that meanders along the north shore of Big Bear Lake. (You'll share this path with joggers, skaters, and strollers.) It starts (or stops) at Stanfield Cutoff and ends (or begins) near the solar observatory, connecting with the BIG BEAR DISCOVERY CENTER (pg. 445), as well.

John Bull Loop Bike Trail

This almost fifteen-mile intermediate loop starts at the base of Van Dusen Canyon, climbs up for several miles to Holcomb Valley, becomes level for a stretch, and then ends with the road being steep and rutted.

Snow Summit Adventure Park

Catch a ride up the mountain and cruise across and down over forty miles of trails. The terrain varies, meaning that trails range from easy, wide, forest service roads to arduous, single-track, dirt trails so there are routes for the novice, intermediate, and advanced riders. The Grand View Pointe Loop, one of the most popular routes, is nine miles long and great for intermediate riders. Seven miles of serious downhill trails await experienced mountain bikers. Those who prefer flatter trails may skip the sky chair entirely and bike beginner-friendly trails running through and from the base area of the resort, including Bristlecone Trail and Towne Trail. See more under SNOW SUMMIT ADVENTURE PARK (pg. 458) and check www.bigbearmountainresorts.com for more details.

BIKE RENTALS

BIG BEAR LAKE:

Bear Valley Bikes - (909) 866-8000 / www.bvbikes.com

40298 Big Bear Boulevard, across Alpine Slide and Magic Mountain Recreation Area

Bear Valley has mountain bikes, tandems cycles, BMX bikes, trailers for children, toddler bikes, and helmets.

Open daily, 10am - 5pm. Call for hours, just to be on the safe side.

Mountain bikes are $10 an hour; tandems are $20 an hour; kids bikes and trailers are $9 an hour.

Chains Required Bike Shop - (909) 878-3280 / www.chainsrequiredbikeshop.com

41869 Big Bear Boulevard

Bicycle repairs as well as rentals of full suspension, $11 - $16 an hour; K2 comfort bike, $9 an hour; Tandem, $15 an hour; and children's K2, $9 an hour.

Open Mon. - Fri., 9am - 6pm; Sat., 8am - 6pm; Sun., 8am - 5pm, weather permitting. Open earlier in the summer, about 7:30am.

Snow Summit Rental Shop - (888)-SUMMIT-1 (786-6481) or (909) 866-5766 / /www.bigbearmountainresorts.com

880 Summit Boulevard, at the base of Snow Summit.

For those serious about mountain biking, the shop has a full line of bikes and protective equipment to rent. Freeride or cross country full suspension bikes, for instance, begin at $69 for 3 hours for bike rental and a lift ticket pass up Snow Summit mountain to ride its trails.
Open mid- April - September, daily.

CHILDREN'S FOREST

(909) 382-2773 or (909) 867-5996- children's forest; (909) 382-2600 - national forest service /
www.mountainsfoundation.org
Keller Peak Road, Running Springs

The small, Children's Forest Visitor Information Center is located at the gateway to the Children's Forest, which is a spread of 3,400 acres within the San Bernardino National Forest. The center, staffed primarily by youths, offers information on recreation opportunities in the forest, education programs, the opportunity to purchase the Adventure Pass, themed workshops, and more. There are a few displays of local flora and fauna and a hands-on nature table.

Drive four very winding miles on the narrow Keller Peak Road (or hike or bike it if you're brave) to reach the Children's Forest Interpretive Trail. Note: Drive another mile on the road to reach KELLER PEAK FIRE LOOKOUT TOWER (pg. 452). At the trailhead there are a few picnic tables and restrooms and a drinking fountain. Use a self-guided brochure as you walk the mildly hilly, three-quarter-miles of looping paved trails that are also readily stroller and wheel-chair accessible; ideal for younger children. Among the scrubs and, further in, the pine trees and by a pretty lake and boulder formations, be on the lookout for wildlife such as birds, deer, squirrels, unusual insects, etc. Interpretive trail signs designed by children help mark the paths and tell stories of the plants and animals. A longer hiking option is the 4.5-mile Exploration Trail that winds through backcountry. More mileage, but still family friendly. Don't forget to pack lunch, water, sunscreen, and binoculars. With all that it offers and set in such beautiful surroundings, I'm glad the Children's Forest is open to adults, too!

The main purpose of the information center is to encourage children to develop a passion for the environment by training youth naturalists and offering opportunities for kids to take a hike. There are several outstanding educational programs offered through this center, both to the public and to school groups. A sampling includes Forest Ecology - learning how plants and animals depend on each other for survival; Finding the Wild Things - learning how animals adapt to the environments, where they live, what they eat, and how to read the signs of their presence; Soil Erosion - physically working to prevent soil erosion; and Charting Your Course - learning map and compass reading techniques. Seasonal snowshoe field trips are available to aid in learning about winter ecology. Get a workout while following animal tracks! School exploration programs are offered Monday through Friday, year round. Each program is four hours long. The majority of the time is spent in the forest, plus there are games and hands-on activities.

Hours: The visitor's center is only open May - September, Sat. - Sun., 9am - 5pm. Keller Peak Road, the paved trail, and this part of the forest are open in the spring, summer, and fall daily, sunrise - sunset. It's closed in winter. Call for a schedule of programs.
Price: $5 per vehicle per day to stop anywhere in the forest. Call for various program prices.
Ages: All for the hiking trails, depending on which one you choose. Age requirements vary for the programs.

COWBOY EXPRESS STEAK HOUSE

(909) 866-1486 / www.cowboyexpresssteakhouse.com
40433 Lake View Drive, Big Bear Lake

Rustle up some good lunch or dinner grub in this rustic, cowboy-themed restaurant. Eat inside and enjoy the ambiance or enjoy the lake view outside. Some enticing entrees include T-bone steaks, $26.95; chicken steak, $21.95; St. Louis bbq beef back ribs, $24.95; fettuccini Alfredo with chicken, $16.95; steak and fried shrimp, $24.95; hamburgers, $9.95; buffalo burgers, $10.95. Children can choose chicken strips, cheeseburger, corn dog, pork ribs, shrimp, or steak for $8.95. All kids' meals come with fries, a drink, and a dessert.

Hours: Open daily, 11am - 9pm. Closed Easter, Thanksgiving, and Christmas.
Price: Menu prices listed above.
Ages: All

GREEN VALLEY LAKE

(909) 867-2009 or (909) 867-2165 - lake info.; (877) 444-6777 - camping reservations /
www.green-valley-lake.com; www.mountaininfo.com

Green Valley Lake Road, Green Valley

Can you keep a secret? This somewhat secluded, small, and pristine, ten-acre, private lake is an ideal and idyllic spot, especially for younger children. Surrounded by pine and oaks trees, families can swim at the little beach that has a lifeguard; rent canoes, kayaks, and peddle boats (no motorized or personal boats allowed); fish for trout (the lake is stocked); enjoy a picnic and/or barbecue meal; and hike or bike on the mile-long, looping, dirt path that goes through the forest and around the lake. At the Sports Court play volleyball, basketball, tennis, and badminton. A convenience store, bait shop, and bike rental place (open July through Labor Day) are available. A fishing license is required for fishermen 16 years and over.

About a half mile from the lake is a campground. The almost forty campsites are snuggled amongst tall pine trees, with a meadow close by. Reservations are recommended. Also, if you're in the area check out the free, small Lilleberg Museum at 33659 Green Valley Lake Road. It displays the history of the mountain area in pictorials and dioramas as well as a few pieces of equipment such as an old telephone system and train apparatus. The museum is open on Saturdays from 2pm to 4pm. Note that the town of Green Valley has only 400 permanent residents.

Hours: The lake is open daily May - October, 5am - 8pm.

Price: Day use is free. The swim beach is $5 for adults; $3 for ages 13 and under. Fishing costs $15 for adults (plus a license); $10 for ages 15 and under. Kayaks are $7 an hour for a single; $10 an hour for a double. Peddle boats are $12 an hour. Row boats are $10 for the first hour. Camping is $20 a night, $2 extra for holiday usage, plus a $9 reservation fee.

Ages: All

HIKING

(909) 866-3437 - Big Bear Discovery Center; (909) 382-2782 - Arrowhead Ranger Station; (909) 382-4802 - national forest / www.mountainsfoundation.org; www.bigbearinfo.com; www.mountaininfo.com

There are many, *many* places to go hiking in the Big Bear Lake and Lake Arrowhead areas. In Big Bear Lake, visit the BIG BEAR DISCOVERY CENTER (pg. 445), a ranger station where you can obtain trail maps. In Lake Arrowhead, visit the Arrowhead Ranger District at 28104 Highway 18 in Skyforest for maps and other information. Several hiking trails are associated with or begin (or end) with some of the campgrounds in Lake Arrowhead and the surrounding areas, as well. Note: Anywhere you park in the national forest for recreational reasons, you must pay $5 a car for an Adventure Pass. Take necessary precautions while hiking and always bring water. I've listed just a few of the trails my family has enjoyed trekking.

Hiking Trails

BIG BEAR LAKE:

(Also see BIKING on page 448, as biking trails can usually be hiked as well, especially the very easy and accessible Alpine Pedal Path.)

Castle Rock:

(FROM HIGHWAY 18, THE TRAILHEAD IS ABOUT ONE MILE EAST PAST THE DAM. PARKING IS VERY LIMITED ON THE HIGHWAY.)

The trail is only eight-tenths of a mile, but it is an uphill walk over some rocky terrain. The destination is Castle Rock, a large rock that kids love to climb on. Its name gives lead to a lot of imaginative play time here. All of my kids wanted to be king - what a surprise! If everyone still has the energy, keep hiking back to the waterfalls, and/or to Devil's Woodpile. The scenery along the way is spectacular.

Cougar Crest Trail:

(THE TRAIL STARTS JUST WEST OF THE BIG BEAR DISCOVERY CENTER - SEE PAGE 445 FOR DIRECTIONS AND DETAILS.)

This four-and-a-half-mile (about three hour) moderate to difficult hike goes up a gentle hill, but it does get you out of breath at this altitude. Note that there is very little shade along this route. It ends at the juncture of the Pacific Crest Trail. (See the next few entries below for more information on this trail.) If you can, however, hike another half mile to reach the summit of Bertha Peak (where the transmitting equipment interferes slightly with the wilderness perspective) for an almost 360-degree view of Bear Valley and Holcomb Valley, and even the Mojave Desert on a clear day.

Pineknot Trail:

(FROM HIGHWAY 18, EXIT SOUTH ON MILL CREEK ROAD AND LOOK FOR THE TRAILHEAD.)

For a panoramic view of Big Bear Lake and the surrounding San Bernardino Mountains, hike this moderate to difficult, six-mile round-trip trail. It begins at the Aspen Glen Picnic Area, winding from the valley amongst white fir and Jeffrey pines up to the ridgeline at Grand View Point, where you deserve to rest and eat snacks that you've packed in.

Snow Summit Adventure Park:

Look up this entry on page 458 for details about the over forty miles of trails around the Snow Summit mountain.

Woodland Trail:

(ON HIGHWAY 38, PARKING IS ALMOST DIRECTLY ACROSS THE STREET FROM M.D. BOAT RAMP, JUST WEST OF THE STANFIELD CUTOFF ROAD.)

This one-and-a-half-mile loop is an easy walk, as the dirt trail follows more along the side of the mountain, rather than into the mountain. Although you can hear the traffic from certain sections of the trail, the changing landscape, from pine trees to coastal shrub to cactus, still offers the sense of being immersed in nature. An interpretative trail guide is available through the Ranger Station. Make it an educational field trip as well as a nice walk!

LAKE ARROWHEAD:

Some of the trails that I've not mentioned below, such as Crab Creek Trail and Seeley Creek Trail, are beautiful, but know that the trail passes crosses through a creek, which can be fun, but can be dangerous for kids when the water runs high.

Children's Forest: (See the entry for CHILDREN'S FOREST on page 449 for details.)

Heap's Peak Arboretum:

(JUST OFF HIGHWAY 18, ABOUT A MILE-AND-A-HALF EAST OF SKYFOREST.)

This almost-a-mile, relatively easy loop begins on pavement and continues on hard-packed dirt the rest of the way. The trail winds through tall Sequoias and pine trees, past wildflowers (depending on the season), over a creek, and alongside numerous native plants. It is never quite completely quiet as the highway noise filters through the forest, but it is still beautiful and serene. Pick up a brochure that highlights the botanical points of interest to make the walk a learning experience as well as a nature excursion.

Indian Rock Trail

(ON HWY. 173, EAST OF ROCK CAMP STATION.)

This very, easy half-mile walk is educational in that it leads to the bedrock mortars used by the Serrano Indians to grind acorns. A stone monument here depicts the encampment of the Serrano Indians.

North Shore Recreational Trail:

(TRAVELING NORTH ON HWY. 18, TURN L. ON HWY. 173 FOR 1.6 MILES, R. AT THE STOP SIGN, STILL ON HWY. 173, R. ON HOSPITAL RD. AND ENTER THE NORTH SHORE CAMPGROUND. OR GO EAST ON TORREY RD., OPPOSITE THE LAKE ARROWHEAD MARINA AND FOLLOW THE DIRT ROAD ½ A MILE UNTIL YOU REACH THE TRAILHEAD.)

Not quite two miles long, this scenic trail is moderately difficult as it takes you over hills, down into the forest, past boulders, and along Little Bear Creek. There you'll catch up to a forest service road.

Pacific Crest National Scenic Trail:

This 2,600-mile long (yes, you read that correctly) trail, reaches from Canada to Mexico - not quite a day hike. About forty miles traverse the Big Bear/Arrowhead Ranger District. If that's still too much of a hike (which it is for me), there are several portions of it to enter and exit and still get in some decent, but not exhausting, hiking time. How fun to be a part of something so huge! Contact the ranger station using the phone numbers or websites listed above for details and maps.

Hours: Open daily, sunrise - sunset.

Price: $5 a day per car for an Adventure Pass. (The pass allows you to park on and hike in national forest land.)

Ages: 4 years and up.

HOLLOWAY'S MARINA AND RV PARK AND BOAT RENTALS

(800) 448-5335 or (909) 866-5706 - Marina and RV; (909) 878-4FUN (4386) - kayaks, canoes, wave runners rentals - North Shore Landing / www.bigbearboating.com

398 Edgemoor Road, Big Bear Lake

Holloway rents flat-bottomed pontoons that hold up to twelve people for $75 an hour. Aluminum motorized fishing boats start at $28 for two hours; waverunners start at $80 an hour; kayaks and canoes start at $20 an hour. Look up TIME BANDIT (pg. 459) for information on taking a tour on board a cool-looking pirate ship that departs from this marina.

The adjacent RV park has all the amenities including a playground, horseshoe pits, basketball court, small convenience store, showers, and place to do laundry.

Hours: Open April - October, 6am - sunset, weather permitting.
Price: Prices are mentioned above, but they vary quite a bit, so call first. RV camping is $25 - $40 a night.
Ages: 2 years and up, depending.

HOT SHOT MINIATURE GOLF COURSE

(909) 866-7333

42143 Big Bear Boulevard, Big Bear Lake

Putt around under shady pine trees and a few building structures such as a lighthouse and log cabin at this basic, but fun miniature golf course. Encourage your kids to be hot shots here!

Hours: Open daily seasonally, weather permitting, 10:30am - dusk, though sometimes they stay open later. Closed during the winter.
Price: $5 for adults; $4 for ages 12 and under and seniors.
Ages: 3 years and up.

KELLER PEAK FIRE LOOKOUT TOWER

(909) 382-2600 / www.mountainsfoundation.org/fire-lookouts/keller-peak

Keller Peak Road, Running Springs

This is a hot ticket: You can see the world, or a good portion of it, from lookout towers, which were originally designed in the 1920's and 1930's to aid rangers in spotting forest fires. The towers were strategically built on the highest points of the mountains. This also means that they are located off the beaten track and incorporate a drive on a winding road. Keller Peak is about five miles off Highway 18; five miles of narrow, winding mountain roads with no guards rails, but breath-taking views. (Or maybe it's the drive that takes your breath away!)

Visitors are now encouraged to visit the towers, climb up the steep ladder (which may be scary for younger kids and older adults), go into the small observation room (only five visitors are allowed in the tower at a time), see the equipment, perhaps even try the Osborne Fire Finder, and enjoy the vista. On a clear day, of which morning times are best, you can see incredibly far. Bring binoculars or borrow ones at the towers. Volunteer staff are on hand to explain the equipment, history of fire lookouts, and the process and procedures for putting them out. Kids receive Smokey Bear fire prevention materials to take home. While you're here, make sure to hike the CHILDREN'S FOREST (pg. 449) trail, which is one mile back on Keller Peak Road. Note - you won't be here long, but it is an interesting stop.

Hours: Open during fire season - Memorial Day through October daily, 9am - 5pm.
Price: $5 for an Adventure Pass
Ages: 6 years and up.

LAKE ARROWHEAD QUEEN

(909) 336-6992 / www.lakearrowheadqueen.com; www.mountaininfo.com

28200 Hwy. 189, Lake Arrowhead

Cruise around beautiful Lake Arrowhead during a fifty-minute narrated tour on board a restored paddle boat. Guides share the history of the 100-year-old lake and the city, and tidbits about some of the old-time celebrities that used to live here. You'll see the many gorgeous homes/mansions that dot the shoreline. Kids are invited to help steer the boat. See the next entry for details about Lake Arrowhead Village.

Hours: Open April - October, daily, 10am - 5pm (last tour); November - May, daily (weather dependent), 11am - 3:30pm (last tour). Tours leave every ninety-minutes.
Price: $16 for adults; $14 for seniors; $12 for ages 2 - 12; children under 2 are free.
Ages: 7 years and up.

LAKE ARROWHEAD VILLAGE

(909) 337-2533 - village info; (909) 337-3715 - visitors's center; (909) 337-2999 - Lollipop Park /
www.thelakearrowheadvillage.com; www.lakearrowhead.net; www.lollipoppark.com

28200 Hwy. 189, Lake Arrowhead

!/$$

Built on the lake's peninsula, this two-level, open-air Village has over fifty shops (including outlet stores) and eateries, plus some fun activities for the family, making it a worthy destination. Some of the kid-friendly shops include Mr. G's for Toys and Rocky Mountain Chocolate Factory, which is an adult-friendly shop as well. From May through Labor Day free concerts are given on the center lawn every Friday and Saturday night, and occasionally on Sundays and Mondays, starting at 6:30pm. The north section of the Village holds a small, fenced-in park with a grass area and free playground, and Lollipop Park, which is a kiddie amusement park. Fun attractions at Lollipop Park include a nine-hole miniature golf course, $4 per person; village train ride, $4; bumper cars; go-carts, $7 for the driver and $3 for a passenger; plus, for little ones only, a small, horse carousel; swing ride; mini train ride; and a pirate ship that swings up and down. The cost is $3 per child per ride, or four rides for $10.

For food, try the family-owned Lake Arrowhead Pizza, Deli and Arcade on the second story. Menu choices include a hand-tossed, medium cheese pizza for about $16, plus pastas, salads, sandwiches, and appetizers. There is an arcade room and eleven TV screens inside, including one huge screen, but a much better picture is found by sitting at an outside table: The view of the lake is stunning. Call (909) 337-0723 for more information.

McKenzies Water-Ski School and LAKE ARROWHEAD QUEEN tour boat (see above entry) are also located and launched here. With all there is to see and do at the Village, you could easier spend a day or two learning, playing, eating, and shopping.

Hours: Most stores are open daily, 10am - 6pm. Closed Christmas. Lollipop Park is open September - May, Thurs. - Sun., 10am - 5pm; open Memorial Day - Labor Day, Sun. - Thurs., 10am - 6pm; Fri. - Sat., 10am - 8pm. It is also open on school holidays - call for hours.
Price: Free, but bring spending money. Prices are listed above for the amusement park.
Ages: All

LAKE GREGORY

(909) 338-2233 - Lake Gregory; (909) 338-2731 - Camp Switzerland / www.sbcounty.gov;
www.campswitzerland.net; www.crestlinechamber.net

24171 Lake Drive, Crestline

$$$

Crestline is a little mountain town that people usually just pass through on their way to Lake Arrowhead or Big Bear Lake. The mid-size Lake Gregory is located near the edge of town, nestled in the foothills of the San Bernardino mountains. During the summer months, a four-acre section of the waveless water is roped off for swimmers and paddle boarders, and is patrolled by lifeguards. The long, thin paddle boards rent for $5 a half hour and must be handled with some finesse if you want to stay topside. Another aquatic option is a 300-foot-long, twisting water slide that ends in a small "pool." Barbecue pits and picnic tables are available at the two smallish swim beaches (across the lake from each other), as are sand volleyball courts, a basketball court, and horseshoe pits. You may bring in ice chests, but no glass containers or alcohol. Two snack bars are here, too.

The rest of the lake is open year round for boating and fishing for trout, bass, catfish, crappie, carp and bluegill. Note that there is free Youth Fishing Derby every June for kids 15 years and under with cash prizes. The on-site bait and tackle shop rents poles. Rowboat rentals are available for $30 for a half day. Seasonal boat rentals include canoes, kayaks, and windsurfers. Pedal boats, which seat four people, and Aqua Cycles (i.e., big-wheel-type water cycles that seat two people) both use pedal power and rent for $10 a half hour, per. They are available daily in the summer and on weekends through October.

There are over two miles of hiking trails that stretch around a good portion of the lake with ten fitness stations along the way. Camping at Camp Switzerland (not the country) is just across the street. This shady canyon and wooded campground offers forty campsites and trailer sites, as well as two adjoining cabins for rent.

Hours: The lake is open daily, sunup to sundown for fishing. Boating activity is open the end of April - September. The swim beach and water slide is open Memorial Day - Labor Day daily, 10am - 5pm.

Price: $5 for ages 4 and up for the swim beach; $2 for seniors; children 3 and under are free. Swim admission and all-day water slide pass is $7. A permit is needed for fishing for ages 16 and up - $11.05. A California state license is not necessary. $5 per vehicle in the gated lots. Camping is $35 for tents; hook-ups start at $40 a night; cabins (they sleep 4) are $85 a night - all prices are slightly higher on holiday weekends.

Ages: All

MCDILL SWIM BEACH and MEADOW PARK

(909) 866-9700 / www.bigbearparks.com; www.bigbearlake.net

41220 Park Avenue, Big Bear Lake

This waveless lagoon, with a lifeguard on duty, offers a refreshing respite during the hot summer months. Kids can play in the water, which is a little warmer than the general lake temperature, or build castles on the sandy beach. Swimmers enjoy going beyond the roped area, out to the floating dock which has a huge inflatable slide (with a triangle-shaped base to climb into), and a floating trampoline. A small playground, a volleyball court, a grass area, picnic tables, barbecue pits, a restroom, and a snack bar (selling candy and drinks) round out the facilities at this beach. And the view of the mountains is spectacular! Children 10 years and under must be supervised by an adult.

Meadow Park is just outside the Swim Beach fence. This large, grassy park has a multi-level playground with twisty, tubular slides, ramps, and other fun elements, plus nice tennis courts, volleyball courts, baseball diamonds, and horseshoe pits. Bring a picnic dinner to cook at the barbecue pits, and enjoy the sunset.

Hours: The swim beach is open Memorial Day - mid-June on weekends only, noon - 5pm; open mid-June - Labor Day, Thurs. - Mon., noon - 5pm (closed Tues. and Wed.). The park is open daily, sunrise - sunset.

Price: The swim beach is $5 for adults; $4 for seniors and ages 3 - 12; $1 for children 2 and under. The park is free.

Ages: All

MILLCREEK MANOR TEA ROOM

(909) 866-8066 / www.bigbeardining.com/teahouse.html

39904 Big Bear Boulevard, Big Bear Lake

Don't wait for serendipi*tea;* make a plan to visit this absolutely charming, English country tea house decorated with antiques. A corner stone fireplace adds to the warm ambiance. Hutches and shelves are filled with tea bric-a-brac, while the pictures, plates, and wallpaper reflect this theme as well. Many of the items on display are for sale.

The Tea Room is not just for tea, as it has an extensive lunch menu, including salad (around $9.75); chili or soup (about $7.95); hot and cold sandwiches, such as barbeque pork, pastrami, chicken salad, or turkey ($9.50 to $11.75); and quiche and crepes. Homemade desserts include scones, cheese, fruit pie, strawberry shortcake, and chocolate fondue. A children's menu offers chicken nuggets with mac and cheese, grilled cheese sandwich, or PB&J ($5.75). High Tea is like a five-course meal. It comes with soup; muffins; a petite salad; assorted finger sandwiches; quiche; scones with dotted cream and jam; gingerbread; and tea. The cost is $26.99 per person. Afternoon Tea is more of a light meal with finger sandwiches, quiche, scones with cream and jam, gingerbread, and tea. The cost is $19.75 per person. Reservations are required for the teas, but not for lunch. A small gift shop with a variety of tea paraphernalia and soaps and such is also in-house.

Hours: Open Wed. - Sun., 11am - 4pm; tea is served at 1:30pm and reservations are needed. Breakfast is served on the weekends from 9am - noon. Closed Mon. and Tues.

Price: See menu prices above.

Ages: 7 years and up.

MOONRIDGE ANIMAL PARK and ZOO

(909) 878-4200 or (909) 584-1299 / www.bigbearzoo.com

43285 Goldmine Drive, Big Bear Lake

Get a little wild up in the mountains! About 150 animals find sanctuary in this small animal park. They are usually from the surrounding mountains and need extra care because they've mostly been orphaned or hurt. Several grizzly bears, plus snow leopards, black bears, timber wolves, fishers, coatimundi, bison, coyotes, bobcats, raccoons, foxes, deer, and birds of prey such as eagles, hawks, and owls now consider this their home. It's just the right size for kids to

walk around easily, and since the enclosures are not too large, it's easy to see the animals up close. You can also walk through a flight enclosure that holds shore and other aquatic birds. And don't missss the reptile room where snakes and tarantulas live.

Special, daily events include animal presentations at noon, where an animal is brought out and talked about, and an animal feeding tour. The forty-five-minute educational feeding tour is given at 3pm daily (except on Wednesdays) most of the year, and on weekends only in the winter. It takes place at each cage. As the animals are fed (mush, dead chicks, and other stuff) a staff member explains why the animal is here, its habits, and more. We've always found the docents and trainers willing, even eager, to answer our kids' questions, so it makes our visit here more memorable. The animal park also offers lots of seasonal special programs, such as Flashlight Safaris, tasty Ice Cream Safaris, and day camps. Traveling exhibits are offered to school groups.

A small, grassy picnic area inside the zoo has a few picnic tables. The lobby doubles as an educational center with a few nature exhibits such as bird eggs and nests, fossils, animal jawbones, and live bunnies and snakes (but not in the same enclosure).

Hours: Open May - August daily, 10am - 5pm. Open September - April daily, Mon. - Fri., 10am - 4pm; Sat. - Sun., 10am - 5pm, weather permitting.
Price: $9 for adults; $6 for seniors and ages 3 - 10; children 2 and under are free.
Ages: All

MOUNTAIN SKIES ASTRONOMICAL SOCIETY ASTRONOMY VILLAGE

(909) 336-1699 / www.mountain-skies.org $$$
2001 Observatory Way, Lake Arrowhead

Observe the universe, or parts of it, from the astronomy village which consists of two main buildings - a combination gift shop/library/research facility, and a 500-square-foot observatory that houses a 16", F/10 Schmidt-Cassegrain with a top mount of a 4" refractor. Purchase a piece of space at the gift shop such as asteroid pieces, blue smoke, and rare, space shuttle memorabilia. The small library/museum has several shelves of books and videos regarding astronomy, as well as a few displays of meteors, Mars rocks, Apollo display models, and signed astronaut photographs. There are picnic tables outside, too.

The best time to visit is on a Saturday night for the Sky Quest Program. This two-and-a-half hour program starts off with a lecture, discussion, and question and answer time. A half-hour slide show follows. A powerful laser pointer is used to point out constellations, specific stars, and other cosmic happenings outside. Finally, guests have the opportunity to look through the telescope. Topic titles include Exploring the Known Universe, Meteorites, Basic Astronomy, and How to Use a Telescope. Ask about school education programs and workshops, other special events, and teacher resource equipment.

Hours: Open Wed., Fri. - Sat., 11am - 2pm. Sky Quest Programs for the public are offered on selected Sat. evenings, usually once a month.
Price: Free to walk around and visit. Sky Quest Programs are $7 for adults; $5 for ages 16 and under. Prepurchase tickets or pay $2 more at the door.
Ages: 6 years and up.

MOUNT WATERMAN SCENIC RIDES

(818) 790-2002; (619) 708-6595 / www.mtwaterman.org $$$
Angeles Crest Hwy/CA 2, La Canada Flintridge

Mount Waterman does have ski lifts, but in the summer time, it's also a great place to go mountain biking on groomed trails, or even just enjoy a fourteen-minute lift ride to the top to take in some fabulous scenery (and fresh air). The Warming Hut at the top serves food and drinks, and has picnic tables outside among the trees.

Hours: Open seasonally, Fri. - Sun., 9am - 4pm.
Price: Scenic lift, no bikes - $10 for adults; $5 for seniors and ages 7 - 12 years; children 6 and under are free. Mt. bike lift tickets are $20 for one ride; $40 for all day.
Ages: 2 years and up for just the scenic lift ride.

NORTH SHORE LANDING

(909) 878-4FUN (4386) / www.bigbearboating.com $$$$$
North Shore Drive, about 2 miles off Hwy 38, Fawnskin

North Shore Landing is associated with Holloways Marina and R.V. Park on the other side of the lake. Boat rentals here include pontoons, that seat up to fourteen people, for $80 an hour; speedboats, starting at $90 an hour; and kayaks and canoes for $20 an hour per.

Hours: Open early April - October, 6am - sunset, weather permitting.
Price: See prices above and note that they may vary.
Ages: 4 years and up, depending on the boat choice.

PINE KNOT LANDING BOAT RENTALS / MISS LIBERTY CRUISE ☼

(909) 866-6463 or (909) 866-7766 or (909) 866-BOAT (2628) / www.pineknotlanding.com; $$$$
www.pineknotmarina.com
400 Pine Knot Avenue, Big Bear Lake

Boat rentals here are "knot" a problem! Cruise around on your own via a ten-passenger pontoon boats at $114 an hour, or a twelve-passenger pontoon for about $125 an hour. Motorized fishing boats start at about $49 an hour for four passengers.

Come on board the double decker *Miss Liberty* paddlewheel boat for a ninety-minute, narrated excursion. Sit inside or out on the deck - the lower deck is enclosed and wheelchair accessible, while the upper deck is out in the open. Learn the history of the lake, famous people who have or still live here, and general information about Big Bear Lake Valley. You'll see million-dollar estates (which are something to gawk at), the Solar Observatory, brown (in the summer) ski slopes, other boaters, and fishermen. The *Miss Liberty* has a snack bar stocked with beverages, chips, cookies, and such. Another special way to tour the lake and enjoy a front row view of the surrounding purple mountains majesty is to go on a sunset cruise, which starts at 7:30pm.

Hours: The rentals are open seasonally, usually April - November, although hours fluctuate: Mon. - Fri., 6am - 7pm; Sat., Sun., and holidays, 6am - 8pm. Always call first! The *Miss Liberty* cruise is available June - September daily, at noon, 2pm, 4pm, and sometimes 6pm. The cruise is offered throughout the year on weekends only, if the minimum quota is met, which is twenty passengers. Note that reservations are necessary for most outings.
Price: The narrated *Miss Liberty* cruise is $20 for adults; $18 for seniors; $12 for ages 5 - 12; children 4 and under are free. Other prices are listed above.
Ages: 4 years and up.

PLEASURE POINT MARINA ☼

(909) 866-2455 / www.pleasurepointbbl.com $$$$
603 Landlock Landing Road, Big Bear Lake

What a pleasure to rent a boat from Pleasure Point Marina and tootle around Big Bear Lake. The starting rental price for pontoon boats (i.e., flat-bottomed) that hold up to eight people is $100 an hour; a twelve passenger, $130. Paddle boats, canoes, and single kayaks are $20 an hour per; double kayaks are $30. Battery-powered canoes are $40 an hour, and electric fun boats (with attached water squirters/cannons that shoot water as you direct the stream and the boat) are $35 an hour. Retail services here include purchasing fishing licenses, lake permits, bait and tackle, and snacks and drinks.

Hours: Open seasonally daily, 7am - 7pm.
Price: See above for prices.
Ages: 4 years and up, depending on the activity.

SKIING, SNOWBOARDING, SNOWSHOEING, SNOW PLAY ☼

The following is a list and quick bites of information on ski slopes and snow play areas in and $$$$$
around the Big Bear/Lake Arrowhead area because there's no business like snow business! The website: www.onthesnow.com/CS/skireport.html, is helpful for up-to-the-minute ski conditions. Also check www.mountaininfo.com. Ask each resort about beginner specials, other special promos, half-day tickets, and even a free lift ticket on your birthday.
SKIING / SNOWBOARDING:
Bear Mountain: 43101 Goldmine Drive - from Hwy. 18 to Big Bear Lake, R. on Moonridge Rd. and follow the signs - (909) 585-2519 or (909) 866-5766 / www.bearmountain.com. Bear Mountain has 12 lifts and 24 runs on 200 acres, with the longest run being 2 miles. Top elevation is 8,800 feet. The Park boasts a Superpipe for airdogs with 195 acres

of freestyle terrain that incorporates jumps, step-ups, step-downs, spines, rollers, a half-pipe, rails, and boxes. Non-holiday rates for all-day skiing are $60 for adults; $50 for ages 13 - 21; $27 for ages 7 - 12; children 6 and under are free, with a paying adult. Holiday rates and peak weekends are $75 for adults; $65 for ages seniors and ages 13 - 19; $32 for ages 7 - 12. (Ski free on your birthday.) Night skiing is available on Friday, Saturday, and holidays, 3pm - 9:30pm. On Friday it is $35 for adults; $30 for ages 13 - 21; $15 for ages 7 - 12. On Saturdays and holidays the prices are $45 for adults; $35 for ages 13 - 21; $25 for ages 7 - 12. Lift tickets are interchangeable with Snow Summit, and a free shuttle runs in between both mountains.

Mountain High: 24510 Hwy. 2 in Wrightwood - (888) 754-7878 or (760) 249-5808 / www.mthigh.com. Wrightwood has mountain conditions without the winding, mountain drive. (It's 20 minutes west off the I-15). It has 13 chairs and 47 runs on 220 acres. The elevation is 8,200 feet. Mt. High has three separate resorts - East, West, and North, offering a variety of skiing and snowboarding. Note: North is mostly beginner and intermediate terrain. Ski the mountains with free shuttles going in between the three resorts. Lift tickets (which are interchangeable among the resorts) Mon. - Fri. are $59 for adults; $49 for ages 13 - 21; $25 for children ages 7 - 12; ages 6 and under are free with a paying adult. On Sat. - Sun., $69 for adults; $49 for ages 13 - 17; $30 for kids. You may also pay incrementally for the number of runs you'll take, and use the unused portion the next time. (Ski free on your birthday.) Night skiing, 5pm - 10pm, is available at $30 - $35 per person.

Mount Baldy: from 10 Fwy, exit N. on Mountain Ave. and go N. on Mt. Baldy Rd. - (909) 981-3344 or (909) 982-0800 / www.mtbaldyskilifts.com. Mt. Baldy has 4 lifts and 26 runs. The elevation is 8,600 ft. Lift tickets are $69 for adults; $29 for seniors and ages 12 and under; $49 for ages 13 - 21. (Ski free on your birthday.) Lift tickets are also available by the hour, using a voucher system. Rides in the sky chairs are also available for non-skiers. Parking is $5. See MOUNT BALDY SCENIC LIFT RIDE (pg. 417) for more info.

Mount Waterman: exit 210 Freeway N. on 2 Fwy; it's E. of Wrightwood - (818) 790-2002 or (619) 708-6595 / www.mtwaterman.org. Mt. Waterman has 3 lifts and 25 runs on over 115 acres. It does not have a snow-making machine, so it isn't always open. The top elevation is a little more than 8,000 feet. Skiers can also go "tree skiing", meaning they can venture off the marked runs and go through the forest. Ski rentals are not available here, but they are just down the hill at Sport Chalet. Lift tickets are $40 (½ day) - $50 (full day) for adults; $20 for seniors; $30 (½ day) and $40 (full day) for ages 13 - 17; $20 for ages 7 - 12. The resort is usually open on weekends only, 9am - 4pm. See MOUNT WATERMAN SCENIC RIDES (pg. 455) for info on the summertime fun.

Snow Summit: 880 Summit Road - exit Big Bear Blvd. R. on Summit Blvd. in Big Bear Lake - (909) 866-5766 / www.snowsummit.com. Summit has 14 chairs and 31 runs on 240 acres. The elevation is 8,000 feet. Family Park is great for beginner snowboarders, while intermediate and advanced terrains are also here. See the Bear Mountain entry, above, as the prices are identical. Lift tickets are interchangeable with Bear Mountain and a free shuttle runs in between both mountains.

Snow Valley: on Hwy. 18, 5 miles E. of Running Springs - (909) 867-2751 / www.snow-valley.com. Snow Valley has 13 lifts and 27 runs on 240 acres. The elevation is 7,440 feet. The snowboarding parks have spines, rails, boxes, tabletops, and banks. Lift tickets are $57 on regular days, $69 on holidays, for adults; $47 - $59 for seniors and ages 13 - 19; $24 - $30 for ages 7 - 12; children 6 and under are free with a paying adult. Night skiing is also available at $12 more per person on select Fridays and Saturdays. Ski free on your birthday.

SNOWSHOEING:

Rim Nordic Ski Areas: on Hwy. 18, miles E. of Running Springs, across from Snow Valley Mt. Sports Park - (909) 867-2600 / www.rimnordic.com. They offer cross country skiing and snowshoeing, plus rentals, and have 10 miles of trails. Trail passes are $19 for adults; $12 for ages 11 - 16 years; children 10 and under are free. Cross country ski rentals (skis, boots and poles) or snowshoe rentals are $17 for ages 11 and up; $10 for children 10 and under. All snowshoers must purchase a trail pass. Open daily, 9am - 4pm. In the summer, the area offers mountain biking. Also see BIG BEAR DISCOVERY CENTER (pg. 445) for more information about trails.

SNOW PLAY:

Note: A National Forest Adventure Pass ($5) is required in the national forest while playing in the snow if you just along the side of the road.

Alpine Slide at Magic Mountain - See page 444 for details.

Big Bear Snow Play: 42825 Big Bear Blvd., Big Bear Lake - (909) 585-0075 / www.bigbearsnowplay.com. Two magic carpet lifts (i.e. like riding an uphill escalator), one covered with plexiglass, take tubers and tobogganers up the hill

where natural snow is helped by snow-making machines. This area has some of the longest tubing runs in Southern California. A heated base lodge is here, too. Open daily, November through Easter, 10am - 4pm. The cost is $25 per person, which includes inner tubes. Children 2 to 6 are free with a paying adult, but must ride on their lap (or purchase a separate ticket).

Mount Baldy: See Mount Baldy in the above section for location. (909) 981-3344 or (909) 982-0800 / www.mtbaldyskilifts.com You must purchase a scenic chair ride ticket to access the tubing park. All day tubing tickets are $15 for 42" and taller + $25 for the lift ticket; $5 for 36" to 42"+ $15 for the lift ticket, who need to ride with an adult. Parking is $5.

North Pole Tubing Park: See Mountain High in the above section for location. (888) 754-7878 or (760) 249-5808 / www.mthigh.com. This 20-acre tubing facility has 6 lanes and handle tows. It's open Sat. - Sun. and holidays, 9am - 4:30 through mid-March. Two-hour tube time (including the use of a tube) is $20 per person; all day is $35. For children 36" - 42", it is $15 all day, and they must accompany a parent in a separate tube; children under 36" are not allowed.

Snowdrift Winter Playground: Hwy. 18, 4 miles E. of Running Springs - (909) 867-2640 / www.snowdrift.net; www.mountaininfo.com/sledding.html. Tube down the 6 hills on your belly, Mon. - Fri., 10am - 4pm; Sat. - Sun., 9am - 5pm. Admission is $12 per person per hour. Children 36" and under are free with a paid adult. Cash only. Tubes are included - no private equipment allowed. No snowman making. Limited parking is available and is $5 on weekends and holidays.

Snow Valley - See Snow Valley in the above section for location. (909) 867-2751 / www.snow-valley.com. At the base of the mountain, Snow Play is open daily (in season), 10am - 4pm. On Fri., Sat., and Sun. the cost, which includes sleds (and a lift ride), is $31 for ages 7 and up; $19 for ages 6 and under. Holidays are $35 for 7 and up; $25 for 6 and under. On weekdays (no lift available), the cost is $19 for ages 7 and up; $15 for ages 6 and under.

SNOW SUMMIT ADVENTURE PARK / SCENIC SKY CHAIR

(909) 866 5766 / www.bigbearmountainresorts.com; www.snowsummit.com $$$$
880 Summit Boulevard, at Snow Summit ski area, Big Bear Lake

Do your kids appreciate the awesome scenery of mountains, trees, and Big Bear Lake, plus breathing clean air? If not, they'll still enjoy the mile-long, almost fifteen-minute (each way) life chair ride up the mountaintop. At the top, there is a picnic and barbecue area, so bring your own food, or purchase a cheeseburger, chicken sandwich, bratwurst, or smoked turkey wrap for about $9.95 each from the View Haus snack bar. What better way to spend a day than up here in a place readily described as "God's country".

As there are over forty miles of trails through the forest and wilderness areas, hikers and biking enthusiasts are in their element up here. The terrain varies, so hiking trails range from easy, wide, forest service roads to arduous, single-track, dirt trails. The most direct route is a service road that is one mile long. The Bike Park has great trails with elements for the intermediate and advanced (black diamond) biker with banked turns, switchbacks, drops, steps ups and bridges. Besides the three top-to-bottom trails for adventuresome bikers (and more on the way), there are also beginner trails at the top and at and around the bottom of the hill. Note that mountain bikes may be transported only up the sky chair; not down. Bike rentals, including those specifically designed for downhill riding, plus helmets (which are required for all riders), elbow and shin guards, chest protectors, etc., are available at the rental shop at the base of mountain, and elsewhere in town.

Hours: The Scenic Sky Chair operates mid-April - mid-June and early September - mid-October (or the beginning of ski season) on Fri. and Sun., 9am - 4pm; Sat., 9am - 5pm. It's open daily, mid-June - early September, Sun. - Fri., 9am - 4pm; Sat., 8am - 5pm, weather permitting.

Price: Round trip (no bike) or a one-way ride (with bike) - $16 for adults; $8 for ages 7 - 12; children 6 and under are free when accompanied by a paying adult. An all-day ride pass (with a bike) is $35 for adults; $22 for kids. The Lift and Lunch Packages starts at $24 for adults and $19 for kids that include a scenic round trip, plus lunch at View Haus, or a one-way ride with a bike and lunch.

Ages: 3 years and up.

STRAWBERRY PEAK FIRE LOOKOUT TOWER

(909) 382-2600 / www.mountainsfoundation.org $
Bear Springs Road, Twin Peaks

See KELLER PEAK FIRE LOOKOUT TOWER (pg. 452) for detailed information on fire towers. I think the

view and bragging rights of being able to say you were in a fire tower make the drive worth it, although you won't be here long. From the top of this tower you can see three lakes - Arrowhead, Gregory, and Silverwood.

Hours: Open a few weeks before Memorial Day through a few weeks after Labor Day on weekends and most weekdays (call first as it is staffed by volunteers), 9am - 5pm.
Price: $5 for an Adventure Pass
Ages: 6 years and up.

SUGARLOAF CORDWOOD CO.
(909) 866-2220
42193 Big Bear Boulevard, Big Bear Lake

!/$

The gigantic, wooden, chain-saw carvings of bears, Indians, and other figures, will attract your attention as you drive along Big Bear Boulevard. This unique store is worth a stop. Take a walk through the lot and inside the rooms to see smaller carvings and other unusual, artistic, gift items. Note that there is a similar store if you head west for a few blocks on Big Bear Boulevard.

Hours: Open most of the year, Mon. - Fri., 10am - 5pm; Sat. - Sun., 9am - 6pm. In the winter, the store is open daily, 10am - 5pm.
Price: Free
Ages: 3 years and up.

SUGARLOAF PARK
(909) 866-9700 / www.bigbearparks.com
44828 Baldwin Lane and Maple Lane, Big Bear Lake

It is a beautiful drive to this well-worn park, but where up here isn't the scenery beautiful? Sugarloaf Park has a softball field, a few tennis courts, a sand volleyball court, a basketball court, and playground equipment with slides, swings, a short rock climbing wall, spirals to climb on and twirl around. A picnic shelters, barbecue pits, and some exercise stations with some solid workout machines let you work off what you just ate. It also features a skate park with ramps, rails, quarter pipes, stairs, boxes, and plenty of skate around room.

Hours: Open daily, sunrise - sunset.
Price: Free
Ages: All

TIME BANDIT
(800) 448-5335 or (909) 878-4040 / www.bigbearboating.com
398 Edgemoor Road at Holloway's Marina, Big Bear Lake

$$$$

If it's adventure you're seekin' matey, then climb aboard and hoist the sails! This jet black, three-masted galleon is a one-third-scale replica of a 16th century pirate ship and it comes complete with its own crew of pirates, well, at least a captain. Sail across Big Bear Lake (which is kind of like sailing the seven seas, just a shorter trip) on a ninety-minute narrated cruise. Stops include the BIG BEAR DISCOVERY CENTER (pg. 445) and Whaler's Pointe restaurant. *Time Bandit*, named after the 1981 movie in which it was featured, often offers live entertainment at night. Overnight charters are available as the ship is equipped with a stateroom and bed, and bunk beds for kids.

Hours: Usually open Memorial Day - October, with tours leaving daily at 2pm. If enough people are signed up (the ship holds 25), tours also depart at 10am, noon, 4pm, and 6pm.
Price: $19 for adults; $16 for seniors; $12 for ages 12 and under. Infants or lap-sitting toddlers are free.
Ages: All

VICTORIA PARK CARRIAGES, LTD. / BEAR VALLEY STAGE LINES
(909) 584-2277 / www.buggies.com
on the corner of Pine Knot and Village Drive, Big Bear Lake

$$$$

There is no more elegant, storybook way to explore Big Bear than by horse and carriage. Take a ride through the village, and down to the lake. Carriages seat from four to seven people. Or, go for a whole different feel by taking on the West - ride a stagecoach! Coaches seat up to fifteen people. Book either vehicle for an hour, or just take a shorter, almost fifteen minute ride around town.

Hours: Shorter rides are available most weekends and holidays from 11am until no one else wants a ride. Call to make a reservation for longer carriage and stagecoach rides.

Price: Shorter rides in the stagecoach are $15 per adult; $8 for ages 13 and under, with a $40 minimum; in the carriage, $20 for adults; $10 for ages 13 and under, with a $40 minimum. Hour-long stagecoach rides are $250 an hour; a carriage ride, $300. Prices might fluctuate depending on date, time of day, and type of carriage.

Ages: 2 years and up.

WILDHAVEN RANCH

(909) 337-7389 or (909) 337-1391 / www.wildhaven.org

29450 Pineridge Drive, Cedar Glen

Wildhaven Ranch is a wildlife sanctuary for over twenty indigenous wild animals. The mission statement proclaims to "serve as stewards of God's creation through rescue, protection, and preservation of the earth's wild creatures." Most of the animals were brought here because they've been orphaned or injured and cannot be rehabilitated and released back to the wild. Others have imprinted with humans, so this is now their home. Species native to the San Bernardino mountains that can be seen include eagles, mule deer, raccoon, coyote, bobcat, black bear, and birds of prey such as owls, hawks, and falcons. Little Bear (who is a bear) is a favorite as this personable creature goes through paces of climbing up on a platform and plays with a ball for a food reward. We learned about California grizzly bears and their extinction; bear habitats and their habits in general; and the American Black bears that have "replaced" them in this ecosystem.

On a guided tour you'll see the animals in their enclosures and learn about their habits and value. Programs are generally a combination of a thirty-minute, or less, raptor presentation held in the barn and an hour walking tour. The Wings & Things presentation allows visitors to observe and learn about falcons, hawks, owls, eagles, and other birds of prey as handlers walk around with them. Paws & Claws features the indigenous mammals of the sanctuary - bear, bobcat, deer, coyote and raccoon. Another program offered during the week is Bear Watch - a time to watch a trainer interact with bears. Classes for schools can be arranged from 11 to 2 pm, before the wildlife are fed. Come to a presentation on the premises or have a presentation come to your school. Creation-based educational programs are available, as well. Volunteer opportunities abound, from helping with small tasks to completing internships.

Hours: Open most of the year for tours and presentations: Bear Watch - Mon., Wed. and Fri. at 1pm. Wings & Things and Paws & Claws - Sat. at 1pm. Reservations are necessary for all visits and tours.

Price: $10 for adults; $5 for ages 8 and under. Private tours for 2 - 10 guests are $100.

Ages: 4 years and up.

YOUNG EAGLES PROGRAM (Big Bear)

(909) 585-3219 / www.bigbearcityairport.com; www.youngeagles.org

501 W. Valley Boulevard, Big Bear City

See the entry for YOUNG EAGLES PROGRAM (Los Angeles County) on page 215 for details. No reservations needed.

Hours: Offered the second Sat. of each month, May - September, 9am - 11am.

Price: Free

Ages: 8- 17 years old.

SAN DIEGO COUNTY

San Diego is the site of the first permanent European settlement on the California coast - the West Coast equivalent of Jamestown. From coastal cities to beaches that are the epitome of California dreaming, the county is also home to Legoland; the extensive military base of Camp Pendleton and other San Diego bases; the enchanting town of Julian; Old Town San Diego, which is steeped in early California heritage; several missions founded by Father Junipero Serra; the resort town of La Jolla; and vast acres of trails to hike. A visit to this county probably wouldn't be complete without seeing the world-class San Diego Zoo, San Diego Zoo Safari Park, and/or SeaWorld, as well as some of the first-class museums located in the massive Balboa Park. Drive just to the south and go over the border to Mexico - into a whole other world.

Tip: Contact the San Diego Convention and Visitors Bureau at (619) 236-1212 / www.sandiego.org. because it offers discount coupons on attractions, tours, harbor cruises, trolley rides, restaurants, hotels, and more.

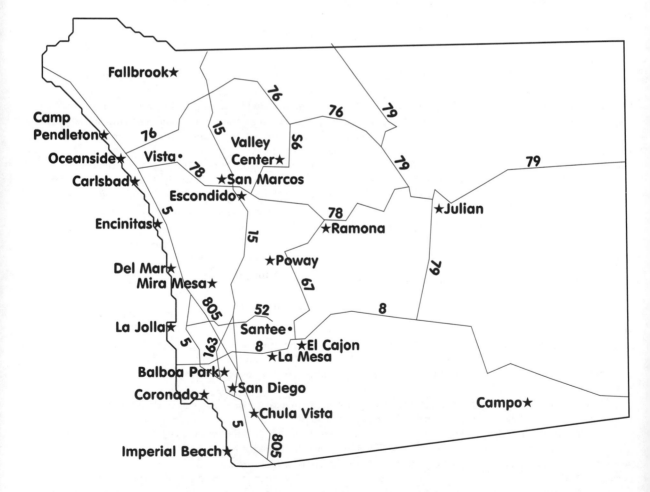

—AMUSEMENT PARKS—

AQUATICA SAN DIEGO

☼
$$$$$

(800) 257-4268 / www.aquaticabyseaworld.com
2052 Entertainment Circle, Chula Vista

G'day mates! Put on your togs (Australian slang for "swimsuit") and enjoy a bit of Australia in Southern California. San Diego's liquid gold attraction is very colorful, beautifully-landscaped, fun, and, most important, very wet. The park is spread over acres and acres of land with several groupings of waterslides. Guests can plunge down the sixteen twisty, water slides; both body and inner-tube raft rides. Some of the tubes are open, some are completely enclosed, and a few are long, straight, speed drops. Tassie's Twister is a two to four person enclosed raft ride that spits out riders into a massive funnel to be spun around and around, and eventually down into an exit pool. Another family-size raft ride, Walhalla Wave, is open-air and more gentle.

Ankle biters (Australian slang for "kids") thrill at the four-story, interactive, water play structure that has water hoses and jets, decent-sized slides, cargo nets to crawl and climb on, and bridges, all in shallow water. And watch out below! A huge bucket fills up and then turns over, dumping hundreds of gallons of water on unsuspecting (and suspecting) visitors. Another section for younger ones, Slippity Dippity, has a few short, wide slides all jutting out from one central rock formation, plus some waterfalls and a splash and swim area. There is also a very small pool just for relaxing. Or, really relax on a tube in Loggerhead Lane - a circular, slow-moving river that has a waterfall, plus palm trees and bushes that line the river banks.

Ride the waves at the enormous Big Surf Shores wave pool, where periodic swells can reach up to five feet high. Don't wipe out! Just outside the Shores area look for the display of live, fresh-water turtles, swimming in their own pool pond.

One of my favorite Sea World elements at Aquatica is the flurry (or flock) of flamingos that greet visitors as soon as they enter. Their (artificial) grassy enclosure also has a mini lagoon and they are just simply fascinating to watch.

The water park has plenty of lounge chairs and other seats mostly placed in sand, giving it an overall beachy feel. Aquatica also has lockers (fees start at $12), private cabanas for rent, free usage of life vests for all ages, and showers. If you get hungry, choose from several full-service eateries, or snack from one of the "stands" scattered throughout the park. No outside food is allowed inside. Have a ripper (i.e. fantastic) time!

Hours: Open Memorial Day - Labor Day daily, usually 10am - 6pm (open 10am - 7pm on certain weekends). Open in September - mid-October, Sat. - Sun., 10am - 5pm. Call or check the website first as hours fluctuate, especially due to concerts at the adjacent Sleep Train Amphitheater.

Price: $38 for ages 10 years and older; $30 for ages 3 - 9; children 2 and under are free. Parking is $15. Check out combo membership to SeaWorld and Aquatica

Ages: 2 years and up.

LEGOLAND

☼
$$$$$

(760) 918-LEGO (5346) / california.legoland.com
One Legoland Drive, Carlsbad

Lego mania reaches an all-time high at the 128-acre Legoland California which features over sixty family rides, shows, and interactive attractions, as well as areas to build and play with Legos™, and restaurants. (There are three other Legolands in the world.) Over thirty-five *million* Legos create the models used in and around this unique amusement park (and you will get tired of reading the word "Lego" by the end of this entry). The Lego builders really are incredible! Note that some of the rides have height restrictions. The following are some highlights of the main attraction areas:

Dino Island features Coastersaurus, which curves around animated and life-size Lego brick dinosaurs. Kids can try out paleontology skills digging for "skeletal" remains in sand pits.

Duplo Village has a boat ride through an enchanted forest, past animated classic fairy tale characters and settings. Take a short ride in a Lego jeep through a "jungle" that has ninety animated animals made of Legos. Choo choo around the railroad track on the Legoland Express. At the waterworks area turn a handle and aim water spray at objects and at pretend animals to bring them to "life." Kids can get wet here, too, as they play in and amongst the fountains that spurt up at unexpected intervals. (Bring a change of clothing.) Younger children can happily while away the day creating and playing at the Duplo playground. It has a maze to crawl through, a train ride, an ambulance, and police motorcycle to "drive," and lots more. At the theater see the live, comedy performances that use people from the

audience and behind-the-scenes from the *Lego Movie* - the sound stage, actual movie footage and some incredible models.

Fun Town offers two driving schools, one for young kids, one for younger kids - no adults allowed. Drive Lego-looking electric cars (not on a track!), complete with stop signs, traffic lights, turns, and traffic jams. (And you'll see there is a reason kids this young do not have licenses.) At the Power Tower, sit in outward-facing seats and pull yourself up a thirty-foot tower, then experience a controlled "free fall" down. For another perspective, pedal the Sky Cyde around an elevated circular track. Other attractions and activities in this area include piloting a kid-size helicopter up and down via a joystick; maneuvering a bumper boat around buoys (and other boats); taking a walk through Adventures' Club building to see ancient lands, the Arctic, and more, all depicted in Legos; touring a small-scale Lego factory to see how the bricks are made and packaged; and playing at the Club House with online games for multiplayers and/or shopping at the bins (and bins) to purchase bulk bricks. Kids can pick out the color and shape of the Lego bricks to create their own specialty masterpiece. The bricks are sold by weight. Get a picture perfect present at the Lego Clubhouse: After a digital photo is taken, you receive all the bricks needed to make the portrait in 3-D. Kids (and adults) belly-laugh at the funny, live Big Test show where acrobatic/clownish firefighters try to teach safety tips. Get a workout by being first in a fire truck and police car that race to a "burning" building. Pump out water fast and furious through a hose and put out the fire. Tip: The Marketplace offers fresh cooked, good, non-fast food.

Pirate Shores has a great seasonal waterzone play area - Swabbie's Deck - where water jets pop up at random times, fountains are fun to frolic in and through, squirt cannons are a blast, and the large Soak-N-Sail play structure is pure water play pleasure with sixty interactive gadgets to spray, pump, and get wet. This shores also has a water log ride; Splash Battle, where mates ride piratey ships on a track and shoot water at bystanders (and each other); Pirate Reef, where two larger boats battle via water cannons with each other; and a huge boat that swings you back and forth and back and forth in the air. So much water and an unarrrrrguably good time! Bring a swimsuit and towel for this area and note that swim diapers are required for children 4 and under.

Past the rocks that sing "we will rock you" is the medieval-themed **Castle Hill.** Ride the roller coaster that takes all-age riders through a castle and into a cave past a fire-breathing dragon. Kids (only) can also mount a "horse" and take part in a simulated joust ride. A real quest is Knights' Tournament where robotic arms swing seated passengers up and down and upside down. This robo-coaster allows riders to choose their own maneuvers and intensity level, so each ride is unique. (I saved my stomach and just observed this one.) Everyone can have adventures at a huge, multi-level playground that has rope ladders, cargo nets, obstacles courses, wooden bridges, and slides. Visitors can also pan for "gold" to be exchanged for a Lego medallion and take a nature walk past models of native animals. You can also swing a club around forty model forest creatures at the eighteen-hole Wild Woods (miniature) Golf course. One round costs $5 per person.

Miniland recreates several areas of the U.S., constructed in 1:20 scale. Each area has fourteen to thirty-three animations and some interactivity such as volcanos erupting in Las Vegas and a man covering himself with a manhole when a vehicle comes around: *New England Harbor* has farmlands, a traditional harbor and a shipyard, and underwater divers exploring a sunken ship. *Washington, D.C.* is impressive with its Lincoln Memorial, Washington Monument, White House, a presidential motorcade, baseball games, and more capital activities. *New York City* showcases the Manhattan and Brooklyn bridges, Central Park (e.g., joggers, the zoo, etc), Times Square complete with police cars with lights and sirens, and the Statue of Liberty. *Southern California* combines beaches and mansions in Beverly Hills with Hollywood, Griffith Observatory, TCL Chinese Theatre (used to be called Grauman's), and sights in San Diego. *San Francisco* boasts cable cars, Pier 39, Ghiradelli Square, Lombard Street, and more. *New Orleans* offers paddle steamers on the river front, plantation houses, Mardi Gras, and the sound of jazz. *Florida* highlights Cape Canaveral and the Daytona International Speedway, where you can race remote Lego cars. Daytona Speedway racers, complete with boaters and jet skiers at Lake Lloyd, speed around the course to cheering fans. *Las Vegas* has all the casinos and glitz, in miniature scale. Not in the U.S. but from a long time ago in a galaxy far, far away, come many *Star Wars* scenes from all six movies and the T.V. show that feature sounds and special effects, just like in the movies! Pose with life-size Lego versions of Darth Vader, Darth Maul and Chewbacca, and see three-foot models of Han Solo, Luke Skywalker, Princess Leia, Yoda and other characters. The *Star Wars* weapons and spacecraft look awesome in Legos, too.

Another picturesque part of Legoland is a large lake where families take a cruise and see - what else - more Lego animals and characters!! The Block of Fame is like a 3-D art gallery with likenesses of George Washington, Abe Lincoln, and more.

The ancient land of Egypt is the theme for **Land of Adventure.** Inside the tented area of Pharaoh's Revenge shoot hundreds of foam balls out of mounted guns at each other. At the interactive Lost Kingdom Adventure take a

jeep ride through the dark temple ruins where guests shoot laser guns at targets and make animated scenes come to "life". There are also a few kiddie rides and slides here.

The mostly hands-on **Imagination Zone** offers both free-play opportunities and structured workshops and contests for all ages. Visual inspiration is all around, such as a Technic T.rex, and a fifteen-foot Einstein. A learning center here allows kids at least 10 years old to build and operate Mindstorms robots. Tip: Sign up first thing on the day of your visit for a class as space fills up. Xbox Family Game Space is gaming fun for everyone. The Hero Factory is for creating and building new heros, and using the ones that Lego built. The Imagination Zone theater shows four different twelve-minute 4-D films on a giant screen, with a favorite for kids starring *Bob the Builder*. I like Racers 4-D: As music and other sounds pulsate, viewers are immersed in the sensations of a car race through different landscapes while actually feeling the wind, snow, water, and tire smoke. Ride the Technic Coaster for a fun and fairly fast (for Legoland standards) trip on the switchback tracks. Take a spin around (and around and around!) on the Bionide Blaster - individual cars that spin around as much as you want them to. Imposing giant Bionides stand guard here. Aquazone participants circle around in power ski-like water vehicles as spectators press buttons that control blasts of water directed toward the riders.

Do try the decadent Granny's Apple Fries - Granny Smith apples covered with batter and fried, then topped with cinnamon sugar and a creamy vanilla sauce. The on-site Legoland store is the largest one in the U.S. It carries everything Lego, including hard-to-find pieces and kits. The store gets mobbed toward the end of the day, so shop early and have them hold your package.

Note to moms (or caregivers) who are looking for get-togethers at Legoland: The first and third Thursday of the month, moms with children 4 years and under meet here and interact via playgroups and stroller strides fitness walks. Look online into the Model Mom Club for details. Check out the variety of educational programs and field trips, plus homeschool days offered here, too - fun learning and great prices. SEA LIFE AQUARIUM (pg. 593) and LEGOLAND WATER PARK (pg. 464) share the same property. If you have a real Lego fanatic, definitely check out the adjacent LEGOLAND HOTEL (563).

Hours: Open most of the year, Mon., Thurs. - Sun., 10am - 5pm. (Often closed on Tues. and Wed., except for holiday periods.) Open daily in the summertime, 10am - 7pm. Check the hours before your visit.

Price: $83 for adults; $73 for ages 3 - 12; children 2 and under are free. Discounts are available online through AAA and through some local stores and restaurants. Parking is $15. Two-day passes, to be used within a 9-day period, are an additional $20 per person. (Well worth it!) Check out combo passes that include Sealife Aquarium and the Water Park. Annual memberships, that you can pay for monthly, are also available.

Ages: Most of the rides and shows are geared for ages 2 - 11, but you are never too old to play with Legos.

LEGOLAND WATER PARK
(760) 918-LEGO (5346) / california.legoland.com
One Legoland Drive, Carlsbad

☼
$$$$$

Not really made out of just Legos, which is good, this water park is definitely Lego-themed and is colorful, creative, and totally fun with an entrance only accessible through Legoland. The centerpiece of the water park is a forty-five-foot tall tower that sports lots of traditional Lego characters and elements. The tower has four slides for those 42" or taller - two enclosed; one open-body, twisting slide; and a slide for up to four riders on a raft. For younger ones who can't ride the big slides, Duplo Splash Safari is the place to be. The large pool (only twenty-four inches deep) has a gradual entrance with the elephant, polar bear and alligator Duplo figures to ride on that also squirt out water; several shorter slides; a lazy river called Kid Creek for little ones; an area to shoot water cannons and listen to a Lego Joker tell jokes and then dump gallons of water; and plenty of pool space to just splash around in. The Splash Zoo is ideal for toddlers: A giant Duplo lion, giraffe, and zebra make their home on a big splash pad that also has fountains, a teeter-totter, and more water-fun toys.

A wild world of adventure awaits at the Legends of Chima areas (based on that same-name Lego hit where animal tribes compete in a mystical land). Go through the lion temple archway to a gentle wave pool for young children; slide down through the head of a massive crocodile, then shoot water cannons and play in the jets; spend hours doing an almost dry activity - making boats from a raft of Legos pieces then testing their seaworthiness; and more. Build-a-raft river adds a unique element to riding a tube around the 800-foot-long lazy river - you get to add on large, soft foam Lego bricks to your raft sides, thereby customizing your raft. Over twenty Lego models are around the edges of the river, some squirting water on you as you drift by. Use Duplos at Imagination Station to build boats, bridges, and more all in a raised, long narrow "table" filled with flowing water. Cover various fountain holes at AquaTune to

create different notes of music.

    Lounge chairs are available on cement and on the beach which has finer sand than you normally find at the beach. You may bring your own umbrella. Private cabanas are also available for rent. Note that proper swimwear must be worn here and wearing just bathing suits is not allowed in the Legoland Park.

Hours: Open mid-March, daily, noon - 5pm; open the bulk of the summer, daily, 10am - 7pm; open weekends only after Labor Day (in September) through October, noon - 5pm. Check for hours first because there are some closures in April and May, as well as longer hours periodically. If you have a real Lego fanatic, definitely check out the adjacent LEGOLAND HOTEL (563). Also see SEA LIFE AQUARIUM (pg. 593) and LEGOLAND (pg. 462) for info on the park.

Price: The entrance to the Water Park is only through Legoland and therefore includes entrance to Legoland - $101 for adults; $91 for ages 3- 12; $10 for ages 1 - 2. Parking is $15. Two-day passes, to be used within a 9-day period, are an additional $20 per person. (Well worth it!) Call or check the website first as discounts are available.

Ages: 2 - 12

THE WAVE

(760) 940-WAVE (9283) / www.thewavewaterpark.com
101 Wave Drive, Vista

    Catch a wave at The Wave on the Flow Rider wave machine. Swoosh on down the four water slides here - two are enclosed, and two are convertible-style (no tops). Some height restrictions apply. Slip 'n slide down the fifth slide, which is short, slopes gently, and ends into Crazy River, a large ring of water that encircles the slide and lounge area. Those 48" and under especially enjoy the multi-story children's water play area with a maze, climbing apparatus that has water spouting out, and slides.

    The large rectangular pool, usually used for lessons and the swim team, is open to the public during Wave hours. There are a limited number of picnic tables here, as well as a few grassy areas for picnicking or sunbathing. You may bring in your own lounge chairs. Lockers ($4), double inner tubes ($8), and cabanas ($45) are available. Use of single inner tubes and body boards are included in your admission price. Outside food is not allowed in, but there is a full-service snack bar here that sells food at very reasonable prices. Have big time fun at this small water park!

Hours: Open the end of May - mid-August, Mon. - Fri., 10am - 4pm; Sat., 11am - 5:30pm; Sun., noon - 5:30pm. Open mid-August - September, weekends only, noon - 5:30pm. Check out the select Fri. splash nights from 4pm - 8pm.

Price: $16.95 for 42" and taller; $11.95 for seniors; $12.95 for 41" and under and spectators; children 3 and under are free. Fri. splash nights are $7.95 per person.

Ages: 1½ years and up.

—ARTS AND CRAFTS—

ART SOUP

(760) 230-2060 / www.artsoupsd.com
191 N. El Camino Real, ste. 203, Encinitas

    Soup is known as a kind of cure all. Art Soup is a cure all for your kids' arts needs as it's part art studio and part social club; a place to hang out and create. The ninety-minute drop-in studio sessions allow free reign of the activities in its large room that's decorated with a huge tree made out of scrunched up paper bags along one wall. Activities include painting (and repainting) a VW bug; using easels; painting both sides of a big glass partition in the center of the room; getting artistic on chalk walls; and a self-serve Craft Bar area at which kids can make up to four art projects from mostly recycled materials. This front area has long tables and chairs, plus lots and lots of bins on shelves offering inspiration in the way of egg cartons, wine corks, puzzle pieces, buttons, stickers, paper tubes, bottles, fabric, boxes, crayons, feathers, beads, tiles, cardboard, paint, glue, and a myriad of other objects to create with, plus staff members to help out. Dress for mess, though smocks are provided, and let the imagining begin!

    Besides the drop-in sessions, there are classes, workshops, toddler-only times, themed projects, art camps, educational field trips, custom murals to decorate and more to get your art on. Another favorite - art-to-go. With a minimum of ten packages, choose from twenty-five themes including race cars, owls, super heros, castles, flower pots, necklaces, wands, tote bags, mini guitars and more.

Hours: Definitely check the calendar for classes and for drop-in sessions which are usually offered at least Tues. - Fri., 9:30am - 1:30pm. Open on weekends for private parties only.

Price: $12 for ninety-minute drop-in sessions.

Ages: 2 - 14 years.

CERAMICAFE

$$$$

Del Mar - (858) 259-9958; La Mesa - (619) 466-4800 / www.ceramicafe.com

Del Mar - 3435 Del Mar Heights Road; La Mesa - 5500 Grossmont Center

These well-lit, paint-your-own ceramics stores have a great array of objects to choose from. We painted dragon figurines, deep mugs, a vase, and a heart-shaped tile. (We were busy!) I used the stencils and stamps, while my boys free-formed it. All the artistic aids, paints, and brushes are included in the price. Finished masterpieces are ready for pick up in about five days. Ceramicafe also offers after-school activities where kids can learn painting techniques, creating with clay, mosaics, and more. Ask about the homeschool art program.

Hours: Del Mar - Open Mon. - Sat., 10am - 9pm; Sun., 10am - 6pm. La Mesa - Open Mon. - Thurs., 10am - 8pm; Fri. - Sat., 10am - 9pm; Sun., 10am - 6pm. Closed Thanksgiving and Christmas.

Price: There is no per-hour studio fee. Prices range from $6 - $60. Mugs, for instance, are $15 - $18; bud vases, $15; and 4 x 4 tiles are four for $20.

Ages: 4 years and up.

CLAY 'N LATTE

$$$$

San Diego - (858) 487-9293; Vista - (760) 726-9293 / www.claynlatte.net

San Diego - 10175 Rancho Carmel Drive; Vista - 20 Main Street, suite H-110

A ceramic piece, some paint, and a little latte goes a long way in making a ceramic masterpiece to take home. Choose from a wide selection of items (over 1,000!), such as plates, bowls, flower pots, goblets, salt and pepper shakers, animal figurines, and more. Kids will have a field day picking out colors (over 100 to choose from) and thinking of ways to design their chosen piece. Warning: This recreational activity can become habit forming! Paints, paintbrushes, and stencils are all provided - you simply provide the artistic creativity (and the money). Look into their summer art camps. Ask about their mosaics and clay imprints as well.

Hours: The San Diego store is open Mon. - Fri., 11am - 8pm; Sat., 10am - 8pm; Sun., noon - 6pm. The Vista store is open Mon. - Thurs., 11am -9pm; Fri., 11am - 10pm; Sat., 10am - 10pm; Sun., noon - 6pm.

Price: $8 studio fee for adults, $6 for children 12 and under, plus the price of item. Ask about specials.

Ages: 4 years and up

CLAYTIME CERAMICS

$$$$

(619) 223-6050 / www.claytime-ceramics.com

1863 Bacon Street, Ocean Beach

A vase with little handprints; a kitty-cat bank; a plate bordered with flowers; or a picture frame in art deco style - these are just a few of the multitude of ideas and items you can paint at this ceramic store. Choose from a variety of objects, get creative, and paint. All the paints, brushes, and aid you need are included in your price. Ask about their painting classes and summer camps where a walk on the beach and tidepool exploration is followed by mosaics, ceramics and other crafts.

Hours: Open Mon. - Thurs., 11am - 7pm; Fri. - Sat., 11am - 9pm; Sun., noon - 5pm.

Price: The price of the object - there is no studio fee.

Ages: 4 years and up.

COLOR ME MINE (San Diego County)

$$$$

(858) 312-5500 / www.colormemine.com

10550 Craftsman Way at 4S Commons Town Center, Rancho Bernardo

See the entry for COLOR ME MINE (Los Angeles County) on page 7 for details.

Hours: Open Sun. - Mon., 11am - 7pm; Tues. - Thurs., 11am - 8pm; Fri. - Sat., 11am - 9pm.

Price: The studio fee is $10 for adults; $6 for ages 12 and under.

FUN DABBLES

(760) 603-9100 / www.fundabbles.com

6102 Avenida Encinas, suite M, Carlsbad

$$$$

Dabbling in fun is what this place does best! One wall in this large, open room is organized by category of what your creative child is going to make and packed with all the supplies to make it - a candle, soap, ceramic piece, or an art masterpiece on canvas. Choose colors of wax cubes to put into your choice of a variety of molds, then customize your **candle** by adding a scent and miniature novelties such as cakes, animals, figurines, glitter, and much more. *Scent*sational fun! Design your own **soap** from a rainbow of colors incorporating playful shape molds such as an ice cream cone or animal, then add a fragrance, and pick some tiny toys from the toy bins to add in a surprise as the soap is used. Part of the fun is the process of watching the item be finished by a staff member, and then, of course, taking it home and using it, or giving it as a gift. Paint your own **ceramic** from a good selection of items, with paint, brushes and stencils provided. Have the kids tell a story with the **canvas** that they paint and as they assimilate patterned papers on their canvases, too. These activities are not just for kids! Glitter tattoos are available, too, as is a wall-sized chalkboard, an indoor bounce and an inflatable slide. Check out the camps and field trips, such as making things with clay, tie dying, sewing, and arts and crafts.

Hours: Open most of the year, Mon. - Thurs., 3pm - 7pm; Fri. and Sun., noon - 5pm; closed Sat. for private parties. Open extended hours on school breaks and in the summer, usually 11am - 6pm. Call first.

Price: $7 for the play area - the inflatables, etc. Candle-making starts at $15; soap-making at $7; ceramics at $12 and canvas art at $10. (This price does not include entrance into the play area.)

Ages: 3 years and up.

MISSUS POTTS

(760) 945-9294 / www.missuspotts.com

4225 Oceanside Boulevard, suite D, Oceanside

$$$$

Missus Potts pottery painting place presents pottery pieces to be procured, personalized and painted! The mid-size, airy room has tables of various heights in the center and walls filled with useful and decorative items to artistically bedeck such as vases, plates, figurines, mugs, picture frames and more. All the materials of paint, brushes, inspiration, staff help, and firing and glazing are included. Clay impressions, classes, parties, and even Clay for Kids, where they learn each step of how clay is formed, molded, etc., are all offered here, too. The studio, parts of it, will even come to you for a minimum of fifteen people.

Hours: Open Mon. - Thurs., 10am - 8pm; Fri. - Sat., 10am - 10pm; Sun., 11am - 6pm.

Price: $8 studio fee for adults, plus the cost of the pottery; $6 for ages 12 and under.

Ages: 4 years and up.

MOUNTAIN BEADWORKS

(760) 765-3100 / www.mountainbeadworks.com

4470 Highway 78, Julian

$$$

Every*beady* can find something fun to make here! This family-owned and family-friendly store is packed with beads and ideas of what to do with them. You'll find strands and bowl fulls of crystal, seed beads, vintage beads, and Czech glass beads, plus silver, leather, wire, and other supplies and tools. Not only do you have a killer selection, but the staff is incredibly helpful. They also offer a slew of classes for individuals and for groups of all ages in their good-sized classroom. When you (and your kids) go home with your newly created, hand-designed piece of jewelry, you won't *bead*ieve your eyes! Note that this store is next door to JULIAN MINING COMPANY (pg. 575).

Hours: Open daily, 10am - 5pmish. Call about holiday hours. Closed Thanksgiving and Christmas.

Ages: 5years and up.

THE HOT SPOT

(619) 223-1339 / www.thehotspotstudio.com

2770 Historic Decatur Road at Liberty Station Barracks 14, San Diego

$$$$

This IS the Hot Spot for candle-making and pottery painting! The large room has wood tables and chairs, plenty of windows, and music playing that all make for an inviting atmosphere to create and do so together with friends. You can even bring your own food and beverages. There are hundreds of pottery pieces to choose from on the wooden shelves - pet dishes, jewelry boxes, mugs, vases, plates, and more. I love watching artistic people design and paint their

masterpieces freehand. I, on the other hand, rely on other's ideas and using stamps and stencils. Either way, it's a great activity and the finished product is always a special keepsake. Leave your item overnight to be fired (which makes it food and microwave safe), or pick a decorative item to paint and take home that same day.

Let your light shine bright by making a very personalized candle. Choose from a variety of shape molds, or a container. Fill that with colorful cubes of wax. Add a fragrance of cotton candy, ocean, Plumeria, bubble gum, etc. Finish it off with a few other special touches of gems or sea shells or glitter. Now, you have a *scent*sational gift! Candle making can also come to your event site.

Hours: Open Sun. - Wed., 10am, - 7pm; Thurs. - Sat., 10am - 9pm. Closed most holidays.
Price: There are no studio fees. Prices range from $15 - $60, with the average being about $20.
Ages: 4 years and up.

WONKARAMICS

(619) 441-0799 / www.wonkaramics.com
771 Parkway Plaza, El Cajon

$$$$$

Express yourself artistically by creating a one-of-a-kind ceramic keepsake or by something a little more unique, via glass fusion. There are over one hundred ceramic objects waiting to be painted and decorated such as vases, plates, mugs, bowls, banks, and gifty items - you might have a hard time picking and choosing! But do, then paint away. Or, create a beautiful and distinct bowl, plate or piece of jewelry out of pre-cut glass by fusion and slumping. Located in the mall, Wonkaramics supplies everything you need, plus paints and brushes, etc. to make your special novelty. Your ceramic piece will be ready for pick up in about a week.

Hours: Open Mon. - Sat., 10am - 9pm; Sun., 11am - 7pm. Closed major holidays.
Price: Ceramic pieces start at $12; slumped glass bottles are $25, jewelry, $20, and up.
Ages: 4 and up for ceramics; 16 and up for glass

—BEACHES—

BUCCANEER BEACH PARK

(760) 435-3065 or (760)435-4500 / www.ci.oceanside.ca.us
1500 S. Pacific Street, Oceanside

Avast ye! This very small, very family-friendly beach park has a beach area designated for swimmers (and water splashers) on the west side of the highway. Surfing is only allowed, then, on either side of this parcel of shoreline. (Go further north for more beach - Tyson Street Beach and Oceanside City Beach.) On the east side of the highway is a grassy park with restrooms, a little playground, and a basketball court, adjacent to railroad tracks. A snack bar here is open during the summer that sells hamburgers, quesadillas, hot dogs, and drinks at reasonable prices. There is even a kid's menu! There are also picnic tables with BBQ grills and outdoor showers here.

Hours: Open daily, sunrise - sunset.
Price: Free
Ages: All

CARDIFF STATE BEACH

(800) 777-0369 or (760) 753-5091 / www.parks.ca.gov
S. Coast Hwy. 101, Cardiff-by-the Sea

$$

We promptly nicknamed one section of this beach "Rocky Beach." There isn't a lot of uncovered sand on that narrow strip (know your tides table!), but there are literally tons of multi-colored, round, smooth rocks here. Wear sandals. Walk a little further north to reach a huge stretch of sand. So, go into the ocean here, the water is just fine. Bathrooms are available and lifeguards are on duty here, too. The tidepools can be pretty amazing to explore during low tide. Note that this beach is adjacent to SAN ELIJO STATE BEACH on the north end (see pg. 470) and TIDE BEACH PARK on the south end (see pg. 472).

Hours: Open daily, sunrise - sunset.
Price: Limited street parking or pay about $15 for parking in the lot.
Ages: 3 years and up.

CARLSBAD STATE BEACH (and SOUTH CARLSBAD STATE BEACH)

(760) 438-3143 / www.parks.ca.gov
7201 Carlsbad Boulevard, Carlsbad

This long, somewhat narrow strip of beach has several different parts to it. In the "center" of the beach, just south and north of Tamarack and Carlsbad boulevards, is a surf beach and in just this area no swimming is allowed. There is a free parking lot here (or park along the streets) and restroom facilities. A cement walkway stretches along a good portion of Carlsbad Beach, with most of the sand accessible via stairs placed every few hundred feet.

There are 110 bluff-top camping sites (220 total sites) available at South Carlsbad Beach, near Solamar Drive, just north of Island Way. The small sites, which remind me of parking lot camping, are bound by the main street on one side and a chain-link fence protecting them from the cliffs on the other. Showers are available with tokens.

Hours: Open daily, sunrise - sunset.
Price: $10 per vehicle in the lot; $15 on special holidays and high peak weekends. Camping is $35 for an inland site; $50 for beachfront.
Ages: All

CORONADO MUNICIPAL BEACH

(619) 437-8788or (866) 599-7242 / www.coronadovisitorcenter.com
Ocean Boulevard, near Avenida de Las Arenas, Coronado

This beach offers a lovely, long stretch of sand, plus a lifeguard station, volleyball courts, a few sand dunes, restroom facilities, stairs to the beach, a view of Navy vessels who use this waterway, and usually Navy personnel working out. If you park or walk southward, toward Flora Avenue, you can climb over a few boulders that line the street and head to the wide expanse of clean, fine sand in front of the famous Hotel Del Coronado, a favorite beach for all ages. Rocks in front of the hotel beach act as a breakwater.

Hours: Open daily, sunrise - sunset.
Price: Free
Ages: All

FLETCHER COVE BEACH PARK

(858) 755-1569 or (858) 720-2400 / www.ci.solana-beach.ca.us
111 S. Sierra Avenue, Solana Beach

A local favorite, this little bluff side beach is reached by a wide, sloping ramp. Its cozy size invites a more personal time, and hopefully one of relaxation as well as play. Lifeguards are here year round for swimmers and surfers.

Topside is a little park with grassy lawns, picnic tables, bbqs, a half basketball court, showers, restrooms, and a small, nice playground with swings, slides, and such, and an impressive view of the ocean and beyond - particularly great for watching sunsets. There are several restaurants within walking distance, too.

Hours: Open daily, 6am - 10pm.
Price: Free, with free parking.
Ages: All

HARBOR BEACH - BREAKWATER WAY

(760) 435-4030 - harbor; (760) 435-4500 - city of Oceanside / www.ci.oceanside.ca.us;
www.oceansidechamber.com
Pacific Street, near Harbor Dr., Oceanside

Adjacent to Oceanside Harbor, this spread of beach (one of the widest in San Diego County) offers amenities such as swimming; kayak rentals and other boat rentals (see OCEANSIDE BOAT RENTALS, pg. 582); barbeque grills and fire rings; picnic tables; a snack bar (open seasonally); volleyball courts (bring your own net and ball); as well as a few shops and eateries. You can also fish from the jetties. Overnight RV camping (no hook-ups) is available for $20.

Breakwater, just south of Harbor Beach, also provides the above "extras", plus the frequent appearance of a sand bar, which is a good surf break. See OCEANSIDE BEACH PIER (560) for more information about the pier, its beaches, and the surrounding area.

Hours: Open daily, sunrise - sunset.
Price: Metered parking and/or paid lots - $8 from 4am - 8am; $20 from 8pm - 4pm..

Ages: All

LA JOLLA SHORES BEACH   ☼

(619) 221-8899 / www.sandiego.gov/lifeguards/beaches

8200 Camino del Oro, La Jolla

This beach comes fully loaded for a full day of fun! The one-mile-plus fairly wide stretch of beach that ends near the Scripps pier and is adjacent to the Underwater Ecological Reserve has a separate area for surfers and for swimmers. Year-round lifeguard service, rest rooms, showers (a parent's essential), cement barbecue pits, and a few playgrounds for the kids, complete with swing sets and climbing apparatus, add up to make this a fun place to go with kids. A temporary rubber walkway allows limited access to the beach for wheelchairs and strollers. A beach wheelchair is available, on a first-come, first-served basis, near the main lifeguard station. Kellogg Park, the adjacent grassy area behind the main lifeguard station, offers another way to enjoy this length of coastline. A cement boardwalk parallels a portion of the beach between the park and the sand.

Look up LA JOLLA COVE KAYAK / SNORKEL ADVENTURE (on page 581) for a kayaking adventure that's just around the "corner." To incorporate a visit to the beach with a drive around picturesque La Jolla, see SCRIPPS PARK (pg. 519) for several other places to visit in the nearby area.

Hours: Open daily, sunrise - sunset.
Price: Free - good luck with parking!
Ages: All

LEUCADIA STATE BEACH (BEACON'S)   ☀

(760) 633-2740 / www.ci.encinitas.ca.us; www.beachcalifornia.com

948 Neptune Avenue, Encinitas

This hidden, non-populated beach is locally known as Beacon's. It is accessible only by walking down a series of steps where a lifeguard stand is stationed here during the summer. The size (or width) of the beach varies with the tide. At low tide, there is plenty of beach under the cliffs. At high tide, the beach is rather skimpy. The beach is a good getaway for swimming and surfing. Note that there are no restrooms here.

Hours: Open daily, sunrise - sunset.
Price: Free
Ages: 4 years and up (because of the steps)

MISSION BAY PARK   ☼

2581 Quivira Court, San Diego

See the entry for MISSION BAY PARK on page 512 for details.

MOONLIGHT BEACH   ☼

(760) 633-2740 / www.ci.encinitas.ca.us; www.beachcalifornia.com

400 B Street, Encinitas

Moonlight can be romantic, but Moonlight Beach is great for the whole family. A short, wide expanse of beach offers clean sand (at least when we visited), three volleyball courts with nets, a great playground for the younger set, cement picnic tables, fire rings, a lifeguard station, restrooms, outdoor showers, and a seasonal snack shop offering hot dogs, hamburgers, chips, and drinks. Forgot your boogie board? No problem - there is a small beach rental shack, also open seasonally, that can equip you with boards, surfboards, wet suits, chairs, and even umbrellas. Note that this beach has a polyethylene walkway that extends toward the ocean for wheelchairs and strollers.

Hours: Open daily, 5am - 10pm.
Price: Free
Ages: All

SAN ELIJO STATE BEACH   ☀

(760) 753-5091 - beach; (800) 444-7275 - camping reservations / www.parks.ca.gov

S. Coast Hwy. 101, near Encinitas Blvd., Cardiff

This beach entrance is a little challenging to find, is accessible via many wooden steps, and is only good at low tide. Having said that, it offers several places for tidepooling, swimming, and snorkeling. Lifeguard stations are manned daily in the summer and mostly on weekends in the spring and fall.

The bluff-side camping spots each have a patch of dirt, separated by a row of trees and bushes. (My youngest thinks that it's worth spending the extra money for camping on the beach side, with direct views of the ocean, versus the "inland" sites right by the side of the road. Of course, it wasn't his money.) A camp store, laundry room, and showers are available here.

The San Elijo Lagoon inlet separates this beach from the next door CARDIFF STATE BEACH. (See pg. 468.)

Hours: Open daily, dawn - dusk.
Price: $10 - $15 per vehicle. Campsites on the bluff are $50; with hook-ups $65. Campsites more inland are $35; with hook-ups $55.
Ages: 3 years and up.

SHELTER ISLAND - SHORELINE PARK BEACH

(619) 686-6200 / www.portofsandiego.org
Shelter Island Drive, San Diego

A stunning view of the skyline and San Diego Harbor awaits visitors at Shelter Island. A marina is on one side of the island while the other side boasts a nice stretch of beach across the water from the boat launch. This area also has a playground, fire pits, restrooms, rocks on the shore to climb, a T-shaped fishing pier with a bait and tackle shop, and shade spots with benches along the paved pathway that hugs the shoreline.

Hours: Open daily, 6am - 10:30pm
Price: Free
Ages: All

SUNSET CLIFFS NATURAL PARK

(619) 525-8213 or (858) 581-9978 / www.sunsetcliffs.info; www.sandiego.gov
1253 Sunset Cliffs Boulevard, San Diego

This natural park runs over a mile, north and south, along Sunset Cliff Boulevard, from Adair to Ladera Streets. It then reaches inland for another fifty acres which are grouped together from the beach to a hillside bordering the 650-acre Point Loma Ecological Reserve, Navy property and Point Loma Nazarene University.

The linear stretch has numerous places to pull over and park (for free!) that parallel Sunset Cliff Boulevard. Visitors can get a front row to admire the incredible (and very popular) view, especially the sunsets - hence the name - and walk along the cliffs - hence the other part of the name. Use caution! A dirt walking/running path follows along the street and shoreline. There are several places to access the beach, such as just north of Hill Street, a lovely section of beach, and at the "corner" of Sunset and Ladera down a steep flight of stairs. Overlooks are by Adair, Osprey, and Froude streets. Note that each patch of sandy beach is surrounded by rocks, making them good places for tide pool exploration. There are also several beach caves, too, but be mindful of high tides. There is a sinkhole (and non-accessible sea caves) across from Monaco St. Head north on the beach, a narrow, but nice tract of sand, for some good , accessible sea caves. There are some to the south as well.

The hillside section of the park has several crisscrossing trails where a biodiversity of native plants, reptiles, small mammals, and birds thrive. Some of the trails lead down to the beach. May the sunset at Sunset Cliffs be a beautiful end of, hopefully, a wonderful day.

Hours: Open daily, sunrise to sunset.
Price: Free
Ages: 4 years and up.

SWAMI'S BEACH

(760) 633-2740 / www.ci.encinitas.ca.us
1298 S. Coast Highway 101, Encinitas

Swami's Beach is not just for mystics! It is worth going down the steep, over 100 wooden stairs to reach the smallish beach, which changes size according to the tide. During low tide the tidepools appear so you can check out the sea anemones, crabs, sea stars, and other critters. Indulge in swimming, or watch the surfers, since this is a popular surfing spot. The kelp beds offshore are supposed to be great for divers, too.

Up top, at Seacliff Roadside Park, is a patch of grass, some shade trees, a few benches to take in the majestic view, a few bbq grills, restrooms, and a small parking lot. You can watch (and hear) the trains roll past behind you, too.

Hours: Open daily, 4am - 2am.
Price: Free

Ages: All

TIDE BEACH PARK

(858) 755-1569 or (858) 720-2400 / www.ci.solana-beach.ca.us

302 Solana Vista Drive, Solana Beach

This is a beach for tidepool explorers and rock collectors. The beach, accessible by stairs at Solana Vista Drive and Pacific Avenue, is under part of a cliff that overhangs and creates small caves, or nooks and crannies, along the shoreline. Don't hang out here during high tide! The tidepools are not the best I've seen for observing marine life, but they are fun nonetheless. We did see lots and lots of limpets, plus mussels, sea anemones, and some small crabs. Just north of the tidepools is CARDIFF STATE BEACH (pg. 468). Tide Beach is life-guarded during the summer and good for swimming and snorkeling.

Hours: Open daily, 6am - 10pm.

Price: Free

Ages: 2 years and up.

TYSON STREET BEACH and PARK

(760) 435-5041 or (760) 435-4500 / www.ci.oceanside.ca.us

Pacific Street and Tyson Street, Oceanside

Accessible by stairs, this pleasant, long stretch of beach is located just south of Oceanside Pier. Amenities include lifeguard stations, bathrooms, patches of grass and some picnic tables, and even a few small playgrounds. The Strand is a driveable strip of pavement between the grass side and beach, so use caution when crossing it. Note that there are beaches, just with different names, north and south of Tyson.

Hours: Open daily, sunrise - sunset.

Price: Parking in the lot is about $5 for the day, or there is metered parking on the street.

Ages: All

—EDIBLE ADVENTURES—

94th AERO SQUADRON (San Diego County)

(858) 560-6771 / www.94thaerosquadron.signonsandiego.com

8885 Balboa Avenue, San Diego

The ivy-covered brick restaurant is a replica of a French WWI-era farmhouse. Outside, cannons are in a semicircle around sandbags. Bales of hay are suspended over wooden carts that look like they're falling apart. A bi-plane, trees, and a wooden fence are also out front. Listen to swing and other older-style music being piped outside.

Inside, the ambiance is just as rustic and charming. Dark wood beam ceilings; huge brick fireplaces with large kettles; and walls and ceiling tastefully lined with helmets, war posters, photos, medals, plane parts, vests, farm implements, and even sandbags add to the somewhat romantic atmosphere. There are even a few pocket booths that contain headphones so diners can listen to the FAA control tower on the adjacent Montgomery Field Airport. Out back, tables on a grassy embankment overlook the airfield, bunkers with camouflage netting, more grounded airplanes, an army jeep, and a duck pond.

The lunch menu includes escargot in mushroom caps ($7.99), fried calamari ($6.99), Cobb salad ($9.99), hamburger ($8.99), French dip sandwich ($12.99), hot crab and artichoke sandwich ($10.99), grilled salmon ($12.95), and pastas. A luncheon buffet is offered for $11.99. The dinner menu includes some of the aforementioned foods plus filet mignon ($25.99), lobster tail (market price), rack of lamb ($32.99), and more. The Sunday buffet brunch has an incredible assortment of delectable foods - blintzes, carved roast beef, crab legs, an omelette bar, a fajita bar, waffles, muffins, crepes, cheesecake, eclairs, and more. Catch the next flight to the 94th Aero Squadron.

Hours: Open Mon. - Thurs., 11am - 9pm; Fri., 11am - 11pm; Sat., 4pm - 10pm; Sun., 9am - 3pm - brunch; 4pm - 9pm - dinner.

Price: Some menu prices are listed above. Brunch is $25.95 for adults; $10.95 for ages 4 - 10; children 3 and under are free.

Ages: 4 years and up.

ANTHONY'S FISH GROTTO

(619) 463-0368 / www.gofishanthonys.com
9530 Murray Drive, La Mesa

$$$

Shell I tell you about this restaurant that resembles an underwater sea cave? It's a pearl of a place. Enter through a giant clam shell. Fish are "swimming" around on the ceiling. Octopus-covered lamps are at the front desk and a fish mosaic covers the wall here. The booths are upholstered with fish designs. Waist-high coral barriers separate the restaurant into sections. (Look for eel and other creatures peeking out from the coral rocks.) The bar is in a cave-like setting. Even the restrooms maintain the theme!

Dining is available inside, or outside under shade trees on patio tables and chairs. Both seating arrangements allow guests to overlook the grotto's small lake. Duck feed is available from the restaurant. A dry-docked boat on the lawn houses a small video arcade.

The Fish Grotto specializes in a wide variety of fresh fish and shellfish, of course, although it offers chicken and steak, as well. Here's a sampling of the menu: Crab stuffed mushrooms ($12.95); clam chowder in a sourdough bread bowl ($7.95); shrimp, scallop and fish kabobs ($17.55); coconut fried shrimp ($20.96); and Alaskan King crab legs ($49.95). The kid's menu offers fish dippers ($6.50), grilled cheese ($5.50), pasta ($5.50), and chicken ($6.50). Drinks are extra. Note: Take some of Anthony's fish home as this location also has a retail market.

Hours: Open Sun. - Thurs., 11am - 8:30pm; Fri. - Sat., 11am - 9pm. Closed all major holidays.
Price: See menu prices above.
Ages: All

AUBREY ROSE TEA ROOM

(619) 461-4TEA (4832) / www.theaubreyrosetearoom.com
8362 La Mesa Boulevard, La Mesa

$$$$

I just fell in love with this place. It's the epitome of a tea room: Covered with pretty wallpaper and without feeling cramped or crowded, almost every imaginable space of the Aubrey Rose Tea Room is decorated with tea accouterments and cupboards that hold tea pots, tea cups and saucers, books, napkins, quaint placards, hats, dolls, jewelry, and collectibles. Almost all of the merchandise is for sale. Each of the table and chair settings are nestled in their own nook, giving a sense of privacy and intimacy. If you forgot to wear a hat or feather boa, you are welcome to borrow one.

The Lady Anne Tea consists of assorted tea sandwiches (served in a style befitting a queen, or lady), along with seasonal fresh fruit, freshly-baked scones with lemon curd and Devonshire-type cream, pastries, and, of course, tea for $25.95 per person. The Queen Victoria Tea is similar, but also offers an additional course of sherry-mushroom turnovers, artichoke heart fondue, and/or something equally scrumptious for $30.95 per person. The Princess Sophia's Tea, for ages 5 through 10 years, includes tea sandwiches (with peanut butter and jelly as a standard), fruit, sconettes, pastries, and a beverage for $23.95 per person. For just a spot of tea, indulge in the Cream Tea of a scone, fruit garnish, and tea for $13.95 per person. Inquire about theme teas, birthdays, or any occasion to celebrate.

Note - Aubrey Rose is located in the midst of La Mesa Village with its numerous antique and collectibles shops.

Hours: Open Wed. - Sat., 10:30am - 5pm, seatings start at 11am and are every half hour until 3:30pm; Sat., seatings are at 11am, 1:30pm, and 4pm. Open on Sun. for Mother's Day and during the month of December. Closed Sun. - Tues. and most holidays. Reservations are always highly recommended.
Price: Menu choices are listed above.
Ages: 5 years and up.

BENIHANA OF TOKYO (San Diego County)

Carlsbad - (760) 929-8311; San Diego - (619) 298-4666 / www.benihana.com
Carlsbad - 755 Raintree Drive, suite 100; San Diego - 477 Camino Del Rio S.

$$$$

See the entry for BENIHANA OF TOKYO (Los Angeles County) on page 14 for details.

BUCA DI BEPPO (San Diego County)

(866) EAT BUCA (328-2822) for all locations; Carlsbad - (760) 479-2533; Mira Mesa - (858) 536-2822; San Diego - (619) 233-7272 / www.bucadibeppo.com

$$$$

Carlsbad - 1921 Calle Barcelona; Mira Mesa - 10749 Westview Parkway; San Diego - 705 6th Avenue

See BUCA DI BEPPO (Los Angeles County) on page 14 for details.

BUGA KOREAN B.B.Q. AND SUSHI BAR

(858) 560-1010 / www.bugabbq.com

$$$$

5580 Clairemont Mesa Boulevard, San Diego

Authentic Korean cuisine (and sushi) is served at this restaurant, but the real reason that I include it in the book is that you can cook your own food (not the sushi) on your own grill in the middle of your own table. A waiter comes by to give instruction. So, yes, you still have to cook dinner, but it's different, it's a fun atmosphere, and the kids enjoy participating.

Menu selections include marinated beef, spicy pork, grilled salmon, prime short ribs, and lots more. If you don't understand what to order, because the food names are hard to decipher, just pick something and be surprised. Try, for example, Bulgogi for around $24; Daiji Samgyubsal (i.e., pork, fresh bacon-style) for about $18; and Seawoo Gui (i.e., grilled king prawn shrimp) for about $23. Buga has a full sushi bar (a California roll is $4) and serves sashimi. Kid's meals are available for $9.95 for beef or chicken teriyaki.

Hours: Open daily, 11am - 10pm.
Price: Some menu prices are listed above.
Ages: 5 years and up.

CHUCK E. CHEESE'S (San Diego County)

See the entry for CHUCK E. CHEESE'S (Los Angeles County) on page 16 for details.

COBBLESTONE COTTAGE TEA SHOPPE

(619) 445-6064 / www.cobblestonecottageteashoppe.com

$$$$

1945 Alpine Boulevard, Alpine

More cute cottage decor than Victorian elegance, Cobblestone Cottage is in a picture-perfect setting with its antique glass windows and miniature gables. It is a delightful place to relax and enjoy life for a bit with friends and family. Each of the tables is set with different color and floral schemes, fine china, and with patio-style chairs. If it's a nice day, have your tea outside amidst a country garden/woods setting underneath a pine tree, with a bubbling fountain and old wooden buildings.

Perk up your attire with a feathery boa, hat, and/or gloves from the Cottage's selection. Feel pampered with the service and the homemade food. High Tea is like a lunch that includes tea (over forty choices), scones (with Devonshire cream, preserves, and lemon curd), fresh fruit, and tea sandwiches (cucumber and cream cheese, ham, and chicken curry) cut into fancy shapes served with fresh flowers on a tiered tray - presentation does count. Tea breads and quiche are followed by dessert. The tea is kept hot, and I've learned to appreciate trying new flavors. High Tea is $19.95 per person. Afternoon Tea is similar to High Tea, minus the tea breads and quiche, at $15.95 per person. If you want tea in the more English tradition of just tea and two scones with embellishments, this can be had for $8.95 per person. You may also order items a la carte, such as a scone with cream and preserves, $3.35; fruit plate, $6.95; chicken salad on lettuce, $8.95; and a full sandwich or quiche with a salad, $8.95.

The attached retail shop has teacups and saucers for sale, as well as plates, jewelry, tea cozies, books, napkin rings, and other gift items. Make time to meander in and around the antique and collectibles shops that are next door to the tea room.

Hours: Open Wed. - Sat., 11am - 4pm. Reservations are highly suggested. Always call first. Closed Sun. - Tues.
Price: Menu prices are listed above.
Ages: 4 years and up.

CORVETTE DINER

(619) 542-1476 / www.cohnrestaurants.com

$$$

2965 Historic Decatur Road, San Diego

This 50's-style diner is a really bebopping place to eat! The central dining room is decorated with posters of musicians and stars from the 50's, old license plates and signs, neon signs, hub caps on the walls, old gas pumps, Bazooka bubble gum displays, and a gleaming vintage car, all while 50's music plays in the background. Some of the padded vinyl booths are sparkly silver and hot pink, and some that particular color of turquoise. Checkered tiles cover the floors and part of the walls. A back room has vintage-shaped TV screens on the walls that play black and white TV shows from that era. Another room is dedicated to the 60's with black-lit flower power and peace signs on the walls

and ceiling, and booths with a streamlined look, from that time period. Most evenings after 6pm a live DJ plays 50's and 60's music and takes requests. Down the hallway lined with more celebrity posters from the 50's, is an arcade room still decorated with the theme of the restaurant, but filled with modern-day video and arcade games, plus air hockey. There is also a prize redemption area.

The food here is great and the menu extensive! Try a Hawaii 5-O chicken sandwich with pineapple ($9.99), Greek salad ($9.50), Rory hamburger with peanut butter ($9.50), Reuben ($9.99), Philly steak sandwich ($10.50), shrimp platter ($13.99), meatloaf ($12.99), or spaghetti and meatballs ($11.99). Other food choices include grilled ribs, blackened chicken pasta, and more. Desserts are delectable. They range from Green Rivers to Wipeout (ocean blue jello with graham cracker sand and gummy fish) to egg cream to peppermint shakes (or twenty other flavors) to brownie hot fudge sundae to cotton candy. Kids' meals are $6.99 for their choice of spaghetti, burger, hot dog, grilled cheese sandwich, mac and cheese, or chicken fingers, plus fries and a soft drink. Was life really this good in the fifties?!

Hours: Open Mon. - Thurs., 11:30am - 9pm; Fri., 11:30am - 11pm; Sat., 11am - 11pm; Sun., 11am - 9pm.
Price: Menu prices are listed above.
Ages: All

FAIROUZ CAFE AND GALLERY

(619) 225-0308 / www.alnashashibi.com

$$$

3166 Midway Drive, #102, San Diego

The aroma of Greek and Lebanese cuisine tantalizes your taste buds the moment you step into this small, storefront restaurant. Ethnic music plays in the background. The booths and tables are surrounded by murals, paintings, and other artwork adorning the walls, as well as clothing items for sale. There is even a small library of books to peruse while eating. Food choices include Greek salad ($7.50), lamb kafta ($18.99), falafels ($7.99), moussaka ($13.99), vegetarian grape leaves ($14.99), and lots more, plus baklava ($3.25) for dessert. The ambiance, the food, the art - it's all Greek to me!

Hours: Open Sun. - Thurs., 11am - 9pm; Fri. - Sat., 11am - 10pm. Closed New Year's Day and Christmas.
Price: Menu prices are listed above.
Ages: 5 years and up.

FARMER'S MARKETS (San Diego County)

See the entry for FARMER'S MARKETS (Los Angeles County) on pg. 18 for details.

HARD ROCK CAFE (San Diego County)

(619) 615-7625 / www.hardrock.com

$$$

801 4th Avenue, near Horton Plaza in the Gaslamp Quarter, San Diego

See the entry for HARD ROCK CAFE (Los Angeles County) on page 21 for details.

Hours: Open Sun. - Thurs., 11;30am - 10pm; Fri. - Sat., 11:30am - 11pm.

HOUSE OF BLUES GOSPEL BRUNCH (San Diego County)

(619) 299-BLUE (2583) / www.houseofblues.com

$$$$$

1055 Fifth Avenue, San Diego

See HOUSE OF BLUES GOSPEL BRUNCH (Los Angeles County) on page 21 for details on this southern sensation. This location's building has different decor, but it follows the theme of eclectic folk art with a hip appeal.

Hours: Gospel Brunch is offered on select Sun., usually twice a month at 11am. Get here earlier. Ask about holiday Sun., such as Easter and Mother's Day. All seating is reserved. Reservations are highly recommended.
Price: $39.50 for ages 13 and up; $17.50 for ages 6 - 12; children 5 and under are free. Prices include tax and gratuity. Parking costs about $10 in a lot across the street.
Ages: 5 years and up.

JANET'S MONTANA CAFE

(619) 659-3874

$$$$

2506 Alpine Boulevard, Alpine

Janet's is a good-sized, authentic, rustic-themed restaurant with ceilings of timber-hewed logs, wooden floors, antler chandeliers, chairs made of tree branches (strong ones!), and decor of stuffed moose and deer heads and

Western art. Outside seating gives an equally country feel while on a covered back porch overlooking lots of shade trees, rocks, a waterfall, old stagecoach, and a little brook with wooden bridges. A few very small shops are also on the premises.

The generously-proportioned, American-style breakfast - usually served with hash browns, home fries, or fresh fruit and a choice of toast, biscuit, muffin or pancakes - consists of: biscuits and gravy ($8.75), ham and cheese omelet ($11.95), waffles with strawberries ($10.25), two pancakes ($7.45), granola French toast ($10.95), and country fried steak. And this is just a sampling of the breakfast menu! For $5.95 kids can order two pancakes, an egg and bacon; French toast; or a ham and cheese omelet with bacon. Hearty lunches and dinners include a buffalo burger ($11.25), turkey melt ($10.95), Reuben ($10.95), chicken quesadilla ($11.95), taco and enchilada ($10.95), roasted turkey breast ($15.45), grilled halibut ($21.95) and baby back ribs ($16.95 - half rack). Kid's meal choices include hamburger, grilled cheese, pizza, popcorn shrimp, or chicken fingers, plus a dessert for $5.95 each.

If it's a nice day, and most are in Southern California, wander over to the adjacent nursery to look at the lovely and unique selection of plants and pottery.

Hours: Open Mon., 6am - 2:30pm; Tues. - Thurs., 6am - 8:30pm; Fri. - Sat., 6am - 9pm; Sun., 6am - 8:30pm. Closed Thanksgiving and Christmas.
Price: Menu prices are listed above.
Ages: All

JOE'S CRAB SHACK (San Diego County)

Oceanside - (760) 722-1345; Pacific Beach - (858) 274-3474; San Diego (Hazard Center) - (619) 574-8617; San Diego (Harbor Dr.) - (619) 233-7391 / www.joescrabshack.com
Oceanside - 314 Harbor Drive; Pacific Beach - 4325 Ocean Boulevard; San Diego - 7610 Hazard Center Drive, #703; San Diego - 525 E. Harbor Drive

See the entry for JOE'S CRAB SHACK (Los Angeles County) on page 22 for details.

JOHN'S INCREDIBLE PIZZA CO. (San Diego County)

(619) 472-5555 / www.johnspizza.com
3010 Plaza Bonita Road in Westfield Plaza Bonita (mall), National City

See JOHN'S INCREDIBLE PIZZA CO. (Orange County) (pg. 248) for details. Also see WESTFIELD PLAZA BONITA (pg. 524) for details about mall offerings.

Hours: Open Mon. - Thurs., 11am - 9pm; Fri., 11am - 10:30pm; Sat., 10am - 10:30pm; Sun., 11am - 9pm.

JULIAN TEA & COTTAGE ARTS

(866) 765-0832 or (760) 765-OTEA (0832) / www.juliantea.com
2124 3rd Street, Julian

This quaint (what in Julian isn't quaint?), 100-year-old house is a *tea*lightful place to take your daughter for an afternoon of one-on-one time, or to go with a group of friends. Although tea is served in the tea room and the front porch, the multi-story cottage also has a several other rooms decorated with a variety of tea paraphernalia and packed with items for sale - china, tea pots, a huge selection of teas, baby gifts, bridal gifts, books on teas, cards, teas, aprons, cooking utensils, food products (i.e. sauces, jams, candies), lace, and cottage arts such as weaving. Such an assemblage!

The traditional and popular Afternoon Tea ($19.95) includes finger sandwiches, scones with jam and whipped cream, desert, and, of course, a pot of tea. Add a cup of homemade soup or a salad for just $2.95 per item. Another option is Cream Tea ($8.95), with two scones with whipped cream, jam, and a pot of tea. More filling teas that include lunch (yea!) include the Drew Bailey Lunch ($16.50) that comes with a sandwich, cup of soup or a salad, dessert, and tea, and the Ploughman's Lunch ($16.50) with green salad, cheese wedges, fruit, bread or cheese scone, cookie, and, of course, tea. Or, just come for dessert. Childrens Tea is available, starting at $8.95, serving PB & J or turkey sandwich, a scone with jam and cream, cookies, and children's tea, apple juice or hot chocolate. Holiday teas, such as ones offered for Valentines' Day, Mother's Day, and the Victorian Tea at Christmas, are always extra special.

Hours: The shop is open Mon., Thurs. - Sat., 9am - 4pm; Sun., 9am - 4pm. Seatings are at 11:30am, 1pm, and 2:30pm. Reservations are recommended and required on weekends. Closed Tues., Wed., New Year's Day, Thanksgiving, and Christmas.
Price: Prices vary depending on the tea.
Ages: 5 years and up.

KILLER PIZZA FROM MARS

Escondido - (760) 741-6277; Oceanside - (760) 722-6060 / www.killerpizzafrommars.com
Escondido - 1040 W. El Norte Parkway; Oceanside - 3772 Mission Avenue

With a name like this, you have to expect something far out of this world! Both of the pizzerias are similar in theme, but have slightly different decor. At the larger and more decorated Oceanside location, first look through the window to be greeted by life-size figures of ET, Darth Mal, Jar Jar Binks, and a few other creatures. Inside, the science fiction/outer space theme is continued throughout this large pizza joint. The black ceilings feature constellations, inflatable aliens and astronauts, and small model space ships from *Stars Wars*, *Star Trek*, and more hanging from the ceiling. Some of the hanging objects glow in the dark.

The walls are covered with an eclectic assortment of anything remotely related to space, such as alien-themed movie posters, magazine covers featuring NASA happenings, and pictures of the cosmos. Bookcases and a large shelf on the wall are packed with more of this type of paraphernalia including games, collectibles, action figures, Jetson figurines, Conehead models, Buzz Lightyear dolls, toys, stuffed animals, more aliens, lunch boxes, glasses, masks, and more. Yoda, a Chewy head, and a few other such items are also featured. T.V. monitors and a couple of arcade-style games complete the kitschy ambiance.

The food is good and ranges from an assortment of pizzas (about $19.41 for a large with one "space partikul") to chicken salads ($7.49) to "spagetty with meetballs" ($6.99). Men might be from Mars, but I daresay that female folk enjoy the offerings from here, too.

Hours: Usually open Sun. - Thurs., 11am - 9pm; Fri. - Sat., 11am - 10pm. Call individual stores for specific hours.
Price: Prices are listed above. Discount coupons are available on the website.
Ages: All

THE OLD SPAGHETTI FACTORY (San Diego County)

San Diego - (619) 233-4323; San Marcos - (760) 471-0155 / www.osf.com
San Diego - 275 Fifth Avenue; San Marcos - 111 N. Twin Oaks Valley Road

See the entry for THE OLD SPAGHETTI FACTORY (Los Angeles County) on page 23 for details.

PARK HYATT AVIARA RESORT

(760) 448-1234 / www.parkaviara.hyatt.com
7100 Four Seasons Point, Carlsbad

All dressed up and nowhere to go? Indulge in an elegant repast of tea time at this fine resort hotel. Tables in the lobby/lounge are covered with white linen, sprinkled with rose petals, and set with fine china. A three-tiered silver cake plate bears scrumptious edibles of finger sandwiches; scones with rose petal jelly, lemon curd, and Devonshire cream; and petit fours and delicate pastries. Sip your choice of teas, including herbal and fruit infusions. A pianist plays during the Friday and Saturday afternoon teas.

Hours: Tea is served Wed. - Sun., 2pm - 4pm.
Price: $30 per person (with champagne - $37). Valet parking is complementary, with the tea.
Ages: 4 years and up.

PETER PIPER PIZZA

El Cajon - (619) 670-5197; National City - (619) 477-1788 / www.peterpiperpizza.com
El Cajon - 2983 Jamacha Road; National City - 3007 Highland Avenue

This huge, fun-filled pizza place is very similar to Chuck E. Cheese's. Obviously the main food offered here is pizza (a large cheese pizza is about $13.99), but chicken wings and a salad bar are also available. For entertainment, there are ball pits, arcade games, lots of skee ball lanes, and a merry-go-round that is free (yea!). The mascot, a green-spotted purple dinosaur, comes on stage a few times throughout the day/night to put on a show. You will have to purchase tokens for the games - twenty tokens for $5. Bring in a good report card and you've earned tokens on the house. The kids love coming here - just cover your ears to block out the din. Note that for a minimum of fifteen kids, one-hour tours are offered where youngsters see the kitchens, learn about dough and oven temperature, and, most importantly, top off their own 7" pizza. A drink and ten tokens are included in the $4.99 per child price. Adults, you're on your own!

Hours: Open Sun. - Thurs., 11am - 9pm; Fri.; 11am - 10pm; Sat., 10am - 10pm. Tours start at 9:30am - call to schedule a date.

Price: Admission is free, but bring money for food and tokens.

Ages: 1½ years and up.

ROCKET FIZZ SODA POPS AND CANDY SHOP (San Diego County)

Pacific Beach - (858) 581-FIZZ (3499); Vista - (760) 806-1050 / www.rocketfizz.com

Pacific Beach - 1414 Garnet Avenue; Vista - 20 Main Street, Suite 120

See ROCKET FIZZ SODA POPS AND CANDY SHOP (Los Angeles) on page 24 for details on this shop with an incredible array of unusual sodas and candy and more.

Price: Technically, free

Ages: 3 years and up.

RUBY'S (San Diego County)

(800) HEY RUBY (439-7829) - for all locations. Note that all the phone numbers end in RUBY (7829): Carlsbad - (760) 931-RUBY; Oceanside - (760) 433-RUBY; San Diego - (619) 294-RUBY / www.rubys.com

Carlsbad - 5630 Paseo Del Norte, suite 130D; Oceanside - 1 Pierview Way on the pier; San Diego - 1640 Camino Del Rio N., suite 360P at Mission Valley Center (this one has a recreation of the 1939 World's Fair pavilion)

See the entry for RUBY'S (Orange County) on page 252 for details.

SHAKESPEARE'S CORNER SHOPPE & AFTERNOON TEA

(619) 683-BRIT (2748) / www.ukcornershoppe.com

3719 India Street, San Diego

"I count myself in nothing else so happy as in a soul rememb'ring my good friends." This Shakespearian quote is appropriate in sharing time with a friend over a spot of tea. Inside Shakespeare's Corner (which is small enough to be about corner size), the shoppe sells a lovely selection of British goods - food, gift items, flags, tea accessories, clothing items, and more.

Seating, for up to fifteen people, is on the outside patio at wrought-iron tables and chairs. Authentic British Afternoon Tea includes finger sandwiches, sausage roll, a home-baked scone with Devon cream and jam, biscuit selection, cake medley, and choice of tea for $23.95. A Child's Afternoon Tea, for ages 12 and under, offers similar fare for $14.95. If you don't want a full tea, order a pot of tea and a scone with cream and jam for $8.95; snacks such as bread pudding with Devon cream for $4.25; or an assortment of finger sandwiches for $5.95. Beverages, besides tea, include British sodas, hot chocolate, and juice. Reservations are required.

Hours: The shoppe is open Mon. - Fri., 10am - 8pm. Tea is served Thurs. - Sun., noon to 4pm. Closed Thanksgiving and Christmas.

Price: Prices are listed above.

Ages: 4 years and up.

SHOGUN (San Diego County)

San Diego - (858) 560-7399; San Marcos - (760) 744-6600 / www.restaurantshogun.com

San Diego - 5451 Kearny Villa Road; San Marcos - 695 S. Rancho Santa Fe Road

See the entry for SHOGUN (Los Angeles County) (pg. 25) for details.

Hours: San Diego - Mon. - Thurs., 11:30am - 9:30pm; Fri., 11:30am - 10pm; Sat., noon - 10pm; Sun., noon - 9:30pm. San Marcos - Mon. - Thurs., 11:30am - 2pm; 5pm - 9pm; Fri., 11:30am - 2pm and 5pm - 9:30pm; Sat., 12:30pm - 9:30pm; Sun., 12:30pm - 9pm.

SUMMER SUNSET LUAU ON MISSION BAY

(858) 539-8774 or (800) 422-8386 / www.catamaranresort.com/luau

3999 Mission Boulevard, Mission Bay.

See Summer Sunset Luau on Mission Bay in the Calendar Section (pg. 478, 736) for more information on this Polynesian experience.

Hours: Open June to August, every Fri., 6pm - 9pm, plus mid-July to mid-August, every Tues., 6pm - 9pm.

Price: Non-hotel guests prices are $64 for adults; $29 for ages 5 - 12; children 4 and under are free.

Ages: 5 years and up.

TEA UPON CHATSWORTH   ☀
(619) 858-CU4T (2848) / www.teauponchatsworth.com $$$$
2180 Chatsworth Boulevard, San Diego

With hard-wood floors and fairly simple decor, this pleasant tearoom has just the right touches: some intimate tables and some longer ones, but not too crowded, set with linen and lace tablecloths under glass, fresh flowers, and pretty, tiered plates for serving delectable food. Music plays softly in the background. High-placed china plates, art, and some odds and ends border the walls. Even though tea is traditionally slanted toward women, menfolk feel comfortable here as well. There are tea items for sale on the window sills, in a few cupboards and behind the counter.

The menu changes seasonally. Here is a sampling, however: The three-course (Afternoon Tea), Windsor Tea, at $25.95 per person, comes with eight different food items - perhaps a parmesan cheese popover; tea sandwiches, such as curried chicken and apricot chutney, and cucumber and dill cream cheese; a mushroom and sherry croissant; a scone with cream and cranberry rose petal jam; a tartlet; tea cake; fresh fruit; and a pot of tea. The selection of tea is wide and varied, so it's great that they encourage you to try several of them. The four-course (High Tea), Queen's Tea, $28.95 per person, comes with twelve food choices. The children's tea, for ages 4 to 10 years old, is $22.95 per child and might come with peanut butter and honey sandwich in the shape of a teapot; petite chicken sandwich; bite-sized desserts; and a scone with jam and cream, plus a tea beverage. Note that a gluten free menu and vegan menu are also available. *Tea* you soon!

Hours: Open Thurs. - Sat., 11am - 5pm; Sun., noon - 5. Tea seatings are generally at 11:30am, 2pm, and 4:30pm. Reservations are advised.
Price: Menu prices are listed above.
Ages: 4 years and up.

—FAMILY PAY AND PLAY—

AIR TIME   ☀
(619) 660-9357 / www.airtimeparty.com $$
2705 Via Orange Way, suite C, Spring Valley

Air Time is 8,000 square feet of carpeted indoor fun! Six giant, colorful inflatables include the Adrenaline Rush II obstacle course; Rock and Roll boxing and jousting ring (a favorite for guys!); Jurassic Adventure with a seventeen-foot volcano and rock climbing wall; and a clubhouse with a slide and basketball hoop. A video arcade and sound system complete the fun. Besides birthday parties, this place is available for team parties, youth groups, adult groups, and more. Mark your calendars for the occasional Mom's Night Out from 6pm to 9pm when you can drop off the kids for three hours (three hours!) of fun and pizza for them, and fun and time for you.

Hours: Open play time is usually at least on Tues. and Thurs., 10:30am - noon, and on certain holidays. Check the online calendar.
Price: $8 per child; adults are free.
Ages: 2 years and up, depending on the event.

ATLANTIS LASER TAG   ☀
(619) 420-3824 / www.atlantislasertag.com $$$
510 Broadway, suites 1-3, Chula Vista

This fantastic, family-friendly, huge (6,000 square feet), multi-level, state-of-the-art laser tag arena is underwater themed. There are cool fish murals (I like the shark ones) that incorporate sea turtles and coral, plus underwater-looking statutes on top of the walls in the arena and hanging from the ceiling. The maze-like setting has walls to shoot around, over, and under, as well as ramps, windows, doorways, pillars, and other hiding spots. Fog, music, blue neon lighting, and never knowing where your enemy will pop out keeps the adrenaline rushing and keeps you coming back for more. Up to forty-four people can play at one time.

Another element that sets this laser tag arena apart is that it offers over twenty different games or strategies, for both individual players and team play. Some of the game options include tag, fugitive, gladiator, time warp, capture the flag, deadaim, and masters. The lightweight, flashing phasers have a variety of settings which can also add to the challenge.

The lobby has video arcade games, with a prize redemption area, plus air hockey and a full-service snack bar that

serves pizza, popcorn, Icees, and soft drinks. Enjoy use of the themed private room for parties.

Hours: Usually open Tues. - Thurs., 4pm - 9pm; Fri., 3pm - midnight; Sat., noon - midnight; Sun., noon - 9pm. Open Mon. by reservation. It is open during the summer and school breaks Mon. - Thurs., 2pm - 9pm; the rest is the same.

Price: $7 for one game; $18 for 3 games. Always call or check the website for specials.

Ages: Must be 7 years old or 48" tall.

AURA SKATEBOARD TRAINING FACILITY

(760) 542-0232 / www.auraskateboarding.com

1074 La Mirada Court, Vista

This mid-size, indoor skatepark is a kid-cool and comfortable place to skateboard, scooter and BMX, and to just hang. Beginners on up enjoy the challenges of the competition style street course and spine ramp, with the extras of lessons, camps, clinics, contests, concerts, and lock-ins offered. Helmets and pads are mandatory. One section of the room has the vibe of being in a big garage that's been converted to a hang out place with some couches, assorted chairs and tables, plus a pool table, foosball, air hockey, original Pac-Man (and other games), and some games and toys for younger kids. The company also designs and builds custom ramps.

Hours: Usually open Mon. - Thurs., 3pm - 8pm; Fri., noon - 9pm; Sat., 10am - 10pm; Sun., noon - 6pm. It's open at noon on school half-days, rainy days or holidays. It's open more hours in the summer - you can see they cater to kids (in a good way).

Price: $10 per day for non-members. The last hour is half price. Check out membership and all that includes.

Ages: 6 years and up.

BELMONT PARK

(858) 228-WAVE (9283) or (858) 488-1549 - park and amusement rides; (858) 488-1971 - arcade, mini golf; or (858) 228-9300 - the Wave House. / www.belmontpark.com; www.wavehousesandiego.com; www.wavehouseathleticclub.com

3146 Mission Boulevard, San Diego

A few shops; restaurants, including the fine dining of Cannonball with seating on the beachfront rooftop; eateries, including an ice cream store and a candy shop; and an arcade and games center encircle the ten, or so, amusement rides and other attractions at Belmont Park. In the center is the Giant Dipper Roller Coaster ($6) which doesn't have any loops, but has plenty of ups and downs! A replica of the Looff Liberty wooden carousel ($2) has horses as well as an ostrich, giraffe, and tiger to ride on. Other amusement rides include traditional Bumper Cars ($4); Krazy Kars, which are bumper cars that bump and spin all around ($4); Tilt-A-Whirl ($4); Beach Blaster, which swings riders standing up sixty feet in the air at randomly occurring G-forces ($5); Control Freak, a vertical ride where riders control the forward, backward and flip motions of the car ($5), which is similar to the Octotron roller coaster ride here in which riders control the motion, as well as the speed ($5); Vertical Plunge, a three-story drop ($3); and the kiddie rides of Crazy Submarine ($3) and Thunder Boats ($2). Certain height restrictions apply to the rides. Play some Midway games that are interspersed among the rides.

Face your fear of heights on Sky Ropes, an outdoors, suspended, obstacle ropes course where you are harnessed in and move over rope bridges and along beams among real and fake tree tops ($6.95). Scale the thirty-foot rock wall of Sky Climb that offers a few different routes ($5.95). Sink your shots at the eighteen-hole Tiki Town Adventure Golf, a mini golf course that is tropically themed. The course is extra fun with some holes that are inside and some that are out. Check out the erupting volcano - one of the best attractions on the course! $8.95 a game. The Vault Laser Maze challenge looks like something from a spy movie as players try to go over and dive/roll under the lasers in a vault setting without breaking them so an alarm won't be tripped. This game can be over quickly as it stops as soon as you "break" a lazer. $2 a game/try. Is there fun to be had in a post-apocalyptic world? According to RUSH Laser Tag and Arcade, which has this motif - yes. This two-story, 3,000 square-foot arena allows all the action of laser tag to be unleashed for $7.95 a game, or $15.95 for unlimited games. Classics and the latest in video and arcade games are also here. Earn tickets and redeem them for prizes at the redemption center.

Besides these other activities, you can continuously surf or body board the perfect five-foot wave via the FlowRider machine at the Wave House Athletic Club. Take lessons or just let it rip. Hourly fees are $20, plus a one-time registration fee of $10 for nonclub members. Feeling adventurous? Try ten-foot waves on the advanced FlowRider called FlowBarrel or Bruticus Maximus (which is definitely tougher sounding). Hourly fees are $40, plus a

one-time registration fee of $20. While at Belmont Park, take a plunge at The Plunge. This large, indoor swimming pool boasts a beautiful underwater/whale mural, painted by renown marine artist, Wyland. The enclosed pool, kept at 84 degrees, is surrounded by huge windows looking out on palm trees, suggesting a tropical atmosphere. Swim sessions are $7 for adults; $6 for seniors and children 6 months to 17 years.

Too nice a day to go swimming inside? Go for a dip outside, as the ocean is just a few steps away. The surf, sand, and bike trail on the beach are "shore" to help make your day at the park a good one!

Hours: The stores and restaurants are open daily, usually 10am - 7pm. In summer, the rides are open Sun. - Wed., 11am - 11pm; Thurs. - Sat., 11am - midnight. The rest of the year the rides are open Mon. - Thurs., 11am - 8pm; Fri. - Sun., 11am - 10pm. Call first as hours fluctuate a lot! Waves are open to ride Mon. - Fri., starting at noon; Sat. - Sun., starting at 11am. The Plunge is open Mon. - Fri., noon - 4pm and 8pm - 10pm; Sat. - Sun., noon - 8pm.

Price: Attractions are priced above. An unlimited rides pass is $26.95 for 48" and taller; $15.95 for 47" and under. Tuesday nights during the summer, beginning at 4pm, most rides at the amusement park are $1 each. Always check the website or call for special deals.

Ages: All, although most of the rides are geared for ages 7 and up.

BOARDWALK

(619) 449-7800 / www.boardwalk-parkway.com

1286 Fletcher Parkway, El Cajon

$$$

This Boardwalk is not made of boards, nor is it by the seaside; it is, however, a large indoor amusement center for kids. It's clean with brightly-colored games and rides that elicited several, "This is FUN!" comments from young kids. Each token costs 25¢. The main attractions are the **carousel** (three tokens), **castle bounce** (three tokens), **frog hopper** (six tokens), **Himalaya** (six tokens) and **soft play gym** (eight tokens). The two-story soft play gym area, for kids 60" and under, has ball pits, a mini zip line, slides, and obstacle courses, plus tubes to crawl through. A decent-size, glow-in-the-dark **Laser tag** arena is another exciting element at the Boardwalk. Almost eight minutes of running around and "zapping" people costs $4 for the first game, $3 for each game thereafter, or $7.95 per person for unlimited play. Numerous arcade and video games are also here with a prize redemption center.

The full-service snack bar offers salads, pizza, pasta, and more, and weekly family deals. Ask about the evening pizza buffet special, such as Monday through Thursday, $6.99 for adults; $3.99 for kids. Kids meals are regularly $2.95 for a choice of corn dog, chicken nuggets, or pizza, plus fries and a drink. If you feel like scoring more fun, strike out to Parkway Bowl, a connecting bowling alley, with sixty lanes of regular or cosmic bowl. Parkway also has a room of video games and a billiards table.

Hours: Open Mon. - Thurs., 11:30am - 9pm; Fri., 11:30am - 11:30pm; Sat., 11am - 11:30pm; Sun., 11am - 9pm. Laser tag is open Mon. - Thurs., 6pm - 9pm; Fri., 6pm - 11pm; Sat., noon - 11pm; Sun., noon - 9pm. Open longer hours during the summer and school break.

Price: Attractions are individually priced above. An unlimited play pass Mon. - Thurs. is $6.75; Fri. - Sun. and holidays, $7.75. Laser tag prices are listed above.

Ages: 1½ years - 12.

BOOMERS! - El Cajon

(619) 593-1155 / www.boomersparks.com

1155 Graves Avenue, El Cajon

$$$$

Come to this family fun center to play for just an hour, or have fun all day. Green fees pay for two rounds at any of the three, nine-hole themed **miniature golf** courses. Choose Memory Lane (fairy tale motif), Iron Horse (western), and/or Lost Crusade (Egyptian) - $9 for adults, $5.99 for seniors and kids 12 years and under. Other attractions include **bumper boats** - $6 for adults, $2 for passengers (height restrictions apply); **go-karts** - $7 for drivers who must be at least 58" tall, $2 for passengers who must be at least 40" tall; **batting cages**; and the **Kid's County Fair**. The latter consists of three rides for young children, 36" to 48" tall: a roller coaster, Ferris wheel, and mini-planes. Each ride costs $3. A **rock wall** costs $6 for two climbs - make the most of them. The two-story arcade and video game building is attractively set up. A full snack bar is also at this fun center, including an all-you-can-eat buffet (pizza, tacos, salad, soup, pasta, and build your own Sundae bar) on weekends for only for $9.99 for adults; $8.99 for seniors; $6.99 for kids. Food and fun - what more could you want?!

Hours: Kids' County Fair is open Mon. - Thurs., 3pm - 7pm; Fri., 3pm - 8pm; Sat., noon - 8pm; Sun., noon - 7pm. Other attractions are open Mon. - Thurs., noon - 8pm; Fri., noon - 11pm; Sat., 11am - 10pm; Sun., 11am - 8pm. Hours fluctuate, especially as they are open longer hours over holidays and school breaks, so please call before you come.

Price: Attractions are individually priced above, or purchase an unlimited use pass for $29.99. The pass is offered daily during the summer; weekends only the rest of the year. The Kid's County Fair is unlimited ride and mini golf for $16.99. Ask about specials.

Ages: 2½ years and up.

BOOMERS! - San Diego

(858) 560-4212 / www.boomersparks.com
6999 Clairemont Mesa Boulevard, San Diego

So much fun can be had at just one place! Choose from two themed **miniature golf** courses: Storybook Land, which has a castle, Cinderella's pumpkin, the shoe from the old woman who lived in one, and more; or Western Town, with a bank, jail, storefront facades, a livery stable, and wagons - $9 per person; ages 4 and under are free. Other attractions include **go karts** - $7 for a five-minute ride (drivers must be at least 58" tall), $2 for a passenger; **bumper boats** - $6 per driver, who must be at least 44" tall, $2 per passenger; **batting cages**; and **Flame Thrower**, a two-person thrill ride. The **Kid's County Fair** has six rides, including teacups, a Ferris wheel, a train ride, a swing, and a fire engine that goes in the air and around and around. Rides cost $3 each or purchase an all-day rides pass for $16.99, which includes unlimited golf, too. Of course there is a video and arcade game area and a prize redemption center. There is also a separate section for less violent kiddie video games. A Boomer's cafe serving pizza and other necessary foods is on-site here, too.

Hours: Open Mon. - Thurs., noon - 8pm; Fri., noon - 10pm; Sat., 10am - 10pm; Sun., 10am - 8pm. Open extended hours in the summer. The Kids County Fair is open Mon. - Thurs., 3pm - 7pm; Fri., 3pm - 8pm; Sat. Sun., noon - 8pm.

Price: Attractions are individually priced above or buy an all-play pass for $29.99..

Ages: 2 years and up.

BOOMERS! - Vista

(760) 945-9474 / www.boomersparks.com
1525 W. Vista Way, Vista

This family fun center really has it all! If you're in a mutinous mood, play the pirate-themed **miniature golf** course with its piratey ship and fountains. If you're feeling rather noble, play King Arthur's course with its huge (relatively speaking) castles and dungeons, and a bridge over water. Golf prices are $9 per person; ages 4 and under are free. **Laser Runner** is an every man/woman/child-for-himself laser tag game played inside an inflatable battleship bounce. There are soft obstacles to hide behind (or jump on) and even small rooms to run around in. The game is action-packed, sweaty, and fun. The cost is $6 for a five-minute game, and children must be 5 years old to play. **Kid's County Fair** is a huge, four-story, soft-play area with slides, obstacle courses, ball pits, tubes and tunnels. This major gerbil run was a major hit with my boys. The cost is $3 for kids, who must be under 50" and wear socks. Other attractions here include **batting cages**; **go karts** - $7 for drivers, who must be at least 58" tall, $2 for passengers, who must be at least 40" tall; and **bumper boats** - $6 a driver, who must be at least 44" tall, $2 for passengers.

The noisy, but attractive, main two-story building houses numerous video and arcade games. A nickel arcade section is upstairs. Boomers Cafe is a full-service restaurant where pizza and other tasty family fare is served along with a fun atmosphere.

Hours: Open Mon. - Thurs., noon - 8pm; Fri., noon - 11pm; Sat., 10am - 11pm; Sun., 10am - 8pm. Open extended hours in the summer and on school breaks.

Price: Attractions are individually priced above, or purchase an unlimited pass for $29.99; $16.99 for unlimited kiddie rides and mini golf. Check the website for discounts and coupons.

Ages: 2 years and up.

CARMEL VALLEY SKATEBOARD PARK / CARMEL VALLEY COMMUNITY PARK

(858) 552-1616 - park; (858) 552-1623 - pool / www.sandiego.gov/park-and-recreation
12600 El Camino Real - skate park; 3777 Townsgate Drive - park and pool, San Diego

Is your child a ripper? This means a really good and consistent skater in skate-speak. At 13,500 square feet, this night-lighted park has what it takes to give your kids the edge. It has a challenge course, a concrete bowl, and urban elements of railings, stairs, banks, and ledges. Amenities include a restroom, shade structure, and observations area. Helmet and knee and elbow pads are required. A parent or legal guardian must accompany kids 12 years and under.

The surrounding park amenities include picnic areas, tennis courts, a multi-purpose athletic field, a recreational center with a game room and gym, and a great playground geared for younger kids with short slides, low bridges, climbing apparatus, and interactive games attached to the main play structure. The adjacent aquatic facility has a main swimming pool and a children's wading pool, plus two large water slides that end in a catch pool.

Hours: The park and skate park are open daily, 10am - 8pm. The pool is open most of the year for recreational swim Mon., Wed., Fri., noon - 3:30pm; Sat., noon - 3pm. It is open in the summer, Mon. - Fri., noon - 3pm; Sat., noon - 4pm. The slides are open Memorial Day through Labor Day.

Price: Free. The pool is $4 for adults; $2 for seniors and ages 15 and under.

Ages: 7 years and up.

CHUCK E. CHEESE'S (San Diego County)

See the entry for CHUCK E. CHEESE'S (Los Angeles County) on page 16 for details.

CHULA VISTA SKATEPARK / LEN MOORE SKATEPARK

(619) 421-4011 / www.chulavista.com
1301 Oleander Avenue, Chula Vista

This supervised skate park is huge at 55,000 square feet of concrete and 10,000 square feet of wood. It also has a courtyard with a park-like ambiance, including picnic tables, and an all-round safe feel to it. (As safe as one can be doing ollies, flips, and other stunts!) The wood section has a mini half-pipe and a series of ramps. The concrete skate area has separate components of bowls, rails, steps, reservoirs, three- to nine-foot banks, a pyramid, ledges, fun boxes, and lots of just-skating space. Well-lit at night and popular at any time, this is one of the best skate parks we've visited.

A pro shop and snack shop, that sells chips and candy, are on the grounds. A helmet and knee and elbow pads are required. Skaters under 18 must have a parent or legal guardian accompany them on their first visit to fill out a waiver. Ask about skate camps, lessons, and numerous special events.

Hours: Open most of the year Wed. - Thurs., 2:45pm - 8pm; Fri., 2:45pm - 9pm; Sat., 11:30am - 9pm; Sun., 11:30am - 5:45pm. Call about possibly extended hours during the summer and school breaks.

Price: $4 per session for members; $10 per nonmember. Membership is $25 a year.

Ages: 6 years and up.

CITY OF SANTEE AQUATIC CENTER at CAMERON FAMILY YMCA

(619) 449-9622 / www.eastcounty.ymca.org
10123 Riverwalk Drive, Santee

Beat the heat at this very fun aquatic center which is part of the YMCA. There are three recreation pools: one is a lap pool, one has a twisty slide for bigger kids (48" and taller), and one is an interactive pool. The separate water play area for younger children is in one-and-a-half-feet of water. The water play area has mini slides, swings (over the water), climbing apparatus, and a structure that squirts out water in all different directions. Bring a picnic to enjoy on the large lawn just outside the gated aquatic center. (There is not much shade around, though.) Note that children 6 years and under must be accompanied by an adult in the water; there is a maximum of two children per adult; and waivers for kids 17 and under must be signed.

Hours: The lap pool is open daily, year round. The interactive pool/slide, etc. is open April - mid-June and September - October, usually on Sat. - Sun., noon - 2pm and 2:30pm - 4:30pm. Open in the summer daily, extended hours and sessions are often 3 hours long, not 2.

Price: $3 per person per two or three-hour swim/water play session for Santee residents; $5 per person for non-residents.

Ages: 2 years and up.

DAVE & BUSTER'S (San Diego County)

(619) 280-7115 / www.daveandbusters.com
2931 Camino del Rio North, San Diego

See DAVE & BUSTER'S (Orange County) (pg. 258) for details.

Hours: Open Sun. - Wed., 11am - midnight; Thurs. - Sat., 11am - 1am.

FUN-4-ALL

(619) 427-1473 / www.fun-4-all.biz
950 Industrial Boulevard, Chula Vista

This small, family amusement park has an older, well-used, **miniature golf** course with a nautical theme - $6.50 a round for adults, $5 for kids 12 years and under; a fun **bumper boat** ride around a few islands - $5 for drivers (must be over 44") and $1.75 for passengers; **go-karts** - $6.50 for drivers and $1.75 for passengers (height restrictions apply); and **batting cages**. There are also several video and arcade games inside the main building, and a full-service snack bar.

Hours: Open Mon. - Fri., 10am - 10pm; Sat. - Sun., 9am - 10pm. Closed Thanksgiving and Christmas.
Price: Attractions are individually priced above. Check the website for coupons.
Ages: 4 years and up.

FUNBELIEVABLE

(619) 456-2474 / www.funbelievableplay.com
11655 Riverside Drive, Suite 155-157, Lakeside

Tropically-themed, this huge indoor play place, is almost as good as an island get-away; almost. The main, tri-level, mega play structure, decorated with surfboards and fake palm trees, sports tiki-faced foam obstacles; side-by-side racing slides; cargo ropes to climb; tubes and tunnels to crawl through; a ball pit; a ball suction dispenser; hop on bounces to swing on; a rock-climbing wall; large balls; a mini zip line; and oversized Lego-like bricks to build things. Socks are required.

An enclosed, Hawaiian-looking area just for toddlers has play surfboards; a tiny ball pit; a short play structure with foam stairs; mini slides; and soft play toys to play on and with.

There is also a basketball and (mini) soccer area, with netting all around, and a lounge and cafe right in front of the play structures for easy viewing. The cafe serves coffee drinks and smoothies, as well as sandwiches, salads, paninis and more. Funbelievable offers fun for parents, too, with Date Night drop offs (only $15 per child) and Family Fun Nights every Friday from 5pm to 8pm. There are also camps and special events - check the website for specific information.

Hours: Open Mon. - Thurs., 10am - 6pm; Fri., 10am - 8pm; Sat. - Sun., 10am- 6pm. Call first as sometimes they are closed for a private event. Closed all major holidays.
Price: $10 for the first child; $8 for a sibling; non-walkers are free with a paid sibling or $5 without; adults are free with paid child.
Ages: 1 - 12 years

GET AIR POWAY (San Diego County)

(858) 848-1AIR (1247) / www.getairpoway.com
12160 Community Road, Poway

See GET AIR TEMECULA (Riverside County) (pg. 343) for a description. This 20,000 square foot facility also features competition style slack line - a thin, flexible plank over the foam pit to walk on or do tricks.

Hours: Open Sun. - Thurs., 10am - 10pm; Fri. - Sat., 10am - midnight.
Price: $14 per person for the first hour; $9 for the second; $7 an hour for 45" and under who use the kid's room only.
Ages: 3 years and up.

GIANT PAINTBALL PARK

(877) GIANT-97 (442-6897) / www.giantsportzoutlet.com
1800 Wildcat Canyon Road, Lakeside

You look like (and probably feel like) a weekend warrior in this game of paintball. Suited up with a full, wrap-around face shield and a paint ball gun (and maybe even some camouflage clothing), you are ready to play an incredibly intense game of "tag" and "capture the flag" at one of several outdoor "battlefields." The fully themed fields include Western, which is not the Old West, but more like urban west with junky, metal vehicles and other things to hide behind; Concrete, that looks like a bombed out city with its numerous concrete tubes and half buildings; Castle, which is a huge castle and its grounds; and Death Valley and Bunker Hill, both of which are heavy on natural terrain

meaning lots of brush and some trees, and some hills. Moving stealthily through the scenarios, using cover, you spy an opponent, then pull the trigger, and splat - he/she has been tagged (ouch!) with a paint ball (or airsoft pellet) and is out of the game. (Realize that this can happen to you, also.) Each game lasts about fifteen minutes. Strategizing and staying focused are key elements. (Oh yea, and having fun, too.)

Your admission fee includes all-day play, which is about fifteen games, and one tank of CO_2. Wear dark clothing that you don't care much about, and expect it to get very dirty. Ask about kids-only events. Participants under 18 must have a waiver signed by a parent or guardian. Airsoft players get their shot of fun here, too, on the same fields (not at the same time), just without all the color of paintballs! Tip: Paint ball and airsoft are great ways to burn calories!

Hours: Open Sat. - Sun., 9am - 4pm.
Price: Field entrance is $20 for paintball or airsoft players with your own equipment. A .50 caliber package is $39 for entry, gun, mask, all-day air and 200 paintballs. Other rentals include masks, $6; .68 caliber assault rifle, $14; etc.
Ages: As young as 10 years old with a parent; 12 years and up on their own.

INFLATABLE WORLD

(619) 216-0199 / www.inflatableworldsd.com
1640 Camino Del Rio North, San Diego

$$$$

Inflatable World is just what it says it is - a world of just inflatables. There are thirteen, giant inflatables with lots of eye appeal such as a massive tiger, menacing dinosaur, chomping shark, and a ferocious King Kong, plus super heros, tropical island themes, and more. Seven of the inflatables are huge slides, four are obstacle courses and two are combo bounce houses. There are a few for younger children, but they are mostly geared for kids 5 years and up (I think). Running and playing on them will wear your kids out and they will get sweaty.

Located in the parking lot of Westfield Mission Valley Mall, this world offers very little shade. Know that. There are a few tables and chairs, and some have umbrellas. The floor between the inflatables is "carpeted" with artificial turf. Be prepared for your time here, too, by bringing water bottles; lots of them, as kids get thirsty while working up a sweat having fun. Water bottles are sold here. No outside food is allowed in, but as you can come and go with your wristband throughout the day, you can leave to grab a bite to eat somewhere else (the mall is right here), and come back. It's recommended to wear long shirts and long pants, even in the summer so participants won't get burned or rashes from the inflatables when they are hot. Adults who are jumping must be under 180lbs.

Hours: Open February - September, Wed. - Fri., noon - 6pm; Sat. - Sun., 10am - 6pm (or 7pm).
Price: $20 for ages 13 and up (non-jumping adults are free); $17 for ages 4 - 12; $15 for ages 2 - 3.
Ages: 5 years and up.

INVASION LASER TAG

(760) 571-9191 / www.invasionlasertag.com
1290 W. San Marcos Boulevard, Suite 101, San Marcos

$$$

Enter the future. Well, just this 5,000 square foot, multi-level laser tag arena that is futuristically and space themed. The black and gray walls and partitions (designed to look like broken stone) have occasional shots of color, mostly from exploding planets, and the props (like robots) and even the ramps are really cool looking. Fog, lights, music, and the adrenaline rush of shooting your opponents with a laser gun while trying to evade getting tagged yourself are all part of the excitement. Call or check the website for specials and info about Midnight Madness games on the weekends.

Ever see spy movies where the spies must step or jump over, and roll or crawl under lasers to get through and reach the goal on the other side of the room? Lazer Frenzy offers you the opportunity to try your skills at dodging laser beams while incorporating mirrors, haze, and neon images into the maze-like challenge. See how high you score (i.e. how fast you complete the course without touching lasers) - mission accomplished.

Hours: Usually open Wed. - Thurs., 3pm - 8pm; Fri., 3pm - midnight; Sat., noon - midnight; Sun., noon - 8pm. Open longer hours, usually at 1pm, on school breaks. Closed Mon., Tues., New Year's Day, Thanksgiving, and Christmas.
Price: Laser tag is $7 for one game; $18 for 3. Lazer Frenzy is $2 for one game; $5 for 3.
Ages: 7 years and up.

JOHN'S INCREDIBLE PIZZA CO. (San Diego County)

(619) 472-5555 / www.johnspizza.com

$$$$

3010 Plaza Bonita Road in Westfield Plaza Bonita (mall), National City

See JOHN'S INCREDIBLE PIZZA CO. (Orange County) (pg. 248) for details. Also see WESTFIELD PLAZA BONITA (pg. 524) for details about mall offerings.

Hours: Open Mon. - Thurs., 11am - 9pm; Fri., 11am - 10:30pm; Sat., 10am - 10:30pm; Sun., 11am - 9pm.

K1 SPEED (San Diego County)

Carlsbad - (760) 929-2225 or (888) 929-2225; San Diego - (619) 241-4740 / www.K1speed.com

$$$$$

Carlsbad - 6212 Carte Del Abet; San Diego - 1709 Main Street

Kids don't have to wait until their sixteenth birthday to drive anymore (that's a scary thought!) to put the pedal to the metal at this large (i.e., 60,000-square-foot) indoor kart track. Kids, accompanied by an adult, between the ages of 5 and 13 (and between 48" to 58" tall) can drive junior karts around while adults (at least 58" tall), in a separate race, accelerate around the corners in the real race cars and go for their best time in fully-computerized, electric-powered karts (no gas fumes!). Head-sock, helmet and a driver's briefing are standard. Leagues, for all ages, are also available. Kids (and adults) can learn about cars and racing - throttle, braking, brake point, and on-track etiquette - in this program, as well as doing some racing.

A public viewing area allows nonparticipants to watch the action, or play some games in the lobby, such as air hockey and video simulations. A Pit Cafe is inside as well. Drivers over 18 must have a valid driver's license. Younger drivers must have a waiver signed by a parent or legal guardian.

Hours: Mon. - Thurs., noon - 10pm; Fri., 11am - 11pm; Sat., 10am - 11pm; Sun., 10am - 8pm. Closed on Thanksgiving and closed early on New Year's Eve, 4th of July, Christmas Eve and Christmas.

Price: $19.99 per race, which is about 14 laps for adults (12 laps for juniors) or 10 minutes, plus a $6 one-time, license registration fee.

Ages: Jr. racers must be at least 48"; adult racers must be at least 4' 10"

KIDSVILLE PLAYGYM

(760) 730-9022 / www.kidsvilleplaygym.com

$$

2375 Marron Road, Carlsbad

Part gym, part indoor play place, and all exploratory, Kidsville is a clean, bright and fun destination just for little ones. Much of the flooring of the large room is padded so children using the colorful padded shapes for gymnastics, the tumbling mats, uneven bars, balance beam, ladder attached to the wall and the three small trampolines won't get hurt.

Towards the back of the room is a large castle wall with a room behind it for kids to play in. It contains a very short rock climbing wall and a ladder that takes climbers up to an enclosed slide. Across the way, a little red schoolhouse has a chalkboard and some toys. A niche room has couches, a round climbing structure, and lots of toys on tot-size tables that sport various scenes. A cute, carpeted room just for little, little ones contains a bitty ball pit, Little Tyke slides and cars, and lots of toys and stuffed animals. A fake rock hill has a slide coming out of it - great for imaginative play. Three small, themed rooms hold an array of costumes for dress-up play, and while the construction junction also has lots of toy trucks and tools, the kitchen is fully supplied.

Another lounge section in the front has couches for parents, plus tables and chairs. Ask about calendar events, story times, classes, membership opportunities, and Parents' Night Out that are offered here. See WESTFIELD PLAZA CAMINO REAL (pg. 524) for info about the mall right across the street.

Hours: Open play is usually Mon., 10:15am - 6pm; Tues. - Fri., 9:30am - 6pm; Sat., 10:15am - 5pm; Sun., 10am - 6pm. Call first, especially on the weekends, as there is no open play when a birthday party is booked.

Price: $10 for the first child; $8 per sibling; non-walking children are $5 or free with full price paid sibling. Adults are free.

Ages: 7 years and under, only.

KID VENTURES 4S RANCH

(858) 207-6088 / www.kidventuresplay.com; www.indoorplaysandiego.com

$$$

10760 Thornmint Road, San Diego

See KID VENTURES PACIFIC BEACH (pg. 487) for details about this fantastic, indoor play place for kids (and adults). Here are a few differences: This location is the biggest one thus far; it has a sitting area in front of a wonderful and inviting beach scene mural that showcases water, a city line and a pier; there are two play castles; a street (for

kid-size cars) is in front of the village buildings; and one of the classes is Super Hero Training.

Hours: Open Mon. - Fri., 9am - 6pm; Sat., 9am - noon. Closed Sat. afternoon and Sun. for private parties.

Price: $15 a child - walking and older; $8 for siblings. Purchase 8 passes for $80. Call for group and military discounts.

Ages: 1 ½ years and up.

KID VENTURES EASTLAKE

(619) 651-8622 / www.indoorplaysandiego.com

851 Showroom Place, Chula Vista

See KID VENTURES PACIFIC BEACH (the next entry) for details about this fantastic, indoor play place for kids (and adults). Here are a few differences: This location is a little bigger than the one in Pacific Beach; its rock climbing wall looks like a craggy mountain (with a friendly skull on background); it has a small enclosure for toddlers; and there is an outside play area with some fake palm trees, "water" with an alligator painted on it, some slides, and a small bounce all on artificial grass.

Hours: Open Mon. - Thurs., 10am - 6:30pm; Fri., 10am - 8:30pm; Sat., 9am - 12:30pm. Closed Sat. afternoon and Sun. for private parties.

Ages: 1 ½ years and up.

KID VENTURES PACIFIC BEACH

(858) 272-2266 / www.indoorplaysandiego.com

5066 Santa Fe Street, Pacific Beach

Sometimes it does take a village - a village to entertain and encourage creative thinking and play for kids to grow and learn. This play village has life-sized sidewalk stores and buildings so that kids immerse themselves in roles as they pretend real life. In the Market, they shop for groceries and use the cash register. Or, they can don an apron in the Coke-inspired, fully-equipped Diner and make meals on the little kitchen appliances and serve them, or be waited on. The Theater offers a place to see a show after a meal - one that kids put on using musical instruments, imagination, a microphone and a stage. The Nursery allows little ones to be big brothers or sisters, or doctors, as they take care of baby dolls and even use stethoscopes and more. Dress up in proper fire attire and then climb aboard the fire truck at the Firestation to turn its wheel and push pedals, and use the hose to rescue someone. Saddle up, partner, on the stick horses and dress up in cowboys duds to mosey on over to the Western Saloon with its hitching post and horse mural. The School House is more fun than most with puzzles, books, puppets, building blocks and other learning toys and games. I love the library look of the walls lined with "books". Paints, stamps, glue, playdough and other art mediums allow every child to be an artist at the Art Studio. A park-life center of the village has benches and tables and comfy chairs for adults to sit, watch, read, chat, etc.

Kid Ventures has added fantasy and exploration elements with its good-sized pirate ship and a castle to play in and on, as well as to slide down. Dress up in princess and knight attire and ride a rocking horse. Young adventurers can also negotiate a rock wall that is designed on a wall painted to look like a grassy hill. Toys throughout the facility include Little Tyke cars, tunnels, balls, and more. Enrichment activities are offered about every hour, such as games, arts and crafts projects, story time, sing-a-longs, and more. And they even can dance in the disco room!

This family play center also caters to parents with its coffee shop/cafe bar in the center of the activity, and counters and stools all around, and free Wi-Fi. The cafe sell specialty teas (like Gingerbread Chai Latte), a variety of coffee drinks, smoothies, juices, muffins, salads, and freshly-made sandwiches. I love the attention to detail at Kid Ventures - the openness of all the areas - all within easy viewing; the colorful, but not cutesy murals; the size of the room and kinds of furnishings and toys; and how kids can have a blast while parents can equally enjoy their time here. Check out camps, classes (cooking, tea parties, wacky science, and more), parties, and other events offered. Note: Socks must be worn by kids and adults. No outside food is allowed in.

Hours: Open Mon. - Fri., 9am - 6pm; Sat., 9am - noon. Closed Sat. afternoon and Sun. for private parties.

Price: $12 a child - walking and older; $8 for siblings. Purchase 8 passes for $75. Call for group and military discounts. Parents are free.

Ages: 1 ½ years and up.

LAZER JOURNEY

(619) 934-4200 / www.lazerjourney.com

871 Showroom Place, Ste 106, Chula Vista

This huge (14,500 square feet!), single story arena is eye-poppingly cool with colorful wall murals and vibrant partitions. Some are also designed to look like stone, with interestingly-shaped cutouts. The fake flowers and plants all around the arena make it look kind of Avatarish. Laser tag is always a fun game and Lazer Journey ratchets it up a few notches. Thirty-two players can engage in a game at one time.

Laser tag isn't the only excitement here. Try your hand (and body) at Lazer Frenzy, a web of laser beams that players must go over or under, but definitely not touch, to get through safely and reach the other side in a timely matter. (Think spy movies.) Video and arcades games abound, including Atomic Rush where competitors race (against time or other opponents) to touch as many of their chosen colored lights on a wall-size board as they can within sixty seconds. The snack bar serves beverages, hot dogs, real pizza (not cardboard-tasting), and other tasty treats.

Hours: Open Mon. - Thurs., 4pm - 9pm; Fri., noon - midnight; Sat., 10am - midnight; Sun., 10am - 7pm. Open extended hours, usually at noon, on school breaks and during the summer.

Price: A game of laser tag is $9. Game cards start at $5 for 20 points.

Ages: 7 years and up.

LAZER TAG GALAXY

(760) 730-9275 / www.lasertaggalaxy.com
2525 El Camino Real in the Westfield Plaza Camino Real, Carlsbad

Zap! Pow! Tag! Seemingly from a galaxy far, far away comes this large (6,000 square feet), space-themed laser tag room with neon-colored markings and alien beings decorating the partitions and walls. Each game is eight minutes long. The private party room is equally themed. Lazer Tag even offers mobile games with inflatable obstacles. Check out WESTFIELD PLAZA CAMINO REAL (pg. 524) for other things to do in the mall.

Hours: Open Mon. - Thurs., 10am - 9pm; Fri. - Sat., 1pm - 10pm; Sun., 11am - 6pm.

Price: $8 per game; $6 per game before 4pm.

Ages: 5 years and up.

LEGO - MINI MODEL BUILD (San Diego County)

(619) 294-9437 / shop.lego.com/en-US/MiniBuilds
7007 Friars Road in the Fashion Valley mall, San Diego

A free LEGO mini model? I'm in! Bring your child, ages 6 to 14 years old (strict age restrictions), to your favorite LEGO store on the first Tuesday of every month and they get to build (and take home) a really cool and unique mini model for free. Unique because the model kits are not available to purchase, per se, and are themed. Quantities are limited. Available from 5pm to 7pm, or whenever supplies run out, kids line up as early as 3pm - when school is out. (They can do homework while they're waiting in line.)

Hours: The first Tues. of each month, usually 5pm - 7pm.

Price: Free

Ages: 6 - 14 years old, only.

MAGDALENA ECKE FAMILY YMCA SKATE PARK

(760) 942-9622 / ecke.ymca.org
200 Saxony Road, Encinitas

This YMCA really knows how to reach active kids. A great, outdoor, 37,000-square-foot skate park at the Y features a thirteen-foot-high vert bowl ramp and six-foot-high double-bowled and double-hipped ramp, a dover bowl, and an eleven-foot kidney bowl, plus a full street course with a handrail station, quarter-pipes, bank ramps, pyramids, roll-in's, and slider station. Street course ramps are layered in Masonite, and half-pipes are layered in steel. The course is challenging for experienced skaters, yet allows less-experienced ones the opportunity to try some more difficult maneuvers. Younger (or beginning) skaters have a separate, gated area with lower ramps so they can build confidence as they attempt trickier moves.

The park requires full safety gear to be supplied by the skaters, and a parent waiver consent form must be signed, on-site, for participants 17 years and under. Sessions are two-and-a-half hours long.

Hours: Open Mon. - Thurs., 2:30pm - 5pm; Fri., 12:45pm - 2:15pm and 2:30pm - 5pm; Sat. - Sun., 9am - 11:30am, 11:45am - 2:15pm, and 2:30pm - 5pm. Open for an extra session (usually 5:15pm - 7pm or so) in the summer and camps are offered then in the morning hours. Closed all major holidays.

Price: Sessions are $5 for members, $10 for nonmembers. Membership is $46 a year and comes with a t-shirt and photo ID card.

Ages: 7 years and up.

MESA RIM CLIMBING AND FITNESS CENTER
(858) 201-4411 / www.mesarim.com
10110 Mesa Rim Road, San Diego
$$$$

   Step by step, rock by rock - a journey up the rock climbing walls is exciting, physically challenging, and self-confidence building. This facility is more than 30,000 square feet huge! It sports numerous rock climbing walls - some of which are short, and some are really, really tall at fifty-two feet; and interesting angles - some are relatively easy and some are just crazy hard, and all of it is good for bouldering, top roping, and lead climbing opportunities. Everyone from novices to experts will find routes that fit their level and even take them to the next. A separate room upstairs has the latest gym equipment, a yoga room with classes, and a party room (I mean for birthday parties and such). The second floor also has a nice overlook room with some comfy chairs and couches, and WiFi.

   A day pass includes the climbing gym, yoga classes, and usage of the fitness equipment. Street shoes are not allowed on the walls. Signed waivers are required for all participants. Mesa Rim offers numerous classes, competitions, and expeditions for adults and kids, including Rock Techs (for ages 12 to 18), Rock Monsters Kids Club (for ages 6 to 11), Home School Programs, and Merit Badge Programs.

   Hours: Open Mon. - Thurs., 6am - 11pm; Fri., 6am - 10pm; Sat. - Sun., 8am - 9pm. Call for the holiday schedule. Rock Techs is offered Tues. and Fri., 4pm - 6pm. Rock Monsters Kids Club is held Wed. and Thurs., 4pm - 6pm; Sat., 10am - 2pm.
   Price: $17 for a day pass for adults; $15 for military, student, and ages 11 - 17; $12 for children 10 and under. Gear package rental, which includes shoes, harness, chalk bag, and belay device, is $6. Rock Techs and Rock Monsters is $25 per session - ask about a free trial session. Ask about deals and memberships.
   Ages: 5 years and up.

MIRAMAR SPEED CIRCUIT
(858) 586-7500 / www.miramarspeedcircuit.com
8123 Miralani Drive, Miramar
$$$$$

   It's all about speed. Well, maybe control and speed. This indoor, quarter-mile, asphalt track allows drivers to race around corners and on the straightaway. Get all geared up with a helmet, racing suit (if you want), and neck guard for your experience. Regular go karts are for drivers 60" and taller, while junior karts are for drivers 48" to 59" tall. Kids 12 years or under and at least 48" tall can sign up for a Saturday or Sunday morning beginning driving class where safety is the focus. Plenty of drive time is included in that $50 fee. Reservations are required.

   Before or after your race, enjoy a game of air hockey or pool, or arcade games. The on-site Monaco Bistro offers a small, but good, selection of food of sandwiches and salads.

   Hours: Open Mon., 11am - 11pm; Tues. - Thurs, 11am - 11pm; Fri., 11am - midnight; Sat., 10am - midnight; Sun., 10am - 11pm.
   Price: $23 per person per race. A head sock is mandatory - $2.
   Ages: 48" height requirement.

MR. PAINTBALL FIELD U.S.A.
(760) 737-8870 - office; (760) 751-2931 - field / www.mrpaintballusa.com
25320 Lake Wohlford Road, Escondido
$$$$$

   Armed with semiautomatic paint guns and dressed in goggles, mask, and layers of clothing (to reduce the somewhat painful impact of the paintballs), you are now ready to play the wildly exhilarating and intense game of paintball. Fifteen different fields on almost 300 acres of land are the playing area where hills, valleys, trees, props, man-made huts, huge spools, villages, natural obstacles, and trenches are used for both offensive and defensive tactical maneuvers. Try to zap your opponents with paintballs, without getting hit yourself. Games last fifteen to thirty minutes. Bring running shoes, a water bottle, and, most of all, stamina. Note: Participants 17 and under must have a signed parental waiver. With all the sport and intensity and just as much fun, though a little less colorful, is the game of airsoft, also played here. Note that there is a pro shop and a snack bar on the premises.

   Hours: Open for paintball and airsoft, Thurs. - Fri., 9am - 3pm; Sat. - Sun. and most holidays, 8:30am - 3:30pm. Closed Christmas. Open during the week over holidays and for groups of 20 or more, with reservations.

Price: $20 per player if you come self-equipped. $45 per person for the basic rentals which includes all-day play, face mask, a Piranha marker, air, and paintballs.

Ages: 10 years and up.

MY KIDS CLUBHOUSE

Bonita - (619) 434-8676; Poway - (858) 668-2838 / www.mykidsclubhouse.com
Bonita - 5034 Bonita Road, Suite C, Bonita; Poway - 12636 Poway Road

The Clubhouse is a very large, open, carpeted room with various pieces of play equipment such as mini kitchen appliances, a kid-size bus, a game center at toddler height with gears and puzzles, and more. At least one-fourth of the room is taken up by a multi-level, net-enclosed, play structure with tubes to crawl through, plastic slides, a small ball pit, a foam obstacle course, and huge balls. What fun! Benches are ideally located for mom and dads to watch and to chat with each other. A small toddler's room has a wooden train set and soft foam blocks. Socks are required for both kids and adults.

A corner cafe offers peanut butter and jelly sandwiches ($2.50), and ice cream, string cheese, cookies, and granola bars. Beverages range from lattes to milk. You are also welcome to bring in your own food and sit at the tables and chairs to munch. Inquire about the kids club (where parents can drop off their children), craft times, camps, and other special events.

Hours: Open Mon. - Fri., 9am - 6pm; Sat. - Sun., 10am - 5:30pm. Closed on most major holidays.

Price: $10 for the first child; $8 for each sibling; infants under 1 and adults are free. Ask about yearly passes.

Ages: 8 months to 8 years.

NED BAUMER AQUATIC CENTER

(858) 538-8083 / www.sandiego.gov
10440 Black Mountain Road, Mira Mesa

Perfect for a hot summer day! The aquatic center has a large main pool for both lap and recreational swim, as well as two shallow pools for kids. The water play structure has hoses with water squirting out from the sides, a short enclosed slide, and other fun apparatus.

Hours: Open for nine months out of the year, usually Mon. - Fri., 11am - 3pm; Sat., noon - 3pm. Open extended hours in the summer.

Price: $4 for adults; $2 for seniors and ages 15 and under.

Ages: 3 years and up.

OUTBACK CLIMBING CENTER

(858) 534-0684 / recreation.ucsd.edu/outb
9500 Gilman Drive at University of California San Diego, La Jolla

Small, but mighty. This tiny rock climbing gym, built from reconstructed racquetball courts, has five main walls with about two top ropes each. A lead cave with angling poses a fun challenge. Stop off here and brush up on some skills, or acquire new ones. The center is also great for kids because the walls are only about thirty-feet high and when kids have conquered the climb, and they will, they feel like they've accomplished a feat. If your child hasn't climbed before, he can receive instruction and even help belaying, if the staff isn't too busy. Parents must belay children under 14 years old, but Outback will give a quick lesson on "how-to." All climbers must have a signed liability form..

Outback Adventures also offers rental equipment for camping, the snow, the beach, and the ocean. They service equipment, too. If you have a group, consider signing up to use the High Ropes Challenge Course.

Hours: Open Mon. - Thurs., 4pm - 10pm; Fri., 4pm - 8pm; Sun., 6pm - 10pm. Closed Sat., holidays, and during school breaks. Summer quarter hours are Mon. - Fri., 5pm - 9pm.

Price: $5 a day for UCSD college students; $7 a day for non-students. Harness and shoe rentals are $2 each. Chalk bags are $1.

Ages: 6 years and up.

PELLY'S MINI GOLF

(858) 481-0363 / www.delmargolfcenter.com
15555 Jimmy Durante Boulevard, Del Mar

Though many of the obstacles on these two rock-lined, mini golf courses are simply twists and turns or bumps on

the blue courseways (i.e. not super challenging), the surrounding themed embellishments are creative and fun. The Ocean Adventure, for instance, sports sculptures of dolphins, seals, an octopus, and a gray whale, including one that spouts water; an almost life-size shark cage on hole #11 (enter through the bars); huge whales tails in a water feature; and a good-sized ship. The Surfing Safari features a wave sculpture with water spurting, surfboards, and more. Other adornments include a large pond and more water elements, bridges, palm trees (for the Southern California feel), and ambiance music.

The courses are eco-friendly in that facts about recycling, water conservation and protecting the environment are posted at holes. There is even developed educational programs on these topics geared for scouts to earn badges and for school groups. A snack bar is on the premises. Note: Older kids might want to try out a bigger back swing at the adjacent driving range with sixty-five teeing stations.

Hours: Open Sun. - Thurs., 9am - 9pm; Fri. - Sat., 9am - 10pm. Closed Christmas.
Price: $9.50 for adults; $7.50 for seniors, military and ages 12 and under for the first round; $4.50 for round two for adults; $3.50 for kids.
Ages: 4 years and up.

PLAYTOWN INDOOR PLAYGROUND

(619) 447-7529 / www.goplaytown.com
858 Jackman Street, El Cajon

Imagine your young children playing in a safe, clean, indoor environment, and having a blast, while meeting new friends, as you keep an eye on them and enjoy socializing with friends, as well. Welcome to Play Town! Geared with young ones in mind the small bounces, toy cars to drive, tubes to crawl through, play treehouse, play houses, mini ride-on coaster, soft play area, castle, and other fun elements keep them busy for hours in one large, brightly-colored room. (Note that everyone must wear socks.) You are welcome to bring in your own food, or purchase beverages here.

Hours: Open Mon. - Wed., 9am - 6pm; Thurs. - Fri., 9am - 8pm; Sun., 8am - noon. Open Sat. - Sun. afternoons for private parties only. Closed New Year's day, Easter, Mother's Day, 4th of July, Thanksgiving, Christmas Eve, and Christmas.
Price: $9 for the first child; $7 for a sibling; non-walking infants or those 11 months and under are free. Adults are free.
Ages: Infant - 6 years.

PLAYWERX

(760) 804-1600 / www.playwerx.com
6060 Avenida Encinas, #B, Carlsbad

PlayWerx is not work at all - it's just fun. The clean, large room has a main, enclosed (with netting), multi-story play structure with foam obstacles; a ball pit; lots of climbing up and down levels; crawling space; rope swings; slides; and some foam blocks. Socks are required. The room is airy as a big portion is open, though gated, to the outdoors via a warehouse-style, rolled up door. Along with shelves of books, this room also has comfy couches and lounge chairs in groupings, making it so easy to keep an eyes on (and ears alert to) your kids. There is a cafe here, too, with an array of coffee beverages, smoothies, pizza, sandwiches, snacks and gluten-free snacks. A smaller offshoot, simple room is for toddlers that contains stuffed animals and other toys. PlayWerx is "next door" to FUNDABBLES (pg. 467) and VITAL CLIMBING GYM (pg. 495).

Hours: Open Tues. - Fri., 10am - 6pm; Sat., 9am - 7pm; Sun., 10am - 6pm. Closed Mon. and some holidays. Check the website for early closings due to private parties.
Price: $10 for ages 4 and up; $7 for ages 3 and under; parents are free.
Ages: 1 - 10 years old.

PUMP IT UP (San Diego County)

Chula Vista - (619) 216-9812; Poway - (858) 679-5867; San Marcos - (760) 510-8000; Sorrento Valley - (858) 658-9968 / www.pumpitupparty.com
Chula Vista - 751 Design Court, Suite A; Poway - 12760 Danielson Court, Suite J; San Marcos - 445 Ryan Drive, suite 103; Sorrento Valley - 9370 Waples Street, Suite 102

The term "pump it up" used to mean getting buff by working out, but now it means "Have a fantastic time playing in this inflatable indoor playground!" Two rooms that are filled with huge, primary-color inflatables, such as giant slides, an obstacle course, a bounce house, a jousting pit (using foam-type lances) and a rock-'em-sock-'em ring,

make this place an absolute blast for kids (and adults). This place has rightly won "best party ever" awards among guests. And, actually, all that bouncing around makes it quite a workout, too.

Open Jump times are offered on select dates and times and, as each location varies, call or check the website of the one you want to visit. These jump times are geared for the after-school crowd of ages 7 to 12 years; for ages 6 and under during Toddler Times; or for ages 2 to 11 to come and play together during Family Jump times. Socks and a signed waiver are required for each person. The rest of the days and times the facilities are available only for parties (for all ages - kids and adults), field trips, boy scout/girl scout badge programs, or other outings. Glow Parties add another element of fun when the regular lights are turned off and the black lights and special effect lighting are turned on. Kids are given glow necklaces as well.

Hours: Open Jump times vary greatly - call the individual location you are interested in visiting. Note that the Sorrento Valley location hosts a Talk About Curing Autism playgroup on the third Wed. of every month from 6pm to 7:30pm.

Price: Open Jump: Chula Vista - $7 per child; Poway - $10 per child, $8 per sibling; San Marcos - $8 per child, $6 for siblings; Sorrento Valley - $8 per child, $6 per sibling. Adults are free. Family Jump Times usually cost another dollar, or two, per child.

Ages: 3 years and up.

RANCHO PENASQUITOS SKATE PARK

(858) 538-8131 / www.sandiego.gov/park-and-recreation/centers/skateparks/index.shtml
10111 Carmel Mountain Road, Rancho Penasquitos

A good mixture of wood and cement, this 22,000-square-foot, unsupervised skate park - labeled an Advanced Street Park - features flat rails, half-pipes, quarter-pipes, a spine, and stairs. A helmet and knee and elbow pads are required by city mandate. A parent or legal guardian must accompany children 12 and under. Rollerbladers and skateboarders are welcome.

Hours: Open daily, 10am - dusk. Closed holidays.
Price: Free
Ages: 7 years and up.

SALVATION ARMY RAY AND JOAN KROC CORPS COMMUNITY CENTER

(619) 287- KROC (5762) / www.kroccenter.org
6845 University Avenue, San Diego

Oh my gosh - this facility is amazing! This long series of buildings contains so many wonderful activities and programs that if it's not offered here, it must not be fun. (That might be a slight exaggeration, but only a slight one.)

The indoor skate park has great ramps, some grinding poles, and other skater favorites. Pads, a helmet, and a parental waiver form for ages 17 and under are required, and children 11 and under must be accompanied by an adult. Check out the recreation field for soccer, flag football, and lacrosse. The field also has a walking track. Feeling challenged? Open to groups, only, is the adjacent outdoor challenge course which offers both high- and low-rope elements. Open to group or individuals is a thirty-foot tall rock climbing tower that allows participants to actually go climb a rock! A parental waiver must be signed for kids 17 years and under.

Join in and play a game of basketball, volleyball, and badminton in the gym. Ages 16 years and up are welcome to use the fitness area for aerobics, weight training, kickboxing, and other exercise equipment and classes. Just hang out in the adjoining recreation room or pick up a game of air hockey, billiards, table tennis, foosball, and/or play a board game. Swim a couple of laps in the twenty-five meter competition pool or just splash around on a hot summer's day in the rec pool. The ice arena is open for general skating sessions, skating lessons, and for hockey leagues. Nonparticipants can watch from ringside seats. (Brrrring a jacket!)

The performing arts center boasts a 600-seat theater where family-appropriate shows are presented, often by youth theater. This is also where Kroc Community Church meets on Sunday mornings at 10:30am - all are welcome. The center also has a dance studio, band and orchestra room, large multi-purpose room, art workshop rooms, and vocal practice room. The adjacent education center is comprised of the Cox Technology Center, Kroc Center Library, visual arts studio, study hall, and tutoring rooms. The Cox Technology Center has twenty-four computer terminals for guests to access the internet and get school or work done. An abundance of programs (e.g., day camps, after-school programs, etc.) for all ages and interests complete this center. Also note that this is the Salvation Army's food and toy distribution center during the holidays. Whew!

Each activity has its own hours, prices, skill levels, and age requirements, so please call first. Note that some

sessions require a minimum number of participants for the session to proceed. Check the website for the many special events held here throughout the year.

Hours: The skateboard park is usually open Mon. - Fri., 4pm - 8pm; Sat. - Sun., noon - 6pm, although sometimes it is closed mid-November through early January for special events. General ice skating sessions are available Mon., 3:30pm - 5:30pm; Wed., 10:30am - 12:45pm, 3:30pm - 5:30pm, and 7:15pm- 8:15pm; Fri., 10:30am - 12:45pm and 3:30pm - 5:30pm; Sat. - Sun., 1pm - 3pm. Rock climbing is open Mon. and Thurs., 4pm - 6pm; Sat., 10am - 1pm. The Challenge course is open by reservation. Recreation swim is open Mon. - Fri., 1pm - 4:30pm; Sat. - Sun., 1pm - 5:30pm. The recreation center is open daily. The Cox Tech Center and library are open Mon. - Sat., 10am - 6pm. Closed Sun. The facility is closed on most holidays.

Price: Day passes are a fantastic deal at $6 for adults; $4 for seniors and ages 17 and under. Day passes include rock climbing, skateboarding, recreational swimming, access to the field, the rec room, the fitness center (age restrictions apply), and the gym (basketball courts, etc. when open). Ice skating and skate rentals are $10, although Wed. night skate and rentals (and sometimes after school) are $5. Ask about membership or about multi-use passes.

Ages: Skateboarders and challenge course users must be at least 6 years old. Swimmers 7 and under must be accompanied by an adult.

SAN DIEGO RC RACEWAY

(858) 831-0477 / www.sdrcraceway.com
8725 Production Avenue, Miramar
$$$

Indoor racing can be a fun activity for the family and it's easy to get hooked on this hobby. The relatively huge, hard-packed dirt track (that gets changed up frequently) always has lots of bumps (i.e. jumps), turns, and banks, making it a great course to race your model cars and trucks. Beginners and kids, particularly, have a class on Saturday mornings (beats watching cartoons!) to learn the how-tos. The class is from 9am to 10am. If you need any automotive parts, the store is fully stocked and the large pit room has plenty of long tables to repair whatever parts need fixin', as well as staff and other people around to help out. Even if you don't race a car (and this facility doesn't have rentals), it's a fun sport to watch.

Hours: Open Tues. - Fri., 2pm - 11pm; Sat., 8am - 9pm, Sun., 9am - 9pm. Race days are usually Wed., Fri. and Sat. Closed Mon.

Price: Free to watch. $20 for non-members to race for the day/night.

Ages: 5 years and up.

SKY HIGH SPORTS (San Diego County)

(858) 693-5867 / sdo.jumpskyhigh.com
8190 Miralani Drive
$$$$

See SKY HIGH SPORTS (pg. 266) for details about this fantastic, indoor trampoline place.

Hours: Open Mon. - Thurs., 10am - 10pm; Fri. - Sat., 10am - midnight; Sun., 10am - 10pm.

Price: $14 per person for the first hour; $9 for the second hour only Mon. - Thurs. (excluding holidays).

Ages: 4 years and up.

SKY ZONE (San Diego County)

(619) 754-9782 / www.skyzone.com
851 Showroom Place #100, Chula Vista
$$$$

See SKY ZONE (Los Angeles) on pg. 41 for details.

Hours: Open Mon. - Thurs., 2pm - 10pm; Fri., noon - midnight; Sat., 10am - midnight; Sun., 10am - 9pm. Open during the summer and holidays extended hours.

Price: $10 for 30 min.; $15 for 60 min.; $20 for 90 min. 10% discount for military.

Ages: 3 years and up.

SOLID ROCK GYM

Poway - (858) 748-9011; San Diego - (619) 299-1124; San Marcos - (760) 480-1429 / www.solidrockgym.com
Poway - 13026 Stowe Dr.; San Diego - 2074 Hancock St.; San Marcos - 992 Rancheros Dr.
$$$$

Experience the thrill and physical challenge (i.e., you'll get sweaty) of rock climbing in a safe, indoor, controlled

atmosphere. Novice climbers can learn the basic skills and importance of a well-placed foot and/or hand, while experienced climbers will enjoy the opportunity to continue training by sharpening their skills. This is a great sport to introduce kids to because it builds confidence, physical fitness, and strategic thinking. (All this just by rock climbing - and we thought school was important!) Staff members are experienced climbers and are always around to instruct and encourage, although everyone must bring their own belayer.

Multi-colored stones mark various routes on the walls, overhangs, and arches for top roping and lead climbing, as well as on the bouldering cave. Although a child may be tentative at the beginning, by the end of the first time, he/she is usually literally climbing the walls, and having a great time doing it. So, if you're looking for a creative way to channel your child's excess energy, turn off the cartoons, then come *rock* and roll! Note: A party room is on the premises. Programs are available at all location for scouts, teen climbing camps, and more. Lessons and membership are available. Signed waivers are required for all climbers.

Hours: Poway and San Marcos are open Mon. - Fri., noon - 9pm; Sat., 10am -9pm; Sun., 11am - 7pm. San Diego is open Mon. - Fri., 9am - 10pm; Sat., 9am - 9pm; Sun., 11am - 7pm. All locations are open national holidays, 9am - 9pm.

Price: An all-day pass, Mon. - Fri. is $13 for any age; weekend and holiday prices are $16 for adults; $14 for ages 16 and under. Harness and equipment rentals are an additional $7.

Ages: 5 years and up.

THE PAINTBALL PARK

(866) 985-4932 / www.thepaintballpark.com
1700 Vandegrift Boulevard (near Rodeo Grounds) Camp Pendleton, Oceanside

$$$$$

Although the paintball park is on in the marine base, anyone can play. The park is thirty acres huge with four turf tournament-size fields that boast of bunkers, buildings, trenches, big trees, sandbag fortifications, and real tanks and other military vehicles to keep play interesting and challenging. There are also ten rec fields, including a 6,000 square foot Castle Field. Capture the Flag is the most common game played, although alternatives include Center Flag, where two teams go for just one flag, and Elimination, where the winning team must annihilate (figuratively speaking) all members of the opposing team. Wear a long-sleeve shirt and long pants, even on summer days. Protective gear is necessary. An alternative to paintball is playing airsoft at the military-like Airsoft Park with two close-combat killhouses, a village marketplace, and tanks and vehicles.

For parties, try Kidsplat, ideal for ages six to ten, where kids are engaged in paintball-type games, running around inflatable bunkers and shooting at targets, but with smaller paintballs and guns that shoot about half as fast. Or, try Splatmaster, which is Kidsplat, but played directly on the paintball fields.

BBQ burgers and hot dogs, pulled pork sandwiches, and more, are offered here on weekends, and there are fast food restaurants just down the road. You are welcome to bring in your own food. Participants under 18 must have a waiver signed by a parent or guardian.

Hours: Open most of the year, Fri. - Sun., 8:30am - 5pm. Paintball is open for night games, Fri. - Sat., 6pm - 10pm. Open in the summer, Wed. - Sun., 8:30am - 5pm. Always call ahead to check on rental gear availability. Open during the week for groups of 15, or more.

Price: Paintball is $30 per person if you have your own equipment; $50 per person with rental equipment - (goggles, semiautomatic paint gun [upgrades available], CO2 refills, and 500 paintballs). Airsoft is $25 for self-equipped walk-ons; $40 for full rental equipment with a pistol; $10 more for a rifle.

Ages: 6 - 8 years for Kidsplat; 8 years and up for Airsoft; 10 years and up for paintball.

ULTRAZONE (San Diego County)

(619) 221-0100 / www.ultrazonesandiego.com
3146 Sports Arena Boulevard, suite 21, San Diego

$$$

Come play laser tag - the tag of the future! Put on your vest, pick up your laser gun, and for fifteen minutes you'll play hard and fast. Laser tag is action packed, and the thrill of the chase really gets your adrenaline pumping! This Ultrazone, with its dark, cave-like setting, is themed "Underground City." The multi-level city, or playing arena, is maze-like and huge. Run up and down ramps; seek cover behind floor-to-ceiling walls; duck into partly hidden doorways; find your way in and around the myriad of partitions and obstacles; and zap your opponents. For more interaction and acceleration of the game there are robotic enemies and targets that allow players to acquire more points. Tip: The best times for younger kids to play is weekday afternoons and early evenings, or during the day on weekends. Older kids come out here in hordes at nighttime.

Hours: Open Mon. - Thurs., 4pm - 10pm; Fri., 2pm - 2am; Sat., 10am - 2am; Sun., 10am - 10m. They are open earlier in the summer and some school holidays. Closed Christmas day.

Price: $7 a game. Although game play is not exclusive for kids at this time, ages 10 and under pay only $5.50 per game Sat. and Sun. from 10am - 2pm. Games must be completed by 2pm. Games are only $5.50 per, too, Fri. - Sat., midnight - 2am.

Ages: Must be at least 7 years old.

VERTICAL HOLD SPORT CLIMBING CENTER, INC.

(858) 586-7572 / www.verticalhold.com

$$$$

9580 Distribution Avenue, San Diego

Indoor rock climbing is rapidly becoming one of the fastest growing indoor sports in America. The multi-colored rocks, embedded in the realistic-looking rock walls, are marked so they can be used as trail guides. Vertical Hold has over 325 routes that are changed every few months. This physically challenging and mentally-stimulating activity is a great way to redirect a child growing up in our couch-potato/video-game society.

Climb vertical walls (of course!), overhangs, and chimney routes, or try your hand (and feet) at bouldering. If you are top rope climbing, you need to bring your own belayer (i.e., the person who stays on the ground attached to your rope so if you should slip or fall, you won't fall far). If you, as an adult, don't know how to belay, an instructor can show you the ropes (literally). You do not need a belayer if you and your kids simply want to boulder. Climbers 17 years and under must have a parental waiver signed to climb and either wear a helmet or sign a waiver for not wearing it.

Free Wi-Fi, showers, lockers (bring your own lock), DJ music (sometimes), and free yoga classes and free technique and climbing clinics are offered (with paid admission), so don't just crawl out from under a rock - go climb it! Notes: A party area is available here. There are several special programs offered here including earning scout merit badges, summer camps, and overnight parties, plus a youth climbing club.

Hours: Open Mon., Wed., Fri., 10am - 11pm; Tues., Thurs., 6am - 11pm; Sat., 8am - 9pm; Sun., 8am - 8pm. Closed Christmas.

Price: $16 for a day pass for adults (it's $16 for kids, too, but includes all the rental gear). $10 per visit at lunchtime (from 10am - 3pm) during the week. Equipment rental of harness, rope, shoes, and chalk is $6.

Ages: 3 years and up.

VITAL CLIMBING GYM (San Diego County)

(760) 689-2651 / www.vitalclimbinggym.com

$$$

6102 Avenida Encinas, suite L, Carlsbad

All that energy and nowhere to go to expend it? Then, it might be Vital to come to this bouldering gym! Bouldering is a little different from straight up rock climbing in that ropes and harnesses aren't necessary - it's a matter of you clinging to (at least I cling to) and climbing the "rocks" with the thick safety crash pads underneath. This type of dynamic exercise is great for the body and mind. Follow any one of the color-coded duct tape routes up the walls and up and over the angles. The walls are about sixteen feet tall and the longest one is about sixty feet. There is a little snack cafe with beverages and snacks, plus a loft/chill area overseeing some of the routes that has a couch and some chairs. Lockers are available here. Ages 15 and under must have a parent present while they climb. Waivers for all ages must be signed. Members perk - These facilities are open 24 hours to its members. The staff leaves at 9pm so members then own the gym - the type of music played, using the equipment, working out, or just hanging out. Note that this gym is right next to FUN DABBLES (pg. 467) and around the corner from PLAYWERX (pg. 491).

Hours: Open daily, 11am - 9pm. (Open 24 hours for members). Holiday hours fluctuate.

Price: The first visit is free for adults; $10 for ages 15 and under. Thereafter, $10 for all ages for a day pass. Optional shoe rentals are $2.

Ages: At least 5 years, and up.

—GREAT OUTDOORS—

AGUA CALIENTE SPRINGS COUNTY PARK

(760) 765-1188- park; (877) 565-3600 - reservation / www.co.san-diego.ca.us/parks

$$

39555 County Route S2, Agua Caliente Hot Springs

For a more therapeutic take on life, come visit Agua Caliente Springs County Park. It features a big, glass-endosed pool with water temperature maintained at 102 degrees as it is fed by underground hot mineral springs. Ahhhh - feels so good! However, only kids 56" and up and adults may use the indoor pool. The two outdoor pools are available, and the fifteen-foot by thirty-foot shallow one is fun for children to use.

The park also has a general store, shuffleboard courts, horseshoe pits, play areas, hiking trails and over 140 campsites. There are several trails to choose from, including a half-mile loop called Ocotillo Ridge Nature Trail and a more arduous 2.5-mile trail called Moonlight Canyon Trail. The park is pretty, and parts of it are lush with lots of plants and trees fed by the natural springs that run throughout. Look for the many species of birds and other wildlife that call it home. Note that this park is adjacent to Anza Borrego State Park. (See the next entry.)

Hours: The park is open Labor Day - Memorial Day for the general public and campers, Sun. - Thurs., 9:30am - 5pm; for overnight campers usage only, Fri. - Sat., 9:30am - 9pm. The outdoor and indoor pools are open daily, 9:30am - 5pm. On Fri. and Sat., the pool is also open 6pm - 9pm for guests 18 years and older. The park is closed June - August.

Price: $3 per vehicle for day use. Use of the pools is $3 per person. Camping costs from $22 (tents) - $33 (full hook-ups) a night. There is an additional $5 fee for camping reservations.

Ages: 3 years and up.

ALGA NORTE COMMUNITY PARK

(760) 268-4777 or (760) 434-2826 / www.carlsbadca.gov   !/$$
6565 Alicante Road, Carlsbad

This wonderful and expansive park features numerous great elements. Dive into the aquatic center that consists of two outdoor pools (a 25-yard instructional one and a 50-meter competition pool), plus a warm water spa for adults, a snack bar, and a small splash pad area for kids. The splash pad has gigantic flowers and pipes that spray water, and fountains that spurt up at random times offering refreshment and squeals of delight. The aquatic area is nicely laid out, too, with palm trees, some huge umbrellas for shade, plenty of space for moving around, and even lights for nighttime swims.

The skate park is one of the largest in San Diego, at 22,200 square feet. Part of it is designated more towards beginners while the majority is for those with higher skills. I describe it as epic as the lighted, unsupervised park boasts a long, straight street course with variously-sized ramps, steps, rails, ledges, a bell tower, and two adjacent, wide and deep, big bowls.

The extra extra large, tri-level, ADA playground, based partly in a hard foam base and partly in sand, has several separate play sections with ramps, slides, climbing poles, slopes, boulders, swings, bridges, walkways, ropes, and all the fun things for kids to expend their considerable energy.

Alga Norte also offers three ball fields; lighted basketball courts (one full and one half); picnic areas; lots of green open space to run, play and throw a frisbee or football; and two sizable dog parks. This community park truly services the entire community.

Hours: The park and skate park are open daily, 8am - 10pm. Recreational swim is open year round, Mon. - Fri., 10am - 7pm; Sat. and holidays, 8am - 3pm; Sun., 10am - 3pm. Hours do fluctuate.

Price: The park and skate park are free. Recreational swim is $5 for adults; $3 for ages 17 and under; $2 for spectators.

Ages: All

ALTA VISTA GARDENS / BRENGLE TERRACE PARK

(760) 945-3954 - Alta Vista; (760) 726-1340 - Brengle / www.altavistagardens.org; www.ci.vista.ca.us   !/$
1270 Vale Terrace Drive (the gardens are on Jim Porter Pkwy), Vista

This is a two-for-one entry as these side-by-side attractions, each with a different emphasis, are both great places to visit. The fourteen-acre Alta Vista botanic gardens are an absolute delight to walk around with their blending of distinct plant sections; colorful and funky artwork interspersed; easy trails that crisscross throughout; places to sit and contemplate; areas designed for kids; and a wonderful view from the hilltop. Children will enjoy running all around, as well as going through short cement drainage tubes; pretend playing at the stone piano and playing real music created from natural elements, like the pebbles chime; incorporating big stone animals based in sand in their imaginative play; and the variety of the unusual plants and flowers. The types of gardens include Desert, Prehistoric, South American, Pan Asian, Jungle, Herb, Rose, and more. A Children's Garden is in the works, as is a water play area and so many

other wonderful projects. The art includes sculptures, mosaics, chimes, statues, and more. Enjoy seeing butterflies, as it's a certified butterfly habitat; sacred lotus; rare pine trees; a pond and its inhabitants; and numerous fruit trees, plus sitting at a patio table and chairs that overlook the view of the valley below and beyond and walking through a small labyrinth. Educational field trips, and classes on farming, the environment and botany are just some of the offerings - check the website for a full listing of those and for special events held here, such as Earth Day celebration.

Adjacent to the gardens is a really tough disc golf course - up and down hills, and one hole is in the midst of a cluster of trees. Brengle Terrace Park offers lighted ball fields, multi-purpose fields, basketball courts, tennis courts, volleyball courts, picnic tables, a tot lot play area, horseshoe pits, and an amphitheater. Come play! See Summer Musicals Under the Stars (pg. 731) for information on the programs at Moonlight Amphitheater.

Hours: The gardens are open Mon. - Fri., 7am - 5pm; Sat. - Sun., 10am - 5pm. The park is open daily, sunrise - sunset.
Price: $2 is asked for entrance to the gardens - put it in the donation box. The park is free.
Ages: All

ANZA BORREGO STATE PARK

(760) 767-5311 - state park; (760) 767-4205 - visitor center; (760) 767-4684 - wildflower hotline; (800) 444-7275 - camping reservations. / www.parks.ca.gov; www.theabf.org
200 Palm Canyon Drive, Borrego Springs

This massive state park is over 600,000 acres of living desert - palm trees, flowers, oases, bighorn sheep, and lizards, plus sand, rocks, mountains, and much more. The following description merely touches on a few of the activities and places that this park has to offer. Remember that this is a desert and the temperatures can reach over 125 degrees during the summer - always bring water!!! Nighttime temperatures can drop drastically, no matter what time of year, so be prepared for anything!

As with any major park, your best bet is to start at the Visitor's Center. Get familiar with the park by watching the slide show that is presented upon request, and looking at the exhibits such as taxidermied animals and photographs. Be sure to pick up trail guides and a map.

Anza Borrego has some of the most incredible scenery in Southern California and although much of it can be seen by driving through the park, the really awe-inspiring vistas and landscape can only be seen by hiking. Within the park, take your choice of hiking trails which range from easy loops to arduous "mountain man" trails. One of the most popular hikes is the three-mile round-trip nature trail from the Borrego Palm Canyon campground up through Borrego Palm Canyon. The end of the trail is a sight for sore eyes (and hot bodies) - a refreshing waterfall with a pool (when there is water)! Parking is available near the trail entrance for $8 per vehicle, cash only.

There are two developed campsites available in this gigantic park, and one, Whittier Horse Camp, for camping with horses. There are places you can also open camp - pull over wherever you choose - for free. Tip: Try to choose a site that has some shelter from the desert winds that blow in seemingly at random times. For more information call the park office at the number above.

See the previous entry, AGUA CALIENTE SPRINGS COUNTY PARK, as it is located at the southern part of Anza Borrego park, as well as OCOTILLO WELLS STATE VEHICULAR RECREATION AREA (pg. 582).

Hours: The park is open for day use daily, dawn - dusk. The Visitor's Center is open October - May, daily, 9am - 5pm. It's open Jun - September on weekends and holidays only, 9am - 5pm.
Price: Free. If you want a camping spot for day use, the fee is $8. Overnight camping prices for developed campgrounds range from $25 - $35 a night, depending on location and facility. Camping reservations are an additional $8.
Ages: 3 years and up.

BALBOA PARK

1549 El Prado in Balboa Park, San Diego
See the entry for BALBOA PARK on page 526 for details.

BATIQUITOS LAGOON ECOLOGICAL RESERVE and NATURE CENTER

(760) 931-0800 / www.batiquitosfoundation.org
7380 Gabbiano Lane, Carlsbad

A nature center, housed in a trailer at this end of the trail, has birds, rocks, and some reference materials. Stop by here if you get a chance. You can also get a free trail guide either inside the center or at the outside bird boxes.

This pretty walking trail (no bikes allowed) is a fairly level hard dirt pathway, for the most part. The trail is sandwiched between a golf course at one end (that boasts a beautiful waterfall) and the lagoon. There is even a branch of the trail that goes closer to the water for short distances. Bring binoculars for a more up-close look at the wide variety of birds that flock here. Along the almost two-mile, non-looping trail are trees, benches, and interpretative signs that describe the critters that call this salt marsh their home. Fishing is allowed at one point, with a permit. School field trips and guided walks of the lagoon are available.

Hours: The lagoon is open daily, dawn - dusk. The nature center is usually open Mon. - Fri., 9am - noon; Sat. - Sun., 9am - 3pm.

Price: Free

Ages: All; strollers/wheelchairs are O.K. for a good part of the path.

BLUE SKY ECOLOGICAL RESERVE

(858) 668-4781 / www.blueskyreserve.org
Espola Road & Green Valley, Poway

Head for the hills! From the parking lot, that is your only option. The large, mostly hard-packed dirt fire road follows along a seasonal creek into the hills. The main trail, leading to 700 acres of nature, is surrounded by tall, leafy oak and sycamore trees, and shrubs. One trail branches off to hook up at the neighboring LAKE POWAY (pg. 509), where trail maps are available. Bring your own water. No bikes allowed. Guided groups hikes, such as Owl Prowl and Star Party, are offered several times throughout the year and wildlife/plant walks are offered every Saturday and Sunday at 9am.

Hours: Open daily, sunrise - sunset.

Price: Free

Ages: 4 years and up.

BORDER FIELD STATE PARK

(619) 575-3613 / www.tijuanaestuary.com; www.trnerr.org; www.parks.ca.gov
1500 Monument Road, San Diego

The best thing, and really the only thing exciting, about the hilltop Border State Park is that its boundaries go up to the border of Mexico. Only a chain-link fence separates the two countries! There is a small monument that is exactly half on U.S. soil and half on Mexican soil. A tall, rusted fence goes down the hillside/cliffside onto the beach and actually out into the water for about fifty feet to divide the lands as well as the peoples. We saw families swimming on the Mexico side, but swimmers are not allowed in the water on the U.S. side, purportedly because of riptides and foul water from the Tijuana River. There are always border patrol officers here, in trucks and in helicopters, encircling the park. This is, also, a great place to go whale watching during their migration season.

The park does have a grassy area for running around, picnic tables, restroom facilities, and pathways to hike into the adjacent Tijuana Estuary. See TIJUANA ESTUARY on page 521 for more information about the estuary and visitor's center.

Hours: Open mid-March - the day before Memorial Day and the day after Labor Day - October daily, 9:30am - 6pm. Open Memorial Day - Labor Day daily, 9:30am - 7pm; November - mid-March daily, 9:30am - 5pm. It is only accessible and open for pedestrians and equestrians - no vehicles, Mon. - Fri. It is also open to vehicles, Sat., Sun., and holidays. The park is closed during and after rain.

Price: $5 per vehicle.

Ages: All

CABRILLO NATIONAL MONUMENT

(619) 557-5450 / cabrillo.areaparks.com; www.nps.gov/cabr
1800 Cabrillo Memorial Drive, at the southern end of Point Loma, San Diego

In 1542 Juan Rodriguez Cabrillo sailed into San Diego Bay and claimed it for Spain. A huge statue of Cabrillo, commemorating his epic voyage along the western coast of the U.S., resides on the tip of the peninsula at this national park. Press the button near the monument to hear the history of Cabrillo and the bay area.

Older kids will appreciate the exhibit hall in the building behind the monument. Displays include maps and drawings of the areas Cabrillo and other explorers "discovered"; lots of written information; examples of food eaten on board ship, like dried fish and hardtack; and models of ships. The adjacent Visitors' Center offers pamphlets, film programs, and guided walks of this area, plus a book shop and an incredible view.

Before walking out to Point Loma Lighthouse, which was used from 1855 to 1891, listen to its history by pressing an outside storyboard button. We listened to it in Japanese and German [as well as English] - just for the fun of it. Kids think it's great to actually climb up the spiral staircase inside the refurbished lighthouse. The odd-shaped bedrooms are fully furnished with period furniture and knickknacks, as is the small living room, kitchen, and dining room. The entrance to the top floor is closed by a grate, but you can look through it and see the huge light that was a beacon to so many sailors.

Take the Bayside Trail, about two miles round trip, to walk further out to the point. Along the way look for remnants of a coastal artillery system used during both world wars. The trail goes down through a coastal sage scrub "forest." Topside of the trail, behind plexiglass, is a whale overlook. From late December through March, catch a glimpse of the gray whales during their annual migration. Audio information is, again, available at the touch of a button. (This time we listened to explanations in French and English.) Even if you don't see a whale, the view is spectacular.

From this viewpoint, look down to see the rocky marine environment of the tidepools. A driveable road from the monument leads down to them. (You must pay the parking fee to enter this area.) Exploring tidepools is always a wondrous adventure for my kids. See and touch (but don't bring home) sea stars, anemones, and limpets, and be on the lookout for crabs and even octopus. Tip: Be sure to bring your camera, wear rubber-soled shoes (the rocks get slippery), and keep a close eye on your little ones! Ask about free, ranger-guided school tours for third to fifth graders for the tidepools, monument, and surrounding parkland.

Hours: Open daily, 9am - 5pm. Open an hour later in the summer. Closed Christmas.
Price: $5 per vehicle (which is valid for up to 7 days); $3 for walk-ins; seniors are free. See Museum Month, San Diego (pg. 708) for details about half-price admission in February.
Ages: 3 years and up.

CACTUS SPORTS COUNTY PARK
(858) 694-3049 - park; (619) 561-3824 - BMX / www.cactusparkbmx.com
10567 or 10610 Ashwood, Lakeside

Cactus County Park has a few memorable features. On the west side of the road this dirt park has baseball fields with stadium seating and a rugged BMX track. BMX practice and racing are held on Mondays and Thursdays from 5:30pm to 7pm. There is a snack shop open then. Note that riding clinics are available. On the east side of the road is a model airplane runway and work station. Bring your own airplane or just come to watch them soar above the surrounding hillsides.

Hours: Open daily, 9:30am - sunset.
Price: Free. Call for BMX prices.

CARLSBAD SKATE PARK
(760) 434-2826 or (760) 602-4684 / www.socalskateparks.com
2560 Orion Way, Carlsbad

This good-sized, non-supervised, lighted skate park features cement bowls and other fun street elements, plus a beginner's area. The park is located between the police and fire departments. Wearing safety gear is enforced by the policemen that drive by. A small circle of grass is across the way and a baseball diamond is just down the hillside.

Hours: Open daily, 8am - 10pm.
Price: Free
Ages: 8 years and up.

CHOLLAS LAKE
(619) 527-7683 / www.sandiego.gov/park-and-recreation/centers
6350 College Grove Drive, San Diego

This sixteen-acre reservoir lake, surrounded by trees, is a designated fishing lake just for youth, ages 15 and under only. How great to be a kid! A short dirt path that goes partially around the lake is popular with bicyclists and joggers. There are picnic tables with barbecue grills, a play area, and a small basketball court. Ask about the fishing clinics and ranger-guided nature walks.

Hours: Open daily, 6:30am - a half hour before sunset. Closed New Year's Day, Thanksgiving, and Christmas. Closes early on state holidays.
Price: Free

Ages: All

COTTONWOOD CREEK PARK   ☼

(760) 633-2740 / www.ci.encinitas.ca.us   ⚑!
95 N. Vulcan Avenue, Encinitas

This delightful park has several appealing facets. The good-sized playground, with sand and foam padded flooring, has several slides; swings; toddler swings; an "M" shaped climbing structure; wiggly stepping stones attached to poles; a tiny house with a sand table; a tiered rock fountain for splashing water; and other creative play equipment. Another fun element is a ten-foot-high large rock designed for kids to climb up and on.

The park also boasts grassy lawns, including one gently sloping hill to roll down; picnic tables and benches scattered throughout; two tennis courts; and two half basketball courts. A creek flows through the south side of the park with several semicircular turnouts that have wooden foot bridges and information panels regarding creek life. There is also a war memorial here.

Hours: Open daily, 5am - 10pm.
Price: Free
Ages: All

COTTONWOOD PARK   ☼

(619) 397-6197 / www.chulavistaca.gov   ⚑!
1778 E. Palomar Street, Chula Vista

This large, traditional park has several noteworthy amenities. The playground, that has a sand and rubber base, has enclosed, twisty slides and other slides; curved, metal climbing ladders; swings (and toddlers' swings); and a large camel and elephant statue to climb. Covered picnic tables, a cement bike/stroller trail that winds throughout, a basketball court, a ball field with stands (for seating, ironically), and restrooms complete this facility.

Hours: Open daily, sunrise - sunset.
Price: Free
Ages: All

CUYAMACA RANCHO STATE PARK / LAKE CUYAMACA   ☼

(760) 765-3020 or (760) 765-0755 - park; (800) 444-7275 - camping reservations / www.parks.ca.gov; $$
www.cuyamaca.us
12551 Cuyamaca Highway [79], Descanso / 13652 Hwy 79, Julian

Retreat from the buildings, noise, and general busyness of city life to this outstanding state park with its 25,000 acres of pristine wilderness - a balm to the mind and soul. Even though the fire in 2003 ravaged most of the land, the land is in process of recovering, so take in the trees, grassy meadows, streams, peaks, and valleys that this park has to offer. There are over 120 miles of hiking trails and forty miles of biking trails along the fire roads and access roads. As the terrain varies, hiking trails vary in their degree of difficulty. Be on the lookout for birds, mule deer, lizards, coyotes, and other critters.

Pick up a trail map ($2) at the park headquarters, or call for one to be sent to you. While at the headquarters, go through its interactive museum which features a taxidermied bobcat, mountain lion, fox, racoon, and rattlesnake. Touch (or wear!) the pelts of some of these animals, too. The museum also has informational panels to lift and learn; a section of a mine with an ore cart; Native American artifacts; a fireman suit and map of the wildfire from 2003; and a video room. Ask about the jr. ranger program. Outside are picnic tables under a shady tree grove.

Seasonal changes at this altitude of 4,000 feet are often drastic and beautiful: Autumn bursts on the scene with its rich colors of gold, red, and orange; winter brings a white blanket of snow; spring explodes with a profusion of brilliant wildflowers; and summer offers refreshment, by sitting near a stream, under a canopy of trees.

Campgrounds in the park, and some near rivers, are available for families at either Paso Picacho or Green Valley. You can hike to waterfalls from the latter campground. The campsites have picnic tables, fire rings, and heated showers (bring lots of quarters!). Paso Picacho also has a few one-room cabins available. You can camp with your horse at specific campgrounds. Note that there are some great trails heading out directly from the campgrounds. We hiked up to the peak, which was arduous, but worth it.

Fishing or boating at Lake Cuyamaca, (760) 765-0515 / www.lakecuyamaca.org, is another way to enjoy this area. Motorboat rentals are $45 a day, *oar* rent a row boat at $20 a day. Pedalboats are $15 an hour. Fishing permits are $8 for adults; $3.50 for kids 8 to 15 years; children 7 years and under are free with a licensed adult. A California license is

also required for ages 16 and up for $14.86 for a day. Depending on the season (and your luck), you can catch trout, catfish, bass, bluegill, and crappie. The lake is at the northern end of the park and a bait-and-tackle shop are located here. There is also a full-service restaurant at the lake - in case you don't catch your own meal! Camping at the lake is $20 for tent camping and $30 for RV.

Hours: The park is open daily, sunrise - sunset. The gift shop and museum are open Sat. - Sun., 10am - 4pm. Fishing and boat rentals are open daily, 6am - sunset. Call for extended summer hours.

Price: There are several designated scenic turn-outs along Hwy. 79 that offer picnic tables and hiking trails; parking here is free. Parking for day use of a campground is $8 per vehicle. Camping is $20 a night per person for primitive camping; $30 per vehicle for developed camping. The camping reservation fee is $8. 12 x 12 cabins are $70 a night.

Ages: 2 years and up.

DALEY RANCH

(760) 839-4680 or (760) 839-4880 / www.escondido.org; www.fodr.org
3024 La Honda Drive, Escondido

This 3,058-acre ranch is a hiking/mountain biking wilderness habitat preserve that offers a variety of terrain, from meadows to open grasslands to hills with rugged boulders. Twenty miles of main trails and offshoots traverse the property and range from wide, easy, paved fire roads to narrow, up and down, dirt trails. We hiked the somewhat steep East Ridge route (1.6 miles) and reached two decent-sized ponds. Boulder Loop Trail (2.5 miles) offers a great view and rock "gardens." The wide Ranch House Loop Trail (2.5 miles) passes the site of Daley's original (unrestored) log cabin. The ranch house, built in 1927, will eventually become an interpretative center. On Sunday, a free shuttle service that runs every half hour, from 8am to 4pm, takes visitors from the parking area up a dirt road to the ranch house. Bring your own water. Note: DIXON LAKE, see the next entry, is just "next door."

Hours: Open daily, dawn - dusk.
Price: Free
Ages: 5 years and up.

DIXON LAKE

(760) 839-4680 - ranger station; (760) 741-3328 - camping / www.dixonlake.com
1700 N. La Honda Drive, Escondido

This beautiful getaway offers year-round fishing with promising areas of the reservoir titled Trout Cove, Catfish Cove, and Bass Point. Fish off the shoreline, off the piers, or rent a motorboat or row boat to try your luck. Paddle boat rentals are also available. The lake is cradled in pines, poplars and other vegetation along the surrounding hillsides. There are a few short walking trails along the lake, and the rocks make it a fun destination for rock climbing. (For longer hikes, go "next door" to DALEY RANCH; see the previous entry.) One picnic area, with a small playground and a patch of grass, is at the entrance of the park. Another larger one, with some picnic shelters and more play equipment, is farther in. A concession stand is open year round.

Camping spots are up on the mountain ridge and overlook the valley on one side, the lake on the other. Some of the sites are a very short hike down from the parking area and therefore a bit more private than other sites. All in all - Dixon Lake is scenic and peaceful. Note: No swimming or biking is allowed.

Hours: Open daily, 6am - dusk.
Price: $5 per vehicle. Fishing is $7 for ages 16 and up; $5 for seniors; $5 for ages 8 - 15; children 7 and under are free. A fishing license is not required. Night fishing is available during summer months. Row boat rentals are $14 for half a day; $17 a full day. Motorboats are $30 for half a day; $35 a full day. Pedal boats are $8 a half hour for up to 4 people. Camping is $25 a night, $35 with RV hook-up, plus an advance registration fee of $5.

Ages: All

DOS PICOS REGIONAL PARK

(858) 694-3049 or (760) 789-2220 / www.sdcounty.ca.gov/parks/
17953 Dos Picos Park Road, Ramona

This is my kind of "secluded" wilderness - close to a small town, yet seventy-eight acres that are mostly au natural. Huge boulders dot the hillsides and a trail leads up amongst them. The valley of the park is filled with numerous oak trees that provide wonderful shade, but there are also open grasslands and chaparral. The park provides a pond (those

over 16 years old need a fishing license), play area, horseshoe pit, picnic area, exercise course, open play areas, and tent and RV camping. Ask about the programs offered here, such as the junior ranger program and the campfires that incorporate some old-fashioned family fun. The town of Ramona is just around the bend.

Hours: Open daily, 9:30am - sunset. Closed Christmas.
Price: $3 per vehicle per day. Tent camping is $24 a night; RV, $29, plus a $5 registration fee.
Ages: All

DOYLE COMMUNITY PARK

(858) 581-7170 or (858) 552-1612 / www.sandiego.gov/park-and-recreation
8175 Regents Road, La Jolla

This has-it-all park goes back much deeper than it first appears. The "bottom level" of the park is composed of a huge playground with different features appealing to various ages. The kiddie playground, geared for ages 2 to 5 years, has a wooden ship, a spiderweb made of nets, and ropes to climb, plus baby and bigger kid swings. The larger, two-story play structure has ramps, bridges, twisty slides, a mini zip line, and tire swings, among other features. The entire playground has a sand base and there are benches all around it along with cement picnic tables and barbecue pits. A basketball court and recreation center offering a myriad of activities are also on this level.

On the upper level there are more basketball courts, a sand volleyball court, a grass area, three ball fields, a small playground, cement picnic tables, a horseshoe pit, and two dog parks; one for smaller dogs and one for larger ones. A cement pathway goes all around the park.

Hours: Open daily, sunrise - sunset. The rec center is open Mon. - Sat. usually at about 11am.
Price: Free
Ages: All

ELFIN FOREST RECREATION RESERVE

(760) 632-4212 - ranger station; (760) 753-6466 - water district / www.olivenhain.com/parks.html
8833 Harmony Grove Road, Encinitas

San Diego always surprises me with all of its city attractions and yet its wealth of natural habitat. Elfin Forest encompasses over 750 acres of open space with oak trees, coastal sage, chaparral, wildlife (such as mule deer, lizards, squirrels, snakes, and such), and scenic hilltop/mountaintop vistas - such a variety of topography! Eleven miles of hiking, biking, and equestrian dirt trails and about six miles of the boulder-lined Escondido Creek meander throughout the reserve.

A main hike from the trailhead is a little over three miles round trip and moderately difficult, which means there are some steep climbs and some level walking areas. There are several switchbacks, many of them in the shade. Bring a fanny pack or backpack for water, and snacks for the kids. The Way Up Trail is tough, but the top-of-the-world scenery makes it worthwhile. An easier, fun, family trail is the self-guided botanical loop trail (about one mile), marked with over twenty-five stops for plant identification. For a more strenuous hike, follow the trail to Lake Hodges. An Interpretive Center is also on the grounds and offers ranger-led hikes and special activities.

Hours: Open daily, 8am to 30 minutes before sunset. The Interpretive Center is open Sat. - Sun., 9am - 3pm. Closed Christmas and on rainy days.
Price: Free
Ages: 5 years and up.

EUCALYPTUS PARK

(619) 397-6197 / www.chulavistaca.gov
4th Ave. and C Street, Chula Vista

The best thing this twenty-one-acre corner park has going for it is the fantastic, very purple playground. Besides the brightly colored twisty slides, tunnels, platforms, ladders, talking tubes, swings, activity panels, curvy metal structures, monkey bars, and little vehicles on giant springs, there is a yellow mini truck and bulldozer to play on, a good-size rock climbing wall, and lots of area to play on and under.

The rest of the park is not so exciting. The baseball diamond, tennis courts, basketball courts, and even the grassy areas and picnic areas are a bit run down, plus it's located on a very busy corner. Maybe the cool playground will be an inspiration to maintain/upgrade the rest of the park?

Hours: Open daily, sunrise - sunset.
Price: Free

Ages: All

FELICITA PARK

(760) 745-4379 / www.sdparks.org; www.co.san-diego.ca.us/parks
742 Clarence Lane, Escondido

This spacious, truly-lovely woodland park beckons guests to play, hike, picnic, and climb on boulders. A large grassy area for running around and several playgrounds help make the park younger-child friendly. Older kids will enjoy the ball fields, horseshoe pits, and volleyball courts. Walk on trails through huge shady oak groves or near the rock-lined seasonal creek. Join in on the many ranger programs offered here that specialize in local and Native American history. For instance, take a tour to the Indian grinding holes and learn about the village life of the local Indian tribes, learn the brutal history of "treeing" a thief, or learn about backcountry safety. This park is also home to the Renaissance Faire (pg. 715).

Hours: Open daily, 9:30am - sunset. Closed Christmas.
Price: $3 per vehicle.
Ages: All

FLINN SPRINGS COUNTY PARK

(858) 565-3600 of (619) 390-1973 / www.sdcounty.ca.gov/parks/
14787 Olde Highway 80, El Cajon

Although the park is just off a main street, it feels more like it's somewhere in the countryside. Lots of old oak trees give the rural park plenty of shade in the picnic areas and along the hiking trails. The dirt paths lead up and around the grassy and rocky hillsides. Be on the lookout for wildlife. A rock-lined, seasonal stream meanders through the park, allowing kids hours of outdoor, imaginative play. Both upper and lower lots have small playgrounds (one is enclosed), picnic tables, and barbecue pits. There is even a grass section, too.

If you're hungry, bring along a picnic lunch or eat next door at the very small Mary Ettas Cafe. Breakfast (eggs, French toast, and other staples) and lunch (hamburgers and such) are served daily from 6am to 1:30pm.

Hours: Open daily, 9:30am - sunset. Closed Thanksgiving and Christmas.
Price: $3 per car.
Ages: All

GLEN PARK

(760) 633-2740 / www.ci.encinitas.ca.us
2149 Orinda Drive, Cardiff-By-The-Sea

This nicely landscaped and maintained park, situated just across the highway from the beach, is a pleasant choice if you're in the neighborhood. The playground, with typical equipment and lots of sand surrounding it, is at the base of the park, along with a basketball court and horseshoe pit. Grassy lawns, palm trees, and large eucalyptus trees follow the gentle slope up toward the back. A few barbecue pits, scattered picnic tables, a cement pathway throughout, a volleyball court, a tennis court, and restrooms complete Glen Park.

Hours: Open daily, 5am - 10pm.
Price: Free
Ages: All

GRAPE DAY PARK

(760) 839-4691 or (760) 743-8207 / www.escondido.org
321 N. Broadway, Escondido

See ESCONDIDO HISTORY CENTER / GRAPE DAY PARK (pg. 531) for details about this grape, I mean great, park with play equipment, historical buildings, and an adjacent children's museum.

Hours: Open daily, sunrise - sunset.
Price: Free
Ages: All

GUAJOME REGIONAL - COUNTY PARK

(760) 724-4489 or (858) 694-3049; (877) 565-3600 - camping reservations / www.co.san-diego.ca.us
3000 Guajome Lake Road, Oceanside

This over 550 acre, mostly nature park has it all! Active visitors can partake in basketball, hiking the 4.5 miles of trails, fishing in the lake, kicking or throwing a ball on the acres of green lawn, and playing at either, or both, of the playgrounds. The mostly flat hiking trails meander through wooded sections, plus some chaparral, marshlands, and grass areas. The playgrounds are new and great - with swings, slides, metal shapes to climb on, and some rock climbing walls. More relaxed-minded visitors can enjoy the beautiful scenery, soak up some nature in the midst of suburbia and read a book under a shade tree.

There are thirty-five campsites with partial hookups for $29 a night (plus a $5 reservation fee). Each of the sites has a picnic table, fire ring, and some large trees for shade and some semblance of privacy. There is also a cabin for rent, $100 a night, on the premises. The cabin sleeps up to six people and has a full kitchen and outside patio and fire pit.

Note that the RANCHO GUAJOME ADOBE (pg. 547) is at the far, far end of the park and that the ANTIQUE GAS & STEAM ENGINE MUSEUM, INC. (pg. 525) is just down the street.

      Hours: Open daily, 9:30am - sunset.
      Price: $3 a car.
      Ages: All

HERITAGE PARK and COMMUNITY CENTER

(619) 421-7032 / www.chulavistaca.gov
1381 E. Palomar Street, Chula Vista

This fairly large park has cement pathways that crisscross throughout (great for bikes and strollers); play equipment with swings, slides, and a good-size sand base, so bring bucket and shovel; lighted basketball courts; open, grassy areas; barbeque pits and picnic tables; and - a big draw - a pond with lots of friendly/hungry ducks. There is also a very small skate park here with the basic elements. The community center is open for all sorts of activities.

      Hours: Open daily, sunrise to sunset.
      Price: Free
      Ages: All

HILTON HEAD COUNTY PARK

(858) 694-3030 or (805) 565-3600 / www.sdcounty.ca.gov
16005 Hilton Head Road, El Cajon

This ten-acre park offers acres of fun. (Ten acres of it, actually.) A basketball court, sports field, exercise stations, picnic area, BBQs, grassy areas, some paved pathways throughout, a boulder-lined dry creek bed, a playground, and an aquatic playground make it ideal for the family. The sand-based playground has a fairly tall tower with enclosed slides, steps, and places to play underneath, plus swings and a tire swing. The big and wide, pulled-apart ship on rubber flooring is a centerpiece play structure to climb in, on, and around. It has slides, port holes, a chain climbing ladder, and a large, purple sea creature that looks likes it's coming up out of the ground. The adjacent water play area has fountains that squirt up from a circular pad and several straight and curved poles that spurt out H2O. Note that there isn't a lot of shade at this park.

      Hours: The park is open daily, 7:30am - dusk. The waterplay area is open May - October daily, 11am - 5pm.
      Price: Free. $3 is asked for kids to play in the water play area.
      Ages: All

HOSP GROVE PARK

(760) 434-2826 / www.carlsbadca.gov
Jefferson Street and Marron Road, Carlsbad

I know the cars are right there, but this 5.5 acre park feels like a little nature refuge. Dirt trails zig zag up (sometimes steeply) and loop around the wooded hillside, for a total of about three miles, offering a nice overlook of the adjacent Buena Vista Lagoon. The trails even continue to the other side of Monroe Street, at the East Grove park.

The base of the park is in eucalyptus groves with a stone-lined seasonal stream and a playground. The sand flooring of the playground supports the swings, slide, play equipment and boulders. Make your mini retreat complete by enjoying a picnic under the shade trees.

      Hours: Open daily 8am - 10pm.
      Price: Free
      Ages: All

IMPERIAL SAND DUNES

(760) 337-4400 / www.blm.gov; www.imperialsanddunes.net; www.californiadesert.gov   !/$$$$

On Highway 78, Glamis

The expansive Imperial Sand Dunes, also referred to as the Algodones Dunes, extend for over forty miles - almost as far as the eye can see. They change in appearance from smooth surfaces to rippling waves, depending on the prevailing winds. They conjure up images of science-fiction flicks, or of a lone, sunburnt person clothed in rags crawling across the dunes crying out desperately, "Water, water!" Tip: Bring your own water.

Stop off first at the Osborne Overlook, located two miles east of Gecko Road along SR78. Here you'll see a great view of the dunes and the surrounding Imperial Valley. The appropriately named "wilderness" area is north of the 78, between Ted Kipf Road and the Coachella lands. A viewing area is two miles north of Glamis along Ted Kipf Road. Awe-inspiring dunes are toward the west side, while the east side has mostly smaller dunes and washes. The region is open for you to walk, run, jump, and roll down the dunes. Horseback riding is also allowed. Note that summer temperatures can rise to 110 degrees, so the most favorable months to visit are October through May. Bring your sunglasses, camera, and a bucket and shovel.

The area south of the highway is open for tent and RV camping (inclusive of the vehicle pass you purchase), off-highway vehicles (OHVs), and all-terrain vehicles (ATVs). Dune buggies are not readily available for rent, so you must bring your own vehicle. Camping is primitive, and trash must be packed out. For more information and an area map, call the BLM (i.e., Bureau of Land Management) at the above number.

Hours: Open daily, sunrise - sunset.
Price: $25 for a week pass.
Ages: It depends on how far you want to hike, or if you are content with just playing in the sand.

JACK'S POND

(760) 591-0827 or (760) 744-9000 / www.san-marcos.net

986 La Moree Road, San Marcos

This clean, small park with two barn-like structures offers a large, fenced in grassy area/corral for kids, not horses; a good playground with slides, tallish towers, a bridge and more; and a Wildlife Discovery Center. The little discovery center has some hands-on exhibits, such as bugs and animals felts; information on the area's natural history; plus activities and programs. Take the quarter-mile, partly-dirt, partly gravel trail which leads back to a pond and around it - a non-looping trail that goes about a half-mile around the perimeter of the pond, and back. Fishing in this natural little nook is allowed and kids under 16 years do not need a fishing license. Be on the look out for lizards, bunnies, bugs and birds.

Hours: The park is open daily, sunrise - sunset. The discovery center is open Sat., 9am - noon.
Price: Free
Ages: 10 years and under.

KEARNY MESA RECREATION CENTER

(858) 573-1387 - park; (858) 573-1389 - pool; (619) 561-3824 - BMX   !/$$
/ www.sandiego.gov; www.kearnybmx.com

3170 Armstrong Street, San Diego

This park has a decent playground (with a tube slide), basketball courts, tennis courts, a recreation building, six ball fields, soccer fields, a BMX course (behind the park), an enclosed dog park, and a swimming pool.

Hours: The park is open daily, sunrise - sunset. The pool is open January - September; call for specific hours of operation. The BMX course usually hosts practices and races Wed. and Fri., starting at 5:30pm; Sun. starting at 11am.
Price: Free to the park. The pool is $4 for adults; $2 for seniors and ages 15 and under.
Ages: All

KIT CARSON PARK / ESCONDIDO SPORTS CENTER

(760) 839-4691 - park; (760) 839-5425 or (855) 372-4255- sports center / www.sportscenter.escondido.org   !/$$

3315 Bear Valley Parkway, Escondido

Come to where the action is! A state-of-the-art, outdoor sports center is located in the heart of Kit Carson Park.

Besides an eighteen-hole disc course (discs are available in the skate shop, in the sports complex), it has an arena soccer field with bleachers, two roller hockey arenas, a 22,000-square-foot skate park, and a pro shop and concession stand. The lighted skate park is complete with variously sized ramps, a full street course with rails, spine, pyramids, quarter-pipes, a bowl, hips, ledges, and much more - impressive! At times the skate park is open for bikers as well as skaters. Bring your own safety equipment because it is mandatory. A parental waiver is required for participants 17 and under. Sign up for leagues, camps, and/or skate sessions, or just come to watch the action. A pond is located across the way from the Sports Center.

Just north of the center is the rest of Kit Carson Park with its 185 undeveloped acres and 100 developed acres. It's very family friendly with pretty landscaping, bridges over a creek, plenty of picnic tables, barbecue pits, green grassy areas for running around, nine ball fields (some with stadium seating), tennis courts, soccer fields, an amphitheater, a fitness course, a fitness trail with markers, hiking trails, and a few playgrounds (plus one just for tots). Whew! The playgrounds feature a gigantic multi-arched cement snake, a Paul Bunyan-sized wagon tilted to slide down, a few climbing trees, and some paved pathways.

Back behind the playground, on the Iris Sankey Magical Garden Trail, or Queen Califa's Magical Circle, is a unique artistic area. Several enormous snakes made of both polished and rough stones and colorful tiles encircle this section of the park. Walk through a maze-like section of black and white tile pieces, interspersed with pieces of mirror to a circular courtyard. This area features several gigantic and brilliantly colorful fantastical sculptures that are, again, created with tile and rock. Queen Califa, perched on a royal blue bird figure is in the center, with other mosaic statues scattered around. There are a few benches in here, but very little shade.

Kit Carson Park handily accommodates all of your family's different activities.

Hours: The park is open daily, dawn - 7pm. Call for hours on the various sporting center activities. The skate park is open November - March, Mon. - Fri., 3pm - 7pm; Sat., 8am - 6pm; Sun., 1pm - 6pm. It is open April - October until 10pm, most nights. Sun. is for bikers only. The skate park is closed New Year's Eve, New Year's Day, Christmas Eve and Christmas Day.

Price: The park is free. Skate/bike sessions are $10 per two-and-a-half-hour session. Year memberships are available at $25 per person, which brings the cost of each session down to $5.

Ages: All

KRAUSE FAMILY BIKE AND SKATE PARK

(858) 246-6731 - skate park; (619) 298-3576 - Y.M.C.A. /
www.missionvalley.ymca.org/programs/skate-park.html
3401 Clairemont Drive, Clairemont

Skateboarders, scooter-riders, BMXers, and roller bladers flip (not literally) for this huge (55,000 square feet!), gated, outdoor skate park that's associated with the Mission Valley Y.M.C.A. It has numerous and variously-sized, mostly wooden ramps and half-pipes, plus grinding boxes, rails, and other street skate elements, as well as areas to simply skate. A large, in-ground, concrete bowl has a maximum ten-foot depth - a favorite feature. There is also a good-sized beginner area. Sessions are about three hours long. The park is supervised and all participants must wear elbow and knee pads and a helmet. There are no rentals available. Bikes are allowed on certain days. Skaters and bikers 17 and under must have a waiver signed by a parent in person, or notarized, for their first session. Ask about skate camps and/or lessons.

Hours: Open Mon. - Fri., 2pm - 5pm, and 5pm - 8pm (after daylight savings time begins); Sat. - Sun., 11am - 2pm, 2pm - 5pm. Check on holidays hours.

Price: $10 per session; or $30 for a membership, then $5 per session. Ask about weekdays specials of $2 per session.

Ages: 7 years and up.

LAGUNA MOUNTAIN RECREATION AREA

(858) 673-6180 or (619) 473-8547 - visitors center; (619) 445-6235 - Laguna Mountain Volunteer Association
/ www.fs.usda.gov/recmain/develand/recreation; www.tourguidetim.com/develand-national-forest.com
10678 Sunrise Highway (this is the address for the centrally-located lodge and general store; the visitors center is just north, next door, at Los Huecos Rd.)

Beautiful! Stunning! So glad we did this! A breath of fresh air (literally). The absolutely lovely drive into the mountains, reaching an elevation of 6,000 feet, entices visitors to pull over and take in the vistas where row after row of mountains are vividly seen on clear days as are majestic panoramas and the valleys below. And come up in the fall

because the leaves change their colors.

The mountain, part of the massive Cleveland National Forest, offers fantastic hiking, mountain biking, sledding and playing in the snow (in the winter!), wildflowers in the spring, and camping.

I advise going to the visitor's center first to purchase a hiking map of the area - I like to know where I'm going. The small visitor's center has some nice displays, too - a number of taxidermied animals, animals pelts to touch, rocks, photos of the area, books, and more. It also has restrooms. Adjacent to the visitor's center is the Laguna Mountain Lodge and General Store. The general store is pretty much that as it is carries a little bit of everything, including food and various sundries. Stay at the lodge a night, or two, in a motel-like room or in a cabin. Call (619) 473-8533 for more info. Another way to spend the night is to stay at either of the two campgrounds, each with over 100 campsites. Burnt Rancheria Campground, open Memorial Day to mid-October, is close to the general store and visitor's center. Laguna Campground, open year round, is closer to the Julian entrance and isn't too far away from Little Laguna Lake.

There are two day use picnic areas here, surrounded by pine and oaks trees. One is just down the road from the visitor's center called Desert View Picnic Area with several picnic tables and bbq pits nestled into the mountainside. Walk the moderately easy trail here and you can peer into the adjacent desert; Anza Borrego Desert State Park. What a difference in topography as you follow along the rim of the mountain! The second day use picnic area is Pioneer Mail which is much further north, closer to Julian.

There are miles and miles (and miles and miles) of hiking/mountain biking trails on the mountain; the mighty 2,650-mile Pacific Crest Trail, which stretches from the border of Mexico through California and Washington and into Canada, even intersects on some of them. The 1.5 mile Wooded Hill Nature Trail reaches the highest peak on the mountain. About two miles south of the visitor's center is an information kiosk for the trails. Park here and start on the not-too-difficult-but-still-challenging Sunset Trail (then onto the 6.7 mile Big Laguna Trail, if you want) to reach sections of the 900-acre Laguna Meadow. Several lakes are found in the meadow lands, as well as a wide variety of plants and animals. All this just to whet your appetite, or get your hiking boots dirty.

Tips: Bring water - always. Bring bug spray in the non-winter months. The climate is almost always cooler up here than down the mountain, so layer up. Bring tire chains in the winter time. In the summer, take advantage of the campfire programs, guided nature walks and other special events. Laguna Mountains is not that long of a drive, but it is seemingly another world away.

Hours: The visitor's center is open Fri., 1 pm - 5pm; Sat. - Sun., 9am - 5pm.

Price: $5 Adventure Pass is required if you stop anywhere along the mountain, which you will.

Ages: 6 years and up.

LAKE HODGES

(619) 668-2050 - park/boat rentals; (619) 465-3474 - recorded fishing info / www.sdrp.org/projects.htm;   !/$$
www.sandiego.gov/water/recreation

Lake Drive, Escondido

This lake and its surrounding green hills (at least in the spring) are stunning; we also visited on a gorgeous day. We followed the shoreline to the boat launch area and saw kayaks, sailboats, and row boats being used. We found a grassy picnic area with tables and were greeted by ducks eagerly awaiting a handout. The island in the lake was most intriguing. You may fish from the lake shoreline or rent a boat to try your luck elsewhere. A fishing license, which is not sold at the lake, is needed for ages 16 and up. A fishing permit is $8 for ages 16 and older; $2.50 for ages 8 to 15; children 7 years and under are free with a paid adult. Row boat rentals are $30 for the day; motor boats are $53. Half-day rentals are also available. Double kayaks are $20 an hour.

It was a delight for us to simply walk around the area as well. In fact, Lake Hodges has several hiking trails. The Piedras Pintadas Trail is 3.8 miles long. Mule Hill, located on the north side of the lake, is an historic site as it's the site of an 1846 Mexican-American battle. There are two interpretive stations along the multi-use trail that tell the story of battle and other interesting facts for history buffs. The trail connects with Sikes Adobe; the trailhead is at Sunset Drive. Kids will especially appreciate the Ruth Merill Children's Interpretive Walk, which is actually the first mile of the Highland Trail, south of the lake. There are numerous markers along the Walk that show and tell about the native plants, animals, and importance of the river systems. Pamphlets with the trail map and more info can be obtained at the River Park office.

Just across the street from the parking lot, drive or take the footbridge, on Lake Drive is a bait-and-tackle shop to supply your fishing needs.

Hours: Open for fishing, February - October, Wed., Sat., and Sun., 30 minutes before sunrise - sunset. Open for walk-ins daily. Boat rentals are available on weekends. Closed New Year's Day, Thanksgiving and Christmas.

Price: Free to the lake. $7 for boat launch. Cash only for boat rentals.

Ages: 3 years and up.

LAKE JENNINGS COUNTY PARK

(619) 443-2510 or (619) 667-6293 or (619) 390-1623 / www.lakejennings.org; camping.lakejennings.org
10108 Bass Road, Lakeside

Fishing is the main attraction here with trout, catfish, bass, and bluegill yours for the catching, depending on the time of year (and your luck). Fish from the shore seven days a week at the various coves, or venture out on the sprawling lake via boat Fridays through Sundays. Row boat rentals are $19 a day, $40 a day for a motorized boat. A daily permit and a California fishing license for those 16 years old and over, which is not sold here, are required. Permits are $8 for adults; $3 for ages 8 to 15; children 7 and under are free with a paying adult. Free classes on how to fish are held on Sundays at 1pm. The Lake Jennings Bait & Tackle Shop sells permits, bait, tackle, snacks, and beverages. Picnic tables overlook the lake.

Miles of hiking across the chaparral-covered hills is another reason to visit Lake Jennings. There is also a large playground on at the park. And don't forget about tent and RV camping. There are some walk-back tent sites which offer a bit more seclusion. Ask about the Saturday programs offered here. They can include making bird feeders, taking a nature walk, seeing and learning about snakes, and more.

Hours: The park and fishing from the campsite area of the lake is open Mon. - Thurs., 9am - 6pm. The park and fishing from any shoreline and from a boat is open Fri. - Sun., sunrise - sunset.

Price: $2 per adult; ages 15 and under are free. Camping fees range from $28 a night for tent - $37 a night for full hook-ups, plus an $8 reservation fee.

Ages: All

LAKE MORENA

(619) 579-4101 - general info; (858) 565-3600 - reservations; (619) 478-5473 - fishing info / www.sdcounty.ca.gov/parks; www.co.san-diego.ca.us; www.lakemorena.com
2550 Lake Morena Drive, Campo

This large, remote reservoir/lake is surrounded by over 3,000 acres of wilderness. The landscape includes chaparral, oak woodlands, marshy grass areas, and more. The land really belongs to the wildlife - bald eagles, mountain lions, mule deer, migratory waterfowl, and others that roam (or fly over) the backcountry. Fishermen are lured to the lake in hopes of catching the big one or, at least, one. Fish from the boulder-lined shore or rent a boat. Hook trout in the winter and bass starting in the spring. Sometimes the fish are tagged so the anglers who catch them win a prize. A fishing license is required, but not sold here.

Hikers have a field day here. Explore the well-known Pacific Crest Trail, but don't try to reach the end of it as the trail terminates in Canada. Overnight tent and RV camping are available. The eighty-five sites are largely located under huge oak trees. Ten primitive cabins (i.e., no electricity, no water, beds but no mattress and cooking must be done outside at the fire ring) sleep four to six people. The lakeside view from the cabins is my kind of roughing it.

Hours: Open daily, 9:30am - sunset. Fishing hours are 30 min. before sunrise to 30 min. after sunset.

Price: $3 per vehicle for day use. Tent camping is $22 a night; RV with hook-up, $27; cabins are $50, plus a $8 reservation fee. Rowboat rentals are $20 a day; motor boat, $40 a day. Fishing for adults is $5 Mon. - Fri., $7 on Sat. - Sun; $3 Mon. - Fri. and $5 on the weekends for seniors and ages 10 - 16; ages 9 and under are free.

Ages: 5 years and up.

LAKE MURRAY

(619) 465-3474 or (619) 668-2050 - lake; (619) 466-4847 - boat rentals / www.mtrp.org/lake_murray.asp; www.sandiego.gov/water/recreation/
5540 Kiowa Drive, La Mesa

At the southern part of MISSION TRAILS REGIONAL PARK (pg. 512) is a beautiful, stocked reservoir allowing fishing and boating activities, with some boats and kayaks for rent, as well. A fishing license is required for ages 16 and up, which is not sold here, plus daily permits which are $8 for ages 16 and up; $2.50 for ages 8 to 15;

children 7 and under are free with a paid adult. There is a concession stand here which sells bait and tackle and some refreshments. A paved trail, 3.2 miles long, goes partly around the lake and is popular for biking, hiking, and walking. Plenty of picnic tables and barbecue pits are also available here.

Hours: The park grounds and shoreline fishing are open daily, sunrise - sunset. Closed New Year's Day, Thanksgiving, and Christmas.

Price: Free. Rowboats are $15 for half a day; kayaks are $10 for a single per hour; $20 for a double per hour.

Ages: All

LAKE POWAY RECREATION AREA

(858) 668-4770 - general info; (858) 668-4778 - concession stand / www.poway.org
14644 Lake Poway Road, Poway

Nestled between mountains, this pretty park features green grassy rolling hills, two playground areas, thirteen exercise stations, ball fields (one that is lighted), a sand volleyball court, picnic tables overlooking the lake, horseshoe pits, an archery range, and miles of dirt pathways and hiking trails. One trail, great for hardy hikers and mountain bikers, is a scenic, three-mile rocky trail that goes a good distance around the lake. More rugged trails include the 2.5-mile hike up to Mt. Woodson, and trails leading into the adjacent BLUE SKY ECOLOGICAL RESERVE (pg. 498). Be on the lookout for wildlife such as red-tail hawks, raccoons, and even deer.

The large Lake Poway is seasonally stocked with trout or catfish. Bait and fishing permits (a fishing license isn't needed) and refreshments can be purchased at the concession stand. Looking for something fun to tackle on summer nights? Try night fishing any Friday and/or Saturday night from 4pm to 11pm, offered early July through mid-September. Boat rentals are available here: Rowboats - $16 a day; motorboats - $24 a day; paddle boats - $13 an hour. Half-day rentals are also available. Ask about the summertime Family Campout programs hosted by Lake Poway.

Hours: Open daily, 6am - dusk. The lake is open for fishing, November - May, Wed. - Sun., 6am - sunset; open June - October, Sat. - Sun., 6am - sunset. Boating is allowed on weekends only. The concession stand is open the same schedule as the park.

Price: Free for Poway residents; $5 per car for nonresidents is charged March - October on weekends and holidays. It's free the rest of the year. Fishing permits are $6 for adults; $3 for seniors and ages 8 - 15; free for ages 7 and under with a paying adult.

Ages: All

LAKEVIEW PARK and DISCOVERY LAKE

(760) 744-9000 / www.san-marcos.net
650 Foxhall Drive, San Marcos

This attractive park has a small, younger children's play area by the parking lot with two wooden trains to climb on, a grassy area, a covered picnic pavilion, and steps leading down to a wading fountain to splash around in on hot days. The fountain turns on for fifteen minutes at 11am, 12:30pm, 2pm, 3:30pm and 5pm - plan your time. An eight-acre lake is ringed by a ¾-mile smooth trail, half of which is paved in asphalt, the other half is hard-packed dirt. The pathway makes for a nice stroll or bike ride. A two-and-a-half-mile trail branches off and leads up to the ridgeline (1,000 foot gain of elevation) for a wonderful view. Another trail, one mile long, follows along Discovery Creek.

Fishing is allowed in the lake, although one has to be fairly optimistic or incredibly lucky to catch anything as the lake is not stocked. You do need a permit.

Hours: Open daily, dawn - dusk.

Price: Free

Ages: All

LAKE WOHLFORD

(760) 839-4346 - lake; (760) 749-6585 - cafe / www.lakewohlford.com
25453 Lake Wohlford Road, Escondido

This beautiful, large, stocked lake offers boating and fishing - catfish, rainbow trout, crappie, bass, and bluegill - but no swimming. Rocks and boulders line the lake. Picnic tables are on the grounds. If you don't catch anything for lunch or dinner, catch something at the Lake Wohlford Cafe, just across from the lake. This is also the place to purchase permits and bait.

Hours: Open most of the year daily, 6am - dusk. Open September - mid-December weekends only, 6am - dusk.

Price: Fishing permits are $7 for adults; $5 for seniors and ages 8 - 15; children 7 years and under are free with a paying adult. Fishing licenses are also required. Row boats are $17 for the day; $14 after 1pm. Motor boats are $35 for the day; $30 after 1pm.

Ages: 5 years and up.

LA MESITA PARK / SKATE MESA

(619) 667-1300 / www.cityoflamesa.com
8855 Dallas Street, La Mesa

This nicely kept-up little park has four lighted tennis courts, a playground with a sand base, grassy lawns for run-around play, horseshoes, picnic tables, and a skate park. This unsupervised skate park is especially good for beginners to intermediate skaters as there aren't any bowls, but plenty of ramps and other challenging features. Helmet, elbow, and knee pads are required and must be brought by the skater as there are no rentals available.

Hours: The park and skate park are open daily, sunrise - sunset.
Price: Free
Ages: All for the park; 7 years and up for the skate park.

LAS POSAS AQUATIC CENTER

(760) 744-9000 or (760) 599-9783 / www.san-marcos.net
1387 W. Borden Road, San Marcos

The park has two tennis courts, a huge treeless field, a soccer field, and a baseball diamond. The main attraction here is summertime fun in the heated pool that has a shallow water area for children and a handicapped access ramp. A small, water play "sprayground" on the deck adjacent to the pool adds to the fun for younger children, and a water play area for slighter older kids aids them in having a "cool" time. Restrooms and showers are here, too.

Hours: The park is open daily, dawn - dusk. The pool and sprayground are open April to mid-May, Sat., 1pm - 4pm; mid-May to mid-June, Mon. - Fri., 2:30pm - 5:30pm; Sat., Sun., and holidays, 1pm - 5:30pm; summer, Mon., - Thurs., 9am - 11am and 2:30pm - 5:30pm; Fri. - Sun., and holidays, 1pm - 5:30pm; through mid-September, Sat. - Sun., 1pm - 4pm.

Price: The park is free. Admission to the pool and sprayground is $2.50 per person Mon. - Thurs.; $3 on Fri. - Sun. and holidays.

Ages: All

LIVE OAK PARK (San Diego County)

(760) 728-2303 - ranger station; (760) 728-1671 - community center / www.co.san-diego.ca.us/parks
2746 Reche Road, Fallbrook

Ah - the pause that refreshes. As its name implies, this inviting rustic park has a bounty of huge, old, shady oak trees. Scattered picnic tables, a few play areas, softball fields, sand volleyball courts, horseshoe pits and a few hiking trails also make this park a worthwhile place to visit. There is also a small botanic garden to meander through, plus a seasonal creek with bridges over it, stroller-friendly pathways, and exercise areas.

Hours: Open daily, 8am - sunset. Closed Christmas.
Price: $3 per vehicle
Ages: All

LOS PENASQUITOS CANYON PRESERVE / CANYONSIDE RECREATION CENTER COMMUNITY PARK

(858) 538-8066 - preserve; (858) 484-7504 - ranch house; (858) 484-3219 - friends of the preserve/hike schedule; (858) 538-8131 - recreation center / www.sandiego.gov/park-and-recreation/parks; www.penasquitos.org
12020 Black Mountain Road / 12350 Black Mountain Road, San Diego

This is a great "combo" destination, meaning it has a combination of elements that appeal to various ages and interests. One part is the Canyonside Recreation Center which has a small playground, ten lighted tennis courts ($5 for nonmembers to play), picnic tables, grassy areas, seven baseball fields, and a community building.

Another aspect of the park/preserve grounds is the 1824 adobe Rancho Santa Maria de los Penasquitos on

Canyonside Drive. Forty-five-minute guided tours are offered on weekends of this second-oldest, standing residence in San Diego. Check out the three-foot-thick walls of the adobe, and the Mexican and Indian artifacts as you tour through the kitchen, bedrooms, office, and mock schoolroom. A natural year-round spring is on this site, too.

The largest portion of this attraction is the thousands of acres and six miles of Canyon Preserve. Hike through chaparral, wildflowers, sage, and riparian woodlands with oaks, sycamores, willows, and cottonwoods. Walk along a year-round creek, among dense canyon vegetation, and past several ponds populated by fish, crayfish, and frogs (and tadpoles in season) to reach the year-round waterfall. The boulder-lined waterfall carves through bedrock. It is reached by hiking inland about three miles, or approximately half the length of the preserve. Coming from the western route, it is also reached by going through a few creek crossings. Bring water. The wildlife at the preserve is as rich and diverse as the plant life. Be on the lookout for mule deer, small mammals, lizards, birds, and, specifically, waterfowl. The crisscrossing trails are frequented by hikers, mountain bikers, and horseback riders. Ask about the numerous naturalist programs such as the geology hike, tracker walks (learn how to track animals), and ecology scavenger hunts.

Hours: The reserve is open daily, 8am - dusk. The ranch is open for guided tours Sat. at 11am and Sun. at 1pm. Call to reserve a school group tour during the week. The community park is open daily, 7am - 10pm.

Price: The preserve is free or $1 per vehicle, depending on where you park. Tours of the ranch free. The community park is free.

Ages: All

LOUIS A. STELZER PARK

(619) 561-0580 - park; (619) 390-7998 - Discovery Kit Program / www.co.san-diego.ca.us./parks
11470 Wild Cat Canyon Road, Lakeside

What a delightful respite! The 310-acre, back-country park has two playgrounds and several clusters of picnic tables with barbecues under sprawling oak and sycamore trees. (My boys also found a few good climbing trees, of course.) Some of the pathways are wheelchair/stroller accessible. A series of short hiking trails almost form a full loop. The .7-mile Riparian Trail begins near the ranger/visitor center and goes over a series of bridges as it follows along the seasonal creek. It connects to the Wooten Loop and then you have a choice: Go left onto the .6-mile Stelzer Ridge Trail, which meanders through oak groves, or go straight, which is a relatively quick climb up to the summit and promontory point.

The small visitor center has a few taxidermied animals and a Discovery Kit program. Each kit features pre- and post-visit materials for teachers and involves hands-on, interactive learning for elementary-aged children to learn about Native Americans, geology, birding, or general ecology.

Hours: Open daily, 7am - sunset. Closed Christmas.
Price: $3 per car; bring quarters.
Ages: All

MAST PARK

(619) 258-4100 / www.ci.santee.ca.us
9125 Carlton Hills Boulevard, Santee

This attractive park, that's located along a bank of the San Diego River, can get very populated. The front of the park is the play area, with a half basketball court, an exercise course, and a small playground with a sand foundation. The large plastic boat-like shape is fun for climbing into. Shade trees, picnic tables, and barbecues add to the family-friendly ambiance. There are two looping paved trails that go around the wooded back side of the park: a shorter trail, and a slightly more extensive one that weaves in and out and amongst the dirt and grassy open areas. We came in autumn as the trees were losing their leaves, crunching them underfoot as we walked the pathway.

Hours: Open daily, sunrise - sunset.
Price: Free
Ages: All

MIRAMAR RESERVOIR

(619) 668-2050 - reservoir / www.sandiego.gov/water/recreation/miramar.shtml
10710 Scripps Lake Drive, Scripps Miramar Ranch

Take a gander at all the geese and ducks waiting for a hand out at the reservoir. B.Y.O.B. (Bring Your Own Bread!) This lovely lake offers fishing and lakeside picnic tables and barbecue areas. Fishermen 16 years and older need

a fishing license and a permit. A paved, non-looping trail extends midway around the lake and, judging by the number of people we saw, it's ideal for walking, biking, rollerblading, and skateboarding.

Hours: Open daily, sunrise - sunset. Closed New Year's Day, Thanksgiving, and Christmas.
Price: Free. Fishing permits are $8 for adults; $2.50 for ages 8 - 15; children 7 and under are free with a paying adult.
Ages: All

MISSION BAY PARK

(858) 581-7602 - ranger station; (619) 235-1169 - reservations / www.sandiego.gov/park-and-recreation/parks/missionbay/index.shtml; www.infosandiego.com+
2688 E. Mission Bay Drive, San Diego

Mission Bay Park is not a singular bay or park like the name implies - it is thousands of acres of incredibly beautiful vistas, and of beaches, water, pathways, playgrounds, grassy areas, and various attractions. Generic things to do include jogging; cycling; in-line skating (especially the three-mile path along Mission Beach Boardwalk which runs along Mission and Pacific Beaches); swimming (there are nineteen miles of beaches here!); picnicking; fishing; kayaking; sailing; paddle boating; and camping. Park at any one of the scenic spots you see along Mission Bay Drive, or Ingraham Street, and enjoy. Hot spots include: **Pacific Beach**, just north of Mission Beach on Mission Boulevard - a favorite hang out for surfers, swimmers, joggers, and others; **Fiesta Island**, just northeast of SeaWorld, and **Vacation Isle**, on Ingraham Street north of Sea World Drive - both have numerous biking trails, delightful picnic areas, and a few playgrounds; **South Mission Beach** and **North Mission Beach**, both along Mission Boulevard - popular beaches for swimming and lying out; and **De Anza Cove**, on E. Mission Bay Drive - a nice area for swimming.

A couple of helpful names and phone numbers in the Mission Bay area include: Campland on the Bay, (800) 4BAY-FUN (422-9386) / www.campland.com, for camping, with over 650 sites; and Seaforth Boat Rentals, (888) 834-2628 / www.seaforthboatrental.com for single kayak ($12 an hour), double kayak ($20 an hour), jet skis ($90 an hour), and other rentals.

Attractions listed separately in Mission Bay Park are: BELMONT PARK (pg. 480), SEAWORLD (pg. 594), and TECOLOTE SHORES PLAY AREA (pg. 520). Check the website for a lot more information on this park.

Hours: Open daily, sunrise - sunset.
Price: Free
Ages: All

MISSION TRAILS REGIONAL PARK

(619) 668-3275 - visitor's center; (619) 668-3281 - park / www.mtrp.org
One Father Junipero Serra Trail, San Diego

This massive, almost 6,000-acre recreational area is composed of several major areas and points of interest and fifty miles of trails. **The Visitor and Interpretive Center** - This architecturally-beautiful building blends in with the natural rock setting of the park, and it is a great starting place for an adventure. Every thirty minutes the small theater presents a film on the park. Pick up trail guides, program information, and/or enjoy some interactive exhibits inside. Kids gravitate to the Indian faces carved from "rocks." Several touch screens offer information about the park - where to go and all about the plants and animals. Walk to the upper story of the center amid bird and animal sounds. See ancient volcanic rock and a great view of your surroundings. Outside the center is a small stage and rocks that are almost irresistible for kids to climb. The kids sweated (I glowed) as we hiked on the moderate looping trail around the Visitors Center, which took us a good hour. Our mission, should we decide to accept it, is to come back to Mission Trails and experience more of what it has to offer! **Lake Murray -** See page 508 for details. **Cowles Mountain -** Hiking is the main sport here. For an outstanding 360-degree view of the city, take the one-and-a-half-mile trail (about two hours) to the top of the mountain. The trail begins at Golfcrest and Navajo. **Old Mission Dam Historic Area -** This is a starting point for several hikes. Picnic tables are here, too. People of all abilities can go on a self-guided, paved pathway from the parking lot to the footbridge across the San Diego River, lush with foliage. Further along is the gorge with rock cliffs. Press buttons along the trail to listen to explanations of the area. Take a longer hike, too. So many trails - so little time! **East Fortuna Mountain -** This area offers some of the most diverse environments of the park. Check out some of the canyons. The smallish Kumeyaay Lake, accessible from Father Junipero Serra Trail, is fun for shoreline fishing. A relatively flat one-and-a-half-mile trail goes around the lake. **West Fortuna Mountain -** You can hike or mountain bike up plateaus and series of canyons. Climb the 100+ steps up to the south portion of the mountain for a breath-taking (literally) view of the area.

Hours: The trails and park are open daily, sunrise - sunset, although the car entry gates are open 9am - 5pm. The Center is open daily, 9am - 5pm. Closed on New Year's Day, Thanksgiving, and Christmas.

Price: Free

Ages: 3 years and up.

MONTEVALLE PARK

(619) 691-5269 / www.chulavistaca.gov

840 Duncan Ranch Road, Chula Vista

Adjacent to Salt Creek Open Space, you'll find plenty to do for the day at this expansive, twenty-nine-acre park, in somewhat of a natural setting. The amenities include three multi-purpose fields; a softball field; tennis courts; basketball courts; off-leash areas - one for large dogs and one for smaller ones; picnic tables and shelters; paved and gravel walking trails lined with a wooden fence that meander through some marshy areas, amongst trees, and over bridges; a community center; a terrific playground; and a skate area. The small skate park has rails and ramps, but no bowls.

It's worth coming here just for the huge playground with its foundation in wood chips and rubber. One section is designed especially for disabled children with long ramps that have lots of interactive gadgets and activities along the ramp walls, plus speaking tubes and a learning Braille section. This area also has a small playhouse with a raised table and several basins on stands filled with sand for wheelchairs to readily fit under. A sand pit is on ground level, too. Toddler swings and swings to accommodate wheelchairs; animals on large springs to ride on; numerous slides; a cargo net to climb; twisted metal pieces to play on; benches; peek-a-boo play spaces under the play platforms; a seasonal water sprayer (that looks like a shower); and two jumbo-size xylophones (one metal and one wood) to make (beautiful?) music complete this playground.

Hours: Open daily, sunrise - sunset.

Price: Free

Ages: All

OCEAN BEACH ATHLETIC AREA / ROBB FIELD SKATEBOARD PARK

(619) 531-1563 / www.sandiego.gov/park-and-recreation/centers

2525 Bacon Street, Ocean Beach

This huge park has something for every athlete in the family. It boasts eight baseball diamonds, soccer fields, racquetball courts, several tennis courts, a football field, lots of grass areas, picnic tables, a bike path that follows along the adjacent San Diego River, and a terrific skate park at the east end.

In front of the skate park are a few very shallow cement pools (more like a toe-dip area than pool) and cement area - a good place for young skaters to practice. The outdoor, smooth concrete-surface skate park has numerous pools of varying depths along with ramps, steps, a split fun box, ledges, blocks, an octagon volcano, and pump bump, plus a few flat areas and a pathway around the perimeter. Benches are just outside for anxious, I mean, observing parents. Vending machines carry beverages; bring your own lunch. Helmet, elbow and knee pads are required by the signs via the signage.

Across the street, Dusty Rhodes Park offers more picnic and run-around area, plus a playground. To the west is Dog Beach, where furry visitors from all over come to romp and play frisbee on this stretch of beach. Tip: Watch where you walk.

Hours: The park is open daily, sunrise - sunset. The skate park is open daily, 10am - dusk.

Price: The park and skate park are free.

Ages: All

OLD POWAY PARK

14134 Midland Road, Poway

See the entry for OLD POWAY PARK on page 565 for details.

OTAY LAKE COUNTY PARK

(619) 482-7361 - park; (619) 668-2050 - boat rentals / www.sandiego.gov/water/recreation

2270 Wueste Road, Chula Vista

The view from atop this small park is beautiful as it overlooks lower Otay Lake. The playground has slides, swings, and climbing equipment, plus talking tubes and a mini zip line. A grassy area, picnic tables, horseshoe pits, a

demonstration garden, and three short hiking trails up the hillside complete this scenic park. Enjoy kayaking, motor or row boating, and fishing in the lake that is stocked once a year with catfish. Note: Visit the nearby U.S. OLYMPIC TRAINING CENTER (pg. 568) on your way to or from the park.

Hours: The park is open Mon. - Fri., 9:30am - 5pm; Sat. - Sun. and holidays, 9:30am - sunset. Closed Christmas. Fishing and boating are available at Lower Otay February - October, Wed., Sat., and Sun., sunrise - sunset. No fishing or boating is allowed November - January. (It's duck season.) Boat rentals are usually available on weekends only. Shore fishing - catch and release only - is allowed at Upper Otay the same schedule as Lower Otay.

Price: $3 per vehicle to the park. Fishing is $8 for adults, plus a fishing license, which isn't sold at the park; $2.50 for ages 8 - 15 (no license necessary); children 7 and under are free with a paying adult. Row boats are $30 for the day; motorboats are $53 for the day and must be reserved in advance. Single kayaks are $10 per hour, tandems are $20.

Ages: All

PALOMAR MOUNTAIN STATE PARK / PALOMAR OBSERVATORY

(760) 742-2119 - observatory; (760) 742-3462 - state park; (800) 444-7275 - camping reservations. / www.parks.ca.gov; www.astro.caltech.edu/palomarpublic; www.fs.fed.us

19952 State Park Drive S6, Palomar Mountain

Up in the Palomar Mountains, at the end of a long and winding road, is the Palomar Observatory. A short hike up to the observatory allows you to see the famed 200" Hale telescope. But forewarn your children - you can only look at the telescope which is housed behind glass panes; you cannot look through it. The telescope is magnificent in size and scope and seeing it is almost worth the drive here! The small one-room museum displays outstanding photos of star dusters, galaxies, and clouds of glowing gas. It also shows a continuously running video about the workings of the telescope and about our universe. Hour-long, public tours are offered on the weekends, April through October, at 11:30am, 1pm, and 2:30pm.

Just a few miles down the road is Palomar Mountain State Park. If you're planning on coming to the observatory, I suggest making the park a destination, too, as just walking around the observatory and museum took us only half an hour. Palomar Mountain General Store, (760) 742-3496, is at the junction of S7 and S6, making it a natural stopping place before going on to the park. The store has a bit of everything, including fossils, gems, Indian jewelry, and artifacts. And if you're hungry, Mother's Kitchen is just next door, serving breakfast and lunch.

Continue about three miles on S7 to reach the park. At 2,000 acres, this Sierra Nevada-like park is incredibly beautiful. It also can get snow in the winter. You'll find several hiking trails through the scenic mountainside. The Boucher Hill Lookout trail, for instance, is a looping four-mile hike with marvelous vistas. Fishing is available at Doane Pond, which is stocked with trout regularly. There is a five-fish limit per day, and those 16 years old and older need a California state license. The park also provides areas for picnicking and overnight camping. Each of the thirty-one family campsites has fire rings and picnic tables, plus community, coin-operated hot showers. Call the ranger station (park office) for more information.

Hours: The museum and the observatory are open mid-March - October, daily, 9am - 4pm; November - mid-March, daily, 9am - 3pm. The museum gift shop is open mid-March - November, Sat. - Sun., 10:15am - 2:45pm, and some weekdays. All are closed Christmas Eve and Christmas Day. The state park is open daily, sunrise - sunset.

Price: Free to the observatory and museum. A $8 vehicle entrance fee is charged for day use of the park. Overnight camping is available at Doane Valley Campground at $30 a night, plus a $8 camping reservation fee or camp at the forty-two site Observatory Campground which is open May - November.

Ages: 8 years and up for the observatory and the museum; ages 3 and up for the park.

POTRERO COUNTY PARK

(619) 478-5212 or (858) 694-3030 / www.sdparks.org; www.sdcounty.ca.gov/parks/

24800 Potrero Park Drive, Campo

Waaay out here is an expansive park (115 acres) that is reminiscent of the olden days in California. Hundreds of enormous oak trees, plus grassy meadows, rocky hillsides, nature trails (look for rocks with holes where the Indians ground acorns into meal), lots of picnic tables, ball fields, playgrounds, exercise stations and machines, and camping and RV sites are here. Be on the lookout for all kinds of wildlife.

Hours: Open daily, 9:30am - sunset. Closed Christmas.
Price: $3 per vehicle. Camping fees range from $22 - $27 a night, plus a $5 reservation fee.
Ages: All

POWAY COMMUNITY PARK

(858) 679-4366 or (858) 668-4671 or (858) 668-4687 - park, skate park, and tennis; (858) 668-4680 - swim
center / www.ci.poway.ca.us; www.powayskate.com
13094 Civic Center Drive, Poway

This park offers something for almost everyone in the community. A mostly unsupervised cement skate park with
bowls, ramps, and stairs is on the corner, just behind the public library. Children must be accompanied by parent or
legal guardian and must be registered to skate. A helmet and pads are necessary. Note that officers of the neighboring
Sheriff's office often drop by for a visit. Drive further in to play on the two lighted tennis courts (call for reservations),
or walk over the grassy embankments to the good-sized Adventure Playground. The playground has swings, a swaying
bridge, several slides, circular monkey bars, and a big wheel to spin around, all on top of a rubberized surface. There
are plenty of picnic tables here as well.

Other park amenities are a dog park (watch where you step), a tot lot, a few ball fields, a soccer field, a basketball
court, bocce ball courts, and a compact exercise "course" with bars for pull ups and sit ups, and pieces of wooden
equipment. The swim center has a fifty-meter pool that is open year round and a wading pool for kiddies, only closed
in the winter. Children 7 years and under must be accompanied by an adult.

Hours: The park is open daily, 8am - sunset. The skate park, unsupervised, is open Mon. - Tues., 8am -
8pm; Wed., 8am - 6pm; Thurs., 8am - 8pm; Fri., 8am - 4pm; Sat. - Sun., 8am - 8pm. The supervised
skate session for ages 14 and under is Fri., 6pm - 8pm. Supervised bike sessions are Wed., 6pm -
8pm and Fri., 4pm - 6pm. The swim center is open April - mid-June and September and October,
Mon., Wed., Fri., 10:30am - 7:30pm; Tues. and Thurs., 8am - 7:30pm; Sat. - Sun., 1pm - 5pm. It's
open mid-June - August, Mon., Wed., Fri., 1pm - 5:30pm; Tues. and Thurs., 1pm - 8pm; Sat. - Sun.,
1pm - 7pm. It's open November - March, Mon. - Fri., 11am - 1:30pm and 3pm - 7pm. Closed on
Sat. and Sun.
Price: The park and skate park are free. The swim center for nonresidents is $5 for adults; $4 for seniors
and ages 17 and under. For residents, $2.50 for adults; $2 for seniors and ages 17 and under.
Ages: All

RANCHO BERNARDO-GLASSMAN RECREATION CENTER

(858) 538-8129 - park; (858) 487-9698 - tennis club / www.rbcommunitypark.com;
www.sandiego.gov/park-and-recreation/centers
18448 W. Bernardo Drive, Rancho Bernardo

This community park has a playground, eight baseball diamonds, basketballs courts, the Bernardo Tennis Center
(with its six courts), two lawn bowling areas, picnic tables, barbecue pits, and lots of grassy areas and paved pathways
throughout for all kinds of wheels. All of this is nice, but what helps make this park stand out is the adjoining open
area with some fairly easy dirt hiking trails. The area has hard-to-resist-climbing-on large rocks scattered throughout,
gentle hills, and a trail that leads to Lake Hodges, a lake within visual range from the park. A portion of the park is also
a leash-free "dog park."

Hours: The park is open daily, sunrise - sunset. The recreation building is open Mon. - Sat., closed Sun. and
holidays. Play tennis daily, 7am - 10pm. (Of course you'd be tired if you played that long.)
Price: Free. Tennis is $5 - you can call to make a reservation.
Ages: All

SALTON SEA STATE RECREATION AREA

(760) 393-3059 - park and camping; (760) 393-3810 - visitor center / www.parks.ca.gov
100-225 State Park Road (for the North Shore), Mecca

Firstly, I know this isn't really in San Diego county, so with that said. . . . Salton Sea is California's largest lake and
is one of the world's lowest spots on earth at -227 feet below sea level. It is also incredibly salty, so while fishing is big
here, a limited type of fish can be caught. And yes, it does smell like rotting fish (sometimes a lot!), especially during
hot days, because fish skeletons/dead fish litter the shores. Walk along the beach and be intrigued by all of the area's
uniqueness and know that the "sand" is made up mostly of crushed bones and shells - wear shoes. The sunsets are

camera-worthy.

Salton Sea is a strange and fascinating place to visit, as there is beauty in the midst of decay. There is a lot to do here, in some respects, but not a lot going on in the immediate surroundings, as many of the buildings are empty/abandoned.

Most of the action takes places at the North End, near Varner's Harbor and the visitor center. Inside the center is a video regarding the Salton Sea, plus photographs of the area and information as to how it was formed, its salinity, preservation efforts, and more. There is also a playground located here and a fishing jetty.

Boating is a preferred recreational sport and there are numerous launching points. Hike on the several trails. Twitching is also immensely popular. Not as in a body part is twitching or jerking around, but as in bird-watching lingo, "the pursuit of a previously located rare bird." The Salton Sea is located along the Pacific Flyway and over 400 species of birds have been counted here including grebes, brown pelicans, great blue herons, ospreys, gulls, owls, tern and many more. Bring your binoculars and make it 401!

Spend the night at one of the over 1,600 campsites, ranging from primitive to full amenities. Note which ones are closed in the summer, though that wouldn't be the best of times to come here, anyway. Make sure to visit SALVATION MOUNTAIN (pg. 566) because it's just down the road a bit.

Hours: Open daily 24/7. The visitor center is open October - May, daily, 10am - 4pm; June - September, Fri. - Sun., 10am - 4pm.

Price: $5 per vehicle for day use during non-peak season (June - September); $8 in season (October - May). Camping is $20 - $30.

Ages: 5 years and up.

SAN DIEGO BOTANIC GARDEN

(760) 436-3036 / www.sdbgarden.org

230 Quail Gardens Drive, Encinitas

$$$$

Desert, exotic tropical, tropical rainforest, palm, bamboo, native California, Mexican, Mediterranean, African, New Zealand, and other garden sections (twenty seven in all!) makes it feel as if you are walking all over parts of the world as you meander the trails throughout these thirty-seven beautifully-landscaped acres.

The bamboo forest, which grows a variety from very thick to quite thin bamboo, contains a pond with lily pads and koi. An array of tropical fruit trees, such as papaya and bananas, grow their fruit upside down, while figs and jujube (not the candy!) are also ripening here. The desert gardens have twisted-looking cactus and other succulents. The Mexican garden features life-size figures made from plants and sculpture parts. The lush foliage of the rainforest showcases the amazing size of some leaves and beyond Crayola colors of green. Throughout the gardens the incredible array of flowers, the wandering trails (some dirt, some paved), the beautiful waterfall, the ponds, the benches under shade trees, and even the fanciful sculptures (for sale) that unexpectedly crop up all invoke the sensation of visiting a secret garden. Add to that the sounds and sights of woodpeckers and a variety of other birds such as wrens, finches, scrub jays, and hermit thrushes, and the outdoors come alive. Take a short hike up to the Overlook Pavilion for a 360-degree view of the gardens, mountains, ocean, and surrounding community.

Kids can spend almost all day in the one-acre Hamilton Children's Garden with its fifteen activities. I'm sure they also become rooted in a love and knowledge of plants here. The colorful sculptures throughout add a touch of whimsy. Bloom with learning at the Spell and Smell Garden where a plant for each letter of the alphabet, and its function, is labeled, such as C is for chocolate mint (smell) and L is for lamb's ear (soft, velvety texture). Check out the Seussian elephant foot tree. Play in dirt and sand at the good-sized Earth Builders portion with logs to build forts, and toys and toy trucks. Go through a little maze to the center where you become the sundial's shadow to tell time. Make music (or noise) with natural elements at Garden Rhythms with a stone xylophone, a drum, bamboo wind chimes, stone pianos and more. Splash a bit in the little, rock-lined stream. Birds and butterflies are attracted to certain plants and in this area you see them as they land and flutter about. Practice chalkboard skills and other artistic endeavors in the Art's Garden, complete with oversized chairs and other objects. The Hamilton Children's Garden also contains an awesome Tree House - a twenty-foot high, multi-platform banyan tree (part real, part man made) with steps up to the separate areas. What kid doesn't dream of living at a place like this? Climb over and through the tree roots and up the rope ladder, too.

The Seeds of Wonder is south of the parking lot and is a small section for preschoolers, especially. It has a few fanciful topiary figures; a hand water pump; animal sculptures to climb on (including some small dinosaurs and some eggs); a small, sandy dig site with buried "bones"; short, hidden pathways for young children to explore; a shed with plants growing on the roof; a miniature train on tracks through a garden area; and a sweet, little playhouse with kitchen

utensils and books inside. Adjacent to this section is a short hiking trail through a representative canyon of sorts - the Native Plants/Native People region. It is reminiscent of the landscape hundreds of years ago with its coastal sage, a pond, and a Native American (Kumeyaay) dwelling.

Plan to be here on a Thursday night in the summer when the garden stays open until 8pm and there are activities and live music included with the price of admission. Ask about guided tours; plant sales; family programs, such as art in the garden, Fairy Festival, or the annual Insect Festival; summer science camps; beautiful Garden of Lights in December; and other listings in the packed calendar of events. Just to let you know that all this write doesn't do this amazing garden justice - it is a "must see".

Hours: Open daily, 9am - 5pm. Closed Christmas.
Price: $14 for adults; $10 for seniors, military, and students; $8 for ages 3 -12; children 2 and under are free. Admission is free on the first Tues. Parking is $2, unless you have 4 or more people in your car, then the parking is free. See Museum Month, San Diego (pg. 708) for details about half-price admission in February. See page x for info on AHS reciprocal memberships.
Ages: 2 years and up.

SAN DIEGUITO COUNTY PARK

(858) 755-2386 / www.co.san-diego.ca.us/parks
1628 Lomas Santa Fe Drive, Del Mar

San Dieguito's 125 acres of nature park offer a variety of trails to hike that crisscross all over the park; lots of grassy, open and wooded spaces to play and picnic; bbq pits; a swinging suspension bridge; two small ponds at one end with ever-present ducks and some turtles; a lookout tower with great views; a basketball court; a seasonal creek; two great playgrounds; exercise stations; and a baseball field that is fully accessible for players with special needs. This park feels, to me, like a great and close by nature retreat. Trees actually change color here in the fall!

Hours: Open daily, 9:30am - 5pm.
Price: Parking is $3.
Ages: All

SAN DIEGUITO RIVER PARK

(858) 674-2270 / www.sdrp.org
18372 Sycamore Creek Road, Escondido

Beautiful and startling scenery await at this enormous natural habitat within San Diego County. The park extends great distances to the west and east - from the ocean at Del Mar, fifty-five miles to Volcan Mountain near Julian - with lots of places from which to access it in-between. Twelve hiking, biking, and equestrian trails crisscross throughout. Check the website for updates on trail openings and trail maps.

Hours: Open daily, sunrise - sunset.
Price: Free
Ages: 5 years and up.

SAN ELIJO LAGOON ECOLOGICAL RESERVE AND NATURE CENTER

(760) 634-3026 - nature center; (760) 436-3944 - lagoon conservancy / www.sanelijo.org
2710 Manchester Avenue, Cardiff-by-the-Sea

One of San Diego's largest coastal wetlands protects nearly 1,000 acres and hundreds of plants, birds, and other animals in the water and on land, even as a highway divides a portion of it. Walk any part, or all, of the seven miles of the eight mostly flat trails that wind through the reserve, past estuaries and salt marshes, and through sagebrush and chaparral, many with interpretive signage. The half-mile loop trail by the nature center is on paved and boardwalk surfaces. The 3.5 mile La Orilla Trail really traverses through distinct areas, including some woodland.

Join in on a free, one-hour, naturalist-led walk every Saturday at 10am and learn about what you are seeing and/or help out with the monthly habitation restoration (i.e. clean up!) School, and other, groups are welcome to set up a time for guided tours.

The green, lovely and airy nature center allows visitors to see a whole new world - well, at least it offers a good view of the lagoon and surroundings from the second-floor Observation Deck. The inside features informational and photographic panels; interactive displays to learn about the surrounding plant and rock and animal life; taxidermied animals such as a bobcat, coyotes, and hawks; and a few live animals such as snakes, lizards, tree frogs, and crabs.

Hours: Trails are open daily, dawn to dusk. The nature center is open daily, 9am - 5pm. Closed Christmas.

Price: Free
Ages: All

SAN PASQUAL BATTLEFIELD STATE HISTORIC PARK

(760) 737-2201 / www.parks.ca.gov
15808 San Pasqual Valley Road (SR78), San Pasqual

This is the site of the worst (i.e., bloodiest) battles in California during the Mexican-American War. Kids need to know this fact for its historical significance, and because it will make their visit here more exciting. The grounds have picnic tables and a quarter-mile, looping trail. The visitors center overlooks the battlefield, which is actually across the highway, on private land. The small center has interpretive panels, a few uniforms, weapons, and a ten-minute video entitled *Mr. Polk's War*. Living History Days are held the first Sunday of each month from 10am to 4pm, October through June. Docents are dressed in period costumes and visitors get to participate in old-fashioned chores, crafts, and other activities. Periodically, you can also see a cannon being fired. Guided school tours are given during the week, by appointment. Note: The battle is reenacted in December. See the Calendar entry, on page 770, for details.

Hours: The park is open Sat. - Sun., 10am - 5pm. Closed New Year's Day and Christmas.
Price: Free
Ages: 6 years and up.

SANTA CORA PARK

(619) 397-6197 / www.chulavistaca.gov
1365 Santa Cora Avenue, Chula Vista

This Chula Vista park has some unique elements such as a hopscotch court, funky playground, rock climbing wall, and a big, wide, grassy hill to roll down, with plenty of run-around space at its bottom. The playground has geometric shapes to climb up and on; poles with seats to twirl around and up; cargo ropes; platforms; ladders; a spinning chair that looks like an upside down plunger; and other fun structures. A separate apparatus looks like a frameless helicopter with a steering wheel.

The sizeable, ten-foot-high (or so), curved, rock climbing wall has colorful hand and foot holds (just like an indoor rock climbing gym), an archway with an overhang, and an accompanying panel with instructions on how to practice bouldering skills. The park also has a tennis court, lighted basketball court, barbecue pits, and several cement picnic tables. Note that there aren't any restroom facilities here. See COTTONWOOD PARK (pg. 500), which is just down the street, for facilities and a different type of park.

Hours: Open daily, sunrise - sunset.
Price: Free
Ages: All

SANTEE LAKES REGIONAL PARK AND CAMPGROUND

(619) 596-3141 / www.santeelakes.com
9310 Fanita Parkway, Santee

This regional park is made up primarily of a series of lakes that are seasonally stocked with trout, catfish, bluegill, and bass. A permit is required and available for purchase at the park entrance. No state fishing license is required. No swimming is allowed. Kayak ($13 for a half hour), paddle boat ($16 and hour for a four-seater), canoe ($17 an hour), and rowboat ($17 an hour) rentals are available. The park also contains miles of paved trails for hiking and biking, and five playgrounds. One playground was specifically designed for children with disabilities, and one is a sprayground with fountains that spurt up sporadically, a shower, a misting ring to run through, and buckets on poles and other apparatus that dump and shoot out water.

Three hundred campsites, a swimming pool (for campers only), a general store, laundry facilities, and a recreation center are on the grounds, too. Full hook-up campgrounds are $41 to $51 a night. Each campsite has a picnic table. Fully-furnished and equipped, lakeside cabins with kitchenettes, that sleep six are $100 a night, Monday through Thursday, and $127, Friday through Sunday. For the ultimate waterbed, rent a similar-type cabin that floats on the water (!) and sleeps four for $122 a night Monday through Thursday; $147, Friday through Sunday.

Hours: The park and fishing are open Mon. - Thurs., 8am - one hour before dusk; Fri. - Sun., 6am - 6:30pm. The pool is open seasonally.
Price: $3 per vehicle during the week; $5 per vehicle on the weekends. Fishing permits are $9 for adults; $6 for ages 7 - 15; children 6 and under are free with a paying adult.

Ages: 2 years and up.

SCRIPPS PARK / LA JOLLA COVE and COASTLINE

(619) 221-8899 / www.sandiego.gov/lifeguards/beaches/cove.shtml
1180 Coast Boulevard, La Jolla

This delightful grassy park overlooks a gorgeous stretch of the California coastline and the Pacific Ocean. The park itself has few amenities - picnic tables, a few palm and cypress trees, and a covered overlook. It's an ideal place for flying a kite and to catch a concert on Sunday afternoons in the summer from 2pm to 4pm. Take a walk on the cement sidewalk that follows up and down a good distance along the coast and revel in the breathtaking scenery and in the variety of landscape.

Just to the north of the park is tiny Shell Beach (good for collecting seashells) and La Jolla Cove, a tiny patch of beach with palm trees swaying in the wind on top of the adjoining sandstone cliffs. There are a few rocks here to climb on and through, like short caves. You may go swimming here. The cove's water visibility can sometimes exceed thirty feet, making this a favorite spot for snorkelers and scuba divers. (Think Hawaiian waters, kind of.) The cove is part of the San Diego La Jolla Underwater Park Ecological Reserve which safeguards marine life in the area, so bring your own snorkel gear and head out to sea.

Further north is the LA JOLLA SHORES BEACH (pg. 470). Heading just south of the park, within easy walking distance, is the SEAL ROCK MARINE MAMMAL RESERVE (pg. 594). Continue on to small South Casa Beach and Wipeout Beach (hard to tell where one stops and the other begins), which has a semicircular portion of sand (embraced by rocks), sea caves, and rocks - large, flat rocks to climb on and jump off (at least the shorter ones). My boys loved this aspect of the beach. Tide pooling is a great activity to do at certain nooks along the coastline.

Note that parking anywhere around this area in the summer time is slightly insane, but worth it. Go "off-season" and enjoy all the same benefits. Look up LA JOLLA CAVE and THE CAVE STORE (pg. 563) and LA JOLLA COVE KAYAK / SNORKEL ADVENTURE (pg. 581) for information on other nearby attractions.

Hours: Open daily, 4am - 8pm.
Price: Free
Ages: All

SHADOW HILL PARK

(619) 258-4100 / www.ci.santee.ca.us
9161 Shadow Hill Road, Santee

If you are in this area, this is a nice little park to release some energy. The sand and rubber-based playground has fun apparatus, plus there is a basketball court, a small lawn, a few picnic tables, a little garden with a picnic nook, short paved pathways for cycling or skating, and a short hiking trail up the hill and around the two tennis courts.

Hours: Open daily, dawn - dusk.
Price: Free
Ages: All

SOUTH CLAIREMONT RECREATION CENTER and POOL

(858) 581-9924 - recreation center; (858) 581-9923 - pool / www.sandiego.gov
3605 Clairemont Drive, Clairemont

This large community park offers various activities for families to enjoy. Green grassy areas and scattered picnic tables provide a picnic atmosphere, while the older-style playground, complete with hopscotch, slides, swings, and climbing apparatus, provides the fun. Check at the community center building for special classes, programs, and events. There is also one tennis court, a basketball court, and a good-sized, outdoor swimming pool, plus a wading pool that is open year round. During the week, only half of the pool is open for public use because the swim team uses the other half. On weekends, the whole pool is open for the public to use.

Hours: The park is open daily, sunrise - sunset. The pool is open daily, Mon. - Fri., noon - 4pm (shallow end only); Sat. - Sun., noon - 3pm (whole pool). Call for hours as they do fluctuate.
Price: The park is free. Swimming sessions cost $4 for adults; $2 for seniors and ages 15 and under.
Ages: All

STAGECOACH COMMUNITY PARK

(760) 434-2826 or (760) 602-4690 / www.carlsbadca.gov

3420 Camino de los Coches, Carlsbad

Although stagecoaches no longer use this park as they once did, there are some preserved adobe ruins from those bygone days. The ruins are housed in a building residing beneath a large, wide expanse of stones set in a spiral for visitors to sit and rest, or play on. The ruins are worth a look. The adjacent community center has a gym.

The park has three multi-use, athletic fields; four lighted tennis courts; a lighted basketball court and some half-courts; paved pathways that traverse throughout the open grassy play areas and trees; picnic tables scattered throughout; and a delightful, stone-lined brook with a wooden bridge - like a mini woodlands area. There is also a short trail towards the back. A good-sized, sand-based playground has several, separate play structures, including one designed to represent a stagecoach. The main playground has lots of slides, including two that are enclosed, plus climbing apparatus, swings, and more.

Hours: Open daily, 8am - 10pm.
Price: Free
Ages: All

SWEETWATER REGIONAL PARK / ROHR PARK

(619) 397-6197 - park; (619) 981-1656 - Chula Vista Live Steamers, Inc.; (877) 565-3600 - camping / www.sdcounty.ca.gov/parks/
3218 Summit Meadow Road / 4548 Sweetwater Road, Chula Vista

Sweetwater Regional Park is a long stretch of land that runs between Sweetwater Road and Bonita Road. Fred Rohr Park is a nice oblong park, within Sweetwater Park, that parallels a golf course. The lake here is home to numerous ducks. Picnic tables are scattered throughout the park along with a few barbecue pits. Entertainment is provided by using swing sets, jungle gyms, volleyball courts, softball fields, basketball courts, grassy areas, shade trees, and cement bike and rollerblade paths. A monthly highlight is a ride on a scale-model steam locomotive around the park. The Live Steamers, who run the locomotive, also operate ⅛-scale diesel and electric trains.

Sweetwater offers a sweet escape from city life. It has over 100 campsites that can accommodate RVs (with full hook-ups) or tents, each with a picnic table and fire ring, and panoramic view of the surrounding mountains. There is even equestrian camping at the summit site of the park that overlooks the reservoir. There are fifteen miles of hiking trails in the area. Sweetwater also has a lakeside (well, reservoir-side) community recreation building with fireplaces, an outdoor deck and amphitheater, and a simple, but imaginative, playground. One section has boulders to climb on and a rock-climbing wall with an archway. Another area has a tower with slides, monkey bar rings, and more climbing apparatus. Down the hill in the day-use area is another playground and a colorful water playground which sports a rainbow with misters; fountains that spurt up water intermittently and a good-size area to run around and squeal; water cannons; and a tall pole with buckets attached that dump out water on people standing below them. An exercise circuit, expanses of grass, and a sense of getting away for a bit add to your day (or weekend) of enjoyment.

Hours: Sweetwater is open daily, 9:30am - sunset. The trains run on the second full weekend of each month (but on Labor Day weekend in September) from noon - 2:30pm.
Price: Free to the park. Train rides are $1 per person. Camping is $29 a night, plus a $5 reservation fee.
Ages: All

TECOLOTE SHORES NORTH PLAY AREA

(619) 236-5555 or (619) 235-1169 / www.sandiego.gov
1590 E. Mission Bay Drive, San Diego

Head for some big time fun at the large Tecolote Shores Play Area. This wonderful playground has a great combination of old and new equipment. In the main area, with its sand-covered grounds, there are slides, swings, and cement turtles to climb on (and under). Other sections include aquatic cement creatures, a good-sized pirate ship, mini-obstacle ropes course, bridges, and various other climbing apparatus. There are plenty of picnic tables and grassy areas here, too. As the playground is right on the bay, the view is beautiful. Tip: There aren't many tall trees here, at least right now, so this is a great place to fly a kite.

Hours: Open daily, sunrise - sunset.
Price: Free
Ages: 1 - 10 years old.

THE PARK AT THE PARK

(619) 795-5000 / www.petcoparkevents.com; www.sandiegopadres.com

100 Park Boulevard, San Diego
See PETCO PARK and THE PARK AT THE PARK (pg. 577) for details.

TIDELANDS PARK / CORONADO SKATE PARK

(619) 686-6200 or (619) 522-7300 - park; (619) 708-8341 - skatepark / www.portofsandiego.org - park;
www.coronado.ca.us - skatepark
2000 Mullinex Drive, Coronado

This delightful, large, corner park offers a spectacular view of San Diego across the bay, plus pathways, a bike path, playgrounds, a fitness course, picnic tables, ball fields, grassy areas, and a sandy beach for swimming (no lifeguards). Fun tip: Check out the Marriot Hotel next to the park as it has real flamingos outside in its front fountain.

A good-sized (16,000 square feet), supervised and gated skate park near the beach has several concrete pools along with steps, rails, ramps, and grinding boxes. A parent or legal guardian must sign a waiver, that is kept on file, for skaters 17 years and under. Helmet, knee, and elbow pads are required. A small snack shop is on the premises, too.

Hours: The park is open daily, 6:30am - 10:30pm. The skate park is open Mon. - Fri., 1pm - dusk; Sat. - Sun., 10am - dusk. It's open daily in the summer and during school holidays, 10am - dusk. Closed New Year's Day morning, Easter morning, Thanksgiving, and Christmas.
Price: The park is free. The skate park has an annual fee of $10 (which includes your first session), then $5 per session after that, or passes. They do have loaner equipment, too.
Ages: All

TIJUANA ESTUARY - VISITORS CENTER

(619) 575-3613 / www.trnerr.org
301 Caspian Way, Imperial Beach

First things first - an estuary is: "The wide part of a river where it flows near the sea; where fresh water and salt water mix." (That's why this book is called *Fun and Educational* . . .) The Visitor's Center has several wonderful interactive exhibits. One of our favorite displays is the ordinary-looking, black-and-white sketched pictures of habitats that magically reveal brightly colored birds, insects, fish, and other animals when viewed through a polarized filter. The touch table contains snake skin, nests, skulls, and a dead sea turtle. The food chain is portrayed through pictures and graphs. The Beneath the Sand exhibit entails pressing the bills of bird puppet heads into holes in various levels of "sand." A light on the side panel displays what birds with shorter beaks eat (insects and plant seed) compared to what birds with longer beaks eat (crabs and worms). Upon request, a small theater shows films such as *Coastal Wetlands of San Diego* and *Tijuana River Watershed.*

Eight miles of walking trails are interspersed throughout the reserve. Ask for a map at the center, as there are different entrance points, and borrow binoculars here, too. Some of the trails follow along the streets, while others go deeper into the coastal dunes and near the Tijuana River. Be on the lookout for terns, egrets, herons, curlews, and other birds and wildlife. On a very short loop around the center, my boys and I saw interesting plants and birds, plus thirteen bunnies! Take a guided walking tour to learn more about the flora and fauna at the estuary, or sign the kids up for one of the numerous programs available. The Jr. Ranger Program, for students 7 to 12 years old, is offered every Thursday from 3:30pm to 4:30pm. During the program kids will enjoy a walk, earn patches or buttons, and/or make a craft - all free of charge! Ask about other educational programs, including one specifically for Scouts, as well as special events.

Just south of the estuary is a park which borders Mexico. See BORDER FIELD STATE PARK (498) for more details.

Hours: The Visitors Center is open Wed. - Sun., 10am - 5pm. Closed New Year's Day, Thanksgiving and Christmas.
Price: Free
Ages: 3 years and up.

TORREY PINES STATE RESERVE

(858) 755-2063 / www.torreypine.org
12600 N. Torrey Pines Park Road, La Jolla

The Torrey pine tree grows only in this and one other reserve (that's also in Southern California) in the whole world! My kids were impressed with this fact and by the beauty of the park. Our favorite trail was the Guy Fleming Trail. It's an easy loop, only two-thirds of a mile, and incredibly scenic through the trees and out to a cliff overlooking

the ocean. Tip: Hold on to younger children! Other trails include the half-mile Parry Grove looping trail; the two-thirds-of-a-mile Razor Point Trail with dramatic views of gorges; the steep, three-quarters-of-a-mile (one way) Beach Trail which ends at the San Diego - La Jolla Underwater Park; and the two demanding Broken Hill Trails.

The Visitor's Center shows a short film that gives an overview of the reserve - just ask to see it. The exhibits here offer good visual information regarding the plants and animal wildlife of the reserve. On display are taxidermied raccoons, skunks, and birds; a pine cone display; a pine needle display; and more. We appreciated Torrey Pines Reserve for its glorious nature trails and its breath of fresh air! A lifeguarded Torrey Pines City Beach is right below the reserve for those who are into sand and surf. Note that the north side of the beach, the state beach also known as Black's Beach, is a clothing-optional beach.

> **Hours:** The reserve is open daily, 7:15am - sunset. It is closed during and immediately after rain. The visitors center is open most of the year, daily, 9am - 5:30pm; open in the winter, daily, 10am - 4pm.
>
> **Price:** The South Beach lot is $10 - $15 per vehicle, depending on the day of the week, low or high season, and if it's a holiday. The North Beach lot is $4 - $6 for the first hour; $6 - $8 for two hours; $12 - $15 for the day, depending on day of the week, etc. Walk-ins are free. There is some free parking down the hill along Hwy. 101.
>
> **Ages:** 3 years and up.

TUBING ON SAN LUIS REY RIVER / LA JOLLA INDIAN RESERVATION CAMPGROUND

(760) 742-1297 or (760) 742-3771 / www.lajollaindians.com
22000 Highway 76, on the La Jolla Indian Reservation, Pauma Valley

Come to the campground just for the day, or spend a night or two here in the lush, semi-wilderness of the foothills of the beautiful Palomar Mountains. Hike amongst the beautiful foliage along the San Luis Rey River; climb the rocks on the river banks; try your luck at fishing; or wade in the river waters.

For more wet thrills, go inner tubing down the river along a two-mile stretch, which takes about an hour. Hike back up to go again, or better yet, come here with a friend who drives and leave one car at each end. Parts of the river are idyllic, while other parts are a bit more exciting (and bumpy) - and the flow depends on the water level. Be prepared for this adventure by wearing a hat, tee shirt, sunscreen, and sneakers (for painlessly stepping on the rocks on the river bottom). B.Y.O.T. (Bring Your Own Tube) or rent an inner tube here for $10. Tip: Tie your inner tube to your child's so you can stay together!

Most of the camping sites are located right by the river. (The water can be soothing or loud, depending on how you interpret its sound.) If you are coming for the day, you are advised to bring your own table, chairs, and barbecues as those items are limited in number in the camp. Chemical toilets are scattered throughout the camp, and hot showers are available at designated places. Campfires are allowed. Firewood, tackle, supplies, and food are available at the small Trading Post on the grounds, but better yet, bring your own. Note that weekends in the summer it gets really packed..

> **Hours:** Open mid-March - November, 8am - sunset for day use. Tubing is usually available daily the end of April - September, 8am - 6pm. Call first.
>
> **Price:** $20 per vehicle for day use for up to four people; an additional $2 per person after that. River tubing is included in this price. Tube rentals are $10. Camping is $25 per vehicle for tent campers for up to four people; $40 for RVs with hook-up. No pets allowed.
>
> **Ages:** 4 years and up.

VOLCAN MOUNTAIN NATURE PRESERVE

(760)765-4098 or (760) 765-2300 / www.volcanmt.org; www.sdcounty.ca.gov/parks/
Near the intersection of Wynola and Farmer Roads, Julian

This preserve has God's fingerprints all over it with its spectacular wilderness scenery. Hikers can go halfway up the mountain, about a mile-and-a-half one way, to the gate, passing through meadows, high chaparral, and forests of oak and pine. If you want to hike the five-mile round trip to the summit for a 360-degree panoramic view of the surrounding area, including the Salton Sea, you'll need to join a guided ranger hike given on selected Saturdays.

> **Hours:** Open daily, sunrise - sunset.
>
> **Price:** Free
>
> **Ages:** 3 years and up.

WATER CONSERVATION GARDEN

(619) 660-0614 / www.thegarden.org
12122 Cuyamaca College Drive West on the campus of Cuyamaca College, El Cajon

Take a leisurely stroll on the stroller/wheelchair-friendly pathways through this eye-appealing five-acre garden. The garden is designed to be an Xeriscape™ demonstration learning center to educate the public on how to create lovely, yet water-wise, landscapes. The front courtyard has a few picnic tables and a cement tube with steam pouring out into a very small pond with plants. Sit on a rock here and meditate.

Sprinkled throughout the garden are a few topiary animals, shade trees, a gazebo, fountains, irrigation options with mini water towers and sluices, and larger-than-life art objects, such as pencils that frame the entrance, huge gardening shears, and a purple sprinkler head (that I thought looked like a lighthouse). The plants are well marked and conservation ideas abound on both placards and by implementation. En route, you'll see an edible garden, fragrance garden (for the visually impaired); practical garden (to aid in soil erosion); wildlife garden (to attract butterflies); a Native American section; cactus and succulent areas; a gazebo and lawn area; a variety of grasses alongside the number of gallons of water they cost to maintain; irrigation systems; and the how-to's of planting on a slope. A few more components of this unique garden experience include mulch displays; concrete bins with a variety of soil aids - manure, fir shavings, compost, and more; an intriguing display of pipes and fittings on raised tables; a tower compass; and a mini weather station. A short children's discovery trail leads to a potting shed, a sand box, and hidden animals to discover. No doubt you'll "leaf" here with more ideas on what to do in your own yard.

A small gift shop and bathrooms are also on the premises. Ask about tours, workshops, and special events. Note that the garden is adjacent to the HERITAGE OF THE AMERICAS MUSEUM (see pg. 534) and the Cuyamaca College Nature Preserve.

Hours: Open daily, 9am - 4pm; open Wed. until 7pm, June - August.
Price: Free. See page x for info on AHS reciprocal memberships.
Ages: All

WILLIAM HEISE COUNTY PARK

(760) 765-0650 - park; (877) 565-3600 - reservations / www.sdcounty.ca.gov/parks/
4945 Heise Park Road, Julian

Consider this forest-like park a family destination. With eight miles of hiking and equestrian trails to choose from, there is bound to be a trail or two suitable for each member of the family. Select an easy pathway that leads through a mountain meadow and a cedar forest; a moderate, three-mile, round-trip trail that goes through canyon live oak; or choose a rugged trail for more experienced hikers, such as the 5.75-mile Kelly Ditch Trail which leads to Lake Cuyamaca. Two shaded picnic areas, a horseshoe pit, a playground, and a pond are all available here, too.

Over forty tent sites, sixty RV sites, and six cabins with electricity and a few furnishings, provide overnight camping in this beautiful area. The campgrounds have piped-in water, showers, barbecues, and fire rings. Bring your own firewood. The small, one-room cabins each have a fireplace and sleep up to six people. Bring your own bedding and know that reservations usually need to be made at least three months ahead of your arrival date.

Hours: Open Mon. - Fri., 9:30am - 5pm; Sat. - Sun., 9:30am - sunset.
Price: $3 per vehicle. Camping is $24 for tents; $294 for RV's and partial hook-ups, plus $5 reservation fee. The cabins are $62 a night.
Ages: All

WILSON MEMORIAL SKATE PARK

(619) 235-1125 or (619) 525-8213 / www.sandiego.gov
702 South 30th Street, San Diego

The unsupervised skate park has 22,000 square feet of cement surface. Railings, stairs, beginner's bowl, and key-hole are some of the park's more fun elements. Helmets and pads are required. Note that police do monitor this area. Adjacent to the skate park is the Memorial Recreation Center and Community Park with a playground, open fields, basketball court, baseball field, and swimming pool that is open seasonally.

Hours: The park is open daily, sunrise - sunset. The skate park is open daily, 10am - dusk.
Price: Free. The pool is $4 for adults; $2 for seniors and ages15 and under.
Ages: 6 years and up.

WOODGLEN VISTA PARK AND SKATE PARK

(619) 258-4100 / www.ci.santee.ca.us
10250 Woodglen Vista Drive, Santee

Woodglen has a little something for everyone. The nice-sized playground with wood chip "flooring" has swings, slides, and big plastic animals to ride. A ball field, tennis court, basketball court, and small skate park motivate the sports enthusiast to get moving. The cement skate park, aptly nicknamed a "pocket," has a half pyramid, grinding wall, rails, spine, steps, and four-foot-high half bowl. Skaters must wear safety equipment and have a signed waiver. There are times just for BMX riders as well. A large grassy area and picnic tables round out this neighborhood park.

Hours: The park is open daily, dawn - dusk. The skate park is open Wed. - Fri., 2pm - sunset; Sat. - Sun., 10am - sunset, with hour long sessions for skaters starting on even hours and bikers sessions starting on odd hours. It is open Mon. and Tues. during school holidays and the summer.

Price: Free for the park. Annual membership fee for the skate and BMX park is $15 for Santee residents; $20 for nonresidents.

Ages: All

WOODLAND PARK AND AQUATIC CENTER

(760) 744-9000 - community services; (760) 746-2028 - pool complex / www.san-marcos.net
671 Woodland Parkway, San Marcos

A large, picturesque fountain and a small, man-made, rock-lined pond decorate the corner section of this park. A short, paved walkway winds around the pond and up through the park inviting strollers to use it. A children's play area and a long grassy area, plus picnic tables and barbecue pits, make the park a fun outing. Try your hand (and foot) at the twenty-five-foot-high rock climbing wall. Up the small hill from the park are three pools, one of which is a wading pool. The swimming pool has a fifty-foot, curvy water slide and the diving pool has a high dive and low diving board - fun features. Showers are available here, too.

Hours: The park is open daily, dawn - dusk. The pool is open Memorial Day - Labor Day. Call for weekday hours; open Sat., Sun., and holidays, 1pm - 5:30pm.

Price: Free for park facilities. $3 per person for pool usage.

Ages: All

—MALLS—

WESTFIELD PLAZA BONITA

(619) 267-2850 / www.westfield.com
3030 Plaza Bonita Road, National City

Have some fun while learning about the rainforest at this mall. The enclosed, soft playground incorporates elements of the rainforest - butterflies, leaves, flowers, ants, and monkeys - so kids can climb up (fake) trees, look at movable termites, go through a short, cave-like bat habitat, and push buttons on educational platforms to hear the sounds and animal noises. This mall also has a trackless train that goes from Target to Macys and back. Seasonal events and activities are hosted here as well, such as visits from the Easter Bunny and Santa Claus; crafts; and special offers, such as free kid's meals, from restaurants. The mall has a few favorite stops, too, like JOHN'S INCREDIBLE PIZZA CO. (pg. 476) and Disney Store National City, (619) 470-3391, which offers not just Disney products, but storytimes, and special activities.

Hours: The train runs Mon. - Sat., noon - 8pm; Sun., 11am - 6pm.

Price: The train is $3 per person.

Ages: 18 months and up.

WESTFIELD PLAZA CAMINO REAL - WFAMILY FUN DAYS

(760) 729-6183 / www.westfield.com
2525 El Camino Real, Carlsbad

Besides the over 150 stores and restaurants, this mall offers a free, soft-play area for young kids, featuring turtles, trees, and other fun elements to climb on and over. There are benches for parents to rest as the kids play.

Family Fun Days are free storytelling times, snacks, games, and make-and-take crafts, such as Valentine's hearts,

decorating aprons, and creating musical instruments. Join in the fun! Note that a carousel is near the 24 Hour Fitness as is LAZER TAG GALAXY (pg. 488). The Family Lounge offers a family restroom with nursing station and comfy place to sit for a spell. See KIDSVILLE PLAYGYM (pg. 486) for a great indoor play place across the street from the mall. Note that there is a Disney store, (760) 730-0337, and Tilt, (760) 730-1322, an arcade and video game play place, here, too.

Hours: Family Fun Days are the second Tues. from 10am - 11am.
Price: Free
Ages: 2 - 10 years.

—MUSEUMS—

AIR GROUP ONE COMMEMORATIVE AIR FORCE WORLD WAR II FLYING MUSEUM
(619) 259-5541 / www.ag1caf.org
1905 North Marshall, Hangar #6, El Cajon

This small aviation museum has two planes on display - an SNJ-5 and an L-5. A wildcat (an airplane, not a cat that's wild) occasionally flies in. The museum, operated by WWII aviation buffs, has a friendly and casual atmosphere. Kids (and other visitors) can tour a C-97 cockpit and get a feel for the instruments. A few army trucks are also on the premises. The art gallery showcases a mural, photographs, posters, and paintings. Display cases around the perimeter of the hangar hold artifacts donated to the museum and include model planes; goggles; equipment; a Norden bombsight, which was once top secret; front pages of newspapers highlighting events from the war; and lots of other paraphernalia. You may schedule a tour, although the workers here are willing to answer questions at any time.

Visitors will also enjoy watching small planes land and take off. Join in on the Friday FlyDays, held the first Friday of each month from 4pm to 8pm where. The Gillespie Field Cafe partners with the museum for dinner, live music, and WWII and antique planes. Make sure to check the Calendar entry for a yearly event, the Airshow San Diego (pg. 725). Would you, or someone you know, enjoy flying in a WWII warbird? The SNJ-5 is available and ready to fly - tailwinds to you. A twenty-five-minute flight, for $350, gives you an incredible view of San Diego in a memorable manner, plus a GoPro video of your flight. For an additional $30, you can even fly the plane some of the time!

Hours: Open Tues., Thurs., Sat., 10am - 2pm.
Price: Free.
Ages: 4 years and up.

ANTIQUE GAS & STEAM ENGINE MUSEUM, INC.
(800) 5-TRACTOR (587-2286) or (760) 941-1791 / www.agsem.com
2040 N. Santa Fe Avenue, Vista

California has a museum for almost any interest. This one answers the age-old question, "Where do engines go when they run out of gas (or steam)?" The forty-acre, mostly outdoor museum, has hundreds of tractors, combines, gas and steam engines (that's a given from the name of the museum), horse-drawn carriages, and equipment used in mining, oil drilling, construction, agriculture, and more. The machines have been (or are in the process of being) restored to working condition. In fact, some of the equipment is used to help farm the adjacent lands. Walk around on your own or make a reservation for a tour, which is offered for preschoolers through college-internship students. Kids will see many of the machines in action and learn a lot about the history of agriculture via harvesting and grinding flour, baking bread in a wood stove, and more. Another option is to visit on the third and fourth weekends of June and October during the Harvest Fairs when they also host the tractor shows and a lot of the engines here come to life. Watch or take part in planting, harvesting, household chores, early American crafts, blacksmithing, log sawing, parades, square dancing, and shopping. We went and it's definitely a good ol' time! See the Calendar entry, on page 731, for more details.

Some of the museum's collection is housed in structures that collectively resemble a small town. Featured buildings include a huge (and complete) blacksmith and wheelwright shop, a farm house with parlor, a sawmill, a one-third-scale train with a telegrapher's office (open Saturdays from 9am to 1pm only), and a barn. A (non-working) gas station is also on the premises. There are picnic tables and even a small playground with two small, stationary tractors to climb on. The museum is interesting to visit any time, but it's especially exciting to visit at exhibition time.

Hours: Open daily, 10am - 4pm. Closed New Year's Day, Christmas, major holidays, and rainy/muddy days.

Price: $5 for adults; $4 for seniors; $3 for ages 6 - 12; children 5 and under are free. Higher admission is charged for special events.

Ages: 4 years and up.

BALBOA PARK

(619) 239-0512 - Visitors Center; (619) 525-8262 - Morely Field Sports Complex / www.balboapark.org; www.sandiego.gov

1549 El Prado Balboa Park, San Diego

This massive, 1,158-acre park is the cultural and recreational heart of San Diego. An incredible number of programs and seasonal events are held here, so see the Calendar section in the back of the book, call or check their website for a schedule of events, or pick up a copy of their bi-monthly events guide. The park has shade trees, grassy areas, several gardens, and picnic areas. The playgrounds are located at Pepper Grove Picnic Area on Park Boulevard, south of the San Diego Zoo (this park is ADA accessible), and at the north end of Balboa Drive. Morley Field Sports Complex, located at 2221 Morely Field Drive in the northeastern section, has twenty-five public, lighted, tennis courts available for all-day use at $6 per person for adults; $4 for seniors; $2 for ages 17 and under. Call the Balboa Tennis Club at (619) 295-9278 / www.balboatennis.com for reservations. Courts are open Mon. - Fri., 8am - 9pm; Sat. - Sun., 8am - 8pm. The park also has a fitness course; bocce ball, which is an Italian sport similar to lawn bowling; a velodrome, that hosts races and offers classes; an archery range; baseball diamonds; lawn bowling for adults; playgrounds; picnic areas; a disc golf course; and a swimming pool that is open seasonally - call for hours. Swim sessions cost $5 for adults, $2 for seniors and children. Call (619) 692-4920 for more pool information.

Balboa Park is home to a majority of the city's best museums, as well as the world famous SAN DIEGO ZOO (pg. 591). Individual museum entries are found elsewhere under the Museums section, listed by their official titles: MINGEI INTERNATIONAL MUSEUM, MUSEUM OF PHOTOGRAPHIC ARTS, MUSEUM OF SAN DIEGO HISTORY, REUBEN H. FLEET SCIENCE CENTER, SAN DIEGO AIR AND SPACE MUSEUM, SAN DIEGO ART INSTITUTE, SAN DIEGO AUTOMOTIVE MUSEUM, SAN DIEGO HALL OF CHAMPIONS SPORTS MUSEUM, SAN DIEGO MODEL RAILROAD MUSEUM, SAN DIEGO MUSEUM OF ART, SAN DIEGO MUSEUM OF MAN, SAN DIEGO NATURAL HISTORY MUSEUM and the VETERANS MUSEUM AND MEMORIAL CENTER, which is across the street. Passports, which are good for one week from the date of purchase, can be bought to visit the fourteen museums (including the Japanese Garden) for $53 for adults, $29 for ages 3 - 12 (note that many museums are free for younger children), or all the museums and the zoo for $89 for adults; $52 for kids. There are also day passes good for visiting any five of the museums in one day for $43 for adults. Below is a list of museums that are free on particular Tuesdays for San Diego County residents and active military and their dependents: First Tuesday: S.D. Natural History (permanent exhibits only), Reuben H. Fleet Science Center, Centro Cultural de la Raza, and S.D. Model Railroad; Second Tuesday: Museum of Photographic Arts, Veterans Museum and Memorial Center, and Museum of S.D. History; Third Tuesday: Japanese Friendship Garden, Mingei International Museum, S.D. Museum of Art (permanent exhibits only), S. D. Art Institute, and S.D. Museum of Man; Fourth Tuesday: S. D. Hall of Champions, S.D. Air and Space Museum (permanent exhibits only), S.D. Automotive Museum, and Cottages and House of Pacific Relations International whose Hall of Nations films, such as *Children Around the World,* show at 11am to 3pm.

The park also offers many other attractions that are worthy of mention. The beautiful, latticed **Botanical Building** is located at the north end of the lily pond next to the San Diego Museum of Art. It has (labeled) tropical and subtropical plants on display. It is open Friday through Wednesday, 10am to 4pm. Admission is free. Ranger-led tours of the gardens are available on Tuesdays and Sundays at 11am. The **Timken Museum of Art** is located next to the Visitors Center. Housed here are collections of works by European Old Masters, eighteenth- and nineteenth-century American paintings, and Russian icons. It is open Tuesday through Saturday, 10am to 4:30pm; Sunday, 1:30pm to 4:30pm. Admission is free. The **Japanese Friendship Garden**, (619) 232-2721 / www.niwa.org, is a small, but beautiful, and serene garden replete with symbols of the Japanese culture. It contains a tea pavilion and Japanese-style exhibit house with a main room that has a traditional table set with (fake) Japanese food. Other elements include a bridge, deck, and a short path leading to the garden, koi pond, stream, and short waterfall, plus a cherry tree grove and places to sit and relax. Admission is $6 for adults, $5 for seniors; ages 6 and under are free. Admission is free on the third Tuesday of every month for San Diego residents. See page x for info on AHS reciprocal memberships. It is open most of the year daily, 10am to 4:30pm. It is closed New Year's Day, Thanksgiving and

Christmas. Free outdoor concerts are given on the famous **Spreckels Pipe Organ,** (619) 702-8138 / www.sosorgan.com, year round on Sundays from 2pm to 3pm, plus on Mondays from 7:30pm to 9:30pm, June through August. The organ is located at an architecturally beautiful building set in a huge half circle. My kids think the steps here are a great place for picnicking. The **House of Pacific Relations,** (619) 234-0739 / www.sdhpr.org, is located behind the United Nations Building, across from the Spreckels Organ. The "House" encompasses seventeen small cottages that are home to thirty different nationalities. Exhibits, such as traditional dress, musical instruments, flags, and furnishings, in each small cottage pertain to specific ethnic groups. Special lawn programs of music, dance, crafts, and ethnic food are held on Sundays from 2pm to 3pm, March through October. Nations are represented on a rotating basis. The cottages are open Sundays from 12pm to 4pm and on the fourth Tuesday from noon to 3pm. Admission is free. The **Spanish Village Art Center**, (619) 233-9050 / www.spanishvillageart.com, is just north of the San Diego Natural History Museum. The "village" has retained its old-world charm with its Spanish architecture and colorful courtyard tiles and flowers. The thirty-seven art studios and galleries include woodcarvings, sculptures, glass blowing, and gems and minerals for show and sale. Oftentimes, the artisans demonstrate their craft, which makes the Spanish Village Center an intriguing stop for slightly older kids. The Villages is open daily, 11am to 4pm; closed New Year's Day, Thanksgiving and Christmas. Three other kid-friendly attractions are the **miniature train ride, carousel,** and **kiddie rides**. The kiddie rides, located just in the entrance of Zoo Place, consist of an airplane and butterfly ride for ages 5 and under - $2.50 per person. Located south of the Zoo and north of the Spanish Village Center are the three-minute train ride, (619) 239-4748 - open daily in the summer 11am to 6:30pm, open weekends and school holidays the rest of the year, 11am to 4:30pm - $3 per person; and an old-fashioned carousel, (619) 239-0512, that, along with horses and other animals to ride on, still offers a chance to grab at the brass ring - $2.50 per person. The carousel and kiddie rides are open daily in the summer, 11am to 5pm; open the same hours the rest of the year on weekends and school holidays. There are a few restaurants and cafes scattered throughout Balboa Park and located inside several of the museums, although we usually bring a picnic lunch. There are a few theaters, such as MARIE HITCHCOCK PUPPET THEATER (pg. 570) and GLOBE THEATRE (pg. 571).

At any time during your visit to the park, you are welcome to hop aboard the Balboa Park Tram. This free, intrapark transportation system can take you from Presidents Way and Park Boulevard, up to the carousel, through where the museums are, to the Visitors Center and House of Hospitality, and up north to 6th Street. It makes several stops along the way, so you can catch it coming or going. It operates November through June - daily, 8:15am to 5:15pm; July through October - Monday, 8:15am to 6:30pm, Tuesday through Sunday, 8:15am to 8pm. Plan to visit Balboa Park many times, as you obviously cannot see it all in one, two, or even three days! Photographer's tip: At night the lighting and beauty of the buildings is wonderful, especially of the Museum of Man edifice, the fountain in front of the science museum and the series of archways of the Spreckels pavilion.

Hours: The park is open daily. The Visitor's Center is open daily, 9:30am - 4:30pm; closed New Year's Day, Thanksgiving, and Christmas. Individual attractions are listed in separate entries.

Price: Entrance to the park itself is free. Parking is free. Individual attractions are listed in separate entries.

Ages: All ages for the park.

BANCROFT RANCH HOUSE MUSEUM

(619) 469-1480 / www.sandiegohistory.org/societies/springvalley/ranchhouse.htm
9050 Memory Lane, Spring Valley

I love visiting old house- museums because I always learn some history about the original owners and the time period that they lived there. With every new tidbit learned, it's like fitting in another piece of a huge, historical puzzle. For instance, in the early 1900's Howe Bancroft, one-time owner of this adobe ranch house, was a renowned historian who wrote and compiled thirty-nine books describing the civilization of the Old West.

A truth window, where visitors can see the layers of original adobe - mostly mud and hay - is one of the first things the guide points out. One small room contains a few display cases of Native American artifacts such as grinding stones, arrowheads, and baskets. Another room contains a straw bed, Bancroft's history books, and few period household goods. A connecting room has an old school desk and a map. The last room holds display cases of boots, clothing, tools, kitchen implements, and, most exciting of all because kids can hold them - ship-to-shore cannon balls, and tumbler balls used to crush rocks. School groups are encouraged to visit.

There are a few picnic tables under shade trees in front of the house and an indigenous garden. Although the surrounding area is a bit rundown and the museum grounds are a work in progress, seeing and hearing a portion of history makes the Bancroft Museum a worthwhile visit.

Hours: Open Fri. - Sun., 1pm- 4pm. Closed Easter and Christmas.

Price: Free, but donations are appreciated.
Ages: 8 years and up.

BARONA CULTURAL CENTER AND MUSEUM

(619) 443-7003 / www.baronamuseum.org
1095 Barona Road, Lakeside

What a classy little museum! A large rock in the lobby features numerous recreated Indian pictographs and the logo of the tribe. The display case contains items from Barona war veterans, such as their uniforms, medals, and personal effects.

Press the buttons located near several of the displays to hear the history and other information about the artifacts. We especially liked hearing the voices of the Bird Singers who sang ceremonial songs, accompanied by gourd rattles. Other exhibits in this area include a small roundish house made of willows; metates and manos (i.e., grind stones) that visitors can actually try out; and baskets. Another section showcases grunion, how to track the sun with stone markers, and how to make paint with natural products. A timeline with informational panels and photos depicts the ceremonies and background of Native Americans in San Diego. A short video describes how the museum was created. The small back room has a stuffed diamondback snake and a few changing displays.

School tours are offered during the week with a minimum of just five kids. The tour encompasses the museum with more insight into the Barona/Kumeyaay people's heritage, and can incorporate a craft or learning a native game. Outreach programs come to other facilities, too. Note that there are picnic facilities south of the museum at Stelzer County Park.

Hours: The museum is open Tues. - Fri., noon - 5pm; Sat., 10am - 4pm. Closed Sun., Mon. and major
              holidays. Other tours are offered by appointment.
Price: Free
Ages: 7 years and up.

BIRCH AQUARIUM

2300 Expedition Way, La Jolla
    See the entry for BIRCH AQUARIUM on page 586 for details.

BUENA VISTA AUDUBON NATURE CENTER

(760) 439-BIRD (2473) / www.bvaudubon.org
2202 S. Coast Highway, Oceanside

This nature center is not just for the birds! The exhibits inside this small building consist mainly of taxidermied birds (some in flight) such as a pelican, a great blue heron, a red-tailed hawk, a colorful yellow western tanager, and more. A stuffed owl has a mouse in its beak and a pellet at its feet that contains partially digested animal parts. Other mounted animals on display include a bobcat, red fox, possum, and more. The touch table has a raccoon skin, petrified wood, and whale bones, among other things. Look through a kid-level porthole on the central display to see fish "swimming" underneath. Spread your arms against a wall to measure your "wing span" up to a variety of birds' span. A book corner for children has a nice selection of nature books to read. Other items of interest are a small rock and mineral display, and a live tarantula.

Outside, take a walk through the marshy reeds to the lagoon. This area is home to a wide variety of birds. Guided field trips are one of the best ways to really learn about the abundant wildlife at Buena Vista. Call for reservations. Migrate over to the picnic tables which are available to make your day just ducky!

Free, one-hour+ tours are offered for kindergartners through 5th graders that cover a variety of topics such as what makes a bird a bird, birds of prey, local history and migration.

Hours: Open Tues. - Sat., 10am - 4pm; Sun., 1pm - 4pm. Closed Mon., Thanksgiving, and Christmas.
Price: Free; donations accepted.
Ages: 3 years and up.

CABRILLO NATIONAL MONUMENT

1800 Cabrillo Memorial Drive, at the southern end of Point Loma, San Diego
    See the entry for CABRILLO NATIONAL MONUMENT on page 498 for details.

CALIFORNIA SURF MUSEUM

(760) 721-6876 / www.surfmuseum.org

312 Pierview Way, Oceanside

$

Surfing is the heart of the Southern California beach culture. This small museum aims to preserve the history and lifestyle of surfing so it won't be wiped out. It displays a diverse selection and variety and a timeline of surfboards. To the inexperienced eye, some might look simply like thick boards, but I'm learning that there is more to the board than meets the eye. A Hawaiian hut made of palm leaves pays homage to surfing's roots, as do the many photographs, art and information regarding surfing. Exhibits rotate yearly and have included a tabletop wave and California surfriders from 1900 to 1940. Check the website for special events.

Hours: Open daily, 10am - 4pm; open Thurs. until 8pm. Closed New Year's Day, Memorial Day, 4th of July, Labor Day, and Christmas.

Price: $5 for adults; $3 for seniors, military and students; ages 12 and under are free. Admission is free on Tues.

Ages: Surfer dudes 8 years and up.

CAMP PENDLETON

(760) 725-5569 - general information; (760) 725-5758 - tours; (760) 763-6081 (weekday #)/(760) 763-6081 (weekend #) - amphibious school battalion / www.pendleton.marines.mil/about/historyandmuseums.aspx; www.themech.org; www.camppendletonhistoricalsociety.org

Oceanside

!

Driving on I-5 between Orange County and Oceanside, it's hard to miss the sprawling Camp Pendleton. At the gate present photo ID, proof of insurance and registration, and a letter of tour confirmation. Then, ask for a newspaper that gives self-driving directions, the camp's history, and information on the buildings. This military training camp is one of the largest, especially for amphibious training. My boys like the thought of being on a real marine base, so taking a "windshield tour" (i.e., driving around in here) was a treat for them. We saw the Marines working out, many military vehicles, and even the helicopter landing pad.

Camp Pendleton is also on an historical site where early Spanish explorers traveled. For a more detailed understanding of this time period, take a ninety-minute tour of the on-site ranch house complex - Santa Margarita Ranch House - comprised of the huge ranch house (once home to Pio Pico, the last governor of Mexican California), the chapel, and the Bunkhouse Museum. (The Las Flores adobe is 14 miles away and needs restoration.) Photos, including one of President Roosevelt's visit, antiques, and other artifacts are visual aids as the buildings retain the essence of yesteryear in both landscaping and interior furnishings. Tours for individuals are available and groups, with a minimum group of twenty people, can call to make a reservation.

Four-hour general, guided group tours, for forty to seventy-five people, are offered of the marine base to learn more about Camp Pendleton and the Marine Corps. (Only one vehicle allowed per tour.) Depending on the day, visitors will see the museums (see the next paragraph), a marital arts demonstration, or a demonstration by the K-9 military working dog unit. Lunch can be arranged for an extra fee at one of the mess halls for $4.55 per person or at South Mesa Club buffet for $8.50.

The Marine Corps Mechanized Museum is located in building 2612 on Vandegrift Boulevard at the base of Rattlesnake Canyon. This museum contains a good number of transport and battle vehicles from Vietnam and Desert Storm era, plus a Vietnamese road marker from the road to Hue City. The one-room World War II and Korea LVT Exhibit is located in Building 21561 in the base's boat basin and maintained by the Assault Amphibious School Battalion. It contains L.V.T.'s (Land Vehicle Tracks) - amphibious vehicles used in combat. These large relics are accompanied by war mementoes such as uniforms, weapons, and personal artifacts. You may ask to watch the video on the history of the L.V.T.'s. You must make reservations to see the museums. Note: THE PAINTBALL PARK (pg. 494) is also located on base.

Hours: Note: Call first to see if the base is currently open to the public. Drive through Camp Pendleton daily during daylight hours. All tours must be made in advance. General guided tours are available the 1st and 3rd Fri., except Fri. before a federal holiday. Tours start at 9am. The Mechanized Museum is open Mon. - Thurs., 8am - 4pm; Fri., 8am - 1pm. Ranch House tours offered on various days during the week, usually at 10am, September - May.

Price: Free

Ages: 6 years and up.

CLASSIC ROTORS - THE RARE AND VINTAGE ROTORCRAFT MUSEUM

(760) 650-9257 / www.rotors.org

2898 Montecito Road at Airport Hangar #G at the Ramona Airport, Ramona

Home to forty-five, or so, rotorcraft, this large hangar holds a collection of some of the most unique helicopters I've ever seen, all kind of packed together, including many Hillers. Come look at a Vertol H-21B Shawnee "Flying Banana" that looks like a Dr. Doolittle PushMe-PullYou; a Monte Copter model 15 Triphibian; a Brantly 305; a Sikorsky S-55/H-19; a gyrocopter; a collapsible copter; and several others. Most of the rotors are flight ready, while others are in the process of being restored, so you'll probably see some being worked on. The star attraction is the unusual-looking Roton Rocket ATV (Atmospheric Test Vehicle) experimental aircraft. It was once used to test and validate a unique spacecraft atmospheric reentry system using helicopter rotors.

As a volunteer takes you on a tour of the aircraft, you learn the history of the machines - where they flew and why - and technical information. Many times, too, visitors are welcome to climb into the helicopters and take it out for a spin; at least an imaginary spin. The museum not only houses the rotors, but it is also a tribute to the pioneers of vertical flight technology.

Hours: Open Fri. - Sat., 10am - 4pm, although call for extended hours. Sometimes the museum isn't open as everyone's at air shows. Call to arrange private tours.

Price: Free; donations gladly accepted.

Ages: 6 years and up.

CRAFTSMANSHIP MUSEUM

(760) 727-9492 / www.craftsmanshipmuseum.com

3190 Lionshead Avenue, Carlsbad

The full name of this museum is *The Joe Martin Foundation for Excellence in Craftsmanship Miniature Engineering Craftsmanship Museum and Machine Shop Facility* (but that's not very miniature is it?). An eclectic collection of hundreds of models and miniatures built by experts, many of them working models, are displayed in rows and rows of glass cases all in one big room. Some of the items include an aluminum Corsair and P-51; plane engines; three miniature V-8 engines; iconic buildings made out of toothpicks, like the Eiffel Tower and Big Ben; a Ferrari V-12; ships; several cases of miniature guns and knives, like a 1854 Smith & Wesson "Volcanic" lever action pistol in ⅓ scale; delicate brass sculptures by Szymon Klimek; a fancy Napoleonic coach; a Curtiss P-40 Warhawk; a motorcycle made from watch parts; steam engines (with sounds and steam); an Epicyclic Train Clock; an electric typewriter; a working 1/14 scale Bridgeport mill model; and a ¼ scale Marmon Coupe built by the factory craftsmen in 1921 - almost every "little" thing you can imagine! Groups tours are welcome - call to make a reservation.

A small, back room is dedicated to an extensive collection of small machine tools, including everything from simple, hand-cranked watchmaker lathes to the electronically-speed-controlled laser engraved machines made today. There are exposed machine tools in the working shop, where a machinist is often at work, so children under 12 must be supervised at all times. If your kids enjoy building things and working with tools, bringing them here would be a constructive use of time.

Hours: Open Mon., Tues., Fri. and Sat., 9am - 4pm.

Price: Free

Ages: 9 years and up.

CREATION AND EARTH HISTORY MUSEUM

(619) 599-1104 / www.creationsd.org

10946 Woodside Avenue North, Santee

Genesis 1:1: "In the beginning, God created the heavens and the earth." This walk-through creation museum is a richly visual way of seeing the biblical account of how the earth and its inhabitants have developed. Each phase of the earth's history is graphically represented by murals, photographs, models, or audio sounds, plus biblical references, questions to ponder, and lots of technical information. Start at the beginning, of course, and proceed through to modern day. Day four (when the sun, moon, stars, and planets were created) is the first dramatic depiction of the unfolding wonders of our universe. This small room is basically dark, with spotlights on stunning photos of the planets, constellations, and our sun. Each photograph is accompanied by factual explanations. Entering the room for days five and six is like entering a small jungle. Greenery abounds alongside a few cages of small live animals such as birds, fish, and snakes. An entire wall shows models of man, his inner workings, diagrams, and pictures of families.

Continue on, and see the fall of man, illustrated by bones, decay, and the sound of crying; and a wood-paneled room with a mural depicting Noah's ark, complete with storm sounds and lightning flashing. The next room has 3-D, touchable walls that are layers of the earth, explaining the flood, along with Grand Canyon murals and mineral and animals fossils (a whale jaw, a sabertooth cat, etc.) in display cases imbedded into the walls. There is also a replicated Mt. St. Helens' erupted volcano that you can walk through with a life-size dinosaur (behemoth?) outside of it. Walk into The Age of the Earth Mineral Cave, a recreated cave complete with stalactites and stalagmites, and an ore cart and tracks. Videos, minerals, and data are inset into cave walls. The cave's purpose is to support the young earth view. Next, is a short blue hallway representing the Ice Age with icicles hanging overhead and models of woolly mammoths. A scale model of the (originally) enormous Tower of Babel takes center stage in the Egyptian room, which also contains several Egyptian artifacts. The Stone Age room comes next; followed by the room of civilization immortalizing (so to speak) Greek and Roman cultures; and the hallway of modern man, including pictures and philosophies of evolutionists and creationists. Most of the rooms offer various free pamphlets that discuss the scientific and biblical ideas and facts presented throughout the museum.

The next large wing, with several long hallways and a few rooms, details more recent scientific advances in the biologic and geologic fields regarding DNA, RNA, cloning, and even plate tectonics. Wall murals, many of which are touchable and are 3-D, as well as models, are of intricate details and thorough renditions of parts of the human body - the eye, ear, cells, body systems, stages of a baby's development in the womb, bones, muscles, and so much more. There are also videos to watch. It's like taking visual anatomy classes! Psalm 139: 14 - ". . . I am fearfully and wonderfully made; your works are wonderful. . ." The Creation Museum is a great, interactive timeline.

The Tabernacle Theatre (which is the actual size of the tabernacle) features a somewhat stark stage divided into three sections, with each "room" housing articles that represent a different component of the tabernacle, such as the Ark of the Covenant; a life-size model of a High Priest in period clothing, Altar of Incense and Golden Lampstand; and animals and other models representing animal sacrifice. A half-hour, pre-recorded narration highlights and explains the objects and their meanings from Old Testament times through modern day, incorporating scripture in the references. The narrations are rendered at 10am, noon, 2pm, and 4pm (or at other times if requested). It's not Disney quality, but's its informative and interesting.   Hour-long, or more, guided tours are available on Fri. and Sat., or at other times for groups with reservations. Two-hour Creation Club workshops are given one Saturday a month that involve a topical presentation, a craft or hands-on animal interaction, and then an hour-long movie pertaining to the day's topic. Afterward, participants can explore the museum on their own. Note: Check out the fairly extensive bookstore/gift shop with the massive, fossil-imbedded rock in the lobby and the dinosaurs on the outside of the building.

Hours: Open Mon. - Sat., 10am - 6pm; Sun., 1pm - 6pm. Closed New Year's Day, Thanksgiving, Christmas Eve and Christmas Day. Much of the museum is geared for at least slightly older children as a lot of the information is very technical; however, the incredible visuals make quite an impact on any age.

Price: $7 for adults; $5 for seniors; $3 for ages 5 - 12; children 4 and under are free. Admission is free on the first Tues. Creation Club workshops are $5 per person.

Ages: 5 and up.

ESCONDIDO HISTORY CENTER / GRAPE DAY PARK

(760) 743-8207 - history center; (760) 839-4691 - park and pool / www.escondido.org; www.grapedaypark.org
321 N. Broadway, Escondido

Grape Day Park has a charming ambiance created by a rose garden, large grassy areas, shade trees, picnic tables, a military tribute in statues and a remembrance wall, Victorian buildings, a restored train depot, and a unique playground. The small playground has a colorful climbing structure that looks like giant grape vines, along with grape leaf seats and a purple slide coming out of the middle of a bunch of grapes. (No sour grapes at this play area.) The park has rocks around the perimeter of the park and five horseshoe pits. Play equipment can be checked out Tuesday through Saturday between 10am and 4pm, including bocce ball, a giant chess board with toddler-size chess pieces, giant checkers, giant dominos and giant pick up sticks. (Parental supervision is required.)

The five buildings that comprise the museum complex were relocated here in 1976, and are open to the public. They are: 1) Escondido's first library; 2) A quaint, completely furnished, two-story 1890's house with a living room, parlor, and kitchen, plus four small bedrooms upstairs; 3) A 1900's barn containing an 1890's popcorn wagon, a 1935 winery truck, a working printing press, and more; 4) A blacksmith's shop (that's only open on Saturdays); and 5) An 1888 Santa Fe Depot. The two-story depot building is nice looking and interesting to explore. Some highlights include a train master's office, a working telegraph station (send a message to someone!), and a Q & A board of Escondido

history. The depot also has a real train car that can be toured. It contains a model train set with an historic layout that makes tracks around realistic-looking landscape.

A tank house and a small herb garden can also be seen on the short walk around the history center. The park is a fun place for kids to play, but bring them sometime to see the museum part of it, also. Call for tour information. Note that the SAN DIEGO CHILDREN'S DISCOVERY MUSEUM (pg. 551) is located right across the street. If you're looking for a place to cool off June through August, the James Stone Municipal pool is just next door. It has a small tube slide and a kiddie wading pool, too. Call for hours and prices, though it's usually $3 for adults.

Hours: The park is open daily, sunrise - sunset. The museum complex is open Tues. - Thurs., Sat., 1pm - 4pm. It's closed Mon., Fri., Sun., Thanksgiving weekend, all major holidays, and during rainy weather.

Price: Free. Donations of $3 for adults and $1 per child for the History Center are requested. School tours are $3 per student for Escondido residents; $5 per for non-residents.

Ages: All for the park; ages 5 and up for the museum.

FALLBROOK GEM AND MINERAL SOCIETY MUSEUM

(760) 728-1130 / www.fgms.org

123 W. Alvarado, suite B, Fallbrook

The small museum has display cases of quartz, feldspar, garnet, topaz, pink rhodochrosite, azurite, beryl, aquamarine, tourmaline, and other very fine specimens. Check out the fluorescent mineral gallery where flecks of bright red, green, orange, blue, and purple show-up on rocks under black lights. A touch table holds a mastodon leg bone, petrified wood, and other objects. There are several types of stones, fossils, and minerals to purchase at decent prices from the small gift shop.

Free, ninety-minute school field trips, usually geared for elementary-aged kids, are given that could include gold panning, arrowhead making, learning about gems, or practicing paleontology by gently chipping away at a fossilized whale head. The kids learn a lot in this casual setting under the direction of an ex-school teacher.

Hours: The museum and gift shop are open Thurs. - Sat., 11am - 3pm, by appointment. Call to make a tour reservation.

Price: Free

Ages: 5 years and up.

FIREHOUSE MUSEUM

(619) 232-3473 / www.sandiegofirehousemuseum.com

1572 Columbia Street, San Diego

Have a hot time in downtown San Diego by visiting the Firehouse Museum! Housed inside an old fire station, the museum features ten antique fire engines from different time periods and other displays in several rooms. Note that sometimes exhibits rotate. Some antique pieces of fire-fighting equipment in the Steamer Hall include a 1905 hand-drawn fire engine and 1841 hand pumper, and tools of the trade like fire helmets, lanterns, and claim buckets (and a cool-looking spiral staircase). A small room off the back features elements to teach children about fire safety, such as a stove and sink to show and tell young visitors how not to grab a pot or pan. A fireman mannequin in full gear is in here, as are escape ladders, to illustrate what to do in case of fire in a multi-story home. School groups are welcome to tour.

The Main Room has several engines, plus collections of helmets, badges, fire nozzles, fire alarms, photos, and speaking trumpets through which chiefs would shout their orders. Another room has old hook-and-ladder trucks, which are really long trucks! A September 11th memorial display includes pictures and World Trade Center artifacts. Most of the staffers are firemen, so they are knowledgeable about the equipment, history, and fire fighting tactics. Note that there is a small gift shop that sells fire fighting apparel here, too.

Hours: Open Thurs. - Fri., 10am - 2pm; Sat. - Sun., 10am - 4pm.

Price: $3 for adults; $2 for seniors and children. Admission is free on the first Thurs. of every month.

Ages: 4 years and up.

FLYING LEATHERNECK AVIATION MUSEUM

(877) FLY-USMC (359-8762) or (858) 693-1723 / www.flyingleathernecks.org

Miramar Road at U. S. Marine Corps Air Station, Miramar

This Marine Corps Aviation Museum is devoted to preserving and promoting the history of the Marine Corp, and

looking to its future. There are thirty aircraft on display (and an army truck) both inside and outside the museum, including a Sikorsky 53A/D cargo helicopter, HOK, Iraqi Bell 2145, MiG-15, Intruder, McDonnell F2H-2 "Banshee," and North American FJ-3 "Fury." The planes and copters date from World War II up to modern day. Several aircraft are undergoing restoration, a process that ranges from a complete overhaul to simply a new coat of paint. Visitors are invited to see the planes, learn their histories, and ask questions of the docents.

The display cases, hallways, and rooms inside the barrack building contain military and aviation artifacts such as uniforms (including a POW uniform), engines, a captured Japanese flag, memorabilia from WWII battlefields, equipment, historic documents, model aircraft, photographs, a collection of patches (2,400!), and more. A favorite item is the F4 flight-simulation cockpit where kids (and adults) can climb into the cockpit to check out all the instruments, gauges, and the joystick. Don't forget to take a look through the great gift shop. Guided tours of the museum are given by appointment. For the more technically oriented, there are numerous videos and documents in the museum's library. Note that there is a playground on the base just down the street from the museum.

Hours: Open Tues. - Sun., 9am - 3:30pm. Closed Mon. and holidays.
Price: Free
Ages: 5 years and up.

GASKILL BROTHERS STONE STORE MUSEUM   ☀

(619) 663-1885- museum #, weekends only; (619) 478-5566 / www.cssmus.org $
31330 Highway 94, Campo

This small museum is exactly as its name implies - a museum created from an old store built out of stones by brothers from 1885 to 1887. The exhibits in the main room consist of a stocked, old-fashioned general store with jars, bottles (filled with tonics) and tins on the shelves; plus dolls, Native American pottery, scales, adding machines, etc.; a small, turn-of-the-century kitchen; tools; appliances; a furnace; a school desk; odds and ends from that time period; and lots of photographs and documents. The back room is a tiny man-made cave blasted from rock, once used for storing food (i.e., a really old-fashioned refrigerator) and other items. Upstairs is a military room, mostly representing the American Legion, with several mannequins in uniforms, including the Buffalo Soldiers Cavalry, plus saddles, some equipment, and photographs and information about this area's military region.

A stream runs in front of the museum and a woods surrounds it. Out back, up a very short hill, is a picnic table under a shade tree. Just around the corner is the PACIFIC SOUTHWEST RAILWAY MUSEUM (pg. 583) and MOTOR TRANSPORT MUSEUM (pg. 540).

Hours: Open Sat. - Sun., 11am - 5pm(ish). Closed during inclement weather.
Price: $2 per person.
Ages: 7 years and up.

GUY B. WOODWARD MUSEUM OF HISTORY   ☀

(760) 789-7644 / www.woodwardmuseum.org $$
645 Main Street, Ramona

A complex of buildings makes up this small, early western museum "town." The outside courtyard has a stage wagon - no springs made for a bumpy ride! A red barn houses an old medicine wagon (an RV prototype). The long garage contains a 1920's tractor, old buggies, an antique fire engine, fire fighting equipment, and lots of old tools, such as saws and wheat scythes, in neat rows on the walls. Just around the corner is a Honey House which contains beekeeping equipment. A narrow Millinery Shoppe features real mink stoles, outrageous feather hats, and a few beaded dresses. Other buildings here include a real jail; an outhouse; a recreated post office; a blacksmith shop complete with all the tools of the trade; a bunkhouse where cowboys used to live; a tack room with dusty, rusty saddles; a one-room schoolhouse; and a hobby room, which is really a catch-all room filled with old typewriters, bottles, and one of the first T.V. sets. Farm machinery is displayed all around the cluster of buildings. See if your kids can recognize washing machines, butter churns, the large incubator, a cream separator, and a machine for bottling milk.

The museum contains the heritage (and furnishings) of the older citizens of Ramona. The 1886 main house has roped-off rooms to look into including a turn-of-the-century doctor's office with a mannequin nurse and a collection of early medical instruments and vials; a beautifully decorated parlor, which is a combination of living room and music room, with mannequins dressed in period clothing; a library; a bedroom; and a kitchen that is packed with irons, dishes, butter churns, and other implements. The screened in back porch is set up like a bedroom - my kids were ready to move in!

The downstairs used to be a wine cellar, and the temperature is still cool here. The conglomeration of "stuff" now

stored and displayed here includes Civil War artifacts, such as uniforms and cannon balls; a collection of cameras; a turkey-feather cape; a six-foot long Red Diamond Rattlesnake skin; Native American artifacts, such as stone mortar and pestle, and pottery; a hair perming machine that looks like something out of a science fiction film; a Casey Tibbs memorial exhibit dedicated to this World Champion rodeo rider; mining equipment; and more.

This unique museum is more than a glimpse into the past - it is a good, long, and interesting look into our ancestors' way of life. Note that school group tours are given by appointment. While you're here, enjoy a stroll around historic Old Town Ramona, located on both sides and across the street from the museum.

Hours:	Open Thurs. - Fri., 1pm - 3pm; Sat. - Sun., 1pm - 4pm. Call first and they can open at other times, too. Closed the month of September and for major holidays.
Price:	$5 for adults; $1 for children 12 and under.
Ages:	5 years and up.

HERITAGE OF THE AMERICAS MUSEUM

(619) 670-5194 / www.cuyamaca.edu/museum
12110 Cuyamaca College Drive West at Cuyamaca College, El Cajon

This museum makes learning about our heritage much more exciting than simply reading about it in a history book. Four different exhibit halls branch off diagonally from the reception desk and four different pamphlets are available that give details about exhibits in each of the halls. The **Natural History Hall** contains rocks and minerals, including a lodestone (i.e., a hunk of rock with a magnetic "personality") with nails sticking out from it. The meteorite display is out of this world. Other favorite items in this wing include a fossilized turtle shell, a Tyrannosaurus rex tooth, Duckbill dinosaur eggs, an Allosaurus claw, trilobites, a rattlesnake skin, a prehistoric bee trapped in amber, shells, coral, and seahorses. The many taxidermied animals include a leopard, deer, coyote, and the head of a cape buffalo.

The **Archaeology Hall** contains an incredible arrowhead collection, gathered from all over the world, and from different periods of time. Some of them are practical, while others are more ornamental. Other displays in the glass cases include stone artifacts, such as hoes and ax heads; Mayan treasures of stone and clay; necklaces (more than 500 are in the collection) made of jade, quartz, and amethyst; and various forms of money, such as shells and copper. Weapons, of course, are always a hit with my boys.

The **Anthropology Hall** showcases impressive Native American artifacts such as eagle feather headdresses, ceremonial costumes, and exquisitely beaded moccasins, gloves, and vests. More intriguing, however, are the elk tooth and eagle claw necklaces; beaded mountain lion paw bag; knife made from a blackfoot bear jaw; shark tooth sword that looks like a small chain saw; and rattles (used for dances) made out of turtle shells and trap door spiders' nests. This section also displays tomahawks, guns from the Old West, and a buffalo robe.

The **Art Hall** features Western art with cowboys and Indians portrayed in drawings, paintings, photographs, and sculptures. It also contains Chinese artifacts dating back over 2,500 years, including a jade burial suit. Two more stunning exhibits are the fifteen-foot long scroll from the Song Dynasty and just above the scroll, a five-foot long carved Jade Dragon Ship from the Qing Dynasty with detailed work of dragons and phoenixes.

Call to schedule a school field trip here for 2nd through 6th graders. The museum gift shop has fossil, beaded items, rocks, and shells at affordable prices. This hilltop museum also has two smallish gardens with picnic tables, plus a stunning 360-degree view. See WATER CONSERVATION GARDEN on page 523 for another great place on the campus.

Hours:	Open Tues. - Fri., 10am - 4pm; Sat., noon - 4pm. Closed Sun., Mon., and major holidays.
Price:	$3 for adults; $2 for seniors; children 17 and under are free. See Museum Month, San Diego (pg. 708) for details about half-price admission in February.
Ages:	5 years and up.

HERITAGE PARK VILLAGE AND MUSEUM

(760) 435-5041 - city; (760) 801-0645 - park caretaker / www.ci.oceanside.ca.us; www.oceansidechamber.com
220 Peyri Drive, Oceanside

This re-creation of an Old West main street came into existence when several original buildings (circa 1893) were relocated to this spot, giving birth to Heritage Park Village and Museum. The park/short main street includes a schoolhouse, newspaper building, a hotel and saloon, general store, blacksmith shop, livery stable, doctor's office, jail, and museum, plus an area for picnicking and a much-photographed gazebo and surrounding grassy area. Amble along the tree-lined street to soak in the ambiance, which won't take long, as, currently, you can only see the outside of the historic buildings, not the insides. Maybe video a fun Old West-type of movie here as the backdrops are already in

place!

Hours: The grounds are open Wed. - Sun., 9am - 4pm.
Price: Free.
Ages: 5 years and up.

HISTORICAL MAGEE PARK

☼

!

(760) 434-9189 / www.carlsbadhistoricalsociety.com; www.carlsbadca.gov/parks/magepark.html
258 Beech Avenue, Carlsbad

This quaint, historic park qualifies as a park with its grassy lawns, picnic tables, barbecues, lovely rose garden, and shuffleboard courts all overlooking the Pacific Ocean. The "historic" part enters the equation because of the 1926 town meeting hall on the grounds and the vintage, 1887 one-story Magee House, a small home open to tour through on the weekends. See the living room with its piano and old-fashioned camera; vintage clothing (which looks like what we're wearing now); the tiny kitchen with its ice box and stove; and bedrooms. The house is decked out in Victorian finery during the month of December. Inside the barn is a buggy, farm tools, and a few more displays. Come enjoy a slice of history.

Hours: The park is open daily, 10am - 8pm. The house is open for tours Fri. - Sat., 10am - 4pm.
Price: The park is free. Donations are requested for the Magee House.
Ages: 8 years and up.

J. A. COOLEY MUSEUM

☼

$$

(619) 295-1611 / www.jacooley.com
4233 Park Boulevard, San Diego

As a book shouldn't be judged by its cover, a museum shouldn't be judged by the way it looks from the outside, at least this one shouldn't. J. A. Cooley's is a treasure trove of collections, with a rotating array of items gathered and garnered by owner and history buff, Jim Cooley. The museum contains over twenty-four rare, vintage, and beautifully restored cars including an 1886 Benz (one of the first cars ever built), 1906 Cadillac, 1936 Ford, 1895 buggy, and a HP 2000 Buick Concept Car. The cars are packed in here on a wooden floor. A plethora of other collections are unassumingly displayed. War posters and other types of posters line the walls.

Over fifty phonographs are here, including a duplex model (like an early stereo!), a 1901 Victor, and an Edison prototype, one of two in the world. (The other is in the Smithsonian.) Most of the phonographs are in working condition, so ask to listen to one. If you have the time, take a look at the numerous clocks. Actually, you can't help but hear them ding dong and tic toc. The eclectic collections also consist of irons, cameras, antique iron toys, train cars, baby carriages, beaded handbags, telephones, wood planes, bells (including a camel bell), bottles, ink "bottles," typewriters, and more. Note that not every item is labeled, so ask Mr. Cooley to show you around - he is a wealth of fascinating information.

Ever-stylish, the working nickelodeons and player pianos are a joy to listen to and fun to watch as the keys move unassisted. Our favorite instrument here is the 1900's Wurlitzer Band Organ. It plays the drums, cymbals, organ, xylophone, and more, all within one glorious machine. The sound makes you want to march or dance, or at least twirl around.

The museum shares its entrance with Mr. Cooley's store, Frank the Trainman. The retail store sells everything train-oriented, especially the Lionel line of cars, tracks, and accessories.

Hours: Open Mon. - Sat., 10am - 4pm; Sun., noon - 4pm. Closed major holidays.
Price: $5 for adults; $2 for ages 12 and under.
Ages: 7 years and up.

JULIAN PIONEER MUSEUM

☼

$

(760) 765-0227 / www.julianca.com
2811 Washington Street, Julian

If I were to clean out my grandparents' and great-grandparents' attics, closets, and garages, I would probably find many articles similar to what is inside this multi-room, pioneer museum made of rock-hewn walls and high, wood-beam ceilings, and a few murals. The wide assortment of items packed in here in display cases and all around include carriages; mannequins dressed in period clothing; guns; saddles; eyeglasses; mining equipment; rocks; bottles; clothing; arrowheads; a ceremonial Indian costume; kitchen implements; a metal bathtub; a potbellied stove; an American flag (with forty-five stars); taxidermied animals; a safe; cannon balls; horseshoes, branding irons and ranching

tools; lanterns; old photographs; fireplaces; rattlesnake skins; Native American baskets; dishes; furniture; lots of old, handmade lace; pianos; a doll collection; and a small touch area with furs, feathers, and animal skulls. One of my favorite exhibits is a perm machine from a 1930's beauty shop. With the wires and rods sticking out all over the mannequin's head, it looks more like something from a science fiction film! Tips: Ask for a pencil scavenger hunt for the kids. Bring a lunch and enjoy a picnic on the tables outside this rustic and interesting museum.

Julian is a charming town with unique shops along Main Street. Your kids will enjoy a stop-off at the Julian Drug Store and Candy Mine for a trip downstairs to the "candy" mine. Go next door to Miner's Diner for an ice cream at its old-fashioned, marble-topped soda counter or enjoy a full breakfast, lunch, or dinner meal. The drug store and diner are located at the corner of Main Street and Washington Street. Note that on Sundays at 1pm, 2pm, and 3pm, Julian Doves & Desperados (a Western-themed reenactment group) performs free, comedic gunfights and skits near the Julian Market & Deli on the main street. Also see EAGLE MINING COMPANY (pg. 574) to take a tour of a real gold mine.

Hours: Open Thurs. - Sun., 10am - 4pm. Closed most major holidays.
Price: Free, but a donation of $3 for adults; $1 for ages 8 - 18 is requested.
Ages: 5 years and up.

LA MESA DEPOT

(619) 465-7776 / www.sdrm.org/la-mesa
4650 Nebo Drive, La Mesa

This restored train station, circa 1894, boasts of a few cars still on the tracks - an engine, and caboose. The small depot building contains several railroad artifacts, including an antique baggage scale.

Hours: Usually open Sat., 1pm - 4pm.
Price: Free
Ages: All

LEO CARRILLO RANCH HISTORIC PARK

(760) 476-1042 or (760) 434-2826 / www.carrillo-ranch.org; www.carlsbadca.gov
6200 Flying LC Lane, Carlsbad

Once a working rancho and once home to actor Leo Carrillo, this sprawling parcel of land currently contains restored ranch structures that pay tribute to Old California culture and architecture. The dirt pathways are uneven and the grounds are fairly extensive and a little hilly so just a walk around is fun and interesting. Take the winding, paved pathway down through the extensive landscaped grounds to the visitor's building, which houses a few of Carrillo's personal effects. As an intro to the ranch, watch a thirteen-minute film on the history of the ranch and life of Leo Carrillo in the adjacent Barn Theater that is lined with old movies posters.

The rest of the delightful grounds are composed of a ¾-mile trail that loops up and around several buildings. These include a wash house; cabana and pool area; U-shaped hacienda and adobe house with several sparsely furnished rooms such as a dining room, kitchen, and bedrooms; stable; barn; and a carriage house with lots of old farm equipment and old vehicles. The interior of the buildings can only be peeked into whenever the park grounds are open, but going inside them is limited to guided tours. The one-hour-or-so tours are the best way, of course, to really learn the history of the ranch and the era it represents.

My kids enjoyed seeing the buildings and courtyard, but they also really enjoyed seeing the numerous peacocks on the grounds (and yes, giving chase occasionally despite my warnings), as well as the lizards, squirrels, and rabbits. Keep your younger kids involved in your visit by having them count the number of times they see the Leo Carrillo brand throughout the park.

Hours: The grounds are open Tues. - Sat., 9am - 5pm; Sun., 11am - 5pm. Closed Mon. Guided tours of the grounds and interiors are offered year round Sat., 11am and 1pm; Sun., noon and 2pm, or at other times by advanced reservation.
Price: Free
Ages: 3 years and up for the grounds; 8 years and up for the tour.

MARINE CORPS RECRUIT DEPOT COMMAND MUSEUM

(619) 524-8431 or (619) 524-6719 or (619) 524-6038 / www.corpshistory.org;
www.mcrdmuseumhistoricalsociety.org
Marine Corps Recruit Depot on Pacific Highway and Washington Street, San Diego

The first thing my kids noticed were the Japanese 70mm Howitzers outside the museum. Inside, the downstairs California Room displays numerous paintings of war, including battles involving Native Americans, blue coats verses gray coats, and more. The hallway has photos of movies and television shows that have featured Marines. An on-going, twenty-minute narrated film is presented in the small theater. It shows all the different phases of Marine training, from boot camp to graduation. Naturally, the "coolest" parts of it, according to my boys, were the army maneuvers where rounds and rounds of ammunition were shot, and the nighttime target practice where spots of light were seen when the guns were fired. After the movie my youngest son, with his eyes shining, declared, "I want to be a Marine!" The visitor's lounge looks like a large living room with couches and chairs. Around the perimeter of the room are exhibits such as helicopter and ship models, various military hats, and small models of physical fitness courses that make me tired just looking at them.

The upstairs rooms are filled with military memorabilia. The extensive exhibits include uniforms, swords, medals, grenades, posters, pictures, flags, mannequins dressed in camouflage, rocket launchers, jeeps, police motorcycles, a collection of knives (including machetes and bayonets), weapons used by Marines or captured from their enemies, and a room devoted to guns and ammunition. The Vietnam gallery and Iraqi Freedom gallery contain photographs, video and audio information, and artifacts from those time periods. Other galleries chronicle the history of the Marine Corps in San Diego; their collective history in wars, including a Ford Ambulance from WWI; and a model of barracks for recruits.

The museum encompasses the history of the Marines from its inception 225 years ago, through WWI and WWII, and up to the present day. Always looking for "a few good men and women," the Marine Corps maintains a museum that is historically important, and that will enlist your child's attention. Educational programs that incorporate world history, geography, current events, the history of the Marine Corps, and the values of honor and courage and commitment are available, as well as guided tours. Tip: Groups may make reservations to eat in the mess hall.

Forty-four Fridays out of the year the Marine Corps holds a brief "morning colors ceremony," where the flag is raised and the *National Anthem* is played. It begins at 8am sharp. During the year, there is also a "pass and review" parade, mini band concert, and a graduation ceremony. The graduation might be long for young kids, but it does stir up patriotism. The public is welcome to attend one or both ceremonies. Call for specific dates.

Hours: Open Mon. - (most) Sat., 0800 - 1600 (8am - 4pm); closed Sun. and most federal holidays.
Price: Free
Ages: 5 years and up.

MARITIME MUSEUM OF SAN DIEGO   ☀

(619) 234-9153 / www.sdmaritime.org $$$$
1492 N. Harbor Drive, San Diego

"I saw a ship a-sailing, a-sailing on the sea; and, oh! it was all laden with pretty things for thee!" (An old rhyme.) The eight historic ships and two submarines that comprise the Maritime Museum - the *Star of India*, *H.M.S. Surprise*, the *Berkeley*, the *Medea*, the *Pilot*, the *Californian*, a *Swift Boat*, the *San Salvador* and the *Dolphin* sub and "Project 641" B-39 Foxtrot sub - are laden with wonderful, nautical artifacts. The 1863 *Star of India*, the flagship of the fleet, is beautiful to behold with its intricate-looking rigging, interesting figurehead, and polished wooden exterior. Inside, kids can look out the portholes; check out the very narrow bunks that once held emigrants; look at the old tools and displays of knots; and marvel at the variations of ships in bottles. Not only are the ships unique, but the shapes of the bottles vary, too. Our favorite is the ship in a lightbulb. A video depicts action at sea. A play boat, below deck, is for youngsters to climb aboard and dress up in the costumes. Top board is the captain's cabin (which is small enough to give me claustrophobia), a few passengers' cabins (which passengers had to furnish themselves), a dining room, and the chart room.

Be your own *Master and Commander* (from) *The Far Side of the World* when you board the *H.M.S. Surprise*, the actual boat used in the above-mentioned movie. Tour this fully rigged replica 18th-century Royal Way frigate and you'll see the costumes, artifacts, weapons (including cannons), props, and furnishings used during the filming, as well as movie clips, the Captain's private quarters, and the gun deck.

Now "home" in former enemy territory, the B-39 Soviet Attack Submarine, classified as "Foxtrot," was once used to track U.S. and NATO warships. It carried twenty-four torpedoes (you can see into the tubes as the hatch doors are open), including some with nuclear warhead capability. The sub is fascinating to explore as you walk past the sonar room, officer's accommodations, galley, and engine room with all the gauges, wheels, and knobs. Be forewarned, though, that the cramped spaces and narrow doorways that must be climbed up and through can make one feel

daustrophobic. A fellow sub, the *U.S.S. Dolphin*, is the last diesel-electric sub in the U.S. Navy, used in undersea naval research because of its extreme diving capacity. Make sure to look through the periscope once on board.

The 1898 ferryboat, *Berkeley*, contains a number of fascinating model ships and yachts. A model ship construction and repair shop is on board, and we watched a builder at work. He told us a model takes an average of five years to complete! Such detailed work! One section of the Berkeley has a whaling gun on exhibit and displays of fish (mostly tuna) and fisheries. Downstairs is the engine room which you can explore on your own. The room is intriguing with its huge machinery and gears, narrow walkways, and slightly spooky ambiance. Also below deck is another room that showcases memorabilia from pleasure boating. The triple expansion steam engine is put to work and demonstrated at various times throughout the day. Cross over the bridge from the *Berkeley* to the 1904 steam yacht, *Medea*, which is a very small vessel. Peek into the elegant, Edwardian-decorated smoking room and into the galley that contains a coal-burning stove, big copper pots, and a wooden ice box.

The *Pilot*, a restored harbor pilot boat, is now used as a teaching vessel. It also sails out around and beyond the bay with students to study marine animals. The public is also invited to take a forty-five-minute tour of the harbor on most days, too. The majestic tallship *Californian* (the official tall ship of California - hence its name) has nine sails that unfurl to catch the wind just as its model did, an 1847 Revenue Cutter. It also has gun ports for fake battles. The *Californian* sails out of port and offers terrific on-board educational living history programs where costumed crew members teach participants about maritime history, about the art of sailing tallships, how shipmates must work together as a team (including swabbing the deck), and how to sing sea chanteys. What a unique way to study the maritime lifestyle! The *Californian* also offers four-hour sails. Reserve your spot online or come early to ensure your spot and explore the other ships. Light snacks and soft drinks are available to purchase on board as coolers are not permitted. Tours and cruises will also be offered on the fifty-foot-long *Swift Boat*, an important training vessel for sailors going off to war, once it is restored and raring to go. The 100-foot-long *San Salvador* with a 100-foot-tall mast (and two other masts) is an historically accurate replica of the first ship, circa 1542, to land in San Diego. It has taken years to build at, fittingly, Spanish Landing Park, to take mateys sailing around the San Diego Bay and up the coast.

The museum offers a full array of classes and programs for kids and adults - from the science of seafaring to living history to elementary physics to docent-guided ship tours via dock side; Pirate Buccaneer Birthday Bash; Sea Chantey Festival; Festival of Sail on Labor Day weekend; day time excursions; and overnight programs, even dockside family sleepovers. One of the daytime sailing trips even ends with a cannon salute. Note that school programs can book up to a year in advance. Ask about Family Fundays where, on certain Sundays, two kids under 12 are admitted free with a paying adult and there are special activities on board such as sing-a-longs and crafts. Note that the USS MIDWAY MUSEUM (pg. 557) is just down the road. Chart your course to have a merry time at the Maritime Museum.

Hours: Open daily, 9am - 8pm. Open one hour later Memorial Day - Labor Day. Four-hour sails board at noon.

Price: $16 for adults; $13 for seniors, students, and active military; $8 for ages 4 - 12; children 3 and under are free for general admission. Ask about AAA discounts. See the internet for other offers. For $5 more per person, add on a forty-five minute excursion on the *Pilot*. Four-hour sails aboard the *Californian*, which include the price of museum admission, are $60 for adults; $57 for seniors and students; $48 for ages 12 and under. School programs vary in price. See Museum Month, San Diego (pg. 708) for details about half-price admission in February. Parking in the lot is $10 for the day; some metered parking is available.

Ages: 5 years and up.

MARSTON HOUSE MUSEUM AND GARDENS

(619) 297-9327 or (619) 298-3142 / www.marstonhouse.org; www.sandiegohistory.org; www.sohosandiego.org $$$

3525 7th Avenue, San Diego

This 1905 mansion was built to provide "function, simplicity and good design." The sixteen various rooms, covering four floors, plus a basement, are decorated in American Arts and Crafts, Oriental, and Native American styles. What a fun and different way to learn the many facets of American history! The forty-five-minute tours are better for older kids who can appreciate the lifestyle changes that occurred during the early twentieth century. Also enjoy touring through the carriage house and the five acres of landscaped grounds that include formal gardens and rustic canyon gardens, a teahouse, and fountain.

Hours: The mansion is open only for guided tours, most of the year, Fri. - Mon., 10am - 5pm; open in the summer, Thurs. - Mon., 10am - 5pm. Tours are given every half hour. Garden tours are self-guided. Closed Thanksgiving and Christmas.

Price: $10 for adults; $7 for seniors; $6 for ages 6 - 12; children 5 and under are free.

Ages: 9 years and up.

MINGEI INTERNATIONAL MUSEUM ☀

(619) 239-0003 / www.mingei.org $$$
Plaza de Panama, Balboa Park, San Diego

"Min" is the Japanese word for "all people"; "gei" means "art," so mingei translates as "art of all people," or folk art. Outside are colorful, fanciful statues made of stone and tile. Fun photo op. A child's enjoyment of this folk art museum depends on the current exhibits. We saw many tapestries, handcrafted furniture, ceremonial masks, currency, Chinese woodblock prints, statues from the Ming Dynasty, and beautiful pieces of jewelry. Past exhibits have included toys and dolls from around the world, Mexican folk art, ceremonial objects, and the horse in folk art. Check out the video rooms that offer in depth glimpses into the countries and their art. Call first, or go on the third Tuesday of the month when admission is free for residents. The museum's gift shop offers colorful and unique items. See BALBOA PARK (pg. 526) for a listing of all the museums and attractions within walking distance.

Hours: Open Tues. - Sun., 10am - 5pm. Closed Mon. and national holidays.

Price: $8 for adults; $5 for seniors, students and ages 6 - 17; children 5 and under are free. Admission on the third Tuesday of every month is free to San Diego County residents. Passports, which are good for one week from the date of purchase, can be bought to visit the fourteen museums in Balboa Park for $53 for adults; $29 for ages 3 - 12 (as many museums are free for younger children). See Museum Month, San Diego (pg. 708) for details about half-price admission in February.

Ages: 8 years and up.

MISSION BASILICA SAN DIEGO DE ALCALA ☀

(619) 283-7319 or (619) 281-8449 / www.missionsandiego.com $$
10818 San Diego Mission Road, San Diego

Father Junipero Serra came to California on a mission - to start missions. The Mission San Diego de Alcala was the first church in California, founded by the Padre in 1769. As with a visit to any of the twenty-one missions, coming here brings the past vividly back to life. The church is long and narrow and, of course, housed in an adobe structure. The gardens here are very small, but pretty. The Padre Luis Jayme Museum, named after the missionary who was killed here by an Indian attack, contains some interesting excavated artifacts such as flintlock pistols, swords, buttons, and pottery. Other exhibits here include vestments, old photos, and small dioramas of all the missions. The monastery ruins have partial walls and the outlines of where the padres living quarters, the library, and other rooms once stood. Tips: Read the pamphlet about the mission as you explore it, because knowing its history makes it much more interesting.

Hours: Open daily, 9am - 4:30pm. Closed Thanksgiving and Christmas.

Price: $5 for adults; $3 for seniors and students over 12; $2 for ages 6 - 11; children 5 and under are free.

Ages: 7 years and up.

MISSION SAN ANTONIO DE PALA ☀

(760) 742-3317 / www.missionsanantonio.org $
3015 Pala Mission Road, Pala

This mission, founded in 1816, is the only remaining Spanish California Mission to continue in its original purpose of proselytizing and serving Native Americans. The adjacent school is for Native American children and the gift shop is run by Native Americans. The small mission is located on an Indian Reservation, a fact that greatly enhanced its value in my children's eyes.

The museum part of the mission consists of two small wings. One contains arrowheads, pottery, clothing with intricate beadwork, the Padre's small quarters, and an altar. Hand-carved religious figures and the Southwestern-style painted ceilings are eye-catching. The other wing is the Mineral Room, showcasing nice specimens of jasper, petrified wood slabs, and amethyst. The room also has a marine display that includes a stuffed puffer fish, corral, huge shells, and a giant clam shell.

The small back courtyard has a nicely landscaped garden, an altar, and a fountain with koi. The old bell tower is

around the side of the mission, next to the cemetery.

Hours: Open Wed. - Fri., 9am - 4pm; Sat., 9am - 5pm; Sun., 8am - 2pm. Closed Mon., Tues. and the week between Christmas and New Years.

Price: $2 for adults; $1 for children 12 and under.

Ages: 6 years and up.

MISSION SAN LUIS REY DE FRANCIA   ☼

(760) 757-3651 / www.sanluisrey.org $$

4050 Mission Avenue, Oceanside

Founded in 1798, this mission has been nicknamed "King of the Missions" because it is the largest of the twenty-one missions. It is also one of the most interesting. The extensive grounds cover nearly six and a half acres, though not all of it is open to the public. The first series of rooms contain several glass-encased displays that document the history of the mission. Next, is the Friar's small bedroom with a knotted rope bed, and monks' robes. (Seven Franciscan friars still live here in a separate section of the mission.) The weavery and work rooms have a loom, spinning wheel, and implements for leather tooling, respectively. The kitchen contains pots, pans, a brick oven, and glassware typical of the Mission period. The next few rooms display embroidered vestments, statues of angels and the Madonna, and other religious art work. The big Mission Church is gorgeous. Exit the church through the Madonna Chapel into the cemetery which contains a large wooden cross to commemorate the 3,000 Indians buried here.

The grounds are equally interesting to explore. Large grassy areas, with plenty of picnic tables, are outside the mission's front doors. Just past this area are ruins of soldiers' barracks. Further down, toward the street, is an ornate stone arch and a tiled stairway that lead to an old mission laundry area and large sunken garden, where Indians bathed. The garden looks like it was left over from Babylonian times; once elegantly landscaped, but now overgrown. Mission San Luis Rey de Francia is a great one to cover for those fourth grade mission reports! Of course, guided tours are available, by reservation. And check out taking a day or overnight individual or group retreat here.

Hours: Open Mon. - Fri., 9:30am - 5pm; Sat. - Sun., 10am - 4:30pm. Closed all major national and federal holidays.

Price: $5 for adults; $4 for seniors and ages 6 - 18; children 5 and under are free, as are active military.

Ages: 5 years and up.

MOTOR TRANSPORT MUSEUM   ☼

(619) 478-2492 / www.motortransportmuseum.org   !

31949 Highway 94, Campo

It might seem like a glorified junkyard, but this outdoor "museum" will make a car enthusiast's heart rev. Located in the building and mostly on the grounds of the old mill, over 200 vehicles from the early days of automobiles to current day, reside here; some waiting to be restored, but in real life, most have found their resting place. Old and rusted vehicles in no particular order are lined up, side by side; cars, buses, trailers, tractors, moving vans, military vehicles, and all kinds of trucks - cargo, fire, fuel, lumber, milk, dump, and more. Manufacturers include Mack, Ford, Nash, Fageol, Garford and many more. Walk the grounds to see the cars close up, but don't get inside them; take photos - great for photo ops!; hold onto little ones as you watch out for tires and other parts lying around; and enjoy this quirky and fascinating display of history.

Inside the massive building are a few prized, restored vehicles and some in process of, such as a Mack truck, WWII jeep and 1917 Nash Quad, plus old gas pumps and lots of tools as this is, basically, a workshop. Tours, clubs and school groups are welcome during the week. Note that just down the road are the GASKILL BROTHERS STONE STORE MUSEUM (pg. 533) and the PACIFIC SOUTHWEST RAILWAY MUSEUM (pg. 583).

Hours: Open Sat., 9am - 5pm,,or, if you're in the area and the gate is open and someone is working, you are usually welcome, then, too.

Price: Free

Ages: 6 years and up.

MUSEUM OF CONTEMPORARY ART - La Jolla   ☼

(858) 454-3541 / www.mcasd.org $$

700 Prospect Street, La Jolla

I admit two things about contemporary art museums: 1) I enjoy visiting them, and 2) I don't always "get" the art on exhibit. I've learned not to step on things lying on the floor or to touch anything, even things as seemingly

innocuous as a pole in the center of the room - it could be an exhibit. Displays here rotate about every three months, so there are new eclectic paintings, sculptures, photos, and other pieces to figure out every few months.

Our favorite past exhibits include a room-size metal spider carrying a nest of eggs; toddler-size figures made out of wax in various stages of melting because of the heat lamps directed on them; the "Reason for the Neutron Bomb," which had 50,000 match tips glued onto nickels on the floor, each one representing a Russian tank; and a darkened room with a large church bell which, when my kids pulled on the rope, triggered a hologram of the Virgin Mary and baby Jesus to appear.

One of the permanent installations is Pleasure Point, a protruding and gravity-defying composition of rowboats, canoes, surfboards, and jet skis hanging overhead outside the west side of the facility.

The M.C.A. offers school tours with reservations and walk-in tours on Sundays at 2pm, plus an additional tour on the third Thursdays at 5:30pm. Pick up a free children's guide (pamphlet) at the reception desk about discovering contemporary art. It asks thought-provoking questions, and gives kids things to do and look for. Don't forget that you can enjoy a light meal at the cafe, or a cappuccino. By the way, the view of the coastline from the museum is spectacular. Also see the following entry, MUSEUM OF CONTEMPORARY ART - San Diego.

Hours: Open Mon. - Tues. and Thurs. - Sun, 11am - 5pm; open the third Thurs. until 7pm. Closed Wed. and major holidays.

Price: $10 for adults; $5 for seniors and older students; ages 25 and under are free. Admission is valid for 7 days at both MCASD locations. Admission is free on the third Thurs. from 5pm - 7pm. See Museum Month, San Diego (pg. 708) for details about half-price admission in February.

Ages: 6 years and up.

MUSEUM OF CONTEMPORARY ART - San Diego

(858) 454-3541 / www.mcasd.org $$
1001 and 1100 Kettner Boulevard, San Diego

Comprised of two artsy-style buildings, across the street from each other, the mood is set for your visit to San Diego's contemporary art museum. What kinds of materials are used in the art that you're looking at? Traditional materials, like paint? Or nuts, bolts, wires, or other improbable materials? These are a few of the questions listed in the (free) children's guide on discovering contemporary art, which is found at the reception desk. The guide helps your child become more involved with the art, and enables him/her to understand the artist's vision in creating their work. Free, guided tours are also available Saturdays at 2pm and the third Thursdays at 5:30pm. Contemporary art is fun because it is eclectic. Some art pieces might be as unusual as a box of cereal, while other paintings, sculptures, and/or photos are a more daring combination of design, light and texture. The museum, which has quarterly rotating exhibits, is a branch of the M.C.A. in La Jolla. (See the previous entry.)

One of the art buildings is three stories, allowing more light-filled gallery space and innovative showings, including large-scale sculptures. There are also multiple-channel video capabilities to gain knowledge and insight as to the works.

Hours: Open Mon. - Tues. and Thurs. - Sun, 11am - 5pm; open the third Thurs. until 7pm. Closed Wed. and major holidays.

Price: $10 for adults; $5 for seniors and older students; ages 25 and under are free. Admission is valid for 7 days at both MCASD locations. Admission is free on the third Thurs. from 5pm - 7pm. See Museum Month, San Diego (pg. 708) for details about half-price admission in February.

Ages: 6 years and up.

MUSEUM OF MAKING MUSIC

(760) 438-5996 / www.museumofmakingmusic.com $$$
5790 Armada Drive, Carlsbad

"It makes no difference if it's sweet or hot, just give that rhythm everything you got." (From *It Don't Mean A Thing* by Irving Mills and Duke Ellington.) This would be a fitting motto for this *note*-worthy museum. The museum is nicely laid out and chronologically traces the history of music from the late 1800's through present day in an audibly and visually stimulating way. Paintings and wall-sized historic photographs of musicians add to the museum's ambiance.

Each section showcases, behind glass, instruments (over 450 total!) typical for that particular era which could include trumpets, banjos, mandolins, harmonicas, guitars, electric guitars (one signed by Stevie Ray Vaughan), keyboards, pianos (one signed by Henry Mancini), horns, and drums. The sections also have listening stations where visitors can, at the press of a button, hear samplings of popular music, sounds of specific instruments, and even some of the key innovations and inventions that changed the style of music being produced. Expose kids to the sound of

ragtime, big bands, jazz, blues, hillbilly, country, and more. Rooms toward the exit emphasize music probably more familiar to them - rock and roll, heavy metal, new wave, jazz infusion, and the Latin scene. Videos, instead of just audios, accompany the latter years of music.

End your visit on an upbeat tune by letting the kids play the instruments in the interactive area. Children are encouraged to try out the drum set, organ, keyboard, African strum stick, theremin (an instrument played by hand movement, without ever touching it!), a banjo, and an electric guitar whose sound, thankfully, can only be heard through headsets. Although the gift shop doesn't sell instruments, it does have a wide variety of them on display and it does sell some unique, music-related gifts. Forty-five-minute to ninety-minute (depending on the size of the group and age level) guided tours for the general public and for school groups are available by advanced reservation.

Hours: Open Tues. - Sun., 10am - 5pm. Closed Mon., New Year's Day, July 4th, Thanksgiving, and Christmas.

Price: $8 for adults; $5 for seniors, students, and ages 6 - 18; children 5 and under are free. See Museum Month, San Diego (pg. 708) for details about half-price admission in February.

Ages: 7 years and up.

MUSEUM OF PHOTOGRAPHIC ARTS

(619) 238-7559 / www.mopa.org $$
1649 El Prado, Balboa Park, San Diego

Your shutterbugs will appreciate this large showroom, with five galleries, that features changing exhibits of photographic works. Some exhibits zoom in on portraiture work or the history of American photography, while others focus more on pictures taken from all over the world. We enjoy the artistry in the pictures as well as comparing styles and choice of subjects. Ask about the Visual Classroom, a student-friendly curriculum supplement and guided tours for groups.

A 200-seat theater shows a variety of movies such as *Matilda*, *Princess Bride*, and *Casablanca*. See BALBOA PARK (pg. 526) for a listing of all the museums and attractions within walking distance.

Hours: The museum is open Tues. - Sun., 10am - 5pm. Closed Mon. and New Year's Day, Martin Luther King Day, Thanksgiving, and Christmas Day. Open some holiday Mon. and other holidays, 10am - 3pm. Call for specific hours for the theater shows.

Price: Museum admission is $8 for adults; $7 for seniors and military; $6 for students; children 12 and under are free. Admission to the museum is free on the second Tues. of every month for San Diego County residents. Passports, which are good for one week from the date of purchase, can be bought to visit the fourteen museums in Balboa Park for $53 for adults; $29 for ages 3 - 12 (as many museums are free for younger children). Theater admission for children's movies is usually free with admission; call for prices for other shows. See Museum Month, San Diego (pg. 708) for details about half-price admission in February. See page xi for info on the Bank of America free weekend program.

Ages: 7 years and up.

MUSEUM OF SAN DIEGO HISTORY

(619) 232-6203 / www.sandiegohistory.org $$
1649 El Prado, Balboa Park, San Diego

This museum presents the history of San Diego, from the 1850's to the present, via numerous photographs, plus maps, works of art, costumes, household goods, furniture, a 1910 railcar, 1901 buggy, and other artifacts. An authentic stagecoach is the first item you'll see and it sets the mood for your visit here. We always enjoy seeing history and understanding more about our past generation's lifestyles. The 100-seat Thornton Theater hosts education programs and more. See BALBOA PARK (pg. 526) for a listing of all the museums and attractions within walking distance.

Hours: Open Mon. - Sun., 10am - 5pm. Closed Thanksgiving and Christmas.

Price: $8 for adults; $6 for seniors, military and students; $4 for ages 6 - 17; children 5 and under are free. Admission the second Tues. of every month is free for San Diego County residents. Passports, which are good for one week from the date of purchase, can be bought to visit the fourteen museums in Balboa Park for $53 for adults; $29 for ages 3 - 12 (as many museums are free for younger children). See Museum Month, San Diego (pg. 708) for details about half-price admission in February.

Ages: 5 years and up.

NATIONAL CITY DEPOT MUSEUM

(619) 474-4400 / www.sdera.org

922 W. 23rd Street, National City

Once a working train depot, the building now houses a few historic railroad artifacts and some merchandise to purchase. The museum also has several rail cars in the process of being restored. The main kid-draw, if you're in the neighborhood, is the huge, multi-track, O-scale model train layout. The trains run through valleys, hills, and towns. All of the "add-ons" that make model trains fun to watch are here. Across the street is a glass-enclosed gazebo that protects a restored 1887 passenger coach. Group tours are given with advanced reservations.

Hours: Open Thurs. - Sun., 9am - 5pm. Closed Thanksgiving and Christmas.

Price: Free

Ages: 3 years and up.

THE NEW CHILDREN'S MUSEUM

(619) 233-8792 / www.thinkplaycreate.org

200 W. Island Avenue, San Diego

This 50,000 square feet, tri-level, modern, environmentally-friendly building is a unique blend of contemporary art museum and interactive children's museum. The spacious rooms have high ceilings that are infused with natural light (even rooms without walls that open directly to the outside), and contain outside-the-box exhibits along with, always, space and inviting nooks to just hang out, a much needed factor. Note that exhibits change because "new" is part of their name! What doesn't change is the quality and excitement that kids express by coming here. Hungry for both a fun and educational place to take your kids? Below is what we recently experienced at the exhibit, "Feast, the art of playing with your food".

The entrance bridge, which is redecorated with every new exhibit, was ap*peel*ingly covered in a banana mural. The lobby/main room had grove of oranges at the ends of ropes which were dangling from the ceiling, plus some curved, metal monkey bars. As kids (and absolutely adults, too) climbed on the bars, and sat and swung on the roped oranges, or even just walked by, their movements produced a cacophony of sounds, amplified by the speakers. The sounds changed according to how fast people moved and what kind of movement was being produced. You can't see wind, only the effects of it. We experientially learned more about wind - movement, interaction and manipulation - in the Wind Vessel section.

The next areas are permanent: A creative arts and craft room with low tables for kids and supplies, and a wall-sized blackboard, and, outside, a large balcony where a vehicle of some sort (I've seen VW bugs and a small tractor) and other items await visitors to paint and repaint and repaint them. Aprons and paint are supplied. Tables and chairs are set up outside here, too, for making clay creations or other art projects. Museums staff post a schedule of their daily art workshops, but also check out the special events and programs, too.

Back inside another room was set up like a mini road/warehouse with play food delivery trucks to drive around a grouping of tires in the center. The next room was like a musical house with kitchen counters made of marimbas; a drum set made of huge pots and cymbals out of lids (ideas for a real homemade band!); cans strung in a row to strike like a xylophones; and recording devices. In another room were building blocks made of dried and compressed mushrooms for both *fungi*s and fun girls.

Across from the lobby is an eating area and cafe that serves chili ($5 to $8), chicken salad ($6 - $9), turkey and Swiss cheese and jalapeno wrap ($6.50), grilled cheese sandwich ($6.50), pasta with chicken meatballs ($5 to $9), and some gluten-free entrees, plus fruit, mini muffins and all natural ice cream. And you gotta love (and contribute to) the wall contraption to put in donation money and watch it go up and down and through a clear tubing system to the end basket. (I have some wall space in my house. . . .)

On the third floor, a huge fruit and vegetable bounce made kids jump for joy regarding eating their veggies. Inside a big, wooden playhouse (which is redecorated according to the museum theme), was a place for kids to play with huge foam puzzles, and relax. A fun, indoor soft play spot had a watermelon boat; a huge piece that looked like Swiss cheese to crawl in and out and through and on; an orange slice to get into; soft foam melon slices to rock on; an enormous water spigot with padded water; and more. More permanent stations of a paper-making studio; a small area with some tables and chairs; and a few more interactive (and clever) toys and exhibits; plus a big bubble station outside with large trays of bubble solution on raised tables make up the rest of this floor.

Down stairs, via stairs or the glass elevator, is a space with bean bags in two big pits to read or watch something on the screen. Look out the window to see a chicken coop. Visitors can pet and feed the chickens via daily workshops.

At the food exhibit we crawled under a gigantic dining room table to play on the carpet and see footage (showing on the tablecloth) of kids eating vegetables and other good-for-you foods. An adjacent room, the Arts Education Center, is for educators as it is stocked with resources. Note: Check the website for great crafts ideas and what else to do at home to extend the learning and creating inspired from these exhibits.

Across the street is a one-acre park. A triangle-shaped grassy lawn proceeds a small stage area, plus a small playground with twisty sculptures to twirl around on and a few swings on cement. A garden project is on one side and an adjoining, enclosed play area, with an abstract climbing structure with fun and imaginative elements, plus a sand pit inside, is on the other. A bike path, train tracks, and across the road, another park with circles of grass, pine trees, and small grassy mounds add to the uniqueness and enjoyment of your outing.

Hours: Open Mon., Wed. - Sat., 10am - 4pm; Sun., noon - 4pm. Closed Tues., New Year's Day, 4th of July, Thanksgiving, and Christmas. Hours fluctuate so call first.
Price: $10 for ages 1 and up; $5 for seniors and military with I.D.; children under 1 are free. The second Sun. of the month is free. Parking in the adjacent lot is $10 or park somewhere else and walk here. There is limited street parking for free on Sunday.
Ages: 1 ½ years and up.

OCEANSIDE MUSEUM OF ART

(760) 435-3720 / www.oma-online.org $$
704 Pier View Way, Oceanside

This pleasing, two-story art museum is located in the heart of the attractive city buildings in "downtown". It contains five galleries with rotating exhibits. Some of the modern and contemporary exhibits will appeal more to kids than others, so check to see what is showing. Some of the exhibits are more traditional in the presentation (i.e., art hanging on walls) and some exhibits are more unusual, such as the pop culture one called Icons of Desire with shiny, tiled, gum-ball machines, ice cream cone, candy and toys. The museum offers several ways for kids (and adults) to get involved with the art via classes and program - take advantage of them! (please)

Hours: Open Tues. - Sat., 10am - 4pm; Sun., 1pm - 4pm. Closed Mon. and major holidays.
Price: $8 for adults; $5 for seniors; students with ID and military are free. Admission is free the first Sun. of each month.
Ages: 8 years and up.

OLAF WIEGHORST MUSEUM AND WESTERN HERITAGE CENTER

(619) 590-3431 / www.wieghorstmuseum.org $
131 Rea Avenue, El Cajon

These lovely grounds, landscaped with a wide variety of cactus and even a small pond, were once the home of Western painter, Olaf Wieghorst. The museum building has two rooms - one features his landscape paintings and the other features his cowboy paintings, plus other objects such as saddles, Native American baskets, photographs, jewelry, Kachina dolls, dream catchers, and a beautiful beaded Indian dress and bag.

Walk outside to his home - a weathered, wooden building from 1947. You can see his period furniture in some of the rooms including the living room couch and old TV set, and several Native American rugs and baskets. A huge mural (twenty feet high) of his is painted on one side of yet another building.

Hours: Open Tues. - Sat., 10am - 3pm. Closed Mon., Sun., and holidays.
Price: $2 suggested donation for adults.
Ages: 8 years and up.

OLD TOWN SAN DIEGO AND STATE HISTORIC PARK

(619) 220-5422 - Robinson-Rose House and park ranger / www.parks.ca.gov;   !/$
www.oldtownmarketsandiego.com; www.oldtownsandiegoguide.com; www.historictours.com
Taylor, Juan, Twiggs, and Congress Sts., Old Town, San Diego

Old Town is a six-block area, which is closed to automotive traffic and bound by Taylor, Juan, Twiggs, and Congress streets. The places mentioned below encompass this area, plus the immediate, walkable vicinity.

This wonderful conglomeration of unique shops, scrumptious places to eat, vintage houses, museums, and Mexican bazaars are all located along dirt "roads" and on paved sidewalks inside the "town." Old Town contains many original and restored buildings from San Diego's Mexican period before 1846, and the early California period. A day here is a combination of history lessons and fun shopping! Just a quick note about some of the stores here: Through

the window at the Cousin's Candy Shop come watch salt water taffy being pulled; then go inside and buy yourself a treat of taffy or homemade fudge. Just a few favorite other stores include Covered Wagon, Urban Seed, Old Town Market Place, and Bazaar Del Mundo.

The route for the attractions listed below starts at the Robinson-Rose House - the park headquarters at the opposite end than Old Town Market - then proceeds east, south, and north before looping back around. Admission is free, unless otherwise noted. All historic buildings are closed on New Year's Day, Thanksgiving, and Christmas. Free maps of the area are available at the park headquarters, in many of the stores in Old Town, and in local hotel lobbies. Free walking tours that cover all of the old buildings, not just the more kid-friendly ones I've listed here, are offered daily at 11am and 2pm, beginning at Robinson-Rose House. Living History activities that could include blacksmithing, carpentry, games, soap-making, card-printing, and more take place on Wednesdays and Saturdays from 10am to 4pm.

ROBINSON-ROSE HOUSE is located at 4002 Wallace Street, on the other side of the parking lot from Taylor Street. This 1853 adobe structure houses the park headquarters/visitors center and has walking tour maps available for purchase. It also has a few exhibits, such as photo murals and a scale model of Old Town as it appeared in the mid 1870's. Open April - September, 10am to 5pm; October - March, 10am - 4pm.

OLD TOWN PLAZA is located directly in front of the Robinson-Rose House. This area is essentially a large grassy area for kids to run around, with olive, fig, cork, and eucalyptus trees providing beauty and shade. A large fountain is in the middle of this park and there are plenty of benches for weary travelers (or shoppers).

The row of stores across from the Plaza are in reconstructed buildings dating from around 1830.

COLORADO HOUSE / WELLS FARGO MUSEUM is located on San Diego Street in the heart of Old Town. This museum has the appeal of the Old West, with an 1868 stagecoach prominently displayed in the center. Other exhibits include a colorful wall display of Wells Fargo featured in comic books, trading cards, and even a board game; rocks with gold, bags of gold found in treasure boxes, and gold coins; mining tools; Old West posters; and more. Try sending a Morse code message, using the provided "how to" sheet, to someone across the room. A video shows and describes this time period and the history of Wells Fargo. A more modern feature is the ATM machine.

CASA DE MACHADO Y STEWART is located almost directly behind the Colorado House/Wells Fargo Museum. This plain-looking adobe is an exact replica of the original house, complete with a dirt walkway leading to it. The brick-floored house contains few furnishings, including a dining table, shelves with dishes and pottery, a sparsely furnished bedroom, and some tools. Just beyond the front porch is a beehive oven and open fire stoves, evidence of the outdoor cooking that pioneers once employed.

MASON STREET SCHOOL is located on Mason Street, diagonal to the Casa de Machado y Stewart. This 1865 red schoolhouse is a child's favorite historical stop in Old Town. It was the first public schoolhouse in San Diego and retains its old-fashioned ambiance with twenty school desks, a school bell, flags, a chalkboard, a wood-burning stove, the dunce's corner (and cap), and old pictures and books. It's open daily, 10am to 4pm.

THE DENTAL MUSEUM is located on San Diego Avenue in front of the schoolhouse. Kids will enjoy a quick peek at the past here as they see a dentist chair, instruments, and even some molds of teeth.

SAN DIEGO UNION BUILDING is located on San Diego Avenue. The first edition of the San Diego Union came off the presses here way back when. Now, kids can see an old Washington handpress (printing press), typeset letters and tools, and the adjacent small newspaper office.

OLD TOWN MARKET is at the other end of the complex at 4010 Twiggs Street. It has a very small museum with historical displays of old San Diego, text panels, a video on this area, and artifacts found while excavating this site. The majority of the market is for shoppers with forty outdoor booths that offer unique gifts, plus artisans who sometimes demonstrate their craft as they work, such as a silversmith, a painter, and a bonsai sculptor. The adjacent stage is used for free shows such as storytelling, concerts, magic shows, and other presentations appealing to families.

WHALEY HOUSE - See WHALEY HOUSE (pg. 559) for details. It's an interesting museum! Take a quick peek into the Old Town Drug Store Museum, located behind this museum. Kids can see an old-time pharmacy containing bottles, patented medicines, and a mortar and pestle.

HERITAGE PARK VICTORIAN VILLAGE, (858) 565-3600 / www.co.san-diego.ca.us/parks/heritage.html is located north of the Whaley House, on Harvey and Juan streets. This group of seven buildings is enchanting to simply look at.

THE MORMON BATTALION VISITOR CENTER, (619) 298-3317 / www.lds.org/locations/san-diego-mormon-battalion-historic-site, is located on 2510 Juan Street. For over half an hour, an informative and costumed tour guide (the only way to see the center) will show your family around this Old West center with a covered wagon in the front. The talking pictures in frames are pretty fun, especially as they leave the frames in each room to continue on with the visitors.

　　The museum has a few themed rooms that are filled with interesting artifacts from the Old West including canons and a big box camera in an adobe-style room, plus several interactive exhibits. One room is set up to look like a campsite in the mountains with logs and tents and trees. Another room, with its wooden floors, walls, and cross beam ceiling, is a general store with barrels, bedrolls, lanterns, and shelves packed with clothing and equipment for "sale". We were led into another room and shown huge paintings of Jesus during various times of his ministry.

　　Although the 500 men of the Mormon Battalion never fought a battle, the 1846 volunteer unit marched 2,000 miles across country to San Diego to help fight in the Mexican/American war. Their arduous trail blazing efforts and accomplishments are reenacted in an interesting fifteen-minute film shown in a room with rocky outcroppings along the perimeters of the walls, plus real plants, and a mural that pulls you into the mountain scenery of the Old West. The staff interact with the videos (and photos in frames), making it a 4-D experience. In the backyard there are activities for visitors including using a water pump, making a brick, dressing up in period clothing and panning for fools gold (that can be kept) in a sluice. You can also get a free souvenir here - an old time photo of yourself. As our tour concluded, we were offered a Book of Mormon and asked if we could have someone call on us regarding the Mormon religion. The visitor center is open daily, 9am to 9pm. Admission is free.

BAZAAR DEL MUNDO, (619) 296-3161 / www.bazaardelmundo.com, is catty-corner to the park, located at 4133 Taylor Street on the corner of Juan and Taylor streets, behind Casa Guadalajara Restaurant. This gaily decorated traditional Mexican courtyard/shopping/eating area is festive in appearance and atmosphere. Occasionally, Mariachi bands play, costumed dancers entertain, and all the colorful storefronts and wares beckon shoppers of all ages. If your tummy is saying, "Tengo hambre" (that's Spanish for "I'm hungry"), sample and savor some of the culinary delights here. Shops are open Tues. - Sat., 10am to 9pm; Sun - Mon.,10am - 5:30pm.

LA CASA DE ESTUDILLO is located at one entrance of Old Town. A good-sized, outer courtyard and garden lead the way to a large, U-shaped, adobe home. Notice the reconstructed beehive oven off to the side. As you tour the furnished house of this once-prominent family, you'll see the kitchen, dining room, several bedrooms, living room, priest's room, chapel, workroom, and study. The house/museum is open daily, 10am - 5pm. Admission is free.

SEELEY STABLES is located on Calhoun Street. This huge, reconstructed barn contains several exhibit stalls. The saddles, bells, and harnesses, plus at least ten stagecoaches, surreys, and carriages, are great visual aids for picturing the past. Free slide shows are presented in the downstairs theater throughout the day, so come and rest, and learn a little history. The upstairs loft has more exhibits of the wild, wild west, such as branding irons, spurs, more saddles, a Mexican cowboy hat, and furniture including an unusual chair made out of steers' horns. A native American display features Kachina dolls, a feather headdress, and baskets. Other exhibits up here include an old-fashioned slot machine, a roller organ, an antique telephone, a case of model horses, and a child's room with toys. Open daily, 10am to 5pm.

　　The backyard of the stables is an open courtyard with early farm equipment around its perimeter, plus several more carriages and stagecoaches in glass-cased enclosures. Also back here, or accessible from Mason Street, is THE BLACK HAWK LIVERY STABLE AND BLACKSMITH. This large blacksmith workshop usually holds demonstrations Tuesday - Thursday, and most Saturdays. Kids might see the hot fires help bend pieces of metal into horseshoes or heavy chains, or they might hear a hammer clank against the anvil to create a sword or branding iron. The stable room is filled with finished pieces and tools.

GEORGE JOHNSON HOUSE is located on Calhoun Street, near Mason Street. This small building has a room to walk through - it took us five minutes, maybe. It displays archaeological findings of the area such as bottles and pottery, plus tools of the trade and pictures showing the painstaking work of excavation and cleaning.

FIESTA DE REYES has nineteen shops and restaurants with strolling mariachis, folklorico dancing, outdoor dining with authentic Mexican food - a taste of across the border. For more info, contact (619) 297-3100 / www.fiestadereyes.com

Look up the SERRA MUSEUM and PRESIDIO PARK (pg. 556), which is located just north of Old Town.

Hours: Most of the attractions are open daily, 10am to 5pm; shops are usually open until 9pm in the spring and summer.

Price: Free, but bring spending money. See individual listings.

Ages: 4 years and up.

PACIFIC SOUTHWEST RAILWAY MUSEUM

Sheridan Road, Campo

See the entry for PACIFIC SOUTHWEST RAILWAY MUSEUM on page 583 for details.

RANCHO BUENA VISTA ADOBE

(760) 639-6164 / www.cityofvista.com

640 Alta Vista Drive, Vista

Follow the signs through the park and over the footbridge to the adobe. Guided tours, the only way to see the inside of the rancho, begin just outside the gift shop in front of an eye-catching, hand-painted map of the surrounding cities. The brick-paved patio and pathways leading to the eleven-room adobe add to the old-time ambiance. The immaculately kept grounds and adobe are often used for weddings, meetings, and other functions.

The first stop is simply to check out the thickness of adobe walls. Walk into each room, all of which are furnished with items donated by area residents. The kitchen is constantly in use and it contains numerous old-fashioned implements. In one bedroom touch cowhide (which is hard) and calf hide (which is supple) draped on a bed. The bathroom has ornate tiles from the 1930's and a cool-looking bathtub. Another room contains a loom and other workman's tools of trade. A living room contains an old piano with candle holders (used before electricity was invented), a phonograph with cylinder "records," pictures, and paintings. My boys especially liked the light fixtures with wood-carved knight figures on them. Outside are a few neatly arranged washing machines and farm tools.

Listen to the fascinating history and stories of this home, from rancho to Hollywood hangout. A few samples to pique your interest: One room supposedly still contains a skeleton in the wall because when it was discovered years and years ago, it was just covered back up again. Once a bandit came to steal a horse and instead, wound up ordering his gang to protect the owner who had befriended him. A few of the rooms were originally not enclosed and used as a thoroughfare for horses. One owner slept with his prize stallion in his room. And so on.

Two-hour California history programs, offered for groups comprising of ten to thirty-three students, include a forty-minute guided tour and two activities. Choose from candle dipping, cooking, branding, roping, weaving, Native American games, and/or Native American crafts. Activities take place in the adobe or in the backyard. Teachers may request a curriculum notebook with lesson plans and worksheets. Three-hour Scout programs are also available.

The small park adjacent to the rancho has a grassy area, picnic tables, and a stage.

Hours: The rancho is open Thurs. - Fri., 10am - 2:15pm (last tour); Sat. at 10am. School programs are offered Mon. - Fri., 9:30am - 11:30am and 11:30pm - 1:30pm with advanced reservations. The park is open daily, dawn - dusk.

Price: The rancho is $4 for nonresident adults; $3 for seniors and Vista residents; $1 for students; 50¢ for ages 12 and under. School programs are $12 per student; $10 for the Scout programs. The park is free.

Ages: 7 years and up.

RANCHO GUAJOME ADOBE

(760) 724-4082 or (858) 694-3030 / www.co.san-diego.ca.us/parks/ranchoguajomeadobe.html; www.sdparks.org

2210 N. Santa Fe Avenue, Vista

This "Cadillac of adobes," built in 1853, contains twenty-two rooms and is one of the finest examples of early California hacienda architecture. (Count all the archways!) It was built for the same reason missions were built; to protect residents from intruders and maintain a small community of family and servants on the grounds.

Encircling a large inner courtyard, the rancho consists of a schoolroom, spacious family living quarters, dining room, a separate chapel, servants' quarters, the kitchen, sheds, stables, and a Victorian-style garden. It has all been beautifully restored. The furnishings, plus the buggy in the carriage courtyard and the docent's information, make the past seem vividly present. You can walk the Santa Fe Trail that goes behind the museum, too.

School groups are offered guided tours that correspond with California state curriculum for third and fourth graders. One of the highlights for students is making adobe bricks. (Dress accordingly!) Note that the ANTIQUE GAS & STEAM ENGINE MUSEUM, INC. (pg. 525) is next door, and GUAJOME REGIONAL PARK (pg. 503), for picnic and playtime, is just down the street.

Hours: Open Wed. - Sun., 9:30am - 4pm for self-guided tours (or guided, if you call in advance). Scheduled guided tours are given Sat. - Sun. at noon and 2pm, except in rainy weather. Closed Thanksgiving and Christmas.

Price: $3 for adults; $1 for children 12 years and under. School tours are $1 per student.

Ages: 7 years and up.

REUBEN H. FLEET SCIENCE CENTER   ☼

(619) 238-1233 / www.rhfleet.org $$$$
1875 El Prado, Balboa Park, San Diego

This huge Science Center is a fascinating place for hands-on exploration, experimentation, and discovery with over eighty permanent exhibits covering perception, astronomy, technology, and science. One permanent exhibit geared specifically for younger kids is the good-size Kid City with a floor that looks like a street. Shop at the grocery store with lots of play food, shopping carts, an interactive food pyramid, and all the accouterments. Climb in an around the factory, which has four levels of climbing and play. Sit in the little fire engine and turn levers and knobs. On the ball wall, push buttons and pull levers and watch balls go down through the see-through chutes, track, and big gears to show cause and effect. Kid City also has soft blocks, computers with educational games, a book nook, funhouse mirrors, magnetic letters, and a craft area. Infants have a separate play area just for them.

Just a few of the several other permanent exhibits and gallery rooms throughout include a periscope that literally goes through the roof to view the outside world; So WATT!, which is an illuminating look at how solar panels generate electricity, visual comparisons of energy resources, and energy conservation; Exploration Bar where interactive demonstrations and scientific experiments take place; Gallery of Illusions and Perceptions which plays games with your brain; Look! Touch! Listen! which engages all the senses; and Aging, where you can use a computer program to simulate aging your face and see how you would look years down the road, incorporating sun exposure, smoking or obesity. (I think I'll avoid those things more than ever, now!) Blockbusters is a place to let the architect or engineer within come out using thousands of uniform KEVA wood pieces to create tower, structures, bridges, and more without glue or connectors. Get the real inside story via Cellular Journey, a hands-on exhibit with oversized 3-D wall models that show cell structures and components. This area also has microscopes to identify different human tissue cells and a realistic lab set up showing how researches learn about stem cells and other medical information.

There are also numerous outstanding temporary exhibits here that rotate every year, or so, such the ExploraZone, courtesy of the Exploratorium in San Francisco. A favorite display here was called Memory, featuring thirty-eight interactive exhibits about making memories, retrieving memories, and . . . I forget what else. Another favorite was Animal Grossology, which featured 3-D and hands-on exploration of a cow's insides, blood-sucking and slime-making creatures, and other disgusting (but intriguing) animal functions. Check the website to see what's currently at the museum. I guarantee that whatever is here is well worth at least one visit, if not several.

The second floor hosts many changing displays as well as TechnoVation, the corporate name for numerous, technology-based exhibits. For instance, watch a film showing laser eye surgery being performed; learn the history of computers from punch card to P.C.; have a video conference with someone across the room; see technological breakthroughs; and find out where water comes from and how it gets clean - from rain water to tap water. Live science demonstrations are also given on this floor. For a whole new world experience for students, the CHALLENGER LEARNING CENTER (pg. 562) is also located here.

The geodesic dome-shaped IMAX theater shows one-hour films on a screen several times the size of screens in regular movie theaters, therefore drawing you into the on-screen action. The shows, including a show once a month in

Spanish, are usually educational and are always interesting. Educators, know that with a minimum of fifty students you can reserve the theater and choose from over twenty-five titles, plus have time in the exhibit gallery for only $7 per student. Other stellar productions include one-hour planetarium shows given on the first Wednesday of every month at 7pm and 8:15pm.

Tip or warning: The gift shop appeals to all ages who are even slightly scientific or hands-on oriented. See BALBOA PARK (pg. 526) for a listing of all the museums and attractions within walking distance.

Hours: The exhibit gallery is open Mon. - Thurs., 10am - 5pm; Fri. - Sun., 10am - 6pm. IMAX films are shown throughout the day.

Price: Exhibit gallery admission is $13 for adults; $12 for seniors; $11 for ages 3 - 12; children 2 and under are free. Admission to the exhibit gallery and an IMAX show or planetarium show is $17 for adults; $15 for seniors; $14 for ages 3 - 12; children 2 and under are free. An additional show is $7 more per person. Admission to the exhibit gallery, only, is free on the first Tues. of every month for San Diego County residents. Passports, which are good for one week from the date of purchase, can be bought to visit the fourteen museums in Balboa Park for $53 for adults; $29 for ages 3 - 12 (as many museums are free for younger children). See Museum Month, San Diego (pg. 708) for details about half-price admission in February. See page xi for info on ASTC reciprocal museum memberships.

Ages: 4 years and up.

SAN DIEGO AIR AND SPACE MUSEUM

(619) 234-8291 / www.sandiegoairandspace.org

2001 Pan American Plaza, Balboa Park, San Diego

Take to the skies in this marvelous museum that visually chronicles the history of aviation from the dawn of flight through the age of space travel with over sixty real, replica, and mock-up aircraft, as well as hundreds of other exhibits. Outside are a Navy Convair Sea Dart and A-12 Blackbird on pedestals. In the lobby is the only flying replica of a NYP-3, as well as the real Apollo 9 command module, plus models hanging overhead, and an XJ-5 simulator ride and two-seater, full-motion, flight simulator called the FS2000. Simulator rides are is $8 per person. The following is information on the permanent exhibits - just know that the museum also hosts fabulous temporary exhibits such as Ripley's Believe It or Not! and the Centennial of Naval Aviation.

The rooms circle around the center pavilion, which contains a PBY-5A Catalina, an F-4S Phantom II, and a Ford 5-AT-B Trimotor, among others. The first few rooms, formally titled the International Aerospace Hall of Fame, give homage to the aero-engineers, pilots, and aviation founders that didn't fly off course in their vision for creating aircrafts and the aerospace industry. The hall contains a hot air balloon, as well as photos, plaques, and medals of aviation heroes. Portraits of Armstrong, Aldrich, and other astronauts, especially, caught my children's eyes. An Apollo XI display features a replica of the plaque left on the moon, the box used to collect lunar samples, and more.

The next rooms are packed with exhibits of early flying machines and models of inventions such as gliders, "birdmen" who used bicycle tires, bi-planes, and the Wright Brother's flyer, plus narrated videos that show pictures of early flying attempts. Consecutive eras are also well defined and enhanced with colorful wall murals, period-dressed mannequins, and other fine details. Wood-paneled rooms, complete with sandbags and army netting, house WWI and WWII planes and other memorabilia such as helmets, goggles, and uniforms. The flying aces and the fighter planes that served them, including the SPAD, the Nieuport, Spitfires, Hellcats, and Zeros, are well represented. In between wars, the U.S. Mail service was introduced. Displays here include a Curtiss JN-4 Jenny, wall posters of stamps blown up in size that commemorate aviation, and a replicated 1918 mail office. Kids love the next exhibits of barnstormers and pictures of daredevils using planes to entertain. These showmen of the air are doing headstands on wings, transferring from a plane to a speeding car, and other feats.

The next series of rooms honor women aviators; house engines, cylinders, and propellers; and display lots of model airplanes. Enter a pilot's ready room to watch the film *Sea Legs*. The armed forces are saluted with their contributions and a scale model of the *U.S.S. Yorktown*, and the *U.S.S. Langley* - the Navy's first carrier.

Enter the Jet Age with the F-4 Phantom, and the spy plane, the Blackbird. This exciting time period is followed by the Space Age. This last set of rooms feature bulky astronaut uniforms, capsules, modules, a moon rock, and more. An adjacent theater room showcases the history of model making.

At the Kid Aviation Action Hangar, tailored for pre-schoolers through elementary age, kids can get blown away at the wind tunnel U-Fly-it ride, which is a flight simulator in a real wind tunnel. There are also two other flight simulators in here, plus pedal planes to pilot around the play airport; a simulated moon surface to walk around in a space suit; mini parachutes to make and launch; a F-104 Starfighter cockpit mock-up to climb into and captain; toys;

games; and more.

Hold on to your seats as they actually bump and jolt you as you engage in an immersive experience at the 3-D/4-D Zable Theater. The various shows are entertaining (and usually flight-oriented) and you are a part of the special effects that take place on screen - with objects flying out at you and feeling the visual sensation of flying - and off screen with the seats moving, misters, and more. The shows are given continuously throughout the day and are included in your price of museum admission.

Soar to new heights as you and your children explore the Aerospace Museum! Behind-the-scenes tours of the aircraft restoration facility are available Mondays and Wednesdays, and sometimes Fridays for an additional $7 for adults; $5 for seniors and kids. Note that family day activities, free with museum admission, are offered on the second Saturday of each month. Activities include take-home projects, plus learning about a particular aviation topic. Summer camp programs, field trips, educational events, paper airplane festivals, book signings, and much more are also available. The museum also has Flight Path Grill, an outdoor restaurant serving hamburgers, pizza hot dogs, salad, and more for about $6 per. See BALBOA PARK (pg. 526) for a listing of all the museums and attractions within walking distance.

Hours: Open most of the year daily, 10am - 4:30pm. Open in the summer daily until 5:30pm. Closed Thanksgiving and Christmas.

Price: $18 for adults; $15 for seniors; $7 for ages 3 - 11; active duty military and children 2 and under are free. Admission is free on the fourth Tues. of every month for San Diego County residents. Passports, which are good for one week from the date of purchase, can be bought to visit the fourteen museums in Balboa Park for $53 for adults; $29 for ages 3 - 12 (as many museums are free for younger children). See Museum Month, San Diego (pg. 708) for details about half-price admission in February.

Ages: 4 years and up.

SAN DIEGO AIR AND SPACE MUSEUM GILLESPIE FIELD ANNEX

(619) 258-1221- direct line; (619) 234-8291 - Air and Space Museum in Balboa Park / www.sandiegoairandspace.org
335 Kenney Street, El Cajon

Even I couldn't miss this museum - it has an Atlas missile on the front lawn! This museum consists of two hangars and lots of outside space that is a depository for "work-in-progress" planes from the SAN DIEGO AIR AND SPACE MUSEUM in Balboa Park as numerous planes here are in the process of being restored or rebuilt. They have completed restoration of a Convair F-102A Delta Dagger and are currently working on a Wright Flyer. What a great "eyes-on" experience young aviators and engineers can gain by visiting this unique museum! There are also several other planes on display inside the hangars, plus a few engines and aeronautical artifacts, and a glass display case of model planes.

Outside, besides the missile, are an F-14A Tomcat, F-86F Sabre, and A-4C Skyhawk, plus an army helicopter and other jet fighters. Exhibits do rotate.

Hours: Open Mon., Wed. - Fri., 7am - 3pm.
Price: Free, but donations gladly accepted.
Ages: 5 years and up.

SAN DIEGO ART INSTITUTE

(619) 236-0011 / www.sandiego-art.org
1439 El Prado, Balboa Park, San Diego

New exhibits showcasing regional artists open every four to six weeks. This small gallery features works in various mediums, depending on the selected artist, including photography, sculpture, oil, watercolor, and more. A small side gallery debuts work from local schoolchildren. See BALBOA PARK (pg. 526) for a listing of all the museums and attractions within walking distance.

Hours: Open Tues. - Sat., 10am - 4pm; Sun., noon - 4pm. Closed Mon., New Year's Day, Thanksgiving and Christmas.

Price: $3 for adults; $2 for seniors and students; children 12 and under are free. Admission to the museum is free on the third Tues. of every month for San Diego County residents. Passports, which are good for one week from the date of purchase, can be bought to visit the fourteen museums in Balboa Park for $53 for adults; $29 for ages 3 - 12 (as many museums are free for younger children).

Ages: 6 years and up.

SAN DIEGO AUTOMOTIVE MUSEUM   ☀

(619) 231- AUTO (2886) / www.sdautomuseum.org $$$
2080 Pan American Plaza, Balboa Park, San Diego

Jump start your child's interest in automobiles at this museum that has more than eighty vehicles on display. Most of the gleaming cars are in a line and readily viewable. Some of the vintage automobiles are on display in appropriate settings, such as a fifties car in front of a backdrop of a drive-through. Understand that the vehicles on display are here on a rotating basis. Classics here range from old-fashioned Model A's to futuristic-looking DeLoreans. Other favorites (that were on display when we visited) include a 1948 Tucker "Torpedo" (only fifty-one were ever built); a 1934 convertible Coupe Roadster; a 1955 Mercedes Benz (300SL Gullwing); a 1957 Chevrolet; and Packards from 1929 to 1936. Prototypes and concept cars, model cars, a race car, a recreated mechanics shop complete with tools, and an engine room for those who want the inside scoop on cars, are also found at this museum. "Gentlemen, start your engines" applied to my boys as they raced over to see the over sixty motorcycles on display. They were particularly elated by the Harley Davidsons, the Indian Chief, and an army cycle.

A kid's corner features a motorcycle to sit on; a frame of a car for kids to sit in and shift gears; a floor mat designed with city streets for youngsters to race around play cars; and car pictures to color. See BALBOA PARK (pg. 526) for a listing of all the museums and attractions within walking distance.

Hours: Open daily, 10am - 5pm. Closed New Year's Day, Thanksgiving, and Christmas.
Price: $8.50 for adults; $6 for seniors; $5 for students; $4 for ages 6 - 15; children 5 and under are free. Admission on the fourth Tues. of every month is free for San Diego County residents. Passports, which are good for one week from the date of purchase, can be bought to visit the fourteen museums in Balboa Park for $53 for adults; $29 for ages 3 - 12 (as many museums are free for younger children). See Museum Month, San Diego (pg. 708) for details about half-price admission in February.
Ages: 6 years and up.

SAN DIEGO CHILDREN'S DISCOVERY MUSEUM   ☽

(760) 233-7755 / www.sdcdm.org $$$
320 North Broadway, Escondido

Come play! Our kids always urged my husband and I to share in playing with them because it's important to them and they like to be with us. (I'm thankful!) This small children's museum is a delightful place to do just that.

The one, good-sized room is divided into various sections to explore and plearn (play/learn) about international cultures, communication, and imagination. The wooden, boat-like play structure has sails, a slide, a tunnel, wheels to spin, and more for sailors to imaginatively travel the oceans. The enclosed (and dry) tiny Toddler Tidepool is an area specifically for ages 3 and under with soft block climbing structures and more. Building is also encouraged with more traditional blocks, wooden Keva planks, and using colorful plastic pieces at the light table. Construct different routes for a ball to race down at the magnetic ball wall. See real science at Aquaponics where water and plants interact to make life possible. Order an exotic something at the Global Village marketplace/cafe counter using pretend money, a cash register and fake food. Dress up in animal costumes or ethnic costumes or in uniforms, like a firefighter, and other career choices. Use props and hats to complete the outfit and enact a story. Or, use the puppet theater to put on a mini play. There are other activities here, too, such as using an air tunnel, beating some drums, looking through large microscopes, and reading books. I also like the fact that there is some created space to be low-key sit and read.

The outdoor patio is green with gardens growing seasonal crops, plants that attract butterflies, and plants to touch and smell - all "fertilized" by composting and by worms. Other things to do out here include painting a huge canvas fabric; manipulating and designing with gigantic large foam blocks, mats, and noodles (I wish I had room for these at my house!); blowing bubbles; climbing the short rock mound; playing with Legos at a water play table; jumping on hay; and digging in a sand pit (i.e. base camp) to brush up on archeological and paleontological skills. Ask about the programs the museum offers such as camps, school field trips, and workshops. Bring a lunch to enjoy at the inside cafe, the picnic tables outback, or even across the street at the GRAPE DAY PARK (pg. 531).

Hours: Open daily, 9:30am - 4:30pm. Closed major holidays.
Price: $6 for ages 1 and up; $3 for military.
Ages: 6 months to 7 years.

SAN DIEGO CHINESE HISTORICAL MUSEUM

(619) 338-9888 / www.sdchm.org $

404 3rd Avenue, San Diego

This very small museum, originally a Chinese mission, contains dishes and bottles dug up from the original Chinatown; replicas of the Terra Cota soldiers; the bed of Feng Yu-hsiang, a warlord of the early Republic of China; some traditional clothing; ancient Chinese coins; a sixteen-panel pictorial history; and more. Changing exhibits have included Chinese opera costumes, calligraphy, paintings, and children's hats. A stone path, outside, leads to a memorial gate and tiny Asian garden with a short waterfall and a fish pond. One-hour guided tours are offered that include this building and the sister building across the street that contains a few more exhibits. Classroom presentations are available that focus on the art of Chinese writing, dragons, or Chinese paper cutting. Extend your time immersed in Chinese culture by going out to a nearby Chinese restaurant.

Hours: Open Tues. - Sat., 10:30am - 4pm; Sun., noon - 4pm. Closed Mon. and holidays.

Price: $2 for adults; children 12 and under are free. Metered parking is available in front of the museum.

Ages: 8 years and up.

SAN DIEGO COUNTY SHERIFF'S MUSEUM

(619) 260-1850 / www.sheriffmuseum.org   !/$

2384 San Diego Avenue, San Diego

Get deputized at this two-story, innocuous-looking adobe building. The museum houses two jails, lots of weapons (all made inoperable), and a wealth of displays and information. The two jails are from different eras: one is a replicated 1850's jail with saddles, guns, an old desk, and a safe all adding ambiance; the other is a more modern-day facility. Just a few minutes behind these bars will hopefully make an impact upon kids so that they won't want to do any time anywhere else. The weapons include Winchester rifles, colt revolvers, a submachine gun, numerous pistols, a pen gun, and a cane gun, among others.

One room contains a booking area with fingerprint and picture-taking stations. Some of the displays in here include inmate art and items that inmates have created to try to escape (e.g., "rope" made from sheets). Other exhibits include billys and cuffs; a roped-off crime scene and information panels on forensics; and a crime laboratory showing target papers revealing various gunshot angles, plus pipe bombs, mortars, and more. Listen to real police scanners. Sit on the police motorcycle that has working sirens and lights.

Upstairs walk through a working metal detector and into a recreated courtroom - you be the judge. A display on gangs, narcotics paraphernalia, and confiscated toy weapons is also here, plus a mannequin in full S.W.A.T. regalia. A corner honoring Search and Rescue teams has a wounded mannequin on a stretcher and a sheriff rendering aid. One display case shows what a washed check is and how to detect counterfeit money. A gallery here is dedicated to the memory of fallen officers and another area salutes the K-9 units. A helicopter (with realistic copter sounds) is outside in the adjacent garage.

A deputy sticker badge, a McGruff coloring book, and other information about the history of San Diego sheriffs and about prevention of crime are available here at no cost. School tours are given that fit in with California fourth-grade curriculum. (Younger and older kids, too, will glean a lot of helpful insight and information with a tour.) Don't forget to patrol the rest of Old Town while you're here. Look up OLD TOWN SAN DIEGO AND STATE HISTORIC PARK (pg. 544) to check out what else there is to see and do in the immediately vicinity.

Hours: Open most of the year, Wed. - Sun., 11am - 5pm; open until 6pm with daylight savings. Closed Mon., Tues. and major holidays.

Price: Free; there is a donation box with a $5 suggested donation for adults.

Ages: 5 years and up.

SAN DIEGO HALL OF CHAMPIONS - SPORTS MUSEUM

(619) 234-2544 / www.sdhoc.com $$$

2131 Pan American Plaza, Balboa Park, San Diego

Give your sports fans something to cheer about by taking them to the immense Hall of Champions. Over forty different sports are represented in this eye-catching, multi-level museum including basketball, hockey, boxing, table tennis, surfing, swimming, boating, fishing, motorsports, fencing, skateboarding, and freestyle motocross. Baseball and football each have their own large galleries filled with memorabilia. The exhibits showcase athletes such as Tony Hawk, Andy MacDonald, Ted Williams and Bill Walton, and teams such as the Padres - all associated with San Diego. What a

winning city this is! You'll see photographs, statues outfitted in sports attire, videos, trophies, medals, and lots of sports equipment such as game jerseys, balls, and even a racing boat and a motorcycle. Use touch screens to look up information on almost any athlete or team represented.

Is your child a sports broadcaster wannabe? He/she can get prepared by watching sports videos at the media center. An almost 150-seat theater is used for presentations, full-length feature films, and sometimes sports films and clips, and bloopers, which kids love. These are usually shown on the free Tuesdays. See BALBOA PARK (pg. 526) for a listing of all the museums and attractions within walking distance.

Hours: Open daily, 10am - 4:30pm. Closed New Year's Day, Thanksgiving, and Christmas.

Price: $8 for adults; $6 for seniors; $5 for ages 3 - 17; children 2 and under are free. Admission on the fourth Tues. of every month is free for San Diego County residents. Passports, which are good for one week from the date of purchase, can be bought to visit the fourteen museums in Balboa Park for $53 for adults; $29 for ages 3 - 12 (as many museums are free for younger children). See Museum Month, San Diego (pg. 708) for details about half-price admission in February.

Ages: 5 years and up.

SAN DIEGO MODEL RAILROAD MUSEUM

(619) 696-0199 / www.sdmrm.org
1649 El Prado, Balboa Park, San Diego

You won't have to railroad your children into coming to this museum. Just one of the things I learned here was the difference between model trains and toy trains. (Hint: The way they operate and the way they look are very different.) The museum houses the largest operating model railroad exhibits in America. Kids (and short adults) can step up onto platforms to get a closer look at the several huge layouts. Watch scale model trains make tracks through and around authentically landscaped hillsides and miniature towns that are complete with scale cars, trees, and people. One of the exhibits depicting the development of railroading in Southern California includes the Tehachapi Pass, and others incorporate the Cabrillo and Southwestern, and a Civil War era live steam locomotive. One of our favorites is the Pacific Desert Line, which has a model train going through a town, citrus groves, and a gorge, all of which can be seen by looking through real train car windows! A huge relief map of San Diego County is accompanied by a touch screen to aid visitors in taking a virtual tour of the area.

Kids will have the most fun in the toy train gallery, which features Lionel type 3-rail trains and more. Turn knobs, push buttons, and pull back on throttles to operate trains, make signal crossers flash, windmills turn, and toy trucks haul "rocks" to a loading dock. One model train even features sounds and smoke. A wooden Brio train set for younger children completes this interactive and at*track*tive room. (Next door is a club room/party room.) The kid's corner, upstairs, hosts storytime, crafts, and games at certain times during the week. As the railroad museum is always in the process of re*model*ing, it is fun and different every time you visit. See BALBOA PARK (pg. 526) for a listing of all the museums and attractions within walking distance.

Hours: Open Tues. - Fri., 11am - 4pm; Sat. - Sun., 11am - 5pm. Closed Mon., Thanksgiving, and Christmas. Call for other holiday hours.

Price: $8 for adults; $6 for seniors; $3 for students; $1 for ages 6 - 14; children 5 and under are free. Admission on the first Tues. of every month is free for San Diego County residents. Passports, which are good for one week from the date of purchase, can be bought to visit the fourteen museums in Balboa Park for $53 for adults; $29 for ages 3 - 12 (as many museums are free for younger children). See Museum Month, San Diego (pg. 708) for details about half-price admission in February.

Ages: 2 years and up.

SAN DIEGO MUSEUM OF ART

(619) 232-7931 / www.sdmart.com
1450 El Prado, Balboa Park, San Diego

This ornately edificed building primarily features European, American, Asian, and twentieth-century art. As with any art museum, my children's interest was sparked by having them look for differences in artistic styles or color, and looking at various choices of subject. Kids need to somehow participate with the art in order to enjoy it. My boys were intrigued most by the statues, especially the fighting Minotaur. The small Image Gallery room has touch screens that introduce and teach children (and adults) more about the paintings and sculptures throughout the museum. (Anything to do with computers draws this generation's interest!)

Although the museum has more appeal for older children, the quarterly Family Festivals, held on Sundays, are geared for all ages. Hands-on activities that relate to a current exhibit and live entertainment, plus free admission to the museum, make this an outing to look forward to. Other great draws include summer camp and free guided tours. Tip: If you're not sure your children will enjoy this museum, come on the third Tuesday of the month, when admission is free for residents. See BALBOA PARK (pg. 526) for a listing of all the museums and attractions within walking distance. A cafe is on the premises, too.

Hours: Open Mon. - Tues., 10am - 5pm; Thurs. - Sat., 10am - 5pm; Sun., noon - 5pm. Open Thurs. in the summer until 9pm. Closed Wed., New Year's Day, Thanksgiving, and Christmas.

Price: $12 for adults; $9 for seniors and military; $8 for students with I.D.; $4.50 for ages 7 - 17; children 6 and under are free. An additional admission fee is sometimes charged for some special exhibitions. Admission on the third Tues. of each month is free to view the permanent collection, for San Diego County residents. Passports, which are good for one week from the date of purchase, can be bought to visit the fourteen museums in Balboa Park for $53 for adults; $29 for ages 3 - 12 (as many museums are free for younger children). See Museum Month, San Diego (pg. 708) for details about half-price admission in February. See page xi for info on the Bank of America free weekend program.

Ages: 8 years and up.

SAN DIEGO MUSEUM OF MAN   ☼

(619) 239-2001 / www.museumofman.org $$$
1350 El Prado, Balboa Park, San Diego

A large portion of this museum is dedicated to the theory of evolution, with other exhibits regarding man's past, future, and his accomplishments over the years. The first floor permanent exhibits are in a jungle-like setting and contain plaster casts of tall, engraved, stone monuments (called stelae) recounting Mayan stories and histories of gods and rulers, in hieroglyphics. The other exhibits that we saw (they do rotate) consisted of tapestry hangings and a weaving demonstration.

Follow the footprints upstairs throughout five galleries that hold numerous, touchable artifacts and replicas with the collective title of Footsteps Through Time: 4 Million Years of Human Evolution. The theory of evolution is displayed via numerous visuals, such as skeletons and skulls of apes and man, side-by-side to compare and contrast; a theoretical timeline; and life-size models depicting what some scientists believe early man looked like. Many of the models are naked (and very hairy). One wall has imbedded fossils that shows how fossils are dated. Here you can walk through a Cro-Magnon cave and listen to the word "hello" in 100 different languages at the language kiosk.

Temporary exhibits reside in the next area. Counter Culture, the Secret Lives of Games was a huge hit with 1,400 games, from classic to board to computer, from all over the world represented here and many able to be played. Race: Are We So Different? incorporates looking at skin under a microscope (no difference in races), and exploring physical cultural differences, including the impact racism has had on history. Strange Bones: Curiosities of the Human Skeleton had bones displaying results of dwarfism, scurvy, neck rings, fused bones, and more. An outside area allows visitors to try their hand at being an archaeologist by uncovering finds in a sand pit.

In the primate hall human visitors can compare their hands and feet to apes and monkeys, and lift flaps to view videos of primates that ultimately ask the question, "Does this behavior look familiar?". One of several dioramas shows a recreation of a Neanderthal burial; another is a replica of the oldest cave painting. Video kiosks feature famous scientists discussing their finds and their work.

Peoples of the Southwest are represented by displays of pottery, Kachina dolls, and jewelry. A full-size, traditional, thatched Kumeyaay "house" is in this section, too. Hunters are represented by displays of weapons, tools, and foods. Our favorite exhibits, pertaining to this latter category, are the rabbit skin blanket, eagle feather skirt, shoes from fibers, and a quiver made out of a raccoon. Ancient Egypt is *tut*tilating with over 400 objects including real mummies, dating from around 330 B.C., plus wooden coffins, coffin masks covered with symbols of Isis, X-rays of mummies, mummified animals, and exotic jewelry. You can even print your name in hieroglyphics.

Experience Ancient Egypt, too, in the well-done, hands-on Children's Discovery Center by dressing up in appropriate clothing and headwear, building pyramids with blocks, trying your hand at hieroglyphics, shopping at a grocery store (with plastic food), and playing ancient games - all in a replicated noble's home. See BALBOA PARK (pg. 526) for a listing of all the museums and attractions within walking distance.

Hours: Open daily, 10am - 5pm. Closed Thanksgiving and Christmas.

Price: $12.50 for adults; $10 for seniors; $8 for ages 13 - 17; $6 for ages 3 - 12; children 2 and under are free. Admission on the third Tues. of every month is free for San Diego County residents. Passports, which are good for one week from the date of purchase, can be bought to visit the fourteen museums in Balboa Park for $53 for adults; $29 for ages 3 - 12 (as many museums are free for younger children). See Museum Month, San Diego (pg. 708) for details about half-price admission in February.

Ages: 5 years and up.

SAN DIEGO NATURAL HISTORY MUSEUM   ☼

(619) 232-3821 / www.sdnhm.org $$$$
1788 El Prado, Balboa Park, San Diego

Naturally, this multi-story museum is a favorite for kids to visit! The south entrance features a giant Foucault pendulum that provides visual proof of the earth's rotation. (Visitors usually stay here for a while, waiting to see if the pendulum will knock down a peg.) This hallway and adjoining rooms feature a child's favorite - dinosaurs, and more. Hanging overhead and standing on display are a thirty-foot model of the extinct megalodon shark; a whale calf; a T.rex; a fossil of an Ankylosaur; "fleshed" out models of dinosaurs; mastodons, saber-toothed cats, and wooly mammoth skeletons; a model of an extinct giant sea cow and baby; a pterosaur (your child will know what this is); compost cast of a lambeosaur; and numerous animal fossils to look at and some to touch, such as skulls and other bones, and a number of shells. You can even sit in the shell of a dinosaur egg. Murals painted by a paleoartist enhance the exhibits.

Take a walk on the wild side through a series of rooms which are recreated rainforests complete with animals, sounds, and hands-on exhibits such as swinging like a gibbon by grabbing the knobs on the wall. Put together a puzzle of dinosaur bones in the fossil lab or dig for bones in the sandy dino pit. Touch really large rocks and minerals on display such as obsidian, petrified wood, amethyst, jade, magma, marine fossils imbedded in marble, and a meteor.

In the downstairs main exhibit room is Water, A California Story. The room contains some taxidermied animals such as a mountain lion, sea otter, owl, and several waterfowl, as well as some insects that live in water plus live rattlesnakes, scorpions, lizards, and tarantulas - all behind glass. There are also photographs, fossils, the massive jaw of a finback whale, the cut-away of a dolphin, and some interactive exhibits that deal specifically with water. The 300-seat, giant-screen theater, also on the lower level, shows twenty-minute and forty-minute movies throughout the day. Past titles have included *Ocean Oasis, Dinosaurs Alive! 3-D,* and *Titans of the Ice Age 3-D.* The Dinosaur Cafe, which is not open every day, offers food for herbivores and carnivores.

The third floor has rotating photography and sculpture exhibits that are stylishly displayed, as you'd see in an art museum. We also saw a display devoted to animal skulls. Call or check the website to see what is currently being showcased. This museum also features standout, major, national traveling exhibits such as the Dead Sea Scrolls, Real Pirates and artifacts from the ancient city of Pompeii.

The museum offers many classes for all ages students (including field trips for minimum ten people for $6 for students, free/$8 for teachers and chaperones), tours, guided nature walks, family programs, camp outs, and even camp-ins. Several lab classrooms are also available here. If you visit on a Sunday, stay for a free (included with price of admission) live performance of Wacky Science Sundays with Ms. Frizzle at 12:15pm and 2:15pm. See BALBOA PARK (pg. 526) for a listing of all the museums and attractions within walking distance.

Hours: Open daily, 10am - 5pm. Closed New Year's Day, Thanksgiving, and Christmas. During special exhibits, daily museum hours are sometimes extended - 9am - 6pm.

Price: $17 for adults; $15 for seniors; $12 for military and ages 13 - 17; $11 for ages 3 - 12; children 2 and under are free. Giant 3-D screen theater shows are included with admission, except on free Tues. when the cost is $5 a show. Special exhibits can cause prices and hours to fluctuate, so always call first. Admission is free on the first Tues. of every month to the permanent exhibits, for San Diego County residents. Passports, which are good for one week from the date of purchase, can be bought to visit the fourteen museums in Balboa Park for $53 for adults; $29 for ages 3 - 12 (as many museums are free for younger children). See Museum Month, San Diego (pg. 708) for details about half-price admission in February. See page xi for info on ASTC reciprocal museum memberships.

Ages: 3 years and up.

SAN DIEGO POLICE MUSEUM   ☀

(619) 726-6151 / www.sdpolicemuseum.com   !

4710 College Avenue, San Diego

You have the right to remain silent, but not about this museum! Each of the several rooms is filled with police artifacts and memorabilia almost from its inception in San Diego to modern day, along with a multitude of mannequins dressed in uniforms from throughout the decades.

The first room has a wooden police desk with lamps, a typewriter, photographs and badges. Lining the upper shelf that goes around the room are police hats from all over the world. There is also a public telephone booth in here. For show, not for use. An open conference room is across the way with a huge display of badges, more photos and posters. The jail cell, a replica of one used until the 1970s, holds two prisoners, a sink, a toilet and a shelf of personal items, plus a bell used in 1913. Outside of the cell is a motorcycle police officer, standing next to his motorcycle. There is also a parking meter, street sign, mural, more photographs and badges.

The large, main room holds a life-size statue of a saddled horse, saddlebags and all, to represent the mounted police. There are also street signs in here; another motorcycle; saddles; the first polygraph machine; manuals from 1889; old photographs; a police switchboard; a jackpot (which are legal if over 25 years old and not used for commercial purposes); helicopter models and uniforms; a tribute to WWII; and several display cases containing police helmets, handcuffs, batons, billy clubs, and lots of bullets and guns and other weapons. One section showcases narcotics and all kinds of drug paraphernalia, evidence kits, and a skull as a reminder of what drugs do. A mini crime lab features all the equipment used in solving a case including fingerprinting identification and composite sketches.

A hallway is lined with plaques honoring policemen killed in the line of duty. The small back room pays homage to S.W.A.T. team members with mannequins wearing gas masks, a sniper on an overhead shelf, shields, weapons, and gas canisters. Don't forget to pull over and check out the on-site gift shop.

Hours: Open Wed. - Fri., noon - 4pm; Sat., 10am - 2pm.
Price: Free
Ages: 5 years and up.

SAN DIEGUITO HERITAGE MUSEUM

(760) 632-9711 / www.sdheritage.org
450 Quail Gardens Drive, Encinitas

With a gas station and a cluster of other buildings at this mostly dirt parcel of land, guests can fill 'er up with history at this ranch house museum. Besides the buildings, some picnic tables and a random collection of vehicles - boat, fire truck and stagecoach - the museum consists of a home that houses displays of cases of tools, a variety of barbed wire, household items, dolls, toys, a mock Indian wickiup, maps, old photos, Mexican Ranchero costumes, a few surfboards, period-dressed mannequins, and a bed. The vintage toys were fun to look at. I appreciate the docent's willingness to explain the items, and the paper and pencil treasure hunt that got the kids involved with the exhibits.

Educational tours are offered to students (and other groups) to learn pioneer and Native American history by a guided tour of the museum and then hands-on learning as participants barter, make butter, make shanties, do a sand painting, and play Native American games. Check the website or call to find out about free family activities often offered on weekends such as soap making, cattle roping, seed planting, adobe brick making and more.

Hours: Open Thurs. - Sun., noon - 4pm.
Price: Free; suggested donations are $4 for adults; $3 for seniors. Special tours are $4 a person.
Ages: 5 years and up.

SERRA MUSEUM - PRESIDIO PARK

(619) 232-6203 / www.sandiegohistory.org
2727 Presidio Drive, San Diego

Located just above OLD TOWN SAN DIEGO AND STATE HISTORIC PARK (pg. 544), picturesque Presidio Park has green rolling hills and lots of old shade trees. Follow the signs and walk along the Old Presidio Historic Trail and you'll be walking in the footsteps of settlers from centuries ago.

On a hilltop in the park sits the mission-style Junipero Serra Museum. It was built in 1929 to commemorate the site where Father Junipero Serra and Captain Gaspar de Portola established California's very first mission and fortified settlement. Outside the museum is an old wine press. Inside, the first floor contains 400-year-old Spanish furniture, some of which is quite elegant. Second story exhibits include clothing, weapons (such as a cannon and cannon balls), art, artifacts from the outside dig site, and house wares that belonged to Native American and early Spanish/Mexican residents. There is also a room dedicated to the founder, Father Serra, that contains personal belongings and items given to him. A seven-minute video is shown throughout the day that describes San Diego's beginnings. Upstairs, in a

bell-like tower, look through the windows for an unparalleled view of San Diego.

Hours: The park is open daily, sunrise - sunset. The museum is open to the public mid-September - May, Sat. - Sun., 10am - 4pm; open June - mid-September, Fri. - Sun., 10am - 5pm. Tours for ten or more people and school tours are given by reservation Tues. - Thurs., September - July.

Price: The park is free. The museum is $6 for adults; $4 for seniors and students; $3 for ages 6 - 17; children 5 and under are free. Guided school tours are $6 per student. See Museum Month, San Diego (pg. 708) for details about half-price admission in February.

Ages: The museum is best suited for ages 7 and up.

SOLANA BEACH HERITAGE MUSEUM

(858) 259-7657 / www.solanabeachcivicandhistoricalsociety.org
715 Valley Avenue, Solana Beach

The house looks like just a regular home from the outside, but it was first built in 1887. Step inside to experience a bit of history with furnishings from that time period. The rooms hold antique treasures such as a wood-burning stove that looks ready to use; an ice box; hand water pump; old fashioned clothes washer and wringer (so NOT fun looking to have to use); treadle sewing machine; phonograph; and more. It's enlightening to compare these implements with those of a 1930's kitchen and living room that are also here. These rooms contain a washing machine with a spin dryer, wall phone (still old-fashioned), player piano, a huge radio, and much more. A photo and informational time line shows the progression of the inhabitants of early California. Note that docents dress in period costumes for school, scout, and seniors tours.

Hours: Open to the public the first and third Sat. from 1pm - 4pm. Group tours can call to arrange a visit at other times.

Price: Free

Ages: 8 years and up.

STEIN FAMILY FARM

(619) 477-4113 / www.thesteinfamilyfarm.org
1806 F. Avenue, National City

Smack in the middle of urban life, this "as-is" farm "museum" is a work-in-progress with its gardening plots and wild grass covering the grounds; a small farmhouse; a weather-beaten stable; and some rusting, dilapidated farm equipment. Informal tours allow visitors a glimpse into the past.

The farm house has original furnishings, such as a potbellied stove, clothing from the 1800's in the bedroom, and a stereo optic view finder. The barnyard animals include a few pigs, chickens, and bunnies. The animals, the information dispensed about yesteryear, and the casual tone of the tour makes the family farm interesting for kids. School and other groups are encouraged to come visit and learn, as well.

Hours: Open to the public Sat., 10am - 2pm. Call for other days and times.

Price: Free

Ages: 5 years and up.

USS MIDWAY MUSEUM

(619) 544-9600 / www.midway.org
910 North Harbor Drive, alongside the Navy Pier, San Diego

At 1,001 feet in length, this floating city is utterly gigantic! The USS Midway, launched in 1945, is the longest-serving carrier in naval history with participation in WWII, the Korean, Vietnam, and Persian Gulf wars. It has supported up to seventy-two aircraft and had a crew of 4,500. Currently, there are over sixty aircraft on display with twenty-nine in the process of being restored. Pick up a free audio guide narrated by various people, many whom have lived and served on board the Midway. They dispense valuable facts and fascinating stories involving the carrier's history and personnel. There are more than thirty labeled stops along the way. Note that there is also a Family Audio Tour that appeals to younger listeners. Kids cans earn jr. pilot wings, too. Live docents are located throughout the museum and they are always eager and willing to share stories and information - wonderful and wonderfully helpful!

Walk up the stairs to the hangar deck to start your tour. Note that the Midway has only been somewhat spruced up as a museum, so it still feels like an authentic aircraft carrier. Climb aboard authentic Navy cockpits and aircraft throughout the museum. First up is a multi-media theater experience to get a better understanding and sensation of the actual Battle of Midway. This hangar deck contains aviation weapons, photo displays, an A-4C Skyhawk, an F-14

Tomcat, and restored SNJ Trainers. Behind the information counter are the berths - confining, triple-layered bunk beds with small, attached metal lockers to store belongings. May your children never quibble about their rooms being too small again. Enter a twelve-person simulator and experience the sensation of being yanked to a stop from 150 mph and engaged in a catapult launch toward the heavens, for $6 per person. The two-seater Air Combat 360 simulator lets you control the rolls, spins, and loops into the wild blue yonder for $8 per person or $16 for single rider. Reservations for simulators can be made in advance.

Below, on the second deck, is the galley, mess hall (low ceilings, so watch your head) complete with tables, machine and metal shop, and post office. Since space was at a premium on warships, sailors had to be careful what they ate because mess decks also served as areas to assemble bombs and missile components, before they were taken topside.

The top "floor," or flight deck, offers a breathtaking view of the San Diego Harbor. On this four-acre deck (equivalent to eight football fields) are numerous military jets and helicopters, including a Huey Gunship assault helicopter, some F-4s Phantom II, an A-6 Intruder, an A-7 Corsair, and an E-2C Hawkeye. Again, there are some planes to actually board (tho not fly!). Line up for two tours, as each destination can hold only about twenty people at a time: With access by metal ladder stairs, one tour goes to the top of the carrier, and the other goes moderately high. Up in the tiny Pri-fly office, you'll learn about the air boss's job as told by ex-navy docents. You may even sit at the control panels and visualize how jets are catapulted into flight and "trapped" when coming back, with a wire. The captain's at-sea cabin, the chart room, and the open-air bridge are also in the immediate vicinity.

One-hour, behind-the-scenes, guided tours are available throughout the day for $30 per person for groups of ten or more. This fee includes entrance to the museum so participants can continue to explore the ship on their own. Youth have numerous options available to them such as two-hour On Board education programs that includes visits to the decks and detailed information about and interactions with the aircraft on display, plus learning labs with an emphasis on science, math, and or social studies for $7 to $10 per student. Experience life as a Navy seaman (or woman) by joining the Overnight Program for $85 per person. This can incorporate the On Board program, plus sleeping in the berths, eating in the mess hall, using the simulators, conducting evening and morning colors on the flight deck, and performing duties such as serving food, mess cooking (is this different than messy cooking?), standing watch, and cleaning compartments. Honorable student discharge includes a program patch. Your pilot wanna-be (no matter the age) can also enjoy a birthday party on board the ship.

The two cafes - one open year round and one on the flight deck open in the summer only - serve snacks, salads, sandwiches ($6 to $11), kids' meals, and beverages. A gift shop that's really ship shape is also on board the carrier. Wheelchair access from the Navy Pier to the hangar deck is readily available; however, the lift from the hangar deck to the flight deck operates only at 10:30am, 2pm, and 4pm. Loaner wheelchairs are available on a first come, first served basis. See MARITIME MUSEUM OF SAN DIEGO (pg. 537) for information on another close-by, waterfront attraction. You can't miss the giant statues closeby, along the waterfront. One is the famous scene of a WWII sailor kissing a nurse. *A National Salute to Bob Hope and the Military* has fifteen life-size bronze statues, representing servicemen and women from different wars, "listening" and cheering on a likeness of Bob Hope as he holds a microphone to entertain the troops.

Hours: Open daily, 10am - 5pm. (The last ticket is issued at 4pm.) Closed Thanksgiving and Christmas.

Price: $20 for adults; $17 for seniors; $13 college students and ages 13 - 17; $8 for retired military and ages 6 - 12; free for children 5 and under and active military personnel. Parking in the lot is $10 for up to 12 hours. Some metered parking is available along N. Harbor Blvd. See the February Calendar section (pg. 708) for details on half-off admission during February.

Ages: 5 years and up.

VALLEY CENTER HISTORICAL MUSEUM

(760) 749-2993 / www.vchistory.org

29200 Cole Grade Road, Valley Center

This small museum's centerpiece is a 100-year-old stuffed grizzly bear. (Grizzly bears have been extinct in California since 1924.) Other exhibits and pieces of history include a 19th-century reed pump organ, a saddle, typewriters, a school desk, and photos of stars who've passed this way. Check out the fully furnished settler's cabin from 1862 that contains a potbelly stove, clothing, furniture, and old kitchen implements and tools. It seems that the famous cook, Betty Crocker, was really Agnes White, a local resident; some of her cook books are featured here as well. A corner niche displays a Native American habitation site with pestle, acorns, baskets, and reed plants. Note that the five-by-eight-foot building outside, crafted in 1898, is listed in the Guinness World Book of Records as the world's

smallest post office. A stagecoach and a few other vintage coaches are also on the grounds.

Friendly docents offer tours to the general public and to school-age children during morning hours, by appointment. The museum is located next to the county library.

Hours: Open Tues. - Sat., 1pm - 4pm. Closed Sun., Mon., and most holidays.
Price: Free
Ages: 7 years and up.

VETERANS MUSEUM AND MEMORIAL CENTER

(619) 239-2300 / www.veteranmuseum.org

2115 Park Boulevard, San Diego

"The nation which forgets its defenders will be itself forgotten." (Calvin Coolidge) The Veterans center is a memorial dedicated to honor all the men and women who have served in all branches of the U.S. Armed Services, including the Merchant Marines.

The small museum is located in the former chapel of the Naval Hospital, which was built in the early 1940's and still retains the original stained glass windows. Display cases contain plaques, medals, gas masks, uniforms, and more memorabilia from WWI, WWII, the Korean War, Vietnam War, and Desert Storm. The Navy Seal's exhibit describes the skills and expertise required in underwater demolition. Several mannequins are dressed in military attire. Multitudes of military flags hang from the ceiling, with several versions of the American flag prominently displayed. A display table has a few uniforms and hats for kids to try on, as well as some war time field phones to use. Docents who have served in the military now serve as tour guides, so the information comes from those who have been there, done that. Memorial plaques are on the back lawn of the museum. Note: BALBOA PARK (pg. 526) is just across the street.

Hours: Open Tues. - Sun., 10am - 4pm. Closed Mon. and most major holidays.
Price: $5 for adults; $4 for seniors and veterans; $2 for students; free for military and children 12 and under. Passports, which are good for one week from the date of purchase, can be bought to visit the fourteen museums in Balboa Park for $53 for adults; $29 for ages 3 - 12 (as many museums are free for younger children). See Museum Month, San Diego (pg. 708) for details about half-price admission in February.
Ages: 7 years and up.

VISTA HISTORICAL MUSEUM

(760) 630-0444 / www.vistahistoricalsociety.com

2317 Old Foothill Drive, Vista

The Vista Historical Museum contains one large hall and four smaller halls with a little bit of everything such as old clothing, gloves, hats, a collection of typewriters, rock specimens, arrows, tools, a hair curler machine that looks like it's out of a science fiction story, and more. Take a self-guided tour around the museum or ask for a docent to explain the items. School groups are welcome.

Hours: Open Wed. - Fri., 10am - 2:30pm; the 1st and 2nd Sat., 10am - 2:30pm. Closed most holidays.
Price: Free
Ages: 7 years and up.

WHALEY HOUSE

(619) 297-7511 / www.whaleyhouse.org

2476 San Diego Avenue, San Diego

Built in 1847, this two-story brick house/museum is definitely worth touring. It has served in the community as a residence, store, theater, and courthouse, and is filled with numerous early California artifacts. It is also one of two authenticated haunted houses in California. The first room you're ushered into, the courthouse room, is fascinating. As you listen to the ten-minute tape explaining the history of the house and this time period, look around. Behind the railing is an old wooden judge's desk, and chairs for the jury. Along one wall is a bookshelf given to Ulysses S. Grant on his inauguration, and an 1860 lifemask (only one of six in existence) of Abraham Lincoln. Display cases in this room feature documents, spurs, pistols, Spanish helmets and swords, clothing, and ornate hair combs and fans. An early copy machine, a letter press, a handmade U.S. flag from 1864 (how many stars does it have?), plus pictures and portraits of George Washington, Abraham Lincoln, Ulysses S. Grant, and Robert E. Lee are also here.

The kitchen, with all of its gadgets, is downstairs, as is the beautifully decorated parlor and a small music room that contains a spinet piano used in the movie, *Gone With the Wind*. There are several bedrooms upstairs that can be

viewed through the protective glass in the doorframes. The bedroom behind the staircase has a decorative wreath, framed on the far wall. It is made from the Whaley girls' hair gathered from hairbrushes and then braided - something to keep the family busy on pre-television nights. The children's bedroom has dolls and toys, while the other bedrooms contain a soldier's dress uniform, mannequins clothed in elegant, ladies' dresses, a lacy quilt covering a canopy bed, and period furniture. I highly recommend taking a guided tour so you don't miss out on any of the background information. Ask about guided school tours. Ghost Tours are given that include going to the cemetery, for ages 12 and up, from 10:30m to midnight for $50 per person.

Exit through the backdoor into a small, picturesque, tree-shaded courtyard. A quick peek into the Old Town Drug Store Museum allows kids to see an old-time pharmacy containing bottles, patented medicines, and a mortar and pestle. Push a button to hear more of the building's history. See OLD TOWN SAN DIEGO AND STATE HISTORIC PARK (pg. 544) for details about other attractions in this immediate area.

Hours: Open Sun. - Tues., 10am - 5pm; Thurs. - Sat., 10am - 9:30pm. Closed Wed., Thanksgiving and Christmas. Call to check the hours for Christmas week.

Price: Daytime admission is: $6 for adults; $5 for seniors; $4 for ages 3 - 12; children 2 and under are free. Evening admission Thurs. - Sat., 5pm - 9:30pm, is $10 for adults; $5 for ages 3 - 12.

Ages: 7 years and up.

—PIERS AND SEAPORTS—

OCEAN BEACH MUNICIPAL PIER

(619) 224-4906 / www.oceanbeachsandiego.com

5099 foot of Niagara Avenue, Ocean Beach

At 1,971 feet into the ocean, the pier is purportedly the longest, T-shaped concrete pier in the world. Drop a fishing line and see what's biting - no license needed. If the fish aren't biting, grab a bite to eat at the Ocean Beach Pier Cafe on the pier, (619) 226-3474, which also has a bait and tackle shop attached to it. Ironically, you can order fish and chips, plus tacos, burgers, and more - and what an ocean view! Just the right ambiance for a cafe on a pier - a little weathered, and views of and over the ocean.

Underneath and just south of the pier, and by the rock jetty, are tidepools - great for exploring during low tide. North of the pier, bordering the sandy beach, is Ocean Beach Park, which is a patch of grass and some palm tress. The beach itself is a long stretch of sand and fairly wide as it kind of goes around a "corner" - popular for swimmers, surfers, and sunbathers.

Ride the Ocean Beach bike path, a separate pathway paralleling the street and part of the 8 freeway. It starts (or ends) at Voltaire Street, where there is a parking lot, and extends to Hotel Circle/Hotel Circle Place.

Hours: The pier is open 24/7.
Price: Free
Ages: All

OCEANSIDE BEACH PIER and HARBOR AREA

(760) 435-4030 - harbor; (760) 435-4500 - city of Oceanside / www.ci.oceanside.ca.us; www.oceansidechamber.com

At the end of Pier View Way at The Strand, Oceanside

The Oceanside Pier is one of the longest piers in San Diego County, and the majority of it is made from wood planks. It stretches out over the ocean almost 2,000 feet, or twenty minutes of walking, depending on the age of your youngest child. The spacious RUBY'S DINER (pg. 478) at the end of the pier is a 40's diner, serving great all-American food at good prices in a very kid-friendly atmosphere. Another pier-related activity is fishing. It doesn't require a license, so reel 'em in! A bait and tackle shop on the pier has pole rentals available. During low tide, look waaay down, over the edge of the pier to see the pylons covered with hundreds of barnacles and sea stars. The other end of the pier (the land end) offers an outdoor amphitheater (used for in-line skating when concerts aren't in session), and a community center.

On the beach is a playground with wooden climbing structures, sand volleyball courts, fire rings, picnic tables, bbqs, and, of course, miles of surf and sand. The beach north of the pier (Pier View North) has more sand than its southern counterpart, so there is more room. Pier View South draws more of a crowd because of the amphitheater and activities here. (Look under "Oceanside" in the city index for adjacent beaches, or just walk south for a little ways.)

Wear shoes with tread to carefully walk along the tidepools and go out on the rock jetties.

Breeze on over to the Oceanside Harbor, just a few streets north of the pier. The Harbor offers a choice of boat rentals at OCEANSIDE BOAT RENTALS (pg. 582). A few eateries, including Joe's Crab Shack restaurant and some shops make up a small "village" here. This area also has HARBOR BEACH / BREAKWATER WAY (pg. 469), offering more fire rings and picnic areas with barbecues, plus covered cabanas and RV camping.

Hours: Most restaurants are open daily, 10am - 6pm. Open extended hours in the summer.

Price: Parking costs about $8 at the beach from 4am - 8pm. There is some metered parking along Pacific St.

Ages: All

SEAPORT VILLAGE

(619) 235-4014 / www.seaportvillage.com

$$

849 W. Harbor Drive at Kettner Boulevard, San Diego

This delightful harbor-side shopping area is in an expansive, beautiful, park-like setting. There are three themed plazas here representing early California, a New England fishing village, and the Victorian era. Along its boardwalk and cobblestone "streets" the Village offers almost fifty unique shops, including Seaport Village Shell Co. and The Toy Cottage. There are several wonderful waterfront restaurants to choose from as well as numerous places for snackers to munch. Kids will enjoy riding a menagerie of fifty-four animals on the 100-year-old Looff Carousel located in the West Plaza. The carousel is open daily, 10am to 9pm. Rides cost $2 per person. Check the online calendar to see what special events are going on.

Hours: Open daily, 10am - 9pm. Open in the summer and on holidays one hour later.

Price: Technically, free. Parking is $3 for the first two hours with validation - a minimum of $10 purchase. Non-validated parking is $8 per hour. Or, take a trolley or bus here - look at the Transportation section for details.

Ages: All

—POTPOURRI—

BATES NUT FARM

(760) 749-3333 or (800) 642-0348 / www.batesnutfarm.biz

!/$

15954 Woods Valley Road, Valley Center

Is your family a little nutty? Then join nuts from all over the world at Bates Nut Farm. This 100-acre ranch features acres of open green grassy areas with shade trees and picnic tables. It is a welcoming and charming place to stop and relax. Nice-sized pens hold a variety of animals to feed (bring your own or purchase a bag here for 50¢) and pet through the fences - sheep, goats, llamas, an emu, ducks, mini donkeys, chickens, peacocks and geese.

The one-hour, Nuts For You tour, with a minimum of fifteen people, is offered year round, except October (when pumpkin tours are in season). The tour includes learning how nuts are grown and harvested and their nutritional value; a walk through the roasting and packaging rooms; going through where fudge is made; around the facilities; and a tractor-drawn hayride. Bring a picnic lunch to enjoy on the grounds. You are invited to seasonally pick your own pumpkins at the eight-acre pumpkin patch (page 747 in the Calendar section) and weave your way through a maze. In fact, groups of fifteen or more can take the Life of a Pumpkin a tour then that includes a walk through the maze, a hayride around the farm, learning all about pumpkins, and taking one home. Check the farm's website for their other great calendar events.

The larger store here has rows and rows of nuts (pecans, cashews, walnuts, and more), dried fruits, and candies, plus antiques, baskets, country crafts, and more. The smaller, adjacent Farmer's Daughter gift boutique sells books, dolls, collectibles, jewelry cards, and more country crafts. Remember, you've got *nut*in' to lose by coming here for a visit!

Hours: Open daily, 9am - 5pm.

Price: Admission is free. Nuts For You tours are $5.50 per person.

Ages: All

BLUES SCHOOLHOUSE (San Diego County)

(619) 299-BLUE (2583) / www.ihobf.org

!/$$

1055 Fifth Avenue, San Diego

See BLUES SCHOOLHOUSE (Los Angeles County) on page 162 for information about this upbeat, innovative school program. Also, see HOUSE OF BLUES GOSPEL BRUNCH (San Diego County) on page 475 for details about a delightfully southern brunch with gospel music.

Hours: The presentations are offered during the week from 10am - noon.
Ages: 5th - 12th grade

BUILD-A-BEAR WORKSHOP (San Diego County)

Chula Visa - (619) 482-9622; San Diego - (619) 542-1565 / www.buildabear.com
Chula Vista - 2015 Birch Road at Otay Ranch Town Center; San Diego - 7007 Friars Road in Fashion Valley

$$$

See the entry for BUILD-A-BEAR WORKSHOP (Orange County) on page 314 for details. The Chula Vista location is part of an outdoor mall, with several restaurants, a myriad of shops, and a movie theater. The San Diego location is also part of a mall that features a DISNEY STORE (pg. 562) and LEGO store (pg. 488), as well as a myriad of others.

Hours: Most stores are open Mon. - Sat., 10am - 9pm; Sun., 11am - 7pm.

CHALLENGER LEARNING CENTER

(619) 238-1233 / www.challenger.org; www.rhfleet.org

$$$$

1875 El Prado in the Reuben H. Fleet Science Center, Balboa Park, San Diego

What did you want to be when you grew up? I'm sure that you, or someone you knew, wanted to be an astronaut. The Challenger Center, established in memory of the Challenger crew and sponsored by NASA, allows school groups the opportunity to live out this dream while stationed on earth.

Students, who, for two hours, are transformed into mission specialists or crew members, work together to solve problems and make decisions at the realistic mock-up of Mission Control and a futuristic space station. Using computer consoles, communication headsets, continuous messages on the loud speakers, electronic messages, teammates they can sometimes only see on video monitors, and emergency sounds and flashing lights, they work to complete tasks on (simulated) space voyages just like astronauts in orbit. Some members use navigation charts to locate celestial objects in the star fields and control lunar landings. Others build, test, and launch probes to gather data and relay data for analysis. The isolation units use robots to handle "hazardous" chemicals and conduct tests, while some workers wear gloves to reach into a glass dome "box" to maneuver and pick up extraterrestrial samples. Life support people monitor and repair the spacecraft's water, air, and electricity while the data team transmits diagrams and info through a computer link. Two scenarios are offered: Voyage to Mars, or Return to the Moon. A third scenario, only an hour long (plus another hour in the main science building) and geared for younger students, is called Micronauts.

Teachers must attend a Mission Prep class and the center provides several weeks worth of curriculum. The center also offers *challeng*ing, week-long summer camps. Let your space pioneer help explore the final frontier! See REUBEN H. FLEET SCIENCE CENTER (pg. 548) for more information about the museum.

Hours: Missions are offered Mon. - Fri., 9am - 11am or noon - 2pm.
Price: Missions are $30 for the teacher training session and $395 (September through June) or $295 (July through August) for a class of 16 - 36 students (and 2 - 8 adults).
Ages: At least 10 years old.

DISNEY STORE (San Diego County)

(619) 299-0652 / www.disneystore.com; www.simon.com

!/$$

7007 Friar Road at the Fashion Valley mall, San Diego

See DISNEY STORE (pg. 314) for details about this interactive, Disney store - it's a whole new world! A BUILD-A-BEAR WORKSHOP (pg. 562), LEGO store (pg. 488) and more stores and restaurants are also at this mall, of course, as well as an occasional kid's event or activity.

Hours: Open Mon. - Sat., 10am -9pm; Sun., 11am - 7pm. Closed Thanksgiving and Christmas.
Price: Free
Ages: 1 - 10 years

FRY'S ELECTRONICS (San Diego County)

(760) 566-1300 / www.frys.com

!

150 Bent Avenue, San Marcos

See the entry for FRY'S ELECTRONICS (Los Angeles County) on page 170 for details.

GEMS OF PALA

☼

(760) 742-1356 / www.mmmgems.com

$$$

35940 Magee Rd., Pala

Located on the Pala Indian Reservation, the small Gems of Pala store offers a flawless selection of rocks and minerals. Both raw and polished emeralds, amethyst, opals, tourmaline, and more is available here. Outside, large bins hold chunks of rocks for sale.

Although the nearby Stewart Mine is no longer open to the public, it is still worked regularly and buckets of mine run, or tailings, are sold at this store. Purchase a bucket of the rocks and dirt, and dump the contents onto a screen on top of the tables outside. A worker will get you started, telling you what to do and what to look for. To look for "treasure," shake the screens and pour water over the rocks, and start sifting. This can be a bit arduous. Kids will be delighted with almost anything they find, although the jackpot is finding tourmaline. This precious stone comes in a rainbow of colors, with pink being the rarest and most highly prized color. The mine also produces kunzite, morganite, lepidolite, and more. Call first to make sure mine run is available and to reserve a bucket, if this is your goal, although reservations aren't necessary.

Hours: Open Sat. - Sun., 10am - 3pm, with buckets ready at 10:30am and 1:30pm, but arrive 15 min. before that time. Closed holidays that fall on a weekend sometimes in the winter - call first.
Price: $20 for a bucket of mine run, cash only.
Ages: 3 years and up.

LA JOLLA CAVE and THE CAVE STORE

◑

(858) 459-0746 / www.cavestore.com

$$

1325 Cave Street, La Jolla

This small building houses a few antiques and artwork. The real draw, literally located in the center of the store, is a natural sea cave locally known as Sunny Jim Cave. It's accessible via a 145-step downward "tunnel" dug in 1902. Once down in the small cave, the only things to see are a view of the ocean through the cave openings, and crabs crawling around on the rocks below. The trip down the steps, which get slippery toward the bottom, was the primary adventure. My boys were excited to tell everyone that they had been inside a real sea cave, though, so it was worth it. The store does also rent snorkel equipment, May through September for $20 for two hours.

Just outside the cave store are steps leading down close to the water's edge, enclosed by a fence. Look for the numerous pelicans on the rocks, the sea lions that frolic in the bay waters below, and the multitude of caves carved out of the cliff side. Facing the ocean and to the right is a quarter mile, or so, dirt trail leading along the hillside overlooking the ocean. Facing the ocean and to the left, just down the street, is the entrance to the sea caves. A fence blocks anyone tempted to go down, but you can see the opening to the caves. Continue walking along the sidewalk just a short distance to SCRIPPS PARK (pg. 519) and further on to reach SEAL ROCK MARINE MAMMAL RESERVE (pg. 594). Look up LA JOLLA SHORES BEACH (pg. 470) and LA JOLLA COVE KAYAK / SNORKEL ADVENTURE (pg. 581) for information on other nearby attractions.

Hours: Open daily, 10am - 5pm (last cave "tour" is at 4:30pm)
Price: Going down to the cave cost $4 for adults; $3 for ages 16 and under. Walking around to the other nearby sites is free.
Ages: 3 years and up.

LEGOLAND HOTEL

☼

(877) 534-6526 / www.legolandhotel.com

$$$$

One Legoland Drive

Just driving up to the three-story, 250 room hotel and you'll know you have arrived at Lego heaven - even the hotel looks like it was constructed out of Legos. It's not - it's sturdier. Enter the lobby, where your kids could play for hours. Beyond the large Lego dragon that is spewing out Lego bricks and an enclosed play area with more bricks, is a room that beckons. Follow the Lego-brick road up to it with its pirate ship, house-size castle and moat filled with Legos. Cross over the drawbridge, under the Lego ogre (pull the lever), and behind castle walls in a carpeted play area with a wall-size chalkboard are more Lego building areas (surprise!). Climb aboard the pirate ship (that looks like it's made from several gigantic Lego blocks) and steer the wheel on a course for adventure. I love the blue sky and cloud murals on the walls and ceilings, and the hot air balloonist hanging from the ceiling. The adjacent sitting area is Mini's

Lounge serving drinks and snacks - cereal, fruit cups, muffins, kids and grown-ups sandwiches, beverages and desserts.

Behind the registration desk in the lobby is a humongous wall of hundreds of Lego figures and an oversized Lego person who moves back and forth along the wall on a bike with wheels that act as magnifying lenses to more clearly (and largely) show all those tiny figures.

Walk past life-sized Lego figures to the buffet-style Bricks Family Restaurant. It features more intricately-made and fanciful characters. The paper tablecloths are designed with Lego shapes and people to color. Crayons are supplied. Food choices include a wide array of breakfast or dinner items - eggs, cereal, yogurt, bacon, potatoes, salad, chicken, Mexican food, pizza, mac and cheese, Chinese food, and more. In primary-colored chairs, outside patio dining is available, too, that is directly in front of the Legoland amusement park entrance. (The Lego dragon in the soap bubble bath out here gently passes gas.) You can also eat at the Skyline Cafe that has an entire glass-enclosed wall containing a 3-D city skyline - impressive. Note: Even the bathrooms downstairs are bedecked in Lego images. Even if you don't stay at the hotel, you are welcome to come and eat at the restaurants, as long as it is not maximized with hotel guests dining, and your kids can play in the lobby rooms. If you are here for dinner, you can even join in on the kid entertainment that usually starts at 6pm in the lobby. Tip: For dinner and play here, you can park in the hotel parking lot - just tell the attendant you are here for a meal.

Each of the three floors of the hotel is themed differently and completely - even the hotel hallways are Lego-themed, from the carpeting to the wall decor to the doorframes! The first floor is Kingdom - castle, knights, and royals; the second floor is Pirate; and the third, Adventure, meaning mostly Egyptian-style digs. Each room has a separate kid's area with two bunk beds and a trundle bed. In this just-for-kids "room" is a kid's treasure chest safe with toys inside - only to be opened after they complete a treasure hunt; a kid's TV; and their own, decorated bathroom. The attached adult sleeping quarters have a queen size bed, (a king size in the suites), with their own TV, plus a mini fridge and other amenities. Lego models prevail in each room - at least seven of them. The wall murals and hangings, pillows, bathrooms, shower curtains, and style of furniture immerse guests in one of the three themes and even more thoroughly in the premium rooms and suites - it's like living out a childhood fantasy.

Ride the elevator (spoiler alert) because when the doors close, disco lights pulsate against the mirrored ball and music blares while kids break out and boogie (and some younger ones get scared). Each floor is given different sound effects, too. What goes on outside the elevator? Umm - electronic whoopee cushions and other kid-giggle surprises.

Hotel guests enjoy nightly kid's entertainment with character visits, games, and brick building contests, plus early access to Legoland. The lovely outdoor pool offers lots of seating and lounge chairs (and more Lego figures - go figure). Build it and they will come. Build it with Lego bricks and they will come with their kids. Check out SEA LIFE AQUARIUM (pg. 593), LEGOLAND WATER PARK (pg. 464) and LEGOLAND (pg. 462) for more details about these attractions as they share the same property.

Hours: Brick Family Restaurant is open for breakfast, 7am – 10:30am and dinner, 5pm – 9pm. Minis Lounge is open 7am - noon and 2pm - 9pm. Skyline Cafe is open 11am – 10pm.

Price: Breakfast is $16.95 for adults and $8.50 for ages 4 to 12. Dinner is $19.95 for adults and $10 for ages 4 to 12. If you are staying at the hotel you can pre-purchase a package for four people, at time of booking, for $50. Children 3 and under eat free. Hotel rates start at $309, but average more in the $400+ range, plus a $25 resort fee.

Ages: 1 year and up.

MOUNT SOLEDAD VETERANS MEMORIAL   ☼

(877) 204-7661 or (858) 459-2314 / www.soledadmemorial.com   !
6905 La Jolla Scenic Drive South / Soledad Road, La Jolla

The twofold goal of this jaunt off the main road is to visit a Veteran's memorial and to get a fantastic, 360-degree view of San Diego county, encompassing the mountains to the ocean (on a clear day). Names and photos are engraved on black granite plaques that honor veterans from all wars. These plaques decorate the walls surrounding steps that lead up to a huge cross at the pinnacle of the mountaintop. We read many of the plaques and then enjoyed the magnificent view. There is a small grass area up here, a few benches, and some walkways that descend into the surrounding chaparral. At annual military-oriented events, bands and political and military speakers are part of the program.

Hours: Open daily, 7am - 10pm.
Price: Free
Ages: 8 years and up

OBSERVER'S INN

(760) 765-0088 / www.observersinn.com

3535 Highway 79, Julian

$$$$

Star light, star bright, first star I see tonight; I wish I may, I wish I might, have this wish I wish tonight. Fulfill a wish by visiting this unique Inn located in the mountains of Julian. Observant guests will see and appreciate the *star* attraction - the night sky displaying all its heavenly beauty. Us city folk rarely get the full picture of the vast array of celestial bodies, but in the mountains the people-manufactured lights fade away and God's lights take over in a dazzling display. A nineteen-foot by twenty-four-foot observatory with a retractable roof, houses several research grade telescopes, although visitors are invited to bring their own, as well. Take a one-hour "sky tour," as the Inn's owner acts as a guide around the visible universe, using a laser pointer to outline constellations and telescopes to focus on a star cluster or ring nebula or other heavenly bodies. The observatory is carpeted, has heat, a sound system, and couches, and is decorated with lots of astronomical photos. Beverages and cookies are offered, too.

This is an Inn, too, which means you may spend the night here. A detached guesthouse has two really nice, private, star-themed rooms (although the rooms can be adjoining) with queen-size beds and full baths decorated with celestial photographs. A living room-like lobby with TV, library, and CDs are also here. Single night booking is allowed Monday through Wednesday; at other times guests must stay for a two-night minimum, unless the weekend isn't booked by the Thursday prior. If you spend the night you are welcome to spend hours on the concrete observing pads just outside the observatory using your own telescope. Bring your 35MM camera to attach to a telescope for great moon pictures. Dress warmly, even during summer months, as nighttime temperatures can drop rapidly. Other activities include hiking on nearby trails, picnicking, resting in a hammock under shady oak trees (although technically, this isn't an activity), and seasonally sledding down hills. (B.Y.O.S. - Bring Your Own Sled.). An on-site gift shop is an authorized Meade dealership.

Hours: Call for hours.

Price: $25 per person for just the sky tour - advanced reservations are required. Guests of the Observer's Inn pay $20 for the sky tour. Nightly rates start at $160 for single or double occupancy, which includes a full, gourmet, Continental breakfast each morning of your stay. (No credit cards.)

Ages: 7 years and up.

OLD POWAY PARK

(858) 668-4575 - park; (858) 486-4063 - Poway-Midland R.R.; (858) 486-4575 - Hamburger Factory / www.ci.poway.ca.us; www.powaymidlandrr.org

!/$

14134 Midland Road, Poway

This charming park is set up like a small historic western village, complete with its own train depot. The two-acre grassy park boasts of shade trees, a gazebo, picnic tables, barbecues, crisscrossing pathways, and bridges over the creek. Come during the week to simply enjoy the park. Come on a weekend, however, for some action, because that's when the "town" is open and everything comes to life! Regular weekend activities include a farmer's market on Saturday mornings from 8am to 1pm; tours through the museum and house; and train rides. There are also arts and crafts booths from 8am to 2pm on the first Saturday of the month from February through May, then most Saturdays the rest of the year. The small Heritage Museum has glass-encased displays containing items from olden times in Poway such as pictures, clothing, a guitar, glassware, and a piano. The small Nelson House contains a turn-of-the century, fully furnished kitchen, living room, music room, and bedrooms. The blacksmith's shop puts on demonstrations of its craft the first and third Saturday of the month from 10:30am to 1:30pm. Last, but not least, take a short ride around town on a genuine steam engine train, trolley, or speeder car. Take a look into the train barn which houses the steam engine, a 1938 Fairmont Speeder, ore cars, and a 1894 Los Angeles Yellow Trolley. Don't forget to check out the many special events that go on here throughout the year, like summer concerts in the park and the Rendezvous in Poway. (See the Calendar section, pg. 746.) During the week, two-hour guided tours to learn the heritage of the park for organized groups of twenty or more are offered for $4 per person.

Bring a picnic lunch, or enjoy good old American food at the on-site Hamburger Factory. The Factory has wood-paneled walls that are decorated with buffalo heads, steer skulls, and more, giving it a rustic ambiance. The restaurant is open daily for breakfast, lunch, and dinner. Kids' meal choices include hamburger, chicken nuggets, a hot dog, or a grilled cheese sandwich. Meals come with fries and a drink for an average of $5.79.

Hours: The park is open daily. Rail cars operate on various weekends on Sat., 10am - 3:45pm; Sun., 11am - 1:45pm. The museum and Nelson house are open Sat., 10am - 2pm; Sun., 11am - 2pm. All of the proceeding attractions are closed the second Sun. of each month, Easter, and the last few weeks in December. The restaurant is open daily, 7am - 9pm.

Price: The park is free. The following pricing for train rides is for adults (as children 12 and under are 50¢) -$1.50 (speeder), $2 (trolley), $2.50 (cable cars), $2.50 (steam) - operates the 1st and 3rd weekends. Donations are requested for the museum and Nelson House.

Ages: All

SALVATION MOUNTAIN

(760) 624-8754 / www.salvationmountaininc.org

601 East Beal Road, Niland (It's actually in Imperial County, east of San Diego County.)

You might not find salvation on this mountain, though the words "God is LOVE" is predominant, but you will find a divinely interesting place to explore. An incredibly eclectic and colorful collage of mostly Bible sayings and pictures "painted" and built on the mountainside by incorporating adobe clay, straw, and found materials, grabs visitors visually and then fills their minds and hearts with a little bit of wonder. You'll see lots of flowers; a painted waterfall going down the mountainside; trees supporting some domed roofs; pictures of some recognizable things; the Lord's Prayer; the nine fruits of the spirit (from the New Testament book of Galatians); and lots and lots of color.

Follow the yellow brick road (i.e. yellow steps) up and around the mountain, which is about 100 feet high and 150 feet across. The view from the top is terrific. You can even walk underneath it all, as it has a few tunnels and caves - all wildly decorated. Call it folk art; call it whimsical; the creator (as well as the Creator) of this Mountain desired to spread the message of God's unconditional love to the world, and this mountain has been his canvas. Note: Make sure to visit SALTON SEA STATE RECREATION AREA (pg. 515) while you are here because it's just down the road a bit.

Hours: Open daily, sunrise - sunset.

Price: Free

Ages: 3 years and up.

SMITH RANCH & JULIAN RAILROAD

(760) 765-2288 / pioneerw.ipower.com

Off Banner Road/ 78 on Ethelwyn Lane, Julian

"Go West, young Man, go West!" and if you are at Smith Ranch, not only are you west, but you are going to experience what life was like in the Old West. The working Smith Ranch is reminiscent of those days with its rural location, numerous fruit trees in the ranch's orchards as well as other mountain trees, dirt trails, and clean air. The ninety-minute Julian Train & Gold Mine Tour is a favorite for "groups" of at least four or more. A fun endeavor in and of itself, visitors board the authentic 18" gauge mining train (with open-air, wooden cars that are wheelchair accessible) and travel a half mile (about twenty minutes) over trestle bridges and through the woods while learning about nature and historic events that took place locally. Disembark at an original 1870 gold rush mine. Ride an authentic ore cart or walk about forty-feet into the mine while hearing the history of it and the Gold Rush. Look for the pick marks. Note that a Christmas train runs starting the Saturday after Thanksgiving through December.

Outside at the miner's camp are a few artifacts discovered when cleaning out the mine, such as an original miner's pick and shovel, a candle, and some other items. Watch a demonstration on mining and then pan for gold, which is not as glamorous as it might seem. Cash in your gold for treats. Cross the rope bridge here and enjoy the mountain scenery. Take the train ride back, and then go into the town of Julian for some fun shopping.

School and other groups, with a minimum of twenty people, are invited to participate in living history field trips. These include the Pioneerways Adventure (3.5 hours long), American Revolution Adventure (3.5 hours), Pilgrim Thanksgiving Adventure (2.5 hours) and Christmas Train Express (1.5 hours). The field trips all include the train ride and a visit to the mine. The pioneer tours include activities such as joining a fire brigade, trying your hand at a hand plow, helping build a fort, caring for horses, joining in the Pony Express, grinding grain, and more. The American Revolution includes witnessing Paul Revere's ride, colonial farming, making hasty pudding, making decisions about signing the Declaration of Independence, or not, serving as a crew member aboard a warship, and making colonial crafts such as tin punching, leather working, and candle dipping. The cost for most tours is about $15 per person. See history. Experience history. Live history.

Hours: The Julian Train & Gold Mine Tour is available Mon. - Sat. at 10am, 11:30am, 1pm, and 2:30pm. Reservations are necessary. Closed Sun. and during inclement weather.

Price: Train & Gold Mine Tour is $15 per person; $12 for ages 3 - 12; children 2 and under are free.
Ages: 3 years and up.

SUMMERS PAST FARMS ☀

(619) 390-1523 / www.summerspastfarms.com !/$
15602 Olde Highway 80, Flinn Springs

Experience a genteel way of life (yes, even with kids) at Summers Past Farms. Although the Farm is not large, its beautifully landscaped gardens, blooming with a variety of flowers and herbs, almost ensure a delightful (and fragrant) *thyme* here. The plants are both for show and sale. One of the small gardens has a little creek with a bridge over it. There is a grassy area with trees, trellises, and white wrought-iron benches. The lavender field has a Provence-style facade. No farm is complete without its resident animals, such as cats, dogs, a few birds, and rabbits.

One of the retail shops, housed in a big red barn, offers potpourri, wreaths, baskets, teas, essential oils, lotions, dried and fresh flowers, and more. Craft classes are available. The other shop is Ye Old Soap Shoppe offering a wide variety of *scent*sational herbal soaps. Pick up a free sample (I chose Lavender/French Vanilla), and maybe you'll even get to see (and smell) the owner mixing essences for his soaps. You may purchase soap-making supplies, or a complete soap-making kit that includes everything you need to make eight pounds of herbal soap for about $72.95.

Check out the Farms website for calendar events like a pumpkin patch and fairy festival, and enjoy coffee, ice tea, and pastries on weekends.

Hours: Open Wed. - Sat., 9am - 5pm; Sun., 10am - 5pm.
Price: Free
Ages: 5 years and up.

TIJUANA, MEXICO ☼

(888) 775-2417 - Tijuana Tourism Board; (800) 44MEXICO (446-3942) / www.tijuana.com; $$$
www.venatijuana.com

Hola! Come spend the day in a foreign country without the European price tag (or luxuries, majestic sights, etc.). YOU MUST HAVE A PASSPORT - not to enter the country; only if you want to get out! There are several ways you can arrive at and enter into Mexico: 1) Drive into Mexico; 2) Take a tram from downtown San Diego to the border, and then take a taxi or walk across; or 3) Drive your own car almost to the border, park on the U.S. side, and then walk or take a shuttle across. Following are more details about the above options: **Option 1** - If you drive into Mexico you must buy Mexican automobile insurance because American insurance doesn't mean anything over there. The border town of San Ysidro has several places to purchase Mexican insurance. The cost depends on the coverage you are buying and the value of your car but about $30 for the day. A few other things to take into account if you drive into Mexico: You will experience lines getting into and especially getting out of Mexico in the afternoon as it's rush hour traffic (actually this occurs no matter what mode of transportation you use); parking can be a problem (I mean challenge); and if you think that Los Angeles drivers are scary - you ain't seen nothing yet! For those who like to live life on the edge - drive into Tijuana. **Option 2** - Take the blue line trolley/bus to Mexico from downtown San Diego, which costs $2.50 one-way for ages 6 and older; $1.50 for seniors. Trolleys run every few minutes, from 5am to 1am. Check the website for all the stations, from American Plaza and downtown at the northern end to San Ysidro. Check (619) 595-4949/(619) 557-4555; www.sdmts.com for locations, maps, and information. There are several stations that offer free parking, like Bayfront and E St. - check the website. The trolley takes you to the border where you can walk across the bridge or take a taxi into Mexico. It's about a mile from the border to the main shopping area in Tijuana. Even if you walk into Tijuana, you might consider taking a cab or shuttle out because you'll be carrying shopping bags, and your children will be tired (and so will you!). Taxis are plentiful, but determine exactly where you are going first, and decide on a price before you get into the cab. The fare is usually $7 to Avenida Revolucion. **Option 3** - This was our personal choice, and it was fairly hassle-free. We parked on this side of the border at Border Station Parking - signs off the freeway direct you to the huge parking lots at 4570 Camino de La Plaza in San Ysidro. The cost is $7 during the week; $10 on weekends for all-day parking, and attendants are on duty twenty-four hours. (Note: Just behind Border Parking are factory outlet stores. More shopping!) Call (619) 428-9477 / www.borderparking.com for more info. Then, we took a Mexicoach shuttle ($6 per person, round trip), which runs every half hour or so from 8am to 9pm, from the parking lot into the heart of the oldest Tijuana shopping district - Avenida Revolucion, which is seven blocks of tourist-shopping heaven. You may buy up to $400 of duty free goods in Tijuana. You then can take the bus back, walk over the border to show your passport, and board the bus again to the parking lot.

Shopping along Avenida Revolucion is an experience. The numerous small shops, most of which are open daily,

10am to 9pm, have goods almost overflowing onto the sidewalks that practically scream at your children to buy them. Vendors are constantly hawking their wares, enticing you, begging you, to come into their store. Be tough. Tips to keep in mind when shopping: 1) Don't feel obligated to buy just because you asked the price. 2) I can almost guarantee that you will see that exact same item at least ten more times. 3) Never pay the original asking price. Bargaining is expected. As a rule of thumb, pay around half (or a little more) of the asking price. Be willing to go higher if it's something you really want or can't live without. (Decide beforehand how much the item is worth to you.) Haggle if you want it, but be prepared to walk away in order to get a better price, or if it isn't the price you want. 4) Prepare your children beforehand that they won't always get the item being bargained for, if the price is still too high, etc. 5) Lastly, and most importantly, teach your children to not say, "I love it - I must have it!" in front of the merchants.

Merchandise that appeals most to kids includes leather vests, hats, boots, purses, gold and silver jewelry, kids' guitars, gaudy ceramic figurines, watches, blankets, ponchos, and knickknacks. The more mature shopper will enjoy leather goods and jewelry, too, as well as perfumes, pharmaceutical supplies, clothing, and more. On every street corner you'll find the touristy-looking carts hooked up to donkeys (painted to look like zebras) along with gaudy sombreros available for you to wear while having your picture taken - $5 for a Polaroid, $1 with your own camera. (Our pictures turned out nice!)

There are other places to shop in Tijuana besides Avenida Revolucion. Try Avenida Constitucion, which is the next street over, and Plaza Rio Tijuana Shopping Center - near the Cultural Center - which has a few major department stores and specialty shops. The latter is a long walk, or a short drive, from Avenida Revolucion. Mercado Hidalgo is only five minutes from the border and often overlooked. It is a true Mexican marketplace where locals shop for produce and specialty items, such as spices and cookware.

We walked around downtown Tijuana, just beyond the shopping district. Tijuana has been cleaned up and renovated in certain areas, but we also saw a lot of poverty, broken sidewalks, and people setting up shop in much less healthy environments than would be allowed in the States. It was an eye-opener for my kids. And, since they couldn't read any of the signs, it gave them an understanding of how difficult it is for foreigners in America to get around. Tip: Bring your own water, still.

There are several nearby attractions in Tijuana. Note: The 01152-664 number designates making an international phone call and the area code; the other digits are the actual phone number. **Bullfights** at Plaza Monumental de Playas, near the border, and on Agua Caliente Blvd. at the Tijuana Bullring: Fourteen fights are held May through September on Sunday afternoons. Tickets range from $16 to $50. Call (01152-664) 680-1808, (01152-664) 686-1510 for more info. **Centro Cultural Tijuana** at Paseo de los Heroes y Mina: The Museum of the Californias is good, although the art gallery wasn't that exciting to my kids. The Centro also has a planetarium/Omnimax theater. (The shows, of course, are in Spanish.) Contact (01152-664) 687-9600 / www.cecut.gob.mx for more info. **Hipodromo Caliente** at Blvd. Agua Caliente y Tapachula: Greyhound races takes place here. There is a small zoo on the grounds, too. Check (01152-664) 682-3110 / bet.caliente.com.mx for more info. **Mexitlan** at Calle 2 and Avenida Ocampo: This city-block-long attraction houses about 200 scale models of Mexico's most important monuments, buildings, churches, plazas, archaeological sites, and more. This is a great way to get an overview of the country. Call (01152-664) 638-4101 for more info. **Mundo Divertido** (Family Entertainment Center) at 2578 Paseo de los Heroes y Jose Ma: This Family Fun Center offers the same fun, and at comparable prices, as the Boomers! fun centers in the States - miniature golf, batting cages, bumper boats, go karts, video and arcade games, and amusement rides such as a roller coaster and a kiddie train. Call (01152-664) 634-3213 for more info. Another **Mundo Divertido** is located at Mundo Divertido Plaza in La Mesa. This facility offers bowling, too. **Rodeos** at Lienzo Charro and Avenida Bravlio Maldonado: Call (01152-664) 680-4185 for dates, times, and prices. **Parque Estatal Morelos** at Blvd. Insurgentes 16000: This state park and ecological reserve has large open spaces, grassy lawns for picnicking, and a Creative Center for children that offers a lake, an open-air theater, botanical gardens, children's rides, and games. Call (01152-664) 625-2469 for more info. **Wax Museum of Tijuana** at First Street 8281 near Avenida Revolucion: This museum is home to over eighty waxy, lifelike historical figures and movie stars such as Mikhail Gorbachev, Emiliano Zapata, Elvis Presley, Marilyn Monroe, and Christopher Columbus. It's open daily from 10am - 6pm. Admission is about $2; children 5 years and under are free. Call (01152-664) 688-2478 for more information.

     Hours: Most shops are open daily, 10am - 9pm.
     Ages: 5 years and up.

U.S. OLYMPIC TRAINING CENTER

(619) 656-1500 / www.chulavistaca.gov; www.teamusa.org
2800 Olympic Parkway, Chula Vista

This beautiful facility is nestled in a mountain range by the blue waters of Otay Lakes. The 155-acre campus is the training grounds for future Olympians (and other athletes) as they prepare for the thrill of victory (not the agony of defeat). Throughout the day, the visitors' center shows a free ten-minute video that arouses the Olympic spirit in all of us.

Free, guided tours of the facility are offered, or just take a detailed map and stroll along the paved Olympic Path on your own. The path slices through the center of the facility. It is elevated so you get a bird's eye view of the sports that are played on both sides, including soccer, field hockey, tennis, track and field, cycling, baseball, beach volleyball, and archery. Water sports, such as rowing, canoeing, and kayaking can also be observed from this vantage point, if there is anyone using the facility. Visitors are asked to stay on the path, which is nine-tenths of a mile each way, as it winds through the training center. Call ahead or check the website to see which athletes are currently training here because seeing them in action makes the center come alive! The facility also has athlete housing, an athlete dining area, a medical facility, and more.

Hours: Open daily, 9am - 4pm. Guided tours are given Sat. at 11am. Call to schedule a group guided tour at another time.

Price: Free

Ages: 6 years and up.

WALTER ANDERSON NURSERY

(858) 513-4900 / www.walterandersen.com

12755 Danielson Court, Poway

Nurseries aren't a normal entry for a children's guidebook, but if you are in the Poway vicinity and your child is a train buff, this is a great little stop off. Walk through the building and then through the abundance of plants (I wish my yard, or any portion of my yard, looked like this) to reach the massive train layout with 1,400 feet of track. Watch the train make tracks around and through an almost magical area of waterfalls, bridges (fifteen of them), a trestle (118 feet), tunnels, a variety of plants, a lake with real pond plants, rocks, and a "populated" city. Delightful!

Hours: The nursery is open daily, 9am - 5pm. The train runs daily, 10:30am - 4pm. Closed New Year's Day, Easter, 4th of July, Thanksgiving, and Christmas.

Price: Free

Ages: All

—SHOWS AND THEATERS—

CALIFORNIA BALLET COMPANY

(858) 560-6741 or (858) 560-5676 / www.californiaballet.org

$$$$

San Diego

This professional ballet company tours throughout San Diego giving performances at the CALIFORNIA CENTER FOR THE ARTS (look at the next entry) and other places, including in-school performances, out-reach performances, backstage tours, and Girl Scout Patch programs. They perform three to four, ninety-minute ballets a year. Past family-oriented shows, usually put on in the spring, have included *Alice in Wonderland* and *Snow White*. The associated junior ballet company, with performers between the ages of 12 and 17 years, put on a yearly show. The company also offers dance classes of ballet and jazz for children 3 years and up.

Hours: Call for a schedule.

Price: Prices depend on the theater venue.

Ages: 6 years and up.

CALIFORNIA CENTER FOR THE ARTS, ESCONDIDO AND FAMILY PERFORMANCES

$$$

(800) 98-TICKETS (988-4253); (760) 839-4138 - museum / www.artcenter.org

340 N. Escondido Boulevard, Escondido

All the world's a stage and kids are invited to come watch the world, or at least a part of it. Broadway musicals, comedies, dramas, dance troupes, classical concerts, operas, and other of the finest, top-name entertainment around is performed at the center. Many productions are perfect for the entire family. Past productions have included *The Sound of Music, Joseph and the Amazing Technicolor Dreamcoat, Late Nite Catechism,* a barbershop quartet, and the singer, Charice.

Special matinee student performances are offered throughout the year for only $4 a show. Past performances for families include *The Magic Schoolbus, Lazer Vaudeville, Bob the Builder Live!,* and *The Hobbit,* which was performed with large puppets. Children's performances can also include art projects, meeting the artists, and museum admission. And check out Wow First Wednesdays when performances are free for the public. They are given on Wednesdays (of course!) at 1pm, 4pm and 7pm, but get here earlier because show seating can fill up fast.

The small museum at the center focuses on contemporary and twentieth-century art. Hour-long, docent-guided tours of the museum are offered for kindergartners to adults. Through the education program, tours are followed by another hour, or so, of making exhibit-related projects. The projects are geared for a maximum of thirty-five kids, at a minimal cost. Take advantage of this terrific way to *really* learn about art - what kids make, they will remember better.

Hours: Call for the names and dates of productions. Family Performances are usually on the weekends. The museum is open Thurs. - Sat., 10am - 4pm; Sun., 1pm - 4pm. Closed Mon. and major holidays. Museum tours are offered by reservation. See the company's website for classes and special events.

Price: Prices vary depending on the show. Family Performance tickets start at $10 per person. The museum is $8 for adults; children 12 and under are free. The museum is free on the first Wed. of every month and often free to ticket holders on the day of performance. See Museum Month, San Diego (pg. 708) for details about half-price admission in February.

Ages: 5 years and up.

CLASSICS FOR KIDS
(619) 231-2311 / www.classics4kids.com
all around San Diego County, with a primary venue of Balboa Theater.

Committed to introducing elementary-school aged kids to and getting them involved with a life-long love for theater arts, Classics for Kids produces professional musical performances at various venues throughout San Diego and Escondido. *The Magic Flute,* for instance, incorporated the Classic Philharmonics, City Ballet of San Diego dancers, and opera vocalists. *Carnival of the Animals* blended ballet and symphony music with a magic art. Concerts for families and for schools, even school assemblies with curriculum supplements, are scheduled throughout the year.

Hours: Call for a schedule.
Price: Family show tickets are $12 - $20 per person. School show tickets are $6 per person for groups of ten or more.
Ages: 6 - 12 years

IMAX DOME THEATER
(619) 238-1233 / www.rhfleet.org
1875 El Prado, Balboa Park, San Diego

See the entry for REUBEN H. FLEET SCIENCE CENTER on page 548 for details as the museum houses the IMAX Theater.

LAMB'S PLAYERS THEATRE
(619) 437-6000 / www.lambsplayers.org
Coronado - 1142 Orange Avenue; San Diego - 444 Fourth Avenue at Horton Grand Theater

This theatre troupe offers five great, usually musical, productions a year and most of them are very kid-friendly. Past shows include *Joseph and the Amazing Technicolor Dreamcoat, You're a Good Man, Charlie Brown, Dracula,* and *American Rhythm,* a journey across America through music. Lamb's Players puts on productions in Coronado and Horton Grand Theater, plus a Christmas show at Hotel del Coronado in December. Inquire about immersion programs the theater offers for school groups and about summer camps for children aspiring to the stage and screen.

Hours: Call for show dates and times.
Price: Tickets usually range from $20 - $74 for adults, depending on the date and time; $5 off for seniors and ages 5 - 17; tickets are half price for active military. Children 4 and under are not admitted. Rush tickets are sometimes available.
Ages: 5 years and up.

MARIE HITCHCOCK PUPPET THEATER
(619) 544-9203 / www.balboaparkpuppets.com
2130 Pan American Place, Balboa Park, San Diego

This intimate theater, located behind the San Diego Automotive Museum, presents kid-approved, half-hour, puppet shows. The type of puppets vary from show to show, and can include hand puppets, marionettes, dummies (for ventriloquists), life-size puppets, and puppets made from anything and everything found around the house. The shows themselves are similar in that they never fail to capture a child's imagination. From *Cinderella* to *The Ugly Duckling* to *The Frog Prince*, stories are told as only puppets can tell them (with a little bit of human help)! Shows change weekly so watch out - bringing the kids here can become habit forming. Note that the theater also hosts birthday parties, as well as puppet-making workshops for ages 3 and up for $7 per person. Contact puppetkidsparties@gmail.com for more info on the workshops. See BALBOA PARK (pg. 526) for a listing of all the museums and attractions within walking distance.

Hours: Most of the year, performances are Wed. - Fri., at 10am and 11:30am; Sat. - Sun., 11am, 1pm, and 2:30pm. Memorial Day - Labor Day, performances are Wed. - Sun., 11am, 1pm and 2:30pm.

Price: $5 general admission; $4 for seniors; children under 2 are free.

Ages: 1½ - 10 years.

NATIONAL COMEDY THEATRE

(619) 295-4999 or (818) 953-4933 / www.nationalcomedy.com

3717 India Street, San Diego

Your belly will be bustin' from laughing so hard at this troupe who perform fast-paced, quick-witted, improvisational comedy. Two teams, usually composed of three comedians each, compete in a series of scenes (i.e., games) which can involve singing, mime, and always fast repartee. The general guidelines of the games are explained, then the audience suggests situations, activities, and more. The audience also judges and picks the winning team. The referee keeps everything in check, including the suggestions. A stand-out feature of the hour to ninety-minute long shows is that material is clean, so they are appropriate for kids (and adults). An audience member or troupe who offers up an inappropriate suggestion must wear a brown paper bag over his/her head for a segment. So, enjoy a hilarious outing with the family. The troupe also offers improv comedy training, high school improv leagues, and summer camps.

Hours: Thurs. at 7:30pm; Fri. and Sat. at 7:30pm and 9:45pm; Sun. at 7:30pm, and the College Team at 9pm.

Price: College Team performances are $10 per person; other shows are Fri. and Sat., $17 for adults; $12 for seniors and students; Thurs. and Sun. (7:30pm show), $12 per person.

Ages: 7 years and up.

OLD GLOBE THEATRE

(619) 23GLOBE (234-5623) or (619) 239-2255 / www.oldglobe.org

1363 Old Globe Way, Balboa Park, San Diego

Originally modeled after Shakespeare's Globe Theatre in London, this 580-seat classic theater is accompanied by two other theaters; the Conrad Prebys Theatre Center and the 612-seat, outdoor Lowell Davies Festival Theatre. Combined, the theater complex puts on about fifteen productions and 600 performances, usually plays, a year. Of course, Shakespeare's plays are a draw, especially during the Shakespeare Festival in summer. Many of the other productions appeal mostly to adults, but the Globe's holiday musical program, *How the Grinch Stole Christmas*, is definitely family fare. It runs November through December.

Call regarding programs, such as Shakespeare Intensive for students, acting workshops, tours (see OLD GLOBE THEATRE (tour), on page 576, for details), and educational opportunities.

Hours: Call for a schedule.

Price: Prices vary depending on show, date, and time.

Ages: Depends on the show.

PALOMAR COLLEGE PLANETARIUM

(760) 744-1150 / www.palomar.edu/planetarium

1140 West Mission Road at Palomar Community College, San Marcos

The fifth largest planetarium in California seats 142 people under a fifty-foot dome for an immersive experience under the nighttime sky. The first show, *The Sky Tonight*, is a live, narrated show highlighting heavenly objects visible from San Diego. The moon, planets, and several constellations and their mythology are discussed. The second feature presentation varies with some being more of a movie and others perhaps more documentary-style. Telescopes are out

on the patio for viewing stars in real life after every show. Purchasing tickets in advance is recommended.

Ninety-minute field trips are offered for schools, 3rd graders and up, year round on Tuesdays and Thursdays, from 10am to 11:30am. A presentation is followed by a time for Q and A. Afterwards, enjoy lunch on campus in a parkish setting   a taste of college at a young age!

Hours: Doors open every Fri. night at 6:30pm. The first show is 7pm - 8pm; the second show is 8:15pm - 9pm. There is no late seating.

Price: Each presentation on Fri. is $6 for adults; $4 for seniors, students and military with ID, and ages 5 - 12. School groups are $120 for groups with less than 30 people; $4 per person for groups of 30 or more.

Ages: 5 years and up only.

POWAY CENTER FOR THE PERFORMING ARTS

(858) 668-4693 - info; (858) 748-0505 - box office / www.powayarts.org; www.powaycenter.com $$$$
15498 Espola Road, Poway

This 800-seat capacity theater offers a variety of family entertainment throughout the year, as well as a few outstanding children's programs. Past productions have included Jim Gamble puppets; a troop that performed juggling, acrobatics, and comedy combined with a laser light show; the Boys Choir of Harlem; *The King and I*; and *Cinderella*. Other performances include Broadway musicals, big band productions, comedy routines, and more.

Hours: Call for performance times.

Price: Ticket prices vary depending on show, date, and time.

Ages: 4 years and up.

SAN DIEGO CIVIC THEATRE

(619) 564-3000 or (619) 570-1100 / www.sandiegotheatres.org $$$$$
1100 Third Avenue at B Street, San Diego

The elegant, almost 3,000-seat theater gives kids (and adults) the opportunity to experience real theater in a formal setting. One of the central companies that consider the Civic Theatre home is Broadway San Diego. Broadway-billed shows and top-name stars perform with this West Coast Broadway company. Past shows include *Phantom of the Opera*, *Stomp, Beauty and the Beast, Doctor Doolittle*, and *Wicked*. Indulge in a show - it is a memorable treat.

Other companies at the Civic, who deserve as much recognition and write-up, include the California Ballet and La Jolla Music Society.

Hours: Call or go online for a show schedule.

Price: Tickets start at $20. Price depends on the performance, time, and date. Parking at the Concourse Mon. - Fri., is $2 per half hour, max $18. After 5:30pm daily and all day Sat., Sun., and holidays, parking is $10.

Ages: 6 years and up, depending on the show.

SAN DIEGO SYMPHONY / COPLEY SYMPHONY HALL

(619) 235-0804 - concert box office; (619) 615-3955 - tour / www.sandiegosymphony.org $$$
750 B Street, San Diego

Performing at the beautiful, classic, and historic 2,250-seat Copley Symphony Hall and at the outdoors amphitheater during the summer for the Summer Pops, the renown symphony plays over 100 concerts a season. Offering a huge range of musical experiences and opportunities, there is a venue that will intrigue almost any age. One-hour family performances on select Sunday afternoons are a terrific way to introduce your children to classical music. Free, preconcert activities can include "What's the Score" conversations, face painting and a musical "petting zoo," which is touching or even playing an instrument to get familiar with it.

School groups, geared for second graders through 8th, are especially welcome at matinee performances (given at 10am and 11:30am) of Young People's Concerts, when tickets are only $5 per person. Reservations are required. Open rehearsals are on select mornings that include over an hour of rehearsal combined with a Q & A time with the musicians, and even a tour for ages 12 and up. Make reservations. Free, one-hour tours are offered once-a-month on Wednesdays starting at noon, the end of October through May, when visitors see and learn about the magnificent building. Check the website for a complete listing of the offerings here.

Hours: Call or go online for concert times.

Price: Prices begin at $10 for a family performance and go up according to performance and date. Discounts are available for students and seniors - check the website for detailed info. Parking at the Parking Palace is $5.

Ages: 5 years and up, depending on the show; 8 years and up for the tour.

ULTRASTAR CINEMAS (San Diego County) ☼ $$$

(619) 685-2841 / www.ultrastarmovies.com
7510 Hazard Center Drive, San Diego

See the ULTRASTAR CINEMAS website, then click the Kids & Family button to see the special offerings. Also see ULTRASTAR GARDEN WALK 14 (Orange County) (pg. 323) for more information on the programs these theaters offer.

WELK RESORT THEATRE ☼

(888) 802-7469 and (760) 749-3000 / www.welktheatresandiego.com; www.welkresort.com $$$$$
8860 Lawrence Welk Drive, Escondido

This "wannaful" (i.e., that's the way Lawrence Welk used to say "wonderful") theater offers five different, full-production Broadway musicals a year, every week of the year. Audiences in the intimate 330-seat theater have seen the likes of *My Fair Lady*, *The King and I*, *Seven Brides for Seven Brothers*, *Forever Plaid*, and its annual, *Welk Musical Christmas Show*. As you can tell by the titles, many of the musicals are family oriented.

Before or during intermission, take a short "tour" around the elegant lobby/museum. It features portions of Welk's life in chronological order via pictures, actual props, bandstands, and instruments from the Lawrence Welk Show.

Grab a bite to eat at one of the restaurants, like the pizzeria, in the Welk Village shopping area. Personally, I was glad we arrived early enough to also shop in the village. The restaurant up the hill from the theater, Canyon Grill, offers a decent buffet lunch and dinner, which is always a good choice for picky eaters. You may combine a meal here with a theater show for a reduced rate.

Hours: Matinee performances are given Wed., Thurs. and Sun. at 1pm. Evening performances are given Thurs. and Sat. at 8pm. No performances are given on Mon., Tues. or Fri. The buffet lunch is served 10:30am - 12:15pm; the buffet dinner, 5:30pm - 6:450pm.

Price: The show, only, on matinees Wed., Thurs. and Sun. is $45 for adults; $29 for ages 3 - 13; with a buffet lunch, $63 for adults; $37 for ages 3 - 13. Evening shows, only, are Thurs. and Sat., $48 for adults; $29 for kids; with a dinner, $66 for adults; $39 for kids. Sun. show and brunch buffet is $66 for adults; $50 for kids. Christmas shows are an additional $10 per.

Ages: 6 years and up. (Children 2 and under are not allowed.)

—TOURS—

BRAILLE INSTITUTE (San Diego County) ☼

(858) 452-1111 / www.brailleinstitute.org !
4555 Executive Drive, San Diego

What would it be like to have limited vision, or not be able to see at all? Take an over hour-long tour of the Braille Institute campus to learn how the visually impaired can get around and learn about the tools that help them be independent. The students also get an introduction to the Braille language by feeling Braille maps and typing on a Braille typewriter. Depending on the availability and the day, visitors might also have the opportunity to talk with a librarian who reads Braille and to see the school's classrooms and computer labs.

Hours: Tours are available Wed. at 1pm and Thurs. at 11am, with advanced reservations, only.
Price: Free
Ages: 8 years and up.

CALIFORNIA PIZZA KITCHEN (San Diego County) ☼

See the entry for CALIFORNIA PIZZA KITCHEN (Los Angeles County) (pg. 197) for more ! information.

DEERING - THE GREAT AMERICAN BANJO COMPANY

(800) 845-7791 / www.deeringbanjos.com
3733 Kenora Drive, Spring Valley

Banjos just have that happy and bright sound to them, don't they? Come and see and learn how that sound is made by taking a one-hour, intimate and casual tour through the factory. The tour begins in the showroom with a brief history of the family-owned company and an explanation about the parts of a banjo. (You get to see the finished product first and then how each component is made.) You'll walk through the various departments along narrow aisles, stopping at each one to look at the skilled craftsmen using machines, which do some of the work, as well as using their hands to fine tune each part. From the various types of wood in choosing the neck and rim, to the metal bands around the banjo head, the hardware, the gluing, the sanding and polishing, the fretting, the spray painting, the intricate detail work (especially the inlays), the strings, and the tuning - there is so much attention to each step of the process, and so many banjos! It takes anywhere from three to twenty man hours to craft a banjo, depending on the elaborateness of it.

The tour ends back at the showroom where you can take your pick of banjos to play, or purchase, as well as other items to buy. You'll have a Goodtime at this factory tour! Note that there is a maximum of fifteen people per tour, so call to make a reservation. The minimum age is 6.

Hours: Tours are given Tues. - Fri. at 1pm.
Price: Free
Ages: At least 6 years old and up.

EAGLE MINING COMPANY

(760) 765-0036 / www.julianca.com
North end of 'C' Street, Julian

Eureka! There's gold in them thar hills! Original mining equipment and a few old buildings make it look like time has stood still here. One of the buildings is a small museum/store with rock specimens, mining tools, and a glass cased display of memorabilia from the early 1900's.

Trek through time on your one-hour, guided walking tour through two genuine gold mines that were founded in 1870: the Eagle Mine and the connecting, High Peak Mine. My kids studied about the forty-niners, but to actually go through a gold mine, walk on ore-cart tracks, see stone tunnels hand carved by picks, and learn the hardships of mining, really made a lasting impact on them. We saw the vein that the miners worked and realized, along with hundreds of other people both past and present, that gold wasn't easily obtainable. It took one ton of rock to yield a sugar-cube-size amount of gold! We went up two of the eleven levels in the mines, saw the hoist room where ore buckets were used as olden-day elevators, and experienced darkness so black that we couldn't see our hands in front of our faces. I admire the fortitude of our early engineers. It's interesting to note the difference between the earlier smooth rock tunnels that were hand drilled and the later jagged edges left from blasting with charges. Don't forget to look up at the amazing shaft tunnels (and duck your head)!

Outside, we saw the milling equipment used to crush rocks, and learned the tedious process of extracting gold. Try your hand at panning for gold (it's harder than it looks) in a "stocked" water trough on the premises. This activity is included in the tour price. And just remember: All that glitters isn't gold.

Julian is a quaint town with unique shops along Main Street. Your kids will enjoy a stop-off at the Julian Drug Store and Candy Mine for a trip downstairs to the "candy" mine. Go next door to Miner's Diner for an ice cream at its old-fashioned, marble-topped soda counter or enjoy a full breakfast, lunch, or dinner meal. The drug store and diner are located on the corner of Main and Washington Sts. Note that every Sunday at 1pm, 2pm, and 3pm, Julian Doves & Desperados (a Western-themed reenactment group) performs free, comedic gunfights and skits near the Julian Market & Deli on the main street. Look up Julian under the city index for other, close-by attractions.

Hours: Open Mon. - Fri., 10am - 3pm; Sat. - Sun., 10am - 4pm; weather permitting and depending on if
              people are here. Closed Thanksgiving and Christmas.
Price: $10 for adults; $5 for ages 4 - 12; $1 for children 3 and under.
Ages: 4 years and up.

GEMOLOGICAL INSTITUTE OF AMERICA

(800) 421-7250 or (760) 603-4116 / www.gia.edu
5345 Armada Drive, Carlsbad

Diamonds are a girl's best friend, but both sexes will enjoy learning more about these and other gemstones. The institute is a school for those interested in learning and applying knowledge about gemology and the jewelry manufacturing arts. Quiz: What are the 4Cs of diamond value? Answer: color, clarity, cut, and carat weight. A one-hour tour begins to familiarize the public with gem analysis and grading, and tools of the trade. The best parts, however, are looking at the numerous stones in raw form and at the finished products of world-class gems. (Sorry, no free samples.)

Many items, such as pearl necklaces, diamond rings, antique tools, and sculptures, are behind glass in the rotunda. Look, too, at the incredibly, intricately carved piece of ivory. Peek through classroom windows to glimpse students of all ages work at computer-aided designs, wax techniques, grading a stone, or other projects. You'll be enthralled by the over sixty labeled window boxes (i.e., glass display cases) lining the hallways that contain rubies, emeralds, aquamarines, garnets (including red, orange, and green ones), zircons, tourmaline, opals, and peridots, plus sculptures made of gems and stunning jewelry pieces.

The guide explains, among other things, the difference between synthetic and real gem stones and how faux ones are produced. You'll also hear interesting stories about royalty and their jewelry. One picture gallery shows the entire diamond process, from mining to the sale of the stone to its cutting to its becoming a piece of glittering jewelry. A small museum showcases rotating exhibits that come from the Smithsonian and from all over the world.

The two-hour Jr. Gemologist program, for fourth through twelfth graders, is a different tour in that it is geared specifically for children; it is hands on, and it meets state standards. Groups, composed of fifteen to forty students, see samples of diamonds in rough and polished forms, as well as other minerals. They use jewelers' loupes and microscopes to examine stones up close. Aided by other visuals, the class includes elements of mineralogy, geology, crystal structure, and an introduction to identifying inclusions. Have kids bring a sack lunch to enjoy at the picnic tables on site. A gift shop is also on the premises. What a gem of a place!

Note that advanced reservations are required for both the general tour and Jr. Gemologist program (fifteen to forty students), and that openings fill up quickly. A photo I.D. is required for everyone.

Hours: Tours are offered Mon. - Fri. with advanced reservations.
Price: Free
Ages: 11 years and up for the general tour; fourth through twelfth graders for the Jr. Gemologist program.

JULIAN MINING COMPANY

(951) 313-0166 / www.julianminingcompany.com
4444 Highway 78, Wynola

Rural America is alive and well at the Julian Mining Company. Open year round for individuals, families, and field trips this outdoor country space offers a variety of "living history" experiences such as panning for gold - which is harder than it looks - at a good-sized "stocked" sluice where you can keep whatever you pan ($9 for adults; $7 for kids 12 and under); panning for gold in a real stream; dipping candles; petting animals at the small petting zoo; pressing cider (in season); riding on a tractor-drawn hayride; picking seasonal fruit (such as apples and raspberries); fossil digs ($5.95 a bag) where participants dig at a fossil site for shark's teeth, coins, arrowheads, and more; throwing a tomahawk; taking a scale model train ride; and participating in Civil and Revolutionary War reenactments (which are excellent).

One of the several, hands-on, school field trips is the two-hour Farm Life Tour which includes cider pressing, visiting the petting zoo, candle dipping, hayride, pioneer chores, wool carding, and pie or butter making. A minimum of twenty-five people is needed and the cost is $9 per student; $5 for adults. At the four-hour Native American Tour, participants make jewelry, shoot a bow and arrow, watch a tanning demonstration, visit a Sioux tipi, and more for a cost of $12 per person. Via lecture and hands-on demonstrations and experiments regarding carbon dating, laws of thermodynamics, micro and macro evolution, archaeological dig, worldwide flood, the creation account, and more the Creation vs. Evolution tour helps to answer the question - What is the origin of life? Note that families or small groups can be added on to these field trips for $15 per person.

Enjoy lunch at the picnic tables and/or purchase additional refreshments at the on-site store. The store also sells old-time toys, animal pelts, unique gifts, books, and other fun stuff. A most popular item is the gem and mineral bag (starting at $11.50) which contains an assortment of tiger eye, pyrite, quartz, agates, shark teeth, and more, that you can just open and enjoy or put on the sluice. Note that MOUNTAIN BEADWORKS (pg. 467) is really close by.

Hours: Generally open to the public on Sat., 10am - 5pm; Sun., noon - 5pm. Open longer during summer and at other times for field trips and private events.

Price: A few hours of activities can cost $10 - $15 per person. See prices above.
Ages: 4 years and up.

KUMEYAAY-IPAI INTERPRETIVE CENTER

(858) 668-1292 / www.poway.org

13104 Ipai Waaypuk Trail (formerly Silver Lake Drive), Poway

Rich in Kumeyaay-Ipai history, a paved trail weaves around and through this six-acre village site. Recreated parts of the village include a house made of reeds, ramadas that provide shade, milling stations where acorns were ground, native plants, and interpretative signs. The docent-led tours, for the general public and for school groups, are wonderfully informative and make the past seem present. A modern building contains exhibits regarding the Kumeyaay such as baskets, photos of rock art, and artifacts from the site.

Hours: Open to the general public for docent-led tours, Sat., 9am - noon.
Price: Free
Ages: 7 years and up.

OLD GLOBE THEATRE (tour)

(619) 23GLOBE (234-5623) or (619) 239-2255; (619) 231-1941- reservations / www.oldglobe.org $$

1363 Old Globe Way, Balboa Park, San Diego

Take a ninety-minute tour of the Old Globe Theatre, which was originally modeled after Shakespeare's Globe Theatre in London. You'll see behind-the-scenes of this theater and the two other ones in the complex while learning their histories, architecture, how sets are built to look like stone castles, costumes and their design, the miniature bug orchestra, and learn about the current plays. Also look up OLD GLOBE THEATRE (pg. 571) for show information. Students and adults can also take an interactive Follow the Bard Tour in which participants learn more about Shakespeare, finding hidden props and costumes around the sets relating to his plays that give insight into the man, himself. Follow-up activities are included in the tour.

Hours: Behind-the-scenes tours are given on selected Sat. and Sun. at 10:30am, no reservation needed; call
             for dates. Follow the Bard Tours are available Mon. - Fri., 9am - 2pm by reservation only.
Price: Behind-the-scene tours are $5 for adults; $3 for seniors and students. Follow the Bard Tours are $5
             per person. School tours are $3 per student for a minimum of ten up to seventy people.
Ages: 9 years and up.

O'S AMERICAN KITCHEN (San Diego County)

Chula Vista - (619) 621-5620; El Cajon - (619) 749-2984; Mira Mesa - (858) 621-6100; Mission Valley - (619)
295-6200; National City - (619) 472-2701; San Diego (Carmel Mt. Ranch) - (858) 592-0222; San Marcos -
(760) 798-7889 / www.osamericankitchen.com

Chula Vista - 872 Eastlake Pkwy.; El Cajon - 375 Parkway Plaza; Mira Mesa - 10673 Westview Pkwy.; Mission Valley -
8590 Rio San Diego Dr.; National City - 3030 Plaza Bonita Rd., Ste. 106 at Plaza Bonita Mall; San Diego (Carmel) - 12045
Carmel Mountain Rd.; San Marcos - 137 S. Los Posas Rd., suite 153

What a delectable aroma! This chain of restaurants serves up great food at affordable prices. Menu selections include four baby back ribs ($10.49); pasta dishes ($6.99); medium Cobb salad ($9.99) half of a barbecued chicken ($7.79); a wide variety of either gourmet pizzas or pizzas you concoct ($11.99 for a large cheese); turkey and provolone sandwich ($5.99); and a cup of soup with bread sticks ($3.29). Kid's menu choices include a mini pizza, chicken wings, or pasta with a side dish for $3.99 each.

Besides being a great and tasty family restaurant, the main reason for its inclusion in the book is the tours offered for elementary-school-aged kids. With a minimum of five kids (though some locations may have different specs), one-hour tours include learning about O's and walking through the restaurant to see how it operates, spending most of the time in the kitchen. Considered a "fast casual" restaurant, the kitchen opens up somewhat into the dining area, making it easy to see the "behind-the-scenes" workings, such as the assembly-line type of fixing and cooking, the dishwashing station, and the walk-in frig. The best part of the tour is making, baking, and eating your own pizza. (Eat a light breakfast before coming, or don't eat one at all!) O's also offers a great way to do fundraisers for school, scout, church, or other youth groups.

Hours: Tours usually begin at 9am or 9:30am as students are encouraged to be finished before 10:30; the
             lunch rush. The restaurants are usually open Sun. - Thurs., 10:30am - 9pmish; Fri. - Sat., 10:30am -
             10pm. (Some locations close earlier.)

Price: Free

Ages: 1st - 6th graders.

PETCO PARK - THE PARK AT THE PARK

(619) 795-5011 - tour; (619) 795-5000 - ball game info; (619) 231-6664 - Omni Hotel / sandiego.padres.mlb.com; www.petcoparkevents.com

100 Park Boulevard, San Diego

Take me out to the ball game, or at least take me out on a tour of a ballpark. Home to the world-famous San Diego Padres, this stadium offers behind-the-scenes tours that last not quite ninety minutes. Fans can see the press box, dugouts, bullpen (maybe warm up your arm with a pitch or two?), a luxury suite, warming track, the Park at the Park, and the team store. All this while learning the history of the team and players, and of the historic Western Metal Supply Co. building, which was constructed in 1909. Although the tour includes climbing stairs and getting a workout by walking about a mile and a half, it is also wheelchair accessible. Families and individuals are welcome to take the tour on a walk-in basis. There is a limit of twenty-five people per tour so groups need to call to make a reservation. Educational tours are also offered with advanced reservations. Note that the Omni Hotel, located next to Petco Park at 675 L Street and actually connected to the ballpark via a skybridge, has awards, autographed baseballs, bats, vintage uniforms, and documents such as contracts and correspondence on display on various floors.

The Park at the Park is a 2.8-acre park just beyond the outfield fence. It boasts a small infield used for supervised wiffle ball games, a grassy hill, a playground for tots with some fun apparatus, and a few picnic tables.

Come see a game via the park as a variety of seating is available. Spots on the hill are the least expensive, as are seats on the side of the giant scoreboard, which actually obstructs the view from the higher-numbered seats. Seats on the picnic terrace where mesh fences are absent (so the view is clear) and small picnic tables or shelves come with the seats to enjoy a picnic lunch or dinner. (These seats are for private parties with reservations.) On game days the park closes about five hours before the game, except for visitors with tickets. Tip: You can even enjoy a tailgate party at Tailgate Park on 12th and Imperial sts. with advance reservation. Spaces cost $20 per. Shuttle buses then take you to the game and bring you back afterward.

Hours: Tours are given off season, about November - March, Sun. - Fri. at 10:30am and 12:30pm; Sat. at 10:30am, 12:30pm and 3pm. Tours are given in season, about April - October, usually the same times as above, but it depends on games and game times. Call ahead to make sure of tour times and avoid disappointment. The park is usually open daily sunrise to sunset and is free.

Price: The tour is $12 for adults; $9 for seniors; $8 for children 12 and under. Parking in lots ranges from $5 - $20, depending on the proximity. There is some metered street parking available for the tour.

Ages: 6 years and up.

SAN DIEGO INTERNATIONAL AIRPORT - TERMINAL TO TARMAC TOUR

(619) 400-2880 / www.san.org; www.airportexplorers.com

Harbor Drive at Lindbergh Field, San Diego

Pilot your way to the airport for a well-organized, two-hour tour of the San Diego International Airport. Tours include a walk through a majority of the facility while learning about architecture, travel, communications, career opportunities, and the history of aviation. Hear about Charles Lindbergh while looking at a replica of the Spirit of St. Louis. See some of the works of art on display, view the endangered-species Least Tern area, and see planes land and take off while driving around the runway. Go through the baggage claim area, find out about courtesy phones, and how to use the maps on the walls. Kids only tours get to see a demonstration of what the on-site fire station does. The tour enables children and adults to find out all about travel without experiencing jet lag, or the cost of a trip! Groups are limited to a maximum of twenty-two people.

Hours: Tours are offered every other Wed. and Fri. at 10am and 1pm.

Price: Free. Parking is validated.

Ages: Kids must be at least 7 years and up.

SAN DIEGO SYMPHONY HALL

750 B Street, San Diego

See SAN DIEGO SYMPHONY HALL (pg. 572) for tour information.

SMITH RANCH & JULIAN RAILROAD   ☼

Off Banner Road/78 on Ethelwyn Lane, Julian $$$$

See SMITH RANCH & JULIAN RAILROAD (pg. 566) for details about riding the rails and experiencing pioneer life in the mountains.

TAYLOR GUITARS   ☼

(619) 258-6957 or (619) 258-1207 / www.taylorguitars.com   !
1980 Gillespie Way, El Cajon

What do Aerosmith, Pearl Jam, President Clinton, and Garth Brooks have in common? They each own Taylor guitars. This over-an-hour-long tour is "Taylor"-made for guitar fans. Starting in the lobby, which features an informational and pictorial timeline of the guitar company, visitors then walk outside to a storage area and through the buildings, into each room and the warehouses to see and learn how a guitar is put together, from start to glossy (or satin) finish. The tour is intimate and casual, and you'll see every aspect of guitar-making up close and get to ask the questions (and get answers) from the workers and tour guide. Cherry, Sapele mahogany, Sitka spruce, Big Leaf maple, cedar, Indian rosewood, Hawaiian koa, and walnut are just a few of the common and exotic woods used in Taylor guitars. Once the wood is cut to precise specifications, it is kept in climate controlled rooms and containers, then carved, sanded, and assembled. Specially designed (loud!) machines, such as the ones that slice grooves in the neck of the guitar, are fascinating to watch as are the workers who are involved in each step of the process. Note: It takes at least a week to ten days to complete just one guitar.

The tour is geared for guitar aficionados (we had some people on ours who asked lots of "technical" questions), but kids will appreciate the different shapes, woods, colors, and sounds of the guitars. I, who am not musically inclined at all, thought it was fascinating and enjoyed seeing every component and the hand crafting still employed. After the tour, guests are invited to purchase a wide selection of merchandise (guitar picks, jackets, etc.) imprinted with the Taylor logo. Guitars are not sold on the premises. The tour is geared for small groups, is not wheelchair friendly, and visitors must stay within specified lines and resist the temptation to touch anything in the factory warehouses. School and other groups are welcome to book a special tour at least two weeks in advance. Photography is permitted.

Hours: Tours are offered Mon. - Fri. at 1pm. Reservations are not required, but suggested. Tours are not given for a week toward the end of June, at the beginning of July, and for a week before Christmas through New Year's Day, and on certain holidays.

Price: Free

Ages: 7 years and up.

—TRANSPORTATION—

AMTRAK (San Diego County)

(800) USA RAIL (872-7245) / www.amtrakcalifornia.com

Ride the rails! See AMTRAK (Los Angeles County) on page 208 for more information.

BARNSTORMING ADVENTURES   ☼

(800) SKY-LOOP (759-5667) / www.barnstorming.com $$$$$
3750 John J. Montgomery Drive, San Diego

Flying in a restored, authentic, open-cockpit biplane, wearing an old-fashioned leather helmet, goggles, and a pilot scarf reminds me of another flying ace, Snoopy, and his adventures with the Red Baron. (Yes, I do know that Snoopy isn't real.) You'll fly over the stunning San Diego coastline for twenty minutes, side-by-side with another passenger (this could be your child), while the pilot sits behind you. It's like riding a motorcycle in the sky!

Another adventure offered here is Air Combat. After a crash course, so to speak, on general aviation and specifically, tactical maneuvers during combat, you'll suit up and take off for the wild blue yonder. When you've gotten a feel for the controls, get ready for combat with a real "enemy." (If you don't have an enemy to bring, the company will provide one for you.) You'll help fly the tandem seating, Varga VG-21 propeller-driven plane with dual joystick controls for over thirty minutes, experiencing high/low yo-yos (where the plane dips abruptly downward and zooms upward and your stomach heads in the opposite direction) and other maneuvers in a dogfight - let the fur fly! This exhilarating experience is one that you'll remember and talk about for the rest of your life.

Warbird Flights allows those who are at least 10 years old (and adhere to the height and weight requirements) to

experience flying in a genuine warbird - a 1941 SNJ-4 Texan, which was an advanced trainer for WWII aviators. If you want to experience real movement, the pilot will do loops, rolls, half-cuban eights, and more acrobatic maneuvers. Hold on to your hat and your stomach. In the You-Fly-It or Cadet Flights, you are flying the plane (with the help of the real pilot). Sitting in the back cockpit, you will takeoff (with some assistance), turn, climb, glide, and FLY!

Hours: Open year round for flights, Tues. - Sun., 11am - 5pm. Call first. Closed Mon., 4th of July, Thanksgiving, Christmas and during inclement weather.

Price: Biplane Adventures start at about $219 total for one or two people for the twenty-minute Barnstormer Hop. Air Combat starts at $596 for one or two people. Warbird Flights start at $495 for a thirty-minute flight. You Fly It starts at $177 for a thirty-minute flight. Ask about current specials. Reservations are required for all flights. The company offers several other flight packages.

Ages: 5 years and up.

BIKE AND KAYAK TOURS ☼

(858) 454-1010 / www.sandiegobikeandkayaktours.com $$$$
Coronado - 1201 1ˢᵗ Street #215; La Jolla - 2158 Avenida De La Playa

There is almost no better way to see the sea than from a kayak: So close to the water, sea creatures and even geological formations - it's a thrill! In La Jolla, kayak the seven caves on a guided tour where the naturalist glides you there and points out the sights along the way. Going through the La Jolla Ecological Reserve you should see sea lions, garibaldi, leopard sharks, and other critters. Ninety-minute tours start at $39 per person. Other tours offered are kayak and snorkel tours, sunset tours, and, for those who want to be on dry land, bike tours.

Rentals are also available for those who want to do it on their own. Single kayak rentals are $24 for ninety-minutes; doubles are $44; triples are $54. Note that prices are less expensive for the first departures in the morning or the last one in the afternoon. Snorkel gear rentals - mask, fins, wetsuit and snorkel - are $29 for the day. Bike rentals are $9 an hour, or $29 for the day.

Hours: Rentals are usually at every hour starting at 10:15am - 3:15pm (last one). Call for specific days.
Price: Prices are listed above.
Ages: 6 years and up and can swim.

BIKE MAPS (San Diego County)

See BIKE MAPS (Orange County) on page 326 for information. Note that bike racks are available on many buses and on Coaster commuter trains.

CALIFORNIA WATER SPORTS - CARLSBAD LAGOON ☼

(888) 5- LAGOON (552-4666); (760) 434-3089 / www.carlsbadlagoon.com $$$
4215 Harrison Street, Carlsbad

This very popular place is located right off the 5 freeway. Three marina/lagoon areas are located here for separate water activities on calm waters. Wave rentals are $95 for an hour. Single kayaks are $15 an hour. Double kayaks, canoes, and pedalboats are $20 an hour, each. Aqua cycles and stand up paddle board rentals are $30 each, per hour. Waterskiing, wakeboarding, and tubing (while being pulled behind a boat) - $95 a half hour and all include a boat, driver and equipment. Liability waivers must be signed for everything. You may not take the equipment out of this marina, but the area is plenty big enough. In between boating activities, lie out on the private beach or play volleyball, eat lunch at the picnic tables, or shop at the pro shop. Enjoy!

Hours: Open the end of March - April(ish) daily, 9am - 5pm; May(ish), daily 9am - 6pm; June - September, daily, 9am (sometimes earlier) - 7pm. Open the rest of the year, Wed. - Fri., 10am - 3pm; Sat. - Sun., 9am - 4pm.
Price: Prices are listed above.
Ages: 6 years and up.

COASTER ☼

(619) 685-4900 - automated system for the coaster, bus, and trolley; (619) 233-3004 - transit office / $$$
www.gonctd.com/coaster/coaster.html; www.sdmts.com
San Diego County

Coast stress-free from Oceanside to Old Town to further south in San Diego, with stops at Carlsbad, Encinitas, Solana Beach, and Sorrento Valley via the sleek transit express rail line. Pick out a destination in the above-mentioned

cities, or let the ride be the adventure as you travel along the shoreline. Note that bike racks area available on the Coaster commuter trains. Automated fare machines (note that only $10 change can be given back) at the Coaster stations make obtaining a ticket a breeze, although calling to find out the schedule on the automated number can drive one a little nuts.

Hours: It operates Mon. - Fri., except major holidays, starting at about 5:30am and ending at about 6:30pm - depending on destination; Sat., 8:30amish - 7:30pmish. Closed most major holidays.

Price: $4 for adults one-way; $2 for seniors; children 5 and under are free.

Ages: All

COUNTRY CARRIAGES

(760) 765-1471 / www.southwestblend.com/countrycarriages; www.julianca.com

$$$$

2134 Main Street at the stop sign, Julian

Clip clop, dip dop - a horse-drawn carriage ride through Julian fits in perfectly with the ambiance of this quaint town. Most of the tours begin in front of the Julian Drug Store, a fun place to stop for a treat at an old-fashioned soda fountain. Any special event - birthday, moonlight rides, and whatever else you think of can incorporate a carriage ride through the countryside.

Hours: Look for the carriage Sat. - Sun., 11am - 7pm or call first as reservations are always recommended.

Price: A 15 min. ride is $20 per couple; 30 min. is $30.

Ages: All

FLAGSHIP CRUISES AND EVENTS

(800) 44CRUISE (442-7847) or (619) 234-4111 / www.flagshipsd.com

$$$$

990 N. Harbor Drive, Broadway Pier, San Diego

Enjoy a one- or two-hour-narrated harbor cruise along San Diego's coast in a nice excursion ship. A snack bar is on board. During a one-hour cruise, you'll explore either the north part of the bay, or the south part. Depending on which cruise you choose, you'll see the *Star of India*, the Naval Air Station, Coronado Bridge, U.S. Navy Seal base, Point Loma Lighthouse, and the San Diego shipyards that hold merchants' vessels, fishing boats, and more. The two-hour cruise encompasses both the north and south parts of the bay. Three-and-a-half-hour whale-watching trips are given the end of December through mid-April. The trips are narrated by a naturalist from the Birch Aquarium. A sighting is guaranteed or you ride again for free. Tip: Bring a jacket or sweater (and camera) on any journey by sea. Note that for fine dining, this cruise line also offers dinner and Sunday brunch cruises.

Hours: Harbor cruises depart daily, 10am to about 5pm. Seasonal three-and-a-half-hour whale-watching cruises depart daily at 9:45am and 1:30pm. Brunch cruises depart year round, Sun. at 10:30am and, Memorial Day - Labor Day, Sat. at 10:30am.

Price: One-hour cruises are $23 for adults; $21 for seniors and active-duty military; $11.50 for ages 4 -12; children 3 and under are free. Two-hour cruises are $28 for adults; $26 for seniors and military; $14 for ages 4 - 12. Whale watching, Mon. - Fri., is $37 for adults, $32 for seniors, $18.50 for ages 4 - 12; on Sat. - Sun. it is $42 for adults, $37 for seniors, $21 for ages 4 - 12. Dinner cruises Sun. - Fri. are $69.50 for adults, $41.70 for ages 4 - 12; Sat. they are $79.50 for adults, $51.70 for kids. Brunch buffet is $64.50 for adults; $38.50 for children. Parking at the Broadway pier is $18 all day.

Ages: 3 years and up.

GONDOLA COMPANY

(619) 429-6317 / www.gondolacompany.com

$$$$$

503 Grand Caribe Causeway, Coronado

This part of Coronado becomes a part of Italy via an authentic gondola cruise through the exclusive waterway of the Coronado Cays. Romantic? Yes, but it can also be a peaceful, almost hour-long adventure with children. The gondolier dresses in the traditional costume of striped shirt and black pants. Italian music plays in the background. An ice bucket and glasses are provided, and you supply your own choice of beverage. Most of the gondolas can take up to six people; a few can up to fourteen passengers.

Hours: Open Mon. - Fri., 3pm - midnight; Sat. - Sun., 11am - midnight.

Price: $95 for two people; $20 per additional person. The Carolina Cruise - for 7 to 14 people - is $29 per person. Children under 3 are free. Reservations are required for all rides.

Ages: 4 years and up.

H & M LANDING
☀
(619) 222-1144 / www.hmlanding.com
$$$$
2803 Emerson, San Diego

San Diego's oldest whale-watching expedition company offers three- and five-hour cruises during whale-watching season, which is late-December through March. Three-hour cruises depart daily at 10am and 1:30pm and head to the coastal waters of Point Loma. Five-hour trips depart Thursday through Sunday, and some holiday Mondays, at 10am and travel to the Coronado Islands and Mexico's marine wildlife sanctuary. Be on the lookout for whales, sea lions, dolphins, and elephant seals.

Hours: Stated above.

Price: The three-hour whale-watching excursion is $45 for adults; $37 for seniors and military; $20 for ages 12 and under; $17.50 for ages 2 - 12. Five-hour cruises are $60 for adults; $50 for seniors and military; $40 for ages 4 - 12 (and pretty long for ages under 4, and even for some adults!). All-day parking is $8.

Ages: 6 years and up.

HORNBLOWER
☀
(888) 467-6256 or (619) 725-8888 / www.hornblower.com
$$$$
970 N. Harbor Drive, San Diego

Hornblower offers one- and two-hour narrated harbor cruises. You'll see numerous ships including air craft carriers and other military vessels, the *Star of India*, the Navy Seals Training base, Hotel Del Coronado, the Coronado Bay Bridge, and (hopefully) lots of marine animals. The company also offers three-and-a-half-hour whale-watching cruises that include narration by the Captain; watching a documentary on whales; viewing sea lions, birds, and whales; indoor/outdoor seating; and a snack bar with hot food and drinks available. Whale sighting is guaranteed or you receive a whale check, good for another cruise. This yacht company also offers other specialty cruises, including brunch and dinner cruises, throughout the year.

Hours: One-hour harbor cruises depart year round, 10am - 4:15pm (during the summer until 5:30pm). Two-hour cruises depart daily, 10am - 3pm (summer until 4:15pm). Whale-watching cruises are offered the mid-December through mid-April daily at 9:30am and 1:30pm. Reservations aren't necessary, but call first (of course!). All cruises are weather dependent.

Price: One-hour harbor tours are $23 for adults; $21 for seniors and active military; $11.50 for ages 4 - 12; children 3 and under are free. Two-hour cruises are $28 for adults; $26 for seniors and military; $14 for ages 4 - 12. Whale watching is $37 for adults, $36 for seniors and military, $18.50 for ages 4 - 12.

Ages: 5 years and up, depending on the tour.

LA JOLLA COVE KAYAK - SNORKEL ADVENTURE
☀
(619) 260-1880 / www.scubasandiego.com
$$$$
Camino del Oro at Kellogg Park, La Jolla

Kayaking is truly an exhilarating adventure, especially around the scenic La Jolla coastline and the La Jolla Underwater Park. For two-and-a-half hours with a naturalist guide, you'll glide in and amongst the sea caves, past cliffs, and through the kelp. Sea lions and harbor seals are often encountered along the cove as well. Now, imagine doing this at nighttime, under the heavenly canvas of stars. Starting in May, these two-hour tours also give you prime viewing for the five-minute firework show set off at Sea World in Mission Bay. Ages 5 and up can experience fun, education, and little snap, crackle, and pop.

Snorkeling at the Underwater Park is an equally exciting excursion. A guide aids you in exploring the near-to-shore, underwater ecosystem and points out some of the most colorful fish off the coast, including the brilliant orange Garibaldi, the California state fish. All gear is provided with the tour. Snorkelers must be able to swim, be at least 13 years old, and weigh at least 100 pounds. You'll be in the water about an hour and a half. A sack lunch and soft drink are provided with both types of tours.

See LA JOLLA SHORES BEACH (on pg. 470) for information on the immediate beach area and SCRIPPS PARK (pg. 519) for more information on the close-by La Jolla area.

Hours: Kayak tours are offered Memorial Day - Labor Day, daily - call to make a reservation. Night Fireworks Kayak tours are available Memorial Day on weekends, only, until Father's Day from 7:30pm - 9:30pm; then from Father's Day - Labor Day, on Wed., Fri. - Sun., 8:30pm - 10:30pm. Snorkel tours are offered daily at 10am.

Price: $70 per person, per tour.

Ages: 5 and up for kayaks; 13 years and up for snorkeling.

LA JOLLA KAYAK

(858) 459-1114 / www.lajollakayak.com

2199 Avenida De La Playa, La Jolla Shores

$$$$$

Come kayak the waters of gorgeous La Jolla on your own or with a guide. You'll paddle past sea cliffs as well as past and through caves. An underwater reserve, featuring reefs and diverse marine life, is in this area, too, so bring or rent snorkel gear. And don't be surprised by the sea lions and harbor seals that swim by your kayak or stop for a friendly visit. Stunning scenery, good exercise, and a fun family excursion - life doesn't get any better than this! Ninety-minute tours include a lesson, life vest, and guide. Wear your swim suit. Note that kids must be at least 6 years old to kayak and with an adult. Note that you can combine your kayak adventure with snorkeling so you see the best of both worlds - above and below the water. The company also offers bike tours and surfboard rentals.

Hours: Tours and rentals are available daily, 8am - sunset, weather permitting. Call for specific tour times.

Price: Kayak rentals are $30 for two hours for a single; $50 for two hours for a double. Snorkel gear is $7 for mask and snorkel; $7 for fins; $15 for wetsuit. Kayak tours are $35 per person; $49 for two people. Two-hour kayak and snorkel tours are $59 per person; $99 for two people.

Ages: 7 years and up.

MAIN STREET CARRIAGE

(760) 765-0438 / www.julianca.com

Corner of Main and Washington, Julian

$$

"When I take you out in the surrey with the fringe on top!" (from *Oklahoma*) During this fifteen-minute, narrated ride you'll see and hear about the history of the small town of Julian, including mining and apple picking, enjoying the sights and sounds of the countryside via a horse-drawn carriage: $7 for adults; $3 for ages 9 and under. Enjoy a longer ride (and more country) - thirty minutes for $45 for two people; an hour for $65 for two people, $5 per additional person.

Hours: Call for reservations during the week. Sat. - Sun., noon - 5:30pm. Open most holidays.

Price: Some prices listed above.

Ages: 3 years and up.

OCEANSIDE BOAT RENTALS

(760) 722-0028 / www.boats4rent.com

256 Harbor Drive South, Oceanside Harbor, Oceanside

$$$$

Rentals includes kayaks - $15 per hour for a single, $25 an hour for a double; pedal boats - $15 to $30 an hour; sailboats - $45 an hour for a fourteen footer; motorboats - $65 an hour for a six-passenger boat that doesn't leave the harbor, and $90 an hour for a six-passenger boat that does (plus a fuel charge); electric boats (which are much quieter than motor boats and seat eight) start at $75 an hour; stand up paddle board - $25 an hour; and wave runners -$105 an hour (plus a fuel charge). Make some time to shop around in the Harbor Village before or after your excursion.

Hours: Open daily, 10am - an hour before sunset, weather permitting.

Price: Prices listed above. The first two hours of parking in the village area are free.

Ages: 4 years and up.

OCOTILLO WELLS STATE VEHICULAR RECREATION AREA

(760) 767-5391- ranger; (760) 767-5393 - district office / ohv.parks.ca.gov

5172 Highway 78, Borrego Springs

!

For a little off-roading fun, try Ocotillo Wells Recreation Area where you can go up hills, over sand dunes, and through dry washes. You must provide your own vehicles (and have them registered), but the entrance is free and so are primitive camping sites. A visitor center is open Friday, Saturday, and Sunday nights for campfires and events such as star gazing, geo caching, and interpretive lectures.

Hours: Open daily.
Price: Free
Ages: 6 years and up.

OLD TOWN TROLLEY TOURS

(619) 298-8687 / www.trolleytours.com
4010 Twiggs Street, San Diego

$$$$$

Ding, ding, ding goes the bell of the trolley! Really get to know the city of San Diego by taking a narrated tour on board an old-fashioned looking trolley. The tour guide will tell you the history of San Diego, plus lots of fun stories. One of the best features about this tour is that you can take a continuous two-hour tour, or jump off (so to speak) and rejoin the tour at any time throughout the day. There are eleven stops covered on the loop, including Old Town, Seaport Village, Horton Plaza, Hotel Del Coronado, San Diego Zoo, and Balboa Park. Appropriately nicknamed "transportainment," we enjoyed the commentary, the freedom of stopping at attractions, staying for a bit, and getting back on board when we were ready. Hassle-free parking to all these attractions is another plus.

Hours: Trolleys run daily most of the year, 9am - 5pm; open in the summer, daily, 9am - 6pm. No tours are given on Thanksgiving or Christmas.
Price: The trolley tour is $36 for adults; $18 for ages 4 - 12; children 3 and under are free. Prices are discounted if booked through the internet.
Ages: 5 years and up.

PACIFIC SOUTHWEST RAILWAY MUSEUM

(619) 465-7776 - recording; (619) 478-9937 - weekends / www.psrm.org; www.sdrm.org
750 Depot Street, Campo

$$$

The sound of a train whistle blowing has always been a signal for adventure! Start your adventure at the old Campo Depot where there are a few stationary push carts, a gift shop, several picnic tables, and even a small playground with swings, old tires, and a sandbox with toys. Then, come aboooard the *Golden State Limited* train for an hour-and-a-half ride (twelve-miles) your children will never forget. You'll depart from the depot/ticket office and ride in restored 1930s passenger coaches. My boys loved the freedom of moving about while traveling. They walked from car to car (parents are asked to accompany minors), watched the scenic mountains and meadows roll past, saw a few cows, and played cards. Tip: We brought a picnic lunch, as only snack food is available to purchase on the train. At the halfway point, kids can view (from the windows) the engine being switched around to pull you back the way you came. The conductors were friendly and shared a lot of information about railroads and the history of the area. If you conduct yourself well, two people per excursion can ride in the locomotive cab for $35 per person ($70 for up to four people - two ride one way and two coming back).

The train stops for all passengers to depart at the museum on the way back. Inside the display building, or museum, are some terrific train treasures - a Southern Pacific Engine, pull carts, photos, tools, a wooden train car desperately awaiting lots of help, and a beautifully restored, oak, segregated passenger (look at the signs above certain seats that say "for colored") and baggage car, built in 1886. Walk through this car and to the attached mailroom car with its cubicles and bags. Outside, on the tracks, are numerous more old and restored rail cars such as passenger, steam and diesel locomotives, cabooses, Pullman, and freight cars. #104, even rusted and sporting some holes, is a classic as it is the last surviving steam locomotive of the SD & A railway. The docents willingly share their knowledge about the history of the cars, people or freight that rode on them and anything else railroad related. Don't hesitate to ask them any questions!

On the walk back to the Depot is more of the outdoors museum, as it is strewn with old and weathered rail cars, some being restored, some not, plus plaques describing the history of this railway. Check out the sign that has hobo codes carved into it.

Ninety-minute school train tours/rides on the 1930's vintage cars are offered on the third Tuesday of every month at 10am, by reservation. (A minimum of thirty students is required.) A train ride is a great "living" classroom. Then, there is time to explore the museum. The general public is welcome to come along if there's room. Check the train website for special excursions such as dinner rides, the Easter Bunny Train, Pumpkin Express, and the North Pole Limited. Note that GASKILL BROTHERS STONE STORE MUSEUM (pg. 533) and MOTOR TRANSPORT MUSEUM (pg. 540) are around the corner.

Hours: The museum is open Sat. - Sun., 9am - 5pm. Trains depart on most Sat. and Sun. at 11am and at 2:30pm. You must have a reservation. Closed New Year's Day, Christmas Eve, Christmas, and New Year's Eve.

Price: Train rides, which include the museum, are $15 for adults; $12 for seniors and active military; $5 for ages 6 - 12; children 5 and under are free. Special event rides might cost more. The student train rides are $5 per person; the general public pays the regular price. Entry to just the museum and grounds are $5 for adults; $2.50 for ages 6 - 12.

Ages: 3 years and up.

SAN DIEGO BAY FERRY and OLD FERRY LANDING

(800) 44CRUISE (442-7847) or (619) 234-4111 / www.flagshipsd.com
990 N. Harbor Drive at the Broadway Pier in downtown San Diego, and the Ferry Landing Marketplace in Coronado

$$$$

Take a fifteen-minute ride over to Coronado (and back) on the San Diego Bay Ferry. Enjoy the Ferry Landing Marketplace on the Coronado side, with its Victorian-style shopping and eating complex. Bike, blade, or walk along the waterfront paved pathways. You can also romp in the grassy lawns along the pathways, or sunbathe on the beach. A farmer's market is held on the island on Tuesdays from 2:30pm to 6pm. TIDELANDS PARK (pg. 521) is next to the Marketplace. If you want to go to Hotel Del Coronado, take the bus (#904) from the landing. It runs approximately every hour from 10am to 6pm, with a few stops along the way. The shuttle is about $2.50 per person; children 5 and under ride free, and all ride for free July through September. Or, enjoy a scenic walk to the hotel (one-and-a-third miles), though it might get a little long for younger children. See FLAGSHIP CRUISES AND EVENTS, the below entry, for information on longer and more scenic boat rides.

Hours: The ferry departs from the pier every hour on the hour, Sun. - Thurs., 9am - 9pm; Fri. - Sat., 9am - 10pm. It leaves Coronado every hour on the half hour.

Price: $4.25 for adults (one-way); children 3 and under are free; bikes are included in the price. Parking at Five Star parking at the Broadway pier is $12 for 10 hours; $18 for the day.

Ages: All

SAN DIEGO PARASAIL ADVENTURES

(619) 223-4(FUN) (4386) / www.goparasailing.com
1548 Quivira Way / 844 W. Mission Bay Drive, San Diego

$$$$$

Experience the thrill of soaring up in the air, "flying" over San Diego waters, and getting a bird's eye view of this lovely city. Rides last about seven minutes, although participants are in the boat for about ninety minutes, to ensure that everyone gets their turn. Take off and land directly on the boat. Single or tandem flights are available.

Hours: Open April - mid-May and mid-September - October, weekends only, 10am - 4pm. Open daily, Memorial Day - Labor Day, 10am - 6pm. Closed November - March.

Price: About $70 per person, plus a fuel charge of $5 per person. Observers can ride in the boat for $25 a person, if there is room.

Ages: At least 90 lbs.; minimum age 7 years old.

SAN DIEGO TROLLEY

(619) 685-4900 - 24-hour information line; (619) 233-3004 - office; (619) 234-5005 - for persons with hearing impairments. / www.sdmts.com/trolley/trolley.asp
San Diego

$$

The San Diego Trolley (and bus) line is a great way to get around San Diego. The Blue line extends from Mission San Diego all the way down to San Ysidro. From this last stop at the border, you can either walk into Mexico, or take a cab. Park for free at the Old Town Transit Center, or all day at the MTS tower garage at 12th and Imperial for $8. The Orange line goes from El Cajon to Santa Fe Depot and downtown. There are several places to catch the trolley line along the routes, with many of the stops being at major attractions. Part of the fun for a child is just the ride. Check out the website for specials such as family weekend deals and friends ride free. Also see OLD TOWN TROLLEY TOURS (pg. 583), for another way to get around San Diego.

Hours: It runs daily, 5am - 1am, with service every fifteen minutes most of the day.

Price: Travel between any two stations is $2.50 for adults; $1.25 for seniors. A day pass is $5, which is also good for most bus routes for one operating day. Up to two children 5 and under ride for free. Family days are every weekend where kids 12 and under ride for free with a paying adult. Tickets are usually dispensed from machines.

Ages: All

SAN DIEGO VINTAGE TROLLEY

(619) 557-4555 / www.sdmts.com; www.sdvintagetrolley.com

12th and Imperial Transit Center, San Diego

Take a "ride back in time" when you board a restored, vintage trolley, circa 1946. Ride the Silver Line trolley past, or stop at, downtown San Diego's most popular destinations including the Gaslamp Quarter, Seaport Village, Petco Park, and along the waterfront. The trolley also has other stops along the way - check the full, 2.7 mile round trip route online. The ride is about twenty-five minutes if you stay on it the whole way. Note that if you disembark and reboard, you pay the fare, again.

Hours: Tues. and Thurs., 9:52am - 1:52pm; Sat. - Sun., 10:52am - 3:22pm - every 30 minutes, from 12th and Imperial Transit Center, and along the way.

Price: $2.50 for adults, round trip; $1.25 for seniors; free for two children 5 years and under with one paying adult. Exact change only.

Ages: All

SEA AND LAND ADVENTURES SEAL TOURS

(619) 298-8687 / www.sealtours.com

500 Kettner Boulevard at Harbor, Seaport Village, San Diego

Is it a bus or a boat? Yes! The amphibious vehicle on this SEAL tour takes passengers on a ninety-minute, narrated ride on the streets through the heart of San Diego, explaining the history of the city and highlighting points of interest. Then, splash! Drive into the waters of Mission Bay (this is an odd sensation at first). You'll spend some more time back up on land before another plunge, this time into the San Diego Bay waters where you'll cruise past (and learn about) the maritime and military history of the area. "Sail" past the sky line, Navy ships, fishing vessels (don't forget to wave), and tugboats. Be on the lookout for sea-lions and other aquatic creatures. The tour is an unforgettable way to learn about San Diego in an exciting manner. And yes, people in cars and all along the land and sea route do stare as the bus/boat is unusual looking. (Or is it the people inside who are unusual looking?!)

Hours: The tour depart November - March, Fri. - Sun. Call for departure times. Tours depart daily the rest of the year, weather permitting.

Price: $36 for adults; $19 for ages 4 - 12; children 3 and under are free, but it's not recommended for them.

Ages: 4 years and up.

TORREY PINES GLIDER PORT

(858) 452-9858 / www.flytorrey.com

2800 Torrey Pines Scenic Drive, La Jolla

Man has had dreams and aspirations to fly since the beginning of time. Hang gliding and paragliding are the closest things we'll get to it in this lifetime (and they are much better than Icarus' attempt!) Kids may participate in this uplifting sport, or come to just watch. We brought a picnic lunch, as there are tables at the cliff tops, although a full-service snack bar, the Cliff Hanger Cafe, is here, too, selling deli sandwiches, salads, and soups. Besides the exhilarating sight of gliders soaring and dipping along the coastline, there is a breathtaking view of the ocean and beach. The small planes you see flying overhead are really remote control planes that have a take-off/landing site right next "door."

Hours: Open daily for flights, 9am - 5pm, although if you're coming to watch, you might want to call first to see if anyone is actually flying that day. Closed Christmas.

Price: Free, unless you're flying! Paragliding tandem flights start at $150, usually take about a half hour, which includes ground school instruction and about 20 minutes of flight time. Hang gliding tandems start at $200. Air conditions determine flight capability. Weight limit is 175 per passenger.

Ages: All to come and watch; 5 years and up for tandem; at least 100 pounds for solo flights.

YOUNG EAGLES PROGRAM (San Diego County)

National number - (877) 806-8902; San Diego - EAAChapter14@gmail.com or (619) 920-8069 - airport / Fallbrook - www.eaa1279.org; San Diego - www.eaa14.org; National - www.youngeagles.org

Fallbrook - 2155 S Mission Road at the Fallbrook Airport; Oceanside - 480 Airport Road; San Diego - 1409 Continental Avenue Hangar 1, Brown Field

See the entry for YOUNG EAGLES PROGRAM (Los Angeles County) on page 215 for details. Fallbrook - This chapter, #1279, usually flies twice a year. Preregister as the fifty spaces available fill up quickly. Their website is very up-to-date. Oceanside - For information on flights with this chapter, #286, check the national website. San Diego - The flight is over the city of San Diego and over the ocean. Younger children who are grounded can ride in a simulator that has a radio, earphones, and all the instruments that are in a cockpit. The ride moves and turns as the wheel is turned. Ask about this chapter's other Young Eagle programs.

Hours: Fallbrook - One Sat. in April and one in October, with registration beginning around 8:30am. Oceanside - Usually once a quarter from 10am to 1pm, or so. San Diego - Usually the second Sat. of each month from 8:30am - noon.

Price: Free

Ages: 8 - 17 years old.

—ZOOS AND ANIMALS—

BIRCH AQUARIUM

(858) 534-FISH (3474) / www.aquarium.ucsd.edu

2300 Expedition Way, La Jolla

Visually exciting statues of leaping, large whales grace the fountain outside the entrance of the Birch Aquarium. There are also picnic tables and a snack stand out here. This outstanding, sizable, aquarium-museum has three main exhibit areas. The aquarium section contains over thirty-three large tanks filled with an incredible variety of creatures found in the Earth's oceans - from monkey face eels to sharks to flashlight fish that glow (or blink on and off) in the dark. Just some of our favorite sea animals showcased here include the almost mesmerizing moon jellies; sunflower starfish; bat rays; very large grouper fish; nurse sharks; odd-looking, longhorn cowfish; the leafy sea dragons or seahorses; garden eels that look like hoses "standing" upright in the sand; the amazing giant octopus; and the beautiful, but venomous, striped lionfish. I also like some of the other colorful fish at the coral reef displays. This exhibit also posts information, coupled with interactive displays, about the harvesting of coral - the harm that's been done and the help that coral can be medically. The largest tank at Birch has a huge kelp forest which makes it easy to view animals that are normally hidden on ocean floors. See divers feed the fish in the forest Tuesdays and Thursdays at 12:30pm, Saturdays at 2pm, and Sundays at 10:30am. (These times may change.)

Outside, the small rocky Tidepool Plaza connects the aquarium and the museum. A wave machine gently creates natural water motion in a simulated tidepool. Kids will see up close (and can gently touch) sea stars, sea urchins, sea cucumbers, and more. Also, take in the magnificent panoramic view of the La Jolla coastline (and the world famous Scripps Institute).

The museum has several fine components. Find out everything you ever wanted to know about seahorses in the incredibly interesting and thoroughly researched Seahorse Exhibit. Did you know that seahorses adapt by changing color to blend in with their environment? See the same type of seahorse in various background settings, and therefore, various colors. Learn about threats to these creatures and how they are dried and ground up to use as medicinal aids. Watch short videos on (seahorse) dating, mating, and giving birth. Note that males give birth - this could make for some very interesting conversation. Look for the tiny baby seahorses in the nursery. And check out the utterly bizarre-looking, weedy and leafy sea dragons - cousins to the seahorse. Note that this exhibit rotates in and out of the museum. One rotating exhibit currently is Whales - Voices in the Sea, where visitors listen to seven types of whales, including humpback, sperm, beaked, gray, and blue whales, and then try to mimic them. (We call this whale karaoke.) Videos here show the elegance of whales in their natural habitat while spotlighting their struggles of survival in an increasingly threatened environment.

Another component of the museum is the rotating oceanographic exhibit with numerous interactive display areas that incorporate touch screens or an activity that shows and explains the integral part that oceans play in relation to how the Earth functions. Kids participate in exhibit experiments to learn about various aspects of ocean sciences such as currents, tides, and waves; and how solar heat falls on the ocean unevenly via a long wave tank. The experiments are

actually quite fun! My kids also really enjoyed a past exhibit called the Ocean Supermarket, where they used scanners on common household products to see which ingredients came from the ocean. (Did you know that ice cream uses carrageenan [i.e., red seaweed] to make it smooth and creamy?!) Another exhibit has been Feeling the Heat: the Climate Challenge which encouraged participants to test their knowledge of if everyday items contribute to climate change and other aspects of global warming.

Kids, especially, will enjoy the Wonders of Water outdoor water play stations where they get to create currents, rapids, and dams by strategically placing (or removing) panels in raised tanks of water. Let them expend energy at Boundless Energy, an educational playground. Power a mechanical fish here with solar energy. Contrast and compare the wind turbine innovations. Ride a teeter-totter. Generate your own electricity to harness solar, wind, and water power.

The back courtyard features a fascinating destination - the shark tank. The large tank is clear so you can easily see all the angles of the many species of shark swimming around. Feeding times are usually at 10:30am on Tuesdays, Thursdays, and Saturdays. There is also a feeding area for humans at the aquarium at the Splash Cafe. The Birch Aquarium has a lot to offer - come "sea" it for yourself! Call about the many special activities, programs, and camps offered through the aquarium including tidepool tours, whale-watching cruises, grunion hunting, snorkeling, sleep overs, and the popular Shark Discovery Days.

Hours: Open daily, 9am - 5pm. Closed New Year's Day, Thanksgiving, and Christmas.

Price: $17 for adults; $13 for seniors; $14 for ages 13 - 17; $12.50 for ages 3 - 12; children 2 and under are free. Parking is free for three hours. See Museum Month, San Diego (pg. 708) for details about half-price admission in February. See page xi for info on the Bank of America free weekend program.

Ages: 3 years and up.

CALIFORNIA WOLF CENTER   ☼

(619) 234-WOLF (9653) or (760) 765-0030 / www.californiawolfcenter.org $$$$
KQ Ranch Road (off Highway 79), Julian

Who's afraid of the big bad wolf? And why? Clear up many misconceptions about Mexican gray wolves and Alaskan gray wolves at the education and conservation wolf center during a two-hour presentation/tour. First, gather in a room filled with wolf paraphernalia for a twenty-minute video presentation. See and learn about what wolves eat; how they communicate (yes they howl, but not at the moon); the pack's pecking order, starting with an alpha (i.e., dominant) male and female; and their predators (man). Learn the difference between a fox, a coyote, and a wolf (this being the largest of the three) via a touch table with skins, skulls, teeth, and plaster footprints. Also hold and learn about tracking collars that researchers use on wolves.

A highlight is going out to the enclosures to actually see these majestic creatures. There are currently about twenty-one wolves here, but you won't get to see them all as several are kept off the main path. The ones seen on the tours and in the education programs are usually more curious and often come close up to the fence where visitors line up - all the better to see you, my dear. There are no guarantees that the wolves will approach, though, as they are wild animals. Bring your camera. Take a short hike up a hill to see the other wolves who may, or may not, come over to check out the group. Two tours are offered and both include the education presentation and seeing two packs of wolves. The Wolf Pack Tour is a smaller group, lending a more intimate time with the guide and more time observing the wolves.

The center also offers private tours, field trips, off-site presentations (wolves "attend" via Skype), and photography tours for ages 18 and up, August through December. Photography tours, for up to two people at a time, are the only way visitors are allowed into an enclosure, animal behavior permitting, although no physical contact is ever allowed. Have a howling good time here!

Hours: Wolf Recovery Today tour is offered mid-September - April, Sat. at 10am and 2pm; Sun. at 10am. That tour is also offered May - mid-September, Sat. at 2pm and 4:30pm; Sun. at 10am. Wolf Pack Tours are offered Mon. at 10am and Fri. at 3pm. Arrive 30 minutes prior to any tour - latecomers will not be admitted because a truck picks you up from the bottom area of a hill for a bumpy ride on a dirt road and through a gate. Reservations are required. Call to set up a time for group programs during the week.

Price: Wolf Recovery Today tours are $20 for adults; $10 for seniors, military, students, and ages 12 and under. Wolf Pack Tours are $30 for adults; $15 for everyone else.

Ages: 7 years and up.

DEL MAR FAIRGROUNDS - RACETRACK

(858) 755-1141 or (858) 793-5533 / www.dmtc.com $$$
2260 Jimmy Durante Boulevard, at Del Mar Fairgrounds, Del Mar

For unbridled fun, check out horse racing season at the famous Del Mar Fairgrounds. Kids have good horse sense - they aren't here to bet, but to enjoy the races. View the races from the stands or go through a tunnel to the infield area. Most weekends bring a special event such as the One and Only Truly Fabulous Hats Contest on opening day, and family day when the infield is transformed to a fun zone for children with pony rides, face painting, an inflatable jump, obstacle course, and more. Admission is free for children, when accompanied by a parent.

Check out Camp Del Mar, where adults watch the races while kids, ages 5 to 12, are supervised by counselors to enjoy activities on the grounds such as an inflatable jump, crafts, mini golf, fun tournaments, air hockey, and/or other games and events, plus lunch and snacks. Camp usually runs from noon to 30 min. after the last race. Also inquire about horse shows, rodeos, and polo games, and know that the fairgrounds are host to the county fair, holiday light shows, and other special events.

> **Hours:** The season runs late July - early September, and some dates in November, Wed. - Sun., 9am - 5pm and special Mon., 9am - 1pm. Post time is usually 2pm, although it's at 4pm on Fri.; and 1pm on Pacific Classic Day. Gates usually open 2 hours before the first post. The track is closed Mon. (except Labor Day Mon.) and Tues.
>
> **Price:** General admission is $6 for adults for the grandstands; $10 for clubhouse admission or reserved seating (which is closer to the finish line) on Sat. and Sun.; free for children 17 and under. Prices vary on Opening Day and weekday tickets - check their website. Camp is $24 a child. Parking is $10.
>
> **Ages:** 5 years and up.

FREE FLIGHT

(858) 481-3148 or (858) 755-9351 / www.freeflightbirds.org $$
2132 Jimmy Durante Boulevard, Del Mar

This permanent little outdoor boarding house is for the birds, literally - about forty-five of them. Some of them are here for behavioral issues and some are rescues for various reasons. There are also birds up for adoption. There are more than thirty perches along the short pathway in this tree-lined and jungle-like "backyard". Look at and even gently touch some of the brilliantly-colored cockatoos, macaws, parrots, and other exotic birds. It's a good place to get some great pictures of birds! Note: Loud squawking of the birds is set off by loud kids who are set off by the loud squawking, etc. Young children might be startled. Also, many of the birds have strong talons which could scare or hurt visitors, so young ones are better off simply looking at and not handling the birds. Children under 13 years must be accompanied by a parent. Bring some change to purchase food to feed the birds. There is also a koi pond here.

Freeflight offers half-hour school tours that explain the different types of birds, their habitats, and educates visitors as to the care of exotic birds, and more. Call to make a reservation. Tip: Visit on sunny days, if possible, as there are more birds brought out then.

> **Hours:** Open Thurs. - Tues., 10am - 4pm; Wed., 10am - 2pm. Closed on rainy days and some holidays.
>
> **Price:** $5 for adults; $2 for ages 12 and under.
>
> **Ages:** 3 years and up.

LEELIN LLAMA TREKS

(800) 6WIKIUP (694-5487) or (760) 765-1890 / www.wikiupbnb.com $$$$$
1645 Whispering Pines Drive, Julian

Looking for an unusual outing? Sign up for a llama trek! Choose from a variety of destinations - to the lake, through the mountains, or through the town of Julian. Each member of your group leads his/her own llama that carries trekkers' lunches and other necessities. Most kids, and adults, aren't used to being around llamas so the intrigue, as well as the scenery, makes the five-mile, four-to-five-hour expeditions unique experiences. The animals are gentle, enjoy being petted, and by the end of the trek, your children will want to take theirs home. They can't. A deli sandwich or salad, chips, cookie, and cold drink are included in your outing. Bring sunscreen and a water bottle. One of the best excursions for kids is the Eagle Mine Trek, which takes about five hours round trip, and includes an almost sixty-minute tour of the gold mine. See EAGLE MINING COMPANY (pg. 574) for details on the mine.

LeeLin Wikiup is a bed and breakfast, geared for couples, owned by LeeLin Llama Treks. (The llamas actually live on the grounds here.) Each room of the Wikiup, although adjacent to each

other, has its own unique, themed decor - Native American, Victorian, Stargazer, or rustic. There is a nice-sized common lounging area with TV, games, book, and tape library. An outdoor hot tub, outdoor deck, horseshoe pits, the llamas, and the lovely surroundings complete this inn's offerings.

Hours: Open year round except during inclement weather. Reservations are required. At least two people must sign up for any of the day treks that begin about 9:30am or 10am.

Price: Prices start at $95. The Eagle Mine trek is $95 for adults; $75 for ages 10 and under. Wikiup rates start at $185 - $195 per couple during the week.

Ages: 7 years and up.

LIONS TIGERS & BEARS

(619) 659-8078 - rescue facility; (800) 979-3370 - reservations; (619) 445-0997 - White Oak overnight Wild Nights / www.lionstigersandbears.org

24402 Martin Way, Alpine

Oh my! This accredited rescue facility is located on a sprawling, ninety-three-acre ranch, only a portion of which currently is being used. There is room for more animals, but funding is needed. Salvation for the animals and education for the public regarding exotic animal trade and care are the main goals. A ten minute intro movie talks about this and states that there are thousands of more tigers in captivity than in the wild. I didn't know that.

About fifty animals, many which have come from abusive residences, find permanent sanctuary here, including (at least at the moment of this writing) eleven big cats (and they are BIG!) - three majestic African lions (one weighs 500 pounds!), two Bengal tigers, a leopard, a serval, a mountain lion and three bobcats.

The big cat, double-fence enclosures are nicely landscaped with natural rock, trees, water (i.e. pools), grass, and even a hammock or two for catnaps. There is also a larger exercise area for the cats with a run around area and rock pool with a waterfall. The facility is also home to six black bears, including the famous Meatball, and several ranch animals.

Ninety-minute (or so) tours are offered for visitors to walk around (on uneven ground) to each enclosure with a knowledgeable and passionate keeper who discusses each animal - their history, their personal habits, and more, in an informal manner, which is great for Q and A. Tip: Feed A Cat sanctuary visits are offered to visitors 18 years and older. For a few minutes, these guests go in between the first and second fence enclosures, stab a piece of meat, or chicken, with a very long fork and then poke it through the fence holes to feed the cat of their choice. For participants, the thrill of being so close to such a powerful animal, and perhaps being roared at, is worth it!

Go into the Animals Encounters where two llamas, a pot-bellied pig, Pygmy goats, a miniature horse, a miniature donkey, a few horses and some other farm animals are waiting to be pet. After all this, walk the grounds on your own and/or even bring a picnic lunch to enjoy here at tables in the shade in front of the cat enclosures.

Hour-long group tours, for up to thirty students (or other age groups), are encouraged to come for even more of an educational outing. They'll see the big cats and learn facts and rescue stories about each of them, while similarities and differences between domestic and wild animals are pointed out and discussed. There is plenty of time for questions and answers. Book a tour in the morning, if possible, as that's when the cats are most active. Waivers must first be filled out by parents of minors.

Tips: Read over the wish list on the website before a visit and bring one or more of the items needed. Check the website for special events, such as elegant overnight stays at the on-site White Oak cottage with all of the amenities; brunches; activities just for kids; photography workshops; and more. Since you're in the area, about ten minutes eastward in Pine Valley are two notable outings: 1) Pine Valley County Park at   28810 Old Hwy 80 - a 17-acre park with oak and pine trees, a seasonal creek, ball fields, tennis courts, shuffleboard, horseshoe pits, and a playground; and 2) Major's Coffee Shop at 28870 Old Hwy 80 / (619) 473-9969 - a cute, 50's decor diner, with indoor and patio outdoor seating, offering good food at reasonable prices. It's open daily, 6am to 8pm.

Hours: Open Tues. - Sat., with tours usually at 9am and 10:15am. You must call first to make a reservation before you visit.

Price: Member-for-a-day is $30 for adults; $15 for ages 12 and under. Annual membership starts at $50 for adults, which includes unlimited visits for the year. Feed A Cat is $130 and includes general admission. Educational visits for school groups (of 20 or more) are $10 per student; $25 for adult chaperones. Girl Scouts are $10 per person.

Ages: 5 years and up.

LIVING COAST DISCOVERY CENTER

(619) 409-5900 / www.thelivingcoast.org

1000 Gunpowder Point Drive, Chula Vista

$$$$

Putting their hands in a pool of sharks is only one of the special things that kids (and adults) are invited to do at the Living Coast Discovery Center, which is located in the Sweetwater Marsh National Wildlife Refuge. You'll start your visit by taking the free trolley into the refuge, as cars are not allowed.

Flanking the entrance are deep-water aquariums with green sea turtles. The medium-sized center is full of interactive exhibits, and plants and animals that correspond to certain environmental zones - the bay, the marsh, and the upland. There are several tanks in the main room containing seahorses, lion fish, piranhas, eels, clown fish, sheephead, crabs, octopus, garibaldi, steelhead trout, and the almost ethereal moon jellies who reside in a glowing blue aquarium. Other live critters that dwell here include snakes, poison frogs, and alligator snapping turtles.

My boys proudly boast that they've touched a shark, and lived! as an adjacent building houses an aquarium with a shallow-water touch tank. It contains leopard and horn sharks, as well as batrays, stingrays, and the odd-looking shovel-nose guitarfish. Some of these creatures actually come within petting distance. There is also a deep water tank for larger sharks and rays that is just for looking at, not touching.

An outside overlook affords an opportunity to observe migrating shore birds such as terns, killdeer, plovers, and more wetlands wildlife. A walk-through bird aviary features snowy egrets, sandpipers, herons, black-necked stilts, and other water birds, as well as some interactive exhibits such as rubbing tables and an oversized clapper rail nest for kids to crawl inside. Other bird enclosures contain non-releasable birds of prey, such as owls, a falcon, hawks, and a bald eagle, whose feeding time is 2:30pm. A hummingbird and a butterfly garden are also on the grounds.

Short, stroller-friendly trails in front of the Center branch off in several directions leading towards the water, allowing visitors to get closer to the bay to see geese and egrets, or smaller water inhabitants. Look for other wildlife along the trail such as bunnies and lizards.

Feel like a Very Important Person? Take one of the five, twenty-minute, VIP Animal Encounters - $50 each for up to 6 people. We did the one with the sea turtles where we saw and touched sea stars and other tidepool animals, saw rescued animals in holding tanks, and then went into the sea turtle area and got to feed them. It was wonderful to see them up close and learn so much about them! We also did another VIP intriguing experience - the encounter of feeding the sharks and rays, which felt like they had slimy lips as they took the food from our fingers. I'm looking forward to doing the falcon one next. The Living Coast offers a variety of other on-site special activities, such as guided tours given Wednesday, Saturday and Sunday; make-it take-it crafts ($1) on most weekend afternoons; day camps; family overnights; and educational programs.

Hours: Open daily, 10am - 4pm. Closed New Year's Day, Easter, Thanksgiving, and Christmas. Trolleys run approximately every fifteen minutes.

Price: $14 for adults; $9 for seniors, students, and ages 4 - 17; military with ID and children 3 and under are free.

Ages: 3 years and up.

OASIS CAMEL DAIRY

(760) 787-0983 / www.cameldairy.com

26757 Julian Rd [78], Ramona

$$$

Do camels spit? Are they mean? Where do they live and why? What do they really store in their humps? Find the answers to these questions and more as you learn about these intriguing animals on a one-hour tour. This first part consists of sitting outside on bleacher seats listening to Nancy, one of the owners, who is both funny and passionate, as she talk about camels, camel care, etc. She also brings out several camels for show and tell. After her talk, go visit the eighteen, or so, camels that roam the acreage and you'll get to see them up close and gently stroke them. You might see a baby camel and even watch one being bottle fed. Thought about riding a camel in the Sahara Desert? Closer, less expensive, and not nearly as lengthy, but still a unique opportunity, visitors can take a short, hand-led camel ride around a ring. The dairy has a few other animals as well, including a donkey, cows, sheep, a bull, a potbellied pig, turtles, and several birds, such as macaws, parrots, kookaburras, turkeys, and an African crowned crane. Don't forget your camera!

Camel milk products are sold here, too, such as lip balm, camel milk chocolate (not made here), and camel milk soap made from the camels milked here. The luxurious soaps come in a variety of scents, including Gold, Frankincense, and Myrrh.

Private group tours are offered whenever you want to make a reservation with a minimum fee of $100 (for up to ten people); $200 for other options and larger groups. Photo safaris and even hands-on camel clinics are also offered. All of these require reservations. Camel rides are available on private group tours for an additional fee.

Hours: Public tours are held one Sun. a month at 1pm; gates open at 12:30pm. Call or check the website for specific dates. The dairy is only open when tours are going on.

Price: Public tours are $10 for adults; $8 for seniors; $7 for ages 14 and under. Camel rides at the public tours are $10 for adults; $5 per child.

Ages: 3 years and up.

SAN DIEGO HUMANE SOCIETY

(619) 299-7012 - society; (619) 243-3432 - education dept. / www.sdhumane.org

5500 Gaines Street, San Diego

Animals and kids have an almost intuitive connection. Via birthday parties, outreach programs, group tours, scout tours, and Animal Adventure Camps, this Humane Society offers ways to foster and deepen that relationship. Week-long Adventure Camps are generally held over school breaks and in the summertime. Guided tours are geared for the age group that is visiting. The tour provides information about guidelines in choosing a pet, being responsible, and pet care. Depending on the animals available, sometimes visitors are allowed to pet or hug a cat or dog. The society also offers ninety-minute classes for elementary-age homeschoolers. Little ones aren't left out as they can join a Tots and Tales story time for preschoolers that's a time of interactive learning and just doggone fun. Note that there is an on-site cafe offering sandwiches, snacks, and beverages. If you're *feline* like it's a dog-eat-dog world and you want to help animals out in some way, unleash your potential and call the society.

Hours: The center is open Mon. - Fri., 9am - 7pm; Sat. - Sun., 9am - 6pm. Call to schedule a tour or sign up for a program or camp.

Price: Prices vary depending on the program.

Ages: 3 years and up, depending on the program.

SAN DIEGO POLO CLUB

(858) 481-9217 / www.sandiegopolo.com

14555 El Camino Real, Rancho Sante Fe

Question: Marco? Answer: Polo! Observe the fast paced, high-energy game of polo (not water polo), where eight players from junior leagues up to the pros compete on horseback. The gated playing field is on seventy-eight-acres of unobstructed, beautiful green grass. Horse and rider thunder past in an intricate game of strategy and skill. Assignment: Find out what the word chukker means.

Watch the hour-long game from the tail gate of your car and bring a picnic; bring a lawn chair field side; or sit at a table by the Player's Club, which is a restaurant and concession area. (No outside food is allowed in the Player's Club.) Admission includes entrance to the Club plus play time in the party jump that is usually on the grounds. Call for other fun, periodic "extras" like a petting zoo or even just the availability of snow cones. Arrive before the featured match to enjoy pre-game activities. Try your hand at the sport via lessons offered here - equipment usage is included with the lesson price.

Hours: Games are played mid-June - September, Sun. at 1pm and 3pm.

Price: General admission to the Player's Club is $12 for adults; children 12 and under are free. Tailgating is $10 per person. Preferred seating is $30 for adults. Parking is $10.

Ages: All

SAN DIEGO ZOO

(619) 234-3153 or (619) 231-1515 / www.sandiegozoo.org

2920 Zoo Drive, San Diego

The world-famous San Diego Zoo is home to some of the rarest animals in captivity and almost every animal imaginable, at least that's what it seems like. Put your walking shoes on because this zoo covers a lot of ground! In fact, you'd be hard pressed to try to see all 4,000 animals in one day, at least with young children in tow. The flamingos, just inside the entrance, are a colorful way to start your day. Personal favorites are the orangutans and siamangs in a naturalistic setting behind a huge glass observation window. I could watch these guys for hours and apparently, vice-versa. The monkey trail has an elevated walkway that allows visitors to walk through a tree canopy (just like in the jungle) and about three acres of exotic habitat. Although the monkeys, especially the mandrills with their colorful faces

(and red behinds), and gorillas are some of the most fascinating creatures here, there are several other species sharing this section including tigers, hippos (be amazed at how enormous they really are), otters, tapir, several other species of mammals, and lots of birds. Enjoy a walk through aviaries to see brilliantly-colored jungle birds amidst tropical foliage; watch the antics of the bears, especially the sun bears; see koalas in their trees; and take the opportunity to observe kangaroos, buffalo, zebra, exotic okapis, camels, giraffes, African lions and other big cats, meerkats, and other animals in enclosures that simulate their natural habitat.

Experience panda-monium and see the giant pandas amidst the bamboo - what unique-looking animals! See the immense polar bears and enjoy other parts of their exhibit area where visitors can read a huge book about polar bears, pop their heads up through fake ice, and learn about real Arctic ice. Elephant Odyssey features an extensive area for the really big stars - elephants. This 2.5-acre habitat for Asian elephants showcases them like never before with an open-sided food area, plus educational panels on their history and culture, and a place to speak with and see their keepers at work. Don't missssssss the Reptile House which contains enormous snakes - anacondas, pythons, boas, and cobras - plus Gila monsters, Komodo dragons, poison frogs, snake-necked turtles, and many more uncommon-looking creatures.

The Discovery Outpost is a children's area, but adults can visit, too. It is always a highlight with its petting zoo; 4-D theater; playground; and insect house with terrariums housing tarantulas, praying mantises, stick insects, scorpions, beetles, and more. This section also features naked mole-rats, spider monkeys, hedgehogs, and alligators. A fun (and funny) show spotlighting sea lions and other animals is a given daily at 11:30am, while other animal-related crafts and even science shows are presented here usually on weekends, during the summer, and seasonal holidays - check the website for detailed info. Interactive animal encounters go on throughout the zoo at various times, daily.

The forty-minute, double-decker, narrated bus tour is not only fun and informative, but it's a great way to get a good overview of most of the animals here. You can also use the Kangaroo Express bus, a vehicle that travels around the zoo enabling riders to hop on and off at five locations, as often as desired, throughout the day. The Skyfari Aerial Tram ride, which is pretty cool, is another way to view a portion of the zoo.

Ask about the many special programs the zoo offers during the year, including sleepovers, which are a great way to see animals at night and during early morning hours when they tend to be more active (the animals, not the kids). During sleepovers, you'll take a bus tour, see a special nighttime show, sing around a campfire, and enjoy dinner, snacks, and a hot breakfast all for $139 for adults, plus the price of zoo admission; $119 for ages 3 to 11. Other programs include the two-hour, Inside Look Tour ($75 + admission) where visitors see off-exhibit areas and take part of animal interactions, and Backstage Pass ($99 + admission), for ages 5 and up, where animal encounters - seeing them close-up and even touching several of them - make the day even more memorable. There are numerous educational programs available to the public and for school groups. Call (619) 718-3000 for tour dates, reservations, and more information for all the above programs, and more.

Hours: Open daily - most of the year, 9am - 5pm; open in the spring and summer, 9am - 6pm or 7pm - check the website calendar or call first.

Price: $46 for adults; $36 for ages 3 - 11; children 2 and under are free, which includes unlimited use of the guided bus tour, Kangaroo Express Bus, and skyfari aerial tram. Certain discounts are available through AAA. Parking is free. Ask about combo packages. For instance, one package includes unlimited entry for 7 consecutive days to the park, the SAN DIEGO ZOO SAFARI PARK, and SEAWORLD - $149 for adults; $119 for age 3 - 9. Admission to the zoo is free during the month of October for ages 3 - 11.

Ages: All

SAN DIEGO ZOO SAFARI PARK

(760) 747-8702 or (619) 231-1515 / www.sdzsafaripark.org
15500 San Pasqual Valley Road, Escondido

Go on a safari and see the exotic animals that live in the African veldt and Asian plains, without ever leaving Southern California. The 2,000-acre Safari Park has tigers, rhinos, lions, elephants, giraffes, lots of birds, a variety of antelope and gazelle, and many more, in atypical zoo enclosures. The animals roam the grasslands freely, in settings that resemble their natural habitats which is why you don't always see them up close. The best way to see a majority of these animals is via the Journey Into Africa tram tour, which is a two-mile, thirty-minute, narrated journey. You ride around the perimeter of (although it seems like through) the African section, stopping for better vantage points and photo ops. I suggest doing the tram tour early in your visit as the lines get longer later in the day.

The ride ends/begins near the Park's pride - the pride of lions, that is, at Lion Camp, which is a terrific place to

see lions close up. The lions frequently use the stripped jeep just on the other side of the glass as a play toy/sleep site. If it's a hot day, you can cool off at the small water play area next to the camp. Also in this area is Heart of Africa, a great starting point for the rest of your wild animal adventure. A paved, circuitous, three-quarters of a mile path winds through some of the thirty acres that comprise this section. The trail leads you past plains that are home to wildebeest and cheetahs, and even a station, open at designated times, where visitors can hand-feed giraffes for an additional fee. Their long, black tongues always elicit a few "eeews" from kids. Cross over a bridge to a small island that has a mock research station and see dart guns and lab equipment. Stop off at Jameson Research Island for stories about animals and some more water play. Walk past warthogs, rhinos, flamingos, and foxes, and into the forestry area to see antelope, the unusual-looking okapi, and a new favorite for me - the secretary bird.

At the northern end of the park, look through telescopes on the observation deck of Condor Ridge to see the habitats of dozens of endangered species, including, obviously, California condors. This area also has prairie dogs, roadrunners, ferrets, and big horned sheep, as well as botanical gardens. Actually, the whole park is like a botanical garden, with brilliant and unusual plants and flowers throughout.

There are numerous other attractions at the Safari Park. Watch the interactions and antics of the monkeys, the glares of the gorillas, and the curiosity of the meerkats. Go batty at the bat exhibit where these odd creatures are kept in their home surroundings - a dark cave. The Petting Kraal has small deer and sheep to pet and feed. Check the time for the animal shows presented here. One of our favorites is the funny and fantastic, Frequent Flyers Bird Show - daily at noon and 2pm. Animals Encounters and Keeper Talks are great ways to visually and auditorily learn about select animals. Hand-feeding rainbow-colored lorikeets, who look like small parrots, is a thrill. Bring your camera to capture your child's expression as the birds land on his arms or even his head. Check for feeding times and bring $3 for a cup of food. I was enchanted by the Hidden Jungle offered in spring because the "room" in here is filled with lush green plants and colorful butterflies fluttering all around. Enjoy some down time at the Discovery Station where children can read books, do puzzles, and work on craft projects. Younger visitors can play on the safari-themed jungle gym or take a twirl on the sixty-one creature carousel for free. Guests 10 years and older can soar on Flightline, a ⅔ mile long zipline over wild parts of the park. The entire experience, orientation and practice, takes an hour and costs $70 per person, in addition to regular park admission. Walk among the treetops for ninety minutes during the Jungle Ropes Safari with rope bridges, aerial tightropes, platforms to negotiate and more in this high ropes challenge course. The cost is $45 per person, plus park admission. Get a ringside seat to watching a cheetah accelerate, and then see this powerful animal close-up, no bars between you - $45 per person. Enjoy all your travels through the animal kingdom.

Want to make your day picture perfect? A variety of Caravan Safaris (ages 6 and up) offer several photo opportunities as you feed some of the animals, learn all about them, and go into some of the animal enclosures on an open, flat-bed truck. The cost is $95 for a two-hour caravan and $150 (for ages 8 and up) for 3.5 hours, plus admission cost to the park. Numerous other family, scout, and other group programs are offered including a favorite - Roar and Snore overnight tent-camping safaris. These are for kids as young as 6 years old and include nature hikes, a campfire, food, photo opportunities, close-up encounters with wild (and more mild) beasts, and more! The cost ranges from $120 to $160 for ages 3 to 11, and $140 to $220 for ages 12 and up (plus park admission), depending on tent size and placement within the park. There is a two person, per tent minimum. Check the website or call (619) 718-3000 for information and a complete schedule of special programs.

Hours: Open daily most of the year, 9am - 5pm; open in the spring and summer, 9am - 6pm or 7pm - check the website calendar or call first.

Price: Admission, which includes park entrance, the Journey into Africa tour, and a ride on the carousel, is $46 for adults; $36 for ages 3 - 11; children 2 and under are free. Certain discounts are available through AAA. Parking is $10. Ask about combo packages. For instance, one package includes unlimited entry for 7 consecutive days to the park, the SAN DIEGO ZOO, and SEAWORLD - $149 for adults; $119 for age 3 - 9. Admission to the zoo is free during the month of October for ages 3 - 11.

Ages: All

SEA LIFE AQUARIUM

(760) 918-LEGO (5346) / www.visitsealife.com/california
One Legoland Drive, Carlsbad

Myth-buster: Although Legoland owns and operates Sea Life, the fish are real, not made out of Legos! Each themed room in this mid-size aquarium appeals to kids, especially, with live fish, colorful wall murals, and some sort of fun activity. Tip: Pick up a quiz trail brochure, find questions along the way, and scratch off the answer on the back to

receive a free sticker at the end of your visit.

Start in the Lake Tahoe room where trout and other fish swim in small brooks and kids can cross a bridge and slide down a short tree trunk slide. In the next rooms are shovelnose guitar fish, stingrays, octopus, leopard sharks, and bright orange Garibaldi (the California state fish) all in eye-level tanks and enclosures that resemble their native habitats. Note that many of the "kelp" and "coral" in the tanks are not real. Listen to sounds of nature piped in, such as sea gulls and waves breaking, and stop to read the fin facts. Did you know that octopus have three hearts and blue blood? Get sucked into the interactive Octopus Gardens to really understand how their camouflage and jet propulsion works. Kids can crawl through tunnels, pop their heads up (via a protective bubble) in a fish tank, look for the Lego figures everywhere, learn, and play.

The centerpiece of the aquarium is the Lost City of Atlantis where sharks swim in the thirty-five foot tunnel overhead and in the gigantic viewing tank, along with rays and a large variety of other tropical fish. Seeing a huge statue of King Neptune, the Lego submarine, and Lego divers in the tank is pretty cool, too. Other highlights include the Mayan-themed seahorse room (such variety even within the species!); the realistic-looking Shipwreck room with eels slinking in and out of the undersea vessel; the tank of rays; the discovery touch pool and tide pool where visitors are encouraged to gently stroke sea stars and sea anemones; and the kelp forest. Besides marine life, household products made from kelp are on display here, such as toothpaste, ice cream, and paint. For an other-worldly feel, stand in the center of the Shoaling Ring room as thousands of silvery fish encircle you, swimming around in the almost 360 degree tank.

Take time to watch a short film on marine animals in the theater; jam over to the jellyfish area where over 100 jellyfish are on display; let the crab exhibit grab your attention with its Japanese spider crabs and lobsters; build a coral reef out of Lego bricks in the cafe area; and definitely check out the schedule of feedings (octopus, seahorse, sharks, rays, and sea stars) and activities (divers cleaning tanks while interacting with visitors and a really funny, interactive puppet show). Look into guided and self-guided educational programs, fields trips, homeschool discount days, youth camps, and scout patch programs, too, at very reasonable prices. There is much to *sea* and do here! Note: This aquarium is towards the entrance of LEGOLAND (462) and LEGOLAND WATER PARK (pg. 404). Also, if you have a real Lego fanatic, definitely check out the adjacent LEGOLAND HOTEL (563).

Hours: Usually open daily, 10am - 5pm; open longer hours on holidays and certain weekends. Summer hours are daily, 9am - 8pm.
Price: $20 per person; children 2 and under are free. Save $ and order tickets online. Parking is $15.
Ages: 1½ - 13 years

SEAL ROCK MARINE MAMMAL RESERVE

(619) 236-5555 / www.sandiego.gov/lifeguards/beaches/pool.shtml
850 Coast Boulevard, La Jolla

From a distance, we saw what looked like lots of lumpy rocks on the beach. As we got closer, however, we could see that they were really seals sprawling on the sand and on the nearby rocks. The seals have taken over what used to be known as Children's Pool Beach, so named because the rocks form a breakwater. My boys and I were thrilled that we were almost close enough to touch the seals, although doing so and getting too close is forbidden. (Even seals are protected by harassment laws!) Walk out on the rock jetty for more of a view. A normal family might be here for just a few minutes; we were here for an hour because we were enthralled. Warning: Seals are not sunbathing here constantly, so seeing them is a hit or miss deal, although they are usually on the beach during cooler months, such as November through June; in the water more frequently the warmer months; and often lay on the rocks for the late afternoon sun. Pupping season is usually February through April.

On either side of the reserve, you'll see beaches, large rocks to climb on, and even grassy park areas. A paved sidewalk trail runs along the coastline. See SCRIPPS PARK (pg. 519) for lots more information about this immediate area.

Hours: Open daily, sunrise - sunset.
Price: Free
Ages: All

SEAWORLD

(800) 25SHAMU(257-4268) or (619) 226-3901 / www.seaworld.com

$$$$$

500 Sea World Drive, San Diego

Submerse yourself into Sea World via a giant wave sculpture that ushers you into the underwater world of animals

and activities, such as Explorer's Reef. This immediate, themed area consists of four touch tanks filled with bamboo sharks and literally thousands of fish.

SeaWorld entertains and educates people of all ages with its wide variety of sea animal exhibits and shows. Do purpose to catch the shows! The dazzling, high-jumping dolphins get top ratings as they are part of a huge, twenty-five minute aquatic production along with human acrobatic performers who are dressed in fanciful costumes. And don't miss the silly sea lion show, where the animals hilariously interact with trainers - arrive early or you will miss out on some of the pre-show antics. The killer-whale show, One Ocean, starring Shamu and friends, is a crowd-pleaser with its thrills - the magnificent animals leap high out of the water - and chills, as those sitting in the splash-zone bleachers get drenched. The shows, the nighttime ones especially, can also feature rock music, water fountains, and special lighting effects. The Pets Rule show is just so darn cute with all the different and funny animal acts. Another unique attraction is Shark Encounter which culminates in a fifty-seven-foot-long, glass-enclosed, people-mover tube that takes you "through" shark-infested waters(!). Another show, especially for the kids, is Madagascar Live! where the costumed characters sing and dance with more human-looking performers inside the theater.

At Rocky Point Preserve visitors can actually touch and feed bottlenose dolphins, but check for feeding times first so you don't miss out. (The food costs about $4.) These mammals feel rubbery. If you stretch your arms far enough, you can touch bat rays and other marine animals at Forbidden Reef and the California Tide Pool. The penguin exhibit features penguins and the penguins' cousins, the funny-looking puffins who fly through the air and sea. A simulated helicopter ride at Wild Arctic lands you at a remote research station. (Actually, you're still at SeaWorld.) Blasts of Arctic air greet you as you view beluga whales, harbor seals, walruses, and polar bears. Journey to Atlantis is a combination roller coaster and water ride that zooms passengers past dolphins as they ride through mist, up the hills, and then plunges them down into mythical waters (that get you actually wet). Another wet activity is the Shipwreck Rapids ride where a nine-passenger raft swirls past several realistic-looking shipwrecks, real sea turtles, through "rapids," and partially (or completely) under a roaring waterfall. Ride a manta, well a Manta roller coaster, a ride that incorporates projection screen images of swimming manta rays to give riders the feeling of being immersed in the water along with the mantas while getting gently sprayed with real water. Learn about and watch more than sixty endangered sea turtles gracefully glide by the immense underwater viewing windows at Turtle Reef, as well as thousands of tropical fish in this exhibit area. Ride Riptide Rescue, an airboat-like ride that goes around (and around) in a big circle. Ride up, up, up and away in the Skytower for a panoramic view, and swing on the Bayside Skyride, a gondola ride over Mission Bay. And don't miss walking around to see the unique fish and other sea creatures in the various aquariums throughout Sea World.

The Sesame Street Bay of Play is two-acres of pure kid delight. It has three rides modeled after Sesame Street characters - Elmo's Flying Fish, Abby's Sea Star Spin (don't get too dizzy!), and Oscar's Rocking Eel mini roller coaster. It also has tubes, slides, ropes, balls, a sandy beach, a moon bounce, an outdoor theater for kid-oriented entertainment, and a large fun water ship for mates to climb aboard and get wet. For those who want (or are allowed) to get wet (more wet?), there are even water fountains to splash in and water tubes to go through. Tip: Bring a towel or change of clothing. Be on the lookout for Sesame Street characters here, too - they love hugs.

The best eater-tainment is Dine with Shamu. This pool-side buffet meal offers truly scrumptious food, such as short ribs, chicken or turkey, potatoes, pollock, penne pasta, shrimp cocktail, shrimp scampi, a variety of salads and vegetables, and an assortment of fresh-baked desserts. (Menu selections do change.) Kids can choose from mac and cheese, chicken, meatballs, fruit salad, and Shamu-shaped cookies. The highlight? The great whale comes out of the water to greet you and a trainer puts him through some of his paces as he/she explains whale behavior. The luncheons and dinners are $42.12 for adults, $20.52 for ages 3 to 9, children 2 and under are free. Reservations are needed. Breakfast, served at 10am or 10:30am, is $28.08 for adults, $17.28 for kids, and offers traditional breakfast foods. Save money by booking in advance/online. If you are planning to be here all day, check out the all-day dining deal for $32.99 for adults and $16.99 for children, at participating restaurants in Sea World.

SeaWorld also offers a lot and a variety of outstanding educational tours, such as a sleep over "with" sharks or other animals, summer camps, marine science investigation, Shamu Adventurers, and more. What fun! The one-hour Dolphin Interaction Program allows visitors, who must be at least 10 years old and 49" tall, to put on a wet suit, wade into waist-high water for about twenty minutes with the dolphins, then touch, feed, and interact with them while learning about their anatomy and personalities. The cost is $215 per person. Interact with penguins and go where guests aren't normally invited on a one-hour tour - $60 for adults; $54 for kids. Call or check the website for information on the times, hours, and admission for all the other unique family and field trips. Ask about the monthly school days specials where admission is greatly reduced for students. Special summertime highlights at SeaWorld

include fireworks and an annual favorite - Cirque de la Mer, a sister act to the mesmerizing Cirque Du Soleil, with dazzling costumes, humor, and seemingly impossible feats of strength and acrobatics.

Although no outside food is allowed inside the park, a picnic area is set up just outside. Spending a day (or night) here is a great way for the whole family to "sea" the world!

Hours: The hours really fluctuate. Open daily most of the year, 10am - 5pm, but sometimes until 7:30pm. Open daily in the summer, 9am - 11pm. Check for seasonality.

Price: $84 for adults; $78 for ages 3 - 9; children 2 and under are free. Get express entrance to rides via Quick Queue for an additional fee. Certain discounts are available through AAA. Check out the Fun Card, where for the price of a single day admission, you get the rest of the calendar year free. Ask about other specials as well. Parking is $15 per day.

Ages: All

WHALE WATCHING

See the TRANSPORTATION section.

WILD WONDERS & ZOOFARI FOUNDATION   ☼

(760) 630-9230 / www.wildwonders.org $$$$$
5712 Via Montellano, Bonsall

A new favorite! About 150 animals consider this almost six-acre animal rescue and wildlife education conservation center home. The mission is to educate the public, especially kids, and rescue injured and non-releasable animals. The one-hour guided tours, given by professional biologists and animal trainers, are informative regarding the animals' stories as to why they are here, descriptions of their personalities, and facts about their species. The numerous different kinds of exotic creatures here aren't readily seen elsewhere, especially this close up and interactive!

The keepers enter most of the enclosures and bring out whatever animals they can to hold and play with so that you are able to touch, feed, and definitely take great photos of or with some of them. You will see binturongs; foxes; alligators (no feeding!); precious-looking kinkajous (what? - look them up); a massive albino Burmese python; a leopard; porcupines (that are really cute!); owls; Arctic foxes; turtles; wallabies; macaws; a serval; tamarins; lynx; coatimundi; wide-eyed bush babies; hedgehogs; and a myriad of insects and reptiles. I had never seen armadillos run around before coming here or been able to pet one! The tours are personal, relaxed, and wonderful.

Most of the enclosures aren't large so it's an easy walk to see them all, though sometimes on uneven, slightly hilly ground and up stairs. The enclosures are nicely kept up with shade, mini pools, trees, and whatever else is needed for care for the animals.

Educational programs (even those that bring animal ambassadors to your school or location) abound, as do zoology day camps for ages 8 to 13 ($80 per day, per child); a zookeeper mentor program; a variety of scouting programs; and other calendar events.

Hours: Reservations are required to visit the facility.

Price: General tours are $25 for adults; $13 for ages 17 and under, with a minimum of $100 for all tours. (Sign up with a friend or check the online calendar to see if you can join another, prescheduled tour!)

Ages: 4 years and up.

SANTA BARBARA COUNTY

Although Chumash Indians were this county's original inhabitants, its name came from a Spanish explorer's party. Seeking shelter in the channel from a severe storm, the fleet was saved on Saint Barbara's feast day. The hub of this multi-faceted county is the compact city of Santa Barbara. The city offers a culturally-rich assortment of things to do and see in a setting that is both elegant and friendly. Visitors are minutes away from the beach or the mountains. The Los Padres National Forest makes up almost half of this county! The hub's spokes, or other cities that complete the county, each have their own distinct "personality." The town of Goleta is home to Santa Barbara's University, as well as miles of coastline. The small town of Lompoc is known for its murals. Solvang is the "Danish Capitol of America." Los Olivos, originally a stagecoach stop, is now a fine arts destination. Santa Ynez boasts of pioneer history. The far flung Santa Maria, with its farming roots, has both a quaint and lively town center, as well as the unique sand dunes.

—AMUSEMENT PARKS—

MUSTANG WATERPARK
(805) 489-8898 / www.mustangwaterpark.com
6800 Lopez Drive, Arroyo Grande
    See LOPEZ LAKE RECREATION AREA / MUSTANG WATERPARK (pg. 614) for details on this waterpark and lake recreation area.

—ARTS AND CRAFTS—

ART FROM SCRAP and EXPLORE ECOLOGY
(805) 884-0459 / www.artfromscrap.org; www.exploreecology.org
302 East Cota Street, Santa Barbara
    Crafters are absolutely in their element at this store with odds and ends and all sorts of stuff ready to be used for art projects, costumes, school endeavors, etc., and all at great prices. Shop for paper, thread, ribbons, tiles, picture frames, beads, sacks, fabric, mirrors, wire, baby food jars, paint, buttons, and more - individually or by the pound. Stock continually changes so you never know what you'll find, but you will find treasures and inspiration.
    Weekly Saturday art workshops are held at the store from 10am to 2pm with different themes each week and with titles such as Shadow Puppets, Make Music, Miniature Universes, Creative Containers, Exquisite Bugs, and more. Ages 5 and under must be accompanied by an adult.
    More than just a store, Art From Scrap leads the way with environmental educational programs, teaching the "new" three R's - reduce, reuse, and recycle. They are closely associated with the WATERSHED RESOURCE CENTER (pg. 636) and hold many classes there, too.
    Check the website calendar for the many other environmental programs that Art From Scrap hosts and co-sponsors including worm composting workshops, beach cleanup days, creek testing kits, teacher's workshops, summer camps, and educational field trips with tile such as Natural Resources, Water Quality, School Gardens, etc.
    Hours: The store is open Tues. - Fri., 11am - 5pm; Sat., 10am - 4pm. Closed Sun., Mon., and many holidays.
    Price: Free, bring spending money. Sat. workshops are $8 per artist.
    Ages: 3 years and up.

—BEACHES—

ARROYO BURRO "HENDRY'S" BEACH PARK
(805) 687-3714 or (805) 681-5650 / www.countyofsb.org
Cliff Drive from Las Positas Rd., Santa Barbara
    This lovely stretch of beach has plenty of sand, plus a lagoon that extends into it and bluffs that hang over a portion of it. Highlights include surfing, tidepooling, swimming, fishing, and whale watching, in season. (Bring your binoculars.) Day-use showers, a small park for picnicking, and bbq grills complete the scene.
    Hours: Open daily, 8am - sunset.
    Price: Free
    Ages: All

CARPINTERIA STATE BEACH
(805) 684-2811 or (805) 968-1033 - beach; (800) 444-7275 - camping reservations / www.parks.ca.gov; www.reserveamerica.com; www.californiasbestbeaches.com
at the south end of Palm Avenue near Carpinteria Ave., Carpinteria
    I know that it depends on the season and even the day, and that most kids don't care much about the scenery around a beach, but Carpinteria has a wonderful shoreline as well as a magnificent view from the beach of inland palm trees and the mountains beyond.
    Dubbed as the "world's safest beach" because a reef helps protect the shoreline from heavy ocean swells, this

beach features very fine sand, sand dunes with vegetation, some volleyball courts, lifeguards during the summer, outdoor showers, reservable covered picnic areas, and large rafts at swimmable distances to climb aboard. The reef to the right of the beach, that circles off from the mouth of Franklin Creek, is great for kayaking or snorkeling. Tip: Kayak and SUP rentals are available at the Boathouse building on Ash Avenue during the summer for $15 an hour for adults; $10 for children 12 and under with a paying adult. Also check Carpinteria Beach Store for rentals or to purchase beach umbrellas, toys, sunscreen etc. Call (805) 566-9482 for more info.

Across from the beach's main parking lot is a small, adjacent Visitor's Center offering an indoor tidepool exhibit, interpretative panels, and programs, such as the Jr. Ranger's Program. One of our favorite parts of the long and wide expanse of Carpinteria State Beach, besides playing in the sand and the water, are the tidepools toward the southern end of the state beach, below San Miguel Campground at Tar Pits Park. A short walk down the stairs and over some tar-covered rocks leads to some wonderful tidepool exploration at low tide. We have found some wonderful shells and some unusual rocks here, too. Guided tidepool walks are offered October through May. Call for more information. At the southernmost end, with very limited parking, is Jellybowl scenic vista, which is a decent place to fish. A fishing license is required. If you feel like a hike or bike ride, keep heading south on the adjacent dirt trail of the CARPINTERIA BLUFFS NATURE PRESERVE AND TRAIL (pg. 608) until you reach the HARBOR SEAL PRESERVE (see pg. 650), and then to the end, about five miles round trip.

About 65 of the 216ish family campsites, for up to eight people per site, allow tent camping, no hook-ups; the others are for RVs with full hook-ups. There are also seven group campsites. Some of the sites are definitely better than others. A majority of the RV sites are literally like setting up camp in a parking lot, although each one still has a fire ring and a picnic table. Choice sites are nestled up to the beach and most of the tent camping spots include a grassy area and a sprawling oak tree or greenery of some kind. The camp offers coin-operated showers. Reservations, which are site-specific, are suggested throughout the year and required in the summer and on weekends and holidays. Note: Railroad tracks parallel the campground and though the trains run about 5 times during the day, starting at 7am and ending at 11pm; they don't run during the night.

Freebies adjacent to and outside of the State Beach boundaries include Linden Field, a decent-size open grassy area that also has chin-up and sit-up bars and a few other pieces of exercise equipment; TOMOL INTERPRETATIVE PLAY AREA (see page 621), a great little park next to Linden Field; and, at the end of Linden Avenue, a beach area with limited free parking in a lot and on the street. There are several cement picnic tables here along with palm trees, volleyball courts, and a good stretch of beach. Since you're in the Carpinteria area, you might want to stop off at the small Robitailles Fine Candies on 900 Linden Avenue. They carry homemade fudge, candies from the 50's (although their stock is fresh), and other goodies. Look up Carpinteria in the Index by City in the back of this book for other area attractions.

Hours: Open daily, 7am - sunset. The Visitor's Center is open Sat. - Sun., 10am - noon in the winter, daily at those times in the summer.

Price: $10 for day-use parking. December - February, camping is $35 - $65 a night, depending if it's tent or full-hook RV, and inland or more toward the beach; March - November, camping is $45 - $80. There is a $8 camping reservation fee.

Ages: All

EAST BEACH   ☼

(805) 564-5433 / www.californiasbestbeaches.com $
E. Cabrillo Boulevard off Castillo, Santa Barbara

Easily one of Santa Barbara's most popular beaches, East Beach stretches from the east, at ANDREE CLARK BIRD REFUGE (pg. 606), to the west, at Stearns Wharf. On the other side of the wharf is the adjacent WEST BEACH (pg. 602).

Miles of white sand; fourteen volleyball courts (come watch a tournament!); a playground; a grassy area; the East Beach Grill full-service restaurant, which serves breakfast and lunch; and the Pacific Ocean - what more could a body want?! At low tide, hike along the beach eastward all the way to Butterfly Beach, which is opposite the Four Seasons Hotel. Look up SANTA BARBARA HARBOR / STEARNS WHARF (pg. 637) for more details as to what else is in the immediate vicinity.

Hours: Open daily, sunrise - 10pm.
Price: Free. Parking in beach lot is $2 an hour; $12 max. There is some free street parking.

Ages: All

EL CAPITAN STATE BEACH   ☼

(805) 968-1033 - beach; (800) 444-7275 - camping reservations / www.parks.ca.gov $$
Refugio Beach Road off the 101, Goleta

The stone-lined stretch of beach offers swimming, a few tidepools toward the southern end, dune trails, and camping. The almost private campsites off the road in El Capitan are an interesting combination of camping near the beach, yet surrounded by sycamore and oak trees, giving them a woodsy atmosphere. Note that while the upper campgrounds are nice, they are closer to the freeway and railroad tracks. Showers are available at a nominal additional cost. Other amendments include open fire pits and a seasonal snack bar. A cycling trail connects El Capitan to REFUGIO STATE BEACH (pg. 601), which is three miles further west. Look for the Monarch butterflies that gather here November through January.

Hours: Open daily, 8am to sunset.
Price: $10 per vehicle for daily use; $9 for seniors. Camping is $35 a night. There is a $8 camping reservation fee.
Ages: All

GAVIOTA STATE PARK   ◐

(805) 968-1033 - park; (800) 444-7275 - camping reservations / www.parks.ca.gov $$
Refugio Beach Road off the 101, Goleta

Just when you think Santa Barbara beaches and vistas can't get any better, visit Gaviota. This beach, though, is better described as a cove that's fenced in by natural rock walls. A creek from the mountains empties into the ocean, making it ideal for wading and fishing. Spend the night in this lovely countryside at any of the thirty-eight campsites which come complete with fire pits and picnic tables. No RV hook-ups. The park also has a playground, grocery store, and snack bar.

Hike inland, on the other side of the road, through the huge park. One trail, across the highway, is called Trespass Road. It's about two-and-a-half miles long and leads to the hot springs in the Los Padres National Forest. Continue on up the trail (and I mean up!), about six miles, round trip, to reach Gaviota Peak.

Hours: Open daily, 7am - sunset.
Price: $10 per vehicle for day use; $9 for seniors; or $10 to hike and bike. Camping is $35, plus a $8 camping reservation fee. Camping is first come, first served, although reservations are required Memorial Day through Labor Day.
Ages: All

GOLETA BEACH PARK   ☼

(805) 967-1300 - beach; (805) 964-7881 - Beachside Cafe / www.countyofsb.org; www.beachside-barcafe.com   !
5968 Sandspit Road, Goleta   ♨

Sand, gentle surf, lifeguards, a long pier (bring your own fishing pole), a playground, a horseshoe pit, volleyball courts, picnic tables on the adjacent lawn, barbecue grills, a paved bike trail - this twenty-nine-acre beach park, complete with palm trees, has it all! Bring food for a picnic lunch or eat at the Beachside Bar and cafe where you can sit and eat at a table while digging your toes into the sand.

Hours: Open daily, 8am - sunset. The cafe is open Mon. - Fri., 11:30am to 10pm; Sat. - Sun., 11am to 11pm.
Price: Free
Ages: All

JALAMA BEACH   ☼

(805) 736-6316 - recorded info; (805) 736-3504 - beach; (805) 736 - 5027 - store & grill / $$
www.jalamabeach.com; www.countyofsb.org; www.jalamabeachstore.net
9999 Jalama Road, Lompoc

The word "windy" means full of wind, which is something that Jalama boasts of quite frequently. After the winding, scenic drive, enjoy the view from a cliff-top vantage point, overlooking the crystal clear ocean waters. You'll see kelp beds, kayakers, surfers, windsurfers, a long stretch of classic California shoreline, and campsites. This isolated

beach, with its fine sand and a few small sand dunes, offers all of the above as well as fishing from the surf or rock outcropping, playing horseshoes or volleyball or basketball, and flying a kite. Bring your own equipment for any activity although there are on-site rentals for fishing - bait, tackle, and fishing license.

Swimming is allowed at the beach, but with waves breaking on the shore and riptides, the surf can be dangerous. There is a small lagoon, and lifeguards are on duty during summer months. Rock hounds will enjoy the rocks that can be found in this area, such as agate and travertine. Also, look for gray whales as they migrate seasonally - January through March, and September through November.

About one hundred campsites, some with RV hookup, are available for reservation and some on a first-come, first-served basis. The few sites directly on the beach are separated by hedges on both sides. Tip: Bring tent pegs because of the wind. The other sites' boundaries aren't as clearly delineated. If you want to camp, but not, rent one of the cabins which can sleep up to six people. Each one has a kitchen and other amenities. Hot showers, a general store, and grill (collectively, the Jalama Beach Store & Grill), are also located here. Known for its Jalama burgers (which cost about $6.50), the beach grill also serves up, for lunch - chicken breast sandwiches ($6.50), fish and chips ($10.50), chili, jalapeno poppers ($6.95), half a pound of deep fried clams ($11.95), and a kid's menu of nuggets, grilled cheese, corn dogs and more. The breakfast menu includes bacon and eggs ($8.95), breakfast burritos ($6.95), and sandwiches ($6.50), pancakes ($5.50) and fruit. Yum!

Hours: The beach is open daily, 8am - sunset. Jalama Beach Store & Grill is open daily at 8am. The grill closes at 4:45pm in off season and at 7pm, or so, during peak season.

Price: $10 per vehicle for day use; $3 for dogs. Camping fees October - March are $23 - $43 (sites on the beach) a night; April - September, $28 - $43. Cabin rentals run from $110 a night on non-peak weekdays to $210 a night on peak weekends, plus a $20 reservation fee.

Ages: 5 years and up.

LEADBETTER BEACH
(805) 564-5433; (805) 568-0064 - cafe / www.californiasbestbeaches.com
Shoreline and Loma Alta drives, Santa Barbara

Located between WEST BEACH (pg. 602) and the adjacent harbor, and under the cliff-top Shoreline Park, this popular beach is noted for swimming because of moderate waves, tidepooling during low tide, beach volleyball courts, a playground, a grassy run-around area, and a picnic area underneath palm trees. A stairway leads from the park down to the beach. When the tide is low, you can walk to the connecting beaches. Note that at the nearby Shoreline Beach cafe you can feast on a battered shrimp taco, grilled seafood burrito or a variety of salads and sandwiches, all while sitting at a table in the sand.

Hours: Open daily, sunrise - 10pm. The cafe is open Mon. - Thurs., 10am (9am in the summer) - sunset; Fri. - Sun., 8am - sunset.

Price: Free. Parking in beach lot is $2 an hour; $12 max. There is some free street parking.

Ages: All

REFUGIO STATE BEACH
(805) 968-1033 - beach; (800) 444-7275 - camping reservations / www.parks.ca.gov;
www.californiasbestbeaches.com
10 Refugio Beach Road, Goleta

The beach offers swimming under the watchful eyes of lifeguards during the summer (watch out for rocks on the shore), some tidepools, a basketball court, a playground, picnic tables, barbecue pits on the beach, a grocery store, a grassy area, a lagoon/marsh inlet, a few palm trees for ambiance, and a beach wheelchair. There are over sixty camp sites nearly on the beach (no RV hook-ups), so be lulled to sleep by the sound of waves. However, you might be startled awake by the sound of the not-too-distant freeway traffic or the very nearby trains as they thunder by. If you're in the mood for pedaling, head east for about three miles on the bike trail that leads to EL CAPITAN STATE BEACH (pg. 600). Take a guided kayak tour, led by a lifeguard, offered from Memorial Day weekend through August and paddle along the coast, seeing and learning.

Hours: Open daily, 8am - sunset.

Price: $10 for day use fee. Camping is $35 - $45 a night. Camping reservations are required April - November. There is an $8 camping reservation fee.

Ages: All

WEST BEACH
☼

(805) 564-5418 or (805) 564-5523 / www.santabarbaraca.gov; www.californiasbestbeaches.com
$$

W. Cabrillo Boulevard by Castillo St., Santa Barbara

EAST BEACH, STEARNS WHARF, WEST BEACH, and LEADBETTER BEACH are all along one strip of land. (Each of these beaches has their own entry.) They are broken up by different names and by different attractions in between beaches. Eleven acres of sandy beach includes some volleyball courts; swimming in the relatively gentle waves; palm trees waving in the wind; the BIKE TRAIL: CABRILLO BEACHWAY (pg. 645) on the beach's perimeter; watercraft, both large and small, sailing in and out of the harbor; launching your own kayak; and a playground. Look up SANTA BARBARA HARBOR / STEARNS WHARF (pg. 637) for details as to what else to do in this immediate area.

Hours: Open daily, sunrise - 10pm.
Price: Free. Parking in beach lot is $2 an hour; $12 max. There is some free street parking.
Ages: All

—EDIBLE ADVENTURES—

AJ SPURS
☀

(805) 686-1655 / www.ajspurs.com
$$$$

350 E. Hwy. 246, Buellton

Hey pardner - if you mosey into town hankering for some good food and have a passion for the West, AJ Spurs is the place to go. It seems like every piece of the Old West is represented and packed into this one restaurant.

Outside, on top of the wooden building, are a few parked stagecoaches. One is also in front, on ground level. Cactus, life-size cowboy cutouts, a small waterfall, a mill wheel, jar lanterns, wooden porch swings with ends made from wagon wheels, antlers, and scenic western murals decorate the outside of this log cabin-style eatery.

Inside, the theme continues. Past the small coin fountain in the lobby, the wood walls and ceilings showcase more murals, mounted animals heads (both deer and buffalo), saddles, stirrups, cowboy hats, dangling horse bits, canteens, branding irons, bearskins, steer skulls, and stuffed ducks - you get the picture. There are also a few taxidermied grizzly bears lurking around corners in ferocious poses.

A smattering of options from the bill of fare includes eight-ounce top sirloin ($22.50); a full rack of ribs ($29.50); bbq chicken ($20.99); burger ($14.99); shrimp scampi ($27.99); lobster tail (market price, about $48); Cajun chicken tortellini ($25.50); and filet mignon ($26.99). All meals come with vaquero soup, tequila beans, salad, and spuds, garlic bread, and a root beer float. Little pardners can order a meal for only $7.99, when an adult meal is ordered. Their choices include popcorn shrimp, chicken tenders, chicken Alfredo, BBQ chicken, hamburger, or ribs. A clean plate earns a trip to the treasure chest. (This applies just to the kids - not the adults.)

Hours: Open Mon. - Fri., 5pm - 9:30pm; Sat. - Sun., 4pm - 9:30pm.
Price: Menu prices are listed above.
Ages: 3 years and up.

CIRCLE BAR B DINNER THEATER
☀

1800 Refugio Road, Goleta
$$$$$

See the entry for CIRCLE BAR B DINNER THEATER on page 640 for details.

COLD SPRING TAVERN
☀

(805) 967-0066 / www.coldspringtavern.com
$$$$

5995 Stagecoach Road, Santa Barbara

Imagine dusty, hungry, and parched travelers arriving over 140 years ago at this stagecoach stop. Not much has changed since then.

Seemingly in the middle of nowhere, and surrounded only by woods and a seasonal stream, is a cluster of buildings with an enchantingly rustic tavern as the centerpiece. The log cabin eatery has several small dining rooms, each with wood-beam ceilings, animals' heads mounted on the walls, and other decor that consists of old tools, jugs,

and other artifacts from bygone days. The small main room has a fireplace and a bar. Outside are a few tables under shady oak trees, as well as some rough-hewn log benches.

Modern-day folk enjoy this rest stop, too, for the ambiance as well as the food. Breakfast (served on the weekends only) - omelettes ($9); N.Y. steak with eggs ($10); homemade whole wheat French toast ($8.25); blueberry pancakes ($8.25); and more. Lunch - wild game chili ($7.57); buffalo burger ($12); venison sandwich ($13.25); French dip ($9.50); Cobb salad ($9.50); baby back ribs ($12); etc. Dinner (which all include an array of fresh breads; soup or salad or chili; vegetables; and potato or rice) - sauteed duck breast ($25); New Zealand rack of lamb ($31); sauteed medallions of rabbit ($24); New York steak ($23.50); and center cut pork chop ($24). Don't miss out on the homemade desserts such as Granny Smith apple cobbler and cheesecake - just like grandma used to make. Note that there is usually live music on the weekends and that weekends, in general, are very crowded. Reservations are highly recommended. Tip: Drive just around the bend to get a good view of the arch bridge.

Hours: Open for breakfast Sat. and Sun., 8am - 11am. Open for lunch daily, 11am - 3pm. Open for dinner nightly, 5pm - 9pm or 10pm. *Closed Christmas.

Price: See above for menu prices.

Ages: 5 years and up.

FARMER'S MARKETS (Santa Barbara County)

See the entry for FARMER'S MARKETS (Los Angeles County) on pg. 18 for details.

INDIA HOUSE

(805) 962-5070 / www.indiahouseusa.com

$$$$

418 State Street, Santa Barbara

I have not been to India, but eating at this restaurant makes me feel like I got a taste of it. (No pun intended.) Colorful and wonderfully gaudy, the floor, walls and ceiling are covered with a mosaic of beautiful fabrics, a myriad of hanging lanterns, fabric banners, rugs of all kinds, statuary and figurines. One section has floor seating with pillows at the back and a patchwork of almost bed-size padding on which to sit next to low tables. Another section of the restaurant has more traditional tables and chairs for eating. The music and aromas of India waft through the restaurant. About half of India House is an Indian bazaar with fun cultural items - clothing, furniture, musical instruments, household goods, and more to purchase.

Menu choices include appetizers of samosa ($3.95) and vegetable pakora ($5.95); vegetarian choices of daal ($9.95) and paneer jelferzl ($13.95); thalis (combo platters) of vegetarian ($11.95) and chef's with three meats ($28.95); chicken curry ($12.95); lamb saag ($16.95); shrimp curry ($18.95); biryanis (spiced rice) with lamb and chicken and vegetables ($16.95); plus breads and desserts. The lunch buffet is $8.95 for all you can eat with six meat and six veggie dishes, Naan bread, rice, and two desserts. Come to Indian House and go global.

Hours: Open daily, 11am - 3pm (for lunch) and then 5pm - 9pm (for dinner).

Price: Menu prices listed above.

Ages: 3 years and up.

KLONDIKE PIZZA

(805) 348-3667 / www.klondikepizza.com

$$$

2059 S. Broadway Street, Santa Maria

Alaskan pizza? It seems to work at Klondike. The family pizzeria is decorated with memorabilia from our 49th state on the walls and on the ceiling. The adornments include a grizzly bear, elk head, Alaskan crabs, a red fox, small totem poles, advertisements about Alaska, skis, sleds, baleen from whales, and more. The sawdust on the floor and the fact that peanuts are given to hungry diners with the understanding that peanut shells are to be tossed on the ground, add to the fun atmosphere. Kids will love ordering (and eating) Road Kill pizza (i.e., all meat), or perhaps trying a pizza topped with reindeer sausage. There are numerous "normal" pizza selections ($18.75 for an extra large pizza with cheese; $25.99 for chicken cordon bleu), as well as burgers ($5.95 for a cheeseburger), chicken entrees ($7.50 for an Hawaiian chicken salad) and sandwiches ($6.99 for a sub sandwich; $5.75 for Alaskan reindeer sandwich). Tuesday night is usually all-you-can-eat. Of course, what good would a place be without arcade games?! There are numerous here.

Hours: Open Sun. - Thurs., 11am - 9pm; Fri. - Sat., 11am - 10pm.

Price: Menu prices are listed above.

Ages: All

PADARO BEACH GRILL

(805) 566-9800 / www.padarobeachgrill.com $$$

3765 Santa Claus Lane, Carpinteria

There is very little seating inside this restaurant because why would you want to sit inside? The enclosed outside area is one, big, delightful, mostly unshaded, grassy space spotted with plenty of wooden picnic tables (some have umbrellas) and some palm trees. While there isn't direct access to the beach, the beach is brought to you via a large sandy zone with buckets, shovels, and other toys. Just like a picnic (but better because you don't have to prepare and lug all the food), you'll be outdoors enjoying a meal while the kids run around on the grass and play in the sand. There is also a pretty little pond here.

Food choices include appetizers of calamari ($9.95) or The Trio of French fries, sweet potato fries and onion rings with bbq sauce and ranch - so healthy! ($5.95); sandwiches or burgers (about $7), fish and chips ($10.50), Cobb salad ($9.50) and more. Kid's choices include a burger, chicken tenders or quesadilla for $5.50 each. Top off your meal with a chocolate fudge or caramel latte shake ($4.75). Enjoy the food; enjoy the scenery. Tip: Before or after your meal, pull over on the side of Santa Claus lane and watch the trains go by.

Hours: Open daily, 10:30am - 8pm, depending on the weather and the season.

Price: Menu prices listed above.

Ages: All

ROCK AND ROLL DINER

(805) 473-2040 / www.rockandrolldiner.com $$$

1300 Railroad Street, Oceano

Come on, baby - let's rock & roll! Two, long, renovated railcars serve as the dining areas for this authentic 50's-themed restaurant serving American and Greek food. Twist and shout (albeit quietly) to the music on the table jukeboxes. Munch on appetizers such as fried zucchini ($6.50); jalapeno poppers ($7.50); or bacon cheese fries ($5.95). Choose from a variety of "real" foods such as a chicken fajita salad ($9.95); cheeseburger ($7.50); French dip ($8.95); meatloaf ($11.75); beef ribs ($13.50); shrimp scampi ($14.50); spaghetti ($9.50); Mexican pizza ($7.95); tacos asada ($10.75); or Greek entries, like gyros ($9.50); falafel ($9.50) and moussaka ($12.95). Save room for a shake. There's a whole other menu for breakfast.

Kid's meals range from $4.50 to $5.50 and include choices of burger, spaghetti, pizza, chicken fingers, or corn dogs. Most meals come with fries. Drinks are extra. Note: I do know this diner isn't really in Santa Barbara county, but if you are visiting the OCEANO DUNES STATE VEHICULAR PARK (pg. 617) or going out to THE GREAT AMERICAN MELODRAMA & VAUDEVILLE (pg. 641), this is a fun place to grab a bite to eat.

Hours: Open Sun. - Thurs., 8am - 8pm; Fri. - Sat., 8am - 8:30pm.

Price: Menu prices are listed above.

Ages: All

SOMETHING'S FISHY

(805) 966-6607 $$$$

502 State Street, Santa Barbara

Yummm - delectable seafood, sushi, and hibachi-style food is served at Something's Fishy. Food cooked with the hibachi is cooked at your table - kind of like food entertainment.

Enjoy the selection of sushi, such as crab rolls, California roll, or octopus at $6.50 each, and lots more. The lunch menu offers hibachi chicken, $13.95; New York steak, $15.95; and shrimp or scallops, $14.95. Dinner prices average $18 to $27. The kid's menu ranges from $6 to $8 for lunch and $9 to $11 for dinner.

Hours: Open Sun. - Thurs., 11:30am - 9 (ish)pm.; Fri. - Sat., 11:30am - 10 (ish)pm.

Price: See menu prices above.

Ages: 4 years and up.

WOODY'S BODACIOUS BARBECUE

(805) 967-3775 / www.woodysbbq.com $$$

5112 Hollister Avenue, Goleta

Wowser! Woody's is a quirky, rustic mix of the Old West and everything else, plus the kitchen sink. The lobby, for lack of a better word, contains an outhouse (just for atmosphere) and an old washtub to wash your hands. Place your order at the counter and go sit at any one of the old wooden benches and tables, covered in red-and-white checkered tablecloths, located in several small rooms where shutters and wood-paneled walls are "decorated" with pots, pans, skis, a toilet, stuffed fish, a lantern, surfboards, and lots of antlers, plus numerous license plates, traffic signs, neon signs, and more stuff. (Look at the ceiling, too.) Most of the rooms also contain a T.V., usually showing rodeos or other sporting events. A few arcade games are scattered throughout. Outdoor seating is available, too.

Bodacious is an appropriate word to describe the savory ribs (pork, beef, and bison) and homemade barbecue sauce that has made Woody's famous. Other menu options include burgers ($7.95 to $10.45); all-you-can eat salad bar ($7.95); grilled chicken breast sandwich ($8.45); tri tip dinner ($15.45); Southern style pork ribs ($11.95); or prime rib ($17.95 for a roadhouse cut). Portions are large, tasty, and usually come with their special, seasoned fries. Also try the nuclear waste buffalo wings if you *really* like hot food ($8.45). The kid's menu offers a hot dog or burger for $4.45, ribs for $9.95, or chicken strips for $6.95. These meals come with fries and a drink. Woody's became an instant favorite with my family.

Hours: Open daily, 11am - 9pm. Closed Easter, 4th of July, and Christmas.
Price: See above menu prices.
Ages: All

—FAMILY PAY AND PLAY—

ADVENTURE CLIMBING CENTER at UNIVERSITY OF CALIFORNIA, SANTA BARBARA

$$$$

(805) 893-3737 or (805) 893-7619 / www.recreation.ucsb.edu;
www.gauchosplay.com/adventure-climbing-center
Ocean Road, Recreation Building #516, University of California Santa Barbara, Goleta

This recreation building on the university campus is open to the public mostly during the summer; call for other times. At certain times, kids may use the two pools, one of the basketball courts, and the rock climbing facility.

The glass-enclosed, indoor rock climbing area has three main sections with walls up to thirty feet tall, over twenty top ropes, a belay edge, six auto-belay stations, three crack features, and a dedicated bouldering section, where a harness is not needed. To climb the walls, so to speak, bring your own belayer, become one by taking a lesson, use the auto belay, or use their staff at certain times offered on Belay Days. Ages 17 and under must have a parent-signed waiver for all activities. If you are interested in doing some team building (or birthday parties), ask about their Ropes Course, available for groups, that includes games, the course (most of which is almost twenty feet in the air) and a short zipline. The cost is $375 for up to 15 people. If you are wondering what to do with your active little darlings during the summer, sign them up for rock climbing summer camp.

Hours: The Rec Center, which contains the rock gym, is open during the academic year for adults, Mon. - Thurs., 11:30am - 10:30pm; Fri. - Sat., 11:30am - 8:30pm; Sun., 11:30am - 9:30pm. It is open mid-June - Labor Day, Mon. - Thurs., 11:30am - 9:30pm; Fri. - Sun., 11:30am - 8:30pm. Closed July 4th and 5th. Note that kids are invited to climb on weekends only from 11:30am - 6pm.
Price: $12 for an adult day pass; $7 for ages 13 - 17; $6 for ages 12 and under. Cost for shoes is $5; the harness is $5, or $8 for both. Parking is about $2.
Ages: 5 years and up.

BOOMERS! (Santa Barbara County)

$$$

(805) 928-4942 / www.boomersparks.com
2250 N. Preisker Lane, Santa Maria

At this family playland try for a hole-in-one at either one of two **miniature golf** courses ($9 for adults; ages 5 and under are free). Both feature fun obstacles and scale buildings, such as a colorful gingerbread house, a windmill, and a castle. Bump and splash each other in **bumper boats** ($7; passengers are $2 - drivers must be at least 44" tall). Big kids, who must be at least 58" tall, can race in **go-karts** ($7; passengers are $2), while younger kids, 40" to 58", can zoom around in their own **lil' thunder road** ($3). Climb the thirty-two-foot **rock wall** ($7 for two climbs). Take a

swing at the **batting cages**. Play over 125 video and sport games at the arcade. A snack bar here offers nachos, pizza, and drinks. Note that Boomers is across the way from PREISKER PARK (pg. 617).

Hours: Open most of the year, Mon.- Thurs., noon - 8pm; Fri., noon - 11pm; Sat., 11am - 11pm; Sun., 11am - 8pm. Open mid June - Labor Day and most school holidays, Mon. - Thurs., 10am - 8pm; Fri. - Sat., 11am - 11pm; Sun., 11am - 8pm. Some attractions close during inclement weather.

Price: Prices listed above.

Ages: 4 years and up.

SANTA BARBARA ROCK GYM

(805) 770-3225 / www.sbrockgym.com
322 State Street, Santa Barbara

This place really rocks! The mid-size (8,500 square foot), airy room offers top roping, and bouldering in a cave and beyond. Gaining in popularity, rock climbing and bouldering give participants a workout physically and mentally as it sharpens one's decision-making processes while literally stretching one physically to reach and be flexible. What's great, too, is that rock climbing is something that can be relished both by those who've never done it before and by skilled climbers. Enjoy climb time on your own or sign up for one of the many classes offered. A signed wavier must be filled out. The Rock Gym location is really nice, on a level just above the main street, and the facility is equally pleasant - it even has a small lounge area inside and patio area outside.

Hours: Open Mon. - Fri., noon - 10pm; Sat., 10am - 9pm; Sun., 10am - 8pm.

Price: $15 for a day pass. $30 for 4 climbs with an instructor, which includes rental harness and auto belay orientation. Rentals are $5 for shoes, $5 for harness, $2 belay device, $2 for chalk bag or $10 for everything.

Ages: 5 years and up.

—GREAT OUTDOORS—

ALICE KECK PARK MEMORIAL GARDENS

(805) 564-5418 or (805) 564-5433 / www.santabarbaraca.gov
1500 Santa Barbara Street, Santa Barbara

This small, 4.6-acre, botanical garden park located in a residential neighborhood, is astoundingly beautiful. Lush grassy expanses are interspersed and bordered by a rich variety of trees, plants, and flowers. The mix includes palm trees, Chinese flame trees, coastal live oaks, Ficus, pink clover blossoms, wisteria, trumpet vines, bougainvillea, camellias, morning glories, roses, Spanish bluebells, and so much more.

A hard-packed dirt path meanders throughout the park and winds around the centerpiece pond. The pond teems with life - blooming lily pads, koi, turtles, ducks, and dragonflies. A few speakers are located around this area that, with the press of a button, quietly tell the history of the park and describe some of the plant life. A rock-lined stream gurgles its way around a portion of the park. Look for and test the sensory garden; plants with particular smells and feels. Check out the butterfly garden that attracts a variety of the beautiful winged insect. Note that KIDS' WORLD / ALAMEDA PARK (pg. 611) is just across the street.

Hours: Open daily, sunrise - 10pm.

Price: Free

Ages: All

ANDREE CLARK BIRD REFUGE

(805) 564-5418 or (805) 564-5433 / www.santabarbaraca.gov/gov/depts/parksrec/parks/features
1400 E. Cabrillo Boulevard, Santa Barbara

This forty-acre, artificial, fresh-water lake and marsh pond attracts native and migratory birds that come here to rest and nest. Bring binoculars and utilize the observation platforms located on the north side of the lake. Don't forget to read the educational panels along the way. A paved pathway encircles the lagoon and is very popular with parents with strollers as well as bicyclists, joggers, and skaters. Take the flat pathway from here, which is part of the BIKE TRAIL: CABRILLO BEACHWAY (pg. 645), the whole three miles to EAST BEACH (pg. 599). Combine an outing here with a visit to the adjacent SANTA BARBARA ZOO (pg. 652), where you can see more exotic birds, and other

animals.

> **Hours:** Open daily, sunrise - 10pm.
> **Price:** Free
> **Ages:** All

ARROYO HONDO PRESERVE

(805) 567-1115 or (805) 966-4520 / www.sblandtrust.org
4 miles W. of Refugio State Beach off Hwy. 101, Gaviota

782 acres of wide open spaces are kept in their natural condition, with the exception of a few added hiking trails. This canyon, surrounded by mountains, sage, shaded streams, oak trees, sycamore trees, yuccas, views of the coastline, and meadows is breathtakingly beautiful. Bring your own water bottles. Picnic tables and portable restrooms are on site.

> **Hours:** Open to the public the first and third full weekends of the month; free, guided nature hikes are held on these days too, at 10am. It is also open every Mon. and Wed., for free, for school and community groups. Advance reservations are required for everyone.
> **Price:** Free for individuals and school groups.
> **Ages:** 4 years and up.

BEATTIE PARK

(805) 875-8100 or (805) 736-1261 / www.cityoflompoc.com
East Olive Avenue and Fifth Street, Lompoc

Located at the southeast corner of town, this fifty-acre park, which is a little tired looking, offers not only a great view of the city, but kid-interesting amenities, as well. Enjoy the basketball courts, sunken soccer/football field, a playground, horseshoe pits, a walking trails, a disc golf course and a picnic pavilion with grills. A small "urban forest" also offers a popular winding dirt fitness trail.

> **Hours:** Open daily, sunrise - sunset.
> **Price:** Free
> **Ages:** All

CACHUMA LAKE RECREATION AREA

(805) 686-5054 or 5055 - general recreation area; (805) 693-0691 - Nature Center; (805) 686-5050 - boat cruise and all camping reservations; (805) 688-4040 - boat rentals / www.countyofsb.org; www.dnaturecenter.org; www.rockymountainrec.com
2225 Highway 154, Santa Barbara

Situated in the mountain footholds and only twenty minutes from both Solvang and Santa Barbara city, this fully-equipped recreation area offers a smorgasbord of activities including boating, fishing (including bow fishing), hiking, camping, and relaxation. The park also has a nature center, two swimming pools that are open in the summer, and nice playgrounds with twisty slides, rock climbing walls, and metal apparatus to climb on. A relatively large (for a campground) general store carries all the necessary accouterments and plenty of just-for-the-fun-of-it items. Other lake amenities include a coin laundry, showers, and a gas station.

Man-made Lake Cachuma is seven miles long with forty-two miles of shoreline. Its marina is open year-round and offers boat rentals such as outboards, rowboats, kayaks, and patio deck boats, as well as launch facilities, a bait and tackle shop. Drop a line off a pier, shoreline, or boat to catch bass, bluegill, perch, catfish, and trout. Ask about the annual fishing derbies.

Other outstanding lake features are the two-hour narrated nature cruises. On the Eagle Cruise tour, given November through February, be on the lookout for migratory bald eagles, Canada geese, teals, and loons. On the Wildlife Cruise, given March through October, the on-board naturalist points out the water fowl such as osprey, great blue herons, plovers, hawks, and mallards, and even the hovering turkey vultures. Tip: Bring binoculars! You'll learn to identify the various birds by their wingspan, nests, and their habits. (We learned that turkey vultures projectile vomit as a defense mechanism.) As the boat maneuvers close to shore look for mule deer, wild turkeys, and the elusive bobcats. The naturalist guide informs listeners of the surrounding, diverse plant life along the shoreline, and in the inaccessible interior land. Both tours are casual in the sense that questions are welcome. The tours are interesting and educational. Tip: Arrive at least a half hour early or you may miss the boat, literally.

The mostly hands-on, surprisingly good-sized nature center has several small rooms branching off from its central room. That room contains a please-touch table and shelves of labeled rocks, fossils, feathers, furs, and a few stuffed animals, including a black bear. Other exhibits include a display of arrowheads, Chumash grind stones, and discovery drawers filled with games and activities. Another room features mounted birds - a great horned owl, an eagle, a snow goose, and more. Compare your wing to other birds against a labeled bird outline on the wall. A display case holds nests and eggs. Look out the two-way mirror and (without scaring them away) observe the numerous species of birds snacking at the outside bird feeders. A plant room showcases indigenous plants and cones, and a tree slab. (Count its rings.) The adjacent room has taxidermied animals such as coyote, mule deer, gray fox, raccoon, and mountain lion. Touch an animal fur and guess what kind of animal it is. (Lift the panel for the answer.) Other exhibits in the center include a light up board to match true statements with pictures of animals; skulls and jawbones of various animals; rocks with geological fact sheets; and stone mortar and pestle to try. The center hosts fishing workshops and educational school field trips throughout the year, including the junior ranger program; free, guided nature walks every Saturday; a trout derby in April; and a live animal program in May.

There are a few short hiking trails within the park. The Sweetwater Trail, an extended 2.5-mile one-way hike, starts here and winds its way between campgrounds to the Bradbury Dam Overlook. Tequepis Trail, directly across the road from the lake, is an eight-mile hike to the Santa Ynez Mountains ridge line. There is no direct access to this trail from the recreation area and a parking permit is required.

Campers can choose from over 520 sites, many with RV hook-ups available. Some sites have trees, most have grass, and numerous have a lake view. Several yurts are on the grounds, too. Yurts, which sleep five to six people, are like canvas-covered cabins. They are insulated, have bunk beds with mattresses, a locking door, inside lighting and heating, and a small table with chairs - not quite camping, but still in the great outdoors. There are also a few one and two-bedroom cabins, with kitchenettes and bathrooms, that boast a front-row lake view.

Horseback riding trail rides and lessons are available just down the road from the lake at Rancho Oso Stables. Minimum age for horseback riding is 8 years, but younger children will enjoy a short, hand-led walk around with the horse. One-hour trail rides are $45 per person; hand-led rides are $20 a child. Call (805) 683-5110 / www.rancho-oso.com for more information.

Hours: Most activities are open year round. Day use hours for the general park are sunrise - sunset; open until 8pm or 8:30pm in the summer. The Nature Center is open Tues. - Sat., 10am - 4pm; Sun., 10am - 2pm; closed Mon. Eagle Cruises are offered November - February, Fri. at 2pm; Sat. at 10am and 2pm; and Sun. at 10am. Wildlife Cruises are offered March - October, Fri. at 3pm; Sat. at 10am and 3pm; Sun. at 10am. The swimming pools are open Memorial Day - Labor Day daily, 10am - 5pm, and open Sat. in September.

Price: Day use entrance is $10 per automobile; $5 for hiker or biker; $3 for dogs. The Nature Center is free, after paying the park entrance fee. Camping starts at $23 (tent - off season) - $48 (with full hook-ups - in season,). There is also a $6.50 camping fee. Yurts are $60 (sleeps 5) - $85 (sleeps 8). Cabins are $90 (weekday - off season) - $135 (weekend - in season). There is also a $20 reservation fee for yurts and cabins. The swimming pools are $3 per person for each two-hour session. Cruises are $15 for adults; $7 for ages 4 - 12; children 3 and under are not allowed; $5 for school groups. Boat rentals are $10 and hour for single kayak and $12 for a double; and $30 for a two-hour rental for a four-passenger motorboat up to $320 for an all day patio deck boat accommodating 20 passengers.

Ages: All

CARPINTERIA BLUFFS NATURE PRESERVE AND TRAIL

(805) 684-5405 / www.carpinteria.ca.us

at the south end of Bailard Avenue, Carpinteria

This bluffs nature preserve is 53 acres of open space with stunning front views of the ocean, coastline, and Channel Islands and Santa Ynez mountains behind.

The trail runs from about 4th Street, at CARPINTERIA STATE BEACH (see page 598), to just south of Bailard Avenue for a total of about five miles, round trip. Much of the trail is hard-packed dirt, while some parts are sandier and some parts are unimproved, so you might have to look for the path. It follows the coastline (and parallels, then crosses, the railroad tracks) mostly along the top of the bluffs, with an ocean view at almost every step. There is some

beach access along the way via stairs. You'll also pass by the HARBOR SEAL PRESERVE (see page 650) so look down to see the seals, as well as whales (as they migrate seasonally), dolphins, and more.

At the eastern end of the preserve is Viola Fields park with athletic fields for baseball/softball and soccer, plus kite flying (and a restroom!).

Hours: Open daily, sunrise to sunset.
Price: Free
Ages: 5 years and up.

CARPINTERIA CREEK PARK

(805) 684-5405 / www.carpinteria.ca.us
Carpinteria Creek Drive from Via Real, Carpinteria

This small (one-acre) park not only has a creek running adjacent to it (hence the name), but unique play structures of two climbing boulders. One is a large, sphere-shaped rock with deliberate cracks and footholds and the other is a taller, thinner rock (more real-looking) with more finger and foot holds - both are easy to climb up and jump down on to a cushy landing. Five picnic tables, grassy space bordered by lovely plants, including some large trees, interpretive signs, and a short paved pathway that runs throughout complete this fun stop off. It is also adjacent to a bike path. There are no bbq or restrooms.

Hours: Open daily, sunrise - sunset.
Price: Free
Ages: 4 - 10 years

CARPINTERIA SALT MARSH NATURE PARK

(805) 684-5405 or (805) 893-4127 / www.sblandtrust.org
Sandyland Road and Ash Avenue, Carpinteria

Appearances can be deceiving. This 230-acre salt marsh preserve is not just a boring, swampy wasteland, as it might appear at first glance, but a thriving, ecological community for a variety of plant and animal species, all bordered by houses, streets, ocean, and train tracks. That said, kids will not find it a thrill a minute, but it is intriguing and educational. Over half of the marsh is a preserve, open only for research, while the other half comprises the nature "park", with several acres open to the public for ready access to walk and view.

You can enjoy the several overlooks and stroll the graveled and boardwalk-style trails that meander along the marsh amid lots of plants, reading its twenty interpretative signs on your own, or, one of the best ways to really experience it - join a docent-led tour offered on Saturdays. Look for the birds that consider the reserve home - herons, egrets, brown pelicans, osprey, and numerous other shore birds. Many birds also stop here during the annual migrations. Numerous plants, fish (including leopard sharks which feed at the mouth of the estuary in the summer), and other sea creatures also reside here. Remember, that CARPINTERIA STATE BEACH (pg. 598) is just a few steps away!

Hours: Open daily, sunrise - sunset.
Price: Free.
Ages: 7 years and up.

CHASE PALM PARK

(805) 564-5418 / www.santabarbaraca.gov
323 E. Cabrillo Boulevard at Garden Street, Santa Barbara

This imaginative park runs parallel to the main street of Cabrillo Boulevard, across the street from EAST BEACH (pg. 599) and SANTA BARBARA HARBOR / STEARNS WHARF (pg. 637). The west end of the park has a fountain and park benches, plus a lovely, traditional carousel with wood-carved animals inside the carousel building. Stroll along the cement and hard-packed dirt pathway as it winds the length of the park, over bridges and through pretty garden landscape, around a scenic pond with a few ducks, along with cement picnic tables and wooden benches scattered throughout.

The east end of the park holds the treasure of a shipwreck playground complete with sand; big cement octopus tentacles; large climbing structures; small bridges; slides; tubes to crawl through, and a few rocks to climb on. One area also has kid-size, adobe-style walls and doors to play hide and seek, and a tepee-like building. Just beyond the playground is a grassy area with gently rolling hills and a stage for outdoor concerts and events. Check out the family

concerts given in the summer. A snack bar here sells hot dogs, churros, popsicles, and other necessary food items in the summer.

Hours: Open daily, sunrise - sunset. The carousel is open Mon. - Thurs., 11am - 6pm; Fri., 11am - 7pm; Sat. - Sun., 10am - 7pm.

Price: Free. Carousel rides are $2 per person; children 9 months and under are free. There is some free street parking, or park at the beach lot for $2 an hour; $12 max.

Ages: 9 months to 14 years.

CHUMASH PAINTED CAVE

(805) 968-1033 / www.parks.ca.gov

Painted Cave Road, Santa Barbara

Almost exactly two miles up a very narrow, sometimes one-lane, winding, woodland-laced road with hairpin turns, is your destination - the Painted Cave. (Be on the lookout for the brown sign that says "park" on the left.) Climb up a few boulders to peer through gratings into the cave. Its walls are covered with still-vivid paintings drawn by Chumash Indians hundreds of years ago. Yes, it's a rather precarious drive for just a few moments of sight-seeing, but to actually view such paintings can be exciting.

A trail, if one can call it that, leads up the boulder-covered hill. Be sure-footed to indulge in this short hike. We also found adventure on the opposite side of the road. A rock-lined dry creek bed (I assume the creek is seasonal!) and the surrounding woods provided my boys with a good deal of entertainment (and made the drive more justifiable).

Hours: Open daily, sunrise - sunset.

Price: Free

Ages: 8 years and up.

COAL OIL POINT RESERVE

(805) 893-5092 - reserve; (805) 893-3703 - tours / coaloilpoint.ucnrs.org

Slough Road, adjacent to the UCSB campus, Goleta

This 158-acre reserve is a rich combination of undisturbed coastal dunes and estuarine habitats. The tidal lagoon area is flooded seasonally and then dries out in the summer to form salt flats and small hypersaline ponds and channels. Thousand of migratory birds, including (and most importantly), the endangered Snowy Plover, rest and nest here. A three+-mile, looping trail goes around the perimeter of the reserve, with eighteen interpretative placards along the way. One trail, the Pond Trail, shortcuts through it. To take a self-guided tour, the entrances to the reserve are at the intersection of Del Playa and Camino Majorca, at Sand's Beach, and at the southern point of the pond trail. The adjacent university offers several guided "tours," or field studies, for students of all ages.

The reserve has great tidepools to explore. Note that the tidepools are closed March through mid-September because they are next to the plover's seasonal nesting grounds. Just around the "corner," on West Campus Beach by the Del Playa entrance, is one of best spots for year-round tidepooling. Peak under small boulders to observe the teeming marine life. Have no *reserv*ations about coming here for an educational and fun day!

Hours: Open daily, dawn - dusk for a self-guided walk. Tours are given on some Sat. from 2pm - 4:15pm. Call to make reservation for a tour at any other time.

Price: Free for a self-guided walk. $5 for adults for a guided tour; students are free. Free parking is on the street outside the campus, or pay $3 for on-campus parking.

Ages: 4 years and up.

FIGUEROA MOUNTAIN

(805) 925-9538 - U.S. Forest Service; (805) 968-6640 - Los Padres National Forest Headquarters; (805) 688-6144 - Solvang Visitors Bureau / www.fs.usda.gov

Figueroa Mountain Road/ Happy Canyon Road, Solvang

This over twenty miles of winding road goes through some of the most gorgeous scenery in all of Santa Barbara County. We drove a good portion of it and stopped at numerous spots along the way, sometimes at marked trails, and sometimes just where the countryside beckoned us. This mountain area, with canyons, waterfalls, chaparral, trees, and more, has over fifteen hiking trails and numerous unmarked "trails". The scenery changes drastically depending on the season. In the spring, the slopes are ablaze with wild flowers, including California poppies, shooting stars, and blue lupines. Indian summers bring fewer people and unmatched beauty. Be forewarned - the road is oftentimes closed

during the rainy season. Snow can sometimes fall during the winter months. Contact the forest service for maps and more information. Fishing is available year-round at Davy Brown Creek, below the Davy Brown campground, and in Manzana Creek from March to mid-May, when it's stocked with trout. Check out Figueroa Campground, which has about thirty sites, to spend more time in this beautiful area.

Hours: Open daily, sunrise - sunset.
Price: Most parking areas require the $5 Adventure Pass to be posted on your windshield.
Ages: 4 years and up.

FLETCHER PARK
(805) 925-0951 / www.cityofsantamaria.org
2200 S. College Drive, Santa Maria

This is a lovely, three-acre corner park with some fun features. An enclosed, portable-looking skatepark sports a variety of ramps, plus rails and boxes and plenty of skate room. Next to this is a half basketball court and then a favorite thing - climbing rocks. These three large, fake boulders are mostly flat on the top and of varying sizes, shapes and configurations. They have finger grips, cracks, and foot holds crafted into them and suggestions for how to climb them most effectively and how to switch up a route. Take the bridge across the drainage ditch to a small playground that has a tire swing, monkey bars, slides, and climbing elements surrounded by some grassy space, a small hill, and a covered picnic area with a bbq. An asphalt pathway goes between the houses and back along the ditch for a ways. Across the street is a sunken field for soccer games.

Hours: Open daily, sunrise - sunset.
Price: Free
Ages: All

HANS CHRISTIAN ANDERSEN PARK
(805) 688-PLAY (7529) / www.cityofsolvang.com
633 Chalk Hill Road, Solvang

Drive through the castle-like turrets (with cool wooden doors) into a delightful, back-to-nature park which has something for everyone. We especially enjoyed the numerous, huge, gnarled oak trees for shade and to climb on, and the seasonal creek. One picnic area has picnic tables and small barbecue pits. Another picnic area has huge charcoal pits, a nice grass area, horseshoe pits (bring your own horseshoes), and a bridge over the creek. The 1.3-mile round-trip dirt trail is great for hikers and horseback riders.

An enclosed, really nice-sized, cement skate park is towards the front of the park. It has several bowls and ramps, rails, steps, a pyramid and other street features. There are two playgrounds, one is tiny and the larger one has several slides, swings, a rock climbing wall, other climbing apparatus, and an activity board. Toward the back of the park are four tennis courts and more climbing trees. After a hard day of shopping in Solvang, give your family a storybook ending by coming to play at the park.

Hours: Open daily, 8am - sunset.
Price: Free
Ages: All

JIM MAY PARK
(805) 925-0951 / www.cityofsantamaria.org
809 Stanford Drive, Santa Maria

The outstanding feature of this park is its medium-size lake, surrounded by homes. A short pier/observation deck allows you to walk out a bit and see the wildlife. I saw a lot of coots. (And I don't mean old coots; I mean birds.) A paved, bike path encircles the lake while another path branches off, paralleling the riverbed. A small playground has some grassy areas with trees behind it. Get more physical by using the exercise stations staggered along the street.

Hours: Open daily, sunrise - sunset.
Price: Free
Ages: 2 - 15 years.

KIDS' WORLD / ALAMEDA PARK
(805) 564-5418 / www.santabarbaraca.gov

1400 Santa Barbara Street, Santa Barbara

Partially designed by kids, and totally designed for them, this part of the park is a favorite - a truly awesome Kid's World. A large, enclosed, multi-level, wooden play fort, with cupolas on top and sawdust on the floor, is the main feature and is packed with imaginative "extras." It has stairways, slides, tube bridges, maze-like crawl spaces (made for kid-size bodies!), a zip line, climbing apparatus, a rope bridge, speaking tubes, and more. In the center of the fort are benches made so that parents can chat with each other while keeping an eye on the kids. A toddler area has swings and a large tic-tac-toe board.

The fort is under a sprawling shade tree, with big roots above ground. Plenty of picnic tables are right outside the fort perimeter, as are a sizable cement beached whale and shark, and more swings.

The rest of the park is pretty and restful, composed of lots of grassy areas and more shade trees, plus a few cement pathways. Look up ALICE KECK PARK MEMORIAL GARDENS (pg. 606), as it is just across the street.

Hours: Open daily, sunrise - 10pm.
Price: Free
Ages: 1 to 12 years.

LAKE LOS CARNEROS PARK

(805) 961-7500 / www.cityofgoleta.org
304 N. Los Carneros Road at Calle Real, Goleta

This large (140 acre) park/nature reserve, just beyond the STOW HOUSE (pg. 635) and SOUTH COAST RAILROAD MUSEUM (pg. 635), is pretty much in its natural state. Depending on the season, you'll find the park to be a green oasis of plants, mostly shrubbery, surrounding a lake, or very dry grass fields with a smaller lake. The ducks and a myriad of birds seem to be plentiful either way. The hard-packed dirt hiking trails branch off in different directions, with the one cutting almost through the center of the park and around the lake being a short, easy walk for most ages. The zig zagging wooden bridge add a special element to the park. Look up STOW GROVE PARK (pg. 621), a neighboring park just north of Los Carneros.

Hours: Open daily, 8am - sunset.
Price: Free
Ages: All

LA PURISIMA MISSION STATE HISTORIC PARK

(805) 733-3713 / www.lapurisimamission.org
2295 Purisima Road, Lompoc

Situated on just a portion of the almost 2,000 acres of undeveloped parkland, this eleventh mission in the California chain was first founded in 1787. It is one of the most authentically-restored missions as the adobe bricks, structures, mission furniture, and decor have been replicated using tools, materials, and construction methods similar to the originals. Even the types of plants in the garden and representative livestock in the corrals harken back to that era.

You're invited to peer into and/or walk through the numerous buildings sprawled over this section of rural land, and to read the informational signs. We began our self-guided tour with the visitors' center. Just beyond this building is a shady picnic grove with California black walnut trees, coastal live oaks, a seasonal creek, and picnic tables. There old building near here once served as an infirmary and still contains rows of beds. Tip: Make sure to look up under the outside rafters at the birds and their mud nests.

The Tule village has three roomy huts made from tule reed. The blacksmith shop displays anvils, tools, and bellows, along with living quarters that has a bed and kitchen. A beehive oven plus kitchen, gourds, a granary, grinding mill stone, storeroom, and pottery shop are some of the components of the next series of rooms. The adjacent long building has a wine cellar; bedrooms; a large living and dining area; guest bedrooms (notice the pre-box-spring ropes across the bed frames); simply furnished padres' quarters; a tanning room (not used for humans to suntan, but to cure animal hides) with several hides; a leather shop; wooden horses with saddles; and a nave with vestments behind glass. Further rooms and items of interest include the mission bell; a Mexican ox yoke; bricks to touch; a large seventeenth-century, hand-written choir book made of sheepskin parchment; a weaving room with looms and spinning wheels; a candle room with strings of hanging candles waiting to be dipped; and military sleeping quarters where weapons hang on the walls, over the heads of beds.

Walk through the long main church with old paintings, outside to the cemetery and on to the huge tallow vats on the "back" side of the mission. The central courtyard is composed of beautiful gardens, a fountain, the lavanderia cistern (used for washing clothes and for bathing), and a corral. Long-horn cattle, horses, four-horn sheep, turkeys, geese, and burros dwell here.

Walking along the dusty paths between buildings gives present-time visitors a real sense of the past, as do the Mission Life Days which are held March through September, one Saturday of the month from 11am to 2pm. These special days feature costumed docents who recreate padres, soldiers, Indians, and other residents from the mission's heyday. Demonstrations can include wool spinning, brick making, candlemaking, and blacksmithing.

One hour guided tours for individuals are offered daily at 1pm (except during Living History Days or special events). Age-appropriate guided tours for groups of school-age children and for adults are offered throughout the year, for a minimum of ten people. Ask about the special evening candlelight tours and other events such as Village Days, Purisima's People Day, El Pastor, Mountain Men, Founding Day, and Sheep Shearing Day. The latter is a one-day event in April where you can see big, fluffy sheep sheared down to look like little naked things, plus learn how wool was processed and used at the mission.

Another pleasure of La Purisima is the miles and miles of hiking, biking, and equestrian trails that crisscross throughout the back country. The terrain varies from rolling hills to canyons to a pond. Trails range from the short climb of the Trail to the Landmark Cross, which does have a cross at the end of the path; to the 2.7 miles of Roadrunner Road, which is a service road forming a loop near the mission; to the miles of trails extending into the heart of the park's chaparral. Be on the lookout for all sorts of animals, especially the numerous birds that use this route for their migration. Pack your own water and/or bring a picnic lunch to enjoy on the mission grounds.

Hours: Open daily, 9am - 5pm. The buildings close at 4:30pm. The visitor center is open Mon., 11am - 3pm; Tues. - Sun., 10am - 4pm. Everything is closed New Year's Day, Thanksgiving, and Christmas.
Price: $6 per vehicle; $5 for seniors.
Ages: 5 years and up.

LOMPOC AQUATIC CENTER / COLLEGE PARK (skate park)
(805) 875-8100 or (805) 736-1261- park; (805) 875-2700 - aquatic center / www.cityoflompoc.com
207 W. College Avenue, Lompoc

This small park's central focus is a 10,000 square-foot skate park. It has ramps and bowls and all the "extras" that make a skate park fun and challenging. Skaters - wear protective safety gear. The surrounding park has shade trees, an open grassy area, a good-sized playground, and picnic tables and BBQs.

The park is next to a state-of-the-art, indoors, aquatic center with glass and aluminum framing and retractable roof panels (i.e. skylights) so it feels like the outdoors. The center has a competition, a therapeutic, and a lap/recreation pool, plus two long and winding water slides and a colorful aquatic play structure. The structure, which has zero depth entry, has enclosed mini slides, steps, water-squirting elements, and space to splash around. There is also a picnic area outside.

Hours: The park is open daily, sunrise - sunset. The aquatics center is open daily for lap swim. For recreational swim (and this includes the water play area), it is open most of the year, Fri., 3:30pm - 5pm; Sat. - Sun., 1pm - 3pm; open daily in the summer, usually 1pm - 3pm. The pool is closed New Years Day, Thanksgiving and Christmas week.
Price: The park is free. The aquatics center is $4 for adults; $3.50 for seniors and ages 13 - 17; $3 for ages 2 - 12.
Ages: 7 years and up.

LOOKOUT COUNTY PARK
(805) 568-2461 or (805) 568-2465 / www.countyofsb.org
2297 Finney Road, Summerland

If you're on the lookout for some fun, this bluff-top park offers an incredible panoramic view of the ocean and shoreline. Kids are most interested in the small playground on rubber-type flooring with its slides, swings, toddler swings, a mini (mini!) zip-line, short "rock" climbing wall, sand pit, and adjacent volleyball court. There are also a few picnic tables, barbecue pits, a strip of grass, shade trees, and an asphalt pathway leading down to the long stretch of beach below. The beach is popular for both swimming and bodysurfing.

Hours: Open daily, 8am - sunset
Price: Free
Ages: All

LOPEZ LAKE RECREATION AREA / MUSTANG WATERPARK

☼
$$$$

(805) 489-1006 - marina and store; (805) 781-5930 or (805) 788-2381 - recreation area/camping; (805) 489-8898 - Mustang Waterpark / www.slocountyparks.com; www.mustangwaterpark.com; www.lopezlakemarina.com
6800 Lopez Drive, Arroyo Grande

Well off the beaten path and snuggled into the surrounding mountains, the 4,600-acre, beautiful, year-round, get-away Lopez Lake is worth the drive from nearby Santa Barbara County. Fishing is a popular activity with rainbow trout, bass, crappie (not crappy, necessarily), and catfish available for catching in their seasons. Fish from the twenty-two miles of lake shoreline or from a boat. The marina boasts a boat launch, tackle shop, restaurant, and convenience store. Kayak rentals are $15 for a single for two hours, $25 for a double. Canoes are $30 for two hours. Stand Up Paddle boards are $15 for two hours. Pedal boats are $30 for two hours. Electric-assist pedal boats (in a pirate or swan style!) are $40 for two hours. Three-person wave runners are $90 for an hour. Motorized fishing boats are $60 for two hours. Ten-passenger, double-decker patio boats are $90 for two hours. There are also pontoon boats, ski boats, cabin boats and more available, too. Two-hour nature boat cruises of the lake are offered one weekend day a month at 9am for $6 for adults; $3 for ages 17 and under, plus the $10 park entrance fee. Hike on the several short, easy trails, or on the few more moderate ones, and be on the lookout for wildlife including deer, wild turkeys, and lots of birds. Or, just enjoy the grassy areas, the vast amount of mature oak trees, and the scattered picnic tables.

Summertime fun includes swimming at the Vista Lago swim area, complete with a beach. For the slightly more adventuresome, the adjacent small Mustang Waterpark offers two, long (600 feet), curvy, water slides that wind through the hillsides, ending in a splash pool. An inner tube ride zips you down one side of a thirty-eight-foot half pipe, back up the other side and back down - backwards. Younger kids, ages 9 and under, are not left out of the water fun as there are two wading pools for them (called pony pools) with mini slides and waterfall trees (that look more like giant mushrooms) embedded in perimeter boulders. A snack bar and lockers are also on the premises - no outside food is allowed in.

For s'more fun, stay at any of the over 350 campsites, from primitive camping to full hook-ups. Most of the sites have a picnic table, a grassy spot, and a huge oak tree at least nearby. Hot shower facilities are at several campgrounds. Look at specific sites online. To avoid some of the noise and for a campsite with a view of the lake, try Conejo or Buck campgrounds.

Hours: The marina is open most of the year daily, 7am - 5pm; open June - September, Mon. - Thurs., 7am - 5pm; Fri., 7am - 8pm; Sat., 6:30am - 8pm; Sun., 7am - 6pm. The recreation area is open daily, 6am - 9pm. The lake is open daily, 6am - dusk. Boat rentals are available daily, 7am - 4pm. Mustang Waterpark is open late March - mid-June and mid-August - mid-September, Sat. - Sun., 11:30am - 5pm (or 6pm, sometimes). It's open mid-June - mid-August, daily, 11:30am - 5pm (or 6pm or 7pm - depending on the day!).

Price: Parking at Lopez Lake is $10. Camping is $23 (primitive, off peak) - $38 (full hook-up, peak), plus a $9 reservation fee. $3.50 per dog. Admission for Mustang Waterpark is $20 for adults; $18 for 48" and taller and under 18 years old; $15 for 42" - 47" (may ride all slides and go double with adult); $12 for 41" and under (restricted to kiddie slides only). A dry observer is $5; a wet assist admission (assisting a small child or special needs patron) is $8. Admission after 2pm, Sun. - Thurs., and after 4pm, Fri. - Sat., is $2 off for 41" and under, and $3 off all other water sliding admissions.

Ages: All

LOS ALAMOS COUNTY PARK

☼
!

(805) 934-6211 / www.countyofsb.org/parks
500 Drum Canyon Road, Los Alamos

Snug up against the hills of Drum Canyon, this lovely fifty-one-acre park is a refreshing place to visit and seemingly far removed from city life. Three group picnic areas encourage families to gather together for a day, or at least a meal. Each "site" has plenty of picnic tables and a huge barbecue grill - big enough to roast a pig!

Plentiful old oak trees spread their mighty (and shady) branches, beckoning kids to climb on them. A large grass area offers run around space. A seasonal creek runs through parts of the park. Horseshoe pits (bring your own shoes), a playground with slides and swings, a ball field, two sand volleyball courts, and hills to hike up and around make this an ideal park as there is something for everyone.

Note: Since you're out this way, and even passed it on the way in, stop off at the historic, wooden 1880 Union Hotel on Bell St. It was rebuilt in the early 1900's and is great for photo ops - both outside and inside. Decorated with a feel of that era - richly wallpapered rooms, lamps, wood accents and even rustic decor of stuffed animal heads and more - are the upstairs hotel rooms, and the downstairs rooms of the gorgeous lobby, saloon, and lounge. Grab a meal on Fridays and Saturdays only, usually (sometimes open more in the summertime), with choices of salads ($11); fish tacos ($12); stuffed mushrooms ($9); a variety of empanadas ($9 - $13); burgers ($14); chicken strips and fries ($8); shrimp ($12); and desserts. Call (805) 344-2744 for more info. There are also several antique shops on Bell St.

Hours: Open daily, 8am - sunset.
Price: Free
Ages: All

LOTUSLAND

(805) 969-9990 / www.lotusland.org

$$$$$

695 Ashley Road, Montecito

Plant it and they will come. This thirty-seven-acre estate boasts a botanical garden of dreams. The main pathway branches off into various themed sections, each one focused on a particular grouping or type of plant in a breathtakingly-beautiful setting. A two-hour walking tour takes visitors through it all.

Begin at the visitor's center, which has oddly bent cactus in the patio courtyard, as well as a small mosaic tile fountain, tile benches, and a garden shop. Enter the Australian Garden, where the plants are native to Australia. The intriguing and serene Japanese Garden features a pond with lily pads and koi that is surrounded by native trees and plants, and a wisteria arbor. The Epiphyllum Garden pathway leads visitors past shady oak trees and eucalyptus tree trunks that are decorated with blooming orchid cacti and other plants. A rock-lined streambed meanders throughout this area. The Cycad (i.e., cone bearing) Garden offers a small pond with lily pads and a little waterfall, all enhanced by encircling palm plants. Feeling blue? The plants in the Blue Garden have silver and blue-gray foliage. The Water Garden was the original swimming pool, but the only thing floating in here now are the numerous Indian lotus plants. Side ponds hold other species of lotus and water lilies.

Cacti, bromeliads, succulents, and aloes all have their own area to call home. The aloe area also has a kidney-shaped pool with a cascading fountain made of giant clam shells. The parterre (i.e., formal planting beds) is divided into two sections by hedges: One side has a rose garden and star-shaped fountain, while the other has an intricate pebble mosaic and fanciful Neptune fountain. The Fern Garden flourishes with giant ferns hanging in baskets from trees, as well as with tree ferns and other species. The garden is bordered by another pool, a sandy "beach" with giant clam shells, and a stone wall lined with succulents. The colorful Butterfly Garden attracts garden-friendly insects, including butterflies. Look for Monarchs, or butterfly wannabes (i.e., caterpillars).

The orchard grows citrus, such as oranges, lemons and limes, as well as deciduous trees - plums, peaches, apples, persimmons, and more. Rows of olive trees, also produced here, end abruptly at a wall fountain with a figure of a mythological horse/sea monster. Last, but not least, is the Topiary Garden which has a twenty-five-foot (in diameter) working clock as its centerpiece. I think it's a bit hard to tell the time this way. The garden also features something particularly fun for kids - a zoo of topiary plants growing in shapes of a camel, gorilla, giraffe, seal, and other animals. Advanced reservation are required for this exotic plant tour as it is located in a residential neighborhood and the maximum number for a group is ten.

Hours: Open mid-February - mid-November, Wed. - Sat. at 10am and 1:30pm. Ask about Family Tours which is the only time children 9 years and under may go on the tour.
Price: $45 for adults; $20 ages 3 - 18; children 2 and under are free. Note that Santa Barbara residents may visit here, at no charge, 18 days a year - these spaces fill up quickly!
Ages: 10 years and up only.

MANNING PARK

(805) 969-0201 or (805) 568-2461 / www.countyofsb.org

!

449 San Ysidro Road, Montecito

There are two different facets to this park. To the west side of San Ysidro Road is a multi-level park that still feels like the estate it once was. This lush little park, with portions that could be classified as botanic gardens, has a green stretch of grass that is dotted with pine and other trees, lots of birds, a few scattered picnic tables and barbecue pits, and a really nice-looking youth center building. Just up the stairs and ramp is a small playground and a few covered picnic sites. There is a tennis court on the south side of this park. No admission is charged.

On the east side of the street is a more typical park, which is accessible by walking across the street, or driving to the other parking lot via Santa Rosa Lane. This medium-size park has a ball field that doubles as a field of grass, plus a volleyball court, a playground, large barbecue pits, and a creek that runs along one side. This park is subject to group reservations.

Hours: Open daily, 8am - sunset.
Price: Free
Ages: All

MINAMI PARK

(805) 925-0951 / www.cityofsantamaria.org

600 West Enos, Santa Maria

This sprawling park has everyone-appeal. There are wide, wide, wide open grass areas and trees interspersed throughout; hard-packed dirt pathways; two sand volleyball courts; softball fields; several lighted tennis courts; bocce ball; a basketball court; and a nice playground. The multi-level playground features long and twisty slides, bridges, short rock climbing walls, metal apparatus to play on and climb, and swings, all in a wood chip base. The community center has a multi-purpose room. Just across the street is a long sunken field for soccer, or other sports.

Hours: Open daily sunrise - sunset.
Price: Free
Ages: All

MORETON BAY FIG TREE

(805) 564-5418 / www.santabarbaraca.gov

Chapala and Montecito streets, Santa Barbara

This is not really an end destination, but it is an interesting, natural wonder to stop off and see. This fig tree, originally a seedling brought over from Australia in 1876, now has a top that spans 160 feet - it's absolutely huge!!! Its roots cover half a city block. The coolest fact for kids? It's listed in the Guinness Book of World Records.

Hours: Open daily, sunrise to half-hour after sunset.
Price: Free
Ages: All

NOJOQUI FALLS

(805) 568-2461 / www.countyofsb.org

3200 Alisal Road, Solvang

Driving the tree-lined road leading to Nojoqui Falls is like a drive in the country. The first part of the park has group picnic areas with both large and small barbecue pits, a small playground, a sand volleyball court, a large grassy area, and <u>lots</u> of trees.

One reason for this beautiful park's popularity is the ten-minute, or so, hike to the limestone cliff waterfall. Located toward the back of the park, walk the dirt-packed, stroller-friendly trail that meanders along a seasonal creek, past boulders, and over bridges to the seasonal 100-foot waterfall. (In the summer and fall, it can become a tricklefall.) The surrounding scenery is admirable in any season.

Hours: Open daily, 8am - sunset.
Price: Free
Ages: All

OAK PARK

(805) 564-5418 / www.santabarbaraca.gov; www.santabarbara.com

300 W. Alamar Street, Santa Barbara

Bordered by a street and a creek (or rocky creek bed during the dry season) this lovely park has numerous old, sprawling oak trees - great for climbing and great for picnicking under. Picnic tables are scattered throughout, with one large picnic area that has a fire pit covered with grates big enough to roast a pig. One of the play areas has a large sandbox and a tire swing, plus a few slides, and critters on big springs for kids to ride and rock back and forth on - all in a wood-chip base. The other playground is for slightly older kids with a swing set, taller slides, monkey bars and rings, and bridges that connect various climbing apparatus, all in a sand base. A very shallow (eighteen-inch) wading pool is open May through September. Other amenities include two tennis courts and horseshoe pits.

Hours: Open daily, sunrise - one-half hour after sunset.
Price: Free
Ages: All

PREISKER PARK

(805) 925-0951 / www.cityofsantamaria.org
330 Hidden Pines Way, Santa Maria

Ahhhhh! This large circular park - one of my favorites - is located at the northern end of the city and has a plethora of mature pine and oak trees (and the possibility of climbing them) that offer shade and a peaceful ambiance. There is also plenty of open, grassy areas to run around, plus gently rolling green hills, a baseball diamond, and two good-sized playgrounds. The playgrounds have a sand base, are dotted with big rocks, and host a few rock climbing walls, slides and swings, and a few other pieces of play equipment. A main attraction is the small wood and cement ship (a little replica of the Santa Maria) for young mateys to climb aboard. Located in a small pond (with a gangplank entrance), it's "armed" with cannon turrets. The pond has a fountain in the middle of it and is home to ducks who quack for handouts. A rock-lined stream with a short waterfall runs through a portion of the park and flows into the pond. Picnic tables are plentiful. This park also has an eighteen-hole disc golf course over mostly flat and lightly-wooded terrain, plus horseshoes, and a decent, paved perimeter walk.

A park within a park is found at North Preisker Ranch Park, just down the street at the corner of Hidden Pines and Railroad Avenue. The park features a large, multi-level children's play area. Besides the main, tall structure with slides, a rock climbing wall, monkey bars, and climbing apparatus, it also has several small railroad cars for your children with an attitoot toot! This area also has a grass area, picnic tables, tennis courts, and basketball courts that are shared with the Junior High School that the public can use when school is not in session. Enjoy a day in these delightful parks.

Hours: Open daily, sunrise - sunset.
Price: Free
Ages: All

RANCHO GUADALUPE-NIPOMO DUNES PRESERVE / OSO FLACO LAKE NATURAL AREA / OCEANO DUNES STATE VEHICULAR RECREATION AREA / DUNES VISITORS CENTER MUSEUM

Dunes Visitors Center Museum - (805) 343-2455 / www.dunescenter.org; Dunes ranger station - (805) 473-7223 or 7220 or (805) 773-7170 / www.ohv.parks.ca.gov; camping reservations at Oceano -(800) 444-7275

There are three entrances/addresses for the dunes: The southern entrance is West Main Street/Hwy. 166 in Guadalupe; the central is Oso Flaco Lake Road in Nipomo; and the northern is Pier Avenue in Oceano. The visitors center museum is located at 1065 Guadalupe Street/Highway 1 in Guadalupe.

Maps of the preserve, an events calendar, and helpful docents make the visitors' center (i.e., Dunes Visitors Center Museum) a good starting point for your trip to the dunes. The center also has interactive displays for kids (and adults) such as a sand pit filled with hidden treasures; skulls and other plaster bones to touch; microscopes and slides; a puppet stage and animal puppets; and award-winning computer programs written specifically to educate and fascinate visitors to the dunes. You can also choose from such video topics as birds of prey, amphibians, geology, and the making of the 1923 Cecil B. DeMille movie, *The Ten Commandments*, which was filmed here. The center has information about the movie set, which still lays buried in the area, intact, under layers of sand. There are also a few taxidermied animals, photographs, and a small gift shop here.

There are three entrances for three very different experiences to the eighteen miles, and acres and acres and acres

of sand dunes. In **Rancho Guadalupe**, the Southern-most entrance, drive past a working sand mine, through marshlands where cattle are grazing, until you almost reach the shoreline of Guadalupe Beach. Spend time exploring the rolling sandy hills, strolling along the beach, and frolicking in the water.

At **Oso Flaco**, park the car in the lot, and walk along the hard-packed dirt path to a long wooden bridge and boardwalk that cross over a portion of one of the fresh-water lakes in the preserve. The pathway extends all the way to the beach (at some points the trail is almost obliterated by sand), making it a total trek of about a mile-and-a-half. Other paths branch off into the dunes. The diversity of plant and animal life here is amazing. The dunes are constantly being resculpted as the wind and water shift the sands to new depths and new heights (up to 500 feet!) We hiked to the beach, but the boys really enjoyed exploring the more dramatic dunes. We took a trail that cut to the right, before the beach, and turned right again at the fence, going "off road" to reach our play area. The kids cavorted, ran, jumped, rolled, slid (with plastic sleds even), and crawled up and down the dunes. I took pictures. They were happy and tired. My pictures were great. When all is said and *dune*, we had a great day.

At the northern, **Oceano** entrance, park right near the beach, or take your four-wheel drive directly onto it! (Mini vans can only go so far.) You can drive quite a few miles on the beach, right up to the waves or dunes. Let the kids go wild! (Within reason, of course.) There are three-and-a-half miles of beach and 1,500 acres of sand dunes in this area available for OHV use. For those without the necessary vehicle you've got a few options. Humvee tours are quite the thrill, zooming up and over the dunes like riding a roller coaster. Prices are $55 an hour per person. Contact Pacific Adventure Tours (805) 481-9330 / www.pacificadventuretours.com. Or, rent an all-terrain vehicle - this is one of our favorite choices. The vehicles rent for about $45 for two hours for the smallest bikes (geared for 9 year olds, or so) on up to $90 for a more powerful model. The following are a few numbers to get you started on this quest: BJ's at (888) 481-5411 / www.bjsatvrentals.com; Arnies at (800) 213-1590 or (805) 474-6060 / www.pismoatvrentals.com; and Steves at (805) 481-2597 / www.stevesatv.com.

Camping is also available at the Oceano Dunes. Swim, surf, and/or fish in the water. This is quite a popular place to be, especially at night. It does get foggy and cold here, even in August, so grab a jacket. Bring your own wood to start a fire directly on the sand. Just outside the Oceano entrance is Pier Avenue, a short street that offers a Nature Center and a fun store stop - the Salt Water Taffy Coffee and Candy House. Delectable candies of all kinds, plus freshly-dipped caramel apples, shaved ice, firewood, and a small gift shop make up the varied selection of items. While in Oceano, which is just north of Santa Barbara County, check out the Pismo State Beach Campground just down the street.

There are numerous, docent-led tours of the dunes and the lakes offered for specific groups and for the general public, including adults, school kids, scouts, and more. Learn about the eco system, history, geology, and preservation of the dunes; wildlife; habitats; and more. Note that dune access is severely limited from March to September because the California least tern and the western snowy plover (birds) nest in the sands. Large sections of the area are fenced off.

Hours: Rancho Guadalupe dunes are open daily, dawn - sunset. Oso Flaco Lake area is open daily, dawn - dusk. Oceano is open daily, 6am - 11pm. The visitor center is open Wed.. - Sun., 10am - 4pm. Dune access is severely restricted March - September.

Price: Rancho Guadalupe is free. Oso Flaco is $5 per vehicle. Oceano is $5 per vehicle for day use; $4 for seniors. Or, find the few spaces on the street if not venturing by car out to the dunes. Dune camping here is $10 a night.

Ages: All

RIVER PARK

(805) 875-8100 or (805) 736-1261 / www.cityoflompoc.com;www.kidsmotopark.com
Highway 246 and Sweeny Road, Lompoc

Shall we gather at the river? River Park, that is? Yes. This mostly natural, linear park runs parallel to the Santa Ynez River (hence the name) and is great for a family gathering. It boasts sand volleyball courts; horseshoe pits; picnic areas; a playground; a walking pathway; chunks of open, grassy play space; and the smallish, man-made Kiwanis Lake. Just right for fishing (and apparently a lot of ducks and other wildlife) the lake also adds a spot of beauty to the park. Adults need to have a fishing license. There are thirty-five campsites with full hook-ups for RVs and tent camping sites, too.

Just when you thought it couldn't get any more fun, it can. There is (on a long-term, temporary basis) a Kids Moto

Fun Park. This OHV facility is here to promote interest in the future Lompoc Valley Motorsports Park. It has a ¼ mile OHV course for motorcycles and ATVs up to 50cc for kids up to 12 years old to ride, for free! (I wish I was younger, for a lot of reasons, but this is one.) Also in the immediate vicinity is a safety class training room, plus benches and a shade area for parents to watch.

Hours: The park is open daily, sunrise - sunset. The Kids Moto Fun Park is open weekends and holidays, 10am - 4pm.
Price: Free. Tent camping is $5 a night for walk-ins, $10 for those who drive in. RV campsites are $20 a night.
Ages: All

ROCKY NOOK COUNTY PARK

(805) 568-2461 / www.countyofsb.org
610 Mission Canyon Road, Santa Barbara

The park is aptly named with its rocks, seemingly strewn throughout, to climb on and jump over, and individual picnic nooks, branching off the main road. Each picnic area has its own barbecue grill.

Oak, sycamore, eucalyptus, and pine trees form a shady "ceiling" and give the park a woodsy feel. The seasonal Mission Creek is almost more fun to explore in the summer, when the water level is low and the numerous exposed rocks lining the sides and bottom, practically beg kids to clamber on and around them. A small playground, a horseshoe pit, some short hiking trails, a few huge fallen logs, and two mosaic alligators near the entrance complete the park's offerings. Note: This park is near MISSION SANTA BARBARA (pg. 627), SANTA BARBARA MUSEUM OF NATURAL HISTORY (pg. 630), and SANTA BARBARA BOTANIC GARDEN (see the next entry).

Hours: Open daily, 8am - sunset.
Price: Free
Ages: 3 years and up.

ROTARY CENTENNIAL PARK

(805) 925-0951 / www.cityofsantamaria.org
2625 South College Drive, Santa Maria

This extensive park has a variety of components. At the northern end is attractive landscaping and a perimeter walking trail encircling an island of grass and a tight circle of trees. The borders also have a variety of ten, legitimate exercise stations. Further south is a great, tri-story play gym with slides, rock climbing walls, learning panels, ramps and bridges. Built-in play space under the equipment is always fun for younger ones. There is a similar, but shorter and smaller, play gym for tots that has speaking tubes and attached musical instruments to play. A basketball court, gazebo, a cluster of picnic tables, open grassy areas, some shade trees, and a massive field for soccer and other sports round out this park.

Hours: Open daily, sunrise - sunset.
Price: Free
Ages: All

SANTA BARBARA BOTANIC GARDEN

(805) 682-4726 / www.sbbg.org
1212 Mission Canyon Road, Santa Barbara

$$$

Picture walking on a dirt trails through a lovely, natural setting of chaparral and oak woodlands, oftentimes alongside the meandering Mission Creek, sometimes branching off in all directions, passing by a waterfall, an authentic Japanese Teahouse and Tea Garden, with an occasional bridge or even the creek to cross (using boulders). It feels like you're out in the woods, surrounded by canyons and hills - I could live here! The 5.5 miles of trails are mostly easy walking and stroller friendly, with a few quarter-mile hiking trails being the exception. You'll find benches and a few drinking fountains along the way, plus a picnic area, so pack a lunch, or at least a snack.

Trees - pine, oak and even a redwood cluster - and shrubbery make up the majority of the 1,000 species of indigenous plants at this mid-size botanic garden. There are also a number of various plants sections - a small desert; a good-size meadow (look for turtles in the pond here); a manzanita section; and more, plus a wide variety of flowers adding brilliant color and beauty. Different seasons bring a variety of wildflowers and wildlife. The Discovery Garden, designed for younger gardeners, has a slab of redwood to inspect the rings, a small pond, a pollination garden, and

other vegetation with either an interactive feature and/or information plaques.

A small nursery is on site if you're interested in purchasing plants. Ask about guided group and school tours. Across the street are a few more trails amidst the plants, so hike up one to see great views of Santa Barbara - the hills and beyond. Enjoy your time at the Garden which is so close to the city, but so far removed from city life.

Hours: Open March - October daily, 9am - 6pm; open November - February daily, 9am - 5pm. Closed New Year's Day, Thanksgiving, Christmas Eve, and Christmas Day. Guided tours for individuals are offered Sat. at 11 and Sun. at 2pm.

Price: $8 for adults; $6 for seniors, students, and ages 13 - 17; $4 for ages 2- 12; children under 2 are free. See page x for info on AHS reciprocal memberships.

Ages: All

SANTA YNEZ RECREATION AREA

(805) 967-3481 - USDA Forest Service / Los Padres National Forest; (805) 967-8766 - Rocky Mountain Recreation - campgrounds / www.fs.usda.gov/lpnf

Paradise Road, Santa Barbara

The Santa Ynez Recreation Area, part of the massive Los Padres National Forest, covers an extensive, accessible portion of Santa Barbara County's wilderness. The above phone numbers are references for the following: Contact the Forest Service for information on field trips, education programs, and publications that enable visitors to enjoy and protect the forest. Contact the Los Padres Forest Association for more information at (805) 640-9060. Rocky Mountain Recreation provides information on campgrounds and picnic areas, and they have a good map of the area trails. Note that trails are open for hikers, equestrians, and to hardy mountain bikers. Stop by the Los Prietos Ranger Station on Paradise Road, within the Lower Santa Ynez Recreation Area, for maps and books that show designated roads, trails, recreation facilities, and more. The ranger station is open year round Monday through Friday from 8am to 4:30pm. It's open the same hours, plus Saturdays, during the summer.

Both the Lower Santa Ynez Recreation Area and the Upper S.Y.R.A. have beautiful scenery, plus trails, camping, and picnic areas. The lower area is easily accessible by car, if it hasn't rained. You do have to cross over a shallow part of the river a few times, which we did in the minivan. The upper is more remote with unpaved roads and more rustic campgrounds. Some lower S.Y.R.A. trail highlights include Aliso National Recreation Trail, which is just east of the Los Prietos Ranger Station. The trail head is at the east end of the Sage Hill campground. Pick up an interpretive brochure here (don't you just love adding to your kids' education?) and take the easy one-mile hike along the seasonal Aliso Creek. If your troops are energetic, and you've packed water, hike the entire, moderately graded, three-and-a-half-mile loop trail.

If you continue driving east on Paradise Road, past Sage Hill, and turn left on the road past the Lower Oso picnic area up to the Upper Oso campgrounds, you'll be near the trail head for the popular Santa Cruz National Recreation Trail. This delightful trail follows along Oso Creek, through a sandstone canyon, and past nature-made pools, which are usually fairly shallow. If the kids are tired (and hungry), Nineteen Oaks Trailcamp makes a good stopping point. (You have to provide the snacks.) Past this spot, the trail ascends up three-and-a-half miles to Little Pine Mountain, and another five miles to another trailcamp.

Another popular trail, Red Rock - Gibraltar, starts at the end of Paradise Road. This area has restrooms. The trail meanders alongside the Santa Ynez River. Going to the right, you'll go uphill, which is very steep at some points, past some tall rocks, encountering some wonderful vistas, with the midway point at Gibralter Dam and Reservoir. Take the same trail back or continue on a loop along a fairly unmaintained dirt trail, which goes briefly through marshland, back to the parking lot. The entire loop is seven miles long and moderately tough. Heading left from the trailhead at the parking lot, a short hike in, is a wading and swimming area in rock pools in the refreshingly cold Santa Ynez River. We hiked a few miles further back and found some very small lakes, surrounded by rocks and lush plant life, almost hidden, that were amazingly delightful - worth the hike.

Fish the stocked river for rainbow trout. A license is required for ages 17 and older. The four family campgrounds at the lower S.Y.R.A. have water, barbecues, fire pits, tables, and toilets. No sites offer full-service hook-ups.

Hours: Open daily, sunrise - sunset.

Price: $5 per automobile for a day-use pass (i.e., Adventure Pass) for stopping anywhere within the national forest. The camping fee is $20 a night.

Ages: 4 years and up.

SKATER'S POINT

(805) 564-5418 / www.santabarbaraca.gov
Cabrillo Boulevard at Garden Street, Santa Barbara

This is where the skate meets the sand. This popular, unsupervised, 14,600-foot concrete playground for skaters is just off the beach, next to Stearn's Wharf. Boarders and bladers work up a sweat on the ledges, rails, quarter-pipes, and bowls, and can then go take a swim in the ocean. A helmet and pads are required.

Hours: Open daily, 8am - sunset.
Price: Free. Parking at the beach lot is $2 an hour; $12 max. There is some free street parking.
Ages: 7 years and up.

STEVENS PARK

(805) 564-5418 / www.santabarbaraca.gov
258 Canon Drive, San Roque

This slightly off-the-beaten path park is a good find. The immediately visible part of the park has shade trees, a rock-lined creek, a playground, some picnic tables, and barbecues. Discover the more hidden part of the park by taking the dirt trail that leads under the road, through San Roque Canyon, and up the hillside to the Santa Ynez mountain range, where it branches off. Either part of the park you choose makes for a fun outing.

Hours: Open daily, sunrise - sunset.
Price: Free
Ages: All

STOW GROVE PARK

(805) 961-7500 / www.cityofgoleta.org
580 N. La Patera Lane, Goleta

This delightful park, which is just up the road from LAKE LOS CARNEROS PARK (pg. 612), STOW HOUSE (pg. 635), and SOUTH COAST RAILROAD MUSEUM (pg. 635), has a redwood grove encircling its picnic area. Other amenities include barbecue pits, a ball field, two volleyball courts, playgrounds, horseshoe pits (bring your own equipment), and a grassy green lawn.

Hours: Open daily, 8am - sunset.
Price: Free
Ages: All

SUNNY FIELDS PARK

(805) 688-PLAY (7529) / www.cityofsolvang.com
Alamo Pintado Road, just past Coyote Creek Rd., Solvang

Bring your sveinbarn (Norse for boy child) and girl child to this huge Viking wonderland of leike (i.e. play), that includes European and Western influences, too. The enclosed, multi-level wooden structures, painted in rich earth tones, form a village that urges imaginations to go wild.

Enter through a castle-like building to run on the wooden ramps that go everywhere; cross over bridges; play in a large Viking bateau (i.e. boat); go into a gingerbread-style house that is decorated on the inside, too; climb medieval towers; put on a show at the puppet theater (bring your own puppets); climb aboard a square, wooden wagon; dance in a Native American structure; enter the several kid-size playhouses; play under the mini buildings; scamper up a rock climbing wall; hang from the monkey bars; go high on the swings, including a tire swing; and enjoy the enclosed and open slides. There are plenty of benches for parents and adjacent covered and uncovered picnic areas; one has a big pit. If that's not enough, there is a baseball field and lots of open, grassy, run-around space, too. Your kids will come, see and conquer!

Hours: Open daily, sunrise - sunset.
Price: Free
Ages: 1 - 12 years old.

TOMOL INTERPRETATIVE PLAY AREA

(805) 684-5405 / www.carpinteria.ca.us

390 Linden Avenue, Carpinteria

A blue walkway, lined by a border wall crawling with life-like and life-size gecko statues, leads under and then onto a rainbow bridge, then into this nicely-landscaped, imaginative playground which is like a kids version of a replicated Chumash village. A central (fake) rock is designed to climb on and walk under. Large cement dolphin, seal and sea lion statues are waiting to be ridden, as is a tomol (in Chumash) - a plank boat. Several small huts, some with coverings, some without, await inhabitants, or at least visitors. A few slides, several boulders (with pictographs) lining the small park perimeters, and a stone bench sitting area complete the village.

This play area is adjacent to a huge open field of Linden Field; a block long, lush walkway with lights and interpretive signage called the Palm to Linden trail that ultimately connects to CARPINTERIA BLUFFS NATURE PRESERVE AND TRAIL (pg. 608); a free beach area at the end of Linden Avenue; and CARPINTERIA STATE BEACH (see page 598). It is also just down the street from CARPINTERIA SALT MARSH NATURE PARK (pg. 609).

> **Hours:** Open daily, sunrise - sunset
> **Price:** Free
> **Ages:** 1 - 10 years

TORO CANYON PARK

(805) 568-2461 / www.countyofsb.org

Toro Canyon Road, Summerland

This beautiful, remote park sports numerous old oak trees along boulder-strewn hillsides. It also has picnic tables, barbecue pits, a horseshoe pit (bring your own equipment), and a dirt/sand volleyball court. Kids can play on man-made play equipment of the playground with swing and slides and/or on God-made play equipment of rocks and trees and a seasonal creek that meanders throughout the park. A short hiking trail leads visitors up a hillside to an overlook gazebo. Longer hiking and equestrian trails can also be accessed through the park.

> **Hours:** Open daily, 8am - sunset.
> **Price:** Free
> **Ages:** All

WALLER PARK

(805) 934-6123 or (805) 934-6211 - park; (805) 925-4964 - pony rides / www.countyofsb.org

3107 Orcutt Road, Santa Maria

Waller Park, located at the south end of town, is 153 acres big and almost bursting with fun things to do, as well as being a very natural park, too. It has two small lakes with fountains in them (and a few rocks that my boys climbed on); several huge parcels of grassy lawns to run around on; shady picnic areas with a slew of picnic tables; basketball and volleyball courts; a disc golf course toward the main entrance; softball fields; barbecue grills; horseshoe pits; plenty of huge, shade trees; and bike trails that branch off throughout the park. The several playgrounds, each a little different, by themselves are worth coming to the park with some great new equipment and apparatus. One has fake boulders with hand and foot holds and twisty slides; another is very colorful and really big with several rock climbing walls, swings, pretend animals on big springs to ride, metal poles and spirals to climb about and hang from, tunnels and ramps; and another is equally large with some enclosed slide, as well as everything else. Just go from playground to playground! There are two small, rock-lined lakes connected by a short waterfall. They are quite pretty with greenery and fountains, plus a walkway around them. The upper one has an island in the middle with a plethora (and I mean that) of ducks, geese, and other fowl. There are also pony rides in a little ring in front of a cute Western facade that are open weekends and holidays only, 11am to 4pm or 5pm. We ran, ate, and played here, making a full day of it. Note that the YMCA SKATEBOARD PARK (see next entry), just off Skyway Drive, is right next door to Waller Park.

Woof-Pac Park, a fenced-off part of Waller Park, is a place for off-leash dogs to race around, sniff, and make new friends. This park is subdivided into enclosed sections for large dogs and a section for smaller dogs. If your dog needs to be cleaned, before or after park usage, use the pet spa - a coin-operated station that has doggie shampoo (more coins), warm-water rinse, and blow dry (more coins). I wonder if we could use this for kids, for a few more coins.

Adjacent to Waller Park is Hagerman Sports Complex with a great, new-style playground surrounded by several lighted ball fields with stadium seats, plus a cafe and inside/outside eating area.

> **Hours:** Open daily, 8am - sunset. Pony rides are $4.

Price: Free
Ages: All

YMCA SKATEBOARD PARK

(805) 937-8521 / www.smvymca.org
3400 Skyway Drive, Santa Maria

Dude - this fenced in, 15,000 square-foot skate park, adjacent to the YMCA and located right next to WALLER PARK (see previous entry), is really cool. The much beloved equipment looks like the portable kind, though it's not. The park features ramps, including a vertical ramp, plus quarter-pipes and half-pipes, as well as rails, jumps, and hills. A sound system is piped in. There is also an area just for beginners to learn the tricks of the trade. It's great that park time is separated into times for just bikes and scooters, and another time period for just skateboarders. The park is supervised. A parental waiver must be on file and a helmet and pads are required. There is also a small playground and small patch of grass adjacent.

Hours: Open Mon., Wed., Fri., 3pm - 4:30pm - bikes and scooters; 4:30pm - 6pm - skateboards. Open Tues. and Thurs., 3pm - 4:30pm - skateboards; 4:30pm - 6pm - bikes and scooters. Open Sat., 10am - 2pm and 4pm - 6pm - skateboards; 2pm - 4pm - bikes and scooters. Open Sun., noon - 2pm and 4pm - 6pm - bikes and scooters; 2pm - 4pm - skateboards.
Price: $5 per day for non-members.
Ages: 7 years and up.

—MUSEUMS—

ART, DESIGN & ARCHITECTURE MUSEUM

(805) 893-2951 / www.museum.ucsb.edu
552 University Road, at University of California, Santa Barbara, Goleta

This picturesque campus by the sea has many special features, such as Storke Tower, which is a 175-foot tower with a sixty-one bell carillon that sounds twice per hour. The campus museum's focus is twofold - one is the fine arts, the other architecture and design. Permanent works in the galleries include those from the 15th through 17th centuries, such as European Old Master Paintings and Renaissance metals and plaquettes; contemporary art, including some Polaroids and gelatin silver prints from Andy Warhol and a selection from local artists; historical photographs and daguerreotypes; writings; and a spotlight on the architectural renderings and design collection. The furniture, model homes, and decorative objects will probably appeal to kids more than drawings. All of this, combined with rotating contemporary exhibits such as drawings and prints from Italian Masters; examples of Greek and Roman art; African sculpture; and Native California baskets, allow the museum to appeal to variety of artistic tastes. One object of the permanent collection is a Renaissance Cabinet (i.e. cabinet of curiosity); a wall-to-wall cabinet concisely representing the world (from the collector's perspective). It is filled with a mixture of items such as shells, stuffed animals, gemstones, musical instruments, and fossils. Remember to check out the outdoor sculpture garden. Look at the museum's calendar of events as some exhibits appeal more to kids than others.

Guided tours are offered for school groups that include curriculum and, for elementary-aged children, an in-class art lesson as well. The maximum number of students is thirty-five.

Hours: Open Wed. - Sun., noon - 5pm. Closed Mon., Tues., school holidays, and major holidays.
Price: Free to the museum. Parking is about $3.
Ages: 7 years and up.

CARPINTERIA VALLEY MUSEUM OF HISTORY

(805) 684-3112 / www.carpinteriahistoricalmuseum.org
956 Maple Avenue, Carpinteria

In the middle of Carpinteria's downtown area is this surprisingly fine historical museum. One long room is separated into smaller rooms that depict segments of early life in this area. The rooms house steamer trunks and pictures of old Carpinteria; old dolls and toys; a living room with furniture, plus a melodeon, spindle, phonograph, and sweeper broom (i.e., an early-day vacuum cleaner); Chumash arrowheads, baskets, and several stone mortar and pestles; a bedroom set; saddles and chaps; and an adobe diorama.

A back room holds old machinery such as a collection of typewriters and cameras, plus a piano, and a butterfly collection. Another small section displays an apple press, washboard, water pump, and wall murals. Warning to the faint-hearted - if you stomp on the platform in this particular area, or clap your hands, the fake rat in the rattrap will twitch!

The museum also contains life-size cutouts of people dressed in period clothing throughout, as well as a stagecoach, an early Ford, and a small classroom with desks, books, slate boards, and a blackboard. A kitchen scenario holds implements such as a butter churn, dishes, and a stove. An adjacent workshop area has old tools and a walnut huller. Outside in the courtyard is an open grassy area, a few old pieces of old farm equipment, and a stagecoach.

Walk around the museum on your own or ask about taking a guided tour. Ask about a calendar of events as the museum is host to numerous community events throughout the year, such as the Flea Market that takes place from 8am to 3pm the last Saturday of each month.

> **Hours:** Open Tues. - Sat., 1pm - 4pm. Closed Sun., Mon., and major holidays.
> **Price:** Free. Suggested donations of $2 for adults; $1 for seniors and children.
> **Ages:** 6 years and up.

THE CARRIAGE AND WESTERN ART MUSEUM

(805) 962-2353 / www.carriagemuseum.org; www.santabarbaraca.gov
129 Castillo Street, Santa Barbara

Almost hidden in a corner of the Pershing Park Ball Field are treasures from California's early golden days contained in the wood and brick building called the Carriage and Western Art Museum. Over seventy horse-drawn conveyances manufactured from 1850 to 1911 have been lovingly restored and are finely displayed. Many of the carriages, buggies, and wagons are used in August for the Old Spanish Days Fiesta (pg. 739) during Santa Barbara's annual Fiesta Celebration. Some of our favorite vehicles include the Hearst carriage, a four-passenger pony runabout, the old fire wagons, surreys, and "typical" covered wagons.

The museum also displays spurs, bits, harnesses, whips, jackets, and over fifty ornately decorated saddles. Some of the more famous saddles include one that belonged to Clark Gable, another that was Will Rogers', and others owned by the Cisco kid and by Jimmy Stewart. The room in the back also has a small stage/restaurant/bar area with western facades and neon signs.

Looking at the carriages was interesting, but taking a tour was more fascinating as we learned from the docent some of the history associated with them and with the equestrian paraphernalia.

The adjacent Pershing Park has several areas of open grassy fields, shade trees, ball fields, and eight tennis courts.

> **Hours:** The museum is open Mon. - Fri., 9am - 3pm to walk through on your own. Guided tours are offered the third Sun., 1pm - 4pm. Call to arrange for a group tour. The park tennis courts are available Mon. - Fri., 5pm - 9pm (they have lights!); Sat. - Sun., during the day.
> **Price:** Free
> **Ages:** 4 years and up.

CASA DE LA GUERRA

(805) 965-0093 / www.sbthp.org
15 East De La Guerra Street, Santa Barbara

This historic adobe, originally built in the 1820's, is now a restored house museum. Once belonging to the commander of El Presidio, it features period rooms and special art. School tours are offered by reservation. The De la Guerra Plaza city park is in front of the Casa and plays host to many of the city festivals and events, such as Cinco de Mayo celebrations and a mercado (i.e., marketplace) during Old Spanish Days.

> **Hours:** Open Sat. - Sun., noon - 4pm. Closed major holidays.
> **Price:** $5 for adults; $4 for seniors; ages 16 and under are free.
> **Ages:** 6 years and up.

CASA DEL HERRERO

(805) 565-5653 / www.casadelherrero.com
1387 E. Valley Road, Montecito

Visit a bygone era when coming to this classy, Spanish-style house located in a residential neighborhood. It was completed in 1925 and shows heavy influences of Islamic and Moorish architecture. Colorful Mediterranean mosaic

tiles are prevalent outside around the courtyard and inside the house, as well. The foyer boasts of tapestries, ornate panels on the ceiling and walls, and church pews for seats. The house is noted for its 13th- to 18th- century Spanish furniture. The living room contains red velvet furniture, pictures, and an early stereo. Walk through the smallish kitchen, bathrooms, formal dining room, enclosed porch with a garden view, and decorative bedrooms. The children's bedrooms have beds, trunks, gold mirrors, and clocks. Look at the sculptures, wood-carved doors and furniture, fireplaces with tiles, and other fine details throughout the two-story house.

The seven acres of cultivated gardens are meticulously groomed and designed in a Moorish fashion. Go through garden gates and an archway that looks like it leads to a secret garden. Take a walk past a rose garden, a little pond, a sundial, a camellia garden, an herb garden, a Spanish patio, and even orange orchards. The tour guide explains the layout of the gardens, the types of plants, and the entertaining that was once done here.

The owner was a blacksmith and his workshop is probably one of the most intriguing stops on the tour for kids. It is filled with his tools, plus workbenches, a casting furnace, forge, and anvils. My boys' fingers were itching to try out, or at least touch, the tools.

A ninety-minute tour includes forty-five minutes inside and forty-five minutes outside in the gardens. Note that the rooms are small and groups cannot be have more than twelve people. Note, too, that the parking lot only holds eight cars. Reservations are required.

Hours: Tours are offered mid-February - mid-November, Wed. and Sat. at 10am and 2pm.
Price: $20 per person. See page x for info on AHS reciprocal memberships.
Ages: Children must be at least 10 years old.

EL PRESIDIO DE SANTA BARBARA STATE HISTORIC PARK
(805) 965-0093 / www.sbthp.org
123 East Canon Perdido Street, Santa Barbara

Originally built in 1792 to protect the mission, the reconstructed presidio (i.e., military fort) was the last Spanish military outpost built in North America. I appreciated the kid's info kit that the docent handed us upon arrival. Take a walk through the courtyards and the buildings and look into the sparsely furnished commander's, padre's, and lieutenant's quarters. The fort also features a decorated chapel and bell tower. Across the street is El Cuartel, the guard's house, which is the second-oldest building in California! (For the oldest building, look up page 307.) Ask about the special events and educational programs offered here throughout the year.

Hours: Open daily, 10:30am - 4:30pm. Closed major holidays.
Price: $5 for adults; $4 for seniors; ages 16 and under are free.
Ages: 6 years and up.

ELVERHOJ MUSEUM
(805) 686-1211 / www.elverhoj.org
1624 Elverhoy Way, Solvang

This quaint museum is tucked away amongst residential houses near the main shopping areas of Solvang. Built in 18th-century Danish-farmhouse style, the inside displays also depict this culture and time period.

The lobby holds a traveling desk and a sample of the red Danish national costume. The country kitchen is designed with typically simple lines and folk paintings. The Early Room contains dogs, shoes made of reeds, thatch (i.e., the plant used for roofs), dresses, a spinning wheel, and furniture. The parlor, or Best Room, features Danish costumes in a display case and furniture from an 1890's Danish farmhouse. Other rooms feature a children's canopy bed with a wonderful dollhouse, and clothing such as a colorful red postman's uniform and a naval officer's uniform. The other wing of the house contains a small art gallery.

On occasion, docents demonstrate a traditional craft from the old country, such as lace making or paper cutting. Guided tours are available by request.

Hours: Open Wed. - Sun., 11am - 4pm. Closed Mon., Tues., and some holidays.
Price: Free; a donation of $3 per adult is suggested.
Ages: 8 years and up.

FABING-MCKAY-SPANNE HISTORICAL HOUSE
(805) 735-4626 / www.lompochistory.org
207 North 'L' Street, Lompoc

This fully restored, two-story, wooden Victorian residence was originally built in 1875 and is furnished with items from that era. The front parlor was a music room of sorts and holds a melodeon, music box, two phonographs, and other musical instruments. Walk through the second parlor with a pump organ and fireplace; the dining room, with a table set for dinner; the kitchen; the pantry - check out the ice box; the bedroom; and the bathroom. Upstairs are more bedrooms filled with period furniture, including a washbasin and stand, and toys, dolls, and books in the children's room. Notice the wreath in the hallway - it's made out of human hair; perhaps an early form of knitting?

Adjacent to the home are three other buildings: The Carriage House houses several buggies and wagons lined up along the walls, and a 1908 Model 'S' Ford, plus saddles, tacks, spurs and more. The Blacksmith Shop has a forge, anvil and all the other necessary tools, plus burned cattle brands on the walls. The Museum Room showcases a 1920's kitchen with all of its implements; a laundry section with washing and drying wringers and other time-consuming machines, plus old-fashioned household items such as bottles, cans, and pans; artifacts from a shipwreck; and a Doctor's Office with shelves of medical tools (some look scary!), a bed, and mannequins.

    Hours: Open Mon. (except legal holidays) and Thurs., 8:30am - 11am and usually the fourth Sat., 10am - 1pm. Closed major holidays, Thanksgiving and Christmas week.
    Price: Free; donations appreciated.
    Ages: 8 years and up.

FERNALD MANSION and TRUSSELL-WINCHESTER ADOBE

(805) 966-1601 / www.santabarbaramuseum.com
414 W. Montecito Street, Santa Barbara

These small, historic homes played an important role in Santa Barbara's history and are worth a look-through. The fourteen-room, Queen Anne-style house, called Fernald Mansion, was constructed in 1862 for Judge Fernald. It contains original furnishings from the nineteenth-century. Although there is not a lot of maneuverability, the forty-five-minute tour will take you through the living room, kitchen, music room with its harp at the ready, and up the curved wooden staircase to the bedrooms and the bathrooms.

Next door is the adobe, built in 1854, which was constructed with timbers from a shipwreck. It contains items salvaged from a sea captain's ship and other furnishings. Note that the museum/homes are located in a residential district.

    Hours: Tours are offered Sat. Call as hours fluctuate.
    Price: Free. Suggested donations of $5 for adults; $1 for ages 12 and under.
    Ages: 10 years and up.

HANS CHRISTIAN ANDERSEN MUSEUM and BOOK LOFT & KAFFE HUS

(805) 688-6010 - book store/museum; (805) 686-9770 - Bulldog Cafe / www.bookloftsolvang.com
1680 Mission Drive, Solvang

Fairytale favorites such as *The Steadfast Tin Soldier*, *The Ugly Duckling*, *Little Mermaid*, *Thumbelina*, *The Emperor's New Clothes*, and *The Princess and the Pea* were all penned by Hans Christian Andersen. This very small museum, located in the second story of Book Loft & Kaffe Hus, is dedicated to the Danish-born author. His books (including first and early editions), manuscripts, letters, paper cuttings (which he did for friends), a bust of Andersen, and pictures of him and of his birthplace, are on display. One glass case is dedicated entirely to the Little Mermaid. You might not be in the museum long, but it is a fun, sentimental adventure. Guided group tours are available by appointment.

The rest of the book store is a book lover's treat! The Book Loft sells both new and used books, as well as classics and rare editions. The children's section is delightful. Make sure to take a look at the small, working model of the Gutenberg Press. Adding to the charm of the store is the attached Bulldog Cafe, where you can sip a cup of coffee and/or enjoy a pastry or sandwich while reading your new/old book.

    Hours: The book store/museum is open Sun. - Mon., 9am - 6pm; Tues. - Thurs., 9am - 8pm; Fri. - Sat., 9am - 9pm. The hours might be shorter in the winter.
    Price: Free
    Ages: 7 years and up.

KARPELES MANUSCRIPT LIBRARY MUSEUM

(805) 962-5322 / www.rain.org/~karpeles
21 West Anapamu, Santa Barbara

View actual pages of history at this museum which has millions of original documents in its archives, and several select ones on display. Each original document is enclosed in glass in a podium-like case, all artfully arranged throughout the museum. Each one also has a description of the contents, including the how, why, and when the document was written. Small busts of well-known people are also on display.

The exhibits rotate every three months. Each feature presentation focuses on a particular person or topic and incorporates about twenty-five documents. Past exhibits have included pages of Webster's dictionary; the final agreement from King Ferdinand and Queen Isabella regarding the New World and Columbus' voyage; scientific manuscripts of Galileo, Newton, and Einstein; and the surrender agreement of World War II. Most of the free pamphlets that correspond to and describe past exhibits also include an insert - a scaled down copy of an original manuscript. What a great teaching tool! One of the small permanent exhibits contains photocopied pages of sheet music from Beethoven, Handel, Mozart, Bach, and others, accompanied by that specific composer's bust. An encouraging observation for kids (and adults) is that those display manuscripts have cross outs, rewrites, or editing notes on them and that means the final, perfect-sounding draft doesn't come out perfect the first time around! Other permanent displays include ancient Egyptian plaques and carvings; models of ships from ancient Rome to the USS Constitution; an original Stone copy of the Declaration of Independence; a replica of the globe used by Christopher Columbus; the computer guidance system used on the first Apollo lander flight to the moon; and other space-related artifacts.

Ask about the Cultural Literacy Program for grades three up to college level, and other educational programs including on-site tours and off-site presentations. Note that there are eleven other such Karpeles museums across the county.

Hours: Open Wed. - Sun., noon - 4pm. Closed Mon., Tues., New Years Day, Thanksgiving, and Christmas.
Price: Free
Ages: 8 years and up.

LA PURISIMA MISSION STATE HISTORIC PARK ☀
2295 Purisima Road, Lompoc $$
See the entry for LA PURISIMA MISSION STATE HISTORIC PARK on page 612 for details.

MISSION SANTA BARBARA ☀
(805) 682-4713 / www.sbmission.org $$
2201 Laguna Street, Santa Barbara
Originally founded in 1786, this tenth mission, in the chain of twenty-one, is considered "Queen of the Missions" and has been occupied consistently by the Franciscan Order. The outside of the handsome mission has long been a favorite of photographers and painters, with its long front building and twin bell towers. Just outside, too, is a Moorish fountain, the basin of which was a lavanderia, used by Indian women to wash clothing.

Take a self-guided tour through the buildings that are open, where one room leads easily into the next. Looking at glass-covered displays visitors see Chumash baskets and tools; a missionary's bedroom (with a tattered tall hat); religious portraits and sculptures; samples of weaving and candle making products; blacksmith's tools; and a kitchen with cookware and dishes. The chapel room contains an exhibit of ornate vestments and musical instruments, and offers a video about the history of the mission. Continue your tour outside through the garden courtyard and into the (still-active) mission church decorated with Mexican art. The door on the other side of the church leads to the cemetery, where early settlers and 4,000 Indians are buried. Juana Maria, the woman portrayed in the book, *Island of the Blue Dolphins*, is also buried here. Guided tours of the mission are available for adult groups and school kids.

Just across the street is Mission Park, with its expanse of green grass and a good-size garden with a plethora of roses. Come for a picnic or to just relax, although the latter can be hard with little ones running around.

Hours: Open daily, 9am - 4:30pm. It closes early on Good Friday and Christmas Eve. Closed Easter, Thanksgiving and Christmas.
Price: $5 for adults; $4 for seniors; $1 for ages 6 - 15; children 5 and under are free.
Ages: 7 years and up.

NATURAL HISTORY MUSEUM OF SANTA MARIA ☀
(805) 614-0806 / www.naturalhistorysantamaria.com   !

412 S. McClelland Street, Santa Maria

This small museum houses quite a decent collection of natural history. Look for the eye-catching head cast of a Tyrannosaurus rex behind the reception desk. The first small room features a terrific, realistic seaside mural with stuffed shore birds and fake kelp, rocks and sea stars giving it a 3-D effect, while beach sounds are piped in. There is a fish quiz board here. A Monarch butterfly display and video is also here.

The next room, and a side room, showcase more murals, of the woodlands, with stuffed animals in the foreground of a roaring grizzly bear, deer, bobcats, birds in flight, foxes, beavers, raccoon, coyote and wild boar, and "music" of animal sounds. There is also a "please touch" table with snake skin sheddings, bobcat fur, feathers, animals tracks, and rocks, plus displays of bird nests, bats, eggs, and more.

The backroom contains display cases of sea shells, crab shells, and sea stars; rocks; arrowheads; butterflies and other insects; a great whale jaw and teeth; a saber tooth cat skull; copies of baleen whale bone; mortar and pestle stones; and the Earth's timeline (with some pretty scary and strange-looking creatures) and quiz board regarding it. A seven-minute video shows the geological history of the Santa Maria region.

The side yard features life-size cut outs of sea mammals such as a Great White shark, orcas, and dolphins, all in a sand base, plus a table imprinted with sea life to do rubbings. The backyard also has a small grassy area and a few picnic tables. Ask about special family programs offered on selected Saturdays, such as a visit with live animals and their handlers.

Hours: Open Wed. - Sat., 11am - 4pm; Sun., 1pm - 4pm. Closed Mon., Tues., and most major holidays. Tours are given by appointment.

Price: Free

Ages: 3 years and up.

OLD MISSION SANTA INES   ☀

(805) 688-4815 / www.missionsantaines.org $

1760 Mission Drive, Solvang

Named in honor of Saint Agnes (the Spanish spelling is Ines), there are only a few rooms of the original mission building, which was completed in 1807, to tour through. Learn the history of the nineteenth mission (out of twenty-one) and its artifacts by pressing the several push buttons that give a narration. The buttons are located throughout the building and the grounds.

The first room is the Vestment Room, which contains numerous ornate vestments from several centuries. Paintings adorn the walls. Walk to the second room that has a wall map of the Spanish Colonial Empire, a 19th-century confessional booth, and old mission bells. An adjoining room displays cases of old nails, candlesticks, pottery, holy implements, branding irons, Bibles, firearms, and stone mortars and pestles. Next are the Madonna Room and the adjacent church, which still holds mass on a regular basis administered by the Franciscan order. The church contains many of the original paintings and wall decorations.

The courtyard, laid out in the shape of a Celtic cross, contains a fountain and a large, lovely garden with grassy areas and a rose garden toward the back. The garden path leads to the mission's cemetery where 1,700 Indians are buried. Along a walkway on the side of the mission are the fourteen stations of the cross, each depicted by a wooden cross and picture of Christ. Note: This mission borders the quaint shopping district of Solvang, so you can combine a history lesson with a day of shopping!

Hours: Open daily 9am - 4:30pm. Closed New Year's Day, Easter, Thanksgiving, and Christmas.

Price: $5 for adults; children 11 years and under are free.

Ages: 6 years and up.

REAGAN RANCH CENTER   ☀

(888) USA-1776 (872-1776) / www.yaf.org   !

217 State Street, Santa Barbara

It helps to like Reagan to appreciate visiting this small center. Santa Barbara, and specifically Rancho del Cielo, Reagan's home for twenty-five years, was known as the Western White House during his presidential years. Step into the lobby of this graceful, multi-storied building and you'll first see a big (5,000 pound) chunk of the Berlin wall, accompanied by a video explaining its importance.

The adjoining, main room's centerpiece is an almost thirty-foot-long interactive "timeline" table with headsets and

touch screens for visitors to learn more about Reagan's Ranch and countryside, plus his history and life as president and beyond. Along the walls are room-size vignettes that each showcase a portion of his life and presidency along with Reagan's belongings and artifacts - his saddle, cowboy hat, living room chair, the desk where he signed the tax cut, his farm tools, favorite books, and his blue Jeep with "Gipper" license plates. All of the exhibits are accompanied by photos, placards, and an audio and/or video explanation, too - very well done. You can also listen to and see some of his speeches, interviews, and more in the theater room and video kiosks. Other displays include letters written by Reagan, info on his Secret Service detail, and campaign memorabilia such as buttons, posters and commemoratives. The second story features a map of the ranch and a small chapel room, just like the one at his ranch. Tip: Ask for the scavenger hunt for kids so they can earn their "Junior Secret Service Clearance" by completing it.

Hours: Open Mon. - Thurs., 11am - 4pm. Closed on most federal holidays.
Price: Free
Ages: 7 years and up.

SANTA BARBARA HISTORICAL MUSEUM

(805) 966-1601 / www.santabarbaramuseum.com
136 East De La Guerra Street, Santa Barbara

This small, simple adobe museum complex offers a sampling of artifacts, photographs, furnishings, costumes, and fine art that represents Santa Barbara's rich multi-cultural history. One room features paintings of all twenty-one California missions. Walk through to the lovely courtyard that has a fountain and large, old pepper trees. The adjacent library contains rare literature, documents, and photographs.

Hours: Open Tues. - Sat., 10am - 5pm; Sun., noon - 5pm. Closed Mon. and holidays. Guided tours are offered Sat. and Sun. at 2pm.
Price: Free
Ages: 6 years and up.

SANTA BARBARA MARITIME MUSEUM

(805) 965-8864 or (805) 962-8404 / www.sbmm.org
113 Harbor Way, Santa Barbara

On the waterfront, surrounded by restaurants and gift shops, is the Maritime Museum, a tribute to this area's maritime past that's worth *seeing*. Out front are statues of a massive harpoon gun and spear, and anchor. Once inside, ask for a treasure map to aid the kids in hunting for certain items in the museum's collection.

The Jimsuit - a one-person, incredibly heavy duty, atmospheric diving suit that looks like something from an old sci-fi movie - is in the entry to greet visitors. Some of the first floor exhibits are a Chumash plank canoe; an explorer's light-up display to aid in learning about early explorers and their routes (great as a supplement to California studies); and displays on otter and seal hunting, and whaling. Feel otter pelts, wool, and the hides of cattle. Lift up flaps to see and smell trade spices. Other exhibits include numerous model boats of various sizes; a fairly extensive diving helmet display from various decades; wall space dedicated to the fishing industry; displays of ranching artifacts; several ships' parts, such as a propeller and wheel; and the huge, restored, 150-year old Point Conception Lighthouse lens, surrounded by information panels and photos that shed light on the details of its history.

The sportfishing chair is one of the most fun exhibits. Sit down, grab onto the stationary fishing pole, and, from the screen, choose the type of fish you are hoping to land. (Hint - read the instructions first.) The salmon, barracuda, marlin, tuna, or bass you choose shows like a movie clip on screen as the fishing pole in your hands starts really jerking around. Reeling in the big one, tension and all, feels very real!

The colorful kids area has a board with various types of knots to try (or tie); life jackets to try on; computers with nautical-themed programs; craft supplies to create; a puppet theater; and a video screen playing in a surfboard.

Look up - you'll see the massive, replicated hull of a schooner, as well as a seaplane and a few other planes in flight. Upstairs, contained within that schooner hull, is an eighty-six-seat theater which presents a continuous series of films regarding El Nino, octopuses, surf movies, documentaries on sharks, and sailing around Cape Horn, as well as movies such as *Shackleton's Antarctic Adventure*. Check the schedule for show times. There are more model boats up here - ranging from a royal barge from China to a Grecian fishing boat to an Inuit canoe. Check out the maritime cannons and cannon balls. Look through a working U.S. Navy periscope to see the ocean, beach, harbor, and houses just outside. An impressive Mark 46 torpedo (inert) is just outside the periscope station. A weather kiosk and radar display

showing real-time image of the Santa Barbara Channel are also here. There are several surfboards here, and a visual and information display of surfing history, but you can't hang ten. At the Survival at Sea exhibit, watch the video of ships out in drastic storm conditions. Don't get steered in the wrong direction at the exhibit where you can virtually pilot a vessel.

The museum has a few other exhibits regarding art, surfing, pilot boats, commercial fisherman, coast guard, weather, and the environment. Ask about activities for kids, such as singing sea chanteys and learning how to tie knots, plus classes and tours for children and adults, live broadcasts, harbor tours, tall ships programs, outreach programs, and a lot more. Tip: Take the elevator up to the fourth floor of this building for an incredible view of the Santa Barbara Harbor and mountains! Also see SANTA BARBARA HARBOR / STEARNS WHARF (pg. 637) for more things to do in this immediate area.

Hours: Open most of the year, Thurs. - Tues., 10am - 5pm. Closed Wed. Open Memorial Day through Labor Day daily, 10am - 6pm. Closed New Year's Day, the first Friday in August, Thanksgiving, and Christmas.

Price: $7 for adults; $4 for seniors, active military, students, and ages 6 - 17; $2 for ages 1 - 5 years; children under 1 year are free. The third Thurs. of every month is free admission. Parking in beach lot is $2 an hour; $12 max. There is some free street parking.

Ages: 3 years and up.

SANTA BARBARA MUSEUM OF ART
(805) 963-4364 / www.sbma.net $$$
1130 State Street, Santa Barbara

The colorful outside museum mural was painted by the world-renowned Mexican artist, David Alfaro Siqueiros. Degas, Matisse, Monet, Picasso, Dali, O'Keeffe, and Chagall all make appearances inside this museum of fine art, as do other masters. A diverse collection of American, 19th-century European, Latin American, and Asian artwork decorate its walls and halls. The museum also features modern art, photography exhibits, and ancient Greek, Roman, and Egyptian sculptures. Ask for a children's activity sheet upon entering the museum because the more that kids are involved with the art, in whatever capacity, the more they will remember. Downstairs is a small, children's gallery featuring rotating artwork and a chance for some hands-on drawing, craft, or other activity.

Take the time to stroll the galleries on your own, or join a free, guided gallery talk usually offered at noon and at 1pm. Age-appropriate guided tours for school kids and other groups are offered by reservation. Family days, studio art classes, workshops, holiday camps, and outreach programs are just a few of the museum's other features. A cafe is on the premises.

Hours: Open Tues. - Sun., 11am - 5pm. Closed Mon., New Year's Day, 4th of July, Thanksgiving Day, and Christmas Day.

Price: $10 for adults; $6 for seniors, students, and ages 6 - 17; children 5 years and under, and Santa Barbara students (with proof of residency), teachers, and active military and their families all with ID, are free. Admission is also free to everyone every Thurs., 5pm - 8pm and there is special programming those nights.

Ages: 6 years and up.

SANTA BARBARA MUSEUM OF NATURAL HISTORY
(805) 682-4711 / www.sbnature.org $$$
2559 Puesta del Sol Road, Santa Barbara

Outside this good-sized, adobe-styled museum that's nestled into a woodland area is an impressive, seventy-three-foot skeleton of the largest animal ever known - the blue whale. Walk under it, into the rib cage. (Think of Jonah from the Old Testament.) Inside, the museum has sections devoted to geology, paleontology, minerals, native wildlife, marine life, and the culture of the Chumash Indians.

The Cartwright Interactions Hall contains small enclosures with live animals such as lizards, salamanders, tarantulas, various snakes (including rattlesnakes), and a few turtles. We liked the X-ray of the snake that swallowed light bulbs. Thousands of pinned butterflies, moths, bees, flies, grasshoppers, and other insects are on display at the insect and plant room. Inquisitive kids can lift panels to find answers to questions. See a termite colony, look at realistic-looking plants and flowers in diorama settings behind glass, and watch short films about ecological

interactions.

The marine building has large dry aquariums showcasing fake fish suspended in air and a Japanese Giant Squid, plus coral, kelp, and other sea life in their "natural" habitats. Other stuffed sea creatures and models include sharks, batrays, octopus, lobsters, jellyfish, and sponges. There is also a real preserved giant squid in this room.

The paleontology/geology rooms hold skeletons of pygmy mammoths, bones of other mammoths and mastodons, a jawbone of a giant-toothed whale, and several fossils. The small Mineral and Gem Gallery showcases a collection of rocks, minerals, and gems. (Learn what the difference is between them.) See tourmaline, crystals, fluorescent specimens (whose characteristics glow under black light) and more. Briefly walk through the crystal mine that holds touchable minerals, including aquamarines and geodes. The Chumash Life displays include dioramas of Indian life, baskets, and tools. The Fleischmann Hall features wonderful changing exhibits such as Dinosaurs, the Next Generation.

The mammal hall showcases traditional dioramas of taxidermied animals in natural poses. The collection includes sea lions, tule elk, bats, a grizzly bear, opossum, mountain lion, raccoon, gray wolf, and several more creatures. The bird habitats room contains hundreds of stuffed birds in "flight", such as a California condor with its nine-foot wingspan, a barn owl with its babies, brown pelicans, orioles, cranes, a golden eagle, and several species of shore birds. This room also contains numerous eggs and nests, as well as habitat dioramas. An art gallery and library are also located in this section of the museum.

Toward the back of the museum is the Space Lab where visitors can test their knowledge of stars, planets, and constellations by pushing buttons to match up the picture with the name of the celestial object. Watch NASA TV that features lift-off to landing coverage of space shuttle missions, as well as frequent live coverage on board the International Space Station. Touch a meteor. Check out the Magic Planet, a four-foot, "floating" globe that changes surface appearance according to if it's showing atmospheric, oceanographic, or geological changes.

The adjacent fifty-five-seat planetarium features forty-minute, or so, programs on the evening sky, as well as specialty programs for young children. These include the fifteen-minute *Twinkle Twinkle for Little Stars* show which changes every week, geared for ages 5 and under, and *Kid's Space Adventure*, a thirty-minute interactive show. Come at a scheduled show time or book a time for a group field trip. Observe the stars for real at the Museum's Palmer Observatory. Join the astronomy club, or just join them in star gazing, especially at the monthly star parties. These parties are for visitors to observe stars and planets through provided telescopes, as well as seeing a show in the planetarium.

The Museum Backyard is wonderful to explore! It is pretty, oak woodland with the Mission Creek running through it, plus some terrific activities to do. Pass through arches made of willow to climb on a pathway of boulders (designed for kids to climb on them!) that form a zig zag trail; build a fort (poles and materials supplied); gaze at a few redwoods; enjoy a presentation at the outdoor amphitheater; eat lunch, or a snack, at the picnic tables; relax and enjoy the beauty; and/or take a short hike on trails, one that actually leaves the museum property. Hundreds of butterflies and moths gracefully fly around in a butterfly house here that is open May through the beginning of September.

A variety of guided tours and programs are available for adult and for school groups. For instance, Nature Adventures, for ages 4 to 10 years old, incorporates lots of hands-on activities along with their classes, workshops, and camps. Traveling astronomy and Audubon Society programs and presentations are available to come to the facility of your choice. Other programs and special exhibitions at the museum often incorporate themed activities for the family. Note: The museum's satellite facility is the TY WARNER SEA CENTER (pg. 653), located on STEARNS WHARF (pg. 637).

Hours: Open daily, 10am - 5pm. Closed New Year's Day, the last Sat. in June, Thanksgiving, and Christmas, with a 3pm closure on Christmas Eve. Planetarium shows are offered Wed. and Fri. at 3pm; Sat. and Sun., 11am - 3pm, on the hour. The 3pm Sun. show is presented in Spanish. *Twinkle Twinkle for Little Stars* is Sat. - Sun. at 11am. *Kid's Space Adventure* is Fri. at 3pm and Sat. - Sun. at 1pm. School planetarium shows are offered October - June, Tues. - Fri. at 10am and 11am, by reservation. Star parties are the second Sat., 7pm - 10pm.

Price: $12 for adults; $8 for seniors and ages 13 - 17; $7 for ages 2 - 12. Summer admission prices are usually $1 more. Admission is free on the third Sun. of each month, for the museum only. Planetarium admission is an additional $4 per person, with paid admission to the museum. Admission for just the star party is $2 for adults; $1 for ages 12 and under; or for the party and a show, $8 for adults; $7 for kids. A nature pass, allowing admission to this museum and to the Ty Warner Sea Center on two consecutive days, is $16 for adults; $11 for seniors and teens; $9 for ages 2 - 13. See page xi for info on ASTC reciprocal museum memberships.

Ages: 3 years and up.

SANTA MARIA MUSEUM OF FLIGHT   ☼

(805) 922-8758 / www.smmof.org $$
3015 Airpark Drive, Santa Maria

Ready to take off to a place where the sky's the limit? This fine museum fills two hangars with small aircraft and flying memorabilia - one specializing in pre-WWII artifacts; the other from WWII to present day. Upon entering, attention is riveted on the bright red plane, a Hunt Special, featured in the movie *Rocketeer*. There is other *Rocketeer* memorabilia, too. Overhead is a replica of the Wright Brothers' glider, as well as a collection of radio control planes. The hangar also contains dioramas of aviation history, a library of books and videos on aviation, model planes in display cases, a WWI gas mask, a skeleton plane that shows the inner workings of a radio control plane, and a gift shop.

Outside are miscellaneous parts of space rockets and a missile launcher, as well as a few small planes, such as the F4 Phantom Fighter, an A4 Skylark and an L5 Observation plane, which are grounded here. This is also a prime spot to watch small planes take off and land.

The metal, second hangar contains a few ejection seats (that look used); the Hughes H-1 Racer used in the movie, *Aviator*; a homebuilt, half-size, Lockheed P-38 Lightning; a small mock up of a space ship launch; one of the few Norden bombsights still around; inert missiles; an army truck; a 1916 Howitzer; a British Gnat Trainer; and a working Link Trainer, which is a vintage instrument flight trainer/early simulator. The hangar also holds WWII displays, such as uniforms; airplane pieces, such as propellers and engines; lots of model airplanes and photos; and a display with mannequins featuring women pilots.

Hour-long, guided, age-appropriate tours of the museum are offered for school-age kids. The minimum number of students needed is fifteen; the maximum, twenty-five. Note that outside the second hanger is a sweet little picnic area/memorial park with tables and benches, trees and flowers, informational panels, and a timeline and a mural, all dedicated to women pilots from past to present.

On the third Saturday of January through July, and again in September through November, the museum hosts fly-in events. There is a cafe on the grounds then, too, serving hot dogs and hamburgers. Note: Ask about the YOUNG EAGLES PROGRAM (Santa Barbara County), on page 649, offered through the adjacent airport.

Hours: Open Fri. - Sun., 10am - 4pm. Closed for special events, New Year's Day, and Christmas.

Price: $5 for adults; $4 for seniors; $3 for ages 12 - 17 and college students; $2 for ages 7 - 11; children 6 years and under are free, as are active military and their dependents.

Ages: 5 years and up.

SANTA MARIA VALLEY DISCOVERY MUSEUM   ☼

(805) 928-8414 / www.smvdiscoverymuseum.org $$$
705 S. McClelland Street, Santa Maria

There is so much for kids to discover at the sizable, terrific, hands-on Discovery Museum, starting with an outside sand pit. Inside, the overarching theme is coastal. There are several other wonderful themed areas or "stations", each one having special activities for young ones to do, accompanied by great murals and props.

A beachy sand area, accompanied by buckets and shovels, is located next to a wooden dock that is part of a ship facade that you can walk up into and steer the big wheel. Kids can crawl under the ship, too (and be stowaways?). A real speed boat is parked next to this "ship" that sailors can board, put on life jackets and spin the captain's wheel to pretend pilot around. There are also glass displays that hold shells, sea stars and other treasures from the ocean. "Shop" at the fish market that sells buckets of the (plastic) catch of the day. A few tanks along a wall contain a variety of real fish, interspersed with information and activities, like a wide choice of magnetic words to make sentences all

against a fish mural. I like the kelp hanging overhead to give that immersion feel.

An insect area features a friendly centipede to climb on, bugs to inspect via microscopes and a huge mural of a insect that shows its body parts. The good-sized 1950's diner next door has tables and chairs and condiments, plus a kitchen, food and menu - be the cook, server, or customer. Put a melody in your heart, or at least in your feet, and dance away the calories on the adjacent floor piano keyboard. At the fire and rescue area, with a mural of firefighters fighting a fire, kids can join in by dressing in fireman uniforms, including boots and helmets, and using the hose. Play a song, of sorts, by using a paddle to strike the pvc-style tubes that ring out different notes. Try your hand at an impromptu play at the tiny puppet theater. Plant a seedling to take home at the Planting Station.

The long crafts bar in the center of the museum supplies everything to create and recycle trash into treasure. I love the seemingly random big tree with fake birds and the real stuffed bear here. The cut-away whale in the center is hard to miss. Walk through its middle to take the short slide down its mouth and even watch a sea-related video towards its tail. Play at the mini indoor playground by going through a tunnel, climbing on ladders to a wooden bridge, and bouncing on a four-person, big spring, safe, see-saw. Climb up and down and sideways at the eight-foot high and fairly long rock wall covered with hand and foot grips.

Things got a little sticky at the real tar pits, but here kids can don helmets and (re)discover fossils and bones in the mock excavation pit. Learn about water flow by going through a tunnel and looking at the 3-D wall mural of a neighborhood. Join the Money Club and learn about money by playing money games, dropping a coin in the top of board to make it go into the charity of your choice, and sitting at the bank teller's desk to be the financial advisor, or the customer.

At the barn and bunkhouse, look at all the brands on the walls; put on some cowboy boots and a hat; saddle up on real saddles; ride rocking horses; gather round a pretend campfire and/or cook at the back end of the wagon; practice your blacksmithing expertise with an anvil, hammer and horseshoe; and sit on a real John Deere tractor and shift gears.

Another big nautical nook, for toddlers, has wonderful undersea murals, and sand and water-colored carpeting. It beckons bitty beachcombers to crawl through plushy "undersea" rocks and caves with portholes. There are also soft block toys to play with and enclosed play "pits", and some manipulatives.

And this list of things to see and do is not comprehensive! The Discovery Museum offers a variety of classes, workshops, and school or group tours, too.

Hours: Open Tues. - Sat., 10am - 5pm; Sun., noon - 4pm. Closed Mon. (except for field trips), and most major holidays.
Price: $4 for adults; $8 per child; children under 2 are free.
Ages: 1 - 11 years.

SANTA MARIA VALLEY HISTORICAL SOCIETY MUSEUM

(805) 922-3130 / www.santamaria.org
616 S. Broadway Street, Santa Maria

For a relatively small museum, this one is packed with a lot of eclectic and wonderful old memorabilia! The first thing to see is a wall of brands, along with a few saddles, and a beautiful wooden organ, followed by a spring wagon and a statue of a cow. The main room is subdivided by representative rooms and mannequins dressed in period costumes. A vintage living room set is front and center. A side room contains portraits, mini trains, musical instruments and a cast of a saber-tooth cat - because somehow they all go together. jk. Towards the back is a wonderful mishmash of old cameras; fossils; fire fighting equipment - buckets, hoses, and cart - and uniforms; a kitchen, of sorts, with furniture and a cast iron stove; an old-fashioned switchboard along with a collection of various telephones; a nineteenth-century buggy; guns and swords; medical tools; a jail cell with a mannequin behind bars wearing an ankle ball and chain; a noose in a display case; and a mini schoolroom with a desk, books, and a copy of teacher's rules from 1872. Guided tours, offered by reservation, lend insight into the exhibits.

Hours: Open Tues. - Sat., noon - 5pm. Closed Sun., Mon., and major holidays.
Price: Free
Ages: 6 years and up.

SANTA MARIA VALLEY RAILWAY HISTORICAL MUSEUM

(805) 863-6645 / www.smvrhm.com
708 S. Miller Street (this address is for the Souza Student Center, just south of the museum), Santa Maria

This is a quick, but fun stop off for railroad buffs. The three restored railcars here include a late 1800's engine used by the Betteravia Union Sugar Company, a 1930's box car, and a 1930's caboose - all of which are a treat to walk through. Inside the box car are several layouts with working model trains that travel past mini mountains, canyons, and cities - always fascinating to watch while learning about old Santa Maria. There is also some train paraphernalia on display and some for sale.

Hours: Open the 2nd and 4th Sat., noon - 4pm.
Price: Free
Ages: 3 years and up.

SANTA YNEZ VALLEY HISTORICAL SOCIETY MUSEUM / PARKS-JANEWAY ☼
CARRIAGE HOUSE $

(805) 688-7889 / www.santaynezmuseum.org
3596 Sagunto Street, Santa Ynez

Go west, young man! On the main street of Santa Ynez, with its western-looking storefronts, dwells a vintage museum. Composed of a small complex of buildings, the museum offers all that the Old West time period held dear.

Outside is a reproduction of a Bodie Stage Line mud wagon. Inside, the lobby showcases a wonderful collections of spurs, bits, bridles, saddles, branding irons, chaps, barbed wire, riata (i.e., rope made of rawhide), and guns, as well as a stuffed golden eagle and a mounted boar's head. It also contains a nice display of Native American baskets, pottery, and stone mortars and pestles, plus samples of beadwork and shell bead money.

Meander back outside to the center courtyard where a fountain and a shady arbor with picnic tables invites visitors to sit and relax a spell. The next series of rooms form a U-shape around the courtyard. First stop is the Pioneer Room, which is divided into three sections - a kitchen, bedroom, and parlor-living room; all furnished with items from the late nineteenth century. Walk through to see butter molds and churns, a cast iron stove, an 1847 sleigh bed, a crib, quilts, a treadle sewing machine, and an organ. The next room features changing displays of period clothing and accessories. We saw elegantly arranged, off-white wedding gowns, along with ornately beaded hand bags. The adjoining Valley Room's changing exhibits highlight the five small, nearby town's beginnings and early development. The exhibits include historical and cultural artifacts, and photos, as well as a narrow gauge train display, with models of the trains that ran through the area from 1887 to 1934, plus a depot, Mattie's Tavern, and more. Outside are farm implements and vehicles such as horse-drawn farm machinery, a 1907 Harvester pickup truck, and an early McCormick-Deering tractor. Forge ahead to look at the complete blacksmith shop also located back here.

Across the courtyard is the fascinating carriage house. Enter this large room and stroll down the streets of time as you admire the over thirty-five carriages parked here. Our favorites include the hunt wagons; a Goddard Buggy; a military supply wagon; the basket-style governesses' carts; surreys; stagecoaches; a still-functioning 1906 popcorn wagon; a hearse; a hitch wagon; a 1927 Model T school bus; and a fancifully-painted donkey cart from Sicily. O.K. - we like them all! There are also some saddles, bits, bridles, and other equestrian gear on display.

Guided tours that allow visitors to gain insight to the memorabilia and time period are available with advanced reservations. Note that the Santa Ynez County Park is just down the street, with the entry off Edison and Numancia Sts. This park offers a few pieces of play equipment, a volleyball court, horseshoe pits, some trees, grassy areas, and picnic tables.

Hours: Open Wed. - Sun., 12pm - 4pm. Closed Mon., Tues., and major holidays.
Price: $4 for adults; children 16 and under are free.
Ages: 6 years and up.

SOLVANG MOTORCYCLE MUSEUM   ☀

(805) 686-9522 / www.motosolvang.com $$$
320 Alisal Road, Solvang

Over ninety vintage, rare, and classic motorcycles in excellent condition are lined up on the showroom floor, seemingly ready to roar to life. Each beautifully-restored vehicle has an accompanying description of its make and history. This eclectic private collection ranges from a 1902 Mitchel to a 1989 custom Harley - the emphasis is on racing motorcycles.

Some of the extra special bikes include an MV Agusta, Brough Superior, 1936 Nimbus sidecar, 1960 Jawa Factory Racer, 1949 Vincent Black Lightning - Supercharged, 1950 Vincent TT Grey Flash (one of four ever made), and 1946

Indian Chief - a classic with fringe on the seat. Note that the museum rotates the bikes on exhibit. The museum also has a replica of the first combustion automobile ever originally built by Karl Benz of Mercedes-Benz.

Hours: Open Sat. - Sun., 11am - 5pm, or by appointment during the week.
Price: $10 for adults; children 9 years and under are free when accompanied by an adult.
Ages: 6 years and up.

SOUTH COAST RAILROAD MUSEUM

(805) 964-3540 / www.goletadepot.org
300 North Los Carneros Road, Goleta

Engineer some time for the kids to conduct their way to this satisfying railroad museum. Walk through an old caboose that shares this section of tracks with a handcar that is powered by passengers. In one of the small rooms at the 1901 depot building, watch a model train making tracks through mountains, over a cut-away bridge, and even past a mini circus. The depot waiting room features an old stove, trunks, and a motor car indicator - a signaling device that warned maintenance crews that a train was coming. You can also see a short slide show about the Goleta Depot project. Look into the ticket office which has several pieces of old equipment in place, and look into the freight office with its roll-top desk, candlestick phone, and scale. Check out the well-stocked gift shop. There is also a pleasant little park on the grounds with picnic tables and shade trees - a spot to rest your *toot*sies!

The highlight of a child's trip here is the nine-minute train ride, of course. The miniature train chugs its way around the depot grounds, past the picnic tables and scattered trees. Adults enjoy it just as much as the kids. Riders must be at least 34" tall for the train ride and 48" for the handcar.

Many special events are held here throughout the year, including the Easter Bunny Express and Depot Day (in September). School and youth group tours include a free ride on the train. Ask for a copy of the self guided tour information sheet. Note that the railroad museum is located right next to STOW HOUSE (pg. 635) and is in LAKE LOS CARNEROS PARK (pg. 612).

Hours: Open Thurs. - Sun., 1pm - 4pm. Mini trains run Thurs. - Fri., 2pm - 3:45pm; Sat. - Sun., 1pm - 3:45pm. Closed New Year's Day, Easter, Thanksgiving, and Christmas.
Price: Admission to the grounds is free. Train rides are $1.50 per person. Train rides are free every Fri. through mid-November and at several other times - call first. Free handcar rides are offered on the third Sat. of each month, or ask for a private ride on other days for a small fee.
Ages: 3 to 14 years.

STOW HOUSE / RANCHO LA PATERA

(805) 681-7216 / www.stowhouse.com
304 N. Los Carneros Road, Goleta

Woodsy surroundings and era-appropriate landscaped grounds make this Rancho and restored 1870's two-story Gothic Revival house, the Stow House, seem as though they have never met up with modern times. I love the porch that practically encircles the huge white house. (Notice the bench under the crossroad "street" signs made from horseshoes welded together.) Take the one-hour tour through the beautiful home to see all the rooms - the six or so upstairs and several more downstairs - that are filled with period furnishings, clothing and hats, toys, knickknacks, china, kitchen gadgets, and more. The dining room is elegantly set for a meal. The laundry room has wringers and washboards, and kids' clothes hanging around. The kitchen has a wonderful old stove, old tins, jars, and kitchen implements. The parlor contains a phonograph, old-fashioned phone, a desk, photos and more. The sewing room and the bedrooms upstairs, especially, while containing all the furniture and things that make a house a lived in home, also allow a closer look at the back-East-style of architecture and decor with alcoves and wallpapering. The docents, dressed in period costume, do an outstanding job of making history be engaging as they show and tell visitors how things work, give the back stories to many of the items, and point out objects that could be overlooked, like the wreath made out of hair, the "port-a-potty", the speaking tube, the unusual refrigerator, and much more.

The ranch grounds are extensive. The back farmyard contains old tractors, a variety of old-fashioned farm machinery, mining cars, and, most importantly, a three-person outhouse - bonding time. Other historic buildings on the ranch grounds are the carriage house with yes, carriages, although the horse stalls in this area contain farm equipment, a fire engine, and a tack display. A blacksmith shop is filled with tools of the trade. On certain days there are blacksmith demonstrations, and visitors can purchase newly-fashioned horseshoes (with their name engraved),

wrought iron items, and more.

Inside the History Education Center building are exhibits, many of them hands-on, that cover local history from indigenous people to modern day, with a focus on ranching and agriculture. Things to do in here include sorting lemons; using carpentry tools; lifting panels to discover the answer to why some eggs are brown and some are white, for instance; writing/branding your name on the wall of brands; watching a slideshow of elementary-school kids from long ago; and lots more.

Call for information about the great educational programs for third graders, as well as other school, youth, and group tours that are offered during the week. Don't miss the small museum room off the visitors center. Note that this land is shared with the SOUTH COAST RAILROAD MUSEUM (pg. 635) and LAKE LOS CARNEROS PARK (pg. 612).

Hours: Open Sat. - Sun., 1pm - 4pm. Call for guided tour during the week. Closed Easter, Thanksgiving, and Christmas.

Price: $8 for adults; ages 11 and under are free.

Ages: 6 years and up.

SUSAN QUINLAN DOLL & TEDDY BEAR MUSEUM & LIBRARY

(805) 730-1707 / www.quinlanmuseum.com $$
122 West Canon Perdido Street, Santa Barbara

There is something about teddy bears and dolls that touch a young (and older) girl's heart and this charming museum has both in spades with over 2,500 dolls and over 500 teddy bears on exhibit. Past the five-foot stuffed warthog on roller skates is a welcoming lounge area with complimentary tea. Sit at a table in front of the playful and colorful wall murals of a teddy picnic and tea party - actually the bears are cavorting at local Santa Barbara spots. Fluffy clouds dot the sky-blue ceiling.

One-of-a-kind dolls, ethnic dolls from all over the world, and dolls of every size (small to near life-size), plus rare bears are arranged here in huge glass display cases with each gallery having a different emphasis. The Historical Gallery traces California's history through a doll timeline starting with the Native American dolls. The Collector's Gallery includes the bear necessities - a tribute to the bear's namesake, Teddy Roosevelt, plus numerous bears in seasonal settings. Puppets and even fairytale characters are here, too. The museum's founder was a children's librarian and this love shows through especially in the Literary Gallery which shows dolls and bears representing literary characters, inspired by books. This is a child's favorite area. Boys aren't left out - there is a collection of space toys, robots, and figures from *Star Wars*, *Star Trek*, *Power Rangers*, and more. Another section contains dolls made of various materials - wood, wax, metal, cloth, and bisque. The children's sewing machines shows how models have changed over the years. Lastly is a Fairy Forest, with more fantasy dolls and teddy bears.

One-hour (or more) tours are offered explaining the history of many of the dolls and a bit about their time periods. Browse the gift shop which offers a variety of dolls, teddy bears, books, and collectibles. Tip: Visit the bathrooms while here as they are theme-decorated with dolls and bears, too.

Hours: Usually open Fri. - Mon., 11am - 5pm. Closed Tues. - Thurs., and most major holidays.

Price: $6.50 for adults; $5.50 for seniors; $3.50 for ages 5 - 12; children 4 and under are free. Groups of 6 or more are $5 for adults; $2.50 for kids.

Ages: 3 years and up.

WATERSHED RESOURCE CENTER

(805) 884-0459 ext.16 / www.artfromscrap.org; www.exploreecology.org   !
2981 Cliff Drive at Arroyo Burro / Hendry's Beach, Santa Barbara

Managed by the ART FROM SCRAP (pg. 598) environmental education program, this model of a green building serves as an education center with a focus on water quality issues. It plays hosts to several groups and programs that the entire family can participate in, such as creek water testing, beach clean ups, demonstrations, and even watching ecological movies. School field trips are offered that teach students about water pollution, solutions, the effect of plastic trash on the ocean and ocean life, watersheds, and more.

The center is open to the public every Sunday. Kids might not be here long, but the small center offers a great opportunity to become environmental aware through interactive games, maps, watershed models, a hands-on wet lab, and by the docents who want to educate youngsters (and us older folk).

Hours: Open to the public every second Sun., 11am - 4pm; help clean up the beach this day, too. Call for a schedule of programs.

Price: Free. Call for program information.

Ages: 5 years and up.

—PIERS AND SEAPORTS—

SANTA BARBARA HARBOR / STEARNS WHARF

(805) 564-5530 - harbor patrol; (805) 966-6676 - Santa Barbara Shellfish Co.; (805) 966-6110 - Los Banos pool; (805) 564-5523 - parking / www.stearnswharf.org; www.santabarbaraca.gov; www.sbfishhouse.com
State Street and Cabrillo Boulevard, Santa Barbara

This harbor is encompassed by long stretches of beach - from EAST BEACH (pg. 599) to WEST BEACH (pg. 602) to LEADBETTER BEACH (pg. 601) - with a lot of fun in the sun in between. Walk or drive onto the wharf's creaky wooden planks. Originally built in 1872, the wharf features the TY WARNER SEA CENTER (pg. 653); several restaurants - be sure to check out Santa Barbara Shellfish Co. at the end because of its tanks of live lobsters and shellfish (which make good food, too); and fun shops that sell shell-encrusted treasures, salt water taffy, and more. Fish from the pier, and during whale-watching seasons - late December through March for gray whales and in the summer for the blue whales - be on the lookout for the mighty marine mammals.

Adjacent to the wharf is the harbor where yachts, commercial fishing boats, and sailboats are moored. Pick up fresh crabs and lobsters from the fishing boats on Market Day, which is Saturdays from 7:30am to 11:30am. The harbor is also the place to book a cruise, rent kayaks, go out whale watching on a boat, and check out other nautical excursions. See the Transportation section for specific places to contact. More restaurants, shops, and the wonderful SANTA BARBARA MARITIME MUSEUM (pg. 629) are also located here. Make sure to visit the tiny visitor's center on the 4th floor of the maritime museum building because it has one of the most incredible views, for free, of all of Santa Barbara, and beyond, plus it carries resources and maps.

Walk, skate, or bike along the waterfront paved path which extends for three miles. See BIKE TRAIL: CABRILLO BEACHWAY (pg. 645) for more information. This area is also home to a skate park (see SKATER'S POINT on page 621); art shows on the sidewalks every Sunday and on select Saturdays; a playground; and the Los Banos swimming pool. This fifty-meter municipal pool has a diving board. It is located at 401 Shoreline Drive, next door to the West Beach Wading Pool which has one-foot-deep water for kiddies. In this vicinity is the Cabrillo Pavilion Boathouse with showers, lockers, beach wheelchair rentals, and volleyball rentals. Across the street from the beach is the fabulous CHASE PALM PARK (pg. 609).

Getting around from State Street to the wharf to the zoo is easy on the SANTA BARBARA WATERFRONT and DOWNTOWN SHUTTLE (pg. 648). It operates daily from 9am to 6pm and costs 50¢ per person; 25¢ for seniors; children 45" and under are free. Also look under SANTA BARBARA TROLLEY COMPANY (pg. 648), as the wharf is one of the many stops along the trolley's route. If you can't decide if you want to tour the city by land or by sea - do both, by way of the amphibious "boat on wheels" of the LAND AND SEA TOURS (pg. 646).

Hours: Open daily. Los Banos Pools are open year-round for lap swim and only in the summer for recreational swim, usually Mon. - Sat., 2:15 - 3:45pm. Call for others hours and sessions.

Price: Recreation swim at Los Banos pool is $4 for adults; $1 for ages 17 and under. The wading pool is free. There is limited street parking. On the east side of the beach, parking is $2 an hour, $12 max with 1½ hours free with validation to the Maritime Museum and/or from a restaurant or store.

Ages: All

—POTPOURRI—

MARINE SCIENCE INSTITUTE

(805) 893-3765 or (805) 893-4093 / www.msi.ucsb.edu
Lagoon Road on the campus of University of California, Santa Barbara, Goleta

Educators, especially: Fantastic marine-based programs are offered via MSI - the REEF (Research Experience and

Education Facility), which hosts thousands of school kids, educators, researchers and more every year. The Outreach Center for Teaching Ocean Science (OCTOS) building, perched on a bluff overlooking the ocean, contains two huge (2,000 gallon) fish tanks in the "wet laboratory"; overhead stuffed sharks and other sea life; an immersive theater; scenario-based activities utilizing a transect of the ocean floor (experience it to understand it); and a "magic planet" (i.e. extra large globe) that allows viewers to see what is going on all over the world, as the surface of it changes according to global conditions based on data input.

Other programs offered include a mobile REEF program (where the aquariums and other equipment come to you), Family Science Night, after school activities, Marine Science 4 Scouts, and Floating Labs. The latter are cruises that take place on the *Condor Express*, whale watching and sight *seeing*. Once anchored, students rotate through a series of stations exploring fields such as marine biology, navigation systems, earth science, oceanography, and more.

Hours: The building is open to the public Sat., 11am - 2pm. Call regarding the program you're interested in.
Price: Free on the public Saturdays. Call for program prices.
Ages: 5 years and up.

MURALS

(800) 240-0999 or (805) 736-4567 - chamber of commerce / www.lompocmurals.com; www.lompoc.com
throughout the city, Lompoc

Mural, mural on the wall, which is the fairest one of all? Lompoc, dubbed "City of Murals in the Valley of Flowers," combines the best of both of these elements, and more, in the over seventy murals gracing the buildings throughout the city. I thought I'd have to drag the kids to view the murals and consider it a quick art experience. While I did make them accompany me, they became enamored with the paintings - with the variety of scenes and collages, characters, time periods, locations, styles, colors, and even sizes. The murals depict flowers, portraits, rocket launches, an old-fashioned train depot, people, and much more.

For a self-guided "tour," pick up a free murals project brochure from the chamber of commerce (also available at www.lompocmurals.com), then drive around to admire and appreciate this free, unique outdoor art exhibit. Note: See the Calendar entry for details about the Flower Fields and Festival (pg. 727) and combine these two attractions in one visit.

Hours: The murals can be seen during any daylight hours. The chamber of commerce is open Mon. - Fri., 8am - 5pm.
Price: Free
Ages: 4 years and up.

PAUL NELSON AQUATIC CENTER and COMMUNITY YOUTH CENTER

(805) 925-0951 / www.cityofsantamaria.org
516 McClelland Street, Santa Maria

Enjoy year-round swimming at this huge pool with a diving board and a short twisting water slide. An adjacent shallow wading pool features a little frog slide and a large mushroom-shaped shower that elicits giggles from young children. Parents can relax pool side in lounge chairs. The field beyond the fence has a grass area with basketball courts and a baseball field.

The indoor community youth center, geared for Jr. and Sr. high schoolers, has pool tables, air hockey, a few arcade games, basketball courts, exercise equipment, and other activities. Just outside, at the adjacent Simas Park, is an expanse of green lawn for baseball, other sports and running around, and a basketball court.

Hours: The pool is open April - August, daily, for recreational swimming, Mon., Wed., and Fri., 3pm - 4:30pm; Sat. 12:30pm - 3:30pm. Hours do fluctuate so call first. The youth center is open daily - the mornings are for adults and kids, but kids, 7th - 12th graders, have it exclusively in the afternoons (after 2:30pm) until closing.
Price: Swimming is $2.50 for adults; $1.25 for ages 6 - 16; seniors and ages 5 and under are free. Ask about purchasing a pool pass. The community center is free.
Ages: 1 year and up.

SANTA BARBARA COUNTY COURTHOUSE

(805) 962-6464 / www.santabarbaracourthouse.org; www.countyofsb.org

1100 Anacapa Street, Santa Barbara

The verdict is in - this magnificent, historic courthouse is one of the city's most fascinating places to tour. The grandiose building, designed in Spanish-Moorish architecture, and its elegant surrounding gardens take up a city block.

Walk around and through the palace-like building on your own to admire the outside fountain, archways, graceful curved staircases inside, ornately carved doors, colorful mosaic tiles, unusual iron and glass hanging lanterns, paintings, and decorative floors, walls, and ceilings. Note that the Courthouse is still used for trials and houses civic offices.

The free, forty-five-minute guided tour is a terrific option as the guide explains the history of California, particularly Santa Barbara, and the history of the Courthouse, including the explanations of the various artistic styles used throughout, especially the Muslim influence. The tour begins in the beautiful mural room, so nicknamed because the walls are covered with murals depicting Chumash Indians, Cabrillo, California under Mexican rule, the building of the mission, and the beginning of the California/American era. Make sure to look at the fancy ceiling beams. Meetings are still held in here. Going into the law library with its painted stars on the ceiling, then down massive hallways, and learn the meaning of the Latin inscriptions over the outside pointed archways. The Hall of Records room is decorated in the original 1920's decor - wild! Other tour highlights (for us) included learning who Saint Barbara (the town's namesake) was; seeing, from across the courtyard, the jail and the solitary confinement quarters in a wing of the Courthouse; and looking at the stained glass window in the lobby. Note that parts of the tour incorporate walking in and out of the building, as well as up and down stairs. Some outside ramps and an inside elevator are available.

While here, take a ride eighty feet up in the elevator, walk up a few stairs, and out onto the balcony of the Courthouse clock tower for a wonderful, panoramic view of Santa Barbara. See the mountains, the ocean, and all the red-tiled roofs in the vicinity.

The meticulously-landscaped sunken garden in the center courtyard has an expansive lawn and bordering bushes, trees, and flowers. It's a peaceful haven for a picnic, and a relaxing place to ponder.

Hours: The Courthouse is open Mon. - Fri., 8am - 4:45pm; Sat. - Sun., 10am - 4:45pm. Closed Christmas. Tours are offered Mon., Tues., Wed., and Fri. at 10:30am and 2pm; Sat. - Sun., 2pm.

Price: Free

Ages: 8 years and up.

SOLVANG   ☼

(800) 468-6765 or (805) 688-6144 - visitor's center; (805) 688-0091 - bike rentals / www.solvangusa.com;   !/$$
www.wheelfunrentals.com

Mission Drive, Alisal Road, Atterdag Road, and Copenhagen Drive form the perimeter of the core of the village, Solvang

Velkommen! The word Solvang is Danish for "sunny field." This sunny field is both an authentic Old World village and a tourist haven. Established in 1911, Solvang, which has become the Danish capitol of America, looks like a page out of one of Hans Christian Andersen's storybooks. Adults, and even kids, will notice and be enamored with the ethnic heritage and Scandinavian architecture including thatched roofs, colorful storefronts, window boxes filled with flowers, windmills, and decorative wood work. It truly is like being in a different country.

The over 300 eateries and shops include antique shops, smorgasbords, clothing stores, bakeries, souvenir shops, cafes, cobbler shops, and restaurants, all within walking distance of one another. Browse the stores to look for unique gifts and collectibles, such as cuckoo clocks, dogs, hand-crafted lace, glasswork, dolls, miniature ceramic windmills, a family coat of arms, and lots more. Snack on an aebleskiver - a Danish pancake ball concoction made with powdered sugar and served with raspberry jam. Just a few of our favorite stops include the Solvang Restaurant at 1672 Copenhagen Drive for great aebleskivers; Solvang Toyland at 1664 Copenhagen Drive for a selection of toys; Ingebrog's Danish Chocolate at 1679 Copenhagen for delectable chocolates and rich ice cream; and the Book Loft at 1680 Mission Drive for new, used, and rare books. The bookstore is also host to the HANS CHRISTIAN ANDERSEN MUSEUM (pg. 626).

Besides driving and walking around the village, other modes of transportation include renting a tandem, or two- to six-passenger surrey to pedal from Wheel Fun Rentals, 475 First Street (open daily, year round, 9am to 6pm, 7pm on the weekends), or taking a carriage ride. For the latter excursion, Belgian draft horses pull a replica 1915 Danish streetcar or *honen* (Danish for "hen") for twenty minutes through the heart of downtown Solvang so visitors can see the town as well as hear about its history. The horse-drawn trolley and carriage rides of Solvang Trolley and Carriage Co. depart from the Visitor's Center on Copenhagen Drive most of the year Fridays through Mondays, noon to 6pm, and during the summer every day, except Tuesday - weather permitting. Call (805) 794-8958 / www.solvangtrolley.com

for more info and other carriage ride options.

Be on the lookout for the town's four windmills, the red and white Danish national flags, the half-scale model of Copenhagen's Little Mermaid (at the intersection of Mission and Alisal streets), and storks (not real ones) on roofs that are supposed to bring good luck. While in Solvang, you can also visit the ELVERHOJ MUSEUM (pg. 625), the SOLVANG MOTORCYCLE MUSEUM (pg. 634), PCPA THEATERFEST (pg. 642, 729) (during the summer only), and OLD MISSION SANTA INES (pg. 628). See the back of this book, under Index by City, for the numerous other nearby attractions, such as parks and places with animals, besides just shopping and eating - although that works fine for our family! Also check the Calendar section for annual events. Mange tak. (Many thanks.)

Hours: The shops are usually open daily, 10am - 6pm. The visitor's center is open daily, 10am - 5pm.
Price: Free entrance and parking to Solvang. Carriage rides are usually $10 for adults; $8 for seniors; $5 for ages 12 and under - they are sometime higher in the summer or on holidays. Bike rentals run from $15 an hour for tandems to $45 an hour for six-passenger surreys.
Ages: All

—SHOWS AND THEATERS—

ARLINGTON THEATER AND CENTER FOR PERFORMING ARTS

(805) 963-4408 / www.thearlingtontheatre.com
1317 State Street, Santa Barbara

Enter via a Spanish courtyard, through a lobby decorated with ceiling murals of fiesta dancers and into the actual theater that was built to resemble a Spanish town, complete with elegant balconies and electronic "stars" twinkling overhead. The theater plays host to Broadway performances, such as *Cats*, plus Metropolitan Opera broadcasts, live headliner entertainers (i.e. Jerry Seinfeld), Michael Bolton, Cirque Wings, and so many more. In between live shows, the theater shows first-run, blockbuster movies.

Hours: Call for specific dates and times.
Price: Prices vary greatly depending on the show and date.
Ages: 8 years and up.

CIRCLE BAR B DINNER THEATER

(805) 967-1962 - dinner theater; (805) 968-3901 - horseback riding; (805) 968-1113 - guest ranch
/ www.circlebarb.com
1800 Refugio Road, Goleta

This rustic-looking, cabin-style dude ranch is tucked away in the middle of horse country in the mountains. The dinner theater, which is just a part of the ranch's offerings, presents three or four different performances a year that are often family-friendly. The shows are usually comedies (although sometimes more adult comedies), with at least one musical in the line-up. Shows are about ninety-minutes long. Dinner theater guests eat outside on a patio overlooking the pool. (Bring a sweater in case it gets cool.) Menu selections include barbecue tri tip, chicken, or a veggie pasta, accompanied by beans, potatoes, rolls, salad, and dessert - all the fixin's. After dinner, the group is then shepherded past the stables into the very intimate 100-seat Old Barn building that serves as the theater.

The ranch also offers horseback riding on trails that crisscross through nearly 1,000 acres of coastal countryside. Horseback riding costs $50 for an hour-and-a-half and riders must be at least 7 years old. Go out for a four hour ride that includes lunch, for $90 per person. Make a day of your outing by riding and then enjoying dinner and a show, or even spend the night at this ranch!

Hours: The season runs April - October, with dinner starting Fri. at 7pm; Sat., 7pm; Sun., 1pm. The show begins one hour after meal times.
Price: $49 per person for dinner and show; $42 for seniors; children 5 years and under are free. If you are staying at the hotel, the cost is $20 just for the show. Room and cabin rates start at about $292 for two people, per night, which includes three meals a day.
Ages: 6 years and up.

ENSEMBLE THEATER COMPANY

(805) 965-5400 / www.ensembletheatre.com

33 West Victoria Street, Santa Barbara

This resident theater troupe performs about four plays or musicals a year in the intimate, 300-seat theater. At least one of the plays is family-appropriate. The Storybook Theater, which shares billing and production space at the theater, puts on at least two plays a year designed specifically for kids. Past play titles include *Snow White and the Seven Dwarfs, Pinocchio,* and *The Mask of Harlequin.* School field trips are invited at the Student Matinee Series in particular, and school assemblies are offered.

Hours: Plays are performed on Tues. - Sat., at 8pm; Sun. at 2pm and sometimes at 7pm. Storybook Theater performs usually in April, on two selected Sat. at noon, 2:30pm, and 4:30pm.

Price: Plays range from $35 - $75, depending on the day, date, and time; usually $20 for youth. Storybook performances are $15 for adults; $10 for ages 11 and under.

Ages: 5 years and up for plays; 2 - 11 years for Storybook performances.

THE GRANADA

(805) 899-2222 - tickets; (805) 899-3000 / www.granadasb.org $$$$$
1214 State Street, Santa Barbara

A blend of old-time and contemporary grand theater, this sophisticated, restored theater is host and home to a wide variety of venues, including State Street Ballet, Broadway musicals, Opera Santa Barbara, Tony award winning musicals, Santa Barbara Choral Society, a family series, national and international touring groups, CAMA, Musical Academy of the West, headlining concerts, and special speaker series. The theater is also home to the Santa Barbara Symphony which performs a repertoire of traditional choral and pops selections throughout the year, including the Classics and Family Series. Educators, look online for information about the Yellow Bus series, where students can attend first-class performances in these stunning surroundings, accompanied by study guides. They sometimes have the opportunity to meet the performers, too. Check out the Visiting Artists Studio, where visiting artist present workshops, classes, and demonstrations.

Hours: Call for a schedule of performances.

Price: Prices vary according to show. Parking is about $5.

Ages: 4 years and up, depending on the production.

THE GREAT AMERICAN MELODRAMA & VAUDEVILLE

(805) 489-2499 / www.americanmelodrama.com $$$$
1863 Front Street, Oceano

For an evening of good, old-fashioned, light-hearted family entertainment, come boo, hiss, and cheer for the villains and heros (and heroines), respectively. (Participation is a must!) The music clues the audience in - if they can't figure out for themselves as to when to do these actions. Each silly storyline is accompanied by lots of music and singing.

Upbeat piano music greets you as soon as you enter through the doors to the melodrama, getting you in the mood for a rollicking good time. Chairs are crowded around small round tables on the sawdust-covered floor. Other seating is available on benches around the raised perimeter of the room. The setting is intimate enough that the actors perform on stage without microphones. The show starts off with a sing along - the words are printed in the newspaper playbill. The hour-and-a-half feature presentation is just plain fun for all ages. Past productions have included *The Mark of Morro, Around the World in 80 Days,* and *Scary Poppins.* After the melodrama, enjoy the half-hour vaudeville revue, with its song, dance, and comedy routine. Are your kids interested in performing on stage? Sign them up for summer Camp Melodrama where they can try out their acting chops.

During intermission, or before the main show, food and drinks are available from the servers, who are also the performers. The bill of fare includes hot dogs ($4.95); salad with chicken breast ($5.95); BBQ beef ($5.95); Polish sausage or pastrami sandwich ($6.50); nachos with cheese ($3.95); baked potato ($3.95 to $4.95); bowl of chili ($4); popcorn ($2.50); and assorted candy ($1.25). Kid's meals of a hot dog, chips, and soda served on a frisbee - $6. Tip: If you are interested in getting dinner elsewhere before you arrive, check out ROCK & ROLL DINER (pg. 604) which is just down the street. Note: I know that this theater isn't in Santa Barbara County, but it's so close to the border and the format was too unique and fun to pass up!

Hours: Show times are usually some Wed., 7pm; Thurs. at 2pm (four times a year) or at 7pm; Fri., 7pm; Sat., 3pm and 7pm; Sun., 6pm. Doors open a half hour before the show.

Price: $18 - $24 for adults, depending on the seat; $16 - $22 for seniors, students, and active military; $14 - $20 for ages 12 and under; children 2 and under are free if they are lap sitting. Prices are slightly higher for the Holiday Extravaganza. A $2 handling fee is charged for all phone reservations.

Ages: 5 years and up.

LOBERO THEATER

(888) 4LOBERO (456-2376) or (805) 963-0761- box office; (805) 966-4946 - tours and other info. / www.lobero.com

$$$$$

33 E. Canon Perdido Street, Santa Barbara

The Lobero is quite a busy theater, as well as the one of the oldest California theaters (originally built in 1873) in continuous operation. Attracting audiences from all age groups and cultural backgrounds, it hosts a wide variety of programming such as the West Coast Ballet (call [805] 687-6086 / www.wcballet.org for more information), Santa Barbara Chamber Orchestra, Santa Barbara Grand Opera, Sings Like Hell concert series, Speaking of Stories performance series, and everything else in between. Come see magic shows, ballet, concerts, dance programs, dramatic presentations, and other first-class performances. The theater also offers fifty-minute behind-the-scenes tours, by reservation only.

Hours: Call for performance schedules.

Price: Tickets prices vary depending on show title and date.

Ages: Depends on performance.

PCPA THEATERFEST

(805) 922-8313 - box office; (805) 928-7731 - bs. office / www.pcpa.org; www.solvangtheaterfest.org

$$$$$

2 locations: Santa Maria - 800 S. College Drive at the Marian and Severson Theaters at the Allan Hancock College (GPS users use 1100 S. Bradley); Solvang - 420 2nd Street at the outdoor Festival Theater.

Put a star next to this entry because the Pacific Conservatory of the Performing Arts (PCPA) knows how to make a theater experience a memorable one! Both theater locations have intimate settings, so the audience feels close to the on-stage action and professional actors. Many of the nine yearly plays and musicals are family friendly. Past shows have included *Hello Dolly!*, *Peter Pan*, *Little Women*, *Forever Plaid*, and *Honk!* - a musical tale of the ugly duckling.

We are especially enchanted by the 700-plus-seat Festival Theater in Solvang because the theater is outdoors; a cozy semi-circle of tiered seats surrounds the center stage. In the middle of this quaint Danish town, under a canopy of trees and starlight, the magic of theater comes to life. Although the Solvang season runs mid-June through October, bring a blanket and/or jacket because the nights can get chilly. Note that last minute tickets are sometimes available.

The PCPA also has Outreach programs and tours that take age-appropriate shows to classrooms or other facilities.

Hours: Call for show dates and times.

Price: Prices range, depending on location and show time, from $25 - $49 for adults; $22.50 - $44.25 for seniors; $17.50 - $35 for students; $15.50 - $31.25 for ages 5 - 18 years. The Solvang location is at least $6 more expensive per person per play. Thursday previews are less expensive. Children 4 and under are not permitted.

Ages: 8 years and up.

SANTA MARIA CIVIC THEATER

(805) 922-4442 / www.smct.org

$$$$

1660 North McClelland Street, Santa Maria

This 100-seat theater is host to nonprofessional actors who produce some good, area theater. Some of the shows are family friendly and some are even interactive; call first.

Hours: Call for specific shows and times.

Price: Call for specific show prices.

Ages: 5 years and up, depending on the performance.

STATE STREET BALLET

(805) 563-3262 - the ballet company; (805) 899-2222 - Granada box office tickets / www.statestreetballet.com; www.granadasb.org

$$$$$

1214 State Street at The Granada, Santa Barbara

This professional company tours nationally and performs at "home", at The Granada, presenting both classic and contemporary ballets. The company also occasionally performs at the Lobero Theatre - www.lobero.com. Make sure to catch at least one of four graceful and passionate shows performed each year. At Christmas time the holiday staple, *Nutcracker* is performed. Ask about the ballet's school and community outreach programs. For instance, students can be invited to performances during school hours when the troupe is in town, or the performers will come to schools for an on-site performance. The public is sometimes invited to open rehearsals.

Hours: Performances are usually given October - April, Sat., 7pm or 8pm; Sun., 2pm or 3pm.
Price: $31 - $53 for adults, depending on the date and the seats; $21 for ages 12 and under. Parking is $5.
Ages: 6 years and up.

—TOURS—

BRAILLE INSTITUTE (Santa Barbara County)

(805) 682-6222 / www.brailleinstitute.org
2031 De La Vina, Santa Barbara

A one-hour, or so, tour of the Braille Institute enables visitors to better understand how well the visually impaired can function in the world. The classrooms, library, art rooms, and computer labs are set up to enable the blind to gain life skills. Try the adaptive computer software which has zoom text and screen reader programs, or type something on the Braille embosser. Ask for permission to sit in on an orientation on how to use the white cane. Kids will definitely like the student store which sells talking watches and calculators, among other products. Note that mobile outreach programs are available to come to elementary schools.

Hours: Call to schedule a tour for a group, or call as they will show individuals around, too. The Institute is open Mon. - Fri., 8:30am - 5pm.
Price: Free
Ages: 8 years old and up.

CALIFORNIA PIZZA KITCHEN (Santa Barbara County)

See the entry for CALIFORNIA PIZZA KITCHEN (Los Angeles County) (pg. 197) for more information.

GOLETA SANITARY DISTRICT

(805) 967-4519 / www.goletasanitary.org
One William Moffett Place, Goleta

Students can take a tour of this sewage treatment plant that complements school standards. (Other groups are welcome as well.) They learn about the water cycle by first listening to a talk on "following" a water stream (such as flushed toilet water) to see what happens to the water along its passage and at its destination. This is a very realistic and functional tour! Then, they visit the lab to analyze water samples and to learn to recognize chemical properties and components. Last, they walk through the treatment plant and huge water tanks to see the mechanics of how it all works. The minimum needed for a tour is ten students.

Hours: Tours are offered Mon. - Fri. Call to make a reservation.
Price: Free
Ages: 4th graders and up.

GOOD LAND ORGANICS

(805) 685-4189 / www.goodlandorganics.com
Goleta

Ahhh - who can resist the smell and taste of freshly-brewed coffee? Become educated about how this morning obsession is made by taking a 2.5 hour, casual tour of Good Land Organics coffee farm - the only commercial grower in California (and possibly the continental United States). Walk the hillside orchards to see the plants growing: It's about a year-long maturation process from the white flower to the dark red "cherry" (i.e., the coffee fruit that contains

the bean), with harvest season June through September. Bite into a coffee fruit and see what you think. (I like mine roasted.) You can help harvest a few beans so you get a real feel for all that goes into your specialty cuppa joe. The certified organic farm boasts 500 mature coffee trees with numerous varieties among them. Jay, the owner, also grows over 100 other fruiting plants, such as avocados and bananas, and several exotic sub-tropical crops such as cherimoyas, dragon fruit, passion fruit, and finger or caviar limes that you break open to see the little "eggs" of lime-tasting fruit. Such diversity!

In the post-harvest coffee process and building, the beans are sorted and put through their paces through the machines. You'll get to sample several types of the home-grown coffee, black (to experience the nuances), or with cream and sugar. Visitors are welcome to bring a picnic lunch to enjoy by the large koi pond and take in the delightful scenery on the farm.

Hours: Tours are offered usually once a month in the summer and the fall - check the website for specific dates and times.

Price: $40 per person.

Ages: 10 years and up.

SANTA BARBARA AVIATION EDUCATION CENTER

(805) 964-7622 or (805) 967-7111 / www.flysba.com/inside_sba/airport_visitors_center
45 Hartley Place, Goleta

Come learn about flying the friendly skies through a very-well presented tour at this airport and visitors center. The guided tour, which is the only way to see this facility, includes on-site classroom time and activities such as making and flying balsa wood airplanes. There are also a few hands-on aviation exhibits such as a small wooden plane to climb aboard, a flight simulator, and a radio-controlled aircraft that students fly in wind tunnels to get the feel for currents and navigation. One wind tunnel is similar to the one in the Smithsonian Air and Space Museum, but better aerodynamically.

The small exhibit hall also contains several model airplanes and lots of literature and videos (over 200 of them!) pertaining to flight. These are great resources for teachers. The local history of aviation and Santa Barbara's contribution to flight and space exploration is also spotlighted. The age-appropriate tours are usually about an hour long, depending on the age and attention span of the attendees. Tours are given for a minimum of ten students and a maximum of fifty. In-class presentations are available upon request, too. Note that once a year the center hosts a wonderful, GATE certified class on aviation for area 6th graders who excel in math and science. The visitors center is also the home base for the Santa Barbara Radio Modelers and for the YOUNG EAGLES PROGRAM (Santa Barbara County) (pg. 649).

Since the visitors center, which is wheelchair and stroller accessible, is adjacent to the airport, guests can also watch small planes land and take off. Note that the Santa Barbara airport is in the city of Santa Barbara on paper, but it's in the heart of Goleta. (I am taking no political stance on this one.)

Hours: Tours are available on Tues., Wed., and Thurs., 9am - 4pm by appointment only. Call at least six to eight weeks ahead of the time you'd like to visit.

Price: Free

Ages: Kindergarten and up.

SANTA MARIA TIMES

(805) 925-2691 / www.santamariatimes.com
3200 Skyway Drive, Santa Maria

Take a tour of this small-town newspaper to see how production is done. Walk through the newsroom seeing various departments to see and learn how a paper is put together. You'll also see old publications, dating from the 1800s, and see "cut and paste" via the computer. Depending on the time of your tour you can view the presses running, from a safe distance. See the papers coming off the conveyor and being set up on pallets. Your group - minimum of four, maximum of fifteen - will receive a fake front page newspaper with a group photo as the starring feature.

Try to set up a tour, which lasts about a half hour, in the afternoon when more of the staff are working. Morning tours will find a skeleton crew.

Hours: Tours are offered by appointment.

Price: Free

Ages: 6 years and up.

—TRANSPORTATION—

AMTRAK (Santa Barbara County)

(800) USA RAIL (872-7245) / www.amtrakcalifornia.com

Ride the rails! See AMTRAK (Los Angeles County) on page 208 for more information.

BIKE MAPS (Santa Barbara County)

See BIKE MAPS (Orange County) on page 326 for information. Also check the Santa Barbara Traffic Solution, (805) 963-SAVE (7283) or (805) 961-8900 / www.sbcag.org.

BIKE TRAIL: CABRILLO BEACHWAY (BIKEWAY)

www.bicyclela.org; www.labikepaths.com

parallel to Cabrillo Boulevard, Santa Barbara

This mostly flat, three-mile, palm-lined path runs along the waterfront, from the LEADBETTER BEACH (pg. 601) parking lot to the ANDREE CLARK BIRD REFUGE (pg. 606) near the SANTA BARBARA ZOO (pg. 652). Note: The paved path gets very crowded on the weekends, especially during the summer.

Hours: Open daily, sunrise - sunset.

Price: Free

Ages: 4 years and up.

CHANNEL ISLANDS OUTFITTERS / PADDLE SPORTS CENTER

(805) 899-4925 - Outfitters; (805) 617-3425 - Paddle Sports Center / www.channelislandso.com; www.islandpackers.com

117-B Harbor Way, Santa Barbara

Kayaks are Channel Islands Outfitters' specialty. Their Paddle Sports Center at Santa Barbara offers a variety of kayaks to rent - $25 for two hours for a single; $40 for a two-seater. Rent stand up paddleboards - $40 for two hours and/or surfboards and boogie boards - $10 each, for two hours. Wet suits are $5 for two hours. Kayaking and SUP lessons, plus classes and summer camps are also available.

Channel Islands Outfitters is owned by guys with a passion to "save the oceans and natural places by fostering an understanding of them through education, adventures, and outdoor experiences." Adventures are led by guides driven to share their knowledge and are the best way to become educated about the environment; soaking in knowledge while soaking in the sun. The History and Wildlife kayak excursion is in the harbor - two hours for $75, gliding in and out of the pier pilings, along the shoreline, getting almost nose to snout with sea lions, and really learning about and *sea*ing the water and all that is in it, on it and near it.

Or, take one of their signature trips to the Channel Islands, such as Santa Cruz Island, the largest of the eight. On the bucket list is a 2.5 hour guided kayaking trip to the Painted Cave - into and through one of the world's largest sea caves, as well as around a portion of the island and perhaps some snorkeling. The trip from Santa Barbara is $140 plus ferry transportation with Truth Aquatics which is $100 for adults; $50 for youth. This excursion also includes a continental breakfast and hot lunch following the incredible kayaking adventure. It is a non-landing trip. A similar-type of trip, called Caves and Coves Classic, is also $140 with an additional $59 for adults; $42 for ages 3 to 12 via using Island Packers as the ferry transportation. It leaves from Ventura Harbor. This awesome opportunity of a lifetime (another one!) goes through volcanic and craggy sea caves. It uses Scorpion Anchorage as a landing point and allows hiking, picnicking and snorkeling post trip. On both (and other trips) a naturalist will teach you about the geology, sea animals, and plant life in the area, as well as the rich history of the Channel Islands. These trips are offered May through September; check the website for several other excursions. Reservations are required. See CHANNEL ISLANDS NATIONAL PARK (from Ventura), on page 668, for more information on the chain of islands just off the coast.

Hours: Generally open daily, 8am - an hour before sunset. Closed in rainy weather. Excursions take place at various times and dates throughout the year - check the website for specific info.

Price: Prices are listed above. Parking is generally $2 an hour; $12 max.

Ages: Must be able to swim.

CLOUD CLIMBERS JEEP TOURS

(805) 646-3200 / www.ccjeeps.com

Departs from Santa Barbara and Solvang

$$$$$

A jeep ride is sometimes simply the best way to see a portion of the world, and I appreciate it when someone else, besides me, does the driving. (It's easier to sightsee!) The three-hour, narrated, Family Discovery Tour is designed with kids in mind. As the jeep climbs up and around the back country and the rugged mountains of Santa Ynez, the driver/tour guide shares the tales and history of the region, including its human and animal inhabitants, and facts about plant life. Kids (and adults) really understand and learn about nature, the Chumash Indians, and early settlers as they travel along portions of the original stagecoach road, and around rock formations and sandstone cliffs while looking and listening for clues during the Discovery Game. This tour also includes a short hike and a stop off at the painted cave, where you can peek in at a cave with Chumash drawings. All this, plus a panoramic view make for a memorable experience. There are several other tours available, too, including Horse-n-Around (which includes horseback riding) and "It's a Blast" which includes a stop at a private gun club.

The open-sided jeeps have canopies and seat five to seven people. Pack sunscreen and/or a hat, and bring a light jacket. Water bottles and blankets are provided.

Hours: Call to make a reservation for tours. The Discovery Tour departs at 9am and 1pm.

Price: The Discovery tour is $375 for up to 5 passengers. The three-hour Santa Ynez Mountain Tour is $89 per person, with a four person minimum.

Ages: Must be at least 6 years old.

CONDOR EXPRESS CRUISES

(888) 77WHALE (779-4253) or (805) 882-0088 / www.condorcruises.com; www.sealanding.net

301 W. Cabrillo Boulevard at Sea Landing, Santa Barbara

$$$$$

Board the *Condor Express*, a seventy-five-foot, double deck, full-service bar and galley, high-speed catamaran to look for gray whales from mid-February through mid-May. A naturalist explains what you see and why you are seeing it on the two-and-a-half hour excursions. Take a four-and-a-half hour trip to the Channel Islands the rest of the year to watch for blue whales and humpbacks, as well as numerous other marine mammals. You'll probably also get to check out the Painted Cave on Santa Cruz Island.

Hours: Gray whale watching trips are daily, in season, at 9am, noon, and 3pm. Cruises out to the islands are offered daily, weather permitting, at 10am.

Price: Gray whale excursions are $50 for adults; $30 for ages 5-12; children 4 and under are free. Island excursions are $89 for adults most of the year ($99 in the summer); $50 for ages 5 - 12; children 4 and under are free. Parking in beach lot is $2 an hour; $12 max; $3 with validation.

Ages: 6 years and up for most cruises.

LAND AND SEA TOURS

(805) 683-7600 / www.out2seesb.com

10 East Cabrillo Boulevard, Santa Barbara

$$$$
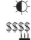

Land Shark! This oversized, forty-nine passenger, odd-looking "bus," or boat with wheels, is amphibious, meaning it is capable of operating on both land and water. Your wonderful, ninety-minute, narrated tour starts off on land, traveling up and down the streets of Santa Barbara and the waterfront, seeing and assimilating information and anecdotes about the history, culture, and people of this town, both past and present. You'll pass by the Moreton Bay Fig tree, historic adobes, the Courthouse, and more landmarks, as well as travel along State Street.

The last half hour is spent in the water - it's a fun adventure just feeling the vehicle dip in! You'll navigate the harbor and hear how it was formed via dredging, learn about the commercial fishing industry, float past expensive yachts and Stearns Wharf, and cruise out to the seal lions. You might see some dolphins, too. Keep an eye out for the various sea birds, such as egrets, gulls, and pelicans.

Throughout your adventure, the captain keeps you well-informed on your surroundings in an entertaining

manner. Visual aids are also incorporated, such as charts and sea urchins, making this an ideal excursion for both kids and adults. Bring a light jacket, regardless of the time of year.

Hours: Tours usually depart daily November - April at noon and 2pm; May - October at noon, 2pm, and 4pm. Trips may be sold out in advance, so call first. Private bookings may call to schedule departure at other times.

Price: $25 for adults; $15 for ages 10 and under; children under 2 are free. Parking at the beach is $2 an hour; $12 max.

Ages: 5 years and up.

METROPOLITAN TRANSIT DISTRICT

(805) 963-3366 - transit center; (805) 683-3364 - bs. office / www.sbmtd.gov $
1020 Chapala Street, Santa Barbara

Catch the inexpensive MTD service that runs from the waterfront to over ten highlights of Santa Barbara, including the Mission, the Botanic Garden, County Courthouse, and Museum of Art. The transit runs from Carpinteria to Goleta. The address given above is for the main station. Pick up a schedule here, on any MTD bus, or online.

Hours: Open daily. Call for hours and scheduled stops. No service on Thanksgiving or Christmas.

Price: One-way fare is $1.75; a day pass is $6. Children under 45" area free.

Ages: All

SANTA BARBARA SAILING CENTER / DOUBLE DOLPHIN CRUISE

(805) 962-2826 / www.sbsail.com $$$$
133 Harbor Way, Santa Barbara

Almost anything water-oriented is offered here. Single kayaks rent for $10 an hour, $5 for college students; double kayaks are $15, $10 for college students. Pedal boats are $20 for an hour. Stand-Up paddle boards are $15 an hour. For rowing champs, rent a rowing scull at $20 an hour. A 22' Capri sailing boat is $50 an hour. For all boats rentals, include $2 to $5 per boat for insurance. Two-and-a-half, narrated whale-watching cruises are available seasonally, mid-February through mid-May for $33 for adults; $11 for college students; $15 for ages 12 and under. On this tour also be on the lookout for dolphins, sea lions, and seals.

Other cruises include a two-hour, buffet-style, sunset dinner cruise, offered Saturday and Sunday evenings April through September at 5pm for $65 for adults, $35 for ages 12 and under. Sunset cruises (no food), are offered at selected times year round, for $27 for adults, $11 for college students. Reservations must be made by 2pm the day of the cruise.

Kids and adults can also learn the ropes of sailing by taking a class, so why *knot*? The center also offers classes on kayaking, plus kids camps, and more. Call for a full schedule.

Hours: The Sailing Center is open daily, March - October, 9am - 6pm; November - February, 9am - 5pm. Whale watching cruises depart daily during the season at 10am and 1pm, although these hours can change.

Price: Some prices are given above. Parking in beach lot is $2 an hour; $12 max; $3 with validation.

Ages: 6 years and up, depending on excursion.

SANTA BARBARA SOARING

(805) 688-2517 / www.sbsoaring.com $$$$$
900 Airport Road, Santa Ynez

Talk about quietly soaring above it all! A breath-taking sensation and scenery adds up to an unforgettable experience as you lift off and up in the two or three-seater glider plane with amazing wingspans. It's like sailing in the sky. It is *almost* as much fun to bring a blanket and some snacks to just watch the pilots and passengers. (Call first to see if anyone is flying, though.)

Hours: Flights are usually offered Sat. - Sun., 10am - 5pm, but call to make a reservation.

Price: $149 for a 10 - 15-minute, 2,500 feet above sea level Scenic Flight with a view of the Santa Ynez Valley and a little beyond; $219 per person for 15 - 20-minute Mountain Adventure; $299 for 5,200 feet, 30-minute Mile High adventure to see the entire Central Coast and points inland.

Ages: 14 years and up to fly; all ages to watch.

SANTA BARBARA TROLLEY COMPANY

(805) 965-0353 / www.sbtrolley.com

22 State Street, Santa Barbara

Clang, dang, dang goes the trolley! Come aboard and see the highlights of Santa Barbara while hearing its history and hearing anecdotes about the town and some of its citizens. Take the ninety-minute narrated tour nonstop, or stop off at Stearns Wharf, the Mission, the Courthouse, downtown (to shop), and/or numerous other places, and reboard any time throughout the day at no extra cost. Remember, too, that for kids, a traditional trolley ride is part of the excursion fun.

Hours: Trolley tours operate daily, leaving once an hour from each of the 15 destinations, starting at 10am to about 5pm. Note that the last 2 tours of the day may have no return trip to pick-up location.

Price: $19 for adults; one child 12 and under is free with each paid adult; additional child day pass is $8; infants are free if they are sitting on your lap. Sometimes the second consecutive day is free. Ask about family deals or check online for discounts for area attractions with the purchase of a trolley ticket. Parking at the beach lot is $2 an hour; $12 max.

Ages: 3 years and up.

SANTA BARBARA WATER TAXI / LIL TOOT

(805) 896-6900 or (888) 316-9363 / www.sbwatertaxi.com

Stearns Wharf off W. Cabrillo Boulevard, Santa Barbara

Board *Lil Toot,* which looks like a tug boat, for a fun, half-hour roundtrip or fifteen minutes one-way excursion in the harbor of Santa Barbara. You'll start (or end) at Stearns Wharf, go past the Sea Center, the pier, and restaurants along the waterfront, and out to the breakwater - what a fantastic view! You'll learn a little local history along the way of the area, the sea life, and the shore birds. Get your cameras ready as kids get to play jr. captain and steer the boat (briefly) and sound the boat's steam whistle. You also cruise among the yachts (some worth millions of dollars) and sailboats at the marina. You can also start (or end) at the harbor near the Maritime Museum, at the end of Harbor Way.

Hours: Open daily, noon - sunset. Shuttles run every half hour.

Price: One-way fare is $4 for adults; $1 for ages 3 - 12; children 2 and under are free. Parking is free for 90 minutes with validation at either boarding point.

Ages: 2 years and up.

SANTA BARBARA WATERFRONT / DOWNTOWN SHUTTLE

(805) 963-3366 / www.sbmtd.gov; www.santabarbara.com

Catch the Waterfront Shuttle, an electric, open-air bus as it runs between the Santa Barbara Zoo and the harbor, along the waterfront, every thirty minutes. The Downtown Shuttle runs the gamut of State Street, from Sola Street to Stearns Wharf, every thirty minutes. Transfers between the two are free, so both are great, cheap, car-less options to get around, making the journey and the destination fun highlights.

Hours: Runs daily, 9am - 6pm.

Price: 50¢ per person; 25¢ for seniors; children 45" and under are free.

Ages: All

SANTA MARIA SPEEDWAY

805-315-2023 / www.racesantamariaspeedway.com

1900 Hutton Road, Santa Maria

Factory stocks, street stocks, sprint cars, minis, and more take to the track seasonally bringing excitement (and noise!) to spectators. The one-third-mile day surface oval track has a three-foot-high concrete crash wall encircling it and a row of trees at the ridgeline, behind the bleachers, that provide a natural windbreak.

Hours: Open April - October on most Sat. nights - the gates open at 3pm; races start at 6pm.

Price: $8 - $25, depending on race and date.

Ages: 5 years and up.

SEA LANDING

(805) 963-3564 or (888) 77WHALE (779-4253) / www.sealanding.com

301 W. Cabrillo Boulevard at Sea Landing, Santa Barbara

Sea Landing is the hub for renting kayaks and jet skis, as well as reserving boat tours for TRUTH AQUATICS (pg. 649) and CONDOR EXPRESS (pg. 646). Jet skis rentals, only available in the summer, are $135 per hour. Kayak rentals, available all year, are for three hours - $15 for a single, $25 for a tandem.

Hours: Open daily, 7:30am - 6pm. Closed some holidays.
Price: See above.
Ages: 6 years and up.

SUNSET KIDD SAILING

(805) 962-8222 / www.sunsetkidd.com

$$$$$

125 Harbor Way, Santa Barbara

Sailing cruises have a whole different feel than that of a more typical, large, noisy passenger cruise. Experience the sea waters on a two-hour morning or afternoon sail; two-and-a-half-hours on a whale watching cruise, available mid-February through mid-May; or ninety-minutes for a lovely sunset cruise.

Hours: Cruises usually set sail most of the year Mon. and Wed. - Sun., at 10am and 2pm, but call for departure times. Closed Tues.
Price: $40 per person. On the morning whale watching cruises, ages 4 - 10 are $25; ages 3 and under are free. Parking in beach lots varies by lot - one is $2 an hour; $12 max.
Ages: 8 years and up.

TRUTH AQUATICS

(805) 962-1127 or (805) 963-3564 - reservation center / www.truthaquatics.com; www.sealanding.net

$$$$$

301 W. Cabrillo Boulevard at Sea Landing, Santa Barbara

This trusted company, in business since 1974, has a fleet of three boats that are primarily designed as dive boats, although anyone will enjoy a single- or multi-day (overnight) excursion to the Channel Islands, particularly Anacapa, Santa Cruz and Santa Rosa islands. The company also specializes in kayaking and standup paddle board trips around the islands and partners with other companies that offer naturalist-guided boating tours as well as hiking tours inland. These are incredible, not-to-be-missed excursions! Snorkeling, kayaking, jet boat, and jet sky equipment rentals can be taken care of before your trip at Sea Landing, the reservation center for Truth Aquatics. See CHANNEL ISLANDS NATIONAL PARK (from Ventura), on page 668, for more information on the chain of islands just off the coast.

Hours: Trips to the Channel Islands depart on selected dates, usually at 8am. Call or check the website.
Price: Prices start at $90 for adults; $50 for ages 12 and under. Rentals are extra. Call for more details. Parking in beach lot is $2 an hour; $12 max.
Ages: 7 years and up.

WHEEL FUN RENTALS

(805) 966-2282 / www.wheelfunrentalssb.com

$$$

22 State Street, Santa Barbara

If you forgot to bring your own, you can still have some *wheel* along Santa Barbara's bike paths and harbor by renting transportation with wheels. Mountain bikes are $11 an hour; $10 for a cruiser; $8 for kids bike; $20 for tandems; and $29 for a single surrey; $39 for a double. They also rent roller blades, boogie boards, wheel chairs, and more. This company has multiple locations in Santa Barbara and throughout Southern California.

Hours: Open November - February, daily, 8am - 6pm; open April - October, daily, 8am - 8pm.
Price: Prices are listed above.
Ages: 3 years and up.

YOUNG EAGLES PROGRAM (Santa Barbara County)

National number - (877) 806-8902; Santa Barbara - (805) 967-2943 - chapter #527; Santa Ynez - (805) 688-3169 - chapter #491 / www.youngeagles.org

Santa Barbara - 45 Hartley Road; Santa Ynez - 900 Airport Road

See the entry for YOUNG EAGLES PROGRAM (Los Angeles County) on page 215 for details.

Hours: Santa Barbara - The program doesn't have set times as it is by reservation only, so call to schedule a time to be flying high! Santa Ynez - Offered usually once in the spring and once in the fall - call for exact dates and times.

Price: Free

Ages: 8 - 17 years.

—ZOOS AND ANIMALS—

CABRILLO HIGH SCHOOL AQUARIUM
(805) 742-2888 / www.cabrilloaquarium.org
4350 Constellation Road, Lompoc

This is an impressive aquarium, especially for a high school campus! The aquarium is composed of several large tanks, a few smaller ones, a theater, computers, murals, and static models fish. Murals, located in a city renowned for its murals, are depictions of Pacific Blue whales, of the local coastline, of the underwater kelp forest with local animals, and of the tropical rainforest. Aquatic-related photographs and artwork also decorate the room. Fish "swimming" overhead include a full-sized dolphin and a ten-foot model of a Great White Shark. Computers record every angle of the aquarium and are available to use for research.

One tank holds jellyfish. Actually, they're called moon jellies, and they look other-worldly. The warm water reef tank is visually exciting because the coral habitat holds brilliantly-colored fish such as clown fish, yellow tangs, damselfish, rainbow wrasse, and firefish. Two tanks hold sea horses, one for potbelly sea horses and another for tropical, lined sea horses. Crustaceans, such as spiny lobsters and crabs, are in another tank; one Pacific spiny lobster is fifteen pounds and eighty-years-old! The tropical marine life tank showcases puffer fish, angelfish, several wrasse, and brittle stars. Other containers hold bass, eels, perch, and sea anemones. An incubator is really a nursery for the main in house food source - brine shrimp. A light shines through swell shark egg casings enabling visitors to see shark embryos. Marine life, such as sea cucumbers, sea stars, and sea urchins, are in a touch tank. The outside of the state-of-the-art, thirty-five-seat theater resembles a weathered lighthouse. Inside, various films are shown on the screen that can also be used as touch screen.

Community outreach programs and tours for schools and other groups are available by reservation.

Hours: Usually open once a month to the public. Call for date and time or to book a tour.

Price: Free

Ages: 3 years and up.

HARBOR SEAL PRESERVE
www.carpinteria.com
at the end of Bailard Avenue, Carpinteria

Seal lovers enjoy a stop-off at this bluff-top observation point. Although the seals are here year long, the best viewing is December through May, during pupping season. (Although one never *really* knows when the seals will decide to visit.) For the half-mile trek, take the CARPINTERIA BLUFFS NATURE PRESERVE AND TRAIL (see page 608) dirt trail south towards the beach, hang a right, follow the path south over the railroad tracks, and go right. (This is not a stroller/wheelchair friendly excursion.) The rookery is located at the south end of the pier - look for its sign and a bench. Note - it is illegal to walk on this section of beach from December through May.

Essentially, you just look down below at the seals, sunning themselves on the beach or splashing around in the water, and listen to their bellows. You can also take the trail and hike north, about two and a half miles round trip, to reach CARPINTERIA STATE BEACH. (pg. 598 for details.)

Hours: Open daily, sunrise - sunset.

Price: Free

Ages: 5 years and up.

OSTRICH LAND USA
(805) 686-9696 / www.ostrichlandusa.com
610 E. Hwy. 246, Buellton

What are the differences between an ostrich and an emu? Stop by and see for yourself! Ostrichland has about fifty

ostriches roaming around in a twenty-acre endosure just off the highway. Pay your money and go behind the store on the walkway in front of the ranch to get a doser peek (not a doser peck). You can also purchase ostrich feed ($1) to bring them within breathing distance. Although you won't be here long (maybe 20 minutes), it's a good opportunity to see ostriches and the ten, or so, emus, which are in a separate endosure, up dose.

Ostriches, one of the world's largest birds, lay equally huge eggs: One ostrich egg is equivalent to about twenty-four chicken eggs. (We purchased one and invited the neighborhood over for a huge omelet.) The small produce stand/gift shop here, which is Ostrich Land's main business, offers fresh ostrich eggs, emu eggs (which are avocado green in color and available in the winter and spring), ostrich meat (which doesn't come from the ostriches on this ranch), feathers, and other ostrich products. A small selection of seasonal fruits and vegetables are also available here. A parting thought: If you are what you eat, consider that ostriches can run forty-five mph, they can live to 100 years old, and they breed three times a day.

Hours: Open most of the year daily, 10am - 5pm.
Price: $4 for adults; $1 for ages 12 and under.
Ages: 3 years and up.

QUICKSILVER RANCH

(805) 686-4002 / www.qsminis.com
1555 Alamo Pintado Road, Solvang

Question: What's small and says "neigh"? Answer: Miniature horses. Quicksilver Ranch is a working breeding facility and home to over eighty miniature horses. (A horse must not exceed thirty-four inches to be registered as a miniature.) The small "so cute!" horses romp and graze in the twenty acres of lush, grassy endosures. Even young visitors will enjoy strolling the grounds as they can get up dose and personal with the animals because the pens are down-scaled. Oftentimes a handler brings out a horse to pet. Please keep in mind that this is not a petting zoo and don't bring food to feed the horses. If you want to see baby miniature horses (making them mini minis), twenty to thirty are usually born during the months of April, May, and June. Note: You'll drive past goats and full-size horses that live on adjacent ranches.

Hours: Open Mon. - Sat., 10am - 3pm. Closed Sun., Thanksgiving and Christmas.
Price: Free.
Ages: 3 years and up.

RETURN TO FREEDOM WILD HORSE SANCTUARY

(805) 737-9246 / www.returntofreedom.org
4115 Jalama Road, Lompoc

$$$$

Picture wild horses running with abandon through tall grasses, past oak trees, and over hills; their manes and tails flowing behind them. Welcome to Return to Freedom, where almost 400 wild mustangs, the last true vestiges of the American West, roam the grounds with their natural (and diverse) herds or family groups on this 310-acre ranch sanctuary. The sanctuary's goals are to preserve these majestic mustangs in their natural habitat and to educate visitors through direct encounters with them. Children and adults have the rare opportunity to observe the wild horses (and their colts) on their own turf, to gently and respectfully approach them, and to develop compassion as they learn the history (and hopefully the future) of the horses. Be prepared to do some walking over hilly terrain and to have romanticized images of cowboy roundups revamped.

Though most of the horses live in herds that free-range the hills, a few of the horses are in open-air paddocks. Some of these animals have come from abusive owners and need special care or supplements. One horse, however, has had a starring role. The beautiful stallion used as the model for Disney's animated movie *Spirit, Stallion of Cimarron* has been retired and now lives at the ranch. Other animals that consider the sanctuary home include burros and a few goats and chickens.

Most "tours" start in the barn area/learning center. Depending on the type of tour, visitors can watch a video about the sanctuary; see maps of where the horse herds are located; hear about the history of the horses, which are descendants of the Spanish conquistador's horses; learn about the government's role in the harsh treatment of mustangs; and learn horse behavior such as grooming, communication, social structure, head tosses, and how a lead horse acts. The two-hour Living History Tours, geared for ages 9 and up, covers this information, plus a walk to the hills to see the horses.

The over three hour Wild Horse Walk (for ages 12 and up, only), entails similar features of the Living History Tours, but more hiking into the hills and the herds, quiet observation of the horses, examination of herd behavior, and perhaps interacting with them, if the horses invite it. Kid's Day at the Ranch is for ages 8 to 16 years, where kids can help out at the ranch feed them, cleaning up manure, grooming the tamer animals, and other ranch chores. Volunteering opportunities for older kids and for adults are available on Volunteer Work Days, the second Saturday of each month from 10am to 4pm. Volunteers do whatever needs to be done - weeding, carpentry, cleaning manure, painting, repairing fences, prepping for events, whatever! A short walk to see the herds is included at the end. Three-hour Photo Safaris, led by an equine photographer, is a unique opportunity to photograph, and learn how to photograph, these beautiful animals. These are just some of the programs offered. If wild horses can't drag you here, hop in your mini van!

Hours: Tours are usually offered May - September: Living History Tours, the first and third Sat. of each month from 10am - 12pm; Wild Horse Walks are the second Sat. from 3:30pm - 6:30pm; Photo Safaris are offered the fourth Sat. Check the online calendar or call for other tours, events, and information.

Price: Living History tours are $25 for adults; $10 for children 12 and under. Kid's Day is $45 per adult/child pair; $15 for each additional child, adult, friend, etc. The Wild Horse Walk is $75 for adults; $20 for ages 12 - 16. Photo Safaris are $150. Call for other event prices.

Ages: 7 years and up, depending on the tour.

SANTA BARBARA POLO

(805) 684-6683 or (805) 684-5819; (805) 684-3093 - clubhouse / www.sbpolo.com
3300 Via Real, Carpinteria

Watching a polo game was an unexpectedly enthralling event. At the start, eight players, four per team, astride their thoroughbreds with long mallets in hand, loosely gathered around the mounted umpire who bowled in the ball. Whack! A player swung the mallet in an arch, connected with the ball and sent it down the field as the other players galloped in pursuit. Each horse and rider pair ran, pivoted, stopped, and maneuvered their way up and down the court with skill and finesse, racing each other, side by side. FYI - the beautifully manicured field is three football fields in length.

We learned a new word, "chukker," which is the seven minutes of playing time per period. There are six chukkers per game, with four minutes in-between each one. At the ten-minute half-time, everyone is invited out onto the field for a Divot Stomp - stomping to help replace the divots (and to run around and socialize, plus a free glass of champagne is included - for adults). Grandstand seats are not shaded at all, so bring sunscreen. They are first come, first served.

Bring your own food to have a tailgate party, or order food from the adjacent snack bar which offers burgers, salads, sandwiches, hot dogs, soda, and more. The clubhouse restaurant, also attached to the stands, is for members only. Note that the club offers polo classes for adults and youth, as well as summer camps.

Hours: Polo season runs May - mid-October. Tournament games are sometimes played on Fri. and Sat., but usually played on Sun. at 1pm and 3pm; gates open at noon. Practice games are sometimes held on Thurs. or Sat.

Price: $10 per person for tournament games; free for the practices.

Ages: 6 years and up.

SANTA BARBARA ZOO

(805) 962-6310 - recording; (805) 962-5339 - live person, Mon. - Fri. or (805) 963-5695 on weekends. / www.sbzoo.org
500 Niños Drive, Santa Barbara

This engaging, mid-size zoo lives up to the zoological gardens part of its description in that the over 500 animals in naturalistic settings dwell in and amongst a myriad of lush plants.

Brightly-colored macaws, although centralized in the parrot garden, are also found in several locations throughout the zoo. The flamingoes have their own lagoon area. Walk through the tropical aviary to view more beautiful birds. For $2 you can feed the red, purple, blue, and green lorikeets, or just go into their aviary and watch them land on your arm or head. Bring a camera!

The nocturnal hall contains a sloth and other nighttime animals. The aquarium and reptile complex houses some unique creatures, such as snake-necked turtles and a matamata turtle with its snorkel-like nose and lizard-like head and neck. A python, some bats, various types of frogs, Madagascar hissing cockroaches, stingrays, and arowana fish - with their fish heads and eel-like bodies - are also in here.

Look at the sea lions, with both above and below ground viewing. Feeding time is usually from 1pm to 2pm. The playful River Otters are also fun to watch, especially at feeding time, which happens four times a day. You can hear the gibbons screeching and hooting before actually reaching their endosure. The Lowland Gorillas, meerkats, anteater, Asian elephants, coatimundi, alligators, monkeys, and even penguins are not only fascinating to observe, but easy to see as their habitats are relatively small. Watch the big cats (lions, snow leopards, Amur leopards, etc.) pace, play around, or indulge in their favorite activity - sleep. Usually on weekends you can hand feed the giraffes from the Giraffe Deck for $6 per person. (Their tongues are long, black, and a little bit sticky!)

A small playground has large, pretend, dinosaur eggs to play in, a rope spider web to climb, an anthill to act like a roly poly and roll down, and more. You can also pet and feed ($2) llamas, goats, and sheep through the fence at the Barnyard. A carousel with wooden animals to ride on costs $1 and is usually open Wednesday through Sunday, 11am to 2pm. For an additional $5 for adults, $4.50 for ages 2 to 12 (children under 2 are free), hop on board a mini train (which is handicap accessible) for a ten-minute ride around the perimeter of the zoo. Picnic grounds are just around the corner and you are allowed to bring outside food inside.

Ask about the zoo's numerous age-appropriate workshops, geared for tiny tots up to junior zookeepers. Other interactive zoo happenings include camp outs, which means spending the night at the zoo and meeting some of the animals, especially nocturnal ones; breakfast with the animals, for members only; behind-the-scenes tours; Backstage Pass, a ninety-minute program for ages 5 and up to work alongside a zookeeper, see how they are cared for, and/or feed some of them - it's all up close and personal; discovery kits for classroom use; and Theater Gone Wild. This theater group puts on performances both at the zoo, and at school or Scout facilities. Note that the ANDREE CLARK BIRD REFUGE (pg. 606) is just outside the zoo perimeter. Have a wild time at this great zoo!

Hours: Open daily, 10am - 5pm. Closed at 3:30pm on Thanksgiving, Christmas Eve., and Christmas.
Price: $15 for adults; $12 for seniors; $10 for ages 2 - 12; children under 2 are free. Parking is $6.
Ages: All

SEEIN' SPOTS FARM

(805) 688-2275 / www.seeinspotsfarm.com
2599 Baseline Avenue, Santa Ynez

This small, family-owned farm's main focus is raising and selling miniature donkeys, which are adorable! The public is invited to enter into the nice-sized petting farm which also has goats, turkeys, ducks (with a little rock-lined pond for them and a bridge), a pot-bellied pig, bunnies, and a giant tortoise. It also has some stone animals to play on, a tractor tire, benches and picnic tables. Definitely check out the unique looking zonkey, which is yes, a cross between a zebra and a donkey. Come with your family or come on a field trip for more of an educational visit. Pick apples here in season and purchase farm fresh eggs anytime. Children can even ride the donkeys for $5.

Hours: Open Wed. - Sun., 10am - 3pm.
Price: By donation - $5 for the family or $3 for individuals is suggested.
Ages: All

TY WARNER SEA CENTER

(805) 962-2526 or (805) 682-4711 / www.sbnature.org
211 Stearns Wharf off W. Cabrillo Boulevard, Santa Barbara

This mid-size, two-story Center, a satellite of the Santa Barbara Museum of Natural History, adds to the *see*worthiness of the wharf. Inside, life-sized models of a California gray whale and her calf are suspended from the ceiling. The simulated tide pool exhibit, where small waves ebb and flow, allows visitors to look at the surface water and to look under the water by crawling through an acrylic-walled viewing tunnel. There are several small "demonstration stations" staffed by knowledgeable volunteers enabling guests to learn about and touch sea stars, sea anemones, urchins, and even small sharks (bite size ones!). One tank in this area holds a live octopus. A larger one contains a Garibaldi (which is the California state fish, but you knew that), rockfish, lobster, ray, and brown smoothhound. The almost glowing jellies floating and undulating up and down are also on exhibit. I appreciate the step

stools everywhere so that younger ones can readily view the animals. The stools also make it easier for them to touch the sea shells and examine particles of sea life (or their own fingers, as kids are wont to do) under microscopes.

The Bio Lab is set up like a working marine laboratory that allows tactile encounters of sea cucumbers and up close observation of swell sharks and other inhabitants. In the back room is a Wet Deck, which means you peer down through an opening in the floor to the water below. Using research equipment, you may help dredge, collect, and sift through samples of the water, sediments, and whatever else gets captured. You might be surprised at what tiny creatures you see. Make sure you open the lockers placed throughout the Center. As you do, you'll hear a recording about the person pictured on the front - what they do and why they became a marine biologist or oceanographer. You'll also see some of the tools of their trade and some personal belongings.

Upstairs you can test water, via a video magnifier, for salinity, pH balance, and temperature. A small theater continuously shows a short film on the sea life in the Santa Barbara channel. Can you sound like an angry orca? How about a romantic sea lion? Tucked in the nook of a wall is a computer kiosk, known as Whale Karaoke. Here you select a mammal, then an emotion, and push play for that recorded sound. Mimic and record your own take on the sound and watch as the computer matches the comparison graphically. One profound exhibit is a preserved pregnant female dolphin who washed on shore. A segment of her is cut away to expose her internal organs and her baby. (Don't get real close because she does have a stench.) While you're up here, don't forget to check out the view of the coastline and ocean.

Even if you live by the sea, you might not know a lot about it or its creatures. The Sea Center offers the opportunity to remedy that in a fairly intimate setting. School tours, birthday parties, and other groups and individuals are welcome. Look up SANTA BARBARA HARBOR / STEARNS WHARF (pg. 637) for details about the immediate area.

Hours: Open daily, 10am - 5pm. Closed first Friday in August for Old Spanish Days Fiesta, as well as New Year's Day, Thanksgiving, Christmas Eve (at noon), and Christmas Day.

Price: $8 for adults; $7 for seniors and ages 13 - 17; $5 for ages 2 - 12; children under 2 are free. A nature pass, allowing admission here and to the Santa Barbara Museum of Natural History on two consecutive days, is $16 for adults; $11 for seniors and teens; $9 for ages 2 - 13. Parking is free for the first ninety minutes with validation. Otherwise, parking in beach lot is about $2 an hour; $12 max. There is some free street parking. Parking on the pier is about $2 an hour.

Ages: 3 years and up.

WHALE WATCHING

See the TRANSPORTATION section.

VENTURA COUNTY

Located between two major tourist markets, Los Angeles and Santa Barbara, Ventura County is a low-key, but worthy destination. As coastal fog along the shores of Oxnard and Ventura lift, the distant Channel Islands are unveiled. Take a cruise out to them. Walk along Main Street in Ventura for a cluster of attractions, as well as some terrific shopping. Inland and northward are the towns of Ojai, with its refined atmosphere, and Santa Paula, with its mid-West open-door policy, but better weather than that part of the U.S.

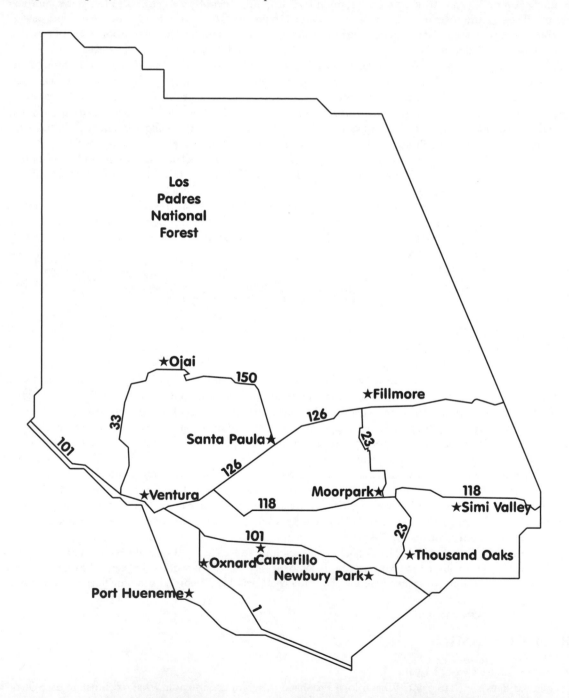

—AMUSEMENT PARKS—

CASITAS WATER ADVENTURE

(805) 649-2233 / www.lakecasitas.info
11311 Santa Ana Road, Ventura

This small, but refreshing water park is located inside LAKE CASITAS RECREATION AREA (pg. 672). The main component of the water park is a spacious, multi-level, colorful, water play area with six slides, chutes, climbing structures, wheels to turn to adjust the water spray, anchored squirt guns, and water spurting out of its pipes - all in only eighteen inches of water. Although designed for children 10 years and under, kids on the upper end of this spectrum will probably find this wading pool too tame. Several lifeguards patrol the pool.

Visitors can also cool off by taking an inner tube ride around on a slow moving "river" that winds through the nicely-landscaped water park. You'll go under bridges, and through waterfalls and jet sprays. Two other small, water play areas contain waterfalls, fountains, and umbrellas that pour water over their sides, deluging those underneath.

Relax on the adjacent grassy areas on the lounge chairs that surround this aquatic playground. A concession stand sells snacks, drinks, and ice cream. Locker rentals are available. Note: If your younger child is not quite potty trained, swim diapers are available to purchase here. Proper swimwear is required for all ages.

Hours: The lake and most amenities are open daily, sunrise - sunset. The water playground is open on weekends only, Memorial Day weekend, mid-August - Labor Day, 11am - 6pm. It is open June - mid-August, Sun. - Thurs., 11am - 6pm; Fri. - Sat., 11am - 7pm.

Price: Most of the year, entrance to the lake is $10 per vehicle; but Easter weekend through Labor Day, on weekends and holidays, it's $15. There is some free parking just outside the main entrance gate. The water playground is an additional $12 per person; children 1 year and under are free. After 5pm, the price drops to $5.

Ages: 1 year and up.

—ARTS AND CRAFTS—

CREATE STUDIO

(818) 575-9566 / www.createstudiofun.com
31826-B Village Center Road, Westlake Village

I walked into Create Studio and immediately exclaimed, "Yes!" The mid-size room exudes inspiration and space for creativity. Paint-splattered tables and benches are in the center while the walls (titled the Wall of Wow) are lined with bins and bins of art projects waiting to happen. They are filled with all sorts of recycled and craft items - buttons, hangars, yarn, bottles, glitter, pom poms, corks, paper punches, plastic thingamajigs (personal favorite), puzzle pieces, cardboard, ribbon, fabric, paint, broken pottery - you get the picture. Aprons, smocks, markers, glue, paint brushes and even easels for those who "just" want to paint are all supplied - all that's missing is you and your kids. Come in to design and craft an open-ended art something or come to work on a school project. Create Studio actually gives back $1 of each student's studio fee to their school if they work on a school appointed project. This studio is like the art space you'd like to set up at home, but you don't have the wide variety of materials available and you want your house to stay clean. Crafters on the go can purchase an Eco Craft Kit consisting of over forty different, new and recycled items packaged in a gallon container for $14 per can.

Hours: Open Tues. - Fri., 11am - 6p; Sat., noon - 5pm. Closed Sun., Mon. and certain holidays.

Price: $13 for adults; $11 for ages 13 - 19; $9 for ages 6 - 12; $7 for toddlers - 5 years. The price includes two hours of studio time and all the materials available. Parents are welcome to assist their kids at no charge.

Ages: 3 years and up.

FIREFLY CERAMICS

(805) 650-1468
1580 Saratoga Avenue, Unit-C, Ventura

Choices, choices - what to paint? What colors? Free-hand design or use a stencil? What size brush to use? Give

the finished product to someone or keep it? Painting your own ceramic piece is supposed to be a stress-free activity! Actually, creating a unique keepsake together with your child is time well spent. Choose from an array of items, decorative and practical, including dinnerware, animal banks, plant stakes, boxes, vases, figurines, and more. It will be glazed, fired, and ready to pick up in just a few days. Precut frames, plaques, clocks, and mirrors can also be purchased to fill in with glass or tile pieces also sold at Firefly. Inquire about summer camp art classes and year-round school fields trips.

Hours: Open Mon. - Sat., 10am - 7pm; Sun., 10am - 4pm. Closed holidays.
Price: The cost of the pieces, plus a studio fee of $7 for adults; $4 for ages 10 and under.
Ages: 4 years and up.

FISH CERAMICS

(805) 581-1109 / www.fishceramics.com
2360 Shasta Way, Unit H, Simi Valley

$$$$

This good-sized studio, which has been in business for over 25 years, focuses on offering a wide variety of classes such as airbrush, clay gourds and pots, glass jewelry, Raku, piping and brush strokes, glass wind chimes, and much more. Visitors are welcome to sign up for a class, join in an open workshop with instructors on hand, or simply "paint-and-go". Set up with long tables and folding chairs, the surrounding shelves are packed with a bonanza of cast greenware, bisque ceramics, and other items. All of the standard tools - brushes, paints, glazes are here, as well as accessories such as lamp cords, sockets, and even fountain pumps needed to complete a project. Note that Girl Scout badges can be earned here.

Hours: Open workshop hours are usually Tues., Wed., Fri., 10am - 5pm; Thurs., 10am - 8pm; Sat., 9am - 5pm. Call first as classes are scheduled at certain times. Closed Sun., Mon., and major holidays.
Price: Paint-and-go (bisque) is $6 per person, plus the cost of an item. Glazing and firing is included. Call for class cost and info.
Ages: 5 years and up.

MAKE MEANING

(805) 852-1107 / www.makemeaning.com
196 W. Hillcrest, Suite #99, in The Oaks Mall, Thousand Oaks

$$$$

Make Meaning(ful) memories while crafting a fun project at this innovative and colorful store. One wall has a section for each different activity offered. It is filled with baskets and containers of items devoted to giving you the all the creative materials and inspiration you need for designing your finished product of a candle, soap, ceramic piece, glassware, or a cake! **Soap Making**: From tasty-looking cupcake soaps to luxury soaps (with jojoba beads, lavender, oatmeal, loofa and other exfoliates and scents, plus customized monogramming) to Soaprizes (toys inside), getting clean has never been so fun. Choose from wide a variety of shapes, colors, toys, and much more - kids will actually want to take a bath. **Candle Making**: Light a fire of "I-can-do-this" by allowing kids to create a very personalized mosaic candle by placing cubes of colored wax and other shapes into the mold. Scents can be added, wax is poured to fill it in, and you can still add an assortment of small candle figures for the top such as flowers, ice cream cones, balloons, cats, and much more. What a great gift idea! **Glasswear and Glassware**: From something as simple as a coaster to a slightly more difficult ring or necklace to a more complex product of a vase or platter, a lovely variety of pre-cut glass shapes and colors can be used to create masterpieces. The glass is then fired and slumped (i.e. fused and shaped over molds) to be picked up in about four days. Glass classes are for ages 9 years and up. **Ceramics**: One option, ideal for anything that could involve food touching it, or for a glossier, baked-on finish, is to choose from a plethora of ceramic objects, such as plates, cups, etc. Paint and/or stencil it, and have it fired for later pick up. Another option, for a last minute gift or for the impatient, is to choose pre-fired, non-food related bisque items, such as picture frames, figurines, banks, and more. Paint and stencil it and take it home that day. Everything is supplied - paints, brushes, and even help. **Cake Decorating** - Happy birthday; happy anniversary; happy whatever! This activity takes the cake as pre-baked four or six inch cakes, covered in fondant icing, are tasty backdrops for edible decorations of fondant-based shapes, edible glitter, edible markers, sprays, and more. Rolling pins, cookie cutters, dull knives and other shape-crafting objects are available to use, too. Note that there is also a glitter temporary tattoo area in the shop.

Pick out all the supplies, go to the other side of the large room to sit at tables and chairs, and Make Meaning. For candles and soap, go over to the Skinny Dip bar to see the project being dipped to cool and finished. Those items are

ready in twenty to forty-five minutes. Glass and ceramic items are ready in five days. You can take home your cake immediately. Walk-ins are always welcome, though making reservations is the best idea. Check the website for classes and events. Note that this store is in The Oaks Mall so there are plenty of fun eating and shopping options around.

Hours: Open Mon. - Thurs., 10am - 8pm; Fri. - Sat., 10am - 9pm; Sun., noon - 6pm.

Price: Soap - $15 and up; candle - $19 and up; glass - $29 and up; ceramics - $10 and up; cake - $39 and up.

Ages: 3 years and up.

PAINT A DREAM (Ventura County)

(805) 520-9500 / www.paintadream.com

1555 Simi Town Center Way #675 at Simi Valley Town Center, Simi Valley

See PAINT A DREAM (Los Angeles County) (pg. 8) for details.

Hours: Open Mon. - Fri., 11am - 8pm; Sat., 10am - 8pm; Sun., 11am - 6pm.

Price: $6 studio fee, plus the cost of your item.

Ages: 4 years and up.

PAINT PALS CLUBHOUSE

(805) 581-4676 / www.paintpalsclubhouse.com

1655 E. Los Angeles Avenue, Simi Valley

Clubhouses weren't this much fun when I was a kid! Paint Pals Clubhouse offers paint-your-own bisque, and more. One section has shelves full of items to paint. Popular items include sunflowers, pigs, jars with ceramic lids, magnets, and picture frames. Long tables in several sections of the store and all the paint, brushes, smocks, and other materials needed are supplied here to create a masterpiece - what a terrific activity!

But, while moms (this one, anyway) sometimes take longer to do a project than kids, there are plenty of other things here to keep the younger set busy. Karaoke is a popular option; whether or not children can actually sing on key seems to be irrelevant. This activity corner also has a few costumes for dressing up. Toward the back of the store is a small black-light maze, with tunnels, that kids enjoy going through and a shadow room where they can make "pictures" on the walls. Other things to do include standing in a giant ring and "blowing" a bubble around themselves; a few arcade games; and Critter Corner, where kids can stuff and fluff a teddy bear, dog, or other animal by picking out a furry animal "skin," and pressing the pedal of the stuffing machine. Viola! - a new best friend is formed. Note that Paint Pals also has a mobile unit where they will come to your party location.

Hours: Open during the school year, Tues. - Sun.,10am - 6pm. Closed Mon., except holiday Mon. Open in the summer daily, 10am - 6pm.

Price: $1 per child (toddlers, too) entrance fee up to 12 years; free to adults. Items cost from $3 on up, which includes use of the paints and other supplies. Karaoke is $1 for one song; $2 for 3 songs. Critter Corner animals are $6 and up; about $7.50 per outfit.

Ages: 3 years and up.

—BEACHES—

EL MATADOR STATE BEACH

(310) 589-3200 / www.lamountains.com

32215 Pacific Coast Highway, Malibu

This is one of a series of small, cove beaches and it is one of the best of the series. Topside are a few picnic tables with an incredible view. Take the dirt trail and steep steps way down to the beach below. There is sand there, but the standout features and main draws, besides the tidepools, are the rock formations on the beach and the sea caves contained within them. (Check out the "secret" passage at the northern end of the beach, but only during low tide!) This beach is great to explore and great for photo ops; no bull!

Hours: Open daily, 8am to sunset.

Price: $8 per vehicle at the drop box. Note that no change is given.

Ages: 4 years and up

MCGRATH STATE BEACH

(805) 968-1033 / www.parks.ca.gov
Harbor Boulevard, Oxnard

There are three main reasons to visit McGrath State Beach: two miles of beach, campsites right by the beach, and bird watching. The two mile stretch of beach and coastline water, dotted with sand dunes, is great for surfing and fishing. Swimming is O.K. here, you just need to be cautious of riptides. Each of the over 170 campsites has a fire ring and picnic table. The most desirable sections (i.e. those closest to the beach) are sites 35 to 37, 41 to 44, and 102 to 107. If you are a bird watcher, this is an ideal spot as over 240 bird species have been recorded here. Grassy areas next to the beach are great for running around and tossing a ball. Picnic tables are here, too, so bring a picnic lunch or dinner.

Hours: Open daily, sunrise - sunset.
Price: $10 per vehicle for day use. Camping starts at $35 a night for tent camping.
Ages: All

OXNARD BEACH PARK / OXNARD - MANDALAY BEACH

(805) 385-7950 / www.oxnardtourism.com; www.parks.ca.gov
1601 South Harbor Boulevard, Oxnard

This all-encompassing beach is where Southern Californians flock in the summer, and even throughout the year. The sizable grass area, ringed with palm trees, next to the parking lot, is perfect for running around and for picnicking. And the playground here is *masterfully* designed for kids to set sail on an adventurous playtime. There are two, huge pirate ships - metal outlines of ships that are filled in with ramps, bridges, lots of play cannons, chain ladders, several slides, speaking tubes, and plenty of play space under the ships as well as on them. There are masts and "pirate only" signs and the kids I observed were completely engaged in make believe. A few, good-sized fake boulders with rock climbing holdings in them; a sea serpent with his head and parts of his body out of the "water" to climb on; swings; animals on large springs to ride; a giant sea turtle; monkey bars; and more, plus a number of benches surrounding it, complete this park.

The pathway separating the lawn from the dunes and beach is ideal for biking, strolling, jogging, and blading. Just over the picturesque dunes (which are great backdrops for photos) is a broad and long stretch of sandy beach. Bring a volleyball to play on the sand courts, or tote a Frisbee, kite, boogie board, or bucket and shovel to enjoy your day of fun in the sun. Note that Rehab Point, adjacent to the park, provides wheelchair/stroller access through the dunes to the ocean.

Hours: Open daily, sunrise - sunset.
Price: Parking costs $1 an hour; $5 max.
Ages: All

POINT DUME STATE BEACH

(310) 457-8143; (805) 488-1827; (818) 597-9192 / www.parks.ca.gov
Westward Beach Road, just of PCH, Malibu

There are two parts, kind of, to this beach area. The free, northern one is a very long and fairly wide stretch of beach, with fine sand and several volleyball courts and nets, plus lifeguard stations. Be on the lookout for the dolphins that frequent these waters. A section of this beach parallels the road, then leads south to a paid area that is almost cove-like as it hugs part of the cliffs. A huge rocky point (hence the name, *Point* Dume) towers over this southern section of beach. We saw people repelling off this rock and there are, apparently, several climbing routes marked on it. Just a short drive down the road is POINT DUME NATURAL PRESERVE (see page 675).

Hours: Open daily, 6am - sunset
Price: Parking at the southern end of the state beach is $3 from 6am - 9am and 4pm - closing; $6 from 9am - 4pm. There is free street parking for the northern part of the beach.
Ages: All

PORT HUENEME BEACH PARK - SURFSIDE SEAFOOD (cafe)

(805) 986-6542 (805) 488-9533 - Surfside / www.ci.port-hueneme.ca.us; www.beachcalifornia.com
at the end of Ventura Road, by E. Surfside Dr., Port Hueneme

There is more to life in Port Hueneme than the Marines - there is marine life! A long fishing pier extends over the ocean. Kids like to race out to its end and play under it, during low tide, of course. This fifty-acre beach (therefore large and very wide) has several cement picnic tables with walls for wind breaks, a few swing sets and volleyball courts, sandy knolls, and a grassy area dotted with palm trees.

At the land end of the pier is an atypical snack bar - Surfside Seafood cafe. This hole-in-the-wall place, with only outside seating surrounded by plexi-glass to keep the wind out, serves up great sea food. Try Surfside's eight-piece breaded shrimp with fries for $14.95; lobster tacos, $12.95; lobster tail, $34.95; bacon cheeseburger, $6.95; corn dog with fries, $6.95; grilled chicken salad, $8.95; and some of our favorites - clam chowder in a bread bowl for $10.95, and two-piece fish and chips for $9.85. All you can eat fish and chips is every Wed., 4pm to 8pm for $10.95 for adults and $8.95 for ages 12 and under. Come here for dinner and watch the sunset. This restaurant's tiny shop also sells tackle and bait, summer beach products, and ice cream - all the beach essentials.

There is a bike/pedestrian path that goes along the beach front and across the road, hooking up to a trail along the green belt of Bubbling Springs Creek. This cement pathway is a lovely ride through green grasses and next to waters that are home to various types of sea birds. At the end of the bike route is a small park, Evergreen Springs Park. Travel a shorter distance, about midway, to arrive at MORANDA PARK (pg. 675).

Hours: Open daily, sunrise - sunset. Surfside is open daily, 10am - 8pm.
Price: Parking at the beach is $2 an hour, $8 max.
Ages: All

SAN BUENAVENTURA STATE BEACH / VENTURA PIER

(805) 968-1033 - park / www.parks.ca.gov
East Harbor Boulevard, Ventura

The best entrance point to the beach, heading southward from the pier on Harbor, is on San Pedro Street. The beach is fairly wide and very long - about two miles! Next to the parking lot is a sizable grass area lined with palm trees, plenty of picnic tables, barbecue pits, and showers. Walk over the dunes to get to the sand where you can frolic in the water and play some volleyball on the sand courts.

At the northern end of the beach is one of California's oldest wooden piers. It was renovated in the 1990's though, so it's O.K. Ventura Pier offers a nice stroll and awesome view of Channel Islands and coastline, plus fishing, so bring your pole. (Tip: It makes for iconic sunset photographs.) The base of the pier features interpretive display panels, a bait shop, snack bar, restrooms, and a nice seafood restaurant called Eric Ericson's on the Pier. Order four pieces of fish, $7; six ounces of clam strips, $8.50; one pound of snow crab, $18; flat iron steak, $13; fresh veggie wrap, $9.50; grilled chicken salad, $10; and more. The restaurant has both inside and patio seating. Call (805) 643-4783 /www.ericericssons.com/web for more info.

A sandy beach stretches beneath the pier and surrounds it. Bikers and pedestrians make good use of the adjacent thirteen-mile Coastal Bikeway. (See pg. 696 for more information about the bike path.) Bike rentals are available on weekends during the summer and on holidays. Several seasonal events occur at the beach, so call to see what's scheduled.

Hours: Open daily, 7am - sunset.
Price: There is some free street parking, or go into the lot and pay $10 for day use. Parking near the pier is $2 an hour; $8 max.
Ages: All

—EDIBLE ADVENTURES—

BENNETT'S HONEY FARM

(805) 521-1375 / www.bennetthoney.com
3176 Honey Lane, Fillmore

Here's the buzz: This honey farm is a fun (and educational) stop off if you are in the area, and if you like honey! The attraction is a small retail store/tasting room that sells games, toys, books, figurines, etc. that have to do with honey. I never knew there was this many honey-related items! It also sells products made from honey such as candles, soap, candy, raw honeycomb, sauces, and granola, as well as a wide array of flavors of very fresh honey. Visitors are

encouraged to sample the honey, so try wildflower, orange, buckwheat, avocado, eucalyptus, and others. Yum! There is also a glass-encased beehive inside with the queen bee dearly marked. Outside are a few round picnic tables and benches under shade trees, with the ranch and mountains in the background, so *bee* seated and indulge your sweet tooth a little bit longer.

      Hours: Open Mon. - Fri., 8am - 4:30pm; Sat. - Sun., 9am - 5pm. Closed on some holidays.
      Price: Free; bring spending money.
      Ages: 2 and up.

BUCA DI BEPPO (Ventura County)

(866) EAT BUCA (328-2822) for all locations; (805) 449-3688 - local / www.bucadibeppo.com $$$$
205 North Moorpark Road, Thousand Oaks
    See BUCA DI BEPPO (Los Angeles County) on page 14 for details.

BUSY BEE CAFE

(805) 643-4864 / www.busybeecafe.biz $$$
478 E. Main Street, Ventura

    This 50's diner is indeed busy - busy with customers and busy in decor with red-and-white-checkered tiles on the walls, black-and-white-checkered tiles on the floor, and splotches of red on lamps, beams, vinyl booth seats, and more. The walls are covered with movie posters featuring stars from the 50's, neon signs, street signs, and pictures. Booths have personal jukeboxes that play two songs for 25¢, while music from the large jukebox plays over the loudspeakers.

    The cafe boasts an extensive menu for all meals. In the am, three eggs any style is $6.99; three pancakes, $4.65; strawberry waffles, $7.25; French toast, $6.55; and omelets start at $7.95. Lunch and dinner items include a cheeseburger, $8.55; tuna sandwich, $8.95; hot pastrami sandwich, $11.95; potato skins, $5.99; pasta primavera, $8.95; Greek salad, $8.95; and hot dip sandwich, $9.45. Tempting desserts and fountain creations are apple dumplings, $6.45; bread pudding, $3.45; lime phosphate, $3.95; egg cream, $2.95; or a malt, $4.45. Kids' meals choices are pancakes, plus an egg and piece of bacon; a Belgian waffle; a peanut butter and jelly sandwich, with fruit; chicken strips; a burger; or junior hot dog with fries. These meals cost $5.69 each and come with a small drink. Note to all antique and thrift store shoppers - you will find numerous shops along Main Street to appease your appetite!

      Hours: Open daily, 7am - 10pm. Closed early on Thanksgiving and closed Christmas day.
      Price: See menu prices above.
      Ages: All

CHUCK E. CHEESE'S (Ventura County)

    See the entry for CHUCK E. CHEESE'S (Los Angeles County) on page 16 for details.

FARMER'S MARKETS (Ventura County)

    See the entry for FARMER'S MARKETS (Los Angeles County) on pg. 18 for details.

FILLMORE & WESTERN RAILWAY COMPANY

364 Main Street, Central Park Depot, Fillmore $$$$
    See the entry for FILLMORE & WESTERN RAILWAY COMPANY on page 698 for details.

JOE'S CRAB SHACK (Ventura County)

(805) 643-3725 / www.joescrabshack.com $$$
567 San Jon Road, Ventura
    See the entry for JOE'S CRAB SHACK (Los Angeles County) on page 22 for details.
      Hours: Open Sun. - Thurs., 11am - 11pm; Fri. - Sat., 11am - midnight.

LAKESIDE DINING at THE LANDING

(818) 865-0095 - Zin Bistro Americana; (818) 889-8300 - Boccacio's / www.zinwestlake.com; $$$$
www.boccaciosonthelake.com
32123 / 32131 Lindero Canyon, Westlake Village
    The above entry name is not a formal title; I'm simply using it to explain these dining experiences. There are

several upscale restaurants along the scenic lake in Westlake Village. Each one offers a small, outside dining section overlooking a patch of grass and a pretty view of the lake, with its bordering homes and private boats. The ducks and geese seem more than a little eager for a hand out. (Signs ask that you don't feed them.) A sidewalk hugs the lake around a few of its curves, so you can go for a short stroll.

The restaurant at the south end of the shopping center is Boccaccio's, which has lunch offerings of lobster bisque ($7); Cobb salad ($13.95); grilled chicken breast ($14); and more. The Landing Grill and Sushi Bar is a few shops in, as is one of my favorites, Zin Bistro Americana. Lunch prices at Zin run from $8 for a Caesar salad to $15 for a build-your-own omelet to $17 for a lobster and crab pot pie to $30 for chicken fried lobster. Bon appetit!

      Hours: The restaurants are usually open from 11am - 9pm or 10pm.
      Price: See menu prices above.
      Ages: 4 years and up.

OLIVIA'S DOLL HOUSE TEA ROOM (Ventura County)

(661) 252-1404 / www.oliviasdollhousetearoom.com
1321 Thousand Oaks Boulevard, Thousand Oaks

    See the entry for OLIVIA'S DOLL HOUSE TEA ROOM (Los Angeles County) on page 23 for details.

      Price: $325

ROCKET FIZZ SODA POPS AND CANDY SHOP (Ventura County)

Camarillo - (805) 987-SODA (7632); Simi Valley - (805) 526-SODA (7632); Thousand Oaks - (805) 494-SODA (7632); Ventura - (805) 641-1222; Westlake Village - (818) TRY-SODA (879-7632) / www.rocketfizz.com
Camarillo - 2619 Ventura Blvd.; Simi Valley - 2432 Erringer Rd.; Thousand Oaks - 593 North Moorpark Road, Suite D;
Ventura - 105 South Oak Street, Suite 100; Westlake Village - 30823 Thousand Oaks Blvd

    See ROCKET FIZZ SODA POPS AND CANDY SHOP (Los Angeles County) on page 24 for details on this shop with an incredible array of unusual sodas and candy and more. The one is Camarillo is the flagship store. It has a small outside patio and inside, a rocket ship fish tank filled with real, bright, candy-color fish. Push the button to hear the countdown for launch.

      Price: Technically, free
      Ages: 3 years and up.

UNDERWOOD FAMILY FARMS - Moorpark

(805) 529-3690 or (805) 523-2957 / www.underwoodfamilyfarms.com
3370 Sunset Valley Road, Moorpark

    Underwood Family Farms is a huge (160-acre) working produce farm, as well as an animal farm. Let's talk food, first. There are two ways to enjoy the crops: 1) Stop by the on-site roadside market to purchase fresh produce (tasty, but boring), or 2) Let the kids pick their own fruits and vegetables. (Ya-hoo - we've got a winner!) There are rows and rows (and rows and rows) of seasonal crops including artichokes, strawberries, blackberries, peaches, squash, potatoes, lettuces, green beans, apricots, apples, onions, garlic, tomatoes, eggplant, peppers, pumpkins, melons, corn, and herbs. Signs here indicate the price per pound and if the crop is ready to be picked. My boys were excited to eat strawberries they picked from the vines, carrots they pulled from the ground, beans they harvested from the stalks, and other good-for-you foods they won't normally eat, proving that kids really enjoy the fruits (and vegetables) of their labor.

    Heavy-duty pull wagons and wheelbarrows are available to transport your prize pickings (or tired little ones) at no extra charge. A grassy picnic area, with tables, is located at the front of the farm, near the restroom facilities. Tips: Wear sunscreen and walking shoes; prepare to get a little muddy if you visit here after a rain; and bring a cooler to store your fresh produce.

    The animal farm and play area is adjacent to the produce farm. This very pleasantly-landscaped area is a superb place to spend some time with your children, especially as there are lots of activities, plus several grassy patches and plenty of benches. Antique and modern farm equipment dotted around add to the atmosphere. Round up your darlings in the Kids Corral that has a small, two-story, mini fort with a slide, swings, and short rock-climbing wall, plus a shaded sand pit. Look up to see pygmy goats walking on skinny wooden ramps over your head - forty feet off the ground! A stationary, scale-size wooden train, with several cars, is great for kids to climb aboard and use their

imaginations, as are a wooden fire truck and bus. Run through a short tunnel built under a hill. Climb up and steer a tractor, whoosh down a combine slide, and even jump up and on a wide and tall stack of hay bales (i.e. the hay pyramid). Enjoy funny and educational twenty-five-minute animal presentations on the weekends at 11:30am, 1:30pm and 3:30pm, featuring mostly barnyard animals. You may also wander around pens to see sheep, bunnies, jersey cows, donkeys, turkeys, alpacas, emus, ponies, and ducks. Check out the chicken coop with its freshly-laid eggs. All of the above is included with the price of admission. Entrance into the Petting Corral is 3 tickets. Other "extras", with per ticket admission price (ticket prices are listed below), include a moonbounce (3 tickets); hand-led pony rides around a small ring (5); a looping trike trail - the bike is supplied (3); tractor-drawn hayrides (3); a three-minute ride on a self-pedaled play tractor in an enclosed area (3); cow train ride - cow-shaped carts pulled by a tractor that go around a portion of the farm (4); gem mining at a sluice (8 tickets for a regular bag); and a mini-electric train ride (3). Experience the animal farm on your own, or take a guided tour.

The farm offers a variety of guided field trips/tours of the fields for groups of twenty or more. The ninety-minute Farm Tour entails picking strawberries or veggies to take home, a tractor-drawn wagon ride, and a visit to the animal farm area. There is plenty of time for a picnic lunch, too. The variety of 2.5 hour to over four-hour Educational Farm Tours include learning about a designated crop (or crops) of strawberries and/or vegetables, their care, growth cycle, and more; picking the crop(s); a tractor-drawn hayride; an animal presentation - learning about the characteristics and behaviors of animals; feeding and petting the animals; and more. All tours include a coloring book. What a great combination of fun and education! Crops do grow seasonally, so call or check the website to see what is currently ready to harvest. Ask about summer farm camps. Tip: See the Calendar entry on page 748 for details about the Fall Harvest Festival. Note: There is also an UNDERWOOD FAMILY FARMS in the nearby city of Somis. (See the next entry.)

Hours: The food and animal farm are open March - November daily, 9am to 6pm and on weekends in December, weather permitting. Closed January and February.

Price: The following price includes entrance to the animal farm, as well as entrance to the fields to pick your own crops: $3 per person Mon. - Fri., $6 per person, Sat. - Sun. and major holidays (which includes a tractor-drawn wagon ride to the fields and admission to the animal show); children under 2 are free. Season passes are available. Prices for crops are charged per pound and change per season/availability. Admission is $12 per person on Sat. - Sun. during the Fall Harvest Festival. Farm Tours start at $6 per student and go up to $14, depending on the tour. Ticket prices for extra activities are $1 = 1 ticket; $20 = 23 tickets, etc.

Ages: 18 months - 10 years for the animal farm; 4 years and up for food tours, and 3 years to pick crops.

UNDERWOOD FAMILY FARMS - Somis

(805) 386-4660 / www.underwoodfamilyfarms.com   !/$
5696 Los Angeles Avenue, Somis

If you're in the area, stop at this roadside stand which sells freshly-picked, seasonal produce. From the end of May to mid-July, you may pick your own blueberries daily, 9am to 4pm. Tractor rides to the fields are offered on weekends only. The biggest draw for kids are the burros, jersey cows, rabbits, guinea pigs, alpacas (i.e., furry llamas that look like they're having a bad hair day), and most fascinating, the pygmy goats. The goats nimbly climb on very narrow wooden ramps that crisscross thirty feet above your head! An adjacent grassy area beckons picnickers. Kids can climb on the wooden vehicle stationed here and play in the sandbox. See the previous entry for UNDERWOOD FAMILY FARMS - Moorpark for a nearby, full-fledged, farm attraction.

Hours: Open April - October daily, 9am to 6pm. Open November - March daily, 9am to 5pm.
Price: Free.
Ages: 2 - 12 years (although those overhead goats are quite a cool sight for all ages).

—FAMILY PAY AND PLAY—

AMBUSH PAINTBALL & AIRSOFT PARK

(805) 259-3200 / www.ambushpaintballpark.com $$$$$
8643 Shekell Road, Moorpark

Both kid and adult friendly, the six different fields/scenarios at this mid-size paintball and airsoft park give you enough variety and space to play ten-minute games of tag and hide and seek, or simply, capture the flag with markers. Not necessarily elaborate, but still a lot of fun, there are buildings, windy dirt trenches, huge spools, hay bales, inflatables, and other objects to run into, around and through in playing each game. Splatmaster games are also available for kids ages 8 to 11 years old. Bring lots of water - it gets hot out here! Pizza can be delivered or you can bring your own food. Players must wear paintball goggles with a full face mask; rentals are available here.

Hours: Open Sat. - Sun., 9am - 4pm.
Price: $20 for full day of paintball or airsoft with your own equipment; $40 for all day admission plus rental equipment for both games.
Ages: 8 - 11 years for Splatmaster; 10 years and up for airsoft and paintball.

BEDFORD PINKARD SKATE PARK

(805) 982-7121 - skate park; (805) 385-7950 - College Park / www.visitoxnard.com; www.socalskateparks.com
3250 South Rose Avenue, Oxnard

Skate 'til your hearts content at this 14,500 square-feet "skate-of-the-art" park with cement bowls, grinding blocks, rails, tombstones, pyramids, and quarter pipes. Helmets are required as is a parent-signed waiver for ages 17 and under. The skate part is in a section of College Park.

Amenities at College Park include basketball courts, a tennis court, volleyball court, picnic area, exercise station, playground, concrete walkways throughout, and nifty dog park (with a dog washing station).

Hours: Both parks are open daily, noon - dusk. Closed on holidays and inclement weather.
Price: Free
Ages: 7 years and up.

BOULDERDASH INDOOR ROCK CLIMBING

(805) 557-1300 / www.boulderdashclimbing.com
880 Hampshire Road, Suite A, Thousand Oaks

Do your kids have you climbing the walls? Then you'll feel right at home at Boulderdash! Both the novice and experienced climber have level-appropriate challenges at this rock climbing center. The beginner has walls that extend up to twenty-five feet, while the more advanced participant can climb walls as high as forty-five feet. The latter section also has a slab, aretes, roofs, and a rappel ledge. (Although these may be familiar terms for climbers, I needed to look up some of those words.) The dedicated bouldering area is good-sized with a traverse of over 100 feet long. Routes change frequently, so there is always something new to try. Rock climbing is not only a fantastic, all-body workout, but almost any age level and any athletic ability can give it a go. Parents can (and dare I say, should?) participate too!

A locker area, soda and snacks area, and pro shop are also on the premises, as is a separate party room. A waiver for all ages (signed by parents for those 17 years and under) is mandatory. One of the most cost effective ways to have your child rock climb is for you, or another adult, to take a two-hour belay class, for $40, so that you may belay your child. Or, make a reservation (only 6 climbers allowed per session) to come to a forty-five minute Open Climb Time when a belayer, and all necessary equipment, is provided for all-age climbers. Have your child join the rock-climbing team, or enroll in a camp or take a class. Safe, exhilarating, and confidence building - if kids are looking for a sport to grab hold of, have them grab the hand and toe holds of a rock climbing wall.

Hours: Open Mon. - Fri., 11am - 10pm; Sat., 10am - 8pm; Sun., 10am - 6pm. Open Climb Time sessions are Mon., Wed., Fri. at 5pm - 5:45pm and 6pm - 6:45pm.
Price: Daily climb fees are $15 for adults, $12 weekdays before 3pm; $13 for students and military; $12 for children 11 and under. An adult belayer (i.e., you or another certified adult that attends) is $5. Rental gear - harness, shoes, and chalk - is $6, inclusive. Open Climb Time is $20 per person.
Ages: 6 years and up.

CHUCK E. CHEESE'S (Ventura County)

See the entry for CHUCK E. CHEESE'S (Los Angeles County) on page 16 for details.

GOLF 'N STUFF (Ventura County)

(805) 644-7131 / www.golfnstuff.com

5555 Walker Drive, Ventura

If you and the kids are in the mood for a little golf 'n stuff, here's the place for you. There are two **miniature golf** courses with windmills, a tower, and other fanciful buildings (I love the castle!), to putt around on at $8.75 per round for adults; children under 3 years play for free with a paying adult. **Indy cars** ($6.75 for drivers) have a height requirement for drivers of 56", while **bumper cars** and **water bumper boats** ($6.75 per ride) both have height requirements for drivers of 48". Passengers for the above attractions are $3.25. Play the action-packed game of **lazer tag** here for $6.50 per game. The center also features a big arcade with over 100 games, even some old-school ones, and a full-service snack bar.

Hours: Open September - mid-June, Mon. - Thurs., noon - 9pm (rides open at 3pm); Fri., noon - midnight (rides open at 3pm); Sat., 10am - midnight (rides and lazer tag open at 11am); Sun., 10am - 10pm (rides and lazer tag open at 11am). Lazer Tag is only available on the weekends in the winter. Open mid-June - August, Sun. - Thurs., 10am - 10pm (rides and lazer tag open at 11am); Fri. - Sat., 10am - midnight (rides and lazer tag open at 11am).

Price: Prices are listed above. Ask about package deals.

Ages: 4 years and up.

KID'S WORLD

(818) 338-8888 / www.kidsworldla.com

618 Lindero Canyon Road, Oak Park

For a world of fun come to one of the best and most colorful indoor play places. There are two, huge, multi-level, mostly-padded, play structures with so many fun elements - a lot of tubes to crawl through (one looks like a shark); cargo netting; a variety of obstacles courses; slides (even three slides side-by-side and a few that are enclosed); things to climb over and under; and lots more. The structure with foam ball blasters provokes lots of giggles, both for the ones shooting and those getting shot. A small, separate soft play room for toddlers has some short slides, foam blocks, and play mats. There are also two basketball rooms (with stands that have adjustable rims); a keyboard station; a mini mini putting green; an arcade room with several games; a fish tank (to look at, not play with); and a place for building blocks in and on a big sparkly silver wall area. A large adjacent room is for crafts or learning time. Separate party rooms are available downstairs and upstairs.

Toward the back is a full service cafe with cheeseburgers ($.8.25); pizza ($7.25); turkey, tuna or veggie sandwich ($8.25); a variety of salads ($8.25); and a choice of kids meals of hot dogs, grilled cheese, chicken tenders, and more ($5.95); plus snack items and beverages. There are table and chairs back here, a real firetruck that kids can climb aboard the cab and "drive", and a small stage.

Everyone must wear socks in the play center. This place is wild, crazy, and sometimes loud, but always fun. I hope a visit here brightens your world!

Hours: Open Mon., 11am - 8pm; Tues. - Thurs., 10am - 8pm; Fri. - Sat., 10am - 9pm; Sun., 10am - 6pm.

Price: $9.75 for 24 months - 16 years; $5 for ages 13 months - 23 months; children 12 months and under are free. Two adults are free with each paying child; $4 each additional adult.

Ages: 18 months - 12 years

LAZERTAG EXTREME

(805) 577-8400 / www.lazertagextreme.com

591A Country Club Drive in the Wood Ranch Shopping Center, Simi Valley

Two teams compete against each other armed with laser guns and wearing a lighted vest in this foggy, large (5,000 square feet), multi-level arena. Futuristically-themed, the grays and blacks of the walls, ramps, partitions, towers and markings are interspersed with some colorful neon lights. Accompanied by pulsating background music, this is a great place to play hide and seek. Zap your opponent with your laser gun to complete your goal of scoring the most points. Mission, not-so-impossible.

For another mission, should you choose to accept it, and more thrills, try Lazer Maze. In this room, the laser beams intersect and cross over each other so that the participant, should he/she be up to the challenge, must crawl, jump and walk over and under the beams and beat the clock - it's a timed laser obstacle course and your time could go by rather quickly if you break a beam.

There is a good selection of current video and arcade games in the lobby, as well as ticket and prize redemption,

plus a snack bar with hot dogs, chips, soda - all the important food groups. Note that Lazertag Extreme is mobile, too, meaning that they can come to you for a party or special event.

Hours: Open Wed. - Thurs., 3pm - 9pm; Fri., 3pm - midnight; Sat., 11am - midnight; Sun., noon - 8pm. Closed Mon., Tues., except for special events, and some holidays.

Price: $9 for one mission. Lazer maze is $3 a mission.

Ages: 5 years and up.

MB2 RACEWAY (Ventura County)

(805) 214-9999 / www.mb2raceway.com

1475 Lawrence Drive, Thousand Oaks

See MB2 RACEWAY (Los Angeles County) on page 36 for details.

Hours: Open Mon. - Thurs., noon - 10pm; Fri. - Sat., 11am - midnight; Sun., 10am - 8pm.

Price: Licensed drivers are $23 for a fourteen-lap race; juniors are $20 for a nine-lap race.

Ages: At least 48" tall.

PUMP IT UP (Ventura County)

(805) 339-9669 / www.pumpitupparty.com

5120 Ralston Street, Ventura

See PUMP IT UP (San Diego County) on page 491 for details.

Hours: Open Jump is Mon. and Thurs., 10am - 11:30am for ages 6 and under only. Family Fun Night is Tues. and Wed., 5pm - 8pm, for ages 2 - 10.

Price: Open Jump is $7 per child; adults are free. Family Fun Nights are $9 for ages 2 - 10; adults are free.

Ages: 3 years and up.

SCOOTER'S JUNGLE (Ventura County)

(805) 203-9200 / www.scootersjungle.com

2250 Union Place, #B, Simi Valley

See SCOOTER'S JUNGLE (Orange County) on page 265 for details.

Hours: Check the website calendar as the event times change every month.

Ages: 2 years and up.

SKATELAB

(805) 578-0040; (805) 578-9928 / www.skatelab.com

4226 Valley Fair Street, Simi Valley

Yeowser! This hip, sprawling (20,000 square feet), indoor skate park has it all, and then some. It has a street section with two half-pipes - one is six feet high and the other is four feet high. It also has grinding boxes, a really large bowl, and much more. There is even a half pipe outside. Family-friendly Skatelab is both popular with kids and adults as parents can go upstairs to the overlook, sit down to watch the action, and enjoy a snack. This park is definitely geared for the intermediate to advanced skater, although there are sessions just for beginners. Bikes, roller blades and scooters are welcome at all times. All skaters and riders 17 years and under must have a waiver signed by their parent or legal guardian at the time of registration. A helmet, elbow, and knee pads are mandatory. Rentals are available.

The entrance hallway to Skatelab is lined with hundreds of skateboards. There is a small museum, upstairs, devoted to vintage skateboards and skateboard paraphernalia, showcasing the history of the sport. I never knew there was so many "extras" in skateboarding!

Hours: Open Mon., 4pm - 7pm, 7pm - 10pm, and 8:30pm - 10pm; Tues. - Fri., 3pm - 6pm, and 4:30pm - 6pm, 7pm -10pm and 8:30pm - 10pm; Sat., 10am - 1pm for beginning skaters; 1pm - 10pm; Sun., 10am - 1pm for beginning skaters; 1pm - 7pm.

Price: $10 each three-hour session; $6 each ninety-minute session Mon. - Thurs.; $8 each ninety-minutes Fri. - Sun.

Ages: 7 years and up.

SKY HIGH SPORTS (Ventura County)

(805) 484-6300 / cam.jumpskyhigh.com

166 Aviador Street, Camarillo

$$$$

See SKY HIGH SPORTS (pg. 266) for details about this fantastic, indoor trampoline place. All jumpers must wear either laced tennis shoes, grip socks or jump in bare feet. This facility also offers ten minute laser tag games, too in an inflatable "room".

Hours: Open most of the year, Sun. - Mon., 11am -9pm; Tues. - Thurs., 2pm - 9pm; Fri. - Sat., 11am - midnight. During school breaks and holidays, it is usually open Sun. - Thurs., 11am - 9pm; Fri. - Sat., 11am - midnight.

Price: $9 per hour per person, Mon. - Thurs., $11 per hour Fri., Sat., and holidays. Summertime prices are $11 an hour. Laser tag is $4 per person, per game.

Ages: 4 years and up.

THE CLUBHOUSE FUN ZONE

(805) 639-0414 / www.theclubhousefunzone.com

4535 McGrath Street, Ventura

$$

Join the club and have fun at this smallish, indoor play place. The main, two-story play structure has a ball pit, tubes, slides, obstacle courses and padding all over. Other fun elements inside the Clubhouse are tyke-size vehicles, mini (mini) racers, a train table, a bounce, and a few toys and small playhouses. There are some comfy couches for adults and some tables and chairs, as well as a computer station and cafe. Socks are required.

Hours: Open Mon. - Fri., 10am - 4pm. Closed Sat. and Sun. for private parties.

Price: $8 per child; adults are free.

Ages: 6 years and under

VENTURA AQUATICS CENTER

(805) 654-7511 / www.cityofventura.net/aquatics

901 S. Kimball Road in the Ventura Community Park, Ventura

$$

It's hot. Question: Where do you go for refreshment? Answer: To the outdoor Ventura Aquatics Center. The Center has a competition pool, with three diving boards; a recreational pool for everyone; a small pool with two, twisty, twenty-five-foot slides - sliders must be 46" tall; and a separate, colorful water playground in shallow water for younger children. It features a short slide, steps, a little tunnel, pipes that burst with water (reminds me of home), a water umbrella, and buckets on tall poles that fill with water and tip over. Lifeguards are on duty.

In between the pools is a lovely patio area with round tables and chairs, surrounded by palm trees. There are also lounge chairs by the pools and the water play pool. Lockers are available to use free of charge, just bring your own lock. Children 9 and under must be accompanied by an adult. You are allowed to bring outside food in - yea! Ahh, now the day isn't unbearably hot.

Hours: Recreational swim is open most of the year Sat. - Sun., noon - 3:30pm; open more hours on school breaks and in the summer. The water playground is open April and September, usually Fri., 1pm - 4pm, Sat. - Sun., noon - 3:30pm. It is open daily in the summer and on school breaks in the spring. Call first or check the changing schedule online.

Price: $5 for ages 6 and up; $3 for seniors and ages 2 - 5; children 2 and under are free and must have a swim diaper.

Ages: 1 ½ years and up.

VERTICAL HEAVEN

(805) 339-9022 / www.climbvh.com

5600 Everglades Street, suite C, Ventura

$$$$

What do monkeys, lizards, bears, and cats all have in common? They all climb trees and walls, although not all with the same grace and/or dexterity. This smallish indoor boulder climbing gym of climbing heaven has walls (up to sixteen-feet tall) covered with hand and foot hold protrusions for over eighty problems/routes. The entire floor is covered with foam padding, so it's all a safe fall zone. It also sports a system wall, hangboard and campus board for those who are serious about climbing as well as cardio equipment and weights.

A special area designed for kids, called the Fun Zone, has a two-story, wooden clubhouse with a fireman's pole inside and a porch all around it, plus netting and a bridge connecting it to a little climbing wall. A short rock climbing wall goes around a good portion of this room. One section even has a cave-like feature with rock climbing holds on the inside of it, too, plus two slides. Thick padding covers the floor. This is a very Fun Zone!

A waiver must be signed by a parent or legal guardian for ages 17 and under. Classes, parties, team-building, after-school programs, camps, and all-night adventures are offered here.

       Hours: Open Mon. - Fri., 11am - 10pm; Sat. - Sun., 11am - 7pm.

       Price: A day pass is $15 for adults; $10 for seniors; $12 for military, students, and ages 17 and under. Ask about their almost daily specials, like the $7 weekday matinees prices (before 3pm). Entrance to the Fun Zone is $10; $5 for ages 3 and under and on weekdays (for all ages) before 3pm. Rental shoes are $5.

       Ages: 5 years and up.

—GREAT OUTDOORS—

CAMINO REAL PARK

(805) 652-4550 / www.cityofventura.net
Dean Drive and Validity Street, Ventura

This sporting park has several ball fields, eight tennis courts, a basketball court, sand volleyball courts, picnic tables, barbecue pits, and three playgrounds. Two of the playgrounds are good-sized with slides, swings, and other play equipment. A paved pathway runs throughout. Although it is right off the freeway, the perimeter of the park has groves of trees and a ravine, giving it *somewhat* of a country feel.

A main draw is the eucalyptus groves because they are roosting places for Monarch butterflies from mid-October - February. The monarchs look like dead leaves hanging from branches, but then they rustle, "come to life," and flutter about - this cycle is a very cool thing to observe.

       Hours: Open daily, sunrise - sunset.

       Price: Free

       Ages: All

CHANNEL ISLANDS NATIONAL PARK

(805) 658-5730 - National Park; (805) 642-7688 or (805) 642-1393 - Island Packers; (805) 987-1301 - Channel Islands Aviation / www.nps.gov/chis; www.islandpackers.com; www.flycia.com

$$$$$

The park headquarters is at 1901 Spinnaker Drive; Island Packers is at 1867 Spinnaker, Ventura

The Channel Islands comprise eight islands off Southern California, five of which make up Channel Islands National Park and marine sanctuary. Prepare your kids for a half or whole day excursion to an island by first obtaining information from the park service. The islands were originally the home of Chumash Indians. Then, hunters came and killed certain otter, seal, and sea lion species almost to extinction. Finally, ranchers settled here. Some parts of the islands are still privately owned. It's important to emphasize to your child that Channel Islands is a national preserve, so "take only memories, leave only footprints."

Climate on the islands is different from mainland climate, even during the summer. The harsher conditions have produced various terrains within the relatively small parcels of land, from sandy beaches to rocky hills. Cruise to the islands and explore nature at its best and wildest. Kids get especially excited about seeing the numerous seals and sea lions that are plentiful because they breed on many of the islands. Be on the lookout for blue sharks and dolphins, and note that whale watching is included with all cruises from the end of December through March. Once on an island, be on the lookout for some unusual birds and animals, like the island fox. Reservations are strongly recommended for all excursions. Bring jackets and your camera; wear sneakers; pack a water bottle; and have a terrific outing!

Here is a very brief overview of the islands (enough to whet your adventuring appetite), along with cruise prices from Island Packers:

Anacapa - This is the closest island to Ventura, only twelve miles away. It is five miles long and one of the most popular islands to visit. On East Anacapa, climb up the 153 steps to a sweeping panoramic view. Enjoy a small visitor's center, and nearly two miles of hiking trails. There is no beach here, but swimming is allowed at the landing cove on

calm summer days, as is scuba and skin diving, and snorkeling. Enjoy the kelp forest! On days of low tide, Frenchy's Cove, towards the western part of the island, is great for tidepooling. Picnicking is always welcomed. This trip, offered year round, takes about seven hours round trip, including approximately sixty minutes for the channel crossing then time on the island to explore. Adult fare is $59; seniors are $54; children 3 - 12 years are $41. Overnight camping is $79 for adults; $74 for seniors; $57 for children.

Santa Cruz - At over ninety-six square miles, this is the largest island off California. Topography varies from sea caves (the Painted Cave here is one of the world's largest known sea caves at almost 100 feet wide!) and steep cliffs, to rolling hills and grasslands. Kayaking, swimming, and snorkeling (particularly in and through the wonderous sea cave and grottoes, and around the kelp) are some favorites pastimes here: Note that you must bring your own equipment, rent it before you head out, or sign up for a guided kayaking tour. Hiking is another favorite. If you land near Scorpion Ranch, the one-mile walk to Cavern Point is easy, but make the most of your trip and time here by going along the bluff on North Bluff Trail for incredible view points. Then go inland (look for the endemic island fox), into oak canyons and groves. Another landing point, Prisoner's Harbor, offers other trails and is more forrested. Going to the island is offered year-round, though excursions to and through the sea cave are offered only spring to early fall. The round trip takes eight to nine hours, including about sixty minutes for the channel crossings, then time on the island for exploration. Adult fare is $59; seniors are $54; children 3 - 12 years are $41. Overnight camping is $79 for adults; $74 for seniors; $57 for kids.

Santa Rosa - This island is fifteen miles long and, although eighty-five percent of it is grasslands, there are still canyons, volcanic formations, and fossil beds that vary the landscape. There is plenty to see and do for those who thrive on being in the midst of nature. Hikes, led by a ranger, are offered as well. Available April through November, the round trip takes about eleven hours, including the channel crossings of almost three hours each way and about four hours on the island. Adult fare is $82; seniors are $74; children 3 - 12 years are $65. Overnight camping is $114 for adults; $104 for seniors; $90 for kids.

San Miguel - This eight-mile-long island has beaches and an incredible number of seals and sea lions. The most popular destination here is the Caliche Forest (i.e., mineral sand castings), which is a 3.5-mile hike from the beach. Be prepared for strong winds, plus rain and fog any time of year. The varying island terrain reflects the assault of weather upon San Miguel. Channel crossings take three-and-a-half to four hours. Weekend camping, offered June through October, and round-trip transportation costs $147 for adults; $136 for seniors; $126 for children 3 - 12 years. Day trips, recommended for hardier kids, are offered September and October. They cost $105 for adults; $95 for seniors; $84 for kids.

Santa Barbara - This is the smallest island, only 640 acres, and is the farthest away from mainland Ventura. It has steep cliffs, a small "museum," and hiking trails. There are no shade trees on the island, so load up with sunscreen. You may stay for three days or longer on this remote island, but bring everything because there is nowhere to obtain any articles once you've arrived. Day-time round trips, offered April through October, take about eleven hours, including about four hours on the island. Adult day fare is $82; seniors are $74; children 3 - 12 years are $65. Camping is $114 for adults; $104 for seniors; $90 for kids.

Note that Island Packers does not rent kayaks or snorkeling equipment. For kayak rentals, contact CHANNEL ISLANDS KAYAKS CENTER. They also offer guided kayak tours. See page 697 for details. There is an additional charge for bringing kayaks on board. Contact CHANNEL ISLANDS OUTFITTERS (see pg. 645) for their numerous guided kayak tours in, through, and around sea caves, and other sea adventures. See Island Packer's website for other companies that they work with who also give guided kayaking tours. Contact TRUTH AQUATICS (pg. 649) and CONDOR EXPRESS CRUISES (pg. 646) for cruising to the islands from Santa Barbara.

If you prefer to fly, check out Channel Islands Aviation located at both the Camarillo Airport and at the Goleta airport. One of their options is, following a half-hour scenic flight over Anacapa and Santa Cruz Islands, to land on Santa Rosa Island and be here for about four-and-a-half hours. A ranger drives around the island where you'll see a century-old cattle ranch and other island highlights. You can hike around a bit, have a picnic lunch (which you supply), and explore more of the island before you fly back. Air fare is $220 per person. Call the aviation company for times and dates and other options.

Also check out CHANNEL ISLANDS NATIONAL PARK VISITOR CENTER (pg. 682) and VENTURA HARBOR VILLAGE (pg. 692) for other things to do while you're in this area.

Hours: Listed under each island.

Price: Listed under each island.

Ages: 6 years and up.

CHARMLEE WILDERNESS PARK   ☼

(310) 317-1364 or (310) 457-7247 / www.malibucity.org $

2577 Encinal Canyon Road, Malibu

Explore the wilds of Malibu (and there are wilds of Malibu!) via Charmlee Park. The park is 532 acres, and eight miles of dirt and fire road hiking trails that meander through the Santa Monica Mountains. Visitors enjoy magnificent views of the coastline, as well as experience oak woodland areas, meadows, chaparral, some interesting rock formations, and seasonal wildflowers. Most of the trails are fairly easy. Download a map route from the website before you head out. There are numerous picnic tables amongst the grove of trees toward the entrance, plus ones that overlook the ocean. A small nature center is the headquarters for several educational programs. Note that docents lead hikes with school children in grades K - 12 on Thursday mornings.

Hours: The park is open daily, 8am - sunset. The nature center is open Sat. - Sun., 9am - 5pm.

Price: $4 per vehicle; sometimes, though, it is free.

Ages: 4 years and up.

CONEJO COMMUNITY PARK / CONEJO VALLEY BOTANIC GARDEN   ☼

(805) 495-2163 - park; (805) 494-7630 - garden / www.crpd.org; www.conejogarden.org   !

350 Gainsborough Road and 1175 Hendrix, Thousand Oaks

This nature park is delightful in size and scope. There are acres and acres of green rolling hills, and a creek running throughout. The creek, by itself, is a major attraction. My boys loved looking for crawdads and, of course, stepping on the rocks, with the possible thrill of slipping and getting a bit wet. Almost a full day's adventure can be had by climbing the gnarled, old oak trees. There are cement pathways throughout the park, making much of it stroller accessible. The ambiance here is peaceful, unless you bring your kids, of course!

The upper field sports a baseball diamond; a basketball court is across the way. A covered picnic area with barbecue pits, a horseshoe pit, and shuffleboard court is also available here, as is a community center. The playgrounds in front of the community center building are great - they have slides, a rope climbing structure, and short climbing wall partially in sand, plus several fake rock formations to climb on, under and through, with connecting ropes to incorporate with imaginative play.

The adjoining botanic garden is thirty-three acres; only part of it is developed and open to walk through. One short path traverses through a variety of landscapes, looping around and covering most of the garden. Another nature trail goes up and around the hillside, following a creek through oak and willow trees before looping back around. Drought-tolerant plants, a meadow section, fruit trees, bird habitats, and a butterfly garden are all part of the landscape. A favorite area is the Kid's Adventure Garden. Children are encouraged to climb up into a tree trunk (or use the ramp) to the treehouse on top; crawl into the beehive (not a real one); walk through the small hydroponic greenhouse (i.e., a soil-less environment for plants); imagine at the zoo garden with animal statues (to play on and just look at) and topiaries; check out the pirates cave; look at the vegetable garden; and make garden-themed crafts. I don't know how much actual plant knowledge my kids gained from our time here, but I hope they are more rooted in appreciating the beautiful gift of nature.

Hours: The park is open daily, dawn - 7pm (8pm in the summer). The botanic garden is open daily, 7am - 5pm. The Kid's Adventure Garden is open Sun., 11am - 3pm. Both are closed on major holidays and during inclement weather. See page x for info on AHS reciprocal memberships.

Price: Free

Ages: All

CONEJO CREEK NORTH PARK   ☼

(805) 495-6471 - park; (805) 449-2660 - library / www.crpd.org   !

1379 E. Janss Road, Thousand Oaks

Around the back of the library, near the freeway, is a long strip of land that is a delightful park. Trees block the view of the freeway, and some of its sound. A rock-lined creek runs through most of the park. My boys could spend hours playing just here, and getting a little wet. There are also two ponds (at each end of the park), sand volleyball

courts, a ball field, picnic shelters, grassy areas, shade trees and natural play areas, an ornamental fountain, and quite a few bridges, one of which leads directly to the library and some join up with walkways. The playgrounds have great amentities - slides (some long and enclosed), bridges, speaking tubes, more rocks to climb on, swings, sand, digger tools, chain ladders, and even a wall featuring the competitive electronic games of Neos. A visit to the library and/or adjacent senior/teen community center can round out your trip.

Hours: Open daily, sunrise - sunset. Call for library hours.
Price: Free
Ages: All

CORRIGANVILLE PARK

(805) 584-4400 / www.rsrpd.org; www.lamountains.com
7001 Smith Road, Simi Valley

Almost 250 acres of rocky parkland was once the setting of thousands of movies and T.V. Westerns and shows. Now, the public can hike the trails past sandstone formations and caves, climb the boulders, and enjoy the rugged landscape. An easy, one-mile-round trip walk for kids is the Interpretation Trail, which is studded with oak trees alongside a small creek and labels telling of the movies produced here. There are even a few remnants from old movie sets, mostly foundations, from *African Queen* and *Robin Hood.* Movie buffs will appreciate it! (Bring your own video camera, use your imagination, and roll 'em!) Picnic tables and huge shade trees make this a great place to enjoy your lunch. There are several other trails throughout the park, including some that parallel the old stagecoach route, one that leads to the wildlife corridor via the Santa Susana Pass Road and onto the mountains, and one that leads to Foothill Park via a quarter mile connector trail. Foothill Park has a half basketball court, bbq, a small playground, and an open, grassy field lined with large shade trees. See FAERY HUNT (pg. 183) for information on a fun, interactive "production" for kids involving fairies and nature held here at certain times throughout the year. Across the driveway is a movie studio with facades (no public access).

Hours: The park is open daily, sunrise - sunset.
Price: Free
Ages: 3 years and up.

DENNISON PARK

(805) 654-3951 / www.ventura.org
7250 Ojai - Santa Paula Rd., Ojai

I recommend the very rural Dennison Park more for the camping than day use as the day use picnic area isn't very big. It contains some trees, a picnic table, a small playground and a horseshoe pit. However, the unspoiled views of the surrounding mountains, valleys, fields, and all of Ojai are quite stunning. And I recommend the campsites for older kids as, because of the view, the sites are high up and many, along the outer ring, are near the edges of hills. Having said all that, it is beautiful here. Most of the sites feel almost private with mature shade trees and shrubbery, and each has a stone or wooden picnic table and bbq pit. There is a park host onsite.

Hours: Open daily, 7:30am - dusk.
Price: $2 per vehicle Mon. - Fri; $4, Sat. - Sun. Camping is $20 per night.
Ages: 6 years and up.

GARDENS OF THE WORLD

(805) 557-1135 / www.gardensoftheworld.info
2001 Thousand Oaks Boulevard, Thousand Oaks

Exit the busy streets through huge wrought iron gates and enter a peaceful and beautiful world of immaculate gardens. This four-and-a-half-acre park features distinctive samplings of gardens, in themed settings, of plants native to Japan, Italy, England, France, and America (specifically, California). The Japanese section evokes a sense of serenity with a koi pond, short brook and waterfall, small bamboo "forest," bridges, lush foliage, and authentic pagoda. The enclosed Mission Courtyard showcases each of the California missions on its walls, along with a fountain in the center. Outside, a life-sized statue of Father Serra beckons visitors. The centerpiece of the French garden is a tiered, horizontal fountain whose waters cascade over large steps into graduated pools. (No wading or splashing - however tempting!) Vibrantly-colored flowers and hedges complete this section. The English garden bursts with a variety of

brilliant blooms and the adjacent rose garden, grouped by color, boasts over 400 bushes. Grape arbors, Cypress trees, and a fountain define the Italian garden.

A centrally-placed bandstand provides a stage for seasonal concerts. Sit and watch the show on the grassy knoll in front of the bandstand. Note that this area is the only place for kids (and adults) to run around in the gardens. This elegant park has strategically placed benches throughout, as well as several cement pathways that crisscross, making the gardens stroller and wheelchair friendly. Bring a lunch to enjoy at the picnic tables under the shade awning. Challenge the kids to a game of chess using the faux stone chess set, with pieces over a foot high, in front of the resource center.

Explore the park leisurely on your own, as all the plants are labeled, or take a forty-minute guided tour, offered to adults and to school children, with a maximum of about fifteen people. Learn about the rock formations at the Japanese garden; add new words, such as "deciduous", to your vocabulary; touch a lamb's ear (plant); and much more.

Hours: Open most of the year, Tues. - Sun., 9am - 5pm. Closed Mon., holidays, and during inclement weather. Guided tours are offered Tues. - Sun.

Price: Free

Ages: 2 years and up

LAKE CASITAS RECREATION AREA

(805) 649-2233 - park; (805) 649-1122 - camping info; (805) 649-2043 - bait, boat rentals and Marina Cafe; (805) 304-6544 - Cydes 4 Rent / www.lakecasitas.info; www.casitasboatrentals.com
11311 Santa Ana Road, Ventura

A day at Lake Casitas is pure pleasure. The main attractions at this beautiful huge lake have traditionally been fishing, biking, and camping. The lake is stocked seasonally with bass, rainbow trout, crappie, and catfish. A fishing license is needed for those 16 years and older. Night fishing from the shoreline until 11pm is offered on full moon weekends throughout the year. If you don't have any luck catching your own meal, catch breakfast or lunch at the lakeside Marina cafe, with its indoor/outdoor seating. The bait and tackle shop has boats for rent. A four passenger aluminum motorboat is $50 an hour, $85 for the day; a ten-passenger pontoon boat is $100 an hour, $205 for the day; single kayaks are $15 an hour; double kayaks, canoes and peddle boats are $20. No waterskiing is allowed.

Play a round of disc golf at the eighteen-hole, lakeside course. See how well you aim as you attempt to fly your disc into each of the chain-link baskets before your opponent does. (Preplan somewhat: If you don't have a disc, purchase one at Real Cheap Sports on East Santa Clara Street in Ventura. They also carry course maps and scorecards.) Park at Campsite M to play this challenging game. Younger kids will probably have more fun on the several playgrounds scattered around the recreation area.

Over 400 campsites range from basic tent camping to full RV hookups and different spots offer different vistas. Each site has a picnic table and fire ring. There is a two-night minimum on weekends. There is a park store on site, too, in case you forget something. Ask for a schedule of events that the lake hosts, such as the Renaissance Fair, Pow Wows, Bass Tournaments, and more. Look in the Calendar section of this book, too. Beat the summer heat with the lake's CASITAS WATER ADVENTURE (pg. 656), a small, but refreshing water park.

Hours: The lake and most amenities, including the Cafe, are open daily, sunrise - sunset.

Price: Most of the year, entrance to the lake is $10 per vehicle; but Easter weekend through Labor Day, on weekends and holidays, it's $15. Pets are $2. There is some free parking just outside the main entrance gate. Walk in and bicycles are free. If you want to just come in and eat at the Cafe, your vehicle admission price will be credited to your Cafe food bill. Camping prices range from $25 - $50, depending on the site and time of year, plus a $8 non-refundable reservation fee.

Ages: 3 years and up.

LAKE PIRU RECREATION AREA

(805) 521-1500 / www.lake-piru.org
4780 Piru Canyon Road, Piru

This beautiful mountain lake is huge at over four miles long and about one mile wide - no wonder there are two floating restrooms (aptly titled S.S. Reliefs) on it. Located at the foothills, Lake Piru offers year-round respite from "real" life. The marina, open daily except Christmas, offers boat rentals, such as pontoons, $140 for four hours; fourteen-foot fishing boats, $60 for four hours; and more. If you want to go waterskiing, you'll need to bring your own boat. No jet skis allowed. You may kayak and canoe in certain areas. The lake is stocked with rainbow trout and bass,

so reel 'em in. A California fishing license is needed for ages 16 and up. Ask about the annual fishing derby held in the spring. A bait and tackle shop are on the premises. Seasonally, the swim beach is open (using imported sand - so very chic!). Lifeguards are on duty in the summer on the weekends.

Day use picnic areas have covered eating areas, a grassy lawn, barbecue grills, a great children's playground and plenty of trees dotting the land. A snack bar is open in the summer, but the general store, which carries bait and tackle, is open year round for business. Over 250 tent and RV camping sites are intertwined with shade trees and great views of the lake. Note that Lake Piru is next to the Sespe Condor Sanctuary, so take a good look at the birds flying overhead. Since this is a natural environment, be on the lookout also for ospreys, geese, deer, skunks, squirrels, and an occasional bobcat.

Hours: Open daily, 7am - sunset.

Price: $10 per vehicle, October - March; $13, April - September. Camping for up to four people ranges from $20 (non-season, tent camping) - $44 (summer, full hook-up) depending on the season and hook-ups. Reservation fees are $8.

Ages: All

LAS FLORES CREEK PARK

(310) 456-2489 / www.malibucity.org
3805 Las Flores Canyon Drive, Malibu

What a creativity-inspiring little park located right off the highway! It has a wooden raft (with sides and handles) on huge springs to create movement of the sea; giant frog and fish statues; a small merry-go-round with a rope tepee structure on it; a wooden teeter-totter; wood blocks and large fake rocks with ropes attaching them to climb on and through; and a wooden boat to climb in. Very fun - very different. There are also sycamore trees with low-hanging branches that beckon climbers, other plants and shade trees, and a seasonal creek on one side of the park. Note: There are picnic tables here, but no restrooms.

Hours: Open daily, 8am - sunset

Price: Free

Ages: 2 - 12 years

LIBBEY PARK

(805) 646-5581 / www.ci.ojai.ca.us; www.libbeybowl.org
Ojai Avenue & Signal Street, Ojai

This sprawling park goes way back off the main street and is like several types of park all in one. Past the cement courtyard with a fountain on the main road is the extra long, metal, play apparatus with ramps, suspension bridges, tunnels, ladders, poles, and slides. A thirty-five-foot long talking tube is mostly underground, with just the funnel-shaped ends above ground, at kid-level. Have your child talk into one end while you listen at the other. There are also swings, pull up bars, and a sand play area. Picnic tables are under enormous oak trees.

An abundant number of tennis courts are here - in the front area and then numerous more towards the back. Some have stadium seating as this is the home of an annual spring tournament that attracts the country's top-ranked collegiate players. Amateurs can play on a first come, first serve basis. The lower courts have lights for nighttime play. Cross under the sound arch with pipes that play a melody when activated by motion. The half-dome-shaped Libbey Bowl has graded seating for concerts, or for your young stars to make their (pretend) debut. The Ojai Music Festival takes place here as does the annual storytelling festival in May, and many other musical forums and programs.

Further back, or entering from Montgomery Street, is the nature section of the park. Kids naturally gravitate to the seasonal creek that is surrounded by glorious old oak and sycamore trees. A natureish trail leads from here to the front and then crisscrosses through the park. For just a little while, perhaps, you'll feel refreshingly removed from civilization. The OJAI VALLEY TRAIL (pg. 697) also begins (or ends) here. Tip: Top off your time with a visit to the ice cream store across Ojai Street. You can also catch a ride around town on the Ojai Trolley which runs daily until about 5pm. The cost is $1 for ages 5 and up; 50¢ for seniors; children 4 and under are free. Call (805) 646-5581 / www.ojaitrolley.com for more information.

Hours: The park is open daily, 6am - 11pm.

Price: Free

Ages: All

LOS PADRES NATIONAL FOREST: MATILIJA WILDERNESS AND SESPE WILDERNESS

(805) 640-9060 - Los Padres Forest Visitors Center; (805) 646-4348 - Ojai Ranger Station / www.lpforest.org; www.fs.usda.gov/lpnf
Highway 33 and beyond, Ojai

I'm already doing you a disservice, dumping thousands of acres of phenomenal hiking and camping terrain into one entry, but I wanted to make sure you at least had a starting point. I mention WHEELER GORGE NATURE TRAIL (pg. 678) in a separate section simply because it is the most accessible trail (just eight miles outside of town) in the national forest. And it's a beaut! The next closest trail is Rose Valley, which has a waterfall and awesome scenery. The country further up and further in is even more spectacular and varied.

Call, check out the website, or visit either the Los Padres Forest Visitors Center or the Ojai Ranger Station for complete information on the trails and territory in these wilderness areas.

Hours: The Visitors Center is open Sat. - Sun., 9am - 3pm. The Ranger Station is open most of the year, Mon. - Fri., 8am - 4:30pm.
Price: $5 per vehicle for an Adventure Pass.
Ages: 6 years and up.

MALIBU BLUFFS PARK

(310) 317-1364 / www.malibucity.org
24250 Pacific Coast Highway, Malibu

As the name suggests, this park is on a bluff top, right across the street from Pepperdine University. The view is fantastic, especially on a clear day, and there are playgrounds here, too. One small, enclosed play area, adjacent to the community center, has one structure with three different slides coming out from it, plus metal twisty things to climb on. Other play elements scattered throughout the park include a mini zip line; a sand area with diggers; a large turtle statue to climb on; and a funky, curved horizontal rock climbing wall with a tube and metal and spherical balls to play on. You can also sit on a whale's fluke bench to whale watch (or use the telescopes). Hike the dirt pathway down and around the surrounding preserve, or all the way down to the beach below.

An ample plot of grass is dotted with a few picnic tables, boulders, and trees, plus a soccer field, two baseball fields (with concession stands that are open on game days), and a cement walkway around the perimeter.

Hours: Open daily, sunrise - sunset.
Price: Free
Ages: All

MARINA PARK

(805) 652-4550 / www.cityofventura.net
at the end of Pierpont Boulevard, Ventura

This very cool park is part beach, part grass. The big expanse of open grass area (no shade trees) has a few picnic tables and precedes a pirate ship themed playground that has fake cannons, portholes, a slide and port and starboard rails. Other elements, all on rubberized flooring, include swings and toddler swings; a series of metal ladders to climb; a good-sized rock climbing wall with holes and holds; a tunnel to climb over and under; and other fun and creative apparatus.

At the adjacent beach part a relatively large, cement and wooden replica Spanish galleon, masts and all, is beached to play in and on. The ship has a zip line, or cable slide, that goes from the ship to a post about fifty feet away on the sand, so whoosh away. The beach also has a volleyball court, and rock jetties with a paved pathway that goes out to a point. Sand dunes along the path, with the ocean and sailboats parading in and out of the marina, make it ideal for taking pictures, or just for meditating. A small cove (with waves) for swimming, and a surfing area are here, too. Note that VENTURA HARBOR VILLAGE (pg. 692) is just around the corner.

Hours: Open daily, sunrise - sunset.
Price: Free
Ages: All

MORANDA PARK

(805) 986 - 6500 or (805) 986-6542 / www.ci.port-hueneme.ca.us
200 Moranda Parkway, Port Hueneme

This hilly green park is spread out and diverse with eight tennis courts, two softball fields, a basketball court, and a good and good-sized playground. A paved path goes around and through the park, making it a great place to stroll, jog, or bike. It also connects about midway with the green belt of Bubbling Springs Creek, a lovely bike/pedestrian path that goes along from the beach front inland along a creek that is home to various types of sea birds. Stop at Moranda Park to play or have a picnic while exploring Oxnard and Ventura.

Hours: Open daily, dawn - dusk. Tennis courts are open daily, 7:30am - 4pm (later in the summer).
Price: Free. Tennis is free, too.
Ages: All

OJAI SKATE PARK

(805) 646-5581 / www.ojaiskatepark.com; www.ci.ojai.ca.us
414 E. Ojai Avenue, Ojai

This good-sized, enclosed, unsupervised cement skate park has several bowls, with a central one that has a small mound in the middle, plus rails, steps, benches and platforms. Practice ollies, boardslides, 50-50 grinds, method air, and more at this popular skate park. A helmet and pads are required.

Hours: Open daily, dawn to dusk.
Price: Free
Ages: 7 years and up.

POINT DUME NATURAL RESERVE

(818) 597-9192; (310) 457-8143 / www.lamountains.com; www.parks.ca.gov
Cliffside Drive, between Birdview Ave. and Dume Dr., Malibu

This overlook of the beach offers great shoreline views, but be careful as not all the cliffs have secure fencing. A dirt trail leads along the topside of the cliffs, while another trail, lined with chain link fence, meanders down to wooden steps that lead to the mostly rocky beach below. The somewhat narrow beach is great for walking and for tidepooling, as well as seeing and hearing seals. See POINT DUME STATE BEACH (page 659) for a nearby swim beach.

Hours: Open daily, sunrise - sunset
Price: Free
Ages: 4 years and up.

POINT MUGU STATE PARK

(805) 488-1827; (805) 488-5223 - park; (800) 444-7275 - camping reservations / www.parks.ca.gov; www.lamountains.com; www.beachcalifornia.com
9000 W. Pacific Coast Highway at Sycamore Cove and Sycamore Canyon, Malibu

This westernmost park in the Santa Monica Mountain Recreation Area consists of miles of beach, plus inland hiking and biking trails; more than seventy miles in all. A passageway under the highway allows visitors access to both parts of the park. The beach is a popular spot for swimming, seasonal whale watching (end of December through March), and viewing flocks of Monarch butterflies (November through January). The inland, mountainside trails vary in length, difficulty, and scenery. Some trail heads are found at the campground.

The La Jolla Valley Loop Trail is about seven miles round trip. It is a relatively easy walk (about ¾ of a mile) to a little waterfall and pond before the trail enters valley grasslands and gets more strenuous. You can follow the Loop trail to reconnect to the canyon, or continue to Mugu Peak Trail and the 1,266-foot summit, which is an additional three miles. Other trails offer high-walled canyons, oak trees groves, fields of wild flowers (in the spring), and more. Note that Backbone Trail, a trail that extends nearly seventy miles across and through the Santa Monica Mountains, has a trailhead here. For more information on Backbone, call the Santa Monica Mountains National Recreation Area at (805) 370-2301 / www.smmc.ca.gov. The rugged ten-mile hike of Boney Mountains State Wilderness Loop, which includes craggy pinnacles, are also part of the Point Mugu system.

Camping is available in Sycamore Canyon, which is part of this park system. Most of the closely-spaced, fifty-eight sites are nestled in the mountainside, where the hiking trails are. These spaces are nice looking and have large shade

trees. Adjacent to the campground is the Sycamore Nature Center, with exhibits housed in a 1928 mission-style bungalow. Very primitive beach camping is available a little over one mile north at the Thornhill Broome exit. There are no showers or chemical toilets here.

Hours: Open daily, 8am - 10pm. The nature center is open Sat. and Sun., 10am - 3pm.

Price: $8 - $12 per vehicle for day use, depending on location. There is limited street parking available. Camping at Sycamore Canyon, which has showers and running water, starts at $45 a night. Camping at Thornhill Broome starts at $25 a night. A $8 camping reservation fee is charged. Admission is free to the nature center with paid vehicle fee.

Ages: All

RANCHO SIERRA VISTA / SATWIWA NATIVE AMERICAN CULTURE CENTER

(805) 370-2300; (805) 370-2301 / www.nps.gov/samo; www.lamountains.com
off Via Goleta Road near Potrero Rd., Newbury Park

Since the cultural center is not visible from the parking area, you need to walk about a quarter of a mile on a tree-lined gravel road to reach it. A small garden, a large reconstructed Chumash ap (i.e., round house dwelling made of willow and tule) to walk through, and the center's building containing informational display panels and a few Native American artifacts, are just the beginning. On Sundays the culture center plays host to traditionally-dressed Native Americans who tell stories, or talk about aspects of their ancestor's life and culture; share tribal songs; demonstrate crafts; and/or lead workshops. Ask or check the website regarding special presentations, and guided, educational hikes.

The trailhead for the two-mile Satwiwa loop trail is just outside the center. This trail traverses amongst oak and sycamore trees, and around the chaparral-covered hillsides that are particularly lovely after the winter rains, and while the spring wildflowers are in bloom. This fairly easy hike is good for almost all ages. Tip: Bring your own water. Go just another mile, round trip, off the loop trail to connect to Boney Mountain trail, which crosses a stream several times to reach a seasonal waterfall. Several other trails intersperse throughout, as this area extends into POINT MUGU STATE PARK (see the above entry). You can even hike to the beach, which is about eight miles each way. A shorter option, and more bike/stroller friendly, is the paved pathway that runs about three miles, one way.

Hours: The park is open daily, dawn - dusk. The Culture Center is open Sat. - Sun., 9am - 5pm.

Price: Free

Ages: 8 years and up.

RANCHO TAPO COMMUNITY PARK

(805) 584-4400 / www.rsrpd.org
3700 Avenida Simi, Simi Valley

Massive and wonderful this park's amenities include four full basketball courts, side-by-side; a baseball diamond; tennis courts; pickleball courts; bocce ball courts (bring your own equipment); a nice-size fitness area with legitimate work out machines and equipment; a .5 walking path frequented by joggers and moms pushing strollers; lots of picnic tables and mature shade trees; shuffleboard courts; a good-sized pond with fountains and lots of ducks, surrounded by a veteran's memorial plaza; and a playground and water spray area. The playground, bordered by rocks, has slides, tunnels, swings, bridges, and metal climbing apparatus. The large, circular water spray area has fountain spurting up from the ground and a rainbow of spheres to run through that squirt water every which way.

Hours: The park is open daily, sunrise - sunset. The water spray area is open Memorial Day - Labor Day, daily, 11am - 5pm.

Price: Free

Ages: All

SANTA SUSANA PARK / SANTA SUSANA DEPOT AND MUSEUM

(805) 584-4400 - park; (805) 581-3462 - depot/museum / www.rsrpd.org; www.santasusannadepot.org
6503 Katherine Road (South of the Railroad bridge), Simi Valley

This great back-to-nature park is right next door to a train depot and museum. The large park is studded with huge, old shade trees. Some run-around grassy areas, picnic tables, a basketball court, baseball diamond, and volleyball court are here, plus a good-sized and fun playground that is reminiscent of a fort with bridges and slides, but what

makes this park a stand out are the large boulders and rock mounds for kids to climb on and play. There is also a tunnel that connects this park to the an untamed area and more rocks on the other side. Trains are always zooming by the park, too, so train lovers get an eye-full.

The quaint railroad depot, authentically restored to how it looked in 1903, is just next door to the park. The old waiting room is now a museum filled with numerous railroad paraphernalia as well as an extensive HO scale model railroad layout. The model trains run through a rural and city representation of Simi Valley as it was in the 1950's - kids and adults are enthralled. The tracks just outside the depot are still quite busy, used by both Amtrak and Metrolink.

Hours: The park is open daily, sunrise - sunset. The depot and museum are open Sat. - Sun. for tours and for the model train to run, 1pm - 4pm.

Price: Free

Ages: All

SHELF ROAD TRAIL / PRATT TRAIL

(805) 654-3951 / www.ventura.org
Shelf Road, near Signal St., Ojai

Shelf Road is a .6 mile old dirt fire road located at the foothills of the mountains that used to be open to cars. Now, it's a trail that leads hikers up and across a portion of the hills, past orange and avocado groves, for a great view of the valley below and mountains on the horizon. The road does tend to get steep at times, but it is wide and well-maintained, so it seems easier, somehow! If you are here around sunset, stop and drink in the "pink moment" that Ojai is famous for. (When the sun is just about to set, the sky blazes pink - really.)

The other trail accessible from this point is Pratt Trail, a more strenuous hike. This "true" hiking trail is almost five miles long, and narrow, with many ups and downs. Certain sections cross over the creek. There are numerous routes branching off from Pratt, so take your pick. It ends at Nordhoff Ridge. Note that the lower end of the trail cuts through private property.

Hours: Open daily, sunrise - sunset.

Price: Free

Ages: 5 years and up.

SOULE PARK

(805) 654-3951 / www.ventura.org
1301 Soule Park Drive, Ojai

Located next to Soule Park Golf Course, this elongated, 223-acre park offers a not-too-far-away get away. Snuggled up against the mountains, so the view is amazing, the park consists of long and fairly wide expanses of grassy areas; lots of mature trees and picnic tables sprinkled throughout; three paddle-tennis courts; a dog park; and a throwback playground. The playground has a metal rocket ship with a slide to launch imaginations; a metal frame of a flying saucer disc to climb up, into and around; a metal frame of a submarine (and yes, its yellow; peeling paint, but yellow); toddler swings; horseshoe pits; and a baseball field towards the entrance.

Hours: Open daily 7:30am - dusk.

Price: $2 per vehicle weekday; $4 on the weekends or holidays.

Ages: 2 years and up.

STECKEL PARK

(805) 654-3951 / www.ventura.org
8080 Mistletoe Road, Santa Paula

This rural park offers an enticing hiatus from city life. The day-use picnic area is along the street, and along the banks of the Santa Paula Creek, which teems with bubbling waters, creek life, and boulders. Bring a fishing pole and see what you catch! Or, just go splashing in it during the summer months. Picnic tables and run-around space are tucked amongst big, shady, oak and walnut woodlands. Entertainment for kids, besides the gorgeous scenery, includes a small playground, a volleyball court, a horseshoe pit, and a field. A small aviary, just past the park office, has several cages holding peacocks, lovebirds, parrots, and other birds that you can peek into the cages and look at.

The adjacent tent campsites, to the west of Santa Paula Creek, each have trees, some shrubbery, and a barbecue pit. Although the campground is just off the highway, the noise is minimal and the surroundings make up for it.

Hours: Open daily, 7:30am - dusk.
Price: $2 per vehicle Mon. - Fri; $4, Sat. - Sun. Camping is $20 - $36 per night, depending on the season and if hook ups are needed.
Ages: All

TRANCAS CANYON PARK

(310) 317-1364 / www.malibucity.org
6050 Trancas Canyon Road, Malibu

Move 'em on, head 'em out, rawhide! This great, Western-themed playground feels like the Old West for young uns. On a plateau, surrounded by mountains with a view of the beach, the playtown has boulders and trees around it, and even some in it. The little town is comprised of a few, two-story buildings on wooden poles, named Rindge Hotel, General Store, Malibu Post Office, and Tile Store. The buildings have slides coming out from them; rock-climbing walls (one has a boot, horseshoe, and sheriff's star as the "rocks"); a series of wagon wheels to climb up; doorways; platforms; and lots of space under the raised buildings with benches and short tunnels for more creative play. Ride the range on play horses and a buffalo on huge springs. Logs, cargo nets, tunnels to crawl through, bridges to cross (one crosses over a blue, recycled rubber area designed to look like water); a configuration of blocks; and swings (including toddler swings) complete this truly out-West little town.

There is a huge expanse of grass (i.e. an athletic field) adjacent to the playground, plus shaded picnic benches. There is a really large, dirt, enclosed dog park (with bridges and other play elements for canines) on an upper level from the playground.

Hours: Open Mon. - Fri., 8am - dusk (or 7pm, whichever is earlier); Sat. - Sun., 9am - dusk (or 7pm)
Price: Free
Ages: 2 - 11 years

WHEELER GORGE VISITORS CENTER, NATURE TRAIL and CAMPGROUND

(805) 640-9060 - Los Padres Forest Visitors Center; (805) 646-4348 - Ojai Ranger Station; (805) 640-1977 - Wheeler Gorge Campground; (877) 444-6777 - camping reservations / www.fs.usda.gov/lpnf; www.lpforest.org; www.reserveamerica.com
17017 Maricopa Highway/State 33, Ojai

"♬ Country roads, take me home to the place I belong ♪. . . ." Just driving the mountain roads lined with oak, sycamore, and cottonwood trees, while listening to the sounds of birds trilling, and breathing in the crisp clean air, feels good. Getting out and walking around feels even better! Make your first stop the Los Padres Forest Wheeler Gorge Visitors Center, located about eight miles out of Ojai on the right-hand side. It is the hub station for going into the Los Padres Forest. Free hiking maps and advice are available here, as are special, interpretative, and educational weekend programs. Just south of this immediate area, you may pull off onto the side of the road and hike around, and/or splash in the Matilija Creek, without having to pay $5 for an Adventure Pass for your vehicle.

Directly across the street from the Visitors Center is Wheeler Gorge Campground, which is not run by rangers, so don't ask them too many questions. Its backcountry sites delight naturalists. Each of the sixty-eight sites (five of which are handicapped accessible) has a fire ring, barbecue pit, and picnic table, but no potable water. Two-night stays are required on the weekend. At the north end of the campground is the trailhead, with limited parking, for the Wheeler Gorge Nature Trail. This narrow, half-mile, looping trail runs along and crosses over Matilija Creek, into the hillsides and up for a breathtaking view. The creek has boulders that line it and are strewn across it at points. Be on the lookout for poison oak. Plant life on the trail changes from cool, shady riparian vegetation to drier chaparral plants. With ten trails that range in length and difficulty, toddlers to hardy hikers will find at least one that suits them.

Hours: The Visitors Center is open Sat. - Sun., 9am - 3pm. Day use for the campground area is open 8am - 6pm. The trail is open daily, sunrise - sunset. The campground is open year round.
Price: Free to the trail. Day use vehicle fee is $10. Tent or RV camping is $23 a night. The camping reservation fee is $10.
Ages: 5 years and up.

WILDWOOD REGIONAL PARK

(805) 495-2163 or (805) 495-6471 / www.crpd.org; www.cosf.org

928 W. Avenue de los Arboles, Thousand Oaks

Take a walk on the wild side at Wildwood Regional Park. The narrow, dirt trails and service roads are great for real hiking. There are two major trail heads that lead to an extensive trail system for hikers, bikers, and equestrians. Come prepared by bringing water bottles, sunscreen, and backpacks with food, for designated picnic areas. Although hiking downhill is easy, plan twice as much time for the hike back up.

Some highlights along the somewhat shorter trails, which are still an almost all-day event, include the Nature Center, Little Falls, and Paradise Falls, which is a forty-foot waterfall that you'll hear before you actually reach it. A hardy 3.2 mile looping hike from the parking lot is down the wooden stairs and over the bridge of Moonridge Trail, into the canyon, past a tepee, to Paradise Falls, then onto Indian Creek Trail (take the side trip to the cave) and along the creek, through the chaparral and woodlands - be on the lookout for wildlife, such as mule deers and lizards - and finally, back up some stairs to the car.

Hike here during the spring months and you'll see an abundance of wildflowers. I encourage you to get a trail map, as different routes have different highlights that you'll want to explore and/or check the second website above for specific trail info. The park offers wonderful, fun, and educational programs, like Saturday Night S'Mores, Full Moon Hikes, and Outdoor Experiential Workshops. Enjoy nature, almost in your backyard!

Hours: Open daily, 7am - dusk.
Price: Free. Some of the programs cost $6 - $8.
Ages: 4 years and up. Kids will tire easily.

—MALLS—

THE LAKES KIDS CLUB

(805) 497-9861 / www.shoplakes.com
2200 E. Thousand Oaks Boulevard, Thousand Oaks

This beautifully-landscaped, upscale, outdoor shopping center (dare I call it a mall?) with two lakes (hence the name), a fountain, and plaza, offers a free kid's club once a week. The productions are first class, featuring name entertainers for your youngsters. Come see marionettes, storytelling, dancing, and singing, and sometimes balloon animals and face painting. Then, grab a bite to eat here. The Lakes also hosts seasonal events and activities, including, ice skating during the winter months. See the Calendar section (pg. 758) for details.

Hours: Every Wed., March - October, 11am - noon.
Price: Free
Ages: 2 - 10 years.

THE OAKS - OK KIDS CLUB

(805) 495-2032 or (805) 495-2031 / www.shoptheoaksmall.com
350 W. Hillcrest Drive, Thousand Oaks

Teaming up with National Geographic Kids, a variety of hour-long shows are presented once a month at the lower level court. Activities or shows could include marionettes, singers, dancers, magicians, and other entertainment. Afterward there is a craft project to make pertaining to the theme. For instance, a pet theme had an animal finger puppets show followed by making one. The mall often hosts special events. It also hosts a Farmer's Market every Thursday from 1:30pm to 6pm. Note that this mall features BUILD-A-BEAR WORKSHOP (pg. 693), and MAKE MEANING (pg. 657), as well as many other fine stores and eateries.

Hours: The first Thurs. of each month at 10am.
Price: Free
Ages: 1½ - 7 years.

—MUSEUMS—

AGRICULTURE MUSEUM

(805) 525-3100 / www.venturamuseum.org
926 Railroad Avenue, Santa Paula

Hoping to plant a seed of interest, the story of agriculture in Ventura is vividly depicted throughout this barn-like museum. A gift shop and Ford Model A farm truck are the first things you see when you enter. Proceed into the spacious main room, with wooden floors, to see old farm machinery such as the first gasoline tractor and several other vintage tractors; a spring wagon; a Holt Caterpillar; a John Deere tractor; and the massive John Deere thresher, circa 1940 - all with explanatory placards. Old farm equipment and tools line the walls, as do old-time photographs, old signs, crates, branding irons, and even saddles, including one that you can sit on. One of the several interactive displays asks questions that you open the panels (via a sprinkler head knob) to find out the answers. Another is a 120-year old warehouse scale originally used to weigh lima beans that you can use, and another is a tractor to sit on. A blacksmith display is in the corner.

The next room is more geared for kids with a fake horse and 1890's real buggy to sit in and pose; a dress up area with old farm clothes; short, wooden trees laden with bean bag oranges, lemons and avocados to pick; lift up panels; an electronic match-the-crop game; a beautiful bee and flower mural with a real (encased) bee hive and bee info; a play cafe; and lots more. Out back are themed garden beds, as well as a planting area for students to participate in. The ninety-minute guided school tours, for K through 8th graders, reap a harvest of knowledge and fun as they include all that the museum has to offer, plus planting a seed to take home, participating in a five sense taste testing and perhaps a related craft. Note that free family fun days are the first Sunday of every month with free craft activities, too.

Don't have a cow when you go into the restrooms, though there is a statue of one right outside the door, along with an old cream separator and packing crate signs. The front of the museum has hitching posts for horses, plus benches, a little garden area, and interpretative signs. The museum is located across the railroad tracks from the historic depot, which is now a visitors center. Check out the CALIFORNIA OIL MUSEUM (pg. 680) and SANTA PAULA ART MUSEUM (pg. 689) that are right around the corner. Take a tour of the nine murals around town that show the history of Santa Paula and its inhabitants. See www.santapaulamurals.org for more info. Note that the FILLMORE & WESTERN RAILWAY COMPANY (see pg. 698) has a regularly-scheduled stop here.

Hours: Open Wed. - Sun., 10am - 4pm. Closed major holidays.

Price: $4 for adults; $3 for seniors; $1 for ages 6 - 17; children 5 and under are free. Guided school tours are $5 per student; self guided school tours are $1 per person. Admission is free on the first Sun. of every month.

Ages: 3 years and up.

AVIATION MUSEUM OF SANTA PAULA

(805) 525-1109 / www.amszp.org

830 E. Santa Maria Street, Santa Paula

Take your child to new heights at this aviation museum, adjacent to the Santa Paula Airport. Watch small planes land and take off. The museum consists of a chain of hangars, each one featuring different exhibits. Inside the first hangar, displays pertain to the history of the Santa Paula airport. See the short video here, too. Other hangars showcase restored vintage, military, classic, and experimental aircraft, plus items from the hangar owner's personal collection. More unusual exhibits (at least unusual for an aviation museum) are vintage and unusual radios, jukeboxes, antique and classic cars, vintage racing cars, paintings, photos, collectibles, and more. You can walk the grounds to the hangars or take a shuttle. The museum's goals are to expand to include other hangars, and to incorporate more historical aircraft, especially from the various war eras. School and other group tours are offered during the week. Call to make a reservation.

Enjoy the numerous classic airplanes that come in for a landing on the first Sunday, coinciding with the museum being open. There are often other "specials" on these days, such as a classic car show, and the gift shop is open. What a great way to spend time with the whole family! See SANTA PAULA AIRPORT and CP AVIATION, INC. (pg. 700) if you're interested in taking an airplane rides and YOUNG EAGLES PROGRAM (Ventura County) (pg. 700) for a free program for the kids.

Hours: Open the first Sun. of every month, 10am - 3pm.

Price: Free

Ages: 4 years and up.

CALIFORNIA OIL MUSEUM

(805) 933-0076 / www.oilmuseum.net

1001 E. Main Street, Santa Paula

The California Oil Museum is housed in the original headquarters of the Union Oil Company. The interior and exterior of the 1890 building has meticulously been restored to its original luster. Outside is a small, enclosed mini park for visitors with a bit of grass, benches and shade trees.

Enter the museum which walls are covered with great pictures and murals regarding the history and technology of the oil industry; of black gold. Quite a few of the exhibits are interactive, such as the Lubricity Exhibit. Kids can turn the gears and see how much easier the figures on bicycles can pedal when the gears are oiled. They can push a button and watch a model rig "drill" for oil through the layers of the earth. With a touch of a button, the Centrifuge Exhibit spins to separate water, and other substances from crude oil. A few touch screens here impart interesting information about how the oil industry affects so many aspects of our lives. See lighter and darker vials of oil depending on how heavy it is; a display of early uses of petroleum; and transporting, pumping and marketing gasoline via models, tubes and a collection of vintage gas pumps. It's all visually well done and interesting.

Since geology is vital to finding oil, several terrific geological displays are in the museum. Some of the fossils on display include shells, dinosaur bones, and shark teeth. Rotating exhibits of science, transportation, history, and art are also presented here throughout the year.

The back room has rotating displays and is used as a classroom for school groups. One exhibit featured small planes - a Kitfox Model 1 and a Flying Flea, and other aviation-themed displays. Another was prehistoric California with a life-size saber-toothed cat with fur, plus numerous skeletons and bones and fossils from that time period.

The upstairs, which can only be seen by a half-hour guided tour, is interesting to older kids. It contains restored 1890s offices, a 1930s-era bedroom, a kitchen, and fireplaces with ornate tiles around them. A walk-in safe here looks like a secret, hidden room.

Walk through the main building to a side gallery room that features rotating displays. I saw an homage to our servicemen and women with mannequins dressed in military uniforms from WWII, plus canteens, medals, photographs, newspaper clippings, and a video. Walk outside to reach the Rig Room. Besides the row of more antique gas pumps, the room is taken up by an immense, full-size drilling rig and a huge cable rig in action. The engine turns the sand wheel that turns the band wheel that moves the wooden walking beam and the huge drill bits. I hope you feel like we did when we visited the museum - like we struck oil! One- to two-hour guided tours (at only $3 per person) are available for adult and school guests.

Just a block down the street, at Ventura Street, is Veteran's Park, which has a gated, cement skate park; play equipment; picnic tables; and a large patch of grass. Check out the AGRICULTURE MUSEUM (pg. 679) and SANTA PAULA ART MUSEUM (pg. 689) that are right around the corner. Take a tour of the nine murals around town that show the history of Santa Paula and its inhabitants. See www.santapaulamurals.org for more info. Note that the FILLMORE & WESTERN RAILWAY COMPANY (see pg. 698) has a regularly-scheduled stop here.

Hours: Open Wed. - Sun., 10am - 4pm. Tours of the upstairs are offered Wed. - Fri., noon - 2pm; Sat. - Sun., noon - 3pm. Closed major holidays.

Price: $4 for adults; $3 for seniors; $1 for ages 6 - 17; children 5 and under are free. Admission is free on the first Wed. of every month.

Ages: 4 years and up.

CAMARILLO RANCH MUSEUM   ☼

(805) 389-8182 / www.camarilloranch.org $$

201 Camarillo Ranch Road, Camarillo

This three-story, fifteen-room house is one of the most lovely restored Victorian homes I've had the pleasure of touring. The distinguished architecture - the archways, twelve-foot-high ceilings, octagon-shaped rooms, beautiful wood staircase, wrap around porch, and other special features, enhance the elegant furniture and colorful wallpaper and borders. On the forty-five-minute tour, the guide explained the past owners' history and all about the house, but truthfully, I mostly enjoyed just looking at all the rooms.

Adjacent to the house is the original mule barn and stables (one of which now houses a gift shop), as well as a huge Moreton Bay Fig tree, and attractively-landscaped grounds. Picnic tables are here, too. The Ranch Museum is now surrounded by a business park, which seems out of place (or time).

Hours: Open Sat. - Mon., 10am - 2pm. Closed on holidays. Group tours may be arranged at other times. School tours are offered Tues., 9am - 11:30am.

Price: Public and group tours are $5 per person. School tours are $1 per student.
Ages: 8 years and up.

CARNEGIE ART MUSEUM   ☀

(805) 385-8157 / www.carnegieam.org; www.ci.oxnard.ca.us $
424 S. 'C' Street, Oxnard

Come see the permanent and rotating exhibits of paintings, photographs, and sculptures at this museum. Have your children draw a picture of their outing! I mention this small, beautiful fine arts museum mainly because of the kid-friendly workshops offered. (Tell your kids the building is done in neo-classical design, though they'll just think the columns look really neat.) I take my kids through art museums, explaining what I can and hoping that some understanding and appreciation for art will take root. However, I think the best way to reach and teach our kids is through guided tours and hands-on workshops.

In a group tour here, kids learn about a particular style, artist, or medium, depending on the current exhibit. Then, they create their own art projects in a workshop taught by a local artist. Reservations are needed. Ask about other classes offered, too.

Hours: Open Thurs. - Sat., 10am - 5pm; Sun., 1am - 5pm. Closed during public holidays and during installation of new exhibits.
Price: $4 for adults; $2 for seniors and students; $1 for age 6 - 18; children 5 and under are free. Admission is free every Fri., 3pm - 5pm. Call for tour and class prices.
Ages: 6 years and up.

CHANNEL ISLANDS MARITIME MUSEUM   ☀

(805) 984-6260 / www.vcmm.org $$
3900 Bluefin Circle, Oxnard

Explore the seas without leaving port! This unique nautical museum focuses on displaying maritime paintings and its outstanding (and massive) collection of model ships all beautifully arrayed and presented in a light and airy building with windows overlooking the picturesque marina. The striking paintings include works from Dutch masters from the 1700's and up. The intricate model ships of all sizes, mostly behind glass cases, are amazing - what attention to detail! Each of the ships is labeled with the specifics of what it is modeled after. Many of ships also feature tiny crewmen and equipment. There are so many models that intrigue, like the Prisoner of War ones made out of animal bones, the clipper ships, and the 1637 *Sovereign of the Seas* with its numerous minute cannons and all that rigging.

Upstairs are more models, including some larger ones and more special ones. There are also flags that the docents here gladly use to teach visitors what they are used for; a steering wheel from a wreck that can be turned; gages to be touched; a board with a variety of knots to try; ships in bottles; whale bones; and scrimshaw. Ask for a paper and pencil scavenger hunt for your kids as they look for objects in the museum and out the windows.

The outside of the museum features an interactive mosaic fountain, plus round tables and chairs, so bring a snack to enjoy here, and soak in the view. Guided tours are offered upon request and the knowledge dispensed is well, indispensable.

Hours: Open daily, 11am - 5pm. Closed New Year's Day, Thanksgiving and Christmas.
Price: $5 for adults; $4 for seniors; $2 for ages 6 - 17; children 5 and under are free. Admission is free the third Thurs. of every month. School tours are $2 per student.
Ages: 4 years and up.

CHANNEL ISLANDS NATIONAL PARK VISITOR CENTER   ☀

(805) 658-5730 / www.nps.gov/chis   !
1901 Spinnaker Drive, Ventura

The Channel Islands Visitor Center is worthy of a trip in itself. You'll pass by beaches and stores (see VENTURA HARBOR VILLAGE on page 692), but pacify the kids with a, "We'll stop there on the way out." The Center is a good combination of museum, store, and resource center. The kids will head straight for the indoor tidepool (not a touch tank), which offers an up-close look at sea stars, anemones, lobsters, and other small, ocean creatures. Other eye-catching displays are the taxidermied animals, such as birds in flight, plus a topographical model of the islands, a life-size replica of an elephant seal, and a cast of a pygmy mammoth skeleton. My boys also enjoyed sifting sand in the

mini-sand pit and grinding pretend meal with a Chumash Indian stone mortar and pestle. Ask about the Jr. Ranger programs. And go up the observation steps outside a few flights up to the top for a panoramic view.

The twenty-five-minute movie, *A Treasure In the Sea,* is shown throughout the day, and is a fun way to learn more about sea life. There are other films shown, as well. Tidepool talks are available on weekends and holidays. Note that rangers lead ninety-minute educational programs here, with a minimum of twelve students, and they also come to local schools for presentations. Look under CHANNEL ISLANDS NATIONAL PARK (from Ventura) on page 668 if you are interested in taking a trip to the islands.

Hours:	Open daily, 8:30am - 5pm. Closed Thanksgiving and Christmas. The weekend and holiday ranger presentations are at 11am and 3pm.
Price:	Free
Ages:	2 years and up.

CHUMASH INDIAN MUSEUM / OAKBROOK REGIONAL PARK

(805) 492-8076 - museum; (805) 449-2505 - park / www.chumashindianmuseum.com; www.conejo-openspace.org
3290 Lang Ranch Parkway, Thousand Oaks

Long ago, the Chumash Indians occupied this area of land, which is now Ventura County, and other surrounding areas. An alcove off the main desk features a large selection of basketry from several Native American tribes, with a majority from the Chumash. There are also mounted deer, rams, and wild boar heads, plus a saddle and historical info and other artifacts from the Lang Ranch.

The small, one-room museum nicely and naturally displays artifacts representative of the Chumash way of life. The glass cases contain a collection stone mortar and pestles; stone, shell and bone tools and jewelry (from 9000 B.C. on); pictures of rock paintings and pigments; plants and herbal remedies; fragments of tomol, or canoe planks; and games using walnuts and other natural game pieces. Paintings and other artwork decorate the walls. There are several taxidermied animals such as a cougar, raccoon, eagle and fox. The centerpiece exhibit is the life-size diorama against the back wall. Five Chumash figures are wearing indigenous clothing and necklaces and are on a sandy beach, obviously done fishing for the day. A recreated tomol is on the beach as are some baskets, shells, and a small (pretend) campfire. The table in front of the diorama holds some items not behind glass. A smaller, encased diorama showcases a young Chumash man in ceremonial paint and dance regalia wearing a deer bone pin, hawk feathers and deer hide.

Don't miss the gift shop, even if you don't come into the museum. It is like a mini-museum with Native American handcrafted articles such as deer antler stone knives, arrowhead necklaces, animal fur, rattles made from turtle shells, dolls, necklaces, beautifully painted stones, and more.

Walk outside .7 miles to see a replicated Chumash village with six different buildings (aps), other structures, and ceremonial grounds all under oak trees. (You don't have to pay the museum fee to see the village.) There are also benches out here for the school programs that take place. School or group tours, minimum twenty-five students, are about two-and-a-half hours long, very informative, and one of the most effective ways to really see and understand what the museum and grounds have to offer. Hear an explanation of the museum exhibits, listen to storytelling, play a few native games, make a craft to take home, and take a guided walk through the park and archaeological preserve, from a Chumash perspective. You'll learn about their way of life, hear how different plants and trees were used, and inspect the village. Guided nature walks, given on select weekends at 10am for the general public, are offered on select weekends. The cost is $10 for adults; $5 for ages 12 and under. It is only via a guided walk that you can see the centuries-old pictographs, or rock paintings, visible from the caves/overhangs as they are protect to preserve them. Note that the annual Chumash celebration is held at the museum and park in September.

The 436-acre Oakbrook Regional Park itself, adjacent to the museum and Lang Ranch Open Space, is beautiful, and can be visited without going into the museum. There are picnic tables, multitudes of mature shady oak trees, and miles of hiking trails, such as the moderate, 4+ mile Lang Ranch Loop.

Hours:	The museum is open Thurs. - Sun., noon - 5pm. Closed Mon. - Wed. and some holidays. The park is open daily, dawn - dusk. School groups are welcome during the week for tours, 10am - 1pm.
Price:	Entrance to the park is free. Admission to the museum is $5 for adults; $3 for seniors, students, and ages 5 - 12; children 4 and under are free. The family price (for up to 5 people) is $10. School tours are $6 per student; $8 with a craft.
Ages:	7 years and up for the museum.

COMMEMORATIVE AIR FORCE MUSEUM (WWII Aviation Heritage Museum) ☀

(805) 482-0064 / www.cafsocal.com $$$
455 Aviation Drive at Camarillo Airport, Camarillo

Several World War II aircraft, and other items, are on display at this two-hangar museum. Most of the artifacts on exhibit date from WWII and include helmets, flags, airplane parts, canteens, maps, posters, swords, remote-controlled planes, uniforms, a teletype machine, and more. Some of the planes are in flyable condition; some are in the process of being restored; and some can be boarded . All of them make this museum-in-process a hit with visitors. Workers explain what they are doing to fix up planes, and it really is interesting to see the metal sheets, rivets, and huge tires that are being used. Volunteers are working on the aircraft on Tuesdays, Thursdays and Saturdays. Come see the permanent and visiting planes such as a YAK-9, a Curtiss C-46-F transport, a Grumman F8F-2 Bearcat fighter, a North American SNJ Navy trainer, a B-25 Mitchell bomber, P51D Mustang Man-O-War, a Japanese Zero (one of three flying ones in the world!), and several others. School or other group guided tours are given on request.

Kids can climb in a cargo airplane cockpit, buckle up, don the heavy WWII helmets, and turn the knobs on the console. They are also invited to put on a headset and practice Morse code; pick up an old field telephone and pretend to call someone; look through a B-29 gunsight; walk through a plane that looks as it did when the Air Force Chief of Staff used it; and look under a B-25 bomber to see where bombs were once lodged. The docents are affable, knowledgeable, and ready to impart aviation facts whenever asked. The museum is involved with air shows and several special events throughout the year. It also offers twenty-minute Warbird rides starting at $250.

Outside, children may climb on a cannon that was originally from a battleship, and look at a few jeeps located between hangars. As the museum is adjacent to the airport, you can spend some time watching small planes take off and land. If you get hungry for breakfast or lunch, jet on over to Waypoint cafe, (805) 388-2535 / www.thewaypointcafe.com, just off the runway, for inside and outside dining. The cafe is decorated with lots of aviation photos, and a few pieces of airplane paraphernalia. At the end of the air field is Freedom Park, which has a large, run-around field, a sports field, a small playground, horseshoe pits, softball fields, roller hockey rink, and a BMX track for practice and competitions. Contact (805) 482-1996 / www.pvrpd.org/freedompark.htm for more info on the park.

Hours: Open Tues. - Sun., 10am - 4pm. Tues., Thurs. and Sat. are work days, so planes are being worked on and even flown. Closed Mon., New Year's Day, Thanksgiving, and Christmas.
Price: $7 for adults; $4 for ages 10 - 18; $3 for ages 6 - 9; children 5 and under are free.
Ages: 4 years and up.

THE DUDLEY HOUSE ☀

(805)-667-8042 or (805) 644-3286 / www.dudleyhouse.org   !
197 N. Ashwood Avenue, Ventura

This historic, gracious, two-and-a-half-story, Queen Anne-style mansion stands on the corner as a monument to days gone by. The grounds hold lemon trees and purple morning glories. Inside the house, which was originally completed in 1892, are furnishings that typify that era. Walk through the bedrooms, living room, dining room, the very old-fashioned kitchen, and other rooms, to get a feel for this time period. Music recorded in the early 1900's (and since copied onto CDs) plays while you take your guided tour.

The museum is host to numerous special events throughout the year, so please check the website or call for more information. For instance, it is decorated with patriotic bunting for 4th of July, and hosts a flea market. A craft boutique is held, along with the usual Open House, on the three weekends following Thanksgiving. Age-appropriate tours are given at times other than the monthly Open House.

Hours: Open the first Sun. of every month, except December, 1pm - 4pm. Open 4th of July, 1pm - 7pm.
Price: Free
Ages: 7 years and up.

FILLMORE HISTORICAL MUSEUM ☀

(805) 524-0948 / www.fillmorehistoricalmuseum.com $$
340 Main Street, Fillmore

Fillmore was founded in 1887 and this museum celebrates its origins in three unique buildings, all dustered

around the FILLMORE & WESTERN RAILWAY (pg. 698). The main museum is a two-story building, the Sespe Bunkhouse, with several small rooms packed with artifacts and history. There are lots of old photographs; clothing, especially dresses, plus hats, shoes, and accessories; furniture, such a roll top desk with an old telephone; farming and ranching tools; dolls, including a porcelain doll collection, and toys; a school desk; books; a Chumash room with baskets, rocks, and stone mortar and pestles; military war uniforms and medals; old cameras; a small weapons collection - guns and swords; musical instruments; an insect collection; items from packing house days with equipment used in harvesting citrus; and lots more. It's an interesting museum to explore and the docents explain many of the displays. I encourage you to take a guided tours to gain more inside info and especially to have students take a tour.

Inside the railroad depot building is a beautiful, wall-to-wall wooden freight room containing old trunks, a mural, a bell, and display cases holding farm tools, household items, lanterns, model railroad collection and more. The front room was an agent's office and still looks like one. The switchboard and old telephones, and the wood-burning stoves, are neat to look at.

The Hinckley House is beautiful and each of its rooms hold furniture and other household items that one would expect to see in the early 1900's. Walk through the front room, with its pump organ and chairs and living room furniture; to the dining room with the table all set; then, the kitchen with all of its old cooking implements, plus an oven and stove; into the bedroom (check out the baby carriage and antique sewing machine); then into Dr. Hinckley's dentist office. (He was the first dentist in Fillmore.) Enjoy relative quiet during the week. It gets busy on the weekends as that's when the railcars come and go.

Hours: Open Tues. - Wed. and Fri., 9am- noon and 1pm - 4pm; Thurs., 1pm- 4pm; Sat., 10am - 3pm. Closed Sun., Mon. and holidays.

Price: $4 for adults; $2 for students; ages 5 and under are free.

Ages: 6 years and up.

GULL WINGS CHILDREN'S MUSEUM

(805) 483-3005 / www.gullwings.org

$$$

418 W. 4th Street, Oxnard

Children's museums strive for the right combination of fun and education. Gull Wings has achieved a delightful balance of these goals. The long building has sectioned off "rooms", each one with a different focus. The first room is ocean themed. It contains a play tiki hut counter cafe, complete with a mini kitchen, plastic food, and cash register for employees and bar stools at the counter for customers. There is also a touch tank with sea stars and urchins, a few fish tanks, and, against the backdrop of a wall sea mural, a puppet theater, a submarine toy to climb into and around, a short wooden pier, and a boat to go merrily down the stream. Permission is granted to board the kid-size boat and sit in the captain's chair to listen to the radio, turn the wheel, or watch a video of a boat cruise to the Channel Islands. Also in this section are some building blocks, and tables and chairs (for parents whose sea legs have given out).

Kids can be the doctor or the patient in the next room. This E.R. has scrubs and masks, a surgery table with play instruments, and an X-ray set up with real X-rays. For hands-on health and science learning, there are plastic models of the body with removable parts, a full skeleton and lots of other bones, and cloth dolls that kids can unlayer to reveal muscles, bones, and organs.

Be a hero! Suit up in real fireman uniforms, boots, and helmets, and use real hoses to attach to the not-working fire hydrant. The back part of an ambulance is open and ready to rescue - all against murals of traffic and a blazing fire.

Lego-A-Go-Go are two small rooms that cleverly combine and correlate science and Legos because "cells are the building blocks of life", DNA are patterns that create physical attributes, etc. Kids are encouraged to create and build here. There are also microscopes with bugs and other things to scrutinize.

Engineer your way to the wonderful, large model train layout next, followed by a kid-proofed Saturn car. Young drivers can get behind the wheel of the Saturn, shift gears, turn on headlights, and, via a plexiglass hood, see the inner workings of an engine. A side door panel is also clear. Then, enter another dimension where a kid-size space shuttle cockpit awaits astronauts to suit up then sit, push buttons and twist dials of mission control, and launch into outer space. Crawl, or crouch down, to go through tunnels and portholes as one small room leads into another on board, then another and another (complete with video monitors of actually being in orbit,) and then into a small black lit room illuminated with stars. The murals of walking on the moon here make visitors part of the scene, especially with the painted dusty footprints on the floor. Outside this space station is a real rocket engine and a mission control board.

A carpeted toddler space is a potpourri of a tiny play market, plus a selection of books, toys and games, and a

table of gears to turn and learn. The back wall is a rock climbing wall painted to look like layers of real rock. In front of this back wall is a real rowboat with oars, life jackets, etc.

Behind this wall is the last series of rooms. Enter Treasure Cavern, a small room that simulates the dark interior of a cave. (Younger kids might get scared.) The displays include stalactites and stalagmites, a real ore cart (against another life-like mural), miners tools, other rocks, and fossils. In the next room future paleontologists (and others) get properly outfitted and then use shovels to dig for bones, and such, through pits of recycled rubber. They can also make fossil rubbings. An adjacent room contains rows stacked with cages of live animals such as geckos, tarantulas, snakes, frogs and bunnies. Ask about the numerous craft and educational classes, as well as special family nights held at the museum. Note that there is a picnic table just outside the museum.

Hours: Open Tues., 9am - 1pm; Wed. - Fri., 9am - 4pm; Sat. - Sun., 10am - 4pm. Closed Mon. and major holidays.

Price: $6 for adults; $5 for seniors and ages 2 - 12; children under 2 are free.

Ages: 2 to 12 years.

MULLIN AUTOMOTIVE MUSEUM

(805) 385-5400 / www.mullinautomotivemuseum.com $$$$
1421 Emerson Avenue, Oxnard

Bonjour. With a nod to the layout and the feel of an elegant art museum, this classy and spacious museum, once owned by Otis Chandler, is home to more than 100 restored French cars exhibited in such a way as to make each one important while still allowing plenty of space to walk in between them and throughout. Also on display are French-stylized furniture, decorative art, and photography from the Art Deco Movement and era. Referred to as "streamlined, symmetrical, and striking", this movement (and museum) showcases cars, such as the 1939 Delage D8-120, 1946 Delage D-6, 1938ish Delahaye T145 Coupe, 1937 Peugeot, 1928 Bugatti, and other extremely fine cars that a classic car enthusiast appreciates (and covets). Most of the cars are gleaming. A 1925 Bugatti was rescued from lake waters after being submerged for seventy years - it's a bit corroded. A few others are also in their somewhat original condition. Race cars are displayed on the second level. Should you see this museum? Oui.

Hours: Usually open the second and fourth Saturday every month (and occasionally other days), 10am - 3pm.

Price: $15 for adults; $10 for seniors; $8 for ages 3 - 11; ages 2 and under are free. There is a $2 per ticket processing fee, as well. Tickets must be purchased in advance. Private visits are allowed at $40 per person.

Ages: 8 years and up.

MURPHY AUTO MUSEUM

(805) 487-4333 / www.murphyautomuseum.org   !/$$$
2230 Statham Boulevard, Oxnard

About forty-five automobiles, mostly on loan from collectors, are in rows, lined up in one room. There are several Packards, ranging from 1927 to 1958, as well as a 1949 Rolls Royce, Ford Model T, 1970 Chrysler 300 Hurst, 1966 Chevrolet Corvette Stingray, and a bright yellow, 1970 Opal GT. There are also rotating displays, such as vintage trailers, all about corvettes, and motorcycles, and special events held in the parking lot. A few vintage gas pumps are sprinkled about the room, and a HUGE scale model train layout (1,800 square feet!) chugs along, delighting onlookers. And shoppers, check out the Atta Boy Vintage shop that has a little bit of everything from the recent (and further back) past. There is something to please everyone at Murphy's.

Hours: Open Sat., 9am - 4pm; Sun., 10am - 5pm. Open by special arrangement for groups and tours on weekdays.

Price: Free; a suggested donation is $9 for adults; free for ages 12 and under and active military.

Ages: 8 years and up.

OJAI VALLEY MUSEUM

(805) 640-1390 / www.ojaivalleymuseum.org $$
130 W. Ojai Avenue, Ojai

This small museum, located inside an old chapel, has a mission - keeping historic Ojai alive by preserving the

valley's cultural and natural heritage. Outside, the grounds are lovely with patches of grass and statues, including a huge condor (which is in front of the adjacent Ojai Visitor Center) and a sleeping bear. Inside, there are two rooms. One houses permanent displays of photos; glassware; Chumash tools, such as arrowheads and mortar and pestle; and a ranchero's or cowboy's equipment, like ropes and spurs. Kids especially like the deer hunter; a Chumash man wearing deer skin. A domed diorama of wildlife includes a wild cat, deer, bears, and a coyote. The second room nicely showcases temporary exhibits. A short video shows Rancho Casitas and its history. Guided tours for students and adults are offered. Call to schedule one.

Hours: Open Tues. - Fri., 10am - 4pm; Sat., 10am - 4pm; Sun., noon - 4pm. Closed Mon. and most holidays.

Price: $5 for adults; $1 for ages 6 - 18; children 5 and under are free.

Ages: 3 years and up.

OLIVAS ADOBE HISTORICAL PARK

(805) 658-4728 or (805) 644-4346 / www.cityofventura.net/olivasadobe   !/$$
4200 Olivas Park Drive, Ventura

The Olivas Adobe is a restored, two-story adobe home built in 1847 that once housed Senor Olivas, his wife, and their twenty-one children! It is representative of the rancho period in California's history and, as such, offers tour to the general public and school tours geared for fourth graders. These latter tours are great and very interactive, as students can participate in making bricks, rope a wooden steer, make tortillas, use stone and mortar pestle, and so much more. The residence has bedrooms, a living room, a large chapel room, and a kitchen to look into that are all furnished just as they were over 100 years ago.

The grounds are beautifully landscaped. The open courtyard, with its lovely bell gate entrance, contains a Spanish beehive oven and some farming equipment, plus it gives younger ones some running-around space. A small exhibit building, across from the rose garden, contains items that relate to this particular time period, such as saddles, pictures, and ranching equipment. While this is not an all-day visit, kids enjoy the opportunity to "see" the past. Ask about the many special programs hosted by the park, such as concerts, and candlelight tours at Christmastime.

Hours: The grounds are open daily, 10am - 4pm. The adobe is open for guided tours Sat. - Sun., 11am - 4pm. Closed Easter and major holidays that fall on weekends.

Price: Free for just the grounds. Docent guided tours of the house are $5 for adults; $3 for seniors and children 11 and under.

Ages: 6 years and up.

PORT HUENEME LIGHTHOUSE

(310) 541-0334 / www.huenemelight.org $
120 W. Port Hueneme Road, Port Hueneme

"Let your light shine before men" (and before ships). (Matthew 5:16a) A Victorian-style lighthouse was originally built on this site in 1874. The forty-eight-foot cement tower you now see was constructed in 1941, and its light still stands guard over this section of sea. While not particularly picturesque, the lure of actually going inside a lighthouse beacons, I mean beckons, many people. A few pieces of old lighthouse gear are on display, and some old photographs of the tower line the walls. Walk up the three sets of stairs that wind around to reach the top, a domed chamber called the lantern room. The focal point is the old-fashioned lens - a beveled, brass-encased set of glass prisms. Up here, too, you can scan the horizon, just as lighthouse keepers of yesteryear. Visitors, often lighthouse afficionados, leave the place beaming.

Hours: Open February - October, the third Sat., 10am - 3pm.

Price: Free. Parking in the promenade is $1 an hour.

Ages: 8 years and up.

RANCHO CAMULOS

(805) 521-1501 / www.ranchocamulos.org $$
5164 E. Telegraph Road, Piru

This forty-acre early rancho, a working citrus ranch, remains in its original countryside setting, so it's just how you picture it would have been in 1853, when it was first built. The lovely grounds include an arbor, rose garden, fish pond,

and brick fountain that all complement the complex of over fifteen buildings. The buildings include the main adobe ranch house, a colonial-style adobe, a free-standing kitchen, olive press, a schoolroom, a barn, a chapel, and a brick winery - a treat to walk through and interesting to inspect. With all of this, the rancho is probably best known for being the setting of Helen Hunt Jackson's novel, *Ramona*.

Guided tours, for all ages, are offered. School kids are invited to do some hands-on activities, as well, and have lunch on the grounds. The Early California History tour shares details of the Tatavian Indians and the family that lived in the rancho during the Mexican/American period. Students tour the home and grounds and see demonstrations of adobe brick making, household chores, and cooking. The Old California Tour is similar, but the emphasis is on taking students back a little bit further in time, when the Spanish were exploring the region. This tour focuses on the Spanish influence and the historical context of the events.

Hours: Open to the public, Sat., 1pm - 4pm; tours are given on the hour. Open for school tours during the week. Closed during rainy weather.

Price: $5 for adults; $3 for ages 6 - 12; children 5 and under are free. School tours are $3 per student.

Ages: 6 years and up.

RONALD REAGAN PRESIDENTIAL LIBRARY AND MUSEUM ☼

(800) 410-8354 or (805) 577-4008 / www.reagan.utexas.edu; www.reaganfoundation.org $$$$
40 Presidential Drive, Simi Valley

The massive, Spanish-style Ronald Reagan Library and Museum sits alone on a hilltop, surrounded by beautifully-landscaped grounds, a gracious courtyard, and gorgeous mountains. The fantastic museum is purposefully arranged to walk visitors through Reagan's road to the presidency. It starts with his growing up years, then his career as an actor, as governor, his terms as president, and his legacy. Videos, a plethora of photos and memorabilia all entertainingly arranged, and interactive exhibits guide visitors along the time line. Although your tour is self-guided, there are numerous docents posted in rooms ready and willing to answer your questions. Interspersed throughout the museum are mini theaters that show inauguration speeches; the tearing down of the Berlin wall; Reagan's meetings with international leaders; his time with Nancy Reagan; a remembrance of the Challenger crew; his assassination attempt; and more - all captivating footage.

Interactive features of the museum include sitting on a model horse, next to Reagan on a horse, so it looks like you're riding together; acting in a movie with the president (before he was the president) via a screen showing the movie and a camera pointed at you; going under and into a crawl section (kids like this) of a large recreation of the Berlin wall which has barbed wire on top and a blaring siren; playing six electronic, educational games on the game table that incorporate Reagan's economic politics; standing at a podium and delivering his inaugural address while people on the wall mural, including Nancy Reagan, cheer you on; and, via video screens built into what looks like an elegant dining room table, seeing more of what goes on in the White House. Use the dining table's screens to view guests that visited the Reagans; food that was served at State dinners; China dishes used on the table (you can even create your own pattern); and more. These are all great features and make the museum that much more interesting.

Other rooms and exhibits include a SIRE (space component for testing missile defense); the suit Reagan had cut off him after his assassination attempt (you can see the bullet hole); a full-size replica of the Oval Office decorated from when he was president; homemade, as well as ultra expensive gifts given to him; a room of Nancy Reagan's gowns and some of her jewelry; a hallway with videos, photos and more, called Peace Through Strength; video information on Reagan's summits; his saddles and other memorabilia from his ranch; and a room that has photos and signatures of most of the past U.S. presidents. A majority of the exhibits are accompanied by both written and audio commentary. If you want to know even more, rent an iPod for $7 (or download a free App beforehand to get a discount), that gives more in-depth information at various stations around the museum, plus you can use it to take photos that are emailed to you.

The Air Force One Pavilion is striking! Watch the video interviewing the President onboard Air Force One as the film details the logistical planning it takes to get a president airborne. The plane is massive! Facing a gigantic glass window that looks out over the mountains, it looks ready for take-off. Feeling presidential? Board this retired Air Force One plane used by seven past presidents, from Nixon to George W. Bush. Dubbed the "flying White House," you'll see the cockpit, communications center (where the "football" was kept), state rooms, Reagan's office, the lounge (this is my kind of airplane travel), and private rooms. Have a friend take a picture of you as you wave when you exit the plane. The pavilion also houses a Marine One helicopter, a bullet-proof limousine, a motorcade with police escort,

a Cold War gallery with photos and videos of signing the treaty, and a copy of a pub Reagan frequented in Ireland.

Out back is a huge, decoratively spray-painted chunk of the actual Berlin wall. There are picnic tables out front, with a beautiful vista, so you could just come here for a picnic, but the museum is too good to miss. A full cafe is on the grounds with views that overlook the valley. Note that the gift shop sells great aids for teaching history. Outstanding school tours are offered. Check the website for the numerous special events held here throughout the year.

Hours: Open daily, 10am - 5pm. Closed New Year's Day, Thanksgiving, and Christmas.

Price: $21 for adults; $18 for seniors; $15 for ages 11 - 17; $12 for ages 5- 10; children 4 and under are free.

Ages: 5 years and up.

SAN BUENAVENTURA MISSION

(805) 643-4318 - mission; (805) 648-4496 - gift shop / www.sanbuenaventuramission.org
211 E. Main Street, Ventura

Built in 1792, and ninth in the chain of California missions, San Buenaventura exudes old-world charm. Although the mission is readily seen from the street, a tour through the rooms and grounds offer a better picture of life during this historical time period. You'll see a small courtyard, artifacts from mission days in the several rooms, and even a small cemetery around the outside. Guided 4th grade school tours are offered during the school year - $35 for up to 35 students and one teacher. The tour includes information about the mission's past inhabitants and usually involves doing a mission-related craft. Teacher tip: If getting a docent doesn't work out they have a guide on line to download.

Hours: Open Mon. - Fri., 10am - 5pm; Sat., 9am - 5pm; Sun., 10am - 4pm. Closed Easter, Thanksgiving, and Christmas.

Price: $4 for adults; $3 for seniors; $1 for ages 17 and under.

Ages: 6 years and up.

SANTA PAULA ART MUSEUM

(805) 525-5554 / www.santapaulaartmuseum.org
117 N. 10ᵗʰ Street, Santa Paula

Fine art finely displayed sums up this small art museum. The main gallery and two small, side rooms showcase local and national artists in this historic bank building. The safe is a tiny gallery and towards the back is another room with rotating exhibits. A kid draw, literally, to the museum are the art trading cards where kids draw pictures of a standard size, as they are traded all over the world, and trade their drawing for someone else's. Guided tours, gallery talks, and other special events help make this museum an artistic destination. Check out the CALIFORNIA OIL MUSEUM (pg. 680) and AGRICULTURE MUSEUM (pg. 679) that are right around the corner. Take a tour of the nine murals around town that show the history of Santa Paula and its inhabitants. See www.santapaulamurals.org for more info.

Hours: Open Wed. - Sat., 10am - 4pm; Sun., noon - 4pm.

Price: $4 for adults; $3 for seniors; free for ages 17 and under.

Ages: 9 years and up.

SANTA SUSANA PARK / SANTA SUSANA DEPOT AND MUSEUM

6503 Katherine Road (South of the Railroad bridge), Simi Valley

See SANTA SUSANA PARK / DEPOT AND MUSEUM on page 676 for information.

STAGECOACH INN MUSEUM

(805) 498-9441 / www.stagecoachmuseum.org
51 N. Ventu Park Road, Newbury Park

This beautiful 1870's hotel and stagecoach stop is both interesting and educational, and seen only by guided tour. The downstairs consists mainly of the parlor, dining room, and kitchen. The furniture, decor, and history are interesting to older kids, but younger kids get antsy. The Anderson Hall houses articles relating to the Chumash, with display cases of arrowheads, tools, weapons, baskets, drawings, and more. The Jungleland exhibit, when a lion and tiger farm was in the area many moons ago, is fun to look at with pictures and memorabilia from that time. (Makes me sad

to have missed it.) Oooooo - a man named Pierre was supposedly shot here and his ghost still haunts the Inn. Now, the Inn becomes fascinating to kids!

A small "cowboy" bedroom has a saddle, bear skin rug, and other western paraphernalia. A child's room is filled with toys of yesteryear (no Xbox!), and contains a bed that Robert Todd Lincoln (Abe's son) slept in.

Outside the hotel, take a short wooded, nature trail, that passes by and leads to other historic points of interest, dotted with old farming equipment. with lots of steps, The Carriage House contains stagecoaches, and the old-looking Pioneer Newbury House, the Spanish Adobe House, and a replica of the first schoolhouse in the area. A beehive oven is also interesting, but explain to your kids that the oven is named for its design, not for cooking bees. Go down to see the The Chumash Indian ap (i.e. home) and then down a flight of wooden steps into a mini forest.

When the kids have seen all they want, head out to the small Stagecoach Park on a grassy hill just above the Inn. The playground fits the theme of the museum as there is a stagecoach-shaped play structure to climb in and on, with a slide and steps attached to it, as well as several black horses on big springs to ride back and forth on - all in a big sand-based play area. There are also a few swings, a basketball court, a picnic table under a shade tree, and a baseball field.

Hours: The Inn is open Wed. - Sun., 1pm - 4pm. The entire complex is open Sat. - Sun., 1pm - 4pm. Closed New Year's Day, Easter, Thanksgiving, and Christmas.

Price: $5 for adults; $4 for seniors and students; $2 for ages 5 - 12; children 4 and under are free.

Ages: 5 years and up.

STRATHEARN HISTORICAL PARK AND MUSEUM

(805) 526-6453 / www.simihistory.com

$$

137 Strathearn Place, Simi Valley

In a lovely, park-like setting, this six-acre, outdoor museum is a conglomeration of several historical buildings moved here from their original locations. Start your one-hour guided tour at the visitor's center, where you learn about the early days of Simi by watching a fifteen-minute video about the Valley's history. Some of the exhibits in the center include saddles, an old-fashioned switchboard, fossils, kitchen gadgets, early laundry equipment, and more.

Next, walk through one of the very first local colony houses. Though the inside decor is from the 1930's, the building itself still retains its original charm. An adobe house, built in the early 1700's, displays an owner's furnishings from the 1950's. The Strathearn House, which is a Victorian house built in 1893, has antique treasures throughout including furniture, clothing, and a pump organ. The library contains some fossils, as well as books. The small church is beautiful and quaint.

Read placards about the corrugated tin garage and the enclosed barn. In an open barn, and around the perimeter of the historic park, see all of the old (and rusted) farm equipment, including several types of wagons, tractors, and threshing tools, plus a few old automobiles. The restoration area is also housed here. Docent-led school tours for 3rd graders help make history come to life for kids.

Hours: The grounds are open Mon. - Fri., 9am - 3pm; Sat. - Sun., 1pm - 4pm. The inside buildings, which can only be seen on a tour, are open Wed. - Fri. at 1pm (sharp); Sat. - Sun., 1pm - 4pm, weather permitting. The last tour starts at about 2:30pm. Open for large groups, and for free, school tours during the week upon request.

Price: $3 per person.

Ages: 5 years and up.

U.S. NAVY SEABEE MUSEUM

(805) 982-5167 / www.history.navy.mil/museums/seabee_museum.htm

!

1001 Addor Street, Port Hueneme

This extensive, state-of-the-art museum is dedicated to documenting, preserving, and displaying material relating to the contributions of the Naval Construction Force, better known as the Seabees, and the U.S. Navy Civil Engineer Corps. While the mission statement is formal sounding, the museum is incredibly rich with fascinating exhibits in several distinctive areas. The Grand Hall is devoted to portraits of heroes, Seabees "firsts", and those killed in action, from World War II to the present. There is also a wall featuring all of the battalion plaques.

The theater continuously shows movies pertaining to the Seabees and the various wars. The larger adjacent gallery walks visitors through the history of Seabees, from its inception in WWII after the bombing of Pearl Harbor, and

through all the wars since then. Each section is accompanied by mural-size photos, placards, medals, war posters, and gear - backpacks, field telephones, gas masks, and more - plus original artifacts significant to that time period or place, like a large bell from a camp park. In addition, there are numerous life-size models of men and women depicted in scenes of battle and peacetime, wearing authentic uniforms and costumes from around the world. Vehicles are also plentiful, particularly jeeps, tanks, and fully-outfitted Humvees, as are weapons - machine guns, rifles, and swords. Everything, in fact, that represents the many facets of a Seabee's life in action. The "We Build/We Fight" section, showcases just some of the accomplishments that Seabees have provided to America.

Another gallery features a 2/3 scale timber tower/guard tower in Afghanistan; a wooden two-hole burnout (latrine); personal items of maps, language guides, coins, books, etc.; a control station with a myriad of dials; a wooden bunkhouse with sandbags and camouflage netting; Antarctic tools; diving helmets; bullets; ship models; and artwork. And - we found Nemo! It actually stands for Naval Experimental Manned Observatory. This submersible is featured against an underseas mural complete with a sand floor and model divers.

"We Help, We Care" is a gallery focusing on the humanitarian efforts around the globe during wartime and in natural disasters. Interactive exhibits allow visitors to get a glimpse of what it's like, and the challenges that come with, managing a huge military construction project. It also allows youth a sense of what being an engineer is, and perhaps inspires them to consider careers in the CEC. Note: Bring a picnic lunch to enjoy outside in the museum's Memorial Garden.

Hours: Open Mon. - Sat., 9am - 4pm; Sun., noon - 4pm. Closed all federal holidays.
Price: Free
Ages: 4 years and up.

WESTERN FOUNDATION OF VERTEBRATE ZOOLOGY

(805) 388-9944 / www.wfvz.org $$

439 Calle San Pablo, Camarillo

If you, or your kids, have ever wanted to be an oologist, this place is *eggactly* what you're looking for. Oology, by the way, is the study of eggs, particularly bird eggs. The Foundation, started by one avid collector, has grown and now contains over 1 million eggs!, 53,000 bird skin specimens!, and 18,000 nests!!

Upon entering the one gigantic room (i.e., the research center/museum), the huge wall mural of sky, sea, and birds, and the incredible variety and number of mounted birds both in "flight" and in glass displays, make quite a visual impact. The birds are condors, owls, penguins, shore birds, mummified falcons, and many, many more. Several of the rows and rows of what look like big filing cabinets are filled with trays of study skins (odd terminology, I think, since they have feathers) of birds. Some of them are on a stick. Guests are invited to gently hold some of the skins/birds, such as brilliantly-colored tanagers, hummingbirds, toucans, and others, as they learn about the species - their design, their habitats, and their way of life.

The egg collection is astounding. They've all been single-hole drilled and drained. You'll see the very rare and enormous elephant bird egg (elephant birds became extinct in the 1600's), teeny tiny hummingbird eggs, fossilized dinosaur eggs, blue eggs, shiny green eggs, and more.

What a variety of nests! There are "typical" nests composed of sticks, as well as mud nests of swallows; intricate woven nests from weavers; shore bird's nests of sand kicked around; nests found in rope (the rope is here, too); and, again - so many more.

The Foundation also has a Kachina doll and spectacles collection, but it is really dedicated to bird conservation. The main objective is to manage this massive ornithological collection - one of the largest in the world, gathered from all parts of the globe - for research purposes. School, civic, and other groups of up to forty people may schedule a private tour. Teaching kits are available to educate the public. Who knows - a career desire might very well be hatched within your child! Bring a jacket as the room is usually kept cool.

Hours: One-hour public tours, for up to twenty people, are scheduled on the last Friday of each month from 3pm - 4pm. Call to reserve your spot. Call to book a group tour at other days and times for fourth graders through college age.
Price: $5 per person; ages 7 and under are free.
Ages: 4th grade and up.

—PIERS AND SEAPORTS—

MALIBU PIER   ☼

(310) 456-8031 - Malibu Beach Co.; (310) 456-1112 - Cafe / parks.ca.gov; www.malibu-farm.com   !
23000 Pacific Coast Highway, Malibu

Malibu Pier is famous first of all because it's in Malibu. And it's the pier. Walk out on the long wooden pier to fish (no license needed) and enjoy the view, and peruse Malibu Beach Supply Co., a gift shop selling not just sundries, clothing, and souvenirs, but also bait and fishing rentals. Grab a bite to eat here at adjacent Malibu Farm Cafe on the Pier. They serve fried egg sandwiches with bacon and arugula, $14; Swedish mini pancakes with whipped cream and berries, $10; yogurt and granola, $8; chicken ricotta and bacon burger, $14; grilled cheese panini, $8; crab cakes and capers aioli, $16; skirt steak sandwich, $18; vegan coconut dish with tofu and veggies, $14; and more. Or, eat at the upscale Malibu Pier Restaurant, located at the base of the pier.

Walk under the pier during low tide and enjoy tidepools at the rocky area on the adjacent beach. This stretch of beach and surf, called Surfrider Beach, is actually quite famous for surfing because of its three-point break.

Hours:	The beach is open daily, sunrise to sunset. Malibu Beach Supply is open Mon. - Fri, 10am - 5pm; Sat. - Sun., 10am - 6pm. The Cafe is open Wed. - Sun., 9am - 3pm.
Price:	Free. There is some free parking north of the pier. Parking at the pier is $10, Mon. - Fri.; $14 on the weekends.
Ages:	All

VENTURA HARBOR VILLAGE   ☼

(805) 642-8538 or (877) 89-HARBOR (894-2726) / www.venturaharborvillage.com   !/$
1583 Spinnaker Drive, Ventura

This harbor harbors a lot of fun. The picturesque "village" has thirty-five unusual gift shops, waterfront restaurants, and cafes. Come for lunch or, my personal favorite, dessert! The Parlor restaurant is small, but fun for kids with its 1920's theme, player piano, tin inlaid ceiling, old ice cream makers on display, and bar stools around the soda fountain. (Tip: Don't call the man behind the soda fountain a jerk.) The restaurant serves burgers, hot dogs, salads, and an array of shakes and malts. The Parlor also has outside seating, overlooking the harbor. I like the fresh seafood restaurant with its tanks of live lobsters and some really big fish. Enjoy a stroll around, look at the boats, and check out all the colorful, ceramic tiled marine murals.

Take a ride on the indoor, thirty-six smallish horse (and other animals) carousel, at $3 a ride. The compact adjacent arcade has mostly benign video games (yeah!), and a kiddie room with a few rides and little kid games. A birthday party room, redemption center, and snack bar with caramel apples, cotton candy, and homemade fudge, help make this place a child magnet. Call (805) 644-3234 for more information.

Free, outdoor concerts are given on most weekends, usually on Sundays, in the summer. A Fisherman's Market is held every Saturday from 8am to 11am in front of Andria's Restaurant. Come early for the catch of the day directly from fishermens' boats - you can even get your fish fileted. The harbor also sponsors numerous annual events, such as the Parade of Lights in December, the tallships in January/February, and Pirates Day Festival in June. (See the Calendar section under corresponding months for details.) Note that adults will probably enjoy the Comedy Club inside Hornblower's Restaurant, depending on who's headlining.

While here, take a whale watching cruise, a cruise around the harbor or one out to the Channel Islands. Look up CHANNEL ISLANDS NATIONAL PARK on page 668 and ISLAND PACKERS on page 699 for more info. For other cruise information, and rentals of kayaks, pedal boats, and SUPs see VENTURA BOAT RENTALS (pg. 700). Enjoy sifting sand between your toes and/or swimming at the small Harbor Cove Beach, which is just across the street from the CHANNEL ISLANDS NATIONAL PARK VISITOR CENTER on page 682. Facilities include restrooms and a children's play area. The waters are protected by rock jetties, which adventuresome kids like to climb on. The rock jetties are not for the faint of heart, however, or for really young kids, as part of the "walkway" on the rocks is washed away. Bring your fishing poles if you have the time and patience. There are picnic areas and barbecues here. You may also play at the nearby MARINA PARK (pg. 674) which has a playground, a play cement ship, a walkway around a harbor, and more. Enjoy your day here with all there is to do and *sea*! Tip: Hop aboard a old-fashioned trolley on the Downtown Ventura Harbor Trolley which tours visitors around from Ventura Harbor Village north to the

Amtrak/Fairgrounds on Harbor Blvd., with several stops along the way. This free, forty-five-minute loop ride is available Memorial Day through Labor Day, Wednesday through Sunday (and holiday Mondays), 11am - 11pm. For more information, call (805) 827-4444 / www.downtownventura.org/downtown-harbor-trolley.

Hours: Most stores are open daily, 11am - 6pm. Many restaurants serve breakfast, lunch and dinner, so they are open earlier and later. The carousel and games are open Mon. - Thurs., 10am - 6pm; Fri. - Sat., 10am - 9pm; Sun., 10am - 8pm. Most places are open extended hours in the summertime.

Price: Technically free, but bring spending money.

Ages: All

—POTPOURRI—

BART'S BOOKS

(805) 646-3755 / www.bartsbooksojai.com

!/$

302 W. Matilija, Ojai

This is one of my happy places. Bart's Books is a large, unique, "outdoor" (i.e. no roof), used bookstore that is worth at least a browse-through, weather permitting. You and your reader-child will delight in this big, Bohemian-style store. It's like exploring an old, comfortable (albeit mostly roofless) house maze, except that most of the "rooms" are created by bookshelves. There are hundreds of books here on every subject, including a small, but packed, children's section and a roofed room of poetry and literature. Sit down on an assortment of benches and chairs, picnic tables, or in a recliner by a fireplace, and even under huge palm trees, to peruse your purchase.

Books that are on shelves on and facing the outside of the store are available for purchase any time of day or night. The trusting (or hopeful) store sign reads: "When closed please throw coins in slot in the door for the amount marked on the book. Thank you." The atmosphere here is worth the trip.

Hours: Open daily, 9:30am - sunset..

Price: Technically, free

Ages: All readers.

BUILD-A-BEAR WORKSHOP (Ventura County)

(805) 449-8704 / www.buildabear.com

$$$

550 W. Hillcrest Drive at The Oaks mall, Thousand Oaks

See the entry for BUILD-A-BEAR WORKSHOP (Orange) on page 314 for details.

Hours: Open Mon. - Sat., 10am - 9pm; Sun., 11am - 7pm.

CHANNEL ISLANDS MARINE FLOATING LAB

(805) 382-4563 / www.floatinglab.com

$$

3900 Bluefin Circle, Oxnard

This floating marine lab (i.e., boat) offers terrific in-harbor and out-of-harbor learning excursions. Students of all ages can book a "tour" here and receive hands-on teaching instruction. The tours incorporate going out of the harbor and dredging to gather whatever from the sea floor, anchoring and then participating in rotating learning stations on board the R/V Coral Sea. This enables students to gain knowledge about marine life, marine environments, and specifically, marine biology. What better way to involve and aid kids in understanding ocean life than for them to inspect it, as close up as under a microscope; to analyze it by investigating samples that they help to haul up from the ocean floor; to touch it by gently stroking live tidepool creatures such as sea stars and sea urchins, plus bat rays, octopus, and more; to explore it by actually being on the ocean; and to hear about it from naturalists.

The learning labs can be combined with whale watching when the Pacific gray whales migrate - January through April. Note that classes on board the boat are usually three-and-a-half hours long, but can be adjusted according to age and interest level. The maximum number of participants is forty. Bring a lunch to enjoy dockside.

Hours: Call to schedule a class, September - June, Mon. - Fri.

Price: Minimum fee of $650 for a three-plus-hour class. Ask about other classes and add-ons.

Ages: Kindergartners and up.

FRY'S ELECTRONICS (Ventura County)

(805) 751-1300 / www.frys.com

1901 E. Ventura Boulevard, Oxnard

See the entry for FRY'S ELECTRONICS (Los Angeles County) on page 170 for details.

—SHOWS AND THEATERS—

FAIRY TALES IN THE PARK

(661) 718-3968 / www.fairytalesinthepark.com

Just like a band of gypsies, this volunteer, roving group of actors and actresses, collectively known as Gypsies in a Trunk, travel from place to place. Their purpose is to put on free, forty-five-minute performances for young children all around Ventura County to promote and inspire a love for live theater. They retell fairy tales and other tales, such as *Jack and the Beanstalk*, *The Hare and the Tortoise*, *Robin Hood*, and *The Wizard of Oz*. Live theater, geared for children, outdoors, for free = perfect! The cities and locations have included outdoor venues at Camarillo, Channel Islands Harbor, Simi Valley, Westlake Village, and Ventura. Bring a blanket or a low-back lawn chair, sunscreen, and some picnicky foods to enjoy.

Hours: Plays are performed May - September at various times throughout the day, depending on the location. Check their calendar website for specific info.

Price: Free; a hat is passed at the end - donations appreciated.

Ages: 3 - 9 years

OXNARD PERFORMING ARTS AND CONVENTION CENTER

(805) 486-2424 / www.oxnardpacc.com

800 Hobson Way at the Oxnard Performing Arts Center, Oxnard

Shows performed at this 1,654-seat theater for the general public include Broadway musicals; concerts; Shangri-La acrobats; and performances by the Ventura County Ballet Company, (805) 648-2080 / www.venturacountyballet.com and the New West Symphony, (805) 497-5800 / www.newwestsymphony.org. Specific kid-friendly acts have included *Sesame Street*, *Nutcracker*, *Anne Frank*, and *Wiggles Live*. School groups often rent the theater to see special performances put on by American Theater for Youth, or other touring groups. Call for a schedule.

Hours: Call for show dates and times.

Price: Varies, depending on the show.

Ages: 3 years and up, depending on the show.

PERFORMANCES TO GROW ON

(805) 646-8907 / www.ptgo.org

various locations in Ventura County

What a refreshing take on theater, in the sense that these shows are geared for families and offer a variety of types of performance. Performances and past titles have included *Anne of Green Gables*; Kuniko Yamamoto, *Japanese Storytelling with Magic, Masks and Mime*; *Puss 'N Boots*, Oregon Shadow Theatre (done with shadow puppets); *Soul Street Dance Co.*; and *Fresh Roasted Concerts*. School groups are welcome to enjoy special performances on a field trip, such as the entertaining and educational *King Tut Theatreworks*, or via a school assemble. Teacher's workshops are also available.

Hours: Call for performance schedules and locations.

Price: $15 - $25 for adults; $10 - $14 for children, depending on the show and location.

Ages: 4 years and up, depending on the show.

THOUSAND OAKS CIVIC ARTS PLAZA / BANK OF AMERICA PERFORMING ARTS CENTER

(805) 449-ARTS (2787) / www.toaks.org; www.civicartsplaza.com

2100 E. Thousand Oaks Boulevard, Thousand Oaks

This arts plaza, with beautiful fountains out front, is home to the Bank of America Performing Arts Center which consists of two theaters: the Scherr Forum Theatre, which seats 400 people, and the Kavli, which seats 1,800. Both

theaters keep a packed calendar of events so there is something going on almost every night. Professional local and national touring production groups put on numerous, first-class shows and presentations including ballet, comedies, juggling, musicals, distinguished speakers (such as David McCullough), concerts, symphonies (a home to New West Symphony, (805) 497-5800 / www.newwestsymphony.org), dance (such as the Moscow dance theater), dramas, and more. A variety of family and children's concerts are offered. Past programs include Jim Gamble's Marionettes, *Do Jump! Acrobatic Theater, Freedom Train, The Music Man, Oregon Trail*, and *Sesame Street Live*. See PERFORMANCES TO GROW ON (pg. 694) for shows that are especially family friendly and inspiring. That company put on shows here as well as at other locations. Note that there are plenty of restaurants in the immediate area at the adjacent mall, The Lakes.

      Hours: Call for show dates and times.
      Price: Prices vary, depending on the show. Parking is $8 at the adjacent six level parking structure.
      Ages: Varies, depending on the show.

VENTURA COUNTY BALLET COMPANY

$$$$

(805) 648-2080 / www.venturacountyballet.com
800 Hobson Way at the Oxnard Performing Arts Center, Oxnard

    All ages grace the stage with performances that are visual treats. Experience shows such as *Jungle Book*, *Sleeping Beauty*, and, of course, *The Nutcracker*.

      Hours: Call for performance times.
      Price: Call for prices.
      Ages: 5 years and up, depending on the show.

—TOURS—

CALIFORNIA PIZZA KITCHEN (Ventura County)

!

    See the entry for CALIFORNIA PIZZA KITCHEN (Los Angeles County) (pg. 197) for more information.

NAVAL BASE VENTURA COUNTY

!

(805) 989-8095 or (805) 989-9234 / www.cnic.navy.mil/Ventura
Construction Battalion Center, Port Hueneme, and Naval Air Station, Point Mugu

    Tours on either base allow citizens the rare opportunity of exploring a military base. Groups of at least ten people, maximum thirty-five, have the opportunity to talk with people who protect our country, find out where tax dollars go in supporting the military, and maybe learn about a future career. The Point Mugu tour selection is larger, and probably more interesting as it has extensive aviation facilities. Some of the tour titles include, Air Traffic Control Tower & Radar Room; Airborne Carrier Command and Control Squadrons; Bird Watching/Ornithology; Fire Station/Crash Crew; VR-55 Minutemen; Naval Satellite Operations Center; and Windshield. Check the website for a complete listing and for descriptions. The Port Hueneme tour titles include Fire Station, Military Working Dogs, and Public Works Engineering Services.

    Tours are usually about an hour in length, so visitors may sign up for more than one tour in the day, as long as they are at the same location. Stipulations include that all participants must be U.S. citizens, groups must provide their own bus for transportation, students must be at least 10 years old, and requests must be made at least three weeks prior to your desired date. Don't miss the boat on taking these tours!

      Hours: Tours can be schedule once a month on Fri., to start at 9am and end at around noon.
      Price: Free
      Ages: Must be 10 years or older.

OJAI OLIVE OIL

!

(805) 646-5964 / www.ojaioliveoil.com
1811 Ladera Road, Ojai

    Learn about olive oil (not Popeye) on this forty-five acre, 3,000 tree ranch. The informal tours, about thirty minutes long, begin when some people gathered for one. Outside, under a grove of trees, the history of the ranch and

the area is explained, as well as how the olives are organically grown and harvested. Olives are hand-picked from mid-October through mid-January and milled for twelve days only in November/December.

Next, come inside to the small room where the machinery is kept. The milling process is explained from the 'Hopper', that cleans off the olives, to the 'Denocciolatore', which removes the pits and pulverizes the fruit, to the mixing containers, where it's churned, and finally to the centrifuge, which separates the oil. The tour guide/owner explains what the difference is in fresh extra virgin olive oil and in the products that is often sold in stores. In the tiny tasting room guests are invited to sample varieties of olive oil, from mild to robust, and some that are flavored. Olive oil is available to purchase, as are cosmetic products made from it such as lip balm, soap and face cream.

Hours: Open for tours Wed., 1pm - 4pm; Sat., 10am - 3pm.
Price: Free
Ages: 8 years and up.

SIMI VALLEY COURTHOUSE

(805) 650-7599 - bar association/tour / www.vcba.org
3855-F Alamo Street, Simi Valley

See the entry for VENTURA COUNTY COURTHOUSE below for details. This tour is two hours long.

Hours: Tours are offered Wed. at 10am, by advanced reservations only.
Ages: 6th and 8th graders, and adults

VENTURA COUNTY COURTHOUSE

(805) 650-7599 - bar association/tour / www.vcba.org
800 S. Victoria Avenue, Ventura

Now students (and adult groups) can have their day in court! This two-and-a-half-hour tour is for groups of twenty to thirty-five people. The process of the Ventura County court system is explained while it is being experienced as participants sit in on and observe a civil and/or criminal case, seeing an actual trial in process. Touring through the courthouse, see and learn about the law library, the ceremonial courtroom, the traffic court, and the jury room. When available, judges, commissioners, attorneys, or other court personnel speak to the group, and answer questions. The tour also consists of seeing the administration building (where residents pay property taxes and obtain licenses), the sheriff's department, and the jail. Here visitors learn what happens when an inmate is incarcerated - from frisking, to showers, to where they eat and sleep.

A highlight of the tour is a grade-appropriate, mock trial of an actual court case. Participants read from scripts as they become members of the jury, lawyers, the bailiff, and even the judge (along with a robe and gavel). The tour ends with a video of the Sheriff's Detention Center. I think this is a fascinating tour, but I'll let you be the judge!

Hours: Tours are given Tues. - Thurs. at 10:30am, by advanced reservations only.
Price: Free
Ages: 6th, 8th, and 12th graders, and adults.

—TRANSPORTATION—

AMTRAK (Ventura County)

(800) USA RAIL (872-7245) / www.amtrakcalifornia.com

Ride the rails! See AMTRAK (Los Angeles County) on page 208 for more information.

BIKE MAPS (Ventura County)

See BIKE MAPS (Orange County) on page 326 for information. Two other contacts include the Ventura County Transportation Commission at (805) 642-1591 / www.goventura.org and County of Ventura Transit Information at (800) 438-1112 - ask for a map.

BIKE TRAIL: COASTAL BIKEWAY

(805) 654-3951 - parks; (805) 648-4127 - ranger office; (805) 646-8126 - Chamber of Commerce; (805) 585-1850 - beach / www.bicycela.org; www.labikepaths.com
One end is on Harbor Boulevard at San Buenaventura State Beach; the other is past Emma Wood State Beach of Hwy. 101.

Thirteen miles of coastal bike trail makes for some beautiful scenery while enjoying a day of family and exercise. Stretching from the south, at SAN BUENAVENTURA STATE BEACH (see pg. 660), northward to Emma Wood State Beach, the trail is popular, especially in the summer.

Surrey cycles, quad sports, choppers, slingshots, and bike rentals are available at Wheel Fun Rentals, (805) 765-5795 / www.wheelfunrentals.com, 850 Harbor Boulevard at the pier. See the next entry for other places to rent bikes, and for another local bike path.

Hours: Open daily, sunrise - sunset.
Price: Free to ride. Parking is $10 at San Buenaventura Beach.
Ages: 4 years and up, depending on how long and far you want to ride.

BIKE TRAIL: OJAI VALLEY TRAIL - VENTURA RIVER TRAIL

(805) 654-3951 - parks; (805) 646-8126 - Chamber of Commerce / www.ventura.org   !/$
One end is on Ojai Avenue in Ojai; the other is at San Buenaventura State Beach in Ventura. Or, start in the middle at Foster County Park in Casitas Springs

This scenic, paved route is about sixteen miles long one way, officially ending (or beginning) on Main Street in Ventura. From the northern end point at Libbey Park, riding to Foster Park is about nine miles. The grade of the trail is a gentle slope from north to south, and therefore noticeably easier to pedal than vice versa. Although the trail follows along the major street of Ventura Avenue (Highway 33), oak and sycamore trees adorn it, making it pretty while shading good portions of it. Major sections are hidden from the main thoroughfare and give it a ride-in-the-country feel. The trail is frequented by bikers, skaters, strollers, equestrians, and joggers. The nine-mile trail from Foster Park to Main Street to the ocean includes a connection to the Coastal Bikeway. (See the previous entry.) That section is not all easy on the eyes, as it goes through industrial areas, but pathway artists have enlivened it somewhat with murals.

Forgot your wheels? Bicycle rentals are available at Bicycles of Ojai, (805) 646-7736 / www.bicyclesofojai.com, at 108 Canada Street, Ojai for $6 an hour. Note: No child-size bikes are available here. Ventura Bike Depot, (805) 652-1114 / www.venturabikedepot.com, near the base of Hwy. 33 at 239 W. Main Street in Ventura, offers rentals for kids and adults starting at $14 for two hours, $10 an hour for tandem. Wheel Fun Rentals, at www.wheelfunrentals.com, has several locations in Ventura and Oxnard.

Hours: The trail is open daily, dawn - dusk.
Price: Free at the Ojai end at Libbey Park; $2 parking at Foster Park during the week, $4 on the weekends.
Ages: 4 years and up, depending on how long and far you want to ride.

CHANNEL ISLANDS KAYAK CENTER

Oxnard - (805) 984-5995; Ventura - (805) 644-9699 / www.cikayak.com $$$$
Oxnard - 3600 S. Harbor Boulevard, suite 2-108 Channel Islands Harbor; Ventura - 1691 Spinnaker Dr. at Ventura Harbor Village

Kayaking is a fun and relatively easy sport for most people to participate in. This company offers hourly, part-day, and full-day, sit-on-top kayak rentals and Stand Up Paddleboard rentals, as well as lessons and tours. If you want to get your feet wet, so to speak, take the two-and-a-half hour, guided History and Wildlife kayak tour, which begins with lessons, then heads out through the channel and around the coast. You'll see tall ships, and seals and other marine animals at almost eye level and enjoy the incredible scenery while learning the history of the area. You'll also be entertained by paddling by a replica of a small Mammoth and through an artificial sea cave, perhaps even finding "pirate" skulls - all in good fun.

The all-day, all-inclusive Channel Islands Kayak guided tour includes transportation out to Anacapa or Santa Cruz Channel Islands, where dolphins and seals are often encountered, as the guide paddles alongside you and shares some of the island's history. Another service that the center offers is kayak rentals to those booking their own passage out to the Channel Islands via Island Packers. (See pg. 668) for details.

Hours: Open daily in the summer, 10am - 5pm. Open the rest of the year, Mon. - Fri., noon - 5pm; Sat. - Sun., 10am - 5pm. Closed some holidays.

Price: Single kayaks rentals are $12.50 an hour; doubles are $20. SUPs are $25 an hour. The History and Wildlife tour is $79.95 per person. The Santa Cruz Island tour is $199.95 per person for a two-person tour. Kayaks rentals to take on your own excursion to the Channel Islands are $35 for a full day for a single; $55 for double.

Ages: 5 years and up.

CHANNEL ISLANDS SPORTFISHING   ☼

(805) 382-1612 / www.channelislandssportfishing.com $$$$$
4151 S. Victoria Avenue, Oxnard

Mature males and pregnant female Pacific gray whales are the first to migrate south to Mexico, and then head back north, toward home. Juvenile whales are the last to make the journey, toward the end of the season. Go out for three hours+ on one of several boats in the fleet with a naturalist and learn about the mammals while, hopefully, seeing some of them. The company also, obviously, offers sport fishing excursions.

Hours: The season runs January - April. Departure times are usually Mon. - Fri., 9am; Sat. - Sun. and holidays at 9am and 1pm.

Price: $50 for adults; $40 for seniors (this doesn't apply on the weekends); $30 for ages 12 and under.

Ages: 6 years and up.

FILLMORE & WESTERN RAILWAY COMPANY   ☼

(805) 524-2546 / www.fwry.com; www.scvrhs.com $$$$
364 Main Street, Central Park Depot, Fillmore

"More powerful than a locomotive"; *The Great Train Robbery*; and *The Little Engine That Could* - what does this potpourri of things bring to mind? A train ride, of course! Riding on a train is a real adventure for children. The countryside is scenic along this route, with citrus groves and beautiful landscapes. This railway line is also a favorite Hollywood location, so many of the trains you see and ride on have appeared in movies and television shows. Ride the rails in an open air railcar, a restored passenger coach (circa 1930); a 1929 parlour car; a restored, 1950's Streamlined diner; or a more modern car.

There are several types of weekend excursions offered. The "regular" ride, or Weekend Scenic Excursion, is a four-hour round trip between Fillmore and Santa Paula, which includes a seventy-five-minute stopover in Santa Paula, where you are invited to tour whatever else is within walking distance, which is most of the town, such as the historic depot, the AGRICULTURE MUSEUM (pg. 679), CALIFORNIA OIL MUSEUM (pg. 680), or the SANTA PAULA ART MUSEUM (pg. 689). A second stopover is at Loose Caboose Garden Center, an eclectic mix of garden art, plants, a koi pond, farm animals, caged birds, fresh seasonal produce and a gift shop. Lunches are offered in the 1929 parlour car en route for an additional fee. (No outside food is allowed on the trains.)

Many specialty train rides are available, too, including Father's Day, Heritage Valley Tour, Pumpkinliner, Headless Horseman, Dinner With Santa, North Pole Express, and more. The Murder Express Lunch Train is a murder mystery comedy offered on select Saturdays and includes a four-hour ride, three-course lunch, and entertainment, plus a stop over at Loose Caboose. Ask about the hour-long School Trains, where students ride the rails to the Fillmore Fish Hatchery (and back), or non-stop enjoy the countryside as they learn about and see the workings of a train, vintage cars, and more. A snack bar and gift shop are on board. Younger children will especially delight in the Thomas the Tank Engine adventure days where guest can take a twenty-five minute ride on Thomas, meet Sir Topham Hatt, and participate in storytelling, crafts and even watching a Thomas movie. See the Calendar entry for details about the wonderful, annual Fillmore Spring RailFest (pg. 710).

The park-like area surrounding the train depot is nicely landscaped with stretches of green grass and a courtyard with a fountain. A few stationary train cars are actually stores that carry antiques and train-related merchandise. An ice cream shop is on the premises, too. Check out the FILLMORE HISTORICAL MUSEUM (pg. 684) near the depot, too. Walk around the block, or on the bike path, and you'll see numerous more train cars, in various states of repair.

Note: Several fresh produce stands dot Hwy. 26, just east of the train depot, which offer an awesome selection of in-season fruit and vegetables, with specialties of oranges and strawberries.

Hours: Weekend Scenic train rides depart January - April, Sat. at noon (boarding at 11:30am), returning at 4pm; May - September and November, every Sat. and some Sun., at noon. Call of check the website for specialty rides.

Price: Round-trip fare for the Weekend Scenic ride is $25 for adults; $23 for seniors; $15 for ages 4 - 12; $10 for ages 3 and under. Murder Express rides are $63 for adults; $34 for ages 7 - 12. School Trains are $8 per person. Thomas trains are $19 per person. Call or check the website for prices for other specialty rides.

Ages: 3 years and up.

HOPPER BOAT RENTALS

(805) 382-1100 / www.hopperboatrentals.com $$$$
2741 Victoria Avenue, Oxnard

Hop to it and rent an ocean kayak, paddle boat, seacyde (which is a water bike on pontoons), a motor or electric boat right on the Channel Islands Harbor. Reservations are recommended.

Hours: Open November - February, Mon. - Fri., 11:30am - 5pm; Sat. - Sun., 10am - 5pm. Open March - October, daily, 10am - 5pm.

Price: All prices are per hour: Single kayaks are $12; doubles are $20. Paddle boats, for one to four passengers, are $15. Electric boats, for one to four passengers, are $50; up to ten passengers, $85. Stand Up Paddle boards are $24 an hour. Cash or check only.

Ages: 3 years and up.

ISLAND PACKERS

(805) 642-7688; (805) 642-1393 / www.islandpackers.com $$$$$
Oxnard - 3600 South Harbor Boulevard at the Marine Emporium Landing; Ventura - 1691 Spinnaker Drive at Ventura Harbor

This is a prime company to use when cruising out to the Channel Islands. See CHANNEL ISLANDS NATIONAL PARK (pg. 668) for complete details on the islands, the price, length of time, and departure times.

View the magnificent Pacific gray whales on their way to Mexico where they breed and give birth before headings home to the Bering Sea. Three hour, or so, excursions begin December 26 and continue through early April. You may also join Island Packers late June through September for an all-day trek out to the north shore of Santa Rosa Island to gaze at the enormous blue and humpback whales. The journey's climax is seeing the whales, but there is much aquatic life to enjoy along the way, as well. Island Packers also offers three-hour Wildlife Watching school group cruises April through December. From June through October set sail on a one-hour Saturday sunset cruise or a two-hour Saturday dinner cruise.

Hours: Departure times for whale watching are usually Sat. - Sun. at , 9:30am and sometimes at 1pm, too. Check the website for all other departure times.

Price: Gray whale watching tours are $36 for adults; $32 for seniors; $26 for children 3 - 12 years. See page 668 for prices for island cruises. Sunset cruises, usually at 6:30pm, are $20 for adults; $12 for children. Dinner cruises, usually 7pm - 9pm, are $56 for adults; $43 for children.

Ages: 6 years and up.

JIM HALL RACING SCHOOL

(805) 654-1329 / www.jimhallkartracing.com $$$$$
2600 Challenger Place, Oxnard

What child doesn't like racing around? Now he/she can learn how to do it in karts and enjoy the thrill of racing without the danger. This racing school offers Parent/Child Learning Days, for kids 10 to 14 who haven't driven before, and Day One Sprint Kart programs minimum 4 feet, 8" tall. Classes range from half-day instruction to a week, or more. Drivers learn safety (yea!), how to drive, braking techniques (this could be especially valuable in just a few years), and banking. Racers will even get timed - watch out, Robby Gordon! Ventura County beaches are just a short drive away from this school.

Hours: Call for class hours. Call two days in advance to reserve for a weekend time.

Price: Varies, depending on the length of class. The Day One Sprint Kart program, which is four hours of instruction and driving, starts at $225.

Ages: 10 years and up.

METROLINK (Ventura County)

(800) 371-LINK (5465) / www.metrolinktrains.com $$$

See the entry for METROLINK (Orange County) on page 329 for details.

SANTA PAULA AIRPORT - CP AVIATION

(805) 525-2138 / www.cpaviation.com $$$$$
830 E. Santa Maria Street, Santa Paula

This small airport is kid-friendly; partly because of its size, and partly because it's always fun to watch planes land and take off. Instead of just watching, however, why not take the kids up for a spin, literally! At the instructor's discretion, if your child is at least 12 years old (and doesn't get motion sickness), he/she can take an exhilarating half-hour acrobatic intro ride with loops, rolls, and G's (better than a roller coaster!), for $145 per person. For those who enjoy a calmer, scenic ride, a Cessna 172, which seats three passengers, is about $150 (total) for a half-hour flight - call as this changes. Other aircraft are available for flights, too. Learn to Fly Instruction is $99 for a half hour. Lunch at the airport restaurant will complete your lofty adventure.

If you're visiting on the first Sunday of the month, take a walk through the adjacent hangars that house the AVIATION MUSEUM OF SANTA PAULA (pg. 680). Check out the YOUNG EAGLES PROGRAM (Ventura County) (pg. 700).

Hours: The airport is open daily. Call for hours for a flight.
Price: Prices listed above.
Ages: 4 years and up for a look around the airport and a scenic flight.

VENTURA BOAT RENTALS

(805) 642-7753 / www.venturaboatrentals.com $$$
1575 Spinnaker Drive, Ventura

Enjoy a forty-minute cruise out of the harbor, past the boats and homes along the coastline. Other options include kayak rentals - $15 an hour for a single, $20 for a double; paddle boats - $15 an hour for a two-passenger, $20 for a four-passenger; stand up paddle boards - $25 an hour; electric boats - $65 for an eight-passenger Duffy with an awning, for an hour. (There are more options available for bigger boats, too.) Ninety-minute California Sleigh Rides (boat cruises) depart twice nightly in December and include seeing other boats and buildings with holiday lights, plus hot chocolate and cookies. See VENTURA HARBOR VILLAGE (pg. 692) for other things to do in this area.

Hours: Cruises depart most of the year, Sat. - Sun. and select holidays, noon - 5pm, every hour on the hour. During the summer, cruises depart Mon. - Fri. at 2pm and 4pm; Sat. - Sun., between noon - 6pm, every hour.
Price: Harbor cruises are $10 for adults; $8 for seniors; $6 for ages 2 - 12; $2 for children under 2. Sleigh Rides are $20 for adults; $10 for children. Paying by credit card is more $ for any boat rental. Other prices are listed above.
Ages: All

YOUNG EAGLES PROGRAM (Ventura County)

National number - (877) 806-8902; Camarillo and Santa Paula - (805) 383-0686 - chapter #723 / www.eaa723.org; www.youngeagles.org
Camarillo - 501 Aviation Drive/Convair Street.; Santa Paula - 830 E. Santa Maria Street

See the entry for YOUNG EAGLES PROGRAM (Los Angeles County) on page 215 for details. Camarillo - Reservations are necessary! Check out the COMMEMORATIVE AIR FORCE MUSEUM (pg. 684) at the airport. Santa Paula - Reservations are necessary! Young Eagle flights coincide with the AVIATION MUSEUM OF SANTA PAULA (pg. 680) being open.

Hours: Camarillo - Offered the first Sat. of every month at 10am, 10:45am and 11:30am. Santa Paula - Offered the first Sun. of every month at 10am, 10:45am and 11:30am.
Price: Free
Ages: 8 - 17 years.

—ZOOS AND ANIMALS—

AMERICA'S TEACHING ZOO

☀
$$$

(805) 378-1441 / zoo.moorparkcollege.edu

7075 Campus Road at Moorpark Community College, Moorpark

Students attend this teaching zoo, that contains 200 exotic animals, to become zoo keepers, veterinarians, and animal trainers. My favorite aspect of this very small zoo is that the knowledgeable staff members throughout (i.e., students) answer any and all of your child's questions. My kids and I learned so much here! As this is a teaching zoo, and not just here for public enjoyment, many of the caged animals are in rows, making it difficult, or impossible, to see most of them. However, the animals that are readily viewed can be seen more up close than at a typical zoo. We saw llamas, American alligator, baboons, a miniature horse, macaws, potbellied pigs, New Guinea singing dogs, spider monkeys, ring-tailed lemurs, lions, foxes, barn owls, hawks, eagles, Galapagos Island tortoises, birds in an aviary, and many more. Siamang primates are very loud when they get agitated! There is also a small reptile house to go into. Tour the tiny kitchen zoo at 12:45 to see how and what the animals eat.

Almost half-hour demonstrations, featuring three to five animals per show, such as primates, hoofed animals, birds, or reptiles, are given on a small outdoor stage. The student trainers give a lot of good information as they talk about the animal's habitats, nutrition, learned behavior, and training. Afterwards, sometimes, kids can touch the animals. One of the reptiles we saw and touched was a huge boa. We were amazed at its strength and its under-belly softness.

Don't miss the 3:30pm feeding of the carnivores! Actually, get there a little early and see animals being fed that aren't on the scheduled program. Trainers feed the lions (go ahead - ask what they're eating) as they "show-off" the lions' learned behavior. Forty-minute school tours, starting at 10am or 10:30am, are given during the week and include animal presentations followed by a half-hour guided tour of the zoo. See the Calendar entry for information on the Spring Spectacular (pg. 713). Ask about the week-long, summer Junior Zoo Safari for kids who like to work with animals. Note: Picnic tables are here for your lunching pleasure on weekends. There is also a park across the street from the college on Campus Drive with a playground and grassy area.

Hours: The Zoo is open weekends, 11am - 5pm. Trainer talks are given throughout the day. Animal presentations are given at noon and 2pm, weather permitting. You can call to see what animals will be shown. Feeding of the carnivores is at 3:30pm.

Price: $8 for adults; $6 for seniors and ages 3 - 12; children 2 and are free. School tours start at $75 minimum or, over 25 students, $3 per person. All admission requires cash or check only.

Ages: All

CHIVAS GOAT MILK SKIN CARE AND GOAT FARM

☀
!/$$$

(805) 727-3121 / www.chivasskincare.com

2220 Bardsdale Avenue, Fillmore

Nineteen French alpine goats are raised and hand-milked to create a line of goat milk soaps, lotions and other beauty products at this small, family-owned farm. Several special events, such as the Spring Fling in April and open houses, are held throughout the year for the public to explore the farm a little, including meeting and feeding the goats, pot-bellied pigs, horses, and tortoises; seeing the the intimate soap workshop; and shopping!

There are two other ways to explore the farm throughout the year. One is to take a ninety-minute school group farm tour, for a minimum of $200. Topics and activities can include interacting with farm animals; learning how to raise goats; playing farm games; exploring edible plants and herbs in the learning garden; hands-on learning of biology via goat milking; and/or the chemistry of soap making by touring the soap workshop. Bring a picnic lunch to enjoy. Note that baby goats are usually born in the spring. The second way is to schedule a private tour. The entrance fee is $8 for adults, $5 for children, with a minimum fee of $200. This minimum can be met by entrance fees, gift shop credit, and/or workshop fees, which range from $10 to $50 per person. Topics include DIY Essential Oil Blending, How to Make Goat Cheese, and more.

Hours: Check the website or call about special events or to schedule a farm tour.

Price: Free for special events; minimum $200 for tours.

Ages: Kindergarten and up.

FILLMORE FISH HATCHERY

(805) 524-0962 / www.dfg.ca.gov

612 Hwy. 126, Fillmore

Stop off and take a quick look around the fish hatchery to see hundreds of thousands of rainbow trout; actually over one million are produced here annually. This hatchery supplies fish to lakes and streams throughout San Luis Obispo, Santa Barbara, Los Angeles, and Ventura counties. The long, narrow, concrete tanks have compartments that are labeled with the various species names. Coin-operated fish food dispensers (10¢) are here and the fish always seem to be hungry. Watch them almost jump out of the water for the food! School field trips on the FILLMORE & WESTERN RAILWAY COMPANY come through the hatchery as part of their train ride. By the way, no fishing allowed.

  Hours: Open daily, 7am - 3:30pm
  Price: Free
  Ages: 2 years and up.

PAINTED PONY

(805) 525-9820 / www.ourpaintedponyfarm.com

15315 Ojai Road, W. of Steckel Park, Santa Paula

Way out here in the country, you won't get to paint a pony, but you will get to spend a few hours on the farm holding baby chicks, milking a goat, and feeding and petting the animals while learning a lot about farming and sustainable living. Just some of the animals include pigs, tortoises, horses, goats, chickens (over seventy-five hens), bunnies, ducks, and sheep - some of which are available for purchase. The farm owners offer a host of seasonal group tours, too, also for a minimum of twenty people, that all include exploring the farm and seeing and feeding the animals. Come apple picking, seasonally; visit the pumpkin patch where about 2,000 pumpkins are growing in the field that you can snip right off the vine; attend week-long spring and summer camps where kids bottle feed baby goats, make cheese from goat's milk, learn about canning, do arts and crafts, and go swimming; and more.

  Hours: Open mid-March - October, Mon. - Fri., by appointment only.
  Price: A farm day tour is usually $5 per person. Call for other options.
  Ages: 3 years and up.

UNDERWOOD FAMILY FARMS

3370 Sunset Valley Road, Moorpark

See UNDERWOOD FAMILY FARMS (Moorpark) on page 662 for details about this adventure with animals for younger children.

WHALE WATCHING

See the TRANSPORTATION section.

CALENDAR
(a listing of annual events)

Many places listed in the main section of this book offer special events throughout the year. Below is a calendar listing of other annual stand outs. Please keep in mind that some events change dates and locations from year to year, so call the attraction a month in advance. The prices and information quoted here are as of April, 2014.

- JANUARY: -

BEN FRANKLIN BIRTHDAY CELEBRATION, Carson. (310) 515-7166 / www.printmuseum.org, 315 Torrance Blvd. at the International Printing Museum. Celebrate Benjamin Franklin's birthday at the International Printing Museum on the 3rd Saturday in January. Come enjoy special tours, hands-on demonstrations, a family show at 11am, and a special program for the older crowd at 1pm. There is a symposium following the 1pm performance. Reservations recommended. See pg. 123 for more information on the INTERNATIONAL PRINTING MUSEUM. Open Sat., 10am - 4pm. $8 per person; $7 for seniors.

CABLE AIR SHOW, Upland. (909) 982-6021 / www.cableairport.com, 1749 W. 13th St. at Cable Airport. Fly bys, aerobatic maneuvers and demonstrations, remote control plane acrobatics, sky divers, community performances (i.e., bands, gymnastics, etc.), an antique car show, vendors, inflatable slides, rock climbing wall, and static displays (such as police and army helicopters) are all part of this wonderful air fair. Take about a fifteen-minute ride in a Cessna ($30 for adults, $20 for kids 12 and under), biplane ($75 per person), or Air Force Harvard T-6 ($175 per person). Or, take a helicopter ride for $35. Bring your own food or eat at the on-site Maniac-Mikes Cafe. There isn't any seating at the air show unless you bring your own chair or blanket, so just wing it! Open Sat., 8am - 4:30pm; Sun., 8am - 4pm. Admission is $10 for adults; $5 for ages 5 - 12; children 4 and under are free. Parking is free.

CABRILLO WHALE WATCH WEEKEND and INTERTIDAL LIFE FESTIVAL, Point Loma. (619) 557-5450 / www.nps.gov/cabr, Cabrillo Memorial Dr. at Cabrillo National Monument. On the second or third weekend in January come watch for Pacific gray whales as they migrate southward. (Whale migration is usually the end of December through March.) Park rangers and authors give presentations about marine life and are on hand to provide information about gray whales, tidepool creatures, and the history of the site. You are invited to also check out the exhibit booths, watch a film about whales, enjoy a puppet show, tour the facilities, and explore the tidepools just below. Open Sat. - Sun., 9am - 5pm. Admission is $3; parking is $5.

CALIFORNIA BABY & KIDZ EXPO, Costa Mesa. (303) 400-3470 / www.babyandkidzexpo.com, 88 Fair Drive at the Orange County Fair and Event Center. This parent, baby, toddler and child expo includes seminars, door prizes, educational resources, camp info, diaper derby, birthday ideas, college planning and so much more. Lots of fun activities for children and live entertainment including kids fashion show, magic show, science show, bubble show and more. Jumpers and train rides (included with admission). Open Sat., 10am - 5pm. Admission is $10 for adults; $5 for srs.; children 12 and under free.

CALIFORNIA BABY & KIDZ EXPO, Pasadena. , 300 East Green Street at the Pasadena Convention Center. See above entry for details.

CHILL AT THE QUEEN MARY, Long Beach. / www.queenmary.com, See December entry (pg. 763) for details.

COIN & COLLECTIBLES EXPO, Long Beach. (888) 743-9316 / www.longbeachexpo.com, 100 S. Pine Ave. at the Long Beach Convention Center. A penny for your thoughts! Over 400 vendors buy and sell rare coins, paper money, foreign currency, collectible postcards, autographs, historical documents, jewelry, and stamps. A free coin and stamp are usually given out to younger children at the Young Numismatists and Young Stampers table, respectively. This event is held late January (or early February), June and September. Open Thurs. - Fri., 10am - 7pm; Sat., 10am - 5pm. Admission is $8 for adults for all three days; $4 for srs. and ages 8 - 16; children 7 and under are free. Parking is about $10 a day.

CORONADO BUTTERFLY RESERVE, Goleta. (805) 966-4520 / www.sblandtrust.org/coronado.html; www.trails.com, Parking at 7731 Hollister Ave., across the street from Ellwood Elementary School. Hundreds of Monarch butterflies come to this grove to rest as they migrate south. The public is welcome on this wooded and coastal land. Park and then hike the ½ mile dirt trail back into the reserve and the specific trees. Take only rugged strollers as ruts and parts are covered with wood chips and tree roots. The trail is well marked and you can take it all the way to the beach. The grove is peaceful - all the butterflies fluttering around and no noise. They look like dead leaves when their wings are folded, but like a stunning orange and black mosaic when they open them and fly. The butterflies arrive in mid-November and usually depart around the end of February. Open daily, dawn to dusk.

Admission is free

FANTASY ON ICE, San Diego. See November entry (pg. 757) for details.

FESTIVAL OF HUMAN ABILITIES, Long Beach. (562) 590-3100 / www.aquariumofpacific.org, 100 Aquarium Way. Billed as "a celebration of the creative spirit of people with disabilities" the festival features dance, music, storytelling and interactive displays for children, and includes interactive classes for people of all ages and abilities. Featured presentations include wheelchair dance, live music, signing choirs, service dog demonstrations and more. The event is held at the Aquarium of the Pacific (pg. 216) and includes interactive classes for people of all ages and abilities. Open 9am - 5pm. Free with admission to the aquarium.

FREE ENTRANCE DAYS IN THE NATIONAL PARKS, / www.nps.gov/findapark/feefreeparks.htm, Entrance to your local National park (and those across the country) is free on the following days: Martin Luther King Jr. Day, Presidents Day weekend, opening weekend of National Park Week (April), National Park Service Birthday (August), National Public Lands Day (September), and Veterans Day. Entrance is free, but other fees, such as camping, reservations, tours, etc. still apply.

GREAT TRAIN EXPO, Anaheim. (630) 608-4988 or (714) 765-8950 / www.greattrainexpo.com; www.anaheimconventioncenter.com, 800 West Katella Ave. at the Anaheim Convention Center. Stop. Look. Listen. A weekend of fun at*track*tions for your family includes oogling huge scale layouts on hundreds of tables, operating some model trains, riding trains for kids, attending free workshops, and more, in this huge hobby marketplace geared for train enthusiasts. Open Sat. - Sun., 10am - 4pm. Admission is $7 for ages 13 and up (good for both days); children 12 and under are free. Parking is $12.

HERITAGE PARK U-PIC ORANGES, La Verne. (909) 293-9005 / www.laverneheritage.org, 5001 Via De Mansion at Heritage Park. Every Saturday, January to mid-March, pick your own oranges at one of the last working orange groves in the area. Now, you can really have fresh squeezed o.j.! The Weber House is also open for free tours. Built in the 1880's, it is one of the oldest remaining houses in La Verne. Open Sat., 9am - 3pm. $5 per bag.

HITS DESERT CIRCUIT, Thermal. (760) 399-9200 or (845) 246-8833 / www.hitsshows.com, 85-555 Airport Blvd. at the HITS Desert Horse Park. For eight weeks horse-lovers can get an eyeful as more than 3,000 horses and riders - the top hunters and jumpers in North America - compete in America's largest horse show with over 1.5 million dollars of total prize money. Professional and amateur riders, both adults and juniors, compete in the show ring. Ask about Kids' Day where crafts, free pony rides, slides, downs, and other kid-oriented activities happen. The circuit begins mid-January and ends mid-March. Open Tues. - Sun., 8am -4pm. Admission is free Tues. - Sat.; Sun., $5 for ages 13 and over; children 12 and under are free. Parking is free.

HOLIDAY ON ICE, Irvine. See November entry (pg. 758) for details.

HOTEL DEL CORONADO ICE RINK, Coronado. See November entry (pg. 759) for details.

ICE AT SANTA MONICA, Santa Monica. See the November entry (pg. 759) for details.

LUNAR FEST RIVERSIDE, Riverside. (951) 453-3548 / www.lunarfestriverside.com, Downtown Riverside at Mission Inn Avenue and Lemon Street. Be transported to the Ancient Orient beginning with the Parade of Nations at 10am, followed by the Opening Ceremonies. The festivities continue with traditional Asian music, including Taiko drums, dance performances, martial arts, and many cultural displays. There is also a children's village, tea pavilions, food and the grand finale of fireworks. Open Sat., 10am - 7pm. Parking and admission is free.

MUSEUMS FREE-FOR-ALL, / www.museumsla.org, Check this website about free admission to over twenty museums on the fourth Saturday in January. Regular parking fees apply. Consult individual museum websites for hours and additional information.

LUNAR NEW YEAR FESTIVAL, Los Angeles. (213) 617-0396 / www.lachinesechamber.org; www.lagoldendragonparade.com, 600 - 900 blocks of Broadway St. in Chinatown. This over 100-year-old, two-day Chinese New Year celebration's main event is the elaborate (and televised) Golden Dragon Parade on Saturday with floats, bands, and dragon dancers in wonderful costumes. The Little King and Queen contest on Sunday is adorable. Other goings-on include a street fair with arts and crafts, live music, and a car show on Sunday. The New Year is celebrated on the first weekend of the Lunar New Year - "Gung Hay Fat Choy" (i.e. Happy New Year.) Open Sat. noon - 8pm and Sun., noon - 5pm. The parade is Sat., 1pm - 4pm. Admission is free, although certain activities cost. Grandstand seating for the parade is $30 per seat pre-sale, and $35 the day of.

MARTIN LUTHER KING JR. DAY, Celebrations take place all over the Southland. Long Beach hosts the Annual Dr. Martin Luther King, Jr. Peace and Unity Parade Celebration - (562) 570-6816. Los Angeles has the MLK Kingdom Day Parade - (310) 250-2891. San Diego hosts a parade, www.alpha-zsl.org. Also see the San Diego Multicultural

Festival (pg. 705).

MONARCH BUTTERFLIES, Ventura. (805) 658-4726 - the Office of Cultural Affairs for "tour" info / www.cityofventura.net, Dean and Varsity Drs. at Camino Real Park. Thousands of Monarch butterflies arrive at the park during this month and hang on the trees at Dean Court. Look at them on your own, or take a one-hour guided tour offered on weekends. Admission is free. Tours are $20 per person.

PISMO BEACH MONARCH GROVE, Pismo Beach. (800) 443-7778 / www.monarchbutterfly.org; www.classiccalifornia.com, off Hwy 1/ S. Dolliver St., at the extreme southern end of the town of Pismo Beach; S. of North Beach State Campground. Every year, from November through February, over 25,000 monarchs come to roost and rest at this grove, the largest gathering in the state and, depending on the year, the largest in the U.S. Sometimes you see what looks like dead leaves as dense clusters of the butterflies hang, wings downward, from the branches. At other times the butterflies flutter around, resplendent in their orange and black markings. This site is staffed with knowledgeable docents, in season, daily, 10am - 4pm (except for holidays). A trailer is here, too, with more info and souvenirs. Talks and a guided walk through the grove are offered daily at 11am and 2pm, weather allowing. Butterflies trees and the beach nearby - an unbeatable combination. Check the website for coloring pages and other activities for kids. The grove is open daily, sunrise to sunrise. Free.

SAN DIEGO CHINESE NEW YEAR FAIR, San Diego. (619) 398-7025 or (619) 234-4447 / www.sdcny.org, 3rd and J sts., downtown San Diego. More than 25,000 people attend these two days of celebrating the Chinese culture. Enjoy demonstrations, such as karate and acrobatics; dances, such as fire dances, Chinese folk dances, the lion dance, and the dragon dance (the dragon is thirty-five feet long!); a craft area where kids make a Chinese lantern and form a lantern parade; and cooking demonstrations with wonderful food. Open Sat. - Sun., 9am - 5pm. Admission is free.

SAN DIEGO MULTICULTURAL FESTIVAL / MARTIN LUTHER KING, JR. PARADE, San Diego. (619) 235-2222, (858) 735-5921 / www.sdmulticultural.com, along Martin Luther King, Jr. Promenade - Fourth Ave. to Market St. on Harbor Dr., adjacent to the outstanding New Children's Museum. Starting the day off with the Martin Luther King, Jr. Parade Saturday at 10am, the celebration continues throughout the day. A feast for the eyes and ears, this festival features stages of multicultural music and dance performances. Kids enjoy all of that, plus storytellers telling tales originating from different continents, hands-on activities, food booths, community information, vending booths with merchandise that span the globe, and more. Ask about Global Villages, an educational program integrating with kids in the classroom. The closest parking is at 6th & K, or take the trolley (see www.sdcommute.com for details). Open 11am - 5pm. The parade begins at 2pm. Admission is free.

SAN DIEGO NEW YEAR TET FESTIVAL, San Diego. (858) 215-4838 / www.sdtet.com, Mira Mesa Community Park, 8575 New Salem Street Celebrated mainly in the Vietnamese community, the coming of spring is ushered in via a three-day festival. Along with a kid's contest, where they are judged on talent, manners, wearing traditional clothing, and more, the cultural village has ethnic performances (i.e. a variety of traditional and modern dancing and singing), calligraphy, workshops, chess competition, crafts, royal impersonators, and vendors, plus a beauty pageant and singing competition for the slightly older crowd. Fri., 5pm - 10pm; Sat., 11am - 10pm; Sun., 11am - 9pm. Admission is free.

TALL SHIPS TOUR, Oceanside, San Diego, Long Beach, San Pedro, Oxnard. (800) 200-LADY (5239) - ship tour / www.historicalseaport.org, The stately, two-masted tall ship *Lady Washington,* a faithful, full-scale reproduction of the first American square rigged ship, and the *Hawaiian Chieftain,* a replica of a typical, nineteenth-century, European merchant trader, glide into port for about six days per port. They usually dock first in San Pedro ([310] 833-6055; Berth 84 at the L.A. Maritime Institute) in late December, then sail to Long Beach (200 Aquarium Way at the Long Beach Harbor), Oceanside ([760] 435-4000; 1540 Harbor Drive S. at Oceanside Harbor), San Diego (1561 Shelter Island Dr.), and back up to Oxnard (Channel Islands Harbor) as they head north in February. Visitors experience the life of sailors first hand, as well as coastal explorers, traders, and missionaries of the 18th century via a one-hour guided dockside tour, or three-hour sailing adventures led by period-dressed crew members. The dockside tour is hands-on, teaching the life of a sailor and of the cultures along the coast. The three-hour, family-oriented adventure sail includes demonstrations of how to handle a tall ship, singing sea shanties, storytelling, and exploring the open seas. Three-hour battle reenactments place you in the history hot seat as the two ships try to out maneuver each other. The highlight is the firing of cannons. (It's not real ammunition - just lots of noise and smoke.) Another three-hour excursion is for students, called the Voyages of Discovery. This is geared for fourth and fifth graders, although older students enjoy it as well. All hands are on deck as students set and trim the sails, steer the ship, and use traditional navigational tools while learning mathematics, cartography, astronomy, and other sciences, as well as how to work together as a team. Note that teachers are sent a packet of suggested pre-trip activities and a bibliography. Programs run rain or shine, just like the sailors of old worked. Whatever option you choose, come sail the high seas of adventure. Check the schedule

for particular times and dates of tours. Dockside tours are offered Tues. - Fri., 4pm - 5pm; Sat. - Sun., 10am - 1pm. The tours are free, but a $3 per person donation is requested. Dockside educational tours, for school groups, are $8 per participant. Family adventure sails begin at 10am and cost $39 per person (including infants). Battle reenactments go to sea at 2pm and cost $63 for adults; $53 for srs., students, and active military; $43 for children 12 and under. Evening sails are $29 Tues. - Thurs.; $39 Fri. - Sat.

TET FESTIVAL, Costa Mesa. (714) 890-1418 / www.tetfestival.org, 88 Fair Drive at the Orange County Fair and Event Center. This three-day festival marks the beginning of spring and is the most widely-celebrated festival in Asian cultures, specifically the Vietnamese community. Arts and crafts, food booths, a fashion show, traditional dances, and other entertainment are just some of the fun "events". Open Fri., 3pm - 10pm; Sat., 10am - 10pm; Sun., 10am - 9pm. Admission is $5; $1 with OCTA bus pass; children 4 and under are free. Carnival rides are an additional fee.

TOURNAMENT OF ROSES PARADE, Pasadena. (626) 449-ROSE (7673) - recording; (626) 449-4100 - real person; (877) 793-9911 - holiday hot line / www.tournamentofroses.com; www.pasadenacal.com, Pasadena City Hall. This two-hour, world-famous parade of fancifully- and elegantly-decorated floral floats, plus bands and equestrian units, is held on New Year's Day. Camp out overnight on the streets to guarantee a viewing spot - check www.cityofpasadena.net for the rules and regulations; try your luck by arriving in the early morning hours on the actual day; or call Sharp Seating Company, (626) 795-4171 / www.sharpseating.com, for grandstand seating. Watching the parade along the sidewalk/curb is free. Prices for grandstand seats range from $48 - $95. Make reservations at least two months in advance. The parade begins at 8am. Call or check the website for the parade route. Parking can cost between $10 - $90, so plan ahead!

TOURNAMENT OF ROSES VIEWING OF FLOATS, Pasadena. (626) 449-ROSE (7673) or (626) 449-4100 / www.tournamentofroses.com; www.pasadenacal.com, along Sierra Madre and Washington blvds., near Sierra Madre Villa Ave. The famous floats can be viewed up close for a few days after the parade. Arrive early in hopes of bypassing some of the hordes of people to let your kids walk around and "oooh" and "aaah" at the intricate workmanship. Bring your camera! It is a one-mile walk to view all the floats. Open Jan. 1, 1pm - 5pm. It's open Jan. 2 and 3 from 7am - 9am for mobility-impaired and srs. only, then from 9am - 5pm for the general public. Admission is $10 per person; children 5 and under are free. Expect to pay at least $5 for parking. Pre purchase tickets at www.sharpseating.com or at the door until 3pm each day.

TRAIN DAYS, Redlands. (909) 307-2669 / www.sbcounty.gov/museum, 2024 N. Orange Tree Lane. Come see model trains and trolleys, real train artifacts, visit with train experts and engineers and make train related crafts. Open Sat. and Sun., 9am - 5pm. $10 for adults; $8 for srs.; $7 for students; $5 for ages 5 - 12; children 4 and under are free.

WHALE WATCHING, See the Transportation section in the main section of the book for places to call to take a whale-watching cruise. The season goes from the end of December through March. Cruises are usually two and a half hours of looking for (and finding!) gray whales as they migrate to and from Baja. Also, be on the lookout for dolphins, pilot whales, and sea lions. Dress warmly.

WOODLAND HILLS ICE, Woodland Hills. See October entry (pg. 756) for details.

- FEBRUARY: -

CALICO CIVIL WAR DAYS, Yermo. (800) TO CALICO (862-2542) or (760) 254-2122 / www.calicotown.com, 36600 Ghost Town Rd. at Calico Ghost Town. Over the three-day President's Day weekend the North meets the South in Civil War reenactments complete with drills, cannon demonstrations, period fashion shows, music, living history displays, Confederate and Union camps, and two battles a day. Lincoln, Grant, and/or Lee might make an appearance, too. The Gettysburg Address is presented on Sun. and Mon. Children's crafts and activities are held throughout the days. Other special events include a cotillion on Saturday night, and Ghost Walks or nighttime tours through the town. Reservations are needed. Open 9am - 5pm. Admission, which includes entrance to the town and most of the activities, is $10 for adults; $5 for ages 6 - 15; children 5 and under are free. Admission on Mon. is $10 per car load. On-site camping (minimum 2 nights) is $30 a night; $45 a night for cabins for 4 people, with a $25 refundable security deposit. Reservations for special events are made typically 3 months in advance.

CAMELLIA FESTIVAL, Temple City. (626) 285-2171 / www.templecitychamber.org, corner of Las Tunas Dr. and Golden West Ave. at Temple City Park. The festival, held the last weekend in February and running for over 70 years, is complete with carnival rides and an art show on Sunday. The highlight, the festival parade, is held on Saturday. Over ninety, camellia-covered floats (which <u>must</u> be finished only with parts of camellias), are designed and made by youth groups. Prizes, including a Sweepstakes Trophy, are given out. Over twenty marching bands and drill teams, plus other

organizations that promote the welfare of children such as Brownies and Cub Scouts, participate. Carnival rides are open Fri., 4pm - 11pm. The parade begins Sat. at 10am and the festivities, including the rides, go on until 11pm. The festival also runs Sun., noon - 8pm. Admission is free. Certain activities cost.

CHINESE NEW YEAR, Chinese New Year can be celebrated in January or February. See entries for this event in the January listings.

CIVIL WAR ENCAMPMENT, Simi Valley. (805) 526-6453 / www.simihistory.com, 137 Strathearn Place at Strathearn Historical Park & Museum The historical park feels like an authentic background for the two day Civil War Encampment (a non-battle event). Union, Confederate and civilian re-enactors realistically show a soldiers' and families' way of life during encampments. As tents are pitched, and cooking, cleaning, firing muskets and life is lived throughout the weekend, guests are invited to visit and interact with the re-enactors. Throughout the days there are artillery, Cavalry, infantry, civilian and other demonstrations, plus skirmishes, President Lincoln giving the Gettysburg Address and more. The park and museum buildings are open for touring - see pg. 690 for more details on them. Open Sat., 10am - 4pm; Sun., 10am - 3pm. $5 for ages 12 and over; $2 for children 5 - 12; ages 4 and under are free.

CORONADO BUTTERFLY RESERVE, Goleta. See January entry (pg. 703) for details.

DICKENS FESTIVAL, Riverside. (800) 430-4140 or (951) 781-3168 / www.dickensfest.com, 9th / Main , in front of City Hall. You'll have a Dickens of a time at this two-day festival! Walk the streets of a re-created London Marketplace where the entertainment, costumes, and food (try shepherd's pie, or fish and chips) are served up Victorian style. The Queen makes an appearance and is available for a meet and greet. Vendors ply their goods - antique jewelry, pottery, toys, hats, and more. A mini faire for kids includes making period crafts, storytelling, learning to juggle, and a scavenger hunt. Carriage rides between venues, for $5, are available. Tea is served at the First Congregational Church on Sat. at 11am & 1:30, and Sat. and Sun. at 12pm & 5pm. Regular tea is $20. The Queen's tea, with more food and a visit from the Queen, is $25 per person. Call (951) 684-2494 for more information and to make a reservation. Other activities and events included dramatic and musical presentations, a costume fashion show, educational workshops, and the Gordon Highlanders encampment - catch at least one drill and fire demonstration, which are accompanied by pipes and drums. Have a night out on the town at the ball at Mr. Fessiwig's place where you can do the (Oliver) Twist. Dance classes are held at a local church for a month before the ball. Fri. is pub night and very bawdy - for adults only. The festival is open Sat., 10am - 6pm; Sun., 10am - 5pm. Entrance to the Marketplace is free. Certain activities cost. The ball is Sat. night at 7:30pm and costs $35 to dance; $10 to come watch; children under 12 may observe free. The Victorian fashion show is Sat. and Sun. at noon and costs $5.Evensong is Sat. night at 5:30pm at the church and costs $10 per person.

FIRST FLIGHT FIELD TRIP, Anaheim. (714) 704-2509 / www.duckscore.com/firstflight.html, 2695 East Katella Ave. in the Honda Center. This free event, put on by the Anaheim Ducks, explores a different theme every year, such as the "Heart of Hockey" which explores the health and fitness of pro hockey players using math and science. There is a "playground" for hands-on activities and a "classroom" with workbooks and demonstrations. Players and coaches from the Ducks participate in all the activities. Open 8am - 12:30pm. Free to all schools.

FREE ENTRANCE DAYS IN THE NATIONAL PARKS, See January entry (pg. 704) for details.

HARLEM GLOBETROTTERS, Anaheim, Los Angeles, Ontario, San Diego. (800) 641-HOOP (4667) / www.harlemglobetrotters.com, Basketball is brought to new heights with incredible plays and performances by the renown Harlem Globetrotters. It is a whole entertainment and sports package 'cause they got game and then some! Audience participation is part of the deal where kids can learn the art of ball spinning and other fun tricks. The Harlem Globetrotters usually play at several locations during this month -Anaheim ([714] 740-2000, Honda Center); Los Angeles ([213] 480-3232, Staples Center); Ontario ([909] 244-5500, Citizens Business Bank Arena); and San Diego ([619] 224-4171, Valley View Casino Center). Call for show times. Tickets range from $16 - $155.

HERITAGE PARK U-PIC ORANGES, La Verne. See January entry (pg. 704) for details.

HITS DESERT CIRCUIT, Thermal. See January entry (pg. 704) for details.

HOLIDAY ON ICE, Irvine. See November entry (pg. 758) for details.

KUUMBA FEST, San Diego. (619) 544-1000 / www.kuumbafest.com, 79 Horton Plaza at the Lyceum Theatre. Kuumba is Swahili for creativity. The San Diego Repertory Theatre celebrates Black History month with this creative three-day fest. Enjoy an ethnic marketplace, educational workshops, a pageant of Egyptian and Zulu monarchs, a fashion show, arts and crafts, dance competitions, children's performances, and music that ranges from gospel to hip-hop. The festivities are Fri. at 5pm - 10pm; Sat., 10am - 11pm; Sun., 2pm - 7:30pm Tickets start at $10.

LINCOLN SHRINE OPEN HOUSE, Redlands. (909) 798-7632 / www.lincolnshrine.org, 125 W. Vine St. at the

Lincoln Memorial Shrine. An encampment with Civil War reenactors, including a surgeon's tent and demonstrations of surgical techniques of the time, are the focal point of this one-day celebration and memorial for President Lincoln. Music includes songs from that era. A gun salute is featured, as well. There is a Watchorn Dinner around this date, too, which includes an evening with a Civil War scholar as the featured speaker. Tickets for the dinner are $40, but reservations are often filled by mid-January. The Shrine also hosts other Civil War reenactments and events throughout the year. Open Sun., 1pm - 4pm. Admission is free.

MUSEUM MONTH, SAN DIEGO, (619) 276-0101 / www.sandiegomuseumcouncil.org; www.balboapark.org., February is Museum Month and more than 40 museums in San Diego County participate. Beginning Feb. 1, pick up a free Museum Month pass at any Macy's and bring it to the participating museums to receive half-off admission during this month. Contact the San Diego Museum Council for a listing of participants and more details.

PISMO BEACH MONARCH GROVE, Pismo Beach. See January entry (pg. 705) for details.

PRESIDENT'S DAY, Simi Valley. (805) 522-2977 / www.reagan.utexas.edu; www.reaganfoundation.org, 40 Presidential Dr. at the Ronald Reagan Presidential Library and Museum. On President's Day Monday, Washington and Lincoln are only two of the presidents honored here. Roving president lookalikes could also include Reagan (of course), as well as Jefferson and Theodore Roosevelt, plus lookalike first ladies. Each year the specific activities change, but there are usually storytellers and few educational presentations, as well as food booths. Note that on Feb. 6, Reagan's birthday, the museum has a tribute with music from the Marine Corp, a twenty-one gun salute, and complementary piece of cake for visitors. The hours for President's Day are from 10am - 3pm. Admission is free for the outside activities. Admission to the museum is $21 for adults; $18 for srs.; $15 for ages 11 - 17; $6 for ages 3 - 10; ages 2 and under are free. Parking is free.

PRESIDENT'S DAY, Yorba Linda. (714) 993-5075 / www.nixonfoundation.org, 18001 Yorba Linda Blvd. at the Richard Nixon Presidential Library and Birthplace. Presidential tributes begin on the Sunday before President's Day and continue through Monday. Actors portraying the Mt. Rushmore presidents will have a round table discussion and tell stories about their lives and times, and pose for pictures. Explore the museum to experience a different presidential era. The first 100 guests receive a free slice of cherry pie. Open Sun., 11am - 5pm; Mon., 10am - 5pm. Admission on Sun. is $11.95 for adults; $8.50 for srs.; $6.95 for students; $4.75 for ages 7 - 11 years; children 6 and under are free. Admission is free on Mon.

PROFESSIONAL BULL RIDERS ANAHEIM CLASSIC, Anaheim. (719) 242-2800 or (800) 745-3000 / www.pbrnow.com; www.hondacenter.com, 2695 E. Katella Ave. at the Honda Center. About forty-five of the world's top bull riders come to town to ride. This indoor rodeo event is enhanced by pyrotechnics, light shows, rock 'n roll music, fireworks, and more. The performances are Fri. at 8pm; Sat. at 6:50pm; Sun. at 2:50pm. Tickets range from $15 - $125. Parking is $15.

RIVERSIDE COUNTY FAIR & NATIONAL DATE FESTIVAL, Indio. (800) 811-FAIR (3247) or (760) 863-8247 / www.datefest.org; www.indiochamber.org, 82-503 Hwy. 111 at the Riverside County Fairgrounds. This ten-day county fair usually begins the Friday before President's Day. There are lots of special exhibits and activities, many with particular kid-appeal. These include the gem and mineral show; carnival-type rides; a model railroad; livestock shows; a petting zoo (we saw the usual array of farm animals as well as llamas, a zebra, and a kangaroo); camel rides; pony rides; and virtual reality rides. The camel and ostrich races (both animals are ridden bareback and also with "chariots") are some of the festival highlights. These races take place a few times a day, and you just never know what is going to happen with two such stubborn species of animals. On President's Day Monday there is a colorful parade starring Queen Scheherazade, that starts at 10am. An hour-and-a-half musical pageant is put on nightly. The festival is open weekdays, 10am - 10pm; weekends, 10am - midnight. Admission is $9 for adults; $8 for srs.; $7 for ages 6 - 12; children 5 and under are free. Rides and some attractions have additional fees. Parking on the fairgrounds is $7.

SCOTTISH FESTIVAL, Long Beach. (562) 499-1771 or (877) 436-9614 / www.queenmary.com, 1126 Queens Hwy, adjacent to and on the Queen Mary. Wear a kilt and bring your bagpipes (although you don't have to) for this two-day event. Over fifty Scottish clans are on hand to entertain visitors with a parade (usually at noon); battle reenactments (on-going, but call); traditional and contemporary music; pipe band competitions; Highland games (e.g. tossing the caber, hammer throw, etc.); sheepdog herding demonstrations; Highland dancing; storytelling; one-hour version of a Shakespearian play; vendors with Scottish wares; a parade of British automobiles; food; evening concerts; and much more. Admission to the festival includes admission to the ship and most of the activities. Open Sat. - Sun., 9am - 6pm. Admission is $22 for adults;$12 for ages 5 - 11; children 4 and under are free. (Advanced tickets are less expensive.) Parking is $17. Tips: Very limited free parking is available on Queensway Dr. and Harbor Plaza in front of the park.

The games, which you may watch for free, take place at the park on the grassy lawn.

TALL SHIPS TOUR, Oceanside, San Diego, Long Beach, San Pedro, Oxnard. See January entry (pg. 705) for details.

TET FESTIVALS, Tet or Vietnamese New Year is the same time as Chinese New Year and can be celebrated in January or February. See entries for this event in the January listings.

WHALE WATCHING, See January entry (pg. 706) for details.

WOODLAND HILLS ICE, Woodland Hills. See October entry (pg. 756) for details.

- MARCH: -

BIG JOHN'S CHERRY ORCHARD, Leona Valley. (661) 270-9565 / www.gatherafruitfulharvest.com, 9258 Leona Ave. This pick-your-own orchard features lilacs in March through May and cherries and lavender throughout the summer. You must call before you come to check on conditions for that day.

BLESSING OF THE ANIMALS, Los Angeles. (213) 485-8372 / www.olvera-street.com, 125 Paseo de la Plaza at El Pueblo de Los Angeles Historical Monument. This event is held on the Saturday before Easter. Children can dress up their pets - all domestic animals are welcome - and bring them to the Plaza Church to be blessed by priests. Some participating zoos bring in more exotic animals. All this is done to honor animals' contributions to the world. It gets wild with all different kinds of animals "held" in children's arms! Open noon - 5pm, with the procession and blessing at about 2pm. Admission is free.

BUBBLEFEST, Santa Ana. (714) 913-5018 / www.discoverycube.org, 2500 N. Main Street Discovery Science Center's Mega Bubblefest Laser Show floats into Orange County for another spring break. International bubble artist and scientist Deni Yang showcases the science of bubbles under a big top in a grand scale production that's like a Las Vegas show for little ones. Open Sat. - Sun., 11am - 5pm. The shows are 11am, 12:30pm, 2pm and 3:30pm. General admission is $15.95 for adults; $12.95 for srs. and ages 3-14; Kids under 3 are free. Parking is $4. Tickets to the show by Deni Yang are $7 for non-members and $5 for members.

BUGS BUNNY EGG HUNT AT THE AERO, Santa Monica. (310) 260-1528 / www.americancinemathequecalendar.com, 1328 Montana Ave. The Aero Theatre celebrates Easter Sunday with an egg hunt paired with a family matinee of classic Warner Brothers cartoon shorts starring the ultimate bunny. The hunt starts at 3:30pm., cartoons at 4pm. Admission $11 for adults, $9 for students, srs. and children ages 3-17.

BUNNY DAYS, Mission Viejo. (949) 460-2725 / www.cityofmissionviejo.org, 24932 Veteran's Way at Norman P. Murray Community and Senior Center. Join the Easter Bunny and friends the Saturday before Easter for egg hunts (divided into age groups for fairness), carnival game booths, family crafts, pony rides and a visit by the Easter Bunny. Open Sat., 11am - 2pm. Admission and the egg hunts are free. Some activities cost.

CELEBRATION OF THE WHALES FESTIVAL, Oxnard. (805) 985-4852 / www.channelislandsharbor.org, at Channel Islands Harbor on Harbor Blvd. near Marine Emporium Landing. It's a whale of a sight! As the majestic ocean mammals migrate, look for them from the shore or take a cruise. This one-day festival includes kayak racing, tide-pool touch tanks, aquarium presentations, an inflatable fun zone, a rock climbing wall, model ship building demonstrations, a farmer's market, and other events and activities. Celebrate on Sun., 10am - 5pm. Admission is free.

EASTER EGG HUNTS, Many parks, schools, churches, and cities put on free Easter egg hunts and/or Easter craft activities the weekend, or Saturday, before Easter. Call the recreation department of your local park, local city hall, or chamber of commerce for more information. Some are small, simply put-together hunts, and others are large *egg*stravaganzas with carnival rides, inflatables bounces, races, and more.

EASTER ON THE FARM, Moorpark. (805) 529-3690 / www.underwoodfamilyfarms.com, 3370 Sunset Valley Rd. at Underwood Family Farms. This yearly *egg*agement at Underwood Family Farms offers a whole farmful of family fun, including animal shows, tractor-drawn wagon rides, face painting, eggy games, balloons, mazes, egg hunts, and a visit with the Easter Bunny. See page 662 for more information about this farm. Open 9am - 6pm. Admission Mon. - Fri. is $3 for ages 2 and up; Sat. - Sun., $6 for ages 2 and up. Some activities may cost extra.

FESTIVAL OF SCIENCE & ENGINEERING, San Diego. (858) 455-0300 / www.sdsciencefestival.com, Each year in March, the San Diego Festival of Science & Engineering hosts a week-long celebration of science and engineering throughout San Diego County. The goal is to inspire the next generation of innovators and researchers. During the week you can find tours, talks, shows, demonstrations and hands on experiments. Past events have included: slime and molecules; building with bones; squid dissection; making ice cream with liquid nitrogen; and a tour

of the Taylor Guitar factory. The week's grand finale, Expo Day, is held at Petco Park with more than 130 organizations providing hands-on activities. Events occur at different times and different venues throughout the week so check the website. Expo Day runs from 10am to 5pm on the last Saturday. Almost all of the events are free.

FESTIVAL OF THE KITE, Redondo Beach. (310) 372-0308 / www.redondopier.com, 110 Fisherman's Wharf On the second Sunday of this month watch brilliantly-colored kites of all shapes and sizes fly high above the shoreline. Hosted by Sunshine Kite Company (a company that really knows and teaches all about kite flying and yo yos), which is located on the pier, there are contests, activities for kids, and synchronized acrobatic flying teams. Come fly 11:30am - 7pm. Beach activities are noon - 5pm. Admission is free.

FESTIVAL OF WHALES, Dana Point. (949) 496-1045 / www.festivalofwhales.org, 34675 Golden Lantern at Dana Point Harbor and the Ocean Institute. It's no fluke - this massive, two-weekend festival celebrates the gray whales' migration. The whole family can enjoy a variety of events offered throughout Dana Point, such as a parade (on the first Sat. at 10am along Pacific Coast Highway); art shows; sand castle workshops; tidepool explorations; street fairs; farmer's market; kid's coloring contests; film festivals; music; lots of food options; evening campfire programs at the adjacent Doheny State Beach; sailing and rowing lessons; sailing regatta; nature walk through Dana Cove with park rangers; kids karnival; rubber ducky race; antique & classic boat show; and a plethora of whale-watching excursions. The Ocean Institute is open during the festival, as is the tallship Pilgrim for living history demonstrations (10am - 2:30pm), and the Doheny State Beach Interpretive Center - whew! Have a whale of a time! Check the websites for specific details. Also see POLYNESIAN CONNECTION FESTIVAL (pg. 712) as this usually coincides. Prices and hours vary depending on the event.

FIESTA DE LAS GOLONDRINAS (Festival of the Swallows), San Juan Capistrano. (949) 493-1976 / www.swallowsparade.com; www.missionsjc.com, Ortega Hwy. at Mission San Juan Capistrano. This three-day festival, celebrating the return of the swallows from their annual migration to Argentina, takes place in different areas throughout San Juan Capistrano, including the mission. The swallows actually return to the mission every year on March 19th, so the festivities happen the weekend before or after this date. A festival highlight is the parade along downtown San Juan with marching bands, horse-drawn carriages, equestrian units, and colorful dancers. The children's pet parade is fun, too, where kids dress up their pets to compete for cutest, most obedient, best team costume, etc. There are also pageants, adobe brick making for kids, demonstrations and the Mercado Street Faire with music, food, family entertainment and a kids play zone. The festival runs 10am to 3pm, with the parade beginning at 11am. (Arrive early.) The mission is open at 8am on the 19th (as the birds usually arrive in the morning) and it closes at 5pm. The street fair runs 8am - 5pm, the festival. Admission at the mission is $10 for adults; $9 for srs., $6 for ages 4 - 11; children 3 and under are free. The street fair, in near-by Historic Town Center is free, but some activities cost money.

FILLMORE SPRING RAILFEST, Fillmore. (800) 773-TRAIN (8724) / www.fwry.com, 364 Main Street The Visitors Center has a huge model train display, plus lots of paraphernalia and collectibles. Antique tractors and equipment, engine demonstrations, craft booths, live entertainment, gunfighters, and barbecue cooking are part of the fun. Check out the open-top speeder cars used to maintain railroad tracks. Miniature live steamer rides cost a minimal fee. Gunslingers come into town have a shootout, rob a bank, and make a getaway on a train. Forty-five-minute rides are offered on an antique steam cars. Two-and-a-half-hour diesel excursions all the way to Santa Paula and back, including a half-hour stop over in town, are also offered. Note: The Santa Paula train ride has food services available. All aboard for the Railfest on Sat. - Sun., 9am - 5pm. Admission is free. Steam train rides, departing at 9am and 11:30am, are $20 for adults; $10 for ages 2 - 12; children under 2 are free. Diesel rides, departing at 10am and 1:30pm, are $24 for adults; $22 for srs.; $14 for ages 4 - 12; $10 for ages 2 - 3. Ask about specialty train rides, too, such as a dinner train with cowboys and other Old West characters.

FLOWER FIELDS, Carlsbad. (760) 431-0352 / www.theflowerfields.com, 5704 Paseo del Norte, off Palomar Airport Rd. Mid-March through mid-May walk through fifty-three acres of rows of blooming ranunculus. The colors are amazing, and the trails lead to bluffs overlooking the shoreline. Call first to make sure the flowers are in full bloom. Adding to your enjoyment are on-site picnic tables; an antique wagon tractor ride ($5 for adults, $3 for kids ages 3-10); a sweet pea maze; poinsettia displays; and a visit to Santa's Playground, which has a few play houses and giant (fake) mushrooms originally from Santa's Village in Lake Arrowhead. Forty-minute guided, educational tours are also available that include a fifteen-minute tractor-drawn wagon ride. School groups are offered three tour options, including one with a one-hour classroom presentation and a guided tour of the Flower Fields for $10 per student. Special events include Easter sunrise service at the Flower Fields; Kids' days; Canon Photography Workshops; Legoland hands-on mosaic building; bubble making; science adventures; puppet shows; and more. There are so many blooming things to do here! Open daily, 9am - 6pm. Admission is $12 for adults; $1 for srs.; $6 for ages 3 - 10; children

2 and under are free.

FREE ICE CREAM CONE DAY, / www.dairyqueen.com. Get your licks in this one day by receiving a free ice cream cone at participating Dairy Queens.

GRUNION RUNS, San Pedro. (831) 649-2870 - official number; (310) 548-7562 - Cabrillo Marine Aquarium / www.dfg.ca.gov/marine/grnindx3.asp; www.cabrillomarineaquarium.org, up and down the coast. Call beaches, the Cabrillo Marine Aquarium (pg. 218), the Ocean Institute (pg. 309), or Birch Aquarium (pg. 586) for more details, dates, and times. Grunions are small, silvery fish that venture out of the waters from March to August to lay their eggs on sandy beaches. They are very particular about when they do this - after every full and new moon, and usually around midnight. You may catch them only on certain months and no nets or gloves are allowed; only bare hands. (Did I mention that the fish are slippery?) Eat what you catch, or let them go, and enjoy a unique night of grunion hunting. Cabrillo Aquarium charges $5 for adults; $1 for srs. and children, which includes a slide presentation and instructions. The beaches are free.

HERITAGE PARK U-PIC ORANGES, La Verne. See January entry (pg. 704) for details.

HERMOSA BEACH ST. PATRICK'S DAY PARADE, Hermosa Beach. (858) 268-9111 / www.hbchamber.net/news_events/st_patricks.aspx, Down Pier Ave. from Valley Drive to 10th and Hermosa. The Hermosa Beach Saint Patrick's Day Parade steps off near the tennis courts on Valley Drive and heads down Pier Avenue. The accompanying festival features a Kiddy Carnival, a petting zoo, international foods, vendors, and Irish music and dancing. The parade begins at 11am. Admission is free.

HITS DESERT CIRCUIT, Thermal. See January entry (pg. 704) for details.

IRON HORSE - FAMILY STEAMPUNK CARNIVALE, Perris. (951) 943-3020 / www.oerm.org, 2201 South "A" St. at the Orange Empire Railway Museum. Steampunk - *a genre of science fiction that typically features steam-powered machinery rather than advanced technology*. What better place to celebrate steampunk than with the backdrop of a live steam powered locomotive. Come for the steampunk costume contest, craft workshops, steam locomotive and vintage trolley rides, games, steampunk artisans, food and various displays. There is also a Victorian Era Tea for $12 ages 12 and up, $10 ages 2 - 11. Sat. and Sun., 9am to 5pm. Admission is $15 for adults, $10 ages 5 - 11, ages 4 and under are free.

ISLA VISTA JUGGLERS FESTIVAL, Isla Vista. / www.sbjuggle.org, Ocean Rd. at the University of California Santa Barbara in Robertson Gym, and at Harold Frank lecture hall. For about thirty years the campus juggling club has hosted this three-day event over a weekend in Spring (usually Easter), so juggle your schedule to try to attend. See beginner and advanced jugglers toss and catch various props - hats, juggling pins, balls, cigar boxes, and more. Also in attendance are clowns on unicycles, magicians, and prop vendors. Sometimes workshops are offered. Open juggling at Robertson Gym is Fri., 6pm - 11pm, Sat. 10am - 6pm, Sun. 10am - 5pm. The show is Sat. 7:30 - 10pm at Harold Frank lecture hall. The festival is free. The Sat. show is $10 for adults; $5 for srs., students, and kids. Parking is about $3.

KITE PARTY, Huntington Beach. (714) 536-3630 / www.kiteparty.com, 200 Pacific Coast Highway at the north and south side of Huntington Beach pier. This two-day "party" is by invitation only to participate, but anyone can watch. About 100 local and international fliers are just-for-the-fun-of-it fliers and some compete in stunt flying (some even have music to accompany their movements), but all fill the sky with their colorful, fanciful flying "machines". The public can pay $20 for a kite and some official flying time, although anyone can fly their own kite outside the roped-off area. Sat. - Sun., 11am - dusk. Free; beach parking costs.

LANTERN FESTIVAL, Los Angeles. (213) 485-8567 / www.camla.org/lantern-festival, 425 N. Los Angeles St. The annual Lantern Festival brings together free arts, culture, and educational activities in a re-created traditional village street fair at the Chinese American Museum. Open noon - 7pm. General admission is free.

LOS ANGELES REGIONAL ROBOTICS COMPETITION, (603) 666-3906 / www.usfirst.org, Working with FIRST (For Inspiration and Recognition of Science and Technology), each team of students has been given the same kit of parts and a six-week time frame to build a robot and solve a common problem. They must strategize, design, build, program, test, and refine. The results are amazing contraptions! The fun part for spectators is watching the intense competition in a sports-like atmosphere as the robots "battle" it out, completing certain tasks, and vying for prizes. Good manners for the team members count here, according to the judges. Participants are certainly the winners with what they've learned, and so is the audience. Check out the Lego League, as well, at www.firstlegoleague.org. Competitions take place in the Los Angeles area and sometimes in the San Diego region, as well. The competition is on Fri. and Sat., 9am - 4pm, with matches in the morning and final rounds in the afternoon. Free admission. There is usually a charge for parking.

LOS ENCINOS EASTER EGG HUNT, Encino. (805) 529-3690 / www.historicparks.org, 16756 Moorpark St.

Come for this *eggciting shellabration*, with an egg hunt (for toddlers to 10-year olds), black smith demonstration, tradition games and old-time music. Tours of the historic adobe home are given by performers in period costume. The hunts are 1:30pm for 2 and under; 2pm for ages 3 - 4; 2:30pm for ages 5 - 10. Remember to bring your own basket. Admission is free.

MCGRATH FAMILY FARMS, Camarillo. U-pic - (805) 983-0333; Tours - (805) 485-4210 / www.mcgrathfamilyfarm.com, 1020 West Ventura Blvd. This family farm sells produce and offers U-pic strawberries, vegetables and pumpkins in-season. Tours are also available throughout most of the year on weekends. Groups of 20 or more can schedule a tour during the week. Open in season, 11am - 4pm. Tour is $5 per person on weekends, $7 for scheduled tours. Fruits are paid for by the pound.

OCEAN BEACH KITE FESTIVAL, San Diego. (619) 531-1527 / www.oceanbeachkiwanis.org, Dusty Rhodes Park The first Sat. of the month offers a colorful, high-flying festival celebrating the joy of kiting. You are invited to build and decorate kites from 9am to 12:30pm. Judging commences across the street at the school from 1pm to 2pm and a parade is at 2pm. From then on, just fly 'em. There is also an on-going crafts fair, with music and food. Open 10am - 4pm. There is no charge for admission or for the materials used for kite making.

PAGEANT OF OUR LORD, Rolling Hills Estates. (310) 521-2520 / www.pageantofourlord.org, 2222 Palos Verdes Dr. N. at Rolling Hills Covenant. Similar to Pageant of the Masters, but on a smaller scale and Christian-based, major works of art come to "life" as people dress up in costume and full make-up to impersonate, albeit statue-like, the people in the original paintings. Music accompanies each presentation. This is an amazingly powerful medium in which to express art. The program is offered for two weeks before Easter at various times - in the mornings, afternoons, and evenings. Admission is $10 - $17 for adults; $8 - $12 for ages 5 - 12; children 4 and under are not admitted.

POLYNESIAN CONNECTION FESTIVAL, Dana Point. (949) 973-7281 / www.hulaconnection.com, 34551 Puerto Place at Dana Point Harbor, at Baby Beach The graceful Hula and Polynesian dances are showcased at this festival that brings the islands to the mainland. Put on by the Hula Connection, that teaches dance, and usually in connection with Dana Point's FESTIVAL OF WHALES (pg. 710), the day consists of educational displays and demonstrations, such as outrigger canoe demonstrations and coconut husking; activities such as lei-making; and entertainment (featuring both kids and adults representing Hawaii, Tahiti, Tonga, Samoa, and New Zealand) dancing the hula, 'fire' knife and hula/Tahitian dancing, poi-ball twirling, and more, all in a natural setting of the beach. The 'kau kau' (food) area offers a taste of Polynesia with Musubi, Hawaiian shaved ice and more delicious menu items. Extend your visit to paradise with an authentic luau at the adjacent OC Sailing and Events Center. A formal dinner is accompanied and followed by exciting professional entertainment. Mahalo. Open Sat., 10am - 4pm for the festival; 5:30pm - 9pm for the luau. Free to the festival. The Luau is $50 per person.

POPPY RESERVE, Lancaster. (661) 946-6092 - state park; (661) 724-1180 - recorded info from the poppy reserve / www.parks.ca.gov, 15101 W. Lancaster Rd. Do you hear echos of the wicked witch's voice in *The Wizard of Oz* cackling, "poppies, poppies"? During the months of March and April our bright orange California state flower blooms in this almost 1,800 acre reserve, as do several other types of wildflowers. (You'll notice wonderful patches of flowers along the roadside, too.) Call first to see how rains have affected the bloom schedule. Hike the seven miles of hilly trails that run through the reserve, including a paved section for stroller/wheelchair access, or go the 2.5-mile round trip from the visitor center to Antelope Butte Vista Point. Don't forget your camera!! Although poppies only bloom seasonally, the reserve is open year round from sun-up to sundown. The Visitors' Center is just open seasonally - mid-March through April, Mon. - Fri., 10am - 4pm; Sat. - Sun., 9am - 5pm. The staff at the center provides orientation to the reserve and educational information. Parking is $10.

RIVERSIDE AIRPORT OPEN HOUSE AND AIR SHOW, Riverside. (951) 351-6113 / www.riversideairshow.com, 6951 Flight Rd. at Arlington and Airport Drs. at the Riverside Airport. Skydivers, aerobatics, and numerous other performances are part of this annual air show. Other activities and events include model aircraft, vintage aircraft, plus military helicopters on display; Riverside Police K-9 demonstrations; rides for kids; and a car show with hot rods, cruisers, and custom cars. The pancake breakfast is at 7am and costs $6. The cafe is also open. The Open House is Sat., 9am - 4pm. Admission is free. Parking is $10 per car.

SAINT PATRICK'S DAY PARADE AND FESTIVAL, San Diego. (858) 268-9111 / www.stpatsparade.org, Sixth Ave. and Maple St. near Balboa Park. On a Saturday around St. Patty's day think of little green men, and I don't mean Martians. Leprechauns, Celtic music, Irish folk dancing, marching bands, clowns, equestrian units, step dancers, floats, kiddie rides, arts and crafts booths, and food are top of the order for this huge, one-day of shenanigans. The parade begins at Juniper St. and Sixth Ave. Park near Balboa Park and take a free shuttle. The two-and-a-half-hour parade begins at 10:30am. The festival is Sat., 9am - 6pm. Admission is free.

SPRING BUSKER FESTIVAL, San Diego. (619) 235-4014 / www.seaportvillage.com/busker, 849 West Harbor Drive at Seaport Village. This is a family-friendly celebration of street performers, including sword swallowers, jugglers, acrobats, comedians, musicians and more. The event takes place throughout the shopping center, Sat. and Sun., noon - 6pm. Admission is free. Parking is $3 an hour, with the first 2 hours free with any purchase in Seaport Village.

SPRING SPECTACULAR, Moorpark. (805) 378-1441 / zoo.moorparkcollege.edu, 7075 Campus Rd. at Moorpark College. Join in on three weekends of animal fun held at AMERICA'S TEACHING ZOO. (See pg. 701 in the main section of the book for details on this place.) These weekends incorporate guest presentations and booths from various animal organizations; behind-the-scenes tours of animals not normally on exhibit; scripted shows with costumes; a kid's zone; up-close educational animal programs and demonstrations; games; and an opportunity to see all the exotic animals. This is a terrific event. Open Sat. - Sun., 10am - 5pm. Admission is $10 for adults; $7 for srs. and ages 3-12; Kids 2 and under are free. Some activities may cost extra.

STRAWBERRIES - CAL POLY POMONA, Pomona. (909) 869-4906 / www.csupomona.edu/~farmstore, 4102 S. University Dr. on the campus of Cal Poly Pomona. Come and U-pic strawberries. Note that there is a pond with ducks close by. The fields are next to the Farm Store at Kellogg Ranch, which sells fresh fruits, vegetables, honey (fill your own bottle from the vat), plants, flowers, and even meats (beef, pork, and lamb) and other grocery products that have been raised on the campus by students. Bring a cooler to pack your goodies. 10am - 6pm, in season.

STRAWBERRY STANDS, Strawberry stands pop up everywhere in season, which starts in February and ends in October - depending on the weather and the year. In Oxnard, call the Oxnard Convention and Visitors Bureau at (800) 269-6273 or (805) 385-7545 / www.visitoxnard.com for a map and guide to local fruit stands. Call the city chamber of commerce that you are in, or near, for more information on established stands. Additionally, check the website www.pickyourown.org.

TANAKA FARMS - STRAWBERRIES, Irvine. (949) 653-2100 / www.tanakafarms.com, 5380¾ University Dr. The time is ripe for tours of strawberry fields and to U-Pic them. Ninety-minute+ field trips, geared for pre-schoolers through fourth graders and for groups of ten or more, can be made with advanced reservations for $10 per person. Tours include info on the plants, a wagon ride around the thirty-acre farm, and picking the delicious fruit to take home and are offered mid-March through June. You are welcome to just come and pick the mouth-watering berries on your own, as well! No reservation needed for weekend tour times every half hour from 9:30am to 2:30pm. Must call and reserve for weekday tour times. The farm and stand is open Mon. - Sun., 9am - 5pm. The tour is $17 per person; children 2 and under free.

TRY HOCKEY FOR FREE DAY, (719) 576-8724 / www.tryhockeyforfree.com, On the first Saturday in March and November many ice rinks around the country make their ice and equipment available for kids, ages 4 to 9, who would like to try hockey. Check the website to find a participating rink. The icing on the cake is it's free!

VENTURA ST. PATRICK'S DAY PARADE, Ventura. (805) 639-0303 / www.venturastpatricksdayparade.com, Main Street The 25th annual County Ventura St. Patrick's Day Parade keeps the spirit with bands, Irish dancers, fire trucks, antique vehicles, four legged pets, and anything else remotely green that can march down Main Street. The parade begins at 10am. Admission is free.

VISIT WITH MICHELANGELO AND LEONARDO DA VINCI, Glendale. (323) 340-4742 / www.forestlawn.com, 1712 S. Glendale Ave. at Forest Lawn Memorial Park in Glendale. A costumed Michelangelo and Da Vinci talk to an audience of up to 350 people for about a half hour about "their" lives, achievements, and who was the better artist - history comes alive! Take a self-guided tour around the premises to view "their" art. (Note: The art does contain some nudity.) See Forest Lawn, on page 170, for details about what else this park has to offer. Check website or call for times. Reservations are necessary. Admission is free.

VISIT WITH MONTEZUMA, Coachella. (800) 204-3131 / www.forestlawn.com, 51990 Jackson Street at Forest Lawn Memorial Park. A costumed Montezuma talks for about thirty minutes at the Plaza of Mexican Heritage about "his" life and accomplishments. Mariachi music and a short, guided explanation of some of the artifacts from the Mexican museum follows the talk. This program takes place on select weekdays at 11am. Reservations are necessary. Admission is free.

VISIT WITH MONTEZUMA, Los Angeles. (800) 204-3131 / www.forestlawn.com, 6300 Forest Lawn Dr. at Forest Lawn Memorial Park at Hollywood Hills. See entry above for details.

VISTA CIVIL WAR REENACTMENT, Vista. Museum - (760) 941-1791; Festival - (805) 496-6036 / www.goldcoastfestivals.com, 2040 N. Santa Fe Ave. at the Antique Gas and Steam Engine Museum. One of the largest

reenactments in the area, meet the soldiers in their encampments and watch the men and horses in great battles with live cannon fire in this rural setting. A great location for this type of event and lots of reenactors in period dress give a real feel for this era. President Lincoln (not the real one) usually shows up, as well. Battles take place both days at noon and 3pm. Admission includes touring the museum. See page 525 for details about the museum. Open Sat. - Sun., 10am - 5pm. Admission is $15 for adults; $13 for srs.; $8 for ages 3 - 13; children 2 and under are free. Parking is $5.

WHALE OF A DAY FESTIVAL, Rancho Palos Verdes. (310) 544-5260 / www.losserenos.org/woad.htm, 31501 Palos Verdes Dr. W. at Pt. Vincente Interpretative Center. Palos Verdes' annual festival celebrating the migration of the Pacific Gray Whale is held on the main grounds of the Point Vicente Interpretive Center and at the adjacent lighthouse. Activities for children include face painting, crafts, stories, games, and whale watching. Tours of the lighthouse are available for kids ages seven and older. The festival commences on the first Sat., 10am - 4pm. Admission is free. Parking is available at Rancho Palos Verdes City Hall located at 30940 Hawthorne Blvd. with free shuttles.

WHALE WATCHING, See January entry (pg. 706) for details.

WHAT'S UP FOR KIDS EXPO, Torrance. (888) 544-1024 or (310) 544-1042 / www.whatsupforkids.com, 3350 Civic Center Dr. at the Torrance Cultural Arts Center. This one-day event is not only a rich resource of fun and educational products and services geared specifically for younger children, but a fun place to bring the family. Some attractions and activities include live entertainment by popular children's singers and dancers, moon bounces, face painting, crafts, a safety expo, and lots of interactive exhibits. Open 10am - 3pm. Admission and parking are free.

- APRIL: -

AMERICA'S FAMILY PET EXPO, Costa Mesa. (800) 999-7295 or (626) 447-2222 / www.petexpooc.com, 88 Fair Dr. at Orange County Fairgrounds. Bark, meow, oink, baaa, sssss, neigh - this three-day weekend is for animals lovers. Over 1,000 animals - dogs, cats, reptiles, goats, rabbits, pigs, fish, snakes, and more - are at the expo. See bird shows; cat shows; a petting zoo; Frisbee dogs; wiener dog races; pet products; search and rescue demonstrations, stage shows, animal competitions; and educational demonstrations. Check out the pet adoption services. (Animals are not for sale here.) Open Fri., 10am - 6pm; Sat., 10am - 7pm; Sun., 10am - 6pm. Admission per day is $13 for adults; $11 for srs.; $8 for ages 6 - 12; children 5 and under are free. (Discount tickets are available online.)

AVOCADO FESTIVAL, Fallbrook. (760) 728-5845 / www.fallbrookchamberofcommerce.org, Main St. Guacamole by the pound. Race cars made from avocados. Thousands of people thronging the streets. A flower show. Avocado croquet. A pit-spitting contest at the Avocado Olympics. These are glimpses of what this one-day festival has in store. Besides arts and crafts, kids activities, and agriculture displays, other happenings include packing house tours of the Del Rey Avocado Company, a walk through the Gem and Mineral Society Museum, and a vintage aircraft show at Fallbrook Airpark. Don't be green with envy; just get green with avocados. The festival is on a Sun., 9am - 5pm. Free admission.

BANNING HERITAGE WEEK, Wilmington. (310) 548-7777 / www.banningmuseum.org, 401 East M St. at the Banning Residence Museum. For one week the museum becomes a living classroom for fourth grade school groups. Intermingle with Victorian-dressed women and men folk; learn dance steps from that era; practice tying sailor knots; pan for gold; do chores such as churning butter and washing clothes by hand; play hoops, and other 19th-century games; learn animal husbandry; take a guided tour of the museum; and more. The program runs Mon. - Fri., 10am - 1pm. Tip: Bring a picnic lunch. Call way in advance for reservations. Admission is free.

BIG JOHN'S CHERRY ORCHARD, Leona Valley. See March entry (pg. 709) for details.

BUBBLEFEST, Santa Ana. See March entry (pg. 709) for details.

BURBANK ON PARADE, Burbank. / www.burbankonparade.com, Each year, the parade has a special theme selected by the Burbank on Parade organizers, and parade marchers build floats and wear outfits that highlight the year's theme. The parade consists of specially decorated floats, high school and independent marching bands, antique and vintage cars, special Burbank VIPs, Burbank organizations, and a parade Grand Marshal. The parade is held annually each spring. Past Grand Marshals include George Lopez, Ron Howard, Andy Griffith, Debbie Reynolds, Alan Hale, Jan & Dean, Donald O'Connor, Danny Bonaducci, Anson Williams, Brooks Gardner, the "Saved By The Bell" cast, Bozo the Clown. Bands as far away at Pennsylvania have traveled to participate in Burbank On Parade as well as the Marine Corps Bands and several other Armed Forces units.

CARLSBAD STRAWBERRY COMPANY, Carlsbad. (760) 603-9608 / www.carlsbadstrawberrycompany.com, 1205 Aviara Pkwy. Pick your own sweet fruit from these 80 acres of strawberry fields, April through July. Pre-picked

strawberries are also available to purchase. Field trips for schools or other organizations are offered, too, for more information and a lesson on strawberries, and then to go strawberry picking. The fields are open daily, 9am - 5pm.

CHILDREN'S DAY, Santa Fe Springs. (562) 946-6476 / www.santafesprings.org, 12100 Mora Dr. at Heritage Park. This day of old-fashioned fun is held around the Week of the Young Child. Kids can churn butter; pan for gold; play turn-of-the-century games; and make crafts. Open Sat., noon - 4pm. Admission and activities are free.

CHILDREN'S EARTH DAY, Culver City. (310) 842-8060 / www.childrensearthday.org, 10101 W. Jefferson Blvd. at the Star Eco Station. This "green" event is wild! Hosted by the STAR ECO STATION (pg. 227), come join the exotic animals here and the fun - games, environmentally-conscious crafts, live entertainment, green shopping, food, celebrity guests, and more. Open Sun., 10am - 4pm. The festival is free. A tour of the Eco Station is $5 per person.

CHUMASH DAY, Malibu. (310) 317-1364 / www.malibucity.org, 24250 Pacific Coast Highway Malibu's annual pow-wow and gathering of the tribes brings native traditions to Malibu Bluffs Park. Open from 11am to 7:30pm. Admission is free.

CICLAVIA, Los Angeles. (213) 355-8500 / www.ciclavia.org. During the CiclAvia, bikes take over the city's streets for a day, creating a family-friendly 15 mile path from downtown Los Angeles to the sea at Venice Beach. See website for map. You may start and end anywhere along the route. Path open from 10am to 3pm Free for anyone to ride.

DEL MAR NATIONAL HORSE SHOW, Del Mar. (858) 792-4288 / www.delmarnational.com, 2260 Jimmy Durante Blvd. at the Del Mar fairgrounds. Saddle up for three weeks of exciting horse competition and Olympic selection. Each weekend features a main equestrian category: Western, Dressage, or Hunter/Jumper. Watch the horses being put through their paces during the week. Note: Check the website for exciting horse shows throughout the year. See website for schedule. Tickets on weeknights and weekend days are $10 per person in the grandstand; $15 for box seats. Saturday night $19 for grandstand. Parking is $10.

DISCOVER RECYCLING, (800) 773-2489 / www.lacitysan.org, Throughout LA One family's garbage is another family's.... favorite annual event. It may sound crazy, but the open houses at LA's sanitation yards are some of the most popular kid-friendly happenings, with tours, prizes, and garbage trucks galore. Events happen at various locations from April through June.

DOO-DAH PARADE, Pasadena. (626) 590-1134 / www.pasadenadoodahparade.info, It's time again for that off-the-wall, definitely-not-the-Rose Parade to march the streets of Pasadena. See the web side for a map of the route. Starts at 11am. The parade is free to watch.

EARTH DAY FESTIVAL, Topanga. (310) 455-0060 / www.topangaearthday.org, 301 Old Topanga Rd. Where better to celebrate Earth Day than in Topanga? Come see the artist, speakers and demonstrations and participate in the workshops. 100% vegetarian, and plenty of earth - friendly food vendors will be at the festival selling all sorts of goodies A $12 donation is suggested. Srs. and children under 5 or free. Hike up the driveway or take the free bio-diesel shuttle.

EARTH DAY, San Diego. (858) 272-7370 / www.earthdayweb.org, Park Blvd. at Balboa Park. Celebrate the preservation of the environment in this huge, one-day event. Over 300 booths and exhibits are featured focusing on alternatives to lighting, power, and energy via goods, services and causes, including wildlife, conservation, organic gardening, ecotourism, alternative energy vehicles, and so much more. The day also features storytelling, a kids' area, crafts, and live entertainment on five stages. Kids (and parents) who attend Earth Day will hopefully become more planet smart. Open 10am to 5pm, with a parade at 10:30am at the Spanish Village. Admission is free.

EASTER, Since Easter can take place in March or April, all of the Easter-related activities are under March.

ESCONDIDO RENAISSANCE FAIRE, Escondido. (805) 496-6036 / www.goldcoastfestivals.com, 742 Clarence Ln. at Felicita Park. The age of chivalry is recreated in a natural setting. Come dressed up, if you want, to experience the glories of the reign of Queen Elizabeth with battle pageants (knights in armor and all), archery demonstrations, jugglers, music in the streets, games, activities, a kid's play area, and entertainment from days of yore, including, perhaps, Shakespeare's plays. Note: As with any enactment from this time period, there are some bawdy events. Open for two weekends, Sat. - Sun., 10am to dusk. Admission is $18 for adults; $15 for srs.; $8 for ages 4 -10; children 3 and under are free. Parking is $5.

FARM WALK, Woodland Hills. (818) 710-4253 / www.piercecollege.edu, 6201 Winnetka Ave. at Pierce College. A farm in the middle of the city - gotta love it. Presented by the agricultural department of this local college, the one-day farmwalk entails a petting zoo, sheep shearing, wool spinning, horse activities, milking cows, animal shows, livestock, nature walks, educational displays, farm equipment, fire engines (to climb aboard), music, crafts, forestry exhibits, booths, food, and more. Open Sun., 9:30am - 4pm. Admission is $5; children 12 and under are free.

FLOWER FIELDS, Carlsbad. See March entry (pg. 710) for details.

FOSSIL FEST, Claremont. (909) 624-2798 / www.alfmuseum.org, 1175 W. Baseline Rd. at the Raymond M. Alf Museum. Come for a behind-the-scenes tour of the Raymond M. Alf Museum (pg. 148) and see how skeletons are prepared, plus make a footprint replica, hear talks on paleontology, and more. You also have the opportunity to explore the museum, with all of its intriguing and prehistoric exhibits. Open Sat., 1pm - 4pm Festival is included in the regular admission price of $3 for ages 5 and up; children 4 and under are free.

FREE CONE DAY, / www.benjerry.com. Life doesn't get any better than free ice cream! You get a scoop of any flavor of Ben & Jerry's ice cream for free on this one day. They call it Customer Appreciation Day, but we are the ones who say "thanks."

FREE ENTRANCE DAYS IN THE NATIONAL PARKS, See January entry (pg. 704) for details.

GILMAN RANCH WILD WEST & WESTERN ART FESTIVAL, Banning. (951) 922-9200; (951) 205-0494 / www.rivcoparks.org, 1901 West Wilson Str. at Gilman Historic Ranch and Wagon Museum. This event features Western reenactments, exhibits, hay rides and hands-on activities. Visit a 1700 to 1800's-era living history encampment and see clothing, tools, and equipment from this time period. The day also includes gold panning, seeing blacksmith demonstrations, tomahawk throwing, and more. Bring your gold dust ($) to use at the trading posts. A tour through the ranch and museum is also available. Food and drink is available. See page 359 for more information on the museum. Opens Sat. 10am - 5pm; Sun. 10am - 4pm. Admission is $3 for adults; $2 for kids; $1 for dogs.

IMAGINATION CELEBRATION, Orange County. (714) 556-5160 / www.icfestival.com; www.artsoc.org, The Orange County Performing Arts Center is a main host for this forty-five day event that's held mid-April through May. At least fifty of Orange County's artistic and educational organizations bring performances, workshops, and exhibitions to over seventy family-friendly events. This festival of arts for families takes place at malls, museums, parks, libraries, schools, etc. Some of the activities include puppet making, family art days, folk tales, band and theater performances, and dancing. Call for a schedule of events. Many events are free in this county-wide celebration of imagination!

INTERNATIONAL SPEEDWAY, Costa Mesa. (949) 492-9933 / www.costamesaspeedway.net, 88 Fair Dr. at the Orange County Fairgrounds. The Speedway roars to life every Saturday night from April through October. Note: Racing in July is limited due to the Orange County Fair. This spectator sport of motorcycle racing can include sidecars, go karts, Quads, a kids' class (ages 6 to 12), and more. After the two-hour show, which can get long for younger ones, take the kids into the pits to get racer's autographs, or, when the bikes cool down, to sit on a cycle or two. Wear jeans and t-shirt (and bring a sweatshirt) as dirt tracks aren't noted for cleanliness. Gates open at 6pm; qualifying races start at 7:30pm. Admission is $15 for adults; $10 for srs. and ages 13 - 17; $5 for ages 3 - 12; children 2 and under are free. Special events are $5 more per person. Parking is $7.

KIDS KRAZY KRAFTS DAY, Carson. (310) 515-7166 / www.printmuseum.org, 315 W. Torrance Blvd. at the International Printing Museum For one day kids of all ages learn by hands-on "playing" to create printing crafts and arts such as origami, cartoon characters, calligraphy, paper (from mushy pulp to paper), silk screen printed t-shirts (bring a clean one of your own to do), cards (using antique printing presses), and so much more. The museum itself is fascinating to tour and these activities make it truly a special day. See pg. 123 for more information on the INTERNATIONAL PRINTING MUSEUM. Krafts and museum touring is 10am - 4pm. $8 per person; $7 for srs..

LA INTERNATIONAL CHILDREN'S FILM FESTIVAL, Santa Monica. (310) 260-1528 / www.americancinemathequecalendar.com, 1328 Montana Ave. American Cinematheque brings the popular east coast film festival to the west for the first time, with two weekends of kids' flicks, opportunities for kids to act as reviewers, and donations to local schools. Check for show times. Admission is $11.

LAKESIDE RODEO & WESTERN DAYS, Lakeside. (619) 561-4331 or (619) 443-8561 - rodeo; (619) 561-1031 - parade info / www.lakesiderodeo.com, 12854 Mapleview and Hwy 67 at the Lakeside Rodeo grounds. Corral your young broncos and bring them to the two-and-a-half-hour rodeo show the last weekend in April. This fantastic three-day rodeo features the major events of bull riding, team roping, calf roping, buckin' horses, barrel racing, bareback riding, saddle broncs, and steer wrestling. A down-home town parade begins at 9:30am on Sat. at Woodside St. and ends at Main St. Rodeo shows are Fri., 7:30pm; Sat., 2pm and 7:30pm; Sun., 2pm. Gates open 90 minutes before the show. Tickets range between $10 - $20 for adults, depending on the day and seat; $5 - $10 for ages 12 and under. Parking is $3.

LA PUPPET FEST, Los Angeles. (310) 356-1008 / www.lapuppetfest.com, This two-week event hosts puppet shows throughout Los Angeles and Hollywood where the fun comes with strings attached. Some of the past shows were *Fun*

with Strings, Live Band Puppet Karaoke, Masters of Puppetry Live!, and *Skirball Puppet Festival*. Note, some of the shows are geared for adults. On Sunday, everyone can join the Million Puppet Parade where you can bring, make, or buy your own puppet then march down the 3rd Street Promenade in Santa Monica. Check the website for show times and cost. The parade is free to join.

LOS ANGELES TIMES FESTIVAL OF BOOKS, Los Angeles. / www.latimes.com/extras/festivalofbooks, Exposition Blvd and S. Figueroa St., University of Southern California campus. This weekend festival is absolutely <u>the</u> place for book lovers of all ages. 150,000 people come to see the over 400 well-known authors, illustrators, and celebrity authors sign their books, do book readings, give seminars, entertain, and participate in panel discussions. Besides the six outdoor stages geared for adults (and several indoor venues), there are special programs on-going at the two children's stages. These include renown storytellers, musicians, singers, character appearances (such as Barney), and book readings by favorite kids' writers. Other activities include free craft-making, clown acts, contests and give-aways by Radio Disney, and much more. Hundreds of publishers, book stores, and other vendors have booths in which they sell their books and related products and services, usually at a discount. This is a "don't miss" event! Open Sat., 10am - 6pm; Sun., 10am - 5pm. Admission is $10 per vehicle. The events are free, but tickets are needed for all indoor panel and speaker sessions, so get them the week before the festival.

MCGRATH FAMILY FARMS, Camarillo. See March entry (pg. 712) for details.

MISSION FEDERAL ARTWALK, San Diego. (619) 615-1090 / www.artwalksandiego.org, along India St. and Kettner Blvd. in the Little Italy neighborhood, downtown San Diego. Hundreds of visual and performing arts exhibitors strut their stuff in a weekend-long celebration of the arts. (Many events happen throughout the month, too.) In cooperation with Museum of Contemporary Art, San Diego Area Dance Alliance, Children's Museum, San Diego Performing Arts League, and others, you'll see paintings, dance, ballet, poetry, photography, sculpture, opera, folkloric dance, divas, and more. Just a few specific activities for kids in the past have included writing poetry, a photo scavenger hunt, creating an origami animal, making a 3-D paper model, and molding a sculpture. Guests of Artwalk can ride the Old Town Trolley for free as it stops off at key places throughout the event. See ARTWALK NTC (pg. 737) for a similar event in August. Open Sat. - Sun., 11am - 6pm. General admission is free.

PASADENA MODEL RAILROAD CLUB'S SPRING OPEN HOUSE, Pasadena. (323) 222-1718 / www.pmrrc.org, 5458 Alhambra Ave. Over a period of two weekends (and a Tues. in between), make tracks to see the largest model railroad layout, which covers 5,000 square feet, as well as lots of other railroad paraphernalia. Open Sat., 1pm - 5pm and 7pm - 9pm; Sun., 1pm - 5pm; Tues., 7:30pm - 9pm. Admission is $5 for adults; $1 for ages 7 - 17; free for children 6 and under.

POPPY FESTIVAL, Lancaster. (661) 723-6077 / www.poppyfestival.com, 43011 N. 10th St W. at Lancaster City Park. The poppy festival, located fifteen miles east of the poppy reserve (see pg. 712 for details), is held for one weekend in April. The festival offers carnival rides; craft vendors; environmental displays; aerospace displays; farmer's market area; live entertainment; circus acts; animals (reptiles and insects, and bird performances); racing remote-controlled NASCAR models; mission's exhibit; dinosaur exhibit; safety zone with police and fire department personnel; and more. Open Sat. and Sun., 10am - 6pm. Admission is $8 for adults; $5 for srs. and ages 6 - 12; children 5 and under are free. (Cash only)

POPPY RESERVE, Lancaster. See March entry (pg. 712) for details.

PRINCESSES AT THE CASTLE, Redlands. (909) 792-2111 / www.kimberlycrest.org, 1325 Prospect Drive at the Kimberly Crest House and Gardens. Treat your little princess to an afternoon of royal activities, refreshments, and photos with other princesses, such as Snow White, Cinderella, Ariel, and even a few fairies, at the beautiful KIMBERLY CREST HOUSE AND GARDENS (pg. 425). Get dressed up and indulge in the crown-shaped cookies, pink-frosted cupcakes, pink lemonade, and popcorn, while getting your face painted and watching balloon animals take shape. A highlight is the procession and proclamation, when your little princess is announced and escorted as she walks down the outside mansion steps, and gives a princess wave to the adoring crowd. This event sells out, so get your tickets early. Sun., 10am - noon and 2pm - 4pm. The price is $65 for princess, age 3 - 10, and one adult.

RAMONA OUTDOOR PLAY, Hemet. (800) 645-4465 / www.ramonabowl.com, 27400 Ramona Bowl Rd. All the world's a stage, or at least all this mountainside is a stage in Hemet. For three weekends a cast of almost 400 (including children and animals) perform on the mountainside to tell the romantic story of Ramona and her Indian hero, Alessandro. The tale, which also reflects our early California heritage, is incredibly well told and fascinating. For more than 85 years this epic play has been presented here. Come early for lunch, or to walk around the Mercado, a Spanish marketplace with folk music, dancers, and artisans. Bring a jacket. Gates open at 1:30pm; preshow activities begin at

1:30; and performances begin at 3.30pm and end at 6:30pm. Tickets range from $32 - $47 for adults, plus a $5 handling fee; $19-$46 for ages 12. There is a $20 discount on some tickets for local residents. Parking is $5

RENAISSANCE PLEASURE FAIRE, Irwindale. (626) 969-4750 / www.renfair.com, 15501 E. Arrow Highway at the Santa Fe Dam Recreation Area. Heare ye, heare ye, this annual faire, one of the largest in Southern California, runs for eight weekends in April through May (sometimes into June), bringing the Renaissance time period to life. Note: Wenches dress accordingly, and there is bawdiness. Eat, drink, and be merry as you cheer on knights; play challenging games from times of yore; be entertained by juggling, dancing, singing, and artisans demonstrations; watch jousting tournaments; see animal shows; participate in children's activities on the weekend; and enjoy the delicious food and fare. Dress up! Meet Queen Elizabeth and her court, plus Sir Francis Drake, William Shakespeare, and other well-known people of the time. Teachers, check out the school day special offered one Fri., from 9:30am - 3:30pm. On this day some of the same activities are offered as during the regular faire, although they are more educationally-oriented and the costumed participants are usually more modestly attired. School-day ticket prices are $14 each and must be purchased ahead of time. The faire is open to the public Sat. - Sun., 10am - 7pm. Admission is $28 for adults; $15 for ages 5 - 12; children 4 and under are free. Parking is $10. Purchase discount tickets online.

SAN BERNARDINO RAILROAD DAYS, San Bernardino. (909) 888-3634; (714) 278-0648 / www.sbdepotmuseum.com, 1170 West 3rd St. at the San Bernardino Santa Fe Depot. The festivities include reenactors with simulated gunfights; live country/western music; vendors; touring the SAN BERNARDINO HISTORY AND RAILROAD MUSEUM (pg. 429); boarding a steam engine and its cars for a free tour; seeing the model railroad displays; working a hand-operated car (nominal fee); and looking at the antique fire apparatus, classic trucks, and classic cars. Train enthusiasts can go one track (i.e. step) further, by riding an actual steam engine (#3751) between Los Angeles and San Bernardino. Start (or end) your two-and-a-half-hour ride at the historic depot. Pay for another one-way ticket back, or take the Metrolink one way. Stay overnight in San Bernardino and make a weekend of it! Open Sat., 9am to 5pm (rides from San Bernardino to Los Angeles); Sun., 9pm to 3pm (rides from Los Angeles to San Bernardino). The festival is free. One-way fare on the steam engine runs $40 to $130.

SAN DIEGO KIDS EXPO AND FAIR, Del Mar. (619) 269 - 9441 / www.sandiegokidsexpo.com, 2260 Jimmy Durante Blvd at the Del Mar Fairgrounds. This event includes activities for all of you kids from toddlers to teens. There are workshops (such as arts, self defense and robotics), activities (zip line, laser tag and bowling) and live music by children's music artists and local musicians. Sat., $8 for adults, 12 and under free. Some activities cost extra.

SANTA BARBARA KITE FESTIVAL, Santa Barbara. (805) 963-2964 or (805) 637-6202 / www.sbkitefest.net, 721 Cliff Dr. on the lawn next to Garvin Theater at Santa Barbara City College's West Campus. A rainbow array of kites take to the skies, although some nose dive, at this annual one-day festival. Kites of all sizes, shapes, and colors fly in various competitions such as sport flying, highest flying, kite fighting, most beautiful, and largest kite. Prizes are awarded. The tail chase event is especially fun for kids as they try to catch the tail of a kite as it alternately dips, dives, and soars. Kites are available for purchase or bring your own. Fly some fun on Sun., 11am - 4pm. Free admission.

SANTA CLARITA COWBOY FESTIVAL, Santa Clarita. (661) 250-3735 / www.cowboyfestival.org, Arch and 12th sts. at Melody Ranch Motion Picture Studio. Howdy-doo! Over 10,000 people attend this four-day event that acknowledges that cowboys are still heroes. Thursday and Friday offer various options at different venues around the area. One highlight is the Western Film Tour which visits several movie sites like Disney's Golden Oak Ranch, Vasquez Rocks, Iverson Ranch and Corriganville. Thursday's and Friday's tours visit different places. The tours cost $45 and leave from William S. Hart at 2pm and return 5:30pm. There are other shows, lectures and demonstrations on Thursday and Friday. Past events have included a demonstration of prairie cooking (and eating), an open mic night for cowboy poets and musicians, a walking tour of Old Town Newhall, a western movie screening and a cowboy fashion show. See website for specific events and prices. Behind-the-Scenes tours of the Melody Ranch studio are offered Sat. and Sun. at 8:30am for $40 per person, which also includes admission to the festival. These tours sell out quickly. Cowboy Church is Sun. at 8am at Master College. Call (661) 268-8863 for more info. At the actual festival, browse in shops at the historic Melody Ranch, which resembles a western town. There are several specifically family-oriented programs offered, including Western farces, trick ropers, panning for gold, steer roping, street shows/performances, magic shows, and more. Come listen to some of the finest poetry, storytelling, and music that the West has to offer. The festival runs Sat. - Sun., 10am - 6pm. Tour the Melody Ranch Motion Picture Museum (where filmmaking still happens) for free. Shop for Western merchandise at the vendors' booths and peruse cowboy art. Tip: Dress up in western duds and don't forget to wear your Stetson. Sat. and Sun., 10am - 6pm. Admission to the festival is $20 for adults; $10 for age 11 and under, which includes a shuttle ride to the ranch as there isn't any public parking on site. Two day tickets are $30 and $15. Note, that while a majority of the shows are included in the admission price, certain

shows are ticketed events and cost extra.

SANTA MARIA VALLEY STRAWBERRY FESTIVAL, Santa Maria. (805) 925-8824 / www.santamariafairpark.com, 937 S. Thornburg at the Santa Maria Fairgrounds. Bring your little shortcakes to this three-day festival to enjoy carnival rides, a petting zoo, train rides, kid's crafts, face painting, safety demonstrations by the police department, an ice sculpting demonstration, a monster truck show, and, most importantly, eating strawberries! Join in on pie eating contests, watch food preparation demonstrations with strawberries, and indulge in this sweet fruit presented in so many scrumptious ways. The festival is open Fri. - Sun., 11am - 10pm; the carnival is open until midnight. General admission is $9 for adults; $7 for srs. and ages 6 - 11; children 5 and under are free. Rides are extra. Check the website for discounts. Parking is $5.

SCANDINAVIAN FESTIVAL, Thousand Oaks. (805) 241-0391 or (805) 493-3151 / www.scandinavianfest.org, 60 W. Olsen Rd. at California Lutheran University. Valkommen! Enjoy a presentation/program of a 16th-century Swedish royal court at this two-day festival which includes a Viking encampment, folk dancing, a colorful parade with authentic costumes, arts and crafts booths, and a replica of Tivoli Gardens, although it's not quite as large as the one in Denmark. Kids will particularly enjoy the jugglers, puppet shows, magicians, clowns, and moon bounces. A smorgasbord is served here, too. The festival is open Sat. and Sun., 10am - 5pm Admission is $8 for adults; $4 ages 13 to 19; 12 and under are free. Certain activities cost extra.

SEA FESTIVAL, Santa Barbara. (805) 962-8404 / www.sbmm.org, 113 Harbor Way, Suite 190. Activities from past festivals include ship tours, storytelling, diving demonstrations, arts and crafts, museum tours, sailing aboard a tall ship, and more. See Santa Barbara Maritime Museum (pg. 629) for more information about this museum. Open Sat. - 11am - 4pm. Tall ship sail 4:30pm to 6:30pm. $7 for adults; ages 6 - 17, seniors and military $4; children 1 - 5 $2. Parking is $2 per hour, $12 max. Tall ship sail $40 for adults, $19 for children ages 4 to 12. Children 3 and under free.

SPRING SPECTACULAR, Moorpark. See March entry (pg. 713) for details.

STRAWBERRIES - CAL POLY POMONA, Pomona. See March entry (pg. 713) for details.

TANAKA FARMS, Irvine. See March entry (pg. 713) for details.

TOYOTA GRAND PRIX, Long Beach. (562) 981-2600; for tickets (888) 82SPEED (827-7333) / www.gplb.com, 3000 Pacific Ave. at Shoreline Dr. This three-day, top-of-the-line racing event includes practice and qualifying runs on Friday; celebrity racing and final qualifying runs on Saturday; and final Champ car racing on Sunday. See you at the races! Gates are open Fri. and Sat. 7am - 9pm, Sun. 7am - 5:30pm. General admission (unreserved seating) for adults is $28 on Fri., $48 on Sat., $55 on Sun. Reserved seating ranges from $62 - $83. There are three-day passes available.

VAN OMMERING DAIRY, Lakeside. (619) 390-2929 / www.omaspumpkinpatch.com, 14950 El Monte Road. K through 6th graders are invited to take an hour-long tour of this family-owned dairy. The tour starts in the commodities shed where seed is stored for the 600 cows that live on the premises. Guests then go through the showers (not literally!) where the cows are washed down before they're milked. From the milking barn, with all of its fascinating modern machinery, the tour visits the maternity pen. Kids are welcome to gently pet the newborns and the animals in the petting zoo. The hay ride, with wheelchair ramps, goes all around the farm. Information is dispensed throughout the tour about the workings of a dairy, cows' eating habits, where the milk goes after it's outside the cows, and more. Visitors leave with lots of knowledge about these milk/meat/leather-producing animals, a greater understanding of how farmers' work affects everyone, an ice cream cup, and a souvenir water bottle. Tours are offered in April and May, Tues., Wed. and Thurs. at 9:30am and 11am. Groups from 15 to 100 people are welcome. Reservations are required. Admission is $6 per person.

VICTORIAN FAIR, City of Industry. (626) 968-8492 / www.homesteadmuseum.org, 15415 East Don Julian Road at the Homestead Museum. Get a taste of what life was like for people living in the Southland during the 1840s, '50s, and '60s through music, dancing, crafts, historic house tours, games, demonstrations, and more! Also see THE HOMESTEAD MUSEUM (pg. 120). Sat. and Sun., 1pm to 5 p.m. Admission free.

VISIT WITH FATHER SERRA, Coachella. (800) 204-3131 / www.forestlawn.com, 51990 Jackson Street at Forest Lawn Memorial Park. Learn California history from a founding father, or rather, a costumed actor who tells about Father Serra's life and time period from a "first person" perspective. This half-hour talk is interesting and educational. The presentation is given at 11am. Call to make a reservation. Admission is free.

YOUTH EXPO, Costa Mesa. (714) 708-1500 / www.ocfair.com, 88 Fair Dr. at the Orange County Fairgrounds. This huge, three-day expo highlights the talents of Orange County kids from elementary through high school age. Their artistic endeavors are showcased in different buildings according to age groups and categories, such as fine arts, photography, woodworking, and ceramics. 4-H Club members also have wonderful exhibits. The Science Fair is a

highlight which draws people from all over the United States who offer money and/or scholarships to students whose experimentally-based research designs are outstanding. The Expo is great for admiring other kids' works, and for sparking the creative genius in your child. Other concurrent events include a petting zoo, wild science presentations, a carnival with rides, and tours of the adjacent Centennial Farm. Educators should check out the Education Resource Center during the expo as it features exhibits and displays from over 100 organizations as well as classroom handouts, posters, and other free, educational tools. Open Fri., 9am - 3pm (this day can get crowded with school tours); Sat. - Sun., 10am - 5pm. Admission is free. Parking is $7.

- MAY: -

AIRPORT DAY, Fullerton. (714) 738-6323 / www.ci.fullerton.ca.us, 4011 W. Commonwealth Avenue Give your spirits a lift on Airport Day, which is celebrated every even year. Come and see how the airport really functions as you tour around it and see displays and demonstrations with the OC Fire Authority, Anaheim Police Department, CA Highway Patrol, Air Combat USA, public library, Fullerton Radio Club and others. Look to the skies for the airplane demonstrations, too. Open Sat., 10am - 4pm Free

ANATOLIAN CULTURES & FOOD FESTIVAL, Costa Mesa. (310) 208-7290 / www.anatolianfestival.org, 88 Fair Drive at the Orange County Fair and Event Center. This event, celebrating the history of people from Asia Minor / Republic of Turkey, is incredible in size and scope. Walk through the massive Gates of Civilization to be greeted by costumed actors/residents of the Ottomans, Romans, Phyrgians, Byzantines, and ten other civilizations. The giant, re-created buildings, with backdrops, are so impressive - the Topkapi Palace, Armenian Cathedral of the Holy Cross, Sultan's Palace in Istanbul, the House of Mary in Izmir, Maiden's Tower, and other landmarks, plus arches, and edifices, as well as the Grand Bazaar (with over 100 vendors hawking their wares of genuine Near Eastern goods). Purchase hand-crafted items of filigree, carpets, calligraphy, stone-carving, and so much more. Turkish coffee abounds as do kebabs, stews, doner (Gyros), dumplings with yogurt sauce, baklava and other delicious baked goods, plus stretchy ice cream. Enjoy performances, crafts, dances, live music and art. 45,000 people attend this four-day event. Open Thurs. - Sun., 10am - 10pm. General admission, per day, is $12 for adults; $9 for srs.; $6 for ages 7 - 12; children 6 and under are free. Students attending with their teachers are free on Thurs. and Fri.

BIG JOHN'S CHERRY ORCHARD, Leona Valley. See March entry (pg. 709) for details.

BUG FAIR, Los Angeles. (213) 763-3499 / www.nhm.org, 900 Exposition Blvd. at the Natural History Museum of Los Angeles. This weekend fair really *bugs* me! Come and gawk at and even touch a wide variety of live insects, such as Madagascar hissing cockroaches, millipedes, and more. Over fifty vendors showcase every kind of insect product available including jewelry, t-shirts, toys, silkworms, live critters, a butterfly house, chocolate-covered crickets (poor Jimminy!), mounted insects, and lots more. The fair includes educational presentations and hands-on activities. Walk through the museum's Insect Zoo while here. See page 139 for a description of the museum. Creep, crawl, or fly here on Sat. - Sun., 9:30am - 5pm. Admission to the museum includes admission to the fair: $12 for adults; $9 for srs., college students, and ages 13 - 17; $5 for ages 3 - 12; children 2 and under are free. Parking is $10 (cash only).

CALIFORNIA STRAWBERRY FESTIVAL, Oxnard. (888) 288-9242 or (805) 385-4739 / www.strawberry-fest.org, 3250 S. Rose Ave. at College Park. This big, juicy festival, held on the third weekend of May, offers unique strawberry culinary delights, an arts and crafts show with over 300 artisans, and contests, including a strawberry shortcake eating contest. Kids enjoy Strawberryland, in particular, because it has a petting zoo, puppet shows, clowns, hands-on arts and crafts, and carnival rides. Have a *berry* good time here! Open Sat. and Sun., 10am - 6pm. Admission is $12 for adults; $8 for srs.; $5 for ages 5 - 12; children 4 and under are free. Certain activities cost extra. Parking at the festival is $10 or there is a free shuttle service.

CARLSBAD STRAWBERRY COMPANY, Carlsbad. See April entry (pg. 714) for details.

CARLSBAD VILLAGE FAIRE SPRING, Carlsbad. (760) 945-9288 / www.carlsbad.org, Carlsbad Village - Grand Ave. from Carlsbad Blvd. to Jefferson St. Held on the first Sunday in May and November, this is the one of the largest one-day fairs held in California. It has over 900 exhibitors, international food, and a variety of live entertainment. This type of fair is especially fun for shoppers of all ages as you never know what kind of unique items you might find and *have* to purchase. It runs from 8am - 5pm. Admission is free, but bring spending money!

CHERRY FESTIVAL / CHERRY PICKING, Beaumont, Cherry Valley. See June entry (pg. 726) for details.

CINCO DE MAYO CELEBRATION, The fifth of May, a national Mexican holiday honoring Mexican victory over the French army at Puebla, is celebrated throughout Southern California with several days of Mexican folk dancing, mariachi music, parades, puppet shows, face painting, storytelling, booths, piñatas, and fun! In Los Angeles, for

instance, contact (213) 628-1274/ www.olvera-street.com at El Pueblo de Los Angeles Historical Monument in downtown. This particular festival runs Sat. - Sun., 10am - 10pm. In Old Town San Diego, contact (619) 296-3236 / www.oldtownsandiego.org. This celebration features a reenactment of the 1862 Battle of Puebla.

DISCOVER RECYCLING, Throughout LA See April entry (pg. 715) for details.

DOWNTOWN HARBOR TROLLEY, Ventura. (805) 827-4444 / www.downtownventura.org, Loops from downtown Ventura to Harbor Village. This trolley runs from Memorial Day to Labor day. See Ventura Harbor Village (pg. 692) for more info. Runs11am - 11pm Wed. - Sun. Runs Thurs. - Mon. if major holiday falls on Monday. Free!

FIESTA MATSURI, Los Angeles. (213) 628-2725 / www.jaccc.org, 244 S. San Pedro in Little Tokyo. Fiesta Matsuri (literally means Festival Festival) is where Kodomo no Hi (children's day in Japanese) and Dia de los Niños (children's day in Spanish) meet. This multiethnic celebration is for families, and particularly children ages 4 to 12. They are invited to participate in a running race, as well as making arts and crafts. Other attractions can include magic shows, sports clinics, calligraphy demonstrations, origami-making, kite-making, dancing, displays of traditional costumes, live entertainment, and more. Kids can even see a samurai armor demonstration and children's mariachi. Open Sat., 11am - 4pm. Admission is free, although certain activities cost.

FLOWER FIELDS, Carlsbad. See March entry (pg. 710) for details.

FREE COMIC BOOK DAY, / www.freecomicbookday.com, Sponsored by the Comic Book Industry, publishers such as Marvel, Dark Horse, DC, Image, and others prepare giveaway editions of their best titles for this one day. Some stores also host comic book creator appearances. Note that it is independent and specialty stores that participate. Check the website or call your local store for the date, which is typically the first Sat. in May.

FULLERTON RAILROAD DAYS, Fullerton. (714) 278-0648 / www.scrmf.org, 120 E. Santa Fe Ave at the Fullerton Train Station. Usually held the first weekend in May, kids and adults go loco over touring through a large steam locomotive, Amtrak passenger cars, and vintage private rail cars. More activities and events include model trains running about the huge and beautifully-landscaped garden layout; more operating train layouts inside a circus tent; children's activities; vendors selling train-related paraphernalia; and a food court. Open Sat. - Sun., 9am - 5pm. Admission is free.

I MADONNARI ART FESTIVAL, Santa Barbara. (800) 793-7666 / www.imadonnarifestival.com, at the corner of Los Olivos and Laguna sts. at Santa Barbara Mission. Since the 16th century, street painting, using chalk as a medium, has been an Italian tradition. Over 200 blank pavement squares in front of the mission will be filled in with colorful drawings by artists and aspiring artists of all ages over the three-day Memorial weekend. The professional works are indeed works of art. (Hope it doesn't rain!) The festival also includes live music and an Italian marketplace. Open Sat. - Sun., 10am - 6pm. Free admission. Young artists who want to paint a patch pay $10, which includes chalk.

IMAGINATION CELEBRATION, Orange County. See April entry (pg. 716) for details.

INTERNATIONAL FESTIVAL, Aliso Viejo. (949) 480-4081 / www.soka.edu, 1 University Dr. at Soka University. Enjoy a day with international flare by tantalizing your taste buds with food from around the world, cultural dances (the costumes are exciting and beautiful) and music (900 performers on three stages), plus games, activities, over 250 exhibitors, and a children's play area. Abierto, ouverte, aperto, offen, or open Sat., 10:30am - 5pm. Admission is free. Parking is $10.

INTERNATIONAL MUSEUM DAY, / imd.icom.museum, Here's a little known fact - May 18th is officially International Museum Day. Each year around that date a theme is selected and many museums offer free admission. Some participants may also sponsor a family day of art and craft activities, storytelling, or other entertainment. Call your local (or favorite) museum and see what they have to offer.

INTERNATIONAL SPEEDWAY, Costa Mesa. See April entry (pg. 716) for details.

KORONEBURG OLD WORLD FESTIVAL, Corona. (951) 735-0101 / www.renfestcorona.com, 14600 Baron Drive at Crossroads Riverview Park. Peasants, lords and ladies, merchants, artisans, craftsmen, nobles, knights, travelers, and everyone else is invited to join in the seven weekends of festivities. The fictitious setting is the Baron's estate, a European Village along the Rhine River via 1450 - 1600. Archery competitions, horse shows, sheep shearing, weaving and spinning demonstrations, great food, and crafts of old are just some of the fun to be had here. Open mid-May through mid-June, Sat., 11am - 7pm (except for some Saturdays with extended hours to 9pm); Sun., 11am - 6pm, and on Memorial Day. Admission is $18 for adults; $15 for srs. and ages 5 - 11; children 4 and under are free. Find discount coupons online. Parking is $5.

LA CANADA FIESTA DAYS, La Canada. (818) 790-4289 / www.lacanadaflintridge.com, Community Center of La Canada Flintridge, 4469 Chevy Chase Dr. La Canada's Memorial Day weekend celebration includes a community

breakfast, live music, a BBQ, a family film, and fireworks - followed by a grand parade down Foothill Boulevard. Memorial day weekend, check website or call for time and events. Most events, excluding meals, are free.

LAFD OPEN HOUSE, / www.lafd.org, The second Sat. in May is "Fire Service Recognition Day" throughout Los Angeles and neighborhood fire stations open their doors to welcome the public. This is an ideal time to meet your local firefighters and thank them. Take a tour of the station and see the equipment and apparatus. Some of the stations have special displays and demonstrations, and some host a pancake breakfast. Check the website to see which ones. Sat., 10am - 4pm. Some stations extend this Open House onto Sun., 10am - 4pm, too. Admission is free.

LOS RANCHEROS VISTADORES, Santa Ynez. (805) 688-4815 / www.missionsantaines.org, 1760 Mission Dr. at Mission Santa Ines. About 500 riders come to have their horses blessed by the padres at the mission on the Saturday afternoon, from 3pm to 4pm, of the Kentucky Derby. If you're in the area and a horse lover, it is a colorful procession to watch. Free to observe.

MANZINITA HIGH MOUNTAIN RENDEZVOUS, Julian. (760) 745-2927 / manzinita.homestead.com, Mesa Grande Rd. at Santa Ysabel Ranch. Experience an authentic 1700's to 1840's Rocky Mountain fur traders' encampment in a rustic mountain setting. Demonstrations of primitive survival skills such as cooking, tool making, tomahawk throwing, and black powder target shooting are given over two weekends, but the real draw is being immersed in this time period. This event is geared for fellow buckskinners and traders, with the public welcome to visit and watch, but not participate. Primitive and modern camping is available on site. Open daily, 10am - 5pm Admission is $5 for adults; ages 10 and under, school groups, military, and scouts in uniform are free.

MCGRATH FAMILY FARMS, Camarillo. See March entry (pg. 712) for details.

MOTA DAY, Pasadena. (213) 740-8687 / www.museumsofthearroyo.com, The five organizations that comprise MOTA - Museums of the Arroyo - open their doors for free one Sunday a year and include fun family activities. The museums include HERITAGE SQUARE MUSEUM (pg. 118) at 3800 Homer St., (Los Angeles); the Lummis Home and Garden at 200 E. Ave. 43; GAMBLE HOUSE (pg. 109) at 4 Westmoreland Pl.; LOS ANGELES POLICE HISTORICAL SOCIETY MUSEUM (pg. 132) at 6045 York Blvd.; PASADENA MUSEUM OF HISTORY (pg. 142) at 470 W. Walnut St. and the Autry Historic Southwest Museum Mt. Washington Campus at 234 Museum Dr. There is a free shuttle service between the museums. The museums are open 11am - 5pm.

MOTHER'S DAY JAZZ & BLUES EXTRAVAGANZA, Los Angeles. / www.mothersdayjazz.com, 2580 Cahuenga Blvd. East Let's see some jazz hands! For 10 years the Ford Amphitheatre has been hosting the hippest, hottest Mothers' Day celebration in town. Bring the kids - or don't... Box Office opens at 1pm, gates at 2pm, show from 3pm to 8pm. $36 per person. Groups of 15 or more are discounted 10%.

NATIONAL PUBLIC GARDENS DAY, / www.nationalpublicgardensday.org, April showers bring May flowers. They also bring a day in May where admission to many botanical gardens and arboretums is free. This annual celebration is designed to raise the awareness of the importance of public gardens. Check the website for a garden near you (and those across the nation). Free

NATIONAL TRAIN DAY (Santa Barbara), Santa Barbara. / www.nationaltrainday.com, 209 State St. Be at the station by 9am to purchase a 9:22am round trip ticket to Carpenteria and return by 10:30am to see a large model train exhibit where there will be food and activities for kids. 9am to noon. Train prices are $8.50 for adults; $7.22 fo srs.; $4.25 ages 2-15.

NATIONAL TRAIN DAY (Los Angeles), Los Angeles. / www.nationaltrainday.com, Union Station - 800 North Alameda St.; Travel Town - 5200 Zoo Drive Enjoy free kids' activities, exhibits, model trains and giveaways at the beautiful Union Station. Tour private luxury cars, freight and commuter trains and other Amtrak equipment. There will also be activities at Travel Town by the LA Zoo, including tours of a railway cars and a sale on all train toys and items in the gift shop. Union Station - 11am to 4pm. Travel Town 10:30am to 3pm. Admission is free.

NATIONAL TRAIN DAY (San Diego), San Diego. / www.nationaltrainday.com, San Diego S-Gaugers - 2445 Truxtun Rd.; San Diego Model Railroad Museum - 1649 El Prado The San Diego S-Gaugers hosts an open house showing S gauge model trains. S gauge trains are 1/64 size with a track width of just under an inch. The SAN DIEGO MODEL RAILROAD MUSEUM (pg. 553) will host train themed activities. S-Gaugers are open 11am to 4pm. The museum is open 11am to 1pm. S-Gaugers admission is free. The museum prices are $8 for adults; $6 for srs.; $3 for students.

OLD TOWN TEMECULA WESTERN DAYS CELEBRATION, Temecula. (951) 694-6480 / www.temeculaevents.org, Front St. and Main St. in Old Town. Happy trails to you as you walk around this wonderful, old Western-style town any day of the week, but particularly this weekend. Goings on include watching gun fighters at

a high noon shoot-out / skit; a Civil War reenactment encampment, with battles twice daily; stagecoach rides; historians and reenactors to talk with; a petting zoo; pony rides; vendor and craftsmen booths; street entertainment; contests; Old Town tours; and more. Come dressed in your best western duds. Open Sat. - Sun., 11am - 5pm. Admission is free.

PLANES OF FAME AIR SHOW, Chino. (909) 597-3722 / www.planesoffame.org, 7000 Merrill Ave. at the Air Museum Planes of Fame at Chino airport. In-air displays of classic and antique aircraft, trainer, liaison, fighter and bomber warbirds, flybys, and jet aircraft are at this weekend event. A crowd favorite is the aerobatic acts in the sky, such as wing walking. Several static (i.e. ground) displays include military aircraft, helicopters, and fighter jets, plus a WWII bomber to tour through. Antique cars and vintage race cars are also on display. Bring a picnic or purchase lunch from food vendors. Gates open at 8am; flying begins around 11am and the show ends about 5pm. Admission is $11 for adults; $4 for ages 5 - 11; children 4 and under are free. Tickets include entrance to the museum.

RAMONA OUTDOOR PLAY, Hemet. See April entry (pg. 717) for details.

RAMONA RODEO, Ramona. (760) 789-1311 or (760) 789-1484 / www.ramonarodeo.com, 5th St. and Aqua Ln. at the Fred Grand Arena. Kick up your heels 'cause the rodeo comes to town the second weekend in May! With a down-home flavor, the rodeo includes all the favorite featured events, plus numerous vendors. Sunday is kids' day, with special activities such as "dummy" steer roping, rope tricks, and cowboy/cowgirl contests. Rodeo shows are Fri., 7:30pm; Sat., 7:30pm; and Sun., 2:30pm. Arrive early. Fri. admission is $10 - $15 for adults, $5 - 15 for children 6 - 12; Sat, $17 - $22 all ages; Sun $12 - $17 for adults and $5 - $17 for children 6 - 12. Children 5 and under are free on Fri. and Sun. Reserved seating is more, but worth it since shows can sell out. Parking is $2.

REDLANDS SHAKESPEARE FESTIVAL, Redlands. (909) 335-7377 / www.redlandsshakespearefestival.com, 25 Grant St. Redlands Shakespeare Festival - The annual free festival occurs each May at the Redlands Bowl outdoor amphitheater in Smiley Park, and features full-scale repertory performances, a University Lecture Series, an Educational Workshop Series, Director's Insight Series, and other special events. Performances and workshops throughout the month. Check for times and days. Free.

RENAISSANCE PLEASURE FAIRE, Irwindale. See April entry (pg. 718) for details.

ROCKET LAUNCH, Huntington Beach. (714) 542-2823 / www.discoverycube.org, 5301 Bolsa Ave. at the Boeing Company. This propelling Rocket Launch competition is one for the whole family to enjoy. Bring a 2-liter plastic soda bottle to design, decorate, build and launch here (or build it at home). The "extras" are provided - fins, parachutes, noses, etc., and even real engineers to help out. Bottles are launched, via water pressure, throughout the day and the ones with longest "hang time" win. There are three categories - K - 6th grade; 7th - 12th grade; and Adult. (Younger children can enter with a parent under Adult.) Prizes include watching an actual rocket launch and gift cards. Bring a lawn chair (and hat - there isn't any shade), compete, or just watch, and enjoy the food trucks that conveniently appear at lunch time. Have a blast! Open Sat., 9am - 2pm. Admission is free. Please register beforehand if you want to participate.

SAN BERNARDINO COUNTY FAIR, Victorville. (760) 951-2200 / www.sbcfair.com, 14800 7th St. For nine days the desert really heats up with excitement when the county fair comes to town. There are eighty-six acres of carnival rides, attractions, farm animals, clowns, family entertainment, and lots more fun. Open Tues. - Thurs., 4pm - 11pm; Fri. - Mon., 2pm - 11pm. Admission is $6 per person. Activities cost extra. Parking is $5.

SCOTTISH FAIR & HIGHLAND GAMES / SCOTSFEST, Costa Mesa. / www.scotsfest.com, 88 Fair Dr. Also known as Scotsfest, the annual festival of Celtic entertainment, food, and Highland games is a two-day event showcasing the best of the Scottish and Celtic heritage. Bagpipes are a given. Saturday & Sunday 9am to 5pm. Adults $18/$25 (1day/2day); srs $16/$22; ages 5-12 $3/$4; military and ages 4 and under free. Parking $5

SCOTTISH FESTIVAL AND HIGHLAND GATHERING, Costa Mesa. (310) 539-4302 / www.scottishfest.com, 88 Fair Drive at the Orange County Fair and Event Center. This Memorial weekend festival, which has been around for over 70 years!, features everything Scottish - caber tossing, hammer throws, shot put, sheepdog herding, good food, opening and closing ceremonies, parades, and a lot of tartan with over sixty clans represented. Bagpipes and Highland Fling dancers, country dancing, pipe bands, and more entertain you and the kids throughout the day. Open Sat. - Sun., 9am - 5pm. One-day admission is $18 for adults; $16 for srs. and students; $6 for ages 5 - 12; children 4 and under are free. Pre-sale discount tickets are available online. Parking is $10.

SEAL DAY, San Pedro. (310) 548-5677 / www.marinemammalcare.org, 3601 S. Gaffey Street at Marine Mammal Care Center. This fund raiser event, hosted by the Marine Mammal Care Center, has tours of the facility, feedings of the animals, demonstrations, speakers, games, special gifts, and raffle prizes. Open Sun., 11am - 4pm. Call for

admission information.

STRAWBERRIES - CAL POLY POMONA, Pomona. See March entry (pg. 713) for details.

STRAWBERRY FESTIVAL, Garden Grove. (714) 638-0981 / www.strawberryfestival.org, between Euclid Ave. and Main St. at Village Green. This four-day event, always held Memorial Day weekend, features carnival rides; games; a parade (Saturday at 10am); arts and crafts booths; entertainment at the amphitheater; dance recitals; kids karaoke contest; a Berry Beautiful Baby Pageant; the annual redhead round-up; and strawberries. Open Fri., 1pm - 10pm; Sat. - Sun., 10am - 10pm; Mon., 10am - 9pm. General admission is free. Certain activities cost. All ride pass $25 Fri., $30 Sat. - Mon.

SUMMER MOVIE EXPRESS, (310) 434-3001 / www.regmovies.com/Movies/Summer-Movie-Express, Regal Theatres throughout Southern California present their Summer Movie Express program, showing family-friendly movies on Tuesday and Wednesday mornings for the barely-there price of $1. There are varying start dates for this program. The program then runs for 9 weeks. Check the website for a list of participating theatres and dates.

TANAKA FARMS, Irvine. See March entry (pg. 713) for details.

TEMECULA BERRY COMPANY, Temecula. (951) 225-5552 / www.temeculaberryco.com, 39700 Cantrell Rd. Blueberries are not just a highly-touted source for anti-oxidants, but they taste great and freeze well. U-pic berries from the ten-acre farm, or just purchase them. Free field trips can be scheduled for pre-schooler and elementary-aged kids. It does get really hot here during peak daylight hours, so wear a hat and bring sunscreen. Plan on coming in the morning or late afternoon to participate in the U-pic. During U-pic season open daily, 8am - 6pm. About $5 per pint.

TEMECULA VALLEY BALLOON AND WINE FESTIVAL, Temecula. (951) 676-6713 / www.tvbwf.com, Warren Rd. at Lake Skinner Recreation Area. Rise and shine for this colorful, three-day festival. On the weekends the balloons are filled with hot air starting around 6am, an event fascinating to watch. Lift-off is around 6:30am, with numerous balloons filling the sky in a kaleidoscope of color. Many of the balloons come back down around 8:30am. Other, less lofty, activities include live entertainment, arts and craft, and a kid's fair with kiddie rides, a petting zoo, free tethered balloon rides, and more. The Friday and Saturday night "glows" (i.e. inflated, lighted balloons that glow almost magically in the evening sky) occur after sunset. Open Fri., 3pm - 10pm; Sat., 6am - 10pm; Sun., 6am - 5pm. Admission for adults is $24 on Fri.,$25 on Sat., and $17 on Sun. Admission for ages 7 - 12 is $5; children 6 and under are free. Parking is $5. Certain activities cost extra. One-hour balloon rides are also available for $210 per person on Sat., $200 on Sun. and includes admission to the festival. Riders must be 48" or taller. Advanced reservations are necessary, so contact (951) 699-9987 / www.agrapeescape.com.

TOPANGA BANJO AND FIDDLE FESTIVAL, Agoura Hills. (805) 370-2301 / www.topangabanjofiddle.org, Paramount Ranch, 2903 Cornell Rd. We dare you to keep your toes from tapping when Paramount Ranch plays host to the annual old-time, blue grass, folk song, folk dancing, and crafts festival. The 3rd Sunday in May, 9am to 6pm. Admission is $15 for adults; $10 for srs. and ages 10-17; under 10 is free.

TURTLE AND TORTOISE SHOW, Long Beach. (562) 570-1745 / www.longbeach.gov/park, 7550 E. Spring St. at the El Dorado Nature Center. Do you know the difference between a turtle or a tortoise? Find out this weekend as members of the California Turtle and Tortoise Society bring their favorites, from the smallest turtle to the large Galapagos Island tortoise. All questions are welcome! Sat., 10am - 3pm. Admission is free. Parking is $5.

VALLEY GREEK FESTIVAL, Northridge. (818) 886-4040 / www.valleygreekfestival.com, St. Nicholas Greek Orthodox Church, 9501 Balboa Boulevard It's all Greek to them, and that inspires this annual cultural event replete with live music, dancing, epic amounts of food, cooking demonstrations, children's activities, and a Greek market. Memorial day weekend, 1pm to 9pm. Admission is free.

VILLAGE OF TALES OJAI STORYTELLING FESTIVAL, Ojai. (805) 646-8907 / www.ojaistoryfest.org, W. Ojai Ave. and Signal St. at Libbey Bowl. Once upon a time. . . . This wonderful time of storytelling, put on by Performances to Grow On, is intertwined with workshops for storytelling, poetry, and movement. Story swaps (with stories from all over the globe) include traditional folk tales, stories of suspense, adventure, and humor from renowned tellers of tales. Check out the student outreach programs for school groups, or groups of at least ten kids. See the schedule for details and to decide which events you want to attend. The student outreach programs are Thurs., while the public is invited Fri & Sat., 9am - 10pm; Sun., 9am - 2:30pm. Admission for specific events is $10 to $32 for adults per session; $8 to $25 for kids. A festival pass is $102 for and adult, $62 for a child and $202 for a family (2 adults and 2 children).

WILD WEST FEST, Carlsbad. (760) 434-2843 / www.carlsbadca.gov, 6200 Flying L.C. Lane. Leo Carrillo Ranch is an authentic background for a festival that celebrates the Old West. Enjoy Western music, a mechanical bull ride,

Rodeo Roper activities, pony rides, entertainment, crafts, a trading post, Western photo backdrops and a salsa contest that visitors can just taste or even compete in. Open Sat., 11am - 2pm. General admission is free. Purchase an activity card for $6, that contains 6 squares, to be used towards bull riding (3 squares), roper ride (3 squares) and crafts (1 - 3 squares each). Pony rides are $6.

- JUNE: -

ADVENTURE PLAYGROUND, Huntington Beach. (714) 842-7442 - playground; (714) 536-5486 / www.huntingtonbeachca.gov, 7111 Talbot at Huntington Beach Central Park. (Park at the Central Library.) Open mid-June through mid-August, young Huck Finns can use a raft (push poles are provided) in the shallow waters of a man-made lake. Kids will also love the slide (i.e. tarp-covered hill) which ends in a little mud pool; a rope bridge leading to a tire swing and mini zip line; sand box; and a work-in-progress kid-built "city" of shacks and clubhouses (only for ages 7 years and up). Lumber, hammers, and nails are provided. All guest must wear tennis shoes; no sandals or water shoes allowed. Note: Day campers usually invade during the morning hours. A shower and changing area are available. Children 9 and under must be accompanied by an adult. Open Mon. - Sat., 10am - 4pm. Admission is $3 per child; free for adults.

AIRSHOW SAN DIEGO, El Cajon. (619) 259-5541 / www.ag1caf.org, 1905 North Marshall Ave. Hanger #6 at the Gillespie Field Airport. Several fly bys and aerial demonstrations, plus displays of more than seventy airplanes, including warbirds and vintage aircraft, decorate the air and airfield the first Friday through Sunday in May. Visitors may also tour through a grounded B-17, view antique cars and motorcycles, purchase memorabilia, and talk with aviation celebrities such as WWII Aces, original Flying Tigers, and Tuskegee Airmen. For an additional cost, you can fly in a vintage aircraft. Students are particularly welcome on Friday when kids are given educational tours regarding the aircraft. Visit the nearby museum, Air Group One (pg. 525). The air show is open 8am - 5pm. Admission is $12 for adults; children 9 and under are free.

BIG BEAR VALLEY COWBOY MUSIC AND POETRY GATHERING, Big Bear. (909) 866-4607 / www.bigbearcowboygathering.net, 40789 Village Dr. The Gathering is a throw-back to the cowboy lifestyle and part of the heritage of this valley. It includes singers, story tellers, comedians and concludes on Sunday with Cowboy Church. Friday's show is $15, Saturday's show is $20. VIP luncheon on Sat. is $35.

BIG IRISH FAIR, Long Beach. / www.irishfair.org, El Dorado Regional Park Top o' the mornin' to ye. This weekend Irish fair, the largest one in the Western U.S., features top-name entertainment, such as Clancy, Hal Roach, and the Fenians, on four different stages; parades; traditional contests, such as fiddle playing and dancing; sheep-herding demonstrations; a dog show featuring Irish breeds; bagpipe music; over 100 vendors of Irish wares; and Leprechaun Kingdom for kids. The Kingdom features storytelling, jugglers, pony rides, and carnival rides. Another favorite at the festival is a recreation of a medieval Irish village, Tara, where sword-yielding performers recount the village's legends and history. The athletic field hosts hurling (might not be what you're thinking) and Gaelic football. Look at the website to get a feel for just how big this festival is and how much there is to do here (and that's no blarney). The festival runs Sat. - Sun., 10am - 7pm. Admission is $15 for adults; $3 for srs. and students; children 12 and under are free with a paid adult. Get tickets online at a discount. Parking is $7.50

BIG JOHN'S CHERRY ORCHARD, Leona Valley. See March entry (pg. 709) for details.

BIG WORLD FUN FAMILY SERIES AT THE FORD, Hollywood. (323) 461-3673 / www.fordamphitheater.org, 2580 Cahuenga Blvd. E. at the John Anson Ford Amphitheater. This outdoor amphitheater presents wonderful, one-hour family performances, geared for ages 4 - 11, on most Saturdays, June through October. Check the schedule for a complete listing, as family-friendly shows are also given sometimes during the week. Enjoy an intimate setting with shows that feature top-name entertainment in magic, puppetry, storytelling, music, dance, or plays designed with the whole family in mind. Stay after the show to have a picnic lunch that you may either bring or purchase on site. The cafe offers pizza, sandwiches, Cobb salad, nachos, and more. Educators note that the website offers curriculum supplement for the show series. Shows on Sat. start at 10am. There are pre-show hands-on activities starting at 9am. Call for a schedule of other show times and dates. Reservations are recommended. Seats cost $5 for adults; children 12 and under are free. Ask about Family Day admission. Parking on site costs $1. Shuttle services from 1718 Cherokee in Hollywood are available.

BRIAN RANCH AIRPORT U-PICK ORCHARD, Llano. (661) 261-3216 / www.brianranch.com, 34810 Largo Vista Rd. off Pearblossom Hwy. You can fly into this ranch, as it does have a small airstrip, though most of us just drive. The 40-acre ranch, waaay down a lonely highway and a mile of dirt road, is a fruit mecca with 600 fruit trees.

Depending on the season, pick cherries (June) - Bing, Lapins, and Sunburst; apricots (mid-June); nectarines (mid-July); peaches (mid-July) - Delight, Fairtime, Nectar, Springcrest, Suncrest and Paradise; apples (mid-July) - Braeburn, Golden Supreme, Red Fuji; and pears (August) - Morettini, Bronze Beauty, Bartlett, and Rosi-Red. Ask about education and scout programs to do with aviation and also with produce. Open in season, Sat. - Sun., 8am - 2pm and by appointment. Fruits are paid for by the pound.

CARLSBAD STRAWBERRY COMPANY, Carlsbad. See April entry (pg. 714) for details.

CELEBRATE PUPPETRY FESTIVAL, Tujunga. (818) 352-5285 / www.balibeyond.com/cp.html, 7570 McGroaty Terrace at McGroaty Arts Center. Some good things do come with strings attached, such as marionettes, and puppets. The art of puppet-making is demystified by attending this outdoor afternoon of workshops where you create your own. The day also includes puppet performances, plus music, and vendors. Bob Baker Marionette Theater puppeteers have also been on hand, so to speak, in the past. Pre-festival workshops are usually held the two Sundays before the festival from noon to 4:30pm (days and times may change) where kids, guided by professionals, can learn to make more detailed puppets. Open Sat., 4pm - 9pm. Admission and activities are free.

CHERRY FESTIVAL / CHERRY PICKING, Beaumont, Cherry Valley. (951) 845-9541 - Beaumont Chamber of Commerce / www.beaumontcachamber.com, I tell you no lie - June is a month ripe for cherry picking, but the season could start in mid-May and go as long as July, depending on the weather. Call first. The three-week, or so, season starts with a four-day festival in Beaumont ($2 admission) that includes a parade, carnival-type rides, game booths, amateur and professional live musical entertainment, and lots of family fun. One place and number to try is Mile High Ranch at Riley's, (951) 797-7534 / www.rileysfarm.coms, at 12929 Mile High Rd. (This ranch has raspberries, too, in August.) Look for roadside signs along Live Oak Avenida, Brookside, and Cherry Ave., announcing other U-Pics and check the website www.pickyourown.org. Note: Dowling Orchard, (951) 845-1217, is not a U-Pic, but it does offer just-picked cherries and a year-round produce market.

CHERRY PICKING, Leona Valley. (661) 266-7116 - Leona Valley Cherry Growers hotline / www.cherriesupic.com, Stop at Rancher's Market at 9001 Elizabeth Lake Rd. for a free map of the two dozen U-Pic orchards. The orchards here don't produce enough of the delicious crop for commercial sale, so the public wins by getting to harvest the cherries themselves! Put a bucket around your neck and start picking, although many orchards also sell pre-picked cherries. The weather-dependent, short season can start as early as May and can last through July. Different types of cherries, such as Bing, Rainier, Cashmere, Montmorency, Tartarians, etc., ripen at various times throughout the season. Call first! We especially enjoy The Cherry House, (661) 622-4480 / www.upickcherryhouse.com, at 10600 Leona Ave. This large orchard of over 2,000 trees also has picnic tables on site and refreshments for sale (weekends only), a small farmer's market, and some of the best cherry prices around. Note that they do charge an admission price of $4 for adults; $2 for children 12 and under. C&D Cherries, (661) 917-4348 / www.cdcherries.com, at 40722 90th St. is open 8am to 5pm on weekends and 8am to 5pm on weekdays, there's plenty of time to pick, then stay to have a cherry-flavored picnic on the shady picnic tables. Tip: If you pick a lot of cherries, purchase a cherry pitter! Checkout the website www.pickyourown.org for a fairly comprehensive list of other orchards.

COIN & COLLECTIBLES EXPO, Long Beach. See January entry (pg. 703) for details.

COLORADO LAGOON MODEL BOAT SHOP, Long Beach. (562) 570-6555 - boat shop in season; (562) 570-1888 - out of season info. / www.lbparks.org, 5119 E. Colorado Ave. and Appian Way at Colorado Lagoon. Pre-packaged craft kits have their place in our instant-gratification society, but they have nothing on actually hand crafting a one-of-a-kind, wooden, 12"- to 40"-long sailboat, that is balanced by a lead keel. Participants, who must be at least 7 years old, glue, sand, file, lacquer, and paint before the final rigging is done and they learn sailing lingo along the way. All materials, including hand tools, are provided. Boats take between five to seven days to complete, consecutively or in whatever increments you choose. Parents can drop kids off (or stay) anytime mid-June through the beginning of August, Mon. - Fri., 10am - 3pm. The small building "shop", staffed mostly by older kids, is a fenced in area just off the beach by the Colorado Lagoon (pg. 10). Bring a picnic lunch and sunscreen. All participants can sail their finished products in the weekly regattas held on Fri. at 2pm. Help your kids chart their course to a great summer! Boats range from $25 for a 12", up to $50 for a 40". There is an additional $60 per child participation fee, too, for the eight-week long program.

CONCERTS, There are numerous venues all over Southern California that offer free, outdoor family concerts during the summer. Check with your local parks and recreations department, or chamber of commerce. For most of them simply bring a blanket, some food, sit back, and enjoy the entertainment. Here are some places to get you started: 1) Dinner and a Concert at Prescott Promenade on Main St. in El Cajon, (619) 401-8858 / www.downtownelcajon.com - Fri. nights May through mid-September, 6pm - 8pm, offers salsa, country, rock, boogie-woogie, and more. 2) Carlsbad

TGIF Jazz in the Park at various parks throughout Carlsbad, (760) 434-2904 / www.carlsbadca.gov - Fri. evenings, 6pm - 8pm. 3) See Summer Concerts (pg. 731) for a location in Pasadena. 4) See Redlands Bowl (pg. 730) for a Redlands venue.

DISCOVER RECYCLING, Throughout LA See April entry (pg. 715) for details.

DOWNTOWN HARBOR TROLLEY, Ventura. See May entry (pg. 721) for details.

ELKS RODEO AND PARADE, Santa Maria. (805) 925-4125 / www.santamariaelks.com/rodeo/rodeo.html, Frontage Rd. at Elks Rodeo grounds. Experience the Old West with a roundup and a Professional Rodeo Cowboys Association event with calf roping, bull riding, saddle bronc riding, steer wrestling, and barrel racing events. Don't forget to try some of Santa Maria's famous BBQ tri-tip. The rodeo parade is held on Sat. at 9am and runs from Broadway Mill to Stowell. Tickets are $15.

FIRE & SAFETY EXPO / FIREFIGHTER DEMOLITION DERBY, Del Mar. (858) 541-2277 / www.burninstitute.org, 2260 Jimmy Durante Boulevard, at Del Mar Fairgrounds Did the title of this event spark your interest? Join firefighters in the largest fire expo held in Southern California. The event is held on a Saturday during the San Diego County Fair. For one-day see live demonstrations of auto extrications and bomb robots; a canine dog demonstration; and a Burn Run where 70+ engines (one from each of the area's stations) converge in a siren blaring, lights flashing parade at 1pm. A highlight is the challenge where firefighters from all over, dressed in full bunker gear and breathing apparatus, which can weight up to 50 pounds, compete in five real-life firefighting tasks. Rides on fire engines, a rock climbing wall, "live" firefighting demonstrations, helicopter fly-overs, a firefighter obstacle course, a kiddie carnival (with puppet shows, clowns, and such), and community service group booths add to this special event. One of the highlights is the Firefighter Demolition Derby, which gives local firefighters the chance to "smash for cash" and everyone else a chance to cheer them on. Open 10pm - 6pm. Admission to the county fair, which includes admission to the expo, is $14 for adults; $8 for srs. and ages 6 - 12; children 5 and under are free. Parking is $10. Free shuttle services from free off-site parking is available.

FLOWER FIELDS / FLOWER FESTIVAL, Lompoc. (805) 736-4567 - flower fields info ; (805) 735-8511 - festival / www.lompocvalleyfestivals.com, The flower fields are usually in peak bloom June through August, sometimes September depending on the weather, so drive your car up and down the numerous roads, especially between Central and Ocean avenues traveling west, to get an eye full of color and nose full of fragrance. (The sweet peas are really aromatic.) Pick up a route map from the chamber of commerce at 111 South I St. Cut flowers and flowers grown for seed include larkspur, stock, marigolds, and many more. You'll also see vegetables and other produce. Stop and smell the flowers, but don't pick them. Make the most of your flower experience by also attending the five-day Flower Festival at Ryon Park the last full weekend in June. The parade, starting Saturday at 10am, goes along H and Ocean avenues. The creative floats must be constructed of flowers or natural materials. The parade also features equestrians, bands, drill teams, and clowns. The festival consists of carnival rides, food booths, an arts and crafts show, and a huge flower show, as well as flower displays and demonstrations. One more thing - look up the entry on Lompoc MURALS (pg. 638) to incorporate seeing them into this *field* trip. The flower fields are open daily. The festival is open daily, but check for hours and specific exhibit times. Admission to the fields and the festival is free; rides at the festival cost extra; minimal fee for parking at the festival.

GREEK FEST, San Diego. (619) 297-4165 / www.stspyridon.org, 3655 Park Blvd. at St. Spyridon Church. Live (and lively) Greek music and dancing, home-made pastries and other Greek food, a tour of this Greek Orthodox church, booths, kids' carnival games, and more are offered at this three-day festival. Open Fri., 5pm - 10pm; Sat., 11am - 10pm; Sun., 11am - 9pm. Free on Friday, $3 for adults; ages 11 and under are free.

GUIDE DOGS OF AMERICA OPEN HOUSE, Sylmar. (818) 362-5834 / www.guidedogsofamerica.org, 13445 Glenoaks Blvd. at the Guide Dogs of America. Come to this once-a-year Open House at GUIDE DOGS OF AMERICA (pg. 199) to tour the facility, see guide dogs demonstrations, and watch puppies in training being put through their paces as they run obstacle courses, and try to stay on task past distractions like food, other animals, and travel situations. A silent auction, vendors, crafts, and food round out the festivities for this worthy cause. The Open House is held on a Sat. - call or check their website for hours. Admission is free admission.

HEROES AIR SHOW, Lake View Terrace. (818) 631-8132 / www.heroes-airshow.com, 11480 Foothill Blvd. at Hansen Dam Recreation and Sports Complex. This one-day show is the premier air show exclusively for helicopters and flight teams, and their vehicles' role in law enforcement, fire service, and search and rescue. See aerial demonstrations of rope/rescue techniques; take a helicopter ride; look at the vintage fire engines, police cars, and emergency service vehicles that make up the "Rolling to the Rescue" exhibit; gather information at the Code 3 Career

Fair; and enjoy the vendors and entertainment. Open Sat., 9am - 4pm. Free admission. Rides cost extra.

HO'OLAULE'A or NATIVE FOR NATURE, San Dimas. (909) 599-7512 / www.sandimascanyonnaturecenter.com, 1628 N. Sycamore Canyon Rd. at the San Dimas County Park Nature Center (pg. 82). For one weekend, enjoy Hawaiian and Native American dances, music, and food, plus nature hikes, face painting, pottery, weaving, beading, games, crafts, and Indian fry bread and sweet corn. The proceeds from the activities provide food and medical care for the animals in the center's sanctuary. Open Sat., 10am - 8pm; Sun., 10am - 4pm. Admission and parking is free. Certain activities cost.

HOPE FOR FIREFIGHTERS, Los Angeles. (310) 776-0933 / www.hopeforfirefighters.org, 333 South Hope St. and Fourth St. When a building is burning, we rush out as firefighters rush in. This celebration/fundraiser is one big way to show appreciation for firefighters, as over 25 stations are represented. Come see fire apparatus and demonstrations, and pet a real dalmatian fire dog. For a really hot time, create your own team to compete at the firefighter "Muster" games, in races that include a bucket brigade; firefighter suit-up, then using a lifenet to save a dummy falling from a building; and an old-fashioned hose pull. Watch out for the water hoses filled up by the fire hydrants! Note to teams: To become proficient in the games, there is a practice held a few weeks beforehand, which includes a picnic for all the teams and their families. This practice includes a tour of the Hollywood station, the Historical Society Museum next door, and getting to meet some of the firefighters. Team sponsorship is $850. There is also live music at the fundraiser, LAFD gift merchandise booths, raffle drawings, and a competition between stations for the "best of" in fire house meals. Open the first Thurs. in June, 11:30am - 2:30pm. Free admission. A fire house meal is $7; dessert is $2 - $4; drinks $1.

HUCK FINN JUBILEE, Ontario. (951) 780-8810 / www.huckfinn.com, 800 N. Archibald Ave. in Cucamonga-Guasti Regional Park. The huge, three-day jubilee is always held on Father's Day weekend. Although known for it's famous Blue Grass music festival, there are lots of other things to do here. It kicks off with a fishing derby at 8am on Friday that goes through Sunday. Ages 16 and over must have a license. The weekend is filled with river raft building contests; egg-tossing contests; a big-top circus; greased pole climbing contests; a mountain man encampment; arts and crafts; a Huck Finn look-alike contest; a Tom Sawyer fence painting contest; and lots more down-home fun. Put on a straw hat and join the throngs of people. Note: Camping is available here, too. The jubilee is open Fri. - Sat., 7am - 11pm; Sun., 7am - 8pm. Admission is $25 for adults; $10 each day for ages 6 - 12; children 5 and under are free. Various attractions cost extra. Parking and fishing is free.

INDIAN FAIR, San Diego. (619) 239-2001 / www.museumofman.org, 1350 El Prado at Museum of Man in Balboa Park. This weekend fair, attended by 1,000 artists and performers representing dozens of tribes, provides one of the largest forums for Native American artistry in the West Coast. It features costumed tribal dancers, traditional storytellers, and a market with arts, crafts, beadwork, pottery, and authentic cuisine. Open Sat. - Sun., 10am - 4:30pm. Admission, which includes admission to the museum, is $12.50 for adults; $10 for srs.; $8 for students; $6 for ages 6 - 17; children 5 and under are free.

INTERNATIONAL SPEEDWAY, Costa Mesa. See April entry (pg. 716) for details.

INTERNATIONAL SUMMER ORGAN FESTIVAL, San Diego. (619) 702-8138 / www.sosorgan.com, Balboa Park at the Spreckels Organ Pavilion. Every Sunday afternoon from mid-June through August enjoy the sounds of Scott Joplin, Charles Tournemire, Maurice Durufle, and others at the Organ Pavilion. Bring a picnic lunch (or at least dessert) to eat on the lawn and listen to the sounds of summer. Note that there are free outdoor concerts often given during the week, too. Concerts start at 7:30pm. Admission is free.

INTERTRIBAL POW WOW, Oceanside. (760) 724-8505 / www.slrmissionindians.org, 4050 Mission Ave. at Mission San Luis Rey de Franca. Join a weekend of tribal dancing, arts and crafts, and American Indian games and food. Open Sat., 9am -11pm; Sun., 9am - 6pm. Admission is free.

JUNETEENTH CELEBRATION, Long Beach. (562) 570-6816 / www.longbeach.gov/park, 1950 Lemon Avenue, at Martin Luther King Jr. Park Community Center. This open-air event celebrates the abolition of slavery in the U.S. and promotes remembrance and awareness with speakers, historians, bands, dance troops and local entertainers. There are a gospel celebration and a reading of the Emancipation Proclamation. Food is available for purchase and there is a children's area with games, jumpers and arts and crafts. Attendees are encouraged to bring chairs and blankets. Sun., noon - 5pm. Free

KINGSMEN SHAKESPEARE FESTIVAL, Thousand Oaks. (805) 493-3014 / www.kingsmenshakespeare.org, 60 Olsen Rd., California Lutheran University, Kingsmen Park. Two of Shakespeare's plays are featured, such as *Taming of the Shrew* or *Merchant of Venice*, during the six-weekend festival. There are also Elizabethan vendors, crafts, foods, and

more. The festival usually runs Fri. - Sun., with pre-show entertainment and food vendors beginning at 5:30pm; performances starting at 8pm. Call for a schedule of pre- and post-performance activities. Bring a low back chair or blanket to sit on, and dress warmly. Admission is $20 for adults; ages 17 and under are free. Lawn Boxes hold six people each and are available for reserve for $70 and up.

KORONEBURG OLD WORLD FESTIVAL, Corona. See May entry (pg. 721) for details.

LIVE OAK MUSIC FESTIVAL, Santa Barbara. (805) 781-3030 / www.liveoakfest.org, Live Oak Camp. Come for the music - folk, blues, jazz, bluegrass, gospel, classical and more - but stay for all the other things you kids will enjoy - crafts, juggling, climbing wall, stories, hikes and a talent show. Live Oak Camp is located about 15 miles from Santa Barbara and is in the beautiful Santa Ynez Valley. The festival is held on Father's Day weekend. Tickets are $55 for adults; $20 for ages 4 - 12. Runs Fri. - Sun.

LONG BEACH SEA FESTIVAL, Long Beach. (562) 570-3204 / www.longbeachseafestival.com, mostly along Ocean Blvd. and Appian Way. This festival runs from June to September and takes place in several areas near the shores of Long Beach. Participants and spectators, landlubbers and seafarers are welcome. Some of the over thirty events include a free fishing rodeo for kids; Moonlight Movies; Oriental cultural craft exhibition; swimming competitions; beach volleyball; a sand sculpture contest (pg. 738) ; day camps for people with disabilities; and boat races. Call or check the web for a schedule of events. Participant fees range according to event; spectators are usually admitted for free.

MARIACHI USA FESTIVAL, Hollywood. (800) MARIACHI (627-4224) or (323) 848-7717 / www.mariachiusa.com; www.hollywoodbowl.org, 2301 N. Highland Ave. at the Hollywood Bowl. This one-day event celebrates family, culture, and tradition. Bring a picnic dinner (note that there are food vendors on site as well) and enjoy Mariachi music, Ballet Folkloric, and a fireworks finale. The four-and-a-half hour performance is given Sat. at 6pm; doors open at 4pm. Tip: Purchase tickets early as the concert is usually sold out. Admission is $46 - $236, depending on seating. Parking is $22-$45. You can also take the Park & Ride shuttle from various parts of the city for $6 round trip if pre-purchased or $10 at the lot. See the Hollywood Bowl website for more info.

MCGRATH FAMILY FARMS, Camarillo. See March entry (pg. 712) for details.

MORRELL NUT & BERRY FARM, Solvang. (805) 688-8969, 1980 Alamo Pintado Road. Fresh, off-the-vine raspberries, olallieberries, boysenberries and blackberries are yours for the picking at this U-Pic farm. Walnuts available mid October through December. Berry season runs June through August; call first. Come pick Thurs. - Sat., 10am - 5pm (closed Mon. - Wed.); Sun., noon - 4pm.

MOVIE NIGHT / OUTDOOR FAMILY FILMS, Many parks offer free, nighttime, out-door family entertainment, G or PG movies. Bring a blanket, picnic dinner, and enjoy a show together! Call your local park for information. Here is a couple of options: Santee Lakes at 9040 Carlton Oaks in Santee, (619) 596-3141 / www.santeelakes.com - 7pm is the time for games and kid's contests, 8pm is the show, parking is $8; and Temecula Berry Company at 39700 Cantrell Rd. Temecula, (951) 225-5552 / www.temeculaberryco.com - their Friday Night movie at the farm begins 8pm.

MOVIES, Movie theaters in the summer often offer incredible bargain rates for G and PG films. UltraStar Movies in San Diego does this. No adults are admitted without a child and the cost is $5 for the entire summer series. Contact www.UltraStarMovies.com for participating theaters. Regal cinemas, www.regalcinemas.com, located all over the Southland, offer a Free Family Film Festival for nine weeks during the summers at 10am on Tuesdays and Wednesdays. AMC Theaters, www.amctheatres.com, at Downtown Disney, Tustin and Torrance offer free features every Wednesday at 10am. The Krikorian Kids' Series offers $1 admission for recent family movies one day a week. See www.kptmovies.com for more info. Harkins Theatres, www.harkinstheatres.com, offer 10 family movies for $5.

PASADENA CHALK FESTIVAL, Pasadena. (626) 795-9100 / www.pasadenachalkfestival.com, 280 East Colorado Boulevard. Chalk it all up to having a good time! Over 600 artists draw marvelous, if temporary, masterpieces out of chalk on the sidewalks of Pasadena at this two-day festival in June or July. A children's chalk area is also set up. Live music and food complete the ambiance. Pull up a piece of sidewalk, Sat. - Sun., 10m - 7pm. Admission is free to watch.

PCPA THEATERFEST, Solvang. (805) 922-8313 - box office; (805) 928-7731 - information / www.solvangtheaterfest.org, 420 2nd St., Solvang at the outdoor Festival Theater and 1100 S. Bradley. In the middle of the quaint town of Solvang, this 750-seat outdoor theater shows plays from mid-June through September. Come watch a musical under the canopy of trees and starlight. Make sure you bring a jacket as summer night air can be unexpectedly chilly. The Theaterfest is a favorite activity for our family for the show and ambiance. See main entry

(pg. 642, 729) for more details. Shows are usually given Wed. - Sun., 8pm, but call for a performance schedule. Prices range, depending on show time, from $31 - $49 for adults; $28 - $44.25 for srs.; $22.25 - $35 for students; $20 - $31.25 for ages 5 - 18 years; children 4 and under are not permitted. Thursday previews are less expensive.

PEARSON PARK AMPHITHEATER, Anaheim. (714) 765-5274 / www.anaheim.net, Lemon and Sycamore sts. The terrific programs put on through the "Just For Kids" series throughout the summer are geared for kids 4 years old through 6th graders. The shows run approximately two hours. Past programs have included Make-a-Circus, magic shows, puppet shows, a wild west show, ballet and jazz troupes, the mad scientist, and audience participation shows with songs or storytellers. Call for specific show information. A concession stand is on site. Fri. shows start at 6:30pm; call for hours for Sat. shows. Tickets usually cost $3 for adults; children 8 and under are free.

REDLANDS BOWL SUMMER MUSIC FESTIVAL, Redlands. (909) 793-7316 / www.redlandsbowl.org, Brookside Ave. between Eureka and Grant sts. Two nights a week, from late June through August, the bowl offers symphony music, jazz, and opera as well as musicals, ballet, and dance ensembles. These are great programs for the family! Note: Don't park in the underground parking since the gates are usually locked at 9pm. Programs are offered Tues. and Fri. evening at 8:15pm and are free - donations are appreciated. Free, forty-five minute music appreciation workshops are given for elementary-aged kids on Tues. at 3pm and Sat. at 10am.

RENAISSANCE PLEASURE FAIRE, Irwindale. See April entry (pg. 718) for details.

SAN DIEGO COUNTY FAIR, Del Mar. (858) 793-5555 - recording; (858) 755-1161 - fairgrounds / www.sdfair.com, 2260 Jimmy Durante Blvd. at the Del Mar Fairgrounds. This major, three-week event features everything wonderful in a county fair - carnival rides; flower and garden shows; gem and minerals exhibits; farm animals; livestock judging; food; craft booths; and a festive atmosphere. Call for a schedule of events. Open Tues. - Thu, 11am - 11pm.; Fri., 11am -midnight, Sat., 10am - midnight; and Sun., 10am - 11pm. Gates and Kids Zone closes 1 hour earlier. Fair close Mon. and first two Tues. Admission is $14 for adults; $8 for srs. and ages 6 - 12 years; children 5 and under are free. Certain activities cost extra. Check the website for discount ticket information. Parking is $10. Free shuttle services from free off-site parking is available.

SAN DIEGO SCOTTISH HIGHLAND GAMES AND GATHERING OF CLANS, Vista. (760)726-3691 or (619) 425-3454 / www.sdhighlandgames.org, 1200 Vale Terrace Dr. at Brengle Terrace Park. For almost thirty years, fifty or so clans have come to participate and enjoy first class entertainment at this gathering. The last weekend in June is the one for Scottish merrymaking, which includes highland dancing, Celtic harping, bagpipe competitions, sheepdog herding trials, athletic competitions (such as caber tossing), a drumming competition, and lots of good food. Open Sat. - Sun., 9am - 5pm. Admission is $14 for adults per day; $10 for srs.; $6 for ages 6 - 16; children 5 and under are free. Ask about two-day passes. Pre-purchased tickets are cheaper. Parking is $4 at Brengle Terrace, or park at Vista High School and take a free shuttle.

SANTA ANITA RACE TRACK CONCERTS, Arcadia. (626) 300-8200 / www.calphil.org, 285 W Huntington Dr at Santa Anita Race Track. The California Philharmonic plays sweet music for six Saturdays that delights older children and adults. Past concerts have included music of Rodgers & Hammerstein (their well-known musicals); Hollywood blockbusters (theme songs from movies); music of Andrew Lloyd Webber; and classical pieces. Kids will be more in tune to the nights that the philharmonic plays music that's familiar or recognizable to them. Concerts are Sat., 7:30pm - 10pm. Gates open at 5:30 for dining and live music. Admission ranges from $20 for lawn spots (no chairs) to $88 for a seat in the conductor's circle.

SAWDUST FESTIVAL, Laguna Beach. (949) 494-3030 / www.sawdustartfestival.org, 935 Laguna Canyon Rd. This three-acre, outdoor arts and crafts festival, with over 180 artisans, goes from the end of June through August (almost simultaneous with the Festival of Arts - see page 732). On-going demonstrations include ceramics, such as throwing pots (so to speak), etching, glass blowing, and more. The Children's Art booth allows kids to create art projects - for free! Family-oriented daytime entertainment includes storytelling and juggling. Nighttime entertainment includes listening and dancing to bands. Restaurants and other food services are on site. Tram service is free. The festival is open daily, 10am - 10pm. Daily admission is $8.50 for adults; $7 for srs.; $4 for ages 6 - 12; children 5 and under are free. A season pass is $18 per person. You can purchase and unlimited pass to this festival the Festival of Arts and the Art-A-Fair, including a day of parking, at www.lagunabeachpassport.com.

SHAKESPEARE BY THE SEA, (310) 217-7596 / www.shakespearebythesea.org, Outdoors, under the stars, free - this is how Shakespeare is meant to be enjoyed. Throughout the summer, usually two plays a season are presented at parks throughout L.A., Orange, and Ventura counties on various nights. Bring a beach chair or blanket (one to sit on and one get warm under) and enjoy the celebrated wordsmith's plays. Most plays start at 7pm but check website. Free,

but donations are appreciated.

SPECIAL OLYMPICS SOUTHERN CALIFORNIA GAMES, Los Angeles. (310) 215-8380 / www.sosc.org, 850 W 37th Street. at University of Southern California. "Let me win, but if I cannot win, let me be brave in the attempt." That is the Special Olympics motto. Come to cheer on hundreds of mentally challenged children and adults as they compete in Olympic-type sports of aquatics, basketball, golf, gymnastics, and more. These are gratifying events to witness. Help run the events if you can volunteer some time. The public also enjoys live entertainment, community exhibits, games, and sports clinics. Games run Sat., 9am - 5pm; Sun., 9am - 5pm, followed by the closing ceremony. Free admission.

SPRING TRACTOR SHOW, Vista. (800) 587-2286 or (760) 941-1791 / www.agsem.com, 2040 N. Santa Fe Ave. at the Antique Gas & Steam Engine Museum. This show is held on two consecutive weekends in June, and again in October. Watch demonstrations of American crafts, farming, log sawing, and blacksmithing, plus see many of the restored tractors in a parade each day at 1pm; a very unusual-looking parade! Join in some of the activities such as hayrides and square dancing, and taste the good, home-cooked food available for purchase. See the main entry (pg. 525) for more information about this museum. Open Sat. - Sun., 9am - 4:30pm. Admission is $10 for adults; $9 for srs.; $7 for ages 6 - 12; children 5 and under are free. Camping, with reservations, is $60 for the weekend and includes admission to the show.

SUMMER CONCERTS, Pasadena. (626) 683-3230 / www.levittpavilionpasadena.org, 87 N. Raymond at Memorial Park at the Levitt Pavilion for the Performing Arts. This park and bandshell are host to over fifty free, evening "concerts" (and shows) during the summer months. Weekly themes encompass Children's nights on Wed., which have included the Bob Baker Marionettes, Circus Skills, West African dancers, Russian folk music, Parachute Express, and others. Thurs. night is World Rhythms; Fri., Dance Beat (from hip hop to Irish); Sat., Musica Latina; and Sun., Jazz and Big Band. Bring your blanket and picnic basket and enjoy the sweet sounds of summer. The concerts are Wed. and Sun., 7pm; Thurs., - Sat., 8pm.

SUMMER MOVIE EXPRESS, See May entry (pg. 724) for details.

SUMMER MUSICALS UNDER THE STARS, Vista. (760) 724-2110 or (760) 639-6199 / www.moonlightstage.com, 1200 Vale Terrace at Brengle Terrace Park at the Moonlight Amphitheater. Four or five Broadway musicals are performed at this outside amphitheater each summer, including one youth theater production. Past performances include *Beauty and the Beast*, *Mary Poppins*, and *Monte Python's Spamalot*. Come see a show under the stars (and moon) and bring a picnic to enjoy on the lawn. Productions run mid-June through mid-September, Wed. - Sun. at 8pm. Call for specific dates and times. Tickets cost between $15 - $52, depending on age of guest and the seat.

SUMMER SOLSTICE PARADE AND FESTIVAL, Santa Barbara. (805) 965-3396 / www.solsticeparade.com, State and Cota sts. to Micheltorenia St. For a really hot time, celebrate the summer solstice with a wacky, goofy, creative, colorful parade. Over 1,000 participants (who pay a fee to participate) dress up in elaborate costumes, incorporating choreographed dancing, giant puppets, people-powered floats, and general silliness. Parade participants can attend workshops in May and June to create their ensembles and get help from artists in residence. Parade watchers grab curb space or set up lawn chairs along the street early. The festival, at Alameda Park, has musical entertainment, drummers, food and refreshment, arts and crafts, storytellers, short theater productions, air bounces, face painting, vendors, and an up-close view of the floats. The parade is at noon on the first Sat. after the summer solstice. The festival is Fri., 4pm - 9pm, Sat., noon - 8pm, Sun., noon - 6pm. Only participants pay an entry fee; admission is free for festival attendees.

SUMMER SOUNDS, Hollywood. (323) 850-2000 / www.hollywoodbowl.com, 2301 N. Highland, at the Hollywood Bowl. For six musically hot weeks, forty-five-minute, somewhat interactive, multi-cultural performances are given at the Bowl on the outside stage in the front Plaza entrance. Bring sunscreen. The performances, which are geared for young children, could incorporate dance, music, storytelling, etc. Past show titles include *Salsa*, *Call of Africa*, *Wild and Crazy Russian Limpopo*, *Everything Celtic Dance Troupe*, and *A Touch of Brass*. An arts and craft project for ages 3 to 10 that pertains to the theme is offered with each performance under a shade awning in the parking lot. Each week brings a different show that is performed twice daily. Shows are Mon. - Fri. at 10am for children 4 and under; 11:15am for ages 5 - 10. Art projects are at 10am for older kids; 11am for younger kids (at least 3 years old). When the orchestra is rehearsing inside the Bowl for a later performance, Summer Sounds visitors are invited to watch the rehearsals at no additional cost. Call for a schedule if you're interested in incorporating the Bowl rehearsal with your experience here. Tickets for Summer Sounds are $7 per person for the seating area. (Babies in laps are free.) There is a $5 materials fee for the art project. Parking is free.

TANAKA FARMS, Irvine. See March entry (pg. 713) for details.

TEMECULA BERRY COMPANY, Temecula. See May entry (pg. 724) for details.

TEMECULA STREET PAINTING/ARTS FESTIVAL, Temecula. (951) 694-6412 / www.temeculaevents.org, Main Street & Town Square in Old Town Temecula. Painting the streets is different than painting the town, especially when it's done with chalk. Come see great works of art on the asphalt created by professionals, and come to see work that simply appeals to proud parents as the festival is open to all participants. Reserve a space or come to look. Entertainment is on-going. Open Fri., 6pm - 9pm; Sat., 8am - 6pm; Sun., 8am - 4pm. Free for artists and the public.

WILL GEER THEATRICUM BOTANICUM, Topanga. (310) 455-3723 / www.theatricum.com, 1419 N. Topanga Blvd. This outdoor theater (dress warmly) produces summertime "edutainment." Family Fundays run June through September. These are programs for young kids featuring name entertainment, such as the Parachute Express. Older audiences enjoy plays such as *The Merry Wives of Windsor* and *St. Joan*. See main entry on page 194. Show times vary. Ticket prices also vary depending on the show, although Kid's Koncerts are usually $8 per person. More mature productions are $13 - $20 for adults; $11 - $14 for srs.; $7 for ages 6 - 12.

- JULY: -

ADVENTURE PLAYGROUND, Huntington Beach. See June entry (pg. 725) for details.

BIG JOHN'S CHERRY ORCHARD, Leona Valley. See March entry (pg. 709) for details.

BIG WORLD FUN FAMILY SERIES AT THE FORD, Hollywood. See June entry (pg. 725) for details.

BRIAN RANCH AIRPORT U-PICK ORCHARD, Llano. See June entry (pg. 725) for details.

CARLSBAD STRAWBERRY COMPANY, Carlsbad. See April entry (pg. 714) for details.

CITRUS CLASSIC BALLOON FESTIVAL, Santa Paula. (805) 525-2057 / www.citrusclassicballoons.com, 18249 East Telegraph Road at Santa Paula Airport Do you glow in the evening? Hot air balloons do. Come join in this two-day festival where more than twenty hot air balloons, of all shapes and sizes, participate in balloon glows on both nights, plus ascensions and races and tethered balloon rides. Other entertainment includes live music; bounces for kids; carnival rides; arts and crafts; vintage and custom car show; vendors; and good food. Fri. 4pm - 11pm; Sat. 6:30am - 11pm. $12 for adults; $7 ages 6 - 14; children 5 and under are free. See website for discount tickets. Park and take a shuttle for free, or pay $7 in the adjacent lot.

COLORADO LAGOON MODEL BOAT SHOP, Long Beach. See June entry (pg. 726) for details.

COMIC-CON, San Diego. (619) 414-1020 / www.comic-con.org, San Diego Convention Center. Simply *Marvel*ous! In*DC*ribable! This four-day, massive comic book convention features comics, graphic novels, original art, toys, movie memorabilia, games, trading cards, clothing, comic book characters, creators (get autographs), film stars, props, shows, and lots more. If a sci-fi, fantasy, and or super hero movie has made it big during the year, there is paraphernalia and models from that movie. The Masquerade, when costumed participants dress up as their favorite comic book characters and compete on Saturday night, is a big event as well, but is geared for older guests. Please note that there are certain elements of adult entertainment at the convention. The edgy components that can make this genre exciting, can also lend itself to scantily clad female models, violent images, etc. Open Wed. night (preview) then Thurs. - Sat., 9:30am - 7pm; Sun., 9:30am - 5pm. These are the hours for the general showroom. Check the website for film showings and other events. Admission on Wed. night is $35 for adults, $16 for srs. and ages 13 - 17, children 12 and under are free; Thurs. - Sat.. is $45 for adults, $23 for srs. and kids; Sun., $30 for adults, $15 for srs. and kids. Tickets are only available online and have been known to sell out months in advance. To purchase tickets you must first become a Comic-Con member, which is free.

CONCERTS, See June entry (pg. 726) for details.

DOWNTOWN HARBOR TROLLEY, Ventura. See May entry (pg. 721) for details.

FESTIVAL OF ARTS / PAGEANT OF THE MASTERS, Laguna Beach. (800) 487-3378 - box office; (949) 494-1145 / www.foapom.com, 650 Laguna Canyon Rd. at Irvine Bowl Park. This event runs from July through August, drawing thousands of visitors. More than 140 artisans and craftsmen display their work here - jewelry, wood crafts, paintings, and more - and at the nearby Sawdust Festival (pg. 730). Kids are particularly drawn to the ongoing demonstrations, such as print making, water color, and Japanese pottery making. Young, aspiring artists should visit the Art Workshop, which is open daily, 11am to 5pm. It supplies free materials for paintings, instruments, paper hat making, and more. The Jr. Art Gallery is juried art work of over 150 school children from Orange County. Kids love looking at other kids' work. Bands play continuously. Call for a schedule of special events. The unique Pageant of the

Masters is comprised of people in full makeup and costume who pose and re-create live "pictures" of well-known art works, both classic and contemporary. Each ninety-second picture is accompanied by a narration and full orchestral music. Note that some of the live art works contain nudity (i.e. real, semi-naked bodies). This one-and-a-half-hour production (with over 250 participants) is staged nightly at 8:30pm. The festival is open daily, 10am - 11:30pm. Pageant tickets range between $15 - $90 per person and includes unlimited festival admission all summer. Festival admission is $7 Mon. - Fri., $10 Sat. & Sun.; students and srs are $4 Mon. - Fri, $6 Sat. & Sun.; children 12 and under, military and Laguna Beach residence are free. Certain activities cost extra. Three-hour-max metered parking is available on the streets, or take a free shuttle from city parking lots on PCH and Laguna Canyon Rd. You can purchase and unlimited pass to this festival (not the pageant), the Sawdust Festival and the Art-A-Fair, including a day of parking, at www.lagunabeachpassport.com.

FIREWORKS and 4th OF JULY SHOWS, Call the recreation departments at your local parks, or call city hall for information. Note: The Hollywood Bowl, (323) 850-2000 / www.hollywoodbowl.org, features a fireworks spectacular, along with outstanding lively music. Channel Islands Harbor in Oxnard, (805) 985-4852 / www.channelislandsharbor.org, has a whole day of fun planned for the family called Fireworks by the Sea. Pony rides, arts, crafts, rock climbing wall, inflatables, water taxi rides, music, parade, and fireworks are just a few of the events.

FLOWER FIELDS / FLOWER FESTIVAL, Lompoc. See June entry (pg. 727) for details.

FREE FISHING DAY, / www.dfg.ca.gov/licensing/fishing/freefishdays.html, One Saturday in July and September there is usually a free fishing day, meaning that no license is required. Call a park or your favorite fishing hole to see if they are participating in this "reel" deal.

FRENCH FESTIVAL, Santa Barbara. (805)-963-8198 / www.frenchfestival.com, 300 W. Alamar at Oak Park. Ooh la la! Join French compatriots across the sea in celebrating Bastille Day (the French Revolution) - or come for the fun of it. Enjoy crepes, decadent pastries, French bread, quiche and escargot (don't tell the kids their more common name) at sidewalk cafes with Parisian ambiance. Continuous, free entertainment on three stages include the Cancan, Moroccan belly dancers, grand opera, Cajun and classical groups, folk dancing, jazz, and cabaret music. Look for artists wearing berets while painting at their easels, as well as mimes, jugglers, accordion players, puppet shows, and storytellers strolling the fair grounds. Kids will also enjoy the large replica of the Eiffel Tower, the classic car show, the poodle parade on Sunday evening, and the wading pool at the park. C'est magnifique! Open Sat. - Sun., 11am - 7pm. Free admission and parking.

GREEK FESTIVAL, Santa Barbara. (203) 795-1347 / www.santabarbaragreekfestival.org, 300 W. Alamar at Oak Park. Come to my big fat Greek festival - well, it's not mine, but it is one of the largest Greek festivals around. Saint Barbara Greek Orthodox Church hosts this party. Baklava, shish-kabob, stuffed grape leaves, gyros, music, authentic Grecian dances, folk dance lessons and demonstrations, and lots of entertainment await festival goers. Open Sat. - Sun., 11am - 7pm. Admission and parking are free.

HOLY SPIRIT FESTIVAL, Artesia. (562) 865-4693 / www.artesiades.org, 11903 Ashworth Ave. at the D.E.S. Plaza. Held for eight days in July, Sunday to Monday, this four-day event celebrates several elements of the Portuguese culture. On Sunday, a grand religious procession is followed by marching bands, food booths (including a free lunch or dinner for every visitor), Mass, and entertainment. Monday night is the three-hour culmination of the festival with bloodless bullfights put on by professional matadors. (Velcro patches are worn by the bull to hold the Velcro tipped spears, but the danger to the matadors still remains.) The festival hours are Fri., 7pm - midnight (which includes the crowning of the festival queen, and then it's mostly a dance); Sat., 5pm - midnight (includes Mass, concert, and dancing); Sun., 11am - midnight; Mon., 6pm - 9pm. Admission is free, except on Mon., when admission is $25 for adults; children 8 and under are free.

INDEPENDENCE DAY CELEBRATION, Torrance. (310) 515-7166 / www.printmuseum.org, 315 W. Torrance Blvd. at the International Printing Museum. Learn a version of how our country got its independence by watching a play in the small theater, *The Confounding Brothers*, featuring Benjamin Franklin, John Adams, and Thomas Jefferson. Attendees also get to print their own keepsake copy of the Declaration of Independence on a colonial press, partake in special crafts, enjoy lunch (hot dogs and apple pie), and take a tour of one of my favorite museums. See pg. 123 for more info on the INTERNATIONAL PRINTING MUSEUM. The Sat. around 4th of July, 10am - 4pm, with performances at 11am and 1pm. Admission is $12 per person, which includes lunch, or $40 for a family of four.

INSECT FESTIVAL, Encinitas. (760) 436-3036 / www.sdbgarden.org, 230 Quail Gardens Dr. at San Diego Botanic Gardens. How about a bug cookie? Or, maybe bug jewelry? This weekend fair also offers live insects and snakes on display, plus crafts, story time, nature walks at the gardens, as well as everything else that could bug guests. Other live

animals, such as snakes, rabbits, owls, and sometimes an anteater or porcupine, come for show and tell, too. See the main entry for information on the gardens (pg. 516). Open Sat. - Sun., 10am - 4pm. Admission allows you to walk around the gardens, as well - $14 for adults; $10 for srs. and students; 8$ children 3 - 12; 2 and under are free. Discount coupons are available online. Parking is $2, or free if four or more people are in the car.

INTERNATIONAL SPEEDWAY, Costa Mesa. See April entry (pg. 716) for details.

KINGSMEN SHAKESPEARE FESTIVAL, Thousand Oaks. See June entry (pg. 728) for details.

LONG BEACH SEA FESTIVAL, Long Beach. See June entry (pg. 729) for details.

LOTUS FESTIVAL, Los Angeles. (213) 485-8745 or (213) 485-1310 / www.laparks.org, Park Ave. and Glendale Blvd. at Echo Park. A blend of Asian and Pacific Island cultures celebrate the symbolism of the lotus flower, which represents divine creative power and purity. All of this at an old-LA. neighborhood park! The park contains a lake filled with an abundance of these flowers in bloom. What a beautiful sight! The lotus stay in bloom until late summer. The two-day festival also usually incorporates music, traditional food, martial arts exhibitions, Polynesian dancing, origami demonstrations, fireworks, dragon-boat races, and children's arts and crafts. One-hour paddle boat rentals are available at the boathouse for $10 for adults and $5 for children. The festival is open Sat., noon - 9pm; Sun., noon - 8pm. Admission is free, although some activities cost.

MCGRATH FAMILY FARMS, Camarillo. See March entry (pg. 712) for details.

MORRELL NUT & BERRY FARM, Solvang. See June entry (pg. 729) for details.

MOVIE NIGHT / OUTDOOR FAMILY FILMS, See June entry (pg. 729) for details.

MOVIES, See June entry (pg. 729) for details.

OLD FORT MACARTHUR DAYS, San Pedro. (310) 548-2631 / www.ftmac.org, 3601 S. Gaffey St. at Angels Gate Park and Fort MacArthur Museum. Multi-period military encampments, set up chronologically, and reenactments, representing time periods from ancient days to modern times, are here on the weekend following the 4th of July weekend. The first event is the Parade of Troops. Observers can mingle with the soldiers and ask questions about their lives, including Roman legionnaires who are in full regalia re-creating a garrison camp circa A.D. 130 - 160. Reenactments of historic military skirmishes can include the Indian wars, the Calvary, both World Wars, and/or the Korean War. There are also marching drills, rifle-loading drills, and firing demonstrations. (It gets loud!) On Sunday, some cannons are shot, too. (More loudness!) Military vehicles are also on the grounds. Bring a sack lunch or purchase food from the vendors. See the Fort MacArthur Museum entry (pg. 109) for more details. Open Sat. - Sun., 10am - 4pm, with skirmishes throughout the day. Admission per day is $10. This includes entrance to the museum, as well.

ORANGE COUNTY FAIR, Costa Mesa. (714) 708-1500 / www.ocfair.com, 88 Fair Dr. at the Orange County Fairgrounds. This huge, twenty-one-day event is great fun for the whole family. There are lots of carnival rides and games; rodeos (that last a few hours); acrobats; headliner concerts; speedway racing; farm animals, featured in shows and races, and to pet; craft booths; exhibits; demonstrations, such as the firefighters combat challenge; and, of course great food. Each day brings new attractions and events. There is so much to see and do that one day might just not be enough! Call or check the website for information on discount days offered during the fair and for the calendar of special events. Open Wed. - Fri., noon - midnight; Sat. - Sun., 10am - midnight; closed Mon. and Tues. Admission is $12 for adults; $7 for srs. and ages 6 - 12; children 5 and under are free. Multi-day passes are available. Discount tickets are available before the fair opens. Parking is $10; a carpool of 4 or more is $3.Most shows cost extra.

PCPA THEATERFEST, Solvang. See June entry (pg. 642, 729) for details.

PEACH PICKING, Sweet, succulent, and juicy - only freshly-picked peaches taste like this. Usually ripe mid-July through early October, contact the following orchards for peaches: •Yingst Ranch, (661) 944-2425 at 35349 80th St. in Littlerock. These 18 acres are open Tues. - Sun., 8am - 5pm. They also sell picked fruit such as apricots, plums, Barlett pears, and Red and Golden delicious apples, in season. •Tyler Family Farm, (661) 724-1735 at 18245 Lancaster Rd. in Lancaster. There are 2,200 dwarf Sprague Last Chance peach trees. The ranch is open Sept. and Oct. daily, 9am - 5pm. •Youngblood Farm, (661) 944-5823 at 7624 East Avenue U in Littlerock. This farm offers fourteen varieties of peaches and two of apples. It is open July through the beginning of November daily, 8am - 1pm. •Brian Ranch Airport U-pick Orchards (pg. 725). Also check www.pickyourown.org for more orchards.

PEARSON PARK AMPHITHEATER, Anaheim. See June entry (pg. 730) for details.

PIRATE DAYS FESTIVAL, Ventura. (805) 642-8538 / www.venturaharborvillage.com, 1500 Spinnaker Dr. at Ventura Harbor Village. This two-day annual festival features pirate reenactors, strolling musicians, a treasure hunt, knott tying and a pirate costume contest. Arrrrr you going to the festival? Of course you arrrrr! Sat. & Sun. 1pm - 4pm. Free, but bring spending money.

RAMONA COUNTY FAIR, Ramona. (760) 789-1311 / www.ramonachamber.com, Aqua Ln. and 5th St. Now this is a good, old-fashioned county fair aided by a rural setting. State fair contests are held with ribbons and prizes in canning, baked goods, science projects, photography, arts and crafts, animal showings, and more. Carnival rides, live entertainment, pie and watermelon eating contest, martial arts demonstrations, vendors, food, and crafts are all part of a *fairly* good day! Note that it is hot here, so bring water and sunscreen. Open Thurs., 5pm - 11pm; Fri., 5pm - midnight; Sat. noon - midnight; Sun. noon - 11pm. General admission is free. Ride wristbands are $15 on Thurs. and Fri.; $18 on Sat. and Sun. at the gate. (Pre-sale prices are cheaper.)

RASPBERRY PICKING, Oak Glen and Moorpark. The tastiest fruits are ones that have just been harvested. Raspberries are usually ripe from mid-July to mid-October. Here is a website - www.oakglen.net - and a few places to call in the Oak Glen area: Los Rios Rancho - (909) 797-1005 / www.losriosrancho.com; Riley's Apple Farm and Log Cabin - (909) 797-4061 / www.rileysapplefarm.com; Riley's Frontier - (909) 790-2364 / www.rileysfrontier.com; Riley's Farm -(909) 797-7534 / www.rileysfarm.com; and Snow Line Orchard - (909) 797-3415 / www.snow-line.com. In Ventura County in Moorpark, call Underwood Family Farms at (805) 529-3690 / www.underwoodfamilyfarms.com. The above entries are also listed in the main section of the book. A great website for finding fruit picking locations all over Southern California is www.pickyourown.org.

REDLANDS BOWL, Redlands. See June entry (pg. 730) for details.

REDLANDS THEATRE FESTIVAL, Redlands. (909) 792-0562 / www.rtfseason.com, Corner of Highland and Cajon in Prospect Park. This outdoor festival has been running for more than 30 years. Each season, that goes the second week of July to the third week of August, features five plays in repertory. Past shows have been *Nunsense*, *Twelfth Night*, *Forever Plaid* and *Man of La Mancha*. The intimate theater sits outside in Prospect Park, and although the festival is in the middle of summer, the evening show times make for more comfortable viewing. The parking is a little way from the theatre which is up a hill, but there is a free tram available for those who want to ride. Guests are encouraged to come early and enjoy a picnic dinner on the grass surrounding the theatre. Note: while most shows are family appropriate, check out any show that you aren't familiar with before bringing kids. Shows start at 8:30pm. Complementary tram service begins at 6:30pm. Admission is $20 for all seats. Student rush is $16, 15 minutes before curtain with ID.

RINGLING BROS. & BARNUM AND BAILEY CIRCUS, Call (800) 745-3000 / www.ringling.com, This is a traditional month for "The Greatest Show on Earth" to come to town. Catch some of the most amazing animal and acrobatic acts ever performed!! Call ahead of time to find out when the parade of circus animals comes through the town. At some locations, come an hour early to participate in free pre-circus activities in the arenas, where visitors can try out a trapeze swing, ride a unicycle (with help), and be a part of a clown act. Some locations have an Animal Open House, too, where guests can see how the animals live, work, and play. Tickets range from $15 - $100, depending on performance date and time, and your seat location.

SANTA ANITA RACE TRACK CONCERTS, Arcadia. See June entry (pg. 730) for details.

SANTA BARBARA COUNTY FAIR, Santa Maria. (805) 925-8824 / www.santamariafairpark.com, 937 S. Thornburg at the Santa Maria Fairpark. Have some family fun at this five-day county fair with the petting zoo; agricultural and livestock exhibits; train rides; top-name entertainment; carnival rides; a Fair Queen Pageant; dancing; booths; Destruction Derby; a rodeo; and much much more. The fair hours are daily, 11am - 10pm; the carnival is open until midnight. Admission is $8 for adults; $6 ages 6 - 11; children 5 and under are free. Pre-sale tickets and season passes are available at a discount. Admission to the Destruction Derby is $12 - $18. Parking is $5.

SANTA BARBARA NATIONAL HORSE SHOW, Santa Barbara. (805) 687-8711 / www.earlwarren.com, Calle Real and Las Positas Rd. at the Earl Warren Showgrounds. *Neigh* doubt about it - this is one of the nation's most highly-regarded horse shows. It takes place on two consecutive, four-day weekends in July. Classes and events include champion hunters and jumpers; American saddle bred; Hackney ponies harnessed to their show buggies; walking horses that strut their stuff; and a Western Horse show. Check the website for a schedule of events. Admission is free.

SAWDUST FESTIVAL, Laguna Beach. See June entry (pg. 730) for details.

SHAKESPEARE BY THE SEA, Se June entry (pg. 730) for details.

SOUTH BAY GREEK FESTIVAL, Redondo Beach. (310) 540-2434 / www.sbgreekfestival.com, 722 Knob Hill at St. Katherine's. Held the first weekend of the month, this thirty-five-year old annual ethnic and religious festival recreates the atmosphere of a Greek fishing village with costumed participants, live Greek music and dancing, fresh-baked pastries, cultural arts and crafts, and food booths. A small kiddie area is on the premises, too. Tours of the church offering insights into Greek Orthodox traditions and Byzantine iconography are also given. I don't know - it's

all Greek to me! Open Fri., 5pm - 10pm; Sat., noon - 10pm; Sun., noon - 9pm. Admission is $2 for adults; $1 for srs.; children 11 and under are free. Check on the website for coupons. Free parking.

STARLIGHT BOWL SUMMER CONCERT SERIES, Burbank. (818) 525-3721 / www.starlightbowl.com, 1249 Lockheed View Dr. Warm summer nights, music wafting through the air, surrounded by family and friends - this is the scene for summer concerts at the bowl. The concerts run the range of musical interests, so check the schedule to see who's playing. Bring a picnic, or purchase food from the indoor cafe or outdoor food court. The season starts with a 4th of July concert (and fireworks) costing $12 - $22 per person for advanced purchases only, and continue through mid-August. Concerts are given on Sun. from 6:30pm - 8:30pm. Gates open at 5:30pm. Admission is $12 for adults; $6 for srs. and ages 3 - 12. Parking is $5. Cash only.

SUMMER MOVIE EXPRESS, See May entry (pg. 724) for details.

SUMMER MUSICALS UNDER THE STARS, Vista. See June entry (pg. 731) for details.

SUMMER SOUNDS, Hollywood. See June entry (pg. 731) for details.

SUMMER SUNSET LUAU ON MISSION BAY, San Diego. (800) 422-8386 or (858) 539-8666 / www.catamaranresort.com/luau, 3999 Mission Blvd. at the Catamaran Resort. You can easily be persuaded that Mission Bay is just like the Hawaiian islands as you enjoy a traditional Hawaiian buffet dinner and beachside show at sunset. After a lei greeting, feast your taste buds on spicy bay shrimp salad; tropical fruit with coconut and grilled pineapple; chicken salad with macadamia nuts; roast Kalua pig; grilled mahi mahi; teriyaki chicken; rice; Hawaiian sweet rolls; and desserts of pineapple flambé with vanilla ice cream; coconut cream pie and fruit tarts; mango sorbet; passion fruit creme brulee; and more. The Pride of Polynesia dancers perform traditional dances - which are so beautiful and graceful to watch - including the hula and one of our favorites, the fire knife performance. Aloha! Enjoy the dinner and show July through August on Fri., 6pm - 9pm. The schedule is as follows: 6pm - 6:45pm, a lei greeting and musical entertainment; 6:45pm - 8pm, a buffet with background music; 8pm - 9pm, the show. Admission is $64 for adults; $29 for ages 5 - 12; children 4 and under are free.

TANAKA FARMS WATERMELON TOURS, Irvine. (949) 653-2100 / www.tanakafarms.com, 5380¾ University Dr. This thirty-acre farm grows all sorts of wonderful crops and offers a variety of tours. This tour includes a guided wagon ride around the working farm, learning about nutrition, tasting select fruits and veggies, and finishing up in the watermelon patch to pick your own. The stand sells pre-picked fresh produce, or you can pick most of the seasonal crops yourself. No reservation needed for weekend tour times every hour from 9:30am to 2:30pm. Must call and reserve for weekday tour times. The farm and stand is open Mon. - Sun., 9am - 5pm. The tour is $17 per person; children 2 and under free.

TEMECULA BERRY COMPANY, Temecula. See May entry (pg. 724) for details.

U.S. OPEN OF SURFING, Huntington Beach. (424) 653-1900 / www.huntingtonbeachevents.com; www.usopenofsurfing.com, Huntington Beach Pier. For over a week, thousands (350,000 or so) flock to the beach as the crowd gets its fill of high competition, world class games. Come see the U.S. Open of Surfing (men's, women's, and jr's); pro beach volleyball; BMX; and skateboarding competitions, plus moto cross demonstrations, concert stages, beach-style fashion shows, and the village (with over 70 vending booths). Wear sunblock. Check the website for a complete schedule of events, which are free to spectators.

VENTURA COUNTY FAIR, Ventura. (805) 648-3376 / www.venturacountyfair.org, 10 W. Harbor Blvd. at Seaside Park. This major event is a week and a half long. The fair offers lots of carnival rides, plus rodeos; pig races; a petting zoo; pony rides; livestock and equestrian events; on-going, first-class entertainment and concerts; and several buildings that have arts and crafts for sale, flower shows, fine arts, gems and minerals, and vendor demonstrations. Whew! The fair is open Mon. - Sun., 11am - 11pm. Carnival opens at noon and closes between 11pm and midnight. A fireworks show is put on nightly at 10pm Sun. - Thurs., and 10:30pm Fri. and Sat. Admission is $12 for adults; $9 for srs. and ages 6 - 12; children 5 and under are free. Rides and certain activities cost extra. Check the website for discount days and coupons. Parking is $10.

VISTA CIVIL WAR REENACTMENT, Vista. See March entry (pg. 713) for details.

WATERMELON FESTIVAL, Pasadena. (818) 353-4554 / www.lionswatermelonfestival.com, 1001 Rose Bowl Dr. Would it surprise you to know there are a lot of watermelon activities here? How about greased watermelon relay races, watermelon-eating and seed-spitting contests and melon-carving demos. But there is also live entertainment, food, carnival rides and games, vendor booths, kids' activities, and, of course, free watermelon samples. 5pm - 10pm; Sat., noon - 10pm; Sun., noon - 10pm. $10 for adults; $5 for ages 3 - 12; Free for children 2 and under. Free parking.

WILL GEER THEATRICUM BOTANICUM, Topanga. See June entry (pg. 732) for details.

YOUTH OUTDOOR SAFARI DAY, Corona. (951) 735-7981 / www.youthsafariday.com, 14995 River Rd. at Mike Raahauge's Shooting Complex. For practice before going on a real safari, to infuse kids with a love for the outdoors, and to introduce or sharpen their skills in recreational shooting, come to Safari Day. Participants can try archery, BB guns, paintball games, and laser shots; go kayaking; make game calls; paint duck decoys; walk through the Sensory Safari Van; and watch shooting exhibitions. (The last few years members of the Olympic Shooting Team have participated.) If that's not enough, kids can fish, chat with mountain men and cowboys in an encampment-type setting, see hawks and falcons up close, and enjoy being outside. The events begin Sat. at 8am sharp. (Preregistration is highly recommended - check the website for forms). The day ends at 3pm. $40 per family ($30 online), which is for 5 people maximum, $10 extra for each additional person. This price includes all the activities, and even lunch.

- AUGUST: -

ADVENTURE PLAYGROUND, Huntington Beach. See June entry (pg. 725) for details.
ANTELOPE VALLEY FAIR, Lancaster. (661) 948-6060 / www.avfair.com, 2551 W. Ave. H at the fair grounds. This ten day af*fair* has all the good stuff - carnival rides, lots of livestock events, a parade, demonstrations from a variety of vendors, booths, great food, and entertainment, including headlining concerts. County fairs are a once-a-year treat. Open during the week around 4pm - midnight; weekends, noon - 1am. Admission is $9 for adults; $7 for srs. and ages 6 - 11; children 5 and under are free. Check the website for discount tickets. Parking is $5.
APPLE PICKING - APPLE LANE FARM, Solvang. (805) 688-5481 / www.applelanesolvang.com, 1200 Alamo Pintado Rd. at Apple Lane Orchards. U-Pic the apples, or just stop by for a bag of freshly-picked fruit. Varieties include gala, golden delicious, red delicious, fuji, and Granny Smith. You know what they say - "An apple a day . . . ." Class tours are available upon request. Open 10am - 5pm during harvest time which is August - October.
ARTWALK NTC @ LIBERTY STATION, San Diego. (619) 615-1090 / www.artwalksandiego.org, 2645 Historic Decatur Rd. This fine art festival brings 16 hours of live music featuring talent from across California. In addition, KidsWalk creates a destination of its own for families; kids can try their hand at various interactive "ARTivities" set to inspire their inner artist to bloom. Bring the whole family and participate in fun, family-friendly art activities ranging from visual art projects to music-making, yoga and more. See MISSION FEDERAL ARTWALK (pg. 717) for a similar event in April. Sat. and Sun., 10am - 6pm. Free Admission
BARONA POWWOW, Lakeside. (619) 443-6612 / www.barona-nsn.gov, 1095 Barona Road, Barona Baseball Field on the Barona Indian Reservation This three-day event, held on Labor Day weekend, will showcase more than 300 Native Americans from across the country competing in traditional Tribal dancing. In addition to beautiful regalia and dancing, spectators will also be able to enjoy the Hand Drum contests, singing and music, authentic Native American cuisine and exquisite handcrafted arts and jewelry. Fri., 6pm-11pm, Gourd Dancing - 6pm; Sat.-Sun., 1pm-midnight, Gourd Dancing - 1pm & 6 pm, Fri.-Sun., Grand Entry - 7pm. Free Admission & Camping on a first come first served basis.
BIG BEAR AIR FAIR, Big Bear City. (909) 585-3219 / www.bigbearcityairport.com, 501 Valley Blvd. at the Big Bear Airport. This bi-annual event takes to the skies for one day. Skydivers make two jumps, at 9am and noon. Keep looking up as vintage aircraft come in for a landing. Back on the ground, there are vintage, static aircraft on display; possibly Blackhawk or Huey helicopters; a U.S. Forestry Service water drop; classic cars; flight simulators; and activities for kids like a bounce house, climbing wall, and inflatable slide. Barbecue food, vendors, and community and military booths complete this fair. Open Sat., 9am - 4pm. $2 per person; free for infants and toddlers in strollers.
BIG BEAR RENAISSANCE FAIRE, Fawnskin. (909) 237-0448 / www.bbvrsinc.org, 39115 Rim of the World Dr. Where hail ye from? Perhaps 16th-century England, as the participants' dress indicates. Merry maids, gentlemen, wenches, knights, and good citizens roam the shire and encampment as the Queen presides over her court. The faire is comprised of four stages of shows; archery tournaments; knights jousting; sword fighting; gypsies belly dancing; Shakespeare's plays presented in shortened versions; birds of prey (from Moonridge Animal Zoo); jugglers; and wandering minstrels. A children's area is set up like a midsummer fairy forest with special activities. Vendors sell pewter steins, potions, Renaissance clothing, swords, and more. Note that bawdy songsters abound. Open first three weekends in August, Sat. - Sun., 10am - 6pm. Admission is $15 per day for adults; $12 for srs., students, and ages 6 - 12; children 5 and under are free. Parking is free
BIG WORLD FUN FAMILY SERIES AT THE FORD, Hollywood. See June entry (pg. 725) for details.
BRIAN RANCH AIRPORT U-PICK ORCHARD, Llano. See June entry (pg. 725) for details.
CAMARILLO AIR SHOW, Camarillo. (805) 419-3530 / www.wingsovercamarillo.com, 555 Airport Way at

Camarillo Airport. Fly bys in the morning and demonstration flights, usually in the afternoon, are highlights of this air show. Other exhibits and activities include WWII warbirds, vintage aircraft, antique farm equipment, over a eighty home-built airplanes, experimental aircraft, custom cars, food vendors, and a kids area with a bounce, a maze, and more. Don't miss touring the AIR GROUP ONE COMMEMORATIVE AIR FORCE WORLD WAR II FLYING MUSEUM (pg. 525) which is on the airfield. Bring a chair and umbrella. Open Sat. - Sun., 9am - 5pm. The air show starts at noon, but vintage plane fly bys start around 9am. Admission is $15 for adults; children 11 and under are free. Parking is free.

CHALK ART FESTIVAL & DOLPHIN DASH, Redondo Beach. (310) 318-0631 / www.redondopier.com, 100 Fisherman's Wharf Come make your own chalk drawing or just look at everyone else's. The event is free to enter and offers prizes in many categories including professional, family and various age groups. For the Dolphin Dash, more than 600 rubber dolphins are dropped into the ocean and "raced" to the shore. The sponsor of the winning dolphin gets a savings bond. Proceeds go to support the library. Chalk Art Festival, 12pm-4pm; Dolphin Dash 4:30 pm. No fee to register for the chalk drawing contest.

CHILDREN'S FESTIVAL OF THE ARTS, Hollywood. (323)871-2787 / www.hollywoodartscouncil.org, 5555 Melrose Ave. Expose kids to arts from around the world with this one-day festival. Attend art workshops and make masks, ribbon shakers, necklaces, puppets, and more. Costumed characters, face painters, and song and dance performances representing Africa, Philippines, America, and several other countries, round out this event. Open Sun., noon - 4:30pm. Admission and the crafts are free.

CIVIL WAR DAYS, Huntington Beach. (714) 842-4481 / hbcivilwar.webs.com, 7111 Talbert Ave. and Golden West Ave. in Huntington Beach Central Park. Live through the Civil War time period, if only for two days. Heralded as one of the best reenactments, come visit with soldiers from the North and South who are authentically dressed in uniform and stay in character throughout the duration. Watch mock battles and wander through the encampments. Open 10am - 4pm. Battles (which get really loud) are Sat. at 1:30pm and 4pm; Sun. at 11am and 2pm. Living history demonstrations follow each battle. A twilight concert follows the 4pm battle on Sat. Church service is Sun. at 9am. Admission is free.

COLORADO LAGOON MODEL BOAT SHOP, Long Beach. See June entry (pg. 726) for details.

CONCERTS, See June entry (pg.726) for details.

DOWNTOWN HARBOR TROLLEY, Ventura. See May entry (pg. 721) for details.

FESTIVAL OF ARTS / PAGEANT OF THE MASTERS, Laguna Beach. See July entry (pg. 732) for details.

FESTIVAL OF SAIL, San Diego. (619) 234-9153 / www.sdmaritime.org, 1492 North Harbor Dr. This Labor Day weekend "rigged" event includes a kids petting zoo, kids craft activities, face painting, beer garden, live on stage entertainment, naval reenactors, arts and craft vendors, plus a multitude of food. Available for an extra fee are Tall Ship cannon battles, mid-day sails, twilight sails, America's Cup sailing experience, and 30 minute bay cruises. Fri. - Sun., 9am - 7pm; Mon., 9am - 5pm. $5 for ages 3 and up, ages 2 and under are free, some activities cost money.

FLOWER FIELDS / FLOWER FESTIVAL, Lompoc. See June entry (pg. 727) for details.

FREE ENTRANCE DAYS IN THE NATIONAL PARKS, See January entry (pg. 704) for details.

GREAT SAND SCULPTURE CONTEST, Long Beach. (562) 477-6820 / www.lbsandcastle.com, The Granada Beach Boat Ramp, 1 Granada Ave. Come see sand sculpture by professionals (how would that look on a resume?) and amateurs. In addition to the sculpture there are arts and crafts, food, live music, vendors, and a kids zone. This is part of the Long Beach Sea Festival (pg. 729). Sat. and Sun., 10am-4pm. Free to come. You must sign up in advance if you want to compete in the contest.

ICE CREAM SOCIAL, Compton. (310) 603-0088 / www.dominguezrancho.org, 18127 S. Alameda St. Come and eat ice cream, what's not to like? Your $5 admission includes a bowl of ice cream and other snacks. You can also play outdoor games including a water balloon toss and "Guess the Flavor", and take a tour of the museum. See DOMINGUEZ RANCHO ADOBE MUSEUM (pg. 106) for more info about this museum. Sun., 12pm - 3pm.

INTERNATIONAL CLOWN WEEK, San Diego. (619) 282-9668 / www.downs.dreamstation.com; www.internationalclownweek.org. Don't stop clowning around! The San Diego All Star Clown Club performs the first week of August in several locations throughout San Diego County. The public is invited to some of these funny functions. Call or check the website for place and time.

INTERNATIONAL SPEEDWAY, Costa Mesa. See April entry (pg. 716) for details.

LA HABRA CORN FESTIVAL, La Habra. (562) 691-3482 / www.lahabracornfestival.com, 201 N. Cypress St. Not to sound corny, but I when I heard about this festival I was all ears. Saturday starts off with a parade at 9:30am,

followed by a carnival with rides, games, music, and food, especially buttery corn on the cob. Shucks, I think you ought to come to this country fair. Open the first weekend in August, Fri., 5:30pm - 11pm; Sat., 11m - 11pm; Sun., 12m - 9m. Admission is free, but rides and some activities cost money.

LONG BEACH GREEK FESTIVAL BY THE SEA, Long Beach. (562) 494-8929 / www.lbgreekfest.org, 5761 E. Colorado St. at the Assumption of the Blessed Virgin Mary Greek Orthodox Church Authentic Greek dance groups, free Greek dance lessons, authentic Greek food and Greek pastries, Greek cooking lessons, snacks, full meals and beverages, vendor booths, childrens area, carnival rides and more. Opa! Labor Day Weekend Sat. - Mon., Noon - 9pm. Admission $3, Children 11 and under are free.

LONG BEACH SEA FESTIVAL, Long Beach. See June entry (pg. 729) for details.

LOS ANGELES IRISH FAIR AND MUSIC FESTIVAL, Long Beach. (562) 618-5558 / www.la-irishfair.com, 1126 Queens Hwy at Queen Mary Event Park Coming to this weekend festival is like finding gold at the end of a rainbow. Ten entertainment stages feature Irish bands and Irish dancing. (I really enjoy the dogging.) Other activities and events include sheep herding demonstrations; Leprechaun Village with rides for wee ones; storytelling; equestrian exhibitions; food; a parade (each day at noon); dance workshops; an Ancient Irish Village; a market place; a Celtic arts center; and Scottish games, including the original extreme sport - caber tossing. (Who thought of this sport?! And why?) Other games include weight, stone, and hammer tossing. Open Sat. - Sun., 10am - 6pm. Admission is $16 for adults; $14 for srs. and students; $5 for children 6-10; children 5 and under are free. A 2 day pass is $25. Parking is $17. Tip: Very limited free parking is available on Queensway Dr. and Harbor Plaza in front of the park.

LOS OLIVOS QUICK DRAW and ARTS FESTIVAL, Los Olivos. (805) 688-1222 / www.losolivosca.com, Los Olivos Park. Not really similar to the quick draw of the Old West, talented artists at Los Olivos must complete a drawing, painting, or sculpture within sixty minutes. (Bronzes are finished at the foundry.) You get caught up in the moment(s) and can't wait to see the outcome. A live auction (gavel and all) for the completed works immediately follows. Enjoy a barbecue in the park, musical entertainment, afternoon sculpture demonstrations, receptions at participating galleries, and browsing around the town. The Sat. festival begins at 10am; the drawing commences from 11am - noon. The work is then framed and auctioned off at 12:30pm; BBQ and live music 2pm to 5pm; Artwalk 1pm to 6pm; demonstrations 2pm - 6pm. Free admission.

MANHATTAN BEACH OPEN, Manhattan Beach. / www.themanhattanbeachopen.com, just south of the Manhattan Beach Pier Called the "Wimbledon of Beach Volleyball", this tournament features top players from all over the world. Fri., Sat., and Sun., 9am - 5pm. Admission is free.

MORRELL NUT & BERRY FARM, Solvang. See June entry (pg. 729) for details.

MOVIE NIGHT / OUTDOOR FAMILY FILMS, See June entry (pg. 729) for details.

MOVIES, See June entry (pg. 729) for details.

MUD MANIA, Long Beach. (562) 570-1755 / www.rancholoscerritos.org, 4600 Virginia Rd. at Rancho Los Cerritos. Get down and dirty at this one-day event. Stomp around in an adobe mud pit, make real adobe bricks, participate in mod relay races, sculpting, archeological adventures, and help whitewash the adobe oven. Tip: Bring a change of clothing and towels - shoes are required. Refreshments and live musical entertainment round out the day. Open Sun., 12:30pm - 4:30pm. Admission is $6 for adults; $4 for ages 4 - 12; children 3 and under are free.

NISEI WEEK JAPANESE FESTIVAL, Los Angeles. (213) 687-7193 / www.niseiweek.org, 244 S. San Pedro St. in Room 303. In Little Tokyo. This two weekend festival, the biggest Japanese festival of the year, takes place at several locations throughout Little Tokyo. A sampling of events and exhibits include martial arts demonstrations, traditional Japanese dancing, games, arts and crafts, Sumo wrestling, hoops tournament, fashion show, Taiko drumming (on huge drums), tofu tasting, calligraphy, bonsai arrangements, and a grand parade with floats held on first Sun. of the event. Most of the activities and programs occur on the weekends, Sat.,10am - 6pm; Sun., 10am - 4pm. Call for a schedule of events. Admission is free, although some activities cost.

NORCO MOUNTED POSSE PRCA RODEO, Norco. (951) 371-1204 / www.norcoprcarodeo.com, 3737 Crestview Ave. This PRCA (Professional Rodeo Cowboys Association) event not only offers bull riding, barrel racing, bareback and bronco riding, team roping, and steer wrestling but also has cowboy dances, music, vendors, and food. On Sun. there is free Cowboy church in the stands at 10am. and at 5pm there is a Challenged Children's Rodeo. Fri. & Sat., gates open at 5pm, rodeo at 7:30; Sun., open at 4pm, rodeo at 6:30pm. Fri. & Sun., admission is $17, children 8 and under free; Sat., admission is $20, children 3 and under free.

OLD SPANISH DAYS FIESTA, Santa Barbara. (805) 962-8101 / www.sbfiesta.org, multiple locations throughout Santa Barbara. This major five-day Santa Barbara party is kicked off Wednesday night with "Little Fiesta" at Mission

Santa Barbara, where a program of early Californian, Spanish and Mexican song and dance features dancers, clicking castanets, and more. Bring lawn chairs. A highlight of the fiesta is the Friday parade. Participants include the queen and her court; mounted color guards; marching bands; colorfully-costumed equestrian riders; numerous antique carriages and wagons; Native American groups; Spanish Colonial reenactors; costumed dancers; and historical figures on elaborate floats decorated with fresh flowers. The parade begins at the corner of Cabrillo Blvd. and Castillo St. at noon. Grab a spot or, for a reserved seat at $15 per person. On Saturday at 10am, the Children's Parade has niñas and niños in fiesta attire parade down State Street in home-constructed wagons and carts that are pushed and pulled by dogs, parents, and siblings. Open-air market places (in De La Guerra Plaza in downtown Santa Barbara and other locations) feature music, dancing, and authentic Mexican and Spanish food. The carnival, located at Mackenzie Park, is open 11am to 10pm daily with rides, midway games, and attractions. Other fair features include a weekend craft fair (10am - 7pm); and a tribute to Vaqueros (i.e. California's cowboys) at the Earl Warren Showgrounds via afternoon and nighttime rodeos with bull and bronc riding, barrel racing, team penning, steer wrestling, and stock horse classes. Watch cowkids do some mutton bustin', and wild cow milking, too. Call (805) 688-5093 / www.sbfiestarodeo.com for more information regarding the rodeo events, running Thurs. - Sun. There is admission charged to some of the performances, generally $15 - $20 for adults and $10 - $15 for children ages 2-11, but there are many free events as well. Nightlife at the sunken gardens of the County Court House showcases a free variety shows of mariachis, flamenco dancers, Mexican folklorico dancers in colorful regional costumes, and other Latin-flavored music. Bring blankets for lawn seating. Again, many of the events are free.

PCPA THEATERFEST, Solvang. See June entry (pg. 642, 729) for details.

PEACH PICKING, See July entry (pg. 734) for details.

PEAR PICKING, Oak Glen. (909) 790-TIME (8463) or (909) 797-7534 / www.rileysfarm.com, 12261 S. Oak Glen Blvd. at Riley's Farm. More flavorful than store bought, Bartlett pears are ready for picking here mid-August to October Mon. - Thurs., 10am - 4pm.; Fri., 10am - 5pm; Sat., 9am - 4pm.

PEARSON PARK AMPHITHEATER, Anaheim. See June entry (pg. 730) for details.

RANCHO MISSION VIEJO PRCA RODEO, San Juan Capistrano. (949) 240-3363 / www.rmvrodeo.com, 30753 La Pata Ave. at Oaks Blenheim Rancho Mission Viejo Riding Park. Ride 'em cowboy - the rodeo's back in town! See bareback riding, saddle bronc riding, bull riding, tie-down roping, team roping, steer wrestling, rodeo clowns, and more at this two-day, large purse (i.e. lots of prize money!) rodeo. There is also a vendor area with shopping, games (like a mechanical bull and rock climbing), and food. Gates open Sat. at 2pm, the rodeo begins at 4pm, and a concert starts at 6pm. Gates open Sun. at 11:30am and the rodeo begins at 1:30pm. Admission is $25 for adults; $10 for ages 4 - 12; children 3 and under are free. Parking is $5.

RASPBERRY PICKING, See July entry (pg. 735) for details.

RINGLING BROS. & BARNUM AND BAILEY CIRCUS, See July entry (pg. 735) for details.

ROBOTICS BY THE SEA, San Pedro. (310) 548-7562 / www.cabrillomarineaquarium.org, 3720 Stephen M. White Dr. This yearly event showcases underwater remotely operated vehicles (ROVs). Also included are demonstrations by local high school robotics clubs, information about land and underwater ROVs, and opportunities to drive an underwater ROV through an obstacle course. Third Sat. of the month, 11am - 3pm. Free

SAN CLEMENTE STREET FESTIVAL, San Clemente. (949) 492-1131 / www.scchamber.com, 3720 Stephen M. White Dr. This festival has everything - food and games booths, live entertainment, contests, a salsa challenge, arts and craft exhibits, a business exposition, children's activities and a classic car & motorcycle show. Second Sun., 9am - 7pm. Free admission and parking.

SANTA ANITA RACE TRACK CONCERTS, Arcadia. See June entry (pg. 730) for details.

SAWDUST FESTIVAL, Laguna Beach. See June entry (pg. 730) for details.

SHAKESPEARE BY THE SEA, Se June entry (pg. 730) for details.

STARLIGHT BOWL SUMMER CONCERT SERIES, Burbank. See July entry (pg. 736) for details.

SUMMER MOVIE EXPRESS, See May entry (pg. 724) for details.

SUMMER MUSICALS UNDER THE STARS, Vista. See June entry (pg. 731) for details.

SUMMER SOUNDS, Hollywood. See June entry (pg. 731) for details.

SUMMER SUNSET LUAU ON MISSION BAY, San Diego. See July entry (pg. 478, 736) for details.

TEHACHAPI MOUNTAIN FESTIVAL, San Clemente. (661) 822-4180 / www.tehachapimountainfestival.com, 3720 Stephen M. White Dr. This event takes place throughout Tehachapi and includes a PRCA rodeo, an arts and

crafts show, a carnival, 5K & 10K runs, Thunder on the Mountain Car Show, food, live entertainment and more. Call or see the website for times, places, events and prices.

TEMECULA BERRY COMPANY, Temecula. See May entry (pg. 724) for details.

TIKI BEACH FESTIVAL, Belmont Shore. (562) 477-6820 / www.alfredosbeachclub.com, 5101 E Ocean Blvd. Like taking a tropical vacation, come experience hundreds of Polynesian dancers, musicians, and fire dancers perform on stage while you sample ono' (delicious) Hawaiian food, shop the island marketplace, check out a tiki museum, and watch outrigger canoe races. Free admission.

VENTURA COUNTY FAIR, Ventura. See July entry (pg. 736) for details.

WHALE FIESTA, San Pedro. (310) 548-7562 / www.cabrillomarineaquarium.org, 3720 Stephen M. White Dr. Celebrate the migration of the Pacific gray whale and the beginning of whale watching season. Enjoy the games, arts and crafts, puppet shows, food and gift vendors, guest speakers, music, sand sculpture contest and duct tape whale sculpture contest. Sun., 10am - 4pm. Free

WILL GEER THEATRICUM BOTANICUM, Topanga. See June entry (pg. 732) for details.

WORLD BODYSURFING CHAMPIONSHIP, Oceanside. (310) 924-5111 / www.worldbodysurfing.org, 1540 Harbor Drive S. at Oceanside Harbor, near the pier. This two-day event has been happening for over two decades! More than 300 participants, including several from foreign countries, equipped with swim fins are judged on length of ride, style, and tricks such as barrel rolls and somersaults. Contestants must be at least 12 years old to enter. Held Sat., 7am - 1pm; the semi-finals and finals are held on Sun., 7am - 3pm. Admission to watch is free; $25 to participate.

- SEPTEMBER: -

ANTELOPE VALLEY FAIR, Lancaster. See August entry (pg. 737) for details.

APPLE PICKING - APPLE LANE ORCHARDS, Solvang. See August entry (pg. 737) for details.

APPLE PICKING - CALICO RANCH, Julian. (858) 586-0392 or (760) 765-3620 / www.calicoranch.com, 4200 Hwy. 78. This twenty-acre apple orchard is one of the only U-Pic orchards left in the Julian area. It boasts of 130 different kinds of apples, although the rarer types have only one tree here. Visitors may enter the orchards to pick apples, or purchase a wide variety of just-picked apples, and sometimes gallons of fresh apple cider (depending on the year). Purchase pre-picked pecks at less per peck than personally picking them (say that five times fast), but then you lose out on the joy of actually picking the apples. The season is short, but tasty - it begins towards the end of September and most of the crop is gone by the beginning of November. The ranch is open seasonally Sat. - Sun., 10am - 4pm. Call first. The cost of the apples - $10 for a ½ peck bag (equal to the volume of a gallon) if you pick.

APPLE PICKING - OAK GLEN, Oak Glen. See the main entry for Oak Glen on page 401. The season runs from mid-September through mid-November.

ARTSPLASH, Carlsbad. (760) 436-2828 / www.carlsbadartsplash.org, Armada Dr., above the flower fields. This free, two-day family event brings together 100 chalk artists who transform regular streets into a visual art gallery - these renditions are incredible! Kids can "purchase" their own square to draw on, too. Other art mediums are represented here as well. A children's area has storytelling and face painting; the stage hosts on-going musical entertainment; and street performers do their thing. Open Sat., 10am - 6pm; Sun., 10am - 5pm.

BANANA FESTIVAL, Port Hueneme. (805) 253-2282 / www.bananaportfest.com, 105 E Port Hueneme Rd. at the Port of Hueneme This festival might *apeel* to you. You will find something here for everyone with live bands, arts and crafts, port tours, educational displays, great food, and, of course, bananas! The kids area features bounce houses, games, a climbing wall, animals and an interactive experience from GULL WINGS CHILDREN'S MUSEUM (pg. 685). Open Sat., 10am - 5pm. Free admission and parking.

BANNING STAGECOACH DAYS, Banning. (951) 849-5290 / www.stagecoachdays.net, 2107. Victory Street at Dysart Park. Commemorating the city as one of the major stops on the transcontinental stagecoach route, this three-day festival pulls out all the stops and features a carnival all four days, and a parade on Saturday at 10am, plus shootouts, dances, Old West-themed gun fights and costume competition, living history encampment, crafts, food, rodeo and junior rodeo. Always weekend after Labor Day, Open Fri., 5pm - 11pm; Sat. 11am - 11pm; Sun., 11am - 9pm. Fri. adults $4, ages 12 and under $2. Sat. - Sun., adults $6, kids $4.

BRIAN RANCH AIRPORT U-PICK ORCHARD, Llano. See June entry (pg. 725) for details.

CABRILLO FESTIVAL, Point Loma. (619) 557-5450 / www.cabrillofestival.org, Ballast Point, Naval Base Point Loma, south end of Rosecrans Street. Journey back in time to commemorate the life and times of Juan Cabrillo, one of

the first explorers of California. Partake in a living history encampment as authentically-dressed Spanish soldiers and sailors from the 16th century give history talks and just live their 16th century lives. You can also enjoy colorful folkloric dancing and music; cultural demonstrations; watching a narrated reenactment of Cabrillo's landing at 1pm; observing weaving and knife-making; and sampling food from Mexico, Portugal, Spain, and Native America. See page 498 for more details on the park and museum. Open Sun., 11am - 4pm. Admission is free. Parking is $5.

CALICO DAYS, Yermo. (800) TO-CALICO (862-2542) / www.calicotown.com, 36600 Ghost Town Rd. at Calico Ghost Town. During a weekend in September or October, relive Calico's glory days and enjoy music, old prospectors burro run, miner's triathlon and more. Walk around the town itself and enjoy its many attractions. See CALICO GHOST TOWN (pg. 433) for more details. Open 9am - 5pm. Admission is $10 for adults; $5 for ages 6- 15 years; children 5 and under are free. On-site camping (minimum 2 nights) is $35 - $40 a night (camping for this weekend books up months in advance); $45 a night for cabins.

CALIFORNIA LEMON FESTIVAL IN GOLETA, Goleta. (805) 967-2500 / www.lemonfestival.com, 7050 Phelps Road at Girsch Park. When life gives you lemons, make lemonade, or lemon chicken, lemon meringue pie, lemon cotton candy, and many other puckery creations. Besides citrus-flavored food, enjoy pony rides; moon bounces; mini golf; police and fire safety and action demonstrations; arts and crafts; a classic car and motorcycle show; vending booths; and bands - country, folk, bluegrass, and pop. Open Sat., 10am - 6pm; Sun., 10am - 5pm. Admission is free.

COIN & COLLECTIBLES EXPO, Long Beach. See January entry (pg. 703) for details.

CONSTITUTION DAY CELEBRATION, Torrance. (310) 515-7166 / www.printmuseum.org, 315 W. Torrance Blvd. at the International Printing Museum. Guests will be able to experience how the Constitution came about by participating as delegates to the Constitutional Convention of 1786 in the Museums' Heritage Theater. Ben Franklin and James Madison help the delegates reach decisions on issues, resulting in the signing of the Constitution. Readers must have 5th grade level reading skills and up. There will also be guided tours and demonstrations. See pg. 123 for more info on the INTERNATIONAL PRINTING MUSEUM. Sat.,10am - 4pm, with performance at 11:30am. Admission is $8 Adults, $7 Students/Seniors 55+.

DANISH DAYS, Solvang. (805) 688-6144 or (800) 468-6765 / www.solvangusa.com, downtown Solvang. Velkommen! Danish Days are good not just for eating Danish, although you must try the aebleskivers, but to celebrate this colorful heritage with old world customs and pageantry. Expect and enjoy lots of folk dancing demonstrations by costumed participants; music; parades (one on Saturday afternoon and a children's one on Sunday); food; a Kids Korner at Solvang Park with games and shows; craft demonstrations, such as woodcarving, paper cutting, dog painting, and making Christmas ornaments; and everything else Danish that can be packed into this three-day festival. Two other note-worthy events that occur at this time are the wonderful PCPA outdoor theater presentations and a (free) visit to the Elverhoj Museum. Look in the SOLVANG entry (pg. 639) for more things to do while here. Open the third weekend in September, Fri. 4pm - 9pm; Sat., 8:30am - 11pm; Sun., 8:30am - 4:30pm. Free admission to most activities.

E HULA MAU, Long Beach. (562) 436-3661 / www.ehulamau.org, 300 E. Ocean Blvd. at the Terrace Theater of the Long Beach Convention Center. Come and treat yourself to an authentically Hawaiian experience that includes hula and chant competitions, food of the islands, and vending booths. The hula is poetry in motion and the competition is both soothing and fun to watch. Cultural workshops for both traditional and contemporary arts, including the hula and slack-key guitar, are $5 - $45 per person, per workshop. Make leis, jewelry, gourd nose flutes, and more. The festival and competition is held the four days of Memorial Day weekend, Fri. noon - midnight; Sat., 8am - midnight; Sun., 8am - midnight; Mon., 9am - 4pm. Admission is $20 per day. Parking is $10.

ENCINITAS OKTOBERFEST, Encinitas. (760) 753-6041 / www.encinitasoktoberfest.com, Mountain Vista Drive and El Camino Real. This festival includes music, Bavarian dancers, a street craft faire featuring over 200 vendors, a family food and refreshment tent, a family fun zone with children's games and family oriented activities. 3rd Sunday in September; Sun., 10am -5pm; ceremonial parade noon. Admission and parking are free.

ENGLISH MOTORS AT FAIRBROOK, Fallbrook. (760) 728-0101 / www.englishmotorsatfairbrook.org, 4949 South Mission Rd. A unique gathering of fine English motor cars and motor bikes, nestled in the Fallbrook hills at Fairbrook Farms, a beautiful twenty-five acre horse ranch. Along with the 250 cars and motorcycles, there are also food and automotive-related booths. Sun., 10am - 3pm. Admission and parking are free.

FALL HARVEST FESTIVAL, Moorpark. (805) 529-3690, 3370 Sunset Valley Rd. at Underwood Family Farms. See October entry (pg. 748) for details.

FESTIVAL OF CHILDREN, Costa Mesa. (877) 492-KIDS (5437) / www.festivalofchildren.org, 333 Bristol St. at

South Coast Plaza. This month-long immersion in arts, culture, and philanthropy involves more than 75 Southern California organizations and local charities. The events, which mostly occur on the weekends (and some Fridays) from noon - 5pm, could include musical and dance performances (Irish, ballet, folk, etc.); art displays; guest appearances by celebrities; exotic animal presentations; health information; cultural presentations; storytelling; circus acts; arts and crafts for kids to make; costumed character appearances; and marionette shows - a bonanza of free activity!

FESTIVAL OF PHILIPPINE ARTS AND CULTURE, San Pedro. (213) 380-3722 / www.filamarts.org, 807 West Paseo Del Mar at Pt. Fermin Park Filipino-cultural celebration with live music, dance performances, comedians, martial arts, contests, dancing, Pinoyvisions films, youth parade, arts and crafts, and Filipino and other Asian cuisine and shopping. Sat. and Sun., 10am - 6pm. Admission $9, children 4 and under are free.

FLEET WEEK / CORONADO SPEED FESTIVAL, San Diego. (619) 858-1545 / www.fleetweeksandiego.org, Naval Air Base on Coronado and throughout San Diego. This tribute to the military, over a few week period, includes activities such as Boot Camp challenge, and Naval ship tours. Guests over 16 years must have a valid government photo ID. The weekend Coronado Speed Festival features over 225 vintage race cars, chosen for authenticity and historical significance, that race a 1.7 mile course on the Naval Air Station North Island in eight classes. Fans are invited to tour the pits and speak with drivers afterwards. A car show is also held on the grounds. Fleet Week coincides with the Miramar Air Show (pg. 752). Check the website for details on specific events, times, places, and prices. The naval tours are held on Sat. and Sun., 10am - 4pm. The Speed Festival is 8am - until the last race. Some events are free, such as the naval tours. The Speed Festival is $25 (in advance, $35 at the gate) for a one-day pass for adults; children 12 and under are free.

FREE ENTRANCE DAYS IN THE NATIONAL PARKS, See January entry (pg. 704) for details.

FREE FISHING DAY, / www.dfg.ca.gov/licensing/fishing/freefishdays.html. One Saturday in July and September there is usually a free fishing day, meaning that no license is required. Call a park or your favorite fishing hole to see if they are participating in this *reel* deal.

GRACEFEST, Palmdale. (661) 942-4111 / www.gracefestav.com, 2723 Rancho Vista Blvd. at the Palmdale Amphitheater Gracefest presents headline Christian music artists, Christian merchants and worldwide compassion ministries. The kid's area provides supervised fun, games and activities for the kids. The Prayer Tent offers many exciting speakers and ministries presenting their programs and messages. Fri., 5pm - 8pm Prayer Rally; Sat., 11am - 9pm. Admission is Free on Fri., Sat. $25 for adults, $10 ages 13 - 19; 12 and under free. Parking is free.

GRAPE DAY PARADE AND FESTIVAL, Palmdale. (760) 743-8207 / www.escondidohistory.org, Grand Avenue and 321 N. Broadway at Grape Day Park The day starts with a 5K run, then there is the historic parade down Grand Ave. After this enjoy the free festival which includes grape stomping, an entertainment stage, vendor booths, a fun zone and free grapes. Sat., 5k run 7:30am, parade 9:30am, festival 9:30am-4pm. Admission and parking are free. There is a fee for the 5K run.

GREEK FESTIVAL, Cardiff-by-the-Sea. (760) 942-0920 / www.stsconstantinehelen.com, 3459 Manchester Ave. Park at the adjoining Mira Costa College. Live Greek music and dancing, Greek cuisine, like dolmathes (i.e. stuffed grape leaves), tiropites (cheese pita), Greek caviar dip and baklava, games, a bazaar, a live auction, and craft booths are a few of the goings-on at this weekend festival. Church tours of Saints Constantine and Helen Greek Orthodox Church are given as requested. The festival is Sat., 10am - 10pm; Sun., 11am - 9pm. Admission is $3 for adults; free for children 11 and under. Free parking.

HALLOWEEN HARVEST FESTIVAL, Woodland Hills. (818) 999-6300 / www.halloweenharvestfestival.com, 20800 Victory Blvd. at Pierce College. This is the season and this festival has it all. A good-sized pumpkin patch; haunted house; hayrides; a petting zoo (1 ticket); kids' activities; scale train ride (2 tickets); carousel (2 tickets); bounces and inflatable slides (1 ticket); bungee bounce (4 tickets); pony rides (2 tickets); bumper boats (2 tickets); gemstone mining (3 tickets); and an elaborate, five-acre corn maze (child 4 tickets, adults 5 tickets) all in a farm-like setting. The Fright Fair, with a huge Factory of Nightmares Haunted House ($13), a two-acre haunted trail called Creatures of the Corn ($13), and nighttime corn maze ($13), for teens and older, begins after 7pm on selected nights. Field trips for schools and other groups are $7 per student and include learning how pumpkins grow (teachers - pick up a curriculum packet); a live stage show; hay ride or corn field maze; pick your own pumpkin; and popcorn. Add a slice of pizza for $3 more per person. Open the end of Sept. through October, Sun. - Thurs., 10am - 10pm; Fri. - Sat., 10am - midnight. General admission is $5 per person; children 2 and under are free. Daytime corn maze is $10 for adults; $8 for children. For $20 per person you get admission, plus 12 activity tickets that can be used at all the rides and attractions for the day. Extra ride tickets are $2 each, or 6 for $10.

"HART" OF THE WEST POW WOW, Newhall. (661) 298-3014 / www.hartmuseum.org, 24151 San Fernando Rd. at the William S. Hart Park and Museum. This celebration of "California is a nation" encompasses many facets of the Old West and usually takes place the last full weekend of the month. A Pow Wow, held at the large picnic area, begins 10am with the Grand Entry, followed by the Blessing, and ongoing dancing (with narration and interpretation) from each of the Indian nations. Native American regalia are for sale at booths. Mountain men, set up in encampments next to the Pow Wow, show how people lived in the mid 1800's, by using period tools, campfire cooking, and display booths. There are also demonstrations for children and adults, Native American storytellers and crafts. Parking is tight. See the entry for this museum (pg. 157) for more information. The celebration hours are Sat. - Sun., 10am - 6pm. Admission is free. Crafts $3 per person. Parking $5 at park, free on the street. You're welcome to bring a blanket and a picnic lunch.

INTERNATIONAL SPEEDWAY, Costa Mesa. See April entry (pg. 716) for details.

JULIAN GRAPE STOMP FESTA, Julian. (760) 765-1857 / www.julianca.com, 1150 Julian Orchards at the Menghini Winery. For one juicy Saturday enjoy a bunch of fun and stomp around in a ton (literally) of grapes - and yes, this means you. Your feet are first sterilized in a vat of vodka and then you can squish the grapes between your toes. (This wine is not sold commercially!) Other activities include listening to Italian bands, dancing, playing Bocce ball (an Italian lawn game), participating in arts and crafts, and sampling wine (this last part is not for children, obviously). Open 11am - 7pm. Admission is $10 for adults; $5 for ages 6 - 20; bambinos 5 and under are gratis (free).

L.A. GREEK FESTIVAL, Los Angeles. (323) 737-2424 / www.lagreekfest.com, 1324 S. Normandie Ave. at Saint Sophia Greek Orthodox Cathedral. This fest features authentic Greek food (sample souvlaki, baklava, gyros, and more); music; traditional folk dances; theatrical performances; cooking demonstrations; Kid's Arcade; game booths; and a marketplace. Open Fri., 5pm - 11pm; Sat., 1pm - 11pm; Sun., noon - 10pm. Admission is $3 on Fri. per person; Sat. - Sun. $5 for adults, $3 for ages 4-12; free for srs. and children 3 and under.

LIVE OAK CANYON PUMPKIN PATCH, Yucaipa. See October entry (pg. 750) for details.

LOBSTER FESTIVAL, San Pedro. (310) 798-7478 / www.lobsterfest.com, 1100 Nagoya Way at Ports O' Call Village. "Here lobster, lobster." A Lobster Call is one of the activities at the three-day festival. (Do they really come?) Street performers, which are always entertaining to watch, lots of musical performances, a kid's area with some games and crafts, and pirate camp *arrrr* some of the things that add to the fun. The *maine* attraction is, of course, the Maine lobster meals - 1.25 oz. of lobster. Other food choices are available, too. Open Fri., 5pm - 11pm; Sat., 11am - 11pm; Sun., 11am - 7pm. General admission is $10 for adults; children 11 and under are free. Coupons are available online.

LOMBARDI'S RANCH, Saugus. See October entry (pg. 751) for details.

LONG BEACH LOBSTER FESTIVAL, Long Beach. (562) 495-5959 / www.originallobsterfestival.com, 400 Shoreline Village Dr. This festival feature live Maine lobsters (of course), live entertainment, storytelling, a giant food court, and a children's stage. Fri., 5pm -11pm; Sat., noon - 11pm; Sun., noon - 10pm. $15 for adults, 12 and under free, does not include food. Packages available that include a lobster feast. Discounts available on-line.

LONG BEACH SEA FESTIVAL, Long Beach. See June entry (pg. 729) for details.

LOS ANGELES COUNTY FAIR, Pomona. (909) 623-3111 / www.lacountyfair.com, 1101 W. McKinley Ave. at Fairplex. Billed as the world's largest county fair, this four-week event is wonderful (and exhausting). It has lots of carnival rides and games, workshops, pig racing, goat and cow milking demonstrations, country contests, headliner concerts, livestock shows, petting zoo, horse-racing, flower and garden shows, music, dancing, booths, and several long buildings filled with exhibits and truly unique items and products for sale. You can also visit the nearby WALLY PARKS NHRA MOTORSPORTS MUSEUM (pg. 155). Come early and plan to spend the whole day - there is a lot to see and do (and buy!). Teachers - ask about the free Fairkids field trips. These field trips comes with curriculum that focus on particular aspects of the fair, such as animals or history, and allow students to enjoy a free day at the fair. Call (909) 865-4075 for more information. Fair hours are Wed., noon - 10pm; Thurs., noon - 11pm; Fri., noon - midnight; Sat., 10am - midnight; Sun., 10am - 10pm. Closed Mon. and Tues., but open Labor Day Mon. Regular admission Wed. - Fri. is $12 for adults; $8 for ages 6 - 12; children 5 and under are free. Admission Sat., Sun. and Labor Day is $19 for adults; $15 srs.; $12 for ages 6 - 12. Call or check the website for discounts. Certain activities cost extra. Parking is $12 Wed. - Fri.; $15 Sat., Sun. and Labor Day.

LOS ANGELES KOREAN FESTIVAL, Los Angeles. (562) 495-5959 / www.lakoreanfestival.org, 3250 San Marino St. at the Seoul International Park. This four-day festival includes a little bit of everything: live cultural performances, traditional dance, Latin band, making paper lanterns, paper folding, camping, international foods, vendors, music, dance, and kids' activities. Thurs. - Sun., 10am - 10pm Free admission.

MUSEUM DAY, / www.smithsonianmag.com/museumday. On one Saturday in September, *Smithsonian Magazine* sponsors Museum Day. Go to the website and download a ticket good for free admission for two to several museums in Southern California.

OKTOBERFEST, Big Bear. See page 752 for details.

OLIVE FESTIVAL, Sylmar. (818) 434-6695 / www.sylmarolivefestival.com, 13100 Hubbard Street; Parking at Los Angeles Mission College parking structure 13356 Eldridge Ave. Celebrate the olive harvest with a sampling of oils and recipes for olives and enjoy the live entertainment, Roman re-enactors and encampment, folklorico dancers, 2 stages, food, Kids Corner, costume contest, eating contests for pizza, tamales, pies, hot dogs, and burritos, and a chalk exhibition with some 50 world-class chalk artists. Sat. and Sun., noon - 8pm. $8 for adults, children 53 inches and under free; Get in free by dressing up in ancient Roman, Greek, or Egyptian costume such as civilian, princess, soldier, or emperor. Parking, $5.

ORANGE COUNTY CHILDREN'S BOOK FESTIVAL, Costa Mesa. (714) 838-4528 - festival info / www.kidsbookfestival.com, 2701 Fairview Dr. at Orange Coast College. This one-day festival is designed to encourage kids to experience the wonder of books. Authors and illustrators do book readings and signings. Stage presentations include a little bit of everything - interactive storytelling; musical entertainment; model trains; Radio Disney deejays and contests; cultural dances; magicians; clown acts; exotic animal presentations that can include boas, birds of prey, wild cats, and camels; and more. Additional kids' activities can include a science and technology area, puppet shows, face paintings, inflatable jumps, and mini train rides. Literary-based vendors and food booths abound. Open Sun., 9:30am - 4:30pm. Admission is free.

ORANGE INTERNATIONAL STREET FAIR, Orange. (714) 633-4816 / www.orangestreetfair.org, 112 E Chapman Ave., Chapman Ave. and Glassell Street at Old Towne Orange Plaza. This street fair boasts nine stages of international entertainment, including a children's stage, international foods, crafts, folk dancing and music. The Street Fair has become known for the variety of food reflecting cuisine from around the world. 3rd weekend in Sept. Fri., 5pm-1am; Sat., noon - 1am; Sun., noon - 10pm. Free admission.

PACIFIC ISLANDER FESTIVAL, San Diego. (619) 699-8797 / www.pifasandiego.com, Ski Beach, Mission Bay. This event invites the thousands of Melanesian, Micronesian, and Polynesian residents of Southern California to celebrate their heritage. Each community sets up their own village as singing and chanting, cultural dances, storytelling, arts, crafts, foods, and even artifacts keep visitors entertained. Open Sat. - Sun., 8am - 4pm. Admission is free.

PASADENA GREEK FESTIVAL, Arcadia. (626) 449-6943 / www.pasadenagreekfest.org, 285 W. Huntington Dr. at the Santa Anita Race Track. This festival celebrates Greek culture with three days of socializing, dancing, and lightning-bolt throwing, plus awesome Greek food such as shish kebabs, lamb chops and gyros! 3rd weekend in Sept., Fri., 5pm-1am; Sat., noon - 1am; Sun., noon - 10pm. $5 for adults; ages 12 and under free. Parking $4.

PCPA THEATERFEST, Solvang. See June entry (pg. 642, 729) for details.

PEACH PICKING, See July entry (pg. 734) for details.

PORTUGUESE BEND NATIONAL HORSE SHOW, Rolling Hills Estates. (310) 318-8258 / www.pbh.net, 25851 Hawthorne Blvd. at Ernie Howlett Park. For over fifty-five years, this classy three-day show has featured numerous equestrian events in two sand rings. Past shows have also included, besides the main feature of horse competitions, a children's carnival, crafts, demonstrations by the Long Beach Mounted Police, puppet shows (Sat. & Sun.), pony rides, a moon bounce, food booths, petting zoo (Sat. & Sun.), Wildlife Safari with animals from around the world (Sun. only) and more. Feel free to bring a picnic lunch. Riding events begin at 8am each day. Children's area open Fri., 10am - 4pm; Sat., 10pm - 3:30pm; Sun. 10am - 4pm. Pony rides are Sat. and Sun. 10:30am to 3:30pm. Admission free on Fri.; Sat. and Sun. it is $5 per person; children 2 and under are free. Ask about reserved seating prices. Parking and shuttle service to the site is free.

POWAY RODEO, Poway. (866) 776-7633 / www.powayrodeo.com, 14336 Tierra Bonita Rd. at the PVRA Arena. This "Brand Above the Rest" rodeo is yet another reason to come to Poway! The PRCA rodeos (i.e., Professional Rodeo Cowboys Association) are some of the best in the nation, with cowboys competing in several categories. Favorite events include kid's mutton bustin', rodeo clown acts, and Jr. barrel races. Behind-the-scenes tours are offered an hour-and-a-half before the show. Pre-rodeo events, that happen days before the rodeo, such as a parade, petting zoo, penned bulls in a parking lot, and a pageant, will have your kids hootin' and hollerin' for more. Rodeos are Fri and Sat. at 7:30pm, gates open at 6pm; Sat. at 1pm, gates open at 11:30am. Admission is $12 - $60 for adults; ages 6 - 12 are $6 - $60; children 5 and under are free.

RASPBERRY PICKING, See July entry (pg. 735) for details.

REDONDO BEACH LOBSTER FESTIVAL, Redondo Beach. (310) 376-6911 / www.lobsterfestival.com, 200 Portofino Way at Seaside Lagoon. Come to this annual *shellabration* and enjoy great Maine lobsters, music and fun for the whole family. Seaside Lagoon is the children's area that has activities, shows, contests and educational exhibits. Open fourth week in September, Fri., 5pm - 11pm; Sat., noon - 11pm; Sun., noon - 8pm. Admission is $15 for adults; $5 ages 6 - 12; children 5 and under are free. Coupons are available online. All military are free with ID.

RENDEZVOUS IN POWAY, Poway. (858) 668-4576 / www..poway.org/oldpowaypark, 14134 Midland Rd. in Old Poway Park. Be a part of history for a weekend as you walk among the twenty-five, or so, interactive encampments and learn about and talk with mountain men, cowboys, buckaroos, and more from the 1820s to 1890s lifestyle. Mock gunfights, Civil War-era cannons, Gatling gun, train rides, crafts, an evening barn dance, train robberies, folk dancing performances, and more await you. Educational tours and train rides are offered to school groups on the Thurs. and Fri. before the rendezvous. Look up Old Poway Park (pg. 565) for more details on the park. Open Sat., 10am - 4pm; Sun., 10am - 2pm. Admission is free.

ROUTE 66 RENDEZVOUS, Ontario. (800) 867-8366 or (909) 891-1151 / www.route66cruisinreunion.com, Euclid Avenue. Let's go cruisin'! Car buffs from all over the country (as evidenced by the 139,000 attendees) come to get their kicks on Route 66 for this three-day rendezvous that encompasses 22 blocks of historic Euclid Avenue. Classics, muscle cars, hot rods, and trucks from 1900 to 1975 can be participating vehicles (usually more than 800!). The cars are cool to watch, but some of the other activities are totally awesome, too. The Neon Light Cruise & Contest is held on Friday, 8pm - 10pm, where neon lights, usually color-coded to match the car, highlight special features on the cars. Throughout the reunion enjoy the cars cruisin', live entertainment, a model car contest, vendors, and wall to wall people, plus kid's activities, and carnival rides. The kid stuff is held in downtown Ontario by Euclid Avenue and D Street. The rendezvous is always held the third weekend in Sept., Fri., 5pm - 10pm; Sat., 9am - 9pm; Sun., 9am - 4pm. Admission is free to spectators to much of the show.

SUMMER MUSICALS UNDER THE STARS, Vista. See June entry (pg. 731) for details.

TANAKA FARMS PUMPKIN PATCH, Irvine. See October entry (pg. 755) for details.

TICKET TO THE TWENTIES, City of Industry. (626) 968-8492 / www.homesteadmuseum.org, 15415 East Don Julian Road at the Homestead Museum. Celebrate the Roaring Twenties as you enjoy music, dancing, crafts, historic house tours, games, demonstrations, and more! Also see THE HOMESTEAD MUSEUM (pg. 120). Sat. and Sun., 3pm - 7pm. Admission free.

TOSHIBA TALLSHIPS FESTIVAL, Dana Point. (949) 496-2274 / www.tallshipsfestival.com; www.ocean-institute.org, 24200 Dana Point Harbor Dr. at the Ocean Institute. This festival, held the weekend after Labor Day, is one of the largest gathering of tall ships on the West Coast. It begins as majestic tall ships sail into port on Thursday at 5pm, entering through a gauntlet of "enemy" cannon blasts. Other days, tour the ships and enjoy demonstrations and exhibits of the sailing arts, such as knot tying, scrimshaw, and wood carvings. Pirate encampment activities include sea chantey concerts, storytelling, mock trials and weddings, and perhaps, walkin' the plank. All this, plus music, crafts, and food make this festival worth *seeing*. Don't forget to explore the touch tank in the Institute. (See pg. 309 for details.) Sunset cruises on board a tallship with mock cannon battle cruises are also available. If you don't take a cruise, watch the battles from the shoreline. Open Sat - Sun., 10am - 5pm. Thursday night is the ship parade from 5pm til sunset. Admission is free to the festival. Tall ship tours are $10 for adults; $8 for kids 3 - 12; children 2 and under are free. Cruise prices vary from $30 - $65 for adults; $25 - $55 for ages 4 - 12. There are various other options for tours and cruises, too.

VISTA VIKING FESTIVAL, Newport Beach. (760) 726-6526 / www.vikingfestivalvista.com, 2006 East Vista Way at the Norway Hall. *Sven* the day indulging in all things Viking at this annual event. Test your strength with the Viking log toss, horn blowing, battle cries, and fish-flinging competitions. Add to this weapon and artisan demonstrations, Norwegian crafts, live entertainment, and ethnic foods, and you have the makings of a great day. Open Sat., 10am - 8pm; Sun., 10am - 6pm. Admission is $8 for adults; $2 ages 6 - 12, ages 5 and under are free. A two-day pass is $11 and parking is $4.

WILL GEER THEATRICUM BOTANICUM, Topanga. See June entry (pg. 732) for details.

- OCTOBER: -

AMERICA'S FINEST CITY LAW ENFORCEMENT EXPO, San Diego. (619) 641-3100 / www.sandiego.gov/qualcomm, 9449 Friars Rd. at Qualcomm Stadium. Ever play cops and robbers? Ever wanted to be the cop? At this expo, your kids (and you) can talk with policemen and find out what it would be like, and/or thank

them for doing such a great job. Attendees are invited to sit in police cars, listen to an all-cop band, get a free child identification kit, and look at the displays ranging from SWAT teams to rescue helicopters. Kid's activities include a rock climbing wall, face painting, and more. Sat., 10am - 2pm. Admission is free.

AMY'S FARM PUMPKIN TOUR, Ontario. (909) 393-2936 / www.amysfarm.com, 7698 Eucalyptus Avenue. Make a reservation to take a one-hour-plus tour of this working calf ranch with about 200 animals, to learn how pumpkins grow, pick a pumpkin from the patch, pet the animals in the petting zoo, feed baby calves bottles of milk, and more. A shaded picnic area with plenty of open grassy space is available. There must be a minimum of ten paying people in a group. See the main entry of Amy's Farm Tours (pg. 441) for more details. Open October and November, Mon. - Fri. in the morning for tours, and on select Sat. at 10:30am. Call to book a date and time. The pumpkin tour is $10 per person, or $8 for adults not picking a pumpkin.

APPLE PICKING - APPLE LANE ORCHARDS, Solvang. See August entry (pg. 737) for details.

APPLE PICKING - CALICO RANCH, Julian. See September entry (pg. 741) for details.

APPLE PICKING - OAK GLEN, Oak Glen. See the main entry for Oak Glen on page 401. The season runs from mid-September through mid-November.

AVOCADO FESTIVAL, Carpinteria. (805) 684-0038 / www.avofest.com, Linden Ave. Holy guacamole! This festival has everything avocado, at least food-wise. Try avocado ice-cream, avocado Key lime tarts, roasted corn with avocado butter, or at least some guacamole from a huge vat. Over forty acts provide entertainment on three stages. Arts and crafts booths as well as commercial booths and an expo tent offering educational information add to the weekend events. At the kids block party, young ones enjoy face painting, a petting zoo, make-and-take crafts, miniature golf, a rock climbing wall, storytelling, and theater performances. At the "best-dressed" avocado contest, your entry could win for best hair, funniest, or scariest. Open Fri., 11am - 10pm; Sat., 10am - 10pm; Sun., 10am - 6pm. Admission is free.

BANNING HERITAGE WEEK, Wilmington. See the April entry (pg. 714) for details.

BATES NUT FARM PUMPKIN PATCH, Valley Center. (760) 749-3333 / www.batesnutfarm.biz, 15954 Woods Valley Rd. Spend a delightful day in the country at this great farm. (See the main entry on pg. 561.) It has an eight-acre (pre-cut) pumpkin patch, along with a straw maze ($2); tractor-drawn hayrides all around the farm ($2 for 18 months and older); petting corral ($3); a moon bounce; pony rides ($5); and a Pumpkin Packages that include a pumpkin, hay ride and straw maze ($9.25). Purchase lunch here (hamburgers and hot dogs) or bring your own to enjoy at the large picnic area. Weekday educational programs are available for school groups. Special weekend events can include live entertainment, face painting, a rock climbing wall, costume contests, and more. Open daily during the month of October, 9am - 5pm. Admission is free.

BOCCALI'S RANCH PUMPKIN PATCH, Ojai. (805) 646-6116 / www.boccalis.com, 3277 Ojai Ave., behind the Boccali's restaurant. For over twenty years this ranch/garden has been an Ojai fixture. The pumpkin patch features home-grown pumpkins (pick them on or off the vine), gourds, and Indian corn in an authentic farm setting. Visitors can also enjoy free, tractor-drawn hay rides on the weekends, and purchasing fruits, vegetables, and herbs from the produce stand at anytime. Note that Haunted Hayrides are offered on select Fri. and Sat. nights, 7pm to 9pm, for $8 per person. As for food, enjoy Boccali's Pizza and Pasta restaurant next door, serving fresh and genuine Italian food. The pumpkin patch is open the month of October daily, 10am - dusk. Open on Fri. and Sat. starting mid-October, until 9pm. Free general admission.

CALABASAS PUMPKIN FESTIVAL, Agoura. (818) 222-5680 / www.calabasaspumpkinfestival.com; www.cityofcalabasas.com, 3701 Lost Hills Rd. at Juan Bautista de Anza Park. Join in contests of pumpkin pie eating, pumpkin seed spitting, pumpkin carving, and pumpkin bowling. Besides picking up a pumpkin, or two, in the pumpkin patch there are inflatables and giant slide, kiddie carnival rides, craft vendors, live stage entertainment, a reptile and bug show, and even a classic car show. Open Sat. and Sun., 10am - 5pm. Admission $5, children under 2 are free. Parking is free.

CALICO DAYS, Yermo. See September entry (pg. 742) for details.

CELEBRATION IN THE PARK, La Mirada. (562) 943-7277 / www.cityoflamirada.org, San Cristobal and San Esteban Drs. at the Neff House at La Mirada Regional Park. For one day return to turn-of-the-century California at the historic Neff House. Learn to tan a hide (I don't mean spankings) and how to quilt; look at antique toys; try your hand (or head) at an authentic barbershop; enjoy a Victorian tea party; participate in traditional games; join in the red wagon parade; drool over the automobiles that are part of the antique car show; picnic on the grounds; and listen to live music. Open Sat., 10:30am- 4pm. Free admission.

CHILDREN'S FALL HARVEST FESTIVAL, Long Beach. (562) 431-3541 / www.rancholosalamitos.com, 6400

Bixby Hill Rd. at Rancho Los Alamitos. In back-at-the-farm surroundings, this geared-for-kids festival offers storytellers, demonstrations, pony rides, a costume parade (have the kids dress up) around the barnyard, crafts, games, and food. See page 147 for more information about this rancho. Open Sun., noon - 4:30pm. Free.

ESCONDIDO RENAISSANCE FAIRE, Escondido. See April entry (pg. 715) for details.

FALL HARVEST FESTIVAL, Moorpark. (805) 529-3690 / www.underwoodfamilyfarms.com, 3370 Sunset Valley Rd. at Underwood Family Farms. See page 662 for more details on this fantastic farm. Entrance to the festival site, live shows (weekends only), the corn maze, gourd tunnel, and tractor-drawn hayride (weekends only), pig races (weekends only) are included with admission. Other attractions and activities include pony rides, moon bounce, trike trail, petting coral, train rides, gem mining, and country games such as building your own scarecrow, shooting a corn cannon, and more. These activities are $2 - $10 per. Each weekend brings a special event such as the Wild West Weekend, which includes gunfighters, stunt ropers, country music, and an old-time medicine show. Farm fresh produce is available for purchase as well as gourds, squash, corn stalks, Indian corn, food, drinks, and much more. The farm has 16 acres of pumpkins, including the Atlantic Giants which can weight more than 500 pounds. Food vendors are here on the weekend serving hamburgers, Mexican food, kettle corn, roasted corn on the cob, and more. School tours, with a minimum of twenty students, vary in price from $6 to $8 per person. (Teachers are free.) Open for the month of October daily, 9am - 6pm. Admission Mon. - Fri. is $3 for ages 2 and up; Sat. - Sun., $12 for ages 2 and up.

FALL TRACTOR SHOW, Vista. See Spring Tractor Show entry in June (pg. 731) for details.

FARMERS MARKET FALL FESTIVAL, Los Angeles. (323) 933-9211 / www.farmersmarketla.com, 3rd St. and Fairfax at Farmers Market. Enjoy this two-day, old-fashioned festival in the heart of historic L.A. See page 18 for info on FARMERS MARKET. Past activities and events (which could change every year) have included a petting zoo; pumpkin patch; live country music, cooking, spinning, gardening, and pottery demonstrations; bobbing for apples; pie-eating contests; and more. Open Sat., 11am - 9pm; Sun., 11am - 8pm. Admission is free. Parking is free for the first 2 hours with merchant validation.

FESTIVAL OF THE KITE, Redondo Beach. See March entry (pg. 710) for details. This one takes place the second Sunday in October.

FLEET WEEK, San Diego. See September entry (pg. 743) for details.

FORNERIS FARMS and MAIZE, Mission Hills. (818) 730-7709 / www.fornerisfarms.com, 15200 Rinaldi Street, Mission Hills. For a month of amazing fun, come play in the corn fields. Walk through the acres of cornstalk maze, trying to find your way out and seeking the CORNundrums (i.e. picture puns and riddles). Other activities include going through the Farm Frolic area (mini hay bale maze, bounce house and hay pyramid - $5), pony rides and petting zoo ($5 each, weekends only), taking a tractor-pulled train ride ($4), picking a pumpkin at the patch, viewing the antique tractors and cars scattered around, and perusing the farm market with fresh produce and fall decorations. Educational field trips are offered for school and scout groups in the morning, during the week. Fresh produce is available at Forneris Farms from April through December. The farm activities are open the month of October, Mon. - Fri., 2pm - 5pm; Sat. - Sun., 9am - 5pm. General admission is free. Maze tickets are $8 per person; children 3 and under are free with a paying adult.

GEM-O-RAMA, Trona. (760) 372-5356 / www1.iwvisp.com/tronagemclub, 3½ hours north of L.A., near Ridgecrest. This two-day event, which occurs the second weekend in the month, is worth the trek! It's explanation deserves a full page, however space in this section is limited. A free gem and mineral show and a free, guided bus trip around the on-site chemical plant are the clean activities. Messy highlights (and I mean messy!) on Saturday morning include mineral collecting for two-and-a-half hours from gooey black mud for hanksite and borax crystals and, in the afternoon, collecting borax and halite from a blow hole. The Sunday highlight is trudging / wading knee to hip deep in the salt lake, which crunches like newly-fallen snow, to chip out halite crystals - small pieces or large chunks. (Note that mineral retailers come here to supply their stores.) Bring sacrificial clothes and shoes, water (to use to wash off), gloves, a heavy hammer, a crowbar (for prying out the specimens), and large boxes lined with trash bags to bring home your treasures. What a unique opportunity to collect saline minerals! Show opens 7:30am on both days and end at 5pm on Sat., 4pm on Sun. Sat. mud trip from 9am - 11:30am; Sat. blow hole from 2:30pm - 5pm; Sun. halite lake from 9am - 1:30pm. Registration is 1½ hour before each trip. Admission is $15 per vehicle on the Sat. mud trip; $15 for the Sat. blow hole; $20 for the Sun. halite lake - such a deal! Note that Pinnacles National Natural Landmark is down the road. Take the time to drive closer and walk around these other-worldly looking formations.

GREENSPOT FARMS, Mentone. (909) 794-7653 / www.greenspotfarms.com, 10133 Ward Wy. I love visiting real farms! Choose and pick your pumpkin in the field and then enjoy a train ride, hay bale maze, corn maze, tractor-pull

hay ride, pony ride, face painting, petting zoo, and refreshments at this twenty-eight acre farm. The nighttime "haunted" hayride is a big draw for those who like to be scared. Note that apples and berries are available here at certain times to U-Pic. School tours are available here, as well. Open the month of October daily, 9am - 6pm. Free general admission. Some activites cost extra.

HALLOWEEN, Lots of "regular" attractions offer something special at Halloween. Zoos, for instance, offer Boo at the Zoo, where spooky, creepy, and crawly fun reign. Aquariums (Scarium of the Pacific instead of Aquarium of the Pacific in Long Beach), amusement parks (i.e. Knott's *Scary* Farm), museums (i.e. the *Queen Mary*), and even botanic gardens (Fullerton Arboretum presents a Haunted Garden) go all out in decorating for Halloween and putting on special events. If you are looking for pumpkin patches and corn mazes check out the events listed in this October section and check the following website for a plethora of places - www.pumpkinpatchesandmore.org.

HALLOWEEN ALTERNATIVES, For alternatives to door-to-door trick or treating, check your local park, mall, or church as many of them offer carnival-type fun, a safer atmosphere, and still plenty of candy!

HALLOWEEN HARVEST FESTIVAL, Woodland Hills. See September entry (pg. 743) for details.

HAUTE DOG HOWL'OWEEN PARADE, Long Beach. (562) 439-3316 / www.hautedogs.org, 5355 East Eliot St. at Marina Vista Park. More than 500 dogs put their best paw forward, decked out in their Halloween best for this ten block, pooch parade. Owners and dogs are often dressed alike as participants vie for best canine costume, best costume on a person, best group, best float (usually a decorated wagon), and more, with great prizes awarded. Yappy hour events have included a kid's costume contest, a bulldog kissing booth, dogs bobbing for hot dogs, a pet adoption fair, and more furry fun. Money raised goes towards a nonprofit organization. Haute Dogs is the Sunday before Halloween, opening at 11am; the parade is at 2:30pm. Free for spectators. Call for info on participating.

HURST RANCH HARVEST FESTIVAL, West Covina. (626) 339-5151 / www.hurstranch.com, 1227 South Orange Ave. Kids will have a great time making butter, pitching hay, pumping water, grinding corn, and doing other farm chores (and yet you can't get them to pick up their socks). The festival affords opportunities to find out about beekeeping, 4H, quilting, weaving, and more. Open Sat., 10am - 2pm Admission is $5 per person; children 2 and under free. Lunch is $5, or bring your own.

INDUSTRY HILLS CHARITY PRO RODEO, City of Industry. (626) 961-6892 / www.industryhillsprorodeo.org, 16200 Temple Ave. at the Industry Hills Center. Everyone benefits from this rodeo - several charities receive needed funds, top performers compete in the rodeo for a large purse, and guests have a great time! Besides the main event of the rodeo with bareback riding, steer wrestling, team roping, saddle bronc riding, bull riding, and tie down roping, visitors enjoy petting zoo, crafts, pony rides, clowns, Western theme booths, a visit by Smokey the Bear, entertainment, and food. Come before the weekend shows start to enjoy the pre-show fun. The rodeo commences Sat. at 6pm; Sun. at 2pm. Gates open 2 hours before show time. Admission is $15 for adults; $10 for srs.; $6 for ages 3 - 11. Prices include parking. A dance, $5 per person, follows the rodeo on Sat. evening.

IRVINE GLOBAL VILLAGE FESTIVAL, Irvine. (949) 724-6606 / www.irvinefestival.org, 4 Civic Center Plaza at Bill Barber Park. Go global right here at home, on the first Saturday in October, with over 100 performances on eight stages - cultural music, dance, martial arts, and so much more; a world of food with over seventy restaurants participating; world religious displays; an international marketplace; crafts; and a Kid's Village. The Village features large inflatables, games, sports, and lots of activities for your worldly child. The festival is Sat., 10am - 6pm. Admission is free.

IRVINE PARK RAILROAD'S PUMPKIN PATCH, Orange. (714) 997-3968 / www.irvineparkrailroad.com, 1 Irvine Park Road inside Irvine Regional Park. *Orange* you looking for some fun this month? This pumpkin patch, located near the train station, offers more than just pumpkins. Take a twelve-minute ride through part of the park ($4); a twenty-minute, tractor-drawn hayride (1 ticket); peddle a kid-size, John Deere tractor racer through an obstacle course (1 ticket); jump in a Halloween-themed bounce for fifteen minutes (1 ticket); enjoy a pony ride (1 ticket) - note that this attraction is not open on Mondays; walk through a not-too-spooky haunted house (free); chart your course through a hay bale maze (free); get your face painted (2 tickets); and eat! Other attractions in this vicinity include paddle boats, bike rentals, and the Orange County Zoo. See IRVINE REGIONAL PARK on page 282 for more details about what this terrific park has to offer. Open Mon. - Fri., 10am - 5pm; Sat. - Sun., 10am - 6pm. Vehicle entry fees are $3, Mon. - Fri.; $5 on weekends; $7 on holidays. General admission to the pumpkin patch is free. Tickets are $5 per ticket or $60 for 15.

JOHNSON BROTHERS PUMPKIN PATCH, Irvine. (949) 733-0650 / www.johnsonbros.net, 15500 Jeffrey Rd. These patches offer pumpkins (from giants to minis); bounce house (2 tickets); inflatable slide (3 tickets); pony rides (4

tickets); a pumpkin graveyard with funny tombstones (1 ticket); barnyard animals; and a kiddie play area with activity gyms, straw ponies to sit on, and bouncing bags to play with. An unusual attraction, but theme-fitting, is an Indian Village replete with tikis, corn grinders to try, and free, do-it-yourself face painting. Johnson Brothers is also a good source for autumn items and decor, such as pre-made scarecrows, gourds, bundles of cornstalks, and more. Open daily in October, 9am - 9pm. Pony rides are offered Mon. - Thurs., 3pm - 8pm; Fri. - Sun., 1pm - 8pm. Free general admission. Tickets are $1.50 each or 30 tickets for $40.

JULIAN MINING COMPANY PUMPKIN PATCH, Julian. (951) 313-0166 / www.julianminingcompany.com, 4444 Hwy. 78. What do giants, minis, and princesses all have in common? They are all types of pumpkins. This terrific place offers an assortment of activities from picking on-the-vine pumpkins to taking a tractor-drawn hayride and train ride; petting the animals at the petting zoo; cider pressing; hand-dipping candles; gold panning; roping; marshmallow "wars" and much more. JULIAN MINING COMPANY is like a farm from the 1800's. See more of what they have to offer on page 575. Open in October, Sat. & Sun, 10am - 5pm. General admission is $3 for adults, $2 for kids 12 and under. Some activities cost extra.

KINETIC SCULPTURE RACE, Ventura. (805) 652-0596 / www.kineticrace.com, Around Ventura Harbor Village. Instead of the rubber meeting the road, art meets engineering in this unique part road, part water, part sand, and part mud race. Racers creatively design their mobile, kinetic, people-powered sculptures to be all-terrain vehicles, and then race 'em. Some look like oversized, flotation bikes; some look like dune buggies; some are themed and riders dress to fit the part. Stay after the race to see the "contestants" up close. The start is at the boat launch ramps behind the Four Points Sheraton Hotel. See web site for the times and location of all the events. Open 10am - 4pm. Free to watch.

LAGUNA MOUNTAIN RENDEZVOUS, Santa Ysabel. (619) 922-9760 / www.lagunamountainrendezvous.com, Mesa Grande Rd. at Santa Ysabel Ranch. Experience an authentic 1700's - 1840's Rocky Mountain fur traders encampment in a rustic mountain setting. Demonstrations of primitive survival skills such as cooking, tool making, tomahawk throwing, and black powder target shooting are given over a period of six days. Beginners and the public are welcome to learn the "how tos" and to purchase items to become mountain men or women. Primitive and modern camping is available on site. Open daily, 8am - 6pm; Fri. until 8pm. Admission is $4 for adults; ages 10 and under, school groups, military, and scouts in uniform are free.

LANE FAMILY FARM PUMPKIN PATCH, Santa Barbara. (805) 964-3773 / www.lanefarmssb.com, 308 Walnut Ln. A long-standing tradition, Lane's has 2½ acres of U-pic pumpkins, plus a small (but worthy of going through) corn maze; horse-drawn, 1901 Studebaker wagon ride (offered weekends only); a petting zoo (with pigs, goats, and donkeys); a talking scarecrow; a fresh-from-the-fields produce stand; and scattered tractors and antique farming equipment. Kids can learn about agriculture and farming by taking a tour which fulfills California curriculum requirements, and it's fun! Open the end of September through October, 9am - 9pm. Free.

LAVENDER HILL PUMPKINS, Fallbrook. (760) 715-8495 / www.lavenderhillpumpkins.com, 1509 E. Mission Rd. At this family-owned farm, it's all about pumpkins; just pumpkins. Thousands of them. And not just the traditional, roundish, orange ones, but tall ones, white ones, ones with "warts", pale orange ones, bright orange ones, colossus kinds, and minis. The variety, the names given to some of their pumpkins, and the opportunity to pick them from the field make this excursion a unique one. Open the end of September through October, Mon. - Fri., 2pm - 5pm; Sat - Sun., 10am - 5pm. Free

LIVE OAK CANYON PUMPKIN PATCH, Yucaipa. (909) 795-TREE (8733) / pumpkins.liveoakcanyon.com, 32335 Live Oak Canyon Rd. This huge (at least in my city eyes) family-operated farm yields bushels of fun in the fall. A petting zoo is on the grounds, with goats, sheep, pigs, donkeys, ponies, chickens, and ducks. Watch the goats surefootedly "walk the plank" for food. Bring money to purchase feed. Tractor-drawn hayrides are available (usually weekends only) and are free. A giant hay "castle" is created from hundreds of bales of hay spread out, as well as staggered on top of each other. Kids are welcome to climb up the castle "walls" (for free) and run through the maze burrowed through the bottom layers. Bring a sack lunch, or purchase food from a refreshment stand (usually open weekends only), and eat at the numerous picnic tables scattered under shade trees. Special weekend events can include live music, pony rides (weekends), bouncing on several inflatables (e.g. bounce house, obstacle course, and giant slide), rock climbing (on a portable wall), playing gourd water drums, a mini quad race, bungee jumping, watching organ grinder monkeys, and other entertainment. Walk along the rows of the best pumpkin patch in Southern California (my opinion), which feature twenty-five acres of vine-cut pumpkins!! There are also huge piles of pre-picked pumpkins that range from giant pumpkins (make pies for everyone in the neighborhood), to sweet-tasting white pumpkins, Cinderellas, and mini pumpkins. Wagons are available to help tote your load. An on-site store sells decorative fall items such as Indian corn (in all colors), corn stalks, scarecrows, pumpkin carving supplies and kits, and numerous gourds,

including the kind used by artists for making instruments, baskets, and other creative endeavors. One-hour, elementary-aged school tours cost $8 and are offered for students to learn all about pumpkins - from seed to pumpkin - as they take a tractor-drawn hayride past pumpkin, corn, and gourd fields; and pick a pumpkin to take home. See page 437 for more details. Open mid-September through October daily, 9am - 9pm. Amusements open at 3pm on weekdays. General admission is free in September and on weekdays, $2 on weekends in October (but you just pay once per season). Some activities cost from $3 to $6. See website for specials.

LOMBARDI'S RANCH, Saugus. (661) 296-8697 / www.lombardiranch.com, 29527 Bouquet Canyon Rd. This family-owned and operated working farm opens its gates at the end of September and continues being open through the month of October. It offers forty-minute school tours during the week that include seeing and learning how pumpkins are grown, harvested, etc.; seeing a variety of vegetables; and walking around the farm to view farm animals. The animals here include a horse, donkey, goats, sheep, llamas, and cows. The tours are designed for ages 4 years and up. Attractions here include a few vehicles to climb in (e.g. a paddy wagon and a real fire truck); a large fiberglass pumpkin slide; a walk through scarecrow alley (with over 100 scarecrows); bales of hay to sit on while munching on a hot dog or caramel apple (sold at the snack bar); and hundreds of pumpkins (up to 150 lb.), squash, gourds, and Indian corn to purchase. Weekend activities include the petting zoo ($3); wagon rides ($5); train rides ($4); corn maze ($4); marching bands, and a variety of other live bands and choral music; and face painting ($3 minimum). Ask about entering the scarecrow contest as it offers hundreds of dollars in cash prizes! The pumpkin-related activities are open daily in October, 9am - 6pm. Admission is free. A self-guided tour is $10 for up to 60 kids. A guided tour is $25 for a minimum of 10 kids and a maximum of 30 (or one class). Fun Passes are $16 for adults and $12 for kids and include petting zoo, train ride, wagon ride and $1 off any pumpkin.

LONDON BRASS RUBBING CENTER, Long Beach. (562) 436-4047 / www.stlukeslb.org/ministries/brass-rubbing, 525 E. 7th Street at St. Luke's Episcopal Church. Cheerio! Your child will thoroughly enjoy making a medieval brass rubbing, offered October through November. On black paper, use a wax rubbing crayon of gold, silver, or bronze to capture the intricate designs. The facsimiles of over sixty tombstones from England vary in size, and depict knights, Lords, ladies in fancy dress, griffins, Shakespeare, and others. Groups of at least ten people can incorporate a half-hour talk, given by a docent in period dress, to learn more about Medieval times and the stories behind some of the people and images in the engravings. A complete English tea can be added on to your time here, too, with advanced reservations and a group of at least ten people. The center is open to the public Wed.. - Sat., 11am - 3pm. It is open to groups during this time, too, as well as Tues. - Sat., 9:30am - 3pm. Teas are served upon request. The price to rub cost between $5 - $15, depending on the size of the brass plate. Groups between ten to twenty people pay $7 per person. Teas are $24 for adults; $14 for ages 17 and under. This price includes a rubbing and a half-hour lesson/talk, too.

LOS ANGELES COUNTY FAIR, Pomona. See September entry (pg. 744) for details. .

LOS ANGELES PRINTERS FAIR, Torrance. (310) 515-7166 / www.printmuseum.org, 315 W. Torrance Blvd. at the International Printing Museum I hope this premier fair makes a good impression on you! Don't just read all about it, experience the world of printing through demonstrations - bookbinding, papermaking, letterpress printing, and more; vendors from all over the country; crafts for kids; and equipment to try your own hand at dating from Gutenberg's time to today. See pg. 123 for more information on the INTERNATIONAL PRINTING MUSEUM. Open Sat., 9am - 4pm. Admission is $8 for all ages.

MCGRATH BROTHERS GREAT PACIFIC PUMPKINS, Ventura. (805) 644-1235 / www.greatpacificpumpkins.com, 5100 Olivas Park Dr. Looking for the Great Pumpkin? Open to the public and for school tours during the month of October, come walk the patch, take a horse- or tractor-drawn hayride ($2), find your way through the hay maze, play a few games, and purchase product from the produce stand. Tours ($4 per person), which last about an hour, are offered for pre-K to elementary-aged school kids to learn about the life cycle of a pumpkin. Visitors are then invited to enjoy the other activities, and pick a pumpkin to take home. Open daily in October, 9am - 6pm. Admission is free.

MCGRATH FAMILY FARMS, Camarillo. See March entry (pg. 712) for details.

MCGRATH STREET PUMPKIN PATCH and GOURD FARM, Ventura. (805) 658-9972 / www.mcgrathstreetpumpkinpatch.com, 5156 McGrath St. During the month of October, walk the fields and choose a vine-cut pumpkin from the patch. Multi-colored Indian corn and gourds (the hard-shell kind used by artists and musicians), are for sale here year round. Free, tractor-drawn hayrides are given on the weekends. A few animals are on the site to look at and gently pet. One weekend, a local school puts on a fair geared for younger children. Groups of ten or more can take a field trip during the week to learn all about pumpkins, Native Americans, and more. Open

daily, 9am - dusk Admission is free.

MIRAMAR AIR SHOW, Miramar. (858) 577-1000 or (858) 577-1011; (858) 577-1016 or (888) 435-9746 for reserved seats / www.miramarairshow.com; www.mccsmiramar.com, Miramar Road at the Marine Corps Air Station. This three-day air show (one of the best!) features the Blue Angels, military, and civilian pilots performing thrilling aviation stunts and maneuvers, including wing walking. On the ground are over 100 displays of airplanes, helicopters, and military equipment, and some simulator rides, plus vendor booths and Consumer Fair exhibits. The Fun Zone includes a Ferris Wheel, climbing wall, obstacle course, mega slides, carousel, train ride, and bungee jump at various prices. You may bring in a cooler, or purchase food here. Note that a valid driver's license, current registration, and proof of insurance are necessary to get onto base. Gates open at 8am; a radio-controlled aircraft demonstration runs 8am - 9:30am, the show runs Fri. - Sun., 9am - 4pm. The Blue Angels usually fly at about 3pm. A twilight show is given Sat., 5:30pm - 9pm, featuring aerial stunts and maneuvers, as well as a pyrotechnic display by the flying aircraft and a great wall of fire. Parking, general admission, and blanket seating are free for all shows. Reserved seating ranges from $6 - $16 for adults, $4 - $10 for ages 3 - 11 for regular grandstand seats; to $85 for adults, $56 per child for tented patio seats, plus two meals and a program. Grandstand seating for the Sat. daytime shows is good for the nighttime show, too. Check the website for details.

MOUNTAIN VALLEY RANCH PUMPKIN PATCH, Ramona. (760) 788-8703 / www.mountainvalleyranch.com, 842 Hwy. 78. You can almost make a day of this outing by visiting fields of pumpkins where you can pick your own, taking a hayride around the farm, trying to find your way out of the large cornfield maze, looking at some of the old farm equipment, and enjoying the petting zoo with pigs, ponies, calves, birds and a corn cannon. Open daily, 9am - 6pm. Call for activity prices.

MR. BONES PUMPKIN PATCH, West Hollywood. (310) 276-9827 / www.mrbonespumpkinpatch.com, 702 North Doheny Drive. Pre-picked pumpkins of all sizes and shapes are available here, as well as farm-fresh goods, Halloween merchandise and decor, carving tools, gourds, and food. Activities for young ones include a pumpkin bounce ($3); face painting ($7 minimum); a straw maze ($3); hay bale tunnels; a petting zoo ($4); and pony rides ($7). Mr. Bones is available for school groups and for birthday parties, too. Open mid-October through October 31 daily, 9am - 8pm. General admission is free.

NANCY'S RANCH, Santa Clarita. (661) 255-6943 / www.nancysranch.com, 25039 ½ W. Magic Mountain Pkwy. Fairytale, lumina, gold rush, and more types of pumpkins are available for the picking' from the vine. (Some of these suckers are really huge!) Straw, bales of hay, and cornstalks surround the pre-picked pumpkin patch adding to the ambiance of autumn. Squash and gourds are also available for purchase. Open the first Sat. in October through Halloween daily, 10am - 7pm.

NATIONAL FIRE PREVENTION WEEK, Call your local fire station to see if they are doing something special this week. Many offer tours of the fire engines and station houses, and sometimes kids can even dress up like firemen. The safety tips are lifesavers.

OAK GLEN - PUMPKIN PATCHES, Oak Glen. See the main entry for Oak Glen on page 401. Many of these orchards, including almost all the Riley's, have pumpkin patches, the kinds where visitors pick the pumpkins fresh from the field.

OKTOBERFEST, Big Bear. (909) 585-3000 / www.bigbearevents.com, 42900 Big Bear Blvd. at the Big Bear Lake Convention Center. This event runs for seven weekends starting in September and has everything you would expect from an Oktoberfest - German Bands, dancing, competitions, kids' contests, arts and crafts, vendors and of course German food and beer. Little Oktoberfest fans will enjoy the Kinder Garten complete with bounce houses, face painting, airbrush tattoos and carnival games. Sat. noon - midnight, Sun. noon - 5:30pm. Check website for prices and the pre-purchase tickets. Special packages are available.

OKTOBERFEST, Torrance. (310) 327-4384 / www.alpinevillage.net, 833 W. Torrance Blvd. at Alpine Village. Bratwurst (yum!), live bands from Germany, watching a cow being milked, wood-sawing demonstrations, authentic German costumes, and beer - what more could a good German want? (Except maybe sauerkraut, pretzels, and sausages, which are also on hand.) This festival is open every Fri. - Sun. for a month, but children are only admitted on Sundays. Hours on Sun. are 1pm - 7pm. Admission is $4 for adults; children 11 and under are free.

OLD TIME MELODRAMA AND OLIO, Julian. (760) 765-1857 / www.julianmelodrama.com, 2129 Main St. at Julian Town Hall. Each weekend during the month of October you are invited to participate in a two-hour, old-time melodrama by booing the villain, cheering the hero, and sighing with the heroine. The shows feature local actors and incorporate a community sing-a-long. Shows are Fri. 7:30pm; Sat., 1:30pm, 3:30pm and 7:30pm; Sun., 1:30pm.

Admission for the matinees is $5 for everyone; evenings are $10 for adults; $5 for ages 4 - 11.

OMA'S PUMPKIN PATCH, Lakeside. (619) 390-2929 / www.omaspumpkinpatch.com, 14950 El Monte Road at Van Ommering Dairy. Admission to this pumpkin patch, located at a genuine dairy farm, includes a Jack pumpkin, a bottle of water, pumpkin education presentation, cottonseed mountain (to climb and dig through), hayrides around the farm and past all the cows, hay bale maze, milk bottle bowling, a petting zoo, playground equipment (with a sand pile and toys), and a shaded place to enjoy a picnic lunch (that you bring). Open the month of October, Tues. - Sat., 10am - 7pm. Reservations are required for groups of twenty or more. Admission is $8 for ages 1 - 15; one free adult for every paying child; additional adults are $4.

ORANGE COUNTY INTERNATIONAL AUTO SHOW, Anaheim. (717) 566-6100 - regional; (714) 765-8950 - local / www.motortrendautoshows.com, 800 W. Katella Ave. at the Anaheim Convention Center. This must be automotive affidonado's paradise! Hundreds of the latest concept cars, muscle cars, sporty imports, luxury, trucks, minivans, sport utility, celebrity rides, hybrids, tricked-out, classics, and exotics (i.e. Lamborghini, Ferrari, and Lotus) are on view for the public to look at, touch, and drool over. Here is where some of the hottest new cars make their debut. Live D.J.'s spin music, although they and some of the car models aren't always entirely clothed. Some of the things for kids include testing their driving at Camp Jeep on mini electric cars or directing a radio-controlled car at RIDEMAKERZ RC Experience. Open Thurs., 4pm - 10pm; Fri., noon - 10pm; Sat., 9am - 10pm; Sun., 9am - 7pm. Admission is $12; $10 for srs.; free for ages 12 and under. Check online for discounts and an exact schedule. Parking is $15 per vehicle. Free offsite weekend parking at Angel stadium with shuttle to show.

PACIFIC BEACHFEST, Pacific Beach. (858) 273-3303 / www.pacificbeachfest.org, between Garnet and Thomas Aves. on and near the boardwalk. This one-day, non-alcoholic event signifies the official end of summer in Southern California. Festival activities include a volleyball competition, sand castle building, dancing to live bands and a pro/am surf competition with surfers from around the world. Purchase food from twenty Pacific Beach restaurants here, such as Asian chicken salads, jambalaya, feta cheese ravioli, and chocolate mousse cake. Kids can be kept busy with face painting, clowns, cookie decorating, clay painting, and a Kids Action Alley with a large slide and dry-land surfboard (for practice). Nearby museums participate by having booths for children. A fire truck is also on hand to explore. A fireworks show from the Crystal Pier caps the day. Open 11am - 7pm. Admission is free. Some activities cost. Beach parking is limited.

PA'S PUMPKIN PATCH, Long Beach. (562) 596-7741 / www.paspumpkinpatch.com, 6701 E. Pacific Coast Highway. Besides the rows and rows of the orange vegetable/fruit, there is a snack bar, fall-related merchandise, petting zoo, train rides, pony rides around a ring, games, a huge tepee, giant inflatable bounces and slides, and some kiddie carnival rides like a little Ferris Wheel and bumper boats. School and scout groups are welcome (as is the general public). Open the month of October daily, usually 10am - 9pm. General admission is free but rides require tickets.

PEACH PICKING, See July entry (pg. 734) for details.

PELTZER FARMS, Temecula. (951) 695-1115 / www.peltzerfarms.com, 39925 Calle Contento. This patch features a real farm experience with pumpkins, naturally, plus pony rides ($5); train rides ($4); a good-size petting zoo with pygmy goats, bunnies, sheep, baby chicks, and more ($2); and free activities of going through a one-acre cornfield maze, watching pig races, climbing the mound-o-hay, and viewing the John Deere Tractor display. Burgers, hot dogs, ice cream, and other food are available on weekends, or bring your own lunch and enjoy a picnic here. School tours, which take about an hour, are offered Mon. - Fri., 9am - 1pm and are $8 per student; teachers and supervising adults are $4. Participants will learn about working on a farm and growing crops. Also included is a booklet, pumpkin, and time in the corn maze and the petting farm. Open the end of September through October daily, 9am - 8pm. Most of the rides are available Mon. - Fri., 3pm - 8pm, plus regular weekend hours. Admission is free.

PIONEER DAYS, Twentynine Palms. (760) 367-3445 / www.visit29.org, Two Mile Road and Utah Trail at Luckie Park. The carnival starts on Thurs.; the parade is Sat. at noon; and the other down home festivities continue through Sun. These include pumpkin patches, decorated bike parade, arm wrestling tournament, haunted house, pet parade, outhouse race, vending booths, and live entertainment. Open Thurs. 5pm - 10pm; Fri., 5pm - midnight; Sat., noon - midnight; Sun., noon - 8pm. General admission is free.

THE PUMPKIN EXPRESS, Campo. (619) 465-7776 / www.psrm.org, Sheridan Rd. off Hwy 94 at the Pacific Southwest Railway Museum. There are a lot of places with miniature train rides for kids, but why not go on a real train ride? In October you can take a train ride from the Pacific Southwest Railway Museum in Campo to the Great Pumpkin Patch. Afterward kids can tour the Haunted Train, and each child can pick out a pumpkin and decorate it.

Trains depart, for the approx. one-hour ride, at 10am, 12:15pm and 2:30pm. The depot opens 2 hours before your trip, plan to arrive at least 45 minutes before departure. Call early to make a reservation. Fares are $15 for adults; $12 for srs.; $10 for ages 6 - 12; $5 for toddlers.

PUMPKIN CITY'S PUMPKIN FARM, Laguna Hills, Rancho Santa Margarita. (949) 586-5862 - Laguna Hills; (949) 589-2075 - Rancho Santa Margarita / www.pumpkincity.com, Laguna Hills - 24203 Avenida de la Carlota at Laguna Hills Mall; Rancho Santa Margarita - 30606 Santa Margarita Pkwy. This fenced-in "farm" takes over part of a parking lot for the month of October. The ground is covered with hay, while tractors, cornstalks and bales of hay all around enhance the autumn mood. There are Indian tepees to go in, and a petting zoo to visit ($2.50), plus kids can take a ride on a pony ($6), a scale train, an elephant (weekends only), and/or a few kiddie rides (1 to 8 tickets at $1.05 per ticket). Not all attractions are at the Rancho Santa Margarita location. Weekend entertainment is provided by costumed characters, country bands, and puppet\eers. Group reservations are offered that include special rates on pumpkins and pony rides. And oh yes, there are thousands of pumpkins here of all shapes and sizes - mini pumpkins to ones that weigh up to 200 pounds! Open Mon. - Thurs., 10:30am - 9pm; Fri., 10:30 - 10pm; Sat. 10am - 10pm; Sun., 10am - 9pm. Admission is free. "Extras" cost.

THE PUMPKIN FACTORY, Corona. (800) 719-4420 / www.thepumpkinfactory.net, 1545 Circle City Dr. Several giant inflatables - thirty-foot slides, bounces, and obstacle courses; an ATV train ride (just like the olden days!); John Deere ride-on vehicles; a petting zoo; child-sized hay bale maze; pony rides; other rides; and pumpkins already gathered from the field make this October outing a fun one. Field trips are offered at 9am and 10:30am, Tues. - Thurs., for $8 per student. The excursion includes a brief educational talk, a small pumpkin to take home, five rides, and a visiting to the petting zoo. Open daily in October usually 4pm - 9pm weekdays; Sat., 10am - 10pm; Sun., 10am - 9pm. Rides are open after 4pm on the weekdays, and all day on weekends.

THE PUMPKIN FACTORY, Westminster. (805) 294-3654, 1025 Westminster Mall. See above entry for details. Not all activities are available at this location.

PUMPKIN FESTIVAL / INSECT FAIR, Pomona. (909) 869-2215 or (909) 869-2200 / www.csupomona.edu, 3801 W. Temple Ave. at Cal Poly University. This two-day pumpkin festival is a very popular local event. Pick your own (pre-cut) pumpkin in the field ($5); pig out at a pancake breakfast ($5 per person); listen to live music; enter the petting zoo; ride a horse; jump in a bounce house; participate in games; get your face painted; and munch on food. Visit the Insect Fair at the Bronco student center which has over 200,000 preserved bugs on display, and 70 tables hosting live critters - millipedes, tarantulas, spiders, and scorpions. The festival is open 10am - 5pm. The Insect Fair is open 9am - 5pm. Admission is free to the pumpkin festival, some activities cost money. Admission to the Insect Fair is $6 for adults; $4 for students with ID and ages 3 - 12.

PUMPKIN LINER, Fillmore. (800) 773-8724 or (805) 524-2546 / www.fwry.com, 364 Main Street Catch a vintage train to ride to a "private" pumpkin patch and then join in the festivities. There are games, haunted hay maze, jumps, a carousel, arts and crafts booths, food booths, and pumpkins. The train company also offers Headless Horseman Family Dinner Train with delicious food, and a train ride that ends at the pumpkin patch. There ARE scary elements to this excursion. Open the month of October, Sat. - Sun., departing 10:30am and 2pm. The Headless Horseman rides are at 7pm on select Fri. and Sat. nights. Pumpkin Liner rides are $20 for adults; $12 for ages 4 - 12; $10 for ages 2 - 3; children under 2 are free, as they occupy a lap, not a seat. Pumpkins are extra. Headless Horseman rides are $49 for adults; $34 for ages 4 - 12; $26 for ages 3 and under. All reservations must be made online or by phone.

PUMPKIN STATION, Bonita. (858) 566-7466 / www.pumpkinstation.com, 5437 Bonita Rd. Pre-picked pumpkins are fine, but there's nothing like getting them straight off the vine. This working farm offers pick-your-own pumpkin; a corn field maze to wander through; tractor-drawn hayrides; farm animals to gently touch; and plenty of space for picnicking. Open the beginning of October - mid-October daily, 9am - 6pm. Open mid-October through Halloween daily, 9am - 8pm. General admission is free, but activities cost.

PUMPKIN STATION, Chula Vista. (858) 566-7466 / www.pumpkinstation.com, 900 Otay Lakes Rd. Halloween is not just about the pumpkins, although this station has plenty of them. Other important elements at this pumpkin patch include train rides, kiddie rides, photo ops, and an inflatable bounce, jump, and play center. Open the end of September through October, Mon. - Thurs., 11am - 9pm; Fri. - Sun., 9am - 9pm. General admission is free, but activities cost.

PUMPKIN STATION, Del Mar. / www.pumpkinstation.com, 15555 Jimmy Durante Blvd. This pumpkin patch looks like a mini carnival. Enjoy train rides, two giant slides, a mini slide, inflatable jump and play center, a carousel, a few kiddie rides, a game zone, a petting zoo, and a slew of pumpkins. From the end of September through October,

it's open Mon. - Thurs., 9am - 7pm; Fri. - Sun., 9am - 9pm. Free general admission, but activities cost.

PUMPKIN STATION, El Cajon. (858) 566-7466 / www.pumpkinstation.com, 415 Parkway Plaza at Westfield. Enjoy train rides; two giant slides; a mini slide; inflatable jump and play center; a carousel; a few kiddie rides; a small Ferris Wheel; a game zone; a petting zoo (with bunnies, llamas, goats, and chickens); and a rows and rows of pumpkins. Shows for youngsters are given on select weekends. Open during the month of October, Mon. - Thurs., 1pm - 9pm; Fri. - Sun., 9am - 9pm. General admission is free, but activities cost.

PUMPKIN STATION, Escondido. (858) 566-7466 / www.pumpkinstation.com, 13421 Highland Valley Rd. Pick your own pumpkin at this location. Try to find your way out of a huge, eight-foot tall corn maze. Take a tractor-drawn hayride. See and pet farm animals. Pack a picnic lunch to enjoy on the premises. Open during the month of October daily, 9am - 8pm. Free general admission, but activities cost.

PUMPKIN STATION, Mission Valley. (858) 566-7466 / www.pumpkinstation.com, 1640½ Camino Del Rio N. at Westfield. This station offers pumpkins galore; a small Ferris Wheel; a petting zoo (of mostly goats and sheep); and inflatable bounces, a jump, Sky Fighter ride, and play center. Come join the fun! Open early through the end of October, Mon. - Thurs., 11am - 9pm; Fri. - Sun., 9am - 9pm. General admission is free, but activities cost.

PUMPKIN STATION, National City. (858) 566-7466 / www.pumpkinstation.com, 3030 Plaza Bonita Rd. at Plaza Bonita Shopping Center. Hundreds of pumpkins, plus a few kiddie rides (i.e. trains, Dino jump, Swing, cars, and boats); carnival-type games; inflatable bounces; play centers; and a petting zoo make this an attractive place to shop for pumpkins and for fun. Open the end of September through October Mon. - Thurs., 11am - 9pm; Fri. - Sun., 9am - 9pm. Admission is free, but activities cost.

RASPBERRY PICKING, See July entry (pg. 735) for details.

SANDCASTLE CONTEST, Newport Beach. (949) 729-4400 / www.newportbeach.com, Near Iris St. and Ocean Blvd. at Corona Del Mar State Beach. Call about participating in this one-day sandy event, or just come to "sea" the most imaginative things created with sand. Both experts and novice builders compete. The contest starts Sun. at 11am. It's free to watch. There is a fee to participate. Parking is $15.

SAN DIEGO ZOO / SAN DIEGO ZOO SAFARI PARK, Escondido, San Diego. (619) 234-3153 or (619) 231-1515 / www.sandiegozoo.org, The Zoo is on Park Blvd. in Balboa Park, San Diego; the Safari Park is at 15500 San Pasqual Valley Road, Escondido. The world-famous Zoo and the Safari Park are both free for ages 11 and under, when accompanied by a paying adult, for the entire month of October. Now, that's wild! See the long write-ups for these wonderful places in the main section of the book.

SAN DIMAS WESTERN DAYS RODEO, San Dimas. (909) 394-RODEO (7633) or (909) 592-3818 / www.sandimasrodeo.com, San Dimas Canyon Rd. at Horsethief Canyon Park. Yee ha! This weekend PRCA rodeo features all a cowboys' (and cowgirls') favorite rodeo events. Come early for pre-rodeo activities, such as a Kid's Korral, then enjoy the shows including bareback riding, tie down roping, steer wrestling, down, bull riding, barrel racing, and more. On Sunday, the Cowboy Church starts at 9am, and the Challenged Buckaroos perform in their own rodeo at 1pm. Shuttles pick up at the Post Office starting at 11am, and run every 15 minutes. Gates open at 11am; pre-show activities on Sat. and Sun. begin at 1pm; the shows starts at 2pm and ends around 4:30pm. Admission is $15 for adults; $8 for ages 3 - 12. Discount tickets available via the website.

SOUTHERN CALIFORNIA FAIR, Perris. (951) 657-4221 / www.socalfair.com, 18700 Lake Perris Dr. at Lake Perris Fairgrounds. For nine days and nights, enjoy top-name entertainment; PRCA rodeos; livestock shows; monster trucks; demolition derby; petting zoo; extreme sports demonstrations; fishing demonstrations; carnival rides and games; and horticulture and fine art exhibits. Open Mon. - Thurs., 4pm - 11pm; Fri., noon - 11pm; Sat. - Sun., 11am - 11pm. Admission on weekdays is $8 for adults; $4 for ages 5 - 11; children 4 and under are free. Rides and some activities cost extra. An unlimited ride wristband is $28. Parking is $8.

STU MILLER'S PUMPKIN PATCH, Thousand Oaks. (805) 532-2333 / www.seasonaladventures.com, Thousand Oaks Blvd. and Lombard St. There are hundreds of pumpkins to choose from here, plus kiddie carnival rides, a bounce house, inflatable slide, and a petting zoo, making this a fun, Halloween stop-off. The location may change so check the website before going. Open the month of October daily, 9am - 9pm. Free

TANAKA FARMS PUMPKIN PATCH, Irvine. (949) 653-2100 / www.tanakafarms.com, 5380 ¾ University Dr. One unique feature of this pumpkin patch is that visitors can pick their pumpkins right off the vine. This thirty-acre working farm, in the heart of Irvine, also offers other autumn fun such as a good-size petting zoo ($3), wagon rides around the farm ($5), and a corn maze (free), plus special weekend activities such as games, crafts, mini ATV rides, and food. Tanaka also offers fresh U-pick vegetables (carrots, onions, green beans, and radishes) and fruit, depending on

what's in season, and a produce stand. Fall items, such as decorative corn and gourds, corn stalks, and painted pumpkins, are also available for purchase. School and other groups, consisting of at least ten children, are welcome for tours and an educational adventure. Check out spring and summer months in this Calendar section to see other Tanaka food offerings. Open the end of September through October daily, 9am - 6pm. Free

TRICK-OR-TREAT FESTIVAL, Costa Mesa. (949) 723-6616 / www.ocmarketplace.com, 88 Fair Drive at the Orange County Fair and Event Center. While this is one of the biggest (and best) swap meets in the area, with plenty of food choices, on the Sunday before Halloween, it is also a trick or treat festival with free face painting; daytime trick or treating for kids in costume; freaky puppet show (geared for kids); strolling entertainment; a pumpkin sculptor; blood drive; show; and a hearse (and ambulance) procession. Shop with the 1,000 vendors and be entertained. Open Sun., 10am - 4pm. Admission is $2 for adults; children 12 and under are free.

THE WICKERD FARM PUMPKIN PATCH, Menifee. (951) 672-3020 or (909) 286-8289 / www.wickerdfarm.com, 26852 Scott Rd. On weekends here you can enjoy the inflatable jump, hay rides, food, craft vendors and various contests like pumpkin seed spitting and pumpkin bowling. There is also a children's costume contest on Sat., starting at 1pm. Open starting second Fri. in October, Sun - Thurs., 10am - 8pm, Fri. - Sat. 10am - 9pm. Admission is free.

WILL GEER THEATRICUM BOTANICUM, Topanga. See June entry (pg. 732) for details.

WOODLAND HILLS ICE, Woodland Hills. (818) 854-4151 / www.woodlandhillsice.com, 6100 Topanga Canyon Blvd. at Westfield Promenade Only in Southern California can you ice skate in a t-shirt and not only not get cold, but get a suntan! This rink is 7,000 square feet of real ice and offers recreational skating, lessons, skating exhibitions, field trips, birthday parties, and more. Nighttime skating, under the stars, is an almost magical treat. Open from Halloween through President's Day, Sun. - Thurs., 10am - 10pm; Fri. - Sat., 10am - 11pm. Per session admission, which includes skate rentals, is $15 for adults; $13.50 for srs. and students; $12 for ages 12 and under. All day, all age pass $18.

- NOVEMBER: -

AMERICAN INDIAN ARTS MARKETPLACE, Los Angeles. (323) 667-2000 / www.theautry.org, 4700 Western Heritage Way at the Autry National Center in Griffith Park. More than 150 nationally-known American Indian artists, traditional dancers, and storytellers, plus a plethora of ethnic food and craft demonstrations, add up to a wonderful weekend marketplace. Explore the AUTRY (pg. 101) while you're here. Open Sat. - Sun., 10am - 5pm. Admission is $10 for adults; $6 for srs. and students; $4 for children 3 - 12; 2 and under are free. This includes admission to the museum.

BLUE AND GRAY, A CIVIL WAR REENACTMENT, Moorpark. (805) 529-3690; (805) 279-5253 - Rotary Club / www.moorparkrotary.com; www.underwoodfamilyfarms.com; www.civilwaralliance.com, 3370 Sunset Valley Rd. at Tierra Rejada Ranch by Underwood Family Farms. Cannons, horses, swords, smoking rifles, stagecoaches, drums, the calvary - this weekend event is one of the largest gatherings of its kind in Southern California, with over 500 reenactors. The fields are transformed into living Union and Confederate encampments. Three battles with ground charges are reenacted on Saturday - at noon, 3pm and 5:15pm (the latter one includes pyrotechnics); and two on Sunday - at noon and 2:30pm. Other happenings include Living History demonstrations such as cooking, soldier school for kids, medical demos, abolitionists rallies, infantry demos, presidential press conferences, music, Victorian ballroom dance classes, conversing with reenactors in character, general stores, and more. A food court serving breakfast, lunch, dinner, and snacks is also on the grounds. Note that a school program commences on Friday. The grounds are open Sat., 10am - 6:15pm; Sun., 10am - 4pm. Admission is $20 for adults; $15 for students (must show I.D.); children 5 and under are free. Check www.moorparkrotary.com for discounts.

CARLSBAD VILLAGE FAIRE FALL, Carlsbad. See May entry for Carlsbad Village Faire Spring (pg. 720) for details.

CASAZZA CHRISTMAS TREE FARM, Etiwanda. (909) 980-2908 / www.cachristmas.com, 6231 East Ave. Seventy acres of trees make this a fun walk and outing with an old-time, country feel. Pick out the perfect tree and have the workers cut it down for you. Open mid-November through mid-December, Mon. - Fri., noon - 5pm; Sat. - Sun., 9am - 5pm. Closed Thanksgiving. Discount coupons are available online.

CHILL AT THE QUEEN MARY, Long Beach. / www.queenmary.com, See December entry (pg. 763) for details.

CHRISTMAS ON THE FARM, Moorpark. (805) 529-3690; (805) 218-0282 / www.underwoodfamilyfarms.com, 3370 Sunset Valley Rd. at Underwood Family Farms. See page 662 for more details on this fantastic farm. Big Wave Dave's Christmas trees are sold here along with wreaths, mistletoe, and lots of Christmas decor. The trees and some

farm activities are available daily, but admission to the animal center, vintage tractor-drawn wagon rides and rides with Santa; most of the farm, and farmer's market are available only on weekends. Note: Wagon rides are only offered on select weekends. Open the weekends after Thanksgiving - December 21, 9:30am - 7:30pm. Wagon rides are available 11am - 4pm. $6 covers the cost of a wagon ride and entry to the animal center.

CHRISTMAS RANCH TREE FARMS, Simi Valley. (805) 527-6412 or (805) 501-0874, 3800 Cochran St. See the entry below for details. This location doesn't offer jeep rides and is two acres big. Open the Sat. after Thanksgiving through mid-December, or so, Mon. - Fri., 2pm - sunset; Sat. - Sun., 9am - sunset.

CHRISTMAS RANCH TREE FARMS, Thousand Oaks. (805) 527-6412 or (805) 501-0874 / www.christmasranchtreefarms.com, 1586 Pederson Rd. Don't just go over the river and through the woods to grandmother's house, but stop in these woods and smell the fresh Christmas trees. For over 37 years going to Christmas Ranch Tree Farms has been a tradition for numerous families. On these fifteen acres, you can choose and cut your own Monterey Pine, Leyland Cypress, Aleppo Pine, and others kinds, via walking the farm or taking a vintage Jeep over a steep hill and to its other side - how fun! Also available here are pre-cut trees, wreaths, garland, and a picnic area. School tours for preschoolers and early elementary age kids, where they learn about trees, what a conifer is, how trees give off oxygen, and more, are offered year round. Open the Friday after Thanksgiving until mid-December, or so, Mon. - Fri., 2pm - 7pm; Sat. - Sun., 9am - 7pm. Admission is free.

CHRISTMAS TRAIN, Orange. See entry (pg. 764) in December.

CHRISTMAS TREE HOLIDAY TRAIN, Fillmore. (800) 773-8724 or (805) 524-2546 / www.fwry.com, 364 Main Street Make a day of picking out a Christmas tree. Starting at Fillmore, take a forty-five minute, vintage train ride to a rural tree farm - Santa Paula Christmas Tree Farm (pg. 761). Choose a tree, have it cut down for you, and enjoy the scenery on the ride back, plus a visit with Santa, while your tree is carried on the train's special flat car. A carousel and other kiddies rides, plus inflatable slides and bounces are at the farm, too. Rides are offered the day after Thanksgiving through December 24 on weekends, leaving at 10am and 2pm. The train ride is $25 for adults; $23 for srs.; $15 for ages 4 - 12; $10 for ages 2 - 3; children under 2 are free. The tree costs extra. Netting is required and available.

CORONADO BUTTERFLY RESERVE, Goleta. See January entry (pg. 703) for details.

FAMILY CHRISTMAS TREE FARM, El Cajon. (619) 448-5331 / www.cachristmas.com, 300 Pepper Dr. Select your own Monterey pine from this ten-acre farm, or choose an already cut Noble, Douglas Fir or Grand Fir tree, or even a potted tree. A petting zoo, hayrides, and a small store with fresh winter greens and wreaths are also on the premises. School tours can be made by reservation. Open the day after Thanksgiving through December 22 daily, 9am - 9pm.

FANTASY ON ICE, San Diego. (619) 234-1031 / www.sdice.com; www.sandiego.org/event, 225 Broadway at Horton Square. Ice skating outside, surrounded by a shopping center, with a huge Christmas tree all lit up is *so* New York, but now it's also so Southern California! The temporary ice rink appears mid-November and welcomes skaters through the beginning of January. You'll probably want to incorporate a visit to Ghiradelli's or another fun food stop at the adjacent Horton Plaza or the nearby Gaslamp District. Open for two-hour sessions, every two hours, daily, 10am - 10pm. The rink is closed Thanksgiving and Christmas, and closes at 5pm on Christmas Eve and New Year's Eve. Admission for the two-hour sessions is $14 for adults; $12 for ages 11 and under. Prices include skate rentals. Parking, with validation, is about $5.

FESTIVAL OF BANDS, Arcadia. / www.arcadiamusic.org, 180 Campus Drv. Come out early on a Sat. morning to watch the procession of more than 40 marching bands down Baldwin Avenue. Immediately following the parade, the bands, with drill teams, color guard, and drum majors, assemble at Salter Stadium at Arcadia High School to face off in percussion performances and precision events that are rousing to watch and listen to. That night, there is an evening field show at Citrus College Stadium in Glendora that showcases competing bands from all over Southern California. The parade begins at 9am. Admission is $12 for adults; $6 for ages 6 - 10; 5 and under free.

FESTIVAL OF LIGHTS / ICE SKATING RINK, Riverside. (951) 826-2370 or (951) 826-2391 / www.riversideca.gov/fol, 3900 Main St. at the Mission Inn Hotel and along Main St. Pedestrian Mall. The Festival of Lights Switch-On Ceremony (self explanatory) begins at 4:30pm, with live band and singing performances, a thank-you ceremony, and finally, the turning on of the 3.5 million twinkling lights and over 400 holiday decorations and animated figures surrounding the historic Mission Inn Hotel and pedestrian mall. What a fantastic sight! This night ends with fireworks and a visit from Santa Claus. Ranked as one of the top lighting festivals in the country, each evening throughout the Festival of Lights features the lights; unique holiday vendors; shopping, (regular shops participate in a window decorating contest); visits with Santa; horse-drawn carriage rides; and outdoor ice-skating. Sometimes strolling

carolers, dance performances, making crafts, and other entertainment are part of the festival fun, too. The ice skating rink is located on the pedestrian mall between University and Mission Inn avenues. Also see the Festival of Trees, the below entry, for another fun event. The Festival of Lights kicks off the Friday after Thanksgiving and continues until the beginning of January. The ice skating rink is open Mon. - Thurs., 4pm - 10pm; Fri., 4pm - 11pm; Sat., noon - 11pm; Sun., noon - 10pm. It is open during Christmas school break daily, noon - 11pm. Closed Christmas day. General admission to the festival is free. Ice skating is $12 per hour and an additional $3 for skate rentals.

FESTIVAL OF TREES, Riverside. (951) 486-4213 or (951) 486-4238 / www.rcmcfoundation.org, 3443 Orange St. at the Riverside Convention Center. Fifty, elaborately-decorated trees, each with a unique theme, are the centerpiece of this four-day Festival of Trees. The trees are a fund raiser, sponsored and pre-purchased with proceeds going to the pediatric unit at Riverside County Regional Medical Center. For kids, the trees are simply magical. The rest of the convention center is equally transformed with an Elves Forest of trees decorated by local schools; singing, dancing, juggling, and other continuous entertainment on the stage; an activity corner for kids to make craft and play games; and a visit and story time with Santa. School field trips are also offered. Special events occurring during the festival include a Teddy Bear Tea Party on Friday from 1pm - 3pm for $20 per person for tea that includes a light snack, and a special show; and Family Day on Saturday from 11am - 7pm, where extra activities include a petting zoo, sidewalk chalk art, scavenger hunt, and entertainment. Also see Festival of Lights, the above entry. The Festival of Trees is Wed., 10am - 4pm; (closed Thanksgiving Thursday); Fri., 9am - 2pm; Sat., 11am - 7pm; Sun., 10am - 4pm. General admission is free.

FREE ENTRANCE DAYS IN THE NATIONAL PARKS, See January entry (pg. 704) for details.

GREENSPOT FARMS, Mentone. (909) 794-7653 / www.greenspotfarms.com, 10133 Ward Wy. This farm is acres upon acres of Christmas trees and just being here generates a family feel, making this place a favorite holiday destination for over twenty years. Walk among the "forest" to pick your own tree - come and tag it early and then come back in December to pick it up, or cut it down and take it home the day you visit. This working ranch, filled with a variety of fruit trees, also has a petting zoo, small gift shop with wreaths and mistletoe, a refreshment stand, and picnic area, bounce house, and, depending on the day and season, tractor rides, scale train rides, and visits with Santa. Check out the honey house where you can look at live honey bees through a window (and purchase honey fresh from the hive). School tours are offered here, too, for $7 per child. Open the Friday after Thanksgiving through most of December daily, 9am - 6pm. Admission is free.

HAGLE TREE FARM, Somis. (805) 386-0254 / www.hagletreefarm.com, 3100 Somis Road Bring a little of the country home by choosing and cutting your own Christmas tree here. Weekend visits with Santa Claus, a hay hill to play on, pony rides, a petting zoo, plus a few picnic tables, and wreaths and garlands for sale can make your Christmas complete. Open the Friday after Thanksgiving through December 24, Mon. - Fri., 10am to dark; Sat. - Sun., 10am to dark. Weekend activities end at 4pm. Admission is free.

HOLIDAY FEST, Yermo. (800) TO-CALICO (862-2542) / www.calicotown.com, 36600 Ghost Town Rd. at Calico Ghost Town. Over Thanksgiving weekend enjoy a rootin' tootin' time at Calico. Live music; staged gun fights; and demonstrations of blacksmithing and rope-making give city slickers a feel for the Old West. Look up Calico Ghost Town (pg. 433) for more details about the museum. Open Fri. - Sun., 9am - 5pm. Admission is $10 for adults; $5 for ages 5-15 years; children 4 and under are free. On-site camping (minimum 2 nights) is $35 - $40 a night (camping for this weekend books up months in advance); $45 a night for cabins.

HOLIDAY ICE RINK, Thousand Oaks. (805) 494-0514 / www.thousandoaksicerink.com, 2200 E. Thousand Oaks Blvd. at The Lakes. Baby, it's cold outside. Well, even if it isn't, you can still go ice skating outside. One of the two man-made lakes at this outdoor shopping complex is frozen over from Thanksgiving to the beginning of January. Enjoy shopping and taking in a restaurant before or after your winter wonderland excursion. Classes are also available and you can rent out the rink for a birthday party or other event. The rink is usually open daily, 10am - 11pm, but check the website or call for specific dates and times. Admission is $10 per one-hour session, plus $4 for skate rentals.

HOLIDAY ON ICE, Irvine. (949) 748-8280 or (949) 753-5180 / www.skatespectrum.com, 71 Fortune Dr. at Irvine Spectrum Center. One of the coolest places to be in Southern California in the winter is at the outdoor ice rink. The skating is fun to do and interesting to watch, plus you can always go eat or shop before or after. Look up IRVINE SPECTRUM CENTER on page 297, in the main section in the book, for details about the mall. Open the beginning of November through the middle of February. Usually open Sun. - Thurs., 11am - 9:15pm; Fri. - Sat., 11am - 12:15am. Admission per one-hour session is $14 per person, plus 4$ for skate rental. Toddlers (size 8T to 12T) are $13 and includes skates.

HOLLYWOOD CHRISTMAS PARADE, Hollywood. (310) 631-0691; (866) 727-2331 - grandstand tickets / www.thehollywoodchristmasparade.com, starting at Hollywood Blvd. and Orange; check to see this year's route. During the day, starting at noon, is Hollywood Christmas Parade with information booths, games, and some live entertainment. All the stars come out at night - I mean the stars of Hollywood - for this celebrity-packed parade that is put on the Sunday after Thanksgiving. There are fantastic floats, live bands, drill units, cartoon characters, equestrian units, and of course, Santa Claus. The two-hour parade goes along a three-mile course through the streets of Hollywood. A concert is given at the end. The parade goes from 5pm to 7pm. Reserved grandstand seating is $45 per person. Standing room is free, but it does get crowded and it's hard to see over people, so get here early. All-day parking in nearby lots runs from $5 - $15. Or, take the metro red line to the Hollywood/Highland exit or Hollywood/Vine.

HOTEL DEL CORONADO ICE RINK, Coronado. (619) 435-6611 / www.hoteldel.com, 1500 Orange Ave. by the Hotel Del Coronado Only in California can you ice skate on a rink ringed by palm trees, right next to the Pacific Ocean from Thanksgiving to the beginning of January! And by a world famous hotel! Two hour skate sessions are available Mon. - Fri. Additional sessions are on Sat. and Sun. and during Christmas break from 11am - 1pm. Admission for the two-hour sessions are $23 for adults; $18 for children 10 and under. The two-hour sessions are $15 for adults; $10 for children. Ice skate rentals are $5 per person.

HOW THE GRINCH STOLE CHRISTMAS, San Diego. (619) 234-5623 / www.oldglobe.org, Balboa Park at the Old Globe Theater. This seventy-five-minute, Dr. Seuss-inspired musical production stars a fuzzy green villain who learns how to have a heart in the magical, musical world of Who-ville. Call for show times. Admission depends on the date and time. Prices start at $37 for adults and $24 for children (17 years and under). Children under 3 are not admitted.

ICE AT SANTA MONICA, Santa Monica. (310) 393-8355 / www.iceatsantamonica.com, 1324 5th St. Chill out by iceskating so close to the ocean. This 8,000 foot ice rink operates daily from the beginning of November through mid-February, so you can skate everyday (you'd be really good if you did that!). There is also a 20' by 20' enclosed Tot Spot rink for ages 6 and under. The rinks are available for birthday parties and lessons. They are open Mon. - Thurs., 2pm - 10pm; Fri., 2pm - midnight; Sat., 10am - midnight; Sun., 10am - 10pm. See WINTERLIT CELEBRATION (pg. 762) for another activity in the immediate vicinity. Admission and skate rental is $12 per person.

INDIO POWWOW, Indio. (760) 238-5770 or (800) 827-2946 / www.fantasyspringsresort.com, 84245 Indio Springs Dr. at Fantasy Springs Casino. Hosted by the Cabazon Band of Mission Indians, this three-day indoor Pow Wow brings together Native Americans and non-Indians in a celebration and competition of music with drum performances, bird singing, and dance contests for all ages, plus food and arts and crafts. Don't miss the "grand entrance" where all the Indians, in elaborate regalia, dance as they come in. The Pow Wow begins Fri., 5pm - midnight (grand entrance at 8pm); Sat., 11am - midnight (grand entrance at 1pm and 8pm); Sun., 11am - 6pm (grand entrance at 1pm). Admission is free.

LIVE OAK CANYON CHRISTMAS TREE FARM, Yucaipa. (909) 795-TREE (8733) / trees.liveoakcanyon.com, 32335 Live Oak Canyon Rd. Come join in the festivities celebrated here around Christmas time. Warm yourself by a large fire pit, visit with Santa Claus (on certain weekends), listen to carolers (usually on the weekends), and enjoy the free hay bale castle and maze; pony rides (weekends only); quad rides; inflatable bounces and slides; refreshment stands, and petting zoo. (See the October entry, on pg. 750, for more details on these attractions.) Walk among a twenty-five acre forest of home-grown Monterey Pines, Sierra Redwoods, and Aleppo Pines. Choose your own Christmas tree here and have a worker cut it down, or purchase a fir tree shipped from Oregon. A tented gift shop sells fresh wreaths, garland, and other decorations and gift items. One-hour, elementary-aged school tours are offered to learn about Christmas trees, enjoy a tractor-drawn hayride, and take home your own Christmas tree seedling. Tours are offered Mon. - Fri., 9am - 3pm and cost $8 per student. Teachers are free. Add on a gourd tour, here, too. See page 437 for details. Open late November - mid-December daily, 9am - 8pm. Admission is free. Some activities cost from $3 to $6.

LOGAN'S CANDIES, Ontario. (909) 984-5410 / www.loganscandies.com, 125 W. "B" St. This small retail candy store makes candy canes starting in November. A limited number of tours are offered to visitors to watch the fascinating process of the striped candy become a sweet reality. During the half-hour tour, first stand outside and listen to a description of the procedure as you peer in through the storefront window. Flavoring is added and kneaded through a huge amber blob which is then stretched and pulled (think taffy pull) to form the white part of the cane. A smaller blob is dyed red. Next, go inside the store to see the two colors twisted together and shaped into variously-sized candy canes. This is one of our favorite seasonal excursions! Tours are given November through the

third week in December, Mon. - Fri. at 5:30pm, 7pm, and 8:30pm. Reservations are needed - book early as they fill up quickly. The cost is $3.75 per person and includes a small bag of candy.

LONDON BRASS RUBBING CENTER, Long Beach. See October entry (pg. 751) for details.

MOTHER GOOSE PARADE, El Cajon. (619) 444-8712 / www.mothergooseparade.com, Main, Chambers, 2nd, and Madison sts. This three-mile mother of parades has been going strong and gaining momentum since 1946. It features over 5,000 participants - marching bands, drill units, equestrian units, specialty units, clown acts, street performers, celebrities, military, dignitaries, vintage automobiles, fire trucks, Santa Claus, and the best part of all - lots of motorized floats depicting Mother Goose rhymes and fairy tales in a different theme each year. The parade takes place the Sun. before Thanksgiving beginning at noon. The pre-parade show/concert begins at 11am in front of the grand stand only. Admission is free.

NORTH POLE EXPRESS, Fillmore. (800) 773-8724 or (805) 524-2546 / www.fwry.com, 364 Main Street Enjoy the train ride to the North Pole to pick up Santa Claus; you can even wear your jammies if you want to. (Actually, it's a much shorter ride to the North Pole than I thought - only forty-five minutes!) There are storytellers, caroling, cookies, and chocolate milk on board, too. Once you get to the destination, there are reindeer, a carousel and other kiddie rides, and a gift shop. Bring your camera. Note that the train company also offers dinner with Santa rides, consisting of turkey or ham, mashed potatoes, and dessert for adults, and chicken fingers, potatoes, and fruit cup for kids. North Pole rides are offered the day after Thanksgiving through December 26, Wed. - Sun., at 4:30pm, 6pm or 7:30pm. Dinner with Santa rides are offered during this time period on Fri. and Sun. evenings at 5:30pm. The train ride is $29 for adults; $19 for ages 2 - 12; children under 2 are free as they sit on your lap. Dinner with Santa is $47 for adults; $26 for ages 2 - 12.

PASADENA MODEL RAILROAD CLUB'S FALL OPEN HOUSE, Pasadena. See April entry (pg. 717) for details.

PELTZER PINES, Brea, Silverado. (714) 649-5291 / www.peltzerpines.com, Brea - 3400 Rose Dr.; Silverado - 7851 Blackstar Canyon Road. Walk among the pine trees on these farms and breath in their fresh pine fragrance - Christmas in the air! You choose the tree - either Monterey Pine or Leyland Cypress - and they will cut it down for you. Open mid-November, Mon. - Fri., 11:30am - 5pm; Sat. and Sun., 9am - 5pm.

PILGRIM PLACE FESTIVAL, Claremont. (909) 621-9581 / www.pilgrimplace.org, 660 Avery Rd. This timely festival takes place on the second Friday and Saturday in November. Thanksgiving is a time to be thankful (and to eat), but do your kids know how this holiday began? Find out by watching the educational highlight here - an hour-long, live reenactment called, *The Pilgrim Story*. This play, which accurately and biblically retells an important story of our heritage, is performed at the outdoor stage at 1:45pm each day by the retired church professionals who live at this center. Call for special school performances, geared for 5th graders or so, given on the prior Tuesday and Wednesday at 10am. Bring a picnic lunch to enjoy at nearby parks. A favorite activity at the festival is called the Glue In. Tables full of recycled items are available for kids to glue onto a piece of cardboard to create a masterpiece (50¢). Other activities include riding the (motorized) Mayflower (50¢); taking a mini-train ride (50¢); visiting the on-site cultural museum; shopping at the bazaar and craft fair; face painting; eating good food; and going to the Wampanoag Indian Village for story time and games. The festival runs from 10am - 4pm. Free admission, and free, but hard-to-come-by, parking. Free shuttles are available.

PINE TREE ACRES, Ramona. (760) 788-5524 / www.pinetreeacres.com, 620-A Haverford Rd. Walk amongst the hundreds of Monterey Pines to choose the perfect one for your family. Cut it down and bring it home. Pine Tree Acres also has fresh pre-harvested trees, potted trees, ornaments and crafts for sale. Weekend fun includes free ornament and cookie decorating, cider, a party jump, visits from Santa and pony rides. Make a day of this excursion! Open the Friday after Thanksgiving through mid-December weekdays, noon - 5pm; weekends, 9am - 5pm. Admission is free, pony rides cost extra.

PISMO BEACH MONARCH GROVE, Pismo Beach. See January entry (pg. 705) for details.

PLANETARIUM SHOWS - CHRISTMAS SHOW / STAR OF BETHLEHEM, Look up planetariums in the main section of this book under Shows and Theaters, in your county. Starting mid-November through mid-December, many of them reset the nighttime skies back to the time of Jesus' birth. For instance, at Tessmann Planetarium in Santa Ana ([714] 564-6356 / www.sac.edu), after an introduction to astronomy, the astronomer/narrator discusses how (and when) the miraculous phenomena called the Star of Bethlehem came about using the planetarium "skies", a slide show, and Bible passages. He includes the possible origins of a nova, comet, star, meteorite, or aligning planets. I won't give away the ending. The one-hour presentation is educational, as well as a wonderful blend of science and faith. See the

main entry (pg. 322) for more information about this planetarium. Tessmann's nighttime shows start at 7pm; daytimes shows at 9:30am and 11am. Tickets are $7 per person. Reserve your space early as shows sell out.

RANCHO CHRISTMAS, Vista. (760) 724-4082 / www.sdcounty.ca.gov, 2210 N. Santa Fe Ave. at Rancho Guajome Adobe. Celebrate Christmas in an atmosphere of yesteryear. The adobe (look up RANCHO GUAJOME ADOBE on pg. 547 for more details) is adorned with seasonal decor from the 1800s. Kids crafts, such as candlemaking, dipping candy apples, and making corn husk angels, plus horse-drawn wagon rides, demonstrations by blacksmiths, panning for gold (for a minimal fee), shopping at vending booths, and other fun activities are all here - most of which are included in the admission price. On Saturday the events culminate in the lighting of the luminaries and a caroling program. Open the last Sat. and Sun. in the month, 10am - 4pm. Admission is $5 for adults; $3 for ages 4 - 12; children 3 and under are free.

RANCHO NOEL POTRERO VALLEY CHRISTMAS TREE FARM, Potrero. (760) 583-5287 / www.ranchonoel.com, 25655 Potrero Park Dr. For a true country excursion, fa la la your way through twenty acres of Christmas trees where you can choose and cut your own Monterey Pine to take home. Bring your own rope to tie down your tree. Open the Friday after Thanksgiving through mid-December daily, 9am - 5pm.

REINDEER ROMP, Los Angeles. (323) 644-4200 / www.lazoo.org, 5300 Zoo Dr., Griffith Park at the Los Angeles Zoo. Reindeer fly in to join their animal and human friends at the zoo (see LOS ANGELES ZOO on page 221) during this season. Guests can visit with the reindeer and learn about them from the keepers; walk around the zoo, of course; take a train ride (extra fee); make paper reindeer antlers; and enjoy special entertainment. Bring your herd! The reindeer are here Thanksgiving through December. Admission is regular zoo admission - $18 for adults; $15 for srs.; $13 for ages 2 - 12.

SANTA PAULA CHRISTMAS TREE FARM, Santa Paula. (805) 933-9569 / www.spctf.com, 18540 E. Telegraph Rd. This Christmas tree farm is slightly off the beaten path, making it a little more like out in the country. Take a stroll around and pick out just the right tree, then cut it down and bring it home. The farm also has camel rides (think *We Three Kings*), pony rides, a petting zoo, and hay stack for the kids. A more fun way to come to the farm is travel by train. See the November entry for Christmas Tree Holiday Train (pg. 757) for more details. Open the Friday after Thanksgiving through mid-December, or so, daily, 9am - dusk. Admission is free - some activities cost.

SANTA'S ELECTRIC LIGHT PARADE, Temecula. (951) 694-6480 / www.cityoftemecula.org, Jefferson Ave., between Del Rio Rd. and Overland Dr. A spectacular Friday evening parade features over fifty entries with lights of home-crafted floats, plus fire engines, marching bands, sheriff's posse, equestrian groups, all kinds of animals, and Santa. Stake out your spot early and bring a blanket and picnic dinner. The shows begins at 7pm. Admission is free.

SANTA'S NORTH POLE LIMITED, Campo. (619) 465-7776 / www.psrm.org, Sheridan Rd. off Hwy 94 at the Pacific Southwest Railway Museum. There are many ways to reach Santa instead of just waiting for a visit from him. From the end of November through latter December on Fri. and Sat. evenings, take a train ride on railcars decked out for the holidays. While on board, you can make your list (and check it twice); enjoy hot chocolate and cookies (you are welcome to bring a picnic dinner on board); listen to a Christmas story read out loud; and sing carols. You disembark at Santa's Village, complete with a sleigh and reindeer. (Good for photo ops). Santa visits with the kids there and on the way back in the train too, and kids are given a jingle bell as a gift and reminder to ring in the Christmas season. Trains depart, for the approx. two-hour ride, at 5pm and 7pm on Sat., 7pm on Fri. The depot opens 2 hours before your trip, plan to arrive at least 45 minutes before your departure. Call early to make a reservation. Fares are $30 - $50 for adults; $20 - 40 for ages 2 - 12; children 1 and under are free.

TRY HOCKEY FOR FREE DAY, See the March entry (pg. 713) for more info.

VETERANS DAY CELEBRATION, Chiriaco Summit. (760) 227-3483 / www.generalpattonmuseum.com, 62510 Chiriaco Summit at the General Patton Memorial Museum. Veterans are remembered and celebrated during this one-day event. Entertainment, which changes from year to year, can include a military band, U.S.O. show, an equestrian unit, an Army chorus, pipes and drums, military reenactments, an appearance by General Patton "himself", an air salute fly-over by WWII aircraft, and definitely a walk through the museum and tank yard. See page 381 for more info on the museum. Open 9:30am - 4:30pm. The U.S.O. Show starts at 11am. Admission is free.

WILDLIGHTS, Palm Desert. (760) 346-5694 / www.livingdesert.org, 47900 Portola Ave. at the Living Desert Wildlife and Botanical Park. Come have a wild night at the park! A special display, up for only six-weeks, features nearly a dozen, larger-than-life animal and other sculptures illuminated in hundreds of thousands of lights. This can include a gigantic teddy bear, a thirty-foot snowman, assorted desert critters, and a golfing Santa. Live entertainment; camel rides; Santa Claus' Village with Candy Cane Lane and a visit with Santa, Prancer's Playland, and Mrs. Claus'

Kitchen serving hot chocolate and s'mores; holiday-themed Wildlife Wonders Shows; wood-burning fireplaces; carousel rides; crafts; and more, add to the holiday festivities. Wildlights is open on weekends only after Thanksgiving, and then daily during Christmas break, 6pm - 9pm. Note that most of the animals are put to bed at nighttime so it's a people-only party. Admission is $10 for adults; $8 for ages 3 - 12.

WINTER FANTASY, Laguna Beach. (949) 494-3030 / www.sawdustartfestival.org, 935 Laguna Canyon Rd. Three acres of fun in the snow and other cool activities are offered for several consecutive weekends, beginning the one before Thanksgiving. (It is open the Friday after Thanksgiving, too.) Real snow is brought in daily, so you can teach your little angels how to make snow angels. There is also a re-created arctic cave to explore. Family entertainment includes jugglers, balloon artists, storytellers, and carolers. Children's art activities, like mask making or creating pottery, are different each day and range from free to $16. Over 150 artists have booths here, with on-going crafting demonstration. Children's Theatre Workshop presents on-going, interactive holiday shows for the family. To complete the fantasy, Santa Claus makes his rounds. Get your holiday shopping done and keep the kids happy - all at the same time! Open weekends (and two Fridays), 10am - 6pm. Admission is $8.50 for adults; $7 for srs.; $4 for ages 6 - 12; children 5 and under are free. A season pass is $18 per person. All military and their family are free with ID. Parking fees vary depending on which lot you choose.

WINTERLIT CELEBRATION, Santa Monica. (310) 393-8355 / www.downtownsm.com, Third St. Promenade. Dramatically lit up Christmas trees, jutting icebergs, icicles dangling from light poles, and lots of twinkling lights are part of this illuminating celebration. Throughout the season (check the website for specifics), visits from Santa Claus, strolling carolers, snow play, and other entertainment keep visitors feeling merry. Winter lights transform this outdoor mall every night from mid-November through mid-January. Look up THIRD STREET PROMENADE (pg. 94) for more details and also Ice at Santa Monica (pg. 759) for a seasonal ice skating rink. Note that Wed. and Sat. you can also enjoy a Farmer's Market in the area.

WOODLAND HILLS ICE, Woodland Hills. See October entry (pg. 756) for details.

- DECEMBER: -

ALTADENA'S CHRISTMAS TREE LANE, Altadena. (626) 403-1123 / www.christmastreelane.net, Santa Rosa Ave., between Woodbury Ave. and Altadena Dr. Usually on the second Saturday in December the lighting ceremony begins at the Altadena Library, at 6pm with the arrival of Santa Claus. Enjoy free hot chocolate, plus a holiday boutique, music by choirs and drum corps, and finally, the lighting of the 150, majestic (huge!), classic Christmas trees (deodras or Himalayan cedars), that stretch along the road for almost a mile. If you miss the ceremony, the lights are on nightly, dusk to midnight. Enjoy an enchanting drive.

ARCTIC LIGHTS SNOW PLAYDAY, Moorpark. (805) 378-1441 / www.moorparkcollege.edu/zoo, 7075 Campus Rd. at Moorpark College. Literally tons of snow are brought in to AMERICA'S TEACHING ZOO (see pg. 701) for both animals and kids to play in. Get guided tours, see animal presentations, and enjoy the imported winter day. The zoo is also decorated with Christmas lights. Open Sat., 11am - 5pm. Admission is $10 for adults; $8 for srs. and ages 2-12; Kids under 2 are free. Some activities may cost extra.

BALBOA PARK DECEMBER NIGHTS, San Diego. (619) 239-0512 / www.balboapark.org, Park Blvd. and President's Way at Balboa Park. This festival marks the opening of the holiday season in San Diego as thousands of people join the celebration. The activities and events include looking at buildings glowing with Christmas lights; tasting holiday fare from around the world; listening to strolling carolers; participating in kid's crafts and carnival-style games; seeing and hearing musical and dance presentations (including ballet, hip hop, Polynesian, bagpipes, country, gospel, jazz, and lots more); being mesmerized by a puppet show; enjoying free admission to the many museums here; watching the Santa Lucia procession (at 6pm and 8pm) at the Museum of Man; delighting in the Singing Christmas Story Tree at the organ pavilion; touring the Old Globe theater; and applauding the holiday favorites performed at the Casa Del Prado Theatre. Visit the re-creation of a Native American village in the heart of the park. Spin, slip, and skate on a full-size ice-skating rink at the Palisades Midway, too, for only $5 per person, which includes skate rentals. Usually open the first weekend in December, Fri., 3pm - 10:30pm; Sat., 11:30am - 10:30pm. Participating museums are free from 5pm - 9pm these evenings. Free parking and shuttle service is available at the downtown County Administration Building and City College. Admission is free.

BELMONT SHORE CHRISTMAS PARADE, Long Beach. (562) 434-3066 / www.belmontshore.org, 2nd St. between Bayshore and Livingston. This two-hour street parade is usually held on the first Saturday in December from 6pm - 9pm. It has over 150 entries, including bands, homemade floats, and Santa Claus. Admission is free.

THE BETHLEHEM EXPERIENCE, Westlake Village. (818) 889-1491 or (805) 496-2394 / www.gotobethlehem.com, 32111 Watergate Rd. at Westminster Presbyterian Church. At this event, which only happens on even years, a centurion greets you as you wait in line in your car (it's a true blend of ancient and modern) to give you a CD. Listen to this as you drive past vignettes of the streets of Bethlehem on the night that Jesus was born. Costumed participants and live animals make this time period come to life. If you want to get out and mingle with the crowd, you must dress in an appropriate costume, that can be provided for you. Then, you can partake in hot chocolate and cookies, pet a sheep, or meet a Magi. Usually open the second weekend in December, Sat. - Sun., around 5pm - 8:30pm. Free admission.

BETHLEHEM STORY, Spring Valley. (619) 461-7451 / www.fchapel.org, 9400 Campo Road at Faith Chapel Experience life as it was on the very first Christmas as re-enactors re-create this pivotal time. Cast members interact with you and engage you in conversation, in character, as you walk about the outdoor town of Bethlehem (i.e. the parking lot of the church) with its tradespeople - potters, blacksmiths, vendors, tanners, candle makers, yarn spinners, carpenters, brick layers, scribes, etc, townsfolk; guards; tax collectors; and even corralled animals - real sheep, chickens and goats. Use the free shekels given you at the entry to purchase samples of authentic food and make a craft. Enjoy the hustle and bustle of the town and the music, try your hand at making some of the wares; play some games; pet the animals; listen to the angels proclaim Jesus's birth; check into the inn to visit the stable where Mary and Joseph and baby Jesus are; and be a part of the story. Free hot chocolate and cider are available. Open for four nights, Thurs. - Sun., 6pm - 9pm. Free

BETHLEHEM VILLAGE, Poway. (858) 748-4642 / www.northcitychurch.com, 1171 Poway Rd. at North City Presbyterian Church. Experience the past today at this recreation of first-century Bethlehem. Mill the grounds with the crowds and encounter Roman guards. See not only a live nativity set, but the nativity play. Kids, especially, enjoy llama rides, a petting zoo, puppet shows, crafts, games, and more. Open Fri. - Sat., 6pm - 9pm. Admission is free.

BETHLEHEM WALK, Escondido. (760) 745-5100 / firstunited.echurch.net, 341 S. Kalmia St. at the First United Methodist Church. Walk the streets of Bethlehem, or at least a re-creation of them, the second weekend in December. Visitors are escorted through a marketplace to experience the bartering of this ancient town and being hassled by soldiers, then onto the inn to try to get accommodations. Being redirected to the stable, guests then see Mary, Joseph, and baby Jesus, and the animals. Afterward, enjoy refreshments in the church's social hall. Reservations (ironically) are highly recommended and can be taken the Sun. after Thanksgiving. Open second weekend of December, Fri., 5:30pm - 9pm; Sat., 4pm - 8:30pm; Sun., 4pm - 8pm. Admission is free, but it is a ticketed/timed event to keep the tour numbers reasonable.

BREAKFAST WITH SANTA, Long Beach. (562) 431-3541 / www.rancholosalamitos.com, 6400 Bixby Hill Rd. at Rancho Los Alamitos. This is a fun adventure for the kids, geared for ages 12 and under. They get to eat a pancake breakfast with Santa while enjoying live performances by such groups as the International Peace Choir. There are activities such as crafts, pony rides, and decorating evergreens to take home. Open 9am - noon. Admission is $25 for adults; $20 for srs. and ages 3 - 14. This price includes entertainment and craft activities.

CAROLING CRUISE, Ventura. (805) 642-1393 / www.islandpackers.com, 1691 Spinnaker Dr. at Ventura Harbor. Sing your favorite Christmas carols (out loud!) while enjoying the harbor, boat, and holiday lights up close, plus snacking on cider and cookies. The cost is $17 for adults; $14 for srs.; $11 for ages 12 and under.

CELEBRATING FAMILY & FRIENDS, Rancho Santa Margarita. (949) 635-1800 / www.cityofrsm.org, 22112 El Paseo at the Civic Plaza. Celebrate the new year with this alcohol-free party that features live stage musical entertainment; children's games and activities; inflatable slides and bounces; visual arts; street entertainers; interactive art booths; food booths; and more. Open December 31, 4:30pm - 9:30pm. Admission is free; some activities cost.

CHANUKAH FESTIVAL AT THE HARBOR, Ventura. (805) 382-4770 / www.chabadofoxnard.com, 1583 Spinnaker Dr. This festival features latkes (yumm), musical entertainment, a Judaica boutique and you get to watch the world's largest balloon menorah being built. Open 2pm to 4:30pm. Free admission.

CHANUKAH WONDERLAND, Manhattan Beach. (310) 372-0941 / www.manhattantorahcenter.com, 1003 N. Sepulveda Blvd. Visit the Manhattan Torah Center during during this celebration and you can play games; make your own latkes, Chanukah candles and dreidels; dress up as Judah Maccabee (who started the whole thing); play games and participate in other activities. Fri. & Sun., 10am - 2pm. Admission is $10 per person.

CHILL AT THE QUEEN MARY, Long Beach. (562) 435-3511 / www.queenmary.com, 1126 Queens Highway at the Queen Mary. CHILL is pretty Chill! The "coolest" experience, literally at 9 degrees, is going inside the Ice Kingdom to walk through the Nutcracker Story, surrounded by figures all carved from ice - some that are almost 3 stories tall! Jackets are provided, but bring your own gloves. It only took us about 20 minutes to do that, including

going down the ice slide. Back outside, ice skating or ice tubing is a treat (there is an extra cost for these activities). You can also ride a huge rocking horse (free), ride a bucking reindeer ($5), create a gingerbread man ($12), go inside an inflatable snow globe (free), eat at the delicious food places, and grab some photo ops. The entrance ticket includes walking through the Queen Mary on your own (i.e. not a guided tour). Open daily, 10am - 11pm. The Ice Kingdom ticket includes access to the ship, entertainment, holiday activities and timed admission to The Ice Kingdom. This ticket is $24.95 for adults, $14.95 ages 4 - 11, 3 and under are free. The Chill Experience includes the features of the Ice Kingdom ticket plus either ice skating or ice tubing. This ticket is $34.95 for adults, $19.95 for kids ages 4 - 11. Discounts are available if you buy your ticket online and there are usually additional discounts in January. Parking is $17 - or park at Shoreline Village for $8 and take the free Passport shuttle.

CHRISTMAS BOAT PARADE OF LIGHTS, Newport Beach. (949) 729-4400 / www.christmasboatparade.com, Newport Beach Harbor. The largest and oldest boat parade (over 100 years!), with more than 200 participants of yachts, boats, kayaks, and more, sets sail for five nights in mid-December. Holiday lights and music fill the air as some owners spend thousands decorating their floating vessels. Consider taking the kids on a cruise to be a part of the parade, and to get a closer look at the beautiful boats. Cruises depart twice nightly at 5:45 pm and 8pm. The cost is $35 for adults; $30 for ages 12 and under. Call (949) 675-0551 for more details and reservations. The Ring of Lights contest goes on simultaneously, where bayside homes and businesses go all out in decorating to compete for prizes in various categories. (It's kind of 2-for-1 nights!) The ideal location for viewing the boat parade is Balboa Island, but you should arrive before 5:30pm, as parking is very limited. If you are going to have dinner in this area, be sure to make reservations. The parade hours are from 6:30pm - 9pm.

CHRISTMAS IN THE PARK, Poway. (858) 486-4063 or (858) 668-4575 / www.powaymidlandrr.org, 14134 Midland Rd. in Old Poway Park. It is the most wonderful time of the year to spend an afternoon in this park. The tree lighting ceremony at 5:15pm is followed by Santa's arrival via train. Caroling and other live musical holiday entertainment, a children's theater performance, a square dancing performance, holiday ornament making, a great model railroad display, and more activities for the family are offered on this second Sat. from 3:30pm - 8:30pm, for free. Refreshments (like hot chocolate and baked goods) and dinner food (like chili, corn dogs, and tamales) are available to purchase. Look up Old Poway Park (pg. 565) for more details on the park.

CHRISTMAS IN THE VILLAGE, La Mesa. (619) 303-5811 or (619) 277-5363 / www.lmvma.com, La Mesa Blvd. between Spring st. and Acacia Ave. One Friday and Saturday the street section is closed to through traffic so this winter wonderland can boast twinkling lights, holiday foods, live music on several stages, strolling carolers, horse-drawn carriage rides, bonfires, and a children's carnival with hayrides, bounces, holiday crafts, puppet shows, and a visit from Santa. Open Fri. - Sat. Parade starts at 5pm, street open until 10pm. General admission is free.

CHRISTMAS ON THE FARM, Moorpark. See page 756 for details.

CHRISTMAS PARADE, Fallbrook. / www.fallbrookchamberofcommerce.org, This one-day Christmas parade, held in early December, includes 130 groups of bands, including marching bands from Camp Pendleton; decorated floats; highway patrol vehicles; fire engines; baton twirlers; Ramona mounted patrol; and more. The parade starts at 5pm on Main Street. Admission is free.

CHRISTMAS RANCH TREE FARMS, Simi Valley, Thousand Oaks. (805) 527-6412; (805) 501-0874See the November entry on page 757 for details about these two farms.

CHRISTMAS TRAIN, Orange. (714) 997-3968 / www.irvineparkrailroad.com, 1 Irvine Park Rd. in Irvine Regional Park. Santa isn't always accessible by train, but he is at this park. While waiting for your turn to ride the scale model train to Santa's Village, which isn't quite as far as the North Pole, enjoy story time with Mrs. Claus, decorate a cookie ($5), jump around in the bounce house ($5), and do some coloring pages (free). When you disembark, meet with Santa (bring your camera!), and purchase some goodies, like hot chocolate and popcorn, at the Elf House snack bar. On your ride back, you see colorful Christmas lights around the park and go through the glowing "Tunnel of Lights". It's like getting an early Christmas present! See IRVINE REGIONAL PARK on page 282 for more details about what this terrific park has to offer. Open the last weekend in November (Fri. - Sun.), and first few weekends of December, 5pm - 8pm. Admission for the Christmas Train is $10 per person; ages 12 months and under are free. Parking is free at the park after 5pm.

CHRISTMAS TREE HOLIDAY TRAIN, Fillmore. See November (pg. 757) entry for details.

CHRISTMAS TREES, If you're looking for Christmas tree farms where you can either choose and have it cut, or ones that offer pre-cut trees (besides store parking lots), and other Christmasy activities, check out www.pickyourownchristmastree.org and www.cachristmas.com. Hope your season is blessed.

CORONADO BUTTERFLY RESERVE, Goleta. See entry (pg. 703) in January.

CRUISE OF LIGHTS, Huntington Beach. (714) 840-7542 / www.cruiseoflights.org, 16889 Algonquin St. by Huntington Harbor. The Philharmonic Society of Orange County sponsors this event, raising money to donate to the youth music programs in Orange County. For ten days in the middle of December, forty-five-minute boat tours are given around the decorated homes of the Huntington Harbor area. These homes have entered a competition, so you will see the creme de la creme, like the Sweepstakes winner, the Most Beautiful, the Most Traditional, etc. You'll also hear interesting commentary. Some boats along the way are also decked out in their Christmas best. Tours are offered at 5:30pm, 6:30pm, 7:30pm and 8:30pm. Call for specific dates. Tickets are $17 for adults, $10 for ages 2 to 12; ages 1 and under are free.

DANA POINT HARBOR BOAT PARADE OF LIGHTS, Dana Point. (949) 923-2255 or (949) 496-5794 / www.danapointharbor.com, 34624 Golden Lantern. This event has been going strong for over 30 years! Each year boats go all-out to compete for awards of Best Theme, Best Use of Lights, Best Animation, Most Colorful, Most Original, and more. The boats can be seen from anywhere in the harbor, or make a reservation at a restaurant for en*light*ening entertainment while you dine! Taking a boat ride to participate in the parade for $29 for adults; $15 for kids. Some daytime activities on these parade nights include visits with Santa Claus, holiday crafts, performances by characters, and a twenty-minute harbor cruise with Santa. The two-weekend show is given Fri. and Sat. at 7:30pm. Watching is free.

DICKEN'S HOLIDAY CELEBRATION, Torrance. (310) 515-7166 / www.printmuseum.org, 315 W. Torrance Blvd. at the International Printing Museum. You'll have the best of times, not the worst of times, at this event designed for the whole family. Characters from *The Christmas Carol, Great Expectations,* and *Tale of Two Cities*, as well as Dickens himself (not really himself, but a guy who plays him incredibly well), come to life as actors play the parts, retell his stories, and interact with the guests. Enjoy music for that time period, food (like Banger and gingerbread), printing holiday cards, and of course, all the wonderful printing presses at this awesome museum (see pg. 123). Ask about a two-hour, more educational version of this program called *The Dickens Holiday Tour* for scheduled groups, available for two weeks in December. Open Sat. and Sun., 10am - 4pm. Admission, including lunch, is $18 per person, or $50 for a family of four. See pg. 123 for more information on the INTERNATIONAL PRINTING MUSEUM.

DOWNTOWN ON ICE, Los Angeles. (213) 847-4970 / www.laparks.org/pershingsquare, 532 S. Olive near Hill St. and 5th and 6th sts. at Pershing Square. On a huge rink surrounded by L.A. skyscrapers, ice skate outside in sunny Southern California mid-November through mid January. As the rink is sponsored by the L.A. Kings, free hockey clinics are given on certain weekends. Live, afternoon concerts and Friday night concerts are free. Check out the weekend Winter Holiday Festival, noon - 8pm, which includes free entertainment, make and take crafts, snow play, puppet shows, and seasonal treats. Open Mon. - Thurs., noon - 9pm; Fri. - Sun., 10am - 10pm. Open over Christmas school break daily, 10am - 10pm. Admission is $10 and includes skate rentals. Parking is $6.

DOWNTOWN SANTA BARBARA HOLIDAY PARADE, Santa Barbara. (805) 962-2098 / www.santabarbaradowntown.com, State St., from Sola to Cota. High-stepping marching bands, floats all decked out for the holidays, performance groups, and of course, an appearance by Santa Claus, add up to an evening of fun and festivities. Usually held the first Fri. in December, 6:30pm - 8:30pm. Admission is free.

FAMILY CHRISTMAS TREE FARM, El Cajon. See the November entry (pg 757) for details.

FANTASY ON ICE, San Diego. See the November entry (pg. 757) for details.

FESTIVAL OF LIGHTS PARADE, Palm Springs. (760) 323-8276 / www.psfestivaloflights.com, on Palm Canyon Dr. between Ramon Rd. and Tamarisk Rd. The one-day holiday parade, held the first Sat. in December, includes over 100 entries including floats, big rigs, marching bands, equestrians, people, vehicles, and even animals festooned in white lights. The parade runs from 5:45pm - 8pm. Admission is free.

FESTIVAL OF LIGHTS / ICE SKATING RINK, Riverside. See the November entry (pg 757) for details.

FIRST NIGHT, Fullerton. (714) 738-6545 / www.cityoffullerton.com, bordered by Lemon, Malden, Chapman, and Commonwealth sts. Bring in the New Year all night long! This alcohol-free event includes entrance to the Fullerton Museum Center, music and dancing in the streets, food booths, and a fun zone for kids that includes kid's karaoke, face painting, train rides ($3), "ice" skating on artificial ice ($7 for 20 minutes) and other rides. Fireworks light up your life at midnight! First Night fun happens between 7pm - midnight. Admission is free. Some activities cost.

GREAT TRAIN EXPO, Del Mar. (630) 608-4988 / www.trainexpoinc.com; www.sdfair.com, 2260 Jimmy Durante Blvd. at Del Mar Fairgrounds. See the January entry for Great Train Expo (pg. 704) for details. Open 10am - 4pm. Admission is $7 for ages 13 and up (good for both days); children 12 and under are free. Parking is $10.

GREENSPOT FARMS, Mentone. See the November entry (pg. 758) for details.

HAGLE TREE FARM, Somis. See the November entry (pg. 758) for details.

HANUKKAH FAMILY FESTIVAL / FESTIVAL OF LIGHTS, Los Angeles. (310) 440-4500 or (310) 440-4636 / www.skirball.org, 2701 N. Sepulveda Blvd. at the Skirball Cultural Center. This is one of the bigger celebrations for the Festival of Lights in the area. It features storytelling, music, a participatory retelling of the story of Hanukkah, playing traditional games, and making crafts such as paper lanterns, clay oil maps, and edible dreidels. Explore the museum, except for Noah's Ark, which is closed for the day. See SKIRBALL CULTURAL CENTER on page 151 for more details on the museum. The one-day event takes place on a Sun., 11am- 4pm. Admission is $10 for adults; $7 for srs. and students; ages 2 - 12 are $5.

HANUKKAH FESTIVAL AT THE ZIMMER CHILDREN'S MUSEUM, Los Angeles. (323) 761-8984 / www.zimmermuseum.org, 6505 Wilshire Boulevard, suite #100 The Zimmer has a Hanukkah Festival each year with a full day of light-themed activities including story time, holiday crafts, and more! The museum is free on this day. See ZIMMER CHILDREN'S MUSEUM on page 158 for more details on the museum. Open Sun., 12:30pm to 5pm.

HANUKKAH HAPPENING, San Diego. (858) 457-3030 / www.lfjcc.org, 4126 Executive Dr. The Lawrence Family Jewish Community Center has a family celebration every year including carnival games, a climbing wall, arts & crafts and more.

HOLIDAY AFLOAT PARADE, San Pedro. (310) 549-8111 / www.sanpedrochamber.com, 1100 Nagoya Way at Ports O' Call. Owners go all out to decorate their boats - tall ships, tugboats, and leisure boats large and small - and compete for the best in a wonderful parade that is put on the first Saturday of December. You can view the ninety-minute parade along the Port's O Call shore from the *S. S. Lane Victory* Los Angeles Maritime Museum, or from other nearby places. Dress warmly. The parade starts at 6pm.

HOLIDAY AT THE RANCH, Goleta. (805) 681-7216 / www.stowhouse.com, 304 N. Los Carneros Rd. This weekend open house beckons visitors to not only see Santa and his "rein-goats", but also to take a guided tour through the historic house beautifully decked out in holiday style, and enjoy story time and live music. Note that SOUTH COAST RAILROAD MUSEUM (on page 635) is just next door, offering scale model train rides. See STOWHOUSE / RANCHO LA PATERA on page 635 for more details about the ranch. Open Sat. - Sun., 11am - 4pm. Admission is $5 for adults; $2 for ages 12 and under.

HOLIDAY FESTIVAL, Coronado. (619) 435-6611 / www.coronadochamber.com; www.ecoronado.com, at First Street at the Ferry Landing Marketplace. On the first Friday in December the party starts when Santa arrives by ferry (the reindeer are taking a rest) at about 4:30pm. A parade commences down Orange Ave. at 6pm, complete with floats, bands, animals, and kids, to Rotary Park. The festivities conclude with a tree lighting ceremony and fireworks. In between time, enjoy snow play; seeing the 100,000 twinkling lights at Hotel Del Coronado; visiting Santa's village, complete with booth, games and prizes; and skating at the outdoor ice rink right by the beach (see page 759 for details). The festival runs from 4pm - 7pm. Admission is free.

HOLIDAY IN THE PARK - LAS POSADAS, San Diego. (619) 220-5422 or (619) 297-9327 / www.parks.ca.gov/oldtownsandiego; www.oldtownsandiegoguide.com, between San Diego Ave. and Twiggs St. in Old Town San Diego State Historic Park. This two-day event celebrates Christmas in an early California manner. Museums, historic homes, stores and restaurants will be decorated in a way befitting the period. There is music and entertainment both nights. On Sun at 5pm is Las Posadas, a retelling of the trek Mary and Joseph made to Bethlehem, looking for lodging. Join in the procession weaving through the park and in the singing of traditional Mexican and American carols. (Or just hum along.) A pinata party for all children follows the parade. Look up page 544 for more info on the park. Open Sat. and Sun., 6pm - 9pm. General admission to the Fiesta and walking around the park is free..

HOLIDAY ON ICE, Irvine. See November entry (pg. 758) for details.

HOLIDAY SPIRIT OF SAN PEDRO PARADE, San Pedro. (310) 832-7272 / www.sanpedrochamber.com, 15th and Pacific in the historic waterfront district. Get in the spirit of Christmas with this holiday parade put on the first Sunday of the month at 1pm. Enjoy local drill teams, floats, bands, fire engines, police motorcycle brigades, and more.

HOTEL DEL CORONADO ICE RINK, Coronado. See November entry (pg. 759) for details.

HOW THE GRINCH STOLE CHRISTMAS, San Diego. See November entry (pg. 759) for details.

ICE AT SANTA MONICA, Santa Monica. See the November entry (pg. 759) for details.

INDIO INTERNATIONAL TAMALE FESTIVAL, Indio. (760) 391-4175 / www.tamalefestival.net, Between Hwy 111 and Indio Blvd., filling the streets of Miles, Towne, Smurr & Requa. Hot tamales, mild tamales and everything in between are cooked and served fresh here at this massively attended festival. Besides just eating, there is a parade (at 10am on Saturday); kid's petting zoo; Rad Rider Bike show; rock climbing wall; inflatable bounces; carnival

rides and games; contests; and traditional Mexican Folkloric dancing and singing, and other entertainment on four stages. Grab your amigos and come fiesta. Open the first weekend in December, Sat. - Sun., 10am - 6pm. Free.

JOURNEY TO BETHLEHEM, Manhattan Beach. (310) 372-4641 / www.journeyoffaith.com, 1243 Artesia Blvd. at Journey of Faith. Over 2,000 years ago Jesus was born in a stable. What was it like? This outside, re-creation tells the story with a presentation and over 170 costumed characters of shepherds, Mary and Joseph, angels, soldiers, live animals (including a camel), and citizens of Bethlehem acting their part. Then, walk the straw-strewn "streets" and mingle with the locals, including Roman soldiers, as they talk to you while in character. Listen as the people haggle for wares. Try your hand at a trade. Kids will also enjoy the petting farm. Each guest is given some shekel-type coins to spend on dried fruit and nuts, authentic food, brick making, creating a clay coil pot, and other ancient crafts. "Experiencing" history helps kids to understand it. Dress warmly as the event is outdoors. Fri. - Sun., 6pm - 9pm. Admission is free.

JULEFEST / WINTERFEST, Solvang. (805) 688-6144 / www.solvangusa.com, This Julefest is really the name for the quaint town of Solvang following Yule traditions and dressing up for Christmas. The town looks like a small European village that twinkle with thousands of lights around and in the shops. Throughout the month, at certain times, there are crafts for kids, carolers, dances performed, carriage rides (for a fee), a parade throughout the streets, and lighting of the Christmas tree. A few other highlights include gawking at a gigantic gingerbread house (8' by 11' by 10') on display at Olsen's Danish Village Bakery at 1529 Mission Drive (you can decorate your own cookie here, too); a Farmer's Markets on Wednesdays; and a Santa Lucia Pageant at Solvang Park at the corner of Mission Dr. / Hwy 246 and First St. This is where theater students parade through the streets, end up at the park, and use verse, movement, and dance, to tell the story of Santa Lucia Day. Look up Nativity Pageant (pg. 769) for details on another special attraction during this fest. General admission is free.

JUNGLE BELLS AT SAN DIEGO ZOO, San Diego. (619) 231-1515 / www.sandiegozoo.org, 2920 Zoo Dr. in Balboa Park. For a few weeks this month, see the zoo in a whole new light! Holiday and animal-themed animated figures move and light up the sky (and some enclosures) to celebrate the holiday season, such as a fifty-two-foot lighted train, six-foot-tall toy soldiers, animated horse and buggy, and a giant teddy bear. Children 16 years and under can slip and slide down a 100-yard hill covered in freshly made snow, create holiday crafts, meet Santa, listen to storytellers, and more. Both the snow play area and lights festival are open mid-December through the end of the month daily, 4pm - 9pm. Closed Christmas Eve and Christmas Day. Admission to these attractions is included with the price of admission to the zoo - $46 for adults; $36 for ages 3 - 11; children 2 and under are free.

KING HARBOR YACHT CLUB CHRISTMAS BOAT PARADE, Redondo Beach. (310) 376-2459 / www.redondo.org, 181 N. Harbor Dr. at King Harbor and Redondo Beach Pier. *Watt* a spectacular sight! Lighted boats parade from King Harbor Marina to the Redondo Beach Pier, with live commentary provided just south of Polly's on the Pier. The parade is in mid-December, 5:30pm - 7pm. Admission is free.

L.A. COUNTY HOLIDAY CELEBRATION, Los Angeles. (213) 972-3099 / www.holidaycelebration.org, 135 N. Grand Ave. at the Dorothy Chandler Pavilion of the Music Center. Think of it as a gift offering: This free holiday extravaganza (even the parking is free) is three hours long and filled with dance and music performances of all nationalities and cultures. Ballet, barbershop quartets, gospel choirs, Chinese Classical Musical Ensemble, folk dance, and soooo much more. You do not have to stay for the entire three hours, but whatever you see and hear, you'll feel the richer for it. December 24, 3pm - 6pm. Doors open at 2:30pm and seating is first come, first served.

LAS POSADAS, Los Angeles. / www.olvera-street.com, Olvera St. For nine consecutive nights, guests are invited to join in this Mexican tradition of singing and a candlelight procession led by actors portraying Mary and Joseph as the couple searches for shelter in Bethlehem. The Christmas pageant also includes a more modern celebration of breaking open a pinata. The festival is open 5:30pm - 8:30pm. Admission is free.

LAS POSADAS, Santa Fe Springs. (562) 946-6476 / www.santafesprings.org, 12100 Mora Dr. at Heritage Park. In step with Mexican traditions, carols in both English and Spanish are sung along the candle lit processional route, as participants (who are encouraged to dress up according to the time period) follow "Mary" and "Joseph" as they seek to find shelter in Bethlehem. Once it is found, the fiesta begins with folkloric dancers and mariachis, and free refreshments. This one-day, Fri. evening procession begins at 6:30pm. Admission is free.

LIGHTED STREETS, Is there a street or two in your neighborhood that the owners have gone all out to decorate every year? A great family tradition is to choose one special night during the Christmas season, go out to a restaurant, and walk up and down the festive streets to enjoy the lights and displays. *Just a few* choice streets include: **Los Angeles County**: *Candy Cane Lane in Woodland Hills - This eight-block neighborhood of Winnetka St. bordered by Corbin Ave. and Victory Blvd goes all out. Gazillions of lights, animated scenes, inflatable snowmen, and more. *Upper

Hastings Ranch in Pasadena - This forty-four block area is bordered by Michillinda Ave., Sierra Madre Blvd. and Riviera Dr. Over 1,000 homes participate and each block decides on and decorates according to a certain theme. Call (626) 793-9911 (a holiday hotline) for other Pasadena light displays. *Santa Fe Springs has an annual Christmas Home Decorating Contest - contact (562) 868-0511 or www.santafesprings.org for winners. *Altadena's Christmas Tree Lane has earned a spot on the National Register of Historic Places - check out www.christmastreelane.net. **Orange County:** *Eagle Hills in Brea has around 100 homes that decorate - enter on E. Birch and S. Starflower Sts. or E. Lambert Rd. and Sunflower St. *Check out www.lakeforestchirsmas.com for a map of houses and streets in south Orange County. **Riverside County:** *Bainbridge Circle in Murieta goes all out for the holidays. **Ventura County**: *Oxnard Historical District in Oxnard - Along F and G sts., between 5th and Palm, and the surrounding area - decorations light up the night in this old and elegant area, nightly. Check (805) 385-7545 / www.visitOxnard.com for more info. **San Diego County**: *Eastlake neighborhood - Off Otay Lakes Rd. & Eastlake Pkwy. homes compete in holiday contest. View winners on www.eastlake.net. **San Bernardino County:** Alta Loma has some great houses - exit 210 fwy N. on Carnelian. **Santa Barbara County:** Old Town Santa Barbara Trolley of Lights Tour - for $25 for adults, $15 for children 12 & under, you can sit back and let the trolley take you on a 90 tour of the best displays in Santa Barbara.

LIGHTS ON TEMPLE CITY, Temple City. (626) 285-2171 / www.ci.temple-city.ca.us, 9701 Las Tunas Dr. at Temple City Park. No matter the weather, twenty-five tons of snow will arrive at the park to help ring in the holidays in this community event. Besides the two play areas and snow run for children 12 and under, there are visits with Santa, crafts for kids, bounce houses, a merry-go-round, scale model train rides, snacks, musical entertainment by the high school, and a lighting of the 100' redwood tree. Festivities are open from 5pm - 9pm, with a mini-parade at 7pm. Admission is free.

LIVE OAK CANYON CHRISTMAS TREE FARM, Yucaipa. See November entry (pg. 759) for details. Don't miss this one!

LOGAN'S CANDIES, Ontario. See November entry (pg. 759) for details.

MARINA DEL REY HOLIDAY BOAT PARADE, Marina del Rey. (310) 670-7130 / www.mdrboatparade.org, Admiralty Way. On the second Sat. of December over eighty boats, decorated to the hilt with Christmas lights and decorations, circle around the marina's main channel. The parade is exciting with winners chosen for Best Theme, Best Humor, Best Music, Best Animation, etc. The best views are at 13650 Mindanao Way at Burton Chase Park (where the "live" action and music is played throughout), or 13755 Fiji Way at Fisherman's Village. Sat. 6pm - 8pm. The festivities begin with a fireworks display.

MENORAH LIGHTING AT FASHION ISLAND, Newport Beach. (949) 721-9800 / www.jewishnewport.com, 401 Newport Center Dr. Along with the lighting of the Jerusalem Stone Menorah; hear live music, enjoy dreidles, doughnuts, balloon animals, face painting, and treats; and make Hannukah crafts. Bring an unwarpped gift for the community toy drive. Start 3pm at the Atrium Garden Court.

MESSIAH SING-ALONG, Los Angeles. (213) 972-7282 / www.lamc.org, 111 South Grand Ave. at Walt Disney Concert Hall. Sing it out (but maybe practice first!) as you join in on one of the most acclaimed chorale presentations; you are part of the chorus. Buy a score in the lobby for $10, or bring your own. This the grandest avenue of all this type of event, but call your local orchestra as several others offer this same opportunity. Two Sun. evenings, at 7pm. Tickets are $24 - $113 per person.

MISSION BAY CHRISTMAS PARADE OF LIGHTS, Mission Bay. (858) 488-0501 / www.mbyc.org, The dazzling, lighted boat parade (the title of the event is self-explanatory) begins at Quivira Basin at 7pm and ends with lighting of the Sea World Sky Tower Tree of Lights and fireworks display at 9pm. The best viewing of these more than 100 boats is along Crown Point, the east side of Vacation Island, or the west side of Fiesta Island. Admission is free.

MONARCH BUTTERFLIES, Ventura. See January entry (pg. 705) for details.

MUSEUMS, Many of your favorite museums get all decked out for the holidays, particularly the historical homes. Many also offer holiday programs, with special family activities.

NANCY'S RANCH, Santa Clarita. (661) 255-6943 / www.nancysranch.com, 25039 ½ W. Magic Mountain Pkwy. For the true Christmas tree ranch experience, walk among the acres of Monterey pine to choose and cut your own. Pre-cut trees are also available. The ranch is open the Friday after Thanksgiving through Christmas Eve, Mon. - Fri., 10am - dusk; Sat. - Sun., 9am - dusk. The pre-cut area is open nightly until 9pm.

NAPLES HOLIDAY BOAT PARADE, Long Beach. (562) 570-5333 or (562) 436-3645 / www.naplesca.com, 5437 E. Ocean Blvd. at Los Alamitos Bay around the Naples Canals, and along 2nd St. by the Long Beach Yacht Club. Boat-owners cover their boats with Christmas lights, and parade past decorated homes along the Naples canals. If you miss the boat (parade), just seeing the homes along here is a special treat (see next entry). Sat., 6pm - 10pm. Admission

is free.

NAPLES ISLAND, Long Beach. This small "island" in Long Beach is always on our list of places to go at Christmas. The homes here are beautiful any time of the year, but from Thanksgiving until New Years, they take on a magical quality with the elaborate and wonderful decorations. This community is known as Naples because it is surrounded by canals, so you can start your walk anywhere along the water and end up back where you started from. The only thing not magical about this place is the parking. Although it is free, you will probably spend several minutes looking for a space. Just do what I do and sing Christmas carols loudly while you look - the kids always enjoy this. See the previous entry for information about the boat parade here. Evenings in December.

NATIVITY PAGEANT, Solvang. (800) 468-6765 or (805) 688-6144 / www.solvangusa.com, 420 2nd Street at the outdoor Festival Theater. The narrated nativity pageant is performed in Solvang's outdoor theater (dress warmly) on a Saturday evening in December. The program features a choir, characters in full costumes, and live animals all accompanied by narration. It is held in conjunction with JULEFEST - see page 767 for details. The first show starts at 5pm; the second at 7pm. Free admission - first come, first served.

NORTH POLE EXPRESS, Fillmore. See November entry (pg. 760) for details.

NUTCRACKER, Numerous venues all over Southern California present this classic ballet to the timeless music of Tchaikovsky. This is an enchanting way to expose your children to the beauty of ballet and classical music because of the costumed characters and gripping storyline. Look in the main section of the book under Shows and Theaters for ballet companies, and/or call your local theater.

OCEANSIDE YACHT CLUB PARADE OF LIGHTS, Oceanside. (760) 722-5751 / www.ci.oceanside.ca.us; www.oceansidechamber.com, 1540 Harbor Drive S. at Oceanside Harbor. For one bright evening, boats decked out in lights go on parade circling the inner harbor. For best viewing, come early and stand near the Harbor Police and fishing dock. The parade runs from 6pm - 9pm - call to find out the exact date. Admission is free.

AN OLD-FASHIONED CHRISTMAS MELODRAMA & ICE CREAM SOCIAL, Costa Mesa. (714) 432-5880 / www.orangecoastcollege.edu; www.octickets.com, 2701 Fairview Rd. at Orange Coast College. Yea for the hero! Boo to the villain! Fa la la with the music! Yum for the ice cream! This annual Christmas Melodrama is great fun for the family to participate in, plus the audience enjoys ice cream with elves at intermission and singing classic Christmas carols. And whohoho do you think comes for a visit at the end of the show? Shows are Fri., 7pm; Sat. and Sun., 2:30pm and 7pm. Tickets are $9 at the door for adults; $7 for children. Parking is free.

OXNARD CHRISTMAS PARADE / TAMALE FESTIVAL, Oxnard. (805) 247-0197 - parade; (805) 766-4906 - tamale / www.downtownoxnard.org, 9th and A sts. to 2nd St. The hometown parade includes floats decorated to a new theme each year, plus marching bands, entertainment, and an awards ceremony. Gobble up authentic homemade tamales during the Tamale Festival, held in conjunction with the parade. Tamale-making demos, live mariachi music, arts and crafts, visits with Santa Claus, and more fun are to be had. The parade is Sat. at 10am. Admission is free.

PARADE OF 1,000 LIGHTS, Long Beach. (562) 435-4093 / www.shorelineyachtclub.com, 429 Shoreline Village Dr. Come enjoy the boats on parade that are adorned with Christmas lights and decorations. Prizes are awarded in several categories. The best views are from Shoreline Village, particularly Parkers Lighthouse, although parking is at a premium. The parade is on a Sat. and starts at 5:30pm. Admission is free.

PARADE OF LIGHTS, Oxnard. (805) 985-4852 or (805) 247-0197 or (800) 269-6273 parade / www.channelislandsharbor.org, 3600 S. Harbor Blvd. at Channel Islands Harbor at Marine Emporium Landing. During this eventful Saturday kids have tons of cold fun at the snowplay area, available from noon until it melts. Live music including carolers; rides and games, such as a rock climbing wall, inflatable fun zones, and water taxi rides; holiday arts and crafts boutique; and visits with Santa and Mrs. Claus are some of the other seasonal offerings. The parade is officially kicked off at 7pm when Santa and his reindeers fly over head (via a helicopter - but don't tell the kids). Watch as numerous boats are decked out for the *hulladays* with lights and animated displays. The parade begins in front of Peninsula Park, heads to the main channel, and loops back around for a second run. Dress warmly (or drink some hot chocolate!). General admission is free.

PARADE OF LIGHTS / SANTA'S VILLAGE, Santa Barbara. (805) 564-5530 / www.santabarbaraca.gov/visitor, Cabrillo Street, at Harbor and along the beach near Stearns Wharf. At 3pm on this Sunday, Santa and his elves arrive escorted by the Harbor Patrol - come by and chat with them. Carolers and special activities from the Maritime Museum add to the enchantment. From 5:30pm - 7pm watch the over thirty decorated boats sail out of the harbor and parade up and down the shoreline, vying for prizes. The evening ends with a firework display. The best vantage point for the parade is on Stearns Wharf. A wonderful fireworks display signals the end of parade. Admission is free.

PARADE OF LIGHTS, Ventura. (805) 642-8538 / www.venturaharborvillage.com, 1500 Spinnaker Dr. at Ventura

Harbor Village. This two-night festive boat parade is usually held the second weekend in December. Pre-parade events include live music, visits with Santa, a fly-by with Santa (via helicopter), carousel rides, games, and indulging in shopping and eating. Located at 1575 Spinnaker Drive and dubbed California Sleigh Rides, Ventura Boat Rentals offers cruises during most of the month to see the boat and shoreline home lights even more close up, traveling along the same route as the parade. Adults are $20; children are $10. Call (805) 642-7753 / www.venturaboatrentals.com for more details. The evening festivities, after the wonderful parade, end with a fireworks display. Fri. and Sat., 5pm for pre-parade fun; 7pm for boat parade. General admission is free.

PELTZER PINES, Brea, Irvine, Silverado. See November entry (pg. 760) for details.

PINE TREE ACRES, Ramona. See Pine Tree Acres (pg. 760) for details.

PISMO BEACH MONARCH GROVE, Pismo Beach. See January entry (pg. 705) for details.

PLANETARIUM SHOWS - CHRISTMAS SHOW / STAR OF BETHLEHEM, See November entry (pg. 760) for details.

POLICE SERVICES CENTER OPEN HOUSE, Santa Fe Springs. (562) 409-1850 / www.santafesprings.org, 11576 E. Telegraph Rd. For about two weeks in the latter part of December, the Police Services Center has staff available for tours of the police station where visitors can meet police officers, detectives, and the public safety team. Coffee, hot chocolate and cookies are available, gratis. Open 10am - 5pm. Admission is free.

PORT OF SAN DIEGO BIG BAY BALLOON PARADE, San Diego. (619) 283-5808 / www.holidaybowl.com, Harbor Dr. Although football is the focal point of this one-day, Holiday Bowl, the colorful, televised parade is also a highlight, especially for kids. Dubbed "America's Largest Balloon Parade" floats, a huge variety of gigantic character and other balloons, numerous marching bands, drill teams, and other entertainment await sports fans of all ages. The two-hour parade begins at 9am. Admission is free. Grandstand seating is $20.

RANCHO NOEL POTRERO VALLEY CHRISTMAS TREE FARM, Potrero. See the November entry on page 761 for details.

REINDEER ROMP, Los Angeles. See November entry (pg. 761) for details.

ROSE PARADE DECORATING, Pasadena. (626) 449-4100 / www.tournamentofroses.com, Volunteers are always needed so call to ask where you can help decorate the Rose Parade floats. Children at least 13 years old and whose parents are Auto Club members can help decorate the AAA float. Check the listed website for other companies who need volunteers as well.

ROSE PARADE FLOAT VIEWING, Pasadena. (626) 449-4100 / www.tournamentofroses.com, Rosemont Pavilion - 700 Seco St.; Rose Palace - 835 S. Raymond Ave.; and Brookside Pavilion - 1001 Rose Bowl Dr. at the Rose Bowl, which has access to those with physical disabilities, on the west side of the Rose Bowl Stadium. Come "backstage" to see the world-famous floats as they are being made. Workers spend weeks meticulously decorating them using plants, seeds, tree bark, flowers, and single petals. Open 3 or 4 days before December 31st. Call to verify dates and times. Admission is $10; free for ages 5 and under.

SAN DIEGO BAY PARADE OF LIGHTS, San Diego. (619) 224-2240 / www.sdparadeoflights.org, San Diego Bay. First - fireworks! Then, over 100 boats decked out with lights participate in a parade from Shelter Island, past the Embarcadero, Seaport Village, and then on to Ferry landing on Coronado, ending at the Navy carrier basin. The parade offers prizes to the "best of" in several categories. It runs on two consecutive Sun., 5:30pm - 9pm. Free viewing from the shoreline.

SAN PASQUAL BATTLE REENACTMENT, San Pasqual. (760) 737-2201 / www.parks.ca.gov, 15808 San Pasqual Valley Rd. at San Pasqual Battlefield State Historic Park. On a Sunday nearest to December 6, reenactors dress up as mountain men and other pivotal figures from the mid-1800's and they pitch tents; provide music, crafts (i.e. adobe brick making, candle making, etc.), and dance of the era; and best of all, they reenact the battle that actually took place here more than 150 years ago (they even fire cannons!) at 11:30am and 2:30pm. See the SAN PASQUAL BATTLEFIELD STATE HISTORIC PARK entry on page 518 for more details on the park. Open 10am - 3:30pm. Admission is free.

SANTA PAULA CHRISTMAS TREE FARM, Santa Paula. See the November entry (pg. 761) for details.

SANTA'S ELECTRIC LIGHT PARADE, Temecula. / www.cityoftemecula.org, See the November entry (pg. 761) for details. This event is either in November or December, depending on the year.

SANTA'S NORTH POLE LIMITED, Campo. See the November entry (pg. 761) for details.

SANTA TRAIN, Perris. (951) 943-3020 / www.oerm.org, 2201 South "A" St. at the Orange Empire Railway Museum. An all-day pass to ride the trains and trolleys is included in your admission price, but on these two weekends,

you also get to visit with Santa on board a specially decked-out train. Share your wish list and receive a free little gift. There are refreshments, Christmas music, and a lots of ho ho hoing. During the day children visit with Santa on the train. The evening train takes passengers to Santa's workshop. See page 371 for more detail about the museum. Open Sat. - Sun., with train trips between 11am - 4pm and 5:30pm - 7:30pm. The daytime Santa Train is $12 for adults; $8 for ages 5 - 11; children 4 and under are free. The evening Train to Santa's Workshop is $15 for adults; $10 for ages 5 - 11, $5 for ages 2 - 4; children 1 and under are free.

SNOW DAYS AT KIDSPACE, Pasadena. (626) 449-9144 / www.kidspacemuseum.org, 480 N. Arroyo Blvd. at Kidspace Museum. Walking, or playing, in a winter wonderland is waay fun! Play in real snow - so bring mittens, boots and warm jackets - in the courtyard of Kidspace Museum
Open after Christmas, 9:30am - 5pm. Price includes admission to the museum: $11 per person; infants under 1 are free.

TOURNAMENT OF ROSES EVENTS, Pasadena. (877) 793-9911 - holiday hotline; (626) 449-4100 / www.tournamentofroses.com, 1001 Rose Bowl Dr. at the Rose Bowl. For three or four days before the big parade and football game, fans can participate in several activities and events that occur at various times at the bowl and off-site. See the **floats being decorated**. (See Rose Parade Float Viewing on pg. 770 for details.) **Bandfest** is the opportunity to watch the practice of the award-winning marching bands from around the world that will be in the parade. It is held at 1570 E. Colorado Blvd. at Pasadena City College. The three shows are Dec. 29, 2pm - 4:30pm; Dec. 30, 10am - 12:30pm; 2pm - 4:30pm. The cost is $15 per person; free for ages 5 and under. **Equestfest** is held at 480 Riverside Drive in Burbank at the Los Angeles Equestrian Center on one day from 10:30am - 3pm. Stroll through the stables, talk with riders, and most of all enjoy the show at noon where riders and mounts perform drills as they practice for their turn in the parade. Trick roping and riding demonstrations, live entertainment, horse-drawn fire wagons, and food round out your day here. The cost is $15 per person; children 5 and under are free. Parking is $5. Ultimate fans can attend the **Rose Bowl Kickoff Luncheon** ($90 per person) and dine with everybody who's anybody in the Rose Parade or game, including the Rose Queen and her court, athletes, coaches, officials, and the grand marshal. Tickets are available through Ticketmaster at (800) 745-3000 or www.ticketmaster.com. Exact events and times change every year, so check the website to plan your outing.

TREE LIGHTING CEREMONY, Long Beach. (562) 435-3511 / www.queenmary.com, 1126 Queens Highway at the Queen Mary. "Deck the hull" with the tree lighting ceremony which includes a holiday sing-a-long and musical performances. Includes complimentary access to Chill (pg. 763). Wed., 3pm - 11pm. Free admission with an unwrapped toy, and the parking price is reduced.

UNA NOCHE DE LAS POSADAS, Santa Barbara. (805) 965-0093 / www.sbthp.org, 123 East Canon Perdido St. at El Presidio de Santa Barbara State Historic Park. A reenactment of Joseph and Mary's search for shelter in Bethlehem] is traditionally celebrated throughout Mexico and South America, and by early California inhabitants. After a short mass and singing of classic Christmas songs, join the procession, led by Joseph and Mary, and walk and sing from State Street, through the Paseo Nuevo mall, and ending at Casa de la Guerra where the young couple finds lodging. Everyone, then, enjoys more singing, hot chocolate, and a pinata (for the kids - just like in Bethlehem over 2,000 years ago!) Fri., starting at 7pm Admission is free.

UPTOWN HOLIDAY PARADE, Whittier. (562) 696-2662 / www.whittieruptown.org, This one-day, uptown parade, for us downtown folks, features more than 120 entries including highschool bands, equestrian and marching units, floats, and Santa Claus. The route is down Greenleaf from Hadley to Mar Vista, ending at Whittier Community Center. The parade in on a Sat., 10am - noon. Admission is free.

VICTORIAN CHRISTMAS, Lake Forest. (949) 923-2230 / www.ocparks.com, 25151 Serrano Rd. at Heritage Hill Historical Park. On the first Saturday in December, experience Christmas as it was during the turn-of-the century. Walk through these four historic buildings, which are festooned with old-fashioned decorations. Over forty exhibits display and demonstrate homemade handicrafts like wooden carvings and lace making. A popular display is the antique engines which include a milking machine, a corn husker, and a corn grinder. A free children's crafts area is available for kids to make their own special creations such as dipping candles and decorating holiday cookies. Genteel entertainment is provided - strolling carolers, jugglers, a silhouette artist, and Saint Nicholas also pays a visit. Shop at the handicraft booths. Children 11 and under can shop at the Children's Shopping Booth, where gifts are less expensive. Note that Heritage Hill also has annual candlelight tours on the second weekend of this month from 5:30pm - 8:30pm. Victorian Christmas is open 11am - 3pm. Admission is $4 for adults; $3 for ages 3 - 12; children 2 and under are free.

VICTORIAN CHRISTMAS, Wilmington. (310) 548-7777 / www.banningmuseum.org, 401 E. M St. at the General

Phineas Banning Residence Museum. Kick off the Yuletide season by immersing yourself in the 19th century on the first weekend in December at the Banning Museum (pg. 101). Docents greet you dressed in period costumes and show you around the beautifully-decorated house/museum. The lavish Victorian adornments are quite lovely and the costumed carolers, bell ringers, and musicians complete the ambiance. You may even take a horse and trolley ride to and from the Drum Barracks Museum (pg. 106), which is just down the street. Open Sat. - Sun., 11am - 4pm. Admission is free.

VICTORIAN HOLIDAY HOUSE TOURS, Oxnard. (805) 247-0197 / www.heritagesquareoxnard.com, 715 S. "A" St. at Heritage Square. Take advantage of this rare opportunity to see the interiors of select Victorian homes as they are decked out for the holidays. Period Christmas music, living history performances, and an old-time ambiance add to the festive atmosphere. Guided tours by docents dressed from that era talk about the pioneers who originally owned the homes, and the architecture. You can also visit the near-by, free, gingerbread house display, at the Heritage Square Hall, 731 S. A Street, Tues. - Sat., 10am - 5pm and Sun., 1pm - 4pm. Tours take place on Sat., 10am - 4pm; Sun., 1pm - 4pm. Reservations are suggested. Admission is $5 per person.

THE WICKERD FARM CHRISTMAS TREES, Menifee. (951) 672-3020 or (909) 286-8289 / www.wickerdfarm.com, 26852 Scott Rd. Cut your own tree at this five-acre farm. There is a giant oak tree with a tire swing, picnic areas, and hayrides. Santa makes an appearance on certain weekends. Open the day after Thanksgiving until Christmas, Sun - Thurs., 10am - 8pm, Fri. - Sat. 10am - 9pm. Admission is free.

WILDLIGHTS, Palm Desert. See November entry (pg. 761) for details.

WINTER FANTASY, Laguna Beach. See November entry (pg. 762) for details.

WINTER FANTASY MUSIC & LIGHT SHOW, Oxnard. (805) 385-2705 / www.downtownoxnard.org, corner of B and Fifth sts. at Plaza Park. Put a little sparkle into your life with this computer-generated music and light show at the Plaza Park Pagoda - a fun add-on to your holiday activities. The show can be seen nightly, every fifteen minutes, throughout the month of December from 5pm - 10pm. Indulge in dinner and/or a movie at the adjacent Centennial Plaza.

WINTERFEST, Garden Grove. (714) 741-5200 / www.ci.garden-grove.ca.us, 13630 Atlantis Way, at Atlantis Park. A lot of holiday fun is packed into the first Saturday of this month: Snow play and sledding; pictures with Santa; games; inflatable bounces; and a crafts area where kids can make a variety of projects such as ornaments, wrapping paper, and Christmas cards. Even a dinner of hot dog, chips and a drink, are included in your admission price. The carnival runs from 4pm - 8pm. Admission is $10; children 2 and under are free.

WINTER FUNDERLAND, Santa Barbara. (805) 682-4711 / www.sbnature.org, 2559 Puesta Del Sol, at the Santa Barbara Museum of Natural History. One Saturday this month enjoy a true winter day complete with snow that you can play in until it melts (bring jackets and mittens), plus Santa and some of his reindeers, Frosty the Snowman, winter-themed crafts, hot chocolate, face painting, and a planetarium show called (at least one year it was called this), *Santa's Starry Ride*. All this and all the fun the museum has to offer! See page 630 for more details on the museum. Open Sat., 10am - 4pm. Admission is $12 for adults; $8 for srs. and teens; $7 ages 3 - 12; children 2 and under are free. Planetarium shows are an additional $4 per person.

WINTER GATHERING AND POW WOW, Coachella. (866) 878-6829 / www.spotlight29.com, 46-200 Harrison Place at Spotlight29 Casino. This three-day annual gathering of the Coachella Valley native peoples is energetic, colorful, and memorable. Traditional dress, dances, and songs take the stage, while Native American arts and crafts and food vie for your attention, too. The Grand Entrance is 7pm Fri. & Sat., and 1pm Sat. & Sun. Open Fri. - Sun., noon - evening. (Call for specific hours.) Free.

WINTER LIGHT PARADE, Twentynine Palms. (760) 367-3445 / www.visit29.org, Adobe Rd./Hwy. 62. This hometown parade is held on Saturday starting at 5:15 p.m. The light parade slogan is - if you can put lights on it, enter it. So, enjoy the floats and entries of all kinds, plus shopping, dining, and entertainment following the parade.

WINTERLIT CELEBRATION, Santa Monica. See November entry (pg. 762) for details.

WINTER WONDERLAND AT THE VENTURA HARBOR, Ventura. (805) 642-8538 / www.venturaharborvillage.com, 1500 Spinnaker Dr. at Ventura Harbor Village. Celebrate the holiday season with this one-day event with snow flurries (faux snow), a visit with Santa and some of his reindeers (I can't tell which ones), strolling carolers, and other live entertainment, ice carving demonstrations, and all the fun - carnival rides and games - that the Village has to offer. Open Sun., 1pm - 5pm. General admission is free.

WOODLAND HILLS ICE, Woodland Hills. See October entry (pg. 756) for details.

IDEAS and RESOURCES
(General ideas of where else to go and what to do, plus where to find specific resource information.)

AIRPLANE or HELICOPTER RIDES: Look in the phone book; call small, local airports for flight information; and/or check the Transportation section in this book for specific flying venues.

ANIMALS

AA Laboratories: (714) 893-5675 / www.egglab.com - They sell fertilized eggs, such as a dozen chick eggs for $12. They also have fertilized duck, quail and goose eggs, and even blown goose eggs for crafts. Incubators rent for $10 a week - home births without the labor pains! Be forewarned, however, that very little instruction comes with your eggs and incubator. Tips: Go to the library to research the process by checking out picture books of developing chicks and ducks. Or, pick up an information sheet and feed at a pet store, such as Blacksmith's Corner, (562) 531-0386 in Bellflower. And yes, if you do not want to raise the birds, AA Labs will (usually) take them back and donate them to farms, zoos, etc.

Insect Lore: (800) LIVE BUG (548-3284) / www.insectlore.com - This website offers living science kits, giving families the opportunity to observe insects and other critters growing and transforming. Our favorite kits are the butterfly; earthworms and compost; praying mantis; silkworm; ladybird beetles (i.e. ladybugs, to lay people); and frog hatchery. Each kit comes with instructions, information, and eggs or embryos. The catalog also offers owl pellets to dissect, plus other science experiments, books, and visual aids.

Wagon Train Feed & Pet in Orange: (714) 639-7932 / www.wagontrainoc.com - This small pet store sells chick, duck, and quail eggs, as well as incubators. (See the Pet Store entry for more details.)

ARCHERY: Look under the Great Outdoors sections in each county for local parks that offer archery ranges. You can also check out USA Archery at www.usarchery.org or call (719) 866-4576. They refer callers to local clubs and places to practice.

ARTS AND CRAFTS: Many places, including libraries and bookstores, offer free or minimal fee classes, or workshops for kids. Also check out craft and handicraft stores such as:

Home Depot: (800) 553-3199 / www.homedepot.com - Most offer free workshops between 9am and noon on the 1st Sat. of each month.

Lakeshore Learning Materials stores: (800) 421-5354 / www.lakeshorelearning.com - Most stores offer free crafts for kids every Sat. from 11am - 3pm for ages 3 and up.

Lowes: (800) 445-6937 / www.lowesbuildandgrow.com - Several offer a free kids' clinic at 10am on the 2nd Sat. of each month. Sign up on their website.

Michaels: (800) MICHAEL (642-4235) / www.michaels.com - Ask about their kids' program, The Knack, which includes free family events and Sat. classes.

Piecemakers Country Store: (714) 641-3112 / www.piecemakers.com - Take a class in needlework, quilting, beading or other old-time country crafts.

AUDIO CDS: The following are some of our favorite, non-singing, CDs

Adventures in Odyssey: (800) A-FAMILY (232-6459) / www.family.org - Focus on the Family puts out this outstanding series consisting of Biblically-based, radio dramas. The stories are centered around a fictional soda shop/Bible room/imagination station/kid's hang-out called Whit's End, and the people that live in the small (made-up) town of Odyssey. Each episode involves kids, families, dilemmas, solutions, morals, wit, and wisdom. I can't recommend these adventures highly enough! TIP: visit www.whitsend.org and follow the links to listen to the current episode on podcast.

Audio Memory: (800)365-7464 / www.audiomemory.com - These CDs, DVDs and MP3 recordings, teach different subjects, like geography, math and history, through song. The creators feel that you never forget what you sing.

Classical Kids Series: (888) 841-3456 / www.rainbowresource.com - These CDs can be found in most larger retail stores or ordered through catalogs such as Rainbow Resource Center. Each hour-long recording in this wonderful series tells the story, in play format, of a famous composer while the composer's music plays in the background. Just some titles include *Beethoven Lives Upstairs*, *Mozart's Magical Fantasy*, and *Tchaikovsky Discovers America*.

Focus on the Family Radio Theatre Drama: (800) A-FAMILY (232-6459) / www.family.org - Put out by Focus on the Family, as are the above-mentioned Adventures in Odyssey, this series presents fantastic dramatizations of classic stories using a variety of voices, sound effects, and music. Some titles include the *Chronicles of Narnia, Squanto, My Secret Garden, Ben Hur, A Christmas Carol*, and more.

Greathall Productions, (800) 477-6234 / www.greathall.com - Be enthralled by award-winning storyteller, Jim Weiss.

Kids (and adults) of all ages will enjoy the masterful retelling of (mostly) classic stories. Some titles of his 47 incredible recordings include *Arabian Nights*, *Sherlock Holmes for Children*, *Three Musketeers*, *Abraham Lincoln*, *Greek Myths*, *Shakespeare for Children*, *Julius Caesar*, *Fairy Tale Favorites in Story and Song*, and *Animal Tales*.

BASEBALL: Call for a game schedule and ask about special days, such as fan appreciation day.

Angels in Anaheim: (888) 796-HALO (4256) / www.angelsbaseball.com

California Winter League: (760) 778-HITS (4487) / www.californiawinterleague.com

Dodgers in Los Angeles: (866) DODGERS (363-4377) / www.dodgers.com

High Desert Heat: (760) 245-4217 / www.scbaseball.com/high-desert-heat-2

High Desert Mavericks near Victorville: (760) 246-6287 / www.hdmavs.com

Inland Empire 66ers in San Bernardino: (909) 888-9922 / www.ie66ers.com

Inland Valley Pirates: (951) 830-3258 / www.scbaseball.com/inland-valley-pirate

Lake Elsinore Storm: (951) 245-HITS (4487) / www.stormbaseball.com

Lancaster Jethawks: (661) 726-5400 / www.jethawks.com

Long Beach Legends: (714) 322-7306 / www.scbaseball.com/long-beach-legends

Padres in San Diego: (877) 374-2784 / www.padres.com

Palm Springs Power: (760) 778-HITS (4487) / www.palmspringspowerbaseball.com

Rancho Cucamonga Quakes: (909) 481-5000 / www.rcquakes.com

Riverside Rebels: (951) 902-5863 / www.scbaseball.com/rebels

Team San Diego: (619) 200-3655 / www.scbaseball.com/team-san-diego

BASKETBALL: Highschool and college games can be fun, too.

Clippers in Los Angeles: (888) 895-8662 / www.clippers.com

Inland Empire Invaders: (855) 434-6823 / www.abaieinvaders.com

Lakers in Los Angeles: (310) 426-6000 / www.lakers.com

Los Angeles D-Fenders: (310) 426-6000 / www.nba.com/dleague/losangeles

Los Angeles Lightning: (310) 770-3960 / www.lalightning.net

Orange County Novastars: (855) 434-6823 / www.novastarbasketball.com

San Diego Surf: (855) 434-6823 / www.surfbasketball.com

Sparks in Los Angeles: (877) 44-SPARKS (447-7275) / www.wnba.com/sparks

BATTING CAGES: "Hey batter batter." Cages are great for hitting practice, in season or out.

BILLIARDS: Many billiard parlors have a family-friendly atmosphere.

BOOKS: Numerous book stores offer story times and/or craft times. Some of the bigger book stores, such as Barnes & Noble and Borders, have a huge children's selection, as well as a children's reading area. Many smaller bookstores cater specifically to kids and are delightful to browse through.

Thrift stores and garage sales are a great resource for used books as are libraries, as they often host sales once or twice a year. Used book stores are also a terrific bargain. Hot tip: There are several $1 bookstores, too, such as the One Dollar Bookstore at 500 Lakewood Center Mall in the Lakewood Mall in Lakewood, (562) 633-2665; a huge one called Piccolo's Books at 101 S. Pine Ave. in Long Beach, (562) 432-2665; and another Piccolo's Books at 22621 Lake Forest Dr. in Lake Forest, (949) 699-2667. The website for all fo them is www.theonedollarbookstore.com.

BOWLING: Many alleys offer bumper bowling for kids, where the gutters are covered so kids almost always knock down a pin or two. (This sounds like something right up my alley, also.) Cosmic Bowling, sometimes known as Rock 'n Roll Bowl, is great fun. Usually played at nighttime, ordinary lights are turned out and neon lights take over. The pins, balls, and lanes glow in the dark and rock music and/or videos play. All this while trying to bowl! Call your local bowling alley.

CAMPING: Campgrounds mentioned in this book are usually listed under the Great Outdoors section. Check your library or local book store for books written just on camping. A starting point are several books put out by Peterson (not me!) and the Guide to ACA-Accredited Camps in Southern California. You can contact Parknet at (800) 444-7275 or www.reserveamerica.com to make camping reservations at any California State Park.

CELEBRITIES: Find out when the next celebrity will be honored with a ceremony dedicating his/her star along the famous "Walk of Fame" in Hollywood, by checking www.hollywoodchamber.net or calling (323) 469-8311. Ceremonies occur almost monthly.

CIRCUS: Check newspapers and sports arenas, or try the following numbers to see when the circus is coming to town. Ask about specials or opening day events.

Carson & Barnes: (580) 743-7292 / www.carsonbarnescircus.com - Features three rings of continual action, with hundreds of animals, international performers, and lots of razzle dazzle.

Circus Vargas: (877) GOTFUN1 (468-3861) / www.circusvargas.com - A real "Big Top" circus. Come early to be invited into the ring to see what it is like to be in a circus.

Cirque Du Solei: www.cirquedusoleil.com - Artsy and eccentric, much-acclaimed productions with frequent theme changes that focus on "impossible" body movements. Very unique! Note: No animals are used in this circus.

Fern Street Circus: (619) 235-9756 / www.fernstreetcircus.org - San Diego-based troupe with aerialists, clowns, and acrobats for whimsical entertainment; from a single clown to a three-ring circus. Ask about programs that teach children circus skills in San Diego.

Great Y Circus: (909) 798-9622 / www.ycircus.org - Not only are small performances given through the year, your kids can actually take classes and learn circus skills. Founded in 1929 through the YMCA, this is oldest community circus in the world.

Ringling Bros. & Barnum and Bailey Circus: www.ringling.com - Still "the greatest show on earth", this multi-ring circus is one of the best known in the Western world. It involves daring animal acts, clowns, and feats of skill presented with theatrical flare and state-of-the-art lighting. At some locations, arrive an hour before show time to get into the arena with the clowns and participate in some of the tricks - swinging on a trapeze swing, riding a unicycle (with lots of help), and more.

CONSTRUCTION SITES: If you're "toolin" around, these sites can give your youngster constructive ideas to build on.

CONVENTION CENTERS: For Kid's Stuff Expos, toy shows, circuses, and much more. Check them intermittently to see what's going on.

Anaheim: (714) 765-8950 / www.anaheimconventioncenter.com

Long Beach,:(562) 436-3636 / www.longbeachcc.com

Los Angeles: (213) 741-1151 / www.lacclink.com

Ontario: (800) 455-5755 / www.ontariocc.com

Pasadena: (626) 795-2122 / www.pasadenacenter.com

Riverside: (951) 222-4700 / www.riversidecb.com

San Diego: (619) 525-5000 / www.sdcc.org

COOKING: There are a lot of kid's cooking classes offered throughout the year through local parks and recreation departments. A few other suggestions are listed below:

Bristol Farms in Manhattan Beach: (310) 233-4752 / www.bristolfarms.com - One to two-hour classes offer a variety of subjects for kids 7 - 12 or teens 13 - 17.

Let's Get Cooking in Westlake Village: (818) 991-3940 / www.letsgetcookin.com - Once-a-month parent/child classes are held on Sat., as well as workshops for pre-teen/teen, and even classes for children ages 6 years and up. Cook up something new and wonderful if you have a birthday party here, too.

San Diego Culinary Institute in La Mesa: (619) 644-2100 / www.sdci-inc.com - Adult and teen cooking classes are available.

Summer Art Academy Cooking Camp: (818) 386-2107 / www.summerartacademy.com - Campuses in La Canada and North Hollywood with classes for kids ages 7- 16.

Sur La Table: Carlsbad - (760) 635-1316; Los Angeles - (323) 954-9190; and Newport Beach - (949) 640-0200 / www.surlatable.com - Classes are offered for ages 6 - 12 and 12 - 16, depending on the location.

COUPONS: Always check the website of the attraction you are visiting, for coupons. Hotel lobbies often have displays with brochures that contain coupons to local attractions. Also, call the visitors center of the city you are planning to visit as they often offer discount coupons. For instance:

Anaheim/Orange County Coupons: (855) 405-5020 / www.anaheimoc.org/coupons - Features savings at over fifty area attractions, hotels, restaurants, and shops.

California Travel and Tourism Commission: www.visitcalifornia.com/Fun-Spots - Check here for on-line coupons to small and large attractions.

San Diego Convention and Visitor's Bureau: (619) 236-1212 / www.sandiego.org/coupons - Offers "coupons" that save on main attractions, harbor cruises, restaurants, and more.

CPR/FIRST AID CLASSES: Call your local Red Cross or hospital for class information. This is a great class for you, your kids (when they are old enough), and babysitters to take.

DRIVE-IN MOVIES: Once a staple of family entertainment, there are not many drive-ins left. However, they can

still be a fun outing. The shows are usually less expensive then a theater and many have double features. A great source for current information about drive-ins is www.drive-ins.com. Use it to find a drive-in theater near you or to reminisce about drive-ins that closed years ago:

Electric Dusk Drive-In: www.electricduskdrivein.com - Not a true drive-in, but has periodic showings using a large inflatable screen.

Hi-Way Drive-In in Santa Maria: (805) 937-3515 / - 1 screen.

Mission Tiki Drive-In in Montclair: (909) 628-0511 / www.missiontiki.com - 4 screens.

Paramount Drive-In: (562) 634-7927 / www.paramountswap.com - 2 screens.

Rubidoux Drive-In in Riverside: (951) 683-4455 / www.rubidouxdrivein.com - 3 screens.

Santa Barbara Drive-In: (805) 964-9050 / www.westwinddriveins.com - 1 screen.

Santee Drive-In: (619) 448-7447 / - 2 screens.

Skyline Drive-In in Barstow: (760) 256-3333 / - 2 screens.

Smith's Ranch Drive-In in Twentynine Palms: (760) 367-7713 / - 1 screen.

South Bay Drive-In in Imperial Beach: (619) 423-2727 / www.southbaydrivein.com - 3 screens.

Van Buren Cinema 3 Drive-In in Riverside: (951) 688-2360 / www.vanburendrivein.com - 3 screens.

Vineland Drive-In in Industry: (626) 961-9262 / www.vinelanddriveintheater.com - 4 screens.

EDUCATIONAL PRESENTATIONS: This section is written for all kinds of educators as most of these programs / presentations travel to schools or other off-site facilities. It is by no means complete, just *some* of the treasures we've discovered.

Amusement Parks: Look under the Amusement Parks section, as they are unexpected places to find educational classes. Knott's Berry Farm (pg. 235), in particular, has over fifteen specialized classes.

California Weekly Explorer, Inc.: (714) 247-2250 / www.californiaweekly.com - This company sends knowledgeable staff members to your school for outstanding, interactive, and educational two-and-a-half-hour presentations. The six different presentations offered are called "walk throughs," as they walk students through particular time periods via costumes, role playing, skits, games, flags, props, music, hands-on quizzes, models, maps, and/or timelines, consistent with the California state framework and requires. Programs are offered Mon. - Fri. and are limited to thirty-five students.

Jim Weiss - Storyteller Extraordinare: (800) 477-6234 / www.greathall.com - Golden-voiced Jim Weiss, with Greathall Productions, is a nationally acclaimed storyteller. He's won over seventy-five prestigious awards retelling (mostly) classic stories such as *Three Musketeers, Sherlock Holmes, American Tall Tales, Famously Funny* and many more. As wonderful as he is to listen to on CD, he is even more enthralling in person. Jim does storytelling as well as workshops for both kids and adults. He explains the twists and turns good stories need, teaching how to choose a topic, map a plot, create and develop characters, use voice inflections masterfully, and more. He is the best!

Jurassic Parties: (714) 500-0593 / www.jurassicparties.com - They bring an assortment animals, including snakes, lizards, tarantulas and scorpions. Great for birthday parties.

Kites for Kids: (800) 431-3339 / www.kitesforkids.com - Presentation includes an educational demonstration and kite making for every participant. Cost is $495 for 1-250 students; per student pricing for groups over 250.

Mad Science: (800) 586-5231 - call to find your local mad scientist! / www.madscience.org - Bubbling potions, rocket launches, magnets, lasers, super bounce ball, cool chemical reactions, slime, and more hands-on learning fun. Programs include after-school enrichment classes, summer camps, school assemblies, and "edu-tainment" birthday parties.

Museums: Numerous museums, especially the art, science and children's museums, have "traveling programs," designed specifically to bring great, hands-on educational programs to your choice of locale. Contact, for example, California Science Center (pg. 103), Discovery Science Center (pg. 301), International Printing Museum (pg. 123), Jurupa Mountains Discovery Center / Earth Science Museum (pg. 360), Children's Museum at La Habra (pg. 301), Raymond M. Alf Museum (pg. 148) and Santa Barbara Museum of Natural History (pg. 630) with it's Waves on Wheels program.

Shows and Theaters: This is another category that often has traveling shows - whether it's a play presented to children, or it's a theatrical workshop of some sort.

Zoos and Animals: Many zoos have fantastic in-house programs as well as traveling presentations. Call the one nearest you for more information.

EDUCATIONAL TOYS: There are numerous stores and catalogs that offer good quality, educational products. Some of our favorite stores include Lakeshore Learning and Learning Express (in Carlsbad). Look in your local

telephone directory for the above listings, and look in the Yellow Pages for two other great resources - teacher supply stores and children's bookstores. Many museum gift shops offer a terrific line of educational (and fun) supplies. The website, www.learningwrapups.com, has a store locator for their product that list many educational stores in the Southland. Also check out some of the following companies that offer catalogs and/or home workshops for their products:

Discovery Toys: (800) 341-8697 / www.discoverytoys.net - A fantastic line of toys, books, games, and computer software.

Dorling Kindersley Books: (212) 213-4800 / us.dk.com - They offer outstanding books.

Usborne Books: (800) 475-4522 / www.edcpub.com - Top-notch, visually-exciting books.

EQUESTRIAN SHOWS: English and Western riding, jumping, and prancing are all part of seeing a horse show. Call your local equestrian center for dates and times and/or check the Calendar section for special event shows.

ETHNIC NEIGHBORHOODS: Where can you take your family to experience another culture? Oftentimes, right in your own neighborhood, where people from other countries have settled and carved out a niche based on their homeland. Here are just a few options to check out, whether it's to try different foods or to shop for items not found in Target.

Armenian foods in Glendale: Located near Colorado St. and Glendale Ave, there are several Armenian cuisine restaurants, including several kabob places, pastries, lamb, quail, chicken, and more.

Chinatown in Los Angeles: www.chinatownla.com - Walk the streets to see a proliferation of red and gold colored buildings with pagoda-style roofs. See Chinatown (pg. 167) for more details.

Little Cambodia in Long Beach: www.littlecambodia.org - Long Beach is home to the largest population of Cambodians in the United States. Located on Anaheim St. between Atlantic Ave. and Junipero Ave., this area has Cambodian restaurants, groceries, gift shops, clothing stores and more.

Little Ethiopia in Los Angeles: www.littleethiopiabusinessassociation.com - Come visit this collection of Ethiopian shops and restaurants along Fairfax Ave., between Olympic Blvd., and Whitworth Dr.

Little India in Artesia: www.artesiaindia.us - Its aromatic restaurants, small grocery stores that carry an array of spices, and shops that prefer brightly-colored saris, among other items, beckon customers along Pioneer Boulevard, between Ashtoreth and South sts.

Little Italy in San Diego: www.littleitalysd.com - Located between Laurel and A sts., W. on of the 5 Fwy. Besides several Italian restaurants, the area offers many programs and festivals throughout the year.

Little Saigon in Westminster: www.easylittlesaigon.com - A mile-long stretch of Bolsa Ave. has bakeries, deli's, supermarkets, and dozens of excellent, inexpensive Vietnamese restaurants.

Little Tokyo in Los Angeles: www.visitlittletokyo.com - This area , near 1st and Central sts., has the Japanese American National Museum (pg. 124), lots of shops and restaurants, and many yearly activities.

FAIR GROUNDS: Numerous events are held at the following locations throughout the year, such as gem shows, reptiles expos, fairs, cat shows, circuses, demolition derbies, Scottish games, horse shows, and lots more. Call or check websites for a schedule:

Los Angeles in Lancaster: (661) 948-6060 / www.avfair.com

Los Angeles in Pomona: (909) 623-3111 / www.fairplex.com

Orange in Costa Mesa: (714) 708-1500 or recorded info: (714) 708-FAIR (3247) / www.ocfair.com

Riverside in Indio: (800) 811-FAIR (3247) / www.datefest.org

Riverside in Lake Perris: (951) 657-4221 / www.socalfair.com

San Bernardino in Victorville: (760) 951-2200 / www.sbcfairevents.com

San Diego in Del Mar: (858) 755-1161 / www.sdfair.com

Santa Barbara in Santa Barbara: (805) 687-0766 / www.earlwarren.com

Santa Barbara in Santa Maria: (805) 925-8824 / www.santamariafairpark.com

Ventura in Ventura: (805) 648-3376 / www.venturacountyfair.org

FARMER'S MARKETS: See Edible Adventures in the main section of the book for details.

FISHING: Here's the hook - you have to look under the Great Outdoors section for places to go fish. You can also call:

Department of Fish and Game: (916) 445-0411 / www.dfg.ca.gov - Free information on fishing, including maps to local lakes, fishing events, hatcheries, stocking guides, fishing clinics, and regulations. They also offer free fishing days during the year.

Fishing Network: www.fishingnetwork.net - This web site is dedicated to provide information on fishing in Southern

California.

Take Me Fishing: www.takemefishing.org - The web site is designed to help families find places to fish and boat.

FOOTBALL: Highschool and college games are exiting, too.

Chargers at Qualcomm Stadium in San Diego: 877-CHARGERS (242-7437) / www.chargers.com

LA KISS - Arena Football Team: (714) 462-KISS (5447) / www.lakissfootball.com

GEOCACHING: www.geocaching.com - This hobby/sport mixes high-tech and adventure. Participants hunt for hidden "treasure" by using a hand-held Global Positioning System (GPS) device. The only thing you need is the GPS and the co-ordinates of a geocache near you. A cache may be a hidden trinket, a log book to write your name in, an interesting place or view, or all three. It may be anywhere in the world, but use discretion when searching. Some park officials frown on hunters veering off established paths to search for the "cache" prize.

GYM CLASSES: There are multitudes of gyms and classes to choose from. Here are just a few:

Creative Kids in Los Angeles: (310) 473-6090 / www.mycreativekids.com - Classes in gymnastics, music, art, fairytale theater, cooking, and more.

Gymboree: (877) 4-GYMWEB (449-6932) / www.gymboreeclasses.com - Check website or your local phone book for listings. Classes are offered for parents and their children - newborns through 4 years old - that include easy exercise, songs, bubbles, and visits from Gymbo, the down.

My Gym: (800) 4-MY-GYMS (469-4967) / www.my-gym.com - Classes in tumbling, songs, games, and gymnastics are offered for the younger set. The franchises are everywhere in Southern California.

HOBBIES AND MODELS: Kids like to collect - anything! For example - dolls, coins, autographs, postcards, rocks, sports cards, figurines, pins, stickers, and stamps. Other hobby ideas include model-making (i.e. cars, planes, rockets, and trains), creating jewelry, and sewing. Look in your phone book for local hobby shops to support your habit.

HOCKEY

Mighty Ducks at Arrowhead Pond in Anaheim: (877) WILDWING (945-3946) / ducks.nhl.com

Kings at Staples Center in Los Angeles,:(888) KINGSLA (546-4752) / kings.nhl.com

San Diego Gulls at the Sports Arena in San Diego: (585) 905-1451 / www.sandiegogullshockeyclub.com

Southern California Bombers in Lakewood: (562) 429-1805 / www.jrbombers.org

Valencia Flyers: (661) 775-8686 / www.valenciaflyers.net

HORSEBACK RIDING: Saddle up for a terrific family outing! Call your local equestrian center.

HOT AIR BALLOON RIDES: Up, up and away! Hot air balloon rides are recommended for ages 8 and up, as younger children might get scared of the flames shooting out (i.e. the "hot air"); they might get bored; and they can't see very well over the basket. All ages, however, are enthralled by watching the balloon being inflated, either in the morning or at sunset! For a real colorful outing, look in the Calendar section for Hot Air Balloon Festivals. Most of the companies listed fly over Del Mar, Palm Springs, and/or Temecula. Flights are about an hour and some include a champagne breakfast. Prices are per person. These are just a few names and numbers to get you started:

California Dreamin' in Del Mar and Temecula; (800) 373-3359 / www.californiadreamin.com - Temecula - $188 per person; Del Mar - $248 per person. Check website for specials.

Fantasy Balloon Flights in Palm Springs; (760) 568-0997 / www.fantasyballoonflight.com - $185 with discounts for groups, families, children and seniors

Skysurfer Balloon Company in San Diego, Del Mar and Temecula; (800) 660-6809 / www.sandiegohotairballoons.com - $175 - $210 per person.

Sunrise Balloons in Temecula: (800) 548-9912 / www.sunriseballoons.com - $219 per person.

ICE SKATING: Go figure! Call, for instance, the arenas listed below:

Anaheim Ice: (714) 535-RINK (7465) / www.anaheimice.com - Offers public sessions, plus figure skating and hockey classes. It's also the rink where the Mighty Ducks practice!

Glacial Garden Skating Arena in Lakewood: (562) 429-1805 / www.glacialgardens.com - Two ice rinks. They also offer broomball which is *fun*tastic!

Salvation Army Ray & Joan Kroc Center: (619) 269-1498 / www.kroccenter.org - A great ice rink along with a ton of other fun things to do.

Toyota Sports Center: (310) 535-4400 / www.toyotasportscenter.com - This ice arena, where the Los Angeles Kings train, has public sessions, hockey, and figure skating.

IMAX THEATRES: www.imax.com - See it BIG! See it in your face! IMAX theaters really intensify your movie-going experience.

JUNKYARDS: One man's trash is another child's treasure. For kids who like to take things apart and make new creations, junkyards are inspiring places to investigate.

KITE FLYING: Go fly a kite! Check the Calendar section for Kite Festivals.

LIBRARIES: Your local library has a lot to offer. Get a group together and ask for a tour. Besides book, video, and audio CD lending, many offer free storytelling on a regular basis and/or finger plays, puppet shows, magic shows, and crafts. Some libraries also encourage your bookworms by offering summer reading programs. A few times throughout the year libraries hold sales where book prices are practically a steal.

MAGAZINES: If you only receive one magazine, make it *Family Fun*. Contact them at www.parents.com/familyfun-magazine or (800) 289-4849. Put out by Disney, each edition is packed with do-able crafts, snacks, party ideas, games, activities, and family-friendly places to travel. Pick it up at the newsstand or get a subscription.

MALLS: Going to the mall can be a fun excursion with kids (honest!), especially if the mall has "extra" features, such as a merry-go-round or fountains, or, if it's spectacular in design, has unique shops and restaurants, etc. See the Malls section in the main part of the book for some of our top picks, that include free kid's clubs.

MONEY: Collect money from foreign countries without the expense of traveling there. Call (800) CURRENCY (287-7362) or check www.travelex.com to find the nearest Travelex location. You may exchange any sum of money for currency from an unlimited number of countries, for only one transaction fee. The fee is usually a $5 service fee or 1% of the U.S. amount, whichever amount is greater. You may also purchase money on-line.

MOVIE THEATERS: An obvious choice, but movies, and especially matinees, can be a relatively inexpensive and fun treat. Check the following theaters. Note that some also offer great bargains in the summertime for kids. See page 729, in the Calendar section, for details.

4 Star Cinemas: (714) 934-6377 / www.4starcinemas.com - $4 tickets before noon every day, before 6pm on Sunday and all day Tues. and Thurs.

Cinemark: (800) 326-3264 / www.cinemark.com - Offers $6 admission all day Tue.

Mommy Movies Mondays: www.kptmovies.com - Stroller check-in, reduced sound levels and dimmed lights (for baby visibility) make these showings idea for a new mom's day out.

Monday Morning Mommy Movies: www.pacifictheatres.com/MMMM.htm - Babies are welcome and expected at these showings.

Picture Show: info - (714) 836-7469; office - (714) 953-8467 / www.pictureshowent.com - Most movies played here have already been released on DVD, but the prices are $2 per ticket and $1 on Tues. with a surcharge of $2 for 3-D.

Regency Theatres: www.regencymovies.com - Some theaters offer discounted days, times and food. Check website for times and prices at specific locations.

Starlight Cinemas: www.starlightcinemas.com - All theaters offer discounted days. Check website for times and prices at specific locations.

Starplex Cinemas: (949) 733-3795- Irvine; (714) 739-1010 - La Mirada / www.starplexcinemas.com - $3 all shows after 6pm and $2 before; $4 for 3-D; $1 Hot Dogs. Wednesday Mommy Matinee - babies welcome.

Tristone Cinemas: www.tristonecinemas.com - All theaters offer discounted rates and some offer further discounts for matinees.

UltraStar Cinemas: (760) 597-5777 / www.ultrastarmovies.com - Early bird and discount Tues. and Thurs. $6 - 3-D add $3.50. At select locations and times their Kidtoon Series shows G-rated family films 11am on Sat. and Sun. for $2.50.

MUSEUMS: ww.museums.bankofamerica.com - If you're a Bank of America cardholder you can get into 150 museums nationwide for free the first full weekend of every month, including 12 great museums in Southern California. Check the Museums on page xi for more great tips.

PARKS: Almost every local park offers classes or sports programs for free, or at a minimal cost. Ask about kid's cooking classes, sidewalk chalk art day, and so much more. Check out www.parks.ca.gov for information about parks throughout California.

PET STORES: This is a fun, mini-outing. Ask about tours. There are several larger chain stores, such as Petco and Petsmart, which are sufficient. However, while cuddly puppies and adorable rabbits are great, unusual and exotic animals can add a unique element to your outing. They can be found at some of the independent stores listed below. Goggle search for fish and bird stores, too. You can also find pet stores by looking up the pet product suppliers and finding local dealers - check out www.nutro.com, for example.

Blacksmith's Corner in Bellflower: (562) 531-0386 / www.blacksmithscorner.com - Like visiting a mini farm, with

its chickens, ducks, pheasants, etc.

Prehistoric Pets in Fountain Valley: (714) 964-3525 / www.prehistoricpets.com - Incredible! See exotic snakes (some twenty-feet long) and monitor lizards from all over the world, plus a small fish pond in the middle of the store, and more. See the main entry on page 334 for more info.

Wagon Train Feed & Pet: (714) 639-7932 / - When we visited this small pet store it had chicks, ducks, a lamb, a pot-bellied pig, turtles, and chinchillas. The stop here was worth a peek and pet. Note: They also sell fertilized chick eggs and incubators.

PHOTO ALBUMS: Tapped dry on how to put together a creative and memorable photo album? This is still a fun project to involve the kids and many stores, such as Aaron Brothers and Michaels, offer acid-free products. Better yet, create a personalized photo book from your digital photographs with such sites as Blurb - one of my favorites - www.blurb.com, Shutterfly - www.shutterfly.com, and Mixbook - www.mixbook.com.

PLAYGROUPS: Check local parks, newspapers, and "Parenting" magazine for information on getting involved with a playgroup. This is a great way to share the joys and trials of raising children. Other resources include:

MOMS: www.momsclub.org - An international, non-profit support group specifically for stay-at-home moms. Weekly meetings, kept at a low number of attendees, consist of talking and eating together, listening to a speaker, and going on various outings. All age children are welcome at all meetings and activities. MOMS groups are everywhere.

MOPS (Mothers Of Preschooler): (888) 910-6677 or (303) 733-5353 / www.mops.org - An international, Christian-based organization that has local meetings in almost every city. Moms usually meet at a church and talk, eat, listen to a speaker, and make a craft while their preschoolers are being cared for by a Moppet helper. Great organization! Call the headquarters to find a MOPS near you.

Tot Lot: A playgroup designed for preschoolers (and their parents) to meet and play together at community parks on a regular basis during the week, building those all-important socialization skills. Registration fees go towards crafts, snacks, and even field trips. Call, for example, Lakewood Recreation and Community Services, (562) 866-9771 / www.lakewoodcity.org for information on Tot Lot at Bolivar, Del Valle, and Mayfair parks. Call your local parks and recreation department to see what programs they offer.

RESTAURANTS: See the Edible Adventures section in the main part of the book. Try eating at some unusual locations, such as at airports, on boats (try the *Queen Mary*), etc. Take your kids out for ethnic foods, too.

ROCKETRY: You can get you in touch with model rocketry classes (for ages 10 and older) and launch sites in Los Angeles and San Bernardino counties by checking the web site home.earthlink.net/~mebowitz or calling (714) 529-1598.

RODEO: Southern California plays host to rodeos throughout the year. Several annual ones are listed in the Calendar section. Check these web sites to find out the schedule of some of the touring events: Pro Bull Riders - www.pbr.com; Professional Rodeo Cowboy Association - www.prorodeo.com; and Rodeoz Authority Guide - www.rodeoz.com.

ROLLER BLADING: Roll at rinks, on the sidewalks, around parks, and along beach fronts. (See Bike Paths, in the main section of the book for specific paved pathways.)

SMART PHONE APPS: You can use your smart phone for more than just games to keep your kids busy. Listed below are a few handy app categories. Because apps change and are added daily you can also search online for new apps that might make your kids safer and your life easier.

Family Finder: There are a lot apps in this field, some just let you check up on the location of another smart phone (that hopefully your kids have with them) and some have messaging, panic buttons, smart alerts (for when your kids leave a certain area or don't arrive), web use monitors and more. A few apps in this category are: Snap Secure - www.mysnapsecure.com; Life360 - www.life360.com; Sygic - www.sygic.com; and Mamabear - www.mamabearapp.com.

First Aid: There are several apps that can be used in medical emergencies or just to answer simple medical questions. Here are a couple: First Aid App by American Red Cross - www.redcross.org ; Pocket First Aid & CPR - www.heart.org.

Swim Guide: www.theswimguide.org - This one is kind of unique. It is a free app that shows beaches that are close to you and whether the water is clean.

SOCCER

Chivas USA: (877) - CHIVAS 1 (244-8271) or (310) 630-4550 / www.cdchivasusa.com

Los Angeles Galaxy: (877) - 3GALAXY (342-5299) or (310) 630-2200 / www.lagalaxy.com

Orange County Blues: (714)738-8011 / www.ocbluesfc.com

San Diego Soccers: (866) 799-GOAL (4625) / www.sdsockers.com

SPORTING EVENTS: Check out high school and college events. These local games are a fun and inexpensive introduction to sports and fun for sports enthusiasts as well.

SPORTS ARENAS: Many special events are held at sports arenas including sporting events like the Harlem Globetrotters, rodeos, concerts, Disney On Ice, circuses, etc.

Honda Center in Anaheim: (714) 704-2400 / www.hondacenter.com

L.A. Memorial Coliseum and Sports Arena in Los Angeles: (213) 747-7111 / www.lacoliseumlive.com

Long Beach Arena in Long Beach: (562) 436-3636 / www.longbeachcc.com

Qualcomm Stadium in San Diego: (619) 641-3100 / www.sandiego.gov/qualcomm

Staples Center in Los Angeles: (213) 742-7340 / www.staplescenter.com

StubHub Center in Carson: (310) 630-2000 / www.stubhubcenter.com

Valley View Casino Center in San Diego: (619) 224-4171 / www.valleyviewcasinocenter.com

SUN CLOTHING: The following companies make a full line of clothing especially designed to block out harmful rays from the sun:

SunGrubbies: (888) 970-1600 / www.sungrubbies.com

Sun Precautions: (800) 882-7860 / www.sunprecautions.com

Sun Protection Zone: (877) 266-7297 / www.sunprotectionzone.com

SWAP MEETS / FLEA MARKETS: Give your kids a dollar or two to call their own, as there are a lot of inexpensive toys or jewelry items for them to choose from at swap meets. Everyone goes home happy with their treasures! Here's a list of just a few good swap meets / flea markets.

Anaheim Marketplace (indoor) in Anaheim: (800) 479-SWAP (7927) / www.anaheimindoormarketplace.com - Over 250 variety shops and a food court. They also have adjacent soccer fields and arcade games. Open Wed. - Mon., 10am - 7pm. Free admission.

College of the Desert Street Fair (outdoor) in Palm Desert: (760) 636-7957 / www.codstreetfair.com - New and used items, antiques, a Farmer's market, arts and crafts courtyard, jewelry, and more make this more of a street fair than swap meet ambiance. Held Sat. - Sun., 7am - 2pm; summer hours are 7am - noon. Admission and parking are free.

Cypress College Swap Meet (outdoor): (714) 952-1847 / www.cypresscollegeswapmeet.com - Open Sat. and Sun, 8am - 4pm. Admission is free.

Glendale Community College Flea Market (outdoor) in Glendale: (818) 240-1000 / www.glendale.edu/swapmeet - A potpourri of new and old items. Open the 3rd Sun. of every month, 8am - 3pm. Free admission.

Golden West College Swap Meet: (714) 895-0888 / www.goldenwestswapmeet.com - New & used items, fresh produce and flowers, antiques. Open Sat. & Sun. 8 a.m. to 3 p.m., rain or shine. Free admission and parking.

Kobey's Swap Meet (outdoor) at the sports arena parking lot in San Diego: (619) 226-0650 / www.kobeyswap.com - The equivalent of twelve footballs fields, this swap meet offers bargains on everything under the sun. Open Fri. - Sun., 7am - 3pm. Admission is $1 on Thurs. and Fri.; $2 on Sat. and Sun. Children 11 and under are free.

Los Angeles City College Swap Meet (outdoor): (323) 913-3931 / www..laccswapmeet.com - Open Sat. and Sun, 9am - 3:30pm. Admission is 75¢ on Sat., $1 on Sun; children 12 and under are free.

Orange County Marketplace (outdoor) in Costa Mesa: (949) 723-6616 / www.ocmarketplace.com - One of the best, with over 1,000 vendors, plus a food court. Open weekends, 7am - 4pm. (Some weekends in July are closed due to the Orange County Fair.) Admission is $2 for adults; children 12 years and under are free.

Pasadena City College Flea Market (outdoor): (626) 585-7906 / www.pasadena.edu/fleamarket - A mishmash mixture of merchandise from about 400 vendors - some great deals, some garage sale items. Open the first Sun. of every month, 8am - 3pm. Admission is free.

Roadium (outdoor) in Torrance: (323) 321-3920 / www.roadium.com - 450 merchants sell new items, some collectibles, bargains, garage-sale stuff, and food daily 7am - 4pm. Admission on Mon. and Fri. is $1 for the driver and 50¢ per person; Tues. and Thurs., 50¢ per person; Wed., $1.25 per person; Sat. and Sun., $1.50 per car, plus 75¢ per person; children 4 and under are always free.

Rosebowl Flea Mart (outdoor) in Pasadena: (323) 560-7469 / www.rgcshows.com - Known for antiques and collectables, the more than 2,500 vendors offer everything you've ever seen and many things you've never heard of. Held the second Sun. of each month. Admission is $20 from 5am - 7am; $15 from 7am - 8am; $10 from 8am - 9am; $8 from 9am until it closes at 4:30pm. Sellers begin leaving at 3pm. Parking is free.

San Bernardino Outdoor Market (outdoor) in San Bernardino: (323) 560-7469 / www.rgcshows.com - A large flea market held at the National Orange Showgrounds. Open Sun., 7am - 3pm. Admission is 50¢ per person, ages 11 and under free. Parking is free.

Santa Fe Springs Swap Meet (indoor) in Santa Fe Springs: (562) 921-4359 / www.sfsswapmeet.com - Over 500 vendors have been meeting here for over thirty years to sell new wares. The meet boasts live entertainment. a food court open daily, and a kiddie ride area open on the weekends. There is a prize drawing and half-price food on Wednesdays. Open Wed. and Thurs., 7am - 2:30pm; Fri., 5pm - 11pm; Sat., 7am - 4:30pm; and Sun., 7am - 5pm. Admission is free for adults Tues. - Thurs.; $1 on Sat.; $1.50 on Fri. and Sun. Children 11 and under are always free.

Saugus Speedway SwapMeet (outdoor) in Saugus: (661) 259-3886 / www.saugusspeedway.com - Over 550 vendors, plus live entertainment, at this huge swap meet held every Sun., 7am - 3pm. The Tues. swap meet, open 7am - 1pm, is smaller. Swap meets are held on Fri. only in the summer. Admission on Tues. is free; Sun., $1.50 for adults; children 11 years and under are free.

Ventura Flea Market (outdoor) in Ventura: (323) 560-7469 / www.rgcshows.com - Antiques, second hand, or used goods for sale. The flea market is held six times a year at Seaside Park (i.e. Ventura County Fairgrounds). Call or check website for dates. Starting at 6am admission is $10; starting at 9am it is $5 for adults, children 11 and under are free. Parking is free.

Vineland Swap Meet (outdoor) in City of Industry: (626)-369-7224 / www.vinelandswapmeet.com - At the Vineland Drive-in with over 600 vendors. Open Mon. and Fri. 7am - 1:30pm; Tues., Wed., Thurs. and Sat. 7am - 3pm; Sun., 7am - 3pm. Admission is 50¢ Mon., Tues., Thurs. and Fri.; $1 on Wed. and Sat.; $1.50 on Sun. Parking is free.

SWIMMING and WADING POOLS: Community pools are open seasonally. Call your local park for information.

THEATER: Check out the Shows and Theaters sections in each county. Below are a few places to get you started. Colleges and high schools are also a great place see shows and plays.

California Theatre - San Bernardino: (909) 885-5152 / www.californiatheatre.net

The Music Center Los Angeles: (213) 972-7211 / www.musicenter.org

Performance Riverside: (951) 222-8100 / www.performanceriverside.org

San Diego County: (858) 381-5595 / www.sdartstix.com

Santa Barbara County: www.santabarbaraca.com/things-to-do/calendar-of-events/performing-arts

Segerstrom Center for the Arts - Orange County: (714) 556-2787 / www.scfta.org

THRIFT STORES: Teach your children the gift of thrift! Give them a few dollars to buy a "new" article of clothing, a toy, or a book. Tip: Main Street, in the city of Ventura, has numerous thrift stores in a row.

TICKETS

Audiences Unlimited: (818) 260-0041 / www.tvtickets.com - Offers free tickets to watch filming of almost all of the network television shows and many of their specials. The minimum age for kids ranges from 10 years old for some shows, to 18 years old for most shows. Call for a schedule or ask them to send you a monthly show schedule.

LAStageTIX: (213) 614-0556 / www.lastagetix.org - Operated by the Theatre League Alliance of Southern California it allows day-of-show tickets (or even a few days before the show) to be purchased for 50% off the regular price. Check the website for a list of the shows and availability.

On-Camera Audiences: (818) 295-2700 / www.on-camera-audiences.com - Is responsible for filling studio audiences for television shows across the country. See the website for a list and go see your favorite.

Times Arts Tix in San Diego next to Horton Plaza: (858) 381-5595 / www.sdartstix.com - Has half-price, day-of-performance, theater tickets available on a first-come, first-served, cash-only basis. Call for a listing of the day's shows.

TOURS: See Tours in the main section of the book. The following are general ideas of where you can go for group tours:

Animal Shelter	Dentist	Newspaper Office
Airport	Factory	Nurseries (plant)
Bakery	Fire Station	Pet Store
Bank	Florist	Police Station
Chiropractor	Grocery Store	Post Office
College/University	Hospital	Printer
Dairy	Hotel	Restaurant

TOYS: Look in this part of the book under Educational Toys (pg. 777). Three other listings worth mentioning are:

Constructive Playthings in Garden Grove: (800) 255-6124 or (714) 636-7831 / www.cptoy.com - Visit their store. They offer top-of-the-line toys, books, games, puzzles, etc., as well as lower priced, carnival-type "prizes."

Oriental Trading Company: (800) 875-8480 / www.orientaltrading.com - This catalog company offers bulk and individual novelty items, usually priced at the lower end of the scale.

U.S. Toy Company: (800) 832-0224 / www.ustoy.com - Contact them for a catalog.

VOLUNTEERING: Volunteering is a terrific way to spend time with your children while teaching them the real values of life - giving and serving. Check with local missions, churches, and temples, as many have regular times when they go to help feed the homeless or serve in some capacity. Here are other volunteer agencies to get you started on your quest:

30-Minute Beach Cleanup in Long Beach: www.beachdeanup.org - Group meets on the third Sat. of each month at 10am at S. Granada Ave. and Ocean Blvd.

4GOOD: www.4goodcommunity.org - A Los Angeles based non-profit organization designed to help families participate in volunteer activities together.

Adopt-a-Park and Adopt-a-Beach in Orange County: (714) 566-3035 or (714) 697-0623 / www.ocparks.com/about/volunteer/adopt - Organizes on-going park and beach cleanups at more than 30 local sites for all age participants.

Big Sunday: (323) 549-9944 / www.bigsunday.org - Their mission is to build community through community service.

California Coastal Cleanup Day: (949) 476-1144 x311 / www.coastal.ca.gov - Every year, on the third Sat. in September, people join together at sites all over CA to take part in the State's largest volunteer event to clean up California's coast. Go to the web site and search for 'cleanup day'.

Children's Hunger Fund: (800) 708-7589 x3009 or (818) 899-5122 / www.chfus.org - Volunteers of all ages assemble care packages for disadvantaged children on Wed. and Sat., 9am - noon, Thurs., 10am - noon.

Corazón de Vida Foundation: (949) 476-1144 x311 / www.corazondevida.org - On selected Sat., volunteers visit one of 14 orphanages in Baja, Mexico to play, work on craft projects, read with the children, help with a building project or simply hold an infant who needs love. Children must be at 8 and those under 16 must be accompanied by an adult. A $40 fee, per person, is required to cover the cost of the bus, food and craft.

Florence Crittenton Services in Yorba Linda: (714) 680-9000 / www.crittentonsocal.org - Abused children living here benefit from volunteers in numerous ways: rocking a baby; fixing a bike; becoming a mentor; planning a party; and more.

Food Finders: (562) 283-1400 / www.foodfinders.org - Families can donate, sort and deliver canned goods, toys, and food year-round.

Habitat For Humanity: (800) 422-4828 / www.habitat.org - This non-profit organization is committed to providing low-income, owner-occupied housing by utilizing volunteer labor and donated materials. (Former President Jimmy Carter is one of the more prominent members.) Volunteers are needed to build homes and serve on committees such as finance, construction, and public relations. Kids must be at least 16 years old to work on construction sites, but younger children can help with off-site activities such as registration, making lunches, etc. Check website for local affiliates or call information.

Heal the Bay, headquartered in Santa Monica: (800) HEAL BAY (432-5229) or (310) 451-1500 / www.healthebay.org - There's nothing like a day at the beach, especially if you're there to help make it cleaner. Clean up pollution in the Santa Monica Bay, San Pedro Bay, Orange County, and adjacent coastal waters. This program works in conjunction with Adopt-A-Beach and Coastal Clean Up. Call (800) COAST-4U (262-7848) / www.coastal.ca.gov/publiced/pendx.html for the annual coastal clean up day and all the other ones in-between.

I Love a Clean San Diego: (619) 291-0103 / www.ilacsd.org - An educational and environmental group sponsoring beach clean-ups, storm drain stenciling, and graffiti removal.

Kids Care Club: (203) 656-8052 / www.kidscare.org - A program designed to encourage service in elementary and middle school kids by joining a local group to work together helping others in their community.

Kids Giving to Kids L.A.: (800) 322-9474 or (310) 788-9474 / www.wishla.org - Started by the Make-A-Wish Foundation, families can come up with creative fund-raising ideas to sponsor a wish for a child facing a life-threatening illness or help out in other areas.

Kids Korps USA: (858) 259-3602 / www.kidskorps.org - Young people, ages 5 - 18, can participate in a wealth of programs from preserving the environment to befriending those in need to helping animals and more. Every child who has a desire to do something to help can find an activity with Kids Korps.

Los Angeles Midnight Mission: (213) 624-9258 / www.midnightmission.org - Volunteer to help set up, decorate, and help serve meals on Thanksgiving or another holiday.

Los Angeles Regional Foodbank in Los Angele:, (323) 234-3030 / www.lafoodbank.org - Ages 14 and up can help maintain 300 garden plots in a low income area, as well as participate in local food drive and food collection.

Make-A-Wish: (800) 722-9474 / www.wish.org

Move a Child Higher in La Canada / Flintridge: (626) 798-1222 / www.moveachildhigher.org - The Riding Club offers therapeutic horseback riding activities to children with disabilities. Volunteers, ages 14 and up, can exercise and groom the horses, and lead and walk alongside the riders.

One OC: (714) 953-5757 / www.oneoc.org - A clearinghouse for a wide variety of age-appropriate opportunities, including feeding the homeless, visiting the elderly, planting trees, cleaning up parks, and removing graffiti. The center even has a guide book on family volunteer activities.

Project Chicken Soup: (310) 836-5402 / www.projectchickensoup.org - Work with the Los Angeles Jewish AIDS Services to prepare and deliver kosher meals to those living with AIDS. All ages are welcome, but children under 12 cannot work in the kitchen and one adult volunteer is needed for every two children under the age of 16.

Ripple Kids: (714) 602-2295 / www.ripplekids.com - Dedicated to inspiring kids to help their community. On the website, kids can find out about volunteering opportunities, read about other and share ideas.

Ronald McDonald House Charities: 630-623-7048 / www.rmhc.com - This house provides a home-away-from-home for up to 20 families who have children receiving treatment for cancer and other serious illnesses at local medical facilities. Opportunities include making or sponsoring a meal, general housekeeping, and clerical opportunities. Note: There are facilities throughout So. Cal. so check the website for information about the one nearest you.

Salvation Army: (562) 436-7000 / www.salvationarmy.org/usw/www_usw.nsf - Volunteers are needed year round, but especially around Christmas time.

San Diego Coastkeeper: (619) 758-7743 / www.sdcoastkeeper.org - This organization provides a listing of more than 40 coastal and inland cleanup sites throughout San Diego.

Second Harvest Foodbank of Orange County: (949) 653-2900 / www.feedoc.org - Kindergartners and up are allowed to actually harvest and glean food from fields in Orange County. The food is delivered to local food banks. Gleaning is usually done Tues. and Fri. from 9am - 11am, with groups of up to 40; Thurs. from 3:15pm - 4:30pm, with groups of up to 15. Sat. and Sun. twice a month, from 9am - 11am, with groups of up to 20. Pre-registration is required.

Soldiers' Angels,:(626) 529-5114 / www.soldiersangels.org - Provides comfort to the men and women of the armed forces and their families.

Southwest Minority Economic Development Association: (714) 547-4073 - Volunteers of all ages participate in serving food to the homeless.

St. Vincent de Paul in San Diego: (619) 645-6411 / www.svdpv.org

Surfrider Foundation: (949) 492-8170 / www.surfrider.org - Help clean up local beaches.

Tierra Del Sol Foundation: (818) 352-1419 / www.tierradelsol.org - Serves adults with developmental and often physical disabilities.

Trails4all: (310) 344-9229 / www.trails4all.org - Coordinates volunteers, who are at least 8 years old, to help with coastal cleanups, trail maintenance, and other activities that are group specific.

Volunteer Agencies L.A.: (323) 450-5080 / www.vda.net - For volunteer opportunities in L.A. and San Fernando Valley.

VolunteerMatch: (415) 241-6872 / www.volunteermatch.org - On-line website that matches volunteers with organizations that need them.

Youth Service America: (202) 296-2992 / www.ysa.org - A national organization "committed to making service the common experience and expectation of all young Americans."

WILDFLOWER HOTLINES

Antelope Valley California Poppy Reserve: (661) 724-1180 or (661) 942-0662 / www.parks.ca.gov

Anza Borrego Desert State Park in Anza Borrego: (760) 767-4684 / www.parks.ca.gov

Joshua Tree National Park in Joshua Tree / Twentynine Palms: (760) 367-5500 / www.nps.gov/jotr

Mojave Desert Information Center: (760) 252-6100 / www.nps.gov/moja

Theodore Payne Foundation for Wildflowers & Native Plants: (818) 768-3533 or (818) 768-1802 / www.theodorepayne.org

INDEX BY NAME

INDEX BY PRICE

Free Occasionally - The following attractions have special days when no admission is charged:

Los Angeles County
  American Military Museum - every Fri., pg.99
  Autry - second Tues., pg.101
  Biotrek - third Sat., pg.195
  George C. Page Museum - first Tues., pg. 109
  Huntington Library, Art Collections and Botanical Gardens - first Thurs., pg. 121
  International City Theatre - a few Sat. a year, pg. 185
  Japanese American National Museum - every Thurs., 5pm - 8pm; third Thurs. all day, pg. 124
  Kidspace Children's Museum - first Tues., 4pm - 8pm, pg. 125
  Long Beach Museum of Art - every Thurs., 3pm - 8pm; every Fri. all day, pg. 128
  Los Angeles County Arboretum & Botanic Garden - third Tues., pg. 71
  Los Angeles County Museum of Art - second Tues.; Mon. - Fri. after 3pm for L.A. County residents; usually holiday
    Mon.; pg. 129
  Museum of Contemporary Art / Geffen - every Thurs., 5pm - 8pm, pg. 136
  Museum of Latin American Art - every Sun.; fourth Fri., 5pm - 9pm, pg.137
  Natural History Museum of L. A. County - first Tues., pg. 139
  Norton Simon Museum - first Fri., 5pm - 8pm, pg. 141
  Skirball Cultural Center - every Thurs., pg.151
  South Coast Botanical Garden - third Tues., pg.85

Orange County
  Bowers Museum - first Sun. for everyone; every Tues. for Santa Ana residents, pg.300
  Discovery Science Center - first Tues. for Santa Ana residents, pg. 301
  Heritage Museum of Orange County - first Sun. for Santa Ana residents, pg.304
  Kidseum - first Sun., pg.305
  Richard Nixon Presidential Library and Museum - President's Day, pg.311
  Santa Ana Zoo - third Sun. for Santa Ana residents, pg. 335

Riverside County
  California Museum of Photography - first Thurs., 6pm - 9pm; first Sun., 1pm - 4pm, pg. 357
  Coachella Valley History Museum - first weekend of every month, pg.377
  Riverside Art Museum - first Thurs., 6pm - 9pm; first Sun., 1pm - 4pm, pg.363
  Palm Springs Art Museum - every Thurs., 4pm - 8pm during the Village Fest; second Sun., pg. 390

San Bernardino County
  Chino Youth Museum - first Fri., 3pm - 5pm, pg.423

San Diego County
  California Surf Museum - every Tues., pg.529
  Creation and Earth History Museum - first Tues., pg.530
  Firehouse Museum - first Thurs., pg. 532
  Japanese Friendship Garden - third Tues. for San Diego County residents, pg.526
  Mingei International Museum - third Tues. for San Diego County residents, pg. 539
  Museum of Photographic Arts - second Tues. for San Diego County residents, pg. 542
  Museum of San Diego History - second Tues. for San Diego County residents, pg. 542
  Museum of Contemporary Art (La Jolla) - third Thurs., 5pm - 7pm, pg. 540
  Museum of Contemporary Art (San Diego) - third Thurs., 5pm - 7pm, pg. 541
  Oceanside Museum of Art - first Sun., pg.544
  The New Children's Museum - second Sun., pg.543
  Reuben H. Fleet Science Center - first Tues. for San Diego County residents , pg.548
  San Diego Air and Space Science Museum - fourth Tues. for San Diego County residents, pg.549
  San Diego Art Institute - third Tues. for San Diego County residents, pg.550
  San Diego Automotive Museum - fourth Tues. for San Diego County residents, pg. 551
  San Diego Botanic Garden - first Tues., pg.516
  San Diego Hall of Champions - Sports Museum - fourth Tues. for San Diego County residents, pg. 552
  San Diego Model Railroad Museum - first Tues. for San Diego County residents, pg. 553

Free !
Los Angeles - !

African American Firefighter Museum, 98
Alex Theatre (tour, 195
Antelope Valley Mall - Antelope Adventures Kid's Club, 90
Anthony C. Beilenson Park, 47
Apollo Community Regional Park, 48
Audubon Center, 58
Averill Park, 48
Baldwin Hills Scenic Overlook, 49
Bayshore Playground, 10
Bellflower Skate Park and Caruthers Park, 49
Belmont Shore Beach or Long Beach City Beach, 10
Bike Trail: Los Angeles River Trail, 209
Bike Trail: San Gabriel River Trail, 209
Bike Trail: South Bay, 210
Blackbird Airpark, 124
Braille Institute (Los Angeles County), 196
Brand Park, 49
Brookside Park - Reese's Retreat, 49
California Institute of Technology - Seismology Tour, 196
California Pizza Kitchen (Los Angeles County), 197
Camera Obscura, 163
Castro Crest, 51
Cerritos Library, 166
Cerritos Regional Park and Sports Complex, 51
Charles Wilson Park, 52
Chatsworth Park, 52
Cheeseboro Canyon, 52

Claremont Skate Park and Cahuilla Park, 53
Colorado Lagoon, 10
Culver City Park, 53
Devil's Punchbowl, 54
Dominguez Rancho Adobe Museum, 106
Douglas Park, 55
Earl Burns Miller Japanese Gardens, 55
East and Rice Canyons, 55
Eaton Canyon County Park, 56
Ed Davis Park in Towsley Canyon, 56
Edwards Air Force Flight Test Center Museum, 197
El Dorado Park West, 57
El Monte Historical Museum, 106
Ernest E. Debs Regional Park, 58
Fairplex Garden Railroad, 169
Fanfare Fountains at Gateway Plaza, 169
Farm Tour, 219
Flight Path Learning Center, 108
Folk Music Center and Museum, 108
Forest Lawn Memorial Park, 170
Fox Hills Park, 59
Franklin Canyon, 60
Fred Hesse Jr. Community Park, 60
Fry's Electronics (Los Angeles County), 170
Gates Canyon Park, 61
George F Canyon Nature Center, 61
Glendale Galleria, 90
Goodwill Industries (Los Angeles County), 199
Gordon R. Howard Museum - Mentzer House, 112
Greystone Mansion and Park, 62
Guide Dogs of America, 199

Hacienda Heights Youth Science Learning Center, 116
Harry M. Dotson Park, 64
Hazard Park, 65
Heritage Junction Historic Park, 117
Heritage Park - Cerritos, 65
Heritage Park - Santa Fe Springs, 117
Higginbotham Park, 65
Hollywood Bowl Museum, 118
Hollywood Forever Cemetery, 172
The Homestead Museum, 120
Hopkins Wilderness Park, 66
Houghton Park, 66
Huntington Skateboard Park, 82
Jet Propulsion Laboratories, 199
Joe Davies Heritage Airpark at Palmdale Plant 42, 124
John Ferraro Building - Los Angeles Department of Water and Power - Headquarters, 125
Johnny Carson Park, 67
Justice Brothers Racing Car Museum, 125
Kids Club, 91
Kid's Club at the Commons, 91
Kyoto Gardens, 68
Lake Balboa, 47
Lakewood Center Kids Club, 91
La Mirada Regional Park, 69
La Pintoresca Park, 69
Lego - Mini Model Build (Los Angeles County), 36
Liberty Park - Cerritos, 69
Lincoln Park, 70
Lindberg Park, 70
Live Oak Park (Los Angeles County), 70
Long Beach Airport Tour, 200
Long Beach Firefighters Museum, 128

Ventura - !

Free; donation; spending money (!/$)

Los Angeles - !/$

Orange - !/$

Riverside - !/$

Riverside International Automotive
  Museum, 364
Sky High Party Zone, 347
Uncle Bud's Car Museum, 369
  San Bernardino - $$
Apple Picking, 401
Barstow Station, 397
Calico Early Man Archaeological
  Site, 413
Hot Shot Miniature Golf Course, 452
John Rains House - Casa De Rancho
  Cucamonga, 425
Jumping Jacks (Riverside
  County), 408
McDill Swim Beach and Meadow
  Park, 454
Mitchell Caverns, 416
Mojave Narrows Regional Park, 416
Mountain Town Reptile Museum, 443
Oak Glen, 401
Party Kingdom, 410
Prado Regional Park, 419
Pump It Up (San Bernardino
  County), 410
San Bernardino Rancho
  Asistencia, 429
Silverwood Lake State Recreational
  Area, 420
Victor Valley Museum, 429
Yorba & Slaughter Families
  Adobe, 431
  San Diego - $$
Agua Caliente Springs County
  Park, 495
Air Time, 479
Antique Gas & Steam Engine
  Museum, Inc, 525
Aura Skateboard Training
  Facility, 480
Cardiff State Beach, 468
Carlsbad State Beach (And South
  Carlsbad State Beach), 469
Chula Vista Skatepark, 483
City of Santee Aquatic Center at
  Cameron Family YMCA, 483
Creation and Earth History
  Museum, 530
Cuyamaca Rancho State Park, 500
Free Flight, 588
FUNBelievable, 484
Guy B. Woodward Museum of
  History, 533
Harbor Beach - Breakwater Way, 469
J. A. Cooley Museum, 535
Kidsville Playgym, 486

Krause Family Bike and Skate
  Park, 506
La Jolla Cave and the Cave Store, 563
Lake Cuyamaca, 500
Las Posas Aquatic Center, 510
Len Moore Skatepark, 483
Magdalena Ecke Family YMCA Skate
  Park, 488
Main Street Carriage, 582
Marie Hitchcock Puppet Theater, 570
Mission Basilica San Diego De
  Alcala, 539
Mission San Luis Rey De Francia, 540
Museum of Contemporary Art - La
  Jolla, 540
Museum of Contemporary Art - San
  Diego, 541
Museum of Photographic Arts, 542
Museum of San Diego History, 542
My Kids Clubhouse, 490
Ned Baumer Aquatic Center, 490
Oceanside Museum of Art, 544
Old Globe Theatre (tour, 576
Palomar College Planetarium, 571
Playtown Indoor Playground, 491
PlayWerx, 491
Pump It Up (San Diego County), 491
Salvation Army Ray and Joan Kroc
  Corps Community Center, 492
San Diego Humane Society, 591
San Diego Model Railroad
  Museum, 553
San Diego Trolley, 584
San Elijo State Beach, 470
Seaport Village, 561
Serra Museum - Presidio Park, 556
Westfield Plaza Bonita, 524
Whaley House, 559
  Santa Barbara - $$
Art from Scrap and Explore
  Ecology, 598
Cachuma Lake Recreation Area, 607
Carpinteria State Beach, 598
El Capitan State Beach, 600
Gaviota State Park, 600
Jalama Beach, 600
La Purisima Mission State Historic
  Park, 612
Lil Toot, 648
Mission Santa Barbara, 627
Rancho La Patera, 635
Refugio State Beach, 601
Santa Barbara Harbor, 637
Santa Barbara Water Taxi, 648
Santa Maria Museum of Flight, 632
Stearns Wharf, 637

Stow House, 635
Susan Quinlan Doll & Teddy Bear
  Museum & Library, 636
West Beach, 602
  Ventura - $$
Camarillo Ranch Museum, 681
Channel Islands Maritime
  Museum, 682
Channel Islands Marine Floating
  Lab, 693
El Matador State Beach, 658
Fillmore Historical Museum, 684
Kid's World, 665
McGrath State Beach, 659
Ojai Valley Museum, 686
Painted Pony, 702
Point Mugu State Park, 675
Pump It Up (Ventura County), 666
Rancho Camulos, 687
San Buenaventura State Beach, 660
Scooter's Jungle (Ventura
  County), 666
Skatelab, 666
Stagecoach Inn Museum, 689
Strathearn Historical Park and
  Museum, 690
The Clubhouse Fun Zone, 667
Underwood Family Farms -
  Moorpark, 662
Ventura Aquatics Center, 667
Ventura Pier, 660
Western Foundation of Vertebrate
  Zoology, 691
Wheeler Gorge Visitors Center,
  Nature Trail and Campground, 678
  $10.01 to $20 ($$$)
  Los Angeles - $$$
Adamson House and Malibu Lagoon
  Museum, 97
Agoura Hills, 27
Air and Space Exhibits, 98
American Cinematheque, 198
Angels Attic, 99
Annenberg Community Beach House
  and Back on the Beach Cafe, 46
Autry, 101
Build-A-Bear Workshop (Los Angeles
  County), 162
Cafe 50's, 15
Calabasas Community Center
  Rockwall, 27
Carney's, 16
Charlie Brown Farms, 16
Chinese American Museum, 168
Chuck E. Cheese's (Los Angeles
  County), 16

INDEX BY CITY

INDEX BY THEME